Financial Accounting and Reporting

An International Approach

Financial Accounting and Reporting

An International Approach

Craig Deegan
Anne Marie Ward

London   Boston   Burr Ridge, IL   Dubuque, IA   Madison, WI   New York   San Francisco   St. Louis
Bangkok   Bogotá   Caracas   Kuala Lumpur   Lisbon   Madrid   Mexico City
Milan   Montreal   New Delhi   Santiago   Seoul   Singapore   Sydney   Taipei   Toronto

Financial Accounting and Reporting: An International Approach
Craig Deegan, Anne Marie Ward
ISBN-13 9780077121716
ISBN-10 0077121716

Published by McGraw-Hill Education
Shoppenhangers Road
Maidenhead
Berkshire
SL6 2QL
Telephone: 44 (0) 1628 502 500
Fax: 44 (0) 1628 770 224
Website: www.mcgraw-hill.co.uk

British Library Cataloguing in Publication Data
A catalogue record for this book is available from the British Library

Library of Congress Cataloguing in Publication Data
The Library of Congress data for this book has been applied for from the Library of Congress

Acquisitions Editor: Leiah Norcott
Development Editor: Tom Hill
Production Editor: James Bishop/Claire Munce
Marketing Manager: Alexis Thomas

Text Design by HL Studios
Cover design by Adam Renvoize
Printed and bound in the UK by Bell & Bain, Glasgow

ISBN-13 9780077121716
ISBN-10 0077121716

Dedication

For my husband Martin and my kids—Thomas, Anna, Mary, Séamus and Barry.
I would never have adapted this textbook if my family did not provide the conditions that make it
much easier to stay locked up in the office working all day and all evening.

Brief Table of Contents

Detailed Table of Contents

About the Authors

Anne Marie Ward, BA(Hons), Macc, PGCUT, FHEA, FCA, PhD

Anne Marie Ward is a Professor of Accounting in the School of Accounting, Finance and Economics at the University of Ulster, Jordanstown. Prior to this she worked in Queen's University Belfast and prior to that as an Audit Manager in Moore Stephens (a chartered accountancy firm). She is a qualified chartered accountant. She currently lectures in the area of managerial finance and financial accounting at the University of Ulster. She also lectures for Chartered Accountants Ireland and Accounting Technicians Ireland and provides CPD courses for the Belfast Solicitors' Association and SLS Publishing.

Anne Marie's current research interests include the development and performance of the UK credit union movement, the motivation behind volunteering in credit unions and corporate governance in credit unions. She has received recognition for her research, being awarded the IAFA Emerging Scholar prize in 2004 and the CHA 'alumni' prize in 2007 for the best paper published from a CHA bursary project. She has written numerous papers in academic journals such as *Journal of Business, Finance and Accounting*, *Financial Accountability and Management*, *British Accounting Review*, *Annals of Public and Cooperative Economics* and *Public Money and Management* as well as several professional articles in professional journals and a variety of technical documents for Chartered Accountants Ireland. She was on the editorial board of the *Encyclopedia of Corporate Social Responsibility* (Springer-Verlag).

Anne Marie is also the co-author of *Introduction to Financial Accounting* (7th edition). She is the sole author of *Finance: Theory and Practice* and *An Introduction to Personal Finance*; both texts are in their third edition.

Craig Deegan, BCom (University of NSW), MCom (Hons) (University of NSW), PhD (University of Queensland), FCA

Craig Deegan is Professor of Financial Accounting in the School of Accounting at RMIT University in Melbourne. Craig has taught at both undergraduate and postgraduate level in Australia for more than 25 years and has presented lectures internationally, including in the United States, France, England, Wales, Scotland, New Zealand, Malaysia, Singapore, South Africa, South Korea, Thailand, Hong Kong and China. Prior to working in the university sector Craig worked as a chartered accountant. His research tends to focus on various social and environmental accountability and financial accounting issues and has been published in a number of leading international accounting journals, including: *Accounting, Organizations and Society*; *Accounting and Business Research*; *Accounting, Accountability and Auditing Journal*; *Accounting and Finance*; *British Accounting Review*; *Australian Accounting Review*; and, *The International Journal of Accounting*.

Further, Craig is the author of the leading financial accounting theory textbook, *Financial Accounting Theory*, which is used widely throughout Australia, and internationally – particularly in the UK and Europe.

Preface

In 2005 I started to teach Advanced Financial Accounting at final-year level and was disappointed that I could not find a textbook that combined both the practical aspects of accounting using International Financial Reporting Standards and the deeper critical evaluative discussion that is required in higher level modules and is best achieved by integrating real-life examples, news stories, professional publications and, of course, academic research. At this point I came across Craig Deegan's Australian textbook and considered that it was exactly what I was looking for; however, it was written using Australian accounting standards, Australian academic articles, Australian companies, etc. Therefore, when I was asked to get involved with a European edition of the textbook I could not turn it down.

This is the first European edition of Craig Deegan's very successful textbook that was originally published in 1995 in Australia. The textbook has already been successfully adapted for the New Zealand market. This European version benefits from the many changes and improvements that occurred to the Australian version as a result of seven review processes that involved in excess of 60 Australian accounting academics (the Australian version is now in its seventh edition).

Though the style, approach and questions have remained consistent with the Australian version, this adaption is shorter and is written using **International Financial Reporting Standards** and specifically makes reference to **European companies**, **European news stories**, **European Union accounting guidance** and **European academic research**. That is not to say that non-European material is not included; indeed, reference has been made to several high-profile news stories that affected US companies and reference to academic articles from a variety of countries from all over the globe have been included, for example from Australia, the US, Africa and the Middle East.

In recent months there has been much change to IFRS. The change has, to an extent, been influenced by criticism of the IFRS in the aftermath of the financial crisis and the on-going 'convergence project' between the IASB and the FASB in which joint work is being undertaken to reduce major differences between the accounting standards being issued by both of these standard-setting bodies. Those changes that have been made at the time of writing this book (writing was completed in April 2012) have been incorporated within the respective chapters of this text. Some of the major changes we cover relate to such areas as financial statement presentation, fair value measurement, accounting for leases, revenue recognition, consolidation accounting and financial instruments. Further, the IASB and the FASB are developing a revised conceptual framework of reporting that will also generate significant changes. To date, a new document entitled *Conceptual Framework for Financial Reporting* has been released (September 2010) and further changes are due. This text describes the nature of these changes and the potential impact they will have on general purpose financial reporting.

Each chapter of this edition contains learning objectives, chapter summaries and a comprehensive end-of-chapter exercise. The book provides material that will enable the reader to gain a thorough grasp of the contents and of the practical application of the majority of financial accounting requirements currently required under IFRS. In the discussion of these requirements, numerous worked examples, with detailed solutions, are provided throughout the text.

However, as mentioned, the most attractive feature of this textbook is the fact that it goes the extra mile. It does not just focus on how to apply the various accounting requirements. This text also encourages readers to critically evaluate the various rules and guidelines. The aim is to develop accountants who are not only able to apply particular accounting requirements, but who will also be able to contribute to the on-going improvement of accounting requirements. The view taken is that it is not only important for students to understand the rules of financial accounting, but to also understand the limitations inherent in many of the existing accounting requirements. For this reason, reference is made to various research studies that consider the merit, implications, and costs and benefits of the various accounting requirements. Various newspaper articles discussing different aspects of the accounting requirements are reproduced in the text for consideration and discussion. The permission of copyright holders to reproduce this material is gratefully acknowledged.

Social responsibility reporting continues to be an important area of accounting, and one that is rapidly developing. While this book predominantly considers financial accounting and reporting, Chapter 26 focuses on social responsibility reporting and provides up-to-date and comprehensive material on this important topic.

Extensive support for lecturers and students is also available online, with additional chapters on topics that are not typically taught on the majority of European accountancy courses, additional questions and answers, and PowerPoint slides.

Anne Marie Ward
January 2013

Acknowledgements

There are many people who must be thanked for their contribution to the first European edition of this book. As a first, I must thank Craig for preparing such a well-written and thorough textbook—this resulted in a very solid foundation from which to start the European edition. In addition, the book has been improved over the course of the many reviews received from a variety of academics from several countries and institutions and I would like to acknowledge the contribution made. These people include:

Qiwei Chen, Brunel University
Bill Collins, University of Stirling
Fiona Dalton, Plymouth University
Ian Dewing, University of East Anglia
Omaima Hassan, Brunel University
Niclas Hellman, Stockholm School of Economics
Loretta Kyne, ITT Dublin
Jing Li, Bradford University
Teye Marra, University of Groningen
Carol Masters, University of Southampton
Kevin McMeeking, University of Exeter
René Ory, Leiden University
Radhq Shiwakoti, University of Kent
Svend Thomson, Handels Hojskole Centret, Denmark

The team at McGraw-Hill London also deserve a great deal of thanks for their guidance and help during the adaptation of this book. In particular, I must mention Tom Hill. I was especially grateful for the flowers which appeared after he received an irate email from me. Getting flowers is an unusual event in my life as my Irish husband only buys me flowers when I have a baby. I am at the stage where the economic (and indeed social) consequences of having another child outweigh the benefit to be gained from having flowers—they usually die within three days and my first child is still in my house after 12 years. So going forward, the plan is to fall out with Tom on a periodic basis instead.

On a serious note I would also like to thank Kate O'Leary, the copy-editor, for doing a thorough job, Claire Munce, the production editor, for keeping me well informed in advance of time-lines and expected duties, and Rosemary Noble, Senior Publisher, McGraw-Hill Australia for co-ordinating writing with Craig in Australia.

Every effort has been made to trace and acknowledge ownership of copyright and to clear permission for material reproduced in this book. The publishers will be pleased to make suitable arrangements to clear permission with any copyright holders whom it has not been possible to contact.

How to use this book

Learning objectives

Upon completing this chapter readers should

LO1   understand the meaning of a 'concept

LO2   understand the need for, and the role

LO3   be able to explain the structure, or bui

LO4   understand the history of the evolutio

LO5   understand the objective of general pu

LO6   understand what is meant by the term
      implications of being classified as a rep

LO7   understand what qualitative characteri
      information if such information is to b

Learning Objectives

Each chapter starts with a list of the chapter's learning objectives. These flag what you should know when you have worked through the chapter. Make these the foundation for your exam revision by using them to test yourself. The end-of-chapter questions also link back to these learning objectives.

Worked Examples

A wide range of detailed scenarios and solutions, some fairly straightforward and some more complex, are provided throughout the text and are a great learning aid, helping to reinforce how the theory is applied in practice and its relevance to actual situations.

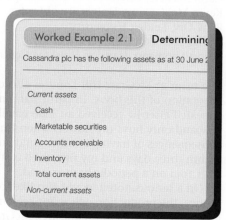

Worked Example 2.1   Determining

Cassandra plc has the following assets as at 30 June 2

Current assets
   Cash
   Marketable securities
   Accounts receivable
   Inventory
   Total current assets
Non-current assets

Financial Accounting in the News
ATION

es and Emirates Airlines

20 nations allow or
listed companies. Of
mented IFRSs. In the
ies are required to
according to IFRSs.[2]
apply IFRSs, partly
P.

mpany from Dubai,
part of the Emirates
by a Dubai govern-
up's financial state-
epared according to

IFRSs. The application of IFRSs may be see
tary, as Emirates Group is not obliged to app
their annual report of 2011–2012 they do not
formal reason for their use of IFRS.

The airlines from the Persian Gulf region, c
Emirates are part, have been accused of unf
tion in the last couple of years,[3] because of a
support. In a statement published on the w
company explains the application of IFRSs a
activity to increase transparency to oppose
tions of state support.

Financial Accounting in the News

Accounting is often a major and controversial part of news items that hit the headlines. Extracts from the media put various aspects of accounting under the spotlight, emphasising how integral it is to business life. They also help students gain a wider grasp of accounting by presenting opposing viewpoints in relation to hot topics. Some show accounting in a historical context; others relate to contemporary issues.

Tables and Figures

Tables provide useful checklists, while figures provide graphical representation of how events and actions link.

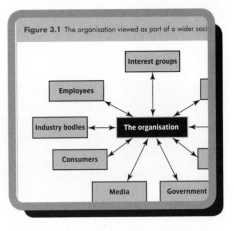

Figure 3.1 The organisation viewed as part of a wider soci

Exhibits

These features contain extracts from actual company reports or documents, or provide a commonly used format for accounting. They highlight the relevance of the chapter content to the practice of accounting, provide another element to the topics covered and help to reinforce learning.

Exhibit 1.1   The institutional frame

Monitoring Board
(of public capital market author

appoints/monitors | reports

IFRS Foundation Trustees
(Governance)

informs | appoints/ oversees
| funds

Standard-setting bodies
IASB (IFRSs/IFRS for SMEs)

IFRS Interpretations Committee

Provide
strategi

Key Terms

Key terms are emboldened in the text the first time they are used, defined in the margin at that point, and listed at the end of each chapter.

Legitimacy Theory
Theory that proposes that organisations always seek to ensure that they operate within the bounds and norms of their societies.

Legitimacy Theory is very
sations continually seek to
their respective societies; t
ceived by outside parties
being fixed, are subject to
environment in which it o
Lindblom (1994) disting
tus or condition, and legiti
an organisation being adjuc

a condition or status which exists when an entity's v
social system of which the entity is a part. When a
systems, there is a threat to the entity's legitimacy.

Legitimacy is a relative concept—it is relative to the s
specific and *place-specific*. Corporate activities that ar
legitimate at a different point in time, or in a differe
country might not be legitimate in another). As Such

SUMMARY

In this chapter we considered the history of internati
framework includes identifying the scope and object
financial information should possess; and defining
number of benefits of conceptual frameworks were
logical; more efficient development of accounting st
tent of accounting standards; and conceptual fram
standard that deals with a specific transaction or ev

The chapter discussed the concept of the 'reporti
entity (which would be determined by whether peo
purposes of decisions relating to the allocation of res
ing standards.

A number of qualitative characteristics were ide

Chapter Summary

Key points of the chapter are summarised in this section. Check through it carefully to make sure you have understood topics covered before moving on.

END-OF-CHAPTER EXE

At the end of each chapter of this book, an exercise will b
Generally, these exercises will be of a practical nature, req
a number of questions of a more theoretical nature will be
tions there is no single right answer, as any response will
The reader is encouraged to contemplate, independently
questions. As a result of reading this chapter you should

1 What is a general purpose financial statement, and who are
2 Are some users of general purpose financial stateme
   assessment?
3 What are the various sources of financial accounting r
   or under-regulated? Why?
4 From the accountant's perspective, what does 'true
   useful, or necessary?

End-of-Chapter Exercise

A comprehensive exercise and worked solution is provided at
the end of each chapter. These are a great revision aid; work
through them before tackling the more challenging questions
to ensure you are on the right track.

REVIEW QUESTIONS

1 Why is it useful for students of financial accounting
2 Why and how might management not act in the int
3 How can we use the output of the accounting syst
   of the owners?
4 How can management expropriate the wealth of de
5 What is corporate social reporting?
6 Why would firms voluntarily present certain informa
   the environment?
7 If firms are voluntarily producing information about th
   ees or about their commitments to the local popu
   'users' of the information are?
8 What are debt covenants and why are they put in p
9 What might be a goal of a well-designed managem

Review Questions

These questions ask you to reflect on key topics within the
chapter, and help cement your learning.

CHALLENGING QUES

21 What is a true and fair override and does it curr
   and against including a true and fair override in
22 The *Application* section of accounting standar
   applied to the extent that the application is cor
   you determine whether an item is material. In d
   statement of financial position, the statement o
23 An organisation has received an interest-free lo
   'loan' be disclosed as debt or as equity, and ho
24 As at the end of the reporting period Ripslash p
   and 54 full-time employees who do not own sh
25 Possies plc considers that its most valuable a
   financial position. Explain this situation

Challenging Questions

These questions require detailed problem analysis and help to
build problem-solving and critical thinking skills.

McGraw-Hill connect™

| ACCOUNTING

Q:

STUDENTS...

Want to get **better grades**? *(Who doesn't?)*

Prefer to do your **homework online**? *(After all, you are online anyway.)*

Need **a better way** to **study** before the big test? *(A little peace of mind is a good thing...)*

A:

With **McGraw-Hill's** *Connect™ Plus Accounting*,

STUDENTS GET:

- **Easy online access** to homework, tests, and quizzes assigned by your instructor.

- **Immediate feedback** on how you're doing. (No more wishing you could call your instructor at 1 a.m.)

- **Quick access** to lectures, practice materials, eBook, and more. (All the material you need to be successful is right at your fingertips.)

- A Self-Quiz and Study tool that **assesses your knowledge** and **recommends** specific readings, supplemental study materials, and additional practice work.

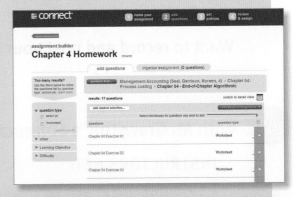

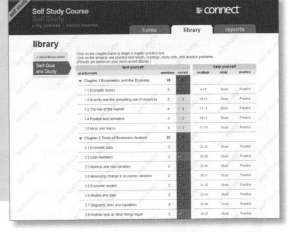

Less managing. More teaching. Greater learning.

 INSTRUCTORS...

Would you like your **students** to show up for class **more prepared**?
(Let's face it, class is much more fun if everyone is engaged and prepared...)

Want an **easy way to assign** homework online and track student **progress**?
(Less time grading means more time teaching...)

Want an **instant view** of student or class performance relative to learning objectives? *(No more wondering if students understand...)*

Need to **collect data and generate reports** required for administration or accreditation? *(Say goodbye to manually tracking student learning outcomes...)*

Want to **record and post your lectures** for students to view online?

 With **McGraw-Hill's *Connect*™ *Plus Accounting*,**

INSTRUCTORS GET:

- Simple **assignment management**, allowing you to spend more time teaching.

- **Auto-graded** assignments, quizzes, and tests.

- **Detailed Visual Reporting** where student and section results can be viewed and analysed.

- Sophisticated **online testing** capability.

- A **filtering and reporting** function that allows you to easily assign and report on materials that are correlated to accreditation standards, learning outcomes, topic and difficulty

- An easy-to-use **lecture capture** tool.

- The option to **upload course documents** for student access.

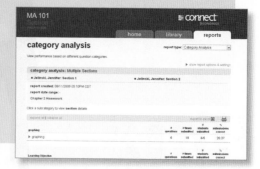

Want an online, **searchable version** of your textbook?

Wish your textbook could be **available online** while you're doing your assignments?

 ***Connect*™ *Plus Accounting* eBook**

If you choose to use *Connect*™ *Plus Accounting*, you have an affordable and searchable online version of your book integrated with your other online tools.

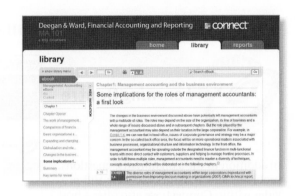

***Connect*™ *Plus Accounting* eBook offers features like:**

- Topic search
- Direct links from assignments
- Adjustable text size
- Jump to page number
- Print by section

 Want to get more **value** from your textbook purchase?

Think learning accounting should be a bit more **interesting**?

 Check out the STUDENT RESOURCES section under the *Connect*™ Library tab.

Here you'll find a wealth of resources designed to help you achieve your goals in the course. You'll find things like **quizzes, PowerPoints, and weblinks** to help you study. Every student has different needs, so explore the STUDENT RESOURCES to find the materials best suited to you.

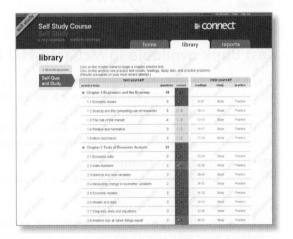

Online Learning Centre

Visit www.mcgraw-hill.co.uk/textbook/deeganward

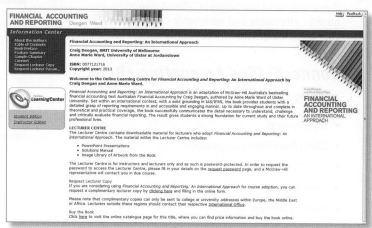

In addition to the assignments, questions, problems and activities McGraw-Hill provides within Connect, we also offer a host of resources to support your teaching.

- PowerPoint presentations *to use in lecture presentations*
- Image Library *of artwork from the textbook*
- Solutions Manual *providing accuracy-tested answers to the problems in the textbook*
- Additional Chapters *covering more specialist topics you may want to explore with your students*

To request your password to access these resources, contact your McGraw-Hill representative or visit: www.mcgraw-hill.co.uk/textbooks/deeganward

EZ TEST ONLINE

Test Bank available in McGraw-Hill EZ Test Online

A test bank of hundreds of questions is available to lecturers adopting this book for their module. For flexibility, this is available for adopters of this book to use through Connect or through the EZ Test online website. For each chapter you will find:
- A range of multiple choice, true or false, short answer or essay questions
- Questions identified by type, difficulty and topic to help you to select questions that best suit your needs

McGraw-Hill EZ Test Online is:
- **Accessible** anywhere with an internet connection – your unique login provides you access to all your tests and material in any location
- **Simple** to set up and easy to use
- **Flexible**, offering a choice from question banks associated with your adopted textbook or allowing you to create your own questions
- **Comprehensive**, with access to hundreds of banks and thousands of questions created for other McGraw-Hill titles
- **Compatible** with Blackboard and other course management systems
- **Time-saving** – students' tests can be immediately marked and results and feedback delivered directly to your students to help them to monitor their progress

To register for this FREE resource, visit www.eztestonline.com

Let us help make our **content** your **solution**

At McGraw-Hill Education our aim is to help lecturers to find the most suitable content for their needs delivered to their students in the most appropriate way. Our **custom publishing solutions** offer the ideal combination of content delivered in the way which best suits lecturer and students.

Our custom publishing programme offers lecturers the opportunity to select just the chapters or sections of material they wish to deliver to their students from a database called CREATE™ at

www.mcgrawhillcreate.co.uk

CREATE™ contains over two million pages of content from:

- textbooks
- professional books
- case books – Harvard Articles, Insead, Ivey, Darden, Thunderbird and BusinessWeek
- Taking Sides – debate materials

Across the following imprints:

- McGraw-Hill Education
- Open University Press
- Harvard Business Publishing
- US and European material

There is also the option to include additional material authored by lecturers in the custom product – this does not necessarily have to be in English.

We will take care of everything from start to finish in the process of developing and delivering a custom product to ensure that lecturers and students receive exactly the material needed in the most suitable way.

With a Custom Publishing Solution, students enjoy the best selection of material deemed to be the most suitable for learning everything they need for their courses – something of real value to support their learning. Teachers are able to use exactly the material they want, in the way they want, to support their teaching on the course.

Please contact your local McGraw-Hill representative with any questions or alternatively contact Warren Eels **e: warren_eels@mcgraw-hill.com**.

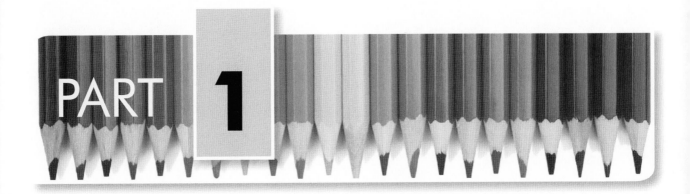

The Accounting Environment

Part contents

Chapter 1

An Overview of the International External Reporting Environment

Learning objectives

Upon completing this chapter readers should:

LO1 understand the scope of regulation relating to external financial reporting;

LO2 understand the typical sources of accounting regulation;

LO3 be able to explain the general functions of the International Accounting Standards Board;

LO4 understand the role of an accounting standard and the process by which it is developed; and

LO5 be able to critically evaluate the arguments for and against the regulation of financial accounting.

1.1 Financial accounting defined

In this book our focus is on financial accounting, which can be considered as a process involving the collection and processing of financial information to meet the decision-making needs of parties external to an organisation. Financial accounting can be contrasted with management accounting. Management accounting focuses on providing information for decision making by parties within the organisation (that is, for internal as opposed to external users) and it is largely unregulated. Financial accounting, by contrast, is subject to many regulations.

Because management accounting relates to the provision of information for parties within an organisation, the view is taken that there generally is no need to protect the information needs or rights of these parties as, being insiders, they can relatively easily access the information they require. By contrast, it is maintained that the information rights of outsiders, who are not involved in the day-to-day operations of an organisation (such as shareholders of a listed company), must be protected. Because financial statements prepared for external parties are often used as a source of information for parties contemplating transferring resources to an organisation, it is arguably important that certain rules be put in place to govern how the information should be compiled. That is, the adoption of a 'pro-regulation' perspective to protect the interests of parties external to a firm requires some regulation relating to the accounting information that such firms should disclose. (We will consider pro-regulation and 'free-market' perspectives in more detail towards the end of this chapter.)

1.2 Users' demand for general purpose financial statements

General purpose financial statements may be used by an array of user groups for many purposes. However, under the Conceptual Framework for Financial Reporting (which was released by the International Accounting Standards Board in September 2010 and replaced the former 'Framework for the Preparation and Presentation of Financial Statements' initially published in 1989), general purpose financial statements are primarily directed towards the information needs of 'existing and potential investors, lenders and other creditors' (paragraph OB2). The Conceptual Framework for Financial Reporting also acknowledges that there are other potential users of financial reports (for example, management, regulators and other members of the public), but they are not deemed to be the 'primary' users of general purpose financial reports and hence these 'secondary' users are not the focus of the prescriptions provided within the Conceptual Framework (paragraphs OB9 and OB10).

> **special purpose financial statement**
> A financial statement designed to meet the needs of a specific group or to satisfy a specific purpose. Can be contrasted with a general purpose financial statement, which is intended to meet the information needs common to users who are unable to command the preparation of reports.

> **general purpose financial statement**
> Financial statements that comply with conceptual framework requirements and accounting standards and meet the information needs common to users who are unable to command the preparation of financial statements tailored specifically to satisfy all their information needs.

Some parties with an interest in the financial affairs of an entity might be in a position to successfully demand financial statements that satisfy their specific information needs. For example, banks might demand, as part of a loan agreement, that a borrowing organisation provide information about its projected cash flows. Such a financial statement would be considered a **special purpose financial statement**—in this case, a financial statement prepared specifically to satisfy the needs of the bank. Other parties with interests in the affairs of an organisation might not have the necessary *power* to demand financial statements that specifically address their own information requirements, having instead to rely on financial statements of a *general nature* released by the reporting entity to meet the needs of a broad cross-section of users, such as investors, potential investors, employees, employee groups, creditors, customers, consumer groups, analysts, media, government bodies and lobby groups. These financial statements are referred to as **general purpose financial statements**, as opposed to special purpose financial statements. As already noted above, general purpose financial statements are produced to primarily meet the needs of existing and potential investors, lenders and other creditors; however, the reports will often also satisfy the information needs of a broader cross-section of users, which might include employees, government, news media, researchers, interest groups and 'the public'.

In this book, we are concerned primarily with general purpose financial reporting. Examples of general purpose financial statements are the financial statements and supporting notes included within an annual report presented to shareholders at a company's annual general meeting (and thereafter typically made available to shareholders and other interested parties on the organisation's website). Our focus in this book will be general purpose financial reporting practices that would typically be used by private-sector profit-seeking entities. However, in recent years there have been moves by governments and government departments towards adopting the kind of accounting procedures that are used by business entities in the private sector. Therefore much of our discussion can be applied to government, particularly government trading enterprises that compete directly with private-sector firms (for example, government-controlled organisations involved in telecommunications, public transport and shipping). Nevertheless, there continue to be some differences between the reporting practices of some government departments and those of private-sector entities.

1.3 Financial reporting regulation

In most European countries there are three sources of regulation for accounting within companies:

1. The accountancy profession including the International Accounting Standards Board (IASB) for international financial reporting standards and the national accounting standards body (if applicable). For example, the Financial Reporting Council in the UK.
2. Company legislation (influenced by European Union Directives).
3. Stock exchange requirements.

Each of these is now discussed in turn.

1.3.1 International financial reporting standards

Global accounting standards are issued by the International Accounting Standards Board (IASB). Standards issued by the IASB are called **International Financial Reporting Standards (IFRSs)**. However, other global standards called International Accounting Standards (IASs) are also in issue. IASs is the name given to the standards that were issued by the International Accounting Standards Committee (IASC), the predecessor of the IASB. The IASB has adopted a number of the IASC's standards and the name (IAS) has not been changed, though the IASB does update the IASs on a regular basis. At the time of writing, approximately 120 countries have either adopted, converged or are committed to converging national accounting standards with IFRSs, particularly for listed companies. Indeed, other companies such as unlisted companies or companies that reside in countries that do not adopt IFRSs are voluntarily adopting IFRSs, as outlined in Financial Accounting in the News 1.1.

> **International Financial Reporting Standards (IFRSs)** A set of international accounting standards stating how particular types of transactions and other events should be reported in financial statements. IFRSs are issued by the International Accounting Standards Board.

Financial Accounting in the News 1.1

IFRS IMPLEMENTATION

United Arab Emirates and Emirates Airlines

According to the AICPA,[1] around 120 nations allow or require the application of IFRSs for listed companies. Of those countries 90 have fully implemented IFRSs. In the United Arab Emirates listed companies are required to prepare their financial statements according to IFRSs.[2] Other companies are allowed to apply IFRSs, partly because of the absence of local GAAP.

Emirates is an international airline company from Dubai, United Arab Emirates. The airline is part of the Emirates Group. The group is privately owned by a Dubai government investment company. The group's financial statements of 2011–2012 have been prepared according to IFRSs. The application of IFRSs may be seen as volun-

tary, as Emirates Group is not obliged to apply IFRSs. In its annual report of 2011–2012 it does not provide any formal reason for its use of IFRS.

The airlines from the Persian Gulf region, of which the Emirates is part, have been accused of unfair competition in the last couple of years,[3] because of alleged state support. In a statement published on the website,[4] the company explains the application of IFRSs as being an activity to increase transparency to oppose the accusations of state support.

Source: Compiled by author from various sources.

The institutional framework for setting IFRSs

The institutional framework for setting IFRSs is shown in Exhibit 1.1.

The current constitution as detailed in Exhibit 1.1 was introduced on 1 March 2010. The IASB is supported by an external 'IFRS Advisory Council' and an 'IFRS Interpretations Committee' that offers guidance where divergence in practice occurs (IFRS Foundation 2012). Some brief detail is now provided on each of the main bodies involved.

The Monitoring Board of Public and Capital Market Authorities

In 2009 the trustees of the IFRS Foundation established the Monitoring Board of Public and Capital Market Authorities (hereafter called the Monitoring Board) to enhance the public accountability of the IFRS Foundation while not impairing the independence of the standard-setting process. The Monitoring Board is an external

---

[1] http://www.ifrs.com/ifrs_faqs.html.

[2] PWC (2011), *IFRS Adoption by Country*.

[3] See 'Rulers of the New Silk Road: The Ambitions of the Three Gulf-based "Super-connecting"Airlines are Bad News for Competitors but Good News For Passengers', *The Economist*, 3 June 2010.

[4] www.emirates.com.

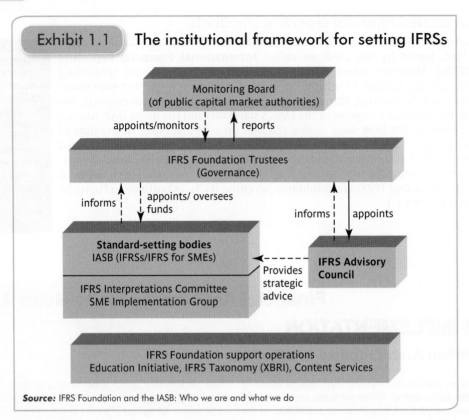

Exhibit 1.1 **The institutional framework for setting IFRSs**

Monitoring Board
(of public capital market authorities)

appoints/monitors ⟶ reports

IFRS Foundation Trustees
(Governance)

informs ⟶ appoints/ oversees funds

informs ⟶ appoints

Standard-setting bodies
IASB (IFRSs/IFRS for SMEs)

IFRS Interpretations Committee
SME Implementation Group

Provides strategic advice

IFRS Advisory Council

IFRS Foundation support operations
Education Initiative, IFRS Taxonomy (XBRI), Content Services

Source: IFRS Foundation and the IASB: Who we are and what we do

body that serves as a formal link and a forum for interaction between representatives of the main capital market authorities worldwide (nominated and appointed to the Board) and the IFRS Foundation. The aim of the Monitoring Board is to appoint members of the IFRS Foundation and to hold them accountable in their role.

The IFRS Foundation trustees

There are 22 trustees and their aim is to promote the work of the IASB and the rigorous application of IFRSs. The trustees are not involved in any technical matters relating to accounting standards. The body has seven committees dealing with matters such as the performance and pay of IASB members, education and content services, internal audit, finance, constitution, executive issues, due process and nominations to the various councils and committees. According to their website (accessed April 2012):

The IFRS Foundation is an independent, not-for-profit private sector organisation working in the public interest. Its principal objectives are:

■ *to develop a single set of high quality, understandable, enforceable and globally accepted international financial reporting standards (IFRSs) through its standard-setting body, the IASB;*
■ *to promote the use and rigorous application of those standards;*
■ *to take account of the financial reporting needs of emerging economies and small and medium-sized entities (SMEs); and*
■ *to bring about convergence of national accounting standards and IFRSs to high quality solutions.*

The governance and oversight of the activities undertaken by the IFRS Foundation and its standard-setting body rests with its Trustees, who are also responsible for safeguarding the independence of the IASB and ensuring the financing of the organisation. The Trustees are publicly accountable to a Monitoring Board of public authorities.

Ultimately the trustees are responsible for the governance of all the bodies that are directly involved in the development of international accounting standards. The IFRS website states that the responsibilities of the trustees include:

1. appointing trustees, members of the IASB, the IFRS Interpretations Committee and the IFRS Advisory Council;
2. establishing and amending the operating procedures, consultative arrangements and due process for the IASB, the Interpretations Committee and the Advisory Council;

3. *reviewing annually the strategy of the IASB and assessing its effectiveness;*
4. *ensuring the financing of the IFRS Foundation and approving annually its budget' (IFRS website, 2012).*

As highlighted by the IFRS Foundation's objectives, responsibility for standard-setting rests with the IASB.

The International Accounting Standards Board

The IASB is described on its website as 'an independent standard-setting body of the IFRS Foundation'. Its members are responsible for developing and issuing IFRSs, the IFRSs for SMEs and the IFRS Interpretations Committee's Interpretations. The IASB is appointed and overseen by the IFRS Foundation trustees, who are publicly accountable to the Monitoring Board of public capital authorities. The IASB is very open with its deliberations, making all correspondence, details of meetings and deliberations available to the public, and invites comment from a variety of stakeholders when publishing standards, including investors, analysts, regulators, business leaders, accounting standard-setters and the accountancy profession.

The predecessor to the IASB, the International Accounting Standards Committee (IASC), was formed in 1973 with the aim of bringing together parties from throughout the world to develop accounting standards that apply internationally. The IASC was governed by representatives from some of its member countries. In April 2001 the IASC was renamed the IASB when it became governed by an independent board whose members are appointed by trustees. The members are drawn from the world's financial community, who represent the public interest. The IASB has 15 full-time members, though this will eventually increase to 16 members under the rules of the new constitution.

Members of the IASB shall be appointed for a term of up to five years, renewable once. These members have a variety of functional backgrounds—from academics, to former chief executives of financial institutions, to former partners in professional accounting firms. Each member has one vote. Until the early 2000s, standards issued by the IASC, and subsequently by the IASB, were not of direct importance to countries that had their own standard-setting processes in place. They would, however, typically be referred to for an indication of possible best practice when accounting standards were being developed within these countries. They were also deemed to provide useful guidance when no domestic standard related to a particular accounting issue. Countries that did not have their own accounting standards in place have been known to adopt directly the standards developed by the IASC and later the IASB. This has been the case especially in developing countries. In more recent times, however, some developed countries have established programmes either to adopt IFRSs or to harmonise their domestic standards with IFRSs. This was done because of the perceived benefits associated with having globally consistent accounting standards.

The website of the IASB explains how accounting standards are issued within the IASB:

- *during the early stages of a project, the IASB may establish an Advisory Committee to give advice on the issues arising in the project. Consultation with the Advisory Committee and the IFRS Advisory Council (also part of the IASB) occurs throughout the project;*
- *the IASB may then develop and publish Discussion Documents for public comment;*
- *following the receipt and review of comments, the IASB could then develop and publish an Exposure Draft for public comment; and*
- *following the receipt and review of comments, the IASB would issue a final IFRS.*

Each IASB member has one vote on technical and other matters. In relation to how many votes are required for an IFRS or exposure draft to be approved, paragraph 36 of the International Accounting Standards Committee Foundation Constitution (as updated December 2010) states:

The publication of an exposure draft, or an International Financial Reporting Standard (including an International Accounting Standard or an Interpretation of the International Financial Reporting Interpretations Committee) shall require approval by nine members of the IASB, if there are fewer than 16 members, or by ten members if there are 16 members. Other decisions of the IASB, including the publication of a discussion paper, shall require a simple majority of the members of the IASB present at a meeting that is attended by at least 60 per cent of the members of the IASB, in person or by telecommunications.

The IASB has full control over its technical agenda. When the IASB publishes a standard, it also publishes a *Basis for Conclusions* to explain publicly how it reached its conclusions and to give background information that might help users of standards to apply them in practice. These *Basis for Conclusions* documents are publicly available. The IASB would also publish dissenting opinions.

The IASB website explains how the Board co-ordinates its activities with national standard-setters, such as the ASB. The Board believes that close co-ordination between the IASB's due process and the due process of national standard-setters is important to the success of the IASB's mission. Further, according to the IASB website, the IASB is exploring ways to integrate its due process more closely with that of its members. Such integration

might grow as the relationship between the IASB and national standard-setters evolves. In particular, the IASB is exploring the following procedure for projects that have international implications:

> **Accounting Standards Board** The UK standard-setting body that develops and publishes UK financial reporting standards.

- IASB and national standard-setters (such as the **Accounting Standards Board** in the UK and Ireland) would co-ordinate their work plans so that when the IASB starts a project, national standard-setters would also add it to their own work plans so that they can play a full part in developing international consensus. Similarly, where national standard-setters start projects, the IASB would consider whether it needs to develop new standards or revise its existing standards. Over a reasonable period, the IASB and national standard-setters should aim to review all standards where there are currently significant differences, giving priority to areas where the differences are greatest.

- National standard-setters would publish their own exposure documents at approximately the same time as IASB exposure drafts are published and would seek specific comments on any significant divergences between the two exposure documents. In some instances, national standard-setters might include in their exposure documents specific comments on issues of particular relevance to their country or include more detailed guidance than is included in the corresponding IASB document.

- National standard-setters would follow fully their own due process, which they would, ideally, choose to integrate with the IASB's due process. Such integration would avoid unnecessary delays in completing standards and would also minimise the likelihood of unnecessary differences between the standards that result.

The IASC issued 41 IASs and a conceptual framework called *The Framework for the Preparation and Presentation of Financial Statements* (IASC 1989). Currently, 29 IASs are still in existence and are promulgated by the IASB, though two are to be withdrawn on 1 January 2013. Thirteen IFRSs have been produced by the IASB, though at the time of writing only nine were applicable. Four standards, namely IFRS 10 *Consolidated Financial Statements*, IFRS 11 *Joint Arrangements,* IFRS 12 *Disclosure of Interests in Other Entities* and IFRS 13 *Fair Value*, become effective on 1 January 2013—early adoption is permitted. IFRS 10 replaces IAS 27 *Consolidated and Separate Financial Statements* and SIC-12 *Consolidation—Special Purpose Entities*. IFRS 11 *Joint Arrangements* supersedes IAS 31 *Interests in Joint Ventures* and SIC-13—*Jointly Controlled Entities—Non-monetary Contributions by Venturers*. IFRS 12 combines, enhances and replaces the disclosure requirements for subsidiaries, joint arrangements, associates and unconsolidated structured entities. As a consequence of these new IFRSs, the IASB also issued amended and retitled IAS 27 *Separate Financial Statements* and IAS 28 *Investments in Associates and Joint Ventures*. The IASB is also currently updating the Conceptual Framework (discussed in Chapter 2). As highlighted earlier, the IASB is answerable to the IFRS Foundation. The IASB has two main sub-groups, the SME Implementation Group and the IFRS Interpretations Committee.

Table 1.1 shows the IASs/IFRSs in place as at early 2012. Remember that the standards issued by the IASC (the IASB's predecessor) were referred to as International Accounting Standards (IASs) and the standards released by the IASB are referred to as IFRSs. At this stage, you should review Table 1.1 to gain an understanding of the many and varied issues addressed by the global accounting standards. Appreciate, however, that even all these accounting standards do not cover every conceivable transaction or event, which is why the UK retains the overriding qualitative reporting requirement that corporations must prepare 'true and fair' financial statements. Many of the accounting standards listed in the table will be covered in depth in other chapters of this text. While Table 1.1 provides a list of the standards in place as at early 2012, it should be appreciated that new standards will be added, and particular accounting standards might be withdrawn, over time. This means that such lists of accounting standards do not remain current for long. Further, the wording and requirements incorporated within particular accounting standards will often change, so interested parties (such as practitioners, students and researchers) should always check the websites of standard-setters for the latest versions of accounting standards. Print copies, which are often made available on an annual basis, will be out of date when the amendments to accounting standards are issued, so the websites of bodies such as the ASB and IASB become increasingly relevant.

SME Implementation Group

The SME Implementation Group (SMEIG) supports the international adoption of the IFRSs for Small and Medium-sized Entities (IFRSs for SMEs) and monitors their implementation. The IFRSs for SMEs are separate IFRSs (most recent revision—July 2009) to cater for the needs of smaller entities that deemed full IFRSs to be too onerous and inappropriate for their needs. In defining an SME, the IASB does not use a benchmark size typology like that used in the UK; instead, it defines an SME in terms of its public accountability, wherein an SME is an entity that does not have public accountability. The IFRSs for SMEs are based on the same principles as full IFRSs, however they contain certain omissions, simplifications, reduced disclosures and have been written for clarity. The SMEIG has been charged with dealing with implementation issues that are raised by users of the IFRSs for SMEs and preparing

Table 1.1 IASB International Financial Reporting Standards (2012)

International Financial Reporting Standards (IFRS)	
IAS 1 Presentation of Financial Statements	IAS 36 Impairment of Assets
IAS 2 Inventories	IAS 37 Provisions, Contingent Liabilities and Contingent Assets
IAS 7 Statement of Cash Flows	IAS 38 Intangible Assets
IAS 8 Accounting Policies, Changes in Accounting Estimates and Errors	IAS 39 Financial Instruments: Recognition and Measurement
IAS 10 Events after the Reporting Period	IAS 40 Investment Property
IAS 11 Construction Contracts	IAS 41 Agriculture
IAS 12 Income Taxes	IFRS 1 First-time Adoption of IFRS
IAS 16 Property, Plant and Equipment	IFRS 2 Share-based Payments
IAS 17 Leases	IFRS 3 Business Combinations
IAS 18 Revenue	IFRS 4 Insurance Contracts
IAS 19 Employee Benefits	IFRS 5 Non-current Assets Held for Sale and Discontinuing Operations
IAS 20 Accounting for Government Grants and Disclosure of Government Grants	IFRS 6 Exploration for and Evaluation of Mineral Resources
IAS 21 The Effects of Changes in Foreign Exchange Rates	IFRS 7 Financial Instruments: Disclosures
IAS 23 Borrowing Costs	IFRS 8 Operating Segments
IAS 24 Related Party Disclosures	IFRS 9 Financial Instruments
IAS 28 Investments in Associates	IFRS 10 Consolidated Financial Statements
IAS 29 Financial Reporting in Hyperinflationary Economies	IFRS 11 Joint Arrangements
IAS 32 Financial Instruments: Presentation	IFRS 12 Disclosure of Interests in Other Entities
IAS 33 Earnings Per Share	IFRS for SMEs
IAS 34 Interim Financial Reporting	

questions and answers based on these issues that offer guidance/advice for approval by the IASB before publication to all users. The group also has to make recommendations to the IASB on the need to amend the IFRSs for SMEs in light of issues that arise and in light of amendments that are made to full IFRSs.

The option of allowing financial statements to be prepared under the IFRSs for SMEs or full IFRSs may result in different approaches being applied to small and large companies. Public companies and large limited companies will typically have to prepare financial statements that comply with IFRSs, have their financial statements audited and send them to the members (shareholders) of the company (or make them available on the company's website if the shareholder has not made a specific request to receive a hard copy). The existence of this differential reporting requirement for small and large limited companies is based on the assumption that the limited number of parties with a material interest in 'small' companies would conceivably be able to request information to satisfy their specific needs. However, it is assumed that the majority of shareholders in 'large' companies do not have this ability. As organisations become larger there tends to be greater separation between ownership and management (or, as this is often termed, between ownership and control) and owners tend to become more reliant on external reports in order to monitor the progress of their investment. Further, as an entity increases in size, its *economic* and *political* importance increase, and in general this increases the demand for financial information about the entity.

The IFRS Interpretations Committee

The IFRS Interpretations Committee is the interpretive body of the IASB. It has 14 members with one vote each, drawn from a variety of countries and professional backgrounds. Like the members of the IASB, they are appointed by IFRS Foundation trustees. The IFRS Interpretations Committee mandate is to 'review on a timely basis widespread accounting issues that have arisen within the context of current IFRSs and to provide authoritative guidance on those issues' (IFRS Foundation 2012). The authoritative guidance is called 'IFRIC Interpretations' (these are published and have the same authority as IFRSs). They cover:

1. *newly identified financial reporting issues not specifically dealt with in IFRSs;*
2. *issues where unsatisfactory or conflicting interpretations have developed, or seem likely to develop in the absence of authoritative guidance.*

(IFRS Foundation 2012)

In developing Interpretations, the IFRIC works closely with similar national committees and meets approximately every six to eight weeks. All technical decisions are taken at sessions that are open to public scrutiny. The IFRIC addresses issues of reasonably widespread importance, and not issues of concern only to a small set of enterprises. Given that so many countries have now adopted IFRSs, a central objective of the IFRIC is to achieve consistent Interpretations of IFRSs by IFRSs-adopters internationally. If IFRSs were interpreted differently within each country, the purpose and benefits of promoting one set of global accounting standards would be diminished. Indeed, the aim of global uniformity in interpreting financial reporting requirements has meant that many national standard-setters have disbanded their own domestic interpretations committees.

According to its website, the primary responsibility for identifying issues to be considered by the IFRIC is that of its members and appointed observers. Preparers, auditors and others with an interest in financial reporting are encouraged to refer issues to the IFRIC when they believe that divergent practices have emerged regarding the accounting for particular transactions or circumstances or when there is doubt about the appropriate accounting treatment and it is important that a standard treatment is established. An issue may be put forward by any individual or organisation. The source of a suggested agenda item is not revealed to the IFRIC or to others.

IFRIC Interpretations are subject to IASB approval and have the same authority as a standard issued by the IASB. The Interpretations can be found on the IASB website, as can more information about the IASB and IFRIC (www.iasb.org).

The IFRS Advisory Council

The IFRS Advisory Council is the formal advisory body to the IASB and the trustees of the IFRS Foundation. It is made up of a wide range of representatives from user groups, preparers, financial analysts, academics, auditors, regulators, professional accounting bodies and investor groups that are affected by and interested in the IASB's work (IFRS 2012). The Advisory Council meets three times per year and its members are approved by the trustees of the IFRS Foundation. The primary objective of the Advisory Council is to give the IASB advice on issues including:

input on the IASB's agenda; input on the IASB's project timetable including project priorities, and consultation on any changes in agenda and priorities; advice on projects, with particular emphasis on practical application and implementation issues, including matters relating to existing standards that may warrant consideration by the IFRS Interpretations Committee.

The IFRS Advisory Council also supports the IASB in the promotion and adoption of IFRS throughout the world.

IFRS Foundation support operations

The support operations promote and support the worldwide use of IFRSs. The IFRS Foundation has a number of supporting initiatives going on, including:

1. the creation of an XBRL taxonomy for IFRSs and the IFRSs for SMEs. The XBRL taxonomy has standardised formats and labels (called tags) which should enable the electronic use, exchange and comparability of financial data across countries;
2. the production of high quality, understandable and up-to-date material (including training material) for the IFRSs for SMEs and the organisation of workshops and conferences on IFRSs;
3. promotion of the IFRS brand and the support of global convergence; and
4. support for the day-to-day management of the IFRS Foundation and communications and improving and expanding external relationships.

For specific information on UK Financial Reporting Standards, access the support material for this chapter on the website at : www.mcgraw-hill.co.uk/textbooks/deeganward.

1.4 Legislation

The European Union (EU) has always supported the standardisation of financial reports. The EU issues directives that require national laws to comply with the principles and criteria included in the directives. The key directives to impact on accounting were the Fourth Directive (prescribed the information to be contained within a set of published financial statements), the Seventh Directive (consolidation issues and group financial statements) and the Eighth Directive (auditors, audit committees, etc.).

The intention of the Commission was to harmonise financial reporting within Europe; however, expansion of the EU is considered to have made this impossible (Roberts *et al.* 1996). As a result, the Accounting Directives were typically not rules but guidelines and principles on content, audit and measurement principles, which allowed diversity of practice within European countries, with countries retaining their own standard-setters (Thorell and Whittington 1994). It was also considered that the creation of European standards might be an obstacle to wider international harmonisation (Haller 2002).

The EU considers that public limited companies would be disadvantaged if their financial statements were not considered to be comparable with the financial statements of companies around the globe and hence, from 2005, EU Regulation 1606/2002 requires that all companies listed on European securities exchanges comply with IFRSs that have been endorsed by the EU when preparing consolidated financial statements (Pope and McLeay 2011).

Therefore, in each European country accounting regulation for plcs is typically provided by legislation on their corporations/companies. For example, in the UK regulation is provided by the Companies Act 2006. Section 395 of this Act gives companies the option of preparing their financial statements in accordance with the guidance provided in Section 396 of the Act or with IFRSs.

Company legislation is particular to each individual country and in some countries, such as Germany, the legislation is very specific about accounting treatments and disclosure requirements; in other countries the legislation makes reference to accounting standards (Ireland/UK) and is less detailed on accounting treatments. Company/corporation legislation also typically provides rules on the conduct of directors, disclosures in financial statements, documentation, audits and auditor liability, creditor and shareholder protection (distribution restrictions, rules on share capital issues and meetings and communication between directors and shareholders) rather than on the accounting framework to adopt. An important requirement of the Companies Act in the UK and Ireland is for directors of public companies, large private companies and some small limited companies to present shareholders with financial statements that are a *true and fair* reflection of the company's performance for a given financial year and its financial position at the reporting period date. (This and other requirements of the Companies Act do not apply to organisations outside the ambit of the Act, for example partnerships.)

It is generally assumed that financial statements are regarded as being true and fair if they have been properly prepared in accordance with accounting standards. Paragraph 10 of accounting standard IAS 1 *Presentation of Financial Statements* states that a complete set of financial statements comprises:

(a) *a statement of financial position as at the end of the period;*
(b) *a statement of comprehensive income for the period;*
(c) *a statement of changes in equity for the period;*
(d) *a statement of cash flows for the period;*
(e) *notes, comprising a summary of significant accounting policies and other explanatory information; and*
(f) *a statement of financial position as at the beginning of the earliest comparative period when an entity applies an accounting policy retrospectively or makes a retrospective restatement of items in its financial statements, or when it reclassifies items in its financial statements.*

An entity may use titles for the statements other than those used in this Standard.

Across time, terminology used in relation to financial statements has changed. For example, within IAS 1 *Presentation of Financial Statements* reference is now made to the 'statement of financial position'. This is equivalent to what many people traditionally called a 'balance sheet'. Further, rather than referring to an 'income statement', as was the case in the earlier versions of IAS 1, reference is now made to a 'statement of comprehensive income'. We will address the components of the statement of comprehensive income in another chapter (Chapter 13), but at this stage we note that paragraph 81 of IAS 1 states that:

An entity shall present all items of income and expense recognised in a period:

(a) *in a single statement of comprehensive income; or*
(b) *in two statements: a statement displaying components of profit or loss (separate statement of profit and loss) and a second statement beginning with profit or loss and displaying components of other comprehensive income (statement of comprehensive income).*

Hence there is still the option to present a 'traditional' statement of profit and loss as long as it is also presented with a 'statement of comprehensive income'. Again, we will return to the statement of comprehensive income later in this book.

As we have noted above, the UK Companies Act requires financial statements to be 'true and fair' (Section 396(2) to (4)).

But why do we need a 'true and fair' requirement? The answer to this is that it is generally accepted that it would be unrealistic to assume that specific disclosure rules or accounting standards could be developed to cover every possible transaction or event. For situations not governed by particular rules or standards, the 'true and fair view' requirement is the *general criterion* to assist directors and auditors to determine what disclosures should be made and to consider alternative recognition and measurement approaches. Although there is no definition of 'true and fair' in the Companies Act—which is perhaps somewhat surprising—it would appear that for financial statements to be considered true and fair, all information of a 'material' nature should be disclosed so that readers of the financial statements are not misled. However, 'materiality' is an assessment calling for a high degree of professional judgement. It is not possible to give a definition of 'material' that covers all circumstances. Paragraph QC11 of the IASB's Conceptual Framework provides that:

> Information is material if omitting it or misstating it could influence decisions that users make on the basis of financial information about a specific reporting entity.

In addition, paragraph 7 of IAS 1 *Presentation of Financial Statements* states:

> Omissions or misstatements of items are material if they could, individually or collectively, influence the economic decisions that users make on the basis of the financial statements. Materiality depends on the size and nature of the omission or misstatement judged in the surrounding circumstances. The size or nature of the item, or a combination of both, could be the determining factor.
>
> Assessing whether an omission or misstatement could influence economic decisions of users, and so be material, requires consideration of the characteristics of those users.

The above requirements make reference to the characteristics of users. Of particular importance would be the accounting knowledge or expertise of accounting that the users of general purpose financial statements are expected to possess. In this regard, paragraph QC 32 of the Conceptual Framework for Financial Reporting states:

> Financial reports are prepared for users who have a reasonable knowledge of business and economic activities and who review and analyse the information diligently. At times, even well-informed and diligent users may need to seek the aid of an adviser to understand information about complex economic phenomena.

A legal view of what constitutes 'true and fair' in the UK was provided by Lord Justice Hoffman and the Honourable Mrs Justice Arden:

> the courts will treat compliance with accepted accounting principles as prima facie evidence that accounts are true and fair. Equally, deviation from accepted principles will be prima facie evidence that they are not. Accounts which depart from the standard without adequate justification or explanation may be held not to be true and fair (Lord Justice Hoffmann (1983) and Hon. Mrs Justice Arden (1984).

(Davies et al. 1999).

As mentioned above the UK Companies Act enables directors to elect not to comply with an accounting standard if non-compliance is deemed necessary to create true and fair accounts. This is referred to as the 'true and fair override'. The perspective taken is that in some isolated cases certain accounting standards might not be appropriate for a particular entity and application of the standards might actually make the financial statements misleading.

Numerous writers argued that, as the true and fair view requirement is not clearly defined, directors could invoke the 'true and fair override' to justify not complying with particular accounting standards. Livne and McNichols (2009) conducted an empirical investigation into the use of the true and fair override by 1,141 UK companies over the period 1998 to 2002 (their analysis was restricted to 307 because of lack of a control sample). The authors ranked the types of override according to cost, wherein they classed overrides that have the greatest authoritative standing as being the most costly. For example, not complying with UK generally accepted accounting principles (GAAP) would have the highest cost as this is likely to cause conflict with auditors, potential intervention by regulatory bodies and litigation as well as criticism by various market participants. The benefits may include being able to satisfy debt covenants. The authors suggest that an override is only likely to occur when the benefit outweighs the cost. A lesser cost is an override of UK law to comply with UK GAAP. The authors found that only 19 per cent of the overrides were non-compliance with UK GAAP, the majority being non-compliance with UK law in favour of UK GAAP. The authors found that firms with weaker performance and lower interest coverage ratios are more likely to invoke the more costly override. This conflicts with the argument that the override results in a financial statement that portrays a more true and fair view as successful companies would be equally as likely to invoke the override. This argument did not hold when the weaker override sample was examined. The most common overrides noted in the sample included not depreciating investment properties, goodwill measurement and amortisation and not showing grants amortised in deferred income.

1.4.1 Directors' Report

A Directors' Report is recommended by the EU's Accounts Modernisation Directive (2003/51/EC), which is incorporated in European countries' national legislation. In the UK the Directors' Report typically contains more information to that required by the Directive. In general, the Directors' Report provides details on the state of the company and how it has complied with accounting regulation and its social responsibilities. Specifically, the Directors' Report should contain the names of the directors and provide an outline of the company's principal activities. It should detail how the directors have discharged their responsibility to promote the success of the company and maintain its business reputation for the long-term benefit of the company's shareholders, employees, the environment and the community. It should also provide an analysis of the business developments over the past year and outline a fair view of the risks and uncertainties that the company faces.

Large companies also need to provide a review of the business and plcs have to provide additional information about business trends, the impact of the company on the environment, on employees and any contractual arrangements with customers or suppliers that are essential to the company. The information provided on the business review, business trends and so on should include key performance indicators. Directors also need to explain their financial statements as part of their business review.

The Directors' Report often includes a great deal of information that is provided by companies on a voluntary basis. That is, while legislation typically stipulates the minimum level of disclosure that must be made in a Directors' Report, many organisations voluntarily produce additional information (which raises a number of interesting issues about *why* they elect to disclose additional information when not required to—we will consider this again in Chapter 3). For example, in recent years it has been common to find companies voluntarily providing information about community-based projects in which they are participating, as well as employee-training schemes and safety initiatives, and company-promoted environmental initiatives.

In many instances, legislation requires the auditor to provide assurance that the Directors' Report is not inconsistent with the financial statements and the legislation may even allow the company to sue the directors personally for making false or misleading statements in the Directors' Report.

At this stage you, the reader, should try to obtain some recent corporate annual reports. Find the Directors' Report in each one. You will see that, in most cases, the Directors' Report will contain the information summarised in the previous paragraphs. As we discuss other accounting requirements throughout this book, make a point of referring to your collection of recent annual reports to see how the companies in your sample are complying with the various requirements that we are discussing. Referring to corporate annual reports as you progress through this book will serve to give the material you read a more 'real-world' feel. Most large, listed, companies provide copies of their annual reports on their websites. Indeed, in recent years companies have provided their annual reports on their websites as an alternative to posting them out to their shareholders. For example, see the websites of:

- KLM Royal Dutch Airlines (www.klm.com)
- Tesco (www.tescoplc.com)
- Unilever (www.unilever.com)
- BP (www. bp.com)
- SAP (www.sap.com)
- Deutsche Bank (www.db.com)
- Volkswagen (www.volkswagen.com or www.volkswagen.co.uk)
- Sainsbury's (www.sainsburys.co.uk)

The annual reports of companies will typically be available by clicking on an 'investors' or 'shareholders' option (or something similar) that is commonly shown on the home page of a company's website.

Finally, the auditors of a company are required to give an opinion on whether the financial statements are true and fair. Exhibit 1.2, presented later in this chapter, shows the opinion section of the auditor's report from Marks and Spencer's 2011 annual report.

1.5 Stock Exchange rules (Listing Rules)

For those reporting entities that have securities listed on a recognised securities exchange such as the London Stock Exchange (LSE) or the NYSE Euronext securities market there are further reporting requirements over and above those provided within accounting standards or in company legislation. For example, the UK Listing Authority (UKLA), part of the Financial Services Authority (FSA), regulates the LSE and provides rules which companies that are publicly traded must comply with. The FSA rules are divided into 20 parts called LRs (Listing Rules). Details of the Listing Rules are available on the FSA website at http://fsahandbook.info/FSA/html/. In particular Listing Rule 9.8 provides details of additional disclosures that are required in the financial statements of listed companies. You would do well to take the time to review the Listing Rules.

1.5.1 More changes ahead as the IASB converges with US rules?

While a number of countries throughout the world are now adopting IFRSs, there are still differences between US generally accepted accounting principles (GAAP) and IFRSs, and these differences are expected to continue for some time. However, there is a joint project between the IASB and the US Financial Accounting Standards Board (FASB) that is aiming at converging IFRS and FASB standards, meaning that further changes in IFRSs and FASB standards are to be expected. There is an expectation (but at the time of writing, not a certainty) that the US will ultimately adopt IFRSs, and the aim of the convergence project is to work towards the time when a 'true' international standardisation of accounting will become a reality. According to the IASB website:

> The IASB and the US Financial Accounting Standards Board (FASB) have been working together since 2002 to achieve convergence of IFRSs and US generally accepted accounting principles (GAAP). A common set of high quality global standards remains a priority of both the IASB and the FASB.
>
> In September 2002 the IASB and the FASB agreed to work together, in consultation with other national and regional bodies, to remove the differences between international standards and US GAAP. This decision was embodied in a Memorandum of Understanding (MoU) between the boards, known as the Norwalk Agreement. The boards' commitment was further strengthened in 2006 when the IASB and FASB set specific milestones to be reached by 2008 (a roadmap for convergence 2006–2008).
>
> In the light of the progress achieved by the boards and other factors, the US Securities and Exchange Commission (SEC) removed in 2007 the requirement for non-US companies registered in the United States to reconcile their financial reports with US GAAP if their accounts complied with IFRSs as issued by the IASB. At the same time, the SEC also published a proposed roadmap on adoption of IFRSs for domestic US companies.
>
> In 2008 the two boards issued an update to the MoU, which identified a series of priorities and milestones to complete the remaining major joint projects by 2011, emphasising the goal of joint projects to produce common, principle-based standards.
>
> The Group of 20 Leaders (G20) called for standard-setters to re-double their efforts to complete convergence in global accounting standards. Following this request, in November 2009 the IASB and the FASB published a progress report describing an intensification of their work programme, including the hosting of monthly joint board meetings and to provide quarterly updates on their progress on convergence projects.
>
> In June 2010 the IASB and the FASB announced a modification to their convergence strategy, responding to concerns from some stakeholders regarding the volume of draft standards due for publication in close proximity. The strategy retained the June 2011 target date to complete those projects for which the need for improvement of IFRSs and US GAAP is the most urgent, whilst identifying those projects for which a later completion date would be appropriate because they address matters that we believe have a relatively lower priority or for which further research and analysis is necessary.

While there appears to be a long-term aim that ultimately there will be one set of standards used internationally, including within the US, the timing as to when the US will adopt IFRSs (and some people still question if it will) is far from certain. Obviously, for the IASB to achieve its aim of developing 'a single set of high-quality, understandable and international financial reporting standards (IFRSs) for general purpose financial statements' (as stated on the IASB website), it will need to encourage the US to adopt its standards. As indicated above, currently the IASB and the FASB are jointly undertaking a process (called the 'convergence project') that seeks to converge the two sets of standards, thereby paving the way for the US ultimately to switch to IFRSs.

However, at this point it should be noted that the US adoption of IFRSs for use by US companies appears to be a number of years away. Ultimately, whether the US adopts IFRSs will be contingent on whether the US Securities Exchange Commission (SEC) and FASB are satisfied with the results generated by the IASB/FASB convergence project.

The ongoing work being undertaken jointly by the IASB and the US FASB will lead to many changes in reporting requirements in the coming years. Financial accountants will continue to work in an environment with evolving requirements, and they will need to keep abreast of the numerous ongoing changes that are likely to occur. As accountants, we need to appreciate that the accounting standards we learn in any given year are always subject to change in future years.

1.5.2 What benefits can we expect from all this international standardisation?

The benefits that have been promoted by harmonisation of standards include an increased ability for European entities to access capital from international sources and, somewhat relatedly, an increased ability of investors to compare the results of European entities with those of overseas entities. There is also the expectation that it will be more efficient for international companies operating in Europe to prepare financial statements internationally on the basis of the same set of accounting standards. In the past, companies that were listed in more than one jurisdiction had to bear the costs of preparing financial statements under more than one accounting system.

All convergence and standardisation benefits come at a cost. Such costs include those of educating accountants to adopt a new set of accounting standards and those associated with changing data-collection and reporting systems. Such costs will be borne by large listed companies, as well as large proprietary companies, not-for-profit entities and local governments. These last three categories of reporting entity are relatively unlikely to benefit from such things as increased capital inflows. Yet they will still incur significant costs.

In relation to the issue of being better able to compare the financial performance of entities from different countries, it is argued that, while there are still differences in the accounting standards issued by different countries, the difficulties inherent in comparing the financial performance of reporting entities from different countries will persist. The differences in accounting rules can have significant implications for profit comparisons. In this regard we can consider research undertaken by Nobes and Parker (2004). They undertook a comparison of the results of a small number of European-based multinationals that reported their results in accordance with both their home nation's accounting rules and US accounting rules. Their comparative analysis shows, for example, that the underlying economic transactions and events of the Anglo-Swedish drug company AstraZeneca in the year 2000 produced a profit of £9,521 million when reported in conformity with UK accounting rules, but the same set of transactions produced a reported profit of £29,707 million when prepared pursuant to US accounting rules—a difference of 212 per cent in reported profits from an identical set of underlying transactions and events! Extending this analysis to a more recent period, the 2006 annual report of AstraZeneca (the final year that companies with a dual home country and US listing had been required to provide a reconciliation between their results using IFRSs and US accounting rules) shows that net income derived from applying IFRSs of $6,043 million became a net income of $4,392 million when calculated in accordance with US accounting rules—this time a difference of 27 per cent compared to the IFRS rules. In its balance sheet (or as it is also known, its statement of financial position), AstraZeneca's shareholders' equity at 31 December 2006 was $15,304 million when reported in accordance with IFRSs, but this became $32,467 million when determined in accordance with US accounting rules, a difference of 112 per cent. Although percentage differences of this size might be unusual, examination of the financial reports of almost any company that reported its results in accordance with more than one nation's set of accounting regulations will have shown differences between the profits reported under each set of regulations and between the financial position reported under each set of regulations.

Having considered how different countries' accounting rules can generate significantly different profits or losses, we should perhaps consider whether such differences are a justification for all the activity that is taking place to standardise accounting standards internationally. What do you think?

The view that harmonisation and subsequent adoption of IFRSs would lead to cost reductions, as well as capital inflows, is not a view that is necessarily supported (or refuted) by any empirical data, but the EU nevertheless held the view that general compliance with IASB standards would lead to significant additional inflows of foreign investment.

1.6 International cultural differences and the harmonisation of accounting standards

As we have emphasised in this chapter, globally countries have adopted, or are moving to adopt, IFRSs rather than accounting standards developed domestically. We now consider some factors that might impact negatively on global harmonisation or convergence of accounting standards. There are a number of potential barriers to global standardisation of accounting standards and these include the influences of different business environments, legal systems, cultures and political environments in different countries.

One of these 'barriers', which we will consider briefly, is cultural differences. Perera (1989, p. 43) describes culture as an expression of norms, values and customs, which reflect typical behavioural characteristics. There are many accounting researchers (for example, Gray 1988; Perera 1989; Fechner and Kilgore 1994; Eddie 1996; Chand and White 2007) who argue that the accounting policies and practices adopted within particular countries are to some extent a direct reflection of the cultural and individual values and beliefs in those countries.

> **conservative accounting policies**
> Policies that tend to understate the value of an entity's net assets. A bias towards understating the carrying value of assets and overstating the carrying value of liabilities.

For example, if a country is deemed to be basically conservative, the argument is that the accounting policies of that country will tend towards conservatism. **Conservative accounting policies** would rely on traditional measurement practices (such as historical cost) and would be more likely to be used in countries in which the society is generally classified as seeking to minimise uncertainty (Perera 1989). Gray (1988, p. 10) argues that the degree of conservatism varies by country, ranging from a strongly conservative approach in the Continental European countries, such as France and Germany, to a much less conservative approach in the US and UK.

1.7 The use and role of audit reports

An audit is the independent examination of financial information of any entity—whether profit-orientated or not and irrespective of its size or legal form—where such an examination is conducted with a view to expressing an opinion on that financial information. The audit opinion is the output of the audit process and is provided in the audit report. The auditor's opinion helps to establish the credibility and reliability of the financial information. The user of this information, however, should not assume that the auditor's opinion is an assurance of the future viability of the entity, or of the efficiency or effectiveness with which management has conducted the affairs of the entity—it is simply an opinion. Also, it cannot be considered with absolute certainty that all transactions have been correctly recorded, even when the auditor provides an unqualified opinion. The auditor does not test/check all transactions; hence there is always the possibility that the financial statements might be materially misstated. It is to be hoped, however, that the probability of material misstatement is kept to a low level. Exhibit 1.2 provides an example of an audit report.

Exhibit 1.2 **Independent audit report to members of Marks and Spencer Group plc**

We have audited the financial statements of Marks and Spencer Group plc for the year ended 2 April 2011 which comprise the Consolidated Income Statement, the Consolidated Statement of Comprehensive Income, the Consolidated and Company Statement of Financial Position, the Consolidated Statement of Changes in Equity and Company Statement of Changes in Shareholders' Equity, the Consolidated and Company Statement of Cash Flows, and the related notes. The financial reporting framework that has been applied in their preparation is applicable law and International Financial Reporting Standards (IFRSs) as adopted by the European Union and, as regards the parent company financial statements, as applied in accordance with the provisions of the Companies Act 2006.

Respective responsibilities of directors and auditors

As explained more fully in the Directors' Responsibilities Statement set out in Other disclosures, the directors are responsible for the preparation of the financial statements and for being satisfied that they give a true and fair view. Our responsibility is to audit and express an opinion on the financial statements in accordance with applicable law and International Standards on Auditing (UK and Ireland). Those standards require us to comply with the Auditing Practices Board's Ethical Standards for Auditors.

This report, including the opinions, has been prepared for and only for the Company's members as a body in accordance with Chapter 3 of Part 16 of the Companies Act 2006 and for no other purpose. We do not, in giving these opinions, accept or assume responsibility for any other purpose or to any other person to whom this report is shown or into whose hands it may come save where expressly agreed by our prior consent in writing.

▶

Scope of the audit of the financial statements

An audit involves obtaining evidence about the amounts and disclosures in the financial statements sufficient to give reasonable assurance that the financial statements are free from material misstatement, whether caused by fraud or error. This includes an assessment of: whether the accounting policies are appropriate to the Group's and the parent company's circumstances and have been consistently applied and adequately disclosed; the reasonableness of significant accounting estimates made by the directors; and the overall presentation of the financial statements. In addition, we read all the financial and non-financial information in the annual report and financial statements 2011 to identify material inconsistencies with the audited financial statements. If we become aware of any apparent material misstatements or inconsistencies we consider the implications for our report.

Opinion on financial statements

In our opinion the financial statements:

- give a true and fair view of the state of the Group's and of the parent company's affairs as at 2 April 2011 and of the Group's profit and Group's and parent company's cash flows for the year then ended;
- have been properly prepared in accordance with IFRSs as adopted by the European Union;
- have been prepared in accordance with the requirements of the Companies Act 2006 and, as regards the Group financial statements, Article 4 of the lAS Regulation.

Opinion on other matters prescribed by the Companies Act 2006

In our opinion:

- the part of the remuneration report to be audited has been properly prepared in accordance with the Companies Act 2006;
- the information given in the directors' report for the financial year for which the financial statements are prepared is consistent with the financial statements.

Matters on which we are required to report by exception

We have nothing to report in respect of the following:

Under the Companies Act 2006 we are required to report to you if, in our opinion:

- adequate accounting records have not been kept by the parent company, or returns adequate for our audit have not been received from branches not visited by us; or
- the parent company's financial statements and the part of the remuneration report to be audited are not in agreement with the accounting records and returns; or
- certain disclosures of directors' remuneration specified by law are not made; or
- we have not received all the information and explanations we require for our audit.

Under the Listing Rules we are required to review:

- the directors' statement, in relation to going concern;
- the parts of the corporate governance statement relating to the company's compliance with the nine provisions of the June 2008 Combined Code specified for our review; and
- certain elements of the report to shareholders by the Board on directors' remuneration.

Stuart Watson (Senior Statutory Auditor) *for and on behalf of PricewaterhouseCoopers LLP Chartered Accountants and Statutory Auditors London 23 May 2011.*

The auditor is not responsible for the preparation of the financial information; that responsibility rests with management. The auditor's responsibility is to form and express an opinion on the financial information. Arguably, the auditor's report is the first item a reader should review when looking at an annual report. A review of the audit report might indicate that the financial statements have not been properly prepared and, perhaps, that they should not be relied upon for making resource-allocation decisions.

Preparers of financial information include the financial managers of enterprises, each of whom might, at times, place primary importance on maximising their own welfare. This frequently results in the goals of the persons preparing the financial information being different from the goals of those using it. This conflict, which

will be further considered in Chapter 3, might cause the preparers of financial information to intentionally or unintentionally introduce misstatements (or bias) into the financial data. Because of the potential bias of management in identifying and presenting such information, there is a need for independent verification of the financial data to assure fairness of presentation.

The users of financial statements need their information to be unbiased in order to reduce the information risk they face. To lessen this risk, users of financial statements are willing to incur an audit fee in return for some assurance that financial statements are fairly presented. The managers of business entities are also generally prepared to subject their financial operations to an audit. Potential investors are thus able to monitor past and future performance in a more reliable manner and this might motivate them to invest more funds at a lower required rate of return than would otherwise be required. Of course, the value of the independent audit will be tied to the reputation of the firm performing the audit.

1.8 All this regulation—is it really necessary?

As preceding sections of this chapter have discussed, financial accounting is fairly heavily regulated within Europe. There are numerous legislative requirements, and there are many accounting standards, with additional standards being issued fairly frequently. But is all this regulation really necessary? What if we had no accounting standards, and reporting entities could report whatever information they wanted in whatever format they considered appropriate?

Opinions on the need for regulation vary, and range from the 'free-market' perspective to the 'pro-regulation' perspective. We will now briefly consider some arguments *for* and *against* regulation.

1.8.1 The 'free-market' perspective

Proponents of the free-market perspective on accounting regulation often believe that accounting information should be treated like other goods, with the forces of demand and supply being allowed to operate to generate an optimal supply of information about an entity. In support of their claims, a number of arguments are provided. One argument, based on the work of authors such as Jensen and Meckling (1976), Watts and Zimmerman (1978), Smith and Warner (1979) and Smith and Watts (1982), is that even in the absence of regulation, there are private economics-based incentives for the organisation to provide credible information about its operations and performance to certain parties outside the organisation, otherwise the costs of the organisation's operations would rise. This view is based on a perspective that the provision of credible information allows other parties to monitor the activities of the organisation. Being able to monitor the activities of an entity reduces the *risk* associated with investing in the entity, and this in turn should lead to a reduction in the cost of attracting capital to the organisation.

It has also been argued that contracts to align the interests of stakeholders, for example profit-related bonuses, are likely to motivate managers to work hard to increase profits, with higher profitability also being in the interests of the owners. To determine profits, accounting reports will be produced, and the owners will demand that these reports be produced in an unbiased manner. Further, depending on the parties involved and the types of asset in place, it has been argued that managers of the organisation will be best placed to determine what information should be produced to increase the confidence of external stakeholders (thereby decreasing the organisation's cost of attracting capital). Regulation that restricts the available set of accounting methods (for example, banning a particular method of amortisation that was used previously by some organisations) will decrease the efficiency with which information will be provided. It has also been argued that certain mandated disclosures will be costly to the organisation if they enable competitors to take advantage of certain proprietary information. Hakansson (1977) used this argument to explain costs that would be imposed as a result of mandating segment disclosures.

While this discussion is about providing financial statements, a related issue is that of external auditing of such reports. It has been argued that even in the absence of regulation, external parties would demand that financial statement audits be undertaken. If such audits are not undertaken, financial statements would not be deemed to have the same *credibility* and, consequently, less reliance would be placed on them. If reliable information is not available, the risk associated with investing in an organisation might be perceived to be higher, and this could lead to increases in the cost of attracting funds to the organisation. It has therefore been argued that managers would have their reports audited even in the absence of regulation (Watts 1977; Watts and Zimmerman 1983; Francis and Wilson 1988).

Another perspective suggests that, even in the absence of regulation, organisations would still be motivated to disclose both *good* and *bad* news about an entity's financial position and performance. It is argued that there is an incentive for managers to release information in the absence of regulation, as failure to do so will have its own implications for the organisation. Drawing upon this argument, Skinner (1994, p. 39) states:

> *Managers may incur reputational costs if they fail to disclose bad news in a timely manner. Money managers, stockholders, security analysts, and other investors dislike adverse earnings surprises, and may impose costs on firms whose managers are less than candid about potential earnings problems. For example, money managers may choose not to hold the stocks of firms whose managers have a reputation for withholding bad news and analysts may choose not to follow these firms' stocks.*

Reviewing previous studies, Skinner (p. 44) notes that there is evidence that managers disclose both good and bad news forecasts voluntarily. These findings are supported by his own empirical research, which shows that when firms are performing well, managers make 'good news disclosures' to distinguish their firms from those doing less well, and when firms are not doing well, managers make pre-emptive bad news disclosures consistent with 'reputational effects' arguments (p. 58).

So, to summarise this point, there are various arguments or mechanisms in favour of reducing accounting regulation as, even in the absence of regulation, firms have incentives to make disclosures. We will now give some consideration to alternative arguments in favour of regulating the practice of financial accounting.

1.8.2 The 'pro-regulation' perspective

In the above discussion we considered a number of reasons that have been proffered in favour of reducing or eliminating regulation. Another perspective is that if information is not produced, there will be greater uncertainty about the performance of the entity and this will translate into increased costs for the organisation. With this in mind, organisations would, it is argued, elect to produce information to reduce costs. However, arguments in favour of a 'free market' rely on users paying for the goods or services that are being produced and consumed. Such arguments can break down when we consider the consumption of 'free' or 'public' goods.

Accounting information is a public good: once it is available, people can use it without paying and can pass it on to others. Parties that use goods or services without incurring some of the associated production costs are referred to as 'free-riders'. In the presence of free-riders, true demand is understated because people know they can get the goods or services without paying for them. Few will have any incentive to pay for the goods or services, as they can be relatively confident of being able to act as free-riders. This dilemma, it is argued, is a disincentive for producers of the particular good or service, which in turn leads to an underproduction of information (Cooper and Keim 1983).

To alleviate this underproduction, regulation is argued to be necessary to reduce the impacts of market failure. In addition, whether an individual is able to obtain information about an entity might depend on the individual's control of scarce resources required by the entity. Although an individual might be affected by the activities of an organisation, without regulation and without control of significant resources, the individual might be unable to obtain the required information.

Regulators often use the 'level playing field' argument to justify putting legislation in place. From a financial accounting perspective, everybody should (on the grounds of fairness) have access to the same information. This is the basis of laws that prohibit insider trading and that rely upon an acceptance of the view that there will not be, or perhaps should not be, transfers of wealth between parties that have access to information and those that do not. There is also a view (Ronen 1977) that extensive insider trading will erode investor confidence to such an extent that market efficiency will be impaired. Putting in place greater disclosure regulations will make external stakeholders more confident that they are on a 'level playing field'. If the community has confidence in the capital markets, regulation is often deemed to be in the 'public interest'. However, we will always be left with the question of what is the socially right level of regulation. Such a question cannot be answered with any degree of certainty. Regulation might also lead to uniform accounting methods being adopted by different entities, and this in itself will enhance comparability of organisational performance.

While we have provided only a fairly brief overview of the free-market versus regulation arguments, it should perhaps be stressed that this debate is ongoing with respect to many activities and industries, with various vested interests putting forward many different and often conflicting arguments for or against regulation. The subject often gives rise to heated debate within many economics and accounting departments throughout the world. What do you, the reader, think? Should financial accounting be regulated and, if so, how much regulation should there be?

While we can argue about the merits or otherwise of accounting regulation, the current extent of regulation can reasonably be expected to be at least maintained and probably increased in the future.

SUMMARY

This chapter provides an overview of the sources of regulation and guidelines relating to financial reporting. As has been indicated, recent years have seen major changes in the accounting standards being used in most European countries and further changes are to be expected in forthcoming years. Since 2005 all plcs in Europe have to prepare their financial statements using the standards developed by the IASB. Hence, the relevance of the IASB to European financial reporting has greatly increased in recent years.

There are numerous rules relating to external reporting. The body of rules is frequently amended, and therefore accountants in practice (and academia) must continually update their knowledge of the rules.

KEY TERMS

Accounting Standards
Board (ASB). 8

conservative accounting
policies 16

general purpose financial
statement 4

International Financial
Reporting Standards (IFRSs) 5

special purpose financial
statement 4

END-OF-CHAPTER EXERCISE

At the end of each chapter of this book, an exercise will be set that addresses particular issues raised within the chapter. Generally, these exercises will be of a practical nature, requiring calculations. However, in some chapters, such as this one, a number of questions of a more theoretical nature will be posed and no answers will be provided. In fact, for some questions there is no single right answer, as any response will be dependent on subjective judgements and personal opinion. The reader is encouraged to contemplate, independently, the various factors that should be considered in answering the questions. As a result of reading this chapter you should be able to provide answers to the following questions:

1 What is a general purpose financial statement, and who are the users of such statements? **LO 1.1**
2 Are some users of general purpose financial statements more important than others? How would you make such an assessment? **LO 1.1**
3 What are the various sources of financial accounting regulation? Would you consider that financial accounting is over- or under-regulated? Why? **LO 1.2**
4 From the accountant's perspective, what does 'true and fair' mean? In your opinion, is the true and fair requirement useful, or necessary? **LO 1.4**
5 How does the conceptual framework for financial reporting contribute to financial accounting practice? **LO 1.4**
6 The UK has adopted IFRSs. As a result, does the Accounting Standards Board still have much relevance, and if so, why? What are some arguments for and against the UK adopting IFRSs? **LO 1.3**

REVIEW QUESTIONS

1 What is the IASB and how does it affect financial reporting regulation in your country? **LO 1.3**
2 What is the role of the independent auditor, and why would the manager or the user of financial statements be prepared to pay for the auditor's services? **LO 1.3**
3 With all the regulations that companies must follow, fulfilling the requirement for corporate reporting is an additional expensive activity. What are some possible arguments for and against disclosure regulation? **LO 1.5**
4 Provide a justification as to why large companies should have to produce financial statements that comply with accounting standards but small companies should not have to do this. **LO 1.1**
5 Define 'generally accepted accounting procedures'. **LO 1.4**

6   What is included within a statement of directors' responsibility report, and what are the implications if a director signs the report and the organisation subsequently fails, owing millions of pounds that it cannot repay? **LO** 1.1

7   What does it mean to say that some financial statements are 'true and fair'? How would a director try to ensure that the financial statements are true and fair before he or she signs the statement of directors' responsibility? **LO** 1.4

8   How are International Financial Reporting Standards developed and revised? Explain the role of the national accounting standard-setting body in your country in that process (if relevant). **LO** 1.3

9   What is the relevance to accounting in your country of Interpretations issued by the International Financial Reporting Interpretations Committee? **LO** 1.2

10 What authority do Interpretations issued by the IASB have in a European/UK financial reporting context? If they do have authority, from where does this authority emanate? **LO** 1.2

11 What are the functions of the IASB? **LO** 1.3

12 What are some of the possible cultural impediments to the international standardisation of accounting standards? **LO** 1.5

13 Why did the European Union decide that European accounting standards needed to be consistent with those being issued by the International Accounting Standards Board? **LO** 1.1

14 Identify major changes to financial reporting practice and financial reporting regulation that resulted following the adoption of International Financial Reporting Standards. **LO** 1.1

CHALLENGING QUESTIONS

15 Because they disagreed with IFRS 5 *Insurance Contracts*, two companies, ABC Insurance and XYZ, elected in 2012 to present two sets of results: one using the rules prescribed by IFRS 5 and the other using their own preferred approach. To justify the additional disclosures, the companies referred to the need for the financial statements to be true and fair and argued that without the additional disclosures the financial statements might be misleading. **LO** 1.1

ABC's directors elected to emphasise the company's results by providing an entire statement of comprehensive income calculated under their preferred approach. Although the directors justified their approach on the basis of the true and fair view, it is obviously not clear whether other factors might have motivated the disclosure policy. XYZ provided an additional column within the statement of comprehensive income on the basis of a disagreement relating to the application of IAS 23. One column was headed 'True and fair profit' and the other 'Accounting standard's profit'.

REQUIRED

(a) Provide a list of possible motivations for directors to adopt a 'third column' approach.

(b) Is the approach adopted by ABC in contravention of the Companies Act?

16 Visit the website of a company listed on the London Stock Exchange (LSE). (*Hint: some company website addresses are provided in this chapter.*) Review the company's corporate governance disclosures and determine whether the company complies with the 'UK Corporate Governance Code' identified by the FSA's Listing Rules. If the company discloses non-compliance, evaluate the reasons provided for non-compliance. **LO** 1.1

17 Has European financial reporting regulation moved away from a self-regulatory model dominated by the accounting profession towards a government-regulated model? **LO** 1.1

18 The decision that Europe would adopt IFRSs was in large part based on the view that European reporting entities, and the European economy, would benefit from adopting accounting methods that are the same as those adopted internationally. Do you think that all European reporting entities have benefited from international standardisation? **LO** 1.5

19 Globally, there are variations in business laws, criminal laws, and so forth. Such international variations in laws will be a result of differences in history, culture, religion and so forth. While we are apparently prepared to accept international differences in various laws, groups such as the IASB expect there to be global uniformity in regulations relating to accounting disclosure—that is, uniformity in accounting standards. Does this make sense? **LO** 1.5

20 It is argued by some researchers that even in the absence of regulation, organisations will have an incentive to provide credible information about their operations and performance to certain parties outside the organisation because the costs of the organisation's operations will otherwise rise. What is the basis of this belief? **LO** 1.5

21 Any efforts towards standardising accounting practices on an international basis imply a belief that a 'one-size-fits-all' approach is appropriate at the international level. That is, it is assumed, for example, that it is just as relevant for a Chinese steel manufacturer to apply IAS 2 *Inventories* as it is for a European car manufacturer. Is this a naive perspective? Explain your answer. **LO** 1.5

22 Provide some arguments for, and some arguments against, the international standardisation of financial reporting. Which arguments do you consider to be more compelling? (In other words, are you more inclined to be 'for' or 'against' the international standardisation of financial reporting?) **LO** 1.5

23 Review a number of accounting standards and then discuss how accounting standards are structured. **LO** 1.4

24 Provide arguments for and against the harmonisation and adoption of IFRSs by the European Union. **LO** 1.5

REFERENCES

CHAND, P. & WHITE, M., 'A Critique of the Influence of Globalization and Convergence of Accounting Standards in Fiji', *Critical Perspectives on Accounting*, vol. 18, 2007, pp. 605–22.

COOPER, K. & KEIM, G., 'The Economic Rationale for the Nature and Extent of Corporate Financial Disclosure Regulation: A Critical Assessment', *Journal of Accounting and Public Policy*, vol. 2, 1983, pp. 189–205.

DAVIES, M., PATERSON, R. & WILSON, W., *UK GAAP*, 6th ed, Surrey, Tolley Publishing Company Ltd. 1999.

EDDIE, I.A., 'The Association between National Cultural Values and Consolidation Disclosures in Annual Reports: An Empirical Study of Asia-Pacific Corporations', unpublished PhD thesis, University of New England, 1996.

FECHNER, H.E. & KILGORE, A., 'The Influence of Cultural Factors on Accounting Practice', *International Journal of Accounting*, vol. 29, 1994, pp. 265–77.

FRANCIS, J.R. & WILSON, E.R., 'Auditor Changes: A Joint Test of Theories Relating to Agency Costs and Auditor Differentiation', *Accounting Review*, October 1988, pp. 663–82.

GRAY, S.J., 'Towards a Theory of Cultural Influence on the Development of Accounting Systems Internationally', *Abacus*, vol. 24, no. 1, 1988, pp. 1–15.

HAKANSSON, N.H., 'Interim Disclosure and Public Forecasts: An Economic Analysis and Framework for Choice', *Accounting Review*, April 1977, pp. 396–416.

HALLER, A., 'Financial Accounting Developments in the European Union: Past Events and Future Prospects', *European Accounting Review*, vol. 11, no. 1, 2002, pp. 153–90.

IFRS, http://www.ifrs.org, 2012.

JENSEN, M.C. & MECKLING, W.H., 'Theory of the Firm: Managerial Behaviour, Agency Costs and Ownership Structure', *Journal of Financial Economics*, vol. 3, 1976, pp. 306–60.

LIVNE, G. & MCNICHOLS, M., 'An Empirical Investigation of the True and Fair Override in the United Kingdom', *Journal of Business Finance and Accounting*, vol. 36, no. 1–2, 2009, pp. 1–30.

NOBES, C. & PARKER, R., *Comparative International Accounting*, eighth edition. London, Pearson Education, 2004.

PERERA, M.H.B., 'Towards a Framework to Analyze the Impact of Culture in Accounting', *International Journal of Accounting*, vol. 24, 1989, pp. 42–56.

POPE, P. & MCLEAY, S., 'The European IFRS Experiment: Objectives, Research Challenges and Some Early Evidence', *Accounting and Business Research*, vol. 41, no. 3, 2011, pp. 233–66.

ROBERTS, C., SALTER, S., & KANTOR, J., 'The IASC Comparability Project and Current Financial Reporting Reality: An Empirical Study of Reporting in Europe', *British Accounting Review*, vol. 28, 1996, pp. 1–22.

RONEN, J., 'The Effect of Insider Trading Rules on Information Generation and Disclosure by Corporations', *Accounting Review*, vol. 52, 1977, pp. 438–49.

SKINNER, D.J., 'Why Firms Voluntarily Disclose Bad News', *Journal of Accounting Research*, vol. 32, no. 1, 1994, pp. 38–60.

SMITH, C.W. & WARNER, J.B., 'On Financial Contracting: An Analysis of Bond Covenants', *Journal of Financial Economics*, June 1979, pp. 117–61.

SMITH, C.W. & WATTS, R., 'Incentive and Tax Effects of Executive Compensation Plans', *Australian Journal of Management*, December 1982, pp. 139–57.

THORELL, P. & WHITTINGTON, G., 'The Harmonisation of Accounting within the EU', *European Accounting Review*, vol. 3, no. 2, 1994, pp. 215–39.

WATTS, R.L., 'Corporate Financial Statements: A Product of the Market and Political Processes', *Australian Journal of Management*, April 1977, pp. 53–75.

WATTS, R.L. & ZIMMERMAN, J.L., 'Towards a Positive Theory of the Determinants of Accounting Standards', *Accounting Review*, January 1978, pp. 112–34.

WATTS, R.L. & ZIMMERMAN, J.L., 'Agency Problems: Auditing and the Theory of the Firm—Some Evidence', *Journal of Law and Economics*, vol. 26, 1983, pp. 613–34.

Chapter 2

The Conceptual Framework of Accounting and its Relevance to Financial Reporting

Learning objectives

Upon completing this chapter readers should:

LO1 understand the meaning of a 'conceptual framework' for financial reporting;

LO2 understand the need for, and the role of, a conceptual framework;

LO3 be able to explain the structure, or building blocks, of a well-designed conceptual framework;

LO4 understand the history of the evolution of the IASB's Conceptual Framework;

LO5 understand the objective of general purpose financial reporting;

LO6 understand what is meant by the term 'reporting entity' and understand the financial reporting implications of being classified as a reporting entity;

LO7 understand what qualitative characteristics should be possessed by financial accounting information if such information is to be considered useful to users of general purpose financial statements;

LO8 understand the concept of materiality and how this influences decisions about the disclosure of financial information;

LO9 be able to define the elements of financial accounting and be able to explain the recognition criteria for the various elements of accounting;

LO10 understand that measurement forms an important component of a conceptual framework and understand that measurement issues remain to be addressed within the IASB Conceptual Framework Project;

LO11 be aware of the joint initiative currently being undertaken by the IASB and the US Financial Accounting Standards Board to develop a revised conceptual framework for financial reporting, and understand some of the changes that might arise as a result of this initiative;

LO12 be able to critically review the existing conceptual framework; and

LO13 understand that a conceptual framework for general purpose financial reporting represents a 'normative' theory of accounting.

2.1   Europe's use of the IASB Conceptual Framework

> **conceptual framework** A framework that seeks to identify the objective of general purpose financial reporting and the qualitative characteristics that financial information should possess.

As International Financial Reporting Standards (IFRSs) have been developed in accordance with the IASB Conceptual Framework, and as Europe has adopted IFRSs, then it makes sense to also adopt the IASB Conceptual Framework. The aim of a **conceptual framework** of accounting is to define the nature, subject, purpose and broad content of general purpose financial reporting. The concept of creating a conceptual framework is not unique to the IASB; conceptual frameworks have been developed in a number of countries, including the US, Canada, the UK, Australia and New Zealand. For example, in the UK the conceptual framework issued by the Accounting Standards Board (ASB) is called the Statement of Principles.

2.2   What is a conceptual framework?

There is no definitive or 'absolute' definition of a conceptual framework. The Financial Accounting Standards Board (FASB) in the US defined its conceptual framework as a coherent system of interrelated objectives and fundamentals that is expected to lead to consistent standards.

It is generally accepted that it is unwise, and perhaps illogical, to develop accounting standards unless there is first some agreement on key and fundamental issues, such as the objectives of general purpose financial reporting; the qualitative characteristics financial information should possess (for example, relevance and representational faithfulness); how and when transactions should be recognised; and who is the audience of general purpose financial statements. Unless we have agreement on such central issues, it is difficult to understand how logically consistent accounting standards can be developed. Conceptual frameworks are developed to provide guidance on key issues, such as objectives, qualitative characteristics, definitions and recognition criteria.

2.3   Benefits of a conceptual framework

Some of the benefits that are expected to result from having a soundly developed international conceptual framework of accounting are summarised as follows:

1. Accounting standards should be more consistent and logical because they are developed from an orderly set of concepts. The view is that, in the absence of a coherent theory, the development of accounting standards could be somewhat ad hoc.
2. Increased international compatibility of accounting standards should occur because they are based on a conceptual framework that is similar to that in other jurisdictions (for example, there is much in common between the IASB and FASB Frameworks).
3. The IASB should be more accountable for its decisions because the thinking behind specific requirements should be more explicit, as should any departures from the concepts that might be included in particular accounting standards.
4. The process of communication between the IASB and its constituents should be enhanced because the conceptual underpinnings of proposed accounting standards should be more apparent when the IASB seeks public comment on them. The view is also held that having a conceptual framework should alleviate some of the political pressure that might otherwise be exerted when accounting standards are developed—the Conceptual Framework could, in a sense, provide a defence against political attack.
5. The development of accounting standards and other authoritative pronouncements should be more economical because the concepts developed within the Conceptual Framework will guide the IASB in its decision making.
6. Where accounting concepts developed within a conceptual framework cover a particular issue, there might be less need to develop additional accounting standards.

2.4 Current initiatives to develop a revised conceptual framework

It is generally accepted that there were numerous shortcomings in the IASB Conceptual Framework. Similarly, the conceptual framework developed and used in the US is also considered to have many shortcomings. With this in mind, the IASB and the FASB embarked on a joint project to develop a revised conceptual framework for international use. Any revised framework issued by the IASB would then be applicable within an international context.

In July 2006 the FASB and the IASB jointly published a discussion paper entitled *Preliminary Views on an Improved Conceptual Framework for Financial Reporting: The Objective of Financial Reporting and Qualitative Characteristics of Decision-useful Financial Reporting Information*. As we have already stressed, determining the objective of general purpose financial reporting needs to be the first step when developing a conceptual framework for general purpose financial reporting. That paper was the first in a series of publications jointly developed by the two Boards as part of a project to develop a common conceptual framework for financial reporting. The Boards received nearly 200 responses to the discussion paper and, after considering the various comments, they released an exposure draft in May 2008. The document was entitled *Exposure Draft of an improved Conceptual Framework for Financial Reporting*, and this phase of the project specifically addressed the objective of financial reporting and the qualitative characteristics and constraints of decision-useful financial reporting information. According to the Exposure Draft, the conceptual framework is:

> *a coherent system of concepts that flow from an objective. The objective of financial reporting is the foundation of the framework. The other concepts provide guidance on identifying the boundaries of financial reporting; selecting the transactions, other events and circumstances to be represented; how they should be recognised and measured (or disclosed); and how they should be summarised and communicated in financial reports.*

> (IASB 2008a)

Again, and as the above definition indicates, the objective of financial reporting is the fundamental building block for the conceptual framework currently being jointly developed by the IASB and the FASB. Hence, if particular individuals or parties disagreed with the objective of financial reporting identified by the IASB and the FASB, then they would most likely disagree with the various prescriptions provided within the balance of the revised conceptual framework.

The first phase of the joint IASB/FASB initiative was completed in September 2010 and the IASB Conceptual Framework was amended. It was renamed the *Conceptual Framework for Financial Reporting*. The October 2010 revised version of the Conceptual Framework includes the first two chapters that the IASB had published as a result of its first phase of the conceptual framework project, these being:

- Chapter 1 *The Objective of Financial Reporting*
- Chapter 3 *Qualitative Characteristics of Useful Financial Information*

Chapter 2, which has not yet been updated, will deal with the reporting entity concept. The IASB published an exposure draft on the reporting entity concept in March 2010. We will consider this exposure draft when discussing the reporting entity concept later in this chapter. Chapter 4 contains the remaining text of the original IASC Conceptual Framework (1989). Therefore, if we look at the *Conceptual Framework for Financial Reporting*, as released by the IASB in September 2010, we find the following sections (but remember, the framework is still incomplete and there are several projects that will be undertaken to address 'missing' chapters of it):

- **Introduction**
  - Purpose and status
  - Scope
- **Chapters**
  1. The objective of general purpose financial reporting
  2. The reporting entity (*to be added at a future date—but to be positioned after the 'objective' chapter*)
  3. Qualitative characteristics of useful financial information
  4. The *Framework* (1989):
  - Underlying assumptions
  - The elements of financial statements
  - Recognition of the elements of financial statements
  - Measurement of the elements of financial statements
  - Concepts of capital and capital maintenance

Following the 2010 amendments to the IASB Framework, the objective of financial reporting is now defined in the following way:

> *The objective of general purpose financial reporting is to provide financial information about the reporting entity that is useful to existing and potential equity investors, lenders and other creditors in making decisions about providing resources to the entity. Those decisions involve buying, selling or holding equity and debt instruments, and providing or settling loans and other forms of credit.*

Hence, pursuant to the IASB Conceptual Framework, information generated through the process of general purpose financial reporting is generated principally to meet the information needs of financial resource providers, as opposed to other stakeholders.

It is generally accepted that conceptual frameworks will evolve over time as information demands change, and as financial systems change. Therefore, it is not surprising that the conceptual frameworks of the FASB and the IASB, both of which were developed more than two decades ago, were considered to be in need of significant revision.

A revised conceptual framework is also necessary because of the Convergence Project (which we discussed in Chapter 1), which the IASB and FASB are undertaking jointly with the aim of converging their two sets of accounting standards. As previously indicated, the ultimate aim is that the accounting standards of both the IASB and FASB will be so comparable that the US will ultimately adopt IFRSs (although as at early 2012 there was no certainty about the timing of when this might happen, or indeed, even whether the US will ultimately make the final decision to adopt IFRSs) and there will be one set of accounting standards (IFRSs) that is used globally.

Given that efforts are underway to converge the accounting standards being released by the IASB with those being released by the FASB, there is a need for one uniform conceptual framework. In explaining the need for a revised conceptual framework, the FASB and IASB (2005, p. 2) stated:

> *The Boards will encounter difficulties converging their standards if they base their decisions on different frameworks ... The FASB's current Concepts Statements and the IASB's Framework, developed mainly during the 1970s and 1980s, articulate concepts that go a long way toward being an adequate foundation for principles-based standards ... Although the current concepts have been helpful, the IASB and FASB will not be able to realise fully their goal of issuing a common set of principles-based standards if those standards are based on the current FASB Concepts Statements and IASB Framework. That is because those documents are in need of refinement, updating, completion, and convergence. There is no real need to change many aspects of the existing frameworks, other than to converge different ways of expressing what are in essence the same concepts. Therefore, the project will not seek to comprehensively reconsider all aspects of the existing Concepts Statements and the Framework. Instead, it will focus on areas that need refinement, updating, or completing, particularly on the conceptual issues that are more likely to yield standard-setting benefits soon.*

The IASB and FASB are undertaking the work on the conceptual framework in eight phases, as listed below. As at early 2012, phase A had been completed and phases B, C and D were active:

Phase	Topic
A	Objectives and qualitative characteristics
B	Definitions of elements, recognition and derecognition
C	Measurement
D	Reporting entity concept
E	Boundaries of financial reporting, and presentation and disclosure
F	Purpose and status of the framework
G	Application of the framework to not-for-profit entities
H	Remaining issues, if any

Details of the progress of the revised conceptual framework can be found on the IASB website (www.ifrs.org) by following the links to the Conceptual Framework Project.

In the rest of this chapter we will focus primarily on the IASB Conceptual Framework for Financial Reporting, as revised and released in October 2010, as this is the conceptual framework that must be applied within countries that have adopted IFRSs.

2.5 Structure of the Conceptual Framework

The Conceptual Framework is not an accounting standard, and as such does not prescribe recognition, measurement or disclosure requirements in relation to specific transactions or events. Rather, the Conceptual Framework provides guidance at a general or conceptual level. Specific transactions and events (such as, for example, how to account for the acquisition of inventory or the acquisition of goodwill) are addressed by particular accounting standards.

Previously, it was generally accepted that the IASB Conceptual Framework was a useful source of guidance, but was not mandatory. However, the inclusion of two paragraphs in the IAS 8 *Accounting Policies, Changes in Accounting Estimates, and Errors* has changed this position so that preparers of general purpose financial statements are now required to follow the Conceptual Framework when a specific issue is not addressed by a particular international reporting standard. Specifically, paragraphs 10 and 11 of IAS 8 state:

10. *In the absence of an IFRS that specifically applies to a transaction, other event or condition, management shall use its judgement in developing and applying an accounting policy that results in information that is*
    (a) relevant to the economic decision-making needs of users; and
    (b) reliable, in that the financial statements
       (i) represent faithfully the financial position, financial performance and cash flows of the entity;
       (ii) reflect the economic substance of transactions, other events and conditions, and not merely the legal form;
       (iii) are neutral, that is, free from bias;
       (iv) are prudent; and
       (v) are complete in all material respects.
11. *In making the judgement described in paragraph 10, management shall refer to, and consider the applicability of, the following sources in descending order:*
    (a) the requirements and guidance in IFRS dealing with similar and related issues; and
    (b) the definitions, recognition criteria and measurement concepts for assets, liabilities, income and expenses in the Conceptual Framework.

The development of a conceptual framework for accounting is considered to involve the assembly of a number of 'building blocks'. The framework must be developed in a particular order, with some matters necessarily requiring agreement before work can move on to subsequent building blocks. Figure 2.1 provides an overview of the framework developed in the late 1980s by the International Accounting Standards Committee (IASC),

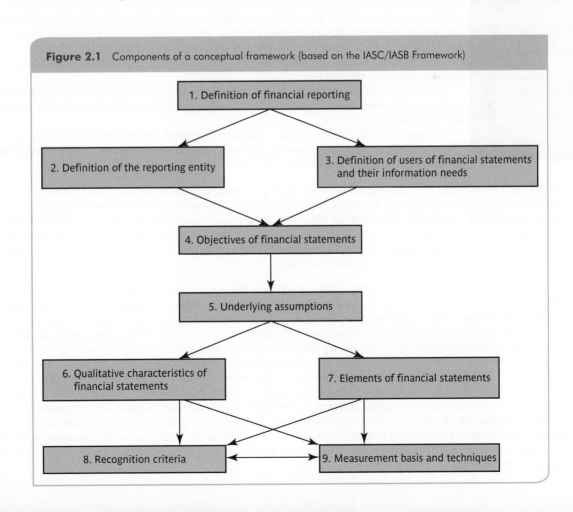

Figure 2.1 Components of a conceptual framework (based on the IASC/IASB Framework)

1. Definition of financial reporting

2. Definition of the reporting entity

3. Definition of users of financial statements and their information needs

4. Objectives of financial statements

5. Underlying assumptions

6. Qualitative characteristics of financial statements

7. Elements of financial statements

8. Recognition criteria

9. Measurement basis and techniques

predecessor of the IASB. Though dated, the building blocks previously identified in the superseded framework are still of relevance.

As represented in Figure 2.1, the first matter to be addressed is the definition of *financial reporting*. Unless there is some agreement on this it would be difficult to construct a framework for financial reporting. Having determined what financial reporting means, we can turn our attention to the *subject* of financial reporting; specifically, which entities are required to produce general purpose financial statements and the likely characteristics of the users of these statements. Then we look at the *objective* of general purpose financial reporting, which we have already briefly discussed in this chapter. Once we have an accepted objective for general purpose financial reporting, the next step is to determine the basic underlying assumptions and qualitative characteristics of financial information necessary to allow users to make 'economic decisions'. We do so later in this chapter.

It is to be expected that over time perspectives on the role of general purpose financial reporting will change. Consistent with this view, many, including accounting standard-setters, expect the development of conceptual frameworks to continue—for them to evolve over time.

2.6   Building blocks of a conceptual framework

In this section we consider the definition of a reporting entity; perceived users of financial statements; the objectives of general purpose financial reporting; the qualitative characteristics that general purpose financial statements should possess; the elements of financial statements; and possible approaches to the recognition and measurement of the elements of financial statements.

2.6.1 Definition of a reporting entity

A key question in any discussion of financial reporting is: what characteristics of an entity signal the need for it to produce general purpose financial statements? Use of the term *general purpose financial statements* signifies that such financial statements comply with accounting standards and other generally accepted accounting principles, and are released by *reporting entities* with the aim of satisfying the general information demands of a varied cross-section of users. See Chapter 1 for a discussion of general purpose and special purpose financial statements. As stated earlier, the guidance that we consider in this chapter relates to general purpose financial statements.

> **reporting entity**
> When users are said to exist who do not have access to information relevant to decision making and who are judged to be dependent on general purpose financial reports, the entity is deemed to be a reporting entity.

The IASB Conceptual Framework subsequently released in 2010 does not address the notion of a **reporting entity** at present; however, the IASB and FASB have been considering the issue.

In May 2008 the IASB released a document entitled *Preliminary Views on an improved Conceptual Framework for Financial Reporting: The Reporting Entity*. In providing background to the report, the IASB stated (2008b: 1):

The boards' existing conceptual frameworks do not include a reporting entity concept. The IASB's Framework for the Preparation and Presentation of Financial Statements defines the reporting entity in one sentence with no further explanation. The FASB's Statements of Financial Accounting Concepts do not contain a definition of a reporting entity or discussion of how to identify one. As a result, neither framework specifically addresses the reporting entity concept. The objective of this phase (Phase D) of the project is to develop a reporting entity concept for inclusion in the boards' common conceptual framework.

If an entity is not deemed to be a 'reporting entity', it will not be required to produce general purpose financial statements—it will not necessarily be required to comply with all accounting standards. Whether an entity is classified as a reporting entity is determined by the extent to which users (of financial information relating to that entity) have the ability to command the preparation of financial statements tailored to their particular information needs. Such a determination depends upon professional judgement. When information relevant to decision making is not otherwise accessible to users who are judged to be dependent upon general purpose financial statements to make and evaluate resource-allocation decisions, the entity is deemed to be a reporting entity.

Company law in the UK, as opposed to the Conceptual Framework, developed more objective criteria for determining when a company is required to provide financial statements that comply with accounting standards. These criteria, which are set out in the Companies Act, relate to measures such as gross revenue, the monetary value of assets and number of employees. Specifically, within the Companies Act a company is deemed to be a large company, and therefore subject to greater disclosure requirements than 'small companies', if it meets two or more of the following tests:

- Gross operating revenue for the financial year of £25.9 million or more.
- Gross assets at the end of the financial year of £12.9 million or more.
- Full-time-equivalent employees numbering 250 or more.

In March 2010 the IASB and FASB released an Exposure Draft in relation to the reporting entity concept entitled *Conceptual Framework for Financial Reporting: The Reporting Entity*. The IASB 2010 Exposure Draft defined a reporting entity as:

> *a circumscribed area of economic activities whose financial information has the potential to be useful to existing and potential equity investors, lenders and other creditors who cannot directly obtain the information they need in making decisions about providing resources to the entity and in assessing whether management and the governing board of that entity have made efficient and effective use of the resources provided.*

Having considered the meaning of a reporting entity, and having learned that reporting entities are required to produce general purpose financial statements, we will now turn our attention to the perceived 'users' of general purpose financial statements.

2.6.2 Users of general purpose financial statements

If general purpose financial statements are to meet their intended purposes, then to be effective, reporting entities need to identify potential users and their respective information needs. Within the IASB Conceptual Framework the primary users of general purpose financial reports are deemed to be 'investors, lenders and other creditors' (Chapter 1, paragraph OB5). Within the IASB Conceptual Framework there appears to be limited consideration of the 'public' as a legitimate user of financial statements. In the previous conceptual framework released by the IASB the 'public' had been identified as a user of general purpose financial statements. However, in the IASB Conceptual Framework released in 2010, even though a primary group of users is identified, it is proposed that accounting information designed to meet the information needs of investors, creditors and other users will usually also meet the needs of the other user groups identified (Chapter 1, paragraph OB10).

In explaining the reasons why the users of financial statements were identified as primarily being investors, lenders and other creditors, the Basis for Conclusions that accompanied the release of the IASB Conceptual Framework stated:

> *The reasons why the Board concluded that the primary user group should be the existing and potential investors, lenders and other creditors of a reporting entity are:*
>
> (a) *Existing and potential investors, lenders and other creditors have the most critical and immediate need for the information in financial reports and many cannot require the entity to provide the information to them directly.*
> (b) *The Board's and the FASB's responsibilities require them to focus on the needs of participants in capital markets, which include not only existing investors but also potential investors and existing and potential lenders and other creditors.*
> (c) *Information that meets the needs of the specified primary users is likely to meet the needs of users both in jurisdictions with a corporate governance model defined in the context of shareholders and those with a corporate governance model defined in the context of all types of stakeholders.*

The issue of which groups should be considered to be legitimate users of financial information about an organisation is one that has attracted a great deal of debate. There are many, such as the authors of *The Corporate Report* (a discussion paper released in 1975 by the Accounting Standards Steering Committee of the Institute of Chartered Accountants in England and Wales), who hold that all groups affected by an organisation's operations have *rights* to information about the reporting entity, including financial information, regardless of whether they are contemplating resource-allocation decisions.

Indeed, many people would question whether the need for information to facilitate users 'making decisions about providing resources to the entity' is the only or dominant issue to consider in determining whether an organisation has a public obligation to provide information about its performance. The activities of organisations, particularly large corporations, impact on society and the environment in many different ways and at many different levels. Such impacts are clearly not restricted to investors or people who are considering investing in the organisation. In large part, the extent to which an organisation impacts on society and the environment, and its ability to minimise harmful impacts, will be tied to the financial resources under its control. As such, a reasonable argument can be made that various groups within society have a legitimate interest in having access to information about the financial position and performance of organisations, and to restrict the definition of users to investors, creditors and other lenders does seem a little too simplistic. In their current work, the IASB and FASB appear to maintain a restricted view of the users of general purpose financial statements and tend

to disregard information rights and the needs of users who do not have a direct financial interest in the organisation. Do you, the reader, consider that this perspective of 'users' of financial reports is too restrictive?

Apart from considering the identity of report users, we also need to consider their expected proficiency in interpreting financial accounting information. In considering the matter of the level of expertise expected of financial statement readers, it has generally been accepted that readers are expected to have some proficiency in financial accounting. As a result, accounting standards are developed on this basis (Chapter 3, paragraph Q32).

So financial statements are written for an audience that is educated to some degree in the workings of accounting—this is an interesting observation given the many hundreds of thousands of financial statements being sent to investors annually, most of whom have no grounding whatsoever in accounting. To usefully consider the required qualitative characteristics financial information should possess (for example, relevance and understandability), some assumptions about the abilities of report users are required. It would appear that those responsible for developing conceptual frameworks have accepted that individuals without any expertise in accounting are not the intended audience of reporting entities' financial statements (even though such people may have a considerable amount of their own wealth invested). Having established the audience for general purpose financial statements, and their expected proficiency in understanding financial accounting information, we now move on to consider the objectives of general purpose financial reporting.

2.6.3 Objectives of general purpose financial reporting

According to Chapter 1 of the IASB Conceptual Framework (which deals with the objective of general purpose financial reporting):

> The objective of general purpose financial reporting forms the foundation of the Conceptual Framework. Other aspects of the Conceptual Framework—a reporting entity concept, the qualitative characteristics of, and the constraint on, useful financial information, elements of financial statements, recognition, measurement, presentation and disclosure—flow logically from the objective.

In terms of the objective of general purpose financial reporting, paragraph OB2 states:

> The objective of general purpose financial reporting is to provide financial information about the reporting entity that is useful to existing and potential investors, lenders and other creditors in making decisions about providing resources to the entity. Those decisions involve buying, selling or holding equity and debt instruments, and providing or settling loans and other forms of credit.

Hence, the whole structure and contents of the IASB Conceptual Framework are based around, and follow on from, the identified objective of general purpose financial reporting.

Before moving on to consider some of the suggested *qualitative characteristics* of financial information, for the sake of completeness we will briefly mention the underlying assumptions identified in the IASB Conceptual Framework. These underlying assumptions are simply that for financial statements to meet the objectives of providing information for economic decision making, they should be prepared on the accrual and going concern basis. Specifically, paragraphs OB17 and 4.1 state:

> OB17   Accrual accounting depicts the effects of transactions and other events and circumstances on a reporting entity's economic resources and claims in the periods in which those effects occur, even if the resulting cash receipts and payments occur in a different period. This is important because information about a reporting entity's economic resources and claims and changes in its economic resources and claims during a period provides a better basis for assessing the entity's past and future performance than information solely about cash receipts and payments during that period.
>
> 4.1   The financial statements are normally prepared on the assumption that an entity is a going concern and will continue in operation for the foreseeable future. Hence, it is assumed that the entity has neither the intention nor the need to liquidate or curtail materially the scale of its operations; if such an intention or need exists, the financial statements may have to be prepared on a different basis and, if so, the basis used is disclosed.

Hence, unless otherwise stated, it is assumed that a general purpose financial statement is prepared on the basis that the entity adopts accrual accounting, and that the entity is a going concern. In practice, most companies state in their accounting policies that the financial statements have been prepared on a going concern basis. Indeed, the Dutch biopharmaceutical company, Pharming Group NV, has provided a statement in the accounting policies section of its 2011 Annual Report to defend its use of the going concern concept. This is included in Financial Accounting in the News 2.1. Pharming was founded in 1988 and has been listed on Euronext Amsterdam since 1999. The company performs research on and development of some niche pharmaceutical products. The company has never shown any profit—at least as far as can be read in publicly available annual

Financial Accounting in the News 2.1

PHARMING GROUP NV – ANNUAL REPORT 2011

Going Concern Assessment

The Board of Management of Pharming has, upon preparing and finalising the 2011 financial statements, assessed the Company's ability to fund its operations for a period of at least one year after the date of these financial statements.

Pharming does not expect to generate sufficient cash from product sales to meet its cash requirements for one year after the date of these financial statements.

To enable continued operations for a period of at least 12 months after the date of these financial statements, several sources to raise or conserve cash in addition to product sales and license agreements have been outlined below:

1. Pharming may raise capital by means of a capital markets transaction, such as non-dilutive (debt) financing issuance of equity or a combination thereof. The timing and proceeds from such a transaction are subject to, for instance, market conditions (e.g. the share price in relation to the nominal value per share), availability of assets to secure debt transactions as well as approvals of boards and/or shareholders (e.g. to issue additional shares).
2. The Company may decide to cancel and/or defer certain activities in order to limit cash outflows until sufficient funding is available to resume them; and
3. Finally, the Company may be able to attract funds through divestment of individual assets or a group

of assets. However, the outcome of such divestment activities is uncertain in view of economic conditions in general and the relatively small market for such specific assets in particular.

This indicates the existence of a material uncertainty which may cast significant doubt about the Company's ability to continue as a going concern.

In case the Company is not able to attract sufficient additional cash from any or a combination of these items, it may ultimately enter into bankruptcy and/or sell all or a part of its assets. Such an event could have a material impact on the carrying value of, in particular, property, plant and equipment as well as inventories.

Overall, based on the outcome of this assessment, these financial statements have been prepared on a going concern basis. Notwithstanding their belief and confidence that Pharming will be able to continue as a going concern, the Board of Management emphasises that the actual cash flows for various reasons may ultimately (significantly) deviate from their projections. Therefore, in a negative scenario (actual cash inflows less than projected and/or actual cash outflows higher than projected) the going concern of the Company could be at risk.

Source: Compiled, with thanks, by René Orij from various sources.

---

reports, since 2003—and that is why doubts may be raised about the going concern of the company. The company cannot finance its operations by its operational cash flows, but it needs to attract funds in the capital markets.

2.6.4 Qualitative characteristics of financial information

If it is accepted that financial information should be useful for economic decision making in terms of making resources available to a reporting entity, as conceptual frameworks indicate, a subsequent element (or building block) to consider is the *qualitative characteristics* (attributes or qualities) that financial information should have if it is to be *useful* for such decisions (implying that an absence of such qualities would mean that the central objectives of general purpose financial statements would not be met).

Conceptual frameworks concentrate quite heavily on identifying the required qualitative characteristics of financial information. The fundamental qualitative characteristics identified in the IASB *Conceptual Framework for Financial Reporting* (as released in 2010) are 'relevance' and 'faithful representation'. This represents a departure from the previous IASB *Framework for the Preparation and Presentation of Financial Statements*, wherein the primary qualitative characteristics were considered to be 'relevance' and 'reliability'. That is, the 'new' framework in place since 2010 has replaced reliability with faithful representation. In discussing the need for information to be relevant and faithfully represented, paragraph QC17 of the IASB Conceptual Framework states:

> *Information must be both relevant and faithfully represented if it is to be useful. Neither a faithful representation of an irrelevant phenomenon nor an unfaithful representation of a relevant phenomenon helps users make good decisions.*

Apart from 'fundamental' qualitative characteristics the IASB Conceptual Framework also identifies a number of 'enhancing qualitative characteristics' (which are important, but rank after fundamental qualitative

characteristics in order of importance). These 'enhancing qualitative characteristics' are outlined in paragraph QC19 of the IASB Conceptual Framework:

> Comparability, verifiability, timeliness and understandability are qualitative characteristics that enhance the usefulness of information that is relevant and faithfully represented. The enhancing qualitative characteristics may also help determine which of two ways should be used to depict a phenomenon if both are considered equally relevant and faithfully represented.

We will consider each of these qualitative characteristics (two primary and four enhancing qualitative characteristics) in turn.

Relevance

Relevance is a fundamental qualitative characteristic of financial reporting. Under the IASB Conceptual Framework, information is regarded as *relevant* if it is considered capable of making a difference to a decision being made by users of the financial statements even if users choose not to act on the information or are aware of the information from a different source (Chapter 3, paragraph QC6).

There are two main aspects to relevance. For information to be relevant, it should have both *predictive value* and *confirmatory value* (or *feedback value*), the latter referring to information's utility in confirming or correcting earlier expectations.

Closely tied to the notion of *relevance* is the notion of *materiality*. This is embodied in various conceptual framework projects. General purpose financial statements are to include all financial information that satisfies the concepts of relevance and faithful representation to the extent that such information is material. Paragraph QC11 of the IASB Conceptual Framework states that an item is material if:

> omitting it or misstating it could influence decisions that users make on the basis of financial information about a specific reporting entity. In other words, materiality is an entity-specific aspect of relevance based on the nature or magnitude, or both, of the items to which the information relates in the context of an individual entity's financial report. Consequently, the Board cannot specify a uniform quantitative threshold for materiality or predetermine what could be material in a particular situation.

Considerations of materiality also provide a basis for restricting the amount of information provided to levels that are comprehensible to financial statement users. It would arguably be poor practice to provide hundreds of pages of potentially relevant and representationally faithful information to financial statement readers—this would only result in an overload of information. Nevertheless, assessing materiality is very much a matter of judgement and at times we might see it being used as a justification for failing to disclose information that could be deemed to be potentially harmful to the reporting entity.

Generally speaking, if an item of information is not deemed material (which is, of course, a matter of professional judgement), the mode of disclosure or even whether or not it is disclosed at all should not affect the decisions of financial statement readers. If an item is not deemed to be material, the general principle is that you do not have to use a particular accounting standard to account for it. In some instances it might be necessary to treat as material an item or an aggregate of items that would not be judged to be material on the basis of the amount involved, because of their nature. An example may be where a change in accounting method has taken place that is expected to affect materially the results of subsequent financial years, even though the effect in the current financial year is negligible.

Worked Example 2.1 provides an example of how we might determine the materiality of an item.

Faithful representation

The other primary qualitative characteristic (other than relevance) is 'faithful representation'. According to the IASB Conceptual Framework, to be useful, financial information must not only represent relevant phenomena, but must also faithfully represent the phenomena that it purports to represent. According to paragraph QC12 of the IASB Conceptual Framework:

> To be a perfectly faithful representation, a depiction would have three characteristics. It would be complete, neutral and free from error. Of course, perfection is seldom, if ever, achievable. The Board's objective is to maximise those qualities to the extent possible.

In terms of the three characteristics of 'complete', 'neutral' and 'free from error', which together reflect faithful representation, paragraphs QC13, 14 and 15 of the IASB Conceptual Framework state:

> QC13   A complete depiction includes all information necessary for a user to understand the phenomenon being depicted, including all necessary descriptions and explanations. For example, a complete depiction of a group

Worked Example 2.1　Determining the materiality of an item

Cassandra plc has the following assets as of 30 June 2013:

	€000
Current assets	
Cash	1,000
Marketable securities	3,000
Accounts receivable	8,000
Inventory	1,100
Total current assets	13,100
Non-current assets	
Investments	6,000
Property, plant and equipment	12,000
Intangible assets	2,000
Total non-current assets	20,000
Total assets	33,100

Profits for the year were €6,000,000 and total shareholders' equity at year end was €12,000,000. Sales for the year were €28,000,000 and related cost of goods sold was €12,000,000. Just before the year-end financial statements were finalised, it was discovered that sales invoices of €900,000 were accidentally excluded from the total transactions of the year. The related cost of goods sold pertaining to these sales was €600,000.

Required
Determine whether this omission is likely to be deemed to be material.

Solution
First, we need to determine the appropriate base amounts. If the sales were properly recorded, sales and accounts receivable would have been €900,000 higher. Inventory would have been €600,000 lower and cost of goods sold would have been €600,000 higher. Profit would have been €300,000 higher.

	Recorded amount (€)	Possible adjustment (€)	Percentage adjustment (%)
Shareholders' equity	12,000,000	300,000	2.5
Profits	6,000,000	300,000	5.0
Sales	28,000,000	900,000	3.2
Cost of goods sold	12,000,000	600,000	5.0
Accounts receivable	8,000,000	900,000	11.3

Determining materiality level is a subjective decision. Changes in most of the items referred to are unlikely to alter the users' decision making; however, an 11.3 per cent change in accounts receivable may have influence. We would therefore argue that the impact on accounts receivable would be material if the transaction was omitted from the financial statements. The impact on the other base amounts would not be deemed to be material, but because the impact on accounts receivable is deemed to be material this is sufficient to warrant the financial statements being adjusted to include the omitted sales.

> *of assets would include, at a minimum, a description of the nature of the assets in the group, a numerical depiction of all of the assets in the group, and a description of what the numerical depiction represents (for example, original cost, adjusted cost or fair value).*
>
> QC14 *A neutral depiction is without bias in the selection or presentation of financial information. A neutral depiction is not slanted, weighted, emphasised, de-emphasised or otherwise manipulated to increase the probability that financial information will be received favourably or unfavourably by users. Neutral information does not mean information with no purpose or no influence on behaviour. On the contrary, relevant financial information is, by definition, capable of making a difference in users' decisions.*
>
> QC15 *Faithful representation does not mean accurate in all respects. Free from error means there are no errors or omissions in the description of the phenomenon, and the process used to produce the reported information has been selected and applied with no errors in the process. In this context, free from error does not mean perfectly accurate in all respects. For example, an estimate of an unobservable price or value cannot be determined to be accurate or inaccurate. However, a representation of that estimate can be faithful if the amount is described clearly and accurately as being an estimate, the nature and limitations of the estimating process are explained, and no errors have been made in selecting and applying an appropriate process for developing the estimate.*

Hence, from the above paragraphs we should understand that financial information that faithfully represents a particular transaction or event will depict the *economic substance* of the underlying transaction or event, which is not necessarily the same as its *legal form*. Further, faithful representation does not mean total absence of error in the depiction of particular transactions, events or circumstances because the economic phenomena presented in financial statements are often, and necessarily, measured under conditions of uncertainty. Hence, most financial reporting measures involve various estimates and instances of professional judgement. To faithfully represent a transaction or event, an estimate must be based on appropriate inputs and each input should reflect the best available information.

In terms of the sequence in which the two fundamental qualitative characteristics of relevance and faithful representation are considered (that is, whether one fundamental qualitative characteristic should be considered before the other), paragraph QC18 of the IASB Conceptual Framework states:

> *The most efficient and effective process for applying the fundamental qualitative characteristics would usually be as follows (subject to the effects of enhancing characteristics and the cost constraint, which are not considered in this example). First, identify an economic phenomenon that has the potential to be useful to users of the reporting entity's financial information. Second, identify the type of information about that phenomenon that would be most relevant if it is available and can be faithfully represented. Third, determine whether that information is available and can be faithfully represented. If so, the process of satisfying the fundamental qualitative characteristics ends at that point. If not, the process is repeated with the next most relevant type of information.*

Of some interest is the fact that when the IASB Conceptual Framework was released in 2010, it identified representational faithfulness as a fundamental qualitative characteristic, rather than using the qualitative characteristic of 'reliability' that was used in the former IASB Framework (that is, reliability was replaced by representational faithfulness when the 2010 document was released by the IASB). In explaining the rationale for this replacement, the IASB argued that the meaning of reliability had not been clearly defined in the previous Framework and attempts to explain it were not successful, therefore a new more representative term was coined (paragraphs BC3.23 and 24 of the Basis for Conclusions that accompanied the release of the IASB Conceptual Framework 2010).

Balancing relevance and representational faithfulness

Ideally, financial information should be both *relevant* and *representationally faithful*. However, it is possible for information to be representationally faithful, but not very relevant, or the other way around. Such information would, in this case, not be deemed to be useful (Chapter 3, paragraph QC17).

For example, while we might be able to quote the acquisition cost of a building reliably (perhaps we have the details of the original contracts and related payments), how relevant would such information be if the building was acquired in 1970? If available, a current valuation of the building might be more relevant. However, until such time as the building is sold, we might not know the amount that would actually be generated on sale. That is, the valuation might not be very reliable or provide a faithful representation of the underlying value (of course, we could try to make it more representationally faithful by obtaining a number of valuations and possibly taking an average). There is often a trade-off between relevance and representational faithfulness. For example, the earlier we can obtain the financial performance results of an entity, the more relevant the information will be in assessing that entity's performance. However, to increase the representational faithfulness of the data, we might prefer to use financial information that has been the subject of an independent audit (therefore, for example, reducing the likelihood of error). The resultant increase in representational faithfulness, or reliability, will mean that we will not receive the information for perhaps ten weeks after the financial year end, at which point the information will not be quite as relevant because of its 'age'. Therefore, there can, in practice, be a matter of balancing one against the other but if the data or information severely lacks one of the characteristics of relevance or faithful representation, then that information should not be provided to financial statement readers.

Another consideration that needs to be addressed when deciding whether to disclose particular information is the potential cost of producing relevant and representationally faithful information, relative to the associated benefits. Paragraphs QC35, 38 and 39 of Chapter 3 suggest that the cost of providing financial information should be justified by the benefits emanating from that information and the IASB will consider this principle when new accounting standards are being developed.

Comparability

As we indicated previously, apart from the two fundamental qualitative characteristics of relevance and faithful representation, there are also four 'enhancing qualitative characteristics'. These enhancing qualitative characteristics are *comparability*, *verifiability*, *timeliness* and *understandability* and each is assumed to enhance the usefulness of information that is both relevant and faithfully represented (Chapter 3, paragraph QC4).

In relation to the enhancing qualitative characteristic of 'comparability', to facilitate the comparison of the financial statements of different entities (and that of the financial statements of a single entity over time), methods of measurement and disclosure must be consistent, but should be changed if no longer relevant to an entity's circumstances. Drawing on studies by Loftus (2003) and Booth (2003), Wells (2003) argues that a key role of a conceptual framework should be to produce consistent accounting standards that lead to comparable accounting information between different entities, as without such comparability it would be difficult for users to evaluate accounting information.

Desirable characteristics such as comparability therefore imply that there are advantages in restricting the number of accounting methods that can be used by reporting entities. However, other academics have argued that steps that result in fewer accounting methods available for use by reporting entities lead potentially to reductions in the efficiency with which organisations operate (Watts and Zimmerman 1986). For example, management might elect to use a particular accounting method because it believes that, for its particular and perhaps unique circumstances, that method best reflects the entity's underlying performance (even though no other entity might use the accounting method in question). Restricting the use of such a method might credibly be held to result in a reduction in the efficiency with which external parties can monitor the performance of the entity, and this in itself has been assumed to lead to increased costs for the reporting entity (this 'efficiency perspective', which has been applied in Positive Accounting Theory, is explored in Chapter 3).

If it is assumed, consistent with the *efficiency perspective* briefly mentioned here, that firms adopt particular accounting methods because those methods best reflect the underlying economic performance of the entity, it is argued by some theorists that the regulation of financial accounting—particularly calls for uniformity in the use of all accounting methods (which enhances comparability)—imposes unwarranted costs on reporting entities. For example, if a new accounting standard is released that bans the use of an accounting method by particular organisations, this will lead to inefficiencies, as the resulting financial statements will no longer provide the best reflection of the performance of those organisations. Many theorists would argue that management is best able to select the appropriate accounting methods in given circumstances and that government and/or others should not intervene by introducing a 'one-size-fits-all' accounting standard. Arguments for and against regulation were provided in Chapter 1. Obviously, the people in charge of developing conceptual frameworks that include comparability as a key qualitative characteristic must believe that the benefits of restricting the number of allowable methods outweigh the potential reductions in efficiency that some organisations may experience as a consequence of their managers not being free to select what they consider to be the most appropriate accounting method.

Verifiability

Verifiability refers to the ability, through consensus among measurers, to ensure that information represents what it purports to represent, or that the chosen method of measurement has been used without error or bias (see Chapter 3, paragraph QC26).

Timeliness

A third 'enhancing' qualitative characteristic is 'timeliness'. The more 'timely' (or up-to-date) that financial information is, the more useful it will be (see Chapter 3, paragraph QC29).

Understandability

The fourth and final 'enhancing' qualitative characteristic is 'understandability', the view being that for information to be useful it obviously needs to be understandable to the users. In the IASB Conceptual Framework, information is considered to be *understandable* if it is likely to be understood by users with some business and accounting knowledge (as discussed earlier). However, this does not mean that complex information that is relevant to economic decision making should be omitted from the financial statements just because it might not be understood by some users (see Chapter 3, paragraph QC32).

Given that conceptual frameworks have been developed in large part to guide accounting standard-setters in the setting of accounting rules (rather than as a set of rules to which entities must refer when compiling their financial statements), this qualitative characteristic of *understandability* is perhaps best seen as a requirement (or challenge) for standard-setters to ensure that the accounting standards they develop for dealing with complex areas produce accounting disclosures that are understandable (irrespective of the complexity of the underlying transactions or events). Based on your knowledge of accounting practice, how successful do you think accounting standard-setters have been at meeting this challenge?

2.6.5 Definition and recognition of the elements of financial statements

The definition and recognition of the elements of accounting are incorporated within Chapter 4 of the IASB *Conceptual Framework for Financial Reporting* as released in 2010. This material was directly taken from the previous IASB *Framework for the Preparation and Presentation of Financial Statements*, hence there have been no recent changes in how the elements of accounting are defined and are to be recognised. Nevertheless, the IASB and FASB plan to review this component of the conceptual framework so future changes in definitions and recognition criteria are probable.

Different approaches can be applied to determining profits (revenues less expenses). Two such approaches are commonly referred to as the *asset/liability approach* and the *revenue/expense approach*. The asset/liability approach links profit to changes that have occurred in the assets and liabilities of the reporting entity, whereas the revenue/expense approach tends to rely on concepts such as the matching principle, which is very much focused on actual transactions and gives limited consideration to changes in the values of assets and liabilities. Most conceptual framework projects, including the IASB Conceptual Framework, adopt the asset/liability approach. Within these frameworks the task of defining the elements of financial statements must start with definitions of assets and liabilities, as the definitions of all the other elements flow from these. This should become apparent as we consider each of the elements of accounting in what follows. In relation to the 'asset and liability view' of profit determination, the FASB and IASB (2005, pp. 7–8) state:

> In both [FASB and IASB] frameworks, the definitions of the elements are consistent with an 'asset and liability view', in which income is a measure of the increase in the net resources of the enterprise during a period, defined primarily in terms of increases in assets and decreases in liabilities. That definition of income is grounded in a theory prevalent in economics: that an entity's income can be objectively determined from the change in its wealth plus what it consumed during a period (Hicks, pp. 178–9, 1946). That view is carried out in definitions of liabilities, equity, and income that are based on the definition of assets, that is, that give 'conceptual primacy' to assets. That view is contrasted with a 'revenue and expense view,' in which income is the difference between outputs from and inputs to the enterprise's earning activities during a period, defined primarily in terms of revenues (appropriately recognised) and expenses (either appropriately matched to them or systematically and rationally allocated to reporting periods in a way that avoids distortion of income).

asset Defined in the IASB Conceptual Framework as a resource controlled by the entity as a result of past events and from which future economic benefits are expected to flow to the entity.

Five elements of financial statements are defined in the IASB Conceptual Framework: assets, liabilities, expenses, income and equity. We will consider each of these in turn, but notice, once again, as the discussion proceeds how the definitions of expenses and income depend directly on the definitions given to assets and liabilities.

Definition and recognition of assets

The IASB Conceptual Framework defines an **asset** as 'a resource controlled by the entity as a result of past events and from which future economic benefits are expected to flow to the entity'. This definition identifies three key characteristics:

1. There must be a future economic benefit.
2. The reporting entity must control the future economic benefits.
3. The transaction or other event giving rise to the reporting entity's control over the future economic benefits must have occurred.

Future economic benefits can be distinguished from the source of the benefit—a particular object or right. The definition refers to the benefit and not the source. Thus whether an object or right is disclosed as an asset will be dependent upon the likely economic benefits flowing from it. In the absence of expected future economic benefits, the object should not be disclosed as an asset. Rather, the expenditure might be construed as an expense.

> **future economic benefits** The scarce capacity to provide benefits to the entities that use them—common to all assets irrespective of their physical or other form.

For example, cash is an asset owing to the benefits that can flow as a result of the purchasing power it generates. A machine is an asset to the extent that economic benefits are anticipated to flow from using it.

Conceptual frameworks do not require an item to have a value in exchange before it can be recognised as an *asset*. The economic benefits may result from its ongoing use (often referred to as *value-in-use*) within the organisation.

As indicated in the above definition of an asset, a resource must be controlled before it can be considered to be an 'asset'. **Control** relates to the capacity of a reporting entity to benefit from an asset and to deny or regulate the access of others to the benefit. The capacity to control would normally stem from legal rights. However, legal enforceability is not a prerequisite for establishing the existence of control. Hence it is important to realise that control, and not legal ownership, is required before an asset can be shown within the body of an entity's statement of financial position. Frequently, controlled assets are owned, but this is not always the case. Organisations frequently disclose leased assets as part of their total assets. For example, the 2011 consolidated statement of financial position of Ryanair plc includes mortgaged aircraft that are not legally owned by Ryanair while the related loan remains outstanding (carrying amount €4,718.7 million), and aircraft that were acquired using finance leases (carrying amount €635.1 million).

> **control** (assets) If an asset is to be recognised, control rather than legal ownership must be established. Control is 'the capacity of the entity to benefit from the asset in the pursuit of the entity's objectives and to deny or regulate the access of others to that benefit'.

There are many resources that generate benefits for an entity but that cannot be recorded owing to the absence of control. For example, the use of the road system generates economic benefits for an entity. However, because the entity does not control the roads, they do not constitute assets of the entity. Similarly, particular waterways will provide economic benefits to entities, but to the extent that such entities do not control the waterways, they are not assets of those entities.

In addition to defining an asset, we also need to consider when we should recognise the existence of an asset. According to the IASB Conceptual Framework, 'recognition is the process of incorporating in the statement of financial position or statement of profit and loss an item that meets the definition of an element and satisfies the criteria for recognition'. In relation to the recognition criteria, the IASB Conceptual Framework provides general recognition criteria for all five elements of financial statements (assets, liabilities, income, expenses and equity), these being:

> *An item that meets the definition of an element should be recognised if:*
>
> *(a) it is probable that any future economic benefit associated with the item will flow to or from the entity; and*
> *(b) the item has a cost or value that can be measured with reliability.*

Hence, for all the five elements of financial accounting, both probability and measurability are key considerations. According to paragraph 4.42 of the IASB Conceptual Framework:

> *We can see from these requirements that the determination of 'probable' is central to the recognition criteria applied to the elements of financial statements. Unfortunately, however, the Conceptual Framework does not define 'probable'. If an asset (or another element of financial statements) fails to meet the recognition criteria in one period but satisfies them in another period, the asset can be reinstated (subject to requirements in particular accounting standards).*

However, it is worth emphasising that while this is a general requirement, the ability to reinstate assets that have been written off will not be available for all assets. Some accounting standards preclude the reinstatement of assets, regardless of whether or not they are subsequently deemed likely to generate future economic benefits. As we have shown, in the hierarchy of rules, accounting standards override the IASB Conceptual Framework. As an example of a prohibition on reinstating assets we can consider the requirements of IAS 38 *Intangible Assets* in

relation to any moves to reinstate previously written-off intangible assets. Specifically, paragraph 71 of IAS 38 states: 'expenditure on an intangible item that was initially recognised as an expense shall not be recognised as part of the cost of an intangible asset at a later date'.

While the above definition of an asset is the definition that currently must be used within countries that have adopted IFRS (such as the UK), it should be noted that this definition might change in future years. Given the central importance of the definition of assets to financial reporting, any change to it will conceivably have broad implications for financial reporting. In relation to joint work being undertaken by the FASB and IASB, the FASB and IASB released a *Project Update: Conceptual Framework—Phase B: Elements and Recognition*, which noted that the existing definition of assets, which relies upon the terms 'control', 'expected' and 'flow' of benefits, has a number of shortcomings. The Boards noted the following (FASB 2008):

> *The Boards agreed that the current frameworks' existing asset definitions have the following shortcomings:*
>
> - *Some users misinterpret the terms 'expected' (IASB definition) and 'probable' (FASB definition) to mean that there must be a high likelihood of future economic benefits for the definition to be met; this excludes asset items with a low likelihood of future economic benefits.*
> - *The definitions place too much emphasis on identifying the future flow of economic benefits, instead of focusing on the item that presently exists, an economic resource.*
> - *Some users misinterpret the term 'control' and use it in the same sense as that used for purposes of consolidation accounting. The term should focus on whether the entity has some rights or privileged access to the economic resource.*
> - *The definitions place undue emphasis on identifying the past transactions or events that gave rise to the asset, instead of focusing on whether the entity had access to the economic resource at the balance sheet date.*

After consulting technical experts, the Boards decided to consider the following working definition of an asset:

> *An asset of an entity is a present economic resource to which the entity has a right or other access that others do not have.*

This proposed definition uses a number of key terms, namely: *specifically present*; *economic resource*; and, *right or other access that others do not have*. The IASB and FASB have provided the following definitions of these key terms:

- *Present* means that on the date of the financial statements both the economic resource exists and the entity has the right or other access that others do not have.
- An *economic resource* is something that is scarce and capable of producing cash inflows or reducing cash outflows, directly or indirectly, alone or together with other economic resources. Economic resources that arise from contracts and other binding arrangements are unconditional promises and other abilities to require provision of economic resources, including through risk protection.
- A *right or other access that others do not have* enables the entity to use the economic resource, and its use by others can be precluded or limited. A right or other access that others do not have is enforceable by legal or equivalent means.

Whether the above definition replaces the existing definition of assets is something that will be revealed in future years. Certainly, the above definition seems to have some limitations of its own. What we need to appreciate is that, given that the definitions of other elements of accounting (equity, income and expenses) rely directly upon the definition of assets, any change to the definition of assets will potentially have a very significant impact on general purpose financial reporting.

> **liability** Defined in the IASB Conceptual Framework as 'a present obligation of the entity arising from past events, the settlement of which is expected to result in an outflow from the entity of resources embodying economic benefits'.

Definition and recognition of liabilities

The IASB Conceptual Framework defines a **liability** as 'a present obligation of the entity arising from past events, the settlement of which is expected to result in an outflow from the entity of resources embodying economic benefits'. As for the definition of assets, three key characteristics are identified in the definition of liabilities (paragraph 4.46) and these characteristics need to exist for recognition in the statement of financial position:

1. There must be an expected future disposition of economic benefits to other entities.
2. There must be a present obligation.
3. A past transaction or other event must have created the obligation.

As indicated, the definition of a liability just provided does not restrict 'liabilities' to situations where there is a legal obligation. Liabilities should also be recognised in certain situations where equity or usual business practice dictates that obligations to external parties currently exist.

Hence the liabilities that appear within an entity's statement of financial position might include obligations that are legally enforceable as well as obligations that are deemed to be equitable or constructive. When determining whether a liability exists, the intentions or actions of management need to be taken into account. That is, the actions or representations of the entity's management or governing body, or changes in the economic environment, directly influence the reasonable expectations or actions of those outside the entity and, although they have no legal entitlement, they might have other sanctions that leave the entity with no realistic alternative but to make certain future sacrifices of economic benefits. Such present obligations are sometimes called 'equitable obligations' or 'constructive obligations'. An equitable obligation is governed by social or moral sanctions or custom rather than legal sanctions. A constructive obligation is created, inferred or construed from the facts in a given situation rather than contracted by agreement with another entity or imposed by government.

Determining whether an equitable or a constructive obligation exists—and therefore whether a liability should be recognised in the statement of financial position—is often more difficult than identifying a legal obligation, and in most cases judgement is required to determine if an equitable or a constructive obligation exists. One consideration is whether the entity has any realistic alternative to making the future sacrifice of economic benefits. If the situation implies that there is no discretion, then a liability would be recognised. In cases where the entity retains discretion to avoid making any future sacrifice of economic benefits, a liability does not exist and is not recognised. It follows that a decision of the entity's management or governing body, of itself, is not sufficient for the recognition of a liability. Such a decision does not mark the inception of a present obligation since, in the absence of something more, the entity retains the ability to reverse the decision and thereby avoid the future sacrifice of economic benefits. For example, an entity's management or governing body may resolve that the entity will offer to repair a defect it has recently discovered in one of its products, even though the nature of the defect is such that the purchasers of the product would not expect the entity to do so. Until the entity makes public that offer, or commits itself in some other way to making the repairs, there is no present obligation, constructive or otherwise, beyond that of satisfying the existing statutory and contractual rights of customers.

As with the other elements of accounting when considering the recognition criteria, probability with respect to liabilities means 'more likely than less likely'. Hence, if Company A is assessed as having a 49 per cent probability of having to pay £100 million, while Company B has a 51 per cent probability of having to pay £1 million, Company A would show no liabilities on the face of the statement of financial position, while Company B would show £1 million. However, given the amount involved and the relatively high probability of payment, Company A would be required to disclose information about the potential obligation in the notes to its financial statements (shown as a contingent liability).

Apart from the consideration of probabilities, where a liability cannot be reliably measured but is potentially material, the liability should be disclosed within the **notes to the financial statements** (again, as a contingent liability).

> **notes to the financial statements** Further explanation or information relating to particular items appearing in financial statements.

As with the definition of assets, the IASB and FASB have recently suggested a revised definition of a liability. As IASB (2008b) states:

The Boards agreed that the current frameworks' existing liability definitions have the following shortcomings:

Some users misinterpret the terms 'expected' (IASB definition) and 'probable' (FASB definition) to mean that there must be a high likelihood of future outflow of economic benefits for the definition to be met; this excludes liability items with a low likelihood of a future outflow of economic benefits.

The definitions place too much emphasis on identifying the future outflow of economic benefits, instead of focusing on the item that presently exists, an economic obligation.

The definitions place undue emphasis on identifying the past transactions or events that gave rise to the liability, instead of focusing on whether the entity has an economic obligation at the balance sheet date. The Boards considered the following working definition of a liability:

A liability of an entity is a present economic obligation for which the entity is the obligor.

This proposed definition uses a number of key terms, specifically *present*, *economic obligation* and *obligor*. The IASB and FASB have provided the following definitions of these key terms:

- *Present* means that on the date of the financial statements both the economic obligation exists and the entity is the obligor.
- An *economic obligation* is an unconditional promise or other requirement to provide or forgo economic resources, including through risk protection.
- An entity is the *obligor* if the entity is required to bear the economic obligation and its requirement to bear the economic obligation is enforceable by legal or equivalent means.

Again, as with the proposed change to the definition of assets, the suggested change to the definition of liability could potentially have significant implications for financial reporting if it was ultimately incorporated within the revised conceptual framework. For example, the above definition could act to exclude constructive or equitable obligations that are not 'enforceable by legal or equivalent means'. This would be a major departure from existing practice. Further, and as with the definition of assets, any change to the definition of liabilities will potentially have a very significant impact on the expenses, income and equity of a reporting entity. Again, whether the above proposed definition ultimately becomes part of the revised conceptual framework is a matter for debate. It should be stressed that, while the IASB and FASB have identified perceived shortcomings in the current definition of liabilities (and assets, as we indicated earlier), their proposed definitions are just that—proposals for change, which might subsequently be rejected.

Definition and recognition of expenses

expenses Defined in the IASB Conceptual Framework as 'decreases in economic benefits during the accounting period in the form of outflows or depletions of assets or incurrences of liabilities that result in decreases of equity, other than those relating to distributions to equity participants'.

The definition of **expenses** is dependent upon the definitions given to assets and liabilities. The IASB Conceptual Framework provides a definition for expenses. It states:

Expenses are decreases in economic benefits during the accounting period in the form of outflows or depletions of assets or incurrences of liabilities that result in decreases in equity, other than those relating to distributions to equity participants.

Therefore, unless we understand what assets and liabilities are, we will not be able to understand what an expense is. Expenses may be considered to be transactions or events that cause reductions in the net assets or equity of the reporting entity, other than those caused by distributions to the owners. The usual tests relating to 'probability' and 'measurability' apply—as they do to all elements of financial statements.

If a resource is used up or damaged by an entity but that entity does not control the resource—that is, it is not an asset of the entity—to the extent that no liabilities or fines are imposed, no expenses will be recorded by the entity. For example, if an entity pollutes the environment but incurs no related fines, no expense will be acknowledged. This issue will be examined further later in this chapter. It is also addressed in Chapter 26.

Definition and recognition of income

income Defined in the IASB Conceptual Framework as 'increases in economic benefits during the accounting period in the form of inflows or enhancements of assets or decreases of liabilities that result in increases in equity, other than those relating to contributions from equity participants'.

As with expenses, the definition of **income** is dependent upon the definitions given to assets and liabilities. The IASB Conceptual Framework defines income as:

increases in economic benefits during the accounting period in the form of inflows or enhancements of assets or decreases of liabilities that result in increases in equity, other than those relating to contributions from equity participants.

Income can therefore be considered to relate to transactions or events that cause an increase in the net assets of the reporting entity, other than increases in net assets that arise as a result of owner contributions.

Income can be recognised from normal trading relations, as well as from non-reciprocal transfers such as grants, donations, bequests or where liabilities are forgiven. Consistent with the recognition of all elements of financial statements, income is to be recognised when, and only when:

(a) it is probable that the inflow or other enhancement or saving in outflows of future economic benefits has occurred; and
(b) the inflow or other enhancement or saving in outflows of future economic benefits can be measured reliably.

It should be noted that the IASB Conceptual Framework draws a distinction between 'revenues' and 'gains'. The category of 'income' consists of *both* revenues and gains. Under the IASB Conceptual Framework, 'revenue' arises in the course of the ordinary activities of an entity and is referred to by a variety of different names, including sales, fees, interest, dividends, royalties and rent. 'Gains' represent other items that meet the definition of income and might, or might not, arise in the course of the ordinary activities of an enterprise. Gains include, for example, those arising on the disposal of non-current assets. Some measure of professional judgement will be involved in determining whether a component of income should be classified as 'revenue' or as a 'gain'.

Revenue is obviously a crucial number to users of the financial statements in assessing a reporting entity's performance and prospects. The IASB and the FASB together initiated a joint project to clarify the principles for recognising revenue from 'contracts with customers'. It applies to all contracts with customers except leases, financial instruments and insurance contracts. As part of the project, an Exposure Draft *Revenue from Contracts with Customers* was released in November 2011. While this Exposure Draft is discussed in depth within Chapter 13 of this book, at this point we can summarise and state that the Exposure Draft adopts a view that revenue recognition should be consistent with the IASB Conceptual Framework guidance. The IASB and FASB have embraced a view that revenue recognition should be a direct function of whether goods and services have been transferred to the *control* of the customer (and not be a function of who holds the risks and rewards of ownership of the asset—something that has been adopted in some accounting standards as the basis for determining whether revenue should be recognised). As paragraph 6.7 of IASB (2008a) states:

> *An entity satisfies a performance obligation when it transfers goods and services to a customer. That principle, which the boards think can be applied consistently to all contracts with customers, is the core of the boards' proposed model for a revenue recognition standard.*

Definition of equity

Paragraph 49(c) of the IASB Conceptual Framework defines **equity** as 'the residual interest in the assets of the entity after deducting all its liabilities'. The residual interest is a claim or right to the net assets of the reporting entity. As a residual interest, equity ranks after liabilities in terms of a claim against the assets of a reporting entity. Consistent with the definitions of income and expenses, the definition of equity is directly a function of the definitions of assets and liabilities. Given that equity represents a residual interest in the assets of an entity, the amount disclosed as equity will correspond to the difference between the amounts assigned to assets and liabilities. As such, the criteria for the recognition of assets and liabilities, in turn, directly govern the recognition of equity. There is no need for a separate recognition criteria for equity.

> **equity** residual interest in the assets of the entity after deduction of its liabilities. The residual interest is a claim or right to the net assets of the reporting entity.

2.7 Measurement principles

While recognition of the elements of financial reporting require that they should be measurable with reasonable accuracy (as well as being 'probable'), conceptual frameworks have tended to provide very limited prescription in relation to measurement issues. Assets and liabilities are often (and certainly in practice under IASs/IFRSs) measured in a variety of ways depending upon the class of assets or liabilities being considered and, given the way assets and liabilities are defined, this has direct implications for reported profits. For example, liabilities are frequently recorded at present value, face value or on some other basis, depending upon the type of liability in question. In relation to assets, these are measured in various ways—for example, inventory is to be measured at the lower of cost and net realisable value; some non-current assets such as property, plant and equipment can be measured at historical cost less a provision for depreciation or can also be measured at fair value; while other assets such as financial assets are to be measured at fair value. The multiplicity of measurement principles currently in use has resulted in us using what is often referred to as a 'mixed attribute accounting model'. This is despite the efforts of many accounting standard-setters and accounting researchers who have argued that it would be more conceptually sound for a single basis of measurement to be applied—for example, measuring all assets based on fair values.

As already indicated a number of times in this chapter, the IASB and the FASB are currently engaged in joint efforts to develop a new, refined conceptual framework. In relation to measurement, the FASB and IASB (2005, p. 12) state:

> *Measurement is one of the most underdeveloped areas of the two frameworks ... Both frameworks (the IASB and FASB Frameworks) contain lists of measurement attributes used in practice. The lists are broadly consistent, comprising historical cost, current cost, gross or net realisable (settlement) value, current market value, and present value of expected future cash flows. Both frameworks indicate that use of different measurement attributes is expected to continue. However, neither provides guidance on how to choose between the listed measurement attributes or consider other theoretical possibilities. In other words, the frameworks lack fully developed measurement concepts ... The long-standing unresolved controversy about which measurement attribute to adopt—particularly between historical-price and current-price measures—and the unresolved puzzle of unit of account are likely to make measurement one of the most challenging parts of this project.*

A further point on the Conceptual Framework is that although very limited work has been undertaken on measurement issues, it is possible that the guidelines set down within future chapters or sections of it might lead to a change in thinking about how assets and liabilities should be measured and represented.

At present, assets and liabilities are measured in a variety of ways, depending on the class of assets or liabilities being considered. Subsequent releases of conceptual framework projects will need to consider such questions as whether liabilities should be recorded at present value, face value or on some other basis. In relation to assets, there are various ways in which these can be measured—on the basis of historical costs, current replacement costs, current selling prices, present value and so forth. Whether the component of the Conceptual Framework that addresses measurement matters will opt for a single method to value all assets is yet to be determined. Certainly, such a change would represent a radical departure from current GAAP. Although the IASB Conceptual Framework has not stipulated a preferred approach to measuring assets or liabilities, it is interesting to note that many recently released accounting standards have adopted a fair value approach to measuring the various assets.

Phase C of the joint IASB and FASB Conceptual Framework Project is to address measurement issues. In this work, the IASB and FASB have identified nine potential measurement bases: *past entry price, past exit price, modified past amount, current entry price, current exit price, current equilibrium price, value in use, future entry price* and *future exit price*. However, it is expected that it will be a number of years before any conclusion is reached about the most appropriate measurement basis or bases for assets and liabilities. As at early 2012 it appeared that work on developing the measurement component of the Conceptual Framework had stalled. Nevertheless the website of the IASB has indicated that when ultimately completed, the measurement chapter of the Conceptual Framework should:

- list and describe possible measurements;
- arrange or classify the measurements in a manner that facilitates standard-setting decisions;
- describe the advantages and disadvantages of each measurement in terms of the qualitative characteristics of useful financial information; and
- discuss at a conceptual level how qualitative characteristics and cost constraints should be considered together in identifying an appropriate measurement approach.

In relation to the issue of measurement, it should be acknowledged that in 2011 the IASB released the accounting standard IFRS 13 *Fair Value Measurement*. While this standard does not prescribe when fair value measurements should be applied (as might be the case within a fully developed conceptual framework), it provides guidance on how fair value shall be determined in those cases where fair value measurement is required by particular accounting standards. IFRS 13 provides:

- a common definition of fair value;
- a common method for measuring fair value; and
- common requirements for disclosures about fair value measurements.

IFRS 13 acts to amend pre-existing fair value provisions within other IASB accounting standards and compiles all fair value measurement and disclosure requirements within a single accounting standard. As already indicated, the new accounting standard does not change which items in the financial statement must, or may be, measured at fair value. Rather, this role is retained within other accounting standards.

The new accounting standard acts to change the definition of fair value used in various accounting standards that require or permit fair value measurements. The new definition of fair value used in IFRS 13 is:

The price that would be received to sell an asset or paid to transfer a liability in an orderly transaction between market participants at the measurement date.

This definition requires that fair value measurements be based on the exit prices associated with statement of financial position items.

2.8 A critical review of conceptual frameworks

There will be many parties who disagree with the points that follow. You will need to consider the merits of the respective arguments.

Some of the criticisms raised relate to the fundamental objectives of conceptual frameworks. As we know, according to the IASB Conceptual Framework, the objective of general purpose financial reporting is to 'provide financial information about the reporting entity that is useful to existing and potential equity investors, lenders and other creditors in making decisions about providing resources to the entity'.

From this, it can perhaps be concluded that annual reports presented by corporations—and these reports would incorporate general purpose financial statements—should be primarily economic in focus. Does this mean that social and environmental issues—such as an organisation's safety record, environmental performance, employee training programmes and the like—should not be included in the annual report? If this is the position taken by those responsible for formulating the contents of a conceptual framework, it would appear to be inconsistent with the views espoused by many accounting academics (for example, Rubenstein 1992; Gray and Bebbington 2001; Gray *et al.* 1996). The dissenting view is that organisations should be accountable for both their economic and their social and environmental performance. Perhaps those responsible for developing the IASB Conceptual Framework believe that evidence of social and environmental accountability is either not necessary, or perhaps can best be provided in places other than general purpose financial statements.

There are many philosophical positions taken in relation to the general/overall responsibilities of business. The view of famous economist Milton Friedman—perhaps an extreme one—is that:

> there is one and only one social responsibility of business—to use its resources and engage in activities designed to increase its profits so long as it stays within the rules of the game, which is to say, engages in open and free competition without deception or fraud.

(1962, reported in Mathews 1993, p. 10)

An individual's view of a business's responsibilities directly impacts on their perceptions of business accountability. Those responsible for developing the Conceptual Framework do appear to take a restricted view of the accountabilities of business (with the primary audience being identified as existing and potential investors, lenders and other creditors)—which is perhaps not too different to the perspective that might have been adopted by Friedman.

In determining whether an entity is a reporting entity, current work being undertaken by the IASB provides that individual reporting entities be identified by reference to the existence of users who are dependent on general purpose financial reports for information for making and evaluating resource-allocation decisions. As indicated previously in this chapter, in a recent exposure draft released by the IASB, a reporting entity is defined as:

> a circumscribed area of economic activities whose financial information has the potential to be useful to existing and potential equity investors, lenders and other creditors who cannot directly obtain the information they need in making decisions about providing resources to the entity and in assessing whether management and the governing board of that entity have made efficient and effective use of the resources provided.

Is it reasonable that the need for information to enable informed decisions 'about providing resources to the entity' should be the only, or dominant, thing to consider in determining whether an entity is a reporting entity and therefore required to produce general purpose financial statements?

Being principally economic in focus, general purpose financial statements typically ignore transactions or events that have not involved market transactions or an exchange of property rights. That is, transactions or events that cannot be linked to a 'cost' or a 'market price' are not recognised. For example, a great deal of recent literature has been critical of traditional financial accounting for its failure to recognise the damage to the environment caused by business (see Rubenstein 1992; Gray *et al.* 1996; Deegan and Rankin 1997). Let us consider a fairly extreme example. Applying generally accepted accounting principles (GAAP), if the environmental consequences of a business's operations were such that they led to a major reduction in local water quality—thereby killing all local sea creatures and coastal vegetation—reported profits would not be directly affected unless fines or other related cash flows were incurred. That is, no externalities would be recognised, and the reported assets/profits of the organisation would not be affected. This is because the waterways are not *controlled* by the entity (and remember, according to the IASB Conceptual Framework's definition of assets, *control* must be established before something is deemed to be an asset of an entity), and therefore their use (or abuse) is not recorded by financial accounting systems. Adopting **conventional financial reporting practices**, consistent with the IASB Conceptual Framework, the performance of such a polluting organisation could, depending upon the financial transactions undertaken, be portrayed as being very successful.

What must be borne in mind by the users of general purpose financial statements, however, is that the financial information included within the statements reflects only the financial performance of the entity as determined by applying the rules incorporated within relevant accounting standards; they do not provide a means of assessing the social or environmental performance of the entity. This in itself is seen by a number of accounting researchers to be a fundamental limitation of accounting.

conventional financial reporting practices Represented by the set of generally accepted accounting principles in place at a point in time. They rely heavily on historical-cost accounting and associated doctrines, such as the doctrine of conservatism.

Following on from the above point, it has been argued that focusing on economic performance in itself further reinforces the importance of economic performance relative to various levels of social and environmental performance. Several writers such as Hines (1988) and Gray and Bebbington (2001) have argued that the accounting profession can play a big part in influencing what forms of social conduct are acceptable to the broader community. Accounting can both *reflect* and *construct* social expectations. For example, if profits and associated financial data are promoted as the *best measure* of organisational success, it could be argued that both the organisation and the community will focus on activities that affect this measure. If accountants embrace other types of performance indicator, including those that relate to the environment and to social factors, this might, conceivably, raise people's expectations about organisational performance. Nevertheless, at present, profitability as indicated by the output of the accounting system is typically used as a guide to an organisation's success.

A review of the financial press indicates that it, too, generally uses financial performance indicators as a guide to the success and health of an organisation. For example, the respected daily financial paper the *Financial Times* each day reports LSE listed companies' earnings per share and price–earnings ratios. Having said this about financial performance indicators, it must be acknowledged that many organisations do provide voluntary social and environmental disclosures within their annual reports, or within stand-alone corporate social responsibility, or sustainability, reports. This practice of reporting will be considered in greater depth in Chapter 26.

Another criticism of conceptual frameworks for accounting is that they represent simply a codification of existing practice (Hines 1989), putting in place a series of documents that describe existing practice rather than prescribing an 'ideal' or logically derived approach to accounting. If the Conceptual Framework is considered to represent a codification of GAAP, can such principles logically be used as a rationale for selecting between alternative accounting methods? Perhaps not. History seems to indicate that proposals for major shifts in current practices are unlikely to succeed. The UK standard, SSAP 16 *Current Cost Accounting* is an example of how significant changes to existing accounting practice were not accepted in practice. This standard was issued in 1980 but withdrawn in 1988 because of lack of support by preparers.

It has been argued that conceptual frameworks have been used as devices to legitimise the ongoing existence of the accounting profession. It is argued that they provide a means of increasing the ability of a profession to self-regulate, thereby counteracting the possibility of government intervention (Hines 1991, p. 328).

Hines (1989) suggests that conceptual frameworks have been developed when accounting professions have been under threat, and that they are a strategic manoeuvre to provide legitimacy to standard-setting bodies during periods of competition or threatened government intervention. In supporting her case, Hines refers to the work undertaken by the Canadian Institute of Chartered Accountants (CICA). CICA had done very little throughout the 1980s in relation to its Conceptual Framework Project. It had begun to develop a framework in approximately 1980, which Hines claims was 'a time of pressures for reform and criticisms of accounting standard-setting in Canada' (1989, p. 88). However, interest waned until another Canadian professional accounting body, the Certified General Accountants Association, through its Accounting Standards Authority of Canada, started to develop a conceptual framework in 1986. This was deemed to represent a threat to CICA, 'who were motivated into action'.

Although the criticisms of conceptual frameworks as set out here are varied, the discussion consistently reflects the political dimensions of the accounting standard-setting process.

2.9 The conceptual framework as a normative theory of accounting

As the following chapter explains, theories can be classified in a number of ways. One way of classifying theories is to label them as either 'positive' or 'normative' theories. While the next chapter covers this issue in some depth, we can briefly point out here that a positive theory of accounting is a theory that seeks to *explain* and *predict* particular accounting practices. That is, a positive theory of accounting will provide explanations of some of the outcomes that might follow the release of a particular accounting requirement (such as an accounting standard), or perhaps predictions about which entities are likely to favour particular accounting methods or adopt particular accounting methods when there are alternatives. By contrast, a normative theory of accounting provides prescription about what accounting methods an organisation *should* adopt. Hence, the difference can be summarised by saying that a positive theory of accounting attempts to *explain* or *predict* accounting practice, whereas a normative theory of accounting *prescribes* particular accounting practice. Conceptual frameworks can be classified as normative theories of accounting as they provide guidance (prescription) to people involved in preparing general purpose financial statements.

SUMMARY

In this chapter we considered the history of international conceptual frameworks. We learned that the role of a conceptual framework includes identifying the scope and objectives of financial reporting; identifying the qualitative characteristics that financial information should possess; and defining the elements of accounting and their respective recognition criteria. A number of benefits of conceptual frameworks were identified, including accounting standards being more consistent and logical; more efficient development of accounting standards; accounting standard-setters being accountable for the content of accounting standards; and conceptual frameworks providing useful guidance in the absence of an accounting standard that deals with a specific transaction or event.

The chapter discussed the concept of the 'reporting entity' and noted that if an organisation is deemed to be a reporting entity (which would be determined by whether people exist who rely upon general purpose financial statements for the purposes of decisions relating to the allocation of resources), it is to release financial statements that comply with accounting standards.

A number of qualitative characteristics were identified as being important in terms of financial information. Two fundamental qualitative characteristics were explained: relevance and representational faithfulness. A further four 'enhancing' qualitative characteristics were also identified: comparability, verifiability, timeliness and understandability. The concept of materiality was also introduced and we learned that materiality is a threshold concept which in turn assists a reporting entity to decide whether particular information needs to be separately disclosed.

The chapter discussed the five elements of accounting: assets, liabilities, income, expenses and equity. We learned that the definitions of income and expenses relied directly upon the definitions given to assets and liabilities. We also learned that the recognition criteria of the respective elements of accounting relied upon judgements about probability and measurability.

We concluded the chapter with a critical analysis of conceptual frameworks.

KEY TERMS

asset 36
conceptual framework 24
control (assets) 37
conventional financial reporting practices 43
equity 41
expenses 40
future economic benefits 37
income 40
liability 38
notes to the financial statements 39
reporting entity 28

END-OF-CHAPTER EXERCISE

Once you have read this chapter you should be able to answer the following:
1 What is the difference in role between the IASB Conceptual Framework and accounting standards? **LO 2.1**
2 What are the benefits that are generated as a result of having a conceptual framework? **LO 2.2**
3 What are the definition and recognition criteria of the five elements of accounting? **LO 2.9**
4 What is the difference between revenues and gains? **LO 2.9**
5 What 'fundamental' and 'enhancing' qualitative characteristics should financial information possess? **LO 2.7**
6 What role does 'materiality' have with respect to deciding whether particular financial information should be disclosed? **LO 2.8**

REVIEW QUESTIONS

1 What is a conceptual framework of accounting? **LO 2.1**
2 What is a general purpose financial statement? **LO 2.5**
3 What is a reporting entity and what factors would you consider in determining whether an entity is a reporting entity? **LO 2.6**

4   What is the history of international conceptual frameworks?   **LO** 2.4

5   Do we need a conceptual framework in Europe? Why?   **LO** 2.2

6   Should the general purpose financial statements of a company be compiled in a manner that is understandable to all investors?   **LO** 2.5

7   What is the difference between revenues and gains and do you think it is useful to subdivide income into revenues and gains? Explain your answer.   **LO** 2.9

8   What is an enhancing qualitative characteristic, and what role do enhancing qualitative characteristics have relative to the role of fundamental qualitative characteristics?   **LO** 2.7

9   What does it mean for financial information to be 'representationally faithful'?   **LO** 2.7

10   Who are the perceived recipients of general purpose financial statements and what knowledge of financial accounting are they presumed to have?   **LO** 2.5

11   If directors of a large listed British company consider that the application of a particular accounting standard is not appropriate to their circumstances, what should they do? Do they have to comply with accounting standards?   **LO** 2.2

12   What force of law does the IASB Conceptual Framework have?   **LO** 2.2

13   The IASB and the FASB are currently undertaking a joint project to develop a revised conceptual project. Explain why any changes they make in the definition of assets and liabilities will subsequently have implications for the profits of reporting entities.   **LO** 2.11

14   Why don't we need separate recognition criteria for equity?   **LO** 2.9

15   Why is it preferable to have a well-developed conceptual framework prior to the development of accounting standards?   **LO** 2.3

16   Define the elements and recognition criteria of financial statements as per the IASB *Conceptual Framework for Financial Reporting*.   **LO** 2.9

17   What do 'probable' and 'measured reliability' mean with respect to the recognition of the elements of financial accounting?   **LO** 2.10

18   Define 'relevance' and 'faithful representation'. Is there a trade-off between the two?   **LO** 2.7

19   Identify and explain some of the perceived shortcomings of the IASB Conceptual Framework.   **LO** 2.12

20   How would you determine whether an item is material?   **LO** 2.8

CHALLENGING QUESTIONS

21   What is a true and fair override and does it currently exist within the UK/Ireland? What are some of the arguments for and against including a true and fair override in the Companies Act?   **LO** 2.7

22   The *Application* section of accounting standards typically states that the respective accounting standard is to be applied to the extent that the application is considered to be 'material'. Explain what material means, including how you determine whether an item is material. In doing so, you should consider the materiality of an item in terms of the statement of financial position, the statement of comprehensive income and the statement of cash flows.   **LO** 2.8

23   An organisation has received an interest-free loan from its parent company with no set repayment date. Should the 'loan' be disclosed as debt or as equity, and how should it be measured?   **LO** 2.10

24   As at the end of the reporting period Ripslash plc has gross assets of £4,000,000, total revenue of £11,000,000 and 54 full-time employees who do not own shares in the organisation. Is Ripslash plc a reporting entity?   **LO** 2.5, 2.6

25   Possies plc considers that its most valuable asset is its employees—yet it has to leave them off the statement of financial position. Explain this situation.   **LO** 2.12

26   For each of the independent situations identified below, consider and conclude whether the entity is required by the Companies Act to prepare financial statements and, if so, whether it is a 'reporting entity'. You should also note the reporting implications of your decision.   **LO** 2.5, 2.6

   (a)   ABC Pty Ltd is a small proprietary company. The shareholders are Mr and Mrs ABC, who also manage the company's day-to-day operations. The company's bankers, The Bank, receive monthly management accounts, budgeted cash-flow information, and the year-end statutory financial statements.

   (b)   F Pty Ltd is a large company—one of only two in the UK—involved in the manufacture of widgets. Although the shares are tightly held—by family members—the company employs more than 200 staff. The company has a small number of major suppliers. The company's sole banker receives the company's statutory financial statements under its borrowing agreement.

(c) E Trust is a private trust wherein up to a maximum of 30 members may deposit amounts to be invested in blue-chip equities. Members' funds consist of units of £1 each. Quarterly reports are produced, which disclose the market value of the trust assets and the values of each member's entitlements.

REFERENCES

ACCOUNTING STANDARDS STEERING COMMITTEE, *The Corporate Report*, ICAEW, London, 1975.

BOOTH, B., 'The Conceptual Framework as a Coherent System for the Development of Accounting Standards', *Abacus*, vol. 39, no. 3, 2003, pp. 310–24.

DEEGAN, C.M. & RANKIN, M., 'The Materiality of Environmental Information to Users of Accounting Reports', *Accounting, Auditing and Accountability Journal*, vol. 10, no. 4, 1997, pp. 562–83.

FINANCIAL ACCOUNTING STANDARDS BOARD, *Project Update: Conceptual Framework—Phase B: Elements and Recognition*, Norwalk, CT, FASB, 2008.

FINANCIAL ACCOUNTING STANDARDS BOARD & INTERNATIONAL ACCOUNTING STANDARDS BOARD, *Revisiting the Concepts: A New Conceptual Framework Project*, Norwalk, CT, FASB, 2005.

GRAY, R. & BEBBINGTON, J., *Accounting for the Environment*, London, Sage, 2001.

GRAY, R., OWEN, D. & ADAMS, C., *Accounting and Accountability*, London, Prentice Hall, 1996.

HICKS, J.R., *Value and Capital*, 2nd edn, Oxford, Clarendon Press, 1946.

HINES, R.D., 'Financial Accounting in Communicating Reality: We Construct Reality', *Accounting, Organizations and Society*, vol. 13, no. 3, 1988, pp. 251–61.

HINES, R.D., 'Financial Accounting Knowledge, Conceptual Framework Projects and the Social Construction of the Accounting Profession', *Accounting, Auditing and Accountability Journal*, vol. 2, no. 2, 1989, pp. 72–92.

HINES, R.D., 'The FASB's Conceptual Framework: Financial Accounting and the Maintenance of the Social World', *Accounting Organizations and Society*, vol. 16, no. 4, 1991, pp. 313–31.

INTERNATIONAL ACCOUNTING STANDARDS BOARD, *Exposure Draft of an Improved Conceptual Framework for Financial Reporting*, London, IASB, 2008a.

INTERNATIONAL ACCOUNTING STANDARDS BOARD, *Discussion Paper—Preliminary Views on an improved Conceptual Framework for Financial Reporting*, London, IASB, 2008b.

INTERNATIONAL ACCOUNTING STANDARDS BOARD, *Exposure Draft ED2010/2: Conceptual Framework for Financial Reporting: The Reporting Entity*, London, IASB, March 2010.

INTERNATIONAL ACCOUNTING STANDARDS BOARD, *Conceptual Framework for Financial Reporting 2010*, London, IASB, September 2010.

INTERNATIONAL ACCOUNTING STANDARDS COMMITTEE, *Framework for the Preparation and Presentation of Financial Statements*, London, IASC, July 1989.

LOFTUS, J.A., 'The CF and Accounting Standards: The Persistence of Discrepancies', *Abacus*, vol. 39, no. 3, 2003, pp. 298–309.

MATHEWS, M.R., *Socially Responsible Accounting*, London, Chapman and Hall, 1993.

RUBENSTEIN, D.B., 'Bridging the Gap Between Green Accounting and Blank Ink', *Accounting Organizations and Society*, vol. 17, no. 5, 1992, pp. 501–8.

WATTS, R.L. & ZIMMERMAN, J.L., *Positive Accounting Theory*, Englewood Cliffs, NJ, Prentice Hall, 1986.

WELLS, M., 'Forum: The Accounting Conceptual Framework', *Abacus*, vol. 39, no. 3, 2003, pp. 273–8.

PART 2

Theories of Accounting

Part content

Chapter 3

Theories of Financial Accounting

Learning objectives

Upon completing this chapter readers should:

LO1 understand what constitutes a 'theory' and appreciate why students of financial accounting should know about various theories of accounting;

LO2 be able to describe various normative and positive theories of financial accounting;

LO3 appreciate that there is no single unified theory of accounting;

LO4 understand what constitutes an 'agency relationship' and be aware of the major aspects of 'agency theory';

LO5 understand the basis of Positive Accounting Theory;

LO6 understand that from a Positive Accounting perspective, accounting-based measures are often used to resolve conflicts between managers and owners, and managers and debt-holders;

LO7 understand the various pressures and motivations that might have an effect on the accounting methods selected by an organisation;

LO8 understand that the choice of alternative accounting methods can often be explained from either an 'efficiency perspective' or an 'opportunistic perspective';

LO9 understand the meaning of 'political costs' and how the choice of particular accounting methods might be used as a strategy to reduce accounting methods;

LO10 understand what is meant by 'creative accounting' and why it might occur;

LO11 be aware of the normative theories of current cost accounting, exit price accounting and deprival value accounting;

LO12 know what a 'systems-based theory' is and understand the basic tenets of stakeholder theory, legitimacy theory and institutional theory as they can be applied to explaining particular accounting disclosures; and

LO13 understand that there are theories that explain why regulation—such as accounting regulation—is introduced and understand the basic tenets of public interest theory, capture theory and the economic interest group theory of regulation.

3.1 Introduction to theories of financial accounting

In the previous two chapters we discussed the bodies responsible for regulating general purpose financial reporting. We also discussed the IASB Conceptual Framework Project and the current activities being undertaken by the IASB and FASB to develop a new conceptual framework. As will be demonstrated in this chapter, a conceptual framework can be described as a *normative theory of accounting*. It prescribes, within a particular framework, the objectives and the qualitative characteristics that financial information *should* possess if it is to fulfil the objectives (as defined within the framework) of general purpose financial reporting. Ultimately, a conceptual framework will also provide guidance on how to measure the elements of accounting.

In this chapter we explore some of the many theories—in addition to conceptual frameworks—that relate to financial accounting. We will see that different accounting theories have different objectives. For example, we will discuss theories that seek to:

- explain and predict which accounting methods or approaches management is likely to select when it has alternatives from which to choose (these theories are commonly referred to as positive theories);
- prescribe which accounting methods should be used in particular circumstances (these theories are commonly referred to as normative theories, the conceptual framework being an example of a normative theory); and
- explain how or why accounting regulation is developed (with some theories arguing that accounting regulation is developed in the public interest and other economics-based theories promoting the view that accounting regulation is introduced to serve the interests of some parties at the expense of those of others).

The theory overview in this chapter will provide readers with knowledge of some of the various accounting theories that have been developed. At present there is no universal agreement on the *objective*, *role* and *scope* of accounting and, consistent with this, there is no single accounting theory that is universally accepted. In this chapter, we will demonstrate that in the decade or so leading up to the 1970s the notable accounting theories being developed were predominantly *normative* in nature; that is, they identified what accounting techniques and methods *should* be applied by reporting entities. Reflecting the higher inflation rates of the time, most of these normative theories were concerned with providing guidelines on how to account for assets and expenses in times of rising prices.

The attention of many accounting researchers continues to focus on the development of normative theories of accounting, such as the conceptual framework. However, in the 1970s a number of accounting researchers developed a theory of accounting known as Positive Accounting Theory, which seeks to *explain* and *predict* the selection of particular accounting policies and their impact, rather than *prescribing* what *should* be done. Positive Accounting Theory therefore has a different emphasis from normative accounting theories.

After reading this chapter, you will realise that, among accounting researchers, there is a great deal of disagreement on the role of accounting and of accounting theory; for example, some people argue that theory should *explain* practice, while others argue that it should *direct* or *guide* practice. These contrasting types of theory have generated considerable debate within accounting literature, and this debate is ongoing.

3.2 Why discuss theories in a book such as this?

The study of financial accounting can be approached in a number of different ways. One approach adopted in some financial accounting textbooks is for the authors to provide an explanation of the rules incorporated within particular financial accounting standards and then illustrate how to apply these rules. That is, a number of texts are predominantly procedural in nature, failing to reflect any deeper thinking about the impact of particular accounting standards and other pronouncements. For example, many financial accounting textbooks elect not to discuss how readers of financial statements might react to the disclosures required by the standards; whether newly mandated disclosures will have positive or negative effects on the organisation; how particular stakeholders affect the disclosure decisions of organisations; and how particular accounting disclosures will influence an organisation's relationships with other parties within society. In contrast to such texts, we believe that not only is it useful to discuss the requirements of the various accounting standards—as we do in depth in the following chapters—but that it is important to provide frameworks—as we do in this chapter—within which to consider the implications of organisations making particular accounting disclosures, whether voluntarily or as a result of a particular mandate. We also think it is useful to consider the various pressures, many of which are political in nature, which influence the accounting standard-setting environment.

Of course, the balance of the material in this book could be studied without reading this chapter. However, because the impact of financial accounting resonates throughout society we believe this chapter provides you with the necessary background to understand the possible implications of an organisation making particular disclosures. The theories in this chapter also provide the basis for understanding the various pressures that drive organisations to make particular disclosures, even in the absence of disclosure requirements pertaining to particular transactions and events. By reading this chapter, together with the material in other chapters of this book, we believe that you will gain a greater understanding of the implications of various accounting standards and other disclosure requirements.

3.3 Definition of theory

Before we consider some of the theories of accounting, it might be useful to discuss what we mean by a **theory**. There is no one definitive meaning of the term 'theory'. The *Macquarie Dictionary* provides a useful definition: 'a coherent group of propositions used as principles of explanation for a class of phenomena'.

> **theory** Coherent set of hypothetical, conceptual and pragmatic principles forming the frame of reference for a field of inquiry.

The accounting researcher Hendriksen (1970, p. 1) defines a theory as 'a coherent set of hypothetical, conceptual and pragmatic principles forming the general framework of reference for a field of inquiry'.

Hendriksen's definition is very similar to the US Financial Accounting Standards Board's definition of their Conceptual Framework Project, discussed in Chapter 1: 'a coherent system of interrelated objectives and fundamentals that is expected to lead to consistent standards'.

It is generally accepted that a 'theory' is much more than simply an idea, or a 'hunch', which is how the term is used in some contexts (for instance, we often hear people say that they have a 'theory' about why something might have occurred when they mean they have a 'hunch').

Accounting theories typically either *explain* and *predict* accounting practice, or they *prescribe* specific accounting practice. As indicated above, such theories are typically referred to as *positive* and *normative* theories respectively. According to Henderson *et al.* (1992, p. 326):

> *A positive theory begins with some assumption(s) and, through logical deduction, enables some prediction(s) to be made about the way things will be. If the prediction is sufficiently accurate when tested against observations of reality, then the story is regarded as having provided an explanation of why things are as they are. For example, in climatology, a positive theory of rainfall may yield a prediction that, if certain conditions are met, then heavy rainfall will be observed. In economics, a positive theory of prices may yield a prediction that, if certain conditions are met, then rapidly rising prices will be observed. Similarly, a positive theory of accounting may yield a prediction that, if certain conditions are met, then particular accounting practices will be observed.*

Because positive theories seek to explain and predict particular phenomena, they are often developed and supported on the basis of observations (that is, they are *empirically based*). The view is that by making numerous observations we will be better placed to predict what will happen in the future (for example, we might study many managers within a particular industry to predict what accounting methods they will elect to use in particular circumstances).

By contrast, normative theories are sometimes referred to as prescriptive theories, because they seek to inform others about particular practices that *should* be followed to achieve particular outcomes. For example, a normative accounting theory might, given certain key assumptions about the nature and objective of accounting, prescribe how assets *should* be valued for financial statement purposes. The prescriptions about what *should* be done might represent significant departures from current accounting practice (for example, for many years Raymond Chambers (1955, 1993) promoted a theory of accounting that prescribed that assets should be valued at market value—at a time when entities were predominantly using historical cost). Therefore, it is not appropriate to assess the validity, or otherwise, of a normative theory on the basis of whether entities are actually using one method or another, although this is a common method of evaluating or testing a positive theory. A normative theory might prescribe a radical departure from current practice.

The dichotomy of *positive* and *normative* accounting theory provides a useful basis for the following discussion.

3.4 Positive Accounting Theory

The name **Positive Accounting Theory** can in itself cause confusion. As outlined above, a positive theory is one that explains and predicts a particular phenomenon. Positive Accounting Theory (PAT) seeks to explain and predict accounting practice. It does not seek to prescribe particular actions. Watts and Zimmerman (1986, p. 7) state:

> **Positive Accounting Theory (PAT)** Seeks to explain and predict accounting practice.

> *[PAT] is concerned with explaining [accounting] practice. It is designed to explain and predict which firms will and which firms will not use a particular [accounting] method . . . but it says nothing as to which method a firm should use.*

According to Watts (1995, p. 334), use of the term 'positive research' was popularised in economics by Friedman (1953) and was used to distinguish research that sought to *explain* and *predict* from research that aimed to provide *prescription*. Positive Accounting Theory, the theory that was popularised by Watts and Zimmerman, is one of several positive theories of accounting. Legitimacy Theory, Institutional Theory and Stakeholder Theory, all discussed in this chapter, are other examples of positive theories. Legitimacy Theory *predicts* that, in certain circumstances, organisations will make information disclosures in an effort to restore the *legitimacy* of the organisation. These other positive theories (Legitimacy Theory, Institutional Theory and Stakeholder Theory) are not grounded in classical economics theory, as is the case with Positive Accounting Theory.

We can refer to the general class of theories that attempt to *explain* and *predict* accounting practice in lowercase letters (that is, as positive theories of accounting), and we can refer to Watts and Zimmerman's particular positive theory of accounting as Positive Accounting Theory (that is, with initial letters in upper case). Hence, while it might be confusing, we must remember that Watts and Zimmerman's Positive Accounting Theory is one specific example of a positive theory of accounting. This confusion might not have arisen had Watts and Zimmerman elected to adopt a different name (or 'trademark') for their particular theory.

Normative accounting theorists have criticised PAT because it does not provide practitioners with guidance, even though it does attempt to explain the possible economic implications of selecting particular accounting policies.

PAT focuses on the relationships between the various individuals involved in providing resources to an organisation. This could be the relationship between the owners (as suppliers of equity capital) and the managers (as suppliers of managerial labour), or between the managers and the firm's debt providers. Many relationships involve the delegation of decision making from one party (the principal) to another party (the agent): this is referred to as an **agency relationship**. The delegation of decision-making authority can lead to a loss of efficiency and, consequently, increased costs. For example, if the owner (the principal) delegates decision-making authority to a manager (the agent), it is possible that the manager will not work as hard as the owner would, given that the manager does not share directly in the results of the organisation. Any loss of profits brought about because the manager underperforms is considered to be a cost of decision-making delegation within this agency relationship—an agency cost. The agency costs that arise as a result of delegating decision-making authority from the owner to the manager are referred to in PAT as *agency costs* of equity.

> **agency relationship** Involving the delegation of decision making from the principal to an agent.

PAT investigates how particular contractual arrangements, many based on accounting numbers, can be put in place to minimise agency costs. One of the most frequently cited expositions of PAT is provided in Watts and Zimmerman (1978). In developing PAT, Watts and Zimmerman relied heavily upon the work of a number of other authors, notably Jensen and Meckling (1976) and Gordon (1964).

PAT, developed by Watts and Zimmerman and others, is based significantly on particular assumptions and methods used in the economics literature and, in particular, on the central assumptions of economics that all individual action is driven by *self-interest* and that individuals will act in an *opportunistic manner* to increase their wealth. Notions of loyalty and morality are not incorporated within the theory (nor, typically, in many other accounting theories). Organisations are considered collections of self-interested individuals who have agreed to co-operate. Such co-operation does not mean that they have abandoned self-interest as an objective; rather, it means only that they have entered into contracts that provide sufficient incentives to gain their co-operation (Henderson *et al.* 1992, p. 327).

Companies try to align the interests of directors and some of these methods of aligning interests will be based on the output of the accounting system, such as providing the manager with a share of the organisation's *profits*—hence the theory's direct application to explaining particular accounting practices. Where such accounting-based alignment mechanisms are in place, financial statements need to be produced. Managers are required to bond themselves to prepare these financial statements. This is costly in itself and under PAT would be referred to as a bonding cost. If we assume that managers (agents) will be responsible for preparing the financial statements, PAT would also predict that there would be a demand for those statements to be audited or monitored. Otherwise, assuming self-interest, agents would attempt to overstate profits, thereby increasing their absolute share of profits. In PAT, the cost of undertaking an audit is referred to as a **monitoring cost**.

> **monitoring cost** Cost incurred monitoring the performance of others.

Various bonding and monitoring costs might be incurred to address the agency problems that arise within an organisation. If it was assumed, contrary to the assumption of 'self-interest' employed by PAT, that individuals always worked for the benefit of their employer, there would be less demand for such activities—other than, perhaps, to review the efficiency with which managers operate businesses. As PAT assumes that not all the opportunistic actions of agents can be controlled by contractual arrangements or otherwise, there will always be some residual costs associated with appointing an agent (known as residual loss).

3.4.1 Efficiency and opportunistic perspectives of PAT

Research that applies PAT typically adopts either an *efficiency perspective* or an *opportunistic perspective*. From the efficiency perspective, researchers explain how various contracting mechanisms can be put in place to minimise the agency costs of the firm—that is, the costs associated with assigning decision-making processes to an agent. The efficiency perspective is often referred to as an *ex ante* perspective—*ex ante* meaning 'before the fact'—as it considers what mechanisms are introduced up-front with the objective of minimising future agency costs. For example, many organisations in Europe and elsewhere voluntarily prepared publicly available financial statements before regulation compelled them to do so. These financial statements were also frequently subject to audit even though there was no statutory requirement to do so (Morris 1984). Researchers such as Jensen and Meckling (1976) argue that the practice of providing audited financial statements leads to real cost savings as it enables organisations to attract funds at lower costs (in other words, it is an efficient use of resources to prepare financial statements and have them audited). As a result of the audit, external parties have reliable information about the resources of the organisation, which is thus perceived to be able to attract funds at a lower cost than would otherwise be possible. This is because, in the absence of information, it would be difficult to assess the ongoing 'health' of an investment in an entity, and this inability to monitor performance would increase the risk associated with an investment. With higher risk, the entity's cost of attracting capital would increase. Providing 'credible' information will arguably lead to a decrease in risk, and a consequent decrease in the costs of attracting capital to the entity.

The *opportunistic perspective* of PAT, on the other hand, takes as given the negotiated contractual arrangements of the firm (some of which are discussed below) and seeks to explain and predict certain opportunistic behaviours that will *subsequently* occur. The opportunistic perspective is often referred to as an *ex post* perspective—*ex post* meaning 'after the fact'—because it considers opportunistic actions that could be taken once various contractual arrangements have been put in place. For example, in an endeavour to minimise agency costs (an efficiency perspective), a contractual arrangement might be negotiated that provides managers with a bonus based on the profits generated by the entity (for example, a manager might be given a bonus that is 5 per cent of profits). This will act to align the interests of the managers with the interests of the owners. Once the contractual arrangement is in place, however, the manager could opportunistically elect to adopt particular accounting methods that increase accounting profits and therefore the size of any bonus (an opportunistic perspective). For example, managers might elect to adopt a particular depreciation method that increases income even though it might not reflect the actual use of the asset. It is assumed within PAT that managers will opportunistically select particular accounting methods whenever they believe that doing so will lead to an increase in their personal wealth (remember, PAT assumes that *all* individuals are driven by self-interest).

The following discussion addresses some of the various contractual arrangements that might exist between owners and managers, and between debt holders and managers, particularly contracts that are based on the output of the accounting system. Again, these contractual arrangements are assumed initially to be put in place to reduce the agency costs of the firm (the *efficiency perspective*). However, it is assumed by positive accounting theorists that once the arrangements are in place, parties will adopt manipulative strategies to generate the greatest economic benefits for themselves (the *opportunistic perspective*).

Owner-manager contracting

A manager who also owns a firm (an owner-manager) bears the costs associated with their own **perquisite consumption**, which could include consumption of the firm's resources for private purposes—acquiring an overly expensive company car or luxurious offices or staying in overly expensive hotel accommodation—or the excessive generation and use of idle time. As the percentage of ownership held by the manager decreases, managers begin to bear less of the cost of their own perquisite consumption. The costs begin to be absorbed by the other owners of the firm.

As noted previously, PAT adopts as a central assumption that all action taken by an individual is driven by self-interest, and that the major interest of all individuals is to maximise their own wealth. Such an assumption is often referred to as the **rational economic person assumption**. If all individuals are assumed to act in their own interests, owners would expect managers (their agents) to undertake activities that might not always be in the interests of the owners (the principals). Further, because of their position within the firm, managers will have access to information that is not available to principals—a problem frequently referred to as **information asymmetry**—thus increasing the potential for managers to take actions that are beneficial to themselves at the expense of the owners. The costs of divergent behaviour that arises as a result of the agency relationship—that is the relationship between the principal and the agent appointed to perform duties on behalf of the principal—are, as indicated previously, referred to as *agency costs* (Jensen and Meckling 1976).

perquisite consumption Consumption by employees of non-salary benefits.

rational economic person assumption That all actions by individuals are driven by self-interest, the prime interest being to maximise personal wealth.

information asymmetry Where some individuals have access to certain information that is not available to others.

It is assumed under PAT that principals expect their agents to undertake activities that might be advantageous to the agents but disadvantageous to the value of the firm (the *opportunistic perspective*). That is, principals assume that agents will be driven by self-interest. As a result, principals will price this into the amounts they are prepared to pay managers. That is, in the absence of controls to reduce the ability of managers to act opportunistically, principals expect such actions and, as a result, will pay their managers a lower salary. This lower salary compensates the principals for, or protects them from, the expected opportunistic behaviour of the agents/managers (often referred to as 'price protection'). Managers, therefore, bear some of the agency costs of the opportunistic behaviours in which they might or might not engage. If it is expected that managers would derive greater satisfaction from additional salary than from the perquisites that they will be predicted to consume, managers might be better off if they are able to commit or bond themselves contractually to reducing their set of available actions, some of which would not be beneficial to owners. To receive greater remuneration, managers must be able to convince owners that they will work in the interests of owners. Of course, before agreeing to increase the amounts paid to managers, the owners of a firm would need to ensure that any contractual commitments could be monitored for compliance. In a market where individuals are perfectly informed, it could be assumed that managers would ultimately bear the costs associated with the bonding and monitoring mechanisms (ibid). Of course, markets are typically not perfectly informed.

Managers could potentially be rewarded:

- on a fixed basis, that is, given a fixed salary independent of performance;
- on the basis of the results achieved; or
- using a combination of the above two methods.

If managers are rewarded purely on a fixed basis, then, assuming self-interest—a central tenet of PAT—they will not want to take great risks because they will not share in any potential gains. There will also be limited incentives for these managers to adopt strategies that increase the value of the firm—unlike equity owners, whose share of the firm might increase in value. Like **debt-holders**, managers with a fixed claim want to protect their fixed income stream. Apart from rejecting risky projects, which might be beneficial to those with equity in the firm, the manager with a fixed income stream is also reluctant to take on optimum levels of debt, as the claims of the debt-holders would compete with the manager's own fixed income claim.

> **debt-holders** Owners of bonds. The firm pays them interest periodically and the principal amount on maturity. The payment must be made before equity holders can extract funds from the firm.
>
> **bonus scheme** Where the manager receives a bonus that is tied to the performance of the organisation.

Assuming self-interest drives the actions of managers, PAT theorists argue that it can be necessary to put in place remuneration schemes that reward managers in a way that is, at least in part, tied to the performance of the firm. This will be in the interests of managers as they will potentially receive greater rewards and will not have to bear the costs of perceived opportunistic behaviours (which might not have been engaged in anyway). If the performance of the firm improves, the rewards paid to managers increase correspondingly. **Bonus schemes** tied to the performance of the firm are put in place to align the interests of owners and managers. If the firm performs well, both parties will benefit.

Bonus schemes generally

It is common practice for managers to be rewarded in terms of movements in share price, earnings per share, the profits of the firm, sales of the firm or return on assets; that is, their remuneration is based on the output of the accounting system (hence, depending upon the terms of the bonus scheme, a change in profits might directly affect a manager's personal wealth).

Accounting-based bonus plans

Given that the amounts paid to managers might be tied directly to accounting numbers—such as profits/sales/assets—any changes in the accounting methods being used by the organisation will affect the bonuses paid. Such changes can occur as a result of a new accounting standard being issued. For example, consider the consequences if a new rule is issued that requires all UK research and development expenditure to be written off, as is the case in the US (within the UK, subject to certain guidelines, development expenditure can be capitalised and subsequently amortised over future periods). With such a change, profits would decline and the bonuses paid to managers could also change. Positive Accounting Theory would argue that, if a change in accounting policy had no impact on the profit/cash flows of the firm, the management of the firm would be indifferent to the change.

Incentives to manipulate accounting numbers

There are a number of costs that might arise if incentive schemes are based on accounting output. For example, it is possible that rewarding managers on the basis of accounting profits can induce them to manipulate the related accounting numbers to improve their apparent performance and, importantly, their related rewards—that is, accounting profits might not always provide an unbiased measure of a firm's performance or value. Healy (1985) provides an illustration of when managers might choose opportunistically to manipulate accounting numbers owing to the presence of **accounting-based bonus schemes** (that is, they adopt an opportunist perspective). He found that when schemes existed that rewarded managers after a prespecified level of earnings had been reached, managers would adopt accounting methods consistent with maximising that bonus. In situations where the profits were not expected to reach the minimum level required by the plan, managers appeared to adopt strategies that further reduced income in that period (frequently referred to as 'taking a bath'). This situation leads to higher income in subsequent periods when the profits might be above the required threshold. For example, a manager might write off an asset in one period when a bonus was not going to be earned anyway so that there would be nothing further to depreciate in future periods when profit-related bonuses might be paid.

> **accounting-based bonus scheme** Employee remuneration scheme where employees receive a bonus tied to accounting numbers.

Market-based bonus schemes

Firms involved in mining or high-tech research and development might have accounting earnings that fluctuate greatly. Successful strategies might be put in place that will not provide accounting earnings for a number of periods. In such industries, positive accounting theorists might argue that it is more appropriate and efficient to reward managers in terms of the market value of the firm's securities, which are assumed to be influenced by expectations about the **net present value** of expected future cash flows. This can be done either by basing a cash bonus on any increases in share prices or by providing managers with shares or options to shares in the firm. If the value of the firm's shares increases, both managers and owners will benefit and, importantly, managers will be given an incentive to increase the value of the firm.

> **net present value** The difference between the present value of the future cash inflows and the present value of the future cash outflows relating to a particular project or object.

As with accounting-based bonus schemes, there are problems associated with managers being rewarded in terms of share price movements. First, the share price will not only be affected by factors that are controlled by the manager but also by outside, market-wide factors; that is, share prices might provide a 'noisy' measure of management performance—'noisy' in the sense that they are affected not only by the actions of management but also largely by general market movements over which the manager has no control. Further, only senior managers would be likely to have a significant effect on the cash flows of the firm and, hence, on the value of the firm's securities. Therefore, market-related incentives might be appropriate for senior management only. Offering shares to lower level management might be demotivating, as their own individual actions would have little likelihood, relative to the actions of senior management, of affecting share prices and, therefore, their personal wealth. Consistent with this, it is more common for senior managers to hold shares in their employer than for other employees to do so.

Accounting-based rewards have the advantage that the accounting results may be based on sub-unit or divisional performance. However, it needs to be ensured that individuals do not focus on their division at the expense of the organisation as a whole.

Positive Accounting Theory assumes that, if a manager is rewarded on the basis of accounting numbers—for example on the basis of a share of profits—the manager will have an incentive to manipulate the accounting numbers in an effort to increase their own personal wealth. Given this assumption, the value of audited financial statements becomes apparent. Rewarding managers in terms of accounting numbers—a strategy aimed at aligning the interests of owners and managers—might not be appropriate if management is solely responsible for compiling those numbers. The auditor will act to arbitrate on the reasonableness of the accounting methods adopted. However, it must be remembered that there will always be scope for opportunism.

The above discussion indicates that incentive-based remuneration contracts might act to motivate managers to take actions that are in the best interests of the owners (that is, to align the interests of managers and owners). Another mechanism, which might complement the employment of efficiently designed management remuneration plans that might motivate managers, is the threat that an underperforming company might be the subject of takeover attempts. The consequence of this is that underperforming managers/agents might lose their jobs when alternative teams of managers target firms with resources that are currently being used inefficiently by the incumbent management team. Given the assumption of an efficient capital market—another central tenet of PAT—managers might be motivated to use their resources efficiently both for the benefit of the owners and because inefficient utilisation might result in the firm being taken over and subsequently in loss of employment for managers.

A well-informed labour market will motivate management to work to maximise the value of their firm. Underperformance might lead to dismissal and, if the labour market is efficient in disseminating data, a 'failed'

manager might have difficulty attracting a position with comparable pay elsewhere. Positive Accounting Theory also assumes that labour markets are efficient.

None of the mechanisms mentioned—private contracting, capital markets and labour market forces—is deemed to be perfectly efficient. However, it is assumed within PAT that the concurrent existence of well-designed management compensation contracts, the market for corporate takeovers and a well-informed labour market should ensure that management, *on average*, will act in the best interests of owners.

Debt contracting

When a party lends funds to another organisation, the recipient of the funds might undertake activities that reduce or even eliminate the probability of the funds being repaid. The costs that relate to the divergent behaviour of the borrower are referred to in PAT as the agency costs of debt. For example, the recipient of the funds might pay excessive dividends, leaving few assets in the organisation to service the debt. Alternatively, the organisation might take on additional and perhaps excessive levels of debt. The new debt-holders would then compete with the original debt-holders for repayment. Smith and Warner (1979) refer to this practice as 'claim dilution'.

Further, the borrowing firm might also invest in very high-risk projects. This strategy would not be beneficial to its debt-holders. They have a fixed claim and therefore if such a project generates high profits they will receive no greater return, unlike the owners who will share in the increased value of the firm. If such a project fails, which is more likely with a risky project, the debt-holders might receive nothing. Therefore, while the debt-holders do not share in any profits (the 'upside'), they do suffer the consequences of any significant losses (the 'downside').

In the absence of safeguards that protect their interests, debt-holders will assume that management will take actions that might not always be in the debt-holders' interest. As a result, in the absence of contractual safeguards, it is assumed that they will require the firm to pay higher costs of interest to compensate for the high-risk exposure (ibid).

If a firm contractually agrees—from an *efficiency perspective*—that it will not pay excessive dividends, not take on high levels of debt and not invest in projects of an excessively risky nature, it is assumed that it will be able to attract debt capital at a lower cost than would otherwise be possible. To the extent that the benefits of lower interest costs exceed the costs that might be associated with restricting how management can use available funds, management will elect to sign agreements that restrict their subsequent actions. These are called negative or restrictive covenants. Begley and Freedman (2004) noted that restrictive covenants typically used five ratios and restrict the firm from particular actions if the accounting-based targets were not maintained. The ratios were as follows:

- Secured and/or priority borrowings/capital and reserves
- Asset disposals/assets
- Interest cover
- Fixed assets/secured debt
- Assets acquired/capital and reserves

Covenants are used in public and private debt issues. A 'public issue' is where a particular security (such as a debenture, unsecured note or convertible note) is made available for the public to invest in (with the terms of the issue typically provided within a publicly available prospectus document). Investors in a public debt issue would have a trustee who is to act in the interests of all the public investors. By contrast, a private debt issue involves an agreement between a limited number of parties (perhaps just one party, such as a bank) to provide debt capital to an organisation.

Barnes and Cahill (2005) note that bank debt is the major source of corporate debt in Europe as the European bond markets are less liquid and not as developed as the US markets. Sakoui (2011), however, noted that there was a shift from bank debt to bond financing amongst corporates as a result of the financial crisis. Standard and Poor's have warned that this restructuring of debt will lead to an increase in the default rates in bonds by European companies in the coming years. Booth and Chua (1995) found that, in the US, corporate bank loans typically used a wide variety of covenants. Many led to an increased loan spread in the event of covenant violation and in some instances the covenants changed throughout the life of the loan agreement, sometimes automatically.

Where covenants restrict the total level of debt that may be issued, this is assumed to lead to a reduction in the risk to existing debt-holders. This is further assumed to translate to lower interest rates being charged by the 'protected' debt-holders. Restrictions on the definition of assets (to exclude the revalued amounts) lessen the ability of firms to loosen debt constraints by revaluing assets. Cotter (1998), in an Australian context, found that, apart from debt-to-assets constraints, interest coverage and current ratio clauses are frequently used in debt agreements. Interest coverage clauses typically require that the ratio of net profit—with interest and tax added back—to interest expense be at least a minimum number of times. In the Cotter study, the number of times interest must be covered ranged from one and a half times to four times. The current ratio clauses reviewed by Cotter required that current assets be between one and two times the size of current liabilities, depending on the size and industry of the borrowing firm.

The purpose of various debt covenants is to provide lenders with regular and timely indicators of the possibility of a borrowing entity defaulting on repaying its debts. A violation of a debt covenant signals an increase in the likelihood of default. However, it needs to be appreciated that the covenant measures are simply indicators of the chances that an organisation will not repay borrowed funds, and simply because an organisation is in technical default of a covenant is not a perfect indicator that the entity would not have repaid the borrowed funds.

When debt contracts are written, and where they utilise accounting numbers, the contract can, as we indicated earlier, rely upon either the accounting rules in place when the contracts were signed (often called 'frozen GAAP') or the contract might rely upon the accounting rules in place at each year's reporting date (referred to as 'rolling GAAP' or 'floating GAAP'). In a study of Australian firms over the period 1991 to 2001, Mather and Peirson (2006) found that in all but one of the public debt contracts, rolling (or floating) GAAP was to be used to calculate the specific ratios used within the contracts. The use of rolling GAAP increases the risk to borrowers in the sense that if the IASB issues a new accounting standard that changes the treatment of particular assets, liabilities, expenses or income, this has the potential to cause an organisation to be in technical default of a loan agreement. For example, a new accounting standard might be released that requires a previously recognised asset to be fully expensed to the income statement (or the statement of comprehensive income). This could have obvious implications for debt to asset constraints, or interest coverage requirements. This in itself could motivate an organisation to actively lobby accounting standard-setters against a particular draft accounting standard.

As with management compensation contracts, PAT assumes that the existence of debt contracts (which are initially put in place as a mechanism to reduce the agency costs of debt and can be explained from an efficiency perspective) provides management with a subsequent (*ex post*) incentive to manipulate accounting numbers—an incentive that increases as the accounting-based constraint approaches violation.

For example, if a firm contractually agreed to a **debt covenant** that stipulated that the ratio of debt to total tangible assets should be kept below a certain figure (and this is considered to reduce the risk of the debt-holders not being repaid), if that figure was likely to be exceeded (constituting a technical default of the loan agreement and thereby potentially requiring the entity to repay the funds immediately) management might have an incentive to either inflate assets (perhaps through an upward asset revaluation) or deflate liabilities. This is consistent with the results reported in Christie (1990) and Watts and Zimmerman (1990). To the extent that such an action was not objective, management would obviously be acting opportunistically and not to the benefit of individuals holding debt claims against the firm. Debt agreements typically require financial statements to be audited.

> **debt covenant**
> Restriction within a trust deed on the operations of a borrowing entity.

Within accounting, management usually has available a number of alternative ways to account for particular items and thus to minimise the effects of existing accounting-based restrictions. The role of external auditors, if appointed, would be to arbitrate on the reasonableness of the accounting methods chosen.

In relation to auditors, and following on from the discussion so far, there would appear to be a particular demand for financial statement auditing when:

- management is rewarded on the basis of numbers generated by the accounting system; and/or
- the firm has borrowed funds and accounting-based covenants are in place to protect the investments of debt holders.

Consistent with the above, it could also be argued that, as the managers' share of equity in the business decreases and as the proportion of debt to total assets increases, there will be a corresponding increase in the demand for auditing. In this regard, Ettredge *et al.* (1994) show that organisations that voluntarily elect to have interim financial statements audited tend to have greater **leverage** and lower management shareholding in the firm.

In summing up our discussion on debt contracting we can see that accounting numbers can have significant implications for the ongoing viability of an organisation. Many organisations borrow funds with the terms of the borrowing being stipulated in contracts that incorporate accounting-based debt covenants. Failure to comply with these negotiated covenants (often referred to as a 'technical breach' of a covenant or contract) can, at the extreme, lead to the operations of the organisation being suspended, or placed in the hands of a party nominated by the lender, while the lenders seek to gain access to their funds. In this regard we can consider an extract from an article that appeared in *Euroweek* in relation to National Express, reproduced in Financial Accounting in the News 3.1.

> **leverage** The relationship between the amount of fixed interest capital (i.e. loan stock, debentures, preference shares, etc.) and the amount of equity capital. It is also referred to as gearing.

Financial Accounting in the News 3.1

NATIONAL EXPRESS LOOSENS ITS DEBT COVENANTS

Euromoney Institutional Investor, *Euroweek*, 19 June 2009

National Express has renegotiated the covenants on £1.26 billion of syndicated loans and loosened its definition of net debt, giving itself more headroom for the next six months. The borrower has been battling to overcome its debt burden in the face of falling revenues on its UK rail franchises.

Its leverage ratio of adjusted net debt to EBITDA was due to fall from four times to 3.5 times on its June 30 test date, but lenders have agreed to retain the looser level. It will revert to the normal level of 3.5 times from December 31. Despite the amendment, the borrower still expects to be leveraged less than 3.5 times at the end of June, it said today. National Express was given more headroom (allowing the ratio to

rise from 3.5 to four times) when it bought Spanish bus company Continental Auto for €680m in 2007.

The borrower has also renegotiated the way it calculates net debt. The weakness of sterling in the latter part of 2008 resulted in a £238m increase in its net debt, much of which is held in dollars and euros. As such, the firm's banks will now allow it to use average currency rates, rather than spot rates, when calculating net debt, thereby reducing foreign exchange volatility.

Source: Euroweek. © Euromoney Institutional Investor PLC
June 2009

While the above material has discussed how accounting-based debt covenants are often negotiated between borrowers and lenders, we could perhaps expect that the level of reliance that lenders place on accounting-based indicators, as a means of protecting the funds advanced to an organisation, will be influenced by the perceived integrity of the accounting systems in place within the borrowing organisation. In this regard, Costello and Wittenberg-Moerman (2011) find that if an organisation discloses information about internal control failures within its accounting system then lenders will tend to decrease their reliance on the use of accounting-based covenants. Rather, borrowers who have had instances of poor internal controls tend to encounter higher interest rates and additional security requirements.

In the discussion that follows, we consider how expectations about the *political process* can also affect managers' choice of accounting methods.

3.4.2 Political costs

political costs Costs that groups external to the firm might be able to impose on the firm as a result of political actions.

The term **political costs** is used to refer to the costs that particular groups external to the firm may be able to impose on the firm, such as the costs associated with increased taxes, increased wage claims or product boycotts.

Organisations are affected by governments, trade unions, environmental lobby groups and consumer groups. Research indicates (Watts and Zimmerman 1978; Wong 1988; Deegan and Hallam 1991) that the demands placed on firms by interest groups might be affected by the accounting results of the firm. For example, if a firm records high profits, this might be used as a justification or an excuse for trade unions to take action to increase their members' share of the profits in the form of increased wages. Publicity such as media coverage is not typically given to the accounting methods used to derive particular accounting numbers. Rather, attention seems to be focused on the final numbers themselves, without regard for how those numbers were determined. On this subject we can consider an extract from the article that appeared in the *The Press and Journal,* reproduced in Financial Accounting in the News 3.2, which refers to a debate between the Unite union and the Scottish bus company First Aberdeen. The 'union boss' identifies the high profits of the company and notes that these profits have not been passed on to any real extent to the employees.

Financial Accounting in the News 3.2

PAY DISPUTE BETWEEN FIRST AND UNIONS BREAKS OUT

Cameron Brooks, *The Press and Journal*, 4 July 2009

A row has broken out between a trade union and a bus company over claims staff are demanding a 52% pay increase. Unite has accused First Aberdeen of trying to mislead the public over how much it is seeking in a new deal for around 500 drivers, cleaners and garage staff. Regional industrial organiser Tommy Campbell said it is 'outrageous' that the company has stated the union is demanding such a hefty increase for 2009/10. He said yesterday that the union, which is threatening to take strike action if the dispute cannot be resolved, has told the company it would encourage members to accept a 4% increase in pay. Mr Campbell said: 'This absurd claim by First is designed to create a smokescreen to hide the fact that their profits are up 38%. This is a greedy company run by fat-cat bosses who only care about lining the pockets of shareholders at the expense of their hard-working employees. A 4% pay increase would not even make a small dent in their huge profits and their continued refusal to award a pay increase shows that they only care about money and not about their staff or passengers.'

In a sense, the reported accounting profits are used as an 'excuse' or justification to make a claim for higher wages. Such a wage push, while perhaps equitable, could be costly for the organisation involved. Perhaps if reported profits were not so high, there would be less chance of demands being made for increased wages.

Within Ireland, banks are using reported losses and the commitment to payment of the public debt which they received as a government bailout as a result of the financial crisis to justify not passing on interest rate cuts to their mortgage customers. For example, in an article entitled '*Three Banks Refuse to Pass on Interest Rate Cut*' (Pope 2011) it was stated:

> *Three of the State's leading banks have refused to pass on the latest European Central Bank rate reduction of 0.25 per cent to variable rate customers, while a fourth has only passed on a portion of the cut. AIB, Ulster Bank and National Irish Bank said they would not pass on the latest rate cut. All three also failed to pass on November's rate cut, although AIB eventually relented after significant pressure was applied.*

> *AIB's executive chairman David Hodgkinson said the capital provided to it by the State meant it had to 'do all that we can to help our customers and support economic revival, while protecting the taxpayers' investment. Today's announcement is in line with those aims'.*

An industry's high profits might be used as a basis for action by groups who lobby politically for increased taxes or decreased subsidies on the grounds of the industry's ability to pay. For example, Watts and Zimmerman (1986) examine the highly publicised claims about US oil companies made by consumers, unions and government within the US in the late 1970s. It was claimed at the time that oil companies were making excessive reported profits and were in effect exploiting the nation. It is considered that such claims could have led to the imposition of additional taxes in the form of 'excess profits' taxes. Indeed this has occurred in the UK. North Sea Oil and Gas accounts for a sizeable portion of the UK's economic output, contributing about £30 billion to the balance of payments, paying about £3.5 billion in taxes and employing approximately 500,000 persons directly and indirectly. This strong performance has led to increased scrutiny from the government as it attempts to raise revenues to deal with the country's debt. In an article by Fiona Harvey in *The Observer* on 27 March 2011, 'Oil giants warn that Osborne's windfall tax would hit North Sea exploration', James Smith, the UK chairman of Shell, argues that the windfall tax, though not having an impact on the price of oil to consumers, is likely to have a major impact on the future investment strategies of the large oil companies in the North Sea. He stated: 'The industry was looking at £60bn in investment over the next 10 years.' That will now be in doubt. In the

same article Derek Leith, oil and gas partner at Ernst & Young, comments on the already high rates of tax being paid by oil companies operating in the North Sea. 'Tax rates on the North Sea industry are already high. Producers from fields opened before 1993 would have paid 75% in tax, and will now expect to pay 81%. Companies with fields opened after that date would have paid about 50%, but that will now be 62%, which ...could mean they reconsider some of their planned investments.'

As already indicated, high profits might be used by consumer groups to justify a position that prices are too high. For example, consider the difficulties a firm might have justifying a price rise for its goods or services if, at the same time, it is recording high profits. Consistent with Watts and Zimmerman (1978), if a firm believes that it is, or might be, subject to political costs, there might be incentives to adopt income-decreasing accounting methods. Watts and Zimmerman (p. 115) state:

> By avoiding the attention that high profits draw because of monopoly rents, management can reduce the likelihood of adverse political actions and, thereby, reduce its expected costs (including the legal costs the firm would incur opposing the political actions). Included in political costs are the costs labour unions impose through increased demands generated by large reported profits.

When the media reports on a company's profitability, it seldom gives any attention to the accounting methods that were used to calculate the profit. In a sense, profit is held out as some form of objective measure of organisational performance (much like government might rely on profits to support a particular action).

In the discussion so far, we have examined how representatives of interest groups might use profits as a justification for particular actions. Lower reported profits might reduce the likelihood of demands for increased wages. Hence, if management considers that there might be claims for increased wages in particular years, or the industry might be the target for increased taxes or consumer calls for price decreases, then managers might elect to adopt income-decreasing accounting methods (for example, managers might depreciate assets over fewer years, thereby increasing depreciation expense and reducing profits). In US-based research, Cahan (1992) undertook an investigation of the accounting methods used by organisations subject to investigation by the US Department of Justice and the Federal Trade Commission and found that firms under investigation tended to adopt income-reducing accounting strategies.

This study represented yet another example of research that sought to confirm the 'political cost hypothesis'—a hypothesis that has been subject to repeated investigation for over 20 years.

3.4.3 PAT in summary

Up to this point, we have shown the following:

- PAT proposes that the selection of particular and alternative accounting methods can be explained either from an *efficiency perspective* or an *opportunistic perspective*. At times, it is very difficult to distinguish which perspective best explains a particular organisation's accounting strategies. The selection of particular accounting methods can affect the cash flows associated with debt contracts, the cash flows associated with management-compensation plans and the political costs of the firm.
- PAT indicates that these effects can be used to explain why firms elect to use particular accounting methods in preference to others. PAT also provides a basis for explaining why particular organisations might lobby for or against particular proposed accounting requirements. As we know from Chapter 1, when new accounting standards are being developed by the IASB, the standard-setters will normally develop a draft accounting standard and then ask for submissions from the public. PAT provides a framework for explaining the lobbying positions taken by the respective respondents.
- PAT indicates that the use of particular accounting methods might have opposing effects. For example, if a firm adopts a policy that increases income by capitalising an item, rather than expensing it as it is incurred, this might reduce the probability of violating a debt constraint and might also increase accounting-related management bonuses. However, it could also increase the political visibility of the firm on account of higher profits. Managers are assumed to select accounting methods that best balance their conflicting effects, while at the same time maximising their own wealth.

3.5 Accounting policy selection and disclosure

As noted earlier in this chapter, a firm might be involved in many agreements that use accounting numbers relating to profits and assets (for example, an organisation might have instituted a bonus plan whereby bonuses paid to managers are based on profits, or it might be subject to a debt covenant that restricts its total debt to a certain percentage of its total assets). Hence the decision to expense or capitalise an item might have important financial implications for the organisation and, potentially, for management.

As a result of the choices that confront the accountant, it is imperative that financial statement u~~~ aware of the accounting policies adopted by reporting entities. Comparing the financial results and positi~~ reporting entities that use different accounting methods might be a misleading exercise unless notional adjus~ ments are made to counter the effects of using these different methods and policies. For such adjustments, knowledge of each firm's accounting policies is necessary.

IAS 1 *Presentation of Financial Statements* requires that a summary of accounting policies be presented in the initial section of the notes to the financial statements (paragraph 117 of IAS 1). In explaining that requirement, paragraph 118 of IAS 1 states:

> It is important for an entity to inform users of the measurement basis or bases used in the financial statements (for example, historical cost, current cost, net realisable value, fair value or recoverable amount) because the basis on which an entity prepares the financial statements significantly affects users' analysis. When an entity uses more than one measurement basis in the financial statements, for example when particular classes of assets are revalued, it is sufficient to provide an indication of the categories of assets and liabilities to which each measurement basis is applied.

Paragraph 119 of IAS 1 further states:

> In deciding whether a particular accounting policy should be disclosed, management considers whether disclosure would assist users in understanding how transactions, other events and conditions are reflected in reported financial performance and financial position. Disclosure of particular accounting policies is especially useful to users when those policies are selected from alternatives allowed in IFRSs.

When a company has changed its accounting policies from one period to the next, comparison of its performance in different periods can become difficult. In this regard, IAS 8 *Accounting Policies, Changes in Accounting Estimates and Errors* requires that, where there is a change in accounting policy used in preparing and presenting financial statements or group financial statements for the current financial year and this change has a material effect on the financial statements or group financial statements, the summary of accounting policies is to disclose, or refer to a note disclosing, the nature of the change, the reason for the change and the financial effect of the change (paragraph 29 of IAS 8).

Financial statements of subsequent periods need not repeat these disclosures. IAS 8, paragraph 14, requires that a change in an accounting policy is to be made only when it:

(a) is required by an IFRS; or
(b) results in the financial statement providing reliable and more relevant information about the effects of transactions, other events or conditions on the entity's position, financial performance or cash flows.

3.6 Accounting policy choice and 'creative accounting'

Those people responsible for selecting between the different accounting techniques—which, as we have seen, should be explained in the **accounting policy notes**—might select the alternatives that they believe most effectively and efficiently report the performance of their firm; in other words, they might approach their selection objectively. As paragraph 10 of IAS 8 states:

accounting policy notes Notes showing accounting principles, bases of recognition and measurement rules adopted in preparing and presenting financial statements.

> In the absence of an IFRS that specifically applies to a transaction, other event or condition, management shall use its judgement in developing and applying an accounting policy that results in information that is:
>
> (a) relevant to the economic decision-making needs of users; and
> (b) reliable, in that the financial statement
>   (i) represents faithfully the financial position, financial performance and cash flows of the entity;
>   (ii) reflects the economic substance of transactions, other events and conditions, and not merely the legal form;
>   (iii) is neutral, that is, free from bias;
>   (iv) is prudent; and
>   (v) is complete in all material respects.

By contrast, it is also possible for such individuals to select the policies that best serve their own interests; in other words, they might approach their selection and application of accounting techniques 'creatively'. The

...ig is frequently used in the media. It refers to where those responsible for the preparation of financial statements select accounting methods that provide the result desired by the preparers. As we have already seen, PAT provides an explanation of why firms might be creative—or opportunistic—with their accounting (perhaps to increase the rewards paid to managers, to loosen the effects of accounting-based debt covenants or to reduce potential political costs).

With the range of accounting techniques available—and these techniques will be highlighted throughout this text—account preparers can be creative, yet at the same time follow accounting standards. Although they might not be *objective*, it might be difficult for parties such as auditors, with an oversight function, to report that the account preparers are doing anything wrong. This may reduce the credibility of accounting.

If the output of the accounting system lacks credibility and assuming that markets such as the capital market are efficient, it would be unlikely that they would use the output of the accounting system in the design of contractual arrangements with such a firm. However, evidence clearly indicates that the market does rely on the output of the accounting system. For example, the debenture trust deeds of large listed firms, as well as negotiated lending agreements with banks, without any apparent exception, use the output of the accounting system to control and monitor the behaviour of corporate management. While we need to acknowledge that creative accounting does exist, it is reasonable to argue that, with the increased number of accounting standards being issued, the scope for being creative should decrease.

Whatever the actual incidence of creative accounting, to consider that all financial statements are developed on an *objective basis* is a naive view. This chapter has discussed how the wealth of the firm, or particular individuals, might be tied to the output of the accounting system. This can be through the existence of accounting-based debt contracts and accounting-based management compensation schemes, both of which are, according to PAT, initially devised to increase the efficient operations of the entity (the efficiency perspective). The existence of political costs, which might be influenced in part by such accounting numbers as 'profits', will also affect the value of an organisation. Adopting the *opportunistic perspective* of PAT, whenever individuals' wealth is at stake, there is always the possibility that opportunistic actions might override the dictates of objectivity. Certainly, PAT assumes that considerations of self-interest would drive the selection of accounting policies. Whatever the case, creativity might be employed, but hopefully not too often!

3.7 Some criticisms of Positive Accounting Theory

Although PAT has received fairly widespread acceptance from a large group of accounting academics, there are nevertheless many researchers who oppose its fundamental tenets. (See Deegan (1997) for further detail.)

Criticism is particularly evident among the normative theorists who see the role of accounting theory as providing *prescription*, rather than *description*. Some of you might not have expected a theory of accounting (such as PAT) to be capable of eliciting such a reaction. As students of accounting, you might find it interesting to ponder why such a theory has made some people so angry—after all, it is just a theory, isn't it?

Although the descriptions of PAT quoted above are extremely negative, it must be kept in mind that there are many researchers and research departments that still favour PAT. What should also be kept in mind is that any theory or model of accounting will be based on certain key underlying assumptions about such things as the purposes of accounting, the purposes of accounting research, what drives individual actions, and so forth. Not all researchers will agree with the assumptions, and hence it is to be expected that there will not be total acceptance of any particular theory of accounting. The discussion below will further highlight some of the perceived shortcomings of PAT. Remember that these 'shortcomings' would conceivably be challenged by those who favour PAT and/or conduct research under the banner of PAT.

One widespread criticism of PAT is that it does not provide prescription and therefore does not provide a means of improving accounting practice. It is argued that simply explaining and predicting accounting practice is not enough.

A second criticism of PAT is that it is not value-free, as it asserts, but rather very value-laden (Tinker *et al.* 1982). If we look at research that has been conducted adopting PAT, we will see a general absence of prescription. There is no guidance on what people *should* do. This is normally justified by positive accounting theorists on the basis that they do not want to impose their own views on others. They would prefer to provide information about the expected implications of particular actions and thereafter let people decide for themselves what they should do. For example, they might provide evidence to support a prediction that organisations that are close to breaching accounting-based debt covenants will adopt accounting methods that increase the firm's reported profits and assets. However, as a number of accounting academics have pointed out, the very act of selecting a theory such as PAT for research purposes is based on a value judgement; deciding what to research is based on a value judgement; believing that all individual action is driven by self-interest is a value judgement; and so on. Hence, no research, whether conducted under PAT or otherwise, is value-free and to assert that it *is* value-free is, arguably, quite wrong.

Following on from the above points, a third criticism of PAT relates to the fundamental assumption that *all* action is driven by a desire to maximise wealth. To many researchers such an assumption represents a perspective of humankind that is far too negative. Another criticism of PAT is that, since its beginnings in the 1970s, the theory has not developed greatly. In Watts and Zimmerman (1978) there were three key hypotheses:

1. *The debt hypothesis*—which typically proposes that organisations that are close to breaching accounting-based debt covenants will select accounting methods that lead to an increase in profits and assets.
2. *The bonus-plan hypothesis*—which typically proposes that managers on accounting-based bonus schemes will select accounting methods that lead to an increase in profits.
3. *The political-cost hypothesis*—which typically proposes that firms subject to political scrutiny will adopt accounting methods that reduce reported income.

These three hypotheses were considered earlier in this chapter. A review of the recent PAT literature reveals that these hypotheses continue to be tested in different environments and in relation to different accounting policy issues—even more than 30 years after Watts and Zimmerman (1978) suggested them.

As a last criticism to consider, it has been argued that PAT is scientifically flawed. As the three hypotheses generated by PAT (mentioned above) are frequently not supported by research but, rather, are falsified, PAT should be rejected from a scientific point of view. Christenson (1983, p. 18) states:

> We are told, for example, that 'we can only expect a positive theory to hold on average' (Watts & Zimmerman 1978, p. 127, n. 37). We are also advised 'to remember that as in all empirical theories we are concerned with general trends' (Watts & Zimmerman 1978, pp. 288–9), where 'general' is used in the weak sense of 'true or applicable in most instances but not all' rather than in the strong sense of 'relating to, concerned with, or applicable to every member of a class' (American Heritage Dictionary 1969, p. 548) . . . A law that admits exceptions has no significance, and knowledge of it is not of the slightest use. By arguing that their theories admit exceptions, Watts and Zimmerman condemn them as insignificant and useless.

However, accounting is a process that is undertaken by people, and the accounting process itself cannot exist in the absence of accountants—it is hard to think of any model or theory that could ever fully explain human action. In fact, to do so would constitute a dehumanising action. Are there any theories of human activity that always hold? What we must appreciate is that theories are simplifications of reality.

While the above criticisms do, arguably, have some merit, PAT continues to be used. A number of accounting research journals continue to publish PAT research. A number of the leading accounting research schools throughout the world continue to teach PAT. What must be remembered is that all theories of accounting will have limitations. They are, of necessity, abstractions of the 'real world'. Whether we individually prefer one theory of accounting to another will depend on our own assumptions about many of the issues raised within this chapter. In the discussion that follows, we turn our attention to normative theories of accounting. As you might expect, such theories are also subject to varied levels of criticism.

3.8 Normative accounting theories

As the discussion so far in this chapter has indicated, PAT seeks to explain and predict the selection of particular accounting policies and the implications of that selection. **Normative accounting theories**, on the other hand, seek to provide guidance to individuals to enable them to select the most appropriate accounting policies for given circumstances. The Conceptual Framework, discussed in Chapter 1, can be considered a normative theory of accounting. Its purpose is to provide guidance to the individuals responsible for preparing general purpose financial statements. The Conceptual Framework Project seeks to identify the objective of general purpose financial reporting and the qualitative characteristics that financial information should possess. The objective of general purpose financial reporting is, according to the IASB Conceptual Framework (as released in September 2010), deemed to be:

normative accounting theories Accounting theories that seek to guide individuals in selecting the most appropriate accounting policies.

> to provide financial information about the reporting entity that is useful to existing and potential investors, lenders and other creditors in making decisions about providing resources to the entity.

This objective serves as a foundation for the various releases that form the output of the Conceptual Framework Project. If we were to disagree with this central objective—and many accounting academics do—we would be unlikely to agree with the subsequent prescriptions provided within the framework. Conceptual frameworks seek to provide recognition and measurement rules within a coherent and consistent framework.

Without a conceptual framework for financial reporting, accounting standards would be developed in a fairly ad hoc manner. There would be inconsistency between the standards, with different standards having different asset valuation principles, different recognition principles, and the like. Conceptual frameworks were initiated as a means of reducing such inconsistencies.

The IASB *Conceptual Framework for Financial Reporting* identifies a number of qualitative characteristics that financial information should possess (as discussed in Chapter 2). Two main qualitative characteristics are identified as *relevance* and *faithful representation*. In relation to faithful representation, the IASB Conceptual Framework states:

> *Financial reports represent economic phenomena in words and numbers. To be useful, financial information must not only represent relevant phenomena, but it must also faithfully represent the phenomena that it purports to represent. To be a perfectly faithful representation, a depiction would have three characteristics. It would be complete, neutral and free from error. Of course, perfection is seldom, if ever, achievable. The Board's objective is to maximise those qualities to the extent possible.*

As you have just read about PAT and how PAT researchers work on the assumption that self-interest drives the actions of all individuals—including those individuals who prepare financial statements—it will now be clear to you that, to be consistent, such researchers consider that managers would not be overly motivated to produce financial statements that are 'complete' and 'neutral' or that 'represent faithfully' the transactions of the business—particularly if there are accounting-based contracts in place with associated cash flow implications. *Objectivity* and *self-interest* are, arguably, mutually exclusive.

The Conceptual Framework does not purport to codify existing practices and hence is not descriptive of practice. Rather, as a prescriptive framework that is intended to be logically developed, it makes many recommendations that represent departures from currently accepted practice. For example, accounting reports have traditionally been prepared by adopting the concept of conservatism, which requires that assets should never be overstated, liabilities should never be understated and revenue recognition should often be deferred until such time as the related cash flows are realised. That is, the concept of conservatism acts to produce financial statements that are biased towards understating the net assets of an entity. The notion of conservatism, however, is not consistent with the recommendations of the IASB Conceptual Framework, which requires a 'neutral depiction without bias in the selection or presentation of financial information'.

Apart from the conceptual framework, there have been a number of other normative accounting theories developed by individual scholars.

Dominant normative theories developed in the 1950s and 1960s, all of which addressed issues associated with changing prices, can be divided into three main classifications (Henderson *et al.* 1992):

1. current-cost accounting
2. exit-price accounting
3. deprival-value accounting

Reflecting the fact that there was no universal agreement on the role of accounting—and there is still none—the alternative normative theories provided conflicting prescriptions. In the discussion that follows, we will briefly consider some of the normative theories. We will not consider the actual applications of the various prescriptions in any great detail but, rather, the main elements of the theories. It should be noted at this point that there is currently little debate on the issues associated with undertaking accounting in periods of changing prices. This might reflect the low rates of inflation we currently experience. Perhaps—and this is sheer conjecture—issues associated with changing prices might again attain prominence if inflation was to reach the heights of some past decades.

3.8.1 Current-cost accounting

current-cost accounting A system of accounting that measures the value of goods and services in terms of their current costs.

Current-cost accounting was advocated by many accounting researchers, including Edwards and Bell in the US (*The Theory and Measurement of Business Income*, 1961). Although there are variations within the different models of current-cost accounting, the general aim of the theory is to provide a calculation of income that, after adjusting for changing prices, could be withdrawn from the entity yet still leave the physical capital of the entity intact. Such measures of income are often promoted as true measures of income (Henderson *et al.* 1992).

For the purposes of illustration, assume that a company started the period with assets of €50,000. Let us assume also that there are no liabilities, so that owners' equity also equals €50,000. During the period, the business sells all of its assets for €70,000. Under historical-cost accounting the profit would be €20,000 and closing owners' equity would be €70,000, which would be matched by assets of €70,000 in the form of cash. If the €20,000 was withdrawn in the form of dividends, under historical-cost accounting the owners' equity of the business would remain as it was at the beginning of the period. However, if we were to adopt current-cost accounting, the profit would not necessarily be the same. If, owing to rising prices, it cost €60,000 to replace the assets that were sold (their 'current cost'), under current-cost accounting profit would be only €10,000, as €60,000 would need to be retained to keep the physical capital of the firm intact. The maintenance of the firm's physical capital or operating capacity is a central goal of current-cost accounting.

Proponents of this normative theory argue that by valuing assets (and this would translate to expense recognition) at their current costs—in some models based on replacement cost—a 'truer' measure of profit is provided than is reflected by the historical-cost system. A frequently raised criticism of current-cost accounting is that it introduces an unacceptable amount of subjectivity into the accounting process, as some assets will not have a readily accessible 'current cost'. However, advocates of the approach argue that the increased relevance of the information more than offsets any disadvantages associated with its reliability, compared with historical-cost data.

3.8.2 Exit-price accounting

One of the most famous expositions of a normative accounting theory was developed by Raymond Chambers. He labelled his theory **Continuously Contemporary Accounting (CoCoA)**. The theory was developed principally between 1955 and 1965 and purports that reported accounting figures should be based on assessments of the exit or selling prices of an entity's assets and liabilities—hence it is labelled an **exit-price theory**.

The development of CoCoA was based on the key assumptions that:

- firms exist to increase the wealth of the owners;
- successful operations are based on the ability of an organisation to adapt to changing circumstances; and
- the *capacity to adapt* will be best reflected by the monetary value of the organisation's assets, liabilities and equities at reporting date, where the monetary value is based on the current exit or selling prices of the organisation's resources (their current cash equivalent).

Capacity to adapt should be reflected by the entity's financial statements, which will highlight adaptive capital. To this end, and as noted above, Chambers prescribed that all assets should be recorded at their **current cash equivalent**. Current cash equivalents were represented by the amounts expected to be generated by selling the assets. The net sales or exit prices were to be determined on the basis of an orderly sale. Within the model, the statement of financial position should clearly show the expected net selling prices of all the entity's assets—net selling prices would acknowledge any costs that would be incurred in making a sale. Adaptive capital would be represented by the total net selling prices of the various assets, less the amount of the firm's liabilities. Profit would reflect the change in the organisation's capacity to adapt that had occurred since the beginning of the period. Because the valuation of assets is to be based on their current cash equivalents, depreciation expenses would not be recognised within CoCoA.

Chambers argued that people can easily understand what valuation on the basis of net selling prices means. Under CoCoA, assets are not valued on the basis of arbitrary cost allocations or amortisation nor on the basis of directors' valuations.

As you would expect, there are many criticisms of CoCoA, such as that it does not consider the 'value in use' of assets; it uses perceived sales price as the valuation basis (which assumes that the firm intends to liquidate the assets); and the assumption that the exit prices are determined by the price that could be achieved in an orderly sale is subjective and variable over time and the resultant financial statements may not be useful for monitoring the firm's management.

3.8.3 Deprival-value accounting

A further normative (or prescriptive) accounting theory that we will briefly consider is deprival-value accounting. Deprival value itself can be defined as the value to the business of particular assets. It represents the amount

> **Continuously Contemporary Accounting (CoCoA)**
> A normative theory that proposes an approach to accounting that relies on measuring the exit prices of the entity's assets and liabilities.
>
> **exit-price theory**
> Normative theory of accounting that prescribes that assets should be valued on the basis of exit prices and that financial statements should function to inform users about an organisation's capacity to adapt.
>
> **current cash equivalent**
> Represented by the amount that would be expected to be generated by selling an asset.

of loss that might be incurred by an entity if it were deprived of the use of an asset and the associated economic benefits the asset generates.

In 1975 deprival-value accounting was recommended by the UK Sandilands Committee. The deprival value of an asset to be reported in the financial statements will be determined by considering: the **net selling price** of the asset; the **present value** of the future cash flows that the asset will generate; or the asset's **current replacement cost**. The deprival value is the lower of replacement cost and the greater of the net selling price and present value (value in use). For example, if an asset could be sold for a net amount of €100 or used to generate a present value of €120, the best use of the asset would be to keep it and use it to generate future cash flows. The deprival value is then the lesser of the present value (€120) and the cost to replace the asset. To adopt this form of accounting would require all assets and liabilities to be considered separately in terms of their deprival value to the business.

> **net selling price** The selling price of an item less the costs that are incidental to making the sale.
>
> **present value** The value of an item to be received or paid for in the future expressed in terms of its value today.
>
> **current replacement cost** A valuation method based on the current replacement cost of an item rather than its historical cost.

Some criticisms of deprival-value accounting have included the concern that different valuation bases would be used within a single financial statement—such as selling prices, present-value calculations and replacement costs. This can be compared with Chambers' CoCoA, which prescribes one method of valuation—net selling prices. It has also been argued that the valuation procedures would be particularly costly and time-consuming, given that more than one method of valuation might have to be used for particular assets. It might also not be clear which valuation approach should be adopted for a particular type of asset.

The aim of the above brief discussion of three different normative theories of accounting (which tell us how we *should* account) is to show the difference between normative and positive theories of accounting.

The following discussion focuses on yet another group of theories, classified as systems-orientated theories.

3.9   Systems-orientated theories to explain accounting practice

Apart from PAT and the normative accounting theories discussed briefly above, there are numerous other theories applicable to the accounting process. What should be stressed is that, as mentioned previously, theories are *abstractions of reality*, and no particular theory can be expected to provide a full account or description of a particular phenomenon. Hence it is sometimes useful to consider the perspectives or insights provided by alternative theories. In some cases, different researchers study the same phenomenon but from different theoretical perspectives. For example, some researchers operating within the PAT paradigm (such as Ness and Mirza 1991) argue that the voluntary disclosure of social responsibility information can be explained as a strategy to reduce political costs. Social responsibility reporting has also been explained from a Legitimacy Theory perspective (for example, Patten 1992) and from a Stakeholder Theory perspective (for example, Roberts 1992). The choice of one theoretical perspective in preference to others will, at least in part, be due to value judgements on the part of the authors involved. As O'Leary (1985, p. 88) states:

> *Theorists' own values or ideological predispositions may be among the factors that determine which side of the argument they will adopt in respect of disputable connections of a theory with evidence.*

> **systems-orientated theories** Theories that explain the role of information and disclosure in managing the relationships between an organisation and the communities with which it interacts.

One branch of accounting-related theories can be referred to as **systems-orientated theories**. According to Gray *et al.* (1996, p. 45):

> *a systems-oriented view of the organisation and society . . . permits us to focus on the role of information and disclosure in the relationship(s) between organisations, the State, individuals and groups.*

From a systems-based perspective, an entity is assumed to be influenced by the society in which it operates and in turn to have an influence on society. This is simplistically represented in Figure 3.1.

Three theories adopting a systems-based perspective are Stakeholder Theory, Legitimacy Theory and Institutional Theory. Within these theories, accounting disclosure policies are considered to constitute a strategy to influence (or, perhaps, *manage*) the relationships between the organisation and other parties with which it interacts. In recent times, Stakeholder Theory and Legitimacy Theory have been applied extensively to explain why organisations might make certain social responsibility disclosures within their annual reports or sustainability reports, rather than why they might elect to adopt particular financial accounting methods. The theories could, however, also be applied to explain, at least in part, why companies adopt particular financial accounting techniques.

Social responsibility disclosures themselves can relate, among other things, to information about the interaction of an organisation with its physical and social environment, including the community, the natural environment, human resources, energy and product safety (Gray *et al.* 1987; Mathews 1993). Stakeholder Theory and Legitimacy Theory are discussed in greater detail in Chapter 26, which considers social disclosures. However, as this chapter considers accounting-related theories, some attention here is warranted. We will briefly consider Stakeholder Theory, Legitimacy Theory and Institutional Theory in turn below.

> **social responsibility disclosures** Disclosures of information about the interaction of an organisation with its physical and social environment.

3.9.1 Stakeholder Theory

Stakeholder Theory has both an ethical (normative) branch and a managerial (positive) branch. The ethical branch adopts the view that all stakeholders have certain intrinsic rights (for example, to safe working conditions and fair pay), and these rights should not be violated. As Hasnas (1998, p. 32) states:

> **Stakeholder Theory** Perspective that considers the importance for an organisation's survival of satisfying the demands of its various stakeholders.

> *When viewed as a normative (ethical) theory, Stakeholder Theory asserts that, regardless of whether stakeholder management leads to improved financial performance, managers should manage the business for the benefit of all stakeholders. It views the firm not as a mechanism for increasing the stockholders' financial returns, but as a vehicle for coordinating stakeholder interests and sees management as having a fiduciary relationship not only to the stockholders, but to all stakeholders. According to the normative Stakeholder Theory, management must give equal consideration to the interests of all stakeholders and, when these interests conflict, manage the business so as to attain the optimal balance among them. This of course implies that there will be times when management is obliged to at least partially sacrifice the interests of the stockholders to those of the other stakeholders. Hence, in its normative form, the Stakeholder Theory does imply that business has true social responsibilities.*

A stakeholder can be defined as 'any group or individual who can affect or is affected by the achievement of the firm's objectives' (Freeman 1984). Stakeholders would include shareholders, employees, customers, lenders, suppliers, local charities, various interest groups and government. From this perspective, the organisation is seen as part of a larger social system, as shown in Figure 3.1. Within the ethical branch of Stakeholder Theory, there is also the view that all stakeholders have a right to be provided with information about how the organisation is affecting them (perhaps through pollution, community sponsorship, provision of employment, safety initiatives, etc.), even if they choose not to use the information, and even if they cannot directly affect the survival of the organisation.

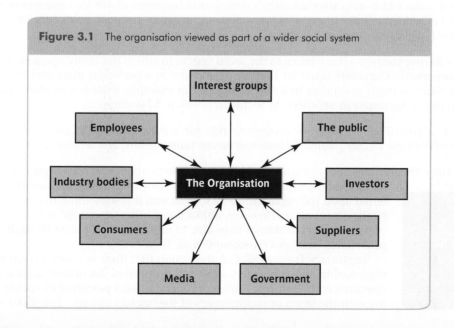

Figure 3.1 The organisation viewed as part of a wider social system

Turning our attention away from the ethical (normative) branch and to the managerial (or positive) branch of Stakeholder Theory, we see that this branch seeks to *explain* and *predict* how an organisation will react to the demands of various stakeholder groups. As the research based on this branch of Stakeholder Theory is used to make predictions, it is reasonable to assess the validity of such research on the basis of its correspondence with actual practice.

Within the managerial branch of Stakeholder Theory (see, for example, Roberts 1992), the organisation identifies its group of stakeholders, particularly those that are considered to be important to the ongoing operations of the business. The greater the importance of the stakeholders, the greater will be the expectation that the management of the firm will take actions to 'manage' the relationships with those stakeholders. As the expectations and power relativities of the various stakeholder groups can change, organisations must continually adapt their operating and disclosure strategies. Roberts (ibid: 598) states that:

> *A major role of corporate management is to assess the importance of meeting stakeholder demands in order to achieve the strategic objectives of the firm. As the level of stakeholder power increases, the importance of meeting stakeholder demands increases, also.*

The power of stakeholders (for example, owners, creditors or regulators) to influence corporate management is viewed as a function of stakeholders' degree of control over resources required by the organisation (Ullmann 1985). The more critical the stakeholder-controlled resources are to the continued viability and success of the organisation, the greater the expectation that stakeholder demands will be addressed. A successful organisation is considered to be one that satisfies the demands (sometimes conflicting) of the various powerful stakeholder groups.

Stakeholder Theory (of the positive, or managerial, variety) does not directly provide prescriptions about what information *should* be disclosed, other than indicating that the provision of information, including information within an annual report, can, if thoughtfully considered, be useful for the continued operations of a business entity. Within the managerial branch of Stakeholder Theory, it is a stakeholder's control over limited resources that are required by an organisation that influences whether specific information is provided to that stakeholder—not issues associated with *rights* to information.

3.9.2 Legitimacy Theory

Legitimacy Theory
Theory that proposes that organisations always seek to ensure that they operate within the bounds and norms of their societies.

Legitimacy Theory is very closely linked to Stakeholder Theory. It posits that organisations continually seek to ensure that they operate within the bounds and norms of their respective societies; that is, they attempt to ensure that their activities are perceived by outside parties to be 'legitimate'. These bounds and norms, rather than being fixed, are subject to change, requiring the organisation to be responsive to the environment in which it operates.

Lindblom (1994) distinguishes between legitimacy, which is considered to be a status or condition, and legitimation, which she considers to be the process that leads to an organisation being adjudged legitimate. According to Lindblom (p. 2), legitimacy is:

> *a condition or status which exists when an entity's value system is congruent with the value system of the larger social system of which the entity is a part. When a disparity, actual or potential, exists between the two value systems, there is a threat to the entity's legitimacy.*

Legitimacy is a relative concept—it is relative to the social system in which the entity operates and is both *time-specific* and *place-specific*. Corporate activities that are 'legitimate' in a particular place and time might not be legitimate at a different point in time, or in a different place (for example, what is legitimate behaviour in one country might not be legitimate in another). As Suchman (1995, p. 574) states:

> *Legitimacy is a generalised perception or assumption that the actions of an entity are desirable, proper, or appropriate within some socially constructed system of norms, values, beliefs, and definitions.*

Within Legitimacy Theory, 'legitimacy' is considered to be a resource upon which an organisation depends for its survival (Dowling and Pfeffer 1975; O'Donovan 2002). It is something that is conferred upon the organisation by society, and it is something that is desired or sought by the organisation. However, unlike many other 'resources', it is a 'resource' that the organisation is considered to be able to impact or manipulate through various disclosure-related strategies (Woodward *et al.* 1996).

social contract
Considered to be an implied contract constituted by the expectations that society holds about the conduct of an organisation.

Legitimacy Theory relies on the notion that there is a **social contract** between an organisation and the society in which it operates. An organisation is deemed to be operating with 'legitimacy' when its operations are perceived by society to be complying with the terms or requirements of the 'social contract'. The social contract is not easy to define, but the concept is used to represent the multitude of implicit and explicit expectations that society has about how an organisation should conduct its operations. The law is considered to provide the explicit terms of the social contract, while other, non-legislated societal expectations embody the implicit terms of the contract. It is assumed that society allows the organisation to continue operations as long as it generally meets society's expectations. Legitimacy Theory emphasises that the organisation must appear to consider the rights of the public at large, not merely those of its investors.

In recognition of the value of maintaining a strong social contract with its customers, Lloyds Banking Group went against the grain of cost-cutting by announcing no branch closures for three years. This they believe gives them a strategic advantage over their rivals as it signals the importance of community and customers to the bank, as explained in the extract reproduced in Financial Accounting in the News 3.3.

Financial Accounting in the News 3.3

LLOYDS PROMISES NO BRANCH CLOSURES FOR THREE YEARS IN A BID TO BECOME UK'S BEST BANK

Dan Hyde, *ThisisMoney.co.uk,*
2 February 2012

State-backed Lloyds Banking Group today pledged to keep all of its 2,902 branches open for at least three years in a bid to 'become the best bank for customers'. Lloyds, which includes the Halifax and Bank of Scotland brands, admitted it has lagged behind its rivals in recent years both in terms of customer service and products. António Horta-Osório, chief executive of the 41 per cent taxpayer-owned monolith, said a strong branch network is 'vital' to the bank's plans to improve. He said: 'We want to put the customer at the heart of everything we do and it is why last year we put a moratorium on branch closures. Today we commit to keeping the same number of branches on a net basis, over the next three years. And we also commit not to close a branch if we are the last one in a community.'

Source: Reproduced with permission from Dan Hyde, Money Mail Reporter.

Given the potential costs associated with conducting operations that are deemed to be outside the terms of the social contract, Dowling and Pfeffer (1975) state that organisations will take various actions to ensure that their operations are perceived to be legitimate. One such action would be—and this is where we get to the theory's relevance to accounting—to provide disclosures, perhaps within the annual report. Hurst (1970) suggests that one of the functions of accounting, and subsequently accounting reports, is to legitimate the existence of the corporation. Within such a perspective, the strategic nature of financial statements and other disclosures is emphasised. From the perspective provided by Legitimacy Theory, it is important not only that an organisation operates in a manner consistent with community expectations (that is, consistent with the terms of the social contract), but also that the organisation discloses information to demonstrate that it is complying with community expectations. That is, if an organisation undertakes actions that conform to community expectations, this in itself is not enough to bring legitimacy to the organisation—it must make disclosures to show clearly that it is complying with community perceptions. It is society's perceptions of an organisation's actions that are important in establishing legitimacy, and not necessarily the actual actions themselves.

A number of studies have identified specific types of social-responsibility disclosures that have appeared within annual reports and that have been explained by the respective researchers as being part of the portfolio of strategies undertaken by accountants and their managers to bring legitimacy to, or to maintain the legitimacy of, their respective organisations.

Within the context of companies that source their products from developing countries, Islam and Deegan (2010) undertook a review of the social and environmental disclosure practices of two leading multinational sportswear and clothing companies, these being Nike and Hennes & Mauritz. Islam and Deegan found a direct relationship between the extent of global news media coverage of a critical nature being given to particular social issues relating to the industry, and the extent of social disclosure. In particular, they found that once the news media started running a campaign that exposed poor working conditions and the use of child labour in developing countries, it appeared that the multinational companies then responded by making various disclosures identifying initiatives that were being undertaken to ensure that the companies did not source their products from factories that had abusive or unsafe working conditions, or used child labour. Islam and Deegan argued that the evidence was

consistent with the view that the news media influenced the expectations of western consumers, thereby causing a legitimacy problem for the companies. The companies then responded to the legitimacy crisis by providing disclosures within their annual report that focused particularly on working conditions and the use of child labour in developing countries. Apart from Stakeholder Theory and Legitimacy Theory, another theory that embraces a systems-oriented perspective and that is applied to the analysis of corporate reporting decisions is Institutional Theory. This theory, which we discuss next, explains that organisations are subject to institutional pressures and as a result of these pressures organisations within a given environment tend to become similar in their forms and practices.

3.9.3 Institutional Theory

> **Institutional Theory**
> Theory that considers the forms organisations assume and explains why organisations within particular 'organisational fields' tend to take on similar characteristics and forms.

Broadly speaking, **Institutional Theory** considers the forms organisations take and provides explanations for why organisations within particular 'organisational fields' tend to take on similar characteristics and forms. DiMaggio and Powell (1983, p. 147) define an 'organisational field' as 'those organizations that, in the aggregate, constitute a recognized area of institutional life: key suppliers, resource and product consumers, regulatory agencies, and other organizations that produce similar services or products'. According to Carpenter and Feroz (2001, p. 565):

Institutional theory views organizations as operating within a social framework of norms, values, and taken-for-granted assumptions about what constitutes appropriate or acceptable economic behaviour (Oliver, 1991). According to Scott (1987), 'organizations, conform [to institutional pressures for change] because they are rewarded for doing so through increased legitimacy, resources, and survival capabilities' (p. 498).

A major paper in the development of Institutional Theory was DiMaggio and Powell (1983). They investigated why there was such a high degree of similarity between organisations. According to DiMaggio and Powell, there are various forces operating within society that cause organisational forms to become similar. As they state (1983, p. 148):

Once disparate organizations in the same line of business are structured into an actual field (as we shall argue, by competition, the state, or the professions), powerful forces emerge that lead them to become more similar to one another.

A key reason why Institutional Theory is relevant to researchers who investigate voluntary corporate reporting practices is that it provides a complementary perspective, to both Stakeholder Theory and Legitimacy Theory, for understanding how organisations interpret and respond to changing social and institutional pressures and expectations. Institutional Theory links organisational practices (such as accounting and corporate reporting) to, among other things, the values of the society in which the organisation operates and the need to maintain organisational legitimacy. The view is held that organisational forms and practices might tend to some form of homogeneity—that is, the structure of the organisation and the practices adopted by different organisations tend to become similar to conform with what is considered to be 'normal'. Organisations that deviate from the form that has become 'normal' or expected will potentially have problems gaining or retaining legitimacy.

There are two main dimensions to Institutional Theory. The first of these is termed *isomorphism* and the second *decoupling*.

Dillard *et al.* (2004, p. 509) explain that, '[i]somorphism refers to the adaptation of an institutional practice by an organisation'. Turning to the other dimension of Institutional Theory, *decoupling* implies that while managers might perceive a need for their organisation to be seen to be adopting certain institutional practices, and might even institute formal processes aimed at implementing these practices, actual organisational practices can be very different from these formally sanctioned and publicly pronounced processes and practices. Thus, the actual practices can be decoupled from the institutionalised (apparent) practices. In terms of voluntary corporate-reporting practices, this decoupling can be linked to some of the insights from Legitimacy Theory whereby social and environmental disclosures can be used to construct an organisational image very different from actual organisational, social and environmental performance. Thus, the organisational image constructed through corporate reports might be one of social and environmental responsibility when the actual managerial imperative is maximisation of profitability or shareholder value (Dillard *et al.* 2004).

From the material provided in this chapter, it can be seen that PAT, Stakeholder Theory, Legitimacy Theory and Institutional Theory all provide different theoretical perspectives on why organisations might elect to make particular disclosures (that is, the theories provide different *explanations*). The relevance of such theories would arguably be greater where there is no regulation prescribing how organisations are to account for a particular transaction or event, or how to disclose particular information. In such a case, particular motivations, and not regulation, might drive what disclosures are made and what accounting methods are adopted. The various theories described above are summarised in Table 3.1.

Table 3.1   Theories of accounting summarised

Theory	Type	Description
Positive Accounting Theory (PAT)	Positive	Seeks to explain and predict particular phenomena, especially the managers' choice of accounting methods. Grounded in classical economics, it focuses on relationships between various individuals within and outside an organisation and explains how financial accounting can be used to minimise the cost implications of each contracting party operating in its own self-interest.
Current-cost accounting	Normative	Aims to provide a prescription for a calculation of income that, after adjustments are made for changing prices, could be withdrawn from the entity while leaving its physical capital intact. The maintenance of the firm's physical capital or operating capacity is central to current-cost accounting.
Exit-price accounting (CoCoA)	Normative	The central objective of CoCoA is to provide information about an entity's 'capacity to adapt' to changing circumstances, with profit being directly related to changes in adaptive capacity. Profit is calculated as the amount that can be distributed while maintaining the entity's adaptive capital intact.
Deprival-value accounting	Normative	Can be defined as the value to the business of particular assets. Deprival value accounting provides the basis for how assets should be measured. Deprival value represents the amount of loss that might be incurred by an entity if it were deprived of the use of an asset and the associated economic benefits generated by the asset.
Stakeholder Theory	Managerial (Positive) branch	Seeks to explain and predict how an organisation will react to the demands of various stakeholders. It predicts that organisations will tend to satisfy the information needs of those stakeholders who are important to the organisation's ongoing survival. Whether a particular stakeholder receives information will depend on how powerful that stakeholder is perceived to be—power often being considered in terms of the scarcity and importance of the resources controlled by the stakeholder concerned.
	Ethical (Normative) branch	All stakeholders have intrinsic rights that should not be violated. Stakeholders have rights to information that should be met regardless of the power of the stakeholders involved. Disclosures are considered to be responsibility driven.
Legitimacy Theory	Positive	Relies on the notion of a social contract, which is an implied contract representing the norms and expectations of the community in which the organisation operates. An organisation is deemed to be legitimate to the extent that it complies with the terms of the social contract. Legitimacy theory predicts that the organisation will make information disclosures to gain, maintain or restore its legitimacy (and thereby its ability to continue operating).
Institutional Theory	Managerial/ Positive	Provides a complementary perspective to Stakeholder Theory and Legitimacy Theory. It provides a framework for understanding how organisations interpret and respond to changing social and institutional pressures. There are two dimensions to Institutional Theory—namely, isomorphism and decoupling. Isomorphism is related to the managerial branch of Stakeholder Theory, while decoupling tends more to be linked to some of the insights of Legitimacy Theory.

While there are numerous theories that can be applied to explain the managers' choice of accounting methods or disclosure strategies (particularly where there are no legislative requirements), there are also a number of theories that have been constructed to explain how and why accounting regulation is developed (including theories explaining the introduction of regulation). As with the other theories discussed in this chapter, there is no one generally accepted theory of regulation. In fact, there is much debate about what drives the introduction of regulation. The following discussion will briefly consider some of this debate.

3.10 Theories that seek to explain why regulation is introduced

As indicated in Chapter 1, general purpose financial reporting is subject to a great deal of regulation. For example, listed companies must comply with a multitude of accounting standards, as well as with the Companies Act 2006 and securities exchange listing requirements. In this section, a brief overview is provided of some of the theories developed to explain why regulation is introduced. Arguments in favour of or against regulation (that is, the *pro-regulation* versus *free-market* arguments) will not be considered here, as they were briefly considered in Chapter 1. In the material that follows, you will see that different accounting researchers have advanced different arguments about what causes regulation to be introduced. Some theories of regulation suggest that regulation is introduced in the *public interest*, while other theories suggest that regulation is introduced to benefit some people at the expense of others, that is, in *self-interest*.

3.10.1 Public Interest Theory

According to Posner (1974, p. 335), Public Interest Theory 'holds that regulation is supplied in response to the demand of the public for the correction of inefficient or inequitable market practices'. That is, regulation is initially put in place to benefit society as a whole, rather than to benefit particular vested interests, and the regulatory body is considered to represent the interests of the society in which it operates, rather than the private interests of the regulators. The enactment of legislation is considered to be a balancing act between the social benefits and the social costs of the regulation. The application of this argument to financial accounting, given the existence of a capitalist economy, implies that society needs confidence in the capital markets to help ensure that resources are directed towards productive assets. Regulation is deemed to be an instrument for creating such confidence.

3.10.2 Capture Theory

Researchers who embrace Capture Theory (capture theorists) would typically argue that, although regulation might be introduced with the aim of protecting the 'public interest' (as argued in Public Interest Theory, as briefly described above), this laudable aim of protecting the public interest will not ultimately be achieved, because in the process of introducing regulation the organisations that are subject to the regulation will ultimately come to control the regulator. The regulated industries will seek to gain control of the regulatory body, because they will know that the decisions made by the regulator will potentially have a significant impact on their industry. The regulated parties or industries will seek to take charge of (capture) the regulator with the intention of ensuring that the regulations subsequently released by the regulator (post-capture) will be advantageous to their industry. As an example of possible regulatory capture, we might consider a submission to *The Independent* newspaper's blog by Ben Chu. This submission discusses the views of the chairman of the UK FSA, Adair Turner, on the perceived lack of independence of US bank regulators and how this was corrosive for the US banking industry.

Financial Accounting In the News 3.4

ADAIR TURNER'S DENUNCIATION OF THE BANKING LOBBY

Ben Chu, *Eagle Eye—Breaking views from Independent commentators*, 10 January 2012

Turner argues that the influence of the US banking lobby was the reason that financial markets were scandalously under-regulated before the 2008 collapse. Turner is very clear that the corrupting power of the banking lobby is still strong, despite the disaster of three years ago:

What worries me, particularly as I look at the US now, is that a political process has gone on to deny to the agencies like the CFTC [Commodity Futures Trading Corporation] and the SEC [the Securities and Exchange Commission] the budget resources that are required for them to do effectively what Dodd–Frank [new legislation to make the US banking system safer] has instructed them to do. Dodd–Frank is an extraordinary piece of legislation, which just says you shall do this and the CFTC shall write a rule. This is an enormous amount of work for these two agencies and for the Federal Reserve Bank in some other areas. What is going on in

▶

*Congress is **deliberate action to starve them of funds**, which I think has a degree of motivation coming out of some financial interests through campaign money to members of Congress.*

Turner is arguing that the banking lobby has subverted the American political system for its own narrow and short term advantage, leaving the ordinary US public dangerously exposed to the economic risk of another financial collapse. Coming from the man who is—for now—Britain's top financial regulator, that's something that ought to alarm us all ...

The British disease was ideological capture of ministers and regulators, according to Turner.

There was a belief that light-touch regulation, or limited-touch, would make the City bigger, and that the City was a source of employment and tax revenue in particular. And therefore there was clear pressure on the FSA at times to say, go easy on the City. The FSA never used the phrase 'light touch',

but politicians did, and they did it in speeches, which were directed at the FSA.

I'm not so sure that political donations can be so easily ruled out as an influence on the thinking of politicians in Britain. The Bureau of Investigative Journalism found that financiers met around 30 per cent of the Conservative Party's costs last year. But I accept that money does not—yet—corrupt our political system in the disgusting manner of the US.

So what led Labour ministers into that trap of ideological capture? Spending too much time with financiers, I would argue, was one of the causes. They learned to see the world through the eyes of the big banks and the City of London. They were persuaded to see Britain's national interest as bound up with the interest of its financiers. And as I pointed out last month, judging from the frequency with which the Treasury has been holding meetings with the same lobby, the Coalition is still in danger of falling into the same trap.

Source: Reproduced with permission from Ben Chu.

3.10.3 Economic Interest Group Theory of Regulation

The Economic Interest Group Theory of Regulation (or, as it is sometimes called, Private Interest Theory of Regulation) assumes that groups will form to protect particular economic interests. Different groups are viewed as often being in conflict with each other, and the different groups will lobby government to put in place legislation that economically benefits them (at the expense of others). For example, consumers might lobby government for price protection, or producers might lobby for tariff protection. This theoretical perspective adopts no notion of *public interest*—rather, private interests are considered to dominate the legislative process. As Posner (1974) states, 'the economic theory of regulation is committed to the strong assumptions of economic theory generally, notably that people seek to advance their self-interest and do so rationally'.

In relation to financial accounting, particular industry groups might lobby the regulator to accept or reject a particular accounting standard. For example, in the UK widespread opposition by preparers to the accounting standard SSAP 16 *Current Cost Accounting* led to its withdrawal in 1985 and an overhaul of the accounting standard-setting body in the UK. To improve its legitimacy a new body was established with members who were independent of the accounting profession and it was been given increased powers (Pong and Whittington 1996; Georgiou and Jack 2011). The IASB has had more success with controversial standards; for example, there was widespread lobbying against IAS 39 *Financial Instruments: Recognition and Measurement*. Banks argued that some of the requirements would add volatility to their reported results that did not reflect the underlying economic reality of the situation. The IASB made minor amendments and continued with the main requirements. However, the EU Accounting Regulatory Committee, the organisation that endorses each IFRS/IAS before requiring European companies to comply with it, put pressure on the IASB to change two of the provisions, one relating to using a full fair value option, the other in respect of hedge accounting. If we accept the Economic Interest Group Theory of Regulation, the lack of initial success in this instance must have been because a more powerful interest group favoured the alternative situation—the use of historical cost.

Reflecting upon the above discussion, do you think that accounting standards are introduced in the public interest, or in the self-interest of particular groups?

While our discussion of 'theories of regulation' (Public Interest Theory, Capture Theory and Economic Interest Group Theory) is brief and certainly does not include all theories pertaining to why regulation is introduced, the discussion does provide some insights into why particular regulations might have been established. Because accounting is subject to a great deal of regulation, it is often interesting to consider why particular regulations were introduced (and perhaps why some other proposed regulation was not ultimately introduced). The theories briefly described above provide some insights that may be helpful in answering such questions.

SUMMARY

This chapter has described various theories that relate to financial accounting. It is stressed that no single accounting theory is universally accepted. A theory itself is defined as a coherent group of propositions used as an explanation for a class of phenomena. The phenomena studied in accounting theory obviously relate to the practice of accounting, but which phenomena are selected for study from the many available will depend on the theoretical approach that is adopted.

The chapter has considered the differences between positive and normative theories of accounting. A positive theory of accounting is one that seeks to *explain* and *predict* particular accounting-related phenomena, whereas a normative theory of accounting prescribes how accounting *should* be practised. The conceptual framework of accounting, which was considered in some depth in Chapter 2 (and will be revisited in other chapters throughout this book), is classified as a normative theory of accounting.

One positive theory of accounting that we described was Positive Accounting Theory, which was popularised by theorists such as Watts and Zimmerman. Researchers who adopt a Positive Accounting Theory perspective typically study issues such as the capital market's reaction to particular accounting policies; what motivates managers to select one method of accounting from among competing alternatives; and the reasons for the existence of particular accounting-based contracts. Positive Accounting Theory proponents typically rely upon a fundamental assumption that individual action can be predicted on the basis that all action is driven by a desire to maximise wealth. As we have seen, such an assumption is often criticised by researchers who adopt alternative theoretical perspectives.

Normative accounting theorists typically argue that it is a central role of accounting theory to provide *prescription*, that is, to inform others about the optimal accounting approach to adopt and why this particular approach is considered optimal. In this view, to fail to provide such prescription is to neglect one's duties as an accounting academic. Normative theories that are considered briefly in this chapter include the Conceptual Framework Project, current-cost accounting, exit-price accounting and deprival-value accounting. Each of the normative theories of accounting differs from the others in its prescriptions, depending on the perspective adopted on how information is used by individuals and, linked to this, what information is actually important to inform decision making.

This chapter also briefly considers systems-based theories. These theories, which include Stakeholder Theory, Legitimacy Theory and Institutional Theory, see the organisation as being firmly embedded within a broader social system. The organisation is considered to be affected by, and to affect, the society in which it operates. According to these theories, accounting disclosures are a way to *manage* relations with particular groups outside the organisation. In a sense, organisational activities and accounting disclosures are perceived to be reactive to community pressures. How the firm operates and what it reports must be determined after a consideration of various stakeholder expectations. Because these 'systems-based' theories seek to explain and predict particular corporate actions, they can also be considered to be 'positive theories' (as opposed to being 'normative theories').

Apart from theories to explain or prescribe the selection of particular accounting methods, we also considered theories that seek to explain how regulation is developed, that is, we considered theories of regulation. We saw that some theories of regulation suggest that regulation is introduced to serve the *public interest* by regulators who work for the *public good*, whereas other theories of regulation assume that the development of regulation is driven by considerations of *self-interest*.

This chapter has emphasised that the selection of one theory in preference to another will depend on the views and expectations of the researcher in question. We have seen that there is often heated debate between individuals from the alternative schools of thought. Theories, as abstractions of reality, cannot be expected to perfectly explain and predict all accounting-related phenomena, nor can they be expected to provide optimal solutions in all cases. No one theory of accounting can—or, perhaps, should—ever be definitively described as the *best* theory. If we accept this, we will see that different theoretical perspectives can, at various times, provide us with valuable insights into accounting issues.

In the rest of this book, accounting requirements as stipulated by the different accounting standards will be considered. As appropriate, reference will be made to the theories discussed in this chapter, thus providing insight into the implications of the various accounting requirements and reporting practices that organisations adopt.

KEY TERMS

END-OF-CHAPTER EXERCISE

This chapter has raised a number of issues in relation to various theories of financial accounting. To test your comprehension of the various issues, try answering the following questions. If you are unable to answer the questions, consider re-reading some of the material provided in the chapter.

1 What is a theory and how would you evaluate whether a theory is a good theory or a bad theory? Is there actually such a thing as a good or a bad theory? **LO** 3.1

2 Do you expect that we will ever have a single universally accepted theory of accounting and, if not, why not? **LO** 3.1

3 What is the difference between a *normative theory* and a *positive theory*? Is one more useful than the other, or do they perform different roles? **LO** 3.2

4 What is the role of Positive Accounting Theory and what are its central assumptions? Given these assumptions, do you think it is realistic for the Conceptual Framework Project to propose that financial statements should be *objective* and *free from bias*? **LO** 3.5

5 Can Positive Accounting Theory explain the existence of *creative accounting*? **LO** 3.10

6 What is a systems-orientated theory of accounting? **LO** 3.12

REVIEW QUESTIONS

1 Why is it useful for students of financial accounting to consider theories such as those discussed in this chapter? **LO** 3.3

2 Why and how might management not act in the interests of the firm? **LO** 3.4

3 How can we use the output of the accounting system to help ensure that management's actions are in the interests of the owners? **LO** 3.4

4 How can management expropriate the wealth of debt-holders? **LO** 3.8

5 What is corporate social reporting? **LO** 3.12

6 Why would firms voluntarily present certain information, such as information about their performance with regard to the environment? **LO** 3.12

7 If firms are voluntarily producing information about the environment, about their initiatives with respect to their employees or about their commitments to the local population, what does this imply about their perceptions of who the 'users' of the information are? **LO** 3.12

8 What are debt covenants and why are they put in place? **LO** 3.6

9 What might be a goal of a well-designed management compensation scheme? **LO** 3.6

10 What mechanisms might be put in place to motivate management to serve the interests of: **LO** 3.7
   (a) the owners?
   (b) the debt-holders?

11 What role does the auditor play in financial reporting? **LO** 3.4

12 Why would a change in accounting policy affect a contractual agreement between a firm and a manager or debt-holder? **LO** 3.6

13 According to Positive Accounting Theory, why would a change in the existing set of accounting standards affect the value of a firm? **LO** 3.8

14 Positive Accounting Theory utilises the concept of political costs. Briefly define political costs. What actions might a firm's management undertake in an attempt to minimise the political costs that might be imposed on the firm? **LO 3.9**

15 Explain why a firm's management might be prepared to expend considerable resources to lobby 'for' or 'against' a proposed accounting standard (for example, one being issued by the International Accounting Standards Board). **LO 3.9**

16 Contrast the role of Positive Accounting Theory with the role of normative accounting theories. **LO 3.2**

17 Under Positive Accounting Theory, what are agency costs of equity and agency costs of debt? Is it possible to put in place mechanisms to reduce all opportunistic action? If not, why not? **LO 3.4**

18 If we accept the assumptions of Positive Accounting Theory, would you expect a manager who is rewarded by way of a profit-sharing bonus scheme to prepare the firm's financial statements in an unbiased manner? Explain your answer. **LO 3.7**

19 How would accounting regulators use the research conducted by positive accounting theorists? **LO 3.13**

20 Legitimacy Theory posits that organisations will attempt to operate within the terms of their 'social contract'. What is a social contract? **LO 3.12**

21 Using Institutional Theory as your theoretical basis, explain why an organisation might voluntarily elect to make particular financial disclosures. **LO 3.12**

22 The IASB's *Conceptual Framework for Financial Reporting* indicates that financial statements should provide unbiased representations of the underlying transactions. Is this realistic? **LO 3.11**

23 Provide some arguments to explain what motivates regulators to introduce particular regulations. **LO 3.13**

CHALLENGING QUESTIONS

24 The introduction of Accounting Standard IAS 38 *Intangible Assets* required companies to expense research expenditure instead of treating it as an asset and spreading the charge against profits over several years. **LO 3.6**

(a) Construct three hypotheses based on each of the three major components of Positive Accounting Theory to predict which companies are more likely to prefer to recognise research expenditure as an asset, rather than being required to treat the related expenditure as an asset.

(b) Suggest how a researcher might test these hypotheses.

25 The British government has decided that no specific regulations would be added to company legislation in respect of corporate social responsibility and that instead, 'market forces' would be relied upon to encourage companies to do the 'right thing' (that is, the view was expressed that if companies did not look after the environment, or did not act in a socially responsible manner, then people would not want to consume the organisations' products, and people would not want to invest in the organisations, work for them, and so forth). **LO 3.13**

You are required to explain the decision of the government that no specific regulation be introduced from the perspective of:

(a) Public Interest Theory

(b) Capture Theory

(c) Economic Interest Group Theory of Regulation

REFERENCES

BARNES, E. & CAHILL, B., 'Private or Public Debt? Drivers of Debt Priority Structure for UK Firms', *Irish Accounting Review*, vol. 12, no. 1, 2005, pp. 1–13.

BEGLEY, J. & FREEDMAN, R., 'The Changing Role of Accounting Numbers in Public Lending Agreements', *Accounting Horizons*, vol. 18, no. 2, 2004, pp. 81–96.

BOOTH, J. & CHUA, L., 'Structure and Pricing of Large Bank Loans', *Economic Review—Federal Reserve Bank of San Francisco*, vol. 3, 1995, pp. 1–52.

CAHAN, S.F., 'The Effect of Antitrust Investigations on Discretionary Accruals: A Refined Test of the Political Cost Hypothesis', *Accounting Review*, January, 1992, pp. 77–95.

CARPENTER, V. & FEROZ, E., 'Institutional Theory and Accounting Rule Choice: An Analysis of Four US State Governments' Decision to Adopt Generally Accepted Accounting Principles', *Accounting, Organizations and Society*, vol. 26, 2001, pp. 565–96.

CHAMBERS, R.J., 'Blueprint for a Theory of Accounting', *Accounting Research*, January, 1955, pp. 17–55.

CHAMBERS, R.J., 'Positive Accounting Theory and the PA Cult', *Abacus*, vol. 29, no. 1, 1993, pp. 1–26.

CHRISTENSON, C., 'The Methodology of Positive Accounting', *Accounting Review*, vol. 58, 1983, pp. 1–22.

CHRISTIE, A., 'Aggregation of Test Statistics: An Evaluation of the Evidence on Contracting and Size Hypotheses', *Journal of*

Accounting and Economics, January, 1990, pp. 15–36.

COSTELLO, A. & WITTENBERG-MOERMAN, R., 'The Impact of Financial Reporting Quality on Debt Contracting: Evidence from Internal Control Weakness Reports', *Journal of Accounting Research*, vol. 49, no. 1, 2011, pp. 97–136.

COTTER, J., 'Utilisation and Restrictiveness of Covenants in Australian Private Debt Contracts', *Accounting and Finance*, vol. 38, no. 2, 1998, pp. 111–38.

DEEGAN, C.M., 'Varied Perceptions of Positive Accounting Theory: A Useful Tool for Explanation and Prediction, Or a Body of Vacuous, Insidious and Discredited Thoughts?', *Accounting Forum*, vol. 20, no. 5, 1997, pp. 63–73.

DEEGAN, C.M. & HALLAM, A., 'The Voluntary Presentation of Value Added Statements in Australia', *Accounting and Finance*, May, 1991, pp. 1–16.

DILLARD, J.F., RIGSBY, J.T., & GOODMAN, C., 'The Making and Remaking of Organization Context: Duality and the Institutionalization Process', *Accounting, Auditing & Accountability Journal*, vol. 17 no. 4, 2004, pp. 506–42.

DIMAGGIO, P.J. & POWELL, W.W., 'The Iron Cage Revisited: Institutional Isomorphism and Collective Rationality in Organizational Fields', *American Sociological Review*, vol. 48, 1983, pp. 146–60.

DOWLING, J. & PFEFFER, J., 'Organisational Legitimacy: Social Values and Organisational Behavior', *Pacific Sociological Review*, vol. 18, no. 1, 1975, pp. 122–36.

ETTREDGE, M., SIMON, D., SMITH, D., & STONE, M., 'Why Do Companies Purchase Timely Quarterly Reviews?', *Journal of Accounting and Economics*, September 1994, pp. 131–56.

FREEMAN, R., *Strategic Management: A Stakeholder Approach*, Marshall, MA, Pitman, 1984.

FRIEDMAN, M., *The Methodology of Positive Economics: Essays in Positive Economics*, Chicago, IL, University of Chicago Press (reprinted in 1966 by Phoenix Books), 1953.

GEORGIOU, O. & JACK, L., 'In Pursuit of Legitimacy: A History Behind Fair Value Accounting', *British Accounting Review*, vol. 43, no. 4, 2011, pp. 311–23.

GORDON, M.J., 'Postulates, Principles, and Research in Accounting', *Accounting Review*, April 1964, pp. 251–63.

GRAY, R., OWEN, D., & ADAMS, C., *Accounting and Accountability*, London, Prentice Hall, 1996.

GRAY, R., OWEN, D., & MAUNDERS, K.T., *Corporate Social Reporting: Accounting and Accountability*, London, Prentice Hall, 1987.

HASNAS, J., 'The Normative Theories of Business Ethics: A Guide for the Perplexed', *Business Ethics Quarterly*, vol. 8, no. 1, 1998, pp. 19–42.

HEALY, P.M., 'The Effect of Bonus Schemes on Accounting Decisions', *Journal of Accounting and Economics*, vol. 7, 1985, pp. 85–107.

HENDERSON, S., PEIRSON, G., & BROWN, R., *Financial Accounting Theory: Its Nature and Development*, 2nd edn, Melbourne, Longman, 1992.

HENDRIKSEN, E., *Accounting Theory*, Sydney, Australia, Richard D. Irwin, 1970.

HURST, J.W., *The Legitimacy of the Business Corporation in the Law of the United States 1780–1970*, Charlottesville, VI, University Press of Virginia, 1970.

ISLAM, M. & DEEGAN, C., 'Media Pressures and Corporate Disclosure of Social Responsibility Performance Information: A Study of Two Global Clothing and Sports Retail Companies', *Accounting and Business Research*, vol. 40, no. 2, 2010, pp. 131–48.

JENSEN, M.C. & MECKLING, W.H., 'Theory of the Firm: Managerial Behavior, Agency Costs and Ownership Structure', *Journal of Financial Economics*, October 1976, pp. 305–60.

LINDBLOM, C.K., 'The Implications of Organisational Legitimacy for Corporate Social Performance and Disclosure', paper presented at the Critical Perspectives in Accounting Conference, New York, 1994.

MATHER, P. & PEIRSON, G., 'Financial Covenants in the Markets for Public and Private Debt', *Accounting and Finance*, vol. 46, 2006, pp. 285–307.

MATHEWS, M.R., *Socially Responsible Accounting*, London, Chapman and Hall, 1993.

MORRIS, R., 'Corporate Disclosure in a Substantially Unregulated Environment', *Abacus*, June 1984, pp. 52–86.

NESS, K. & MIRZA, A., 'Corporate Social Disclosure: A Note on a Test of Agency Theory', *British Accounting Review*, vol. 23, 1991, pp. 211–17.

O'DONOVAN, G., 'Environmental Disclosures in the Annual Report: Extending the Applicability and Predictive Power of Legitimacy Theory', *Accounting, Auditing and Accountability Journal*, vol. 15, no. 3, 2002, pp. 344–71.

O'LEARY, T., 'Observations on Corporate Financial Reporting in the Name of Politics', *Accounting, Organizations and Society*, vol. 10, no. 1, 1985, pp. 87–102.

PATTEN, D.M., 'Intra-industry Environmental Disclosures in Response to the Alaskan Oil Spill: A Note on Legitimacy Theory', *Accounting, Organizations and Society*, vol. 15, no. 5, 1992, pp. 471–5.

PONG, C.K. & WHITTINGTON, G., 'The Withdrawal of Current Cost Accounting in the United Kingdom: A Study of the Accounting Standards Committee', *Abacus*, vol. 32, no. 1, 1996, pp. 30–54.

POPE, C., 'Three Banks Refuse to Pass On Interest Rate Cut', *Irish Times*, 9 December 2011.

POSNER, R.A., 'Theories of Economic Regulation', *Bell Journal of Economics and Management Science*, Autumn 1974, pp. 335–58.

ROBERTS, R., 'Determinants of Corporate Social Responsibility Disclosure: An Application of Stakeholder Theory', *Accounting, Organizations and Society*, vol. 17, no. 6, 1992, pp. 595–612.

SAKOUI, A., 'S&P Warns of Increase in Debt Defaults by European Countries', *Financial Times*, 4 May 2011.

SMITH, C.W. & WARNER, J.B., 'On Financial Contracting: An Analysis of Bond Covenants', *Journal of Financial Economics*, June 1979, pp. 117–61.

SUCHMAN, M.C., 'Managing Legitimacy: Strategic and Institutional Approaches', *Academy of Management Review*, vol. 20, no. 3, 1995, pp. 571–610.

TINKER, T., MERINO, B., & NIEMARK, N., 'The Normative Origins of Positive Theories: Ideology and Accounting Thought', *Accounting Organizations and Society*, vol. 7, 1982, pp. 167–200.

ULLMANN, A., 'Data in Search of a Theory: A Critical Examination of the Relationships among Social Performance, Social Disclosure, and Economic Performance of US firms', *Academy of Management Review*, vol. 10, no. 3, 1985, pp. 540–57.

WATTS, R.L., 'Nature and Origins of Positive Research in Accounting', in S. Jones, C. Romano & J. Ratnatunga, eds. *Accounting Theory: A Contemporary Review*, Sydney, Australia, Harcourt Brace, 1995, pp. 295–353.

WATTS, R.L. & ZIMMERMAN, J.L., 'Towards a Positive Theory of the Determination of Accounting Standards', *Accounting Review*, January 1978, pp. 112–34.

WATTS, R.L. & ZIMMERMAN, J.L., *Positive Accounting Theory*, Englewood Cliffs, NJ, Prentice Hall, 1986.

WATTS, R.L. & ZIMMERMAN, J.L., 'Positive Accounting Theory: A Ten Year Perspective', *Accounting Review*, vol. 65, no. 1, 1990, pp. 131–56.

WONG, J., 'Economic Incentives for the Voluntary Disclosure of Current Cost Financial Statements', *Journal of Accounting and Economics*, April 1988, pp. 151–67.

WOODWARD, D.G., EDWARDS, P., & Birkin, F., 'Organizational Legitimacy and Stakeholder Information Provision', *British Journal of Management*, vol. 7, 1996, pp. 329–47.

PART **3**

Accounting for Assets

Part contents

4

An Overview of Accounting for Assets

Learning objectives

Upon completing this chapter readers should:

LO1 understand the definition of an asset and the asset recognition criteria;

LO2 understand the process involved in determining whether particular expenditures should be recognised as assets (that is, capitalised) or expensed;

LO3 be able to describe some of the various asset measurement rules allowable under IFRS;

LO4 be aware of the disclosure requirements embodied within IAS 1 *Presentation of Financial Statements* as they pertain to a reporting entity's assets;

LO5 be able to explain how to calculate the acquisition cost of an asset; and

LO6 be able to discuss various issues surrounding the capitalisation of interest.

4.1 Introduction to accounting for assets

In this book we will cover a range of issues associated with accounting for assets. To begin with, in this chapter we will consider:

- how we define assets;
- an overview of how we might measure various classes of asset;
- how assets are classified and disclosed within the statement of financial position; and
- how we determine the acquisition costs of assets.

While the material provided in this chapter has general application to assets, in subsequent chapters we will examine how to account for specific types of asset. For example, in Chapter 7 we will address how to account for inventory and in Chapter 8 we will address how to account for intangible assets. As we will learn, there are different rules to apply when we account for different types of asset. Conceptually, you might have thought that all assets should be measured in the same way, for example at fair value or at cost, but this is not the case as measurement rules vary depending upon the type of asset in question.

Across time, the value of the majority of assets will either increase or decrease. Where the value decreases, we will need to understand how to allocate the cost of that asset across its useful life. To this end, Chapter 5

will address how we depreciate non-current assets for accounting purposes. We will also need to know how to account for valuation increases and decreases. Chapter 6 will discuss how we undertake revaluations of non-current assets, and how we account for impairment losses (which are deemed to exist when an asset's carrying amount exceeds its recoverable amount). This chapter commences with a definition of assets.

4.2 Definition of assets

As we learned in Chapter 2, the IASB *Conceptual Framework for Financial Reporting* (hereafter referred to as the Conceptual Framework) provides definitions of the elements of accounting, these being assets, liabilities, equity, income and expenses. The Conceptual Framework defines an asset as: 'a resource controlled by the entity as a result of past events and from which economic benefits are expected to flow to the entity'.

Considering the above asset definition, an asset of an entity should have three fundamental characteristics:

1. An asset is expected to provide future economic benefits to the entity.
2. An asset must be controlled by the entity (but does not have to be legally owned).
3. The transaction or event giving rise to the control must already have occurred.

As we can see from the definition of assets provided above, 'future economic benefits' is the essence of assets. Future economic benefits represent the scarce capacity of assets to provide benefits to the organisations that control them and they provide the basis for organisations to achieve their objectives. These characteristics are common to all assets regardless of their physical form. In relation to the physical form of an asset, paragraph 4.11 of the Conceptual Framework states:

> *Many assets, for example property, plant and equipment, have a physical form. However, physical form is not essential to the existence of an asset; hence patents and copyrights, for example, are assets if future economic benefits are expected to flow from them to the entity and if they are controlled by the entity.*

Assets can take a variety of forms. For example, cash is an asset because of the command over future economic benefits it provides. It can be easily exchanged for other goods and services which in turn might provide economic benefits. Trade receivables are assets because of the cash inflows that are expected to occur when customers pay their accounts. Prepayments—such as prepaid rent or prepaid insurance—are assets because they represent existing rights to receive services. Plant, property and equipment are assets because they can be used to provide goods or services. Paragraph 4.10 of the Conceptual Framework discusses the ways in which assets can generate economic benefits. It states:

> *The future economic benefits embodied in an asset may flow to the entity in a number of ways. For example, an asset may be:*
>
> *(a) used singly or in combination with other assets in the production of goods or services to be sold by the entity;*
> *(b) exchanged for other assets;*
> *(c) used to settle a liability; or*
> *(d) distributed to the owners of the entity.*

We can draw a distinction between future economic benefits and the source of those benefits. The definition of an asset refers to the benefits; therefore, in the absence of expected economic benefits, the object or right will not be considered to be an asset. The consequence of this is that any assumption that a particular object or right will always be an asset is incorrect. For example, while a building would normally be expected to generate future economic benefits, if it becomes obsolete, unusable or is abandoned and has no resale value then the building would no longer represent an asset (an example here might be a mining town that is subsequently abandoned as a result of no economically recoverable reserves remaining within the mine site).

control (assets) If an asset is to be recognised, control rather than legal ownership must be established. Control is the capacity of an entity to benefit from an asset in the pursuit of the entity's objectives and to deny or regulate the access of others to that benefit.

As indicated in relation to the definition of an asset provided earlier, a reporting entity does not have to have legal ownership of an asset to record the asset within its statement of financial position. What is important is that the entity is able to 'control' the item's use. **Control** represents the capacity of the entity to benefit from the asset in the pursuit of the entity's objectives and to deny or regulate the access of others to that benefit. Therefore, because ownership is not essential, items like leased assets are often included as part of the assets of entities even though another organisation has legal title to them. Leased assets will be discussed further in Chapter 10.

4.2.1 Recognition issues

Although the Conceptual Framework defines assets, such a definition on its own is not operational. We need further guidance. Paragraph 4.44 of the Conceptual Framework provides criteria for the *recognition* of assets. Specifically:

> *An asset is recognised in the balance sheet when it is:*
>
> ■ *probable that the future economic benefits will flow to the entity; and*
> ■ *the asset has a cost or value that can be measured reliably.*

The recognition criteria are discussed in detail in Chapter 2, starting on page 36). A change in company policies could mean that items once considered assets might need to be written off in subsequent periods—that is, expensed. For example, a mining company might be involved in mining operations in a remote location around which a town has grown up. As a result of particular circumstances, a decision might be made by the organisation to abandon the mine site. The remote town might then effectively become a ghost town. The buildings owned by the mining company might once have generated economic benefits and were therefore considered assets. However, if they are of no further use to the reporting entity and there is no resale market for the assets, they should be written off. The write-off of the buildings should be treated as an expense of the company and would typically be referred to as an impairment loss.

Given recognition criteria such as 'probable', a high degree of professional judgement might be necessary. It is, therefore, possible that an expenditure that is deemed an asset by one financial statement preparer might be considered an expense by another. Such differences of opinion will have obvious consequences for the reported profits of reporting entities. They will also have implications for asset-based ratios such as the net asset backing per share ratio (see Worked Example 4.1).

Worked Example 4.1	Asset recognition and consideration of probable economic benefits

Assume that Kirra plc has assets of €1 million, liabilities of €300,000 and, therefore, shareholders' funds of €700,000. It has issued a total of 100,000 equity shares. Assume that the company then designs and manufactures an item of machinery at a cost of €150,000. The machinery produces a new type of flexible, transparent fin for surfboards. The cost of €150,000 comprises wages of €90,000, raw materials of €35,000 and depreciation of €25,000. The depreciation relates to other plant and machinery used to make the fin-making machine. The wages are to be paid at a future date.

Required

(a) Provide the accounting entry for the construction of the machinery, assuming that the machinery satisfies the criteria for recognition of an asset.
(b) Provide the accounting entry, assuming that the machinery is subsequently revealed not to be an asset because future economic benefits are not considered probable.

Solution

(a) For this expenditure to be recognised as an asset (that is, for it to be capitalised), it must be considered *probable* that the item will generate net cash flows at least equal to €150,000. In this case, if economic benefits of at least €150,000 are considered probable, the aggregated accounting entry would be:

Dr	Machinery—fin-making machine (an asset) (SOFP)	€150,000	
Cr	Wages payable (SOFP)		€90,000
Cr	Raw materials inventory (SOFP)		€35,000
Cr	Accumulated depreciation—plant and machinery (SOFP)		€25,000

Net assets will not change as a result of treating the expenditure as an asset. That is, before the expenditure, the net assets were €700,000 (which equals assets less liabilities = €1,000,000 – €300,000). After the expenditure on the machine, the net assets will still be €700,000. The manufacture of the machine led to an increase in assets of €90,000 (the increase in machinery of €150,000, less the raw materials consumed, and less the increased provision for depreciation). It also led to an increase in liabilities of €90,000 (the wages payable), and hence net assets (assets less liabilities) did not change. Net asset backing per share would be €700,000 ÷ 100,000 = €7 per share.

▶

> (b) If the probability that the machine will generate any positive net cash flows is subsequently assessed to be below 50 per cent (that is, economic benefits are not *probable*), the expenditure on the machine would be treated as an expense at the time such an assessment is made. The loss would typically be referred to as an impairment loss. The accounting entry would be:
>
> | | | | |
> |---|---|---|---|
> | Dr | Impairment loss—machinery (SOP&L) | €150,000 | |
> | Cr | Accumulated impairment loss—machinery (SOFP) | | €150,000 |
>
> If the asset is treated as being fully impaired, the net assets will fall to €550,000 and the net asset backing per share of Kirra plc would become €5.50 per share. The implications of a reduction in net asset backing per share are not always clear, but it would seem to be a reasonable proposition that a reduction in net asset backing per share from €7.00 to €5.50 would reduce the amount that potential investors would be prepared to pay for securities issued by Kirra plc.

Again, it is emphasised that if, at a given time, expenditure is not deemed likely to generate future economic benefits, that expenditure should be expensed in the period in which it becomes apparent that insufficient benefits will be realised. We will cover the impairment of assets more fully in Chapter 6.

Following the recognition of an impairment loss in an earlier period, it is possible that the recoverable amount of an asset might subsequently increase up to former levels; for example, in a subsequent period, when additional information becomes available that indicates that economic benefits are now probable. In these instances, paragraph 114 of IAS 36 *Impairment of Assets* requires that the asset be reinstated so long as certain conditions are met:

> *An impairment loss recognised in prior periods for an asset other than goodwill shall be reversed if, and only if, there has been a change in the estimates used to determine the asset's recoverable amount since the last impairment loss was recognised. When this is the case, the carrying amount of the asset shall, except as described in paragraph 117, be increased to its recoverable amount. That increase is a reversal of an impairment loss.*

Therefore the subsequent recognition of an asset will require a credit to the entity's statement of profit and loss, perhaps labelled something like 'gain from asset previously derecognised' or 'gain from reversal of previous impairment loss'. The restriction imposed by paragraph 117 is that the reversal (the gain) is limited to the initial impairment amount. Increases in value beyond this point do not affect the 'Statement of Profit and Loss' as they are unrealised gains that are included in 'Other Comprehensive Income'. For an example of a reversal of a prior period impairment loss we can return to Worked Example 4.1. Let us assume that new information became available in a subsequent period that indicated that the machine referred to in Worked Example 4.1 would generate net cash flows equal to at least €150,000 (and assuming it had already been subject to the recognition of an impairment loss), then the adjusting accounting entry would be:

Dr	Accumulated impairment loss—machinery (SOFP)	€150,000	
Cr	Gain from reversal of previous impairment loss (SOP&L)		€150,000

While this is a general principle, which is supported by IAS 36, that assets that have been subject to an impairment loss in previous periods can subsequently be recognised again as assets (such as in the illustration given above), it needs to be appreciated that some accounting standards specifically exclude this reversal for specific types of asset. As Chapter 8 will demonstrate, pursuant to IAS 38 *Intangible Assets*, expenditure on an intangible item that was initially recognised as an expense shall not be recognised as part of the cost of an intangible asset at a later date. In effect, such requirements (which can be deemed to be quite conservative) will cause the statement of financial position to understate the assets controlled by the entity.

As noted in Chapter 3, the firm may be involved in many contractual arrangements that use the accounting numbers relating to profits and assets. For example, there might be *interest coverage clauses*; clauses that restrict dividend payments to some designated fraction of earnings; management compensation clauses tying managers' rewards to reported profits; or clauses that specify debt-to-asset constraints. Hence the decision to expense or capitalise an item might be one that has direct implications for the value of the organisation and for the wealth of the managers. As noted in Chapter 2, however, there is an expectation that general purpose financial statements should be prepared in an unbiased manner (see the Conceptual Framework), regardless of any accounting-based contractual relationships that the organisation and/or its managers might have entered.

For an asset to be recognised, it is required to possess a cost or other value that can be *measured reliably*. At this stage, it should be appreciated that the asset measurement rules may vary depending on the class of assets being measured.

Table 4.1 Some classes of assets and their associated measurement rules

Asset	Measurement rule
Cash	Face value
Trade receivables	Face value less a provision for loan losses
Inventories	Lower of cost and net realisable value
Goodwill	At cost when acquired less any impairments—internally generated goodwill is not to be recognised
Property, plant and equipment	At cost, recoverable amount or revalued amount. If revaluations are undertaken, the requirement is that the valuations be based on 'fair value'
Marketable securities held by general insurers, life insurers and superannuation funds	Net market value
Marketable securities held by entities other than superannuation funds, life insurance businesses or general insurers	At cost or market value. Cost is frequently used to the extent it is not above market value
Assets leased by way of a finance lease	At the present value of the minimum lease payments
Biological assets	At fair value less estimated point of sale costs

Table 4.1 provides a summary of some of the various asset measurement rules currently used under IFRS. Because different classes of asset are typically measured in different ways (and some intangible assets are not permitted to be recognised as assets in the first place), the sum of the total assets of an entity will not reflect the cost of the assets or their net market value.

It would seem that the global accounting standard-setters (the IASB) are paving the way for a single preferred method of valuation to be applied for all assets—market value or fair value (which would mean that it would be more appropriate to add together the various asset values as they would be measured on the same basis). Recent changes to the IASB Conceptual Framework have shown a distinct move towards ranking relevance above reliability, and neutrality above prudence, when considering the qualitative characteristics of financial information. According to Henry and Holzmann (2011), the IASB's Conceptual Framework revisions (in 2010) 'say goodbye to reliability and stewardship'. They note that the term 'faithful presentation' is now used as a desirable characteristic of quality information instead of the term 'reliability'; the term 'stewardship' is omitted when the objectives of financial statements are outlined; and conservatism and prudence are no longer considered to be desirable characteristics of financial reporting, as they are considered to conflict with the concept of neutrality. This reduces the relevance of arguments put forward by supporters of the historic-cost concept, who have always argued that this concept provides more reliable information as the figures can be easily audited whereas fair value measurements may be determined using assumptions (for example, the present value of the asset's future cash flows). Similarly, Henry and Holzmann (ibid) also argue that the removal of the stewardship function of accounting has also weakened the case for the historic-cost measurement basis as it was deemed to have been 'more useful than fair value when assessing management's stewardship'.

If the future of accounting is to move to a preferred single method of valuation, then this would result in many changes to the existing international accounting standards. If measurement practices and related accounting standards were to be changed, much debate would result and it is questionable whether it is realistic to make any major changes to existing accounting practices that provide a multiplicity of measurement bases for different classes of asset.

Further, the accounting standard-setting process is considered to be very political in nature (Watts and Zimmerman 1986). Throughout the process of developing an accounting standard, the public is invited to make submissions—typically at the exposure draft stage. High levels of disagreement with a particular proposal might reduce the probability of the standard ultimately being implemented. Significant changes to generally accepted accounting practice are likely to be opposed by a significant proportion of financial statement preparers. Academic research has noted that the preparers are the most vocal lobbyists in relation to accounting standard-setters and this situation is expected by the users of the information. For example, Georgiou (2010) surveyed the users of financial accounting information in the UK and reported that they consider the national accounting professional bodies and the European and US accounting standard-setters to have the most influence on IASB standard-setting.

In the US similar results were reported by Hochberg et al. (2009) (preparers represented 32.2 per cent of the letters received when the Sarbanes–Oxley Act was being drawn up; users only accounted for 6.4 per cent).

Though academic literature has reported support for the historical-cost accounting approach from the preparers of accounting information, Houghton and Tan (1995) also report that the level of support for historical-cost or present value and market value is industry specific. Individuals working in financial institutions typically have a preference for present-value measures while non-financial institution representatives have a significantly stronger preference for historical-cost. Foster and Shastri (2010) suggest that the historical support from financial institutions may be influenced by the readily available markets for many of their assets, hence the cost of using fair values is not as great as it would be for other entities that may have to use more subjective means of obtaining the fair value (such as using estimated present values). Financial institutions are more likely to support a fair value approach when markets are stable or increasing but the recent financial crisis is likely to have weakened support from that industry. Many of the securities that were once easily valued are now more difficult as many markets became illiquid and the reliability of the relevant fair value measurement basis can be called into question (ibid). In addition, obtaining fair values for market-based instruments that lack transparent substance (for example, securities that include subprime debt obligations) is very difficult and again the value is no longer easily determined.

Support for fair value accounting is emerging in other sectors; for example, Navarro-Galera and Rodríguez-Bolívar (2010) reported positive support for fair value accounting by the chief financial officers of public sector organisations in Spain. They considered that fair value accounting would improve 'the accountability of government financial statements in terms of transparency, understandability, objectivity and reliability of financial reporting', though this is only possible if two conditions are met for the assets being valued : 'there needs to be a liquid market and the fair value estimations need to be practical'. Navarro-Galera and Rodríguez-Bolívar go on to explain how they think practical valuations can be achieved: the government needs to 'develop reliable estimations techniques and reliable measurement criteria; ensure adequate training of the personnel responsible; and have the financial capacity to fund the implementation of generally accepted valuation methods' (p. 383). Other writers also express concern, not about the use of fair value but about valuation of certain assets; for example, Bretherton (2011), in an article on the valuation of council roads, discusses how 'tricky' it is to determine their true value. Another area focused on by academics is whether pressure conditions, such as debt covenants or debt financing, cause the preparers of accounting information to show a preference for a particular basis. Gox and Wagenhofer (2010), for example, found a significant relationship between the ease of obtaining finance and the measurement basis used for valuing assets; specifically they found that firms that could raise finance with ease had a preference for the historical-cost basis of measurement whereas firms that had difficulties in raising finance preferred the fair value measurement basis. They also concluded that use of fair value accounting increases accounting risk. So it would seem that the preparers are more likely to support fair value measurement if it is not costly (time and expertise), is more reliable, is more likely to portray the company in a stronger light or will reduce constraints on management.

At the present time, the statement of financial position aggregated total, referred to as 'total assets', typically represents a summation of numerous asset classes—cash, trade receivables, inventory, land, buildings and marketable securities. See, for example, Exhibit 4.1, which shows the details of assets held by the BMW AG Group (in € millions), taken from BMW AG's statement of financial position as at 31 December 2010. Each asset class might have been measured on the basis of a different approach from that used for the other asset classes, yet we simply add them all together (perhaps like adding apples to oranges?). The use of different measurement classes within a single financial statement is in marked contrast to suggestions made by accounting researchers such as Chambers (see Chapter 3), but this is nevertheless a generally accepted approach.

In relation to the measurement of assets, classes of asset other than those briefly considered above may cause further problems in determining appropriate measurement bases. For example, what would be the appropriate basis of asset measurement for a building such as a museum or an art gallery? How would we measure the value of a botanical garden or a collection of ancient artefacts? The IASB Conceptual Framework definition of assets depends upon the probable generation of **future economic benefits**. Do museums, art galleries, botanical gardens or artefact collections generate 'economic benefits'? Certainly, many people accept that they provide social and cultural benefits. Such items are frequently referred to as **heritage assets**, which are typically held by government authorities for the use of current and future generations. There is usually no expectation that they will ever be sold, and any receipts, for example from visitors, are generally less than the ongoing expenses of maintaining such resources. They are often considered to generate negative net cash flows. Are such resources *assets* in accordance with the IASB Conceptual Framework definitions? Do you consider that a resource such as a museum collection, which has restrictions on its sale and use, is an asset? Why? How would you value it? The Mona Lisa, commonly considered to be the most valuable painting in the world, certainly the most famous, has no assigned value as the Louvre consider it to be priceless. The Louvre spent €4.8 million renovating its room, the Salle

Exhibit 4.1	Details of total assets from the BMW AG statement of financial position (balance sheet) at 31 December (in € million)

	2010	2009
Assets		
Intangible assets	**141**	145
Property, plant and equipment	**6,257**	5,536
Investments	**1,875**	1,303
Tangible, intangible and investment assets	**8,273**	**6,984**
Inventories	**3,259**	2,620
Trade receivables	**667**	690
Receivables from subsidiaries	**6,448**	6,197
Other receivables and other assets	**1,122**	882
Marketable securities	**2,556**	4,987
Cash and cash equivalents	**1,574**	2,195
Current assets	**15,626**	**17,571**
Prepayments	106	92
Surplus of pension and similar plan assets over liabilities	341	–
Total assets	**24,346**	**24,647**

des Etats. The painting is not insured as it belongs to the French state, which is its own insurer. In terms of valuation, it will never be sold so determining a valuation is difficult. When it left France on a tour of the US in 1962 it was insured for $100 million (taking inflation into account this would be $738 million in 2012!) But can the French Government record a value of $738 million? They are not going to sell it. The cost of running the Louvre probably exceeds the revenues obtained from admissions and other related income so the economic value may even be negative—yet the painting has value that goes beyond what is economic and measurable and is more intrinsic in nature. For this reason, the French Government consider it to be an asset that is priceless.

As a further issue to consider, how should assets such as trees be valued? Many businesses rely upon trees to generate future cash flows, perhaps through the sale of timber or paper. For example, an organisation might plant some pine tree seedlings with the expectation that they will generate commercially saleable timber in 14 years' time. To assess the financial position of the business, there might be an expectation that the trees should be shown as assets in the statement of financial position, but how would we measure their value? Should they be valued at the cost of the seedlings; at the cost of the seedlings plus further direct costs such as water, fertilisers and so on; or at present value, which will include assumptions about the timing of the milling, cash receipts, tree survival rate and appropriate discount rates? If the same sort of tree is in a botanical garden, or on the side of a road maintained by a local council, as opposed to being in a timber forest, would or should it have the same value? Should it be considered to be an asset? Should trees on the side of the road be considered assets?

4.3 General classification of assets

4.3.1 Definition of current assets

Most of us would be familiar with a definition of current assets as assets that, in the ordinary course of business, would be consumed or converted into cash within 12 months after the end of the financial period (the '12-month test'). This is what is often taught in introductory courses in financial accounting. However, IAS 1 *Presentation of Financial Statements* requires us to consider an entity's *normal operating cycle* when determining whether assets (and liabilities) should be classified as current or non-current for the purposes of presentation in the statement of financial position. According to paragraph 66 of IAS 1:

An entity shall classify an asset as current when:

(a) *it expects to realise the asset, or intends to sell or consume it, in its normal operating cycle;*
(b) *it holds the asset primarily for the purpose of trading;*
(c) *it expects to realise the asset within twelve months after the reporting period; or*
(d) *the asset is cash or a cash equivalent (as defined in IAS 7) unless the asset is restricted from being exchanged or used to settle a liability for at least twelve months after the reporting period.*

An entity shall classify all other assets as non-current.

According to IAS 1, the operating cycle of an entity is the time between the acquisition of assets for processing and their realisation in cash or cash equivalents. When the entity's normal operating cycle is not clearly identifiable, its duration is assumed to be 12 months. As an entity's 'operating cycle' might be greater than 12 months, assets that might not be converted to cash for a period in excess of 12 months can now be considered 'current' within such entities (IAS 1, paragraph 68). Assets held for trading purposes should also be classified as current in nature.

current ratio
Determined by dividing current assets by current liabilities. A measure of the short-term liquidity or solvency of an organisation.

Hence, unlike the traditional approach to classifying assets as current or non-current, which used the 12-month test, some professional judgement is now called for to determine the entity's 'normal operating cycle'. The classification of assets into current and non-current elements has implications for assessing the liquidity of the reporting entity. For example, analysts typically use ratios such as the **current ratio** (current assets divided by current liabilities) to assess the ability of the firm to pay its debts as and when they fall due. The decision relating to an entity's operating cycle will have implications for accounting ratios such as this.

4.3.2 Definition of current liabilities

In this chapter our focus is on assets. However, since we are discussing the statement of financial position, we will also briefly consider the definition of current liabilities. While we would probably be familiar with a definition of current liabilities in terms of an obligation being due for payment within 12 months of the end of the financial period (also a 12-month test), IAS 1 requires us to consider the entity's normal operating cycle. Consistent with the approach taken to define current assets, which considers the 'normal operating cycle', paragraph 69 of IASB 1 provides that a liability is to be classified as current when it satisfies any of the following criteria:

(a) *it expects to settle the liability in its normal operating cycle;*
(b) *it holds the liability primarily for the purpose of trading;*
(c) *the liability is due to be settled within twelve months after the end of the reporting period; or*
(d) *the entity does not have an unconditional right to defer settlement of the liability for at least twelve months after the reporting period.*

An entity shall classify all other liabilities as non-current.

So, in contrast to traditional approaches, something might now be disclosed as a current liability when that liability is not expected to be settled for a period in excess of 12 months.

intangible assets
Non-monetary assets without physical substance. Common forms of intangible assets include patents, goodwill, brand names and trademarks.

If there is no single, clearly identifiable operating cycle, or if the cycle is less than 12 months, the 12-month period must be used as the basis for classifying current assets and current liabilities.

Apart from the current/non-current dichotomy, there are other ways in which we classify assets. Assets may also be classified as 'tangible' and 'intangible', both of which could be current or non-current. **Intangible assets** can be defined as non-monetary assets without physical substance, and include brand names, copyrights, franchises, intellectual property, licences, mastheads, patents and trademarks. Chapter 8 describes how to account for intangible assets, including goodwill and research and development.

4.4 How to present a statement of financial position

As the discussion below will demonstrate, currently there are two basic approaches to presenting a statement of financial position. IAS 1 (paragraph 60) requires that, for the purposes of statement of financial position presentation:

An entity shall present current and non-current assets, and current and non-current liabilities, as separate classifications in its statement of financial position in accordance with paragraphs 66–76 except when a presentation based on liquidity provides information that is reliable and more relevant. When that exception applies, an entity shall present all assets and liabilities in order of liquidity.

Relevance and faithful representation considerations are important in determining whether the statement of financial position should be presented in a way that separates current assets from non-current assets and current liabilities from non-current liabilities (which could be considered to be the 'traditional' approach), or in a way that lists the assets and liabilities in terms of their order of liquidity without any segregation between current and non-current portions.

Therefore, IAS 1 does not prescribe a single format for the presentation of the statement of financial position. In determining which format to use, the commentary to IAS 1 provides some useful assistance. According to paragraphs 62 and 63 of IAS 1:

62. *When an entity supplies goods or services within a clearly identifiable operating cycle, separate classification of current and non-current assets and liabilities in the statement of financial position provides useful information by distinguishing the net assets that are continuously circulating as working capital (the current portion) from those used in the entity's long-term operations (the non-current portion). It also highlights assets that are expected to be realised within the current operating cycle, and liabilities that are due for settlement within the same period.*
63. *For some entities, such as financial institutions, a presentation of assets and liabilities in increasing or decreasing order of liquidity provides information that is reliable and is more relevant than a current/non-current presentation because the entity does not supply goods or services within a clearly identifiable operating cycle.*

IAS 1 also requires specific disclosures in relation to the duration of an entity's operating cycle. It requires that, where the entity presents current assets separately from non-current assets and current liabilities separately from non-current liabilities, and the entity has a single clearly identifiable operating cycle greater than 12 months, the length of that operating cycle must be disclosed.

Banking institutions such as the Bank of Ireland and Deutsche Bank have elected for some years to adopt the liquidity approach to presentation. Exhibit 4.2 shows how the Bank of Ireland structured its statement of financial position (which it referred to as a 'consolidated balance sheet') in its 2010 annual report.

4.4.1 Specific disclosures to be made on the face of the statement of financial position

Paragraph 54 of IAS 1 requires, as a minimum, that the face of the statement of financial position is to include line items that present the following amounts (these line items represent the aggregates of a number of accounts and would typically be supported by additional detail within the notes to the financial statements):

(a) *property, plant and equipment;*
(b) *investment property;*
(c) *intangible assets;*
(d) *financial assets (excluding amounts shown under (e), (h) and (i));*
(e) *investments accounted for using the equity method;*
(f) *biological assets;*
(g) *inventories;*
(h) *trade and other receivables;*
(i) *cash and cash equivalents;*
(j) *the total of assets classified as held for sale and assets included in disposal groups classified as held for sale in accordance with IFRS 5* Non-current Assets Held for Sale and Discontinued Operations;
(k) *trade and other payables;*
(l) *provisions;*
(m) *financial liabilities (excluding amounts shown under (k) and (l));*
(n) *liabilities and assets for current tax, as defined in IAS 12* Income Taxes;

| | Exhibit 4.2 | Illustration of the liquidity approach to statement of financial position disclosure (assets only) |

Bank of Ireland Consolidated Balance Sheet as at 31 December

	Note	2010 €m	2009 €m
ASSETS			
Cash and balances at central banks		1,014	4,241
Items in the course of collection from other banks		491	400
Trading securities	21	151	403
Derivative financial instruments	22	6,375	5,824
Other financial assets at FV through profit or loss	23	10,045	9,679
Loans and advances to banks	24	7,458	5,031
Available for sale financial assets	25	15,576	20,940
NAMA senior bonds	26	5,075	–
Loans and advances to customers	27	114,457	119,439
Assets held for sale to NAMA	28	804	9,581
Interest in associates	30	26	23
Interest in joint ventures	31	199	194
Intangible assets—goodwill	32	44	48
Intangible assets—other	32	408	459
Investment properties	33	1,304	1,265
Property, plant and equipment	34	372	404
Current tax assets		125	134
Deferred tax assets	44	1,128	865
Other assets	35	2,291	2,170
Retirement benefit asset	45	11	6
Other assets classified as held for sale	36	119	–
Total assets		167,473	181,106

(o) deferred tax liabilities and deferred tax assets, as defined in IAS 12;
(p) liabilities included in disposal groups classified as held for sale in accordance with IFRS 5;
(q) minority interest, presented within equity; and
(r) issued capital and reserves attributable to equity holders of the parent.

Additional line items can also be disclosed on the face of the statement of financial position. According to paragraph 58 of IAS 1, judgement on whether additional items are presented separately on the face of the statement of financial position is based on an assessment of:

(a) the nature and liquidity of assets;
(b) the function of assets within the entity; and
(c) the amounts, nature and timing of liabilities.

4.4.2 Examples of presentation formats

Entities may choose to provide other subtotals in addition to those shown in the above exhibit. For example, the statement of financial position could be presented to show:

(a) *total assets less total liabilities equals net assets/equity; or*
(b) *total assets equals total liabilities plus total equity.*

While the above approach to presenting a statement of financial position is the approach currently required by IAS 1, it should be noted that in October 2008 the IASB issued a Discussion Paper entitled *Preliminary Views on Financial Statement Presentation*. This Discussion Paper suggests some significant changes to the way the statement of financial position, statement of comprehensive income and statement of cash flows shall be presented. It is anticipated that a revised accounting standard will not be issued for a number of years. Given the significant nature of the revisions to financial statement presentation that are being proposed, the final section of this chapter provides a brief overview of the proposals made within the IASB Discussion Paper.

4.5   Determination of future economic benefits

As described earlier in this chapter, the IASB Conceptual Framework indicates that the essence of an asset is the 'future economic benefits' that the item will generate. Further, it must be 'probable' that these economic benefits will be generated and the asset must possess a cost or a value that can be measured reliably.

Generally speaking, the economic benefits themselves can be considered to come from two sources. The benefits can be derived from the use of the asset within the reporting entity or through the sale of the asset to an external party. If the expected benefits to be derived from the use of the asset within the organisation—often referred to as 'value in use'—exceed the market value, it would be expected that the entity would retain the asset. Conversely, if the expected sales price exceeds the asset's expected value in use, it would be expected that the entity would dispose of the asset.

Typically, assets are recorded initially at cost. Some assets, such as property, plant and equipment, may subsequently be revalued upwards if the net amount that is expected to be recovered through the cash inflows and outflows arising from their use and subsequent disposal exceeds their cost. (Revaluations are covered in Chapter 6.) Where the recoverable amount of an asset is less than the asset's cost ('recoverable amount' is defined in IAS 36 *Impairment of Assets* as the 'higher of an asset's net selling price and its value in use'), according to generally accepted accounting practice, the asset should be written down to its **recoverable amount**. This write-down is referred to as the recognition of an 'impairment loss'. Where the recoverable amount of an asset is to be based on its market value—perhaps there is an intention to sell it—to the extent that the asset is not of a specialised nature, it should be relatively easy to determine the value of the future cash flows. If the asset's value is to be determined by its value in use, determining this value can be highly subjective. This might be the case if the asset is very specialised in nature and there is no market for it. Further, if the 'value in use' is calculated by reference to the cash flows in a number of future periods, should those cash flows be discounted to their present value? If so, how should the appropriate discount rate be determined? IAS 36 (paragraph 6) requires that, in determining 'value in use' for the purpose of calculating 'recoverable amount' (and, therefore, possible impairment losses), the expected cash flows should be discounted to their present value.

> **recoverable amount** The net amount expected to be recovered through the cash inflows and outflows arising from the continued use and subsequent disposal of an item. Represented by the higher of an asset's fair value less costs to sell, and its value in use.

The value in use is, according to paragraph 31 of IAS 36, determined by:

(a) *estimating the future cash inflows and outflows to be derived from continuing use of the asset and from its ultimate disposal; and*
(b) *applying the appropriate discount rate to those future cash flows.*

We will return to the subject of impairment of assets in Chapter 6.

For the purposes of illustration, and ignoring issues associated with calculating the present value of expected future cash flows, let us assume that a reporting entity has acquired an asset at a cost of £25,000. It is expected that the asset will generate an income stream over the next few years that has a present value of only £18,000, after which time the asset will be scrapped. In this event, it will be necessary for the asset to be written down to its recoverable amount. Its expected future economic benefits from use (that is, its 'value in use') are less than the asset's cost, and the write-down will be treated as an impairment loss of the reporting entity. This write-down would not be considered to be depreciation. Depreciation involves the allocation of the cost (or revalued amount) of an asset over its expected **useful life**.

> **useful life** Estimated period over which future economic benefits embodied in a depreciable asset are expected to be consumed by the entity, or the estimated total service to be obtained from the asset by the entity.

If an asset is to be held for a number of periods, the service potential of the asset would be expected to decline over time. This should be recognised in the financial statements as an expense. Remember that the definition of an expense relies, in part, on there being a consumption or loss of a future economic benefit. It is generally accepted that the asset should be amortised or depreciated over the period of its useful life. If the expenditure on an item results in a uniform flow of economic benefits to the business over a fixed period, that asset should be expensed on a time basis. This applies, for example, to prepaid property rates and land tax, prepaid insurance premiums and prepaid rent.

Where the expenditure results in a benefit to the business for an indefinite period with a specified minimum term, the expenditure should be amortised over the minimum term. If the time over which the future benefits are to be derived is indeterminate or so extended that it is not practicable to determine an apportionment of the expenditure based on assessments of expected related revenue, the **amortisation** should be done on a time basis over a short period (for example, an arbitrary period of five years might be selected).

> **amortisation** The allocation of the cost of an asset, or its revalued amount, over the periods in which benefits are expected to be derived from this asset. Intangible assets are amortised; tangible assets are depreciated.

It will not always be clear whether future revenue will be generated by current expenditures. Consider advertising expenditure—obviously it would be economically irrational to undertake such expenditure except with a view to generating future benefits. Therefore, this would seem to fit the definition of an asset. However, the linkage between expenditure on advertising and future returns is not well defined. Because the returns are uncertain, it is usual for expenditure such as advertising to be written off as incurred. The future economic benefits to be derived from advertising cannot generally be 'measured reliably', which is one of the criteria for asset recognition in the Conceptual Framework. IAS 38 *Intangible Assets* would also act to preclude the recognition of advertising expenditures as an asset—we will consider intangible assets more fully in Chapter 8. If an advertising campaign has been paid for upfront but the advertising services have not been provided by the end of the reporting period, the expenditure would typically be treated as a current asset in the form of a prepayment.

> **capitalise** To carry forward (defer) some expenditure as an asset (as opposed to writing it off as an expense) on the basis that it will generate future economic benefits.

If a firm **capitalises** certain expenditures, rather than writing them off as incurred, its assets and profits will be higher in the year of deferral and lower in subsequent years as amortisation or impairment is expensed to profit and loss. Vice versa, when the expenditures are expensed when incurred, its assets and profits will be lower in that year

---

Financial Accounting In the News 4.1

WHAT WENT WRONG? ACCOUNTING FRAUD AND LESSONS FROM THE RECENT SCANDALS

Gary Giroux, *Social Research*, **22 December 2008**

Early in 2002, an internal audit found operating expenses charged as capital expenditures, double counting of revenues and undisclosed debt. New auditor KPMG reviewed the books; old auditor Arthur Andersen was fired. Ebbers resigned in April. On June 25, 2002, WorldCom announced $3.8 billion in accounting errors ($3.1 billion for 2001 and $800 million for first quarter 2002), mainly by capitalizing 'line costs,' which are fees to other telecom companies for network access rights. These are operating expenses. With the required restatements, net losses were now reported for both 2001 and first quarter 2002. CFO Scott Sullivan was fired on the same day.

Further review found over $10 billion in operating expenses that were fraudulently capitalized. WorldCom filed for bankruptcy in July 2002.

CFO Sullivan pleaded guilty to securities fraud and agreed to cooperate with prosecutors. Ebbers was indicted on securities fraud and making false statements to the SEC and convicted. WorldCom emerged from bankruptcy in 2004 as MCI, with debt reduced to less than $6 billion and about that much cash. Debtors ultimately received about 35 cents in the dollar in new bonds and stock; the original stockholders received nothing. MCI agreed to pay the SEC some $750 million to repay investors wiped out by the scandal.

but will be higher in subsequent years as there will be no amortisation or impairment entries relating to the expense.

There are many instances in which the capitalisation of expenditure, other than advertising, has solely been used to manipulate the perceived earnings and financial performance of an entity; WorldCom is probably one of the most famous accounting scandals of the last decade (see Financial Accounting in the News 4.1). As can be seen from the WorldCom article, the economic and social consequence of incorrectly classifying expenditure as assets (whether by fraud or error) can be great. Many employees lost their jobs and many investors lost their savings, so it is important that standard-setters provide strong guidance on recognition and measurement.

4.6 Acquisition cost of assets

There are a number of accounting standards that are relevant when determining the acquisition cost of assets. In situations where there is a business combination, which is defined as the bringing together of separate entities or operations of entities into one reporting entity, there is a specific accounting standard that deals with related asset acquisitions.

In relation to intangible assets, which can be defined as non-monetary assets without physical substance, a specific accounting standard, IAS 38 *Intangible Assets*, deals with how to determine the costs of such assets (see Worked Example 4.2). Intangible assets are the subject of Chapter 8, so we will limit our remarks on intangibles at this point. IAS 38 provides guidance on accounting for intangible assets other than goodwill (with goodwill being covered by the standard on business combinations). According to IAS 38, an intangible asset is initially to be measured at cost.

As we will see in Chapter 8, IAS 38 *Intangible Assets* specifically excludes the recognition of certain intangible assets for statement of financial position purposes. For example, internally generated goodwill, research expenditure, and expenditure on internally generated brands, mastheads, publishing titles, customer lists and items of similar substance are not to be recognised as intangible assets. Such assets can only be recognised if they are purchased from another party. For intangible assets that can be recognised for statement of financial position purposes (for example, development expenditure), the cost of an internally generated intangible asset comprises all expenditure that can be directly attributed and is necessary to creating,

---

Worked Example 4.2   Accounting for the cost of an intangible asset

Trigger Ltd is developing a new process for producing its major product—surfboards. During 2013 related expenditure amounted to €90,000. This expenditure related to salaries of staff involved in developing the process. It also included the costs of materials consumed in developing the process.

In 2014 the related expenditure amounted to €10,000. This related to wages of the staff involved in developing the process. Some general administrative overheads were also allocated to the development process.

It was only in 2014 that the entity was able to demonstrate that the new process met the necessary conditions for being considered an asset. The recoverable amount of the asset is estimated as exceeding €10,000.

Required
Determine what the carrying amount of the asset should be in 2014.

Solution
At the end of 2014 the asset pertaining to expenditure incurred in developing the new production process would be recorded at €10,000. The carrying amount of €10,000 does not exceed the recoverable amount of the asset. Because the allocation of administrative overheads does not relate directly to the development of the new production process, it would not be included in the cost of the asset. The expenditure incurred in 2013 would have been expensed at that time because the recognition criteria for assets could not be met. Because expenditure on such intangible assets cannot be reinstated after being expensed—a requirement of paragraph 71 of IAS 38 *Intangible Assets* (which states that 'expenditure on an intangible item that was initially recognised as an expense shall not be recognised as part of the cost of an intangible asset at a later date')—the €90,000 expenditure incurred in 2013 will never form part of the cost of the new production process recognised in the statement of financial position.

producing and preparing the asset for it to be capable of operating in the manner intended by management. The cost includes, if applicable:

- expenditure on material and services used or consumed in generating the intangible asset;
- the salaries, wages and other employment-related costs of personnel directly engaged in generating the asset; and
- any expenditure that is directly attributable to generating the asset, such as fees to register a legal right and the amortisation of patents and licences that are used to generate the asset.

Apart from determining the cost of intangible assets, we also have standards that specifically address the 'cost' of assets such as inventory (IAS 2), property, plant and equipment (IAS 16) and biological assets (IAS 41). The determination of the cost of inventories is covered in Chapter 7. We will therefore restrict the following discussion to determining the acquisition cost of property, plant and equipment.

4.7 Accounting for property, plant and equipment—an introduction

IAS 16 *Property, Plant and Equipment* deals with various issues associated with the recognition, measurement and disclosure of property, plant and equipment. IAS 16 is not applicable to property, plant and equipment that has been classified as being held for sale. There is a separate accounting standard, IFRS 5 *Non-current Assets Held for Sale and Discontinued Operations* that deals with such assets.

Property, plant and equipment are tangible assets and are deemed to be non-current assets because they will be held beyond the next 12 months or beyond the normal operating cycle of the entity. Consistent with the recognition criteria applicable to assets generally, paragraph 7 of IAS 16 requires that the cost of an item of property, plant and equipment be recognised as an asset if, and only if:

(a) it is probable that future economic benefits associated with the item will flow to the entity; and
(b) the cost of the item can be measured reliably.

Paragraph 15 of IAS 16 requires an item of property, plant and equipment that qualifies for recognition as an asset (see above test) to be measured initially at its cost. However, after the initial recognition of the asset at cost, the entity may decide to adopt either the 'cost model' or the 'fair value' model in measuring the asset (IAS 16, paragraph 29). We will consider the cost model versus the revaluation model in Chapter 6.

4.7.1 Historical cost

Since property, plant and equipment can be measured at cost, clearly we need to determine what is meant by 'cost'. According to paragraph 16 of IAS 16, the cost of an item of property, plant and equipment is to comprise:

(a) its purchase price, including import duties and non-refundable purchase taxes, after deducting trade discounts and rebates;
(b) any costs directly attributable to bringing the asset to the location and condition necessary for it to be capable of operating in the manner intended by management; and
(c) the initial estimate of the costs of dismantling and removing the item and restoring the site on which it is located, the obligation for which an entity incurs either when the item is acquired or as a consequence of having used the item during a particular period for purposes other than to produce inventories during that period.

According to paragraph 17 of IAS 16, 'directly attributable costs' would include:

(a) costs of employee benefits (as defined in IAS 19 Employee Benefits) arising directly from the construction or acquisition of the item of property, plant and equipment;
(b) costs of site preparation;
(c) initial delivery and handling costs;
(d) installation and assembly costs;
(e) costs of testing whether the asset is functioning properly, after deducting the net proceeds from selling any items produced while bringing the asset to that location and condition (such as samples produced when testing equipment); and
(f) professional fees.

As also indicated above, the cost of an asset should include installation and assembly costs. For example, consider a computer network that cost €250,000 to acquire initially, plus €2,000 to transport the equipment to its place of use, plus an additional €50,000 paid to computer consultants to make the equipment ready for use. The acquisition cost of the asset would typically be treated as the aggregate amount of the expenditure for the computer—€302,000. This total amount would subsequently be depreciated over the future periods in which the benefits were expected to be derived. Paragraph 19 of IAS 16 provides examples of costs that do not form part of the cost of an item of property, plant or equipment, these being:

(a) costs of opening a new facility;
(b) costs of introducing a new product or service (including costs of advertising and promotional activities);
(c) costs of conducting business in a new location or with a new class of customer (including costs of staff training); and
(d) administration and other general overhead costs.

4.7.2 Fair value

While we would expect that the majority of the costs associated with acquiring an item of property, plant and equipment would be met with cash, property, plant and equipment can also be acquired by other means, such as by exchanging shares of the company for the assets or exchanging other types of asset for the property, plant and equipment. This raises questions in relation to determining 'cost'.

IAS 16 requires that, if an item of property, plant and equipment is acquired in exchange for equity instruments of the entity (for example, by issuing additional shares), then the cost of the item of property, plant and equipment is the fair value of the equity instruments issued, with fair value being defined as the amount for which an asset could be exchanged between knowledgeable, willing parties in an arm's length transaction.

Usually, the fair value of the consideration ('consideration' being what is given in exchange to acquire a particular asset) is used to measure the acquisition cost of an asset. However, when the consideration is the purchaser's own equity instruments (such as shares that are not listed on a stock exchange) the fair value of the asset acquired is used to measure the value of the equity issue because it is considered that the fair value of the asset acquired can be measured more reliably.

An item of property, plant and equipment may also be acquired through the exchange of another item of property, plant and equipment. The cost of the acquired asset is measured at the fair value of the asset given up, adjusted by the amount of any cash, or cash equivalents, that are transferred. That is, when an asset is exchanged for another asset, the carrying amount (book value) of the asset given in exchange is not generally relevant for determining the 'cost' of the acquired asset—it is the fair value of the asset given in exchange that is relevant (IAS 16, paragraphs 6 and 26).

Where an entity acquires an item of property, plant and equipment by exchanging another asset, then a gain or loss on disposal will be recognised, with the gain or loss being the difference between the carrying amount of the asset being exchanged, and its fair value. For example, let us assume that we are acquiring some land in exchange for a ship we currently own. If the carrying amount of the ship was £600,000 (and IAS 16 defines carrying amount as 'the amount at which an asset is recognised after deducting any accumulated depreciation and accumulated impairment losses'), made up by an original cost of £800,000 less accumulated depreciation of £200,000, but its fair value was £750,000, then we would record the land being acquired at a cost of £750,000 and show a net gain of £150,000 on disposal of the ship. Our journal entries would be:

Dr	Land	£750,000	
Dr	Accumulated depreciation—ship	£200,000	
Cr	Ship		£800,000
Cr	Gain on disposal of ship		£150,000

The net gain would be the difference between the proceeds from the disposal of the ship (which is equated to the fair value of the land) and the carrying amount of the ship.

In situations where the fair value of the asset being given up is difficult to determine, perhaps because the asset is of a type that is not commonly traded, it is permissible to use the fair value of the asset being acquired as its cost. However, there might be cases where neither the fair value of the asset being given up nor that of the asset being acquired can be reliably determined. Perhaps the assets are unique or highly specialised and there is no active market for them. In such cases, the accounting standard permits the cost of the property, plant and equipment acquired in exchange for a similar asset to be measured at the carrying amount of the asset given up in the exchange.

While we have been discussing the initial acquisition cost of the asset, it should be appreciated that subsequent accounting periods will require adjustments to the value of the assets by way of depreciation, recognition of impairment losses or, perhaps, through asset revaluations. Subsequent chapters of this book will consider how to account for such changes in value. Again, it is emphasised that for property, plant and equipment there

is a requirement that assets initially be recorded at cost. However, following initial recognition, the entity may elect either to continue to measure the asset at cost (less appropriate depreciation), or to revalue the asset to its fair value.

As a further example of the 'fair value rule' provided above, let us assume that a reporting entity exchanged a block of land (carrying value of £20,000) with another entity for a truck (recorded in the other entity's books at £30,000). Is the reporting entity better off after the transaction? Not necessarily. It is the fair value that is relevant and not the carrying value. If the block of land had a fair value of £35,000, the truck would initially be recorded at £35,000. If the truck's carrying value and fair value were both £30,000, the truck would be recorded at only £30,000, which is less than the fair value of the exchanged land. In real terms, the reporting entity might actually be worse off, as it could have sold the block of land for £35,000 (assuming a ready market), acquired the truck for £30,000 and had a balance in cash of £5,000. However, from an accounting perspective, if the truck's recorded value is based on historical cost, the reporting entity has made a net gain of £10,000 if the truck is considered to have a fair value of £30,000. Opportunity costs are not recognised. This £10,000 gain would be represented by the difference between the fair value of the truck and the carrying amount of the land. Worked Example 4.3 gives another example of how to determine the acquisition cost of assets.

As indicated in Worked Example 4.3, where the purchase consideration comprises shares or other securities, the acquired asset should be recorded at the fair value of those securities. Where the securities are listed on a securities exchange, the price at which they could be placed on the market will usually be an indication of fair value. However, it would be necessary to make a valuation of the securities of an unlisted company.

As indicated, if the valuation of the assets being given up in the exchange is difficult to determine (say, in Worked Example 4.3, we realise that the valuation of the shares is difficult owing to non-listing or a 'thin market'), an alternative approach is to value the acquired asset at its fair value if that amount is more clearly determinable than what was given in exchange.

4.7.3 Safety and environmental expenditure

Certain items of property, plant and equipment might be acquired for safety or environmental reasons. While these items might not produce any direct economic benefits, the expenditure on them might be necessary for the entity to obtain future economic benefits from its other non-current assets. In this regard, paragraph 11 of IAS 16 states:

> Such items of property, plant and equipment qualify for recognition as assets because they enable an entity to derive future economic benefits from related assets in excess of what could be derived had it not been acquired. For example, a chemical manufacturer may install new chemical handling processes to comply with environmental requirements for the production and storage of dangerous chemicals; related plant enhancements are recognised as an asset because, without them, the entity is unable to manufacture and sell chemicals. However, the resulting carrying amount of such an asset and related assets is reviewed for impairment in accordance with IAS 36 Impairment of Assets.

Where expenditure, such as that referred to above, must be incurred to enable an asset to continue to be used and future periods in which the asset is used are expected to benefit from the expenditure, the expenditure shall be capitalised. If the expenditure was not incurred, then the service potential of the related asset, or assets, might not be realised. For example, legislation might be promulgated requiring machinery to comply with a minimum level of safety standards, or to fit a device to limit harmful environmental impacts. This safety or environmental expenditure is capitalised because it is necessary (owing to legislative requirements) for the entity to continue its manufacturing process and failure to comply would mean that the economic benefits embodied in the original asset would not be obtained.

Another issue we need to consider in determining the costs of an asset are any estimates of costs that might be required in relation to dismantling or removing the asset, or restoring sites as a result of using the asset. As we saw previously, paragraph 16 of IAS 16 states that the cost of property, plant and equipment is to include 'the initial estimate of the costs of dismantling and removing the item and restoring the site on which it is located, the obligation for which an entity incurs either when the item is acquired or as a consequence of having used the item during a particular period for purposes other than to produce inventories during that period'. As an example of how this requirement applies, an oil company might construct an offshore oil-drilling platform. Before establishing the platform there would be an expectation that the platform would be removed at the completion of the project and any environmental disturbances rehabilitated. These expected future costs would be estimated at the commencement of the project and a liability would be recorded in accordance with IAS 37 *Provisions, Contingent Liabilities, and Contingent Assets*. The expected costs would be measured at their expected

| Worked Example 4.3 | Determining the acquisition costs of assets |

Assume that Joy plc is acquiring a portable building from Davies plc for the following consideration:

Cash	£150,000
Shares	100,000 shares with a market value per share of £1.90
Land	Joy is going to transfer title of some rural land to Davies (carrying value of £120,000; market value of £95,000)
Liabilities	Joy has agreed to take legal responsibility for Davies' bank loan of £65,000
Legal fees pertaining to the acquisition: £9,000, which will be paid one month later	

Required

Determine the acquisition cost of the asset.

Solution

In determining the cost of the acquisition, it is the fair value of the consideration that is relevant, not the historical book values.

Joy plc should account for the cost of the building as follows:

Cost	£
Cash	150,000
Shares	190,000
Land	95,000
Legal fees	9,000
Liabilities (bank loan)	65,000
	509,000

The journal entry to record the acquisition would be:

		£	£
Dr	Building	509,000	
Dr	Loss on disposal of land	25,000	
Cr	Bank loan		65,000
Cr	Cash		150,000
Cr	Legal fees accrued		9,000
Cr	Land		120,000
Cr	Share capital		190,000

The asset—in this case, the building—has a limited life and therefore should subsequently be depreciated over the periods in which the benefits are expected to be derived.

---

present value and the amount would be included as part of the cost of the asset—the drilling platform. The total amount of the asset, including the estimated costs for dismantling and removal, would be depreciated over the expected useful life of the asset. One rationale for including the costs of dismantling and removal would be that agreeing to undertake such actions might be a necessary precondition for enabling the asset to be available for use. An illustration of this is provided in Worked Example 4.4.

4.7.4 Allocation of cost to individual items of property, plant and equipment

From time to time, a group of items of property, plant and equipment might be acquired and paid for in a single payment. For example, a number of computers could be acquired at the same time for the development of a

Worked Example 4.4	Capitalisation of expenditure to be incurred subsequent to the acquisition of an asset

During the reporting period ending 30 June 2014, Garratt Limited erected an on-land oil rig in Germany. The cost of the exploration rig and associated technology amounted to €6,567,000. Other costs associated with the erection of the oil rig amounted to:

	€
Costs incurred in obtaining access to the site	2,324,900
Transport	856,300
Erection	445,640
Resource consent	1,657,000
Engineers' fees	900,200
	6,184,040

The oil rig was ready to start production on 1 July 2014, with actual production starting on 1 October 2014. At the end of the rig's useful life, which is expected to be 5 years, Garratt Limited is required by its resource consent to dismantle the oil rig, remove it, and return the site to its original condition. After consulting its own engineers and environmentalists, Garratt Limited estimates these costs to be:

	€
Dismantling the oil rig	199,400
Transport	355,800
Environmental clean-up costs	4,854,500
Replacement of flora and fauna	690,300
	6,100,000

Garratt Limited plans to provide for these costs over the expected life of the oil well. It uses a discount rate of 8 per cent.

Required

Prepare the journal entries necessary to account for the oil rig for the years ended 30 June 2014, 30 June 2015 and 30 June 2016. Ignore depreciation.

Solution

30 June 2014

Dr	Oil rig	€16,902,700	
Cr	Cash/Accounts payable (€6,567,0000 + €6,184,040)		€12,751,040
Cr	Provision for restoration costs		€4,151,660

As we can see above, at the end of the reporting year of 30 June 2014, a provision for restoration costs must be created. The provision is the best estimate of the expenditure required to settle the obligation. Provisions are to be recorded at present value, pursuant to paragraph 45 of IAS 37 *Provisions, Contingent Liabilities, and Contingent Assets*.

The estimated site restoration costs of €4,151,660 (€6,100,000, payable in 5 years, discounted at 8 per cent, which equals €6,100,000 × 0.6806) are added to the cost of the oil rig. The costs incurred in dismantling the rig, removing it and restoring the site to its original condition are costs that are necessary to realise the future economic benefits embodied in the asset, and the required expenditure has been included in the cost of the asset.

Discounting the future obligation creates interest costs for future years. As paragraph 60 of IAS 37 states:

> Where discounting is used, the carrying amount of a provision increases in each period to reflect the passage of time. This increase is recognised as borrowing cost.

▶

The borrowing (interest) costs are allocated to specific years, as follows:

Date	Opening balance	Interest at 8%	Balance of site restoration costs
	€	€	€
1 July 2014	–	-	4,151,660
30 June 2015	4,151,660	332,133*	4,483,793
30 June 2016	4,483,793	358,703	4,842,496
30 June 2017	4,842,496	387,400	5,229,896
30 June 2018	5,229,896	418,392	5,648,288
30 June 2019	5,648,288	451,712**	6,100,000

*€4,151,660 x 8% = €332,133
**includes rounding difference

The journal entries to recognise the periodic interest charges are:

30 June 2015
Dr   Interest expense   €332,133
Cr   Provision for restoration costs   €332,133

30 June 2015
Dr   Interest expense   €358,703
Cr   Provision for restoration costs   €358,703

As we can see from the above entries, at the end of each period the amount recorded for the provision of restoration costs increases. By the end of the final period of the project the balance of the provision will be €6,100,000. This amount will then be eliminated when Garratt Limited undertakes the actual restoration work.

computer laboratory to be used by students. These computers would generally be indistinguishable, so the allocation of the purchase price is straightforward. For example, if 25 computers were acquired at a cost of €145,000, the cost attributable to each computer would be €5,800.

However, where a number of individual items of property, plant and equipment are acquired and a lump-sum payment is made, the cost of the assets is still determined according to the requirements of IAS 16; that is, pursuant to paragraph 16, the cost would include the fair value of the consideration given, together with any directly attributable costs. How the costs are to be allocated to individual items is not directly addressed by IAS 16. However, generally accepted practice would be for the cost to be allocated to the individual items in proportion to their fair values at the time of acquisition. This is demonstrated in Worked Example 4.5.

4.7.5 Components approach

Certain classes of property, plant and equipment, for example aircraft and ships, might comprise a number of individual component parts, each of which has a different useful life. For example, an aircraft might comprise a number of components, including the airframe, the engines and internal fittings. IAS 16 does not prescribe the unit of measurement for recognition of individual components making up an item of property, plant and equipment. Rather, it is left to the professional judgement of the financial statement preparers (IAS 16, paragraph 9). Each of the components might have a different useful life or provide economic benefits to the entity in different patterns. They may be owned or subject to a finance lease. As these individual components have different lives, each might require different depreciation rates and methods (IAS 16, paragraph 44). To ensure that the individual components are accounted for separately, paragraph 43 of IAS 16 requires:

Each part of an item of property, plant and equipment with a cost that is significant in relation to the total cost of the item shall be depreciated separately.

Worked Example 4.5	Allocation of cost to individual assets

On 15 July 2015, Gilmore Limited acquired a manufacturing plant for €3,900,500. The purchase price included the land, building, machinery and inventory of raw materials. An external valuer employed by Gilmore Limited believes the cost can be allocated to the individual items in the following proportions:

	%
Land	55
Building	35
Machinery	8
Inventory	2
	100

Required

Prepare the journal entry as at 15 July 2015 to record the acquisition of the assets.

Solution

Allocation of purchase price:

	%	€
Land	55	2,145,275
Building	35	1,365,175
Machinery	8	312,040
Inventory	2	78,010
	100	3,900,500

15 July 2015			
Dr	Land	€2,145,275	
Dr	Building	€1,365,175	
Dr	Machinery	€312,040	
Dr	Inventory	€78,010	
Cr	Bank		€3,900,500

4.7.6 Deferred payments

It is possible for an entity to acquire an item of property, plant and equipment and arrange with the vendor of the equipment that payment will not be made for some time into the future. In this instance, the cost of the item must be determined by discounting the amounts payable in the future to their present value at the date of acquisition (IAS 23, paragraph 16). The difference between the cash price equivalent and the total payment is recognised as interest expense over the period of credit unless such interest is recognised in the carrying amount of a qualifying asset—we will consider qualifying assets in the next section of the chapter. The discount rate to be used is the rate at which the acquirer can borrow the amount under similar terms and conditions. An example of how deferred payments are accounted for is provided in Worked Example 4.6.

4.7.7 Accounting for borrowing costs incurred when constructing an item of property, plant and equipment

An area in which there has been some disparity in accounting treatment is that of interest expenses incurred during the construction of an asset. For example, an organisation might need to borrow funds to finance the ongoing construction of an asset such as a building. At issue would be whether the related interest expenses should be treated as a cost of the asset or whether the interest expenses should be expensed in the period in which they are incurred. How do you think the borrowing costs should be treated? Such a decision could have a significant impact on the organisation's reported profits and assets. IAS 23 *Borrowing Costs* provides guidance

Worked Example 4.6   Accounting for the deferred payment of an asset

On 1 July 2014, Cornwall Point Limited acquired a sand-dredging machine. Cornwall Point Limited paid an initial amount of £100,000 on the date of acquisition and agreed to make a further eight annual payments of £150,000, starting on 30 June 2015. Cornwall Point Limited could borrow funds at 9 per cent per annum.

Required
Prepare the journal entries as at 1 July 2014 and 30 June 2015 to account for the acquisition of the asset.

Solution

Present value of £100,000 initial payment	£100,000
Present value of £150,000 for 8 years discounted at 9% (£150,000 × 5.5348—see Appendix B)	£830,220
	£930,220

1 July 2014

Dr	Sand-dredging machine	£930,220	
Cr	Bank		£100,000
Cr	Loan		£830,220

30 June 2015

Dr	Interest expense—(£830,220 × 9%)	£74,720	
Dr	Loan	£75,280	
Cr	Bank		£150,000

---

on how to account for borrowing costs that are incurred when an asset is being constructed. IAS 23 defines borrowing costs as 'interest and other costs incurred by an entity in connection with the borrowing of funds'. According to paragraph 6 of IAS 23, 'borrowing costs' may include:

(a) *interest on bank overdrafts and short-term and long-term borrowings;*
(b) *amortisation of discounts or premiums relating to borrowings;*
(c) *amortisation of ancillary costs incurred in connection with the arrangement of borrowings;*
(d) *finance charges in respect of finance leases recognised in accordance with IAS 17* Leases; *and*
(e) *exchange differences arising from foreign currency borrowings to the extent that they are regarded as an adjustment to interest costs.*

When an asset is deemed to be a 'qualifying asset' and borrowing costs have been incurred to acquire, construct or produce the asset, then such costs must be included as part of the cost of the asset (IAS 23, paragraph 1). Conversely, if the borrowing costs cannot be attributed to a qualifying asset, then they would be expensed in the period in which the borrowing costs were incurred. Obviously, the above requirement calls for a definition of 'qualifying asset'. A 'qualifying asset' is defined in IAS 23 as:

an asset that necessarily takes a substantial period of time to get ready for its intended use or sale.

A 'substantial period of time' is generally regarded as being more than 12 months. The borrowing costs to be included would be those that would have been avoided if the expenditure on the asset had not been made. The capitalisation of the borrowing costs is to cease when substantially all the activities necessary to prepare the asset for its intended use or sale are complete.

Paragraph 7 of IAS 23 provides further guidance in relation to identifying whether a particular asset is a qualifying asset. It states:

Depending on the circumstances, any of the following may be qualifying assets:

(a) *inventories*
(b) *manufacturing plants*

(c) power generation facilities
(d) intangible assets
(e) investment properties.

Financial assets, and inventories that are manufactured, or otherwise produced, over a short period of time, are not qualifying assets. Assets that are ready for their intended use or sale when acquired are not qualifying assets.

The consequence of including costs such as interest costs in the cost of an asset is an increase in depreciation expenses in subsequent years (assuming the asset is not being constructed for sale). To the extent that the asset is being produced to sell, the cost of sales will rise as a result of the inclusion of borrowing costs in the cost of the asset. Hence the capitalisation of borrowing costs simply acts to defer the ultimate recognition of those costs.

The capitalisation of borrowing costs as part of the cost of a qualifying asset begins on the 'commencement date'. According to paragraph 17 of IAS 23:

The commencement date for capitalisation is the date when the entity first meets all of the following conditions:

(a) *it incurs expenditures for the asset;*
(b) *it incurs borrowing costs; and*
(c) *it undertakes activities that are necessary to prepare the asset for its intended use or sale.*

As long as the above conditions are met, borrowing costs continue to be capitalised and included as part of the cost of the asset. An entity should cease to include borrowing costs as part of the cost of an asset when it suspends development of the qualifying asset (IAS 23, paragraph 20) or when substantially all the activities necessary to prepare the asset for sale or use are complete (IAS 23, paragraph 22).

When a qualifying asset is acquired with borrowed funds, either such funds can be borrowed specifically for the purpose of acquiring or constructing the asset, or the borrowed funds might come from funds the organisation has borrowed for general purposes.

Where funds are borrowed specifically for the purpose of acquiring an item of property, plant and equipment, and the asset is considered to be a 'qualifying asset', the amount to be capitalised is the actual interest paid within the period. For example, assume that on 1 July 2015 Manheim Limited borrowed €500,000 at 12 per cent per annum, for two years, for the specific purpose of constructing an item of plant. The amount of interest capitalised as at June 2016 would be €60,000, which is €500,000 × 12%. The journal entry to capitalise the interest borrowed would be:

Dr	Plant	€60,000	
Cr	Interest payable		€60,000

If funds that have been borrowed are temporarily invested, perhaps owing to a delay in the construction or acquisition of the qualifying asset, then any investment income earned is deducted from the borrowing costs incurred (IAS 23, paragraph 12).

By contrast, where funds are borrowed for general purposes and to fund various activities, and some of these funds are used to acquire or construct a qualifying asset, then related interest is still to be capitalised so long as the capitalised amount does not exceed the amount of borrowing costs the entity incurred in the period. (IAS 23, paragraph 14)

For example, assume the same example above where on 1 July 2015 Manheim Limited contracted to construct an item of plant at a cost of €500,000. Let us further assume that the organisation had previously borrowed €1,000,000 at 13 per cent per annum, as well as another €2,000,000 at 10 per cent per annum, and that these available funds were used to construct the asset. The weighted average cost of the available funds would be:

Loan €	Interest rate %	Interest €
1,000,000	13	130,000
2,000,000	10	200,000
		330,000

The average interest rate would be €330,000/€3,000,000 = 11 per cent. Therefore, the amount of interest capitalised would be €55,000, which is €500,000 × 11%. The journal entry to capitalise the interest borrowed would be:

Dr	Plant	€55,000	
Cr	Interest payable		€55,000

4.7.8 Prior research on interest capitalisation

While borrowing costs relating to assets that are constructed over a substantial period of time must now be capitalised (to the extent that the capitalisation does not cause the carrying amount of the asset to exceed its recoverable amount), this has not always been the case. Historically, managers had a choice about how to treat such borrowing costs. One study that considered what motivates organisations to voluntarily adopt a particular accounting treatment for dealing with interest expenses incurred during the construction of assets was that of Bowen *et al.* (1981). Adopting Positive Accounting Theory (which is explained in Chapter 3), they proposed that the choice to expense or capitalise interest might be affected by the existence of management compensation agreements tied to reported earnings, accounting-based debt covenant constraints or political costs associated with higher reported earnings.

The results of Bowen *et al.*'s study indicated that firms with management compensation contracts are no more likely to capitalise interest than other firms. This was contrary to the researchers' expectations, but could in part be the result of the potentially naive assumption that the remuneration contracts did not specify whether interest was to be capitalised or expensed. In fact, the remuneration contracts might well have limited the managers' choice. However, Bowen *et al.* did find, as expected, that organisations that capitalised their interest, thereby increasing reported profits and assets, had financial ratios consistent with being closer to the violation of debt covenants. The act of capitalising the interest was, therefore, considered a means of loosening the restrictions of the debt agreements and of moving the firm away from a potentially costly default on its debt contracts. Bowen *et al.* also found that the largest firms in the oil industry elected to expense interest, rather than capitalise it. The effect of this was to decrease reported income. The explanation for this seems to have been that, in the period under investigation, the petroleum industry was under intense public scrutiny and it was felt that higher profits could attract more adverse attention for the organisations. This potentially adverse attention could have led to wealth transfers away from the firms (for example by windfall taxes). By adopting a method of accounting that reduces reported income, the attention focused on the organisation should, according to Positive Accounting Theory, be reduced.

4.7.9 Repairs and additions to property, plant and equipment

Following the acquisition of a non-current asset, additional expenditure may be incurred. These costs can range from ordinary repairs to significant additions. The major problem in this area is the decision whether or not to capitalise these expenses and, if the expenses *are* capitalised, determining the number of periods over which the expenditure should be amortised. A general approach is to capitalise expenditures that result in increased future benefits, but expense those expenditures that simply maintain a given level of service. Expenditure on periodic overhauls or repairs would generally be expensed on the basis that such expenditure does not improve the asset from its former state (IAS 16 *Property, Plant and Equipment*, paragraph 12).

The capitalised value of an item of property, plant and equipment, together with the costs associated with any subsequent improvements of the asset, will be depreciated over future periods, given that it is usual for non-current assets to have a limited useful life; however, land can be an exception to this general rule.

4.8 Assets acquired at no cost

Resources may also be acquired at no cost, for example through a donation. In such a case, if nothing is paid for an item, can it be recognised as an asset? To the extent that the item is expected to provide probable and measurable future economic benefits, it should be recognised as an asset (Conceptual Framework, paragraph 4.14).

But what would the other side (the credit side) of the accounting journal entry be? As we know, the Conceptual Framework defines income as 'increases in economic benefits during the accounting period in the form of inflows or other enhancements of assets or decreases of liabilities that result in increases in equity, other than relating to contributions from equity participants'. Since a donated asset would increase the assets of the entity without increasing its liabilities, the consequent increase in equity would mean that income would be recognised (Conceptual Framework, paragraph 4.47).

Worked Example 4.7 considers how to account for an asset acquired at no cost.

It should be appreciated that while it appears conceptually correct for an organisation to recognise an asset for the purpose of its statement of financial position (as we have discussed above) even when the asset has been donated to the organisation, this treatment is not embraced by IAS 16 *Property, Plant and Equipment*. The

> ### Worked Example 4.7   Accounting for an asset acquired at no cost
>
> Crescent Head Ltd decides as a goodwill gesture to give Point Plummer Ltd, at no cost, a truck with a market value of €90,000. Point Plummer Ltd is a local not-for-profit organisation that teaches children about water safety. The carrying value of the truck in the books of Crescent Head Ltd is €80,000 (cost of €100,000; accumulated depreciation of €20,000).
>
> #### Required
>
> Provide the journal entries to record the asset transfer for:
> (a) Point Plummer Ltd; and
> (b) Crescent Head Ltd.
>
> #### Solution
>
> (a) The entry in the books of Point Plummer Ltd would be:
>
> | | | | |
> |---|---|---|---|
> | Dr | Truck | €90,000 | |
> | Cr | Donation income (or something similar) | | €90,000 |
>
> (b) Before providing the journal entry in the books of Crescent Head Ltd, we need to determine whether the act of giving up the asset represents an expense. Conceptually, it *would* appear to represent an expense. It appears to be a 'loss on disposal' of an asset. Any associated benefits of donating the asset would be too uncertain to allow them to be recognised as an asset. While the Conceptual Framework is silent on the issue of gifts or donations, it does state in paragraph 4.49:
>
> *Expenses are recognised in the income statement when a decrease in future economic benefits related to a decrease in an asset or an increase of a liability has arisen that can be measured reliably. This means, in effect, that recognition of expenses occurs simultaneously with the recognition of an increase in liabilities or a decrease in assets.*
>
> Hence the accounting entry in the books of Crescent Head Ltd:
>
> | | | | |
> |---|---|---|---|
> | Dr | Donation expense (or something similar) | €80,000 | |
> | Dr | Provision for depreciation—truck | €20,000 | |
> | Cr | Asset—truck | | €100,000 |
>
> *Note:* Because of the difference between carrying amount and market value, there is a difference between the expense recognised by Crescent Head Ltd and the revenue recognised by Point Plummer Ltd.

requirements of accounting standards override the requirements within conceptual frameworks. Specifically, paragraph 15 of IAS 16 states that: 'An item of property, plant and equipment that qualifies for recognition as an asset shall be measured at its cost.'

It would appear therefore that a strict application of the standard would mean that if the item of property, plant and equipment has been received as a result of a donation, no cost would initially be recognised for the asset (which would mean that no revenue would be recognised either). However, there would be nothing to prevent the organisation from subsequently revaluing the asset to its fair value. Revaluations are considered in Chapter 6.

4.9   Discovery of errors in prior period financial statements

The last thing we will discuss in this chapter on assets is errors made in measuring assets. It is possible that errors made in valuing assets and other elements of financial statements might not be discovered until subsequent periods. For example, it might become known in 2014 that in the previous year ending 30 June 2013 the inventory of an organisation was valued in excess of its net realisable value and hence was overstated. This would have meant that assets and profits in the previous periods were overstated (because inventory should have been written down with a related expense being recognised in the 2013 financial year). At issue is how we treat this

error from an accounting perspective, keeping in mind that the error was not discovered until the next financial period. We have a number of options for dealing with an error made in a previous financial year. For example, in such a situation, we could:

- reissue the 2013 financial statements with the error corrected (but this would be quite expensive and is often deemed impractical);
- make retrospective adjustments, that is, we could decrease opening retained earnings and reduce the balance of opening inventory (thus changing prior period comparatives); or
- recognise the adjustment as an expense of the current period rather than making retrospective adjustments to prior period balances (for example, debit an inventory write-down expense and credit the balance of inventory).

Where an error in an account balance is discovered after financial statements have been issued, IAS 8 *Accounting Policies, Changes in Accounting Estimates and Errors* mandates a retrospective basis for the correction of errors, adopting the perspective that the financial statements be presented as though the error never occurred. That is, where prior period errors are discovered, the requirements dictate the use of the second option listed above (IAS 8, paragraph 42). This is considered in Worked Example 4.8.

| Worked Example 4.8 | **Discovery of a prior period error in the value of an asset** |

Torquay Ltd is completing its financial statements for the year ended 30 June 2014. In undertaking the accounting work it became apparent that an item of machinery that was thought to be on hand at the end of the previous financial year had actually been destroyed in a fire on 28 June 2013. The machinery had a cost of £90,000 and accumulated depreciation of £12,000.

Required

Provide the accounting entries to account for the discovery of this prior period error.

Solution

In this case we will need to reduce opening retained earnings and reduce the value of property, plant and equipment in line with the requirements of paragraph 42 of IAS 8. The accounting entry in 2014 would be:

Dr	Opening retained earnings	£78,000	
Dr	Accumulated depreciation—machinery	£12,000	
Cr	Machinery		£90,000

 4.10 **Possible changes in the requirements pertaining to financial statement presentation**

As noted earlier in this chapter, in October 2008 the IASB issued a Discussion Paper entitled *Preliminary Views on Financial Statement Presentation*. The Discussion Paper proposes some significant changes to the way financial statements are to be presented. The project is being undertaken jointly by the IASB and the US Financial Accounting Standards Board (FASB). In July 2010 a 'staff draft' of an Exposure Draft of a new Financial Statement Presentation accounting standard was prepared (because it was a 'staff draft' it was not open for public comment) and some amendments were issued in July 2011 with a final standard to follow some years later. The Discussion Paper and the Staff Draft represent the initial steps towards creating a new accounting standard that would ultimately replace IAS 1 (interested readers should look at the IASB website for further information on the financial statement presentation project). Because of the major implications these proposals could have for how we present financial statements, it is worthwhile giving a brief overview of the proposals, particularly given that they may culminate in an accounting standard that requires statements of financial position to be presented very differently from the current presentation formats.

The project was motivated by the IASB's and FASB's concerns that financial statements can currently be presented in many alternative ways. This, in turn, makes it difficult for analysts, investors and other users to compare the financial statements of different reporting entities. Further, the formats of the various financial statements do not make it easy for users to see how the information in the respective statements is linked. For example, the statement of cash flows separates operating activities from financing activities, but that distinction is not always apparent in the statement of financial position and the statement of comprehensive income. This makes it difficult to compare operating income with operating cash flows—a step often taken in assessing the quality of an entity's earnings.

To provide more useful information, the IASB and FASB intend making the financial statements more 'cohesive'; that is, the objective is to format the information in financial statements so that a reader can follow the flow of information through the various financial statements (IASB 2008, p. 16). The aim is to provide a cohesive financial picture as stated in IASB (2008, p. 30):

A cohesive financial picture means that the relationship between items across financial statements is clear and that an entity's financial statements complement each other as much as possible. Financial statements that are consistent with the cohesiveness objective would display data in a way that clearly associates related information across the statements so that the information is understandable. The cohesiveness objective responds to the existing lack of consistency in the way information is presented in an entity's financial statements. For example, cash flows from operating activities are separated in the statement of cash flows, but there is no similar separation of operating activities in the statements of comprehensive income and financial position. This makes it difficult for a user to compare operating income with operating cash flows—a comparison often made in assessing earnings quality. Similarly, separating operating assets and liabilities in the statement of financial position will provide users with more complete data for calculating some key financial ratios, such as return on net operating assets.

The IASB and FASB are also proposing that financial statements should be presented in a more disaggregated manner. In particular, it is proposed that financial statements are prepared in way that separates an entity's financing activities from its business and other activities and, further, separates financing activities between transactions with owners in their capacity as owners and all other financing activities. The 'Business' section of the financial statements would include all items related to assets and liabilities that management views as part of its continuing business activities. Business activities are those activities conducted with the intent of creating value, such as producing goods or providing services. It is proposed that the 'Business' section be further disaggregated into an *Operating category* and an *Investing category*. According to paragraph 62 of the Staff Draft of the Exposure Draft released in 2010:

An entity's financial statements shall include the following sections, categories and subcategory if applicable:

(a) a business section, containing:
    (i) (1) an operating category;
         (2) an operating finance subcategory; and
    (ii) an investing category.
(b) a financing section, containing:
    (i) a debt category; and
    (ii) an equity category.
(c) an income tax section.
(d) a discontinued operation section.
(e) a multi-category transaction section.

The 'Financing' section would include only financial assets and financial liabilities that management views as part of the financing of the entity's business activities (referred to as 'financing assets and liabilities'). Amounts relating to financing liabilities would be presented in the *financing liabilities category* and amounts relating to financing assets would be presented in the *financing assets category* in each of the financial statements. In determining whether a financial asset or liability should be included in the financing section, an entity should consider whether the item is interchangeable with other sources of financing and whether the item can be characterised as independent of specific business activities.

Table 4.2 represents the proposed format for presenting information within the financial statements, excluding the notes. (The section names are in **_bold italics_**; bullet points indicate required categories within sections.)

Table 4.2 Proposed format for the presentation of financial statements

Statement of financial position	Statement of comprehensive income	Statement of cash flows
Business • Operating assets and liabilities • Investing assets and liabilities	*Business* • Operating income and expenses • Investing income and expenses	*Business* • Operating cash flows • Investing cash flows
Financing • Financing assets • Financing liabilities	*Financing* • Financing asset income • Financing liability expenses	*Financing* • Financing asset cash flows • Financing liability cash flows
Income taxes	*Income taxes* On continuing operations (business and financing)	*Income taxes*
Discontinued operations	*Discontinued operations* Net of tax	*Discontinued operations*
	Other comprehensive income Net of tax	
Equity		*Equity*

According to the IASB (2010), each entity would decide the order of the sections and categories but would use the same order in each individual statement. Each entity would decide how to classify its assets and liabilities into the sections and categories on the basis of how an item is used (the 'management approach'). The entity would disclose why it chose those classifications. In explaining the use of the management approach, IASB (2008, 2010) notes that, because functional activities vary from entity to entity, an entity would choose the classification that best reflects management's view of what constitutes its business (operating and investing) and financing activities. Thus, a manufacturing entity may classify the exact same asset (or liability) differently from a financial institution because of differences in the businesses in which those entities engage. In relation to the presentation format proposed for the statement of comprehensive income, IASB (2008, p. 17) states:

> The proposed presentation model eliminates the choice an entity currently has of presenting components of income and expense in an income statement and a statement of comprehensive income (two-statement approach). All entities would present a single statement of comprehensive income, with items of other comprehensive income presented in a separate section. This statement would include a subtotal of profit or loss or net income and a total for comprehensive income for the period. Because the statement of comprehensive income would include the same sections and categories used in the other financial statements, it would include more subtotals than are currently presented in an income statement or a statement of comprehensive income. Those additional subtotals will allow for the comparison of effects across the financial statements. For example, users will be able to assess how changes in operating assets and liabilities generate operating income and cash flows.

While the above discussion is only a brief overview of current proposals, it is nevertheless hoped that it provides an indication of the extent of change that might occur in future years in terms of how we present financial statements. At the time of writing, it was not anticipated that any significant changes in presentation formats would be required before 2014. Again, the above material helps to emphasise that, as accountants, we must not assume that the rules we learn now will necessarily be in operation in the future— accounting today seems to be a profession with rapidly changing rules.

SUMMARY

The chapter explored a number of general issues that relate to assets. Assets, we saw, are defined as resources controlled by an entity as a result of past events and from which future economic benefits are expected to flow to the entity. To apply the asset definition, recognition criteria are necessary. The Conceptual Framework states that, for an asset to be recognised, future economic benefits must be both probable and capable of reliable measurement.

Given that the recognition criteria are based on assessments of measurability and probability, the recognition of an asset will frequently depend on professional judgement. This means that accountants may differ in their judgements of whether particular expenditure should be accounted for as an expense or as an asset. While the recognition criteria of *measurability* and *probability* are the general criteria for assets, subsequent chapters of this book will show that other recognition criteria will need to be applied for various classes of asset, pursuant to the relevant accounting standards.

The chapter emphasised that classes of asset are typically measured using different measurement rules. This, in itself, raises questions about the meaning of the aggregated total ('Total assets'). The IASB Conceptual Framework contains no general guidance on measurement rules for assets other than noting that, 'a number of different measurement bases are employed to different degrees and in varying combinations in financial statements' (paragraph 4.55). Instead, the accounting standards that address individual methods of accounting for particular classes of asset typically provide measurement rules specific to those classes. There is some overlap between the various accounting standards, for example a number of accounting standards now require particular assets to be measured at fair value.

The chapter also considered the accounting standards on the acquisition costs of assets. Specifically considered were IAS 16 *Property, Plant and Equipment* and IAS 38 *Intangible Assets*. We noted the general principle that the cost of acquisition of an asset is considered to be the purchase consideration plus any costs incidental to the acquisition. Purchase consideration is typically measured in terms of the fair value of the assets given in exchange.

KEY TERMS

END-OF-CHAPTER EXERCISE

Consider the following example. Cabarita plc acquired a parcel of land, with a building thereon, in exchange for the following consideration: **LO** 4.5

Cash	£125,000
Shares in Cabarita plc	200,000 ordinary shares with a market value of £1.50 per share
Computing machinery	Cost of £50,000; accumulated depreciation of £15,000; market value of £20,000

The value of the land is considered to be equivalent to the value of the building.

REQUIRED

(a) What are the cost of the land and the cost of the building?
(b) Provide the accounting journal entry in the books of Cabarita plc.

SOLUTION TO END-OF-CHAPTER EXERCISE

(a) The cost of the land and the cost of the building are calculated as follows:

Fair value of the purchase consideration	£
Cash	125,000
Shares at market value—200,000 at £1.50	300,000
Computing machinery at market value	20,000
Total	445,000

Therefore, as both the land and the building are of equal value, the value of each is £222,500.

(b) The accounting entry in the books of Cabarita plc is:

Dr Land	£222,500	
Dr Building	£222,500	
Dr Loss on disposal of computer	£15,000	
Dr Accumulated depreciation—computer	£15,000	
Cr Cash		£125,000
Cr Share capital and share premium		£300,000
Cr Computer machinery		£50,000

REVIEW QUESTIONS

1 Differentiate between the 'definition of assets' and the 'criteria for recognition of assets' provided in the IASB Conceptual Framework. **LO** 4.1

2 Should all expenditure carried forward to future periods be amortised/depreciated? Why? **LO** 4.1

3 If an asset is expensed in one financial year because future economic benefits were not deemed to be 'probable', can the same asset be reinstated in future periods if the benefits are subsequently assessed as probable? In this respect, does the ability to reinstate assets apply to all assets? **LO** 4.2

4 Why would advertising expenditure typically be expensed in the period incurred? What would be an exception to this general rule? **LO** 4.2

5 Should borrowing costs associated with the construction of a building be treated as part of the cost of the building, or should the borrowing costs be expensed as incurred? **LO** 4.6

6 What is the difference between value-in-use and value-in-exchange and of what relevance is either to the determination of the amount at which an asset is to be disclosed within the statement of financial position (balance sheet)? **LO** 4.3

7 Assume that, in a particular year, a reporting entity acquires a patent for a solar-powered toothbrush, but the probability of future economic benefits being generated by the patent is considered to be less than 50 per cent. As a result of changed circumstances in a subsequent year, the outlook is that the benefits are more than 50 per cent probable. **LO** 4.2

REQUIRED

Explain whether the patent may be recognised as an asset (i) when acquired, or (ii) when the probability subsequently exceeds 50 per cent.

8 How are current assets defined for the purpose of presentation in a statement of financial position? **LO** 4.1

9 Tea Tree Bay Ltd acquires a Gizmo Machine from Jetsons Ltd for the following consideration: **LO** 4.5
Cash €20,000
Land In the books of Tea Tree Bay Ltd the land is recorded at its cost of €100,000. It has a fair value of €140,000. Tea Tree Bay Ltd also agrees to assume the liability of Jetsons Ltd's bank loan of €30,000 as part of the Gizmo Machine acquisition.

REQUIRED

(a) Calculate the acquisition cost of the Gizmo Machine.
(b) Provide the journal entries that would appear in Tea Tree Bay Ltd's books to account for the acquisition of the Gizmo Machine.

10 What are some of the various asset measurement rules currently recommended under IFRS? **LO** 4.3

11 What are intangible assets and how, according to IAS 1 and IAS 38, should they be disclosed in a reporting entity's statement of financial position? **LO** 4.1

12 IAS 1 provides alternative presentation formats for a reporting entity's statement of financial position. Explain the alternative presentation formats, and describe the issues to consider as part of the process of selecting from the alternative presentation formats. **LO** 4.4

13 According to IAS 16, would you expense or capitalise expenditure incurred in repairing an asset? Explain your answer. **LO** 4.2

14 Assume that Wallingford Rugby Club signs up five promising recruits by offering each of them a five-year player's contract. As an additional incentive, it also offers each of the players a substantial sign-on fee. Do you think these players, or the associated economic benefits that they will generate, are 'assets' of Wallingford Rugby Club? How would you account for the sign-on fee? **LO** 4.1

15 Point Addis Ltd is in the process of preparing its financial statements for the year ended 30 June 2014. In preparing the financial statements, the managers of Point Addis discover that a storage facility at a remote location was destroyed by fire on 10 June 2013. However, because the destruction was not known to them, no adjustments were made in the 2013 financial statements. How will this loss of an asset be accounted for when the 2014 financial statements are prepared? **LO** 4.4

16 Cactus Ltd acquires some printing machinery. The amount paid to the manufacturer is £85,000, plus an additional £2,000 for delivery. Once the machinery is delivered, it needs some modifications before it can be used. The modifications amount to £7,000. An additional amount of £2,000 is paid for installation. **LO** 4.5

REQUIRED

(a) For accounting purposes, what is the 'cost' of the machinery?

(b) Could other costs be included in the measurement of the cost of acquiring the printing machinery if its construction and installation took a substantial period of time?

CHALLENGING QUESTIONS

17 What factors would you consider when determining the format to use in disclosing a reporting entity's statement of financial position? **LO** 4.4

18 In an article on the BBC News website on 6 October 2011 ('*Can Apple Stay Ahead without Jobs at Its Core?*' by Rebecca Marston, 2010) it was reported that Apple's share price tumbled by 5 per cent after the announcement that Steve Jobs, co-founder and figurehead of Apple, had passed away. **LO** 4.1

REQUIRED

The fact that the share prices fell following the sad death of Steve Jobs is consistent with the view that the man 'Steve Jobs' was an 'asset' to the company. How do you think this 'asset' would have been disclosed in the financial statements of Apple in previous years?

19 During the reporting period ending 30 June 2014, Midnight Boil Limited constructed a nuclear power generator. The cost of the power generator and associated technology amounted to £12,550,000. Other costs associated with the construction amounted to:

	£
Costs incurred in obtaining access to the site	2,500,500
Power permits	400,500
Engineers' fees	1,100,500
	4,001,500

The plant was ready to start generating power on 1 July 2014, with actual generation starting on 1 October 2014. At the end of the power plant's useful life, which is expected to be 10 years, Midnight Boil Limited is required by government to dismantle the plant, remove it and return the site to its original condition. After consulting its own engineers and environmentalists, Midnight Boil Limited estimates these costs to be:

	£
Dismantling the plant	750,500
Environmental remediation costs	1,249,500
Replacement of flora and fauna	100,000
	2,100,000

Midnight Boil Limited plans to provide for these costs over the expected life of the power-generating facility. It uses a discount rate of 10 per cent. **LO** 4.5

REQUIRED

Prepare the journal entries necessary to account for the power plant for the years ended 30 June 2014, 30 June 2015 and 30 June 2020. Ignore depreciation.

20 In an article in *Public Finance* in June 2011 on the accounting for council roads in the UK, *The Road to the Code*, Mandy Bretherton, a technical manager for local government finance at CIPFA (a UK public sector accountancy body), discusses the valuation of current transport infrastructure in the UK, noting that at present historical cost is used, but a move to equivalent asset replacement less deductions for all physical deterioration and impairment is being phased in. **LO 4.3**

REQUIRED

Discuss the relative merits of both valuation techniques, highlighting the practical issues and provide your opinions on the usefulness of the resultant valuations.

21 On 1 July 2014, Point Lookout Limited acquired a boat to use in its surfing holidays business. Point Lookout Limited paid an initial amount of €250,000 on the date of acquisition and agreed to make a further five annual payments of €300,000, starting on 30 June 2015. Point Lookout Limited can borrow funds at 8 per cent per annum. **LO 4.6**

REQUIRED

Prepare the journal entries as at 1 July 2014 and 30 June 2019 to account for the acquisition of the asset.

22 If we look at a reporting entity's statement of financial position, we will see a total given for all the entity's assets (this is a requirement of IAS 1). This aggregate total is derived by adding together the various classes of current and non-current assets. Do you think it is appropriate that the various classes of asset are simply added together, even though they have probably been measured on a number of quite different measurement bases? Justify your answer. **LO 4.3**

23 Does the statement of financial position item 'Total assets' represent the value of a reporting entity's assets? Explain your answer. **LO 4.3**

24 Double Island Ltd constructed a Whizbang Machine and incurred the following costs in doing so: **LO 4.5**

Amounts paid to employees to build the machine	€120,000
Raw materials consumed in building the machine	€45,000
Depreciation of manufacturing equipment attributed to the construction of the Whizbang Machine	€25,000

REQUIRED

(a) Provide the journal entries that Double Island Ltd would use to account for the construction of the asset.

(b) Assume that immediately after the journal entries in part (a) have been made, new information becomes available that indicates that the recoverable amount of the Whizbang Machine is only €160,000. Provide the adjusting journal entries.

25 Lighthouse Ltd acquired land for the purpose of building Lighthouse Point, a health and beauty spa. The following costs were incurred:

Purchase price of land paid in cash	£1,000,000
Stamp duty and legal fees	£80,000
Removal of pre-existing buildings	£20,000
Application to local government bodies for development	£10,000
Expenses incurred in evaluating a different site found to be unsuitable	£30,000
Architects' fees	£100,000
Construction of spa buildings	£1,500,000
Salary of manager overseeing the Lighthouse Point project for 18 months	£120,000
Borrowing costs (interest) incurred in relation to the project	£180,000

The original buildings on the site were removed by Lighthouse Ltd and sold for £50,000 **LO 4.5**

REQUIRED

(a) Determine the cost of the Lighthouse Point health and beauty spa.

(b) Allocate costs between land and building so that a depreciable cost can be determined for the buildings. (It is not necessary to calculate depreciation.) Identify those items for which an arbitrary or estimated allocation between land and building was required.

26 On 15 September 2012, Tweed Ltd acquired land on a remote island at a cost of €100,000. The land was held for future development as a resort when transport to the island was made available. At each reporting date, Tweed Ltd made the following assessments of the net selling price of the land and the value of the land to the business if kept for future use: **LO** 4.3

Date	Net selling price	Value in use
31 December 2012	€110,000	€130,000
30 June 2013	€90,000	€120,000
31 December 2013	€80,000	€90,000
30 June 2014	€120,000	€110,000

REQUIRED

(a) At what amount should the land be recorded in the statement of financial position (balance sheet) of Tweed Ltd for each reporting date?

(b) Assume that on 30 September 2014 the government cancelled all plans to provide transport to the island. There is no prospect of selling the land. The cost to Tweed Ltd of developing transport exceeds the present value of expected future benefits of operating the resort. How should Tweed Ltd account for this event?

REFERENCES

BANK OF IRELAND, *Annual Report 2010*, http://www.bankofireland. com/fs/doc/publications/investor-relations/annual-report-for-the-twelve-month-period-ended-31-december-20102.pdf.

BMW AG, *Annual Report 2010*, http://annual-report.bmwgroup. com/2010/gb/files/pdf/en/ BMW_Group_AR2010.pdf.

BOWEN, R.M., NOREEN, E.W., & LACEY, J.M., 'Determinants of the Corporate Decision to Capitalise Interest', *Journal of Accounting and Economics*, August 1981, pp. 151–79.

BRETHERTON, M., 'On Account: The Road to the Code', *Public Finance*, June 2011, p. 43.

FOSTER, B.P. & SHASTRI, T., 'The Subprime Lending Crisis and Reliable Reporting: Limitations to the Use of Fair Value in Unstable Markets', *CPA Journal*, vol. 80, no. 4, 2010, pp. 20–5.

GEORGIOU, G., 'The IASB Standard-setting Process: Participation and Perceptions of Financial Statement Users', *British Accounting Review*, vol. 42, 2010, pp. 103–18.

GOX, R.F. & WAGENHOFER, A., 'Optimal Precision of Accounting in Debt Financing', *European Accounting Review*, vol. 19, no. 3, 2010, pp. 579–602.

HENRY, E. & HOLZMANN, O.O., 'Conceptual Framework Revisions: Say Goodbye to "Reliability" and "Stewardship", *Journal of Corporate Accounting and Finance*, March/April 2011, pp. 91–4.

HOCHBERG, Y.V., SAPIENZA, P., & VISSING-JØRGENSEN, A., 'A Lobbying Approach to Evaluating the Sarbanes–Oxley Act

of 2002', *Journal of Accounting Research*, vol. 47, no. 2, 2009, pp. 519–83.

HOUGHTON, K. & TAN, C., *Measurement in Accounting: Present Value and Historical Cost—A Report on the Attitudes and Policy Positions of Australia's Largest Businesses*, Melbourne, Group of 100, 1995.

INTERNATIONAL ACCOUNTING STANDARDS BOARD, *Discussion Paper: Preliminary Views on Financial Statement Presentation*, London, IASB, October 2008.

INTERNATIONAL ACCOUNTING STANDARDS BOARD, *Staff Draft of Exposure Draft IFRS X Financial Statement Presentation*, London, IASB, July 2010.

MARSTON, R., 'Can Apple Stay Ahead without Jobs at Its Core?', BBC News Business, 6 October 2011, http://www.bbc.co.uk/ news/business-15194356.

NAVARRO-GALERA, A. & RODRÍGUEZ-BOLÍVAR, M.P., 'Can Government Accountability be Enhanced with International Financial Reporting Standards?', *Public Money & Management*, November 2010, pp. 379–84.

WATTS, R.L. & ZIMMERMAN, J.L., *Positive Accounting Theory*, Englewood Cliffs, NJ, Prentice Hall, 1986.

Chapter 5

Depreciation of Property, Plant and Equipment

Learning objectives

Upon completing this chapter readers should:

LO1 understand the role of accounting in allocating the depreciable amount of a non-current asset over the asset's expected useful life;

LO2 be aware of factors that must be considered in determining the useful life of a depreciable asset;

LO3 understand the various approaches (straight line, sum of digits, declining balance, production basis) for allocating the depreciable amount of a non-current asset to particular financial periods;

LO4 understand when to start depreciating a depreciable asset; and

LO5 know the disclosure requirements of IAS 16 *Property, Plant and Equipment* as they pertain to depreciation.

5.1 Introduction to accounting for depreciation of property, plant and equipment

Subsequent to their acquisition, non-current assets with limited useful lives will typically need to be depreciated over the period during which economic benefits are expected to be derived. This chapter will consider the accounting requirements pertaining to depreciation. **Depreciation** expense represents a recognition of the decrease in the service potential of an asset across time. When non-current assets (apart from land, perhaps) are acquired, there is a general expectation that the economic benefits related to the acquisition will not last indefinitely. With this in mind, a proportion of the acquisition cost of the asset will be allocated to particular financial periods throughout the asset's useful life. As the IASB *Conceptual Framework for Financial Reporting*, paragraph 4.51, states:

> **depreciation**
> Allocation of the cost of an asset, or its revalued amount, over the periods in which benefits are expected to be derived.

> *Where economic benefits are expected to arise over several accounting periods and the association with income can only be broadly or indirectly determined, expenses are recognised in the income statement on the basis of systematical and rational allocation procedures. This is often necessary in recognising the expenses associated with the using up of assets such as property, plant and equipment, goodwill, patents and trademarks; in such cases the expense is referred to as depreciation or amortisation. These allocation procedures are intended to recognise expenses in the accounting periods in which the economic benefits associated with these items are consumed or expire.*

As the **depreciable assets** of a business might comprise a significant proportion of the firm's total assets, the choice of depreciation policies can have a significant impact on the profits of a business. The potential magnitude of depreciation expense is evident from, for example, a review of BMW AG's consolidated results for the 2010 financial year, which indicated that the total of the depreciation and amortisation expenses amounted to €6,678 million,[1] in a year when total comprehensive income attributable to shareholders—after consideration of amortisation and depreciation—was €3,351 million, and when total assets were €108,867 million. Another example, in the 2010 financial year, is Tesco PLC's depreciation and amortisation expenses, which totalled £1,389 million[2] in a year when the total comprehensive income totalled £2,757 million, and reported assets amounted to £35,337 million. As we can see, depreciation expense can be quite significant.

> **depreciable asset**
> A non-current asset having a limited useful life.

The international accounting standard relating to the depreciation of property, plant and equipment is IAS 16 *Property, Plant and Equipment*. The standard provides a set of comprehensive instructions on how to account for tangible non-current assets. IAS 16 addresses issues such as the acquisition costs of property, plant and equipment (which we addressed in Chapter 4) and subsequent measurement, including the revaluation of property, plant and equipment (which we address in Chapter 6), depreciation, and disposal and derecognition.

While IAS 16 covers depreciation issues as they relate to property, plant and equipment, IAS 38 *Intangible Assets* provides rules in relation to the amortisation of intangible assets. We consider intangible assets in more depth in Chapter 8.

From an accountant's perspective, depreciation represents the allocation of the cost of an asset, or its revalued amount, over the periods in which benefits are expected to be derived. Depreciation is defined in IAS 16 as 'the systematic allocation of the depreciable amount of an asset over its useful life'.

Depreciation should not be confused with the decline in the market value of an asset across time. An asset might even increase in value over time, but a depreciation charge might need to be recognised to take into account the wear and tear that the asset might have undergone. As paragraph 52 of IAS 16 states:

> *Depreciation is recognised even if the fair value of the asset exceeds its carrying amount, as long as the asset's residual value does not exceed its carrying amount. Repair and maintenance of an asset do not negate the need to depreciate it.*

Depreciation is typically applied when historical-cost accounting is being used (or perhaps a modified version of historical-cost accounting that utilises revaluations of non-current assets). If 'market-value accounting' (also sometimes referred to as 'exit-price accounting') is applied, changes in the market value of non-current assets are treated as expenses (if the market price falls), or as income gains (if the market price increases). If market-value accounting is being used, depreciation is typically not recognised.

The accounting standard on property, plant and equipment, as it relates to depreciation, treats depreciation as an allocation process, rather than one of considering variations in valuations. Determining the valuation of an asset would generally require consideration of the discounted cash flows that would be generated from using the asset, or the cash flows that would result from selling the asset. Such a calculation requires many assumptions and assessments. Using an allocation process eliminates the necessity for making such assessments.

In determining how to allocate the cost of the asset to the period's profit or loss, three issues must be addressed:

1. What depreciable base should be used for the asset?
2. What is the asset's useful life?
3. What method of cost apportionment is most appropriate for the asset?

While depreciation will frequently be treated as an expense in the period in which it is recognised, at times the depreciation of one asset will contribute to an increase in the value of another asset. For example, an item of machinery might be used to construct a particular item that will subsequently be sold or used by the reporting entity. In such an instance, the depreciation would be recognised by increasing the costs of the asset being constructed, rather than simply treating the depreciation as an expense of the period (IAS 16, paragraph 48). Examples where this can occur include depreciation of manufacturing equipment that is used to generate inventory or depreciation of property, plant and equipment that is used for development activities under IAS 38 *Intangible Assets* (IAS 16, paragraph 49).

An example of this treatment for depreciation is evident in whisky distillation companies as highlighted in Financial Accounting in the News 5.1 by Mary O'Brien, who discusses the accounting of the depreciation on whiskey storage casks.

---

[1] The total depreciation and amortisation of €6,678 million is made up of allocations from the following asset types: intangible assets €1,379 million; property, plant and equipment €2,303 million; leased assets €2,817 million, and other investments €179 million.

[2] The total depreciation and amortisation of £1,389 million is made up of allocations from the following asset types: intangible assets £195 million and property, plant and equipment £1,194 million.

Financial Accounting in the News 5.1

DEPRECIATION: CORRECT TO ADD BACK?

Mary O'Brien, *Accountancy Ireland*,
August 2007

I recall coming across a case of a distillery business which consisted of the distillation and maturation of whiskey. As part of the maturation process, the whiskey was stored in a number of casks for years. The depreciation of the casks was included in the figure for stock. The effect was that the depreciation of those casks was not charged to the profit and loss account in the years that the whiskey was stored in the casks. When the whiskey was sold, the depreciation of the casks that had stored the whiskey was charged to the profit and loss account in that year.

As an example of the requirement to capitalise the depreciation charge, consider Worked Example 5.1.

| Worked Example 5.1 | **Depreciation charge included in the carrying amount of another asset** |

Point Impossible Ltd constructs and sells boats. In making a boat, an electric sander was used. The cost of the electric sander is €9,000 and it is expected to have a useful life of 500 hours, and no residual value. During the financial year the sander was used for 50 hours on the boat.

Required
Provide the journal entry to account for the depreciation of the electric sander.

Solution
The depreciation expense in this case would be based on the expected life of 500 hours and would equal €9,000 × 50/500 = €900.
The journal entry would be:

Dr Boat—inventory   €900
Cr Accumulated depreciation—sander   €900

5.2   Depreciable amount (base) of an asset

As we have noted, in order to determine depreciation expense we need to consider the depreciable base, the useful life and the most appropriate method of cost apportionment. First, we will consider the depreciable base. The **depreciable amount** or, as it is also called, the depreciable base, is the cost of a depreciable asset, or other amount substituted for cost in the financial statement, less its residual value. Paragraph 6 of IAS 16 defines residual value as:

> the estimated amount that an entity would currently obtain from disposal of the asset, after deducting the estimated costs of disposal, if the asset were already of the age and in the condition expected at the end of its useful life.

For example, if an asset had a cost of £50,000 and it is expected that the asset will be disposed of in five years' time for £10,000, the 'depreciable amount' (or base) is £40,000; that is, £50,000 less the residual of £10,000. Determining the amount to be recovered on disposal—the residual amount—will typically be based on professional judgement,

depreciable amount
Historical cost or revalued amount of a depreciable asset less the net amount expected to be recovered on disposal of the asset at the end of its useful life.

unless perhaps a forward exchange arrangement is already in place in which there is an agreement on how much will be received from the sale of the asset at a future point. Therefore, various estimates might be possible. If an asset is relatively unique, then it will be more difficult to determine residual value relative to assets that are commonly bought and sold. It should also be appreciated that residual value is determined by reference to what the entity would currently expect to obtain from the asset's disposal based on its projected age and condition (again, refer to the above definition), and not what it expects to actually obtain at a future date. The choice of a particular residual value will have direct implications for future profits and recorded assets. A higher estimate for the residual value will lead to lower depreciation charges and a lower balance of accumulated depreciation and, thus, a larger amount for total assets. For example, in the case of the asset described above, if we depreciate it on a straight-line basis over its expected useful life of five years, given a residual value of £10,000, the yearly depreciation charge would be £8,000. At the end of year 2, the accumulated depreciation of the asset would be £16,000 and the carrying amount of the asset would be £34,000. However, if we estimate that the residual value is £20,000, the yearly depreciation charge would be £6,000. At the end of year 2, the accumulated depreciation would be £12,000 and the carrying amount of the asset would be £38,000.

If the residual value of an asset increases so that it is equal to, or greater than, the carrying amount of the asset, no further depreciation is charged (IAS 16, paragraph 54).

5.3 Determination of useful life

Having determined the depreciable amount of an asset, we need to consider its useful life. For the purposes of IAS 16, the useful life of a depreciable asset is to reflect its useful life for the entity holding the asset, rather than simply its economic life per se. IAS 16 defines useful life as:

(a) *the period over which an asset is expected to be available for use by an entity; or*
(b) *the number of production or similar units expected to be obtained from the asset by an entity.*

In Worked Example 5.1 we utilised production hours as the basis of the asset's useful life. The definition of useful life provided above reflects the view that an asset's useful life for one entity may be different from its useful life within another entity. In determining useful life, IAS 16 provides some useful guidance. Paragraph 56 states:

The future economic benefits embodied in an asset are consumed by an entity principally through its use. However, other factors, such as technical or commercial obsolescence and wear and tear while an asset remains idle, often result in the diminution of the economic benefits that might have been obtained from the asset. Consequently, all the following factors are considered in determining the useful life of an asset:

(a) *expected usage of the asset. Usage is assessed by reference to the asset's expected capacity or physical output.*
(b) *expected physical wear and tear, which depends on operational factors such as the number of shifts for which the asset is to be used and the repair and maintenance programme, and the care and maintenance of the asset while idle.*
(c) *technical or commercial obsolescence arising from changes or improvements in production, or from a change in the market demand for the product or service output of the asset.*
(d) *legal or similar limits on the use of the asset, such as the expiry dates of related leases.*

The possibility of obsolescence, both technical and commercial, is a factor regardless of the physical use of an asset. Worked Example 5.2 helps to make this clearer.

Another factor that should be considered in some cases is the legal life of the asset. For intangible assets (non-monetary assets without physical substance), such as patents, licences, franchises or copyrights, the legal life of the contract period might be the limiting factor in the firm's use of the asset.

Having determined the depreciable amount of the asset and its useful life, it is necessary to determine how the depreciable amount should be allocated or apportioned to future periods. That is, what is the expected pattern of benefits? As with many things in accounting, determining the useful life and the pattern of benefits will depend heavily upon professional judgement.

5.4 Method of cost apportionment

Having considered the depreciable base and the useful life of a depreciable asset, we will now consider the method of cost apportionment to be applied to the depreciable asset. The method of apportionment should best reflect the economic reality of the asset's use. IAS 16 does not mandate the use of a particular method of

Worked Example 5.2   Determination of useful life

Assume that a business has an item of plant with the following characteristics:

- The plant should continue to produce output in its current manner for the next 12 years.
- Demand for the output of the plant is expected to be maintained for the next seven years, after which time the demand will fall to such a low level that it will not be viable to produce the goods.
- A more technically advanced machine will probably be available in five years' time and the firm believes that it will need to switch to the new plant in order to remain competitive.

Required

Determine the period of time that should be used in the depreciation calculation.

Solution

Given the above information, the firm would use a period of depreciation of five years being the shortest of the following periods:

- physical life—12 years
- commercial life—7 years
- technical life—5 years

Five years would represent the period of time the entity expects to hold the asset. Before determining the periodic depreciation expense, consideration should be given to the expected residual value of the plant in five years' time so that the 'depreciable amount' can be determined. Consideration also needs to be given to the expected pattern of the benefits. Evidently, many judgements have to be made about depreciation, and these judgements will have a direct effect on depreciation expenses, and therefore upon reported profits.

---

depreciation—rather, it indicates that the basis chosen should be that which best reflects the underlying physical, technical, commercial and, where appropriate, legal facts. There are two general approaches to cost apportionment. These are categorised as time-based and activity-based depreciation methods. If the decline in the asset's value depends on its use, rather than on issues of technical, legal or commercial concern, an activity-based depreciation method should be used. If the decline in value is going to be greatest in early periods, owing to issues such as technical obsolescence, a method that provides for greatest depreciation charges in early years should be used, such as the **sum-of-digits method** or the **declining-balance/reducing-balance method** (both of which are time-based). If the asset has a defined life, perhaps legally defined by contract, and it is expected that it will be used uniformly, the **straight-line method** of depreciation should perhaps be used. Again, it is emphasised that the depreciation method chosen should best reflect the underlying economic reality. As paragraph 60 of IAS 16 states:

> The depreciation method used shall reflect the pattern in which the asset's future economic benefits are expected to be consumed by the entity.

The choice of depreciation method may impact on other financial decision-making by management. Jackson (2008) found that there was a relationship between the depreciation method selected by management and capital investment decision-making. Jackson reported that, when management invested in capital and used the straight-line method of depreciation, this resulted in higher profits in earlier years; however, the resultant larger capital base meant that the entity reported an overall lower profit ratio. This, he concluded, caused managers to make economically inefficient decisions by delaying capital investment decisions that would bring larger economic gains. He concluded that the choice made for accounting purposes may cause managers to make non-value-maximising capital investment decisions. Therefore, the choice of depreciation method might have a significant effect on the firm's profits and total assets. You can see the differences in expense that might result from calculating depreciation expense in various ways by reviewing Worked Example 5.3.

sum-of-digits method Method of depreciation that allocates a greater amount of depreciation in the early years of an asset's life.

declining-balance method Method of depreciation to be used when the economic benefits to be derived from a depreciable asset are expected to be greater in the early years than the later years.

straight-line method Method of amortisation or depreciation where the cost or revalued amount of an asset, less its expected residual value, is uniformly depreciated over its expected useful life.

| Worked Example 5.3 | A review of alternative depreciation methods |

Noosa Ltd acquires an asset for €25,000. It is expected to have a residual value of €5,000 in five years' time—its expected useful life to the entity.

Required

Calculate each period's depreciation, using:
(a) the straight-line method
(b) the sum-of-digits method
(c) the declining-balance method (also known as the reducing-balance method)
(d) the units-of-production method

Solution

(a) *Straight-line depreciation*

This is a time-based depreciation method and is the most easily understood and widely used depreciation method. With this approach, the depreciable amount is divided by the number of years in the asset's useful life, as follows:

$$\boxed{\text{(Cost – residual value)} \div \text{useful life}} = (€25,000 – €5,000) \div 5 = €4,000 \text{ per year}$$

This method of depreciation would be appropriate when the pattern of benefits derived from the asset is expected to be uniform throughout the asset's useful life.

(b) *Sum-of-digits depreciation*

The sum-of-digits method of depreciation is a time-based depreciation method and, like the declining-balance method considered below, is an accelerated form of depreciation. The use of accelerated methods assumes that the asset will provide greater economic benefits in its earlier years than in later years. In these circumstances, higher depreciation charges are allocated in earlier years, with the depreciation expense decreasing in later years. In this example, the asset is expected to be used for five years. The digits from 1 to the end of the asset's life, in this case 5, are summed:

$$1 + 2 + 3 + 4 + 5 = 15$$

Or we could use the formula $n(n + 1) \div 2$, which gives

$$(5 \times 6) \div 2 = 15$$

Year		Depreciation
1	$5 \div 15 \times (€25,000 – €5,000) =$	€6,667
2	$4 \div 15 \times (€25,000 – €5,000) =$	€5,333
3	$3 \div 15 \times (€25,000 – €5,000) =$	€4,000
4	$2 \div 15 \times (€25,000 – €5,000) =$	€2,667
5	$1 \div 15 \times (€25,000 – €5,000) =$	€1,333
		€20,000

Depreciation based on the sum-of-digits method would be appropriate where the economic benefits expected to be derived from the asset will be greater in the early years than the later years.

(c) *Declining-balance depreciation* (also referred to as the diminishing-balance method/reducing-balance method)

The declining-balance method is an accelerated method of depreciation. Rather than multiplying a consistent balance (in this example, €20,000) by a reducing fraction, a consistent percentage is applied to a decreasing carrying amount. The percentage to be applied to the opening written-down value (or carrying amount) of the asset is determined by using the following formula:

$$\boxed{\text{percentage} = 1 – \text{the nth root of (salvage value} \div \text{cost)}}$$

where n = the life of the asset, which in this case is 5

$$= 1.0 – \sqrt[5]{0.2}$$

$$= 1.0 – 0.72477$$

$$= 0.27523$$

Year		Depreciation
1	0.27523 × (€25,000)	= €6,881
2	0.27523 × (€25,000 – €6,881)	= €4,987
3	0.27523 × (€25,000 – €11,868)	= €3,614
4	0.27523 × (€25,000 – €15,482)	= €2,620
5	0.27523 × (€25,000 – €18,102)	= €1,898
		€20,000

As with the sum-of-digits approach, depreciation based on the declining-balance approach would be appropriate where the economic benefits expected to be derived from the asset will be greater in the early years than the later years.

(d) *Units-of-production method*

To use this method—which is an activity-based depreciation method—we would need additional information. The units-of-production method results in a depreciation charge based on the expected use or output of the asset. Therefore we need more details about total expected use or output related to the asset, and the use or output for the current accounting period. For this asset we will use expected use denominated in hours and we will assume that the asset is expected to be used for a total of 1,000 hours before its useful life is at an end. We will further assume that, in the current financial period, the asset has been used for 210 hours. Depreciation, therefore, would be calculated as:

units-of-production method / production basis Method of depreciation that allocates the depreciable amount of an asset according to the use or output of the asset.

Actual usage for the year divided by total expected usage multiplied by depreciable amount
$$= (210 \div 1,000) \times (€25,000 – €5,000) = €4,200.$$

The different methods of depreciation just outlined will clearly lead to differences in accounting profits and reported assets. Therefore, and as stressed throughout this book, the choice of an accounting policy might be a choice with cash-flow implications for the organisation, particularly if specific agreements, such as management bonus schemes or debt contracts with restrictive accounting-based covenants, are tied to accounting profits. It is hoped, however, that management will be objective and select the depreciation method that best reflects the pattern of benefits to be derived from the asset. Again, objectivity and the expectation that accounting information should be free from bias is one of the key qualitative characteristics of general purpose financial statements (according to the Conceptual Framework). An example of the variety of depreciation methods used is evident from the accounting policies of Tesco PLC, a UK retail company. As can be seen from Exhibit 5.1, it uses the straight-line method for properties and leased assets and the declining-balance method with a variety of different rates for other tangible assets.

Exhibit 5.1	Details of the accounting policy for tangible assets in the financial statements of Tesco PLC for the year ended 26 February 2011

Property, plant and equipment

Property, plant and equipment is carried at cost less accumulated depreciation and any recognised impairment in value.

Property, plant and equipment is depreciated on a straight-line basis to its residual value over its anticipated useful economic life.

The following depreciation rates are applied for the Group:

- freehold and leasehold buildings with greater than 40 years unexpired – at 2.5% of cost;
- leasehold properties with less than 40 years unexpired are depreciated by equal annual instalments over the unexpired period of the lease; and
- plant, equipment, fixtures and fittings and motor vehicles – at rates varying from 9% to 50%.

Assets held under finance leases are depreciated over their expected useful lives on the same basis as owned assets or, when shorter, over the term of the relevant lease.

Given the discussion on the type of asset, its use and resultant 'most appropriate' depreciation method, it might be reasonable to assume that consistent approaches are taken by companies; however, research suggests that this is not the case. A study by Jaafar and McLeay (2007) found that, though the straight-line method was the most popular, there were statistical differences in the methods used across countries. In particular, declining-balance methods of allocating depreciation, such as diminishing-value or sum-of-digits methods, were more common in Germany, France and Belgium. This the authors put down to the tax considerations, as in these countries depreciation is a tax-deductible expense, whereas in some countries, such as the UK and Ireland, depreciation is independent of tax. They also found that the units-of-production method of depreciation was limited to the resources sector.

5.5   Depreciation of separate components

As was indicated in Chapter 4, IAS 16 requires the 'components approach' to be used when accounting for items of property, plant and equipment. This requires the cost of an item of property, plant and equipment to be allocated to its various components and, where these individual components have different lives or where the consumption of economic benefits embodied in the components differs, each component must be accounted for separately. An example of this would be an aircraft, where the engines, internal fittings and airframe would be accounted for separately as they all have different useful lives (IAS 16, paragraph 44).

An example of the components approach to depreciation is provided in Worked Example 5.4.

Worked Example 5.4   A components approach to depreciation

At the beginning of the financial period, De Lange Limited acquired an aircraft for use in its travel business. The aircraft cost £3,569,000. De Lange Limited's maintenance and engineering department has provided the accounting department with the following list of component parts and useful lives.

	Useful life (years)	Component cost (£)
Airframe	15	1,830,000
Engines	10	1,324,000
Interior fixtures and fittings	5	415,000
		3,569,000

These components and lives are consistent with those previously used, and with what is currently used within the industry.

Required

Assuming that the individual components of the aircraft are depreciated on a straight-line basis over their useful lives, prepare the journal entries necessary to account for the depreciation expense at the end of the 12-month reporting period.

Solution

Calculating the depreciation expense:

	Component cost £	Useful life (years)	Depreciation expense (£)
Airframe	1,830,000	15	122,000
Engines	1,324,000	10	132,400
Interior fixtures and fittings	415,000	5	83,000
	3,569,000		337,400

Journal entry

Dr	Depreciation expense	£337,400	
Cr	Accumulated depreciation—airframe		£122,000
Cr	Accumulated depreciation—engines		£132,400
Cr	Accumulated depreciation—interior fixtures and fittings		£83,000

5.6 When to start depreciating an asset

Having considered the depreciable base, useful life and method of cost apportionment, the next step is to consider when we should start depreciating the asset. The rule provided in IAS 16 is that depreciation charges are to be made from the date when a depreciable asset is first put into use or held ready for use. Therefore, an asset being constructed would not be depreciated until it is ready for use. If an item is able to be used but will not actually be used for a number of periods, the asset would nonetheless be required to be depreciated once it is completed, even though it is not being used. Such depreciation would account for the possibility of decreases in service potential not caused by use but perhaps by technical or commercial obsolescence (IAS 16, paragraph 55). Depreciation ceases when the asset is sold, or when the asset is derecognised and classified as held for sale under IFRS 5 (IAS 16, paragraph 55).

5.7 Revision of depreciation rate and depreciation method

The depreciation expense charged to each accounting period is an estimate that involves the exercise of judgement. As it takes into account technical, commercial and other considerations, the basis for calculating the depreciation expense should be reviewed annually to take changing circumstances into account. For this to be achieved, two issues must be considered: the useful life of the asset and the depreciation method used. How these two factors affect the assessment of the annual depreciation charge is considered below.

If it becomes apparent that the expected useful life of a non-current asset has changed, the entity concerned is required to revise its depreciation rate. It might be decided that the useful life of a non-current asset is different from that originally expected because of a number of factors. For example, the useful life might be extended because of certain expenditures that improve the asset and lengthen its life. Alternatively, technological changes or changes in the market for the products of the asset might reduce the useful life of the asset. Changes in the repair and maintenance policy of the entity might also impact on the expected useful life of the asset. In relation to expectations about the useful life (and the residual value) of a non-current asset, paragraph 51 of IAS 16 requires that:

> The residual value and the useful life of an asset shall be reviewed at least at the end of each annual reporting period and, if expectations differ from previous estimates, the change(s) shall be accounted for as a change in an accounting estimate in accordance with IAS 8 Accounting Policies, Changes in Accounting Estimates and Errors.

Apart from revisions of expectations about the useful life of an asset, there might also be changes in expectations about the pattern of benefits expected to be derived from the asset. In this regard, paragraph 61 of IAS 16 requires the following:

> The depreciation method applied to an asset shall be reviewed at least at the end of each annual reporting period and, if there has been a significant change in the expected pattern of consumption of the future economic benefits embodied in the asset, the method shall be changed to reflect the changed pattern. Such a change shall be accounted for as a change in an accounting estimate in accordance with IAS 8.

Revisions of depreciation rates can have very significant impacts on profits. IAS 16 requires that, if a revision of useful life or of the amounts expected on disposal causes a material change in the depreciation charges of a firm, the financial effect of that material change should be disclosed. As with most disclosure requirements, materiality is to be determined in accordance with the Conceptual Framework. As emphasised earlier in this text and referred to in the Conceptual Framework, decisions pertaining to materiality are based upon professional judgement; therefore, what is considered material by one party might not be considered to be material by another.

5.8 Land and buildings

Where land and buildings are acquired together, IAS 16 requires that the cost be apportioned between the land and the buildings, and that the buildings be systematically depreciated over time. Land itself would not usually be depreciated, given its usually indefinite life. As paragraph 58 of IAS 16 states:

> Land and buildings are separable assets and are accounted for separately, even when they are acquired together. With some exceptions, such as quarries and sites used for landfill, land has an unlimited useful life and therefore

is not depreciated. Buildings have a limited useful life and therefore are depreciable assets. An increase in the value of the land on which a building stands does not affect the determination of the depreciable amount of the building.

Paragraph 59 of IAS 16 further states:

If the cost of land includes the costs of site dismantlement, removal and restoration, that portion of the land asset is depreciated over the period of benefits obtained by incurring those costs. In some cases, the land itself may have a limited useful life, in which case it is depreciated in a manner that reflects the benefits to be derived from it.

For example, if a land and building package is acquired at a cost of £400,000 and it is considered that the land has a value of £150,000, £250,000 would be attributed to the building and this amount of £250,000 would need to be depreciated over the useful life of the building (after consideration of its ultimate residual value).

Company directors have been known to complain about having to depreciate buildings on the grounds that buildings' value typically increases over time. This argument, however, is invalid. Generally, it is the land that increases in value, not the buildings. Buildings have a limited useful life and this must be recognised through depreciation charges. Again, it should be emphasised that directors must depreciate their buildings under existing accounting standards. Electing not to depreciate buildings (and therefore failing to act in compliance with IAS 16) will have the effect of increasing the profits and total assets of the firm. However, these effects may be reversed on the ultimate sale of the depreciable asset. In relation to calculating the gain or loss on disposal of a depreciable asset, paragraph 71 of IAS 16 states:

The gain or loss arising from the derecognition of an item of property, plant and equipment shall be determined as the difference between the net disposal proceeds, if any, and the carrying amount of the item.

The standard also states that:

The gain or loss arising from the derecognition of an item of property, plant and equipment shall be included in profit or loss when the item is derecognised.

As can be seen from the above material extracted from IAS 16, the standard adopts the term 'derecognition'. The term incorporates the retirement and disposal of an asset. According to IAS 16, the carrying amount of an item of property, plant and equipment is to be derecognised:

(a) on disposal; or
(b) when no future economic benefits are expected from its use or disposal.

From the above requirements, we can see that knowledge of the 'carrying amount' of an item is necessary to determine the gain or loss on 'derecognition' of an asset. As previously indicated, the carrying amount of an asset is defined by IAS 16 as the amount at which an asset is recognised after deducting any accumulated depreciation and accumulated impairment losses. Therefore, if a firm has decided not to depreciate an asset (meaning the carrying amount will be higher), its profit on sale would be lower than for a firm that had been depreciating the asset.

For example, assume that a firm buys an item of plant for €25,000. It is expected to have a useful life of five years and no salvage value. The firm sells the asset at the end of the third year for €12,000. If the item has been depreciated according to the straight-line method for three years, total depreciation would amount to €15,000 and the carrying amount would be €10,000. The profit on sale would be €2,000. Hence the net effect on profits over the three years would be negative €13,000 (profit on sale of €2,000 less the accumulated depreciation of €15,000). If the item is not depreciated, its book value would still be €25,000, and the loss on sale would be €13,000. The difference in expense recognition would be a matter of timing.

Although the above discussion has related to property, plant and equipment, which are tangible assets, intangible assets should also be systematically amortised over their useful lives. As we know, 'intangible assets' are non-monetary assets without physical substance and would include brand names, copyrights, franchises, intellectual property, licences, mastheads, patents and trademarks. The term 'depreciation' is often used interchangeably with the term 'amortisation'. The terms have the same meaning; however, depreciation is generally used in relation to non-current assets that have physical substance (such as property, plant and equipment), while amortisation is generally used in relation to intangible non-current assets. We will consider intangible assets in more depth in Chapter 8. However, at this stage we note that IAS 38 *Intangible Assets* applies to intangible assets. IAS 38 requires that entities determine whether an intangible asset has an indefinite or a finite useful life. For the purposes of IAS 38, an intangible asset is regarded as having an indefinite useful life when, based on an analysis of the relevant factors, there is no foreseeable limit on the period over which the asset is expected to generate net cash inflows for the entity. Where an intangible asset is considered to have a finite life, its depreciable amount should be allocated on a systematic basis over its useful life in a similar manner to that outlined for depreciation earlier (IAS 38, paragraph 97).

Conversely, if an intangible asset is considered to have an indefinite useful life, paragraph 107 of IAS 36 states: 'an intangible asset with an indefinite useful life shall not be amortised'. Rather, the asset would be subject to annual impairment testing. Worked Example 5.5 further illustrates some of the issues that we need to consider when determining how to depreciate assets.

Worked Example 5.5 — A further consideration of depreciable life

(a) Ochillupo Ltd purchases a canning machine from a major supplier holding a clearance sale. The machine will start to be used in two years' time, when Ochillupo Ltd plans to expand the current business to include a fruit-canning operation. The machine costs €150,000 at the sale, a saving of €50,000 on its recommended retail price. The machine will be kept in storage until it is needed. It is reported to have a useful life of ten years if operating at full capacity.

(b) Ochillupo Ltd recently purchased some new commercial vehicles at a cost of €220,000. The documentation that came with the vehicles boasts that the useful economic life of these vehicles when they are worked hard is approximately 150,000 km. Given the size of the orchard in which the vehicles are to be used, management estimates that it will take approximately 15 years to reach this level of usage. A new model vehicle with exceptional advantages over the current model is expected on the market within five years. The company will probably update its vehicles when this new model is released.

(c) An asset purchased six years ago for €100,000 had an estimated useful life of seven years and accordingly will be fully written off at the end of the next financial year. The asset is being carried in the financial statements as follows:

	€
Cost	100,000
less: Accumulated depreciation	(85,716)
	14,284

A review by Ochillupo Ltd indicates that the machine can be used effectively within the business for a further five years. It has been established that the carrying value of the asset is a good approximation of the recoverable amount of that asset.

Required
Determine the appropriate depreciation treatment for the three cases described.

Solution

(a) Canning machine
The 'depreciable amount' will be the cost of the asset. The recommended retail price is not relevant. The asset is not earning revenue at present and is not expected to be used for two years.
Depreciation should be charged from the time a depreciable asset is first put into use or is held ready for use. Since the canning machine is being held ready for use, it would seem that depreciation should be charged immediately and allocated over a period of 12 years.

(b) Commercial vehicles
These vehicles have a physical life of 15 years. However, they are expected to be used by the present owner for only five years—their technical life. Therefore the company should depreciate the assets over five years.
The depreciable amount is the difference between the carrying amount and the expected residual value. An estimate of the residual value in five years is necessary.

(c) Other assets
IAS 16 requires that an asset's useful life be reviewed regularly. The company believes that the asset has a useful life of five years and that the current carrying amount is a good approximation of the recoverable amount of that asset. Thus the carrying value of €14,284 should be depreciated over a revised estimated useful life of five years, providing a revised depreciation charge of €2,857 per year.

5.9 Modifying existing non-current assets

As indicated in Chapter 4, when modifications or improvements are made to existing non-current assets and the expenditure is material and considered to enhance the service potential of the asset, such expenditure should be capitalised to the extent that particular accounting standards do not preclude such capitalisation (for example, IAS 38 prohibits the capitalisation of expenditures on certain types of intangible asset). Where expenditure is capitalised, the expenditure would subsequently be depreciated to the entity's statement of comprehensive income.

How we depreciate the modification or improvement will depend upon whether the improvement or modification retains a separate identity (perhaps an asset's life is enhanced by adding a component to the asset and that component can be removed and used elsewhere if desired), or whether the expenditure relates to something that becomes an integral part of the asset and is not feasibly removable.

The depreciable amount of any addition or extension to an existing depreciable asset that becomes an integral part of that asset must be allocated over the remaining useful life of that asset. The depreciable amount of any addition or extension to an existing depreciable asset that retains a separate identity and will be capable of being used after that asset is disposed of must be allocated independently of the existing asset, and on the basis of its own useful life.

5.10 Disposition of a depreciable asset

Items of property, plant and equipment can cease to be used for a number of reasons. These include sale, exchange, permanent withdrawal or destruction. Irrespective of the method of disposal, the accounting treatments follow three basic steps, these being:

- eliminate the cost or revalued amount and the accumulated depreciation;
- record the consideration received (if any); and
- record the gain or loss on disposal.

5.10.1 Sale

When an asset is sold, there will generally be either a profit or a loss on the sale. The profit or loss derived on the sale of a depreciable asset is the difference between the carrying amount of the asset, that is, its cost or revalued amount less the accumulated depreciation and any accumulated impairment losses, and the amount received for the asset as measured at fair value. Pursuant to IAS 16, the profit or loss on disposal is referred to as a gain or loss on derecognition and is recognised on a 'net basis'. Using a 'net basis' means that the proceeds from the disposal should not be separately treated as revenue. Worked Example 5.6 looks at the disposal of a depreciable asset.

Worked Example 5.6 **Disposal of a depreciable asset**

Sandon Point Ltd acquires an item of machinery on 1 July 2012 for a cost of £100,000. When the asset is acquired, it is considered to have a useful life for the entity of five years. After this time, the machine will have no residual value. It is believed that the pattern of economic benefits would best be reflected by applying the sum-of-digits method of depreciation. However, contrary to expectations, on 1 July 2014 the asset is sold for £70,000.

Required

Calculate the profit on disposal of the asset and provide the appropriate journal entries in the books of Sandon Point Ltd to record the disposal.

Solution

For an asset with a useful life of five years, the sum-of-digits depreciation is:

$n(n + 1) \div 2 = 5 \times 6 \div 2 = 15$

First year depreciation = 5 ÷ 15 × £100,000   = £33,333

Second year depreciation = 4 ÷ 15 × £100,000 = £26,667

Total accumulated depreciation at 1 July 2007 = £60,000

Therefore, the carrying amount of the asset is £40,000 as at 30 June 2014, made up of the historical cost of £100,000 less the accumulated depreciation of £60,000. The profit on the sale of the asset would therefore be £30,000, that is, the amount of the consideration less the carrying amount.

The gain on the machinery would be represented by the difference between the proceeds of the sale and the carrying amount of the machinery. The accounting entry would be:

Dr	Cash at bank	£70,000	
Dr	Accumulated depreciation — machinery	£60,000	
Cr	Gain on sale of machinery		£30,000
Cr	Machinery		£100,000

5.10.2 Sale proceeds deferred

When the receipt of the sale proceeds on the disposal of an item of property, plant and equipment is deferred for a period of time, paragraph 72 of IAS 16 requires the fair value of the consideration to be recognised initially at its 'cash price equivalent' (present value), with the difference between the cash price equivalent and the consideration received being treated as interest revenue in accordance with IAS 18.

The discount rate to be used is the rate at which the vendor could invest the amount under similar terms and conditions. An example of deferred sales proceeds is provided in Worked Example 5.7.

Worked Example 5.7 **Sale proceeds deferred**

Assume the same information provided for Sandon Point Ltd in Worked Example 5.6 but this time the sale proceeds of £70,000 will be received in two years' time, on 30 June 2016. The applicable interest rate is 8 per cent.

Required

Provide the journal entries necessary to account for the sale of the asset.

Solution

Calculation of the present value of the consideration receivable:

$$£70,000 \text{ in 2 years at } 8\% = £70,000 \times 0.85734 = £60,014$$

The journal entry at the date of the disposal is:

1 July 2014

Dr	Loan receivable	£60,014	
Dr	Accumulated depreciation — machinery	£60,000	
Cr	Machinery		£100,000
Cr	Gain on sale of machinery		£20,014

At the end of the financial year, the increase in the value of the loan receivable must be recognised. It will be calculated as £60,014 × 8% = £4,801.

30 June 2015

Dr	Loan receivable	£4,801	
Cr	Interest revenue		£4,801

Again, at the end of the second year, the increase in the value of the receivable must be recognised, and then the receipt of cash must be accounted for. The interest revenue to be recognised equals (£60,014 + £4,801) × 8% = £5,185.

30 June 2016

Dr	Loan receivable	£5,185	
Cr	Interest revenue		£5,185
Dr	Cash at bank	£70,000	
Cr	Loan receivable		£70,000

5.11 Contractual implications of building depreciation

As mentioned previously, reporting entities are frequently involved in contractual arrangements that are tied to reported accounting numbers. Compliance with IAS 16 in relation to building depreciation will lead to lower reported profits than would failing to recognise any building depreciation. As previously indicated, however—ignoring the possibility of revaluations—the subsequent profit on sale of the building will be higher in the presence of depreciation. The recognition of building depreciation will increase expenses (depreciation expense) and therefore reduce profits. It will also lead to a reduction in net assets. Assets and profits are frequently used within some of the accounting-based ratios used in debt covenants. Building depreciation will increase debt-to-equity ratios, reduce times interest covered ratios and reduce profit available for dividends. Therefore, managers facing possible debt covenant violations are less likely to want to comply with IAS 16. An example of how the change to international accounting standards affected many companies that operate in building intensive industries is provided in Financial Accounting in the News 5.2. This article shows how a change to FRS 15 (which is the UK equivalent of IAS 16) impacted on a UK company, SFI (in the hotel and entertainment business).

Financial Accounting In the News 5.2

DEPRECIATION SWITCH FLATTENS SFI'S FIGURES

David Blackwell, *Financial Times*, 27 January 2000

A change in depreciation policy under the FRS 15 accounting standard left SFI, the pub and restaurant group, with a fall in pre-tax profits in spite of strong first-half trading.

Tony Hill, chairman and chief executive, said sales, free cash flow and earnings before interest, tax, depreciation and amortisation were all well ahead in the first half. The estate had almost doubled in size to 79 pubs in a little more than two years, and was set to expand to 140 by the end of 2002.

SFI, which owns the Litten Tree and Bar Med pub chains, and operates three table-dancing clubs, reported a fall in pre-tax profits in the 24 weeks to 20 November to £3.1m from £3.3m in the previous 25 weeks. The drop came after a rise in the depreciation charge from £854,000 to £1.4m under FRS 15, which requires the depreciation of freeholds and long leases.

Sales rose from £17.8m to £23.8m, generating an 18 per cent rise in pre-tax profits to £3.66m under the former accounting standards with earnings before interest, tax, depreciation and amortisation rising 30 per cent under the old rules to £5.6m.

Source: Extract from *Financial Times*. © THE FINANCIAL TIMES LIMITED 2012

Clinch (1983) undertook a study of reporting entities' building depreciation policies from a Positive Accounting Theory perspective (Positive Accounting Theory is described in Chapter 3). He found support for the view that there are cash-flow effects associated with a decision to comply with the requirement to depreciate buildings. He found strong support for the contention that non-compliance with the requirement to depreciate buildings leads to greater auditing costs. The increased auditing costs are explained on the basis that non-compliance with accounting standards leads to extended discussions with auditors, who usually base their fees on the time taken on the audit. Clinch also found evidence that the possible benefits of non-compliance stem from cost savings associated with avoiding violations of debt covenants. Providing depreciation might, at the extreme, lead to the violation of an existing covenant that might, in turn, lead to costly debt renegotiations.

Now that international accounting standards are moving more towards a fair value approach, changes may be afoot again. More specific guidance on valuation and fair value is likely to harmonise accounting within Europe. At the moment, different methods of obtaining a current valuation are used throughout different countries in Europe. French and Gabrielli (2007) note that the principal approach used in continental Europe is the depreciated replacement cost (DRC), whereas in the UK the principal basis is market value. The DRC is defined as 'the current cost of reproduction or replacement of an asset less a deduction for physical deterioration and all relevant forms of obsolescence and optimisation'. The market value is defined in the RICS Appraisal and Valuation Standards as the 'estimated amount for which a property should exchange on the date of the valuation between a willing buyer and a willing seller in an arm's length transaction after proper marketing wherein the parties had each acted knowledgably, prudently and without compulsion'.

Non-compliance with accounting requirements, however, must be considered in the light of the negative implications such actions can have, for example, for the reputation of the firm and potentially for costs that firms will subsequently incur in order to attract funds. Also, in the presence of non-compliance with accounting standards, assuming non-compliance is detected, contractual restrictions might be based on numbers adjusted in accordance with applicable accounting standards rather than the numbers initially provided by the reporting entity.

5.12 Depreciation as a process of allocating the cost of an asset over its useful life: further considerations

As we have seen in this chapter, when we depreciate an asset we are effectively allocating the cost (or revalued amount) of an asset over its expected **useful life**. For example, if we acquire a machine for €1,000,000 that has an expected useful life of ten years with no expected residual value, we would recognise €100,000 in depreciation each year (assuming that the pattern of benefits is expected to be uniform across the useful life of the asset and assuming we have not revalued the asset). The effect of this is that, across the useful life of the asset, we have reduced profits by the cost of the machine, which was €1,000,000. What must be appreciated, however, is that the cost of replacing the machine might have increased across time so that it is greater than the aggregate amount that we have recognised as depreciation expense. For example, if the cost of replacing the machine after ten years has doubled to €2,000,000, it could be argued that we have not recognised sufficient expenses and might have distributed to shareholders too much in dividends (dividends being distributed out of profits).

> **useful life** Estimated period over which future economic benefits embodied in a depreciable asset are expected to be consumed by the entity, or the estimated total service to be obtained from the asset by the entity.

Indeed, this is one of the main criticisms of historical-cost accounting (Chapter 3 briefly considered some alternative approaches to historical-cost accounting, which take into account current valuations of assets). We will address asset revaluations in the next chapter; however, at this stage we should note that, if assets are revalued to fair value at regular intervals, this has the effect of increasing the total amount of depreciation being recognised, thereby reducing profits and hence the amount available to distribute in the form of dividends.

5.13 Disclosure requirements

IAS 16 provides a number of disclosure requirements in relation to depreciation. Specifically, paragraph 73 requires (and these disclosures would be made in the notes to the financial statements) the following:

> The financial statements shall disclose, for each class of property, plant and equipment:
>
> (a) the measurement bases used for determining the gross carrying amount;
> (b) the depreciation methods used;
> (c) the useful lives or the depreciation rates used;
> (d) the gross carrying amount and the accumulated depreciation (aggregated with accumulated impairment losses) at the beginning and end of the period; and
> (e) a reconciliation of the carrying amount at the beginning and end of the period showing:
> (i) additions;
> (ii) disposals;
> (iii) acquisitions through business combinations;
> (iv) increases or decreases resulting from revaluations and from impairment losses recognised or reversed directly in equity in accordance with IAS 36;
> (v) impairment losses recognised in profit or loss in accordance with IAS 36;
> (vi) impairment losses reversed in profit or loss in accordance with IAS 36;
> (vii) depreciation;
> (viii) the net exchange differences arising on the translation of the financial statements from the functional currency into a different presentation currency, including the translation of a foreign operation into the presentation currency of the reporting entity; and
> (ix) other changes.

SUMMARY

The chapter considered a number of issues relating to the depreciation of non-current assets. It made specific reference to the applicable accounting standard, IAS 16 *Property, Plant and Equipment*, for depreciation requirements as they pertain to property, plant and equipment. The chapter also referred briefly to IAS 38 *Intangible Assets* for details of how intangible assets should be amortised. The focus in this chapter was predominantly on property, plant and equipment.

From an accounting perspective, depreciation represents the allocation of the cost of an asset, or its revalued amount, over the accounting periods expected to benefit from its use. That is, depreciation is an allocation process rather than a valuation process.

Three general issues arise when accounting for depreciation: determination of the *depreciable base* of the asset; the *useful life* of the asset; and the method to be used in *allocating the cost* of the asset over the various accounting periods. There is also a decision to be made about when to start depreciating an asset. The depreciable base of the asset will be its historical cost, or its revalued amount, less any anticipated residual to be received from the ultimate disposal of the asset at the end of its useful life, less any impairment losses that have been recognised. The determination of useful life will depend on judgements relating to the physical, technical and commercial life of the asset. The method used to allocate the cost of the asset should reflect the pattern of benefits being derived from its use, taking into account issues associated with the physical wear and tear of the asset and technical and commercial obsolescence. There are various methods of depreciation, including the straight-line method; sum-of-digits method; declining-balance method; and depreciation calculated on a production basis. The method used should reflect the pattern of benefits being generated by the asset.

Depreciation itself should start from the time when a depreciable asset is first put into use or is held ready for use. When a depreciable asset is ultimately sold, the difference between the net amount received on disposal and its historical cost or other revalued amount substituted for historical cost, less accumulated depreciation and less any accumulated impairment losses, must be recognised in the profit or loss of the period.

KEY TERMS

END-OF-CHAPTER EXERCISE

Fistral Ltd acquires a blank-making machine—blanks are the inner foam core of a surfboard—for the following amounts:

- Initial price paid to the supplier on 1 July 2013: £70,000
- Cost to deliver the machine to the site: £5,000
- Amount paid to an engineer to make the machine work: £35,000

The engineer completes her work on 31 December 2013.

It is expected that the benefits from the blank-making machine will be derived uniformly over ten years and that the machine will have no residual value.

On 1 July 2014, an additional component is acquired at a cost of £60,000 and is attached to the blank-making machine acquired on 1 July 2013. Although this does not extend the life of the blank-making machine, it makes the machine more efficient. The additional component is expected to have a useful life of 20 years, and to be able to be used on other machines when the useful life of the existing blank-making machine is over. At the end of 20 years, the component will have no residual value. **LO** 5.3

REQUIRED

Determine the total depreciation expense for the blank-making machine and attachment for the year ended 30 June 2015.

SOLUTION TO END-OF-CHAPTER EXERCISE

As the additional component can continue to be used beyond the life of the blank-making machine, the two items should be depreciated independently. As the benefits are expected to be derived uniformly, it is appropriate to use the straight-line method of depreciation.

The depreciable amount of the blank-making machine should include the initial cost, delivery cost and the amount paid to the engineer—that is, the costs necessary to get the machine into a usable state. This gives a total cost of £110,000. One year's depreciation of this, assuming no residual value and a life of ten years, is £11,000.

The depreciation expense of the additional component will be its cost allocated over 20 years. This gives an amount of £3,000. Hence the total depreciation expense for the year to 30 June 2015 is £14,000.

REVIEW QUESTIONS

1   Does depreciation reflect a change in the market value of an asset?   **LO** 5.1
2   Define 'useful life' in terms of the decision to depreciate an asset.   **LO** 5.2
3   What effect does depreciation have on the statement of comprehensive income and the statement of financial position?   **LO** 5.1
4   An item of plant is acquired at a direct cost of £110,000. It requires installation and modifications amounting to £20,000 and £10,000, respectively, before it is efficiently operational. It is expected to have a useful life of six years, at which point it will have a residual value of £15,000.   **LO** 5.3

   REQUIRED
   Provide the depreciation entries for the first two years using:
   (a) the sum-of-digits method
   (b) the declining-balance method (reducing-balance method)
   (c) the straight-line method
5   What is the difference between amortisation and depreciation?   **LO** 5.1
6   You have been appointed the accountant of a new organisation that is preparing its first set of financial statements. In determining the depreciation for the first year, what sorts of information would you need?   **LO** 5.2
7   The financial statements of ABC Ltd indicate that the directors did not depreciate their buildings on the basis that an increase in the value of the associated land was not treated as revenue. Is this a valid argument?   **LO** 5.1
8   Staunton Ltd acquires a new tractor for its pineapple farm. The tractor is expected to be operational for a period of 18 years, although a more economical version, which Staunton Ltd's competitors will probably acquire, will be available in six years. It is envisaged that Staunton Ltd will close down in 15 years, as its existing lease will expire.   **LO** 5.2

   REQUIRED
   Determine the number of periods over which the tractor should be depreciated.
9   What could motivate management to use one method of depreciation in preference to another?   **LO** 5.3
10   How is the gain or loss on the disposal of a non-current asset determined?   **LO** 5.4
11   Winkipop Ltd acquires an item of machinery on 1 July 2011 for a total acquisition cost of €90,000. The life of the asset is assessed as being six years, after which time Winkipop Ltd expects to be able to dispose of the asset for €10,000. It is expected that the benefits will be generated in a pattern that is best reflected by the sum-of-digits depreciation approach. On 1 July 2014, owing to unforeseen circumstances, the machinery is exchanged for a motor vehicle. The motor vehicle is two years old, originally cost €30,000 and has a market value of €20,000.   **LO** 5.4

   REQUIRED
   Provide the journal entry to record the disposal of the machinery on 1 July 2014.
12   What considerations would you take into account when deciding to use one depreciation method, for example the straight-line method, in preference to another?   **LO** 5.3
13   If a company depreciates its property, plant and equipment, what are the associated disclosure requirements?   **LO** 5.5
14   Can an organisation switch depreciation methods from one financial period to the next?   **LO** 5.3

15 On 1 July 2013, Bells Tourist Operations acquired an aircraft that can be used for taking wealthy tourists to remote beaches with lovely sands and limited crowds. The aircraft cost €12,000,000. An engineer's analysis commissioned by the company determined that the aircraft could be broken down into the following components: airframe, engines and fittings. The airframe comprised 55 per cent of the cost, the engines comprised 40 per cent and the fittings comprised 5 per cent.

The airframe is estimated to have a useful life of 15 years. At the end of its useful life it will have an estimated scrap value of €150,000. The engines have an estimated useful life of 20,000 hours, while fixtures and fittings are expected to have a useful life of five years. Both the engines and fixtures and fittings are expected to have no residual value at the end of their useful lives. During the first year the aircraft was operating for 2920 hours.   **LO 5.4**

REQUIRED

Prepare all journal entries necessary to account for the acquisition of the aircraft, and its depreciation, for the year ending 30 June 2014.

CHALLENGING QUESTIONS

16 Is depreciation an allocation process or a valuation process? Provide reasons for your answer.   **LO 5.1**

17 At the beginning of 2011 Lorne Ltd acquired an item of machinery at a cost of £100,000. At the time it was expected that the machinery would have a useful life of ten years and a residual value of £10,000. Until the end of the 2013 financial year the depreciation expense was recognised on a straight-line basis. At the beginning of the 2014 financial year, the remaining useful life was reassessed as being 11 years and the residual value was reassessed at £14,000.   **LO 5.3**

REQUIRED

Calculate the depreciation expense for the 2011, 2013 and 2014 financial years.

18 Anglesea Ltd constructed a building in 2010 for a cost of £960,000. The building was expected to have a useful life of 25 years, after which time it would be demolished at an expected demolition cost of £100,000. Being on the coast, the building was sometimes subject to wild winds. At the end of the 2014 financial year, the roof of the building was blown away and a replacement was constructed at a cost of £200,000. It was predicted that, by replacing the building's roof, its expected useful life would be extended a further 25 years after the end of the 2014 financial year.   **LO 5.3**

REQUIRED

Calculate the depreciation cost for the 2013, 2014 and 2015 financial years.

19 Wastewater Limited acquired an item of plant on 1 July 2012 for €3,660,000. When the item of plant was acquired, it was initially assessed as having a life of 10,000 hours. During the reporting period ending 30 June 2013 the plant was operated for 3,000 hours.

At 1 July 2013 the plant had a remaining useful life of 7,000 hours. On 1 July 2013 the plant underwent a major upgrade costing €234,600. Management believes that this upgrade will add a further 2,000 hours of operating time to the plant's life. During the reporting period ended 30 June 2014 the plant was operated for 4,000 hours.

On 1 July 2014 the plant underwent a further major upgrade, the cost of which amounted to €344,900, and this added a further 3,100 hours' operating time to its life. During the reporting period ending 30 June 2015 the plant was operated for 3,800 hours.   **LO 5.2**

REQUIRED

Prepare all the journal entries that Wastewater Limited would prepare for the years ending 30 June 2013, 30 June 2014 and 30 June 2015 to account for the acquisition, subsequent expenditure and depreciation on the asset.

20 On 1 July 2011 Sprintfast Couriers, which has a year-end of 30 June, purchased a delivery truck for use in its courier operations at a cost of €65,000. At the end of the truck's useful life it is expected to have a residual value of €5,000. During its six-year useful life, Sprintfast Couriers Limited expect the truck to be driven 246,000 km.   **LO 5.3**

REQUIRED

Calculate the annual depreciation charge for each of the six years of the truck's life using the following methods:
- **(a)** the straight-line method
- **(b)** the sum-of-digits method
- **(c)** the declining-balance method (reducing-balance method)

(d) the units-of-production method using kilometres as the basis of use and assuming the following usage:

Year	Kilometres
2012	28,000
2013	34,000
2014	42,000
2015	55,000
2016	68,000
2017	19,000
	246,000

21 Gazza Ltd acquires a machine for a cost of £29,000. It is expected that the machine will continue to be operational for seven years, during which time it is expected to run for 35,000 hours. The estimated residual value of the machine is £7,000 at the end of its useful life. **LO** 5.3

REQUIRED

Calculate the depreciation charge for each of the first three years, using the following methods:
(a) the straight-line method
(b) the sum-of-digits method
(c) the declining-balance method, using a 33 per cent rate
(d) the units-of-production method, based on hours of operation, given that operating times are as follows:

year 1	6,000 hours
year 2	7,000 hours
year 3	5,500 hours

22 First Point Ltd acquires an item of machinery on 1 July 2011 for a cost of €250,000. When the asset is acquired, it is considered to have a useful life for the entity of six years. After this time, the machine will have no residual value. It is believed that the pattern of economic benefits would best be reflected by applying the sum-of-digits method of depreciation. However, contrary to expectations, on 1 July 2014 the asset is sold for €110,000. The amount is to be received as follows: €60,000 on 30 June 2015 and €50,000 on 30 June 2016. The applicable interest rate is 6 per cent. **LO** 5.3

REQUIRED

Calculate the profit on disposal of the asset and provide the appropriate journal entries in the books of First Point Ltd to record the disposal and the subsequent receipts of cash.

23 Amsterdam Ltd purchased a property ten years ago for €3,000,000. Included in this amount is €350,000 that relates to buildings constructed on the land. A recent valuation has shown that the property is now valued at €5,400,000. The valuer has suggested that the location of the property and the quality of the soil are such that it is unlikely that the value will ever drop below the initial cost of acquisition. The buildings on the property are of a general nature. **LO** 5.1

REQUIRED

Describe the appropriate depreciation treatment.

24 On 1 July 2012 Long Boards Ltd acquired a printing machine at a cost of €120,000. At acquisition the machine had an expected useful life of 12,000 machine hours and was expected to be in operation for four years, after which it would have €nil residual value. Actual machine hours were 3,000 in the year ended 30 June 2013 and 3,400 in the year ended 30 June 2014. On 1 July 2014 the machine was sold for €50,000. **LO** 5.3

REQUIRED

(a) Prepare journal entries to record depreciation of the printing machine for each of the years ended 30 June 2013 and 30 June 2014 using the straight-line method. State the carrying amount of the machine at the end of each period. Prepare the journal entry to record the sale of the machine on 1 July 2014.
(b) Prepare journal entries to record depreciation of the printing machine for each of the years ended 30 June 2013 and 30 June 2014 using the declining-balance method (reducing-balance method) with a depreciation rate of 40 per cent. State the carrying amount of the machine at the end of each period. Prepare the journal entry to record the sale of the machine on 1 July 2014.
(c) Prepare journal entries to record depreciation of the printing machine for each of the years ended 30 June 2013 and 30 June 2014 using the sum-of-digits method. State the carrying amount of the machine at the end of each period. Prepare the journal entry to record the sale of the machine on 1 July 2014.

(d) Prepare journal entries to record depreciation of the printing machine for each of the years ended 30 June 2013 and 30 June 2014 using the production basis. State the carrying amount of the machine at the end of each period. Prepare the journal entry to record the sale of the machine on 1 July 2014.

25 Malibu Ltd acquired a building on 1 July 2007 at a cost of £800,000. The useful life of the building was estimated as 20 years with no residual value. Malibu Ltd used the straight-line method of depreciation. On 30 June 2013 the estimate of the useful life of the building was revised to 15 years. **LO** 5.3

REQUIRED

Prepare journal entries for depreciation of the building for the years ended 30 June 2012, 2013 and 2014, and state the carrying amount of the building at the end of each of the three reporting periods.

26 Possoes Ltd acquired an aeroplane in 2012 for £75 million. Possoes does not revalue its assets, but instead measures its aeroplanes at cost less accumulated depreciation. If the cost of the same type of aeroplane increases to £110 million over the next three years, and assuming that the organisation distributes all of its profits to shareholders (in the form of dividends), then does the practice of basing depreciation on historical cost create any possible problems for the organisation? If, by contrast, the organisation periodically revalues its assets to fair value, would this have acted to alleviate such problems? **LO** 5.1

REFERENCES

CLINCH, G., 'Alternative Hypotheses Concerning Depreciation of Buildings', *Abacus*, vol. 19, no. 2, 1983, pp. 139–47.

FRENCH, N. & GABRIELLI, L., 'Market Value and Depreciated Replacement Cost: Contradictory or Complementary?', *Journal of Property Investment and Finance*, vol. 25, no. 5, 2007, pp. 515–24.

JAAFAR, A. & MCLEAY, S., 'Country Effects and Sector Effects on the Harmonization of Accounting Policy Choice', *Abacus*, vol. 43, no. 2, 2007, pp. 156–88.

JACKSON, S.B., 'The Effects of Firms' Depreciation Method Choice on Managers' Capital Investment Decisions', *Accounting Review*, vol. 83, no. 2, 2008, pp. 351–76.

TESCO PLC, *Annual Report and Financial Statements 2011*, http://www.tescoplc.com/media/417/tesco_annual_report_2011_final.pdf.

Chapter 6

Revaluations and Impairment Testing of Non-current Assets

Learning objectives

Upon completing this chapter readers should:

LO1 understand how and when to revalue an item of property, plant and equipment in accordance with IAS 16 *Property, Plant and Equipment*;

LO2 understand how and when to revalue an intangible asset in accordance with IAS 38 *Intangible Assets*;

LO3 understand the difference in accounting treatments for upward revaluations to 'fair value', as opposed to write-downs to 'recoverable amount';

LO4 understand what an 'impairment loss' is and know how to account for one in accordance with IAS 36 *Impairment of Assets*;

LO5 understand how to account for revaluations that reverse previous revaluation increments or decrements;

LO6 understand how to account for accumulated depreciation when a non-current depreciable asset is revalued, and understand that, subsequent to revaluation, new depreciation charges will be based on the revalued amount of the non-current asset;

LO7 know how the profit on disposal of a revalued non-current asset is determined and understand how asset revaluations can affect an organisation's profits owing to changes in depreciation expenses and in final profits or losses on the sale of the revalued asset;

LO8 be able to explain possible motivations that might drive an organisation to elect to, or not to, revalue its non-current assets to fair value; and

LO9 know the disclosure requirements pertaining to asset revaluations.

6.1 Introduction to revaluations and impairment testing of non-current assets

Financial statements prepared under the historical-cost accounting convention are frequently criticised on the ground that recorded historical cost might bear no relation to the current value of the assets concerned. Under IFRSs, entities are permitted to revalue many of their non-current assets, either upwards or downwards, to reflect their fair value. However, while many non-current assets may be revalued, the revaluing of certain types of asset

is specifically excluded by virtue of some accounting standards. For example, IAS 38 *Intangible Assets* will permit some intangible assets to be revalued upwards only when there is an 'active market' for the asset. An active market is deemed to exist when the items being traded within the market are homogeneous, willing buyers and sellers can normally be found at any time, and prices are available to the public. IAS 38 also specifically excludes the revaluation of many types of internally generated intangibles, such as brand names, publishing titles and so forth. We concentrate on intangible assets in Chapter 8. The requirements for undertaking revaluations of property, plant and equipment (covered by IAS 16) are not as strict as those imposed for intangibles, and an item of property, plant and equipment may be revalued to the extent that a 'fair value' can be determined. In this chapter our discussion will relate chiefly to the revaluation of property, plant and equipment.

The accounting for property, plant and equipment under IAS 16 can be described as a modified historical-cost system—a system that does allow many non-current assets to be revalued from cost to fair value. Interestingly, while upward **asset revaluations** are not permitted in some countries, such as the US, they *are* permitted in others, in particular those countries that have adopted accounting standards released by the IASB (such as the UK and those in the European Union). Revaluations have been permitted in the UK for many years.

> **asset revaluation**
> Recognising a reassessment of the carrying amount of a non-current asset to its fair value as at a particular date, excluding recoverable amount write-downs.

Where revaluations are undertaken, directors should be prudent and not revalue an asset to an amount in excess of what would appear reasonable. In this regard, it is generally accepted that directors should ascertain whether the carrying amount of any non-current asset—taking into consideration the asset's value to the company as a going concern—exceeds the amount that is expected to be recovered through the ongoing use and subsequent disposal of the asset (often referred to as the **recoverable amount**). Where the carrying value of an asset exceeds the recoverable amount, paragraph 59 of IAS 36 *Impairment of Assets* requires that the non-current asset be written down to its recoverable amount.

> **recoverable amount**
> The higher of an asset's fair value less costs to sell and its value in use.

Impairment losses should not be confused with depreciation (which was covered in the previous chapter). Depreciation is recognised even if the recoverable amount of an asset exceeds its carrying amount.

In some cases it will not be appropriate to consider the expected net cash inflows applicable to individual assets where a group of assets working together supports the generation of net cash flows relevant to the determination of recoverable amount. In such cases, IAS 36 states that, in order to identify whether there has been a decline in the future economic benefits represented by particular assets, it might be necessary to estimate the net cash inflows for the relevant group of assets—with the group typically being referred to as a 'cash-generating unit'—and compare that amount with the carrying amount of the combined group of assets.

6.2 Measuring property, plant and equipment at cost or at fair value—the choice

The relevant accounting standard is IAS 16 *Property, Plant and Equipment*. IAS 16 covers a number of issues, including determining the cost of property, plant and equipment and the depreciation, derecognition and revaluation of property, plant and equipment. In this chapter we will concentrate on revaluations and impairment of property, plant and equipment.

Once an item of property, plant and equipment has been recognised by an entity, paragraph 29 of IAS 16 requires each class of property, plant and equipment to be measured either at *cost* (referred to in the standard as the 'cost model') or at *fair value* (referred to as applying the 'revaluation model').

It is permissible for some classes of property, plant and equipment to be valued at cost and other classes to be valued at fair value, but an entire class must be measured consistently on the same basis (IAS 16, paragraphs 30, 31 and 36).

IAS 16 defines a class of property, plant and equipment as a grouping of assets with a similar nature and use within an entity's operations. The following are examples of separate classes:

- land
- ships
- furniture and fittings

- buildings
- aircraft
- office equipment

- machinery
- motor vehicles

Once an entity elects to value a class of assets on the basis of fair value—that is, it adopts the revaluation model—it is expected to maintain this basis of valuation for this class of assets. However, IAS 16 allows an entity to switch from the fair value basis of valuation back to the cost basis as long as the change generates financial information that is more relevant and reliable and as long as adequate disclosures of the change in accounting policy are made.

Clearly, by permitting some classes of non-current assets to be valued on the cost basis and others to be valued at fair value, we have not eliminated the confusion associated with understanding what the total balance of non-current assets actually represents. It is neither *cost* nor *fair value*, but a combination of the two. How meaningful do you think this aggregated number is?

6.3 Recognition of impairment losses

Where an entity elects to change from the cost basis to a fair value basis for measuring a class of non-current assets, and that class has previously been the subject of an impairment loss, any increase in the carrying amount of the asset must first be recognised as income (thereby reversing the previous expense) to the extent that the increase in value does not exceed the amount that would have been recorded for the asset had no write-down previously occurred. Any increase in the fair value of the asset above the amount that would have been recorded for the asset, had no impairment loss been recognised, is to be transferred to an account known as the revaluation surplus. The revaluation surplus is part of owners' equity.

For example, let us assume that we have an item of land acquired in 2011 for €1 million. If the recoverable value of the land in 2013 is considered to be €800,000, an expense of €200,000 would be recognised in 2013 (an impairment loss). If the value of the land has increased to €1.3 million in 2015 and a revaluation is undertaken, €200,000 would be recognised as income (effectively reversing the previous €200,000 impairment loss) and €300,000 would be transferred to the revaluation surplus.

Worked Example 6.1 provides an illustration of an asset revaluation where there has been a previous impairment loss.

Worked Example 6.1 — Reversal of a previous impairment loss

Point Impossible Ltd acquired some land in 2013 at a cost of €2.5 million. In 2014 it was determined that the recoverable amount of the land was €2.0 million. In 2015 it was decided to revalue the land to its fair value, which was then assessed as having increased to €2.8 million.

Required
Provide the journal entries to record the above movements in value.

Solution

2014

Dr	Impairment loss—land (expense)	€500,000	
Cr	Accumulated impairment cost—land		€500,000

2015

Dr	Land	€300,000	
Dr	Accumulated impairment cost—land	€500,000	
Cr	Reversal of previous impairment loss—land (income)		€500,000
Cr	Revaluation surplus		€300,000

As indicated, the above impairment reversal would be treated as part of income in 2015. The revaluation surplus is part of equity.

IAS 36 *Impairment of Assets* imposes the general requirement that a non-current asset should be written down to its recoverable amount when its *carrying amount* is greater than its *recoverable amount*. IAS 36 defines an impairment loss as: 'the amount by which the carrying amount of an asset or a cash-generating unit exceeds its recoverable amount'.

Pursuant to IAS 36, different approaches to accounting for an impairment loss of property, plant and equipment will be required depending upon whether the cost model or revaluation model has been adopted. As paragraph 60 of IAS 36 states:

> An impairment loss shall be recognised immediately in profit or loss, unless the asset is carried at revalued amount in accordance with another Standard (e.g. in accordance with the revaluation model in IAS 16). Any impairment loss of a revalued asset shall be treated as a revaluation decrease in accordance with that other Standard.

Therefore, if an asset has been revalued, the impairment loss will be recognised by reducing (debiting) the balance of the revaluation surplus as it pertains to the previous revaluation. Otherwise, the impairment loss is taken into account by recognising an expense directly. Worked Example 6.2 provides an example of this difference.

Worked Example 6.2 — Recognition of an impairment loss where either the cost model or fair value model is used

Coogee Ltd has a machine, which has a carrying value of €500,000. As at the end of the reporting period, the recoverable amount of the asset has been determined as being equal to €350,000.

If we assume use of the cost model to account for this class of asset, the entry would be:

Dr	Impairment loss	€150,000	
Cr	Accumulated impairment losses—machinery		€150,000

However, if the machine was measured at fair value by way of an asset revaluation (that is, the revaluation model was previously adopted) and if we assume that the previous revaluation increment was €60 000, we would first eliminate the respective balance in the revaluation surplus and then recognise an impairment loss as follows:

Dr	Impairment loss	€90,000	
Dr	Revaluation surplus	€60,000	
Cr	Accumulated impairment losses—machinery		€90,000
Cr	Machine		€60,000

Where a non-current asset is measured on the cost basis, any write-downs to recoverable amounts are not considered to be *revaluations*. They are 'impairment losses'. Hence the recognition of an impairment loss in respect of a non-current asset does not oblige the entity to revalue the whole class of non-current assets to which that asset belongs. Paragraph 12 of IAS 36 identifies the following factors as signs of potential impairment:

External sources of information

(a) *during the period, an asset's market value has declined significantly more than would be expected as a result of the passage of time or normal use;*

(b) *significant changes with an adverse effect on the entity have taken place during the period, or will take place in the near future, in the technological, market, economic or legal environment in which the entity operates or in the market to which an asset is dedicated;*

(c) *market interest rates or other market rates of return on investments have increased during the period, and those increases are likely to affect the discount rate used in calculating an asset's value-in-use and decrease the asset's recoverable amount materially;*

(d) *the carrying amount of the net assets of the entity is more than its market capitalisation;*

Internal sources of information

(e) *evidence is available of obsolescence or physical damage of an asset;*

(f) *significant changes with an adverse effect on the entity have taken place during the period, or are expected to take place in the near future, in the extent to which, or manner in which, an asset is used or is expected to be used. These changes include the asset becoming idle, plans to discontinue or restructure the operation to which an asset belongs, plans to dispose of an asset before the previously expected date, and reassessing the useful life of an asset as finite rather than indefinite; and*

(g) *evidence is available from internal reporting that indicates that the economic performance of an asset is, or will be, worse than expected.*

6.3.1 Determining the recoverable amount of an asset

As indicated in the definition of an impairment loss (that being: the amount by which the carrying amount of an asset or a cash-generating unit exceeds its recoverable amount), a consideration of both the 'carrying amount' and the 'recoverable amount' is necessary in determining the impairment loss. Within IAS 36 *Impairment of Assets*, 'carrying amount' and 'recoverable amount' are defined in paragraph 6 as follows:

> **Carrying amount** *is the amount at which an asset is recognised after deducting any accumulated depreciation (amortisation) and accumulated impairment losses thereon.*
> *The recoverable amount of an asset or a cash-generating unit is the higher of its fair value less costs to sell and its value-in-use.*

> **carrying amount** The amount at which an asset is recognised after deducting any accumulated depreciation (amortisation) and accumulated impairment losses thereon.

The above definition of recoverable amount further requires definitions of 'fair value less costs to sell' and 'value-in-use'. We will consider these definitions in more depth soon; however, at this stage we can note that 'fair value less costs to sell' is defined in paragraph 6 as 'the amount obtainable from the sale of an asset or cash-generating unit in an arm's length transaction between knowledgeable, willing parties, less the costs of disposal'. 'Value-in-use' is defined as 'the present value of the future cash flows expected to be derived from an asset or cash-generating unit'. These definitions further require us to consider the meanings of 'cash-generating unit' as well as how cash flows and present values are to be determined for the purpose of determining value-in-use. Assumptions need to be made in respect of the timing of the expected future cash flows and when selecting the appropriate discount rate. Paragraph 33 of IAS 36 states that these projected cash flows should be based on management's best estimate, should not include expected restructuring and should not assume growth in excess of the long-term expected growth rate for the industry, products, etc.

6.3.2 Present values

In relation to present values, we can see that, from the above definition of 'recoverable amount' and its reference to 'present values', it is apparent that IAS 36 requires the cash flows assessed in determining recoverable amount to be discounted where the recoverable amount is determined by reference to expectations relating to the asset's value-in-use. Discounting the future cash flows will have direct implications for the calculated value of recoverable amount and perhaps the need to change the value of an asset in a downward direction. The process of discounting the expected future cash flows will reduce the calculated recoverable amount. For example, assume that an entity has land with a carrying value of €5 million, but a current market value of only €4 million. Further, assume that the organisation is not using the land, so that there are no cash flows being generated from its use. Management considers that the land will be able to be sold in five years' time for €6 million. Perhaps there is already a forward agreement to sell the asset. Pursuant to IAS 36, we need to determine the present value of expected future cash flows. Assuming a discount rate of 8 per cent for the purposes of illustration, the present value of the future sales price is only €4.084 million (€6 million × 0.6806, where €0.6806 would represent the present value of €1 received in five years, discounted at a rate of 8 per cent per annum). As the recoverable amount of €4.084 million is less than the carrying amount of the asset, IAS 36 requires the recognition of an impairment loss.

Any discussion of present values raises the obvious issue of what discount rate should be used to discount the expected future cash flows when determining 'value-in-use'. Paragraph 55 of IAS 36 *Impairment of Assets* requires:

> *The discount rate (rates) shall be a pre-tax rate (rates) that reflect(s) current market assessments of:*
>
> *(a) the time value of money; and*
> *(b) the risks specific to the asset for which the future cash flow estimates have not been adjusted.*

Current practice therefore requires a two-step process in determining 'value-in-use'. First, we estimate the future cash inflows and outflows to be derived from the expected continued use of the asset and its subsequent disposal. Second, we apply the appropriate discount rate to the cash flows. Worked Example 6.3 provides an illustration of the use of the cost model with an associated impairment loss.

Following an impairment loss, future depreciation charges will also need to be adjusted to the allocated asset's revised carrying amount, less its residual value, over the asset's useful life on a systematic basis (IAS 36, paragraph 63).

> ### Worked Example 6.3 — Use of the cost model and determination of an impairment loss
>
> Point Lookout acquired some machinery at a cost of €1 million. As at 30 June 2014 the machinery had accumulated depreciation of €200,000.
>
> On 30 June 2014 it was determined that the machinery could be sold for a price of €650,000 and the costs associated with making the sale would be €20,000. Alternatively, the machinery is expected to be useful for another five years and the net cash flows expected to be generated from the machine would be €180,000 over each of the next five years.
>
> As at 30 June 2014 it is assessed that the market would require a rate of return of 7 per cent on this type of machinery.
>
> #### Required
>
> Determine whether an impairment loss needs to be recognised in relation to the machinery and, if so, provide the appropriate journal entry.
>
> #### Solution
>
> In accordance with IAS 36, an impairment loss is to be recognised when the recoverable amount of an asset is less than its carrying amount.
>
> The carrying amount of the machinery is its cost less accumulated depreciation and any accumulated impairment losses. In this example, this equates to €800,000.
>
> The recoverable amount is determined as the higher of the asset's net selling price and its value-in-use. The net selling price is €650,000 less €20,000, which is €630,000.
>
> The value-in-use is determined by discounting the expected future net cash flows to be generated by the asset using a discount rate relevant to the asset. Utilising the tables provided in Appendix B, we find that the present value of an annuity of €1 for five years discounted at 7 per cent is €4.1002. Hence, the value-in-use is determined as €180,000 multiplied by 4.1002, which gives us €738,036. According to IAS 36, recoverable amount is the higher of the value-in-use and the net sales price, which in this case is €738,036. Therefore the impairment loss is €800,000 less €738,036, which equals €61,964. The journal entry would be:
>
> | | | | |
> |---|---|---|---|
> | Dr | Impairment loss—machinery | €61,964 | |
> | Cr | Accumulated impairment losses—machinery | | €61,964 |
>
> In the above entry we used an account entitled accumulated impairment losses. This is similar to how we depreciate assets by crediting the adjustment to an accumulated depreciation account, rather than crediting the amount directly against the asset.

6.3.3 Cash-generating units

As we noted above, 'fair value less costs to sell' and 'value-in-use' are determined by reference either to a specific asset or to a cash-generating unit. IAS 36 defines a cash-generating unit as the 'smallest identifiable group of assets that generates cash inflows that are largely independent of the cash inflows from other assets or groups of assets'.

The reason we are sometimes required to consider values for a cash-generating unit instead of an individual asset is that in some circumstances it might not be possible to separately determine the recoverable amount of an individual asset because of the way it is combined in a larger unit or collection of assets. That is, the cash flows being generated might be dependent upon a combination of assets and it might not be possible to determine the expected cash flows specific to a particular asset. Worked Example 6.4 provides an illustration of how we might account for an impairment loss by reference to a cash-generating asset.

Determination of the recoverable amount and value-in-use can be quite subjective and we found different methods being used by different companies in Europe. For example, Ambrian Capital plc uses historical price earnings data and the earnings of its subsidiaries to determine recoverable value. Tesco, Parmalat and TDK use discounted future cash flows to determine value-in-use. Tesco considers cash flows over the coming five years, Parmalat over the life of the asset and TDK does not provide detail on the extent of the period considered. Details of the specific accounting policies for Tesco and Parmalat are included in Exhibit 6.1, details of the accounting policies for Ambrian Capital plc and TDK are provided in the support material for this chapter, which can be accessed at www.mcgraw-hill.co.uk/textbooks/deeganward.

An exception occurs when the revaluation reverses a previous impairment of the same asset (discussed later). The general form of the entry for a straightforward revaluation increment would be:

Dr	Asset	X
Cr	Revaluation surplus	X

The format of the statement of comprehensive income is explored and discussed in Chapter 16. However, at this stage you need to remember that, while some gains and losses are required to be included in profit or loss, some other gains or losses are explicitly excluded by virtue of particular accounting standards. Rather, the excluded gains or losses are to be included in 'other comprehensive income'. Figure 6.1 provides an example of a statement of comprehensive income and shows where a revaluation increment would be shown.

Figure 6.1 Statement of comprehensive income

XYZ Limited

Statement of comprehensive income for the year ended 31 December 2014

	2014 (€/£000)	2013 (€/£000)
Revenue	390,000	355,000
Cost of sales	(245,000)	(230,000)
Gross profit	145,000	125,000
Distribution costs	(9,000)	(8,700)
Administrative expenses	(20,000)	(21,000)
Other expenses	(2,100)	(1,200)
Finance costs	(8,000)	(7,500)
Profit before tax	105,900	86,600
Income tax expense	(31,770)	(25,980)
Profit for the year	74,130	60,620
Other comprehensive income:		
Exchange differences on translating foreign operations	5,003	10,667
Gains on property revaluation	20,000	4,000
Income tax relating to components of other comprehensive income	(6,000)	(1,200)
Other comprehensive income for the year, net of tax	19,003	13,647
Total comprehensive income for the year	93,133	74,087

In this chapter we will not consider the income-tax effects of recognising revaluations as this relies upon material that is introduced in Chapter 18. Chapter 18 will provide further illustrations of the revaluation of non-current assets, with consideration being given to related tax effects.

6.6 Treatment of balances of accumulated depreciation upon revaluation

There are two general approaches to dealing with accumulated depreciation at the date of a revaluation. The most commonly used approach, which is referred to as the net method, requires that, if the revalued assets are

> **accumulated depreciation**
> Total amount of depreciation recorded for an asset, or a class of assets. For statement of financial position purposes, shown as a deduction from the relevant class of assets.
>
> **revaluation decrement** When an asset is revalued downwards, the revaluation decrement represents the difference between the carrying amount of the asset and the amount based on its current valuation.

depreciable assets, any balances of **accumulated depreciation** existing for those assets at the revaluation date be credited in full to the asset accounts to which they relate. The asset accounts are then to be increased or decreased by the amount of the revaluation increments or **revaluation decrements**. Specifically, paragraph 35(b) of IAS 16 directs that, when an item of property, plant and equipment is revalued, the accumulated depreciation at the date of the revaluation is to be eliminated against the carrying amount of the asset and the net amount restated to the revalued amount of the asset. The amount of the adjustment arising on the elimination of accumulated depreciation forms part of the increase or decrease in the carrying amount.

For example, assume we have a machine with a cost of €10,000 and accumulated depreciation of €1,000 (giving a *carrying amount* of €9,000). Let us further assume that it is decided to revalue the machine to its fair value of €14,000. To take account of the accumulated depreciation we would initially debit accumulated depreciation by €1,000—thus causing the balance of accumulated depreciation as it relates to this asset to be zero—and credit the asset account by €1,000. That is, the journal entry would be:

Dr	Accumulated depreciation	€1,000	
Cr	Machine		€1,000

We would then debit the machine account by €5,000 and credit the revaluation surplus by €5,000. This would cause the carrying value of the asset to be €14,000, which is its fair value. That is, the journal entry would be:

Dr	Machine	€5,000	
Cr	Revaluation surplus		€5,000

Subsequent depreciation after a revaluation is based on the revalued amount of the non-current asset. It should be noted that an entity cannot account for a downward revaluation simply by increasing the amount of the accumulated depreciation by the amount of the revaluation decrement, even though the net effect would be the same. Worked Example 6.5 illustrates the use of the 'net method'—which nets off accumulated depreciation against the asset prior to recognition of the fair value increment or decrement.

Worked Example 6.5 — Revaluation of a depreciable asset using the net-amount method

Assume that, as at 1 July 2014, Farrelly Ltd has an item of machinery that originally cost £40,000 and has accumulated depreciation of £15,000. Its remaining life is assessed to be five years, after which time it will have no residual value. While completing a regular revaluation of all machinery, Farrelly decided on 1 July 2014 that the item should be revalued to its current fair value, which was assessed as £45,000.

Required

Provide the appropriate journal entries to account for the revaluation using the net-amount method.

Solution

The total revaluation increment will represent the difference between the carrying amount and the fair value of the asset at the date of the revaluation. In this case, it would be:

$$£45,000 - (£40,000 - £15,000) = £20,000$$

The appropriate journal entries on 1 July 2014 would be:

Dr	Accumulated depreciation—machinery	£15,000	
Cr	Machinery		£15,000
Dr	Machinery	£20,000	
Cr	Revaluation surplus		£20,000

According to IAS 16, future depreciation should be based on the revalued amount of the asset. The depreciation charge for the year to 30 June 2015 would be £9,000 (the new carrying amount of £45,000 divided by the remaining useful life of five years). Where the depreciation charges for any financial period have changed materially owing to a revaluation, the financial effect of the change (that is, the increase or decrease in the depreciation charges) should be disclosed in the notes to the financial statements for that financial period.

While the demonstrated net method is the general approach to be followed for revaluations of property, plant and equipment, paragraph 35(a) of IAS 16 provides an alternative treatment called the 'gross method'. This treatment requires that both the gross amount of the asset and the accumulated depreciation at the date of the revaluation be 'restated proportionately with the change in the gross carrying amount of the asset so that the carrying amount of the asset after revaluation equals its revalued amount'. The gross method of revaluation is applied in Worked Example 6.6.

Worked Example 6.6 — Revaluation of a depreciable asset—the use of the gross method

Assume as in Worked Example 6.5 that on 1 July 2014 Farrelly Ltd has an item of machinery, which originally cost £40,000 and has accumulated depreciation of £15,000. Its remaining life is assessed to be five years. It is decided on 1 July 2014 that the item should be revalued to its current fair value, assessed as £45,000.

A review of a newer but comparable item of machinery indicates that the newer machine has a market value of £72,000.

Required

Adopting the gross method, provide the appropriate journal entries to account for the revaluation.

Solution

The gross carrying amount of the asset and the accumulated depreciation account are to be restated proportionately, which is the requirement of paragraph 35(a) of IAS 16. The following steps show how this asset can be revalued using the gross method.

STEP 1: Calculate the ratio of accumulated depreciation (AD) over gross amount of the asset (GA) immediately prior to the revaluation.
The calculation is: £15,000/£40,000 = 0.375

The ratio is 0.375, which means 37.5 per cent of the gross amount has been reduced by depreciation charges just before revaluation. In other words, the accumulated depreciation balance is 0.375 of the gross amount of the asset balance. This ratio must be the same just after the revaluation.

STEP 2: Solve the equation: GA – AD = £45,000
We know from STEP 1 that:

$$AD = 0.375 \times GA$$

therefore:

$$GA - (0.375GA) = £45,000$$
$$0.625GA = £45,000$$
$$GA = £72,000$$

We just worked out what the balance of the GA should be. It is simple to work out the AD balance because GA – AD = £45,000, so AD = £27,000. Now we know what the balance of the AD account should be.

Notes:

• £45,000 is the amount the asset is being revalued to = GA – AD = the carrying amount
• £27,000/£72,000 = 0.375 = the ratio calculated at STEP 1, so we know we are correct

STEP 3: Do the journal entries to make the balances of GA and AD equal to the balances that we calculated at STEP 2.

Dr	Machinery	£32,000	
Cr	Accumulated depreciation		£12,000
Cr	Revaluation surplus		£20,000

It should be noted that whether the net-amount method or the gross method is used, the carrying amount of the non-current assets will be the same. For example, the balances under both methods after revaluation would be:

	Net-amount method £	Gross method £
Machinery	45,000	72,000
Accumulated depreciation	0	27,000
Carrying amount	45,000	45,000

6.7   Revaluation decrements

conservatism
Traditional approach
requiring asset values
never to be overstated
and liabilities never to
be understated.

The concept of **conservatism**, which has traditionally been applied in practice (but is not consistent with the principles espoused in the IASB Conceptual Framework, particularly the notion that financial statements should be prepared without *bias*), holds that losses should generally be recognised in the financial statements as they become probable and measurable, and that gains should not be recognised as part of profit or loss until realised. It is the concept of conservatism that requires that, if a class of non-current assets is revalued, the revaluation decrement should be treated as an expense of the period and referred to as a loss on revaluation (remember, the revaluation increment went to the revaluation surplus, which is part of equity but which is not recognised in profit or loss but rather is treated as an item of 'other comprehensive income'). The first part of paragraph 40 of IAS 16 requires that: 'If an asset's carrying amount is decreased as a result of a revaluation, the decrease shall be recognised in profit or loss.'

The accounting treatment for a revaluation decrement is examined in Worked Example 6.7. An exception to this general rule, to be considered after Worked Example 6.7, is the case where the decrement reverses a previous increment relating to the same asset.

Worked Example 6.7   A revaluation decrement

Young Ltd acquires some machinery at a cost of €150,000 on 1 July 2013. On 30 June 2014, the machinery, which has an accumulated depreciation balance of €20,000, is assessed as having a fair value equal to €100,000. Young Ltd carries machinery at fair value.

Required
Provide the journal entries to reflect the revaluation decrement.

Solution
As noted previously, upon revaluation we would need to offset the accumulated depreciation against the asset account (unless reference is being made to a newer asset and the gross method is used) before recognising the revaluation decrement. The accounting entry would be:

Dr	Accumulated depreciation	€20,000	
Cr	Machinery		€20,000
Dr	Loss on revaluation of machinery	€30,000	
Cr	Machinery		€30,000

The loss of €30,000 represents the difference between the carrying value of the revalued non-current asset (in this case, €130,000) and the fair value. This loss would be recognised as an expense and would cause a reduction in profits.

6.8   Reversal of revaluation decrements and increments

With respect to a class of assets, reversals of previous revaluations should, as far as possible, be accounted for by entries that are the reverse of those bringing the previous revaluations to account. For example, where a revaluation decrement reverses a previous increment (or cumulative increment) for an individual asset, it would be debited to the revaluation surplus previously credited for that asset, rather than being debited to the period's profit or loss. The reduction in the revaluation surplus would be shown as a negative item in 'other comprehensive income' within the statement of comprehensive income. Any excess over the previous revaluation increment would then be debited to the profit or loss. That is, if there had previously been no downward revaluation, the revaluation decrement would be treated as an expense and therefore as a part of profit or loss (as indicated

in Worked Example 6.5). However, if there has previously been a revaluation increment for the same asset, the subsequent decrement for that asset is to be adjusted against the balance in the revaluation surplus as it pertains to that asset (IAS 16, paragraph 40).

Similarly, where a revaluation increment reverses a previous decrement (or cumulative decrement), it would be credited to the profit or loss (that is, treated as income). Any excess over and above the previous revaluation decrement would then be credited to the revaluation surplus (IAS 16, paragraph 39).

Consider Worked Example 6.8, which gives an example of reversals of previous revaluation increments and decrements.

Worked Example 6.8 — Reversals of previous revaluation increments and decrements

PK Ltd acquires a block of land on 1 January 2013 for €200,000 in cash. As the result of increased housing demand in the area, the land has a market value of €290,000 on 1 January 2014. Some time later, however, it becomes known that the land and its surrounding area were previously the site of a toxic dump. As a result, the market value falls to €140,000 on 30 June 2016.

Required

Assuming the firm makes revaluations on both 1 January 2014 and 30 June 2016, provide the appropriate journal entries.

Solution

1 January 2013

Dr	Land	€200,000	
Cr	Cash		€200,000

(to record the initial acquisition of land)

1 January 2014

Dr	Land	€90,000	
Cr	Revaluation surplus		€90,000

(to represent the increment in the fair value of land; this increase would be treated as part of 'other comprehensive income' but not as part of profit or loss)

30 June 2016

Dr	Revaluation surplus	€90,000	
Dr	Loss on revaluation of land	€60,000	
Cr	Land		€150,000

(fair value of land falls from €290,000 to €140,000; the loss of €60,000 represents the reduction over and above the previous revaluation increment. The amount of €90,000 would be a reduction in 'other comprehensive income' while the amount of €60,000 would be a reduction to profit or loss)

It should be noted that if the above land had not been revalued in January 2014—that is, if it had been recorded at cost—impairment testing would be required pursuant to IAS 36 *Impairment of Assets*. An impairment loss would be recognised if the recoverable amount of the asset declines below its carrying amount. That is, regardless of whether the cost model or the revaluation model is used, an item of property, plant and equipment shall not have a carrying value in excess of its recoverable amount. As we know, the recoverable amount is determined as the greater of the value-in-use and the net selling price of the asset. In this example, if the recoverable amount of the asset is assumed to be the same as the net selling price—in this case, €140,000—and to the extent that this is below the carrying amount of the asset (which would be €200,000 if no revaluation was undertaken in 2014), an impairment loss of €60,000 must be recognised.

A real-life example of the reversal of revaluation decrements and increments can be seen from the accounting policy adopted by Parmalat, an Italian-based company that also has businesses in Portugal, Romania and Russia. An extract from its Accounting Policies is reproduced overleaf in Exhibit 6.2.

Exhibit 6.2   **Accounting policies used by Parmalat S.p.A. in 2010**

PARMALAT S.p.A.

Accounting policies (Financial Statements at 31 December 2010)

Tangible assets (relevant extract)
When the reason for a writedown ceases to apply, the affected asset is revalued and the adjustment is recognised in the income statement as a revaluation (reversal of write-down) at an amount equal to the write-down made or the lower of the asset's recoverable value or its carrying value before previous write-downs, but reduced by the depreciation that would have been taken had the asset not been written down.

6.9 Accounting for the gain or loss on the disposal or derecognition of a revalued non-current asset

Paragraph 71 of IAS 16 provides that:

> *The gain or loss arising from the derecognition of an item of property, plant and equipment shall be determined as the difference between the net disposal proceeds, if any, and the carrying amount of the item.*

In relation to the timing of the gain or loss, paragraph 68 of IAS 16 states that: 'The gain or loss arising from derecognition of an item of property, plant and equipment shall be included in profit or loss when the item is derecognised.' Paragraph 68 therefore does not require the separate disclosure of the proceeds of the sale as revenue and the presentation of the carrying amount of the asset as an expense—only the net amount, the gain or the loss, is to be presented. The term 'derecognition' as used in paragraph 68 refers to the point in time at which an item is removed from the statement of financial position—that is, when it is no longer recognised. According to paragraph 67 of IAS 16, the carrying amount of an item of property, plant and equipment is to be derecognised on disposal or when no future economic benefits are expected from its use or disposal.

Worked Example 6.9 sets out how to account for the gain or loss on disposal of a revalued item of property, plant and equipment.

Worked Example 6.9   **Accounting for a gain or loss on disposal of a revalued non-current asset**

On 1 July 2013 Bombo Ltd acquires a block of land at a cost of €60,000. On 1 July 2014 it is revalued to €75,000. On 30 June 2015 the land is sold for €90,000.

Required
Determine the gain or loss on the sale of the land according to IAS 16 and prepare the journal entry to record the sale.

Solution
As the carrying amount of the land at the date of disposal is €75,000 (owing to the earlier revaluation increment), the gain on the sale of the land is €15,000. If the land had not previously been revalued, the gain on the sale would have been €30,000.

The gain on the sale of the land—which would be included as part of profit or loss—would be represented by the difference between the proceeds of the sale and the carrying amount of the land. The gain on the sale would also need to be disclosed.

The accounting entry would be:

Dr	Cash at bank	€90,000	
Cr	Gain on sale of land		€15,000
Cr	Land		€75,000

The accounting entries for the sale of revalued land, as shown in Worked Example 6.9, do not remove the balance of the asset revaluation that is in the revaluation surplus as a result of the revaluation undertaken on 1 July 2014. That is, there is still a balance of €15,000 in the revaluation surplus, even though the asset to which the revaluation relates has been sold. What should be done with the remaining balance in the revaluation surplus? Paragraph 41 of IAS 16 provides some guidance in this regard:

> *The revaluation surplus included in equity in respect of an item of property, plant and equipment may be transferred directly to retained earnings when the asset is derecognised (that is, eliminated from the statement of financial position). This may involve transferring the whole of the surplus when the asset is retired or disposed of.*

So, to eliminate the balance of the revaluation surplus that relates to the land disposed of, the following entry may be made (it is emphasised that, in the terminology of the accounting standard, the entry *may* be made, which implies an option to leave amounts in the revaluation surplus for assets that have been derecognised!):

Dr	Revaluation surplus	€15,000
Cr	Retained earnings	€15,000

Paragraph 41 of IAS 16 specifically prohibits transfers from the revaluation surplus to profit or loss. That is, when a revalued asset is subsequently sold, any existing revaluation is not to be eliminated by treating it as part of profits. The revaluation increment would previously have been included in 'other comprehensive income'. Worked Example 6.10 provides another example of how to account for the revaluation surplus on the sale of an item of property, plant and equipment.

Worked Example 6.10 — Sale of a revalued item of property, plant and equipment

Gunnamatta Ltd acquired a printing machine on 1 July 2013 for €100,000. It is expected to have a useful life of ten years, with the benefits being derived on a straight-line basis. The residual is expected to be €nil. On 1 July 2015 the machine is deemed to have a fair value of €96,000 and a revaluation is undertaken in accordance with Gunnamatta Ltd's policy of measuring property, plant and equipment at fair value. The asset is sold for €89,000 on 1 July 2017.

Required

Provide the journal entries necessary to account for the above transactions and events.

Solution

1 July 2013

Dr	Printing machine	€100,000	
Cr	Cash/Payables		€100,000

(to recognise the acquisition of the machine)

1 July 2015

Dr	Accumulated depreciation	€20,000	
Cr	Printing machine		€20,000

(to offset two years' depreciation against the cost of the asset)

Dr	Printing machine	€16,000	
Cr	Revaluation surplus		€16,000

(to revalue the asset to its fair value of €96,000)

1 July 2017

Dr	Cash at bank	€89,000	
Dr	Accumulated depreciation	€24,000	
Cr	Printing machine		€96,000
Cr	Gain on sale of printing machine		€17,000

(to account for the sale of the asset)

1 July 2017

Dr	Revaluation surplus	€16,000	
Cr	Retained earnings		€16,000

(to transfer the balance of the revaluation surplus to retained earnings following the disposal of the asset)

In determining the gain on sale in Worked Example 6.10, we need to calculate the difference between the net sales proceeds and the carrying value of the machine. At 1 July 2017 there would have been two years of accumulated depreciation since the revaluation was undertaken in 2015. At that point, the asset was valued at €96,000 and it was expected to have a remaining useful life of eight years. With no residual value, this means that the annual depreciation charge would be €12,000 per year. It should also be noted that had the revaluation not been undertaken in 2015, the written-down value of the asset would have been €60,000 in 2017 and the gain on sale would have been €29,000 rather than €17,000—the difference being the amount of the revaluation less the additional depreciation in the following two years, or €16,000 − [2 × (€12,000 − €10,000)].

6.9.1 Consequences of revaluation

If a company revalues a non-current asset, any subsequent gain on sale (the gain being determined as the difference between the carrying value of the asset at the date of sale and the consideration received, and which would be included in profit or loss for the period) will be reduced, compared with the gain obtained if the asset had not been revalued. This was demonstrated in Worked Example 6.9.

Further, if the asset is depreciable, subsequent depreciation charges will be increased. Depreciation charges are based on cost or, if the depreciable non-current asset has been revalued, on the revalued amount. So increasing the value of the asset will increase subsequent depreciation charges. This was demonstrated in Worked Example 6.10 when the yearly depreciation charge increased from €10,000 to €12,000.

In some cases, firms might prefer to show lower profits; perhaps because they are being accused of being monopolistic and of earning excessively high profits. In such cases an asset revaluation might be a preferred option, even though a decision to revalue made on this basis would constitute 'creative accounting' and would therefore not be consistent with the basic tenets espoused in the IASB Conceptual Framework.

Managers might also elect to measure their property, plant and equipment at fair value (and therefore undertake periodic revaluations) because the valuations better reflect the value of the organisation's assets. It might also make the organisation less likely to be taken over owing to undervalued assets. Directors might consider that undertaking periodic revaluations provides more relevant information for financial statement readers' decision making.

6.10 Offsetting revaluation increments and decrements

Revaluation increments and decrements may be offset only to the extent that they pertain to a specific, individual asset. For example, if one block of land had a fair value that increased by £1 million and another decreased in fair value by £800,000, the requirement is to take £1 million to the revaluation surplus in respect of one of the items of land, and recognise a loss on revaluation of £800,000 in respect of the other block of land. In relation to revaluation increments, as already indicated in this chapter, paragraph 39 of IAS 16 requires:

> *If an asset's carrying amount is increased as a result of a revaluation, the increase shall be recognised in other comprehensive income and accumulated in equity under the heading of a revaluation surplus. However, the increase shall be recognised in profit or loss to the extent that it reverses a revaluation decrease of the same asset previously recognised in profit or loss.*

6.11 Investment properties

While our focus in this chapter has been on property, plant and equipment in general, it is worth noting the existence of an accounting standard that relates specifically to investment properties: IAS 40 *Investment Properties*. An investment property is defined in IAS 40 as property (land, buildings—or part of a building, or both) that is held by the owner or by the lessees under a finance lease to earn rentals, or for a capital appreciation, or both. An investment property is considered to generate cash flows that are largely independent of the other assets of the entity. This can be contrasted with owner-occupied property, where the related cash flows would not only be attributable to the property, but would also be attributable to the other assets used in the operations of the entity. Investment properties would include land that is held for capital appreciation (and which is currently unused by the entity) or land that is leased to other entities on a shorter-term basis. Property being developed for sale in the ordinary course of business would be deemed to be 'inventory' and not an investment property. Also, property that is held for the purpose of long-term rentals would not be considered to be investment property. For example, a building that is leased to another entity under a lease contract that stipulates that the lease period is for the major part of the building's life would not be construed to be an investment property.

Once an item is deemed to be an investment property, it is initially to be recorded at the cost of acquisition—as is the case for other property, plant and equipment. Subsequent to initial measurement, IAS 40 requires that investment properties are measured either at fair value (the fair value model) or at cost (the cost model). If the fair value model is adopted, changes in the fair value of investment properties are recognised directly in profit or loss, and not in the revaluation surplus, as would be the case under IAS 16. This represents an interesting requirement and one that is probably justifiable on the ground that any gains or losses on an investment property are more likely to be realised in the near future compared to any changes in the fair value of other property, plant and equipment.

6.12   Economic consequences of asset revaluations

Some academic research suggests that fair value is superior to historical cost as a means of valuing assets (Herrmann *et al.* 2005) as they argue it has predictive value, feedback value, timeliness, neutrality, representational faithfulness, comparability and consistency. Other academics have tested the value relevance of revaluing assets and found that in some countries revaluation reserves contribute significantly to explaining the market value of equity (Piak 2009). Another focus is on the behavioural implications of asset revaluations. If a business has contracts in place that are tied to reported profits, such as profit-based management bonuses and interest-coverage clauses, management might have incentives not to revalue its assets because to do so would reduce future reported profits. A revaluation would also reduce measures such as return on assets, given that asset bases will increase. Remember, of course, that if management is selecting a revaluation policy on an opportunistic rather than an objective basis, such a strategy might, if it materially affects the financial statements, be noted and reported on by the auditors.

However, if assets are increased, an asset revaluation might loosen constraints such as debt-to-asset restrictions, possibly imposed by the debt holders of the firm. For example, a firm's unadjusted statement of financial position might show total assets of €100 million and total liabilities of €55 million. If that firm had an agreement with lenders that its **debt-to-assets ratio** was not to exceed 50 per cent, it would be in technical default of the agreement and could, at the extreme, be subject to closure. Now assume that, before finalising the financial statements, the firm revalues its non-current assets by €15 million. The effect of this would be to increase assets to €115 million. Liabilities would remain at €55 million (the credit side of the journal entry would be to the revaluation surplus, which is part of shareholders' funds) and the revised debt-to-assets ratio would be 47.8 per cent. The firm would no longer be in technical default of its debt agreement.

> **debt-to-assets ratio**
> Derived by dividing the total debt of an organisation by its total assets.

Debt-holders are aware that asset revaluations act to loosen debt-to-asset constraints. As such, it is not surprising that there are restrictions placed on revaluations. In their review of public trust deeds, Whittred and Zimmer (1986) found:

> *The trust deeds permitted asset revaluations. However, most were specific as to which assets may be revalued and who may conduct the revaluation. Typically, the trust deeds excluded 'any amount [by] which the book value of any tangible asset is written up subsequent to the annual balance date immediately preceding the date of the Deed, except where such writing up is made in accordance with, and so that the book value does not exceed a valuation by, an independent valuer approved by the trustee.*

Brown *et al.* (1992) investigated management incentives associated with choosing to revalue non-current assets upwards. They argue that, as the process of undertaking a revaluation is costly, there must be some real expected benefits associated with the revaluation. (Revaluation costs are considered to include fees charged by a valuer; opportunity and out-of-pocket costs of time spent by directors in reviewing the figures being reported and discussing them with auditors; the record-keeping costs; and the costs charged by auditors for the additional review.) Empirical evidence in support of this argument can be found in the study by Missonier-Piera (2007). He reported a positive association between asset revaluations and the implied creditworthiness of Swedish industrial and commercial firms that rely on debt financing. They concluded that revaluations increase firms' borrowing capacity. Consistent with this, Nichols and Buerger (2002) found that German banks give significantly higher loans to companies that use fair value to value their tangible fixed assets.

Other benefits to the organisation are deemed to relate to the ability to loosen restrictive debt covenants as a result of an upward revaluation. Brown *et al.* (1992) contend that the higher the ratio of debt to total tangible assets (a ratio frequently used in debt contracts), the more likely it is that a firm will revalue its assets. They further propose that a firm with a debt covenant in place is more likely to revalue than a firm without a debt

covenant. Empirical evidence to support this contention can be found in a study on Belgian unlisted industrial companies by Gaeremynck and Veugelers (1999). They found that successful firms with a high variance of performance or with low equity-to-debt ratios are less likely to revalue assets, and firms that move closer to technical default or come close to breaching covenants are more likely to revalue assets.

Brown *et al.* (1992) also maintain that, as upward revaluations will lead to a reduction in profits (through increased depreciation and reduced gain on sale of the revalued non-current asset), firms subject to political scrutiny, either from government or other interest groups, will be relatively more likely to revalue assets upwards.

In relation to asset revaluations and their implications for reducing political costs (through reducing reported income), Whittred and Chan (1992) pose the question (p. 63) of whether it is rate of return or size that makes a firm politically visible. The effects of a revaluation can work in opposite directions in this regard. A revaluation acts to increase the reported asset size of the organisation, which could make the organisation more visible. However, a revaluation of non-current assets also acts to reduce income, which, in a sense, can make the organisation less visible.

Leaving aside this possible impasse (about whether political visibility is related to reported profits or assets) and returning to Brown *et al.* (1992), we find that these researchers assume that a reduction in profits resulting from the discretionary adoption of an upward asset revaluation will lead to a reduction in the propensity for outside parties to transfer wealth away from the organisation. This assumption necessarily relies upon another key assumption, that regulators, and other parties in the political process, focus on the reported profit figures rather than the accounting methods used to derive those profits. As the authors state: 'Underlying the political process theory is the crucial assumption that regulators and other interested parties do not incorporate into their decisions the substantive effect of an accounting change' (p. 39).

Assumptions such as this are frequently made in the Positive Accounting Theory literature—particularly in studies that consider 'political costs' (see Chapter 3). It is typically assumed (often without this assumption being made clear) that regulators either do not understand the implications of adopting different accounting methods or that they do not consider it justifiable to unravel the effects of alternative accounting methods. Remember, the revaluation of non-current assets is undertaken simply via a book entry, which in turn causes the increase in reported assets and the subsequent reduction in reported profits (through increased depreciation charges and reduced profit on disposal). Whether these assumptions about regulators are realistic is clearly a matter of personal opinion. That said, Brown *et al.* (ibid) further propose that firms operating in strike-prone industries are more likely to revalue their non-current assets upwards than firms operating in other industries. It is argued that, if an organisation reduces reported income, unions will feel that they have less justification for demanding increased salaries. The results of the Brown *et al.* study generally supported their predictions. From the sample of companies reviewed, they found that revaluers were more highly geared, closer to violating debt covenant constraints, and larger. Revaluers were also found to be more likely to be operating in strike-prone industries. Though not focusing on the political implications of revaluations, Lin and Peasnell (2000) found that revaluations were associated with depletion of equity, indebtedness, poor liquidity, size and fixed asset intensity in a sample of UK companies. These results are consistent with the theory that management use asset revaluation to improve the reported strength of the business when more highly geared.

IAS 16 requires that, where a class of non-current assets has been revalued to fair value in accordance with an independent valuation, this must be disclosed within the notes to the financial statements. Conceivably, this would be useful information to the readers of financial statements, as an **independent valuation** would arguably be deemed to be more impartial or objective than a valuation undertaken by employees of the entity.

> **independent valuation** For non-current assets, a valuation made by an expert in valuations of that class of assets whose pecuniary or other interests could not be capable of affecting that person's ability to give an unbiased opinion on that valuation.

Considering issues such as the competence of the valuer, Goodwin and Trotman (1996) undertook a study of external auditors' judgements in relation to non-current asset revaluations undertaken by their clients. The results indicated that the amount of time spent on the audit of the revalued non-current assets related directly to the perceived competence of the independent valuer. As perceived competence increased, the time spent on auditing the balance of the revalued assets decreased.

Goodwin and Trotman also considered the implications of whether the organisation being audited was proposing to make a public share issue. The authors argue that a proposal to make a public share issue might provide management with an incentive to revalue non-current assets to 'strengthen the balance sheet prior to issue', thereby increasing the inherent risk of the non-current assets being misstated. The results of the study indicated that auditors spend more time on the audit of revalued non-current assets when management proposes to issue shares to the public.

Cotter and Richardson (2002) examined the reliability of asset revaluations in a sample of Australian firms over the period 1981 to 1999 and found that revaluations by independent assessors were more reliable. They measured reliability as reversals of the upward revaluations in subsequent years.

6.13 Disclosure requirements

IAS 16 includes a number of disclosure requirements pertaining to the revaluation of non-current assets. We discussed these requirements earlier in this chapter in Section 6.4.1, 'How does an entity determine fair value?' As we showed in that section, information such as dates of revaluation, whether an independent valuer was involved in determining valuations and the approach used to determine fair value must be disclosed in the notes to the financial statements.

IAS 16 also has disclosure requirements relating to the depreciation methods used, and assumptions made about the useful lives of property, plant and equipment. IAS 16 also requires a reconciliation of the opening and closing carrying amounts of property, plant and equipment, as shown in the statement of financial position. Specifically, paragraph 73 of IAS 16 states:

The financial statement shall disclose, for each class of property, plant and equipment:

(a) *the measurement bases used for determining the gross carrying amount;*
(b) *the depreciation methods used;*
(c) *the useful lives or the depreciation rates used;*
(d) *the gross carrying amount and the accumulated depreciation (aggregated with accumulated impairment losses) at the beginning and end of the period; and*
(e) *a reconciliation of the carrying amount at the beginning and end of the period showing:*
   (i) *additions;*
   (ii) *assets classified as held for sale or included in a disposal group classified as held for sale in accordance with IFRS 5 and other disposals;*
   (iii) *acquisitions through business combinations;*
   (iv) *increases or decreases resulting from revaluations under paragraphs 31, 39, 40 and from impairment losses recognised or reversed directly in equity in accordance with IAS 36;*
   (v) *impairment losses recognised in profit or loss in accordance with IAS 36 (paragraph 126);*
   (vi) *impairment losses reversed in profit or loss in accordance with IAS 36 (paragraph 126);*
   (vii) *depreciation;*
   (viii) *the net exchange differences arising on the translation of the financial statements from the functional currency into a different presentation currency, including the translation of a foreign operation into the presentation currency of the reporting entity; and*
   (ix) *other changes.*

There are also a number of required disclosures that a reporting entity is required to make if impairment losses have been recognised. The extensive disclosure requirements are stipulated in paragraphs 126 to 137 of IAS 36 *Impairment of Assets*. In addition to those noted above, separate disclosure is required for the following:

126. An entity shall disclose the following for each class of assets:

(c) *the amount of impairment losses on revalued assets recognised directly in equity during the period; and*
(d) *the amount of reversals of impairment losses on revalued assets recognised directly in equity during the period.*

130. An entity shall disclose the following for each material impairment loss recognised or reversed during the period for an individual asset, including goodwill, or a cash-generating unit:

(a) *the events and circumstances that led to the recognition or reversal of the impairment loss;*
(b) *the amount of the impairment loss recognised or reversed; and*
(c) *for an individual asset:*
   (i) *the nature of the asset; and*
   (ii) *if the entity reports segment information in accordance with IFRS 8, the reportable segment to which the asset belongs;*
(d) *for a cash-generating unit:*
   (i) *a description of the cash-generating unit (such as whether it is a product line, a plant, a business operation, a geographical area, or a reportable segment as defined in IFRS 8);*
   (ii) *the amount of the impairment loss recognised or reversed by class of assets and, if the entity reports segment information in accordance with IFRS 8, by reportable segment; and*
   (iii) *if the aggregation of assets for identifying the cash-generating unit has changed since the previous estimate of the cash-generating unit's recoverable amount (if any), a description of the current and former way of aggregating assets and the reasons for changing the way the cash-generating unit is identified; and*

 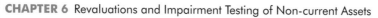
(e) *whether the recoverable amount of the asset (cash-generating unit) is its fair value less costs to sell or its value-in-use;*

(f) *if recoverable amount is fair value less costs to sell, the basis used to determine fair value less costs to sell (such as whether fair value was determined by reference to an active market); and*

(g) *if recoverable amount is value-in-use, the discount rate(s) used in the current estimate and previous estimate (if any) of value-in-use.*

131. *An entity shall disclose the following information for the aggregate impairment losses and the aggregate reversals of impairment losses recognised during the period for which no information is disclosed in accordance with paragraph 130:*

(a) *the main classes of assets affected by impairment losses and the main classes of assets affected by reversals of impairment losses; and*

(b) *the main events and circumstances that led to the recognition of these impairment losses and reversals of impairment losses.*

SUMMARY

The chapter considered the revaluation of non-current assets, with the emphasis on property, plant and equipment. A revaluation can be defined as the act of recognising a reassessment of the carrying amount of a non-current asset to its fair value as at a particular date. When a non-current asset has a recoverable amount in excess of its carrying amount, there is no requirement to perform an upward revaluation. On the other hand, if the recoverable amount is below the carrying amount, a non-current asset should be the subject of an impairment loss. This is consistent with the traditionally conservative approach adopted in accounting to the valuation of assets, that is, that assets may be understated but should never be overstated in the financial statements. The recoverable amount of an asset is defined as the higher of an asset's net selling price and its value-in-use.

Where an upward revaluation of property, plant and equipment is undertaken, the asset is to be revalued to its fair value. Revaluations should be undertaken as part of a process that revalues the entire class of assets to which the revalued non-current asset belongs. Where an asset is revalued upwards, the increase in the recorded value of the asset is not treated as part of profit or loss but is transferred to a revaluation surplus and included as part of 'other comprehensive income'. The only exception to this rule is where the revaluation increment reverses a previous revaluation decrement, in which case the revaluation increment will be treated as part of the financial period's profit or loss.

Where an asset is revalued downwards, the decrease in the recorded value of the asset is to be treated as an expense and included within profit or loss. The only exception to this rule is where the revaluation decrement reverses a previous revaluation increment, in which case the revaluation decrement will be debited against (deducted from) the existing revaluation surplus and the related movement included as a reduction to 'other comprehensive income'.

When a revaluation of a depreciable non-current asset is undertaken, the most common approach is to adopt the 'net method' whereby we credit any existing accumulated depreciation against the non-current asset to be revalued, and subsequently increase the non-current asset account (debit the account) by the amount of the revaluation. Where a revalued non-current asset is subsequently sold, the gain or loss on disposal is to be measured as the difference between the carrying amount of the revalued asset as at the time of the disposal, and the net proceeds, if any, from disposal. The gain or loss must be recognised in the profit or loss for the financial year in which the disposal of the non-current asset occurs.

The chapter has also considered how revaluations can, at times, loosen certain accounting-based debt covenants, such as restrictions written around an organisation's debt-to-assets ratio.

KEY TERMS

END-OF-CHAPTER EXERCISE

Van Bommel N. V. is a Dutch diversified industrial company with its major business activity being to manufacture flotation devices for babies and toddlers. Over the past decade, the business has been very profitable and the directors, Ruud Van Bommel and Liza Van Bommel, have kept payment of dividends to a minimum to allow the company to diversify into other activities. The following is a list of property, plant and equipment held by the company:

Investments in companies	Carrying value (€)	Current fair value (€)
Property, plant and equipment		
Factory (Netherlands)		
Land	100,000	150,000
Buildings		
– Cost	70,000	80,000
– Accumulated depreciation	(20,000)	–
Factory (Austria)		
Land	150,000	120,000
Buildings		
– Cost	125,000	70,000
– Accumulated depreciation	(45,000)	–

Mr Van Bommel informs you that the directors intend to revalue the property, plant and equipment during the year. The company has not revalued any assets in the past.   **LO** 6.1

REQUIRED

(a) How would you account for the revaluation of the above assets?

(b) What would the relevant journal entries be?

SOLUTION TO END-OF-CHAPTER EXERCISE

(a) As shown below, it is considered that two classes of assets exist in this case: land used in the organisation's operations; and buildings used in the organisation's operations. The calculations for determining increments and decrements are as follows:

Investments in companies	Carrying amount (€)	Current fair value (€)	Increment/(Decrement) (€)
Property, plant and equipment			
Land			
– Factory (Netherlands)	100,000	150,000	50,000
– Factory (Austria)	150,000	120,000	(30,000)
Buildings—net			
– Factory (Netherlands)	50,000	80,000	30,000
– Factory (Austria)	80,000	70,000	(10,000)

(b) The relevant journal entries are as follows:

Dr	Land—factory (Netherlands)	€50,000	
Cr	Revaluation surplus		€50,000
Dr	Loss on revaluation of land	€30,000	
Cr	Land—factory (Austria)		€30,000
Dr	Accumulated depreciation (Netherlands)	€20,000	
Dr	Accumulated depreciation (Austria)	€45,000	
Cr	Buildings—factory (Netherlands)		€20,000
Cr	Buildings—factory (Austria)		€45,000
Dr	Buildings—factory (Netherlands)	€30,000	
Cr	Revaluation surplus		€30,000
Dr	Loss on revaluation of buildings	€10,000	
Cr	Buildings—factory (Austria)		€10,000

REVIEW QUESTIONS

1 What effect will an asset revaluation have on subsequent periods' profits? Explain your answer. **LO** 6.7

2 Explain the difference in the accounting treatment for revaluation increments and revaluation decrements. Do you consider that this difference is 'conceptually sound'? **LO** 6.3

3 When should a revaluation increment be credited to the statement of comprehensive income? **LO** 6.4

4 For the purposes of IAS 16 or IAS 36, how is 'recoverable amount' determined? **LO** 6.4

5 When would you determine the recoverable amount for a cash-generating unit rather than for an individual item of property, plant and equipment? **LO** 6.1

6 If an item of property, plant and equipment is measured at cost, but the recoverable amount of the asset is determined to be less than cost, what action must be taken? **LO** 6.4

7 If a reporting entity decides to revalue its property, plant and equipment, what basis of valuation must be adopted? **LO** 6.1

8 If a reporting entity elects to use either cost or fair value as the basis for measuring its property, plant and equipment, can it elect to switch to the other method at a later time? **LO** 6.1

9 For the purposes of IAS 16, how is a 'class of assets' defined? Would residential land and farming land be included in the same class of assets? **LO** 6.1

10 How could a revaluation of a non-current asset minimise or loosen the effects of a restrictive debt covenant? **LO** 6.8

11 An item of depreciable machinery is acquired on 1 July 2011 for £120,000. It is expected to have a useful life of ten years and a zero residual value. On 1 July 2015 it is decided to revalue the asset to its fair value of £110,000. **LO** 6.1

REQUIRED

Provide journal entries to account for the revaluation.

12 How should the reversal of an impairment loss be accounted for? **LO** 6.5

13 An asset having a cost of £100,000 and accumulated depreciation of £20,000 is revalued to £120,000 at the beginning of the year. Depreciation for the year is based on the revalued amount and the remaining useful life of eight years. Shareholders' equity, before adjusting for the above revaluation and subsequent depreciation, is as follows: **LO** 6.6

	£
Share capital	300,000
Revaluation surplus	45,000
Capital profits reserve	85,000
Retained profits	70,000
	500,000

REQUIRED

Prepare journal entries to reflect the revaluation of the asset and the subsequent depreciation of the revalued asset. Which of the equity accounts would be affected directly or indirectly by the revaluation?

14 Townend Ltd has the following assets in its statement of financial position as at 30 June 2014. **LO** 6.5

	€
Plant and equipment, at independent valuation	2,000,000
Less accumulated depreciation	400,000
Carrying amount	1,600,000

The plant and equipment originally cost Townend €600,000 in 2012, but as a result of market conditions the fair value of the plant and equipment has increased. The directors of Townend Ltd are concerned about the effects of the higher book value on profits—owing to the higher depreciation, it is reducing profits. They ask you, the accountant, to reverse the previous revaluation. Concerned to behave ethically, what would you do?

15 Bad Company Ltd has some machinery that it acquired in 2013 at a cost of €4,000,000. In 2014 it is concerned about high reported profits—the labour union is considering pushing for additional wages, but Bad Company Ltd does not want to pay them and is consequently considering ways to reduce profits. Recently, it has acquired some identical machinery to that acquired in 2013. The machinery has been acquired in a liquidation sale of a business that is in the hands of the bank (owing to the business defaulting on a loan) and the cost is €500,000. After this purchase, Bad

Company Ltd writes down to €500,000 the machinery acquired in 2013 at a cost of €4,000,000. Is this an appropriate course of action? **LO** 6.8

16 Petersen Ltd has the following land and buildings in its financial statements as at 30 June 2014: **LO** 6.1

	€
Residential land, at cost	1,000,000
Factory land, at valuation 2011	900,000
Buildings, at valuation 2010	800,000
Accumulated depreciation	(100,000)

At 30 June 2014, the balance of the revaluation surplus is €400,000, of which €300,000 relates to the factory land and €100,000 to the buildings. On this same date, independent valuations of the land and buildings are obtained. In relation to the above assets, the assessed fair values at 30 June 2014 are:

	€
Residential land, previously recorded at cost	1,100,000
Factory land, previously revalued in 2011	700,000
Buildings, previously revalued in 2010	900,000

REQUIRED

Provide the journal entries to account for the revaluation on 30 June 2014. Petersen Ltd classifies the residential land and the factory land as different classes of asset.

CHALLENGING QUESTIONS

17 What, if anything, is the difference between recoverable amount and fair value? Where revaluations are undertaken, can a reporting entity use 'value-in-use' as the basis for the revaluation? **LO** 6.1

18 Helnik Housing Ltd owns two blocks of land, acquired in 2011 for the purposes of future residential development. Block A cost €250,000 and Block B cost €350,000. **LO** 6.3

Valuations of the blocks are undertaken by an independent valuer on 30 June 2013 and 30 June 2015. The assessed values are:

	2013 valuation (€)	2015 valuation (€)
Block A	230,000	290,000
Block B	370,000	340,000

REQUIRED

Assuming asset revaluations were undertaken for the land in both 2013 and 2015, provide the journal entries for both years.

19 Warren Ltd acquires a four-wheel-drive bus on 1 July 2011 for €300,000. The bus is expected to have a useful life to Warren Ltd of seven years, after which time it will be towed out to sea and sunk to make an artificial reef for marine life (after all oils and solvents have been removed). **LO** 6.4

The straight-line method of depreciation is used.

On 1 July 2013 the bus is revalued to €250,000 and its useful life is reassessed: it is expected, at that date, to have a remaining useful life of six years.

On 1 July 2014 it is unexpectedly sold for €220,000.

REQUIRED

Provide the journal entries to record the revaluation on 1 July 2013 and the subsequent sale on 1 July 2014.

20 On 1 July 2013, Ocean Grove Limited acquired and installed an item of machinery for use in its manufacturing business. When acquired, the machinery cost £1,200,000, had an estimated useful life of ten years and an expected residual value of £200,000. Ocean Grove Limited depreciates machinery on a straight-line basis over its useful life. At 30 June 2015 the machinery had a carrying amount of £1,000,000.

At the end of the 2015 reporting period, the annual review of all machinery found that this particular item of machinery had incurred significant damage as a result of being rolled down a sand dune. As a result of the damage, the engineering

department estimated the fair value less costs to sell the machinery at the end of the reporting period was £710,000. As the machinery can operate in a limited capacity, it could be expected to provide annual net cash flows of £105,000 for the next eight years. The expected residual value will remain unchanged. The management of Ocean Grove Limited uses a discount rate of 8 per cent for calculations of this kind. **LO 6.4**

REQUIRED

Determine whether Ocean Grove Limited has incurred an impairment loss in relation to the asset. If so, determine the amount of the impairment loss, and provide the journal entry necessary to recognise any impairment in the machine.

21 Endless Summer Ltd purchased two parcels of land (Bruce and Brown) for €2,000,000 each on 1 July 2012. Subsequent to initial measurement, Endless Summer revalued the land. Fair values are as follows: **LO 6.3**

Parcel of land	Fair value 30 June 2013	Fair value 30 June 2014
Bruce	€1,800,000	€1,600,000
Brown	€2,500,000	€2,200,000

REQUIRED

(a) Prepare journal entries to record the revaluations on 30 June 2013 and 30 June 2014.

(b) The manager claims, 'There should be no adjustment for the decline in fair value because the recoverable amount of each parcel of land exceeds €2,000,000 at 30 June 2014.' Explain whether this is consistent with accounting standards.

22 Superbank Ltd acquired some machinery at a cost of €2,000,000. As at 30 June 2014 the machinery had accumulated depreciation of €400,000 and an expected remaining useful life of four years.

On 30 June 2014 it was determined that the machinery could be sold at a price of €1,200,000 and that the costs associated with making the sale would be €50,000. Alternatively, the machinery is expected to be useful for another four years and it is expected that the net cash flows to be generated from the machine will be €390,000 over each of the next four years.

It is assessed that at 30 June 2014 the market would require a rate of return of 6 per cent on this type of machinery. **LO 6.3**

REQUIRED

Determine whether any impairment loss needs to be recognised in relation to the machinery and, if so, provide the appropriate journal entry at 30 June 2014. Also, provide the journal entry to account for depreciation in 2015.

REFERENCES

BROWN, P., IZAN, H.Y., & LOH, A., 'Fixed Asset Revaluations and Managerial Incentives', *Abacus*, vol. 28, no. 1, 1992, pp. 36–57.

COTTER, J. & RICHARDSON, S., 'Reliability of Asset Revaluations: The Impact of Appraiser Independence', *Review of Accounting Studies*, vol. 7, no, 4, 2002, pp. 435–57.

GAEREMYNCK, A. & VEUGELERS, R., 'The Revaluation of Assets as a Signaling Device: A Theoretical and an Empirical Analysis', *Accounting and Business Research*, vol. 29, no. 2, 1999, pp. 123–38.

GOODWIN, J. & TROTMAN, K., 'Factors Affecting the Audit of Revalued Non-current Assets: Initial Public Offerings and Source Reliability', *Accounting and Finance*, vol. 36, no. 2, 1996, pp. 151–70.

HERRMANN, D., SAUDAGARAN, S., & THOMAS, W., 'The Quality of Fair Value Measure for Property, Plant and Equipment', *Accounting Forum*, vol. 30, 2005, pp. 43–59.

LIN, Y. & PEASNELL, K., 'Fixed Asset Revaluation and Equity Depletion in the UK', *Journal of Business Finance and Accounting*, vol. 27, no.

3–4, 2000, pp. 359–94.

MISSONIER-PIERA, F., 'Motives for Fixed-asset Revaluations: An Empirical Analysis with Swiss Data', *International Journal of Accounting*, vol. 42, no. 2, 2007, pp. 186–205.

NICHOLS, L. & BUERGER, K., 'An Investigation of the Effect of Valuation Alternatives for Fixed Assets on the Decision of Statement Users in the United States and Germany', *Journal of International Accounting, Auditing & Taxation*, vol. 11, 2002, pp. 155–63.

PIAK, G., 'The Value Relevance of Fixed Asset Revaluation Reserves in International Accounting', *International Management Review*, vol. 5, no. 2, 2009, pp. 73–80.

WHITTRED, G. & CHAN, Y.K., 'Asset Revaluations and the Mitigation of Underinvestment', *Abacus*, vol. 28, no. 1, 1992, pp. 58–74.

WHITTRED, G. & ZIMMER, I., 'Accounting in the Market for Debt', *Accounting and Finance*, November 1986, pp. 1–12.

Chapter 7

Inventory

Learning objectives

Upon completing this chapter readers should:

LO1 be able to calculate the cost of inventory pursuant to IAS 2 *Inventories*;

LO2 understand how to apply the lower of cost and net realisable value rule for measuring inventory;

LO3 understand why there is typically a necessity to make inventory cost-flow assumptions;

LO4 be able to apply the inventory cost-flow assumptions permitted by IAS 2; and

LO5 know the disclosure requirements of IAS 2.

7.1 Introduction to inventory

For a large proportion of businesses, the asset known as **inventory**—which is also sometimes known as stock—accounts for a significant proportion of total assets. The related expense, **cost of goods sold**, accounts for a significant amount of the total expenses of many firms. For example, the 2010 annual report of IKEA[1] (see www.ikea.com) indicates that inventories totalled €3,415 million. IKEA's cost of goods sold in 2010 was €12,454 million when profits after tax amounted to €2,696 million. Therefore, for companies such as IKEA (which controls a variety of retail stores across 41 countries and two industrial groups—Swedwood and Swedspan), the accounting methods relating to inventories will be of great importance in terms of their impact on reported assets and profits.

The relevant international accounting standard is IAS 2 *Inventories*. As stated in paragraph 2 of IAS 2:

> *IAS 2 applies to all inventories except:*
>
> *(a) work in progress arising under construction contracts, including directly related service contracts [covered by IAS 11 Construction Contracts, which is described in Chapter 13];*
> *(b) financial instruments; and*
> *(c) biological assets related to agricultural activity and agricultural produce at the point of harvest [covered by IAS 14 Agriculture].*

inventory Goods, other property and services held for sale in the ordinary course of business; or in the process of production, preparation or conversion for such sale; or in the form of materials or supplies to be consumed in the production of goods or services available for sale.

cost of goods sold Cost of inventory sold during the financial period. Can be determined either on a periodic basis or on a perpetual (continuous) basis.

---

[1] A subsidiary of the Stichting INGKA Foundation based in the Netherlands.

As further indicated in paragraph 3, nor does IAS 2 apply to the measurement of inventories held by:

(a) *producers of agricultural and forest products, agricultural produce after harvest, and mineral and mineral products, to the extent that they are measured at net realisable value in accordance with well-established practices in those industries. When such inventories are measured at net realisable value, changes in that value are recognised in profit or loss in the period of the change; and*

(b) *commodity broker-traders who measure their inventories at fair value less costs to sell. When such inventories are measured at fair value less costs to sell, changes in fair value less costs to sell are recognised in profit or loss in the period of the change.*

7.2 Definition of inventory

Inventories are defined in paragraph 6 of IAS 2 as assets:

- *held for sale in the ordinary course of business; or*
- *in the process of production for such sale; or*
- *in the form of materials or supplies to be consumed in the production process or in the rendering of services.*

Therefore, inventories include finished goods, raw materials and stores, and work-in-progress. The above definition specifically requires that assets held for sale be held for sale 'in the ordinary course of business'. Therefore, if an item is being held for sale, but not in the ordinary course of business, that asset is not deemed to be inventory, and IAS 2 does not apply. Rather, if the asset is a non-current asset, IAS 5 *Non-current Assets Held for Sale and Discontinued Operations* applies.

There are two main purposes of accounting for inventory. The first is to provide a measure of 'inventory' for statement of financial position purposes and the second is to determine the cost of goods sold for inclusion in the reporting entity's statement of comprehensive income.

7.3 The general basis of inventory measurement

lower of cost and net realisable value Cost is the aggregate of costs such as purchase and conversion; net realisable value is the estimated proceeds of sale less costs to completion and costs to sell.

IAS 2, paragraph 9, requires that inventories are to be measured at the **lower of cost and net realisable value** and such measurement would usually be undertaken on an item-by-item basis. However, paragraph 29 of IAS 2 provides that in some circumstances it might be appropriate to group similar or related items together when determining the lower of cost and net realisable value, such as assets relating to the same product line that have similar purposes or end uses and are produced and marketed in the same region and cannot be practically evaluated separately from the other items of that product line.

The requirement to measure inventory at the lower of cost and net realisable value is a rule that is generally applicable to all for-profit entities. There are, however, some limited exceptions to this general rule. For example, the international accounting standard that pertains to retirement benefit plans, IAS 26 *Accounting and Reporting by Retirement Benefit Plans*, requires that all assets of defined benefit plans are to be measured at fair value, where fair value is taken as market value for marketable securities as at reporting date. Any changes in the net market value of a retirement benefit plan's assets—including inventory—since the beginning of the reporting period are to be included as a component of revenue, or expense, for the reporting period. This is a clear departure from the general rule that inventory is to be measured at the lower of cost and net realisable value.

IAS 2 provides that not-for-profit entities may also adopt a different treatment for measuring inventory. In respect of not-for-profit entities, inventories held for distribution are to be measured at the lower of cost and current replacement cost.

Returning to the rule that applies to most reporting entities—that inventories be measured at the lower of cost and net realisable value—it would obviously be useful to define what we mean by 'cost' and 'net realisable value'. First we will consider 'cost'. Paragraph 10 of IAS 2 states:

The cost of inventories shall comprise all costs of purchase, costs of conversion and other costs incurred in bringing the inventories to their present location and condition.

According to IAS 2:

- The 'cost of purchase' comprises the purchase price, import duties and other taxes, as well as transport, handling and other costs directly attributable to the acquisition of finished goods, material and services. Trade discounts, rebates and other similar items are deducted in determining the costs of purchase.

- The 'costs of conversion' of inventories include costs directly related to the units of production, such as direct labour. They also include a systematic allocation of fixed and variable production overheads that are incurred in converting materials into finished goods.
- 'Other costs' are included to the extent that they are incurred in bringing the inventories to their present location and condition. For example, it may be appropriate to include non-production overheads or the costs of designing products for specific customers in the cost of inventories.

7.3.1 Items excluded from the cost of inventory

In relation to what should *not* be included in the cost of inventory, paragraph 16 of IAS 2 requires that costs of inventory exclude costs that relate to:

- *abnormal amounts of wasted materials, labour or other production costs;*
- *storage costs, unless those costs are necessary in the production process prior to a further production stage;*
- *administrative overheads that do not contribute to bringing inventories to their present location and condition; and*
- *selling costs.*

When acquiring inventory it is quite common for the purchaser to be offered a discount for early payment. The discount would be considered to relate to the management of accounts receivable and would be treated as a revenue item by the purchasing company, perhaps labelled something like 'discount received'. The discount for early payment would not be accounted for by reducing the cost of the inventory being acquired. Similarly, if a penalty for late payment is imposed, this would not be included as part of the cost of inventory. Instead, it would be treated as a 'late payment expense'.

7.3.2 Allocating costs to inventory

In allocating costs to inventories, a decision must be made on how to treat **fixed production costs**. Fixed production costs are costs of production that remain relatively constant from financial period to financial period irrespective of variations, within normal operating limits, in the volume of production. They would include costs such as those relating to the depreciation of factory buildings, and costs of factory management and administration. Where more than one product is being produced it might be necessary to allocate fixed manufacturing costs between different products. As paragraph 14 of IAS 2 states:

> A production process may result in more than one product being produced simultaneously. This is the case, for example, when joint products are produced or when there is a main product and a by-product. When the costs of conversion of each product are not separately identifiable, they are allocated between the products on a rational and consistent basis. The allocation may be based, for example, on the relative sales value of each product either at the stage in the production process when the products become separately identifiable, or at the completion of production. Most by-products, by their nature, are immaterial. When this is the case, they are often measured at net realisable value and this value is deducted from the cost of the main product. As a result, the carrying amount of the main product is not materially different from its cost.

The two main methods for dealing with manufacturing **fixed costs** are **direct costing** and **absorption costing**. IAS 2 requires the adoption of absorption costing. Under absorption costing, fixed manufacturing costs are included in the cost of inventories because they are considered to be as much a part of the cost of conversion as are direct labour and other variable costs. Under direct costing, fixed production costs are treated as **period costs** (that is, they are recognised as expenses in the financial period in which they are incurred) and are excluded from the cost of inventories. Although direct costing is frequently used for internal management purposes, it is not permitted for external reporting purposes. Again, absorption costing is required by IAS 2.

Pursuant to IAS 2, the cost of inventory is to include both variable and fixed production overheads. Production overheads are indirect costs of production, preparation or

fixed production costs Costs of production that are not expected to fluctuate as levels of production change.

fixed costs Costs that do not fluctuate (at least in the shorter term) as levels of production/activity change.

direct costing Where fixed production costs are treated as period costs (brought to account as expenses in the financial period in which they are incurred) and thus excluded from the cost of inventories.

absorption costing Where the cost of inventory includes variable production costs and fixed production costs. Often referred to as 'full costing'.

period costs Costs that are written off in the period in which they are incurred since they are not expected to provide economic benefits beyond the end of the current financial period.

conversion that cannot be identified specifically or traced to the individual goods or services being produced in an economically feasible manner. Paragraph 13 of IAS 2 requires that:

The allocation of fixed production overheads to the costs of conversion is based on the normal capacity of the production facilities. Normal capacity is the production expected to be achieved on average over a number of periods or seasons under normal circumstances, taking into account the loss of capacity resulting from planned maintenance. The actual level of production may be used if it approximates normal capacity. The amount of fixed overhead allocated to each unit of production is not increased as a consequence of low production or idle plant. Unallocated overheads are recognised as an expense in the period in which they are incurred. In periods of abnormally high production, the amount of fixed overhead allocated to each unit is decreased so that inventories are not measured above cost. Variable production overheads are allocated to each unit of production on the basis of the actual use of production facilities.

standard costs
Used to assign costs to inventory, they are predetermined product costs established on the basis of planned products and/or operations, planned cost and efficiency levels and expected capacity utilisation.

Many organisations also use standard costs to allocate costs to inventory. Pursuant to IAS 2, standard costs may be used to arrive at the cost of inventory only where the standards are realistically attainable, reviewed regularly and, where necessary, revised in the light of current conditions. **Standard costs** are predetermined product costs established on the basis of, among other things, planned products and/or operations, planned cost and efficiency levels, and expected capacity utilisation. Under a standard-cost accounting system, inventories are costed at a standard cost and the computation of cost variances becomes part of the accounting cycle. If standards have been properly set and maintained, they are a sound basis for the purpose of inventory valuation and all variances from standard can be charged or credited to profit or loss in the period in which they arise. Costs arising from exceptional wastage should be excluded from the cost of inventories.

As an example of determining the cost of inventory, consider Worked Example 7.1.

Worked Example 7.1 Determination of the cost of inventory

The following list relates to expenditure incurred by Burridge Ltd for the latest financial year. Burridge Ltd makes a standard, one-design skateboard referred to as a 'pop-out'. Standard costing is not applied. Rather, fixed manufacturing costs are allocated to inventory, on the basis of normal operating capacity.

Item of expenditure	€000
Advertising	10
Loan losses (bad debts)	15
Depreciation—administrative equipment	20
Depreciation—factory equipment	30
Directors' salary	90
Electricity—administration building	10
Electricity—factory	30
Freight in of raw material	30
Freight out of inventory	20
Insurance—administration building	10
Insurance—factory	15
Interest expense	30

Item of expenditure	€000
Purchase of materials used to make pop-outs	400
Purchase of office stationery and supplies	70
Rates—administration building	20
Rates—factory	20
Rent—administration building	100
Rent—factory	200
Repairs and maintenance—administration building	10
Repairs and maintenance—factory	30
Salaries—administrative personnel	150
Wages—factory personnel	300
Sales commissions	180
	1,790

Other information
(i) 10,000 pop-outs are made during the year.
(ii) There is no opening inventory at the beginning of the year.
(iii) Normal operating capacity is 10,000 pop-outs.
(iv) Burridge received a discount of 2 per cent for paying early for the €400,000 of raw materials used to make the pop-outs.

Required
Pursuant to IAS 2, what is the unit 'cost' of a pop-out?

Solution
Costs need to be divided into those that relate to inventory, and those that do not. Any costs of an administrative nature or related to the sale of the products are not to be included in the 'cost' of inventory.

Item of expenditure	Costs that relate to inventory (€000)	Other costs (€000)
Advertising		10
Loan loss write-off (bad debts)		15
Depreciation—administrative equipment		20
Depreciation—factory equipment	30	
Directors' salary		90
Electricity—administration building		10
Electricity—factory	30	
Freight in of raw material (carriage in)	30	
Freight out of inventory (carriage out)		20

Item of expenditure	Costs that relate to inventory (€000)	Other costs (€000)
Insurance—administration building		10
Insurance—factory	15	
Interest expense		30
Purchase of materials used to make pop-outs	400	
Purchase of office stationery and supplies		70
Rates—administration building		20
Rates—factory	20	
Rent—administration building		100
Rent—factory	200	
Repairs and maintenance—administration building		10
Repairs and maintenance—factory	30	
Salaries—administrative personnel		150
Wages—factory personnel	300	
Sales commissions		180
Total	1,055	735

Pursuant to IAS 2, fixed factory overheads must be allocated to inventory on the basis of normal capacity. As the current period's output is considered to be 'normal', we can simply add all the production costs together, including the fixed manufacturing overheads (such as the factory rent, rates and insurance) and divide the total cost by the level of output. The cost per pop-out, therefore, is:

$$€1,055,000 \div 10,000 = €105.50$$

In Worked Example 7.1 note that we have not deducted the 2 per cent early discount received by Burridge from the cost of the inventory. Rather, this would be shown separately as an income item, perhaps labelled something like 'discounts received' (for early payment). Nor have we included the interest expense as part of inventory. As we will discuss later in this chapter, costs associated with borrowing can sometimes be included in the cost of inventory. Such treatment is governed by IAS 23 *Borrowing Costs*. Paragraph 11 of IAS 23 does allow interest costs to be included in the cost of inventory, but only when the inventory is considered to be a 'qualifying asset'.

IAS 23 defines a *qualifying asset* as 'an asset that necessarily takes a substantial period of time to get ready for its intended use or sale'. A 'substantial period of time' is generally regarded as being more than 12 months. The borrowing costs to be included would be those that would have been avoided if the expenditure on the asset had not been made. If it is assumed that the inventory of Burridge Ltd did not take Burridge more than 12 months to complete—as would often be the case—the cost of inventory would exclude the interest expenses.

As we have noted, inventory is to be valued at the lower of cost and net realisable value. We have just considered one illustration of the determination of 'cost'. We consider net realisable value in Worked Example 7.2. 'Net realisable value' is defined in IAS 2 as the estimated selling price in the ordinary course of business less the estimated costs of completion and the estimated costs necessary to make the sale.

Worked Example 7.2 — Lower of cost and net realisable value

Rayday Ltd holds four lines of inventory. The total production costs of each item of inventory on hand at the end of the financial period are shown below. Apart from the production costs, estimates of future packaging costs and transportation costs are also provided. It is considered that the items are not saleable unless they are packaged in crates and transported to market.

Product line	Production costs (€000)	Transport costs (€000)	Packaging costs (€000)	Expected sales proceeds (€000)
Gidgets	20	2	3	35
Widgets	30	4	4	30
Didgets	15	1	1.5	22
Sidgets	25	2.5	2.5	35

Required

Determine the closing value of inventory for Rayday Ltd.

Solution

As indicated earlier, where practical to do so, the lower of cost and net realisable value rule must be applied on an item-by-item basis. It is not permissible to net the differences between the items. The net realisable value of the items is determined by subtracting the additional future transportation costs and packaging costs from the expected sales proceeds.

Product line	Net realisable value (€)	Cost (€)	Lower of cost and net realisable value (€)
Gidgets	30,000	20,000	20,000
Widgets	22,000	30,000	22,000
Didgets	19,500	15,000	15,000
Sidgets	30,000	25,000	25,000
Total	101,500	90,000	82,000

The value of closing inventory would therefore be disclosed as €82,000. A review of the data above shows that €82,000 is well below the net realisable value of the total inventory. Lower of cost and net realisable value can provide a very conservative reflection of the value of inventory, with the result that the amount reported in the entity's financial statements may be a great deal less than its market value. This treatment, as espoused in IAS 2, is generally consistent with the accountant's somewhat dated 'Doctrine of Conservatism'. This doctrine holds that gains should not generally be recognised until they are realised, while losses should be recognised in the period in which they first become foreseeable—that is, losses do not have to be realised to be recognised for accounting purposes. This asymmetric approach to the recognition of expenses and income is not consistent with the IASB Conceptual Framework. The IASB Conceptual Framework requires that the recognition of revenues/income and expenses should be made on the same basis, with due recognition given to issues such as the probability that the inflow or outflow of economic benefits has occurred, and whether the inflow or outflow can be reliably measured. However, as we have noted before, accounting standards such as IAS 2 have precedence over the IASB Conceptual Framework.

As a further point, it should also be remembered that, although expenditures associated with such activities as marketing, selling and distribution are not to be included in the 'cost' of inventory for statement of financial position purposes, they must necessarily be considered when calculating 'net realisable value'.

Worked Example 7.3 provides another example of inventory cost determination.

Worked Example 7.3 | Inventory cost determination

Scottie Thomson Ltd commenced business at the beginning of the current financial year. The company manufactures life-size dolls. Relevant data are:

Normal operating capacity (units)	100,000
Goods produced (units)	100,000
Opening finished goods inventory (units)	Nil
Closing finished goods inventory (units)	20,000
Opening value of raw materials inventory	Nil
Closing value of raw materials inventory	£100,000
Factory salaries	£250,000
Administration salaries	£90,000
Factory rent	£120,000
Depreciation of factory equipment	£80,000
Rental of office equipment	£60,000
Raw materials purchased	£300,000
Sales price per unit	£9.00 per unit
Delivery costs of finished goods	£1.00 per unit

At the end of the year there are no partly finished goods.

Required

Determine the value at which inventory should be disclosed in the year-end statement of financial position.

Solution

Under IAS 2, absorption costing is required. Under absorption costing, any fixed production costs are assigned to inventory on the basis of normal capacity, that is, they are treated as product costs. Pursuant to paragraph 16 of IAS 2, other fixed costs, such as those relating to administration, are expensed in the period incurred, and are thus treated as period costs, not product costs.

The company in this illustration is operating at normal capacity of 100,000 units.

Costs of inventory

Variable costs			
Factory salaries		£250,000	
Raw material purchased	£300,000		
less Closing inventory	£100,000	£200,000	
Total variable costs		£450,000	
divided by Units produced		100,000	
Per unit variable costs			£4.50
Fixed costs			
Factory rent	£120,000		
Factory depreciation	£80,000		
Total fixed costs	£200,000		
divided by Normal operating capacity	100,000		
Per unit fixed costs			£2.00
Total cost per unit			£6.50
Net realisable value			
Sales price per unit		£9.00	
less Delivery costs per unit		£1.00	
		£8.00	

▶

◀ **Closing value of inventory**

As inventory is to be valued at the lower of cost and net realisable, and as cost is lower than net realisable value, the value of inventory on hand at reporting date would be:

$$20,000 \times £6.50 = £130,000$$

Inventory has commonly been used by wayward management to manipulate reported performance in companies. The Committee of Sponsoring Organisations of the Treadway Commission examined fraudulent financial reporting practices in US public companies over the period 1987–1997 and reported in 1999 that about half of the frauds committed involved asset-value manipulation and the majority of these were in respect of inventory. A real-life example that resulted in heavy fines for the auditor and jail sentences for the directors/managers is now outlined.

Financial Accounting in the News 7.1

GHOST GOODS: HOW TO SPOT PHANTOM INVENTORY

Joseph T. Wells, *Journal of Accountancy*
June 2001

Generating phony profits over an entire decade was no easy feat. Phar-Mor's CFO said the company was losing serious money because it was selling goods for less than it had paid for them. But Monus argued that through Phar-Mor's power buying it would get so large that it could sell its way out of trouble. Eventually, the CFO caved in—under extreme pressure from Monus—and for the next several years, he and some of his staff kept two sets of books—the ones they showed the auditors and the ones that reflected the awful truth.

They dumped the losses into the 'bucket account' and then reallocated the sums to one of the company's hundreds of stores in the form of increases in inventory costs. They issued fake invoices for merchandise purchases, made phony journal entries to increase inventory and decrease cost of sales, recognized inventory purchases but failed to accrue a liability and over-counted and double-counted merchandise. The finance department was able to conceal the inventory shortages because the auditors observed inventory in only four stores out of 300, and they informed Phar-Mor, months in advance, which stores they would visit. Phar-Mor executives fully stocked the four selected stores but allocated the phony inventory increases to the other 296 stores. Regardless of the accounting tricks, Phar-Mor was heading for collapse. During the last audit, cash was so tight suppliers threatened to cut the company off for non-payment of bills.

The auditors never uncovered the fraud, for which they paid dearly. This failure cost the audit firm over $300 million in civil judgments. The CFO, who did not profit personally, was sentenced to 33 months in prison. Monus went to jail for 5 years.

Source: Journal of Accountancy. © 2012 American Institute of Certified Public Accountants.

It should be noted that, for inventory covered by IAS 2, upward revaluations are not permitted. Therefore, if an item is worth more than cost, it should be left at cost. If it is worth less, it should be written down and the **write-down** treated as an expense in the period of write-down (consistent with the 'Doctrine of Conservatism'). That is, the rule about the lower of cost and net realisable value must be adhered to and cannot be circumvented by asset revaluations. As indicated in Chapter 6, the accounting standards pertaining to revaluations specifically exclude inventories. However, if in a subsequent period the circumstances that caused the inventory to be written down below cost no longer exist, then paragraph 33 of IAS 2 requires the inventories to be reinstated to the extent that the new carrying amount does not exceed the lower of the original cost or the net realisable value in the current period.

> **write-down** Reducing the carrying value of an asset.

Inventory held in the form of marketable securities, explicitly not covered by the inventory standard IAS 2, may be deemed to be a 'trading security', which is a security held for sale in the normal course of business. It is becoming usual practice for firms to value trading securities at fair value, the most common measure of which is market value (often referred to as 'marked to market') with the valuation increments and decrements both being included in the period's profit or loss. A trading security would include such things as shares listed on a stock exchange. The requirement to recognise the gain or loss arising from a change in the fair value of a 'financial asset' is stipulated in IFRS 9 *Financial Instruments*.

Returning to inventories covered by IAS 2, as stipulated by paragraph 15 of IAS 2, other costs will also often be incurred in bringing inventories to their present location and condition. These costs might include additional costs necessary to meet the needs of specific customers—for example, some customers might require that inventory be packaged in a particular way, or be slightly modified relative to the inventory being sold to other purchasers. Such 'other costs' would be included in the cost of inventory. As we indicated earlier in this chapter, it is also possible for borrowing costs to be incurred by an entity in the process of producing inventory. For example, an entity might need to borrow funds to acquire particular raw materials used to produce its inventory. At issue here is whether we should include the borrowing costs—such as the interest expenses—in the costs of the inventory. We can look to IAS 23 *Borrowing Costs* for guidance. As we saw in Worked Example 7.1, paragraph 11 of IAS 23 requires that interest be included in the cost of inventory only when the inventories are qualifying assets, that is, inventory that 'takes a substantial period of time' to be completed. We would expect that most inventory items would not satisfy the requirements of IAS 23, and hence borrowing costs would not be included in the cost of inventory. However, for an item such as a ship under construction, borrowing costs might be included in the cost of the inventory—the inventory being the ship. IAS 23 provides a number of examples of assets that could be considered as 'qualifying'—and that therefore could include interest expenses as part of their 'cost'. Specifically, paragraph 2 of IAS 23 states:

Depending on the circumstances, any of the following may be qualifying assets:

(a) inventories
(b) manufacturing plants
(c) power generation facilities
(d) intangible assets
(e) investment properties.

Financial assets, and inventories that are manufactured, or otherwise produced, over a short period of time, are not qualifying assets. Assets that are ready for their intended use or sale when acquired are not qualifying assets.

7.4   Inventory cost-flow assumptions

In Worked Example 7.3 we assumed that all units cost the same amount and we performed the calculation at year end. However, if the costs of the individual inventory items fluctuate throughout the year, which would be likely in most organisations where items are manufactured or acquired at various times throughout the year, and we cannot or do not wish to identify the specific 'cost' of each individual item, certain cost-flow assumptions must be made.

During the year, inventory is likely to be purchased or manufactured at several different prices/costs. If inventories are to be measured at cost and numerous purchases have been made at different unit costs, the question arises of which of the various cost prices should be assigned to each transaction.

Instead of attempting to identify items specifically, a cost-flow assumption is frequently made and consistently applied in determining cost of goods sold and closing inventory. Thus, the actual physical flow of goods and the flow of goods according to the cost-flow assumption might be quite different.

In selecting a cost-flow method, management must exercise judgement to ensure that the method chosen provides the most practical accounting reflection of the real situation. For example, it might be inappropriate to apply averages based on costs incurred over a whole financial period in circumstances where there was a complete turnover of inventories several times during that financial period.

According to IAS 2, costs of inventories should be assigned to particular items of inventory by one or more of the following methods:

■ *specific identification—this method assigns specific costs to identified units of inventory;*
■ *weighted average cost—this method assigns weighted average costs, arrived at by means of either a continuous calculation, a periodic calculation or a moving periodic calculation; and*
■ *first-in, first-out (FIFO)—this method assigns costs on the assumption that the inventory quantities on hand represent those last purchased or produced.*

If the production costs or purchase prices of inventory items did not change, the above three methods would generate the same costs, but steady prices would rarely be expected across time. The method adopted should be appropriate to the circumstances and be applied consistently from financial period to financial period. An entity is to use the same method for all inventories having a similar nature or use. For inventories with a different nature or use, different methods may be applied (so long as the method chosen is one of the three options just listed).

Conceptually, a specific identification of the items sold and the items on hand at reporting date seems optimal, but this approach might be impractical to apply. Under the **specific-identification method** of inventory valuation, and assuming items being sold are similar or identical, the seller determines which item is sold and the cost of that specific item is expensed to cost of sales. This could lend itself to profit manipulation. The ending inventory is costed at the cost of the specific individual items on hand at the end of the year. For example, a seller has for sale three identical inventory items with costs of €100, €150 and €200. Since the inventory items are identical, purchasers will have no preference for a particular item. The seller can manipulate ending inventory (assets) and income (profit) by selecting different items for sale. If the seller chooses to sell the €100 item, profits and closing inventory will be €100 greater than if the €200 item had been sold.

Items with a significant monetary value, such as motor vehicles, are frequently accounted for by the specific-identification method, particularly when the items have a unique characteristic, such as a unique product or identification number. When items have different characteristics, and the buyers are not indifferent about which item they select, the ability to manipulate profits is reduced. Paragraph 23 of IAS 2 requires that specific identification be used to assign costs to inventory items that are:

(a) *not ordinarily interchangeable; or*
(b) *goods or services produced and segregated for specific projects.*

Paragraph 24 of IAS 2 states that specific identification is not appropriate when there are large numbers of inventory items that are ordinarily interchangeable, as the selection of items remaining in inventory could be made to obtain predetermined effects on the result for the reporting period.

For goods that are ordinarily interchangeable, or are not produced and segregated for specific projects, IAS 2 requires that the costs be assigned using the weighted-average cost or the first-in, first-out (FIFO) formulas.

Under the **weighted-average approach**, an average cost is determined based on the cost of beginning inventory and the costs of items purchased or manufactured during the period. The various costs of the individual units are weighted by the number of units at a particular purchase price. The units in ending inventory and units sold are costed at this average cost. The weighted-average cost method is appropriate where the goods are homogeneous in nature and the turnover of items is high.

Under the **first-in, first-out cost-flow method (FIFO)** of inventory valuation, the goods from beginning inventory and the earliest purchases are assumed to be the goods sold first. This would seem to be the pattern of selling behaviour in most entities. Ending inventory is assumed to be made up of the more recent purchases, or the more recently manufactured items, and thus represents a more current value of the inventory for the statement of financial position. It should be noted that this cost-flow assumption may be used even when it does not match the physical flow of goods. While FIFO is commonly used within Europe, it is often criticised because it tends to match old or outdated inventory costs with current sales prices and by doing so tends to result in inflated profits relative to what would be recorded if current up-to-date costs were used to determine cost of goods sold.

The **last-in, first-out cost-flow method (LIFO)** of inventory valuation is not acceptable under IAS 2; however, it is discussed here for the sake of completeness. Under the LIFO cost-flow method, the most recent items purchased or manufactured are assumed to be the first goods sold. Therefore, ending inventory is assumed to be composed of the oldest goods. This could result in inventory being valued at costs that were paid or incurred some years before. The cost of sales contains relatively current costs, thus achieving a potentially better matching of current costs to revenues. In a period of rising prices, LIFO adopters would show lower profits and lower closing inventory than FIFO adopters. Allowing the adoption of LIFO would potentially open the door to profit manipulation, as acquiring inventory at year end might alter the period's profit, even if those items acquired are still on hand at year end.

Interestingly, LIFO may be used in the US for external reporting purposes. If it is used for these purposes it may also be used for the purposes of calculating the entity's taxation liability. In a period of rising prices, adopting LIFO effectively results in higher

specific-identification method Method of accounting for the cost flow of inventory. Significant euro/sterling value items are often accounted for in this way, particularly where they have a unique characteristic such as a unique product number.

weighted-average approach An average cost is determined for inventory based on beginning inventory and items purchased during the period. The costs of the individual units are weighted by the number of units acquired or manufactured at a particular price. The units in ending inventory and units sold are costed at this average cost.

first-in, first-out cost-flow method (FIFO) Method of assigning costs to inventory where it is assumed that the first inventory that enters an organisation's stores is the first inventory that is sold.

last-in, first-out cost-flow method (LIFO) Method of assigning costs to inventory where it is assumed that the last inventory item that enters an organisation's stores is the first inventory that is sold.

cost of goods sold, lower profits and, consequently, lower taxes. This is particularly attractive to US firms. Further, the choice of an inventory cost-flow assumption does not have to reflect the underlying physical flow of inventory. LIFO is prohibited in countries that adopt the standards produced by the IASB.

The benefits of lower taxes that are available to US firms that adopt LIFO have to be traded off against other implications of reporting lower profits. Conceivably, reporting lower profits and lower closing inventory might have implications for certain accounting-based contractual arrangements, such as accounting-based management bonus schemes, and debt-to-asset constraints or interest-coverage clauses contained in negotiated debt agreements.

As discussed in previous chapters of this book, management can often choose between particular accounting procedures, for example:

- revaluing or not revaluing non-current assets;
- capitalising or expensing a particular expenditure; and
- using the straight-line or sum-of-digits method of depreciation.

Accounting researchers often seek to explain why management chooses one method of accounting in preference to another. Many researchers working within the Positive Accounting Theory paradigm have attempted to explain accounting policy choices in terms of the debt hypothesis, the management-bonus hypothesis and the political-cost hypothesis (see Chapter 3 for an overview of these hypotheses and of Positive Accounting Theory). Hunt (1985) reports that organisations within the US that elect not to adopt LIFO—and therefore report higher profits and assets in periods of increasing prices—typically have higher leverage and lower interest-coverage ratios. His results were consistent with the frequently used 'debt hypothesis', which holds that organisations potentially close to breaching debt covenants (such as maximum debt-to-asset ratios and minimum interest-coverage ratios) will adopt income-increasing (which is also equity increasing) and, hence, asset-increasing accounting methods. Some support for the debt hypothesis explaining the selection of particular inventory cost-flow assumptions was provided by Cushing and LeCleare (1992).

Returning to the treatment of inventory under IAS 2 (which prohibits the use of the LIFO method discussed above), the determination of cost of sales and closing inventory under each of the cost-flow assumptions further depends on the method used to record movements in the inventory, that is, whether the **periodic** or the **perpetual inventory system** is used. We use either the perpetual or the periodic inventory method to work out the number of units of inventory on hand. So in determining cost of goods sold (for the statement of profit and loss) and the cost of closing inventory (for the statement of financial position) we not only need to consider what cost-flow assumptions have been made (for example, FIFO, specific-identification or weighted-average approach), we also need to determine whether the perpetual or periodic system is being employed to determine the actual number of units of inventory on hand. Under the periodic inventory system, inventory is counted periodically (for example, at year end) and then costed. By contrast, under the perpetual inventory system, a running total is kept of the units on hand (and possibly their value) by recording all increases and decreases as they occur. Some inventory cost-flow examples and methods are reviewed in Worked Examples 7.4 and 7.5.

periodic inventory system Also known as the physical inventory method, this is a method of accounting for inventory where inventory is counted periodically and then priced.

perpetual inventory system Also known as the continuous method, this is a method of accounting for inventory where a running total is kept of the units on hand by recording all increases and decreases as they occur

Worked Example 7.4 **Inventory cost-flow example**

Bernie Ltd has the following inventory transactions for the year ending 30 June 2014:

Opening inventory at 1 July 2013	2,000 units @ €5	€10,000
Purchases on 1 October 2013	6,000 units @ €6	€36,000
Purchases on 1 February 2014	8,000 units @ €8	€64,000
Purchases on 1 June 2014	4,000 units @ €10	€40,000
Total	20,000 units	€150,000

During the year Bernie Ltd sells 15,000 units, and has 5,000 units on hand at year end. Bernie Ltd uses the periodic system to record inventory.

Required

Compute the cost of sales and ending inventory amounts under the following cost-flow methods:
(a) First-in, first-out (FIFO)
(b) Weighted average
(c) Last-in, first-out (LIFO)

Solution

(a) FIFO

The cost of sales comprises the beginning inventory of 2,000 units and the next 13,000 units purchased. That is, the first items of inventory that came in were assumed to be the first ones that went out—first in, first out. The ending inventory comprises the last 5,000 units purchased.

$$\text{Cost of sales} = (2{,}000 @ €5) + (6{,}000 @ €6) + (7{,}000 @ €8) = €102{,}000$$

$$\text{Ending inventory} = (1{,}000 @ €8) + (4{,}000 @ €10) = €48{,}000$$

(b) Weighted average

The cost of sales and ending inventory are costed at the weighted-average price of beginning inventory and purchases.

$$\text{Weighted-average cost} = €150{,}000 \div 20{,}000 \text{ units} = €7.50 \text{ per unit}$$

$$\text{Cost of sales} = (15{,}000 @ €7.50) = €112{,}500$$

$$\text{Ending inventory} = (5{,}000 @ €7.50) = €37{,}500$$

(c) LIFO

The cost of sales comprises the last 15,000 units purchased. The ending inventory comprises the beginning inventory of 2,000 units and 3,000 units purchased on 1 October 2013.

$$\text{Cost of sales} = (4{,}000 @ €10) + (8{,}000 @ €8) + (3{,}000 @ €6) = €122{,}000$$

$$\text{Ending inventory} = (2{,}000 @ €5) + (3{,}000 @ €6) = €28{,}000$$

From Worked Example 7.4 we can see how the selection of a particular inventory cost-flow assumption creates a different cost of goods sold, and different balances of closing inventory for use within the statement of financial position. In times of rising prices, LIFO will generate the highest cost of goods sold and the lowest closing inventory whereas FIFO will generate the lowest cost of goods sold and the highest closing inventory. Weighted-average cost will generate results in-between those generated by LIFO and FIFO.

Worked Example 7.5 — Inventory cost-flow methods

Bakehouse Ltd begins selling rolling pins in 2013. Each rolling pin looks the same; however, the unit costs of manufacturing rolling pins (which is done in batches) have fluctuated because of rising material costs. Bakehouse Ltd adopts a FIFO cost-flow assumption and employs a perpetual inventory system. Details of costs are as follows.

Date completed	Number completed	Unit costs (€)
10 July 2013	100	2.50
10 August 2013	300	2.70
5 December 2013	250	2.80
1 March 2014	300	3.00
1 June 2014	200	3.10
	1,150	

Details of sales are as follows:

Date of sale	Number sold	Unit costs (€)
12 July 2013	90	5.00
15 August 2013	210	5.00
10 December 2013	300	5.10
25 March 2014	200	5.00
15 June 2014	150	5.20
	950	

Required

What is the cost of sales for the year ended 30 June 2014 and what is the value of inventory for statement of financial position purposes as at 30 June 2014?

Solution

Because the inventory items, which are rolling pins, are identical we cannot precisely determine the cost of each specific item sold. For example, is the firm selling items in December that were in fact produced in July, August or December? We typically would not know. We need to make cost-flow assumptions. For example, we may assume that the first rolling pins produced are the first ones sold, that is we could adopt the FIFO cost-flow assumption. With this assumption, cost of goods sold would be €2,660, reconciled as follows (assuming a perpetual inventory system is employed in which inventory records are updated each time an item is sold or manufactured):

Date	Manufactured	Sold	Balance
10 July	100 @ €2.50 = €250		100 @ €2.50
12 July		90 @ €2.50 = €225	10 @ €2.50
10 August	300 @ €2.70 = €810		10 @ €2.50 300 @ €2.70
15 August		10 @ €2.50 = €25 200 @ €2.70 = €540	100 @ €2.70
5 December	250 @ €2.80 = €700		100 @ €2.70 250 @ €2.80
10 December		100 @ €2.70 = €270 200 @ €2.80 = €560	50 @ €2.80
1 March	300 @ €3.00 = €900		50 @ €2.80 300 @ €3.00
25 March		50 @ €2.80 = €140 150 @ €3.00 = €450	150 @ €3.00
1 June	200 @ €3.10 = €620		150 @ €3.00 200 @ €3.10
15 June		150 @ €3.00 = €450	200 @ €3.10
	1,150 €3,280	950 €2,660	

Closing inventory would therefore be valued at €620 (200 × €3.10).

The periodic system was used for the calculations in Worked Example 7.4. The implication of this is that calculations of cost of goods sold are done periodically, for example at the end of the financial period, rather than each time a sale is made. Contrast these calculations with those shown in Worked Example 7.5, where the perpetual inventory system is used, and cost of goods sold and inventory balances are updated each time a sale occurs. As we can see from this example, if the perpetual system is used the balance of inventory on hand is kept up to date. In Worked Example 7.6 we consider, for comparative purposes, the journal entries that are needed under both a periodic and a perpetual inventory system. As we will see, when the periodic system is used we use a 'purchases' account and cost of goods sold will be determined at the end of the period using the following formula:

> Cost of goods sold = Opening inventory + Purchases − Purchase returns (if any) − Closing inventory

Worked Example 7.6

Journal entries to be used in accounting for inventory: a comparison of the periodic and perpetual systems of accounting for inventory

Hoy Ltd sells Yellow Jersey road bikes acquired from Wiggins Cycles Ltd. At the beginning of July 2013 Hoy Ltd had 100 Yellow Jersey road bikes that cost £600 each. During the year the following transactions took place:
(a) On 10 July 2013 Hoy Ltd sold 50 Yellow Jersey road bikes for cash at £800 each.
(b) On 5 August 2013 Hoy Ltd purchased 70 Yellow Jersey road bikes at £700 each and this cost included freight costs.
(c) On 10 August 2013 Hoy Ltd paid for the purchases and received a 2 per cent discount for early payment.
(d) On 5 September 2013 Hoy Ltd sold 60 Yellow Jersey road bikes at £900 each.
(e) On 15 September 2013 Hoy Ltd returned 10 defective Yellow Jersey road bikes to the supplier; the brakes on the bikes were loose.
(f) On 10 June 2014 Hoy Ltd sold 40 Yellow Jersey road bikes at £1,000 each.

Required
(a) Provide the journal entries to account for the above transactions using first the periodic system and then the perpetual system. Hoy Ltd uses the FIFO cost-flow assumption.
(b) Determine cost of goods sold and the balance of closing inventory.

Solution
(a) **Perpetual inventory system**   **Periodic inventory system**

10 July 2013

Dr	Cash	£40,000		Dr	Cash	£40,000	
Cr	Sales revenue		£40,000	Cr	Sales revenue		£40,000
Dr	Cost of goods sold	£30,000					
Cr	Inventory		£30,000				

5 August 2013

Dr	Inventory	£49,000		Dr	Purchases	£49,000	
Cr	Accounts payable		£49,000	Cr	Accounts payable		£49,000

10 August 2013

Dr	Accounts payable	£49,000		Dr	Accounts payable	£49,000	
Cr	Cash		£48,020	Cr	Cash		£48,020
Cr	Discount revenue		£980	Cr	Discount revenue		£980

5 September 2013

Dr	Cash	£54,000		Dr	Cash	£54,000	
Cr	Sales revenue		£54,000	Cr	Sales revenue		£54,000
Dr	Cost of goods sold	£37,000					
Cr	Inventory		£37,000				

▶

Perpetual inventory system (continued)   **Periodic inventory system (continued)**

15 September 2013

Dr	Accounts receivable	£7,000			Dr	Accounts receivable	£7,000	
Cr	Inventory		£7,000		Cr	Purchase returns		£7,000

10 June 2014

Dr	Cash	£40,000			Dr	Cash	£40,000	
Cr	Sales revenue		£40,000		Cr	Sales revenue		£40,000

Dr	Cost of goods sold	£28,000	
Cr	Inventory		£28,000

Here we can see that different accounts are used. Under the perpetual system, when purchases are made the asset account of inventory is updated immediately. By contrast, under the periodic system, when purchases are made the purchases go to an expense account called 'purchases'. Under the perpetual system, each time a sale is made the inventory account is updated and a related cost of goods sold is recorded. Under the periodic system, cost of goods sold is determined at the end of the accounting period rather than throughout the period.

(b) To determine cost of goods sold under the periodic system, we would provide the following journal entry at the end of the period:

Dr	Opening inventory (cost of goods sold)	£60,000	
Cr	Inventory (statement of financial position)		£60,000

Dr	Inventory (statement of financial position)	£7,000	
Cr	Closing inventory (cost of goods sold)		£7,000

(closing inventory is made up of 10 units at £700 each)

Cost of goods sold under the periodic system would therefore equal:

	£
Opening inventory	60,000
Purchases	49,000
	109,000
Purchase returns	(7,000)
	102,000
Closing inventory	7,000
Cost of goods sold	95,000

As we can see, in this example the amount determined for cost of goods sold under the periodic system is the same as the total amounts debited to 'cost of goods sold' under the perpetual system (£30,000 + £37,000 + £28,000).

Before concluding our discussion of the differences between the periodic and perpetual inventory systems we should perhaps briefly consider the role of an end-of-period stocktake using the perpetual and periodic methods of accounting for inventory. Under the *perpetual system,* we constantly update our records of inventory as sales, purchases and returns are made. The role of the stocktake in this case would be to determine whether what is on hand actually corresponds with what our accounting records indicate. A difference might indicate, for example, that a theft has occurred. The stocktake might also reveal obsolete or damaged inventory. Where a *periodic system* is utilised, the stocktake is needed to tell us how much inventory is on hand as under this system we do not update inventory each time an inventory movement occurs.

7.5 Reversal of previous inventory write-downs

As previously indicated in this chapter, if in a subsequent period information becomes available that indicates that inventory previously written down to net realisable amount has subsequently increased in value, it is permissible to reverse the previous write-down. However, in keeping with the rule that inventory is to be valued at the lower of cost and net realisable value, any subsequent increase in value is to be restricted to the

amount that was previously written down, that is, the value of the inventory must not be increased above its original cost.

Where there is a reversal of a previous inventory write-down, the entry would involve a debit to the inventory account and a credit to an income account labelled 'Reversal of previous inventory write-down' or its equivalent.

For the purposes of illustration, consider Worked Example 7.7.

Worked Example 7.7   Reversal of a previous inventory write-down

Froome Ltd has 500,000 pairs of swimming goggles in inventory. The goggles cost Froome £2 each. At 30 June 2013, and because of a pollution scare that has worried swimmers, the net realisable value of the goggles was reassessed at £1.40 each. As a result, at 30 June 2013 the following entry would be required:

Dr	Inventory write-down expense	£300,000
Cr	Inventory		£300,000

Required

If in August of the next financial year the pollution problems have been resolved and it is determined that the net realisable value has risen to £2.90, what accounting entry would be required (remember, the write-back would be restricted to the amount of the original write-down as inventory is not permitted to be valued in excess of cost)?

Solution

Dr	Inventory	£300,000
Cr	Reversal of previous inventory write-down (income)		£300,000

7.6   Disclosure requirements

Where the information is material, paragraph 36 of IAS 2 requires that the financial statements disclose the following information:

(a) *the accounting policies adopted for measuring inventories, including the cost formulas used;*
(b) *the total carrying amount of inventories and the carrying amount in classifications appropriate to the entity;*
(c) *the carrying amount of inventories carried at fair value less costs to sell;*
(d) *the amount of inventories recognised as an expense during the period;*
(e) *the amount of any write-down of inventories recognised as an expense in the period;*
(f) *the amount of any reversal of any write-down that is recognised as a reduction in the amount of inventories recognised as an expense in the period;*
(g) *the circumstances or events that led to the reversal of write-downs of inventories; and*
(h) *the carrying amount of inventories pledged as securities for liabilities.*

See Exhibit 7.1 for an example of an accounting policy note, in this case provided by Volkswagon in its 2010 annual report.

Exhibit 7.1   Accounting policy note from the 2010 annual report of Volkswagen

ACCOUNTING POLICIES

INVENTORIES

Raw materials, consumables and supplies, merchandise, work-in-progress and self-produced finished goods reported in inventories are carried at the lower of cost of net realizable value. Cost is determined on the basis of the direct and indirect costs that are directly attributable. Borrowing costs are not capitalized. The measurement of same or similar inventories is based on the weighted average cost method.

Volkswagen is involved in the manufacture and sale of vehicles and its accounting policy for inventories is specific to this type of business environment.

SUMMARY

The chapter addressed the topic of accounting for inventory. Inventory is defined as assets held for sale in the ordinary course of business, in the process of production for sale or to be used in the production of goods; and other property or services for sale, including consumable stores and supplies.

Pursuant to IAS 2, inventory is to be measured at the lower of cost and net realisable value on an item-by-item basis. Cost itself is defined as the aggregate of the cost of purchase, the cost of conversion and other costs incurred in the normal course of operations in bringing the inventories to their present location and condition. Net realisable value is the estimated proceeds of sale less, where applicable, all further costs to the stage of completion and less all costs to be incurred in marketing, selling and distribution to customers.

For the purposes of financial statement presentation, it is a requirement of the accounting standard that inventory should include an allocation of fixed manufacturing costs—that is, absorption costing and not direct costing should be applied.

In accounting for the flow of inventory (which is necessary to determine the value of inventory and the cost of goods sold for the period), it is typically necessary to make some cost-flow assumptions, as it is not possible or practical to trace the flow of particular items of inventory through the system. The cost-flow method adopted by management must be the most practical accounting reflection of the reality of the inventory flow. Under IAS 2, costs may be assigned to inventory using the specific-identification method, the weighted-average method or the first-in, first-out method. Use of the last-in, first-out method is specifically prohibited by IAS 2. Organisations also need to choose between using the perpetual or periodic system to determine the number of units of inventory on hand.

KEY TERMS

END-OF-CHAPTER EXERCISE

Toulon Ltd started business at the commencement of the current financial year. The company manufactures rugby balls. The following information is available in relation to its production activities: **LO 7.1**

Normal operating capacity (units)	200,000
Goods produced (units)	200,000
Opening finished goods inventory (units)	Nil
Closing finished goods inventory (units)	50,000

Opening value of raw materials inventory		Nil
Closing value of raw materials inventory		€200,000
Factory wages		€1,550,000
Administration salaries		€100,000
Salespersons' salaries (€/£1 per unit sold)		€150,000
Factory rent		€150,000
Depreciation of factory equipment		€100,000
Factory supervisor's salary		€50,000
Rental of office equipment		€50,000
Raw materials purchased		€600,000
Sales price per unit		€13.00 per unit
Delivery and advertising costs per unit sold		€2.00

At the end of the year there are no partly finished goods.

REQUIRED

Determine the value at which inventory should be disclosed in the year-end statement of financial position.

SOLUTION TO END-OF-CHAPTER EXERCISE

As indicated earlier in this chapter, pursuant to IAS 2, absorption costing is required when valuing inventory for general-purpose financial reporting. Under absorption costing, any fixed production costs, such as the supervisor's salary and factory rent, are assigned to inventory on the basis of normal operating capacity—that is, they are treated as product costs. Other fixed costs, such as those relating to administration, are treated as period costs, not product costs, and are expensed in the period incurred.

Costs of inventory

Variable costs			
Factory wages		€1,550,000	
Raw material purchased	€600,000		
less Closing inventory	€200,000	€400,000	
Total variable costs		€1,950,000	
divided by Units produced		200,000	
Per unit variable costs			€9.75
Fixed costs			
Factory rent	€150,000		
Factory supervisor's salary	€50,000		
Factory depreciation	€100,000		
Total fixed costs		€300,000	
divided by Normal operating capacity		200,000	
Per unit fixed costs			€1.50
Total cost per unit			€11.25
Net realisable value per unit			
Sales price per unit			€13.00
less Delivery and selling costs		€2.00	
less Salespersons' salary per unit		€1.00	€3.00
			€10.00

Closing value of inventory

As inventory is to be valued at the lower of cost and net realisable value, the value of inventory on hand at reporting date would be:

$$50,000 \times €10.00 = €500,000$$

REVIEW QUESTIONS

1 Outline arguments for and against the use of the lower of cost and net realisable value rule. **LO** 7.2
2 Is it permissible to revalue inventory to its fair value? Do you think the requirements in relation to inventory valuation are overly conservative? **LO** 7.1
3 What should be included in the 'cost' of inventories? **LO** 7.1
4 What does net realisable value mean as it pertains to inventory? **LO** 7.2
5 What is an inventory cost-flow assumption and why is one necessary? **LO** 7.3
6 What inventory cost-flow assumptions are permitted under IAS 2? **LO** 7.4
7 Distinguish between the periodic and perpetual inventory methods. **LO** 7.1
8 Explain the difference between absorption and direct costing. **LO** 7.1
9 Assuming that costs of inventory are rising across time, you are required to determine which of either the first-in first-out or the weighted-average cost approach will generate the highest cost of goods sold. **LO** 7.4
10 What is a 'standard cost'? According to IAS 2, when may standard costs be used to assign costs to inventory? **LO** 7.1
11 Explain how it is possible for profits to be manipulated through the use of the specific-identification and LIFO inventory cost-flow assumptions. **LO** 7.3
12 IAS 2 prohibits the use of the LIFO method. What is the argument against the use of LIFO? **LO** 7.4
13 Moondoggie Ltd holds four lines of inventory. The total production costs of each item are shown below. Apart from the production costs, estimates of future packaging costs and transportation costs are provided. It is considered that the items are not saleable unless they are packaged and transported to market. **LO** 7.2

Product line	Production costs (€)	Transport costs (€)	Packaging costs (€)	Sales proceeds (€)
Wetsuits	5,000	1,000	1,000	9,000
Blocks of wax	3,000	1,000	2,000	5,000
Flippers	10,000	2,000	1,500	13,000
Board shorts	20,000	2,000	2,500	25,000

REQUIRED

Determine the closing value of inventory for Moondoggie Ltd.

14 Shelley Ltd starts selling bowling balls in 2013. Although each ball looks the same, the unit cost of manufacture (which is done in batches) has fluctuated during the period. Shelley Ltd adopts a FIFO cost-flow assumption and employs a perpetual inventory system. Details of costs are as follows: **LO** 7.4

Date completed	Number completed	Unit costs (€)
2 July 2013	200	75
1 August 2013	300	80
24 December 2013	150	88
15 March 2014	200	90
15 June 2014	200	88
	1,050	

Details of sales are as follows:

Date of sale	Number sold	Unit price (€)
5 July 2013	100	100
10 August 2013	230	110
30 December 2013	100	105
16 March 2014	300	120
25 June 2014	100	130
	830	

REQUIRED

What is the cost of sales for the year ended 30 June 2014 and what is the value of inventory as at 30 June 2014?

CHALLENGING QUESTIONS

15 Explain in which circumstances it would be appropriate to use the following cost-flow assumptions: **LO** 7.3
   (a) specific-identification assumption
   (b) weighted-average cost assumption
   (c) first-in, first-out assumption

16 Lynch Ltd has some inventory of wetsuits on hand at 30 June 2014. Costs for making the wetsuits comprise material worth €10,000, labour of €8,000 and factory overheads applied on the basis of normal operating capacity amounting to €4,000.

   Lynch Ltd considers that only one customer, Wayne Ltd, will buy the wetsuits, which are all bright pink with fluorescent green inserts. Wayne Ltd is prepared to buy them all in July 2014 for a total amount of €20,000, provided Lynch Ltd sews a smiley face on the right arm of each suit at a total cost to Lynch Ltd of €2,000. Lynch Ltd will also be required to pay for the freight charges to get the inventory to Wayne Ltd. This freight cost will be €1000.   **LO** 7.2

REQUIRED

As at 30 June 2014, at what amount should inventory be recorded in the books of Lynch Ltd?

17 Horan Ltd has the following inventory transactions for the year ending 30 June 2014. All inventory items are identical.

Opening inventory at 1 July 2013	1,000 units @ £10
Purchases on 1 September 2013	3,000 units @ £12
Purchases on 12 February 2014	4,000 units @ £14
Purchases on 21 June 2014	2,000 units @ £15

Horan Ltd sells 8,000 units during the year, and has 2,000 units on hand at year end. The company uses the periodic system to record inventory. At year end, the net realisable value of each inventory item is £20 per unit.   **LO** 7.4

REQUIRED

Compute the cost of sales and ending inventory amounts under the following cost-flow methods:
   (a) first-in, first-out (FIFO) method
   (b) weighted-average cost method
   (c) last-in, first-out (LIFO) method

18 Coolum Pty Ltd manufactures sunglasses that are sold to department stores, pharmacies, optical dispensers and optometrists. During the current year Coolum Pty Ltd produced 60,000 pairs of sunglasses. Owing to increased competition and unseasonally wet weather affecting sales of sunglasses, the company operated at only 60 per cent of its

normal capacity. Other than costs associated with raw materials, variable costs are indicated by (V) and fixed costs are indicated by (F). **LO** 7.2

Opening finished goods inventory (units)	5,000
Opening finished goods inventory	€40,000
Closing finished goods inventory (units)	15,000
Opening value of raw materials inventory	€20,000
Closing value of raw materials inventory	€10,000
Raw materials purchased	€290,000
Factory wages (V)	€90,000
Factory supervisor's salary (F)	€35,000
Administration salaries (F)	€80,000
Cleaning of factory (V)	€5,000
Maintenance of factory equipment (V)	€25,000
Selling expenses (F)	€30,000
Depreciation of factory equipment (F)	€65,000
Rental of office equipment (F)	€15,000
Factory insurance (F)	€50,000
Freight outward (V) (€0.16 per unit sold)	€8,000
Sales price per unit	€12

Coolum Pty Ltd uses the first-in, first-out cost-flow method.

REQUIRED

(a) Prepare a statement showing the cost of goods manufactured.

(b) Prepare a statement of comprehensive income extract showing the cost of goods sold and identifying those costs that are recognised as expenses in the current period.

19 As at 30 June 2014, which is the end of the financial year, Rincon Limited has 100,000 hats in inventory, all of the same type and size. The hats cost Rincon Limited €4 each. At 30 June 2014, and because of a decrease in demand for hats, the sales price of the hats was assessed as being €2.50 each. There would be an average sales cost of €0.30 per hat. **LO** 7.2

Subsequently, in August 2014, and because of the drastic onset of global warming, there was an unexpected surge in the demand for hats such that each hat can be sold for €30. In August 2014 there were still 100,000 hats in inventory; however, it was expected that these would be sold within the following months.

REQUIRED

You are required to provide the accounting entry that would be made in August 2014 to measure inventory at the lower of cost and net realisable value and which takes into account the information about the surge in demand for hats.

20 Billybang Pty Ltd imports shorts and sells them to department stores throughout Europe. At 1 July 2013 opening inventory comprised ten units at €22.00 each. Throughout the quarter ended 30 September 2013 the sales price of surf shorts was €30.00 and distribution costs were €0.50 per unit. Extracts from Billybang's inventory record reveal the following transactions: **LO** 7.4

Date	Purchases	Sales
31 July	20 units @ €20.00	
2 August		5 units
4 August		16 units
31 August	15 units @ €18.00	
3 September		12 units
10 September	10 units @ €21.00	
29 September		11 units

REQUIRED

(a) Calculate the cost of goods sold and ending inventory assuming that Billybang Pty Ltd uses the:
- periodic inventory system with the weighted-average cost-flow method;
- periodic inventory system with the FIFO cost-flow method;
- periodic inventory system with the LIFO cost-flow method;
- perpetual inventory system with the weighted-average cost-flow method;
- perpetual inventory system with the FIFO cost-flow method; and
- perpetual inventory system with the LIFO cost-flow method.

(b) Explain why some entities might prefer a perpetual inventory system to a periodic inventory system.

(c) In the US the LIFO cost-flow method has been permitted for a long time and some companies carry inventory at purchase costs that existed decades ago. Why do you think that such companies are typically reluctant to allow inventory to fall to levels that would mean using the longstanding LIFO layers?

21 Strapper Ltd sells one type of mountain bike. Its financial year ends on 30 June and it commenced the financial year with 50 bikes that cost £450 each. Strapper Ltd uses the FIFO method and it had the following transactions throughout the financial year: **LO 7.4**

(i) On 30 July it acquired 60 bikes at £400 each.

(ii) On 4 August it paid for the purchase on 30 July and received a discount of 2 per cent for early payment.

(iii) On 28 August it sold 40 bikes for £700 each; the sales were made for cash.

(iv) On 23 September it acquired 30 bikes for £420 each, less a trade discount of 4 per cent.

(v) On 1 November it paid for the purchases made on 23 September. Because of the late payment Strapper Ltd was charged a penalty of 1 per cent.

(vi) On 24 December Strapper Ltd sold 15 bikes for £900 each.

(vii) On 1 March Strapper Ltd purchased another 40 bikes for £500 each. No trade discount was received.

(viii) On 5 March the amount due for the 1 March purchase was paid and a 2 per cent discount was received for early payment.

(ix) On 30 June it was assessed that there was a downturn in the demand for bikes and as a result the net realisable value of the bikes was assessed as being £350 each.

REQUIRED

(a) Using the periodic system of accounting provide the journal entries for the above transactions and determine the balance of cost of goods sold for the year and the value of closing inventory.

(b) Using the perpetual system of accounting provide the journal entries for the above transactions and determine the balance of cost of goods sold for the year and the value of closing inventory.

REFERENCES

COMMITTEE OF SPONSORING ORGANISATIONS OF THE TREADWAY COMMISSION, *Fraudulent Financial Reporting: 1987–1997—An Analysis of U.S. Public Companies*, 1999, http://www.coso.org/FFR-Analysis_Summary.htm

CUSHING, B.J. & LeCLEARE, M.J., 'Evidence on the Determinants of Inventory Accounting Policy Choice', *Accounting Review*, April 1992, pp. 355–67.

HUNT, H.G., 'Potential Determinants of Corporate Inventory Accounting Decisions', *Journal of Accounting Research*, Autumn 1985, pp. 448–67.

IKEA, *IKEA Annual Report 2010*, http://www.ikea.com/ms/cs_CZ/pdf/Welcome_inside_2010_final.pdf

WELLS, J.T., 'Ghost Goods: How to Spot Phantom Inventory', *Journal of Accountancy,* June 2001, http://www.journalofaccountancy.com/Issues/2001/Jun/GhostGoodsHowToSpotPhantomInventory.htm

Chapter 8

Accounting for Intangibles

Learning objectives

Upon completing this chapter readers should:

LO1 understand what types of asset can be considered intangible assets and understand the differences between intangible and tangible assets;

LO2 understand when expenditure on intangible assets should be recognised as an asset;

LO3 understand when expenditure on intangible assets must be expensed;

LO4 understand that intangible assets will need to either be systematically amortised or be the subject of impairment testing and that this choice will depend upon whether the asset is expected to have a limited useful life or an indefinite life;

LO5 understand how to account for research and development expenditure;

LO6 be able to describe some empirical research that has been undertaken on corporate accounting practices relating to research and development; and

LO7 be able to define goodwill and explain how it is calculated for accounting purposes.

8.1 Introduction to accounting for intangible assets

The major accounting standard dealing with intangible assets is IAS 38 *Intangible Assets*. It defines an intangible asset as 'an identifiable non-monetary asset without physical substance'. Common forms of intangible asset include patents, goodwill, mastheads, brand names, copyrights, research and development, and trademarks. From this definition we can see that the lack of physical substance does not preclude an item from being considered an asset. As paragraph 56 of the IASB Conceptual Framework states:

> Many assets, for example property, plant and equipment, have a physical form. However, physical form is not essential to the existence of an asset; hence patents and copyrights, for example, are assets if future economic benefits are expected to flow from them to the entity and if they are controlled by the entity.

According to paragraph 54 of IAS 1 *Presentation of Financial Statements*, intangible assets, as a category, must be separately disclosed in an entity's statement of financial position. For example, the 2010 statement of financial position of SAP Group shows that there was €2,376 million in intangible assets in 2010. Exhibit 8.1 provides the details about intangibles as shown in Note 16 to SAP Group's 2010 consolidated financial statements. But, as we will see in this chapter, many intangible assets will not be shown within the financial statements because of the restrictions placed on recognition within our accounting standards. Therefore, total intangible assets as reported by organisations will typically be considered to be understated relative to what the 'true' value of intangible assets might be.

Exhibit 8.1	Intangible asset note provided in the 2010 consolidated financial statements of SAP Group

NOTE 16. INTANGIBLE ASSETS

€millions	Goodwill	Software and database licences	Acquired technology/ IPRD	Customer relationship and other intangibles	Total
Purchase cost					
January 1, 2009	5,070	323	646	763	6,802
Foreign currency exchange differences	–23	1	–6	–4	–32
Additions from business combinations	41	0	29	3	73
Other additions	0	19	0	0	19
Retirements/disposals	0	–9	–6	–4	–19
December 31, 2009	**5,088**	**334**	**663**	**758**	**6,843**
Foreign currency exchange differences	38	3	7	–5	43
Additions from business combinations	3,401	11	569	1,155	5,136
Other additions	0	79	0	0	79
Retirements/Disposals	0	–10	1	–5	–14
December 31, 2010	**8,527**	**417**	**1,240**	**1,903**	**12,087**
Accumulated amortization					
January 1, 2009	95	191	250	151	687
Foreign currency exchange differences	–1	1	–3	–2	–5
Additions depreciation	0	36	135	121	292
Impairments	0	0	0	0	0
Retirements/disposals	0	–9	–6	–4	–19
December 31, 2009	**94**	**219**	**376**	**266**	**955**
Foreign currency exchange differences	2	4	7	5	18
Additions depreciation	0	36	143	142	321
Impairments	0	0	0	0	0
Retirements/disposals	0	–10	1	–5	–14
December 31, 2010	**96**	**249**	**527**	**408**	**1,280**
Carrying value December 31, 2009	**4,994**	**115**	**287**	**492**	**5,888**
Carrying value December 31, 2010	**8,431**	**168**	**713**	**1,495**	**10,807**

The additions to goodwill result from our acquisitions (€3,405 million) and adjustments to goodwill of previous acquisitions (€4 million) due to changes of expected contingent consideration payments that had previously been accounted for under IFRS 3 (2004).

Software and database licences consist primarily of technology for internal use, whereas acquired technology consists primarily of purchased software to be incorporated into our product offerings and in-process research and development. The additions to software and database licences in 2010 and 2009 were individually acquired from third parties and include cross-licence agreements and patents, whereas the additions to acquired technology and other intangibles primarily result from our business combinations discussed in Note (4).

Other intangibles consist primarily of acquired trademark licences and customer contracts.

Intangible assets can have significant value. An organisation known as Interbrand provides details of the value of the world's top 100 brand names on its website (www.interbrand.com). The top ten values attributed to various global brand names in 2010 were the following: Coca-Cola, US$70.45 billion; IBM, US$64.73 billion; Microsoft, US$60.90 billion; Google, US$43.56 billion; General Electric, US$42.81 billion; McDonald's, US$33.58 billion; Intel, US$32.02 billion; Nokia, US$29.50 billion; Disney, US$28.37 billion; and HP US$26.87 billion. What is interesting is that the top three brands remained constant from 2008 to 2010, as did the top ten brands other than HP, which came in at number ten thereby replacing Toyota in the top ten (Toyota was number 11 in 2010). Google's brand name increased in value in the two years to 2010 by a greater amount than the other organisations in the top ten. What we will also learn in this chapter is that, while these brand names are obviously considered to have very high values, in situations where these names have been developed by the organisation itself (and not acquired), then they cannot be recognised within the organisation's financial statements. IASB 38 specifically excludes such recognition.

> **identifiable intangible assets**
> Include patents, trademarks, brand names and copyrights. Can be considered identifiable as a specific value can be placed on each asset, and they can be separately identified and sold.

Intangible assets are frequently classified as either identifiable or unidentifiable. **Identifiable intangible assets** include patents, trademarks, licences, research and development, brand names (as discussed above), mastheads and copyrights. In a sense, such intangibles can be considered identifiable because a specific value can be placed on each individual asset, and they can be separately identified and sold.

Unidentifiable intangible assets, on the other hand, would be those intangible assets that cannot be separately sold. For example, an organisation might be particularly successful because of factors such as loyal customers, established reputation and good employees. Although they are valuable to the business, they cannot be individually measured with acceptable levels of reliability. Rather, we may treat them as a composite asset entitled **goodwill**. As we will see later in this chapter, the unidentifiable intangible asset goodwill is permitted to be recognised for accounting purposes only when it has been externally acquired, not when it has been internally generated. As we will also see, this prohibition on recognising internally generated goodwill has proved very unpopular from the perspective of many reporting entities.

> **unidentifiable intangible assets**
> Intangible assets that cannot be separately sold, such as loyal customers and established reputation. Cannot be individually measured with acceptable levels of reliability.

For the purposes of IAS 38, three conditions need to be established before we can contemplate recognising an item as an intangible asset. The item must be:

- non-monetary;
- identifiable; and
- lack physical substance.

> **goodwill**
> Unidentifiable intangible assets representing the future economic benefits associated with an existing customer base, efficient management, reliable suppliers and the like.

IAS 38 defines monetary assets as 'money held and assets to be received in fixed or determinable amounts of money'. In requiring that an item be 'identifiable', IAS 38 distinguishes other intangible assets from goodwill. Goodwill is an unidentifiable asset that IAS 38 does not permit to be recognised (bear in mind, however, that IFRS 3 *Business Combinations* does allow goodwill to be recognised subject to certain conditions). In relation to the requirement that an item be identifiable before it is recognised as an intangible asset, paragraph 12 of IAS 38 states:

An asset meets the identifiability criterion in the definition of an intangible asset when it:

(a) *is separable, that is, is capable of being separated or divided from the entity and sold, transferred, licensed, rented or exchanged, either individually or together with a related contract, asset or liability; or*

(b) *arises from contractual or other legal rights, regardless of whether those rights are transferable or separable from the entity or from other rights and obligations.*

In recent times it would seem that the value of more and more companies is being based increasingly on their intangible assets, rather than on their tangible assets. Hence issues associated with the valuation of intangible assets are tending to become more important across time. As Moodie (2000, p. 42) states:

What makes the current market so radically different is that in the old mining boom days, investors were at least placing bets on a tangible asset—an unexplored ore body. But the new breed of cyber-investors are placing their bets fairly and squarely on an intangible asset—a company's intellectual capital.

With greater value being attributed to intangible assets, there is a consequent need for sound financial information about such assets. As we have indicated, the accounting requirements in place from 2005 require expenditure on many intangible assets to be expensed, with the result that many valuable intangible assets will not appear in statements of financial position. This means that financial statement readers will not be able to know about certain intangible assets—for example, about the value of copyrights or brand names—because the related expenditure to develop the 'assets' internally has to be expensed (written off) as incurred. This is despite the fact that such 'assets' will in many cases be expected to generate future economic benefits. It is questionable whether an accounting rule that requires all internally generated intangibles (with the exception of development expenditure) to be written off, even when there is an expectation that future economic benefits will be derived, will result in more relevant information for financial statement users.

As with the majority of other assets, intangible assets, whether identifiable or unidentifiable, typically have a limited life. Those that are not considered to have a limited life are deemed to have an indefinite life. Pursuant to IAS 38, the assessment of whether an intangible asset has a limited life or an indefinite life affects in turn how we amortise the asset in subsequent years (as we explain in what follows).

8.2 Which intangible assets can be recognised and included in the statement of financial position?

Pursuant to IAS 38 *Intangible Assets*, many internally generated intangible assets are specifically precluded from being carried forward as assets regardless of the future economic benefits that might be expected to be generated. For example, paragraph 54 of IAS 38 states that no intangible asset arising from research (or from the research phase of an internal project) shall be recognised. Expenditure on research (or on the research phase of an internal project) shall be recognised as an expense when it is incurred. Further, paragraph 63 states:

> Internally generated brands, mastheads, publishing titles, customer lists and items similar in substance shall not be recognised as intangible assets.

For other intangible assets, they may be recognised only where there is an associated 'cost'. This cost is to include purchase price (including taxes, legal fees and deducting discounts provided) and the costs associated with getting the asset ready for its use (which could include employee costs associated with work undertaken to get the asset ready for use). Initial recognition of an intangible asset at an amount other than cost is not permitted. In addition, unrecognised intangibles cannot subsequently be recognised through revaluation.

Pursuant to IAS 38, intangible assets (other than goodwill, which is also addressed in IFRS 3) are required to be separable (which, as we saw earlier, is one of the attributes associated with an item being deemed to be 'identifiable') if they are to be recognised as assets for statement of financial position purposes. 'Separable' means that the organisation could rent, sell, exchange or distribute the specific future economic benefits attributable to the asset without also disposing of future economic benefits that flow from other assets used in the same revenue-earning activity. The implication of this is that intangible assets such as the formation or start-up costs of an organisation can no longer be shown as an asset.

Consistent with the recognition of assets generally, an intangible asset must be recognised when it is probable that the future economic benefits that are attributable to the asset will flow to the entity, and the cost of the asset can be measured reliably. There is also an imperative that the entity have control over the future economic benefits that are expected to flow from the asset.

8.3 What is the initial basis of measurement of intangible assets?

Expenditure on many internally generated intangibles does not qualify for deferral (that is, for inclusion as an asset) and therefore must be treated as an expense. If an intangible asset is acquired separately, and not as part of a business acquisition (and in a business combination, many assets would be acquired), the costs of the intangible asset are to include the costs associated with acquiring the asset and preparing the asset for its intended use. As paragraph 27 of IAS 38 states:

> The cost of a separately acquired intangible asset comprises:
>
> (a) its purchase price, including import duties and non-refundable purchase taxes, after deducting trade discounts and rebates; and
> (b) any directly attributable cost of preparing the asset for its intended use.

Once an intangible asset has been acquired and made ready for use, any subsequent expenditure is to be recognised as an expense unless both the following conditions are met:

1. It is probable that the expenditure will increase the future economic benefits embodied in the asset in excess of the standard of performance assessed immediately before the expenditure was made.
2. The expenditure can be measured and attributed reliably to the asset.

As indicated above, intangible assets can also be acquired as part of a business combination. IFRS 3 *Business Combinations* defines a business combination as follows:

> *A transaction or other event in which an acquirer obtains control of one or more businesses. Transactions sometimes referred to as 'true mergers' or 'mergers of equals' are also business combinations as that term is used in this Standard.*

For example, one company may acquire all the shares of another company and then consolidate all the assets and liabilities of the acquired company with those assets and liabilities that it held prior to the acquisition. Paragraph 33 of IAS 38 states that where intangible assets are acquired as part of a business combination, rather than as a separate acquisition of an asset, the various assets—including identifiable intangible assets—will initially be recognised at their 'fair value'. This can be contrasted with individual acquisitions of intangible assets, where they are recognised at 'cost'. Paragraph 33 of IAS 38 states:

> *In accordance with IFRS 3* Business Combinations, *if an intangible asset is acquired in a business combination, the cost of that intangible asset is its fair value at the acquisition date. The fair value of an intangible asset reflects market expectations about the probability that the future economic benefits embodied in the asset will flow to the entity. In other words, the effect of probability is reflected in the fair value measurement of the intangible asset. Therefore, the probability recognition criterion in paragraph 21(a) is always considered to be satisfied for intangible assets acquired in business combinations.*

The above requirement is interesting, particularly the statement that 'the probability criterion is always considered to be satisfied for intangible assets acquired in a business combination'. This seems to be a simplistic assumption and not in accord with the asset recognition criteria in the IASB Conceptual Framework, which require consideration to be given to the probability of future economic benefits being generated.

This apparent inconsistency is to be addressed in future work by the IASB (paragraph 18 of 'Basis for Conclusions to IAS 38'). For our purposes, however, we need to appreciate that different recognition criteria apply to intangible assets, depending upon whether an intangible asset is acquired individually, or as part of a business combination. Again, if an intangible asset is acquired as part of a business combination it is to be recognised at its fair value even if internally generated by the other company. However, if it is acquired separately it is to be recognised at 'cost'.

For example, if a publisher has developed a successful list of publishing titles internally they are not to recognise the list as an asset, but if their organisation is acquired, the list of titles may in fact be recognised by the acquiring party (IAS 38, paragraph 34).

So, although paragraph 63 of IAS 38 stipulates that certain intangible assets may not be recognised if they have been internally developed, if an entity is acquired by another entity its (unrecognised) assets may be recognised by the acquirer. On why internally developed intangible assets cannot be recognised within the original entity, paragraph 64 of IAS 38 states:

> *Expenditure on internally generated brands, mastheads, publishing titles, customer lists and items similar in substance cannot be distinguished from the cost of developing the business as a whole. Therefore, such items are not recognised as intangible assets.*

We are left to wonder how the case is conceptually different in a business combination. How are we able to distinguish various intangible assets from goodwill when we acquire a business when we are assumed to be unable to do so when developing such assets internally? Certainly IAS 38 does appear to be vulnerable in a number of respects to criticism on logical grounds. Moreover, some of its requirements seem to be inconsistent with others within the standard.

IAS 38 also requires that, when some expenditure related to an intangible asset has been recognised as an expense in a previous financial period, the subsequent recognition of this expenditure as part of the cost of an intangible asset is prohibited (IAS 38, paragraph 71).

Here again, we can question the logic that if expenditure incurred on an intangible asset is initially expensed, then it cannot be recognised at a subsequent date. This requirement is not consistent with the IAS Conceptual Framework, which prescribes that if information subsequently comes to light to suggest that future economic benefits that were previously in doubt are deemed to be probable, an asset should be reinstated. Worked Example 8.1 provides an example of when to carry forward expenditure on intangible assets.

Worked Example 8.1 Capitalising expenditure on intangible assets

During the financial year Point Leo Ltd made the following expenditures:
(a) Point Leo Ltd spent €250,000 promoting the recognition of its brand name;
(b) Point Leo Ltd acquired a patent (a right to produce a certain product) for a cost of €400,000; and
(c) Point Leo Ltd spent €90,000 acquiring a customer database but after further consideration is not sure that the list will provide very many new customers.

Required
In relation to the above expenditures, which items will be carried forward to future periods as intangible assets?

Solution
Point Leo Ltd is permitted to carry forward expenditure on intangible assets (that is, capitalise expenditure on intangible assets) only where such expenditure represents the acquisition of intangible assets, and where associated economic benefits are deemed to be 'probable'. Therefore, the only expenditure that would be carried forward as an intangible asset would relate to the patent—and only to the extent that the amount is considered to be recoverable from future operations. The expenditure on the brand name would be expensed as it related to an expenditure that is specifically precluded from asset recognition by virtue of paragraph 63 of IAS 38. The expenditure on the customer list would be expensed because the associated economic benefits would not be considered to be 'probable'.

8.4 General amortisation requirements for intangible assets

Intangible assets (other than goodwill) that are considered to have a limited usefYul life are required to be amortised over their useful lives (we will consider goodwill in more depth in due course). The useful life of an intangible asset is defined in paragraph 8 of IAS 38 as:

> the period of time over which the asset is expected to be used by the entity, or the number of production or similar units expected to be obtained from the asset by the entity.

Amortisation methods based on time would be applied to intangible assets whose lives are limited by time. For example, if an intangible asset is acquired that has a life of ten years (perhaps stipulated by a contract), the asset could be amortised over ten years on a straight-line basis. Alternatively, if an intangible asset's life is limited to the production of a certain number of units of product, amortisation on a production basis would be appropriate. For example, if an intangible asset is acquired that allows an expected production of 10,000 units and if 2,200 units are produced in the first year, 22 per cent of the asset would be amortised. Where the pattern of benefits is uncertain, the straight-line method is required to be used (IAS 38, paragraph 97). Consistent with the accounting treatment of a tangible asset's cost, paragraph 97 of IAS 38 states:

> The depreciable amount of an intangible asset with a finite useful life shall be allocated on a systematic basis over its useful life. Amortisation shall begin when the asset is available for use, that is, when it is in the location and condition necessary for it to be capable of operating in the manner intended by management. Amortisation shall cease at the earlier of the date that the asset is classified as held for sale (or included in a disposal group that is classified as held for sale) in accordance with IFRS 5 Non-current Assets Held for Sale and Discontinued Operations and the date that the asset is derecognised.

In determining the amortisation charge of an asset, we generally need to consider what the residual value of the asset is expected to be. The total sum of amortisation charges pertaining to an asset will equal the cost (or revalued amount where a revaluation is permitted) less the expected residual. Pursuant to IAS 38, the residual value of intangible assets with finite lives is generally considered to be zero unless:

- there is a commitment by a third party to purchase the asset at the end of its useful life; or
- there is an active market for the asset, and the residual amount can be determined by reference to that market, and it is probable that the market will still exist at the end of the useful life of the asset.

In many cases these conditions will not be met, with the result that no residual value will be recognised.

IAS 38 requires the useful life residual value and the amortisation method and period to be reviewed annually. In some circumstances an intangible asset may be considered to have an indefinite useful life. The accounting standard defines an indefinite useful life as occurring where '[t]here is no foreseeable limit on the period over which the asset is expected to generate cash flows'. Where an asset is considered to have an indefinite life there is no requirement to amortise the asset (IAS 38, paragraph 107).

An indefinite life does not mean the same thing as an infinite life—an infinite life would imply that the asset was expected to last forever. As paragraph 91 states:

> The term 'indefinite' does not mean 'infinite'. The useful life of an intangible asset reflects only that level of future maintenance expenditure required to maintain the asset at its standard of performance assessed at the time of estimating the asset's useful life, and the entity's ability and intention to reach such a level. A conclusion that the useful life of an intangible asset is indefinite should not depend on planned future expenditure in excess of that required to maintain the asset at that standard of performance.

Although there is no requirement to amortise intangible assets that are considered to have an indefinite life, such assets are required to be subject to impairment testing at the end of each reporting period. If there is deemed to be an impairment in the value of the asset (its recoverable amount is less than its carrying amount), this amount of impairment is shown as an expense. IAS 38 requires the assumption that the asset has an indefinite life to be reviewed annually. Further, the entity has to disclose the reasons supporting its view that the asset has an indefinite life.

Amortisation charges must be expensed unless another standard requires the amount to be included in the carrying amount of another asset. For example, and as paragraph 99 of IAS 38 explains, the cost of amortisation of an intangible asset might be included in the cost of inventory and therefore not be recognised as an expense until the item is ultimately sold (in which case the expense would be included within the cost of goods sold). Worked Example 8.2 illustrates how to arrive at the amortisation expense for intangible assets.

Worked Example 8.2   Determining amortisation expense

During the year ending 30 June 2014, Shoreham Ltd acquired the following intangible assets:

(a) A patent at a cost of £500,000. This patent allows the production of 200,000 units. During the year ended 30 June 2014, Shoreham Ltd produced 40,000 units.

(b) The right to use the trade name 'Coca Cooler' in the local district for a cost of £700,000. Coca Cooler is a highly recognised brand of ice-cream that has been popular for more than 50 years and is expected to be popular indefinitely. As at 30 June 2014, it is considered that Shoreham Ltd would easily be able to obtain £700,000 if it wanted to dispose of the trade name.

Required

Determine the amortisation expense for Shoreham Ltd for the year ended 30 June 2014.

Solution

The patent would be amortised on the basis of the amount of production as it appears that production units rather than time is the factor that determines the useful life of the asset. Therefore, amortisation for the patent would be 20 per cent (that is, 40 divided by 200) multiplied by £500,000, which equals £100,000.

The trade name is considered to have an indefinite useful life and would therefore be subject to annual impairment testing. As the value of the trade name has not been impaired, no impairment expense would be recognised.

Many in the corporate world disagree with the general requirement that most internally developed intangibles are not allowed to be recognised as assets in the statement of financial position. An extract from Richard Brass' news story on small businesses in the UK in Financial Accounting in the News 8.1 argues that the inability to include the value of internally generated intangible assets can cause problems in small companies in respect of business succession.

Financial Accounting in the News 8.1

WHITEHALL ATTACKS BARRIERS THAT BLOCK FIRMS SELLING UP

Richard Brass, *The Telegraph*
17 January 2005

People are the most difficult asset to value, writes Richard Brass

For many small business owners, it's the thought that gets them out of bed in the morning. Build your business up, get it rolling along nicely, then sell it for a tidy sum that will fund your retirement, with something left over for the grandchildren.

Today, it's an idea that should beat a pension hands-down. But every year it proves a mirage for up to 100,000 businesses that fail to find a buyer and are forced to close, leaving their owners without the nest egg they dreamed of.

The high level of closure of viable businesses due to the lack of a buyer has become a serious enough problem for the Department of Trade and Industry to try to dismantle the barriers to business transfers.

A review last November by the DTI's Small Business Service found a major barrier to transfer of businesses, particularly small ones, is valuing intangible assets.

Intangible assets are at the heart of a growing number of small businesses in an increasingly service-based economy but the lack of a common method of valuation has made buying a business a minefield. It makes the value of a business hard to nail down and often denies buyers access to funding from the banks, which will not lend against intangible property.

Source: The Telegraph © Telegraph Media Group Limited 2012

8.5 Revaluation of intangible assets

The requirements of IAS 38 state that intangibles may be revalued only if there is an 'active market'. Therefore, most intangible assets will not be able to be revalued as there is no active market for them given that most intangible assets are unique in nature. An active market is defined in the accounting standard as: 'A market exhibiting all of the following: the items traded are homogeneous; willing buyers and sellers can normally be found; and prices are publicly available.' Further, the fact that only assets that have been acquired at a cost can subsequently be revalued places a prohibition on the revaluation of many internally generated intangible assets. Where a revaluation occurs, it is to be to the fair value of the asset.

Because of the unique nature of many intangible assets, in most cases an 'active market' will not exist. As paragraph 78 of IAS 38 states:

> It is uncommon for an active market with the characteristics described in paragraph 8 to exist for an intangible asset, although this may happen. For example, in some jurisdictions, an active market may exist for freely transferable taxi licences, fishing licences or production quotas. However, an active market cannot exist for brands, newspaper mastheads, music and film publishing rights, patents or trademarks, because each such asset is unique. Also, although intangible assets are bought and sold, contracts are negotiated between individual buyers and sellers, and transactions are relatively infrequent. For these reasons, the price paid for one asset may not provide sufficient evidence of the fair value of another. Moreover, prices are often not available to the public.

The complexities of identifying what is an active market can be explained using football players. David Beckham, ex-England captain and currently a midfield player for LA Galaxy (a US soccer team), who previously played for Manchester United, Real Madrid and AC Milan, is probably one of Europe's most famous soccer players, not only for his abilities on the pitch but also for his business acumen off the pitch. He has consistently been one of the highest earning footballers in the world for the past decade. He is clearly an asset to any club not just because of his football skills but also because of his ability to generate funds for the club in terms of increased merchandising. However, placing a value on him each year would be very difficult. He may get injured, he is getting older and his value is arguably impacted on by his actions off the pitch. Though a market for footballers does exist, contracts are negotiated between buyers and sellers, each footballer is different and transactions are too relatively infrequent to enable comparisons to be made. For this reason, the price paid for one player will not provide sufficient evidence of the fair value of another player (as stipulated under paragraph 78 of IAS 38). Information of the value-generating abilities of footballers is provided in Financial Accounting in the News 8.2. Though this information is not from their respective clubs' perspectives, it does provide evidence of the value that each player has created for their own personal brand, their name.

Financial Accounting in the News 8.2

BARCELONA STAR MESSI BEATS BECKHAM AND RONALDO TO TOP THE FOOTBALL RICH LIST

Mail Online, 20 March 2012

Lionel Messi can add the accolade of the world's best-paid footballer to his huge haul of awards and medals. The three-time World Player of the Year topped the latest rich list after pocketing £27.4 million from wages, bonuses, sponsorships and endorsements.

The Barcelona star topped his £13m annual salary from the Spanish giants with sponsorship deals from the likes of Adidas and Pepsi. Messi pipped former England captain David Beckham to the top spot in the survey by *France Football* magazine.

Becks, 36, collected £26m and maintained his high profile despite plying his trade in America with LA Galaxy. Real Madrid star Cristiano Ronaldo had to settle for third and £24m despite leading the scoring charts in La Liga with 32 goals in 26 games this season.

Manchester United striker Wayne Rooney was the Premier League's top earner with £17m.

Source: © Associated Newspapers Ltd

Where there is an active market (for example, for milk quotas) the accounting standard requires revaluations to be done regularly so that the recorded value does not differ materially from fair value at reporting date. Subsequent to revaluation, any amortisation charges are to be based on the revalued amount of the intangible asset after taking into account the remaining useful life. According to paragraph 87 of IAS 38, where revaluations are undertaken they are to be done the same way as for property, plant and equipment, as explained in Chapter 6. That is, where there is a revaluation increment, the increase is credited to a revaluation surplus account (and the amount is shown as part of 'other comprehensive income'), except where it reverses a previous revaluation decrement, in which case the revaluation increment would be recognised as income and be included in profit or loss. Where there is a revaluation decrement, the decrement will be recognised as an expense (and included in profit or loss) unless there has been a previous revaluation increment, in which case the decrement would be debited to the revaluation surplus (with this also representing a deduction to 'other comprehensive income'). Where there has been a revaluation increment to an asset, and that asset is subsequently sold, the relevant balance in the revaluation surplus may be transferred to retained earnings. Alternatively, the balance in the revaluation surplus may be transferred to retained earnings throughout the life of the asset in proportion to the amortisation of the asset.

Worked Example 8.3 provides some insight into how to approach revaluing intangible assets.

8.6 Gain or loss on disposal of intangible assets

According to paragraph 113 of IAS 38, the gain or loss on the disposal of intangible assets will be determined as the difference between the net proceeds from the disposal, if any, and the carrying amount of the asset. The

Worked Example 8.3   Revaluation of intangible assets

Grove Ltd wants your advice on which of the following intangible assets may be revalued and, if a revaluation can be done, what the accounting entry would be.

(a) The company has developed its brand name to the point where it is a very valuable asset. It would appear that if it were to sell the brand name it would receive at least €2 million for it.

(b) The company acquired a patent two years previously for €1 million. The associated production process is quite specialised; however, there is one other manufacturer who has the necessary knowledge to utilise the patent. That other manufacturer would probably be prepared to pay at least €1.5 million for the patent.

(c) The company acquired a franchise—McDingbat Hamburgers—for €500,000. There is great demand for this franchise as evidenced by the 'wanted' advertisements placed in a number of franchise journals. The current market price for such a franchise is €670,000.

Solution

IAS 38 requires that intangible assets may be revalued but only where there is an active market. As the expenditure on the brand name would be expensed by virtue of paragraph 63 of IAS 38, and is not permitted to be recognised as an asset because it was internally generated, then no revaluation is permitted. In relation to the patent, there is an absence of an active market, therefore a revaluation is prohibited. In relation to the franchise, the intangible asset was acquired from an external party and there is an active market. Hence the only intangible asset that is permitted to be revalued would be the franchise. The accounting entry—ignoring taxation effects—would be:

Dr	McDingbat franchise	€170,000	
Cr	Revaluation surplus		€170,000

carrying amount of the asset is defined in the accounting standard as: 'The amount at which an asset is recognised in the statement of financial position after deducting any accumulated amortisation and accumulated impairment losses therefrom.' This determination of the gain or loss is consistent with how the gain or loss on the sale of tangible assets, such as property, plant and equipment, would be determined.

8.7   Required disclosures in relation to intangible assets

IAS 38 contains numerous disclosure requirements. Among them is a requirement for the financial statements to disclose the following for each class of intangible assets, distinguishing between internally generated intangible assets and other intangible assets (paragraph 118):

(a) whether the useful lives are indefinite or finite and, if finite, the useful lives or the amortisation rates used;

(b) the amortisation methods used for intangible assets with finite useful lives;

(c) the gross carrying amount and any accumulated amortisation (aggregated with accumulated impairment losses) at the beginning and end of the period;

(d) the line item(s) of the statement of comprehensive income in which any amortisation of intangible assets is included;

(e) a reconciliation of the carrying amount at the beginning and end of the period showing:

  (i) additions, indicating separately those from internal development, those acquired separately, and those acquired through business combinations;

  (ii) retirements and disposals;

  (iii) increases or decreases during the period resulting from revaluations and from impairment losses recognised or reversed directly in equity;

  (iv) impairment losses recognised in the statement of comprehensive income during the period;

  (v) impairment losses reversed in the statement of comprehensive income during the period;

  (vi) any amortisation recognised during the period;

  (vii) net exchange differences arising on the translation of the financial statements into the presentation currency, and on the translation of a foreign operation into the presentation currency of the entity; and

  (viii) other changes in the carrying amount during the period.

Examples of different classes of intangible asset include:

- brand names;
- mastheads and publishing titles;
- computer software;
- licences and franchises;
- copyrights, patents and other industrial property rights, services and operating rights;
- recipes, formulas, models, designs and prototypes; and
- intangible assets under development.

Paragraph 122 of IAS 38 also requires the financial statements to disclose:

(a) *if an intangible asset is assessed as having an indefinite useful life, the carrying amount of that asset and the reasons supporting the assessment of an indefinite useful life. In giving these reasons, the entity shall describe the factor(s) that played a significant role in determining that it has an indefinite useful life;*

(b) *a description, the carrying amount and remaining amortisation period of any individual intangible asset that is material to the financial statements of the entity as a whole;*

(c) *for intangible assets acquired by way of a government grant and initially recognised at fair value:*
   (i) *the fair value initially recognised for these assets;*
   (ii) *their carrying amount; and*
   (iii) *whether they are carried under the benchmark or the allowed alternative treatment for subsequent measurement;*

(d) *the existence and carrying amounts of intangible assets whose title is restricted and the carrying amounts of intangible assets pledged as security for liabilities; and*

(e) *the amount of contractual commitments for the acquisition of intangible assets.*

The standard also requires a number of disclosures in relation to research and development expenditure. Although we will consider research and development more fully in the next section of this chapter, it should be appreciated at this stage that the accounting standard contains disclosure requirements that are specific to research and development. For example, the financial statements are required to disclose the aggregate amount of research and development expenditure recognised as an expense during the period.

8.8 Research on the value relevance of accounting for intangible assets

The introduction of IAS 38 and its requirement to account for purchased goodwill at fair value, which is subsequently reviewed for impairment, provides fertile ground for determining if fair value accounting for intangibles materially improves the quality of information that is available to the users of financial statements. Lhaopadchan (2010) examined empirical evidence in this area and found that the weighting of evidence would suggest that managerial self-interest and earnings management concerns appear to motivate many goodwill impairment decisions. Lhaopadchan does not commit to a view on the value relevance of the fair value adjustments, concluding that investors/users have a long history of amending accounting figures for interpretation.

Having discussed intangible assets generally, we will now specifically examine two types of intangible asset. First, we will discuss research and development, and second, accounting for goodwill.

8.9 Research and development

research and development
Research is original investigation, while development is defined as activities undertaken with specific commercial objectives, and involves the translation of research knowledge into designs for new products.

IAS 38 *Intangible Assets* applies to intangible assets generally (as discussed in this chapter), although there are a number of paragraphs that relate specifically to **research and development**.

Research and development expenditures might account for a large proportion of the total expenditures of many entities. The accounting problem is one of determining whether the expenditure will, with reasonable probability, provide future economic benefits. At times there would be a high degree of uncertainty about whether expenditure incurred through research and development would ultimately generate future economic benefits.

Accounting standard IAS 38 makes a simplifying assumption—it requires the immediate expensing of all expenditure undertaken on the research component of research and development (IAS 38, paragraph 54). *Research* is required to be considered separately from development. Research generally precedes development and is defined in IAS 38 as:

original and planned investigation undertaken with the prospect of gaining new scientific or technical knowledge and understanding.

The expensing of research is justified by the fact that it is undertaken in the early stages of developing a new product or process and that the likelihood of it being possible to link the expenditure with future economic benefits is deemed to be uncertain (IAS 38, paragraph 55).

As we progress towards the subsequent stage (development), this uncertainty is deemed to reduce to levels that are acceptable for the purpose of asset recognition (at least in the minds of those responsible for developing the accounting standard). Development, which generally follows research, is defined in paragraph 8 of IAS 38 as:

the application of research findings or other knowledge to a plan or design for the production of new or substantially improved materials, devices, products, processes, systems or services prior to the commencement of commercial production or use.

Development typically involves the commercial application of 'knowledge' generated in earlier research phases. The accounting standard provides a number of examples of development activities. These include:

(a)   *the design, construction and testing of pre-production or pre-use prototypes and models;*
(b)   *the design of tools, jigs, moulds and dies involving new technology;*
(c)   *the design, construction and operation of a pilot plant that is not of a scale economically feasible for commercial production; and*
(d)   *the design, construction and testing of a chosen alternative for new or improved materials, devices, products, processes or systems.*

Under paragraph 57 of IAS 38 development expenditure may be deferred (capitalised) if the entity can demonstrate all of the following:

(a)   *the technical feasibility of completing the intangible asset so that it will be available for use or sale;*
(b)   *its intention to complete the intangible asset, and use or sell it;*
(c)   *its ability to use or sell the intangible asset;*
(d)   *how the intangible asset will generate probable future economic benefits. Among other things, the entity can demonstrate the existence of a market for the output of the intangible asset, or the intangible asset itself, or if it is to be used internally, the usefulness of the intangible asset; and*
(e)   *the availability of adequate technical, financial and other resources to complete the development and use or sell the intangible asset; and*
(f)   *the ability to measure reliably expenditure on the intangible asset during its development.*

The test for deferral is the same that applies to other intangible assets. Specifically, paragraph 21 of IAS 38 requires that:

An intangible asset should be recognised if, and only if:

(a)   *it is probable that the future economic benefits that are attributable to the asset will flow to the enterprise; and*
(b)   *the cost of the asset can be measured reliably.*

This is consistent with the asset recognition criteria provided within the IASB Conceptual Framework. Where the total of the deferred development costs carried forward exceeds the expected recoverable amount, the deferred costs must be written down to the recoverable amount. This would be referred to as an *impairment loss*. An example of the amortisation of research and development expenditure is given in Worked Example 8.4.

The requirement that all research must be written off as incurred does mean that much research activity that does in fact lead to subsequent economic benefits will nevertheless be required to be expensed. This has major implications for the reported profits of organisations that are heavily involved in research and development. While the requirement to write off all research as incurred does appear relatively 'harsh' (or conservative), this treatment is not as harsh as the treatment required within the US, where all research and development expenditure must be expensed as incurred (pursuant to SFAS 2, which was issued by the Financial Accounting Standards Board in 1974), regardless of whether or not it generates, or is expected to generate, economic benefits (an exception is software development and website costs; PWC 2010). This US position is extremely conservative.

| Worked Example 8.4 | Amortisation of research and development |

Portsea Ltd is developing a new product called a burble. The company spent £300,000 researching the demand for the burble. It then spent £250,000 working out whether the compounds out of which the burble is made will biodegrade in less than 50 years.

As a result of the knowledge gained in the preceding steps, the company designed machinery to produce the burbles. This design phase cost £600,000. It is expected that millions of burbles will be sold for at least £10 each. All the expenditure was incurred within the one reporting period.

Required

How much of the above expenditure would qualify to be shown as an intangible asset?

Solution

The accounting standard requires the expensing of all research expenditure. The first two expenditures above would be considered to constitute research and therefore £550,000 would be expensed as incurred. The funds spent designing the machinery would be considered to constitute development. Hence to the extent that the future economic benefits are measurable with reasonable accuracy and are probable, £600,000 would be recognised in the statement of financial position. This amount would be subject to future amortisation charges unless it could be justified that the life of the asset was indefinite.

8.9.1 Costs included as part of research and development

In relation to the costs that would be included in research and development, IAS 38 provides general guidance. It notes in paragraph 66 that the costs of internally generated intangible assets (a great deal of research and development would be internally generated) would comprise all directly attributable costs necessary to create, produce and prepare the asset to be capable of operating in the manner intended by management. Examples of directly attributable costs are:

(a) costs of materials and services used or consumed in generating the intangible asset;
(b) costs of employee benefits (as defined in IAS 19 Employee Benefits) arising from generation of the intangible asset;
(c) fees to register a legal right; and
(d) amortisation of patents and rights that are used to generate the intangible asset.

8.9.2 Amortisation of deferred development costs

IAS 38 provides a number of requirements for the amortisation of intangibles. These requirements therefore also apply to any development expenditure that has been capitalised and deferred to future periods. Paragraph 97 applies to intangible assets that are deemed to have a finite useful life. We discussed paragraph 97 earlier in this chapter.

Amortisation, which is to commence when the asset is available for use, might be based on output levels, or upon the expiration of time—whichever is the more appropriate. In relation to assessing the useful life of an intangible asset, paragraph 90 of IAS 38 provides some useful guidance:

Many factors need to be considered in determining the useful life of an intangible asset, including:

(a) the expected usage of the asset by the entity and whether the asset could be managed efficiently by another management team;
(b) typical product life cycles for the asset and public information on estimates of useful lives of similar types of assets that are used in a similar way;
(c) technical, technological, commercial, or other types of obsolescence;
(d) the stability of the industry in which the asset operates and changes in the market demand for the products or services output from the asset;
(e) expected actions by competitors or potential competitors;
(f) the level of maintenance expenditure required to obtain the expected future economic benefits from the asset and the entity's ability and intent to reach such a level;

(g) the period of control over the asset and legal or similar limits on the use of the asset, such as the expiry dates of related leases; and

(h) whether the useful life of the asset is dependent on the useful life of other assets of the entity.

Paragraph 104 of IAS 38 requires that the amortisation period and the amortisation method be reviewed yearly (at least) and changed to reflect the new circumstances. These changes should be accounted for as changes in accounting estimates in line with IAS 8. Where the intangible asset is not being amortised, because it is deemed to have an indefinite life, it should be reviewed regularly and impaired when the recoverable amount falls below its carrying amount. If the indefinite life classification no longer applies, then the accounting standard further requires that the assumption that an asset has an indefinite life be reviewed regularly. The accounting standard requires:

The change in the useful life assessment from indefinite to finite shall be accounted for as a change in an accounting estimate in accordance with IAS 8 Accounting Policies, Changes in Accounting Estimates and Errors.

An example of the amortisation of deferred development costs is given in Worked Example 8.5.

Worked Example 8.5   Amortisation of deferred development costs

Streaky Bay Ltd is involved in research and development. For the year ended 30 June 2014, research and development on Project X is incurred as follows:

Research	€185,000
Development	€300,000

Project X is expected to return profits of €250,000 over the next four years (with about €62,500 expected to be recognised each year), starting from 1 July 2014. Streaky Bay Ltd uses a discount rate of 8 per cent.

Required

(a) How much research and development should be expensed in the year to 30 June 2014?
(b) How much research and development should be amortised in the year to 30 June 2015?

Solution

(a) As noted above, IAS 38 requires that research be written off as incurred. The balance of the development expenditure should be carried forward only to the extent that it is expected to be recouped from future operations.

	€	€
Research		185,000
Development	300,000	
Amount expected to be recouped	(207,006)	92,994
Research and development expensed in 2014		277,994

As was detailed in Chapter 6, the recoverable amount of an asset is defined in paragraph 6 of IAS 36 as the 'higher of its fair value less costs to sell and its value-in-use'. The 'value-in-use' is the present value of the future cash flows that the entity expects to derive from the asset. The present value of future cash flows needs to be determined using an appropriate discount rate. In this example, the amount expected to be recouped from future operations—which is the recoverable amount—is the present value of future cash flows expected to be derived from the asset. Relying upon the present value table provided in Appendix B, the amount expected to be recouped is €62,500 × 3.3121 = €207,006.

(b) As development has a limited life when considered as an asset, it should be amortised over its useful life, with the amortisation commencing from when it is ready to use. So, in this case, the amortisation in 2015 is calculated by dividing the deferred expenditure (present value of €207,006) by the number of periods in which the benefits are expected to be generated. Straight-line amortisation is adopted on the assumption that the pattern of benefits will be uniform throughout the four years. The amortisation is therefore:
€207,006 ÷ 4 = €51,751.50.

8.9.3 Empirical research on accounting for research and development

As stated previously, within the US, research and development expenditure typically must be expensed as incurred. The position adopted by the FASB is a most conservative position and one that does not enable differentiation between entities that have valuable research and development projects and those that do not.

Requiring firms to write off research and development as incurred reduces both profits and assets in the period of the write-off. It is conceivable that, when SFAS 2 initially became operative within the US, firms faced difficulties associated with contractual arrangements they had previously entered into, such as interest-coverage clauses and debt-to-asset constraints (although the definition of 'assets' within particular debt contracts may exclude intangibles). This might have been the case particularly for smaller research and development firms that were involved in a limited number of projects. Horwitz and Kolodny (1980) tested this proposition and found support for the view that smaller research and development firms reduced their research and development expenditure around the time SFAS 2 was introduced. The results, however, were not replicated in a similar study undertaken by Dukes et al. (1980).

Requiring all research and development to be written off, as is the case in the US, might potentially affect managers' decisions if they are rewarded on the basis of accounting earnings. For example, Baber et al. (1991) found evidence to support the view that managers might reduce their research and development expenditure in periods where such a strategy is necessary to report positive or increasing profits (see Horwitz & Kolodny 1980). In comparison with the treatment under IAS, which allows the carrying forward of development expenditure (to the extent that certain tests based on 'probability' are met), the immediate write-off rule removes any latitude for judgement that might, at different times, be used opportunistically to manipulate profits. Empirical evidence from countries that have historically followed rules similar to those required by IAS 38 would suggest that the accounting for research and development may be used for earnings-smoothing purposes—for example, Markarian et al. (2008) found that Italian companies tended to use cost capitalisation for earnings-smoothing purposes. However, Cazavan-Jeny et al. (2011), in a study of French companies, were unable to unambiguously establish whether their findings implied that management used research and development capitalisation to manage earnings or because it was unable to estimate the earning power of research and development expenditures. They concluded that management was unable to truthfully convey information about future performance through its decision to capitalise research and development. This means that management's capitalisation behaviour cannot be taken as a signal about future performance. However, they found a significant and negative relationship between research and development expensed and future performance. This supports the case for a dual approach (capitalising and expensing) as there is no clear evidence of future economic benefits being gained from this expenditure; hence it provides support for an immediate charge against profit. A similar relation between expensed research and development and future performance was reported by Tsoligkas and Tsalavoutas (2011) for UK companies.

Research and development expenditures might take a number of periods to translate into higher earnings. The motivation to manipulate such expenditures and, in the process, related profits might be particularly strong if a manager who is rewarded principally on the basis of 'profits' is also approaching retirement (this is frequently referred to as a 'horizon problem').

It has been assumed by some researchers that the incentive for a manager approaching retirement to manipulate discretionary expenditures, such as deciding to undertake new research and development activities, will be tempered if the manager holds shares in the firm or is rewarded on the basis of the market's valuation of the firm (Lewellen et al. 1987). They suggest that:

> Stock based compensation therefore can assist in aligning managerial and shareholder interests, by increasing the cost to managers of investments that decrease share prices and raising the pay-off to them from variance-increasing investments (if the firm is levered).

This view is consistent with the findings of Dechow and Sloan (1991), who reviewed expenditures on research and development by US firms. They found that, in a sample of firms with managers responsible for determining expenditure on research and development and also approaching retirement, managers with stronger stock-price-based incentives were less likely to cut research and development expenditures. Assuming that managers are motivated primarily by a desire to maximise their own wealth (although we know from Chapter 3 that there are a number of notable accounting researchers who strongly disagree with this assumption), there will be a trade-off between any expected increase in wealth brought about by manipulating earnings and related bonuses and any expected decreases in wealth brought about by changes in the market value of the firm. Among the managers reviewed by Dechow and Sloan, those who elected not to manipulate accounting earnings are assumed to have considered that any expected gains from accounting-based rewards would have been more than offset by the reduction in wealth caused by reductions in the market value of the firm's securities.

In a further study, Goodacre and McGrath (1997) investigated whether UK investment analysts would react differently to the two treatments for accounting for research and development (capitalising or expensing the research and development expenditure). Goodacre and McGrath constructed a set of financial statements, complete with supporting notes, for a hypothetical electronics company. Different versions of the financial statements were prepared. One scenario involved a company that spends an industry-average amount each year on research and development, and immediately expenses all research and development expenditure. The second scenario involves a company that also spends an industry-average amount on research and development but capitalises all research and development expenditure and writes off the resulting asset over the anticipated life of the asset, which is assumed to be four years. In all other respects, the 'expensing' and 'capitalising' companies were identical. On the basis of the financial statements and supporting notes that were supplied, investment analysts (drawn from UK stockbrokers, banks and other investment intermediaries) were asked to forecast a share price for the company as at the date of the current year end. The results of the study showed that the mean market value for both the capitalising and the expensing companies was not significantly different. Goodacre and McGrath state that:

> On balance, it can be concluded that the analysts' valuation of the companies' shares, on average, does not appear to be significantly affected by the accounting treatment of R & D expenditure. This result supports previous market based research (Dukes 1976 and others) which suggests that investors see through R & D accounting differences and value companies appropriately. It also confirms similar experimental studies which have focused on different, but related, accounting issues such as capitalisation of leases (Wilkins and Zimmer 1983; Abdel-Khalik, Thomson and Taylor 1978 and 1981) in which analysts and bankers have not been 'fooled' by different accounting treatments.
>
> (1997, p. 171)

Goodacre and McGrath's claim that the choice of a particular accounting method in preference to another will not affect the value of the firm—because investors can 'see through' the effects of the accounting method choice—is dependent upon full disclosure of information about the accounting methods employed. (Perhaps this should be in the accounting policy section, which typically is included as an initial note in the notes to the financial statements.) In contrast to Goodacre and McGrath's experiment, empirical investigation by Oliveira *et al.* (2010) found that the change of accounting for intangibles in Portuguese firms in 2005, when IFRS were adopted, had no impact on the value relevance of intangibles as a whole; however, when subclasses including research and development and goodwill were considered separately, an increase in value relevance was reported. Consistent with this finding, Tsoligkas and Tsalavoutas (2011) found support for an increase in the value relevance of accounting for research and development after the introduction of IFRS in UK firms. However, these studies ignore the contractual issues discussed in Chapter 3.

We considered in Chapter 3 how organisations are frequently involved in accounting-based contractual arrangements, such as debt-to-assets constraints and interest-coverage requirements. Such restrictions are frequently part of agreements between organisations and providers of debt capital. The choice of the accounting method to be used to account for research and development can affect these agreements, although it should be noted that intangible assets such as research and development are often not included in the definition of 'assets' for the purposes of such agreements (Whittred & Zimmer 1986). Some accounting researchers argue that, if the agreements are affected and there are associated cash-flow consequences, the accounting-based agreements might have to be renegotiated—in itself often a costly exercise—and the choice of accounting method might well affect the value of the organisation and hence that of its shares. Such a view necessarily assumes that the value of the firm in itself will be a function of expected future cash flows and that a change in accounting method is anticipated to affect such cash flows. In a study of Italian firms, Markarian *et al.* (2008) reported no link between the capitalisation of research and development expenditure and the risk of violating debt covenants.

In Worked Example 8.6 we take a closer look at calculating deferred development balances.

Having considered how to account for research and development, we will now focus our attention on another intangible asset—goodwill.

8.10 Accounting for goodwill

8.10.1 What is goodwill?

Goodwill arises when one entity acquires another entity, or part thereof. For example, if one company acquires a controlling interest in another entity (the acquired entity becoming a subsidiary) goodwill might arise. In this section we consider the main issues associated with accounting for goodwill. However, we will defer consideration of issues that arise on the consolidation of a group of entities until Chapter 20.

| Worked Example 8.6 | Calculating deferred development balances |

Slater Ltd is currently working on four research and development projects. Summarised data relating to each project's expenditure and recoverable amount is provided below:

	Actual (€000)		Budgeted (€000)		
Project	2014	2015	2016	2017	2018
A R&D expenditure	15	15	20	20	0
Expected revenue inflows	10	10	10	0	0
B R&D expenditure	40	40	70	0	0
Expected revenue inflows	0	0	100	250	100
C R&D expenditure	300	100	50	0	0
Expected revenue inflows	0	0	350	350	150
D R&D expenditure	0	300	0	0	0
Expected revenue inflows	0	0	100	50	50

All revenue and expenditure predictions are deemed to be 'probable'. A discount rate of 9 per cent is used. In relation to the specific projects, the following information is also available:

Project A
This project involves documenting existing knowledge about the migratory behaviour of deep-sea tuna. The revenue inflows of €10,000 per year represent a three-year government grant.

Project B
This project relates to the ultimate development of surfboard wax that will be easy to apply on the coldest winter day, but will not melt even if left in the sun on the hottest summer day. The expenditure in 2014 was considered to represent research and the expenditure in 2015 was deemed to represent development.

Project C
This project involves the development of medication to stop ear infections. A significant breakthrough at the beginning of 2015 caused the researchers to believe that all costs would be recouped through future production and sales. Before 2015, the viability of the project had appeared doubtful. Only €50,000 of the expenditure in 2014 was deemed to represent research and the balance of all other expenditure was deemed to be development.

Project D
This project involves the development of a new fluorescent long-sleeved 'bikie' for wearing while cycling. €50,000 has been spent on research and the balance on development relating to this garment. It is expected that only €200,000 will be recoverable.

Required
Determine how much research and development expenditure should be deferred as at the end of 2015.

Solution
We can consider each of the projects separately, as follows:

▶

Project A

As the work being undertaken relates only to the documentation of existing knowledge, the associated expenditure would probably not be considered to constitute development. The expenditure would consequently be written off as incurred. As such, there is no need to determine the recoverable amount.

Project B

This project would meet the definition of research and development. The recoverable amount is determined by discounting the future cash flows at the discount rate of 9 per cent, as follows:

€100,000	×	0.9174	=	€91,740
€250,000	×	0.8417	=	€210,425
€100,000	×	0.7722	=	€77,220
				€379,385

Given that the recoverable amount of €379,385 is expected to exceed the sum of the actual and budgeted costs, all expenditure incurred to date on development (€40,000) can be carried forward. The amount spent on research will be expensed as incurred in accordance with the accounting standard.

Project C

This project would meet the definition of research and development. However, since it is not until the beginning of 2015 that the future economic benefits are deemed to be probable, none of the expenditure incurred before 2015 can be carried forward. Further, the accounting standard specifically states that expenditure on intangible assets that failed previously to meet the criterion for deferral (based on the assessment of probability) and were charged to the profit or loss are not to be written back in the light of subsequent events. The recoverable amount of Project C is determined by discounting the future cash flows at the discount rate of 9 per cent, as follows:

€350,000	×	0.9174	=	€321,090
€350,000	×	0.8417	=	€294,595
€150,000	×	0.7722	=	€115,830
				€731,515

As the recoverable amount of €731,515 exceeds the development expenditure, €100,000 may be capitalised and carried forward.

Project D

The recoverable amount of Project D is determined by discounting the future cash flows at the discount rate of 9 per cent, as follows:

€100,000	×	0.9174	=	€91,740
€50,000	×	0.8417	=	€42,085
€50,000	×	0.7722	=	€38,610
				€172,435

As the development expenditure incurred of €250,000 is more than the recoverable amount of €172,435, the full amount of the development expenditure should not be carried forward. The research expenditure would be written off as incurred. As at the end of 2015 the remaining recoverable amount is €172,435.

Therefore, for Projects A, B, C and D, as at the end of 2015, the amount of €312,435 can be deferred to future periods, summarised as follows:

Project	Amount carried forward (€)
A	0
B	40,000
C	100,000
D	172,435
	312,435

Goodwill itself is an unidentifiable intangible asset. It cannot be individually identified and is an intrinsic part of a business. It cannot be purchased or sold separately, but only as part of an entity in its entirety. Because goodwill is not separable, it fails to meet the criteria provided in IAS 38, which requires that an intangible asset be identifiable as well as non-monetary and non-physical in nature. Goodwill represents the future economic benefits associated with an existing customer base, efficient management, reliable suppliers and the like. However, each of these individual factors is not usually separately valued or identified within an entity's statement of financial position. Rather, they are typically combined into the composite asset of goodwill. Appendix A of IFRS 3 *Business Combinations*, defines goodwill as:

> *An asset representing the future economic benefits arising from other assets acquired in a business combination that are not individually identified and separately recognised.*

Goodwill might be built up over a number of periods or obtained by acquiring an existing business. Many individuals or organisations buy businesses with the intention of making them successful and then selling them at a higher price, taking into account the goodwill that they will have built up within the business.

Therefore, goodwill may be *internally generated* or *acquired* by purchasing an existing business. Under IFRS, internally generated goodwill is not to be recognised as an asset for the purpose of disclosure within the statement of financial position. The reason for this is that, according to the accounting standard-setters, **purchased goodwill** can be measured more objectively on the basis of the amount paid for it than internally generated goodwill, which is not capable of being reliably measured. Consequently, the accounting treatment for purchased goodwill differs from that for internally generated goodwill.

purchased goodwill
Goodwill that has been acquired through a transaction with an external party, as opposed to goodwill that is generated by the reporting entity itself. Under IFRS, purchased goodwill must be shown as an asset of the reporting entity.

Within IAS 38, paragraph 48 states 'internally generated goodwill shall not be recognised as an asset' as it is not an identifiable resource that is controlled by the entity that can be measured reliably at cost (IAS 38, paragraph 49).

Therefore, goodwill can only be recognised where it is acquired as part of a business acquisition. This means that a company may have extremely valuable goodwill, yet be unable to show any value for the asset. Yet, as soon as another party buys the business, that acquiring party can disclose that goodwill as an asset. Again, we can question the logic of this requirement. If an asset exists, should not it exist regardless of its source, that is, regardless of whether it is acquired or internally generated? However, the argument of the standard-setters is that it is simply too difficult to reliably measure the value of goodwill unless it has been acquired in a market transaction. Of course, there would be ways to measure the value of internally generated goodwill. For example, we might obtain a valuation of the business as a whole (perhaps its market capitalisation if it is a listed company) from which we would deduct the fair value of the entity's identifiable net assets to thereafter give the balance of goodwill. However, while this is possible in principle, we are still left with the rather harsh requirement that no internally generated goodwill may be recognised for accounting purposes.

8.10.2 How is goodwill measured?

Pursuant to IFRS 3 *Business Combinations*, purchased goodwill is measured as the excess of the cost of acquisition incurred by the acquirer over the fair value of the identifiable net assets and contingent liabilities acquired. Purchase consideration should be measured at the fair value of what is given up in exchange. As an example of calculating goodwill, consider Worked Example 8.7.

It is sometimes questioned whether or not goodwill is actually an asset. Unlike other assets, it cannot be sold separately from the business to which it belongs. Hence those individuals in favour of some form of current-cost or market-based accounting argue that, because goodwill is not individually saleable, it should not be shown as an asset. For example, in Chapter 3 we considered Chambers' model of accounting, *Continuously Contemporary Accounting* (CoCoA). According to CoCoA, assets are valued on the basis of their individual exit prices. The total of the exit values of the individual assets is then, in turn, used as a guide to determining the entity's 'capacity to adapt' to changing circumstances. If the net assets of the organisation have a low aggregated exit value, the organisation may be considered to have a low capacity to adapt. That is, in the short term, the organisation would be relatively unable to switch its activities into alternative pursuits, as it does not have sufficient liquid assets to enable such a change. As goodwill cannot be sold separately, in such a model of accounting it would be given zero value. Having said this, however, if we accept that goodwill is an asset, the next issue to consider is how (or if) to amortise it.

> ### Worked Example 8.7   Calculation of goodwill
>
> Horan Ltd purchases the Coolum Store for the consideration of:
>
> Cash   £150,000
> Land   Horan Ltd is going to transfer title of some land to the owners of the Coolum Store (book value of the land is £120,000; market value is £195,000).
>
> The statement of financial position of the Coolum Store as at the date of acquisition shows assets of £290,000 and liabilities of £95,000. All assets are fairly valued except the Coolum Store's building, which is in the financial statements at £60,000, but has a fair value of £85,000. There are no contingent liabilities.
>
> #### Required
> What is the value of goodwill?
>
> #### Solution
>
> | | £ | £ |
> | --- | --- | --- |
> | *Fair value of purchase consideration* | | |
> | Cash | 150,000 | |
> | Land (at fair value) | 195,000 | 345,000 |
> | *Fair value of net assets acquired* | | |
> | Carrying value of assets | 290,000 | |
> | Excess of fair value over carrying value | 25,000 | |
> | | 315,000 | |
> | *less* Liabilities | 95,000 | 220,000 |
> | Goodwill | | 125,000 |
>
> Therefore, following the above acquisition, Horan Ltd will show goodwill in its financial statements totalling £125,000. Yet, pursuant to IAS 38, before the acquisition no amount could be shown for goodwill in the financial statements of the Coolum Store. Therefore, if we are to accept that goodwill is an asset, the assets of the Coolum Store, at the date of acquisition, are understated owing to the non-recognition of the internally generated goodwill. However, as noted above, the accounting standard justifies this non-recognition of goodwill on the basis of the difficulties encountered, or expected to be encountered, in reliably measuring goodwill that in itself has not been the subject of a market transaction.

8.10.3 Goodwill amortisation versus impairment

In the years up to the implementation of IFRS in 2005, many countries amortised purchased goodwill, typically for periods that did not exceed a predetermined maximum period. Arguably, the requirement to amortise purchased goodwill has been one of the most controversial accounting issues. Most of the opposition to amortisation related to the requirement that purchased goodwill be amortised over a period of no more than say 20 years. Most businesses felt that they would actually be building up the value of goodwill across time through activities including advertising, which would typically be written-off as incurred. They thought it inappropriate to ignore the internally generated goodwill, while at the same time being required to amortise the purchased goodwill. The accounting standard-setters usually defended the arbitrary time limit by arguing that it is too difficult to determine the period from which economic benefits are expected to flow. However, is this not also the case for many other non-current assets? For example, there are obvious problems in determining the economic life of a building, particularly when the building is unique in nature. Nevertheless, there were typically no maximum depreciation time limits for buildings. Nor were there maximum amortisation or depreciation periods for any other assets. So is it really appropriate to set an upper limit for goodwill amortisation? Adopting defensible positions on such questions is difficult.

In addition, many countries stipulated that the straight-line amortisation method be used. This also caused debate. We may question the logic of ever imposing the use of a single amortisation method, such as the straight-line method, on all companies, given that the flow of benefits to all companies would not be the same. If it was considered logical to impose one method of amortisation on goodwill, why did the regulators not impose particular amortisation methods on other intangibles, such as development expenditure? When IFRS 3 *Business Combinations* became relevant for many European companies in 2005, the requirement to systematically amortise goodwill was abandoned. This was to please many corporate managers as the periodic amortisation of goodwill in some organisations meant the recognition of many millions of euros/pounds of expenses. The requirement to amortise goodwill was replaced with the requirement to undertake annual impairment testing.

Regarding the impairment losses relating to goodwill, paragraph 124 of IAS 36 *Impairment of Assets* states: 'An impairment loss recognised for goodwill shall not be reversed in a subsequent period.' An impairment loss is defined in IAS 36 as the amount by which the carrying amount of an asset or a cash-generating unit exceeds its recoverable amount. The recoverable amount of an asset is defined in IAS 36 as the higher of its fair value less costs to sell and its value-in-use. If the recoverable amount of an asset is lower than its carrying amount, this difference is deemed by IAS 36 to be an impairment loss, which should be recognised by debiting an expense (impairment loss) and crediting an asset (in this case, goodwill). There is a prohibition on revaluing goodwill, so if the recoverable amount of goodwill is assessed as being greater than its carrying value, no revaluation may be made.

Worked Example 8.8 provides an example of how to account for the impairment of goodwill.

Worked Example 8.8   Impairment of goodwill

Rip plc acquires Curl plc on 1 July 2014 for €5,000,000, this being the fair value of the consideration transferred. At that date, Curl plc's net identifiable assets have a fair value of €4,400,000. Goodwill of €600,000 is therefore the difference between the aggregate of the consideration transferred and the net identifiable assets acquired.
The fair value of the net identifiable assets of Curl plc are determined as follows:

	(€000)
Patent rights	200
Machinery	1,000
Buildings	1,500
Land	2,300
	5,000
Bank loan	(600)
Net assets	4,400

At the end of the reporting period of 30 June 2015, the management of Rip plc determines that the recoverable amount of the cash-generating unit, which is considered to be Curl plc, totals €4,500,000. The carrying amount of the net identifiable assets of Curl plc, excluding goodwill, is unchanged and remains €4,400,000.

Required

(a) Prepare the journal entry to account for any impairment of goodwill.
(b) Assume instead that, at the end of the reporting period, the management of Rip plc determines that the recoverable amount of the cash-generating unit, which is considered to be Curl plc, totals €4,100,000. Prepare the journal entry to account for the impairment.

Solution

We will consider a number of issues before ultimately providing the solution. First, we need to consider the level of aggregation we use when considering the asset that is subject to possible impairment. That is, should we consider it separately or as part of a larger 'cash-generating unit'?

In terms of whether an asset should be considered separately, or in combination with other assets, for the purposes of recognising an impairment, paragraph 66 of IAS 36 states:

> If there is any indication that an asset may be impaired, a recoverable amount shall be estimated for the individual asset. If it is not possible to estimate the recoverable amount of the individual asset, an entity shall determine the recoverable amount of the cash-generating unit to which the asset belongs (the asset's cash-generating unit).

The recoverable amount of goodwill cannot be considered independently of other assets which it supports. While the above requirements relate to the impairment of assets in general, there are some requirements within IAS 36 that specifically relate to goodwill. Of particular relevance is paragraph 80, which requires that rather than treating goodwill as an asset of the overall organisation, goodwill should be allocated to the relevant sub-component of the organisation.

Sometimes, however, the goodwill may relate to a number of cash-generating units within the organisation. As paragraph 81 of IAS 36 explains:

Goodwill sometimes cannot be allocated on a non-arbitrary basis to individual cash-generating units, but only to groups of cash-generating units. As a result, the lowest level within the entity at which the goodwill is monitored for internal management purposes sometimes comprises a number of cash-generating units to which the goodwill relates, but to which it cannot be allocated.

In this worked example, the assets of Curl plc are deemed to be the smallest group of assets that generate cash inflows that are largely independent of the cash inflows from other assets or groups of assets. Therefore, Curl plc is a cash-generating unit. The cash-generating unit comprising Curl plc includes goodwill within its carrying amount. As such, under paragraph 90 of IAS 36, it must be tested annually for impairment (or more frequently if there is an indication that it may be impaired) and impaired in accordance with paragraph 104 where the carrying amount is found to exceed the recoverable amount of the cash generating unit.

(a)

	Goodwill of Curl plc (€000)	Net identifiable assets (€000)	Total (€000)
Carrying amount	600	4,400	5,000
Recoverable amount			4,500
Impairment loss			500

Journal entry

Dr	Impairment loss—goodwill	€500,000	
Cr	Accumulated impairment loss—goodwill		€500,000

(b)

	Goodwill of Curl plc (€000)	Net identifiable assets (€000)	Total (€000)
Carrying amount	600	4,400	5,000
Recoverable amount			4,100
Impairment loss			900

Paragraph 104 of IAS 36 requires the impairment loss of €900,000 to be allocated to the assets in the cash-generating unit (Curl plc) by first reducing the carrying amount of goodwill. Once the balance of goodwill is fully eliminated, the balance of the impairment loss must be allocated on a pro-rata basis against the identifiable assets within the respective cash-generating unit.

Hence, €600,000 of the total impairment loss (see above) of €900,000 can be offset against the goodwill, leaving a balance of the impairment loss of €300,000. The remaining impairment loss of €300,000 is recognised by reducing the carrying amounts of Curl plc's identifiable assets, as follows:

	Goodwill of Curl plc (€000)	Net identifiable assets (€000)	Total (€000)
Carrying amount	600	4,400	5,000
Impairment loss	(600)	(300)	(900)
	–	4,100	4,100

◀ Allocating the €300,000 balance of the impairment loss pro-rata against the identifiable assets of the cash-generating unit on the basis of carrying values provides the following calculations:

	(€000)	Allocation of impairment loss (€000)	
Patent rights	200	x 300/5,000	12
Machinery	1,000	x 300/5,000	60
Buildings	1,500	x 300/5,000	90
Land	2,300	x 300/5,000	138
	5,000		300

Journal entry (in €000):

Dr	Impairment loss—goodwill	€600	
Dr	Impairment loss—identifiable assets	€300	
Cr	Accumulated impairment loss—goodwill		€600
Cr	Accumulated impairment loss—patent rights		€12
Cr	Accumulated impairment loss—machinery		€60
Cr	Accumulated impairment loss—buildings		€90
Cr	Accumulated impairment loss—land		€138

As already noted, an impairment loss recognised in relation to goodwill is not permitted to be reversed in subsequent periods.

The impairment of goodwill is subjective. Lhaopadchan (2010) used the case of the Royal Bank of Scotland (RBS) in the UK to highlight how risky the intangible asset 'goodwill' can be. He noted that, in 2008, RBS had net assets of £91.5 billion including goodwill of £48.5 billion and he argues that management were resistant to recognising asset impairments as this highlights poor acquisition strategies. However, he suggests that many managers are using the financial crisis and the declining market as an opportunity to camouflage and correct these past acquisition blunders. For example, Vodafone wrote off £26 billion of goodwill in 2006. This impairment resulted from its acquisition of Mannesman, a Germany-based company, in 2000. Again, in 2008 it impaired goodwill amounting to £5.9 billion as a result of its acquisition of Turkey's second-largest mobile operator in December 2005.

SUMMARY

The chapter addressed issues relating to intangible assets. It considered how to account for intangible assets generally, as well as how to account specifically for research and development, and goodwill. Intangible assets themselves are considered to be non-monetary assets without physical substance and include patents, goodwill, mastheads, brand names, copyrights, research and development, and trademarks. There is a specific requirement that expenditure associated with many internally generated intangible assets (including research expenditure and expenditure on internally generated brands, mastheads, publishing titles, customer lists and items similar in substance) be expensed as incurred. Such internally generated intangibles are also not permitted to be revalued.

Where intangible assets are revalued, such revaluations can only be undertaken where there is an 'active market' for such assets and fair values can be ascertained.

Intangible assets can be classified as either identifiable intangible assets or unidentifiable intangible assets. Goodwill is an example of an unidentifiable intangible asset. Intangible assets can be considered to have either a limited useful life or an indefinite life. Where intangible assets are considered to have a limited (finite) life, there is a need to allocate their cost, or revalued amount, over their useful lives by way of periodic amortisation. Where an intangible asset is considered to have an indefinite life, amortisation charges do not apply. Rather, the asset is subject to annual impairment testing.

In relation to research and development expenditure, this chapter explained that research and development comprise various expenditures, including the costs of material and services consumed in research and development activities;

salaries and wages; and depreciation of research-related equipment. Research must be considered separately from development. Research expenditure is required to be expensed as incurred. Development expenditure may be carried forward as an asset to the extent that future economic benefits are deemed probable, and such benefits are measurable with reasonable accuracy. Development expenditure would need to be amortised in subsequent periods.

The other specific intangible asset addressed in this chapter is goodwill. Goodwill is defined as the future benefits from unidentifiable assets, where unidentifiable assets are assets that are not capable of being both individually identified and specifically recognised. Only purchased goodwill can be recognised for external reporting purposes. Purchased goodwill is measured as the excess of the cost of acquisition incurred by an entity over the fair value of the identifiable net assets and contingent liabilities acquired. Goodwill carried forward to future periods is subject to annual impairment testing rather than requiring periodic amortisation.

KEY TERMS

goodwill . . . . **184**   purchased goodwill . . . . **200**   unidentifiable intangible assets . **184**

identifiable intangible assets . . . **184**   research and development **192**

END-OF-CHAPTER EXERCISE

Slipstream plc operates a road bike manufacturing plant. It has decided to purchase a 100 per cent interest in Dion Ltd, a fibreglass manufacturing business. The cost of the acquisition is €1,000,000 plus associated legal costs of €50,000. As at the date of acquisition, the statement of financial position of Dion Ltd shows: **LO 8.7**

	€	€	€
ASSETS			
Current assets			
Cash		10,000	
Accounts receivable	60,000		
Provision for doubtful debts	(10,000)	50,000	
Inventory		140,000	
Total current assets		200,000	
Non-current assets			
Land and buildings, at cost	700,000		
Accumulated depreciation—land and buildings	(150,000)	550,000	
Plant and equipment	400,000		
Accumulated depreciation—plant and equipment	(100,000)	300,000	
Total non-current assets		850,000	
Total assets			1,050,000
Liabilities			
Current liabilities			
Accounts payable		70,000	
Bank overdraft		30,000	
Total current liabilities		100,000	

Non-current liabilities

Bank loan	200,000
Total liabilities	300,000
Net assets	750,000

Additional information

The assets and liabilities of Dion Ltd are fairly stated, except for the following:
* Land and buildings have a fair value of €700,000.
* Some of the fibreglass has been water-damaged, so that total inventory has a fair value of €110,000.
* Dion Ltd has a patent over a particular manufacturing process. This is not recorded in the statement of financial position, but has a market value of €80,000.
* There are no contingent liabilities.

REQUIRED

Determine, for accounting purposes, the amount of goodwill that has been acquired by Slipstream plc.

SOLUTION TO END-OF-CHAPTER EXERCISE

	€
Acquisition cost	1,000,000
Net assets shown in the statement of financial position as at the date of acquisition	750,000
Adjustments	
Excess of fair value of land and buildings over the carrying value	150,000
Excess of carrying value of inventory over the fair value	(30,000)
Patent at fair value, unrecorded in the statement of financial position	80,000
Fair value of the identifiable net assets being acquired	950,000
Goodwill acquired in transaction	50,000

Notes

1 Although the acquisition cost of assets would normally include legal fees, paragraph 53 of IFRS 3 specifically notes that in a business combination, acquisition-related costs, such as legal fees, are to be treated as expenses.

2 The identifiable assets must be measured at their fair values, with goodwill being measured as the excess of the cost of the acquisition over the fair value of the identifiable net assets acquired. So valuation adjustments are required for the land and buildings, and the inventory. The patent must be recognised even though it is not recognised in the statement of financial position of Dion Ltd.

REVIEW QUESTIONS

1 We have a separate accounting standard, IAS 38, that specifically deals with intangible assets and it provides different requirements from those for property, plant and equipment (the rules for which appear in IAS 16). What is it about intangible assets that requires them to have a separate accounting standard? Do you think the differences in requirements are logical?　**LO 8.1**

2 Provide an argument in support of the accounting requirement that research is to be written off as incurred. Do you think this requirement is overly 'conservative'?　**LO 8.5**

3 Explain the difference in how you measure intangible assets that are individually acquired compared with those that are acquired as part of a business combination.　**LO 8.3**

4 What activities should be included in the cost of research and development? In your answer differentiate between research activities and development activities.　**LO 8.5**

5 Explain the difference between tangible assets and intangible assets. Is it necessary to have different accounting rules for tangible and intangible assets?　**LO 8.1**

6 How is the value of goodwill determined for accounting purposes?　**LO 8.7**

7 Would goodwill be considered an 'asset' according to the IASB Conceptual Framework?　**LO 8.2**

8 Which of the following costs would be included as part of (i) research costs, or (ii) development costs for a project to improve the production process of a confectionery plant? **LO** 8.5

(a) depreciation of administrative equipment during the research phase of the project;

(b) salaries of administrative staff during the development phase of the project;

(c) salaries of staff working half-time on the research project and half-time on other work;

(d) depreciation of laboratory equipment used to undertake development of the new production process;

(e) consulting fees paid to outside consultants used in the research phase and development phase of the project; and

(f) raw materials used in the research phase and development phase of the project.

9 What are possible arguments for and against the prohibition of recognition of internally generated goodwill? **LO** 8.3

10 What is an active market, and is an active market likely to exist for intangible assets such as brand names or development-related expenditures? Explain your answer. **LO** 8.2

11 Evidence in Whittred and Zimmer (1986) indicates that intangibles are typically excluded from the definitions of 'assets' employed in debenture trust deeds. Why do you think this is the case? **LO** 8.6

12 (a) If an accounting standard is introduced that requires certain types of expenditures to be written-off rather than capitalised, and that type of expenditure is discretionary, would you expect management to change their expenditure patterns from what they would have been in the absence of the standard? Use the results of empirical research described in this chapter to support your argument. **LO** 8.3

(b) Would your expectation in the above situation be different if the manager is rewarded primarily on the basis of accounting earnings?

(c) What effect would the further knowledge that the manager is approaching retirement have on your views?

13 Energy plc is involved in the research and development of a new type of aerodynamic racing bicycle. For this R&D, it has incurred the following expenditure:

- £50,000 obtaining a general understanding of wind flow dynamics;
- £30,000 on understanding what local cyclists expect from a racing bicycle;
- £90,000 on testing and refining a certain shape of bicycle; and
- £190,000 on developing and testing a full prototype of the aerodynamic racing bicycle, to be called the 'Speedator'.

There is expected to be a very large market for the product, which will generate many millions of pounds in revenue. **LO** 8.2

REQUIRED

Determine how the above expenditure would be treated for accounting purposes.

14 Tamarama plc acquires 100 per cent of Bronte plc on 1 July 2013. Tamarama plc pays the shareholders of Bronte plc the following consideration:

Cash	€70,000
Plant and equipment	fair value €250,000; carrying amount in the books of Tamarama plc €170,000
Land	fair value €300,000; carrying amount in the books of Tamarama plc €200,000

There are also legal fees of €35,000 involved in acquiring Bronte plc.

On 1 July 2013 Bronte plc's statement of financial position shows total assets of €700,000 and liabilities of €300,000. The fair value of the assets is €800,000. **LO** 8.7

REQUIRED

Has any goodwill been acquired and, if so, how much?

15 Nat plc purchases a 100 per cent interest in Angourie plc. The cost of the acquisition is €1,400,000 plus associated legal costs of €70,000. As at the date of acquisition, the statement of financial position of Angourie plc shows: **LO** 8.7

	€	€	€
Assets			
Current assets			
Cash		20,000	
Accounts receivable	80,000		
Provision for doubtful debts	(10,000)	70,000	
Inventory		100,000	
Total current assets		190,000	
Non-current assets			
Land and buildings, at cost	850,000		

Accumulated depreciation—land and buildings	(150,000)	700,000	
Plant and equipment	510,000		
Accumulated depreciation—plant and equipment	(100,000)	410,000	
Total non-current assets		1,110,000	
Total assets			1,300,000
Liabilities			
Current liabilities			
Accounts payable		90,000	
Bank overdraft		20,000	
Total current liabilities		110,000	
Non-current liabilities			
Bank loan		190,000	
Total liabilities			300,000
Net assets			1,000,000

Additional information

- The assets and liabilities of Angourie plc are fairly stated except for land and buildings, which have a fair value of €800,000.
- Angourie plc has a brand name that is not recognised on the statement of financial position and that has a fair value of €50,000.
- There are no contingent liabilities.

REQUIRED

(a) Determine, for accounting purposes, the amount of goodwill that has been acquired by Nat plc.

(b) Why do you think that Nat plc would have been prepared to pay for goodwill?

(c) Can Nat plc revalue the goodwill upwards in a subsequent period?

16 The following abstract by Amir and Livne (2005) refers to their empirical findings in respect of the relationship between future performance benefits and capitalisation of footballers. Obtain and read the article and comment briefly on the merits of the current accounting for footballers under IAS 38 relative to the practice of amortisation over a certain time period. **LO 8.6**

Accounting, Valuation and Duration of Football Player Contracts
Eli Amir and Gilad Livne

Abstract

FRS 10 requires investments in player contracts by football companies to be capitalized and amortized. Given the high degree of uncertainty associated with such contracts, it is not clear that this treatment is consistent with asset capitalization criteria. The evidence provided in this paper does not support inconclusively this capitalization requirement in that it indicates weak association of investment in player contracts with three measures of future benefits. In particular, the duration of this association is at most two years, which is shorter than the duration implied by the amortization period reported by sample companies. Nonetheless, other findings suggest that market participants seem to agree with the treatment prescribed by FRS 10. These results should be of interest to practitioner and standard setters who (axiomatically) regard intangibles acquired in an arm's length transaction as assets.

---

17 In 2013 McGoy plc decided to develop a bicycle out of a new type of material that was resistant to damage. The material to be used was more like plastic than the fibreglass that was traditionally used on bicycles. In 2013 McGoy plc spent £510,000 on research aimed at understanding the properties of different types of plastic. This knowledge provided what the company considered to be a significant breakthrough, which if utilised should lead to significant future economic benefits.

In 2014 McGoy plc developed a prototype of its bicycle. It asked several leading cyclists to ride its bicycle at the annual Tour de France. Costs involved in developing the prototype in 2014 were £780,000. The reaction to the new bicycle was positive and many major retailers put in orders for bicycles. Anticipating the demand, McGoy plc had spent £25,000 on legal costs to register a patent for the bicycle. The patent has a life of five years, after which time other producers may copy the bicycle design.

Because of the positive reaction, in 2015 McGoy plc undertook worldwide marketing of the bicycle at a cost of £2,200,000. It became apparent that demand for this new bicycle was huge, and within four months, orders for over £40 million worth of the bicycles were received. McGoy plc employed a firm of accountants to work out the present value of the new bicycle and they believed that the product had a present value of at least £200 million. The managing director of McGoy plc then decided that he would like to have the present value of the bicycle reflected in the company's financial statements, that is, he wanted it to be valued at its fair value. While his accountants considered that the present value was £200 million, a major competitor made a legally binding offer to buy the patent for the product for a price of £150 million. **LO** 8.5

REQUIRED

Describe how to account for the above transactions and events and provide appropriate journal entries.

18 Kelly plc is currently working on four research and development projects. Summarised data relating to each project's expenditure and recoverable amount is provided below:

Project	Actual (€000)		Budgeted (€000)		
	2014	2015	2016	2017	2018
Alpha R&D expenditure	75	75	100	100	0
Expected revenue inflows	50	50	50	0	0
Beta R&D expenditure	200	200	350	0	0
Expected revenue inflows	0	0	500	1,250	500
Gamma R & D expenditure	1,500	500	250	0	0
Expected revenue inflows	0	0	1,750	1,750	750
Delta R&D expenditure	0	1,500	0	0	0
Expected revenue inflows	0	0	500	250	250

All revenue and expenditure predictions are deemed to be 'probable'. A discount rate of 6 per cent is used.

In relation to the specific projects, the following information is also available:

Project Alpha

This project involves the compilation of all known information about the abrasive nature of different types of seaweed. The revenue inflows of €50,000 per year are being provided by a major shipping company.

Project Beta

This project relates to the ultimate development of a surfboard that will allow surfers to do more radical manoeuvres. Fifty per cent of the expenditure in 2014 was considered to represent research, while the balance of the related expenditures represents development.

Project Gamma

This project involves the development of a wetsuit with a rechargeable heat-pack. Initially, surfers rejected the concept because they believed it would create pain because of small electric shocks, and sales prospects looked poor. However, in 2015, surfers changed their minds and large-scale demand for the product was created. Only €250,000 of the expenditure in 2014 was deemed to represent research and the balance of all other expenditure was deemed to be development.

Project Delta

This project involves the development of a new wristwatch that predicts the height of waves. €250,000 has been spent on research and the balance on development. It is expected that only €1,000,000 will be recoverable. **LO** 8.5

REQUIRED

Determine how much research and development expenditure should be deferred as at the end of 2015.

19 Paragraph 23 of an earlier version of IAS 38 *Intangible Assets* stated that: **LO** 8.2

The Board's view, consistently reflected in previous proposals for intangible assets, is that there should be no difference between the requirements for: (a) intangible assets that are acquired externally; and (b) internally generated intangible assets, whether they arise from development activities or other types of activities.

REQUIRED

Evaluate the above view. Identify and explain inconsistencies between this view and the current requirements of IAS 38.

CHALLENGING QUESTIONS

20 Should computer software be classified as an intangible asset or as part of property, plant and equipment? **LO 8.1**

21 Inglis plc has a number of taxi licences that are shown in the financial statements at cost. Can these licences be revalued to fair value and, if so, do they also need to be subject to periodic amortisation? **LO 8.4**

22 Sir David Tweedie, past chairperson of the IASB, when talking about internally generated intangible assets, stated: **LO 8.4**

> *As we get smarter, perhaps we'll allow some of them back on, but the rest of the world doesn't believe in them at the moment because of their unreliability and arguments over how they should be measured, so we've said that until that's settled, they should be off-balance sheet.*

Evaluate Sir David's comments in light of the current accounting practice for intangible assets.

23 As goodwill is not to be amortised, does this mean that the balance of goodwill can be carried forward indefinitely? **LO 8.7**

24 IP plc reports the following intangible assets: **LO 8.1**

	£m
Patents at directors' valuation	160
less Accumulated amortisation	(40)
	120
Trademarks, at cost	15
Goodwill, at cost	50
less Accumulated amortisation	(10)
	40
Brand name	100
Licence at cost	10
less Accumulated amortisation	(1)
	9

Patents were acquired at a cost of £80 million and were revalued soon afterwards. They have an estimated life of 16 years, of which 12 years remain.

The trademark can be renewed indefinitely, subject to continued use. The cost represents registration fees, which were initially expensed but recognised five years later after the trademark had started to become recognised by consumers.

Goodwill has been purchased and amortised on the straight-line basis.

The brand name is stated at fair value and is internally generated.

The licence has a ten-year life, of which nine years remain. The licence can be traded in an active market and has a fair value of £17 million.

REQUIRED

(a) State how each asset, or class of assets, should be reported in accordance with IAS 38.

(b) State the carrying amount and whether each asset/asset class should be amortised. Specify any choice of methods permitted for IP plc.

25 In Paragraph 1.4 of Accounting Interpretation (AI) 1 *Amortisation of Intangible Assets* released by the IAS in June 1999, it is stated: **LO 8.4**

> *Some commentators have suggested that the useful lives of certain identifiable intangible assets such as brand names, mastheads, licences and trademarks are indeterminate and that, as a result, such assets are not depreciable assets. It has also been suggested that because the values of such assets are not expected to diminish over time, the assets have no depreciable amount.*

REQUIRED

Evaluate the above view.

26 State whether the following assets may be revalued. Prepare journal entries for any revaluations permitted by accounting standards. Assume that each item listed below represents a separate class of assets. **LO** 8.1

(a) A company has developed a masthead for its newspaper to the point where it is a very valuable asset. Although the masthead is not currently recognised, management believes it could be sold for at least €3 million.

(b) A company purchased a publishing title two years ago for €1.2 million when another publisher went into liquidation. The book has been very successful and management believes that it could probably sell it for €1.5 million if ever they put it on the market.

(c) A company acquired a franchise for an ice-cream stand at a beach at a cost of €100,000. There is great demand for this type of franchise as evidenced by recent sales of equivalent franchises at other beaches. The current market price for such a franchise is €200,000.

(d) A company has deferred development costs of €520,000 and the estimated recoverable amount for the development project is €860,000.

27 Innovator plc incurred expenditure researching and developing a cure for a common disease found in turnips. At the end of 2013 management determined that the research and development project was unlikely to succeed because trials of the prototype had been unsuccessful. During 2014 a breakthrough in agricultural science improved chances of the product succeeding and development resumed. The project was completed in 2014. At the end of 2014 costs incurred on the project were expected to be recoverable. Innovator expects that 10 per cent of the project revenue will be received in 2015, 20 per cent in 2016, 30 per cent in 2017, 30 per cent in 2018 and 10 per cent in 2019. After five years the product will be at the end of its useful life because the disease found in turnips will have been eradicated. Costs incurred were as follows: **LO** 8.5

	Research (€000)	Development (€000)
2013	40,000	10,000
2014	12,000	60,000

REQUIRED

(a) How much research expenditure and development expenditure should be recognised as an expense in 2013?

(b) How much research and development expenditure should be recognised as an expense in 2014?

(c) State how much expenditure should be carried forward (deferred) and reported in the statement of financial position at the end of 2013 and 2014.

(d) Prepare journal entries for the amortisation of deferred costs in 2015 and 2016, assuming that actual revenues are as expected. State the amount of deferred expenditure carried forward in the statement of financial position in relation to the deferred costs.

(e) Assume that, after charging amortisation based on sales revenue at the end of 2014, the discounted net cash flows expected to be generated from the deferred expenditure were estimated as €15,000. Prepare any journal entries required to account for this information.

REFERENCES

AMIR, E. & LIVNE, G., 'Accounting, Valuation and Duration of Football Player Contracts', *Journal of Business Finance and Accounting*, vol. 32, no. 3–4, 2005, pp. 549–86.

BABER, W., FAIRFIELD, P., & HAGGARD, J., 'The Effect of Concern about Reported Income on Discretionary Spending Decisions: The Case of Research and Development', *Accounting Review*, October 1991, pp. 818–29.

CAZAVAN-JENY, A., JEANJEAN, T., & JOOS, P., 'Accounting Choice and Future Performance: The Case of R&D Accounting in France', *Journal of Accounting and Public Policy*, vol. 30, no. 2, 2011, pp. 145–65.

DECHOW, P. & SLOAN, R., 'Executive Incentives and the Horizon Problem', *Journal of Accounting and Economics*, vol. 14, 1991, pp. 51–89.

DUKES, T., DYCKMAN, T., & ELLIOT, J., 'Accounting for Research and Development Expenditures', *Journal of Accounting Research*, 1980 Supplement, pp. 1–26.

GOODACRE, A. & MCGRATH, J., 'An Experimental Study of Analysts' Reactions to Corporate R&D Expenditure', *British Accounting Review*, vol. 29, 1997, pp. 159–79.

HORWITZ, B. & KOLODNY, R., 'The Economic Effects of Involuntary Uniformity in the Financial Reporting of Research and Development Expenditures', *Journal of Accounting Research*, 1980 Supplement, pp. 38–74.

LEWELLEN, W., LODERER, C., & MARTIN, K., 'Executive Compensation and Executive Incentive Problems', *Journal of Accounting and Economics*, vol. 9, 1987, pp. 287–310.

LHAOPADCHAN, S., 'Fair Value Accounting and Intangible Assets: Goodwill Impairment and Managerial Choice', *Journal of Financial Regulation and Compliance*, vol. 18, no. 2, 2010, pp. 120–30.

MARKARIAN, G., POZZA, L., & PRENCIPE, A., 'Capitalisation of R&D Costs and Earnings Management: Evidence from Italian Listed Companies', *International Journal of Accounting*, vol. 43, no. 3, 2008, pp. 246–67.

MOODIE, D., 'Banking on Thin Air', *Charter*, vol. 71, May 2000, pp. 42–5.

OLIVEIRA, L., LIMA RODRIGUES, L., & CRAIG, R., 'Intangible Assets and Value Relevance: Evidence from the Portuguese Stock Exchange', *British Accounting Review*, vol. 24, no. 4, 2010.

PWC, 'Accounting for Innovation: The Impact on Technology Companies of Accounting for Research and Development under IFRS (Executive summary)', PricewaterhouseCoopers LLP, 2010, http://www.pwc.com/en_US/us/issues/ifrs-reporting/assets/ifrs-technology-accounting-r-d.pdf.

TSOLIGKAS, F. & TSALAVOUTAS, I., 'Value Relevance of R&D in the UK after IFRS Mandatory Implementation', *Applied Financial Economics*, vol. 21, no. 13, 2011, pp. 957–80.

WHITTRED, G. & ZIMMER, I., 'Accounting in the Market for Debt', *Accounting and Finance*, November 1986, pp. 1–12.

PART 4

Accounting for Liabilities and Owners' Equity

Part contents

Chapter 9

An Overview of Accounting for Liabilities

Learning objectives

Upon completing this chapter readers should:

LO1 know the definition of a liability and understand how to apply the recognition criteria provided in the IASB Conceptual Framework;

LO2 understand what a contingent liability represents and understand how it should be disclosed within the notes to a reporting entity's financial statements;

LO3 understand which 'provisions' should be treated as liabilities;

LO4 understand why, with certain transactions, professional judgement is required to determine whether the transaction gives rise to a liability, or should be recognised as part of equity;

LO5 understand some of the reasons why firms would typically prefer to disclose a transaction as part of equity, rather than as a liability;

LO6 understand how to calculate the issue price of securities such as debentures; and

LO7 know how to account for any premium or discount that arises on the issue of debentures.

9.1 Liabilities defined

IAS 37 *Provisions, Contingent Liabilities, and Contingent Assets* defines a **liability** as 'a present obligation of the entity arising from past events, the settlement of which is expected to result in an outflow from the entity of resources embodying economic benefits'.

The above definition is the same as the definition of liabilities provided in the *Conceptual Framework for Financial Reporting*.

As we know from previous chapters, in particular Chapter 2, there are three key components in the above definition of 'liability', these being:

1. There must be a future disposition of economic benefits to other entities.
2. There must be a present obligation.
3. A past transaction or other event must have created the obligation.

> **liability** Defined in the IASB Conceptual Framework as 'a present obligation of the entity arising from past events, the settlement of which is expected to result in an outflow from the entity of resources embodying economic benefits'.

In addition to defining liabilities, the IASB Conceptual Framework provides recognition criteria for liabilities. For a liability to be recognised and disclosed in a reporting entity's statement of financial position, it must, according to paragraph 4.38, be *probable* that the sacrifice of economic benefits will be required, and the amount of the liability must be able to be *reliably measured* (IASB Conceptual Framework, paragraph 4.38).

The above recognition criteria refer to an 'element'. In relation to the five elements of financial statements, paragraph 4.2 of the IASB Conceptual Framework states:

> Financial statements portray the financial effects of transactions and other events by grouping them into broad classes according to their economic characteristics. These broad classes are termed the elements of financial statements. The elements directly related to the measurement of financial position in the balance sheet are assets, liabilities and equity. The elements directly related to the measurement of performance in the income statement are income and expenses. The cash flow statement usually reflects income statement elements and changes in balance sheet elements; accordingly, this Conceptual Framework identifies no elements that are unique to this statement.

The element we focus on in this chapter is liabilities. The recognition of liabilities is not to be restricted to situations where there is a legal obligation. Liabilities should also be recognised in certain cases where equity or usual business practice dictates that obligations to external parties currently exist; for example a liability is required for the amounts expected to be expended for goods sold where the entity has a policy of rectifying faults in the goods even after the warranty lapses (IASB Conceptual Framework, paragraph 60).

So the liabilities that appear within an entity's statement of financial position might include obligations that are legally enforceable as well as obligations that are deemed to be equitable or constructive. When determining whether a liability exists, the intentions or actions of management need to be taken into account. That is, the actions or representations of the entity's management or governing body or changes in the economic environment directly influence the reasonable expectations or actions of those outside the entity and, although they have no legal entitlement, they might have other sanctions that leave the entity with no realistic alternative but to make certain future sacrifices of economic benefits. Such present obligations are sometimes called 'equitable obligations' or 'constructive obligations'. An equitable obligation is governed by social or moral sanctions or custom rather than legal sanctions. A constructive obligation is created, inferred or construed from the facts in a particular situation rather than contracted by agreement with another entity or imposed by government. Some examples of entities with equitable or constructive obligations include the following:

- A retail store that habitually refunds purchases by dissatisfied customers even though it is under no legal obligation to do so. The store could not change its policy without incurring unacceptable damage to its reputation.
- An entity that has identified contamination in land surrounding one of its production sites. The entity might not be legally obliged to clean up the surrounding land but, because of concern for its long-term reputation and relationship with the local community and because of its published policies or past actions, is presently obliged to do so.
- A government that makes a public commitment to provide financial assistance to victims of a natural disaster and, because of custom and moral considerations, has no realistic alternative but to provide the assistance.

Determining whether an equitable or a constructive obligation exists is often more difficult than identifying a legal obligation, and in most situations calls for professional judgement. As noted above, one consideration is that the entity should have no realistic alternative to making the future sacrifice of economic benefits and this implies that there is no discretion. In cases where the entity retains discretion to avoid making any future sacrifice of economic benefits, no liability exists or is recognised. It follows that a decision of the entity's management or governing body is not in itself sufficient for the recognition of a provision. Such a decision does not mark the inception of a present obligation since, in the absence of something more, the entity retains the ability to reverse the decision and thereby avoid the future sacrifice of economic benefits. For example, an entity's management or governing body might resolve that the entity will offer to repair a defect it has recently discovered in one of its products, even though the nature of the defect is such that the purchasers of the product would not expect the entity to do so. Until the entity makes public that offer, or commits itself in some other way to making the repairs, there is no present obligation, constructive or otherwise, beyond that of satisfying the existing statutory and contractual rights of customers. What is being emphasised here is that in some cases (for example, where there is a possible constructive or equitable obligation) some degree of professional judgement might be required in determining whether a liability should be recognised. Where a liability is based on a legal obligation there is less reliance on professional judgement.

9.2   Classification of liabilities as 'current' or 'non-current'

In disclosing liabilities, a reporting entity has a choice, based on notions of relevance and faithful representation, to disclose liabilities either on the basis of a current/non-current liability dichotomy or on the basis of order of liquidity if that approach provides information that is more relevant (IAS 1 *Presentation of Financial Statements*, paragraph 60).

Hence, reporting entities have a choice of how to disclose their liabilities—but the choice must be governed by which presentation format provides more relevant and reliable information. In explaining the benefits of using the respective approaches to disclosing liabilities, paragraphs 62 and 63 of IAS 1 state:

62. *When an entity supplies goods or services within a clearly identifiable operating cycle, separate classification of current and non-current assets and liabilities in the statement of financial position provides useful information by distinguishing the net assets that are continuously circulating as working capital from those used in the entity's long-term operations. It also highlights assets that are expected to be realised within the current operating cycle, and liabilities that are due for settlement within the same period.*

63. *For some entities, such as financial institutions, a presentation of assets and liabilities in increasing or decreasing order of liquidity provides information that is reliable and is more relevant than a current/non-current presentation because the entity does not supply goods or services within a clearly identifiable operating cycle.*

In relation to disclosure it is also possible that some organisations might disclose some of their liabilities separately as current and non-current, while the same organisations might disclose other liabilities on the basis of order of liquidity. This can happen when the firm has diverse operations, some of which do not have a clearly identifiable operating cycle (IAS 1, paragraph 64).

In considering the **current/non-current liability** dichotomy, we would probably be familiar with a definition of current liabilities in terms of an obligation being due for payment within 12 months of the end of the financial period (referred to as the 12-month test). This was the traditional approach to defining current liabilities. The new definition as stipulated in IAS 1 *Presentation of Financial Statements* focuses on the 'operating cycle'. Paragraph 69 of IAS 1 states:

> **current liability**
> Liabilities that satisfy any of the four criteria provided by IAS 1.
>
> **non-current liability**
> Any liability that does not pass the test provided within IAS 1 for a current liability.

An entity shall classify a liability as current when:

(a) *it expects to settle the liability in its normal operating cycle;*
(b) *it holds the liability primarily for the purpose of trading;*
(c) *the liability is due to be settled within twelve months after the end of the reporting period; or*
(d) *the entity does not have an unconditional right to defer settlement of the liability for at least twelve months after the reporting period.*

An entity shall classify all other liabilities as non-current.

We see that, in contrast with traditional approaches, a liability may now be disclosed as a current liability when it is not expected to be settled for more than 12 months. If liabilities are disclosed as current on the basis of the entity's operating cycle, and this cycle is greater than 12 months, the reporting entity should disclose the length of its operating cycle.

In explaining the use of the entity's 'operating cycle', paragraphs 70 and 71 of IAS 1 state the following:

70. *Some current liabilities, such as trade payables and some accruals for employee and other operating costs, are part of the working capital used in the entity's normal operating cycle. An entity classifies such operating items as current liabilities even if they are due to be settled more than twelve months after the reporting period. The same normal operating cycle applies to the classification of an entity's assets and liabilities. When the entity's normal operating cycle is not clearly identifiable, it is assumed to be twelve months.*

71. *Other current liabilities are not settled as part of the normal operating cycle, but are due for settlement within twelve months after the reporting date or held primarily for the purpose of trading. Examples are financial liabilities classified as held for trading in accordance with IAS 39, bank overdrafts, and the current portion of non-current financial liabilities, dividends payable, income taxes and other non-trade payables. Financial liabilities that provide financing on a long-term basis (i.e. are not part of the working capital used in the entity's normal operating cycle) and are not due for settlement within twelve months after the reporting period are non-current liabilities, subject to paragraphs 74 and 75.*

While the above discussion identifies how liabilities should be disclosed pursuant to IAS 1, in terms of a current/non-current dichotomy, it should be appreciated that in October 2008 the IASB released a Discussion Paper entitled *Preliminary Views on Financial Statement Presentation*. This Discussion Paper was then followed by an

Exposure Draft that was released in 2010. The Discussion Paper and Exposure Draft reflect joint work being undertaken by the IASB and the US Financial Accounting Standards Board (FASB). The work is expected ultimately to culminate in a revised version of IAS 1 being issued. The Discussion Paper recommends significant changes to how financial statements should be presented. For example, it has been proposed that the statement of financial position would be grouped by major activities (operating, investing and financing), not by assets, liabilities and equity, as it is today. Interested readers should refer to Chapter 4 (Section 4.10) for further details of the proposed changes to financial statement presentation.

9.3 Contingent liabilities

Where the recognition criteria for a liability are not satisfied (that is, the future outflow is perhaps not probable and/or reliably measurable), the item should not be included within the statement of financial position (that is, a liability should not be recognised). However, if it is possible that the firm will be obliged (although not currently obliged) to transfer resources in the future as a result of an agreement that has already been entered into—and the possibility is not deemed to be 'remote'—and the amount is potentially material, disclosure in the notes to the financial statements is appropriate. Further, if there is an existing obligation, but the obligation cannot be measured with reasonable accuracy, then while the item cannot be disclosed in the statement of financial position it would be appropriate to disclose it in the notes to the financial statements to the extent it is potentially material.

> **contingent liability**
> Where an obligation is dependent upon a future event or where the amount of the obligation cannot be measured reliably at a given point in time.

In the circumstances just described, where an obligation is dependent upon a future event (for example, a future court ruling pertaining to a claim already made against the reporting entity), or where the amount of the obligation cannot be measured reliably at a given point in time, the associated obligation is referred to as a **contingent liability**. As there is either no probable obligation at reporting date or no obligation that can be measured reliably, it would be inappropriate to include contingent liabilities within the statement of financial position itself. That is why disclosure of contingent liabilities is relegated to the notes to the financial statements. Paragraph 10 of IAS 37 defines a contingent liability as arising when there is:

(a) *a possible obligation that arises from past events and whose existence will be confirmed only by the occurrence or non-occurrence of one or more uncertain future events not wholly within the control of the entity; or*

(b) *a present obligation that arises from past events but is not recognised because:*
   (i) *it is not probable that an outflow of resources embodying economic benefits will be required to settle the obligation; or*
   (ii) *the amount of the obligation cannot be measured with sufficient reliability.*

Worked Example 9.1 provides an illustration relating to when a contingent liability should be recognised.

Worked Example 9.1 **Recognition of a contingent liability**

During 2013 Mark Richards plc, whose reporting period ends on 30 June each year, guarantees the bank overdraft of Shawn Thomson plc. At the time of providing the guarantee, Shawn Thomson plc was in a sound financial position. During 2015 international trading conditions deteriorated to such an extent that Shawn Thomson plc incurred substantial losses. Finally, on 28 June 2015, Shawn Thomson plc was forced to file for protection from its creditors.

Required

How would Mark Richards plc report the guarantee provided to Shawn Thomson plc in its financial statements ending 30 June 2014 and 30 June 2015?

Solution

In this illustration, the obligating event is the provision of the guarantee, which gives rise to a legal obligation. At 30 June 2014, it is unlikely that an outflow of resources embodying economic benefits will occur. No provision is recognised. However, the guarantee is disclosed as a contingent liability.

At 30 June 2015, it is probable that an outflow of resources embodying economic benefits will be required to settle the obligation. A provision—which is a liability which must be recognised within the financial statements—for the best estimate of the obligation must be recognised.

Some authors have speculated that companies sometimes seek to project a view that particular obligations cannot be measured reliably as justification for keeping particular liabilities off the statement of financial position (as we know from the above discussion, a liability is not to be recognised if it cannot be measured reliably). For example, Ji and Deegan (2011) reviewed the disclosure practices of a number of large Australian companies to document how the companies disclosed information about their obligations to clean up contaminated sites. The authors found that it was very common for companies to argue that they were unable to reliably estimate the magnitude of the costs necessary to clean up particular contaminated sites and, as a result, the companies did not recognise the associated liabilities for the purposes of the statement of financial position, preferring instead to provide information about the potential liability in a note entitled 'Contingent Liabilities'. As an example of some disclosures pertaining to an obligation for site remediation, the 2010 Annual Report of Orica Ltd stated in the notes to the financial statements (note 33, p. 100):

In accordance with the current accounting policy, provisions have been created for all known environmental liabilities that can be reliably estimated. For sites where the requirements have been assessed and are capable of reliable measurement, estimated regulatory and remediation costs have been capitalised, expensed as incurred or provided for. For environmental matters where there are significant uncertainties with respect to Orica's remediation obligations or the remediation techniques that might be approved, no reliable estimate can presently be made of regulatory and remediation costs.

Contingent liabilities would include potential liabilities associated with guarantees that have been given to cover the debts of other organisations or potential obligations associated with legal actions taken, or to be taken, against the firm.

Appendix B to IAS 37 provides a useful decision tree for determining whether a transaction or event should be recognised as a provision and therefore included within the statement of financial position, or disclosed as a contingent liability within the notes to the financial statements. The decision tree is reproduced in Figure 9.1.

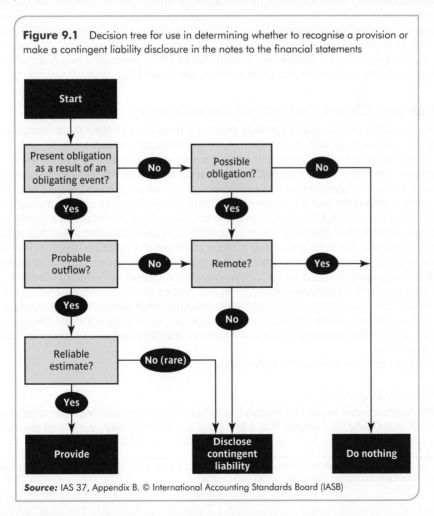

Figure 9.1 Decision tree for use in determining whether to recognise a provision or make a contingent liability disclosure in the notes to the financial statements

Source: IAS 37, Appendix B. © International Accounting Standards Board (IASB)

The disclosure requirements for contingent liabilities are detailed in IAS 37. These disclosures should be made in the notes to the financial statements unless the possibility of any outflow of economic benefits in settlement is considered to be 'remote'. At the end of the reporting period, an entity should disclose each class of contingent liability, together with a brief description of the nature of the contingent liability. Specifically, paragraph 86 of IAS 37 states:

Unless the possibility of any outflow in settlement is remote, an entity shall disclose for each class of contingent liability at the reporting date a brief description of the nature of the contingent liability and, where practicable:

(a) an estimate of its financial effect, measured under paragraphs 36–52;
(b) an indication of the uncertainties relating to the amount or timing of any outflow; and
(c) the possibility of any reimbursement.

Exhibit 9.1 reproduces an extract of the contingent liability note from the 2010 financial statements of SAP.

Exhibit 9.1 Contingent liability note from the 2010 annual report of SAP

(23) Other Financial Commitments and Contingent Liabilities
Contingent Liabilities
In the normal course of business, we usually indemnify our customers against liabilities arising from a claim that our software products infringe a third party's patent, copyright, trade secret, or other proprietary rights. In addition, we occasionally grant function or performance guarantees in routine consulting contracts or development arrangements. Also, our software license agreements generally include a clause guaranteeing that the software substantially conforms to the specifications as described in applicable documentation for a period of six to 12 months from delivery. Our product and service warranty liability, which is measured based on historical experience and evaluation, is included in other provisions (see Note (19b)).

For contingent liabilities related to litigation matters, see Note (24).

(24) Litigation and Claims (first part of the note only)
We are subject to a variety of claims and lawsuits that arise from time to time in the ordinary course of our business, including proceedings and claims that relate to companies which we have acquired, and claims that relate to customers demanding indemnification for proceedings initiated against them based on their use of SAP software. We will continue to vigorously defend against all claims and lawsuits against us. We record a provision for such matters when it is probable that we have a present obligation that results from a past event, is reliably estimable and the settlement of which is probable to require an outflow of resources embodying economic benefits. For the TomorrowNow litigation, we have recorded a provision of €997 million. We currently believe that resolving all other claims and lawsuits against us, individually or in the aggregate, did not and will not have a material adverse effect on our business, financial position, profit, or cash flows. Consequently, the provisions currently recorded for these other claims and lawsuits are neither individually nor in aggregate material to SAP. However, all claims and lawsuits involve risk and could lead to significant financial and reputational damage to the parties involved. Because of significant inherent uncertainties related to these matters, there can be no assurance that our business, financial position, profit or cash flows will not be materially adversely affected nor can we reliably estimate the maximum possible loss in case of an unfavorable outcome. For a description of the development of the provisions recorded for litigation, see Note (19b).

Among the claims and lawsuits are the following:

Intellectual Property Litigation[1]
In October 2006, United States-based Sky Technologies LLC (Sky) instituted legal proceedings in the United States against SAP and Oracle. Sky alleges that SAP's products infringe one or more of the claims in each of

▶

---

[1] Only three cases are included in this exhibit. If you want to read about all the legal proceedings that SAP is involved in, then you should access their financial statements for details on all their actions.

five patents held by Sky. In its complaint, Sky sought unspecified monetary damages and permanent injunctive relief. In September 2010, SAP and Sky resolved this dispute for an amount not material to SAP's business, financial position, profit, or cash flows.

In January 2007, German-based CSB-Systems AG (CSB) instituted legal proceedings in Germany against SAP. CSB alleges that SAP's products infringe one or more of the claims of a German patent and a German utility model held by CSB. In its complaint, CSB has set the amount in dispute at €1 million and is seeking permanent injunctive relief. Within these proceedings CSB is not precluded from requesting damages in excess of the amount in dispute. In July 2007, SAP filed its response in the legal proceedings including a nullity action and cancellation proceeding against the patent and utility model, respectively. The nullity hearing on the German patent was held in January 2009 and the German court determined that the patent is invalid. The cancellation hearing for the utility model was held in May 2009 and the court determined that the utility model was invalid. CSB is appealing; however, the infringement hearing has been stayed pending the appeals.

In May 2010, CSB-Systems International, Inc. (CSB) instituted legal proceedings in the United States against SAP. CSB alleges that SAP's products infringe one or more of the claims in one patent held by CSB. In its complaint, CSB seeks unspecified monetary damages and permanent injunctive relief. The trial has not yet been scheduled.

In rare circumstances it is possible that disclosure of the information required by IAS 37 might seriously prejudice an entity engaged in a dispute with another party on the subject matter of the provision, contingent liability or contingent asset. In these circumstances, paragraph 92 of IAS 37 states that the information need not be disclosed but the entity is required to disclose the nature of the dispute, together with the fact that, and reasons why, the information has not been disclosed.

Contingent liabilities can potentially be very material. Failure to be aware of the potential and material liabilities a firm might be subject to—for example, the firm might have guaranteed the debts of a related entity—can make the financial statements misleading.

Again, it is emphasised that if an obligation is contingent on a future event, there is no 'present obligation' and therefore no liability would need to be disclosed in a reporting entity's statement of financial position. This explains why organisations such as SAP (see Exhibit 9.1) do not treat items such as potential legal damages as liabilities but rather as contingent liabilities, which are disclosed in the notes to the financial statements (and not included within the statement of financial position).

9.4   Liability provisions

It is accepted that liabilities will include such items as accounts payable, bank overdrafts, loans and leases. Traditionally, various types of 'provision' have also been included among an entity's liabilities and disclosed as such in its statement of financial position. These include provisions for annual leave, provisions for long-service leave, provisions for warranty repairs and provisions for maintenance. While 'provisions' for such items as future repairs and maintenance had traditionally been created and recognised, and while such provisions had traditionally been considered liabilities in the statement of financial position, this practice is no longer permitted. Amounts that are 'provided' for future expenditure, but that do not constitute an obligation to an external party—such as provisions for repairs and maintenance—are not liabilities. For an item to be disclosed as a 'provision' it must be a liability. Therefore, one consideration in assessing whether a 'provision' exists is whether the entity has a present obligation to an external party to make a future sacrifice of economic benefits. Because the entity cannot be both the recipient of the economic benefits and the party under the duty to perform, a present obligation implies the involvement of two separate parties: the entity and another party. However, it is not necessary to know the identity of the party to whom the present obligation is owed in order for a present obligation to exist. In describing 'provisions', paragraph 19 of IAS 37 *Provisions, Contingent Liabilities, and Contingent Assets* states:

> It is only those obligations arising from past events existing independently of an entity's future actions (that is, the future conduct of its business) that are recognised as provisions. Examples of such obligations are penalties or clean-up costs for unlawful environmental damage, both of which would lead to an outflow of resources embodying economic benefits in settlement regardless of the future actions of the entity. Similarly, an entity recognises a

provision for the decommissioning costs of an oil installation or a nuclear power station to the extent that the entity is obliged to rectify damage already caused. In contrast, because of commercial pressures or legal requirements, an entity may intend or need to carry out expenditure to operate in a particular way in the future (for example, by fitting smoke filters in a certain type of factory). Because the entity can avoid the future expenditure by its future actions, for example by changing its method of operation, it has no present obligation for that future expenditure and no provision is recognised.

The defining characteristic of a 'provision' as opposed to other 'liabilities' is that the timing of the ultimate payment, and perhaps the amount of the ultimate payment, are uncertain. That is, something is labelled a provision if it is a liability of uncertain timing and/or amount. Therefore if something is disclosed as a provision this should alert the reader to the uncertainties inherent in its ultimate payment. Indeed, paragraph 10 of IAS 37 defines a provision as 'a liability of uncertain timing or amount'. In describing provisions, paragraph 11 of IAS 37 states:

Provisions can be distinguished from other liabilities such as trade payables and accruals because there is uncertainty about the timing or amount of the future expenditure required in settlement. By contrast:

(a) *trade payables are liabilities to pay for goods or services that have been received or supplied and have been invoiced or formally agreed with the supplier; and*
(b) *accruals are liabilities to pay for goods or services that have been received or supplied but have not been paid, invoiced or formally agreed with the supplier, including amounts due to employees (for example, amounts relating to accrued vacation pay). Although it is sometimes necessary to estimate the amount or timing of accruals, the uncertainty is generally much less than for provisions.*

Accruals are often reported as part of trade and other payables, whereas provisions are reported separately.

In relation to when provisions are to be recognised, paragraph 14 of IAS 37 states:

A provision shall be recognised when:

(a) *an entity has a present obligation (legal or constructive) as a result of a past event;*
(b) *it is probable that an outflow of resources embodying economic benefits will be required to settle the obligation; and*
(c) *a reliable estimate can be made of the amount of the obligation.*

If these conditions are not met, no provision shall be recognised.

Now that we have considered the rules pertaining to the recognition of a provision, we also need to look at the rules relating to measurement. In relation to the measurement of a provision, paragraph 36 of IAS 37 requires that the:

amount recognised as a provision shall be the best estimate of the expenditure required to settle the present obligation at the reporting date.

The above requirement makes reference to the 'best estimate'. The best estimate is the amount the entity would pay to settle this obligation at the end of the reporting period or to transfer it to a third party at that time. Estimates of outcomes and financial effects are determined by the judgement of management of the entity, supplemented by experience of similar transactions and possibly by reports of independent experts. Events after the end of the reporting period provide further supplementary evidence as to the existence of provisions.

Uncertainties surrounding the amount to be recognised as a provision are dealt with by various means according to the circumstances. Where a single obligation is measured, the individual most likely outcome might be the best estimate of the liability. Other possible outcomes should also be considered. For example, an entity might be required to rectify a fault in an item of plant it constructed for a customer. The single most likely outcome might be for the fault to be repaired at the first attempt at a cost of £10,000. However, a provision would need to be made for a greater amount if there is a significant chance that further attempts at repair are likely.

Where a large population of items is involved, the provision is measured by weighting all possible outcomes by their associated possibilities. This is known as the expected-value method of estimation. Using this basis, the amount of the provision will depend on the possibility of a loss. An example of this is provided in Worked Example 9.2.

Worked Example 9.2 Calculating a provision using the expected value method

Quicksliver Limited sells 'four-slice' pop-up toasters. The toasters are sold with a six-month warranty that covers the costs of repairing any manufacturing defects that become apparent within six months of purchase. If minor defects are detected in all products sold, repair costs of £1,050,000 would result. If major defects are detected in all products sold, repair costs of £6,500,000 would result.

Based on past experience and future expectations, Quicksliver Limited is able to estimate that 80 per cent of all toasters sold will have no defects, 12 per cent of goods sold will have minor defects and 8 per cent will have major defects.

Required

Establish the expected costs of repairs and prepare the journal entry to record them.

Solution

In this situation, IAS 37 requires Quicksliver Limited to assess the probability of outflow for the warranty obligation as a whole. The expected cost of repairs is ([80% of nil] + [12% of £1,050,000] + [8% of £6,500,000]) = £646,000.

Dr	Warranty expense	£646,000	
Cr	Provision for warranty expense		£646,000

Provision for warranty expense on toasters

Paragraph 42 of IAS 37 requires the risks and uncertainties that inevitably attend many events and circumstances to be taken into account in reaching the best estimate of a provision. Two matters need to be considered: the risks and uncertainties surrounding the provision; and the time value of money.

Risk describes the variability of outcome. An increase in risk might increase the amount at which a liability is measured. The existence of uncertainty, however, does not justify the creation of excess provisions or a deliberate overstatement of liabilities.

In relation to measuring the amount of a provision, if materially different to its undiscounted amount, a provision shall be recognised at its present value. Specifically, paragraph 45 of IAS 37 states:

Where the effect of the time value of money is material, the amount of a provision shall be the present value of the expenditures expected to be required to settle the obligation.

As paragraph 46 of IAS 37 explains, provisions are discounted to reflect the fact that provisions relating to cash flows that arise soon after reporting date are more onerous than when the same cash flows arise later, because of the time value of money. If cash flows are not discounted, two provisions giving rise to the same cash flows but with different timing would be recorded at the same value, although rational economic appraisal would regard them as different.

Paragraph 47 of IAS 37 identifies what rate should be used to discount expected future cash flows. It states:

The discount rate (or rates) shall be a pre-tax rate (or rates) that reflect(s) current market assessments of the time value of money and the risks specific to the liability. The discount rate(s) shall not reflect risks for which future cash flow estimates have been adjusted.

Provisions are required to be reviewed regularly. As paragraph 59 of IAS 37 states:

Provisions shall be reviewed at each reporting date and adjusted to reflect the current best estimate. If it is no longer probable that an outflow of resources embodying economic benefits will be required to settle the obligation, the provisions shall be reversed.

If an entity is discounting its provisions to present value, even if the absolute amount of a provision does not change, the present value of the provision can be expected to change across time. Where the change in the carrying amount of a provision is due to the impacts of using present values, IAS 37 requires that the change be recognised as a borrowing cost (IAS 37, paragraph 60).

Exhibit 9.2 reproduces the provision note from the 2010 financial statements of Deutsche Lufthansa AG Cologne, a European parent company with many subsidiaries including Swiss, Austrian Airlines and Germanwings.

| Exhibit 9.2 | Provision note from the 2010 annual report of Deutsche Lufthansa AG Cologne |

Note 37. OTHER PROVISIONS

In €m	31.12.2010			31.12.2009		
	Total	Non-current	Current	Total	Non-current	Current
Obligations under partial retirement contracts	41	6	35	64	10	54
Other staff costs	279	219	60	284	214	70
Onerous contracts	197	126	71	142	73	69
Environmental restoration	32	28	4	30	25	5
Legal proceedings	72	17	55	77	15	62
Restructuring/severance payments	61	3	58	199	4	195
Fixed-price customer maintenance contracts	104	19	85	139	22	117
Maintenance of aircraft on operating leases	363	175	188	402	209	193
Warranties	38	–	38	30	–	30
Other provisions	337	50	287	375	48	327
Total	**1,524**	**643**	**881**	**1,742**	**620**	**1,122**

Provisions for staff costs mainly relate to staff anniversary bonuses, variable payment portions and other current obligations. Expected losses from onerous contracts result from ongoing obligations or other contractual relationships in which performance and consideration are out of balance. Provisions for environmental restoration are based on surveyors' findings and the assumption that all contamination is removed within ten years without any further legal requirements. Provision for legal proceedings is based on an assessment of the likely outcome of the proceedings.

Changes in groups of individual provisions in 2010 were as follows:

In €m	Obligations under partial retirement contracts	Other staff costs	Onerous contracts	Environmental contracts	Legal proceedings	Restructuring/ severance payments
As of 1.1.2010	64	284	142	30	77	199
Changes in the group of consolidated companies	–	0*	–	–	–	–
Currency translation differences	–	2	7	0*	1	0*
Utilisation	– 64	– 36	– 59	– 2	– 7	– 109
Increase/ additional provisions	34	39	112	3	17	27
Interest added back	7	16	2	1	0*	0*
Reversal	0*	– 11	– 7	0*	– 16	– 56
Transfers	0*	– 15	–	–	0*	0*
As of 31.12.2010	**41**	**279**	**197**	**32**	**72**	**61**

* Rounded below EUR 1m.

Table showing movements on Fixed-price customer maintenance contracts, Maintenance of aircraft on operating leases, Warranties, other provision and the total has not been reproduced—as the disclosures are the same as in the above table.

The funding status for provisions for obligations to staff under partial retirement agreements is as follows:

Funding status

In €m	2010	2009
Present value of funded obligations under partial retirement agreements	190	219
External plan assets	– 149	– 155
	41	**64**

In 2005 EUR 97m was transferred to an external trust fund as insolvency insurance for employer's performance arrears, under phased retirement agreements under which the employee at first works full-time for less pay and then retires early on the same reduced pay. In 2007 and 2009 a further EUR 39m and EUR 2m were transferred respectively. These assets, which fulfil the requirements for plan assets and therefore reduce the net amount of obligations accordingly, are measured at market value on the balance sheet date.

Obligations under partial retirement agreements were calculated on the basis of the following assumptions:

Assumptions

In %	2010	2009	2008
Interest rate	2.2	5.5	6.0
Projected earnings from external plan assets	3.1	3.2	6.0

The following cash outflows are estimated for the non-current portion of the other groups of provisions:[2]

In €m	2012	2013	2014	2015 and thereafter
Onerous contracts	43	18	16	57
Environmental restoration	4	3	3	20
Restructuring/severance payments	2	0*	0*	0*
Fixed-price customer maintenance contracts	11	7	0*	2
Maintenance of aircraft on operating leases	89	42	22	35
Other provisions	22	18	5	47

* Rounded below EUR 1m.

At this stage you have examined liabilities, provisions and contingent liabilities. In Worked Example 9.3 you put this theoretical knowledge into practice by determining whether a transaction is a liability, a provision or a contingent liability and explaining how to account for it.

Worked Example 9.3 — Classification of a transaction as a liability, a provision or as a contingent liability

The draft financial statements for the year ended 30 September 2014 for Donnard plc report a profit before tax of €350,000 and turnover of €5 million. During the conduct of the audit you are informed that a senior manager who was dismissed in December 2013 commenced an action against the company alleging wrongful dismissal and claiming damages of €50,000. The company's solicitors estimate that the manager has a 25 per cent chance of success in her claim. Irrecoverable legal costs of €10,000 will be incurred by Donnard regardless of the outcome.

Required

Explain how the above matter should be treated in the financial statements of Donnard plc for the year ended 30 September 2014 and, where appropriate, show by journal entry the effect on its profit for the year.

Solution

This scenario falls within the scope of IAS 37 *Provisions, Contingent Assets and Contingent Liabilities*. Remember a provision is a liability of uncertain timing or amount. Under the Conceptual Framework, a liability occurs where there is a present obligation as a result of a past (obligating) event, which will result if a probable outflow of economic benefits can be reliably estimated.

First, the action has commenced before the end of the year—hence the past event criteria is met. Is it obligating? The solicitors estimate that the manager has a 25 per cent chance of success. This is not probable/reasonably certain. It is more like a 'possible obligation'. Therefore under this condition the claim for damages should not be recognised, but disclosed in a note to the financial statements. The disclosure should cover the nature and timing of the economic outflows (i.e. a legal case against the company with a 25 per cent chance of success may result in the

---

[2] Comparatives omitted for this table; see their financial statements for the full disclosure.

company having to pay €50,000); also the timing of the outflows should be disclosed if appropriate (i.e. the case will be heard within six months) and any reimbursements expected if relevant (none in this case).

The €10,000 legal costs are irrecoverable and will be incurred by Donnard plc regardless of the action. This is a clear liability. The past event is the legal action. The obligating nature of it is the contract to hire the solicitors/time incurred by them. It is stronger than probable—the liability is certain. It is the timing that is uncertain and indeed the accruals concept becomes relevant as some of the €10,000 may relate to this year and some to the next accounting period. If the law firm can provide a time to date (liability to date), then this is an accrual, with a provision being created for the balance that will be consumed in the future.

Dr	Legal costs in relation to court case	€XX	
Cr	Trade and other payables (accrual)		€XX
Dr	Legal costs in relation to court case	€10,000–€XX	
Cr	Provision for legal fees		€10,000–€XX

Profits will have fallen from €310,000 to €300,000.

9.5 Some implications of reporting liabilities

As we saw in Chapter 3, organisations commonly enter into contractual arrangements that are tied in part to the liabilities of the firm—for example, debt-to-assets constraints. So how liabilities are measured and disclosed can be of great importance to the ongoing survival of the organisation. For example, organisations might borrow funds from external sources, and the ongoing availability of these funds might depend on the organisation maintaining, at a minimum, certain pre-specified levels of performance—for example, ensuring by way of an interest-coverage clause that the organisation's profits, perhaps after some adjustments, exceed interest expense by a certain minimum number of times. The ongoing availability of the funds might also depend on the firm ensuring that it does not exceed an agreed maximum level of debt—for example, through a pre-specified debt-to-assets constraint. As we know, such contractual requirements are based on numbers generated through an organisation's financial accounting system. So whether something is disclosed as an asset, a liability, an expense or income can be very important for an organisation. For example, if a firm has determined that a transaction will not generate probable future economic benefits—a decision that, as we know, depends on professional judgement—the transaction will be treated as an expense. Compared with treating the expenditure as an asset, this will have a detrimental effect on a firm's debt-to-assets ratio and interest-coverage ratio. These clauses may be included within the contractual arrangements of the organisation, which might influence whether the organisation will comply with, or breach, specific contractual arrangements.

Researchers working within the Positive Accounting Theory paradigm (see Chapter 3) typically hypothesise that managers in organisations close to breaching particular accounting-based debt covenants will choose, where there is a choice, accounting methods that increase income, and thereby assets and equity, or decrease debt, thereby reducing the probability of debt covenant violation. To the extent that potential violation of debt covenants drives the selection of one accounting method in preference to another, such practices could be considered to represent creative accounting. They would also represent a departure from the principles espoused in the IASB Conceptual Framework, where it is argued that financial information included within a general purpose financial statement should be *relevant* and should *faithfully represent* the underlying transactions (IASB Conceptual Framework, paragraph 12).

The view that managers will adopt particular accounting methods to circumvent the coming into effect of debt restrictions necessarily assumes that there are costs associated with breaching debt-covenant restrictions and that lenders or their trustees will take action to impose costs on covenant-defaulting firms. Frequently, where a firm does breach a debt-related contractual requirement, it is given a period of time (a grace period) within which to remedy the breach before any action is taken (Chen & Wei 1993). Alternatively, when a breach occurs, lenders can insist upon early repayment; restrictions on the firm borrowing further funds; the firm selling some of its assets; and so on. It should also be acknowledged that the debt-related contractual restrictions are typically written around accounting numbers that are prepared for the purpose of inclusion in half-yearly or yearly financial statements. Hence, it is possible for a firm to default on a particular accounts-based debt clause but be able to remedy the breach prior to the reporting date (DeFond & Jiambalvo 1994).

As we know, generally accepted accounting principles change frequently. Such changes can result from the release of accounting standards prohibiting the use of accounting methods that were previously permitted.

Certainly there was an immense number of changes in 2005 as a result of companies adopting IFRSs. The release of a new accounting standard can, in itself, have an adverse effect on a firm's leverage, and therefore on whether the firm complies with particular debt covenants. For example, an accounting standard might be released that precludes a certain transaction from being capitalised, instead requiring it to be expensed as incurred. Alternatively, an accounting standard might be released that mandates a maximum period of amortisation. Both of these potential changes could have adverse cash-flow effects on an organisation, particularly if the organisation is subject to accounting-based debt covenants, and the debt contract in question does not pre-specify the accounting rules to be used for a particular class of transactions.

When an accounting-based debt covenant is breached, perhaps as a result of the issue of a new accounting standard, it is possible that management might be able to negotiate with the lenders to relax the restriction. Such negotiation can in itself be costly, but might be particularly appropriate when a change in financial accounting requirements was not anticipated by any of the parties to a contractual arrangement. However, renegotiation of a debt contract might not always be possible. It is generally argued (for example, see Smith 1993) that the greater the number of lenders within a loan syndicate, the harder and more costly it is to renegotiate a clause when a technical default has occurred. Consistent with this, it is also argued that it is easier to renegotiate private debt agreements than those entered into for public debt issues (which might include thousands of debt-holders). However, if a firm is in financial distress, debt-holders might not want to renegotiate their debt contracts. Instead, they might wish to extract assets from the defaulting organisation before it becomes even more debt-laden.

Interestingly, there are some researchers who write at length about the benefits that should flow if a firm finds itself in financial distress. They argue that being highly debt-laden, having difficulty servicing interest and principal payment schedules and being close to breaching debt agreements need not necessarily be considered all bad news. For example, Gilson (1989, 1990) argues that financial stress can cause an organisation to rethink its strategies, which might result in a shift in the activities of the organisation. These refocused activities might, in turn, lead to an increase in cash flows and, hence, in the value of the organisation. Gilson (1989) and others also argue that financial stress can be good because it provides the necessary stimulus to remove existing managers and replace them with a new and more efficient management team. Certainly such a change will potentially lead to improvements in profitability so that, in strict financial terms, such a management change will appear successful. However, as we noted in Chapter 3, financial accounting does not consider social costs. For example, some researchers would argue that the social costs of creating unemployed managers must be considered before espousing the (economic) virtues of replacing a management team. They would argue, perhaps rightly, that organisations have many social obligations that are not reflected in financial performance and that some consideration should be given to these responsibilities when agreeing on future corporate strategies. However, further discussion of social issues of this nature is deferred until Chapter 26.

While the above discussion relates to the use of debt covenants in lending agreements, it does not directly consider the securities market reaction to disclosures of debt covenant violation. It would be reasonable to expect that, if debt covenants are violated, then this could be viewed quite negatively by the market. As Griffin *et al.* (2011, p. 1) state:

> A debt covenant violation can be a significant and costly event for a company's shareholders with uncertain consequences, primarily because a violation shifts control rights to creditors who, through the threat of bankruptcy, can exert substantial influence on loan terms, corporate governance, and management decision making. Creditors' options depend on the severity of the violation and may range at one extreme from calling the loan and demanding repayment to less onerous actions such as changing the loan terms, modifying the covenant, and/or waiving the violation for a period during which they can exercise their control rights to improve the situation.

In the study of how insiders might gain from trading as a result of having information about covenant violations, Griffin *et al.* predict that insiders who have special access to information will sell their shares in the company before the debt covenant violation is disclosed (because disclosure of the violation provides information about a significant adverse event therefore leading to a price decline) and will buy back shortly after the violation (at a time when actions are being taken to address the violation). In relation to the results of their study, Griffin *et al.* (2011, p. 15) state that the market's reaction to disclosure of debt covenant violation is 'prompt, negative, and arguably efficient'. In discussing their results, they state (p. 38):

> Our results suggest that insiders benefit by selling shares before a covenant disclosure (to avoid the loss from a price decline) and benefit further by purchasing shares after such disclosure, although the losses avoided from the earlier selling exceed the gains from the later buying. Our results also suggest that insiders base their trades on an information advantage derived from access to debt and/or covenant renegotiations, in that a regression analysis suggests that insiders may gain by selling at least one month prior to a pre-disclosure drop in market-adjusted stock price and by buying at least one month prior to a post-disclosure stock price increase.

9.6 Debt equity debate

All things being equal, firms would typically prefer to disclose low levels of debt. Where firms are close to breaching existing debt restrictions—perhaps they have a debt-to-assets constraint they are approaching—but, nonetheless, need an injection of funds, additional debt might lead to a technical breach of their contractual agreements and therefore possibly the winding up of the company. Deegan (1986) documented how firms might, when faced with a need for additional funds, issue debt-like securities, labelling them equity. Examples are provided of firms issuing securities, labelled redeemable **preference shares** (preference shares are discussed in Chapter 12), which:

> **preference shares** Shares that receive preferential treatment relative to ordinary shares, with the preferential treatment relating to various things, such as dividend entitlements or order of entitlement to any distribution of capital on the dissolution of the company.

- are redeemable (exchangeable for cash) at a specified date;
- provide a fixed rate of dividend payment;
- do not provide voting rights; and
- are guaranteed by related organisations.

Such securities are obviously very debt-like—consider the three key components of a liability provided at the beginning of the chapter. Nevertheless, such securities were found to be typically disclosed as equity.

This treatment is not allowed under IFRS. IAS 32 *Financial Instruments: Presentation* adopts a more logical substance-over-form approach (see Chapter 12 and paragraphs 18, AG25 and AG26 of IAS 32 for a discussion of the substance of different types of preference share).

Preference shares that are redeemable at a scheduled redemption date, and so exhibit characteristics of liabilities, should be differentiated from preference shares that are redeemable at the option of the issuer (and so exhibit characteristics of **share capital**).

As can be seen from Worked Example 9.4, the requirement to treat preference shares as debt can have significant implications for a firm's debt-to-assets ratios. It is only in recent years that preference shares that are debt-like have been required to be disclosed as debt. Although the issue of preference shares has been a limited phenomenon in recent years, one would expect that the recent move by most countries to converge their accounting standards with IFRS will further reduce the issuing of such shares.

> **share capital** The balance of owners' equity within a company which constitutes the capital contributions made by the owners.

Firms have been known to take on debt in such a manner that it is disclosed as neither debt nor equity—that is, it is kept off the statement of financial position. One past

---

Worked Example 9.4 — Impact of classifying preference shares as debt, rather than equity

As at 30 June 2015 Burridge plc has total assets of €2.5 million and total liabilities of €1.6 million. On the same date, Burridge issues €800,000 in preference shares. These shares are redeemable in two years' time at the option of the shareholder and offer a dividend rate of 10 per cent. They do not include voting rights.

Required

Calculate the debt-to-assets ratio for Burridge plc as at 30 June 2015, assuming that:
(a) the preference shares are treated as equity
(b) the preference shares are treated as debt

Solution

If the preference shares are issued, assets will increase by €800,000 to €3.3 million to reflect the additional €800,000 in cash.
(a) If the preference shares are treated as equity, the debt-to-assets ratio is calculated as:
€1.6m ÷ €3.3m = 48.48 per cent
(b) If the preference shares are treated as debt, the debt-to-assets ratio is calculated as:
€2.4m ÷ €3.3m = 72.73 per cent
While the above calculations show how the alternative classification as debt or equity will impact on the debt-to-assets ratio, because the redemption is at the option of the shareholder the correct treatment would see the preference shares being treated as debt.

example of 'off-balance-sheet financing' was leasing. Before the introduction of an accounting standard on leasing (to be discussed in the next chapter) firms would, rather than borrowing to buy an asset, enter into a long-term lease and leave both the asset and the associated obligation off the statement of financial position. As we will see in Chapter 10, this loophole has been closed.

9.7   Accounting for debentures

> **debenture** A written promise to pay a principal amount at a specified time, as well as interest calculated at a specific rate.

A **debenture** is a written promise to pay a principal amount at a specified time in the future, as well as interest calculated at a specified rate. Debenture liabilities are typically secured over the assets of the entity issuing the debentures. That is, if the entity issuing the debentures (the borrower) defaults on the agreement and does not make the agreed payments, the entity acquiring the debentures (the lender) can have the right to seize assets that were provided as security. Debentures may be issued at par, at a premium, or at a discount. Debentures are also referred to as 'bonds'.

Within Europe, corporations are responsible for issuing significant amounts of debt in the form of debentures/bonds. With the large amounts being issued, valuation is an important issue, since how debentures/bonds are valued will have direct implications for reported liabilities and expenses. The article from AFME's website reproduced in Financial Accounting in the News 9.1 provides some insight into the magnitude of the European bond market relative to other securities.

Financial Accounting in the News 9.1

OVERVIEW: THE EUROPEAN AND GLOBAL BOND MARKETS

Association for Financial Markets in Europe (AFME), 2011

Globalisation and the rise of multiple types of European bond markets including a European corporate bond market have changed the opportunities for European bond investors—and everyone else.

Although the US has traditionally dominated the world's bond markets, bonds issued in the US now account for less than half—about 44%—of the global bond market volume. In Europe, bonds are about 2/3 of the total amount of securities outstanding in bonds and shares; in the US, the bond market is about the same size as the stock market. Historically fragmented, the bond markets of the world comprise a great variety of bond products with complex and different characteristics. About 60% of the European bond market is government bond debt, 29% is corporate, and 11% is asset-backed; in the US, the proportion of bonds issued by the corporate sector is much larger.

Bond markets are open to both institutional and individual investors, but there is much more participation generally by institutional investors than individual investors. European individual investors in bonds represent less than 5% of the direct investment in the European bond markets. The majority of bond market participants in Europe are institutional investors, such as pension funds, insurance companies and banks.

Direct holdings of bonds by individual investors nevertheless vary a lot between European countries. In Italy,

individual investor holdings of bonds comprise 20% or more (in 2004, average more than €12,000) of total financial holdings. In Germany, the equivalent percentage is between 10–15% (in 2004, some €5,800) and in other countries it will be typically lower than 5%; the lowest figure being that for the UK (just 1.5%). (In 2004, average British, Spanish and French individual investors held around €1,000 worth of bonds.)

In comparison in the US, individual holdings of bonds amount to circa 6.9% of total financial holdings. The US bond markets have significant participation by individual investors in the local municipal government bond market (sub-sovereign bonds) where about 20–25% of investor participants are individuals.

Where deposits and cash are excluded from total financial holdings to take into account only investment in financial products, the portion of bonds in Italian individual investor portfolios rises to 30.7% (against 2% for Britain and 7.9% for the US).

In Belgium, Germany and Italy, individual investors prefer to invest in bonds directly while in other European countries such investments take place primarily through funds.

Source: AFME. © 2012 AFME

9.7.1 Debentures issued at par

The **par (or face) value** of a debenture/bond represents the amount that the debenture holders will receive on maturity of the debentures. Investors will be prepared to pay the par value if they believe that the rate of interest offered by the issuing company on the debentures—this would be written on the debenture certificate and is often referred to as the **coupon rate**—matches what they believe the rate of interest should be. The fair value of the debentures would, in this instance, be the same as the face value of the debentures. As will be indicated below, if the market believes that the firm is not offering a high enough rate of interest it will not be prepared to pay the full par value—it will demand a discount. That is, the fair value (which is defined in IAS 39 *Financial Instruments: Recognition and Measurement*, and other accounting standards, as 'the amount for which an asset could be exchanged or a liability settled, between knowledgeable willing parties in an arm's length transaction') will be less than its face value. Conversely, if the market believes that the firm is offering a relatively high rate of interest, they will be prepared to pay more than the full par value, offering to pay a premium (the fair value will be greater than its 'face value'). Worked Example 9.5 provides an example of debentures being issued at par value.

> **par (or face) value** The amount debenture holders receive on maturity of debentures.
>
> **coupon rate** The rate of interest specified on the face of a security.

Worked Example 9.5 — Issue of debentures at par value

Company C issues £10 million of five-year, 10 per cent, semi-annual coupon debentures to the public (which pay interest each six months). The market also requires a rate of return of 10 per cent. Assume that the funds are received and the debentures are allotted on the same day: 30 June 2015.

Required

Provide the accounting entries at 30 June 2015, 31 December 2015 and 30 June 2020 to record:

(a) the receipt of funds
(b) the first payment of interest
(c) the redemption of the debentures

Solution

Because Company C is issuing bonds that provide a rate of return matching the rate of return expected by the market, there is no need to issue the securities at a discount or a premium—they can be issued at their face value.

(a) On receipt of funds, the firm places the cash from a public issue in trust until such time as it allots the debentures.

30 June 2015

Dr	Cash trust	£10,000,000	
Cr	Application—debentures		£10,000,000

(to record the receipt of funds from the investors)

Dr	Cash at bank	£10,000,000	
Cr	Cash trust		£10,000,000

(to transfer funds to the entity's operating account following the allocation of the debentures)

Dr	Application—debentures	£10,000,000	
Cr	Debentures		£10,000,000

(to record the allocation of the debentures, and to eliminate the 'application' account)

The application account is considered to be a liability, as are the debentures. When the debentures have been issued, the issuing organisation has fulfilled its obligation and thereafter the application account can be closed.

(b) The entry to record the first payment of interest would be:

31 December 2015

Dr	Interest expense	£500,000	
Cr	Cash at bank		£500,000

(interest expense for six months = £10m × 10% ÷ 2)

►

◄ (c) When the debentures are redeemed on 30 June 2020, the entry to record the redemption would be:

30 June 2020

| Dr | Debentures | £10,000,000 | |
| Cr | Cash at bank | | £10,000,000 |

(to recognise the repayment of the face value of the debentures)

9.7.2 Debentures issued at a discount

It is worth noting that the following discussion relies upon the reader having some knowledge of how to calculate present values. For those readers with limited knowledge in this area, Appendix C provides a brief explanation of how to calculate present values. In financial accounting, a number of different categories of liability must be discounted to their present value, so accountants must know how to calculate present values.

The rate of return required by the market might fluctuate daily; hence it is usual for debentures not to be issued at par (face value). Remember, regardless of what investors pay for the debenture, they will receive the face value (or par value) on redemption; and the interest received will equal the rate written on the debenture certificate, referred to as the coupon rate, multiplied by the par value of the security (regardless of the actual price paid for the debentures). That is, the amount received on redemption and the periodic interest receipts will not change, regardless of what is paid for the security. If the market requires a rate of return in excess of the coupon rate of the debentures, the issue price of the debentures must be reduced to the price at which the cash flows to the investor—in the form of the periodic interest receipts and the final repayment of principal— represent a rate of return equivalent to that required by the market. That is, the debentures will be issued at a discount. Worked Example 9.6 provides an illustration of debentures being issued at a discount.

Worked Example 9.6   Debentures issued at a discount

Assume that the market requires 12 per cent for the debentures considered in Worked Example 9.5.

Required

Calculate the issue price of the debentures and include the relevant accounting entries.

Solution

We need to work out the present value of the future receipts, discounted at the market's required rate of return—in this example it is 12 per cent.

As the market rate exceeds the coupon rate, we should realise that the securities will be issued at a discount. That is, they will be issued for an amount less than their face value. To determine the issue price of the securities, and for the sake of simplicity, we will divide the market's required annual rate of return (12 per cent) by 2 to provide the rate of return required for each six-month period (given that the securities are semi-annual). The present value of the annuity and the present value of the principal can be calculated by referring to the present value tables provided in the appendices to this book (although for this example we have used present value calculations that go to 7 decimal places).

Present value of interest payments
£500,000 for 10 periods @ 6 per cent
£500,000 × 7.3600866　　　　=　　　£3,680,043
Present value of principal repayment
£10,000,000 in 10 periods @ 6 per cent
£10,000,000 × 0.5583948　　=　　　<u>£5,583,948</u>
Present value of future cash flows　　　<u>£9,263,991</u>

The price of £9,263,991 represents the fair value of the securities (that is, the amount for which an asset could be exchanged or a liability settled, between knowledgeable, willing parties in an arm's length transaction), and it is the fair value of the securities that must be disclosed as a liability in the statement of financial position pursuant to paragraph 46 of IAS 39. The journal entry on the issue of debentures would be:

30 June 2015

| Dr | Cash | £9,263,991 | |
| Cr | Debentures | | £9,263,991 |

In the past, the discount (or premium) that arises on a debenture issue would have been separately disclosed and accounted for, but pursuant to IAS 39, separate disclosure is no longer made. Rather, the present value of the liability shall be disclosed within the statement of financial position. It is a requirement of IAS 39 that the effective interest method is used to account for a financial liability such as a debenture. IAS 39 provides the following definition of effective-interest method:

> The effective interest method *is a method of calculating the amortised cost of a financial asset or a financial liability (or group of financial assets or financial liabilities) and of allocating the interest income or interest expense over the relevant period. The effective interest rate is the rate that exactly discounts estimated future cash payments or receipts through the expected life of the financial instrument or, when appropriate, a shorter period to the net carrying amount of the financial asset or financial liability.*

Pursuant to the effective interest method, the interest expense for a period is calculated by multiplying the present value of the outstanding liability at the beginning of the period by the market's required rate of return (interest rate). In the example being used here, the rate is 6 per cent. Using the effective interest method, the carrying amount of the debenture at the end of the debenture's life will equal the face value of the debenture, as Table 9.1 demonstrates.

Table 9.1 Determining the periodic interest expense under the effective-interest method

Period	Opening liability	Effective interest @ 6 per cent	Coupon rate	Net liability
	£	£	£	£
0				9,263,991.0
1	9,263,991	555,839.5	500,000	9,319,830.5
2	9,319,830.5	559,189.8	500,000	9,379,020.3
3	9,379,020.3	562,741.2	500,000	9,441,761.5
4	9,441,761.5	566,505.7	500,000	9,508,267.2
5	9,508,267.2	570,496.0	500,000	9,578,763.2
6	9,578,763.2	574,725.9	500,000	9,653,489.1
7	9,653,489.1	579,209.4	500,000	9,732,698.5
8	9,732,698.5	583,962.0	500,000	9,816,660.5
9	9,816,660.5	588,999.7	500,000	9,905,660.2
10	9,905,660.2	594,339.8	500,000	10,000,000.0

9.7.3 Effective-interest method

We can use a table to determine the interest expense calculated using the **effective-interest method**.

As shown in Table 9.1, the amount of the liability increased each period using this method equals the difference between the present value of the opening liability, multiplied by the market rate of interest (which gives the interest expense), and the actual payment being made (based on the coupon rate).

Adopting the effective-interest method means that the balance of the debenture liability represents the present value of the liability throughout the debenture term (adopting the market's required rate of return at the date the debentures were issued as the discount rate). Using the effective-interest method, the accounting entries would be:

effective-interest method Calculating interest expense for a period by multiplying the opening present value of a liability by the appropriate market rate of interest.

31 December 2015

Dr	Interest expense	£555,839	
Cr	Debentures		£55,839
Cr	Cash		£500,000

30 June 2016

Dr	Interest expense	£559,190	
Cr	Debentures		£59,190
Cr	Cash		£500,000

31 December 2016

Dr	Interest expense	£562,741	
Cr	Debentures		£62,741
Cr	Cash		£500,000

As we can see above, the interest expense increases across time as the present value of the liability increases.

9.7.4 Debentures issued at a premium

> **premium** The amount paid per debenture in excess of the par or face value.

If debentures are issued that provide a coupon rate in excess of that demanded by the market, then investors will be prepared to pay a **premium** (that is, more than the face value of the bonds). In this case, when the returns are compared with the higher price paid for the debentures, the effective rate of return on the debentures equates with the return required by the market. That is, whatever coupon rate is offered, it is

---

Worked Example 9.7   Debentures issued at a premium

The debenture issue is the same as that in Worked Example 9.6, except that the market demands 8 per cent on such debentures.

Required

Calculate the issue price (fair value) of the debentures and provide the accounting journal entries for 30 June 2015, 31 December 2015 and 30 June 2016.

Solution

Present value of interest payments

£500,000 for 10 periods @ 4 per cent
£500,000 x 8.1108925   =   £4,055,446

Present value of principal repayment
£10,000,000 in 10 periods @ 4 per cent
£10,000,000 x 0.6755643   =   £6,755,643
Issue price   =   £10,811,089

Hence the premium is £811,089. We will also assume that this is a direct private placement and therefore we will not use a trust or application account.

30 June 2015

Dr	Cash	£10,811,089	
Cr	Debentures		£10,811,089

Using the effective-interest rate method

31 December 2015

Dr	Interest expense	£432,444	
Dr	Debentures	£67,556	
Cr	Cash		£500,000

(interest expense = £10,811,089 x 0.04 = £432,444)

30 June 2016

Dr	Interest expense	£429,741	
Dr	Debenture premium	£70,259	
Cr	Cash		£500,000

[interest expense = (£10,811,089 – £67,556) x 0.04 = £429,741]

assumed that the actual issue price of the securities will be adjusted by the market so that the actual cash flows generated from the investment will provide a rate of return equivalent to that required by the market (the **market rate of return**). This is examined more closely in Worked Example 9.7.

> **market rate of return**
> The rate of return that the market, typically the capital market, requires from a particular investment.

9.8 Hybrid securities

Although a more detailed description of financial instruments is provided in Chapter 12, it should be noted at this point that reporting entities will sometimes issue **hybrid securities**, which have both debt and equity characteristics. We have already discussed how preference shares can have both debt and equity characteristics. Some companies also issue debt that allows conversion, at the debt-holder's option, into shares of the issuing company. That is, the securities may be converted or redeemed for cash. These are commonly referred to as *convertible notes*.

> **hybrid securities**
> Securities exhibiting both debt and equity characteristics.

An issue that arises in the case of convertible notes is whether they should be treated as debt or equity—or perhaps part debt and part equity. If conversion of the securities to shares is probable, they would have an equity component. They would also have a liability component relating to the payment obligations that exist prior to conversion. If redemption of the securities for cash is the probable outcome, they would need to be partly classified as liabilities.

While we will be covering hybrid securities in more depth in Chapter 12, we can note here that IAS 32 stresses that financial instruments such as convertible notes should be disclosed partially as debt and partially as equity (paragraph 29).

With regard to determining the amount to be assigned to the equity component and the amount to be assigned to the debt component, paragraph 32 of IAS 32 states:

> *The issuer of a bond convertible into ordinary shares first determines the carrying amount of the liability component by measuring the fair value of a similar liability (including any embedded non-equity derivative features) that does not have an associated equity component. The carrying amount of the equity instrument represented by the option to convert the instrument into ordinary shares is then determined by deducting the fair value of the financial liability from the fair value of the compound financial instrument as a whole.*

SUMMARY

The chapter addressed the general issues pertaining to liabilities. A liability is defined in the IASB Conceptual Framework as a present obligation of an entity arising from past events, the settlement of which is expected to result in an outflow from the entity of resources embodying economic benefits. Liabilities are to be recognised when the future transfer of economic benefits is considered to be probable and the amount of the obligation can be measured reliably.

For statement of financial position purposes, liabilities can be classified as current or non-current. Current liabilities are those that are repayable within 12 months of the reporting date or within the entity's 'normal operating cycle'.

This chapter considers the accounting treatment of preference shares and convertible notes, and indicates that the way such securities are disclosed should be dependent upon whether they are of the substance of debt or of equity. 'Provisions' are also considered, and it is stressed that, for a provision to be considered a liability, there must be a present obligation (legal, moral or constructive) to other entities, with the result that provisions for such things as future repairs do not constitute liabilities.

Accounting for the issue of debentures is also discussed. Where the coupon rate of the debentures is the same as the required market rate, debentures will be issued at their par or face value; where the required market rate of the debentures is less than the coupon rate, debentures will be issued at a premium; and where the required market rate of the debentures is greater than the coupon rate, debentures will be issued at a discount.

KEY TERMS

contingent liability **218**	hybrid securities **235**	preference shares **229**
coupon rate **231**	liability **215**	premium **234**
current liability **217**	market rate of return **235**	share capital **229**
debenture **230**	non-current liability **217**	
effective-interest method **233**	par (or face) value **231**	

END-OF-CHAPTER EXERCISE

On 1 July 2015 Kruger plc privately issues €1 million in six-year debentures, which pay interest each six months at a coupon rate of 6 per cent per annum. At the time of issuing the securities, the market requires a rate of return of 4 per cent. Consistent with the requirements of IAS 39, the debentures are accounted for using the effective interest method.   **LO 9.6**

REQUIRED

(a) Determine the fair value of the debentures at the time of issue (which will also be their issue price).

(b) Provide the journal entries at:

    (i) 1 July 2015

    (ii) 31 December 2015

    (iii) 30 June 2016

SOLUTION TO END-OF-CHAPTER EXERCISE

In this question, the interest payments of 6 per cent per annum are made each six months for six years. Therefore we will treat the debentures as offering a coupon rate of 3 per cent over 12 periods. Similarly, the market rate will be calculated as 2 per cent for 12 periods.

(a) The issue price is equal to the present value of the interest annuity and the principal repayment. The discount rate is the market's required rate of return, in this case, 2 per cent per six-month period.

Present value of principal	=	€1,000,000 × 0.7885	=	€788,500
Present value of annuity	=	€30,000 × 10.5753	=	€317,259
Issue price			=	€1,105,759

Because the market rate of the debentures is less than their coupon rate, the debentures' fair value is assessed as being greater than their face value, that is, they are issued at a premium, as shown above.

(b) Journal entries

1 July 2015

Dr	Cash	€1,105,759	
Cr	Debentures		€1,105,759

The interest expense in each period will be the present value of the liability at the commencement of the period, multiplied by the market's required rate of return. In this case, it will be €/£1,105,759 × 0.02 = €/£22,115.

31 December 2015

Dr	Interest expense	€22,115	
Dr	Debentures	€7,885	
Cr	Cash		€30,000

30 June 2016

Dr	Interest expense	€21,957	
Dr	Debentures	€8,043	
Cr	Cash		€30,000

Interest = (€1,105,759 − €7,885) × 0.02 = €21,957

REVIEW QUESTIONS

1 What attributes should an item or transaction exhibit in order to be classified a liability? **LO** 9.1

2 What is a contingent liability and how should it be disclosed for financial reporting purposes? **LO** 9.2

3 If a reporting entity has an obligation to clean up a contaminated site, but does not believe it can measure the liability with any reliability, then should the obligation be disclosed at all within the financial statements and accompanying notes? If so, how would it be disclosed? **LO** 9.2

4 An entity has determined that it will cost approximately €15 million to clean up a site that it previously contaminated as a result of its operations. Pursuant to IAS 37, what attributes should this proposed clean-up have if it is to satisfy the requirements necessary for labelling it a provision? **LO** 9.4

5 Determine whether the following items would be classified and recorded as liabilities: **LO** 9.1
   (a) provision for repairs
   (b) provision for long-service leave
   (c) dividends payable
   (d) a guarantee for the debts of a subsidiary

6 What factors may cause the price of a debenture at issue date to be different from its face value? **LO** 9.6

7 It is often argued that managers would prefer to show lower levels of debt than higher levels of debt. Why do you think this might be so? **LO** 9.5

8 Some researchers argue that it would be harder to renegotiate a public debt agreement than a private debt agreement. Why do you think this might be the case? **LO** 9.5

9 If a company is in financial distress, some accounting researchers argue that this is not necessarily all bad news. The fact that the company is in distress might signal that the incumbent management team is inefficient, thereby providing the mechanism or impetus to remove it and replace it with a new, more efficient team. This is a good outcome. **LO** 9.5

REQUIRED
Evaluate this view.

10 How would you determine the discount or premium on a debenture issue? **LO** 9.7

11 Company X recognises the following instruments within the 'Shareholders' equity' section of its statement of financial position: **LO** 9.4
   • redeemable preference shares
   • perpetual convertible notes
   • preference shares
   • subordinated loans

REQUIRED
How would these instruments be disclosed pursuant to IAS 1, IAS 37 and the IASB Conceptual Framework?

12 Brighton Ltd is a manufacturer of boats and gives warranties at the time of sale to purchasers of the boats. Pursuant to the warranty terms, Brighton Ltd undertakes to make good, by repair or replacement, manufacturing defects that become apparent within a period of three years from the date of sale. **LO** 9.3

REQUIRED
Should a liability in the form of a provision be recorded? How would it be measured and how should it be presented to financial statement users?

13 Hampton Ltd has a number of non-current assets, some of which require, in addition to normal ongoing maintenance, substantial expenditure on major refits/refurbishment at certain intervals or on major components that require replacement at regular intervals. **LO** 9.3

REQUIRED
Should a liability in the form of a provision be recorded? How would it be measured and how should it be presented to financial statement users?

14 Sandringham Mining Ltd has been mining in a particular coastal area. A requirement of the local Environmental Protection Authority is that the area be restored to a state that is beneficial to the local fauna. **LO** 9.3

REQUIRED

Does a liability exist and, if so, when should a provision for restoration be recognised?

15 Elwood Chemicals Ltd has, as a result of its ongoing operations, contaminated the land on which it operates. There is no legal requirement to clean up the land. **LO 9.2**

REQUIRED

Should Elwood Chemicals Ltd recognise a liability?

16 Explain how the release of a new accounting standard could potentially cause a reporting entity to violate an existing debt covenant. **LO 9.5**

17 Midnight Boil Limited sells electricity generated from its nuclear power plant. Its managing director, Peter Polly, is not overly concerned about the environment but nevertheless knows that the company has a legal obligation to clean up the site in 20 years' time when the plant is shut on 30 June 2035. As at 30 June 2015, the best estimate to clean up the site (in 2035) is €10,500,000. **LO 9.3**

One year later, on 30 June 2016, the best estimate at cleaning up the site (in 19 years' time) is still considered to be €10,500,000.

The pre-tax rates that reflect current market assessments of the time value of money and the risks specific to the liability were 7 per cent as at 30 June 2015 and 6 per cent as at 30 June 2016.

REQUIRED

Provide the journal entries in relation to the above obligation for the years ending 30 June 2015 and 30 June 2016.

18 Cactus plc issues some convertible notes in 2015. These notes are issued for £20 each and allow note-holders the option to convert each note to one ordinary share in Cactus plc. The date for conversion is 31 July 2016. If the conversion option is not exercised, cash of £20 per note will be paid to the note-holders. At 30 June 2016 the price of Cactus plc's shares is £18.00. Would you disclose the notes as debt or as equity as at 30 June 2016? **LO 9.4**

19 On 1 July 2014 Michaela plc issues £1 million in five-year debentures that pay interest each six months at a coupon rate of 10 per cent. At the time of issuing the securities, the market requires a rate of return of 8 per cent. Interest expense is determined using the effective-interest method. **LO 9.6**

REQUIRED

(a) Determine the issue price.

(b) Provide the journal entries at:

    (i) 1 July 2014

    (ii) 30 June 2015

    (iii) 30 June 2016

20 On 1 July 2014 Bombo plc issues £2 million in six-year debentures that pay interest each six months at a coupon rate of 8 per cent. At the time of issuing the securities, the market requires a rate of return of 6 per cent. Interest expense is determined using the effective interest method. **LO 9.6**

REQUIRED

(a) Determine the issue price.

(b) Provide the journal entries at:

    (i) 1 July 2014

    (ii) 30 June 2015

    (iii) 30 June 2016

21 On 1 July 2014 Rankin plc issues €1 million in ten-year debentures that pay interest each six months at a coupon rate of 10 per cent. At the time of issuing the securities, the market requires a rate of return of 12 per cent. Interest expense is determined using the effective interest method. **LO 9.6**

REQUIRED

(a) Determine the issue price.

(b) Provide the journal entries at:

    (i) 1 July 2014

    (ii) 30 June 2015

    (iii) 30 June 2016

CHALLENGING QUESTIONS

22 The article by Antonella Ciancio reproduced below provides information about claims that might arise as a result of the collapse of Parmalat in 2003. **LO** 9.2

REQUIRED

(a) In the light of the information in the article, do you believe that it is appropriate for the four banks to utilise a contingent liability note as the vehicle to provide information about the organisations' potential liability in relation to the claims?

(b) Alternatively, are there any grounds to suggest that the banks should recognise a provision in relation to the claims?

(c) Search the web to determine the outcome of the case. Then, review the annual reports of the banks for the period before the court case to determine the actual disclosures that had been made by the banks in relation to the Parmalat case. You are to discuss whether you agree with the disclosure policy adopted by the banks in advance of the court case ruling.

MILAN COURT TO RULE IN PARMALAT CASE ON MONDAY

Antonella Ciancio, *Reuters* US edition, 15 April 2011

A Milan judge is due to rule on Monday in Milan in a market-rigging trial against four major foreign banks and six of their employees for their alleged role in the 2003 collapse of Italian food giant Parmalat (PLT.MI). Banks Citigroup Inc (C.N), Bank of America Corp (BAC.N), Morgan Stanley (MS.N) and Deutsche Bank (DBKGn.DE) have been charged for allegedly helping the food group mislead investors.

If guilty, the banks could face the impounding of about 120 million euros. The banks have repeatedly denied any wrongdoing.

Here are some facts about the Parmalat court cases:

* There have been three main trials into Parmalat's collapse in 2003, dubbed 'Europe's Enron': two in Italy's financial hub Milan and the other in Parma, close to the group's headquarters.

* Charges against the people involved in the trial could be dropped under the Italian statute of limitations which sets a time limit for legal proceedings, a judicial source said on Friday. However, this possibility does not apply to the banks as companies are subject to different legislation in Italy.

If considered guilty, the banks face the impounding of a total of about 120 million euros of profit.

Prosecutors have also asked for the four banks to be fined 900,000 euros each in case they are sentenced.

* In Parma, Parmalat's founder Calisto Tanzi, who was the group's chief executive at the time, has been sentenced to

18 years in prison on charges of fraudulent bankruptcy and criminal conspiracy. A total of 56 people were originally charged but most sought plea bargains or accelerated trials or had charges dropped.

* In a separate trial in Milan, Tanzi has been sentenced to 10 years in prison for market rigging and obstructing market regulators. He is appealing against the ruling.

* Parmalat collapsed at the end of 2003 with a 14 billion euros hole in its accounts. The crisis erupted in December 2003, when it said a 4 billion euro bank account held by a Cayman Islands unit did not exist, forcing management to seek bankruptcy protection and triggering a criminal fraud probe.

* Despite the company's investment-grade credit rating, concerns had swirled for months over Parmalat's failure to say why it did not use cash shown on its balance sheet to cut debt.

* A streamlined version of the dairy group, stripped of loss-making foreign units, relisted on Milan's bourse in 2005.

* Parmalat's collapse sparked litigation worldwide against dozens of banks by current Parmalat management and by investors.

* Parmalat has recouped more than 2 billion euros from settlements with banks including Morgan Stanley (MS.N) and the former Merrill Lynch, now part of Bank of America.

REFERENCES

CHEN, K.C.W. & WEI, K.C.J., 'Creditors' Decisions to Waive Violations of Accounting-based Debt Covenants', *Accounting Review*, April 1993, pp. 218–32.

DEEGAN, C.M., 'Preference Shares—Issues Relating to their Use and Disclosure', *Chartered Accountant in Australia*, October 1986, pp. 48–53.

DEFOND, M.L. & JIAMBALVO, J., 'Debt Covenant Violation and Manipulation of Accruals', *Journal of Accounting and Economics*, vol. 17, 1994, pp. 145–76.

GILSON, S.C., 'Management Turnover and Financial Distress', *Journal of Financial Economics*, vol. 25, 1989, pp. 241–62.

GILSON, S.C., 'Bankruptcy, Boards, Banks, and Block Holders', *Journal of Financial Economics*, vol. 27, 1990, pp. 355–87.

GRIFFIN, P.A, LONT, D., & MCCLUNE K., 'Insightful Insiders? Insider Trading and Stock Return around Debt Covenant Violation Disclosures', *Accounting and Finance Association of Australia and New Zealand Annual Conference,* Darwin, July 2011.

JI, S. & DEEGAN, C., 'Contaminated Sites within Australia: Many Sites, but Minimal Corporate Disclosures', *Critical Perspectives on Accounting Annual Conference,* New York, April 2011.

SMITH, C.W., 'A Perspective on Accounting-based Debt Covenant Violations', *Accounting Review*, April 1993, pp. 289–303.

Chapter 10

Accounting for Leases

Learning objectives

Upon completing this chapter readers should:

LO1 understand what a lease represents;

LO2 understand the differences between operating leases and financial leases;

LO3 understand how lessors and lessees should account for financial leases;

LO4 understand how lessors and lessees should account for operating leases;

LO5 understand the implications of lease recognition for a reporting entity's financial statements; and

LO6 be aware of joint efforts currently being undertaken by the IASB and the FASB to develop a revised accounting standard that will lead to significant changes in how leases are to be accounted for.

10.1 Introduction to accounting for leases

The international accounting standard pertaining to **leases** is IAS 17 *Leases*. This standard applies to all leases except for 'leases to explore for or use minerals, oil, natural gas and similar non-generative resources; and licensing agreements for such items as motion picture films, video recordings, plays, manuscripts, patents and copyrights' (IAS 17, paragraph 2). It also does not apply to items that are covered by another standard such as leases on investment property (covered by IAS 40 *Investment Property*) or biological assets (covered by IAS 41 *Agriculture*). According to paragraph 4 of IAS 17, a lease is:

> *an agreement whereby the lessor conveys to the lessee in return for a payment or series of payments the right to use an asset for an agreed period of time.*

> **lease** An agreement conveying the right from a lessor to a lessee to use property for a stated period in return for a series of payments.

Lessees may have access to a large and diverse array of assets by means of leases. The central accounting issue is whether or not the leased assets and the associated commitments relating to the lease arrangement should appear in the reporting entity's statement of financial position. A lessee does not have legal title to the leased asset during the lease term. However, should lack of legal ownership preclude the lessee's reporting of the asset, and related liability, in the statement of financial position?

As the discussion in Chapter 4 indicated, it is *control* of an asset that is relevant, not *legal ownership*. As the IASB Conceptual Framework indicates, assets are future economic benefits controlled by the entity as a result of past transactions or other past events. Hence a firm will recognise assets it does not *own*, as long as it is able to *control* the use of those assets. But do leases transfer control of assets to the lessee? As we will see, depending upon the terms of the lease agreement, control of the asset can in fact be vested in the lessee.

If a firm has entered into a long-term lease, disclosure of the lease obligation as a liability in the statement of financial position of the lessee would also be appropriate (subject to certain requirements, to be discussed below). The economic substance of acquiring an asset by way of a lease can, depending upon the terms of the lease, be essentially the same as 'acquiring' an asset by borrowing funds, even though legal title does not pass to the lessee upon signing the lease. For certain types of leases, failure to disclose the leased asset, and the related lease obligation, may cause the financial statements to be misleading. As paragraph 21 of IAS 17 states:

> *Transactions and other events are accounted for and presented in accordance with their substance and financial reality and not merely with legal form. Although the legal form of a lease agreement is that the lessee may acquire no legal title to the leased asset, in the case of finance leases the substance and financial reality are that the lessee acquires the economic benefits of the use of the leased asset for the major part of its economic life in return for entering into an obligation to pay for that right an amount approximating, at the inception of the lease, the fair value of the asset and the related finance charge.*

According to IAS 17, certain leases must be disclosed in the statement of financial position (as a leased asset and a lease liability), while others will not appear in the statement of financial position. Specifically, leases that are classified as finance leases must be disclosed in the statement of financial position, whereas leases that are considered to be operating leases will not appear in the financial statements.

At this point it needs to be emphasised that the following discussion relates to the accounting requirements in place at the time of writing this chapter. That is, we will be discussing the accounting requirements incorporated within IAS 17. There is much discussion about the accounting for leases and a revised accounting standard is expected to be released in 2013 or 2014 with an application date expected to be in 2015, or later. We will discuss the probable contents of the new accounting standard towards the end of this chapter, but one of the key likely changes is that the requirement to differentiate between operating and financial leases—as is required under IAS 17 and described below—will ultimately be removed, and there will be a requirement that all leases (other than short-term leases of 12 months or less) be shown on the statement of financial position both as a lease liability and as an asset, which will be referred to as a 'right-of-use asset'. The consequence will be that, when the new accounting standard is finally released, more leased assets and associated liabilities will appear in the statement of financial position than is currently the case. We will defer further discussion on the likely new accounting standard and will now return to our discussion of IAS 17.

finance lease A lease in which the terms of the lease agreement transfer the risks and benefits of ownership from the lessor to the lessee.

operating lease Lease in which the risks and rewards of ownership stay with the lessor.

IAS 17 defines a **finance lease** as a lease that 'transfers substantially all the risks and rewards incidental to ownership of an asset. Title may or may not eventually be transferred.' Finance leases are also sometimes referred to as capital or financial leases. A lease that is not a finance lease is an operating lease. Indeed, IAS 17 defines an **operating lease** as 'a lease other than a finance lease'. An operating lease does not transfer substantially all the risks and rewards incidental to ownership of the asset to the lessee.

Where substantially all the risks and rewards of ownership pass to the lessee (a finance lease) and if the financial effects of the lease are material, paragraph 20 of IAS 17 requires the lessee to record, as at the beginning of the lease term, an initial asset and liability equal to the fair value of the leased property or, if lower, the present value of the minimum lease payments (we will define 'minimum lease payments' shortly).

For a finance lease, the lease payments paid by the lessee to the lessor will comprise both the payment of principal and the payment of interest. As paragraph 25 of IAS 17 states:

> *Minimum lease payments shall be apportioned between the finance charge and the reduction of the outstanding liability. The finance charge shall be allocated to each period during the lease term so as to produce a constant periodic rate of interest on the remaining balance of the liability. Contingent rents shall be charged as expenses in the periods in which they are incurred.*

Contingent rents are defined in IAS 17 as, 'that portion of the lease payments that is not fixed in amount but is based on the future amount of a factor that changes other than with the passage of time (e.g. percentage of future sales, amount of future use, future price indices, future market rates of interest)'. As already indicated, if the risks and rewards of ownership are not transferred, the lease is referred to as an operating lease. For an operating lease, no lease liability or asset should be shown in the statement of financial position of the lessee (although some disclosures will be required in the notes to the financial statements). In effect, the lease payments relating to an operating lease are simply treated as rental expenses, which go through the statement of profit and loss.

To determine whether a lease is a finance lease or an operating lease, we need to determine the **risks and rewards of ownership**. Again, the central rule is that, if the risks and rewards (or benefits) of ownership transfer to the lessee, the leased asset, and the associated liabilities for the minimum lease payments, are recognised and disclosed in the statement of financial position of the lessee (the lease would be a finance lease). If we are to recognise the lease for statement of financial position purposes (that is, capitalise the lease), we need to be able to calculate the **minimum lease payments** (given that assets and liabilities are recognised at the fair value of the asset or the present value of the minimum lease payments, whichever is the lower). This and other important terms are defined in what follows.

> **risks and rewards of ownership** Risks include those associated with idle capacity and obsolescence and benefits include gains in realisable value.
>
> **minimum lease payments** Rental payments over the lease term including the amount of any bargain purchase option, premium and any guaranteed residual value and excluding any rental relating to costs to be met by the lessor and any contingent rentals.

10.2 Key terms used in accounting for leases

10.2.1 Risks and rewards of ownership

From the preceding discussion it should be clear that consideration of the risks and rewards of ownership is central to the application of IAS 17. Paragraph 7 of IAS 17 addresses the risks and rewards of ownership. It states:

> *Risks include the possibilities of losses from idle capacity or technological obsolescence and of variations in return because of changing economic conditions. Rewards may be represented by the expectation of profitable operation over the asset's economic life and of gain from appreciation in value or realisation of a residual value.*

If the lessee holds the risks and rewards of ownership, the lessee's risk exposure is basically what it would be if the lessee acquired the asset by way of a purchase transaction. Therefore, if the risks and rewards of ownership are transferred *in substance* to the lessee, the lessee's risk exposure in relation to holding the asset is basically equivalent to what it would have been if the lessee had acquired the asset for cash or by way of a loan.

It is not always a straightforward exercise to determine whether the risks and rewards incidental to ownership have passed substantially to the lessee. Professional judgement might be required. As a result, IAS 17 dedicates paragraphs 10 to 12 to assisting determination of whether a lease is a finance lease or an operating lease. These paragraphs explain:

10. *Whether a lease is a finance lease or an operating lease depends on the substance of the transaction rather than the form of the contract. Examples of situations that individually or in combination would normally lead to a lease being classified as a finance lease are:*
    (a) *the lease transfers ownership of the asset to the lessee by the end of the lease term;*
    (b) *the lessee has the option to purchase the asset at a price that is expected to be sufficiently lower than the fair value at the date the option becomes exercisable for it to be reasonably certain, at the inception of the lease, that the option will be exercised;*
    (c) *the lease term is for the major part of the economic life of the asset even if title is not transferred;*
    (d) *at the inception of the lease the present value of the minimum lease payments amounts to at least substantially all of the fair value of the leased asset; and*
    (e) *the leased assets are of such a specialised nature that only the lessee can use them without major modifications.*
11. *Indicators of situations that individually or in combination could also lead to a lease being classified as a finance lease are:*
    (a) *if the lessee can cancel the lease, the lessor's losses associated with the cancellation are borne by the lessee;*
    (b) *gains or losses from the fluctuation in the fair value of the residual accrue to the lessee (for example, in the form of a rent rebate equalling most of the sales proceeds at the end of the lease); and*
    (c) *the lessee has the ability to continue the lease for a secondary period at a rent that is substantially lower than market rent.*
12. *The examples and indicators in paragraphs 10 and 11 are not always conclusive. If it is clear from other features of the lease that the lease does not transfer substantially all risks and rewards incidental to ownership, the lease is classified as an operating lease. For example, this may be the case if ownership of the asset transfers at the end of the lease for a variable payment equal to its then fair value, or if there are contingent rents, as a result of which the lessee does not have substantially all such risks and rewards.*

If a lease is cancellable at limited cost to the lessee, the lessee has limited risks and the lease is considered to be an operating lease. For the lessee to be considered to bear the risks associated with asset ownership, it is logical that there should be costs for the lessee should the lessee choose to cancel the lease. This is why paragraph 11(a) is considered to be an important consideration in determining whether a lease should be classified a finance lease. How a lease is classified will depend on the *economic substance* of the lease agreement and, as already indicated, the exercise of professional judgement is required. Leases that do not appear to satisfy any of the above criteria (in paragraphs 10 to 12) will typically be classified and accounted for by the lessee as operating leases (which means that they do not require disclosure within the statement of financial position as an asset and liability will not be recognised, and lease payments are typically treated as rental expenses). At this stage of the discussion, further clarification of some of the above terms (and others) might be useful; notably such terms as:

- fair value
- non-cancellability
- contingent rent
- transfer of ownership
- bargain purchase option
- lease term
- economic life
- minimum lease payments

Fair value

As we know, consideration of the fair value of a leased asset is necessary in determining the amount to be included for the leased asset in the statement of financial position of the lessee. IAS 17 defines 'fair value' as 'the amount for which an asset could be exchanged or a liability settled, between knowledgeable, willing parties in an arm's length transaction'. This definition of the term is consistent with those adopted in other accounting standards.

Non-cancellability

As already indicated, if a lessee was able to cancel a lease at short notice with limited penalty, the lessee would not be considered to be holding the risks and rewards associated with asset ownership and so the lease would be considered to be an operating lease. Hence, it is important to determine that the lease is non-cancellable before it is considered to be a finance lease. IAS 17 states that:

A non-cancellable lease *is a lease that is cancellable only:*
(a) upon the occurrence of some remote contingency;
(b) with the permission of the lessor;
(c) if the lessee enters into a new lease for the same or an equivalent asset with the same lessor; or
(d) upon payment by the lessee of such an additional amount that, at inception of the lease, continuation of the lease is reasonably certain.

Again, if a lease is considered to be cancellable it would, regardless of the remaining terms of the lease, be classified an operating lease. Cancellability has the effect of minimising the risks to the lessee.

Contingent rent

The existence of contingent rents is a factor that works against a lease being considered a finance lease, as the variability in future potential payments effectively shifts some of the risks and rewards of ownership back to the lessor.

Transfer of ownership

Transfer of ownership is referred to in paragraph 10(a) in IAS 17. Logically, if the lease includes transfer of ownership of the asset to the lessee at the end of the lease term and the lease is non-cancellable, the lease agreement is really just another type of debt agreement with title transfer occurring after the final payment has been made. As with any other purchase of an asset financed by debt, both the asset and the liability should be recognised in the books of the purchaser/lessee. Consequently, the asset and the liability should be accounted for separately. Again, remember that in accounting for leases we consider the *economic substance* of the underlying transaction. If the *substance* of the lease transaction is similar to what would be involved if an entity borrowed to acquire an asset, the lease transaction should be dealt with for accounting purposes in a fashion similar to the 'borrow and buy' transaction.

Bargain purchase option

While it is not a term that is used explicitly within IAS 17, a **bargain purchase option** is a provision that allows the lessee to purchase the leased asset for a price that is expected to be significantly lower than the expected fair value of the asset at the date the purchase option becomes exercisable. This is effectively what paragraph 10(b) of IAS 17 (reproduced above) is referring to. The difference between the option price and the expected fair market value must be large enough to make exercise of the option reasonably assured. This evaluation is made at the inception of the lease. If the exercise of the option is likely (by definition, a rational party would not forgo a 'bargain'), it is also likely that transfer of ownership will occur, and the risks and rewards of ownership are therefore assumed to be transferred.

> **bargain purchase option** Provision that allows a lessee to purchase leased property for a price expected to be far lower than the expected fair value of the property at the date the option becomes exercisable.

Lease term

'Lease term' is defined in IAS 17 as the non-cancellable period for which the lessee has contracted to lease the asset, together with any further terms for which the lessee has the option to continue to lease the asset, with or without further payment, when at the inception of the lease it is reasonably certain that the lessee will exercise the option.

Economic life

'Economic life' is either:

- the period over which an asset is expected to be economically usable by one or more users; or
- the number of production or similar units expected to be obtained from the asset by one or more users.

It follows that the lease term and the economic life of the asset might not be the same. As already indicated (paragraph 10(c) of IAS 17), if the non-cancellable lease term is for the major part of the economic life of the asset, the lease is generally considered to be a finance lease. IAS 17 does not define 'major part' and therefore requires accountants to exercise professional judgement. However, it is generally accepted that if the lease term is greater than, or equal to, 75 per cent of the economic life of the leased asset, the risks and rewards of ownership are effectively transferred to the lessee (that is, it is a finance lease).

As we will see shortly, in determining the period over which the leased asset is depreciated we need to consider the shorter of the lease term and the economic life of the asset.

Minimum lease payments

The determination of the minimum lease payments and the present value of those payments are important in that:

- the present value of the minimum lease payments is used in determining whether a lease is a finance or an operating lease (refer to paragraph 10(d) of IAS 17, reproduced earlier), and
- if the lease is considered to be a finance lease, the amount to be initially recognised in the statement of financial position for the asset and liability is, pursuant to paragraph 20, the fair value of the leased property or, if lower, the present value of the minimum lease payments as determined at the inception of the lease.

Therefore the determination of minimum lease payments is a very important part of applying IAS 17. Minimum lease payments themselves are defined at paragraph 4 of IAS 17 as:

> the payments over the lease term that the lessee is or can be required to make, excluding contingent rent, costs for services and taxes to be paid by and reimbursed to the lessor, together with:
>
> (a) for a lessee, any amounts guaranteed by the lessee or by a party related to the lessee; or
> (b) for a lessor, any residual value guaranteed to the lessor by:
>   (i) the lessee;
>   (ii) a party related to the lessee; or
>   (iii) a third party unrelated to the lessor that is financially capable of discharging the obligations under the guarantee.

For the lessee, as we have seen above, minimum lease payments include guaranteed residual values. Lease contracts will sometimes include residual value guarantees. Under these guarantees, the lessee will compensate the lessor if the value of the leased item at the end of the lease falls below a specified value. A residual value guarantee may require the lessee to purchase the property for a certain or determinable amount or make up a deficiency

below a stated amount upon termination of the lease. Residual value guarantees are used to protect the lessor's expected return.

For the lessee, IAS 17 defines the guaranteed residual value as:

> that part of the residual value that is guaranteed by the lessee or by a party related to the lessee (the amount of the guarantee being the maximum amount that could, in any event, become payable).

That is, payment of the guaranteed residual is contractually required. From the perspective of the lessor, IAS 17 defines the guaranteed residual as:

> that part of the residual value that is guaranteed by the lessee or by a third party unrelated to the lessor that is financially capable of discharging the obligations under the guarantee.

If something is 'guaranteed' obviously there is the expectation that it will be paid. A residual might or might not be guaranteed. The payment of this guaranteed residual will often lead to the asset being legally transferred to the lessee. If there is a *guaranteed residual* (the maximum amount that could become payable), then, as noted above, this amount is included in the minimum lease payments, as its payment is reasonably assured. *Unguaranteed residuals* are not included in the minimum lease payments, as there is not sufficient certainty that the amount will be paid. In IAS 17 they are defined as 'that portion of the residual value of the leased asset, the realisation of which by the lessor is not assured or guaranteed solely by a party related to the lessor'.

Lease contracts often include a bargain purchase option (defined earlier). A bargain purchase option would be included as part of the minimum lease payments because the exercise of a 'bargain' option is reasonably assured and it is therefore probable that the amount will ultimately be paid by the lessee (stipulated in paragraph 4 of IAS 17).

The definition of minimum lease payments adopted within IAS 17 excludes costs for services and taxes (often referred to as executory costs) that are paid to the lessor in reimbursement. The exclusion of such costs is consistent with the general capitalisation principles used for assets. Periodic repairs, insurance and rates would not typically be recognised as part of the cost of an asset, as they merely maintain the asset in the state it was in at the beginning of the period, rather than increasing its service potential.

10.3 Interest rate for determining the present value of the minimum lease payments

When determining the present values to measure leased assets and lease liabilities (IAS 17, paragraph 20) we need to use a discount rate. IAS 17 stipulates that the discount rate to be used in calculating the present value of the minimum lease payments is the interest rate implicit in the lease, if this is practicable to determine; if not, the lessee's incremental borrowing rate is to be used (IAS 17, paragraph 20).

According to IAS 17, the interest rate implicit in the lease is:

> the discount rate that, at the commencement of the lease term, causes the aggregate present value of:
> (a) the minimum lease payments; and
> (b) the unguaranteed residual value to be equal to the sum of:
>   (i) the fair value of the leased asset; and
>   (ii) any initial direct costs of the lessor.

While not certain, the unguaranteed residual (discussed earlier) represents the expected recoverable amount of the asset at the end of the lease term. An example of how a discount rate is computed is given in Worked Example 10.1, while classifying a lease as a finance lease or an operating lease is explained in Worked Example 10.2.

Given that we have satisfied this test (paragraph 10(c)), we really do not need to consider the test of whether the present value of the minimum lease payments *amounts to at least substantially all* of the fair value of the asset. This is because we have already largely satisfied ourselves that the risks and rewards of ownership have been transferred to the lessee. However, for the sake of completeness we will consider this test.

It is not clear from the standard what 'substantially all of the fair value of the leased asset' means. It would seem to be a higher amount than 'major part'. Again, accountants are required to exercise professional judgement. 'Substantially all' would appear to mean an amount very close to 100 per cent of fair value. This is supported by paragraph 21 of IAS 17, which refers to the present value approximating the fair value of the leased asset at the inception of the lease. But the standard does not provide any precise guidelines or percentages. However, it is generally considered that, if the present value of the minimum lease payments amounts to at least 90 per cent

Worked Example 10.1 — Example of computing discount rate

McTavish plc decides to lease some machinery from Nielsen plc on the following terms:

Date of entering lease	1 July 2015
Duration of lease	10 years
Life of leased asset	11 years
Unguaranteed residual value	£2,000
Lease payments	£4,000 at lease inception, £3,500 on 30 June each year (that is, 10 yearly payments of £3,500 each)
Fair value of leased asset at date of lease inception	£26,277

Required
Determine the interest rate implicit in the lease.

Solution
The implicit rate is the rate that, when used to discount the minimum lease payments plus any unguaranteed residual, equates the sum of the discounted minimum lease payments and the discounted unguaranteed residual to the fair value of the asset at the commencement of the lease. The present value of an annuity of £1 in arrears ('in arrears' means the amount is received, or paid, at the end of each year) for ten years discounted at 10 per cent is £6.1446 (see the present value tables in the appendices). The present value of £1 in ten years, discounted at 10 per cent, is £0.3855. Hence, the present value of the ten payments of £3,500 discounted at 10 per cent is £3,500 multiplied by 6.1446, which equals £21,506, and the present value of the unguaranteed residual discounted at 10 per cent is £771, which is £2,000 multiplied by 0.3855. The present value of the up-front payment of £4,000 is not discounted. Therefore, using a rate of 10 per cent for discounting purposes, the present value of the minimum lease payments and the unguaranteed residual is:

Present value of payment on 1 July 2015	£4,000
Present value of 10 yearly payments	£21,506
Present value of unguaranteed residual	£771
	£26,277

The discounted value of £26,277 is the same as the fair value of the asset at lease inception. Thus, 10 per cent is the implicit rate in this example. Note that some degree of trial and error might be involved in determining the discount rate.

The rate of interest is then used to determine the interest expense incurred each period. The present value of the liability at the beginning of the period is multiplied by the rate of interest to determine the interest expense for the period. The balance of the lease payment is then treated as a reduction of the lease liability.

Worked Example 10.2 — Classification of a lease as a finance lease or an operating lease

Lonsdale plc has entered into a lease arrangement with Queenscliffe plc in which it has agreed to lease an item of machinery from Queenscliffe plc on the following terms:

Date of commencement of lease	1 July 2015
Duration of lease	8 years
Fair value of machine at lease inception	€871,172
Initial up-front payment	€200,000
Lease payments at the end of each year	€100,000
Implicit rate of interest	6 per cent

The lease is considered to be non-cancellable. The economic life of the machinery is considered to be ten years. However, Lonsdale plc will return the machinery to Queenscliffe plc at the end of the lease term. At this stage it is expected that the machinery will have a residual (unguaranteed) value of €80,000 at the end of the lease term.

Required

(a) Determine what the minimum lease payments are.
(b) Prove that the rate of interest implicit in the lease is 6 per cent.
(c) Determine whether the lease should be classified an operating lease or a finance lease.

Solution

(a) Minimum lease payments are the payments over the lease term that the lessee is or can be required to make. They exclude contingent rent, costs for services and taxes to be paid by and reimbursed to the lessor. They include any amounts guaranteed by the lessee or by a party related to the lessee. Minimum lease payments would include any bargain purchase option that is included. In this case the minimum lease payments would also include the up-front payment of €200,000 plus the subsequent lease payments of €100,000 per annum.

(b) The implicit rate is the rate that, when applied to the minimum lease payments plus any unguaranteed residual, causes the sum of these present values to equal the fair value of the asset at lease inception. It is emphasised that unguaranteed residuals are not part of the minimum lease payments because the lessor is not required to make such payments. Nevertheless, knowledge of the unguaranteed residual is necessary to determine the interest rate implicit in the lease. Using 6 per cent, the present value of the minimum lease payments, plus the unguaranteed residual, is:

$$
\begin{array}{lll}
€200,000 \times 1.00 & = & €200,000 \\
€100,000 \times 6.2098 & = & €620,980 \\
€80,000 \times 0.6274 & = & \underline{€50,192} \\
& & \underline{€871,172}
\end{array}
$$

Given that the above amount of €871,172 is equivalent to the fair value of the asset at lease inception, 6 per cent is the rate of interest implicit in the lease.

(c) For a lease to be considered a finance lease, it must first be considered to be non-cancellable. The lease agreement between Lonsdale plc and Queenscliffe plc satisfies this requirement. If the lease was cancellable at minimum cost to the lessee, it would not have effectively transferred the risks inherent in asset ownership to the lessee. For the lease to be considered a finance lease, it must also satisfy the test of whether the risks and rewards of ownership have effectively been transferred to the lessee. Some of the indicators of this are provided in paragraphs 10 to 12 of IAS 17. Had the lease transferred ownership or included a bargain purchase option, it would be a fairly straightforward matter to conclude the lease to be a finance lease (see parts (a) and (b) of paragraph 10 of IAS 17). As this is not the case, we have to consider some of the other indicators provided by paragraph 10 of IAS 17. In this case, two important tests are the following (either of which should be met before we can conclude it is a finance lease):

(i) The lease term is for the major part of the economic life of the asset, even if title is not transferred.

(ii) At the inception of the lease the present value of the minimum lease payments amounts to at least substantially all of the fair value of the leased asset.

The two key terms above are 'major part' and 'substantially all'. It is not clear from the standard what the 'major part' of the economic life of the asset actually means. 'Major part' clearly means considerably more than 50 per cent of the economic life of the asset, but also clearly means considerably less than 'substantially all'. The exact percentage is a matter for interpretation and professional judgement. The standard does not provide a precise guideline but it is generally held that a lease term of 75 per cent or more of the economic life of the asset would be sufficient. In this case, the lease term is for 80 per cent of the economic life of the asset. On this basis, we would argue that the lease is a finance lease.

of the fair value of the leased asset (which in itself means that any unguaranteed residual value is relatively small), the lease is a finance lease. Nevertheless, it needs to be appreciated that given the ambiguity of the requirements stipulated in the accounting standard, it could be argued that 85 per cent is close enough, or that 90 per cent is not enough, and it should be at least 95 per cent. It is not clear where to draw the line, but it is clear that it must be a very high percentage.

In this case, the present value of the minimum lease payments is €200,000 plus €620,980, which equals €820,980. This amount is 94 per cent of €871,172, so this test, included in paragraph 10(d), is satisfied. Because the present value of the leased asset at the conclusion of the lease is assumed to be only €50,192, the majority of the asset's service potential has been consumed by the lessee.

Given that the lease is non-cancellable and that at least one of the above tests has been satisfied, the lease is classified as a finance lease.

In some circumstances the lessee might be unable to determine the fair value of the asset at the inception of the lease (perhaps because the asset has unique attributes), or the lessee might not be able to reliably estimate the residual value. In such circumstances it would not be possible to determine the **implicit interest rate**. In these circumstances the lessee is to discount the minimum lease payments by using the lessee's incremental borrowing rate. The **incremental borrowing rate** can be defined as the rate of interest the lessee would have to pay on a similar lease or, if that is not determinable, the rate that, at the inception of the lease, the lessee would incur to borrow over a similar term, and with a similar security, the funds necessary to purchase the asset.

> **implicit interest rate** The discount rate that causes the aggregate present value of the minimum lease payments plus any unguaranteed residual to be equal to the fair value of the leased property at the inception of the lease.
>
> **incremental borrowing rate** Rate of interest the lessee would have to pay on a similar lease or the rate that the lessee would incur to borrow the funds to purchase the asset.

10.4 Lessee accounting for finance leases

In substance, where a lessee enters a finance lease arrangement, it is essentially the same as acquiring an asset by way of a long-term loan. The lessee will record an asset (a leased asset) and a lease liability. As we have stated, the asset and liability will be recorded at the fair value of the leased asset or, where lower, at the present value of the minimum lease payments. The present value of the minimum lease payments will be lower where there are such things as unguaranteed residuals in place (unguaranteed residuals do not form part of the minimum lease payments).

Hence, the accounting standard pertaining to leases specifically requires that consideration be given to the present value of the future cash flows. As we know, for many liabilities that are due beyond 12 months there is a requirement that present values be used. Again, please note that the unguaranteed residual is excluded from the amount recognised for the lease asset and lease liability in the financial statements of the lessee. It was included in the above worked examples to enable the determination of the rate implicit in the lease. Therefore, where there is an unguaranteed residual value, the amount recorded in the lessee's statement of financial position as a leased asset at the inception of the lease will be less than the asset's fair value—the difference being the present value of the unguaranteed residual.

Over the term of the lease, the rental payments to the lessor constitute a payment of principal plus interest, and the lessee should apportion each payment between the two. The interest expense is computed by applying the interest rate implicit in the lease to the outstanding lease liability at the beginning of each lease payment period. The balance of the payment is considered a reduction of the principal of the lease liability.

So, for Worked Example 10.1 relating to McTavish plc, the initial lease liability would be £25,506. (We have excluded the unguaranteed residual.) As the first payment of £4,000 was made on the first day of the lease, there would be no interest element and the lease liability would be reduced by £4,000. To determine the interest expense component included within the first year-end payment of £3,500, the opening liability of £21,506— that is, £25,506 less the up-front payment of £4,000—must be multiplied by the implicit rate of 10 per cent. The interest expense for the first year would therefore be £2,151, and £1,349 would be offset against the liability. The entries for the year ending 30 June 2016 would be:

1 July 2015

| Dr | Leased machinery | £25,506 | |
| Cr | Lease liability | | £25,506 |

(to record the leased asset and lease liability at the present value of the minimum lease payments)

| Dr | Lease liability | £4,000 | |
| Cr | Cash | | £4,000 |

(to record the initial up-front lease payment)

30 June 2016

Dr	Interest expense	£2,151	
Dr	Lease liability	£1,349	
Cr	Cash		£3,500

(to recognise the first annual lease payment)

The interest expense for the year ended 30 June 2017 would be determined by multiplying the liability at the beginning of the year (£25,506 – £4,000 – £1,349) by the *implicit rate* of 10 per cent. This provides an interest expense of £2,016. The lease payment schedule for the life of the lease is provided in Exhibit 10.1. As we can see, the interest expense declines across the period of the lease as the outstanding principal decreases in amount.

Exhibit 10.1 **Lease Payment Schedule for McTavish plc (Worked Example 10.1)**

	Lease expense (£)	Interest expense (£)	Principal reduction (£)	Present value of lease liability (£)
01 July 2015				21,506
30 June 2016	3,500	2,151	1,349	20,157
30 June 2017	3,500	2,016	1,484	18,673
30 June 2018	3,500	1,867	1,633	17,040
30 June 2019	3,500	1,704	1,796	15,244
30 June 2020	3,500	1,524	1,976	13,268
30 June 2021	3,500	1,327	2,173	11,095
30 June 2022	3,500	1,109	2,391	8,704
30 June 2023	3,500	870	2,630	6,074
30 June 2024	3,500	607	2,893	3,182
30 June 2025	3,500	318	3,182	0

10.4.1 Depreciation of leased assets

A leased asset should be depreciated using the depreciation (amortisation) policies normally followed by the lessee in relation to the assets that are owned (IAS 17, paragraph 27). The period of amortisation/depreciation should be the number of accounting periods that are expected to benefit from the asset's use. Where there is reasonable assurance at the inception of the lease that the lessee will obtain ownership of the asset at the end of the lease term (the lease might provide for transfer of the asset to the lessee or it might contain a bargain purchase option), the asset should be depreciated over its useful life; otherwise, the asset should be depreciated over the lease term (IAS 17, paragraph 27). If the asset has a **residual value**, this is subtracted from the capitalised value of the leased asset to determine the depreciable base.

> **residual value** The actual or estimated net realisable value of a depreciable asset at the end of its useful life.

Referring again to Worked Example 10.1 and assuming straight-line depreciation is used, the depreciation on 30 June each year would be £2,551 (£25,506/10). As the lease agreement does not transfer ownership at the end of the lease, the depreciation period would be the term of the lease agreement. The accounting entries on 30 June each year would be:

Dr	Lease depreciation expense	£2,551
Cr	Accumulated depreciation—leased machinery	£2,551

Although the amount capitalised as an asset and the amount recorded as an obligation at the inception of the lease are computed at the same present value, the depreciation of the asset and the discharge of the obligation are independent accounting processes during the term of the lease. Hence the carrying amount of the asset and the carrying amount of the liability will not be equal after the initial entry.

10.4.2 Lessee's journal entries for a finance lease

Following on from the above discussion and worked examples, we can now usefully provide general pro forma entries for finance leases in the books of the lessee. These are:

| Dr | Leased asset | £XXX | |
| Cr | Lease liability | | £XXX |

(to record the leased asset and the lease liability at the inception of the lease term)

| Dr | Lease depreciation expense | £XXX | |
| Cr | Accumulated depreciation—leased asset | | £XXX |

(to record the lease depreciation expense at the end of each reporting period)

Dr	Lease liability	£XXX	
Dr	Interest expense	£XXX	
Cr	Cash		£XXX

(to record the lease payment, with the payment being allocated between principal and interest)

| Dr | Executory expenses | £XXX | |
| Cr | Cash | | £XXX |

(to record the payment of executory costs by the lessee such as rates and maintenance; this journal entry is required only if the lessee is responsible for the payment of these costs; executory costs are not considered to constitute part of the minimum lease payments)

The last three sets of journal entries provided above are repeated throughout the term of the lease, although the amounts recorded for interest expense and lease liability will change. The depreciation expense will also change from period to period if a depreciation method other than the straight-line method is used.

10.4.3 Initial direct costs

Initial direct costs are defined in IAS 17 as incremental costs that are directly attributable to negotiating and arranging a lease. They would include commissions, legal fees and costs of preparing and processing documentation for new leases. Paragraph 24 of IAS 17 requires that a lessee capitalise their *initial direct costs* that relate to a finance lease as part of the cost of the leased asset. Therefore, where such costs are incurred, the lease asset comprises the present value of the minimum lease payments and the amount of initial direct costs incurred. The total amount would be subject to regular depreciation.

10.5 Lessee accounting for operating leases

As already indicated, an operating lease is a lease that does not transfer substantially all the risks and rewards incidental to ownership of the asset to the lessee. IAS 17 requires that, when a lease is classified as an operating lease by the lessee, the lease payments should be expensed on a basis that is representative of the pattern of benefits derived from the leased asset. If the lease payments do not represent prepayments, they should be expensed in the period in which they are made. Specifically, paragraph 33 of IAS 17 requires:

Lease payments under an operating lease shall be recognised as an expense on a straight-line basis over the lease term unless another systematic basis is more representative of the time pattern of the user's benefit.

If lease payments are made in arrears, recognition of year-end rental liabilities might be required. Worked Example 10.3 provides an example of accounting for an operating lease.

10.6 Lessee accounting for sale and leaseback transactions

sale and leaseback transaction A transaction in which an entity sells an asset and immediately leases it back.

A **sale and leaseback transaction** occurs when the owner of a property (seller/lessee) sells the property to another party, and simultaneously leases it back from the purchaser/lessor (the legal owner). The seller/lessee does not lose control of the asset if the subsequent

> ### Worked Example 10.3   Example of accounting for an operating lease
>
> On 1 July 2015 Margaret plc enters a lease agreement with River plc for the lease of a building. The length of the lease is for five years and the terms require annual payments of €60,000. The lease is non-cancellable and the estimated economic life of the building is 20 years. The market value of the building is €2 million. Lease payments are made at the end of each financial year.
>
> #### Required
> Provide the journal entries that would be made in the books of Margaret plc to account for the lease.
>
> #### Solution
> First, we must determine whether the lease is a finance lease or an operating lease. Even though the lease is non-cancellable, the lease period is too short for the risks and rewards of ownership of the asset to be considered to have transferred to the lessee. Hence the lease is to be treated as an operating lease. As a result, each payment can be treated as a rental payment, there will be no interest expense and the lessee will not have any depreciation expenses. The aggregated accounting entry each period in the books of Margaret plc would be:
>
> | | | |
> |---|---|---|
> | Dr Rental expense—building | €60,000 | |
> | Cr Cash | | €60,000 |
>
> If Margaret plc had not paid the lease payment by the end of the reporting period, an amount would need to be accrued as a lease expense payable (a liability), rather than there being a credit to cash.
>
> If we consider the above operating lease, then we will see that, although the organisation has committed to making lease payments for the next five years, and therefore has a probable obligation as well as a right to use an asset for five years, neither the obligation nor the related asset will appear in the financial statements. However, if we consider the definition of a liability as provided within the IASB Conceptual Framework, we see that a liability is defined as:
>
> > *A present obligation of the entity arising from past events, the settlement of which is expected to result in an outflow from the entity of resources embodying economic benefits.*
>
> The obligation relating to the five-year lease arrangement discussed above would certainly seem to fit the definition above, and the obligation would be both *probable* and *measurable* with reasonable accuracy (these being the recognition criteria of the elements of financial reporting). Therefore, while IAS 17 would treat the above lease as an operating lease thereby precluding the associated liability and asset from appearing on the statement of financial position, this exclusion does not appear conceptually sound. This is one of the issues that the IASB and FASB have addressed in their project relating to lease accounting, and as we will see at the end of this chapter, when the new accounting standard is finally issued, it will require leases such as that described above to be included in the statement of financial position. Classifying leases as operating leases will be abandoned under new rules likely to be mandated from 2015.

lease is a finance lease. Generally, in such a transaction the property is sold at a price equal to or greater than current market value, and is leased back for a term approximating the property's useful life, and for lease payments sufficient to repay the buyer for the cash invested plus a reasonable return on investment. In addition, the lessee typically pays all executory costs just as if title had remained with the lessee. A sale and leaseback is often considered to represent a useful way of obtaining funds while still allowing the recipient of the funds to maintain control of a particular asset. Sale and leaseback transactions are quite common. Financial Accounting in the News 10.1 provides some information about the use of sale and leasebacks as a means of corporations raising necessary funds.

Where substantially all of the risks and rewards incidental to ownership of the leased property remain with the lessee, the leaseback is classified as a finance lease, as the transaction represents the refinancing of an asset. The same criteria as discussed earlier are applied to determine whether a sale and leaseback transaction should be classified as a finance lease. Where the lessee classifies the leaseback as a finance lease, any profit on the sale should be deferred in the statement of financial position and amortised to the statement of comprehensive income over the term of the lease (IAS 17, paragraph 59).

Financial Accounting in the News 10.1

LEASEBACK: QUICK WAY TO RAISE CASH

Carolyn Cummins, *Sydney Morning Herald*
25 October 2008

THE pending recession in Europe and Britain has forced many companies to review how to raise cash from alternative sources rather than trying a bank or the sharemarket. This has led to a huge increase in corporate sale and leaseback transactions.

A report from CB Richard Ellis says that between 2004 and 2007 the total value of this type of transaction rose from 6.7 billion euros to 46 billion euros.

This represented an increase from 6 per cent to 21 per cent of the European investment market for this type of transaction.

The report says that against the backdrop of economic uncertainty and a substantial increase in the cost of corporate debt, these transactions are gaining momentum across Europe and accounted for 21 per cent of all invest-

ment activity in the first half of 2008—their highest percentage contribution ever.

The head of corporate strategies with CBRE's global corporate services, John Wilson, said a company's decision to proceed with a sale and leaseback was motivated by a range of factors. These include the increased pressure to raise capital, the high cost of debt, the need for more flexible lease structures and the growing acceptability of a company selling its real estate.

'The wave of sale and leasebacks in the banking sector in recent years eradicated the "last resort" stigma previously attached to this type of transaction, transforming it into another viable choice for corporates looking to raise capital,' Mr Wilson said.

Source: *Sydney Morning Herald* 2008

In a sense it is assumed that, as a result of the sale and leaseback (where the lease is a financial lease), the asset has not really been 'sold' to the lessor and therefore it would be inappropriate to recognise fully any profit related to the 'sale'. As paragraph 60 of IAS 17 puts it:

> *If the leaseback is a finance lease, the transaction is a means whereby the lessor provides finance to the lessee, with the asset as security. For this reason it is not appropriate to regard an excess of sales proceeds over the carrying amount as income. Such excess is deferred and amortised over the lease term.*

Where substantially all of the risks and rewards incidental to ownership effectively pass to the lessor as a result of a sale and leaseback transaction, the lease will be classified as an operating lease. If the selling price for the property is established at fair value at the date of sale, there has, in effect, been a normal sale transaction and any profit or loss is to be recognised immediately (as required by paragraph 61 of IAS 17). Where, however, the selling price is more or less than fair value, financial independence between the sale and leaseback cannot be presumed. That is, the sale is not a 'normal' arm's length sales transaction, but rather forms part of a leasing arrangement. IAS 17 provides for different scenarios and treatments when a sale and leaseback involves an operating lease and the sales price of the asset does not equal its fair value. Specifically, paragraph 61 of IAS 17 states:

> *If a sale and leaseback transaction results in an operating lease, and it is clear that the transaction is established at fair value, any profit or loss shall be recognised immediately. If the sale price is below fair value, any profit or loss shall be recognised immediately except that, if the loss is compensated for by future lease payments at below market price, it shall be deferred and amortised in proportion to the lease payments over the period for which the asset is expected to be used. If the sale price is above fair value, the excess over fair value shall be deferred and amortised over the period for which the asset is expected to be used.*

Paragraph 63 further states:

> *For operating leases, if the fair value at the time of a sale and leaseback transaction is less than the carrying amount of the asset, a loss equal to the amount of the difference between the carrying amount and fair value shall be recognised immediately.*

An example of a sale and leaseback transaction is provided in Worked Example 10.4.

Worked Example 10.4   Example of a sale and leaseback transaction

As at 1 July 2015, Winki Company owns a building that cost €5 million and has accumulated depreciation of €3.5 million. The building is sold on 1 July 2015 to Pop plc for €2,007,250, and then immediately leased back by Winki Company for ten years (the remaining life). Lease payments are €400,000 per year, paid at the end of the year. The lease is non-cancellable. The implicit rate is 15 per cent.

Required

(a) Verify that the interest rate implicit in the lease is 15 per cent.
(b) Provide the accounting entries in the books of Winki Company for the year ending 30 June 2016.
(c) Provide the accounting entries in the books of Pop plc for the year ending 30 June 2016.

Solution

(a) As paragraph 4 of IAS 17 states, the *interest rate implicit in the lease* is the discount rate that, at the commencement of the lease term, causes the aggregate present value of the minimum lease payments and the unguaranteed residual value to be equal to the sum of:
   (i) the fair value of the leased asset, and
   (ii) any initial direct costs of the lessor.

   To verify that the interest rate implicit in the lease is 15 per cent:

   €400,000 × 5.0188 = €2,007,250

   As the discounted present value of the future lease payments at 15 per cent equals the fair value of the asset at lease inception, 15 per cent is the rate implicit in the lease.

(b) Journal entries in the books of Winki Company

   1 July 2015

Dr	Cash	€2,007,520	
Dr	Accumulated depreciation	€3,500,000	
Cr	Building		€5,000,000
Cr	Deferred gain		€507,520

   (to record the sale of the building to Pop plc; as the lease is a finance lease, any profit on 'sale' is to be deferred and amortised throughout the lease term in accordance with paragraph 59 of IAS 17; profit recognition is typically undertaken using the asset's depreciation policy)

Dr	Leased building	€2,007,520	
Cr	Lease liability		€2,007,520

   (to recognise the finance lease)

   30 June 2016

Dr	Interest expense	€301,128	
Dr	Lease liability	€98,872	
Cr	Cash		€400,000

   (to recognise the periodic lease payment; interest = €2,007,520 × 15%)

Dr	Depreciation of leased asset	€200,752	
Cr	Accumulated lease depreciation		€200,752

   (to record depreciation of the leased asset assuming the straight-line method is used)

Dr	Deferred gain	€50,752	
Cr	Profit on sale of leased asset		€50,752

   (to recognise the deferred gain on a straight-line basis)

(c) Journal entries in the books of Pop plc

   1 July 2015

Dr	Building	€2,007,520	
Cr	Cash		€2,007,520

   (to record acquisition of the building from Winki Company)

Dr	Lease receivable	€2,007,520	
Cr	Building		€2,007,520

   (entry on commencement of finance lease, wherein the lease receivable is substituted for the building)

►

30 June 2016		
Dr Cash	€400,000	
Cr Interest revenue		€301,128
Cr Lease receivable		€98,872
(to record receipt of periodic lease payment)		

10.7 Lessee disclosure requirements

IAS 17 requires that numerous disclosures be made. For a finance lease, the lessee must disclose the following information within the notes to the financial statements (IAS 17, paragraph 31):

Lessees shall, in addition to meeting the requirements of IFRS 7 Financial Instruments: Disclosures, *make the following disclosures for finance leases:*

(a) *for each class of asset, the net carrying amount at the reporting date;*
(b) *a reconciliation between the total of future minimum lease payments at the reporting date, and their present value. In addition, an entity shall disclose the total of future minimum lease payments at the reporting date, and their present value, for each of the following periods:*
   (i) *not later than one year;*
   (ii) *later than one year and not later than five years;*
   (iii) *later than five years;*
(c) *contingent rents recognised as an expense in the period;*
(d) *the total of future minimum sublease payments expected to be received under non-cancellable subleases at the reporting date; and*
(e) *a general description of the lessee's material leasing arrangements including, but not limited to, the following:*
   (i) *the basis on which contingent rent payable is determined;*
   (ii) *the existence and terms of renewal or purchase options and escalation clauses; and*
   (iii) *restrictions imposed by lease arrangements, such as those concerning dividends, additional debt, and further leasing.*

Although operating leases are not capitalised for the purposes of inclusion in the statement of financial position, IAS 17 nevertheless requires numerous disclosures with regard to operating leases. Pursuant to paragraph 35 of IAS 17, the following disclosures should be made:

Lessees shall, in addition to meeting the requirements of IAS 17, make the following disclosures for operating leases:

(a) *the total of future minimum lease payments under non-cancellable operating leases for each of the following periods:*
   (i) *not later than one year;*
   (ii) *later than one year and not later than five years;*
   (iii) *later than five years;*
(b) *the total of future minimum sublease payments expected to be received under non-cancellable subleases at the reporting date;*
(c) *lease and sublease payments recognised as an expense in the period, with separate amounts for minimum lease payments, contingent rents, and sublease payments;*
(d) *a general description of the lessee's significant leasing arrangements including, but not limited to, the following:*
   (i) *the basis on which contingent rent payable is determined;*
   (ii) *the existence and terms of renewal or purchase options and escalation clauses; and*
   (iii) *restrictions imposed by lease arrangements, such as those concerning dividends, additional debt, and further leasing.*

As an illustration of a lease disclosure note, consider Exhibit 10.2, which reproduces the accounting policy lease note relating to lease commitments that appeared in the 2011 annual report of Ryanair plc. The note provides details not only of the finance lease commitments but also about the organisation's commitments in relation to operating leases (which, as we know, do not appear on the statement of financial position).

Exhibit 10.2 **Lease commitment note appearing in the 2011 annual report of Ryanair plc**

NOTE 1 BASIS OF PREPARATION AND SIGNIFICANT ACCOUNTING POLICIES (extract)

Leases

Leases under which the Company assumes substantially all of the risks and rewards of ownership are classified as finance leases. Assets held under finance leases are capitalised in the balance sheet, at an amount equal to the lower of their fair value and the present value of the minimum lease payments, and are depreciated over their estimated useful lives. The present values of the future lease payments are recorded as obligations under finance leases and the interest element of a lease obligation is charged to the income statement over the period of the lease in proportion to the balances outstanding.

Other leases are operating leases and the associated leased assets are not recognised on the Company's balance sheet. Expenditure arising under operating leases is charged to the income statement as incurred. The Company also enters into sale-and-leaseback transactions whereby it sells the rights to acquire an aircraft to an external party and subsequently leases the aircraft back, by way of an operating lease. Any profit or loss on the disposal where the price achieved is not considered to be at fair value is spread over the period during which the asset is expected to be used. The profit or loss amount deferred is included within 'other creditors' and divided into components of greater than and less than one year.

NOTE 23 COMMITMENTS AND CONTINGENCIES (extract)

(a) Finance leases

The Company financed 30 of the Boeing 737-800 aircraft delivered between March 2005 and March 2011 with 13-year euro-denominated Japanese Operating Leases with Call Options ('JOLCOs'). These structures are accounted for as finance leases and are initially recorded at fair value in the Company's balance sheet. Under each of these contracts, Ryanair has a call option to purchase the aircraft at a pre-determined price after a period of 10.5 years, which it may exercise. The following table sets out the total future minimum payments of leasing 30 aircraft (2010: 20 aircraft; 2009: 20 aircraft) under JOLCOs at March 31, 2011, 2010 and 2009, respectively:

| | At March 31, | | | | | |
| | 2011 | | 2010 | | 2009 | |
	Minimum payments	Present value of minimum payments	Minimum payments	Present value of minimum payments	Minimum payments	Present value of minimum payments
	€M	€M	€M	€M	€M	€M
Due within one year	61.9	48.7	38.9	32.5	45.1	31.1
Due between one and five years	305.2	262.8	203.7	183.7	184.5	139.3
Due after five years	556.3	535.7	353.7	345.3	443.0	417.4
Total minimum lease payments	923.4	847.2	596.3	561.5	672.6	587.8
Less amounts allocated to future financing costs	(76.2)	–	(34.8)	–	(84.8)	–
Present value of minimum lease payments	847.2	847.2	561.5	561.5	587.8	587.8

▶

Commitments resulting from the use of derivative financial instruments by the Company are described in Notes 5 and 11 to the consolidated financial statements.

Operating leases

The Company financed 61 of the Boeing 737–800 aircraft delivered between December 2003 and March 2011 under seven-year, sale-and-leaseback arrangements with a number of international leasing companies, pursuant to which each lessor purchased an aircraft and leased it to Ryanair under an operating lease. Between October 2010 and March 2011, 10 operating lease aircraft were returned to the lessor at the agreed maturity date of the lease. At March 31, 2011 Ryanair had 51 operating lease aircraft in the fleet. As a result, Ryanair operates, but does not own, these aircraft. Ryanair has no right or obligation to acquire these aircraft at the end of the relevant lease terms. 5 of these leases are denominated in euro and require Ryanair to make variable rental payments that are linked to EURIBOR. Through the use of interest rate swaps, Ryanair has effectively converted the floating-rate rental payments due under 2 of these leases into fixed-rate rental payments. Another 30 leases are also denominated in euro and require Ryanair to make fixed rental payments over the term of the leases. 16 remaining operating leases are U.S. dollar-denominated, of which two require Ryanair to make variable rental payments that are linked to U.S. dollar LIBOR, while the remaining 14 require Ryanair to make fixed rental payments. The Company has an option to extend the initial period of seven years on 28 of the 51 remaining operating lease aircraft as at March 31, 2011, on pre-determined terms. 3 operating lease arrangements will mature during the year ended March 31, 2012. The Company has decided not to extend any of these operating leases for a secondary lease period. The following table sets out the total future minimum payments of leasing 51 aircraft (2010: 55 aircraft; 2009: 43 aircraft), ignoring interest, foreign currency and hedging arrangements, at March 31, 2011, 2010 and 2009, respectively:

	At March 31,					
	2011		2010		2009	
	Minimum payments	Present value of minimum payments	Minimum payments	Present value of minimum payments	Minimum payments	Present value of minimum payments
	€M	€M	€M	€M	€M	€M
Due within one year	100.2	91.7	77.8	71.5	85.8	78.8
Due between one and five years	325.5	248.5	208.8	160.3	177.8	134.9
Due after five years	164.8	91.8	112.2	64.3	29.1	17.2
Total	590.5	432.0	398.8	296.1	292.7	230.9

Exhibit 10.3 provides details of the information that must be disclosed in respect of the tangible assets that are leased. The net carrying amounts of the aircraft controlled by Ryanair plc that have been obtained using finance leases as at the end of the reporting period are provided for each year (note the cost and associated cumulative depreciation are not required). This exhibit is useful because it shows the extent to which leased assets are used by large organisations such as Ryanair. As we can see, organisations can lease hundreds of millions of euros worth of assets, and therefore how we account for such assets, and related liabilities, has a major effect on corporate financial statements.

> ### Exhibit 10.3 — Property, plant and equipment note appearing in the 2011 annual report of Ryanair plc, with specific disclosure of leased assets
>
> #### NOTE 2 TANGIBLE ASSETS (extract)
> The net book value of assets held under finance leases at March 31, 2011, 2010 and 2009 was €635.1 million, €422.8 million and €435.5 million, respectively.

An example of accounting for leases by a lessee is provided in Worked Example 10.5.

> ### Worked Example 10.5 — Comprehensive example of accounting for leases by a lessee
>
> Trigger plc enters into a non-cancellable five-year lease agreement with Brothers plc on 1 July 2015. The lease is for an item of machinery that, at the inception of the lease, has a fair value of €369,824.
>
> The machinery is expected to have an economic life of six years, after which time it will have an expected salvage value of €60,000. There is a bargain purchase option that Trigger plc will be able to exercise at the end of the fifth year for €80,000.
>
> There are to be five annual payments of €100,000, the first being made on 30 June 2016. Included within the €100,000 lease payments is an amount of €10,000 representing payment to the lessor for the insurance and maintenance of the equipment. The equipment is to be depreciated on a straight-line basis.
>
> A review of the appendices to this book shows that the present value of an annuity in arrears of €1 for five years at 12 per cent is €3.6048, while the present value of an annuity of €1 for five years at 14 per cent is €3.4331. Further, the present value of €1 in five years discounted at 12 per cent is €0.5674, while the present value of €1 in five years discounted at 14 per cent is €0.5194.
>
> #### Required
> (a) Determine the rate of interest implicit in the lease and calculate the present value of the minimum lease payments.
> (b) Prepare the journal entries for the years ending 30 June 2016 and 30 June 2017.
> (c) Prepare the portion of the statement of financial position relating to the leased asset and lease liability for the years ending 30 June 2016 and 30 June 2017.
> (d) Prepare the journal entries for the years ending 30 June 2016 and 30 June 2017, assuming (for purposes of illustration) that the lessee classifies the lease an operating lease.
>
> #### Solution
> (a) First, as the lease is non-cancellable and the present value of the minimum lease payments amounts to at least substantially all of the fair value of the leased asset (calculations provided below), the lease is a finance lease.
>
> The interest rate implicit in the lease agreement is the interest rate that results in the present value of the minimum lease payments, and any unguaranteed residual value, being equal to the fair value of the leased property at the inception of the lease. The minimum lease payments include any bargain purchase option. If we use a rate of interest of 12 per cent, the discounted value of the payments is €369,824, determined as:
>
> | | |
> |---|---|
> | Present value of five lease payments of €90,000 discounted at 12 per cent (we eliminate the executory costs) | = €90,000 × 3.6048 = €324,432 |
> | Present value of the bargain purchase option | = €80,000 × 0.5674 = €45,392 |
> | | €369,824 |
>
> As the amount of the minimum lease payments discounted at 12 per cent equates to the fair value of the asset at lease inception, the interest rate implicit in the lease is 12 per cent.
> (b) When preparing the journal entries it is often convenient to produce a table such as that provided below. Interest expense in the table is determined by multiplying the opening liability for a period by the rate of interest implicit in the lease.

►

Date	Lease payment (exclusive of executory costs)	Interest expense	Principal reduction	Outstanding balance
	€	€	€	€
1 July 2015				369,824
30 June 2016	90,000	44,379	45,621	324,203
30 June 2017	90,000	38,904	51,096	273,107
30 June 2018	90,000	32,773	57,227	215,880
30 June 2019	90,000	25,906	64,094	151,786
30 June 2020	170,000*	18,214	151,786	0

*Includes bargain purchase option

1 July 2015

| Dr | Leased machinery | €369,824 | |
| Cr | Lease liability | | €369,824 |

(to record the leased asset and liability at the inception of the finance lease)

30 June 2016

Dr	Executory expenses	€10,000	
Dr	Interest expense	€44,379	
Dr	Lease liability	€45,621	
Cr	Cash		€100,000

(to record the lease payment of €100,000)

| Dr | Lease depreciation expense | €51,637 | |
| Cr | Accumulated lease depreciation | | €51,637 |

(to record depreciation expense [(€369,824 – €60,000) ÷ 6])

As the lessee will most probably retain the asset after the lease period as a result of the bargain purchase option, the economic life of the asset, and not the lease term, is used for depreciation purposes.

30 June 2017

Dr	Executory expenses	€10,000	
Dr	Interest expense	€38,904	
Dr	Lease liability	€51,096	
Cr	Cash		€100,000

(to record the lease payment of €100,000)

| Dr | Lease depreciation expense | €51,637 | |
| Cr | Accumulated lease depreciation | | €51,637 |

(€369,824 less €60,000 divided by six years)

(c) Portion of the statement of financial position for years ending 30 June 2016 and 30 June 2017

	2016	2017
	(€)	(€)
Assets		
Leased asset	369,824	369,824
less Accumulated depreciation	51,637	103,274
	318,187	266,550
Current liabilities		
Lease liability	51,096	57,227
Non-current liabilities		
Lease liability	273,107	215,880

As at 30 June 2016, the present value of the outstanding lease liability is €324,203. The current portion of the liability (€51,096) is the amount by which the lease liability will be reduced by the lease payments in the next 12 months (from the lease payments schedule).

(d) Journal entries for years ending 30 June 2016 and 30 June 2017, assuming that the lease is an operating lease

30 June 2016

Dr	Executory expenses	€10,000	
Dr	Lease expenses	€90,000	
Cr	Cash		€100,000

(to record lease payment for 2016)

30 June 2017

Dr	Executory expenses	€10,000	
Dr	Lease expenses	€90,000	
Cr	Cash		€100,000

(to record lease payment for 2017)

10.8 Accounting by lessors

From the lessor's perspective, pursuant to IAS 17, leases are classified for accounting purposes as operating leases or finance leases (as they are from the lessee's perspective). In deciding whether a non-cancellable lease is a finance lease or an operating lease, the lessor can apply the same criteria as were discussed for the lessee. The factors to consider are included in paragraphs 10 to 12 of IAS 17. Among these are the requirements that for a lease to be considered a finance lease it needs to be non-cancellable, and:

- the lease term must be for the major part of the economic life of the asset (though based on professional judgement this condition would generally be considered to be satisfied where the lease term is greater than or equal to 75 per cent of the economic life of the leased asset); or
- the present value of the minimum lease payments must amount to at least substantially all of the fair value of the leased asset (though, again, based on professional judgement, this condition would generally be considered to be satisfied where the present value of the minimum lease payments amounts to greater than or equal to 90 per cent of the fair market value of the leased asset at the inception of the lease).

From the perspective of the lessor, finance leases can be further classified into:

- leases involving manufacturers or dealers; and
- direct-finance leases.

> **direct-financing lease**
> A finance lease that is not a lease involving a manufacturer or dealer in which the lessor acquires legal title to an asset then transfers the risks and rewards of ownership of the asset to a lessee for lease payments.
>
> **lease receivable** A receivable recorded in the books of a lessor; for a finance lease it is the present value of the minimum lease payments plus the present value of any unguaranteed residual.

Details on accounting for manufacturers or dealers that also provide lessor facilities for their customers is provided on the OLC (www.mcgraw-hill.co.uk/textbooks/deeganward). The direct-finance classification of lessor is now discussed further.

10.9 Lessor accounting for direct-financing leases

A **direct-financing lease** is a lease in which the lessor provides the financial resources to acquire the asset. The lessor typically acquires the asset, giving the lessor legal title, and then enters a lease agreement to lease the asset to the lessee, who may subsequently *control* the asset. No sale is recorded. Rather, the lessor derives income through periodic interest revenue. Where the risks and rewards of ownership are held by the lessee, the lessor substitutes a **lease receivable** for the underlying asset. The lease receivable is recorded as the net investment amount (IAS 17, paragraph 36).

This is defined in paragraph 4 of IAS 17 as, 'the gross investment in the lease discounted at the interest rate implicit in the lease'.

IAS 17 defines the 'gross investment in the lease' as the aggregate of:

(a) the minimum lease payments receivable by the lessor under a finance lease and
(b) any unguaranteed residual value accruing to the lessor.

The interest to be earned by the lessor over the lease term will be represented by the difference between the fair value of the leased asset and the sum of the undiscounted minimum lease payments and any unguaranteed residual value. Consistent with the interest expense for the lessee, the interest revenue for the lessor is determined by multiplying the opening present value of the lease receivable by the interest rate implicit in the lease.

At the inception of the lease, the lessor might incur **initial direct costs** (explained earlier). Under a direct-finance lease, the initial direct costs are, if material, to be included in the lessor's investment in the lease (IAS 17, paragraph 38).

Lease rentals representing a recovery of executory costs, being those costs that are related specifically to the operation and maintenance of the leased property, including insurance, maintenance and repairs, should be treated as revenue by the lessor in the financial years in which the related costs are incurred. This provides a proper matching of expenses to revenues because the revenues associated with providing the executory costs are matched to the period in which those costs are incurred.

> **initial direct costs**
> Costs that are directly associated with negotiating and executing a lease agreement.

10.9.1 Lessor's journal entries for a direct-financing lease

The net method or the gross method can be used to record the lease from the perspective of the lessor. If the **gross method** is adopted, the lease receivable is recorded as the sum of the undiscounted minimum lease payments and the unguaranteed residual. An account, unearned interest revenue, is created and amortised to interest revenue over the term of the lease. The unearned interest revenue is subtracted from lease receivable to arrive at the carrying (present) value of the lease receivable.

The **net method**, which appears to be the method most commonly used, records the lease receivable at its present value and does not use a contra account (unearned interest revenue). If the gross method is used, the balance of the lease receivable less the unearned interest will equal the balance of the lease receivable recorded using the net method. The pro forma entries for both methods would be as set out below.

> **gross method**
> Lease receivable is recorded at the sum of the undiscounted minimum lease payments and the unguaranteed residual.
>
> **net method** Lease receivable is recorded at the present value of the minimum lease payments plus the present value of any unguaranteed residual value and initial direct costs.

Net method

Dr	Asset	€XXX	
Cr	Cash/payables, etc.		€XXX

(to record the initial acquisition of the asset by the lessor)

Dr	Lease receivable	€XXX	
Cr	Asset		€XXX

(to record the present value of the lease receivable at the inception of the lease)

Dr	Cash	€XXX	
Cr	Lease receivable		€XXX
Cr	Interest revenue		€XXX

(to record the receipt of a lease payment)

Gross method

Dr	Asset	€XXX	
Cr	Cash/payables, etc.		€XXX

(to record the initial acquisition of the asset by the lessor)

Dr	Lease receivable	€XXX	
Cr	Asset		€XXX
Cr	Unearned interest revenue		€XXX

(to record the lease receivable at the inception of the lease)

Dr	Cash	€XXX	
Cr	Lease receivable		€XXX

Dr   Unearned interest revenue   €XXX
Cr   Interest revenue   €XXX
(to record the receipt of a lease payment)

It should be noted that, as the asset itself (for example, a building or an item of machinery) is not recorded in the financial statements of the lessor, no depreciation for accounting purposes will be recorded in the financial statements of the lessor. If the asset has been leased by way of a finance lease, *control* will be passed to the lessee. Hence, consistent with the IASB Conceptual Framework's definition of assets, the lessor will not show the leased asset within its statement of financial position. Rather, it will show a lease receivable.

10.9.2 Lessor disclosure requirements

Paragraph 47 of IAS 17 requires that for a finance lease the lessor must make the following disclosures:

Lessors shall, in addition to meeting the requirements in IFRS 7, disclose the following for finance leases:

(a) *a reconciliation between the gross investment in the lease at the end of the reporting period, and the present value of minimum lease payments receivable at the end of the reporting period. In addition, an entity shall disclose the gross investment in the lease and the present value of minimum lease payments receivable at the end of the reporting period, for each of the following periods:*
   (i)   *not later than one year;*
   (ii) *later than one year and not later than five years;*
   (iii) *later than five years;*
(b) *unearned finance income;*
(c) *the unguaranteed residual values accruing to the benefit of the lessor;*
(d) *the accumulated allowance for uncollectible minimum lease payments receivable;*
(e) *contingent rents recognised as income in the period; and*
(f) *a general description of the lessor's material leasing arrangements.*

Worked Example 10.6 is a further example of accounting for leases, but this time from the perspective of the lessor.

| **Worked Example 10.6** | **Comprehensive example of accounting for leases by a lessor** |

To show how the entries for a lessor compare with the entries made by the lessee, we will use the same data as that used in Worked Example 10.5, except this time we will be doing the exercise from the perspective of Brothers plc.

Required

(a) Determine the interest rate implicit in the lease, and calculate the present value of the minimum lease payments.
(b) Prepare the journal entries for the years ending 30 June 2016 and 30 June 2017 using the net method.
(c) Prepare the journal entries for the years ending 30 June 2016 and 30 June 2017 using the gross method.

Solution

(a) As for the lessee, the lessor will capitalise the present value of the minimum lease payments, but as a lease receivable rather than as a leased asset. We have already determined that the present value of the minimum lease payments is €369,824, and that the implicit rate is 12 per cent. In this example, there is no unguaranteed residual value expected to accrue to the benefit of the lessor at the end of the lease term. Had there been an unguaranteed residual, the present value of the residual would be added to the lease receivable.
(b) As when preparing the entries for the lessee, we typically use a table to determine the allocation between interest revenue and principal reduction. This table is reproduced below from the perspective of the lessor—the figures are of course the same as in Worked Example 10.5. Note that, from the lessor's perspective, no depreciation entries are made for accounting purposes.

▶

Date	Lease payment (exclusive of executory costs)	Interest revenue	Principal reduction	Outstanding balance
	€	€	€	€
1 July 2015				369,824
30 June 2016	90,000	44,379	45,621	324,203
30 June 2017	90,000	38,904	51,096	273,107
30 June 2018	90,000	32,773	57,227	215,880
30 June 2019	90,000	25,906	64,094	151,786
30 June 2020	170,000	18,214	151,786	0
	530,000	160,176	369,824	

Using the net method

1 July 2015

| Dr | Machinery | €369,824 | |
| Cr | Cash | | €369,824 |

(to recognise the initial acquisition of the machinery by the lessor)

| Dr | Lease receivable | €369,824 | |
| Cr | Machinery | | €369,824 |

(to substitute the lease receivable for the asset; it would be inappropriate to continue to show the machinery in the statement of financial position since the lessor no longer 'controls' it)

30 June 2016

Dr	Cash	€100,000	
Cr	Executory expense recoupment (part of profit or loss)		€10,000
Cr	Interest revenue		€44,379
Cr	Lease receivable		€45,621

(to record the lease receipt of €100,000)

30 June 2017

Dr	Cash	€100,000	
Cr	Executory expense recoupment (part of profit or loss)		€10,000
Cr	Interest revenue		€38,904
Cr	Lease receivable		€51,096

(to record the lease receipt of €100,000)

(c) Using the gross method

1 July 2015

| Dr | Machinery | €369,824 | |
| Cr | Cash | | €369,824 |

(to recognise the initial acquisition of the machinery by the lessor)

Dr	Lease receivable	€530,000	
Cr	Unearned interest revenue		€160,176
Cr	Machinery		€369,824

(to substitute the asset for a lease receivable and to recognise the total of unearned revenue)

30 June 2016

Dr	Cash	€100,000	
Cr	Exectury expense recoupment (part of profit or loss)		€10,000
Cr	Lease receivable		€90,000
Dr	Unearned interest revenue	€44,379	
Cr	Interest revenue		€44,379

(to record the lease receipt of €100,000 and yearly interest payment)

30 June 2017

Dr	Cash	€100,000	
Cr	Exectury expense recoupment (part of profit or loss)		€10,000
Cr	Lease receivable		€90,000
Dr	Unearned interest revenue	€38,904	
Cr	Interest revenue		€38,904

(to record the lease receipt of €100,000 and yearly interest payment)

10.10 Lessor accounting for operating leases

Where a lease is classified by the lessor as an operating lease, the leased property subject to the lease is to be accounted for as a non-current asset to the extent that such an asset satisfies the usual requirements to be considered a non-current asset. As paragraph 49 of IAS 17 states: 'Lessors shall present assets subject to operating leases in their statements of financial position according to the nature of the asset'. That is, the lessor effectively retains control of the asset in the presence of an operating lease and, therefore, should disclose the asset that has been leased to another party. Further, if the asset is depreciable, the lessor involved in an operating lease is required to depreciate the asset. As paragraph 53 of IAS 17 states:

> The depreciation policy for depreciable leased assets shall be consistent with the lessor's normal depreciation policy for similar assets, and depreciation shall be calculated in accordance with IAS 16 and IAS 38.

For operating leases, the lease receipts are treated as rental revenue.

10.11 Leases involving land and buildings

As land is an asset that normally has an indefinite life, IAS 17 asserts that the risks and rewards of land cannot be transferred to the lessee unless the lease will, at its completion, transfer ownership or the lease contains a bargain purchase option. Hence, unless the lease is reasonably assured of transferring ownership to the lessee, a lease of land would be treated as an operating lease by both the lessee and the lessor. As paragraph 14 of IAS 17 states:

> Leases of land and of buildings are classified as operating or finance leases in the same way as leases of other assets. However, a characteristic of land is that it normally has an indefinite economic life and, if title is not expected to pass to the lessee by the end of the lease term, the lessee normally does not receive substantially all of the risks and rewards incidental to ownership in which case the lease of land will be an operating lease.

The above requirement is interesting. If, for example, a lessee were to enter a 100-year non-cancellable lease arrangement for some land, then despite the length of the lease, and the fact that the lease might be non-cancellable, the lessee would not be required to include a liability (or asset) within its statement of financial position regardless of the present value of the next 100 years of probable lease payments. As mentioned earlier in this chapter, requirements such as this are not consistent with the requirements incorporated within the IASB

Conceptual Framework in terms of the definition and recognition criteria of liabilities and assets. Nevertheless, applying the requirements of IAS 17, where a lease involves both land and buildings, the minimum lease payments must be allocated between the land and buildings in proportion to their relative fair values at the inception of the lease. Consistent with the above, if the lease is not assured of transferring ownership of the land and buildings to the lessee at the completion of the lease, the lease payments allocated to the land component are to be treated as if the lease were an operating lease. Whether the payments allocated to the building(s) are classified as pertaining to an operating lease or a financial lease will depend on whether the lease transfers the risks and rewards of ownership of the building(s) to the lessee. The usual tests for determining whether a lease is a finance or operating lease would be applied.

An exception to the above general rule would be where the fair value of the land at the inception of the lease is immaterial to the fair value of the total property. In such a case, the property may be treated as a unit for the purposes of the lease classification and the land component may effectively be ignored. If the lease of the buildings then appears to transfer the risks and rewards of ownership, the total lease for the land and buildings may be treated as a finance lease; otherwise it would be treated as an operating lease (paragraph 17 of IAS 17).

Accounting for a lease involving land and buildings is examined more closely in Worked Example 10.7.

Worked Example 10.7	Accounting by the lessee for a lease involving land and buildings

On 1 July 2015 Musgrave plc signs a non-cancellable agreement to lease a land and buildings package from Thom plc. The lease agreement requires seven annual payments of £75,000, with the first payment being made on 30 June 2016; £5,000 of each of these payments represents a payment to Thom plc for rates and maintenance of the property.

Owing to harsh climatic conditions, the buildings are expected to have a life of only nine years, after which time they will have no residual value.

At 1 July 2015 the land and buildings have a fair value of £117,632 and £274,476, respectively, providing a total for land and buildings of £392,108. The buildings are expected to have a value (unguaranteed by the lessee) of £100,000 at the end of year 7. The rate of interest implicit in the lease is 10 per cent.

Required

(a) Prove that the rate of interest implicit in the lease is 10 per cent.
(b) Allocate the lease payments between the land and buildings.
(c) Provide the journal entries for the years ending 30 June 2016 and 30 June 2017 as shown in the books of Musgrave plc.

Solution

(a) The interest rate implicit in the lease agreement is the interest rate that causes the present value of the minimum lease payments and any unguaranteed residual value to be equal to the fair value of the leased property at the inception of the lease.

Present value of seven lease payments of £70,000
discounted at 10 per cent (we eliminate
the executory costs) = £70,000 × 4.8684 = £340,788
Present value of the
unguaranteed residual = £100,000 × 0.5132 = <u>£51,320</u>
<u>£392,108</u>

As the minimum lease payments plus the unguaranteed residual discounted at 10 per cent equates to the fair value of the asset at lease inception, the interest rate implicit in the lease is 10 per cent.

(b) The lease payments should be allocated on the basis of the fair values of the assets at the inception of the lease. Therefore the allocation of lease payments is:

Land   = £70,000 × (£117,632 ÷ £392,108) = £21,000
Buildings = £70,000 × (£274,476 ÷ £392,108) = £49,000

▶

In this illustration, as the fair value of the land is greater than 25 per cent of the fair value of the total land and buildings, and as the lease does not transfer the land to the lessee at completion of the lease period, the portion of the lease attributable to the land will be treated as an operating lease.

The present value of the minimum lease payments relating to the buildings is:

£49,000 × 4.8684 = £238,551

As the terms of the lease agreement transfer the risks and rewards of ownership of the buildings to Musgrave plc, Musgrave plc will treat the payments allocated to the buildings as a finance lease.

(c) Journal entries for the years ending 30 June 2016 and 30 June 2017:

Date	Lease payment for building	Interest expense	Principal reduction	Outstanding balance
	£	£	£	£
1 July 2015				238,551
30 June 2016	49,000	23,855	25,145	213,406
30 June 2017	49,000	21,341	27,659	185,747
30 June 2018	49,000	18,575	30,425	155,322
30 June 2019	49,000	15,532	33,468	121,854
30 June 2020	49,000	12,185	36,815	85,039
30 June 2021	49,000	8,504	40,496	44,543
30 June 2022	49,000	4,455	44,545	0*
	343,000	104,447	238,553	

Note: There is a £2 rounding error due to the use of only 4 decimal places in the calculations.

1 July 2015

| Dr | Leased buildings | £238,551 | |
| Cr | Lease liability | | £238,551 |

(to record the leased asset and associated liability at the inception of the finance lease)

30 June 2016

Dr	Executory expenses	£5,000	
Dr	Interest expense	£23,855	
Dr	Lease liability	£25,145	
Dr	Lease rental expense—land	£21,000	
Cr	Cash		£75,000

(to record the lease payment of £75,000)

| Dr | Lease depreciation expense | £34,079 | |
| Cr | Accumulated lease depreciation | | £34,079 |

(to record depreciation expense (£238,551 ÷ 7); as the lessee does not appear likely to retain the asset at the end of the lease, the life of the lease is used for depreciation)

30 June 2017

Dr	Executory expenses	£5,000	
Dr	Interest expense	£21,341	
Dr	Lease liability	£27,659	
Dr	Lease rental expense—land	£21,000	
Cr	Cash		£75,000

(to record the lease payment of £75,000)

| Dr | Lease depreciation expense | £34,079 | |
| Cr | Accumulated lease depreciation | | £34,079 |

(to record periodic lease amortisation expense)

10.12 Lessee accounting for lease incentives under a non-cancellable operating lease

Accounting standard IAS 17 does not deal specifically with the treatment of **lease incentives**, with the result that in practice many divergent accounting approaches have been adopted. It is quite common for potential lessees, particularly potential lessees of buildings, to be offered incentives to enter non-cancellable operating leases. (Remember the tests that are required before a lease is classified as a finance lease—most leases for buildings, or parts thereof, would not satisfy these tests as the lease would typically be taken out for a limited proportion of the total life of the asset.) Lease incentives might include

> **lease incentives**
> Incentive provided to a lessee to encourage the lessee to sign the lease.

initial rent-free periods, financial assistance for fitting out offices, up-front cash incentives or financial assistance to terminate existing lease agreements. It is commonly accepted that such up-front incentives are typically not 'free' to the lessee but instead are paid for over the term of the lease. Interpretation SIC-15 *Operating Leases—Incentives*, issued by the IASB, provides guidance in relation to accounting for lease incentives by both lessors and lessees. Paragraph 3 of SIC-15 requires:

> *All incentives for the agreement of a new or renewed operating lease shall be recognised as an integral part of the net consideration agreed for the use of the leased asset, irrespective of the incentive's nature or form or the timing of payments.*

What this means is that the lessor should recognise the aggregate cost of incentives as a reduction of rental income over the lease term. Lessees should recognise the aggregate benefit as a reduction of the rental expense over the lease term. For both lessors and lessees, this recognition should be on the straight-line basis, unless another systematic basis is representative of the time pattern over which the benefit of the leased asset is diminished. The rental expense component of lease rental payments will be calculated and recognised on a basis representative of the pattern of benefits to be derived from the leased property. This is detailed in Worked Example 10.8.

Worked Example 10.8   Accounting for a lease incentive under an operating lease

Point plc enters into a lease agreement with Roadnight plc on 1 July 2012. Under the terms of this agreement, Point plc agreed to lease a central Torquay property from Roadnight plc for a period of ten years. In order to finalise the agreement, and as an incentive to enter into the agreement, Roadnight plc agreed to an initial three-year rent-free period. Under the terms of the agreement, the annual rental for years 4 to 10 amounted to €96,000 per annum.

Required

(a) Prepare the journal entries for Point plc for the reporting periods ending 30 June 2013 and 30 June 2017.
(b) Prepare the journal entries for Roadnight plc for the reporting periods ending 30 June 2013 and 30 June 2017.

Solution

Effectively, what is happening is that the lessee is making seven payments of €96,000 to lease the property for ten years. The total amount to be paid is therefore 7 × €96,000, which equals €672,000. Across the 10-year lease period, this equates to €67,200 per year. From the lessor's perspective, the incentive acts to reduce the rental income across the term of the lease. Similarly, the incentive acts to reduce the rental expense over the lease term from the perspective of the lessee. The incentive is allocated throughout the lease term on a straight-line basis.

(a) Journal entries in the books of Point plc

30 June 2013

Dr	Lease expense	€67,200	
Cr	Accrued lease expenses		€67,200

(recognising lease expense for first year)

After three years (the rent-free period) there would be a balance of €201,600 in 'accrued lease expenses' (3 × €67,200), which is a liability. This balance will then be reduced by €28,800 in each of the remaining seven years, thereby leaving a €0 balance in 'accrued lease expenses' at the end of the lease term.

▶

31 March 2017

Dr	Lease expense	€67,200	
Dr	Accrued lease expenses	€28,800	
Cr	Cash		€96,000
(receipt of lease payment)			

(b) Journal entries in the books of Roadnight plc

31 March 2013

Dr	Lease revenue receivable	€67,200	
Cr	Lease revenue		€67,200
(recognising lease revenue for first year)			

31 March 2017

Dr	Cash	€96,000	
Cr	Lease revenue		€67,200
Cr	Lease revenue receivable		€28,800
(receipt of lease payment)			

What is less clear, however, is how incentives provided by the lessor in the form of leasehold improvements should be accounted for. Although SIC-15, paragraph 6, requires costs in connection with a pre-existing lease (for example, termination, relocation or leasehold improvements) to be accounted for by the lessee in accordance with the applicable accounting standard, including costs that are effectively reimbursed through an incentive arrangement, no guidance is provided on how leasehold improvement costs incurred by the lessor in terms of a lease agreement should be accounted for.

If a lessor has agreed to, and undertaken, leasehold improvements as part of a lease incentive, what does the lease incentive represent from the perspective of the lessee? Is it revenue or is it a liability? It is reasonable to conclude that such incentives are to be considered to be borrowings, which will be repaid by the lessee as part of the future lease rentals. The rental expense component of lease rental payments will be calculated and recognised on a basis that is representative of the pattern of benefits to be derived from the leased property. The remainder of the payments (after allowing for interest, if applicable) will be applied to reduce the lease incentive liability. In most instances, this method of allocation will result in the liability being reduced on a straight-line basis over the term of the lease.

For example, assume that Lessee Company enters into a non-cancellable, seven-year lease for office space in the London Canary Wharf district (and the building has an expected life of 60 years). To entice Lessee Company to enter the lease, Lessor Company agrees to fit out the office. This fit-out would have cost Lessee Company £140,000 had it undertaken or commissioned the work itself. The lease rental expense is £300,000 per annum.

Based on the facts provided, the entry in the books of Lessee Company on signing the lease would be:

Dr	Fixtures and fittings	£140,000	
Cr	Lease incentive liability		£140,000

(to recognise the cost of the office fit-out as an asset and the related liability, which will be repaid over the term of the lease)

If we assume that the benefits are to be recognised on a straight-line basis, the accumulated entry to recognise the payments in the first year would be:

Dr	Lease incentive liability	£20,000	
Dr	Lease rental expense	£280,000	
Cr	Cash		£300,000

(to recognise the periodic lease payments)

Of course, the fittings would also need to be depreciated, as follows:

Dr	Depreciation expense—fixtures and fittings	£20,000	
Cr	Provision for depreciation—fixtures and fittings		£20,000

(to recognise periodic depreciation of the assets)

10.13 Future changes in accounting for leases

As at the time of completing this first edition of *Financial Accounting and Reporting: An International Edition,* it was apparent that there will be fundamental changes in how reporting entities will be required to account for leases. However, because the International Accounting Standards Board (IASB) and the US Financial Accounting Standards Board (FASB) are still considering a number of issues, it is not possible to predict with total accuracy the final contents of the new accounting standard that is expected to be released in 2013 (or perhaps later depending upon the levels of agreement on certain key issues). When the new accounting standard is released it is anticipated that it will not have an application date prior to 2015. This section provides some insights into the likely changes in how reporting entities will be required to account for their leases.

As a first step towards releasing a revised accounting standard, the two Boards initially issued a Discussion Paper in 2009. Exhibit 10.4 is a copy of an early media statement jointly released by the IASB and FASB in December 2006 in relation to work being undertaken to develop a revised accounting standard.

Exhibit 10.4 **Joint media statement released by the IASB and FASB on lease accounting**

IASB and FASB announce membership of international working group on lease accounting (extract)

7 December 2006

Leasing is a major international industry and an important source of finance for a wide range of entities. The current international accounting requirements, set out in IAS 17 Leases, and the US standard FASB Statement No. 13, Accounting for Leases, were developed some 25–30 years ago and have been criticised for allowing similar transactions to be accounted for in very different ways. At the same time, while the world leasing volume amounted to US$579 billion in 2004, many leasing transactions are not reported on balance sheets. The boards have been told that investors and other users of financial statements routinely make adjustments to the financial statements for analytical purposes using incomplete footnote disclosures, raising questions about the usefulness of the current lease accounting model. The project will be conducted jointly by the IASB and the FASB, and both boards will comprehensively reconsider current lease accounting guidance. For more information about the project on lease accounting, please see the IASB and FASB Websites.

As a motivating factor to developing a new accounting standard, the IASB and FASB noted a number of criticisms of the existing accounting requirements, including the following (IASB & FASB 2009, paragraphs 1.12 to 1.15):

1.12 *The existing accounting model for leases (as reflected in IAS 17) has been criticised for failing to meet the needs of users of financial statements. In particular:*

  (a) *many users think that operating leases give rise to assets and liabilities that should be recognised in the financial statements of lessees. Consequently, users routinely adjust the recognised amounts in an attempt to recognise those assets and liabilities and reflect the effect of lease contracts in profit or loss. However, the information available to users in the notes to the financial statements is insufficient for them to make reliable adjustments to the recognised amounts.*

  (b) *the existence of two very different accounting models for leases (the finance lease model and the operating lease model) means that similar transactions can be accounted for very differently. This reduces comparability for users.*

  (c) *the existing standards provide opportunities to structure transactions so as to achieve a particular lease classification. If the lease is classified as an operating lease, the lessee obtains a source of unrecognised financing that can be difficult for users to understand.*

1.13 *Preparers and auditors have criticised the existing model for its complexity. In particular, it has proved difficult to define the dividing line between finance leases and operating leases in a principled way. Consequently, the standards use a mixture of subjective judgements and 'bright-line' tests that can be difficult to apply.*

1.14 *Some have argued that the existing accounting model is conceptually flawed. In particular:*

    (a) *on entering a lease contract, the lessee obtains a valuable right (the right to use the leased item). This right meets the boards' definitions of an asset. Similarly, the lessee assumes an obligation (the obligation to pay rentals) that meets the boards' definitions of a liability. However, if the lessee classifies the lease as an operating lease, that right and obligation are not recognised.*

    (b) *there are significant and growing differences between the accounting model for leases and other contractual arrangements. This has led to inconsistent accounting for arrangements that meet the definition of a lease and similar arrangements that do not.*

1.15 *The US Securities and Exchange Commission (SEC) recognised the inadequacies of the existing lease accounting standards in its June 2005 Report, Report and Recommendations Pursuant to Section 401(c) of the* Sarbanes–Oxley Act of 2002 Arrangements with Off-Balance Sheet Implications, Special Purpose Entities, and Transparency of Filings by Issuers *and recommended that the FASB undertake a project to reconsider the leasing standards, preferably as a joint project with the IASB.*

The process of creating a new standard for lease accounting has been controversial, hence the long period of consultation. The standard will ultimately have very significant implications for many reporting entities and will significantly increase the amount of liabilities (and assets) being reported; hence it is important to hear the views of all stakeholders. While an Exposure Draft *Leases* was released in August 2010 (with comments requested by mid-December 2010), in July 2011 the IASB and FASB announced an intention to re-expose their leasing proposals via another exposure draft to be released in 2012, before the expected release of an accounting standard in 2013. Table 10.1 represents expectations about what is likely to appear in the accounting standard—however, it is emphasised that these are expectations based on material that was available as at the beginning of 2012 and we can never be fully sure what will ultimately appear within a forthcoming accounting standard, particularly when a further exposure draft is about to be issued.

While Table 10.1 provides only a brief coverage of some expected changes to how reporting entities shall account for leases—and it must be emphasised again that the contents of Table 10.1 are based on material

Table 10.1 Expectations about the contents of the future leasing standard

Issue	Likely accounting requirement
When should the lease be recognised?	A lessee and a lessor shall measure lease assets and lease liabilities at the date of commencement of the lease. The date of commencement of the lease is the date on which the lessor makes the underlying asset available for use by the lessee.
How should the lease be measured?	The lessee would initially recognise a liability to make lease payments and a right-of-use asset, both measured at the present value of lease payments. The right-of-use asset is defined as an asset that represents the lessee's right to use, or control the use of, a specified asset for the lease term. The liability shall subsequently be measured using the effective interest method whereby lease payments are allocated between interest expense and a reduction of the lease obligation (as under IAS 17). The lessee shall amortise the right-of-use asset on a systematic basis that reflects the pattern of consumption of the expected future economic benefits.
What are included in the capitalised lease payments?	Lease payments shall include payments arising under a lease including fixed rentals and rentals subject to uncertainty, including, but not limited to, contingent rentals and amounts payable by the lessee under residual value guarantees and term option penalties. The lessee's liability and lessor's receivable should include lease payments that depend on an index or rate and lease payments that meet a high recognition threshold (such as 'reasonably certain').

▶

Table 10.1 Expectations about the contents of the future leasing standard (*Continued*)

Issue	Likely accounting requirement
What is the lease term?	The lease term is to be defined as the non-cancellable period for which the lessee has contracted with the lessor to lease the underlying asset, together with any options to extend or terminate the lease when there is a significant economic incentive for an entity to exercise an option to extend the lease, or for an entity not to exercise an option to terminate the lease. This means that the lease term will include optional renewal periods that are more likely than not to be exercised.
What is the required discount rate?	The lessee would use the rate the lessor charges the lessee when that rate is available, otherwise the lessee is to use its incremental borrowing rate. The lessee's incremental borrowing rate is the rate of interest that, at the date of inception of the lease, the lessee would have to pay to borrow over a similar term, and with a similar security, the funds necessary to purchase a similar underlying asset.
How are initial direct costs to be accounted for?	Initial direct costs are defined as recoverable costs that are directly attributable to negotiating and arranging a lease that would not have been incurred had the lease transaction not been made. Lessees and lessors should capitalise initial direct costs by adding them to the carrying amount of the right-of-use asset and the right to receive lease payments, respectively.
What if there are variable lease payments that depend on an index or a rate?	Some leases have variable components; for example, across time a lease payment might partly be based on the rate of inflation. The boards discussed the measurement of lease payments that depend on an index or a rate included in the lessee's liability to make lease payments and the lessor's right to receive lease payments and decided that: 1. Lease payments that depend on an index or a rate should be initially measured using the index or rate that exists at the date of commencement of the lease. 2. Lease payments that depend on an index or a rate should be reassessed using the index or rate that exists at the end of each reporting period. 3. Lessees should reflect changes in the measurement of lease payments that depend on an index or a rate (a) in net income to the extent that those changes relate to the current reporting period and (b) as an adjustment to the right-of-use asset to the extent that those changes relate to future reporting periods. 4. Lessors should recognise changes in the right to receive lease payments due to reassessments of variable lease payments that depend on an index or a rate immediately in profit or loss.
Residual value guarantees	Lease payments should include residual value guarantees in the measurement of the lessee's liability to make lease payments and the lessor's right to receive lease payments.
Purchase option	Lease payments should include the exercise price of a purchase option (including bargain purchase options) in the measurement of the lessee's liability to make lease payments and the lessor's right to receive lease payments, if the lessee has a significant economic incentive to exercise the purchase option. This represents a departure from the exposure draft released in 2010, which proposed that the exercise price of a purchase option is not a lease payment and therefore should be excluded from a lessee's lease liability and a lessor's lease receivable.

Table 10.1 Expectations about the contents of the future leasing standard (*Continued*)

Issue	Likely accounting requirement
Amortisation of right-of-use asset	If it is determined that the lessee has a significant economic incentive to exercise a purchase option, the right-of-use asset recognised by the lessee should be amortised over the economic life of the underlying asset, otherwise the right-of-use asset should be amortised over the lease term.
Lessor recognition of a residual asset	At the end of the lease term the lessor might have rights to a residual asset if the lease term is not for the life of the underlying asset. Where a residual asset will exist: 1. The lessor would recognise a right to receive lease payments and a residual asset at the date of the commencement of the lease. 2. The lessor would initially measure the right to receive lease payments at the sum of the present value of the lease payments, discounted using the rate that the lessor charges the lessee. 3. The lessor would initially measure the residual asset as an allocation of the carrying amount of the underlying asset and would subsequently measure the residual asset by accreting it over the lease term using the rate that the lessor charges the lessee. The increase in the value of the residual asset across time (which in part would be due to the effects of discounting) would be included in profit or loss as interest income.
Are there exclusions for short-term leases?	Initially there were to be no exceptions for short-term leases; however, this has now changed. A short-term lease is defined as a lease that, at the date of commencement of the lease, has a maximum possible term, including any options to renew, of 12 months or less. The boards decided that, for short-term leases, a lessee need not recognise lease assets or lease liabilities. For those leases, the lessee should recognise lease payments in profit or loss on a straight-line basis over the lease term, unless another systematic and rational basis is more representative of the time pattern in which use is derived from the underlying asset. For those excluded leases, a lessor should continue to recognise and depreciate the underlying asset and recognise lease income over the lease term on a systematic basis.

available in early 2012 and might not accurately reflect the requirements that might ultimately be included in the new standard—it does nevertheless indicate that significant changes are likely when a revised accounting standard is eventually issued. How reporting entities will respond to these changes will be interesting. Clearly, many more leases, which we have traditionally referred to as operating leases, will have to be included in the statement of financial position. The removal of the requirement that a lease must transfer the risks and rewards of ownership to the lessee before an asset and liability are recognised will have obvious implications for reporting entities' assets and liabilities, and therefore for their gearing ratios and so forth. Accounting for leases has been in the work-in-progress tray for standard-setters for a long time. Vivian Beattie and Alan Goodacre studied the impact of the suggested changes to lease accounting in the UK in the 1990s. They discuss the potential impact of this in an article in the *Financial Times* in 1997, reproduced in Financial Accounting in the News 10.2.

More detail of the study reported in Financial Accounting in the News 10.2 can be found in Beattie *et al.* (1998), though the results were extended to include 300 UK companies. Consistent with the results reported in Financial Accounting in the News 10.2, they found that capitalising operating leases had a significant impact on the magnitude of six out of nine key accounting ratios. The affected ratios were: profit margin, return on assets, asset turnover and three measures of gearing. They concluded that the unrecorded long-term liability represented 39 per cent of reported long-term debt, while the unrecorded asset represented 6 per cent of total assets. The adjustments changed the ranking of the companies in respect of company performance, suggesting that the proposed changes have relevance for stakeholders.

Financial Accounting in the News 10.2

A LESSON FROM THE LEASING SHOP

Vivian Beattie and Alan Goodacre, *Financial Times,* 4 September 1997

Standard-setters in the UK, US, Australia and New Zealand, together with the International Accounting Standards Committee, have recently taken the unusual step of publishing a joint discussion paper, Accounting for Leases: A New Approach, which proposes that all leases be capitalised.

If adopted, this would mean that leases currently classified as operating leases would have the asset (and related liability) recorded on the balance sheet of the lessee.

To estimate the impact that this is likely to have on the balance sheets of UK companies and, in particular, on performance ratios, we used a method of constructive capitalisation. Results for 1994 for a large random sample of 232 listed companies showed that operating leases represent a major source of long-term debt-type financing in the UK. On average, the unrecorded lease liability per company was £51m, of which £8m would be classified as short-term debt and £43m as long-term debt. The latter represented 39 per cent of reported long-term debt before capitalisation.

There was wide variation in the importance of operating leases across broad sectors, with the greatest impact in the services sector; this had an average long-term lease liability of £88m, representing 69 per cent of long-term debt. The smallest impact was observed in the mineral extraction sector with an average long-term lease liability of £5m (just 3 per cent of long-term debt).

Capitalisation had a significant impact on six of nine performance ratios investigated (profit margin, return on assets, asset turnover and three measures of gearing). For example, the net debt to equity gearing ratio, often favoured by company management, would change from a mean of 20 per cent to a staggering 72 per cent following capitalisation, while the profit margin would increase from 8.8 per cent to 9.8 per cent on average. What is more, the ranking of companies, both across the broad sectors and even within sectors, would change significantly as a result of differential use of operating leases by companies; again the services sector would be most affected.

These findings suggest that a policy change requiring operating lease capitalisation is likely to have serious economic consequences. Significant changes in the magnitude of key accounting ratios and a major shift in company performance rankings imply that interested parties' decisions and company cash flows are likely to be affected.

The off-balance sheet attraction of leasing finance would be drastically reduced, which would tip the balance towards purchasing. Alternatively, to lessen the impact of such a policy, company management could elect for shorter lease terms so that the lease asset and liability required to be capitalised would be smaller. Apparently, this has already caused some concern to lessors in the property sector as it would have a detrimental effect on the valuation of leased properties.

The good news for affected parties is that the proposal is only at the discussion stage and the UK Accounting Standards Board has a very busy programme ahead of it before it gets to leasing.

Further, the supporting logic for including operating leased 'assets' on the balance sheet is not without its problems; its wholesale adoption would extend to human assets as well as capital assets (since employees are also leased assets). Partial adoption is therefore more likely.

Source: Extract from *Financial Times*. © THE FINANCIAL TIMES LIMITED 2012

10.14 Implications for accounting-based contracts

As we know, entities frequently enter into contracts with other parties that encumber them with contractual conditions tied to the accounting numbers of the firm. To restrict the amount of debt that the firm can take on, existing debt-holders typically contract to restrict debt by stipulating maximum debt-to-asset ratios that the entity should not exceed (Whittred and Zimmer 1986).

Assume that a company has assets of €10 million and liabilities of €5.5 million. Also assume that the **debt-to-asset constraint** imposed on the firm as a result of agreements signed with lenders requires the debt-to-asset ratio to be kept below 0.6. Now assume

> **debt-to-asset constraint** A restriction included in a debt agreement limiting the amount of debt an entity may have relative to its total assets.

technical default
When a borrowing
entity has failed
to comply with
certain restrictive
covenants that have
been negotiated with
lenders.

that the firm wishes to lease some assets valued at €1.5 million. If the lease is treated as an operating lease (which, under existing accounting standards, means that it will not be recognised for the purposes of the statement of financial position), debt and assets will not be affected, so the debt-to-asset ratio will not be affected. However, if the lease is treated as a finance lease, the debt-to-asset ratio would become 0.609 (€7,000,000 ÷ €11,500,000) and the company would be in **technical default** of the loan agreement—potentially a costly situation for the company.

It is, therefore, generally accepted that highly geared companies subject to accounting-based debt contracts would prefer to keep leases off the statement of financial position—perhaps by constructing the clauses of the lease agreement in such a way that the company can justifiably classify the lease as an operating lease. If the lease agreements are constructed in such a way that the lease becomes an operating lease, this will mean that the risks and rewards of ownership will be held by the lessor. In consequence of holding the risks and rewards of ownership, the lessor will be expected to require a higher return (higher lease payments) than would be the case if the lease was a finance lease.

El Gazaar (1993) considered the effects that US accounting standard SFAS 13 (released in 1976) had on US firms. SFAS 13 required US firms to capitalise leases of a finance nature. Where restrictive debt covenants were in place (for example, debt-to-asset constraints and/or interest-coverage requirements), the effect of SFAS 13 was to make those covenants more binding. Capitalising off-balance sheet leases increases assets and liabilities, which increases the likelihood of violating debt covenant restrictions if the debt agreements use rolling generally accepted accounting principles. 'Rolling principles' means that the accounting-based covenants are based on the accounting numbers generated by the rules in place at reporting date—rules that might change. El Gazaar argues that the introduction of an accounting standard requiring the capitalisation of finance leases increases the probability of a company ending up in technical default and has negative cash-flow effects on the firm as management have to take action to alleviate the impact of additional debt such as raising additional equity, redeeming debt or renegotiating debt (all costly options).

The increase in the tightness of debt covenants is considered to have negative cash-flow effects and, consistent with this, it was found that tighter debt covenant restrictions correlated with negative changes in security prices around the time of the release of SFAS 13.

Just as the introduction of previous leasing standards (which utilised the concept of financial versus operating leases) created concerns for reporting entities and led to various strategies being undertaken to devise leases that were construed as operating leases, it will be interesting to see how reporting entities will react to a future accounting standard that abandons the concept of finance leases versus operating leases and therefore requires even more leases to be shown within the statement of financial position. Beattie *et al.* (2006) surveyed 132 expert users and preparers in the UK to find out their opinion on the suggested changes to the accounting for leases (i.e. the capitalisation of operating leases). Both types of stakeholder (user and preparer) agreed that the current leasing standard was not of high quality. There was a view that it allowed transactions to be deliberately structured for classification as off-balance sheet operating leases, thereby enabling similar transactions to be accounted for in different ways. However, the preparers considered that this did not impair user decision-making (a view not held by the users). Both stakeholders agreed that the assets, liabilities and subsequent gearing ratios would change and this would have knock-on effects for companies. On the downside it was suggested that companies may have to renegotiate borrowing covenants, may experience a downgrading in credit rating and would incur compliance costs. On the upside, users considered that it would improve users' evaluation of a company's long-term commitments and their ability to make comparisons across companies. It was also considered that the accounting change may have an adverse impact on the leasing industry as its benefit (an off-balance sheet form of finance) over other forms of debt finance is removed and it was suggested that managers may negotiate very short lease contracts to minimise the impact on the statement of financial position.

As we know, when the new accounting standard is ultimately introduced, lessees' statements of financial position will need to incorporate right-of-use assets and obligations to make lease payments which previously were not recognised. This will impact the reported gearing of reporting entities and this will likely have an impact on various loan covenants, such as those that incorporate debt-to-asset constraints. In terms of the statement of comprehensive income, the recognition of leases will require lessees to recognise interest expense (which is typically higher in the early years of a lease) and also to recognise amortisation expenses related to the right-of-use asset. Amortising the right-to-use asset and recognising the interest expenses on the liability will lead to a pattern of lease expense recognition that is 'front loaded'—that is, the new standard will reduce profits in earlier years and will have an impact on key ratios such as interest coverage ratios.

SUMMARY

The chapter addressed the accounting treatment of leases. As explained, a major issue in accounting for leases is whether the leased asset and the related liability should appear on the statement of financial position of the lessee.

While there will be changes in future years, leases are currently to be classified as operating leases or finance leases. A lease that transfers the risks and rewards of ownership from the lessor to the lessee is considered to be a finance lease. Where a finance lease exists, the leased asset and lease liability must appear in the statement of financial position of the lessee.

Where a lease is capitalised (placed within the statement of financial position), the amount to be capitalised is the present value of the minimum lease payments or the fair value of the leased asset, whichever is the lower. Where a lessee has capitalised a lease, lease payments are to be apportioned between interest expense and the repayment of the lease liability. Further, the lessee must depreciate the leased asset over its expected useful life to the lessee.

Where a lease does not transfer the risks and rewards of ownership to the lessee, it is currently classified as an operating lease and no asset or liability is recognised in the financial statements of the lessee (unless periodic lease payments are made in advance, or in arrears). The periodic lease payments on an operating lease are treated as an expense in the financial statements of the lessee and as revenue in the financial statements of the lessor.

Leases also have to be classified as either finance or operating leases from the perspective of the lessor. For the lessor, finance leases can be further broken down into leases involving dealers or manufacturers, or direct-finance leases.

Where a lease is classified as a finance lease, the lessor will remove the underlying asset from the statement of financial position, and replace the asset with a lease receivable. Periodic lease receipts from the lessee will be apportioned between interest revenue and the recoupment of the lease receivable.

This chapter has also provided an insight into future changes on how reporting entities shall account for leases. As we have seen, the IASB and FASB are jointly working on proposals which aim at removing the financial lease and operating lease classifications currently in use. Their proposals will act to require reporting entities to recognise, for statement of financial position purposes, many leased assets and associated obligations that were previously considered to be operating leases (and which were therefore previously omitted from the statement of financial position).

KEY TERMS

END-OF-CHAPTER EXERCISE

On account of his continued inability to keep up with other riders when cycling, Scott Thomson decides to take action to reduce the popularity of cycling. To this end, he decides to pursue the development of motorised roller blades, a product some might see as offering an alternative to cycling. To do so, he forms Thomson plc. To make the roller blades, Thomson plc needs to acquire some machinery from Fernster plc, which designs and manufactures the machinery. To manufacture the equipment, which has an estimated economic life of eight years, costs Fernster plc £200,000. Fernster plc sells the equipment to parties such as Thomson plc for £263,948.

Thomson plc decides to lease the equipment from Fernster plc for a period of seven years, by way of a non-cancellable lease. The lease commences on 1 July 2015. The lease payments are made at the end of each year and amount to £55,000. The lease payments include reimbursement of Fernster plc's executory costs of £5,000 per annum. There is an unguaranteed residual at the end of the lease term of £40,000. **LO** **10.2**

REQUIRED

(a) Determine whether the lease is an operating lease or a finance lease.
(b) Determine the interest rate implicit in the lease.
(c) Provide the journal entries in the books of Thomson plc as at 1 July 2015 and 30 June 2016.
(d) Provide the journal entries in the books of Fernster plc as at 1 July 2015 and 30 June 2016.

SOLUTION TO END-OF-CHAPTER EXERCISE

(a) As the lease is non-cancellable and the lease term is for the major part of the economic life of the asset (for example, a period in excess of 75 per cent of the machinery's useful life), the lease is a finance lease.
(b) The interest rate implicit in the lease is that which, when used to discount the minimum lease payments and any unguaranteed residual, causes the combined present value to equal the fair value of the asset at lease inception. If we use a discount rate of 10 per cent, the present value of the minimum lease payments over seven years and the unguaranteed residual are as follows:

Minimum lease payments	£50,000 × 4.8684	=	£243,420
Unguaranteed residual	£40,000 × 0.5132	=	£20,528
			£263,948

As the discounted value equals the fair value of the asset at lease inception, 10 per cent must be the rate of interest implicit in the lease.

(c) Journal entries in the books of Thomson plc

1 July 2015

Dr	Leased machinery	£243,420	
Cr	Lease liability		£243,420

(to recognise the leased asset and lease liability at the commencement of the lease; the lessee does not include the unguaranteed residual)

30 June 2016

Dr	Executory costs	£5,000	
Dr	Interest expense	£24,342	
Dr	Lease liability	£25,658	
Cr	Cash		£55,000

(to recognise the first lease payment)

Dr	Depreciation expense	£34,774	
Cr	Accumulated lease depreciation		£34,774

(to recognise the period depreciation expense = £243,420 ÷ 7)

(d) Journal entries in the books of Fernster plc

1 July 2015

Dr	Lease receivable	£263,948	
Dr	Cost of goods sold	£179,472	
Cr	Inventory		£200,000
Cr	Sales revenue		£243,420

(to recognise the sale of inventory to Thomson plc and the related lease receivable). The cost of goods sold represents the cost of the equipment to Fernster plc less the present value of the unguaranteed residual at the end of the lease. The sales revenue represents the present value of the minimum lease payments (which by definition excludes unguaranteed residuals).

30 June 2016

Dr	Cash	£55,000	
Cr	Lease receivable		£23,605
Cr	Interest revenue		£26,395
Cr	Recoupment of executory costs		£5,000

(to recognise the receipt of the periodic lease payment)

It should be noted that, in the above exercise, owing to the existence of the unguaranteed residual, the lease liability in the books of the lessee will be different from the lease receivable in the books of the lessor. As IAS 17 specifies, where a lease is classified by the lessee as a finance lease, the lessee is to record, if material, as at the beginning of the lease term, an initial asset and liability equal in amount to the lower of the fair value of the asset and the present value of the minimum lease payments. Minimum lease payments exclude the unguaranteed residual.

In relation to lessors, where a lease is classified as a finance lease by the lessor (either a direct-finance lease or a lease involving a dealer or manufacturer), the lessor's investment in the lease, comprising the present value of the minimum lease payments receivable plus the present value of any unguaranteed residual value expected to accrue to the benefit of the lessor at the end of the lease term, shall, if material, be brought to account as a receivable, as at the beginning of the lease term.

As the lease receivable in the financial statements of the lessor and the lease payable in the financial statements of the lessee will not be the same amount (because of the unguaranteed residual), the interest revenue recorded in the financial statements of the lessor will be different from the interest expense recorded in the financial statements of the lessee.

REVIEW QUESTIONS

1 What is a lease? **LO** 10.1
2 When should we capitalise a lease transaction? **LO** 10.3
3 If a lease transaction is to be capitalised, how do we determine the value of the leased asset and the lease liability? **LO** 10.3
4 Would there be circumstances in which a lessee would prefer to treat a lease as an operating lease rather than a finance lease? **LO** 10.5
5 As this chapter explains, the IASB and FASB are currently working on the development of a new accounting standard for leases. In this regard, you are required to answer the following: **LO** 10.6
   (a) What are some of the major changes that might occur as a result of the new accounting standard?
   (b) Is it expected that all leases will be required to be shown on the statement of financial position?
   (c) What discount rate is to be used to determine present value?
   (d) Will the new leasing requirements positively or adversely impact reporting entities' gearing ratios and reported profits?
6 The following was in the notes (Note 18) to the 1990 financial statements of Incitec Ltd:
   On 12th October 1989 a subsidiary, Eastern Nitrogen Limited, entered into a Sale and Leaseback arrangement whereby an ammonia plant located in Newcastle with a net book value of €13,983,000 was sold for a cash consideration of €71,400,000 of which a deposit of €5,000,000 had been received in the previous financial year. The profit on the sale is being brought to account over the estimated useful life of the plant. The deferred gain has been disclosed in these financial statements as a deduction from the gross cost of plant and equipment.

   Is the accounting policy adopted by Incitec in accordance with the current requirements of IAS 17? In answering this question, state any assumptions you are making about the sale transaction and the type of lease. **LO** 10.5
7 At the inception of a lease, in what circumstances would the lease receivable recorded by the lessor not be equivalent to the lease payable recorded by the lessee? **LO** 10.5
8 What are minimum lease payments and what do they include? **LO** 10.3
9 Determine for each of the following arrangements the manner in which the relevant lease should be classified, by both the lessor and the lessee, under IAS 17. Give reasons for your answers. **LO** 10.2
   (a) Company A enters into a non-cancellable lease with a five-year term for an item of plant, which has an expected useful life of eight years. The lease is renewable for a further two-year period at commercial rates prevailing at the time of renewal. The present value of the minimum lease payments is equal to 80 per cent of the fair value of the

leased property at the inception of the lease. The remaining 20 per cent of the fair value is represented by the guaranteed residual value. The residual value has been guaranteed by an independent third party, an insurance company, which is unrelated to either the lessor or the lessee.

(b) Company B enters into a non-cancellable lease with a seven-year term for an item of plant, which has an expected useful life of ten years. The present value of minimum lease payments is equal to 75 per cent of the fair value of the asset at the date of inception of the lease. The residual value accounts for the remaining 25 per cent. So confident is the lessor that the plant will retain its value that it is guaranteeing 50 per cent of the residual value, with the lessee being responsible for guaranteeing the remaining 50 per cent of the residual value.

(c) Company C enters into a non-cancellable lease with a five-year term for a large commercial vehicle, which has an expected useful life of eight years. The lease is renewable for a further two years at commercial rates prevailing at the time of renewal. The present value of minimum lease payments is equal to 65 per cent of the fair value of the asset at the date of inception of the lease. The residual value is not guaranteed by the lessee and the vehicle will revert to the lessor. In a separate agreement the lessee has written a put option, which entitles the lessor to put the leased vehicle to the lessee in five years' time on payment of an amount equal to the residual value of the lease.

(d) Company D enters into a non-cancellable lease for plant with a term of eight years. The plant has a useful economic life of 12 years. Company D has an option to renew the lease with the same rental for a further four years, even though market rentals are expected to increase with inflation over the next decade. The present value of the minimum lease payments is 70 per cent of the sum of the fair value of the plant.

10 Lessee plc, on 1 July 2015, sells a tractor having a carrying amount on its books of €100,000 to Lessor plc for €140,000 and immediately leases the tractor back under the following conditions: **LO 10.3**
- The term of the lease is ten years, non-cancellable, and requires rental payments of €22,784 at the end of each year.
- The estimated economic life of the tractor is ten years.
- There is no residual value.
- Lessee plc pays all executory costs (that is, these are not included in the lease payments).
- The implicit rate of interest in the lease is 10 per cent.

(a) Classify the lease for both the lessee and the lessor.
(b) Prove the interest rate implicit in the lease is 10 per cent.
(c) Prepare the journal entries for the lessee for the first year of the lease.
(d) Prepare the journal entries for the lessee for the second year of the lease.

11 Using the data provided in Review Question 10, answer the following questions from the perspective of the lessor. **LO 10.3**
(a) Prove that the rate of interest implicit in the lease is 10 per cent.
(b) Prepare the journal entries for 2015 and 2016 using the net method.
(c) Prepare the journal entries for 2015 and 2016 using the gross method.

12 Rankin plc has entered into an agreement to lease an item of equipment that produces teddy bears. The terms of the lease are as follows: **LO 10.3**
- Date of entering lease: 1 July 2015.
- Duration of lease: 10 years.
- Life of leased asset: 10 years.
- There is no residual value.
- Lease payments: €5,000 at lease inception, €5,500 on 30 June each year (that is, ten payments).
- Included within the lease payments are executory costs of €500.
- Fair value of the machine at lease inception: €27,470.
Determine the interest rate implicit in the lease.

13 Burt plc enters into a non-cancellable five-year lease agreement with Earnie plc on 1 July 2015. The lease is for an item of machinery that, at the inception of the lease, has a fair value of £1,294,384.

The machinery is expected to have an economic life of six years, after which time it will have an expected residual value of £210,000. There is a bargain purchase option that Burt plc will be able to exercise at the end of the fifth year for £280,000.

There are to be five annual payments of £350,000, the first being made on 30 June 2016. Included within the £350,000 lease payments is an amount of £35,000 representing payment to the lessor for the insurance and maintenance of the equipment. The equipment is to be depreciated on a straight-line basis. **LO 10.3**

(a) Determine the rate of interest implicit in the lease and calculate the present value of the minimum lease payments.

(b) Prepare the journal entries in the books of Burt plc for the years ending 30 June 2016 and 30 June 2017.

(c) Prepare the portion of the statement of financial position for the year ending 30 June 2017 relating to the lease asset and lease liability.

(d) Prepare the journal entries of Burt plc for the years ending 30 June 2016 and 30 June 2017 assuming that Burt plc classifies the lease an operating lease.

14 Gregory plc enters into a non-cancellable five-year lease agreement with Sanders plc on 1 July 2015. The lease is for an item of machinery that, at the inception of the lease, has a fair value of £231,140. The machinery is expected to have an economic life of seven years, after which time it will have no residual value. There is a bargain purchase option, which Gregory plc will be able to exercise at the end of the fifth year, for £50,000. **LO 10.3**

Sanders plc manufactures the machinery. The cost of the machinery to Sanders plc is £200,000. There are to be five annual payments of £62,500, the first being made on 30 June 2016. Included within the £62,500 lease payments is an amount of £6,250 representing payment to the lessor for the insurance and maintenance of the machinery. The machinery is to be depreciated on a straight-line basis. The rate of interest implicit in the lease is 12 per cent.

(a) Calculate the present value of the minimum lease payments.

(b) Prepare the journal entries for the years ending 30 June 2016 and 30 June 2017 in the books of:
  (i) Sanders plc
  (ii) Gregory plc

15 On 1 July 2015 Iselin plc signs a non-cancellable agreement to lease land and a building from Weber plc. The lease agreement requires seven annual payments of €375,000, with the first payment being made on 30 June 2016. Within each of these payments €25,000 represents a payment to Weber plc for rates and maintenance of the property. The building is expected to have a life of only nine years, after which time it will have no salvage value. At 1 July 2015 the land and building have a fair value of €588,160 and €1,372,370, respectively. The building is expected to have a value (unguaranteed by the lessee) of €500,000 at the end of year 7. The rate of interest implicit in the lease is 10 per cent. **LO 10.3**

(a) Prove that the rate of interest implicit in the lease is 10 per cent.

(b) Allocate the lease payments between the land and building.

(c) Provide the journal entries for the years ending 30 June 2016 and 30 June 2017 for Iselin plc.

(d) Provide the journal entries for the years ending 30 June 2016 and 30 June 2017 for Weber plc.

16 On 2 November 2006 *The Gold Coast Bulletin* published an article by Chalpat Sonti entitled 'HQ Sale Lifts Bartercard' in which it was stated: **LO 10.2**

Bartercard International has posted a tidy profit on the sale and leaseback of its Southport headquarters, a bright spot in an otherwise turbulent week for the company . . . Bartercard's Southport property, in Scarborough St, had a book value of about €3.5 million, and the sale represented a tidy profit for the company, said chairman Wayne Sharpe. Proceeds from the sale would be used to repay all long-term debt in the group, with the balance to finance Bartercard's further expansion in Bartercard UK and the United Arab Emirates.

Determine whether you think the Southport property was leased back by Bartercard by way of a finance lease or an operating lease.

CHALLENGING QUESTIONS

17 The IASB and FASB have been developing a revised accounting standard for leasing which will act to eliminate the concept of financial leases versus operating leases. If their proposals (some of which have been described in this chapter) are incorporated within a revised accounting standard, then how do you think the management of reporting entities will respond to the new accounting requirements? Do you think it will impact how or whether they lease assets and, if so, why? **LO 10.6**

18 Mark Richards plc enters a finance lease to lease an asset from Michael Petersen plc. The lease term is for seven years and the leased asset is initially recorded in Mark Richards plc's financial statements for £250,000 at the date of lease inception. The asset is expected to have a useful life of eight years. The lease terms include a guaranteed residual of £20,000, and that the asset is expected to have a residual value of £10,000 at the end of its useful life. **LO 10.4**

Determine the lease depreciation expense assuming that:

(a) Mark Richards plc is expected to get ownership of the asset at the end of the lease term.

(b) Mark Richards plc is not expected to get ownership of the asset at the end of the lease term.

19 Owing to low liquidity, Lisa plc decides on 1 July 2015 to sell its land and buildings to Anderson plc. The carrying values of the land and buildings in the books of Lisa plc, at 1 July 2015, are: **LO 10.3**

Land, at cost	€1,800,000
Buildings, at cost	€1,750,000
Accumulated depreciation	€350,000

The land and buildings are sold for €4,334,700 (their fair value), with the amount being allocated equally as follows:

Land	€2,167,350
Buildings	€2,167,350

Immediately following the sale, Lisa plc decides to lease back the land and buildings from Anderson plc. The term of the lease is 20 years. The implicit interest rate in the lease is 12 per cent. It is expected that the buildings will be demolished at the end of the lease term. The lease is non-cancellable, returns the land and buildings to Anderson plc at the end of the lease and requires the following lease payments:

Payment on inception of the lease on 1 July 2015	€600,000
Payment on 30 June each year starting 30 June 2016	€500,000

There is no residual payment required.
(a) Provide the entries for the sale and lease in the books of Lisa plc as at 1 July 2015.
(b) Provide the entries for the purchase and lease in the books of Anderson plc as at 1 July 2015.
(c) Provide the entries in the books of Lisa plc as at 30 June 2025.
(d) Provide the entries in the books of Anderson plc as at 30 June 2025.

20 On 1 July 2015 Flyer plc decides to lease an aeroplane from Finance plc. The term of the lease is 20 years. The implicit interest rate in the lease is 10 per cent. It is expected that the aeroplane will be scrapped at the end of the lease term. The fair value of the aeroplane at the commencement of the lease is €2,428,400. The lease is non-cancellable, returns the aeroplane to Finance plc at the end of the lease and requires a lease payment of €300,000 on inception of the lease (on 1 July 2015) and lease payments of €250,000 on 30 June each year (starting 30 June 2016). There is no residual payment required. **LO 10.3**
(a) Provide the entries for the lease in the books of Flyer plc as at 1 July 2015.
(b) Provide the entries for the lease in the books of Finance plc as at 1 July 2015.
(c) Provide the journal entries in the books of Flyer plc for the final year of the lease (that is, the entry in 20 years' time).
(d) Provide the journal entries in the books of Finance plc for the final year of the lease (that is, the entry in 20 years' time).

21 Deliveries plc leased a truck from a truck dealer, City Vans plc. City Vans plc acquired the truck at a cost of £180,000. The truck will be painted with Deliveries plc's logo and advertising and the cost of repainting the truck to make it suitable for another owner four years later is estimated to be £40,000. Deliveries plc plans to keep the truck after the lease but has not made any commitment to the lessor to purchase it. The terms of the lease are as follows: **LO 10.3**
• Date of entering lease: 1 July 2015.
• Duration of lease: four years.
• Life of leased asset: five years, after which it will have no residual value.
• Lease payments: £100,000 at the end of each year.
• Interest rate implicit in the lease: 10 per cent.
• Unguaranteed residual: £50,000.
• Fair value of truck at inception of the lease: £351,140.
(a) Demonstrate that the interest rate implicit in the lease is 10 per cent.
(b) Prepare the journal entries to account for the lease transaction in the books of the lessor, City Vans plc, at 1 July 2015 and 30 June 2016.
(c) Prepare the journal entries to account for the lease transaction in the books of the lessee, Deliveries plc, at 1 July 2015 and 30 June 2016.
(d) On 30 June 2019 Deliveries plc pays the residual of £50,000 and purchases the truck. Prepare all journal entries in the books of Deliveries plc for 30 June 2019 in relation to the termination of the lease and the purchase of the truck.

22 Hopeful plc leased a portable sound recording studio from Lessor plc. Lessor has no material initial direct costs. Hopeful plc does not plan to acquire the portable studio at the end of the lease because it expects that, by then, it will need a larger studio. The terms of the lease are as follows: **LO 10.3**

- Date of entering lease: 1 July 2015.
- Duration of lease: four years.
- Life of leased asset: five years.
- Lease payments: €50,000 at the beginning of each year.
- First lease payment: 1 July 2015.
- Lease expires: 1 July 2019.
- Interest rate implicit in the lease: 8 per cent.
- Guaranteed residual: €40,000.

(a) Determine the fair value of the portable sound recording studio at 1 July 2015.

(b) Prepare a schedule for the lease payments incorporating accrued interest expense.

(c) Prepare the journal entries to account for the lease in the books of Hopeful plc at 1 July 2015, 30 June 2016 and 1 July 2016.

(d) At the termination of the lease Hopeful plc returns the portable sound recording studio to Lessor plc but its fair value at that time is €25,000. What must Hopeful plc do to comply with the terms of the lease? Prepare the journal entries in the books of Hopeful plc for return of the asset to Lessor plc and the settlement of all obligations under the lease on 1 July 2019.

REFERENCES

BEATTIE, V., EDWARDS, K., & GOODACRE, A., 'The Impact of Constructive Operating Lease Capitalisation on Key Accounting Ratios', *Accounting and Business Research*, vol. 28, no. 4, 1998, pp. 233–54.

BEATTIE, V., GOODACRE, A., & THOMSON, S.J., 'International Lease-accounting Reform and Economic Consequences: The Views of UK Users and Preparers', *International Journal of Accounting*, vol. 41, no. 1, 2006, pp. 75–103.

EL GAZAAR, S.M., 'Stock Market Effects of the Closeness to Debt Covenant Restrictions Resulting from Capitalisation of Leases', *Accounting Review*, April 1993, pp. 258–72.

INTERNATIONAL ACCOUNTING STANDARDS BOARD & FINANCIAL ACCOUNTING STANDARDS BOARD, *Draft Discussion Paper on Leases*, London, IASB and FASB, October 2008.

INTERNATIONAL ACCOUNTING STANDARDS BOARD & FINANCIAL ACCOUNTING STANDARDS BOARD, *Discussion Paper DP/2009/01, Leases: Preliminary Views*, London, IASB and FASB, March 2009.

WHITTRED, G. & ZIMMER, I., 'Accounting Information in the Market for Debt', *Accounting and Finance*, November 1986, pp. 1–12.

Chapter 11

Share Capital, Reserves and Share Options (Employee Bonus Schemes)

Learning objectives

Upon completing this chapter readers should:

LO1   understand that the equity of an organisation can consist of several different accounts;

LO2   understand that within equity there can be various classes of shares, each affording different rights to holders;

LO3   be able to provide the journal entries to recognise the issue of both fully paid and partly paid shares by a company;

LO4   be able to provide the journal entries to account for distributions;

LO5   be able to provide the journal entries necessary when preference shares are to be redeemed;

LO6   be able to provide the journal entries necessary when shares are forfeited by their owners;

LO7   be able to provide the journal entries necessary to account for rights issues and option issues;

LO8   understand what constitutes a share split and a bonus issue of shares;

LO9   understand the effect of various vesting conditions on the accounting treatments required for share-based payments; and

LO10   know the disclosure requirements of IAS 1 *Presentation of Financial Statements* in relation to share capital and reserves

11.1 Introduction to accounting for share capital and reserves

Equity/owners' equity is known as **shareholders' funds** in a company. Under conventional double-entry accounting, equity equals the total assets of the organisation, less its total liabilities (that is, Equity = Assets minus Liabilities). Alternatively, we can say that the total assets of an organisation will be matched by the total of the claims held by external parties (liabilities) plus claims held by the owners (that is, Assets = Liabilities plus Equity).

The IASB Conceptual Framework defines equity as the 'residual interest in the assets of the entity after deducting all its liabilities'. The residual interest is a claim or right to the net assets (assets minus liabilities) of the reporting entity. As a residual interest, equity ranks after liabilities in terms of a claim against the assets of a reporting entity. As noted in Chapter 2, the definition of equity is directly a function of the definitions of assets and liabilities. Given that equity is the residual interest in the assets of the entity and given that the amount assigned to equity will always correspond to the excess of the amounts assigned to its assets over the amounts assigned to its liabilities, the criteria for the recognition of assets and liabilities provide the criteria for the recognition of equity.

> **equity** The owners' share of the business calculated by subtracting the liabilities of the entity from its assets.
>
> **shareholders' funds** In a company, shareholders' funds represent the difference between total assets and total liabilities.

In previous chapters we have considered how to account for different assets and liabilities. As noted above, how we do this will have a direct impact on the balance of equity. For example, a decision to revalue non-current assets upwards above their historical cost will increase equity by increasing the revaluation surplus account (which is part of equity). Similarly, valuing all marketable securities at their market value will change the value of those assets, and hence the value of equity through changes in reported profits—if the increments or decrements are taken to the statement of comprehensive income, as is often the case.

New requirements to recognise particular liabilities that were traditionally not recognised will also lead to a negative change in equity. Changes in the measurement of particular liabilities will also affect the balance of equity (for example, changes from face value to present value in the measurement of liabilities). Hence the adoption of particular measurement techniques for assets and liabilities, perhaps as a result of a change in accounting standards, will directly affect the balance of equity given that equity equals assets minus liabilities.

The total of equity is typically made up of a number of different accounts. Within a company, equity—or shareholders' funds—can comprise:

- Share capital relating to one class or several classes of shares—for example, ordinary shares plus various classes of preference shares.
- Reserves such as a revaluation surplus, foreign currency translation reserve, capital redemption reserve, general reserve or forfeited shares reserve.
- Retained earnings (or accumulated losses).

As an illustration of the various accounts that can make up shareholders' funds, consider Exhibit 11.1. It shows an extract from the consolidated statement of financial position (balance sheet) for Nutreco as at 31 December 2010 (and 2009). Only the part of the statement of financial position that relates to equity is shown. Supporting the numbers that appear in the statement of financial position will be notes to the financial statements. For example, there will be notes to the financial statements that provide further details on issued shares, as well as on the movements in all the other reserve accounts.

As is the case for Nutreco (see Exhibit 11.1), retained earnings often make up a significant proportion of total shareholders' funds. Retained earnings, which we will consider in more depth in Chapter 14, represent the accumulation of prior periods' profits or losses, less any dividends declared and paid and less any transfers that might be made out of retained earnings to other reserves. Retained earnings might also be used (reduced) for the purpose of a bonus issue of shares, as we will see in this chapter.

The total reserves of a company will also often include a revaluation surplus. We discussed the revaluation surplus in Chapter 6. As we learned, when certain classes of non-current assets are revalued in an upward direction, this increase is not treated as part of profit or loss (but is included as part of 'other comprehensive income'), but rather, any increase in the fair value of the asset is transferred directly to revaluation surplus. However, while the amount of an upward revaluation of a non-current asset is not treated as part of the period's profit or loss (as explained in Chapter 6, when a non-current asset is revalued to fair value there is a debit to the asset account and a credit to revaluation surplus), the amount of the asset revaluation is included within 'other comprehensive income', and is included within 'total comprehensive income for the year' (IAS 1, paragraph 7).

The statement of comprehensive income is examined in detail in Chapter 14.

11.2 Different classes of shares

Companies can have on issue various classes of shares. For example, many companies issue both ordinary shares and preference shares.

Exhibit 11.1	Components of Nutreco plc's equity as at 31 December			
Equity (€m)	**Note**	**2010**	**2009**	
Issued and paid-up share capital	22	8.4	8.4	
Share premium	22	159.5	159.5	
Treasury shares	22	−7.3	−1.2	
Hedging reserve	22	−8.7	−13.5	
Retained earnings	22	547.0	507.9	
Undistributed result	22	111.4	90.3	
Translation reserve	22	−0.9	−21.2	
Equity attributable to owners of Nutreco		809.4	730.2	
Non-controlling interests	22	10.2	10.5	
Total equity		819.6	740.7	

11.2.1 Ordinary shares

ordinary/equity shares A class of shares that typically ranks behind the claims of creditors and some preference shareholders.

Ordinary shares (also known as **equity shares**) might be composed of issues of shares made at different times so that some shares may be fully paid, while others are partly paid to various amounts. Further, even though all ordinary shares might have the same rights, ordinary shares might be issued at different prices, depending on the market's demand for the shares at the time of the share issue.

Ordinary shares confer voting rights—except in certain circumstances, such as when the company is in financial distress—and owners are entitled to a distribution of profits in the form of dividends. However, they are not assured of **dividends**, and in particular years they might receive no cash payments. Failure to receive dividends in one year does not mean that a right to dividends will accrue until dividends are ultimately paid. Holders of ordinary shares typically rank last in any distribution of assets when a company is wound up.

preference shares Shares that receive preferential treatment relative to ordinary shares, with the preferential treatment relating to various things, such as dividend entitlements or order of entitlement to any distribution of capital on the dissolution of the company.

11.2.2 Preference shares

Preference shares are so called because of preferential treatment their holders might receive over and above ordinary shareholders. The preferential treatment may be in relation to the receipt of dividends or the order of ranking in relation to asset distributions on the winding up of a company. Some preference shares confer voting rights, some confer voting rights only if dividend entitlements have not been paid, while others do not confer voting rights at any time. There is such a plethora of different forms of preference share that it is not possible to describe them all. Deegan (1986) describes some forms of preference shares, including:

dividend A distribution of the profits of an entity to the owners of that entity, typically in the form of cash.

- non-redeemable, participating preference shares
- convertible, redeemable, participating preference shares
- convertible, redeemable preference shares
- redeemable preference shares secured by a letter of credit or other security
- short-term, redeemable preference shares secured by a put option backed by a letter of credit

From the first to the last type in the above list, the preference shares become progressively more debt-like. If preference shares are described as 'participating', this indicates that, after they have received the preference

dividend at a fixed rate, the preference shareholders may then participate with the ordinary shareholders in any further profits that are to be distributed. Preference shares also sometimes come with the right of conversion to ordinary shares according to some prespecified terms (that is, convertible preference shares); they might also enable the holder to redeem the shares for cash at the option either of the company or of the shareholder (that is, redeemable preference shares).

As noted above and within previous chapters, some preference shares can take on the characteristics of equity, while others can take on the characteristics of debt. As will be shown in Chapter 12, on financial instruments, where preference shares have the characteristics of debt they must, according to IAS 32 *Financial Instruments: Presentation*, be disclosed as debt, and the related payments are to be considered expenses rather than a distribution of profits; that is, as interest expense rather than dividends (IAS 32, paragraph 36). Normally, preference shares that are redeemable on a fixed date, or at the option of the shareholder, and provide a fixed rate of return and provide no voting rights will be considered to be of the same substance as debt, and therefore should be disclosed as debt (IAS 32, paragraph 18).

Nutreco is an example of a company classifying its cumulative preference shares as debt. Nutreco's 2010 group annual report shows, at Note 23 'Interest Bearing Borrowings', that €54.5 million of preference shares have been classified as non-current liabilities in 2009. These were redeemed in the year. The preference shares are described within the notes to the financial statements as follows:

Nutreco Annual Report 2010

Extract from Note 23 'Interest Bearing Borrowings'

Cumulative preference shares 'A'

Prior to the Initial Public Offering in 1997, Nutreco issued cumulative preference shares 'A', which under IFRS classify as interest-bearing borrowings. Under the agreement between Nutreco and the holders of the cumulative preference shares 'A', the latter receive a fixed annual dividend of 6.66%.

Nutreco has repurchased the cumulative preference shares 'A' for an amount of EUR 54.5 million by the end of the current dividend period (31 December 2010) and the shares will be cancelled in the first quarter of 2011.

11.3   Accounting for the issue of share capital

The **share capital** (also referred to as contributed equity) of a company represents the amounts that owners have contributed to the organisation. Traditionally, when shares were issued, we needed to consider their **par value** (or notional value). Shares were normally not issued below par value but they could be, and usually were, issued in excess of par. If shares were issued at a price in excess of par, this excess amount was referred to as a **share premium**. For example, if a company issued its shares at an amount of €1.80 each and they had a par value of €1.00, the share premium on the issue would have been €0.80 per share.

Worked Example 11.1 considers the determination of share capital.

11.3.1 Shares issued for cash

On **application** it is usual for applicants to be required to send money representing part, but not all, of the price of the shares for which they apply (known as 'application money'). Once the closing date for applications is reached, the number of shares applied for must be compared with the number on offer. If applications are lower than the number on offer, the issue is undersubscribed and the company will be required either to cancel the offer and refund the application money or to call upon the underwriters to take up the remaining shares. If the issue is oversubscribed, then a basis for allotting shares must be established. Some applications may be rejected and the application money must be refunded; some may receive a reduced allocation and their excess application money used as further payment towards the price of the shares.

> **share capital** The balance of owners' equity within a company, which constitutes the capital contributions made by the owners.
>
> **par (or face or nominal) value** The amount debenture holders receive on maturity of debentures.
>
> **share premium** The difference between the issue price of a share and the par value of that share.
>
> **application** Process whereby potential equity investors provide an expression of interest, by way of a monetary deposit, for shares in an entity.

Worked Example 11.1   Determination of share capital

Coolum plc commences its life by issuing 1 million €1 ordinary shares at an issue price of €1.40 per share. Hence, Coolum plc receives €1.4 million in total.

Required

Prepare the equity section of the statement of financial position immediately after the issue of the shares.

Solution

Following the issue, the shareholders' equity section of the statement of financial position would be represented as:
Shareholders' equity

Share capital	€1,000,000
Share premium	€400,000
Total shareholders' equity	€1,400,000

---

allotment Process whereby an entity allocates shares to the successful applicants of the shares.

Having established the basis for allocation, shares can then be issued to those who are to get them — this is known as **allotment**. The balance of the price is, typically, payable in instalments, perhaps some on allotment (known as 'allotment money'). Worked Example 11.2 considers the accounting for a public issue of shares. Quite frequently, there will be an oversubscription for shares when there is an IPO. That is, more shares will be applied for than the number to be issued. Where there has been an oversubscription, the company needs to consider what to do with the excess applications. We will consider how to account for oversubscriptions later in this chapter.

Worked Example 11.2   Public issue of shares

As a result of an offer to the public, Peregian plc receives applications for 5 million shares during July 2015. Peregian plc subsequently issues 5 million shares on 1 August 2015. The shares are issued at a price of €2.10 each.

Required

Provide the accounting entries to recognise the receipt of the application monies and the subsequent allotment of shares.

Solution

The accounting entries to recognise the receipt of the application monies and the subsequent allotment of shares would be:

1–31 July 2015

Dr Bank account	€10,500,000	
Cr Application and allotment account		€10,500,000

(to recognise the aggregated receipt of application monies during July 2015)

When companies make an initial offer of shares to the public (which will require the compilation of a prospectus), this is typically referred to as an initial public offering (IPO). IPOs are often managed by another party, such as a financial institution or a stockbroker because such organisations have expertise in managing the public issue of shares. The financial institution or stockbroker might also employ the services of an underwriter. The underwriter gives advice on various matters, such as how to market the securities and what prices to ask for the securities. The underwriter also typically agrees to acquire all the available shares that were made available to the public but for which the public did not subscribe. Therefore, in the presence of an underwriter any risks associated with undersubscription are shifted from the company to the underwriter.

1 August 2015

Dr Application and allotment account	€10,500,000	
Cr Share capital		€10,500,000

(to recognise the issue of shares and to close off the application account)

The amount in share capital is determined by multiplying the issue price of the shares by the number of shares issued. In this example we have assumed that there has been no oversubscription.

11.3.2 Partly paid shares

A company may issue shares on an instalment basis. This will require an amount to be paid on issue and a further amount at some specified future date (known as 'call money'). There may be more than one instalment, so there would be a first call, a second call, etc. Anyone failing to pay a call is liable to forfeit their partly paid shares and, once forfeited, these may be reissued to others on terms agreed for this purpose. These are referred to as **forfeited shares** and **reissued shares**, respectively.

When shares are partly paid, the paid portion of the shares is accounted for in the same manner as fully paid shares, while the balance, the deferred consideration, is of the nature of a receivable. This deferred consideration meets the IASB Conceptual Framework definition of an asset because the company has a future economic benefit, the benefit is controlled by the directors, as they have determined when it is to be receivable, and the benefit arose as a result of a past event, the issue of the shares. Furthermore, it is probable that the future economic benefit can be measured with reliability.

> **forfeited shares**
> Shares that have been cancelled due to failure of the investors to pay all amounts due.
>
> **reissued shares**
> Forfeited shares that have been purchased by investors.

Where no future date has been specified for calling up the unpaid portion, an asset is not recognised until the company has specified a future date or dates for calling up the unpaid portion and informs shareholders of these dates. However, where shares have been issued on an instalment basis, with an amount to be paid on issue and with further amounts payable at specified future dates, a receivable must be recognised. This is shown in Worked Example 11.3.

In Worked Example 11.3 the receivable is measured at its estimated realisable value. Where the collection of the receivable becomes doubtful, an allowance for doubtful debts should be raised.

Worked Example 11.3   Issue of partly paid shares

Yeates plc commenced operations on 1 July 2015 by issuing 15 million £1 ordinary shares by way of a direct private placement and at an issue price of £1.50 per share. Shareholders were required to pay £1.00 on application, with a further £0.35 payable on 1 September 2015 and a further £0.15 payable on 1 December 2015.

Required
Prepare the journal entries in the books of Yeates plc to account for the issue of the shares.

Solution
1 July 2015

Application

Dr	Cash account	£15,000,000	
Cr	Application and allotment account		£15,000,000

(cash received for shares)

Allotment

Dr	Application and allotment account	£15,000,000	
Cr	Share capital account		£15,000,000

(issue of shares partly paid)

Call 1 July 2015

Dr	First call account	£5,250,000	
Dr	Second call account	£2,250,000	
Cr	Share premium account		£7,500,000

(recognising equity receivable—the call accounts are considered to be receivables)

1 September 2015

Dr	Cash account	£5,250,000	
Cr	First call account		£5,250,000

(receipt of cash for first call of £0.35 per share)

◄

1 December 2015

Dr	Cash account	£2,250,000
Cr	Second call account		£2,250,000

(receipt of cash for second call of £0.15 per share)

The call accounts, which are amounts receivable in the future by Yeates plc for the shares, meet the IASB Conceptual Framework definition of an asset. Clearly, Yeates plc has a future economic benefit that is controlled—the directors have already determined when it is receivable, and the benefit arose from a past event, the issue of the shares.

11.3.3 Issue of shares other than for cash

Shares in a company may be issued for a consideration other than cash. This consideration may take the form of:

- promissory notes
- contracts for future services
- real or personal property, or
- other securities of the company (for example, convertible debentures)

Where shares are to be issued for a consideration other than cash, the directors of the company must determine the fair value of the consideration for the issue. Fair value is defined in the accounting standards as 'the amount for which an asset can be exchanged between knowledgeable, willing parties in an arm's length transaction'. The issue of shares other than for cash is shown in Worked Example 11.4.

Worked Example 11.4   Issue of shares other than for cash

On 1 July 2014 Joel plc invited Parkinson plc to purchase 700,000 shares at €2.50 per share. At the time of accepting the offer, Parkinson plc only had cash resources available of €900,000. The balance of the purchase price would be made up of future consulting services that Parkinson plc would supply to Joel plc.

By 30 June 2015 Parkinson plc had supplied €400,000 worth of services to Joel plc. This is not a public share sale and hence the double entry does not have to go through the application and allotment account.

Required
Provide the accounting entries to record the issue of the Joel plc shares.

Solution
The entries to reflect the sale of the shares by Joel plc would be:

1 July 2014

Dr	Cash	€900,000	
Dr	Future consulting services receivable	€850,000	
Cr	Share capital		€1,750,000

(issuing of shares for cash and for future services)

30 June 2015

Dr	Consulting fees expense (statement of comprehensive income)	€400,000	
Cr	Future consulting services receivable		€400,000

(recording portion of services received)

The above entry assumed that the services consumed by Joel plc were not used in the manufacture of inventory or in the construction of particular non-current assets. Had they been used for such purposes, then the cost of the services would have been included within the cost of the respective assets rather than being expensed to the statement of comprehensive income.

11.3.4 Shares oversubscribed

Quite frequently, there will be an oversubscription for shares. That is, more shares will be applied for than the number to be issued. Where there has been an oversubscription, the company needs to consider what to do with the excess applications. Worked Example 11.5 provides an illustration of accounting for an oversubscription of shares.

Worked Example 11.5   **Oversubscription for shares issued as partly paid**

In July 2015 Mooloolaba plc calls for public subscriptions for 10 million €1 ordinary shares. The issue price per ordinary share is €1.20, to be paid in three parts, these being €0.50 on application, €0.40 within one month of the shares being allotted and €0.30 within two months of the first and final call, with the call for final payment being payable on 1 September 2015. By the end of July, when applications close, applications have been received for 12 million shares; that is, 2 million in excess of the amount to be allotted.

Required

Provide the accounting entries to record the issue of Mooloolaba plc's shares.

Solution

The accounting entries to record the receipts of the monies and the subsequent issue would be as follows.

1–31 July 2015

Dr	Bank account	€6,000,000	
Cr	Application and allotment account		€6,000,000

There has been an oversubscription for shares, and a number of approaches can be adopted to manage this oversubscription. The approach to be adopted would normally be prescribed in the prospectus related to the share issue (for a public issue of shares). Two approaches that could be adopted in the case of an oversubscription are:

1. Satisfying the full demand of a certain number of subscribers and refunding the funds advanced by the other subscribers. This approach can be adopted where the shares are issued through an underwriter and the underwriter seeks to look after some favoured clients. Typically, where a publicly listed issue is oversubscribed, gains will be made by the initial investors on the first day of share trading (demand exceeds supply, leading to a price increase).
2. Issuing shares to all subscribers on a pro rata basis. If shares are issued on a pro rata basis, the excess monies on application can either be refunded to all subscribers or they can be used to reduce any further amounts that might be owing on allotment (if shares are issued as partly paid).

In this example, we will assume that the excess funds are used to offset the amount due on allotment (€0.40 per share), and that all subscribers will receive an allotment of shares on a pro rata basis. This means that if somebody has subscribed for 10,000 shares, they will receive 8,333 shares: that is, 10,000 x 10 ÷ 12 shares. Allotment of shares is made on 1 August.

1 August 2015

Dr	Application and allotment account	€5,000,000	
Cr	Share capital account		€5,000,000

(to allot the shares as partly paid to €0.50)

Dr	Application and allotment account	€4,000,000	
Dr	Call account	€3,000,000	
Cr	Share capital		€5,000,000
Cr	Share premium		€2,000,000

(to recognise the amount due on allotment at €0.40 per share and the amount due on the first and final call of €0.30 per share; the allotment account and the call account are receivables, but are typically disclosed in the statement of financial position as a reduction against share capital)

▶

Note: sometimes the application and allotment accounts are kept separate. Where this happens, the allotment account would be treated in the same manner as a call account and the following entry would be made to remove the application funds from the application account to the allotment account as follows:

Dr	Allotment	€1,000,000
Cr	Application	€1,000,000

The effect of this is to offset the excess funds received on application against the amount due on allotment, rather than providing a refund to the subscribers. Following this entry, each subscriber is considered to owe the company a further €0.30 per share as a result of the share allotment. When this is received, the following transaction will occur:

Dr	Bank account	€3,000,000
Cr	Application and allotment account	€3,000,000

When the final call is received, the following transaction will result:

1 September 2015

Dr	Cash at bank	€3,000,000
Cr	Call account	€3,000,000

(to recognise the receipt of amounts due on the first and final calls)

It is assumed that all amounts due on allotment are paid. In practice, however, it is common for some investors to fail to pay the amounts due on allotment. Such a failure can result in the shares being forfeited. (We will consider the accounting treatment of forfeited shares later in this chapter.) Forfeiture would be very common where the market price of the share has fallen to the extent that what remains to be paid on the partly paid shares exceeds their current market value.

11.3.5 Share issue costs

When a company sells shares, various costs are incurred that are directly associated with the issue of the equity instruments. These include legal, promotional, accounting, underwriting and brokerage fees directly related to the issue of the shares. These costs are necessary to ensure the legal requirements associated with the sale are complied with, and would not have been incurred had the shares not been issued. Share issue costs directly incurred as a result of the issue of shares are deducted from the proceeds of the share issue.

A company can also incur various indirect costs during a share issue. These costs include the costs of management time, costs associated with researching and negotiating sources of finance and costs of feasibility studies, as well as the allocation of various internal costs. These indirect costs are not deducted from the proceeds of the share issue. Finally, the costs of an equity transaction that is abandoned are recognised as an expense (IAS 32, paragraph 37).

An example of the allocation of costs associated with a share issue is detailed in Worked Example 11.6.

Worked Example 11.6 **Accounting for share issue costs**

On 1 July 2015 Swellnet plc publicly issued 1,000,000 £2 ordinary shares at £2.50 each. All the shares were subscribed for. Swellnet plc incurred the following costs that were associated with the share issue:

	£
Advertising of share issue and prospectus	8,500
Accounting fees associated with drafting of prospectus	2,800
Legal expenses associated with share issue	3,600
Brokerage fees	1,080
Administration costs of existing staff members and other overheads	2,300
Costs associated with negotiating sources of finance	3,020
	21,300

◀ **Required**

Prepare the journal entries necessary to account for the issue of the shares.

Solution

Journal entries

1 July 2015

Dr	Bank account	£2,500,000	
Cr	Application and allotment account		£2,500,000

(to recognise the cash received on applications for the shares)

Dr	Application and allotment account	£2,500,000	
Cr	Share capital account		£2,000,000
Cr	Share premium account		£500,000

(to allot the shares)

Dr	Share premium account	£15,980	
Dr	Administration overheads (statement of comprehensive income)	£5,320	
Cr	Cash		£21,300

(allocating costs associated with share issue)

The administration costs and costs associated with negotiating sources of finance are not deducted from the proceeds of the share issue.

11.4 Accounting for distributions

Distributions made by a company to its shareholders may take a number of forms. Although the usual form of distribution is a cash dividend, distributions can also be made in the form of a redemption of shares or the repurchase and cancellation of shares. Distributions can also be made in the form of cash, other assets or the conversion of equity to a liability. Where distributions are not made in the form of cash, they must be recorded at the fair value of the consideration at the date of distribution.

11.4.1 Accounting for cash dividends

Dividends are a distribution of profits to shareholders. They are authorised by the directors of the company subject to any conditions that might be contained in the constitution of the company. Usually, a dividend is paid during the course of the year. An interim dividend is paid in anticipation of the current year's profit and can be paid at any time during the year. A final dividend is authorised and typically paid after the end of the reporting period, and once the financial statements have been completed.

Whether or not a shareholder receives a dividend depends largely on the type of shares held. For example, holding ordinary shares does not automatically entitle a shareholder to a dividend. Dividends are paid at the discretion of the directors, and subject to the broad requirement that dividends can only be paid if the company's assets exceed its liabilities immediately before the dividend is declared and the excess is sufficient for the payment of the dividend; that the payment of the dividend is fair and reasonable to the company's shareholders as a whole; and that the payment of the dividend does not materially prejudice the company's ability to pay its creditors (as is required under company law in many European countries).

The journal entries associated with the payment of dividends depend on whether the company draws a distinction between the various components of equity for financial reporting purposes. Where no distinction is held between the various components of equity, the entry to record the distribution of dividends is:

Dr	Dividends paid	XXX
Cr	Cash	XXX

At the end of the reporting period, the dividends paid will be closed off to equity.

Dr	Retained earnings	XXX
Cr	Dividends paid	XXX

It should be noted that some entities might simply debit retained earnings and credit cash, rather than performing the two separate sets of entries above. The net effect is the same.

11.4.2 Interim dividends

When the directors pay an interim dividend, an appropriation is recorded in the records of the company.

Dr	Interim dividends	XXX	
Cr	Cash		XXX

At the financial year end, the appropriation of interim dividends is closed to retained earnings.

Dr	Retained earnings	XXX	
Cr	Interim dividends		XXX

11.4.3 Final dividends

Once the final profit for the year has been calculated, which is after the end of the financial year, the directors are in a position to decide on the amount of final dividends to allocate to shareholders. International Financial Reporting Standards prohibit the recognition of a dividend at the end of the reporting period unless the dividend has been declared prior to year end and the payment of the dividend does not require further ratification by other parties, such as by the shareholders at the annual general meeting (which is typically held after the year end).

IAS 10 *Events After the Reporting Period* specifically prohibits the recognition of dividends as a liability at the end of the reporting period if the dividends have been declared after the end of the reporting period. As paragraphs 12 and 13 state:

> 12. *If an entity declares dividends to holders of equity instruments (as defined in IAS 32* Financial Instruments: Presentation) *after the end of the reporting period, the entity shall not recognise those dividends as a liability at the reporting date.*
> 13. *If dividends are declared (i.e. the dividends are appropriately authorised and no longer at the discretion of the entity) after the reporting date but before the financial report is authorised for issue, the dividends are not recognised as a liability at the reporting date because they do not meet the criteria of a present obligation in IAS 37. Such dividends are disclosed in the notes in the financial report in accordance with IAS 1* Presentation of Financial Statements.

The rationale behind this is that dividends declared after the reporting period do not meet the definition of a present obligation at the end of the reporting period because the entity has the discretion rather than an unavoidable commitment at the end of the reporting period to pay the dividends. However, it is again stressed that, if a final dividend is declared at or before the end of the reporting period and requires no further ratification (the payment is binding), then it should be recorded as a liability. The entries would be of the form:

Dr	Final dividend declared	XXX	
Cr	Dividend payable		XXX

Dr	Retained earnings	XXX	
Cr	Final dividend declared		XXX

11.4.4 Accounting for the distribution of assets other than cash

When a distribution made by a company does not take the form of cash, the value that the distribution is recorded at is the fair value of the consideration at the date of the distribution. If the fair value of the asset being distributed is different from its carrying amount, the difference is recognised as an income or expense item. For example, assume that because of cash-flow considerations the directors of a company decided to pay a dividend in the form of a truck. At the date of distribution the fair value of the asset was €100,000. It had originally cost €150,000 and had a carrying value of €80,000. The journal entry to record the distribution would be:

Dr	Dividends paid	€100,000	
Dr	Accumulated depreciation	€70,000	
Cr	Truck		€150,000
Cr	Gain on disposal of asset		€20,000

In this example, the €20,000 gain on the disposal of the asset is the fair value adjustment recognised as a component of income or expense in the statement of comprehensive income.

11.5 Redemption of preference shares

Financing of the redemption of preference shares is typically controlled by law in European countries. The aim of the legislation is to protect creditors by ensuring that the capital investment in the company remains intact and repayments are not being made to shareholders which will put the creditors at risk of not receiving their funds from the company. In the UK, preference shares can be redeemed out of profits that would otherwise be available for dividends, or out of the proceeds of a fresh issue of shares made for the purposes of the redemption. Regardless of the source of financing, the total undistributable capital is typically maintained by establishing an undistributable equity reserve called the Capital Redemption Reserve (CRR) and transferring an amount from distributable reserves to this undistributable reserve to ensure that the total shareholder fund balance before the redemption equals the total shareholder fund balance after the redemption.

Where the redemption is out of the proceeds of a fresh issue of shares, the entries would be as follows (assuming the fresh issue of shares and redemption are satisfied by cash and are equal in size—this means that a CRR does not have to be created):

DR	Cash	XXX	
CR	Share capital (equity/liability)		XXX

(the issue of shares)

DR	Share capital—redeemable preference shares (liability)	XXX	
CR	Cash		XXX

(the redemption of the preference shares)

When the new share issue is less than the redemption value, then an amount representing the difference will have to be transferred from revenue reserves to the capital redemption reserve.

DR	Revenue reserves	XXX	
CR	CRR		XXX

(This will ensure that the undistributable total capital balance is maintained)

While the above entries relate to a redemption of preference shares by means of a 'fresh' issue of shares, preference shares can also be redeemed out of accumulated profits (retained earnings), as follows:

DR	Retained earnings	XXX	
CR	Share capital (equity)		XXX

(to transfer retained earnings to share capital)

DR	Share capital—redeemable preference shares (liability)	XXX	
CR	Cash		XXX

(to redeem the preference shares)

The accounting for the redemption of preference shares is covered in Worked Example 11.7.

11.6 Forfeited shares

As noted previously in this chapter, if shares are issued as partly paid and some shareholders subsequently fail to pay the amounts due on allotment or on subsequent calls, their shares can be forfeited. If the forfeiture of shares results from non-payment of amounts owing, the shareholder will thereafter cease to be a member of the company. The shareholder may be entitled to a full or partial refund of the monies paid before the forfeiture of the shares. There are various possible outcomes:

> **forfeited shares account** An account reflecting the amounts paid by investors for partly paid shares and where those shares have been cancelled owing to failure of investors to pay all amounts due.

- A company's operating rules (within its constitution) may state that refunds are to be made to the investor or the stock exchange may require this practice. In either case, the amount refunded, might not represent the full amount paid by the investor, as the company will typically deduct the costs incurred in reissuing the shares. Amounts paid by defaulting investors are recorded within a **forfeited shares account**. This account is a liability and will exist until such time as the monies are refunded to the former shareholders.

> ### Worked Example 11.7 Redemption of preference shares
>
> On 1 July 2015 Granite Bay plc makes a private placement of redeemable preference shares to Noosa National Park plc. Ten million preference shares are issued at a price of €3.00 per share, and they are redeemable at a fixed date, this being 30 June 2018. On 30 June 2018 the shares are redeemed as expected.
>
> #### Required
>
> Provide the accounting entries to reflect the issue and subsequent redemption of Granite Bay plc's redeemable preference shares.
>
> #### Solution
>
> The accounting entries to reflect the issue and the subsequent redemption would be:
>
> *1 July 2015*
>
> | | | | |
> |---|---|---|---|
> | Dr | Cash at bank | €30,000,000 | |
> | Cr | Share capital—preference shares | | €30,000,000 |
>
> *(to recognise the issue of 10 million preference shares at a price of €3.00 per share)*
>
> Given the substance of the issue, the shares would be considered debt. The share capital account would be listed under the liabilities of Granite Bay plc, with a suitable note explaining why they have been classified as debt and not as equity. The returns paid to the holders would be recognised as an interest expense rather than dividends. However, regardless of the accounting, under company law preference shares are regarded as shareholder capital, which forms part of the legal total shareholder funds. It is this total that must be maintained, under law. Therefore, the following entry is required on redemption to maintain the overall capital balance:
>
> *30 June 2018*
>
> | | | | |
> |---|---|---|---|
> | Dr | Share capital—preference shares | €30,000,000 | |
> | Cr | CRR | | €30,000,000 |
>
> This entry has the effect of eliminating the preference shares and creating a capital redemption account.
>
> | | | | |
> |---|---|---|---|
> | Dr | Retained earnings | €30,000,000 | |
> | Cr | Cash | | €30,000,000 |
>
> The preference shares must be redeemed only out of profits or out of the proceeds of a new issue made for the purposes of the redemption. Hence, following the above entry, shareholders' equity has been reduced by the book value of the preference shares. Company law typically requires that a redemption of preference shares should not reduce total share capital. The balance in the capital redemption account *can* be transferred to share capital. The entry would be:
>
> | | | | |
> |---|---|---|---|
> | Dr | CRR | €30,000,000 | |
> | Cr | Share capital | | €30,000,000 |
>
> Further, the requirement would also mean that, although we have redeemed preference shares (meaning there are fewer shares on issue), total share capital will not change.

■ Where a company's constitution makes no mention of refunding amounts previously paid by defaulting investors and the stock exchange has no rule on the matter, then the company is entitled to retain the amounts paid by the former shareholders, less any amounts incurred to reissue the shares. In this case, the amounts paid by the defaulting investors are recorded within a **forfeited shares reserve**, which would be shown as part of the shareholders' funds of the company.

forfeited shares reserve A reserve for non-refundable amounts paid by defaulting shareholders, shown as part of shareholders' funds of the company.

To illustrate the use of a forfeited shares account, assume, for example, that Coogee plc has issued 10 million £1 shares at a price of £2.00 per share. The investors are required to pay £1.00 on application and a further £1.00 when a call is made some months later. Following the call for £1.00 per share, it becomes apparent that the holder(s) of 100,000 shares have failed to pay the amount due on the call. As a result, the directors of the company elect to forfeit the shares. The accounting entry to record the forfeiture would be:

Dr	Share capital	£100,000	
Dr	Share premium	£100,000	
Cr	Call		£100,000
Cr	Forfeited shares account		£100,000

Assume that a refund must be made to the defaulting investors. But this refund will be made only after the costs of the reissue have been deducted.

Let us also assume that Coogee plc reissues the shares as fully paid for an amount of £1.60; that is, £0.40 below the original issue price. We will suppose that the costs involved in generating the sale of the shares amount to £2,500. The accounting entries would be:

Dr	Cash at bank	£160,000	
Dr	Forfeited shares account	£40,000	
Cr	Share capital		£100,000
Cr	Share premium		£100,000
Dr	Forfeited shares account	£2,500	
Cr	Cash at bank		£2,500

The forfeited shares account is used to make up any shortfall on the issue of the shares and to fund the costs of the share reissue. Following the above journal entries, there would be a balance of £57,500 in the forfeited shares account. This represents a liability that must be paid to the former shareholders. The accounting entry relating to the refund would be:

| Dr | Forfeited shares account | £57,500 | |
| Cr | Cash at bank | | £57,500 |

Note: If the company is not listed on a stock exchange that requires repayment and its constitution is silent on the refunding of monies associated with forfeited shares, the net amount of £57,500 in the above illustration could be retained by the company. The amount would be transferred from the forfeited shares account to the forfeited shares reserve and would form part of shareholders' funds. Another illustration of share forfeiture is considered in Worked Example 11.8.

Worked Example 11.8 Forfeiture of shares

On 1 July 2015 Torquay plc allots 1 million shares for a price of £1.00 as partly paid to £0.50 per share. A call for the balance of the share price—£0.50—is made on 1 October 2015. By 1 December 2015 the holders of 900,000 shares have made the payment that is due on the call. The directors decide to forfeit the remaining 100,000 shares.

The shares are reissued on 14 December 2015 as fully paid. The company receives £0.70 per share when the shares are reissued. The costs of conducting the sale amount to £500. The surplus amounts are returned to the original shareholders after payment of all the expenses associated with reissuing the shares.

Required

Provide the journal entries necessary to account for the call, forfeiture and subsequent reissue of Torquay plc's shares.

Solution

Journal entries to account for the call, forfeiture and subsequent reissue of Torquay plc's shares are as follows:

1 October 2015

| Dr | Call | £500,000 | |
| Cr | Share capital | | £500,000 |

(to record the call of £0.50 per share on one million shares)

1 December 2015

| Dr | Cash at bank | £450,000 | |
| Cr | Call | | £450,000 |

(to record the aggregated receipt of call monies received from the holders of 900,000 shares)

Dr	Share capital	£100,000	
Cr	Call		£50,000
Cr	Forfeited shares account		£50,000

(to record the forfeiture of 100,000 shares)

14 December 2015

Dr	Cash at bank	£70,000	
Dr	Forfeited shares account	£30,000	
Cr	Share capital		£100,000

(to recognise the amount received on the subsequent sale of the forfeited shares)

| Dr | Forfeited shares account | £500 | |
| Cr | Cash at bank | | £500 |

(to recognise the payment of costs incurred in relation to the sale of the shares)

| Dr | Forfeited shares account (shareholders) | £19,500 | |
| Cr | Cash at bank | | £19,500 |

(to recognise the return of remaining monies to the original shareholders)

11.7 Share splits and bonus issues

share split When a company reduces the par/nominal value of its shares and issues more shares to make up the total original par/nominal value. For example, changing the par/nominal value of shares from € 1 to € 0.50 and issuing an extra € 0.50 share to each shareholder.

From time to time, particular companies might elect, pursuant to a resolution passed at a general meeting, to undertake a **share split**. A share split involves the subdivision of the company's shares into shares of a smaller value. For example, a company that has issued 100 million shares might elect to subdivide these shares to create 200 million shares. Companies might undertake a share split because they feel that the lower priced shares will make the securities more marketable—but there is limited empirical research to support such a view.

When a share split occurs, there is no change to owners' equity. The balance of the share capital remains the same. A share split does not require any accounting journal entries, but it does require the company to amend its share registers, which in itself will create some costs. Therefore, management must believe that there are some benefits associated with share splits.

If a company performs a share split, and the shares to be split are partly paid, the share split must be done in such a way as to divide the uncalled portion equally among the shares issued. For example, if a company has issued 1 million shares on which there was an amount of 50 cents uncalled per share, and the company splits its shares in two, the company would have 2 million shares on which 25 cents can be called per share.

bonus shares Shares received from a bonus issue.

Companies can also issue **bonus shares**. When a bonus issue is made, existing shareholders receive additional shares, at no cost, in proportion to their shareholding at the date of the bonus issue. For example, a company might have issued 10 million ordinary shares. On a given date it decides to issue one million bonus shares out of retained profits (a 'one-for-ten' bonus issue). If the market price per share is €1.00, the accounting journal entry to record the bonus issue may be summarised as:

| Dr | Retained earnings | €1,000,000 | |
| Cr | Share capital—ordinary shares | | €1,000,000 |

The effect of the above entry is that one equity account—share capital—increases, while another equity account—retained earnings—decreases. There is no net effect on owners' equity; however, the procedure does effectively 'lock in' the retained earnings, making them unavailable for future cash dividends.

bonus share dividend A distribution to existing shareholders in the form of additional shares in the entity, normally on a pro rata basis.

When bonus issues are made out of retained earnings, they are commonly referred to as a **bonus share dividend**. Although shareholders typically feel as though they have gained from a bonus issue, what must be remembered is that their proportional share in the net assets of the business does not change. For example, if the company referred to above has total assets of €100 million, and liabilities of €23 million, the net asset backing per share would be €7.70 per share before the bonus issue. This is calculated by dividing the net assets of the company by the number of shares on issue (€77,000,000 ÷ 10,000,000). Therefore an individual holding of 10,000 shares would have a total claim against the net assets of the business of €77,000.

Following the bonus issue, the net asset backing per share would be €7.00 per share (€77,000,000 ÷ 11,000,000—the assets of the business do not change, but the issued shares increase by 1 million). The individual initially holding 10,000 shares would hold 11,000 shares following the bonus issue, and the investor's share of the net assets of the business would still be €77,000 (11,000 × €7.00). So although the shareholders might be happy with a bonus issue, are they really any better off after such an issue compared with before the issue? Interestingly, there is some evidence to suggest that the **total market capitalisation** of a company after a bonus issue tends, on average, to be greater than it was before the bonus issue. (Market capitalisation of a company is calculated by multiplying the number of shares on issue by their market price.) In part, this might be due to a signalling effect. Evidence, such as that provided in Bechmann and Raaballe (2007), suggests that the majority of share splits and stock dividends are accompanied by increases in the total dividends paid by the companies. This study examined the dividend behaviour of firms on the Copenhagen Stock Exchange post each type of event. This might indicate to investors that the company is going to be in a position to pay greater dividends, which, in itself, might warrant a reappraisal of the value of the organisation. Of course, undertaking a bonus issue or share split is a very indirect way for a company to signal increased dividends—it could more easily simply announce that total dividend payments will increase in the future.

> **total market capitalisation**
> Calculated by multiplying the number of issued shares in a company by their latest market price.

Another approach to issuing shares is by way of either rights issues or by releasing share options. We will briefly consider these in the following sections.

11.8   Rights issues

A rights issue generally involves providing existing shareholders with the rights to acquire additional shares in the entity for a specified—and often quite attractive—price. For example, a company might offer existing shareholders the right to acquire one additional share in the company for each ten shares currently held. The acquisition price would be specified. If all current shareholders acquired the shares available under the rights issue, the proportional ownership interest of each shareholder would not change.

Some rights issues may be tradeable, and others not. If the rights are tradeable (often referred to as 'renounceable'), the recipients of the rights (shareholders) will have the ability to sell the rights to others. Rights that cannot be transferred or traded are referred to as non-renounceable rights. The accounting entries for a rights issue are similar to those for a share issue. Worked Example 11.9 considers a rights issue.

Issuing additional shares, whether through a rights issue or otherwise, can lead to individual shareholders having a diluted interest in a company in situations where new investors are offered the opportunity to buy new shares in the company. In many European countries shareholder rights are protected by company law as they have pre-emptive priority when the company issues new shares. This right gives the existing shareholders the option to buy any shares that are being issued in proportion to their current holding so that their control is not diluted by the new share issue. However, the recent financial crisis has called into question this practice, as it is argued that it places an unnecessary delay on the fundraising process. The article in Financial Accounting in the News 11.1 discusses the pros and cons of pre-emptive rights.

Worked Example 11.9   **A rights issue**

Coolum plc required additional equity funding and decided to issue a renounceable rights offer. To reduce the risks associated with the rights issue, Coolum plc appointed an underwriter.

Coolum sent out details of the rights issue to existing shareholders on 1 July 2015 and it offered existing shareholders the right to acquire an additional share in Coolum plc for €2.20 per share. The shares were to be fully paid on application and all applications had to be received by 1 September 2015. The total shares on offer through the rights issue were 10 million (meaning total subscriptions of €22 million).

By 1 September 2015 applications had been received for 9 million shares, meaning that the underwriter was responsible for acquiring the remaining 1 million shares. The shares were issued on 7 September 2015, with this also being the date on which amounts due from the underwriter were received.

Required

Provide the journal entries to account for the Coolum plc rights issue.

Solution

1 September 2015

Dr	Bank account	€19,800,000	
Cr	Application and allotment account		€19,800,000

Because of the undersubscription, the underwriter is required to acquire the additional 1 million shares. The amount due from the underwriter is a receivable.

Dr	Receivable—underwriter	€2,200,000	
Cr	Application and allotment account		€2,200,000

9 September 2015

Dr	Cash at bank	€2,200,000	
Cr	Receivable—underwriter		€2,200,000
Dr	Application and allotment account	€22,000,000	
Cr	Share capital		€22,000,000

Financial Accounting in the News 11.1

SHARE DILUTION AND PRE-EMPTIVE RIGHTS (extract)

Brooke Masters, *Financial Times*
19 June 2008

The capacity of shareholders to slow down capital raising is coming under increasing scrutiny, says Brooke Masters. What are shareholder rights really worth? In the UK, shareholders prize their pre-emptive right not to be diluted by new equity as a fundamental principle. Most US investors lost that right in the 1960s and do not miss it.

Ordinarily, this transatlantic culture clash would simply be a curiosity. But the contrast between the recent troubles encountered by UK banks' rights issues and rapid capital-raising by a slew of US banks has raised new questions about the UK regime. As a result, the Treasury and the Financial Services Authority are reviewing the rights issues process.

A big issue on the table as authorities meet with shareholders and City representatives will be whether pre-emptive rights can be harmonised with the need by companies to raise capital quickly. Rights issues, which give existing shareholders time to buy new shares or sell off their right to do so, can take weeks to approve and execute. During the process, UK banks Bradford & Bingley and HBOS found themselves dangerously exposed to short-sellers and other sceptics.

By contrast, US banks including Wachovia, Merrill Lynch and Citigroup were able to bring in overseas investors or issue new shares almost overnight.

'Investors in the US don't have any expectation that they can maintain their share in the company,' says Chris

Walton, an attorney at Clifford Chance. 'It's a trade-off for the ability of companies to control the process and drive through better execution.'

Pre-emptive rights were once the norm in the US, dating back to an early 19th century court case. But in 1967, the state of Delaware, where more than half of all large US companies are incorporated, changed its company laws so that shareholders stopped having automatic protection against dilution. While Delaware companies were still permitted to explicitly grant their shareholders pre-emptive rights, few did. Other states quickly followed in Delaware's footsteps and the right has largely disappeared.

The contrast reflects a larger difference between US and UK shareholder laws. UK investors generally have more explicit protections built into their company law, while those in the US have the ultimate trump card of filing a shareholder lawsuit if they believe the company has failed to keep their interests in mind. US investors also have additional protection because corporate boards have an explicit fiduciary duty to shareholders, while UK directors owe their duty to the company.

The UK has considered limiting pre-emptive rights several times in the past couple of decades, particularly in times of economic stress when companies have needed to raise cash quickly. But each time the proposal has been beaten back.

Source: Financial Times. © FINANCIAL TIMES LIMITED 2012.

11.9   Share options (in brief)

A share option will give the holder the right to acquire shares at a particular price in the future. In this respect, they are similar to rights issues. However, options are often sold by the entity or are provided as part of a salary package provided to employees. Some options also have a life of a number of years before they are either exercised or expire. Rights issues, by contrast, typically have quite short lives. Share options are considered to be *equity-settled share-based payment transactions* (discussed in detail in WebChapter 3). These are defined as transactions in which the reporting entity receives goods or services as consideration for equity instruments of the entity, and the equity instruments can include shares or share options. In relation to how equity-settled share-based transactions are to be measured, a general rule is provided in paragraph 10 of IFRS 2 *Share-Based Payments*, as follows:

> *For equity-settled, share-based, payment transactions, the entity shall measure the goods or services received, and the corresponding increase in equity, directly, at the fair value of the goods or services received, unless that fair value cannot be estimated reliably. If the entity cannot estimate reliably the fair value of the goods or services received, the entity shall measure their value, and the corresponding increase in equity, indirectly, by reference to the fair value of the equity instruments granted.*

Once share options are issued, the actual options may or may not be exercised in the future. They will be exercised to the extent they are 'in the money'. An option is deemed to be 'in the money' to the extent that the exercise price (the price to acquire the share) is less than the market price of the share. Accounting for option issues—particularly putting a cost on them—can be a difficult exercise. IFRS 2 *Share-Based Payments* provides the rules for accounting for share options. Accounting for share options is a particularly controversial topic—particularly the issue of placing a cost on the share options that were issued to employees. Many companies argued that such options cost the company nothing and therefore they recognised no expenses in relation to the issue. Pursuant to IFRS 2, a cost must now be attributed to the options. Worked Example 11.10 provides a relatively straightforward example of accounting for share options provided to employees. In this example we nominate a cost for each option, thereby avoiding the tricky valuation issue.

Worked Example 11.10   Share options provided to employees

On 1 July 2015 Caloundra plc provided a total of 5 million options to three of its key managers. The options were valued at 50 pence each and allowed the executives to acquire shares in Caloundra plc for £5 each. The executives are not permitted to exercise the options before 30 June 2017 but then may exercise them any time between 1 July 2017 and 30 June 2018. The market price of Caloundra plc shares on 1 July 2015 was £4.40. Therefore, if the executives are unable to formulate strategies to increase the value of the firm's shares the options will be 'out of the money' and therefore of limited value.

It is assumed that on 31 December 2017 the share price reaches £6.00 and all the executives exercise their options and acquire the shares in Caloundra plc.

Required

Account for the issue and exercise of the options in Caloundra plc.

Solution

The initial provision of options to the executives is to be treated as part of total salaries cost. Therefore the entry is:

1 July 2015

Dr	Salaries expense	£2,500,000	
Cr	Share options account		£2,500,000

The share option account would be considered to be part of total equity and would be disclosed separately from share capital. Should the options ultimately not be exercised—because the market price of the shares does not exceed £5 throughout the period in which the right to exercise has vested—paragraph 23 of IFRS 2 *Share-Based Payments* allows the entity to transfer the balance in the share option account to another equity account (the initial transaction should not be reversed).

However, in this example the options are in fact exercised by the managers, which leads to the following entries:

▶

31 December 2017

Dr	Cash at bank	£25,000,000	
Cr	Share capital		£25,000,000
Dr	Share options	£2,500,000	
Cr	Share capital		£2,500,000

As we can see from the above entry, the cost attributed to the options at the date of their issue will be transferred to share capital when the options are exercised.

11.10 Share options (in more detail)

There is a general presumption that, apart from transactions with employees, the fair value of the goods and services provided by parties other than employees can be measured reliably. If this is not the case, the transactions are to be measured by reference to the fair value of the equity instruments granted (IFRS 2, paragraphs 10 and 11). As we will discuss shortly, if market prices are not available because there is no 'active market' for the equity instruments—as would often be the case for options being issued to employees—fair value would be assessed by using a valuation approach such as an option pricing model.

11.10.1 Have the entitlements vested?

In relation to the provision of services, consideration needs to be given to whether the equity instruments vest immediately or whether they vest at a later time, perhaps conditional on the completion of a particular period of service. This has implications for when the associated asset or expense will be recognised. According to IFRS 2, if something vests it has become an unconditional entitlement. Specifically, IFRS 2 defines to 'vest' as:

> *To become an entitlement. Under a share-based payment arrangement, a counterparty's right to receive cash, other assets, or equity instruments of the entity vests when the counterparty's entitlement is no longer conditional on the satisfaction of any vesting conditions.*

The 'counterparty', as referred to in the above paragraph, is the party providing the goods or services to the reporting entity. The above definition of 'vest' requires in its turn a definition of 'vesting conditions'. As indicated previously in this chapter, and according to IFRS 2, vesting conditions are:

> *The conditions that determine whether the entity receives the services that entitle the counterparty to receive cash, other assets or equity instruments of the entity, under a share-based payment arrangement. Vesting conditions are either service conditions or performance conditions. Service conditions require the counterparty to complete a specified period of service. Performance conditions require the counterparty to complete a specified period of service and specified performance targets to be met (such as a specified increase in the entity's profit over a specified period of time). A performance condition might include a market condition.*

If the equity instruments vest at grant date, the reporting entity will recognise the whole transaction on that date. The reason for this treatment is that the counterparty (the other party to the transaction) is not required to complete a specified period of service before becoming unconditionally entitled to the equity instruments. The reporting entity assumes that the counterparty has rendered services in full in return for the equity instruments. Therefore the entity should recognise the services received in full with a corresponding increase in equity (IFRS 2, paragraph 14). Should the equity instruments not vest at grant date, or where equity instruments are granted subject to vesting conditions, for example the employee is required to complete a predetermined period of service, paragraph 15 of IFRS 2 creates a presumption that they are a payment for services to be received during the vesting period, hence they are recognised during the vesting period with a corresponding increase in equity (IFRS 2, paragraph 15). Examples of this scenario are provided in part of paragraph 15 of IFRS 2:

> 15 ... For example:
>
> (a) if an employee is granted share options conditional upon completing three years' service, then the entity shall presume that the services to be rendered by the employee as consideration for the share options will be received in the future, over that three-year vesting period; or

(b) *if an employee is granted share options conditional upon the achievement of a performance condition and remaining in the entity's employ until that performance condition is satisfied, and the length of the vesting period varies depending on when that performance condition is satisfied, the entity shall presume that the services to be rendered by the employee as consideration for the share options will be received in the future, over the expected vesting period. The entity shall estimate the length of the expected vesting period at grant date, based on the most likely outcome of the performance condition. If the performance condition is a market condition, the estimate of the length of the expected vesting period shall be consistent with the assumptions used in estimating the fair value of the options granted, and shall not be subsequently revised. If the performance condition is not a market condition, the entity shall revise its estimate of the length of the vesting period, if necessary, if subsequent information indicates that the length of the vesting period differs from previous estimates.*

To illustrate the above requirements, let us assume that a reporting entity grants its managing director share options with a fair value at grant date of £100,000. We will further assume that the options will vest should the managing director see out his five-year contract. Over the period of the contract, the reporting entity will recognise an employment expense of £20,000 per year in the statement of comprehensive income and an increase in equity as follows:

Dr	Employee benefits expenses	£20,000	
Cr	Share capital		£20,000

Worked Example 11.11 considers how to account for employee service costs where the ultimate payment vests in full if the employee works for the entity for three years. The example is adapted from one provided in IFRS 2.

Worked Example 11.11 Employee costs with a vesting period

An entity grants 100 share options to each of its 500 employees. Each grant is conditional upon the employee working for the entity for the next three years. The entity estimates that the fair value of each share option is €15.00 (perhaps this value was determined as a result of applying an option pricing model).

At *grant date* the entity estimates that 20 per cent of employees will leave during the three-year period and therefore forfeit their rights to the share options (that is, the right to the options would not have vested).

We will consider applying the requirements of IFRS 2 in two scenarios, the first being that everything turns out as expected. In the second scenario there is a revision of employee departures.

Scenario 1

Assuming everything turns out exactly as expected, the entity recognises the following amounts during the vesting period for services received as consideration for the share options. As can be seen, the total amount of the expense is recognised uniformly over the vesting period. There would be an increase in remuneration expense, and an increase in equity of €200,000 each period.

Year	Calculation	Remuneration expense for period	Cumulative remuneration expense
1	100 × 500 × 80% × €15 × 1 year/3 years	€200,000	€200,000
2	100 × 500 × 80% × €15 × 2 years/3 years – €200 000	€200,000	€400,000
3	100 × 500 × 80% × €15 – €400,000	€200,000	€600,000

The related accounting entries at the end of each of the next three years (assuming the salaries expense is not treated as an asset; perhaps in the form of work-in-progress inventory) would be:

Dr	Employee benefits expense	€200,000	
Cr	Share capital (equity)		€200,000

Scenario 2

In this scenario, things do not turn out as expected. During year 1, 20 employees leave, which is fewer than anticipated. In view of this, at the end of year 1 the entity revises its estimate of total employee departures over the three-year period from 20 per cent (that is, 100 employees expected to leave) to 15 per cent (that is, 75 employees expected to leave).

During year 2, a further 22 employees leave. So at the end of year 2 the entity revises its estimate of total employee departures over the three-year period from 15 per cent down to 12 per cent (that is, 60 employees expected to leave).

During year 3, a further 15 employees leave. Therefore, a total of 57 employees forfeited their rights to the share options during the three-year period, and a total of 44,300 share options (443 employees x 100 options per employee) vested at the end of year 3. Knowing the actual number of departures allows the 'correct' aggregated amount to be recognised at the end of year 3, with an adjustment to be made for amounts previously recognised. Because the actual number of options to be issued is known at the end of year 3, the final year-3 calculation does not need to take probabilities into account.

Employee turnover during the vesting period:

	Year 1	Year 2	Year 3
Number of employees at grant date	500	500	500
Actual resignations			
Year 1	–20	–20	–20
Year 2		–22	–22
Year 3			–15
Expected resignations	–55	–18	–
Total expected number of employees to vest	425	440	443

Year	Expected number of employees to vest	Shares per employee	Fair value of equity instruments	Portion of vesting period	Remuneration expense for period	Cumulative remuneration expense
1	425	100	€15.00	1/3	€212,500	€212,500
2	440	100	€15.00	2/3	€227,500	€440,000
3	443	100	€15.00	3/3	€224,500	€664,500

The accounting entries would be:

End of year 1

| Dr Employee benefits expense | €212,500 | |
| Cr Share capital (equity) | | €212,500 |

End of year 2

| Dr Employee benefits expense | €227,500 | |
| Cr Share capital (equity) | | €227,500 |

End of year 3

| Dr Employee benefits expense | €224,500 | |
| Cr Share capital (equity) | | €224,500 |

As shown in Worked Example 11.11, at the end of each reporting period the cumulative expense must be adjusted to reflect the number of shares or options that are ultimately expected to vest. This process of re-adjusting the amounts based on the latest available information is referred to as 'truing up'. It should be noted that, in Worked Example 11.11, we treated all the employees the same and did not try to differentiate between them on the basis of the probabilities of their ultimately leaving the organisation. In practice, reporting entities would consider stratifying their employees into different groups on the basis of the likelihood of their leaving the organisation within the vesting period. For example, management might be deemed to have a lower probability of leaving the organisation relative to other staff.

In Worked Example 11.11 the vesting conditions were quite straightforward and depended upon the expiration of time. However, an award may be subject to other conditions, say a certain level of earnings over a particular period, with the award vesting immediately the target is reached. In such cases, the reporting entity is required to estimate the length of the vesting period at grant date based on the most likely outcome of the performance condition (paragraph 15(b) of IFRS 2).

Worked Example 11.12 illustrates the accounting treatment of an equity-settled share-based payment transaction with performance conditions where the length of the vesting period varies.

Worked Example 11.12 — Award with non-market conditions and varying vesting period

On 1 July 2015 Point plc awards 200 shares each to 300 employees subject to certain non-market vesting conditions. The shares are to vest if:

■ at 30 June 2016 Point plc's earnings have increased by more than 12 per cent
■ at 30 June 2017 Point plc's earnings have increased by an average of 10 per cent or more over the two-year period since grant date
■ at 30 June 2018 earnings have increased by an average of 8 per cent over the three-year period since grant date

The shares have a fair value of €12.00 at 1 July 2015, which equals the share price at grant date. No dividends are expected to be paid over the three-year period.

During the year ending 30 June 2016, 20 employees leave the organisation. Based on prior experience, Point plc believes that a further 30 employees will leave during the remainder of the vesting period. At 30 June 2016 earnings have increased by 11 per cent. It is expected that earnings will continue at a similar rate of increase for 2017. Point plc therefore expects the shares to vest on 30 June 2017.

By 30 June 2017, 25 employees have resigned. Point plc expects a further 25 employees to leave by the end of the vesting period. During the year ended 30 June 2017 earnings increase by 7 per cent. Point plc expects that during the year ending 30 June 2018 earnings will increase by at least 8 per cent, meaning that earnings will have increased by more than the average of 8 per cent over the three-year period.

At 30 June 2018, 32 employees had left during the year, and Point plc's earnings had increased by 9 per cent during the year.

Required

Prepare the accounting journal entries for the years ending 30 June 2016, 2017 and 2018.

Solution

Employee turnover during the vesting period is calculated as follows:

	30 June 2016	30 June 2017	30 June 2018
Number of employees at grant date	300	300	300
Actual resignations			
Year to 30 June 2016	(20)	(20)	(20)
Year to 30 June 2017		(25)	(25)
Year to 30 June 2018			(32)
Expected future resignations	(30)	(25)	–
	250	230	223
Actual increase in earnings	11.0%	7.0%	9.0%
Average increase in earnings	11.0%	9.0%	9.0%
Expected average increase over vesting period	11.0%	8.0%	

▶

Year	Expected number of employees to vest	Shares per employee	Fair value of equity instruments	Expected portion of vesting period	Cumulative remuneration expense up to previous period	Cumulative remuneration expense	Remuneration expense for period
30 June 2016	250	200	€12.00	1/3	–	€300,000	€300,000
30 June 2017	230	200	€12.00	2/3	€300,000	€368,000	€68,000*
30 June 2018	223	200	€12.00	3/3	€368,000	€535,200	€167,200**

* €68,000 = (230 × 200 × €12 × 2/3) − €300,000

** €167,200 = (223 × 200 × €12 × 3/3) − €368,000

The above calculations are based on the expectations held at the end of each reporting period. For example, at the end of 2016 it was anticipated that the share entitlement would vest at the end of 2017.

The accounting journal entries for the years ending 30 June 2016, 2017 and 2018:

30 June 2016

Dr	Employee benefits expense	€300,000	
Cr	Share capital		€300,000

30 June 2017

Dr	Employee benefits expense	€68,000	
Cr	Share capital		€68,000

30 June 2018

Dr	Employee benefits expense	€167,200	
Cr	Share capital		€167,200

11.11 Required disclosures for share capital

IAS 1 *Presentation of Financial Statements* requires a number of disclosures to be made in relation to share capital. For example, paragraph 78(e) requires an entity to disclose, either on the face of the statement of financial position or in the notes, further subclassifications of equity capital and reserves so that the information is disaggregated into various classes, such as paid-in capital and reserves.

According to paragraph 79 of IAS 1:

An entity shall disclose the following, either in the statement of financial position or the statement of changes in equity, or in the notes:

(a) for each class of share capital:
   (i)   the number of shares authorised;
   (ii) the number of shares issued and fully paid, and issued but not fully paid;
   (iii) par value per share, or that the shares have no par value;
   (iv) a reconciliation of the number of shares outstanding at the beginning and at the end of the period;
   (v)   the rights, preferences and restrictions attaching to that class including restrictions on the distribution of dividends and the repayment of capital;
   (vi) shares in the entity held by the entity or by its subsidiaries or associates; and
   (vii) shares reserved for issue under options and contracts for the sale of shares, including the terms and amounts; and

(b) a description of the nature and purpose of each reserve within equity.

11.12   Reserves

As we know, companies can have numerous types of reserve forming part of their shareholders' funds. In Chapter 6, as well as previously within this chapter, we considered the revaluation surplus, which forms part of the shareholders' funds of a company. The revaluation surplus is created through the upward revaluation of non-current assets. For example, if an organisation revalues its land from €700,000 to €850,000, and ignoring tax implications, the accounting entry to record the revaluation would be:

Dr	Land	€150,000
Cr	Revaluation surplus	€150,000

Apart from the revaluation surplus, companies often create reserves that they label **general reserves**. Such titles are not overly informative, as the reserves could have been created for any number of reasons. Some companies establish general reserves as a means of transferring profits out of retained earnings for future expansion plans. For example, a company might consider that it needs to put aside €750,000 per year for three years to fund the restructuring of the organisation in three years' time. The entry each year would be:

> **general reserve**
> Reserve that is part of shareholders' funds and is created for various reasons—sometimes as a means of transferring profits for future expansion plans.

Dr	Retained earnings	€750,000
Cr	General reserve	€750,000

The net effect of the above entry on shareholders' funds is nil. The purpose of this entry might be that directors want to signal, by reducing retained earnings, that they do not intend to pay, as dividends, the amount transferred to the general reserve.

There are many other reserves that companies can have in addition to those discussed above. The majority will be created by transferring amounts from retained earnings. In relation to equity, IAS 1 *Presentation of Financial Statements* requires the entity to present a statement that shows all changes in equity that have occurred throughout the reporting period. This 'statement of changes in equity' is to be produced along with the statement of financial position, statement of comprehensive income, statement of cash flows and notes to the financial statements.

In relation to the required content of a statement of changes in equity, paragraph 106 of IAS 1 states:

> *An entity shall present a statement of changes in equity showing in the statement:*
>
> (a) *total comprehensive income for the period, showing separately the total amounts attributable to owners of the parent and to minority interest;*
> (b) *for each component of equity, the effects of retrospective application or retrospective restatement recognised in accordance with IAS 8;*
> (c) *the amounts of transactions with owners in their capacity as owners, showing separately contributions by and distributions to owners; and*
> (d) *for each component of equity, a reconciliation between the carrying amount at the beginning and the end of the period, separately disclosing each change.*

Paragraph 107 of IAS 1 further requires:

> *An entity shall present, either in the statement of changes in equity or in the notes, the amount of dividends recognised as distributions to owners during the period, and the related amount per share.*

SUMMARY

The chapter addressed a number of accounting issues associated with share capital and reserves, which are themselves components of owners' equity (or shareholders' funds, as companies commonly refer to owners' equity).

Owners' equity is defined as the residual interest in the assets of an entity after deduction of its liabilities. The balance of owners' equity will be directly affected by the various rules for asset and liability recognition and measurement adopted by the reporting entity. For a company, shareholders' funds can comprise many accounts, including revaluation surplus, general reserves, retained earnings and share capital.

Where shares are issued to the public, additional amounts due from subscribers following the share allotment are considered assets of the share-issuing company.

The chapter also noted that, as well as ordinary shares, companies can issue preference shares. Preference shares should be disclosed as debt or equity (or perhaps as part debt and part equity), depending upon the conditions associated with their issue.

Forfeiture of shares, share splits and bonus issues were also discussed. As indicated, share splits and bonus issues have no effect on the total of shareholders' funds in a company.

KEY TERMS

END-OF-CHAPTER EXERCISE

Noosa plc makes an offer of shares to the public. In its prospectus it notes that the shares are to be issued at €1.00 per share. The shares are to be paid in three instalments. The first payment, to be made on application, is €0.40. A second amount of €0.40 will be due within one month of allotment, and the third amount of €0.20 will be due within one month of the first and final call, which will be made within six months of the shares being allotted. Noosa plc will seek to issue 10,000,000 shares. The closing date for applications is 31 August 2015.

By the closing date, applications have been received for 14 million shares. To deal with the oversubscription, Noosa plc has decided to issue shares to all subscribers on a pro rata basis.

All amounts due on allotment are paid by the due date. The final call for €0.20 is made on 30 November 2015, with the amounts being due by 31 December 2015. Holders of 2 million shares fail to pay the amount due on the call by the due date, and on 15 January 2016 these holders have their shares forfeited. The forfeited shares are auctioned on 15 February 2016. An amount of €0.70 per share is received. The cost of holding the auction is €5,000. The shares are sold as 'fully paid'. **LO 11.3**

REQUIRED

Provide the accounting journal entries necessary to account for the above transactions and events.

SOLUTION TO END-OF-CHAPTER EXERCISE

The accounting entries to record the above transactions and events would be as follows:

31 August 2015

Dr Bank	€5,600,000	
Cr Application and allotment account		€5,600,000

(to recognise the total amounts received on application for shares)

An amount of €0.40 per share was received on 14 million shares. The application and allotment account is considered to be a liability.

Dr Application and allotment account	€4,000,000	
Cr Share capital		€4,000,000

(to recognise the issue of the shares at €0.40 per share)

Dr Application and allotment account	€4,000,000	
Dr Call account	€2,000,000	
Cr Share capital		€6,000,000

(to recognise the amount of €0.40, which is due within one month of the allotment and the call which will be due for an amount of €0.20 per share payable on 30 November 2015)

It is assumed that the company has decided to issue the shares on a pro rata basis, and that it is permitted to offset the additional amounts paid on application against the amounts due on allotment.

30 September 2015

Dr Cash at bank	€2,400,000	
Cr Application and allotment account		€2,400,000

(the aggregated entry to record the receipt of the amounts due on allotment)

31 December 2015

Dr Cash at bank	€1,600,000	
Cr Call account		€1,600,000

(the aggregated entry to recognise the receipt of monies due from the holders of 8 million of the shares)

15 January 2016

Dr Share capital	€2,000,000	
Cr Call account		€400,000
Cr Forfeited shares account		€1,600,000

(to record the forfeiture of those 2 million shares on which the call of €0.20 was not paid; the amount of €1.6 million represents the amount that has already been paid by the defaulting shareholders)

15 February 2016

Dr Cash at bank	€1,400,000	
Dr Forfeited shares account	€600,000	
Cr Share capital		€2,000,000

(to recognise the receipt of €0.70 per share on those shares sold as fully paid to €1.00)

Dr Forfeited shares account	€5,000	
Cr Cash at bank		€5,000

(to recognise the cost of the auction.)

Dr Forfeited shares account	€995,000	
Cr Cash at bank		€995,000

(to refund the balance remaining in the forfeited shares account to the former shareholders)

REVIEW QUESTIONS

1 What are share splits and what accounting entries are necessary when a share split is undertaken? **LO 11.8**

2 Would you expect the total market capitalisation of an entity to increase following a share split? **LO 11.8**

3 When shares are issued, accounts such as the application, allotment and call accounts are used. **LO 11.1**

REQUIRED

Describe, respectively, whether these accounts are assets or liabilities (or neither).

4 Bronte Plc has 50 million £1 shares on issue. It decides to do a 'one-for-five' bonus issue from retained earnings. **LO 11.8**

REQUIRED

Provide the necessary journal entries.

5 Assuming that there is an oversubscription for shares in a company, how can the directors of the company deal with the funds that have been oversubscribed? **LO 11.3**

6 Explain why owners' equity is affected by the choice of particular asset and liability measurement practices. **LO 11.1**

7 How do International Financial Reporting Standards require preference shares to be disclosed? **LO 11.10**

8 Clovelly plc issues some preference shares. They provide a rate of return of 6 per cent and are redeemable at the option of the company. Would you disclose these preference shares as debt or equity? Explain your decision.   **LO 11.2**

9 What forms of preferential treatment can the holders of preference shares receive over and above the rights of holders of ordinary shares?   **LO 11.2**

10 Are preference shares debt or equity?   **LO 11.2**

11 What disclosures are required in relation to the reserves of a company?   **LO 11.10**

12 What is the role of the statement of changes in equity?   **LO 11.10**

13 First Point plc commences operations by issuing 1 million £1 shares at a price of £1.40 per share, payable in full on application. Application monies are received on 31 July 2015 and the shares are allotted on 4 August 2015. The share issue is made as a result of an offer being made to the public.   **LO 11.3**

REQUIRED

Provide the journal entries to account for the receipt of the application monies and the subsequent allotment of the shares.

14 On 1 July 2014 Mick plc invited Fanning plc to purchase 1,000,000 €1 ordinary shares at €3.00 per share. At the time of accepting the offer, Fanning plc—which is an insurance company—only had cash resources available of €2,600,000. The balance of the purchase price would be made up of insurance to be provided by Fanning plc to Mick plc. By 30 June 2015, Fanning plc had supplied €280,000 worth of insurance to Mick Plc.   **LO 11.3**

REQUIRED

Provide the accounting entries to record the issue of the Mick plc shares.

15 On 1 July 2015 Coastalwatch plc issued 5,000,000 shares at £5.00 each. All the shares were subscribed for. Coastalwatch plc incurred the following costs that were associated with the share issue: **LO 11.3**

	£
Advertising of share issue and prospectus	10,000
Accounting fees associated with drafting of prospectus	4,000
Legal expenses associated with share issue	5,000

REQUIRED

Prepare the journal entries necessary to account for the issue of the shares.

16 Tewantin plc makes an offer to the public for investors to subscribe for 10 million €1 ordinary shares. The shares are issued at €2.00 per share. Applications for shares close on 15 July 2015, with €1.00 being paid on application and a further €1.00 being payable within one month of allotment.   **LO 11.6**

By 15 July 2015 applications have been received for 11 million shares, and it is decided that all subscribers will receive shares on a pro rata basis, with any excess paid on application to be offset against the amount due on allotment. The shares are allotted on 20 July 2015.

Subsequently, holders of 1 million shares fail to make their payments due on allotment by 20 August 2015. On 31 August the 1 million shares are forfeited and auctioned as fully paid. An amount of €1.50 is received for each share sold.

REQUIRED

Provide the journal entries to account for the above events.

17 Byron plc required additional equity funding and decided to issue a renounceable rights offer. To reduce risks associated with the rights issue, Byron plc appointed an underwriter.

Byron plc sent out details of the rights issue to existing shareholders on 1 July 2015 and it offered existing shareholders the right to acquire an additional €1 share in Byron plc for €3.00 per share. The shares were to be fully paid on application and all applications had to be received by 10 September 2015. The total shares on offer through the rights issue were 15 million.

By 10 September 2015 applications had been received for 13 million shares, meaning that the underwriter was responsible for acquiring the remaining 2 million shares. The shares were issued on 17 September 2015, with this also being the date on which amounts due from the underwriter were received.   **LO 11.7**

REQUIRED

Provide the journal entries to account for the Byron plc rights issue.

18 On 1 July 2015 Cooloola plc provided 1 million options to its chief executive officer. The options were valued at €1.00 each and allowed the chief executive officer to acquire €1 shares in Cooloola plc for €7 each. The chief executive officer is not permitted to exercise the options before 30 June 2017 but then may exercise them any time between 1 July 2017 and 30 June 2019. The market price of the Cooloola plc shares on 1 July 2015 was €6.50.

On 31 December 2017 the share price reaches €7.70 and the chief executive officer decides to exercise her options and acquire the shares in Cooloola plc. **LO** **11.9**

REQUIRED
Account for the issue and exercise of the options in Cooloola plc.

CHALLENGING QUESTIONS

19 If a company declares a final dividend to shareholders, then under what conditions would such a dividend declaration create a liability that would be required to be disclosed in the statement of financial position? **LO** **11.4**

20 Tamarama plc issues 1 million redeemable preference shares of £2.00 each on 1 July 2015. The shares offer a rate of return of 7 per cent per annum. The shares are later redeemed at the option of the shareholders on 30 June 2017. **LO** **11.5**

REQUIRED
(a) Would you classify these preference shares as debt or equity? Why?
(b) Provide the journal entries necessary to record the issue and subsequent redemption of the shares.

21 Brighton plc issues a prospectus inviting the public to subscribe for 10 million £1 ordinary shares of £2.00 each. The terms of the issue are that £1.00 is to be paid on application and the remaining £1.00 within one month of allotment.

Applications are received for 12 million shares during July 2015. The directors allot 10 million shares on 5 August 2015. All applicants receive shares on a pro rata basis. The amounts payable on allotment are due by 5 September 2015.

By 5 September 2015 the holders of 2 million shares have failed to pay the amounts due on allotment. The directors forfeit the shares on 10 September 2015. The shares are resold on 15 September 2015 as fully paid. An amount of £1.80 per share is received. **LO** **11.6**

REQUIRED
Provide the journal entries necessary to account for the above transactions and events.

22 On 1 July 2015 Lurline plc provides its managing director with a share-based incentive according to which she is offered a bonus that is calculated as 100,000 times the increase in the fair value of the entity's share price above €5.00. When the bonus was offered the share price was €4.50. If the managing director does not leave the organisation the accrued entitlement will be paid after three years. However, if she leaves the organisation the accrued entitlement will be paid out upon departure—that is, the benefit will not be forfeited. **LO** **11.9**

Other Information
- The share price at 30 June 2016 is €4.00.
- The share price at 30 June 2017 is €5.50.
- The share price at 30 June 2018 is €6.00.
- The managing director stays for three years and is paid the bonus on 1 July 2018.

Prepare the journal entries that would appear in the accounting records of Lurline plc to account for the issue of the share appreciation rights.

23 On 1 July 2015 Maroubra plc granted its managing director the right to choose either 30,000 phantom shares (that is, the right to receive a cash payment equivalent to the value of 30,000 shares) or 35,000 shares in the company. The grant is conditional upon the completion of three years' service as managing director of Maroubra plc. In addition, should the managing director choose the shares alternative, the shares must be held for an additional two years after the vesting date. **LO** **11.9**

On 1 July 2015 Maroubra plc's share price was €19.00. The subsequent share prices were as follows:

- 30 June 2016   €16.00
- 30 June 2017   €21.00
- 30 June 2018   €23.00

At grant date Maroubra plc does not expect to pay any dividends during the term of the arrangement with the managing director, as all profits are being reinvested. This policy is maintained for the duration of the arrangement.

After taking into account the effects of the post-vesting restrictions, Maroubra plc estimated that the fair value of the share alternative as at 1 July 2015 was €15.00 per share.

Prepare the journal entries for the years ending 30 June 2016, 2017 and 2018 to account for the share-based transaction.

REFERENCES

BECHMANN, K.L. & RAABALLE, J., 'The Differences Between Stock Splits and Stock Dividends: Evidence on the Retained Earnings Hypothesis, *Journal of Business Finance and Accounting*, vol. 34, no. 3/4, 2007, pp. 574–604.

DEEGAN, C., 'Preference Shares—Issues Relating to their Use and Disclosure', *Chartered Accountant in Australia*, vol. 57, no. 4, October 1986, pp. 48–53.

Chapter 12

Accounting for Financial Instruments

Learning objectives

Upon completing this chapter readers should be able to:

LO1 describe what a financial instrument is, and when a financial instrument shall be recognised;

LO2 know what constitutes a financial asset, a financial liability and an equity instrument;

LO3 identify the factors that determine whether a financial instrument shall be presented as debt or equity, in the financial statements of the issuing entity;

LO4 explain the difference between a primary financial instrument and a derivative financial instrument;

LO5 describe what a compound financial instrument is and how the debt and equity components of a compound equity instrument are to be determined;

LO6 discuss what a 'set off' represents, when it is permitted and what benefits it generates;

LO7 explain how to measure financial instruments, and know that financial instruments are initially to be recorded at fair value;

LO8 describe the measurement rules for financial instruments subsequent to initial recognition and know that financial assets shall subsequently be measured at either fair value or amortised cost, with the basis of measurement depending upon both the entity's business model for managing financial assets, and the contractual cash flow characteristics of the financial asset;

LO9 know how to account for gains and losses on financial instruments measured at fair value;

LO10 understand how to account for derivatives, and the assets and liabilities that are part of a hedging arrangement;

LO11 explain the difference between a fair-value hedge and a cash-flow hedge, and know how to account for the respective hedged items and hedging instruments;

LO12 discuss that some derivative financial instruments can significantly increase the risk exposure of an organisation—and so appreciate the necessity for full disclosure in relation to such instruments; and

LO13 have a general understanding of the disclosure requirements embodied in IFRS 7 *Financial Instruments: Disclosure*.

12.1 Introduction to accounting for financial instruments

Accounting for financial instruments has, in recent years, been a controversial area of accounting. In fact, so strong was the opposition in Europe to the accounting standard IAS 39 *Financial Instruments: Recognition and Measurement* that the European Union's very adoption, in 2005, of accounting standards released by the International Accounting Standards Board was jeopardised. In response to the concerns of the European Union—voiced particularly by European banks—the IASB made amendments to IAS 39, in part to appease the European banks.

Accounting for financial instruments can be a rather complicated matter given the myriad of forms that financial instruments can take (for example, shares, bonds, share options, interest rate futures, currency futures, compound financial instruments, and so forth). While IAS 39—as briefly discussed above—initially incorporated most of the accounting requirements in relation to financial instruments, there are now a number of accounting standards that apply to financial instruments.

Until 2009 the major accounting standard dealing with financial instruments was IAS 39 *Financial Instruments: Recognition and Measurement*. However, the IASB embarked on a project to improve the usefulness for users of financial statements by simplifying the classifications and measurement requirements for financial instruments. The project, which at the time of writing this chapter was incomplete, comprised three phases. These are:

- Phase 1: Classification and measurement
- Phase 2: Impairment methodology
- Phase 3: Hedge accounting

In June 2010 the IASB added a fourth component on offsetting. As part of the improvement project, IFRS 9 *Financial Instruments* was issued in 2009 and subsequently revised and reissued in October 2010 with a mandatory effective date (revised in July 2011) of 1 January 2015 (although early adoption is permitted). IFRS 9 incorporates the decisions made as part of Phase 1 above (that is, the phase that deals with *classification* and *measurement* of financial instruments). IFRS 9 includes requirements for the classification and measurement of financial instruments, as well as the recognition and de-recognition requirements for financial instruments. At the time of writing this chapter, IFRS 9 was considered to represent a 'work-in-progress' and once all three phases identified above are completed, then it shall replace IAS 39 in its entirety. However, until such time as all phases are complete, IAS 39 will retain relevance for issues not addressed in IFRS 9.

Another relevant standard is IAS 32 *Financial Instruments: Presentation*. IAS 32 acts as a companion to IFRS 9. It sets out principles for the presentation of financial instruments as liabilities or equity and for offsetting financial assets and financial liabilities (paragraphs 2 and 3 of IAS 32).

Apart from determining whether particular financial instruments should be presented as liabilities or as equity from the perspective of the issuer (with this issue being addressed in IAS 32—and the classification as debt or equity will in turn have implications for whether the related payments are classified as dividends or interest expense), there will also be various disclosure requirements (for example, the entity might be expected to disclose information about the nature and extent of risks arising from financial instruments to which the entity is exposed, or the total interest income derived from financial instruments). Various required disclosures are identified in IFRS 7 *Financial Instruments: Disclosures*. Paragraphs 1 and 2 of IFRS 7 identify the objectives of IFRS 7, and these are:

1. *The objective of this Standard is to require entities to provide disclosures in their financial statements that enable users to evaluate:*
   (a) *the significance of financial instruments for the entity's financial position and performance; and*
   (b) *the nature and extent of risks arising from financial instruments to which the entity is exposed during the period and at the end of the reporting period, and how the entity manages those risks.*
2. *The principles in this Standard complement the principles for recognising, measuring and presenting financial assets and financial liabilities in IAS 32* Financial Instruments: Presentation *and IFRS 9* Financial Instruments.

Hence, while it perhaps is somewhat confusing, when we account for financial instruments we currently need to consider four accounting standards, these being IFRS 7 and 9 and IAS 32 and 39, albeit that IAS 39 is to be removed in due course.

12.2   Financial instruments defined

This chapter addresses issues associated with **financial instruments**. For the purposes of this discussion, we adopt the definition of financial instruments provided in paragraph 11 of IAS 32 *Financial Instruments: Presentation*. According to paragraph 11, a financial instrument is:

> *any contract that gives rise to both a financial asset of one entity and a financial liability or equity instrument of another entity.*

If these components do not exist, the item is not deemed to be a financial instrument. It is stressed that a 'financial instrument' has two sides—one party to the contract must have a financial asset, whereas the other party to the contract holds a financial liability or equity instrument. As the definition of 'financial instrument' just provided indicates, there must be a contractual right or obligation in existence for something to be deemed to be a financial instrument. If there is no contractual right or obligation, then there is no financial instrument.

The above definition of a financial instrument calls for us to define, in turn, a **financial asset**, a **financial liability** and an **equity instrument** (given that these terms are used in the definition of 'financial instrument'). Financial assets are defined from the perspective of the holder of the financial instrument, whereas financial liabilities and equity instruments are defined from the perspective of the issuing organisation.

According to paragraph 11 of IAS 32, 'financial asset' means any asset that is:

(a) *cash;*
(b) *an equity instrument of another entity;*
(c) *a contractual right:*
  (i) *to receive cash or another financial asset from another entity; or*
  (ii) *to exchange financial assets or financial liabilities with another entity under conditions that are potentially favourable to the entity; or*
(d) *a contract that will or may be settled in the entity's own equity instruments and is:*
  (i) *a non-derivative for which the entity is or may be obliged to receive a variable number of the entity's own equity instruments; or*
  (ii) *a derivative that will or may be settled other than by the exchange of a fixed amount of cash or another financial asset for a fixed number of the entity's own equity instruments. For this purpose the entity's own equity instruments do not include puttable financial instruments that are classified as equity instruments in accordance with paragraphs 16A and 16B, instruments that impose on the entity an obligation to deliver to another party a pro rata share of the net assets of the entity only on liquidation and are classified as equity instruments in accordance with paragraphs 16C and 16D, or instruments that are contracts for the future receipt or delivery of the entity's own equity instruments.*

financial instrument Any contract that gives rise to both a financial asset of one entity and a financial liability or equity instrument of another entity.

financial asset An asset that is cash or a contractual right to receive cash from or exchange financial instruments with another entity.

financial liability A contractual obligation to deliver cash or another financial asset to another entity, or to exchange financial assets or financial liabilities with another entity under conditions that are potentially unfavourable to the entity.

equity instrument Financial instrument that provides the holder with a residual interest in an entity after deduction of its liabilities.

Physical assets (for example, inventories or leased assets) and intangible assets (for example, patents) are not financial assets because they provide an opportunity to generate an inflow of cash or another financial asset, but they do not give rise to a present right to receive cash or another financial asset (paragraph AG10 of IAS 32).

'Financial liability', on the other hand (and remember, a financial liability and equity instrument are defined from the perspective of the issuing entity), means any liability that is:

(a) *a contractual obligation:*
  (i) *to deliver cash or another financial asset to another entity; or*
  (ii) *to exchange financial assets or financial liabilities with another entity under conditions that are potentially unfavourable to the entity; or*
(b) *a contract that will or may be settled in the entity's own equity instruments and is:*
  (i) *a non-derivative for which the entity is or may be obliged to deliver a variable number of the entity's own equity instruments; or*
  (ii) *a derivative that will or may be settled other than by the exchange of a fixed amount of cash or another financial asset for a fixed number of the entity's own equity instruments. For this purpose, rights, options or warrants to acquire a fixed number of the entity's own equity instruments for a fixed amount of any currency*

are equity instruments if the entity offers the rights, options or warrants pro rata to all of its existing owners of the same class of its own non-derivative equity instruments. Also, for these purposes the entity's own equity instruments do not include puttable financial instruments that are classified as equity instruments in accordance with paragraphs 16A and 16B, instruments that impose on the entity an obligation to deliver to another party a pro rata share of the net assets of the entity only on liquidation and are classified as equity instruments in accordance with paragraphs 16C and 16D, or instruments that are contracts for the future receipt or delivery of the entity's own equity instruments.

'Equity instrument' is defined in IAS 32 as, 'any contract that evidences a residual interest in the assets of an entity after deducting all of its liabilities'. The most commonly issued equity instrument would be an ordinary share in a company. An attribute of an equity instrument is that the holder is not entitled to a fixed-rate return.

The above definitions make reference to derivatives (also termed derivative financial instruments). Derivatives (such as share options, futures and currency swaps) derive their value from other underlying items (such as receivables or ordinary shares). Derivatives are discussed in paragraph AG16 of IAS 32. This paragraph states:

Derivative financial instruments create rights and obligations that have the effect of transferring between the parties to the instrument one or more of the financial risks inherent in an underlying primary financial instrument. On inception, derivative financial instruments give one party a contractual right to exchange financial assets or financial liabilities with another party under conditions that are potentially favourable, or a contractual obligation to exchange financial assets or financial liabilities with another party under conditions that are potentially unfavourable. However, they generally do not result in a transfer of the underlying primary financial instrument on inception of the contract, nor does such a transfer necessarily take place on maturity of the contract. Some instruments embody both a right and an obligation to make an exchange. Because the terms of the exchange are determined on inception of the derivative instrument, as prices in financial markets change those terms may become either favourable or unfavourable.

In determining the classification of a financial instrument as either a financial liability or an equity instrument, we know that a central issue is the existence of a 'contractual obligation'. If a financial instrument does not give rise to a contractual obligation on the part of the issuer to deliver cash or another financial asset, or to exchange another financial instrument under conditions that are potentially unfavourable, it is considered to be an equity instrument (paragraph 17 of IAS 32).

Evidently, then, the definitions of 'financial asset' and 'financial liability' are tied to a determination of whether one party to the contractual arrangement will be required to exchange financial assets or financial liabilities with another entity under conditions that are *potentially favourable* to the entity (meaning it would be a financial asset), or whether the party will be required to exchange financial assets or financial liabilities with another entity under conditions that are *potentially unfavourable* to the entity (in which case it would be a financial liability). But what is meant by favourable and unfavourable in this context? The distinction is illustrated in Worked Example 12.1 in which a contractual arrangement is entered into, with one party to a contract buying an option contract from another entity.

The likelihood of an option being exercised does not impact on its classification as a financial liability (paragraph AG17 of IAS 32).

Worked Example 12.1	Share options and determining whether a financial asset or a financial liability exists

On 1 July 2015 Buyer plc purchases an option contract from Seller plc for €1,000 that gives Buyer plc the right (or 'option') to acquire 10,000 shares in Bells plc for a price (exercise price) of €5.00 per share. When the contract was exchanged the price of Bells plc's shares was €4.50 each. The option entitles Buyer plc to exercise the options to buy the shares any time within the next six months. If the options are not exercised within the six-month period, they will expire on 31 December 2015.

Required

Determine whether a financial liability or financial asset exists.

Solution

This options contract establishes a financial instrument that gives Buyer plc the right to acquire 10,000 shares in Bells plc for €5.00 a share, and creates an obligation for Seller plc to sell 10,000 shares in Bells plc to Buyer plc for €5.00 a share.

▶

From Buyer plc's perspective it has a financial asset. The contract gives Buyer plc the right to exchange financial assets (cash for shares) under conditions that are potentially favourable. Should the price of Bells plc's shares increase beyond €5.00, Buyer plc would exercise the options and make a profit. The worst case scenario for Buyer plc would be that the shares in Bells plc do not increase beyond €5.00 (they would be 'out of the money'). Then Buyer plc would let the options lapse, and simply lose the original payment of €1,000.

From Seller plc's perspective, it has a financial liability. Seller plc has entered a contract to exchange financial assets (shares for cash) under conditions that are potentially unfavourable to the entity. For example, if the shares in Bells plc increase to €6.00, Seller plc will be required to acquire 10,000 shares from the market for €6.00 each, and sell them to Buyer plc for €5.00 each.

As the discussion so far has shown, the term 'financial instrument' encompasses a wide range of items, including cash at bank, bank overdrafts, term deposits, trade receivables and payables, dividends payable, borrowings, loans receivable, notes receivable, notes payable, bonds receivable, bonds payable, investments, options, forward foreign exchange agreements, foreign currency swaps and interest rate swaps. For example, cash at bank would be considered to be a financial instrument, given that it represents for one party a right to demand cash at a future date and an obligation by another party to provide cash (refer to the definitions applicable to financial instruments provided earlier). Similarly, trade receivables fits the definition of a financial instrument because it represents for one party a right to receive cash and an obligation on the part of another party to provide cash.

As the name 'financial instrument' would suggest, the ultimate transfer of a financial asset is involved: if an arrangement does *not* involve the ultimate transfer of a financial asset, it is not considered to be a financial instrument. For example, if a contractual commitment is to be satisfied through the delivery of a non-financial asset, such as inventory, or through the provision of services, it is not a financial instrument. Similarly, prepayments are not financial instruments because they typically provide a right to future goods or services and not to cash or another financial instrument.

Financial instruments can be further classified as either primary financial instruments or derivative (sometimes called 'secondary') financial instruments. Examples of primary financial instruments would include receivables, payables and equity securities such as ordinary shares. The accounting treatment of primary financial instruments is either fairly straightforward or is covered in other chapters of this book. Hence this chapter will tend to focus more on accounting for **derivative financial instruments**.

Derivative financial instruments include financial options, futures, forward contracts and interest rate and currency swaps. (The accounting treatment of these instruments is considered in the support material for this chapter on www.mcgraw-hill.co.uk/text-books/deeganward). As an example of a derivative financial instrument consider Worked Example 12.2.

> **derivative financial instrument** Instrument that creates rights and obligations with the effect of transferring one or more of the financial risks inherent in an underlying primary financial instrument.

Worked Example 12.2   Derivative financial instrument

Assume that McCoy plc, an English company, imports fibreglass from the United States. On 1 February 2015 it acquires the material at a cost of US$500,000, payable in two months' time. The exchange rate at the time is £1 = US$1.55. The actual debt would be considered to be a trade payable and to be a primary financial instrument.

Required

(a) As the debt is payable in two months' time, describe the potential risk to McCoy plc.
(b) Assuming that McCoy plc is worried about possible adverse exchange rate movements, what action could the company take?

Solution

(a) As the debt is denominated in US dollars, fluctuations in the exchange rate, which typically occur daily, will change the amount that will ultimately be paid in sterling. For example, if the exchange rate falls from £1 = US$1.55 to £1 = US$1.40, the payable denominated in sterling will increase from £322,580 (which is $500,000 ÷ $1.55) to £357,143 (which is $500,000 ÷ $1.40). This would be considered to be a foreign exchange loss.

(b) Assuming that McCoy plc is worried about possible adverse exchange rate movements, the company could approach a bank on 1 February 2015 with the intention of entering into a forward-rate agreement. The bank could agree, for example, to supply McCoy plc with US$500,000 in two months' time at an agreed forward rate of £1 = US$1.52. This agreement means that if the exchange rate changes, McCoy plc will still receive US$500,000 from the bank at an agreed cost of £328,947. Therefore McCoy plc has 'locked in' the actual price of the material at £328,947 (which is $500,000 ÷ $1.52) and the bank will have to absorb any adverse movements in the exchange rate that might occur in the future. The agreement with the bank is considered to be a derivative financial instrument, with the financial risks inherent in the underlying financial instrument (the trade payable) having been transferred from McCoy plc to the bank. McCoy plc would have both a foreign currency receivable (a financial asset) with the bank and a foreign currency payable (a financial liability) with the overseas supplier. From the perspective of McCoy plc, gains on one would be offset by losses on the other (and vice versa). McCoy plc would be considered to have entered a hedging arrangement.

The use and development of alternative forms of financial instruments has increased markedly in the past decade, particularly the use of derivative financial instruments. This increase has provided accounting regulators with numerous issues to address. For many years it was common for many financial instruments to be kept 'off balance sheet', with minimal or no disclosure about their actual existence. This is now changing with the new disclosure requirements. Commonly, there was minimal disclosure pertaining to instruments such as futures, swaps and options (all to be further discussed in this chapter). This meant that many readers of financial statements were unaware of the risks an organisation was exposed to, particularly if the instruments concerned were in the form of securities such as futures. Where organisations failed to disclose details of material financial instruments it is difficult to understand how such financial statements could have been considered to be true and fair pursuant to the Companies Act.

The newer forms of financial instrument seem to have been developed with the main focus on reducing risk, particularly where there are high levels of volatility in the values of the underlying instruments. They can also be useful as a means of attracting additional funds into an organisation. If interest rates or foreign currency exchange rates are predicted to be volatile, financial instruments (typically derivative instruments) will likely be developed and used to minimise the financial impacts of the potential volatility. Parties that acquire financial instruments might also do so speculatively, with the potential to make substantial gains or substantial losses. This can be the case particularly for parties that elect to speculate with various forms of futures contract.

12.3 Debt versus equity components of financial instruments

When financial instruments are issued that are to be placed on the statement of financial position, the issuer is required to determine whether the item should be disclosed as a liability or as equity (or in some circumstances, perhaps as part debt and part equity). All things being equal, corporate managers would prefer to disclose financial instruments as equity rather than debt. There are many reasons for this. Gearing ratios (for example, total debts divided by total assets) are often used as indicators of corporate risk, hence the lower the reported debt, the lower the apparent risk. Organisations also typically have numerous contracts with their debt providers, which include certain restrictions on the amount of additional debt the organisation can raise (see Chapter 3 for an overview of debt contracts and their related restrictions). Following the initial release of IAS 32, many corporations developed financial instruments to comply with the IAS 32 definition of equity. In substance, many of the financial instruments were liabilities, but from a technical perspective they complied with the classifications of equity provided in IAS 32. Many of these instruments were very complex, and the IASB responded by coming up with equally complicated rules to cover the complex financial instruments (many of these rules being quite difficult for many accountants to understand). The aim of the amendments to the standard was that if something was of the substance of a financial liability, then it should be disclosed as such.

In determining whether a financial instrument is debt or equity, consideration should be given to the *economic substance* of the instrument, rather than simply its *legal form* (paragraph 15 of IAS 32).

Paragraph 16 of IAS 32 provides further guidance on whether a financial instrument is debt or equity. For a financial instrument to be classified as an equity instrument (the preferred outcome for most reporting entities), it must satisfy the conditions identified at both subparagraph (a) and (b) of paragraph 16, these being:

(a) *The instrument includes no contractual obligation:*
  (i) to deliver cash or another financial asset to another entity; or
  (ii) to exchange financial assets or financial liabilities with another entity under conditions that are potentially unfavourable to the issuer.

(b) If the instrument will or may be settled in the issuer's own equity instruments, it is:

    (i) a non-derivative that includes no contractual obligation for the issuer to deliver a variable number of its own equity instruments; or

    (ii) a derivative that will be settled only by the issuer exchanging a fixed amount of cash or another financial asset for a fixed number of its own equity instruments. For this purpose, rights, options or warrants to acquire a fixed number of the entity's own equity instruments for a fixed amount of any currency are equity instruments if the entity offers the rights, options or warrants pro rata to all of its existing owners of the same class of its own non-derivative equity instruments.

In paragraph 21 of IAS 32 it is emphasised that something is not an equity instrument simply because it may result in the delivery of an entity's own equity instruments. Where the number of equity instruments required to satisfy a contract is variable, the contract does not evidence a residual interest in the entity's assets after deducting all its liabilities.

In considering paragraph 16(b)(i) above, let us assume, for example, that Bombora plc has entered an agreement to provide Rocky Outcrop plc with €1 million of shares in Bombora plc (based on market value at the time of payment). If the price of the shares was €2.50 at the time the instrument was created, Bombora plc would have to provide 400,000 shares if the market price remains static. However, if the market price falls to €2.00 Bombora plc would have to provide 500,000 shares. The risk remains with Bombora plc, and Rocky Outcrop plc will receive €1 million in shares regardless of the market price. Given these conditions, the instrument that provides that Bombora plc will transfer shares to Rocky Outcrop plc would fail the test of paragraph 16(b)(i) and therefore would be considered to be a financial liability from Bombora plc's perspective. From Rocky Outcrop plc's perspective, it is a financial asset.

IAS 32 provides a great deal of guidance for determining whether a financial instrument is a financial liability or an equity instrument. For example, paragraph 18 highlights the importance of 'substance over form' when classifying a financial instrument. Therefore, if the legal form is equity but the substance of the instrument is that it meets the definition of a financial liability, then it should be treated as a financial liability. For example, a fixed dividend preference share that is redeemable is more like a financial liability than equity. However, if the distributions to the holders, whether cumulative or not, are discretionary, then the shares are equity instruments (IAS 32, paragraph AG26). Another example is where a financial instrument that gives the holder the right to redeem it with the issuer for cash or another financial instrument (a puttable instrument) is in substance a financial liability.

As we have shown, the critical feature in differentiating a financial liability from an equity instrument is the existence of a contractual obligation on the part of one party to the financial instrument (the issuer) either to deliver cash or another financial asset to, or to exchange another financial instrument with, the other party (the holder). According to paragraph 35 of IAS 32:

A consequence of classifying a financial instrument as debt, rather than equity, is that the related periodic payments would be classified as interest expenses, rather than as dividends (dividends being an appropriation of profits). Hence, not only will the classification of a financial instrument as a financial liability impact on the statement of financial position, it will also impact negatively on the statement of comprehensive income by making the associated payments an expense (interest expense), rather than distributions of profits (dividends).

Further, paragraph 36 of IAS 32 states:

Hence, payments related to liabilities impact directly on reported profits or losses. Payments made in relation to equity (dividends) do not impact on profits. The classification of interest, dividends, gains and losses as expenses or revenues or as direct debits or credits to equity must be consistent with the statement of financial position classification of the related financial instrument or component as at the date on which the interest, dividends, gains or losses are recognised.

While many financial instruments are wholly financial liabilities or equity instruments, an entity might also issue securities that have both equity and liability characteristics. For example, an organisation might issue **convertible notes**. These can be described as debt that gives the holder the right to convert the securities into ordinary shares of the issuer. Such securities are frequently classified as **compound financial instruments**, as they can include equity instruments and financial liabilities. The debt and equity components of a compound security should be accounted for and disclosed separately on the basis of the economic substance of the security at the time of its initial recognition (IAS 32, paragraph 29 and AG31).

IAS 32 does not allow a financial instrument, or the equity and liability components of a compound instrument, to be reclassified by the issuer after initial recognition, unless a transaction or other specific action by the issuer or holder of the instrument alters the substance of the financial instrument (IAS 32, paragraph 30).

convertible note
Debt that gives the holder the right to convert securities into ordinary shares of the issuer.

compound financial instrument A financial instrument that contains both a financial liability and an equity element.

Hence, a change in the likelihood that a conversion option will be exercised will not lead to a change in classification of a financial instrument; a subsequent transaction may lead to a change in classification. To illustrate a transaction or action that changes the classification of an instrument, we can again consider preference shares. As indicated in IAS 32, if a preference share has no maturity or redemption date but gives an option to the issuer to redeem the share for cash, the share will not satisfy the definition of a financial liability because the issuer does not have a present obligation to transfer financial assets to the shareholder or to take any other specific action. The issuer can keep such shares on issue without redemption. A financial liability arises, however, when the issuer of the shares exercises its option, usually by notifying the shareholders formally of the impending redemption of the shares. At that time, the instrument is reclassified from equity to liability.

The requirement that the issuer should not reclassify the instrument, unless a transaction or other specific action alters the substance of the financial instrument, represents a departure from the IASB Conceptual Framework, which would allow for the debt or equity classification to change from period to period on the basis of revisions of perceived probabilities. As we know, for a liability to be recognised there is a requirement within the Conceptual Framework that, 'it is probable that an outflow of resources embodying economic benefits will result from the settlement of a present obligation and the amount at which the settlement will take place can be measured reliably'.

For example, if convertible notes are issued giving the holder the right to seek repayment in cash or to convert the notes to equity, and the market price of the shares is high, on the balance of probabilities the likelihood of conversion to equity would be high. The securities would be considered to be equity pursuant to the IASB Conceptual Framework. Conversely, if the share price is low, application of the IASB Conceptual Framework would see the securities classified as debt. With low share prices, the note-holders would be unlikely to convert the notes to shares but would instead seek repayment.

In contrast, IAS 32 would require convertible notes to be disclosed on the basis of the holder's ability to contractually require the company either to repay the principal or convert to shares, regardless of the perceived probabilities of the respective actions. Hence, IAS 32 would require convertible notes to be classified as having both equity and liability components. According to paragraphs 31 and 32 of IAS 32:

> *Since we know that the debt and equity components must be recognised separately we need to determine the respective amounts to be recognised. We must determine the fair value of the liability component—which is recognised within the financial statements—and allocate the difference between the fair value of the liability component and the fair value of the entire instrument to the equity component. That is, the amount attributed to the equity component is the residual.*

Hence, if an entity issued a compound financial instrument such as a convertible note (effectively a debt instrument, which provides an option for the holder to convert the debt to an equity share in the entity) at a price of €22.00, and it was determined that a debt instrument of similar risk and yielding the same rate of interest—but without the option of converting to equity—could be sold for €18.00, €18.00 would be the liability component of the convertible note. The equity component would be the residual, which is €4.00.

We have now considered various issues in relation to whether a financial instrument is of the nature of debt or equity. If a financial instrument has debt characteristics, then it shall be disclosed as a liability in the statement of financial position. At this point it should be acknowledged that in certain circumstances financial assets and financial liabilities can be set off against each other and only a net amount is to be shown. This practice, which we now briefly discuss, can have positive benefits for the statement of financial position in terms of reducing reported gearing based on such ratios as debt to equity, debt to assets, and so forth. The accounting for compound financial instruments is included in the support material for this chapter, available at www.mcgraw-hill.co.uk/textbooks/deeganward.

12.4 Set-off of financial assets and financial liabilities

set-off/offsetting
Financial assets and liabilities are offset where there is a legally enforceable right to set off, and there is an intention to settle on a net basis, or to realise the asset and settle the liability simultaneously.

A set-off can be defined as the reduction of an asset by a liability or of a liability by an asset in the presentation of a statement of financial position, so that the net amount only is presented.

Requirements relating to the **set-off** of assets and liabilities are incorporated within IAS 32 *Financial Instruments: Presentation*. IAS 32 requires assets and liabilities to be set off against each other for statement of financial position disclosure purposes when a legally recognised right of set-off for these items exists, and the reporting entity intends to settle on a net basis, or to realise the asset and settle the liability simultaneously (IAS 32, paragraphs 42, 45 and 46).

Assume, for example, that Entity A owes Entity B an amount of £1.2 million and Entity B owes Entity A an amount of £1 million. Assume also that both parties intend to settle on a net basis. As a result of the set-off, Entity A would be required to show a pay-

Worked Example 12.3   Setting off debt

Assume that Grommet plc has the following statement of financial position before set-off:

Grommet plc: Statement of financial position at 30 June 2015	€
ASSETS	
Property, plant and equipment (net)	400,000
Loans receivable	600,000
Total assets	1,000,000
EQUITY AND LIABILITIES	
Equity and reserves	
Share capital	400,000
Retained earnings	100,000
	500,000
Liabilities	
Loans payable	500,000
Total equity and liabilities	1,000,000

Assume that Grommet plc has an amount of €200,000 owing to Goofyfoot plc and an amount of €240,000 receivable from Goofyfoot plc. Assume also that a legal right of set-off exists, that there is an intention to exercise the right to settle simultaneously and that Grommet plc offsets the payable of €200,000 against the receivable of €240,000.

Required

Prepare a revised statement of financial position that incorporates the set-off.

Solution

Statement of financial position post-set-off:

Grommet plc	
Statement of financial position at 30 June 2015	€
ASSETS	
Property, plant and equipment	400,000
Loans receivable	400,000
Total assets	800,000
EQUITY AND LIABILITIES	
Equity and reserves	
Share capital	400,000
Retained earnings	100,000
	500,000
Liabilities	
Loans payable	300,000
Total equity and reserves	800,000

As a result of the set-off, the gearing ratio of debt to total assets has dropped from 50 per cent to 37.5 per cent. Utilising a right of set-off would constitute a reasonably inexpensive method of reducing a firm's gearing, compared with such activities as buying back the debt. As such, a set-off represents a low-cost way of loosening debt constraints (if they exist). More simply, it represents an easy way to produce a statement of financial position that shows an improved financial position in terms of such indicators as leverage.

able of only £200,000 in its statement of financial position, and Entity B would show a receivable of £200,000 in its statement of financial position. Whenever a right to offset exists, and it is intended that the right will be exercised, disclosure on a net basis is required.

Performing a set-off will improve an entity's gearing ratio, which might be of importance if a firm is subject to constraints imposed by debt agreements, as shown in Worked Example 12.3.

We will now consider various aspects of the measurement of financial instruments. However, as a concluding comment on the disclosure of financial instruments, it should now be clear that there are numerous issues to consider in determining whether a financial instrument is a financial liability or an equity instrument from the perspective of the issuing entity. This will impact on the gearing and reported profitability of an entity.

12.5 Recognition and measurement of financial instruments

The general principle applied for the initial recognition of financial assets is detailed in paragraph 3.1.1 of IFRS 9. This paragraph requires an entity to recognise a financial instrument in its statement of financial position at the point in time 'when the entity becomes party to the contractual provisions of the instrument'. The general measurement principle applied within IFRS 9 is that financial instruments are to be measured initially at fair value plus or minus transaction costs that are attributable to the acquisition/issue of the financial instrument (IFRS 9, paragraph 5.1.1). Although all financial instruments, including investments in equity instruments, must initially be measured at fair value, in limited circumstances for equity instruments and, pursuant to IFRS 9, cost may be deemed to be an appropriate *estimate* of fair value. That may be the case if, since acquisition, there is insufficient information available to determine the fair value of the equity instruments, or perhaps there are a wide range of possible fair value measurements such that cost represents the best estimate of fair value within that range.

Fair value is defined in IFRS 13 as:

the price that would be received to sell an asset or paid to transfer a liability in an orderly transaction between market participants at the measurement date.

The above definition of fair value uses a number of important terms, for example 'orderly transaction' and 'market participants'. Pursuant to IFRS 13, an 'orderly transaction' is:

A transaction that assumes exposure to the market for a period before the measurement date to allow for marketing activities that are usual and customary for transactions involving such assets or liabilities; it is not a forced transaction (e.g. a forced liquidation or distress sale).

'Market participants', another key term in the definition of fair value, are deemed to be:

- *independent of each other, that is, they are not related*
- *knowledgeable, having a reasonable understanding about the asset or liability and the transaction using all available information*
- *able to enter into a transaction for the asset or liability, and*
- *willing to enter into a transaction for the asset or liability, that is, they are motivated but not forced or otherwise compelled to do so.*

12.5.1 Measurement of financial assets following initial recognition

Following initial recognition—which as we now know must be at fair value—financial assets shall subsequently either be measured at *fair value* or at *amortised cost* (IFRS 9, paragraph 5.2.1). Classification is made at the time the financial asset is initially recognised and the use of either measurement basis (fair value or amortised cost) will be dependent on *both*:

(a) the entity's business model for managing the financial assets; and
(b) the contractual cash flow characteristics of the financial asset (IFRS 9, paragraph 4.1.1).

Further, in relation to using amortised cost as the basis of measurement subsequent to acquisition, paragraph 4.1.2 of IFRS 9 requires:

A financial asset shall be measured at amortised cost if both of the following conditions are met:

(a) The asset is held within a business model whose objective is to hold assets in order to collect contractual cash flows.

(b) The contractual terms of the financial asset give rise on specified dates to cash flows that are solely payments of principal and interest on the principal amount outstanding.

We will now briefly consider each of the above tests —namely, the 'business models test' and the 'contractual cash flow characteristics test'. Debt instruments that do not meet both of these conditions, or 'tests', must be measured at fair value.

Entity's business model for managing financial assets (business model test)

Under the business model test, an entity is required to assess whether its business objective for a debt instrument is to collect contractual cash flows of the instrument, rather than realising its fair value change from the sale of the instrument prior to its contractual maturity.

If an entity holds assets to realise fair value changes, then it should measure the asset at fair value. Conversely, if assets are held to receive periodic interest payments and principal repayment, then the assets shall be recorded at amortised cost. An entity may have different business units that are managed differently. For example, an entity may have a business unit (A) where the objective is to collect the contractual cash flows of loan assets, while the objective of another business unit (B) would be to realise fair value changes through the sale of loan assets prior to their maturity. The financial instruments that give rise to cash flows that are payments of principal and interest (see the cash flow characteristic test below), in business unit (A) may qualify for amortised cost measurement even if similar financial instruments in business unit (B) do not. Instruments that are held for trading would be measured at fair value as they are not held to collect the contractual cash flows of the instrument.

It should be noted that, although the objective of an entity's business model may be to hold financial assets in order to collect contractual cash flows, the entity need not hold all of those assets until maturity. The entity can sell the financial assets. As an example, an entity's assessment that it holds investments to collect their contractual cash flows remains valid even if the entity disposes of the investments to fund capital expenditure. However, if more than an infrequent number of sales are made out of a portfolio, the entity would need to assess whether and how such sales are consistent with an objective of collecting contractual cash flows.

The following examples of when the objective of the entity's business model may be to hold financial assets to collect the contractual cash flows (meaning that the use of amortised cost might be appropriate) are adapted from IFRS 9 *Application Guidance* and include:

- an entity holding investments to collect their contractual cash flows but prepared to sell an investment in particular circumstances;
- where an entity's business model is to purchase portfolios of financial assets, such as loans. Those portfolios may or may not include financial assets with incurred credit losses. If payment on the loans is not made on a timely basis, the entity attempts to extract the contractual cash flows through various means—for example, by making contact with the debtor by mail, telephone or other methods.

Contractual cash flows that are solely payments of principal and interest on the principal amount outstanding (contractual cash flow characteristics test)

Having established which financial assets are held for the collection of contractual cash flows, paragraph B4.8 of IFRS 9 requires an entity to 'assess whether contractual cash flows are solely payments of principal and interest on the principal amount outstanding for the currency in which the financial asset is denominated'.

One factor to consider is 'leverage'. In terms of IFRS 9, leverage is a contractual cash flow characteristic of some financial assets. Leverage increases the variability of the contractual cash flows with the result that the cash flows do not have the economic characteristics of interest. Stand-alone option, forward and swap contracts are examples of financial assets that include leverage. For example, a forward exchange contract (also often

referred to as a 'futures contract') on interest rates or foreign currency rates can increase or decrease dramatically in value as a result of relatively small increases or decreases in relevant interest or exchange rates (as we shall show later in this chapter). Therefore, such returns are considered to be highly 'leveraged'. Therefore, should the contractual terms of the financial asset include leverage (for example, a stand-alone option or a forward or swap contract), this will result in economic characteristics that are not interest (for example, the economic characteristics may represent price differentials from a market source such as an index, an exchange rate or an interest rate, not interest on a principal sum). The reason for this is that leverage increases the variability of cash flows (for example, one which changes an interest rate by a multiplier of a benchmark rate). Contracts that include leverage fail to meet the condition of being solely payments of principal and interest on the principal amount outstanding. Therefore, as paragraph B4.1.9 of IFRS 9 explains, contracts containing leverage cannot be measured at amortised cost and shall be measured at fair value.

Examples of contractual cash flows that are solely payments of principal and interest on the principal amount outstanding (and therefore would require the entity to use amortised cost) include:

- A bond with a stated maturity date where payments of principal and interest on the principal amount outstanding are linked to an inflation index of the currency in which the instrument is issued. The inflation link is not leveraged and the principal is protected.
- A variable interest rate instrument with a stated maturity date that permits the borrower to choose the market interest rate on an ongoing basis. For example, at each interest rate reset date, the borrower can choose to pay three-month Bank Bill Rate (BBR) for a three-month term or one-month BBR for a one-month term.
- A bond with a stated maturity date and that pays a variable market interest rate. That variable interest rate is capped.
- A full recourse loan that is secured by collateral.

Examples of contractual cash flows that are not payments of principal and interest on the principal amount outstanding include:

- A bond that is convertible into equity instruments of the issuer.
- A loan that pays an inverse floating interest rate (that is, the interest rate has an inverse relationship to market interest rates; for example, 8 per cent minus the BBR).

So, as an example, if an entity were to acquire a financial asset, such as a government bond, with the intention of receiving a fixed flow of interest revenue throughout the period, then the bond would be measured at amortised cost in the period after acquisition. Conversely, if an organisation acquired some shares in a company for the purpose of selling them at a gain in the future, then that financial asset shall be recorded at fair value subsequent to acquisition.

While we understand what fair value means, and while we should now have some reasonable understanding of when amortised cost shall be used to subsequently measure a financial asset, some consideration of the actual meaning of 'amortised cost' would be useful. Paragraph 9 of IAS 39 defines amortised cost as follows:

> *The amortised cost of a financial asset or financial liability is the amount at which the financial asset or financial liability is measured at initial recognition minus principal repayments, plus or minus the cumulative amortisation using the effective interest method of any difference between that initial amount and the maturity amount, and minus any reduction (directly or through the use of an allowance account) for impairment or uncollectibility.*

In determining amortised cost as described above, we are required to use the effective-interest method. IAS 39 provides the following definition of effective-interest method:

> *The effective interest method is a method of calculating the amortised cost of a financial asset or a financial liability (or group of financial assets or financial liabilities) and of allocating the interest income or interest expense over the relevant period. The effective interest rate is the rate that exactly discounts estimated future cash payments or receipts through the expected life of the financial instrument or, when appropriate, a shorter period to the net carrying amount of the financial asset or financial liability.*

Worked Example 12.4 provides an example of how to determine the amortised cost of a financial asset.

Worked Example 12.4 **Determining the amortised cost of a financial asset**

On 1 July 2014 Jack plc acquired some corporate bonds issued by McCoy plc. These bonds cost £1,066,242, they had a 'face value' of £1 million and offered a coupon rate of 10 per cent paid annually (£100,000 per year, paid on 30 June). The bonds would repay the principal of £1 million on 30 June 2018. At the time the market only required a rate of return of 8 per cent on such bonds. Assume that there were no direct costs associated with acquiring the bonds.

Required

(a) Explain why the company was prepared to pay £1,066,242 for the bonds given that they only expect to receive £1 million back in four years' time.

(b) Calculate the amortised cost of the bonds as at 30 June 2015, 2016, 2017 and 2018.

Solution

(a) In this instance the market was requiring 8 per cent. However McCoy plc was offering a 10 per cent return. When the market's required rate of return is less than the rate being offered on a bond, the price of that bond will be above its face value. That is, it will be issued at a premium and at an amount that then causes the effective interest rate provided by the investment to become 8 per cent. In this case, and using the present values, the issue price will be £1,066,242, determined as follows:

Present value of interest stream of four payments of £100,000 per year at the end of the next 4 years	£100,000 × 3.312126 =	£331,213
Present value of the principal to be received in 4 years:	£1,000,000 × 0.735029 =	£735,029
Fair value at 1 July 2014		£1,066,242

Note: While we have used present value calculations based on 6 decimal points, there are present value tables in the appendices to this book that are calculated to 4 decimal points.

(b) To determine the amortised cost of the financial asset, we use the effective-interest method. With the effective-interest method, the interest revenue for the period would be calculated by multiplying the opening present value of the asset by the market rate of interest, which in this case is 8 per cent. The payment of £100,000 received by Jack plc each year would constitute both interest revenue and repayment of the principal. In the last period (2018), a total of £1,100,000 is received by Jack plc, representing the periodic payment of £100,000 (which is both interest and principal repayment) and the repayment of the principal at the end of the life of the bond, this being £1 million.

Date	Opening present value (£)	Interest (£)	Principal repayment (£)	Closing present value (£)
1 July 2014	–	–	–	1,066,242
30 June 2015	1,066,242	85,299	14,701	1,051,541
30 June 2016	1,051,541	84,123	15,877	1,035,664
30 June 2017	1,035,664	82,853	17,147	1,018,517
30 June 2018	1,018,517	81,483	1,018,517	0

Worked Example 12.4 did not consider the possibility that the financial instrument had been impaired. We will now consider this possibility.

12.5.2 Impairment of financial assets measured at amortised cost

At the end of each reporting period an entity is required to assess whether there is any evidence that a financial asset, or group of financial assets, measured at amortised cost has been impaired. According to paragraph 59 of IAS 39, impairment of a financial asset or group of financial assets may be evidenced by the following loss events:

(a) *significant financial difficulty of the issuer or obligor;*

(b) a breach of contract, such as a default or delinquency in interest or principal payments;

(c) the lender, for economic or legal reasons relating to the borrower's financial difficulty, granting to the borrower a concession that the lender would not otherwise consider;

(d) it becoming probable that the borrower will enter bankruptcy or other financial reorganisation;

(e) the disappearance of an active market for that financial asset because of financial difficulties; or

(f) observable data indicating that there is a measurable decrease in the estimated future cash flows from a group of financial assets since the initial recognition of those assets, although the decrease cannot yet be identified with the individual financial assets in the group, including:

  (i) adverse changes in the payment status of borrowers in the group (e.g. an increased number of delayed payments or an increased number of credit card borrowers who have reached their credit limit and are paying the minimum monthly amount); or

  (ii) national or local economic conditions that correlate with defaults on the assets in the group (e.g. an increase in the unemployment rate in the geographical area of the borrowers, a decrease in property prices for mortgages in the relevant area, a decrease in oil prices for loan assets to oil producers, or adverse changes in industry conditions that affect the borrowers in the group).

According to paragraph 63 of IAS 39:

> Where evidence of impairment exists, the carrying amount of the asset should be written down to the present value of the expected future net cash flows discounted using the asset's original effective interest rate with the write down amount being recognised in profit or loss.

For the purpose of illustrating the application of the above requirement, assume that an entity acquires a three-year debenture in another entity at a cost of €1 million, which pays interest at a rate of 10 per cent per annum and which provides an effective rate of interest of 10 per cent (meaning that the debenture has been issued at its face value with no premium or discount on issue). The carrying amount of this asset at the date of its original recognition would be €1 million. If at the end of year 1 (with two years to go on the debenture) the issuer of the debenture has liquidity problems and an agreement is reached that only half of the principal and interest is to be paid, the present value of the future payments will be recalculated and the change will be taken to the period's profit and loss. In this case, the present value of the future cash flows (and the original discount rate must be used) would amount to €500,000 × 0.8264 (for the principal) plus €50,000 × 1.7355 (for the two years of interest payments), which adds to €500,000. The value of the debenture asset would be reduced from €1 million to €500,000 (either directly or through an allowance for accumulated impairment losses) and a loss of €500,000 would be recorded in the period's profit or loss.

While the above discussion has indicated when a financial asset shall be measured at amortised cost, there is an allowable exception. As paragraph 4.1.5 of IFRS 9 states:

> An entity may, at initial recognition, irrevocably designate a financial asset as measured at fair value through profit or loss if doing so eliminates or significantly reduces a measurement or recognition inconsistency (sometimes referred to as an 'accounting mismatch') that would otherwise arise from measuring assets or liabilities or recognising the gains and losses on them on different bases.

hedging A process that involves entering into a contract to reduce the risk involved with a transaction.

Therefore, if a financial asset and a financial liability are somehow related and the gains on one perhaps offset the losses on the other, then the argument is that the gains and losses should both be taken to profit or loss, else there would be an 'accounting mismatch'. This is typical in **hedging** transactions. The accounting mismatch would remain if the fair value gains on one financial instrument went to profit or loss while the other related financial instrument was measured at amortised cost.

12.5.3 Gains of financial assets measured at fair value

So far we have learned that financial assets shall be measured at fair value at transaction date, and thereafter they are to be recorded at either fair value or amortised cost. We have also learned that, while some assets might satisfy the conditions to be measured at amortised cost, they can be measured at fair value if there would otherwise be deemed to be an 'accounting mismatch'. An issue that we now need to consider is how to account for any gains on financial instruments measured at fair value.

Paragraph 5.7.1 of IFRS 9 requires that a gain or loss on a financial asset or financial liability that is measured at fair value shall be recognised in profit or loss. However, there are a number of exceptions to this requirement. One exception is if the asset held is part of a hedging relationship. We will address accounting issues associated with hedges later in this chapter.

12.5.4 Fair value changes (equity instruments not held for trading)

Another exception to the requirement that gains or losses in fair value go to profit or loss occurs if it is an investment in an equity instrument, that is not held for trading, and the entity has elected to present gains and losses on that investment in other comprehensive income in accordance with paragraph 5.7.5 of IFRS 9, which states:

> *At initial recognition, an entity may make an irrevocable election to present in other comprehensive income subsequent changes in the fair value of an investment in an equity instrument within the scope of this Standard that is not held for trading.*

As we know, when an entity produces a statement of comprehensive income, the profit or loss is presented first, then 'other items of comprehensive income' are presented. A total of 'other comprehensive income' is then presented, after which it is then added to 'profit or loss' to then provide 'total comprehensive income'. Hence, making the election under paragraph 5.7.5 will not impact 'total comprehensive income'; rather, it will shift the change in fair value to 'other comprehensive income', rather than including it within 'profit or loss'. However, while the gains or losses might be reported within 'other comprehensive income', any related dividends from the investment must be included within profit or loss (IFRS 9, paragraph 5.7.6).

12.5.5 Fair value changes (equity instruments held for trading)

Gains or losses on equity investments held for trading must be included in profit or loss. 'Held for trading' is defined in IFRS 9 as:

> *A financial asset or financial liability that:*
>
> *(a) is acquired or incurred principally for the purpose of selling or repurchasing it in the near term;*
> *(b) on initial recognition is part of a portfolio of identified financial instruments that are managed together and for which there is evidence of a recent actual pattern of short-term profit-taking; or*
> *(c) is a derivative (except for a derivative that is a financial guarantee contract or a designated and effective hedging instrument).*

Therefore, if an organisation has equity investments measured at fair value which satisfy any of the conditions in parts (a) to (c) above, then the gain will be taken to profit or loss, as demonstrated in Worked Example 12.5. Worked Example 12.6 then provides an example of a situation where an entity has made an election to present the change in fair value of an equity instrument in other comprehensive income (regarded as not held for trading).

Where a financial instrument is measured at fair value and its fair value decreases below zero, it then becomes a financial liability measured in accordance with paragraph 4.2.1 of IFRS 9.

Worked Example 12.5 — Increase in the fair value of an equity investment (held for trading)

On 1 July 2014 Peter plc acquired 100,000 shares in Drouyn plc for €9.00 each. On 30 June 2015 they had a fair value of €11.50 each.

Required

Prepare the journal entries at 1 July 2014 and 30 June 2015 to account for Peter plc's investment.

Solution

1 July 2015

Dr Investment in Drouyn plc	€900,000	
Cr Cash		€900,000

30 June 2015

Dr Investment in Drouyn plc	€250,000	
Cr Gain on equity investments		€250,000

| **Worked Example 12.6** | **Increase in the fair value of an equity investment (not held for trading)** |

On 29 June 2014 Larry plc acquires shares in Bertleman plc for €200,000 plus a purchase commission of €4,000. On 30 June 2014 the quoted market price of the investment is €200,000. If the investment were sold a commission of €6,000 would be payable. The asset is to be measured at fair value with changes in fair value being included in other comprehensive income in accordance with an election made pursuant to paragraph 5.7.5 of IFRS 9.

Required

(a) At what amount should the investment initially be recorded by Larry plc on 29 June 2014?
(b) At what amount should the investment initially be recorded by Larry plc on 30 June 2014?

Solution

(a) On 29 June 2014 Larry plc recognises the asset at €204,000. The commission expense would be included as part of the carrying amount of the asset (see paragraph 5.1.1 of IFRS 9).
(b) On 30 June 2014 Larry plc measures the asset at €200,000 (without regard to the possible commission on sale) and recognises a loss of €4,000 in other comprehensive income.

Initial recognition of financial liabilities

As we have already indicated, paragraph 3.1.1 of IFRS 9 requires financial instruments, and therefore financial liabilities, to be initially recognised in a statement of financial position 'when the entity becomes a party to the contractual provisions of the instrument'.

When a financial liability is initially recognised, it is measured at its fair value or at amortised cost plus or minus transaction costs that are directly attributable to the acquisition/issue of the financial liability (IFRS 9, paragraph 5.1.1).

Subsequent measurements of financial liabilities

Paragraph 4.2.1 of IFRS 9 provides the following rules for subsequent measurement of financial liabilities where it states:

An entity shall classify all financial liabilities as subsequently measured at amortised cost using the effective interest method, except for:

(a) *financial liabilities at fair value through profit or loss. Such liabilities, including derivatives that are liabilities, shall be subsequently measured at fair value.*
(b) *financial liabilities that arise when a transfer of a financial asset does not qualify for derecognition or when the continuing involvement approach applies.*
(c) *financial guarantee contracts as defined in Appendix A. After initial recognition, an issuer of such a contract shall (unless paragraph 4.2.1(a) or (b) applies) subsequently measure it at the higher of:*
  (i) *the amount determined in accordance with IAS 37 Provisions, Contingent Liabilities, and Contingent Assets; and*
  (ii) *the amount initially recognised (see paragraph 5.1.1) less, when appropriate, cumulative amortisation recognised in accordance with IAS 18 Revenue.*
(d) *commitments to provide a loan at a below-market interest rate. After initial recognition, an issuer of such a commitment shall (unless paragraph 4.2.1(a) applies) subsequently measure it at the higher of:*
  (i) *the amount determined in accordance with IAS 37; and*
  (ii) *the amount initially recognised (see paragraph 5.1.1) less, when appropriate, cumulative amortisation recognised in accordance with IAS 18.*

How a financial liability is recognised at amortised cost is demonstrated in Worked Example 12.7.

Gains or losses on financial liabilities measured at fair value

For a financial liability measured at fair value through profit or loss, any gain or loss arising from a change in the fair value that is not part of a hedging relationship is generally recognised in profit or loss. However,

| Worked Example 12.7 | **Financial liabilities other than those measured at fair value** |

On 1 July 2014 Slater plc issued four-year bonds with a total face value of £100,000 and a coupon interest rate of 10 per cent per annum, payable annually in arrears. The market interest rate for Slater's bonds was 12 per cent and so the company had to discount the issue price to its fair value of £93,923. As explained in Chapter 9, whenever the market's required rate of return exceeds the coupon rate being offered, then bonds will be issued at a discount to their face value.

Required

Prepare the journal entry to issue the bond at 1 July 2014, and the entry at 30 June 2015 to record the interest paid.

Solution

The table below demonstrates the amortised cost using the effective-interest method.

1 Year ended	2 Opening bond payable (£)	3 Payment (£)	4 Interest at 12% (column 2 × 12%) (£)	5 Increase in bond payable (column 4 – column 3) (£)	6 Amortised cost of bond payable (column 2 + column 5) (£)
30 June 2015	93,923	10,000	11,272	1,272	95,195
30 June 2016	95,195	10,000	11,423	1,423	96,618
30 June 2017	96,618	10,000	11,594	1,594	98,212
30 June 2018	98,212	10,000	11,788	1,788	100,000

The annual interest cost is measured by multiplying the effective interest rate by the amount of the liability at the beginning of each period. Any excess of interest cost over the amount of interest paid is accounted for as an increase in the carrying amount of the liability (which is its present value). By the maturity date, the liability will be increased to an amount equal to the principal, as the discount reduces to zero. Notice the similarity between accounting for financial liabilities at amortised cost using the effective-interest method and accounting for lease liabilities in Chapter 9.

Journal entries

1 July 2014

| Dr | Cash | £93,923 | |
| Cr | Bond payable | | £93,923 |

(issuing bonds for £93,923)

30 June 2015

Dr	Interest expense	£11,272	
Cr	Bond payable		£1,272
Cr	Bank		£10,000

(interest payment and amortisation of bond payable using effective-interest rate of 12 per cent)

paragraphs 7.7.7 and 7.7.8 of IFRS 9 require that gains or losses on financial liabilities designated as at fair value through profit or loss are to be split into the amount of the change in fair value that relates to changes in the credit risk of the liability, which shall be presented in the 'other comprehensive income' section of the statement of comprehensive income, and the remaining amount of the change in fair value of the liability shall be presented in profit or loss. The full amount of the change in the fair value of the liability is permitted to be included within profit or loss only if the recognition of changes in the liability's credit risk in other comprehensive income would create or enlarge an 'accounting mismatch' in profit or loss. Such determination is made at the time of initial recognition of the liability.

Where the financial liability is measured at amortised cost, any gain or loss arising from derecognition of the financial liability and through the amortisation process is recognised in profit or loss.

IAS 39 also prescribes specific accounting treatment for financial assets and financial liabilities that are 'hedging instruments' or 'designated hedged items'. The rest of this chapter will concentrate on derivatives (as previously defined). As can be seen from the above requirement, unless the derivative has been acquired to 'hedge' the value of other financial instruments (and the entity has from the date of acquiring the derivative designated the derivative as a hedge and the hedge passes certain tests in relation to its 'effectiveness'), the derivative is to be measured at its fair value with any changes therein to be included within the period's profit or loss. The only exception to this treatment is where the entity designates the derivative as a cash-flow hedge. Where the derivative is a cash-flow hedge, the portion of the gain or loss on the hedging instrument that is determined to be an effective hedge is recognised in other comprehensive income, while the ineffective portion of the gain or loss on the hedging instruments is recognised in profit or loss.

12.6 Derivative financial instruments and their use as hedging instruments

Derivative financial instruments can take many forms and include futures contracts, options contracts, interest rate swaps, foreign currency swaps and forward rate contracts. We will consider each of these in the pages that follow. Derivative financial instruments are one type of financial instrument addressed in IAS 39. As indicated earlier in this chapter, there is currently a project in place at the IASB to improve the usefulness of financial information for users of financial statements by simplifying the classifications and measurement requirements for financial instruments. Therefore, changes to this topic are expected in the near future. At present, though, IAS 39 provides most of the guidance on this topic.

Consistent with other financial instruments, derivatives are initially to be recognised at fair value in accordance with paragraph 43 of IAS 39. The value of a derivative is directly related to another underlying item. For example, a share option—which is a derivative—derives its value from the market value of the underlying shares. Derivatives transfer risks between the parties to the derivative-related contract in respect of the underlying securities concerned. According to paragraph 9 of IAS 39:

A derivative is a financial instrument or other contract within the scope of this Standard (see paragraphs 2–7) with all three of the following characteristics:

(a) *its value changes in response to the change in a specified interest rate, financial instrument price, commodity price, foreign exchange rate, index of prices or rates, credit rating or credit index, or other variable, provided in the case of a non-financial variable that the variable is not specific to a party to the contract (sometimes called the 'underlying');*

(b) *it requires no initial net investment or an initial net investment that is smaller than would be required for other types of contracts that would be expected to have a similar response to changes in market factors; and*

(c) *it is settled at a future date.*

12.6.1 Derivatives used within a hedging arrangement

hedge contract
Arrangement with another party in which that party accepts the risks associated with changing commodity prices, cash flows or exchange rates.

Derivatives are often used as a means of hedging the gains or losses that might arise in the future in relation to other assets and liabilities—as we will demonstrate in what follows. To minimise the risk associated with particular assets or liabilities, an entity may enter a **hedge contract**. By entering into an agreement that takes a position opposite to the original transaction, an entity can minimise its exposure to gains and losses on particular assets and liabilities.

As an example of a hedging arrangement, we can consider Worked Example 12.8.

According to IAS 39, the purpose of 'hedge accounting', as defined in paragraph 85, is to recognise 'the offsetting effects on profit or loss of changes in the fair values of the hedging instrument and the hedged item'. This definition refers to a hedging instrument and a hedged item—two terms we considered in Worked Example 12.8. A hedging instrument is a designated derivative or designated financial asset/liability whose fair value or cash flows are designed to be opposite in sign relative to the fair value changes or cash flows from the underlying hedged item. A hedged item can be an asset, liability or even a commitment that exposes the entity to risk due to changes in its fair value or future cash flows and is designated at the outset as being hedged (IAS 39, paragraph 9).

According to paragraph 86 of IAS 39, there are three principal types of hedge:

1. fair-value hedges;
2. cash-flow hedges; and
3. hedges of net investments in a foreign operation.

Worked Example 12.8　Hedging arrangement

A UK company, Mungo plc, orders some inventory from a US supplier, Barry Inc., on 1 May 2014 for US$200,000 (when the exchange rate is £1.00 = US$0.75) at a cost in sterling of £266,667 ($200,000 ÷ 0.75). The goods are to be supplied and paid for on 30 June 2014. As at 1 May 2014 the forward rate for the delivery of US dollars on 30 June 2014 was £1.00 = US$0.72. Mungo plc enters a forward-rate agreement with its bank.

Required

(a) How could Mungo plc safeguard against exchange rate fluctuations?
(b) Identify the hedged item and the hedged instrument.
(c) What is a forward rate and how would this benefit Mungo plc?
(d) Assuming that sterling decreases in value relative to the US dollar so that £1.00 buys only US$0.60 on 30 June 2014, in the absence of a forward-rate agreement, how would this impact Mungo plc?

Solution

(a) To safeguard against exchange rate fluctuations, on the date it placed the order Mungo plc could also enter into a forward exchange rate contract to buy US$200,000 on 30 June 2014 from another party (typically a bank) at a **forward rate** of £1.00 = US$0.72.
(b) In this situation the amount to be paid by Mungo plc to Barry Inc. is the *hedged item*. The forward rate arrangement made by Mungo plc with the bank is the *hedging instrument*.
(c) A forward rate is the exchange rate for delivery of a currency at a specified date in the future. It is a guaranteed rate of exchange that will be provided at a future date regardless of what happens with exchange rates. With this forward-rate agreement, the entity has locked in the price of the goods at £277,778 ($200,000 ÷ $0.72). That is, it has hedged the future payment. The entity has contracted to buy a specified number of US dollars at a future date (probably from a bank) at a predetermined rate. This is sometimes referred to as a 'buy hedge'.

> **forward rate** The exchange rate that is currently offered for the future acquisition or sale of a specific currency.

(d) Let us assume that sterling decreases in value relative to the US dollar so that £1.00 buys only US$0.60 on 30 June 2014. In the absence of a forward-rate agreement (which we have designated the *hedging instrument*), the entity would pay the US supplier £333,333 ($200,000 ÷ $0.60). This is £66,666 more than the original sterling obligation. However, given the forward exchange rate agreement, the entity can obtain US$200,000 at an agreed cost of £277,778. This amount is significantly below the fair value of the US dollars given the new exchange rate—so there is a gain on the agreement with the bank (that is, the hedging arrangement with the bank would be considered to have a positive fair value). The gain on the hedging instrument offsets the losses on the hedged item. Both gains and losses have to be accounted for separately.

The most common forms of hedges are fair-value hedges and cash-flow hedges. Fair-value hedges would be used to hedge the value of particular assets or liabilities—for example, to hedge the value of a share portfolio (the value of a share portfolio might be hedged by acquiring share price index (SPI) futures as a hedging instrument; we will look at SPI futures later in this chapter). A cash-flow hedge, on the other hand, would be used to hedge a future expected cash flow—for example, to hedge an amount that is payable to a foreign supplier, where that amount is denominated in US dollars.

If a hedging instrument does not satisfy certain strict requirements identified in IAS 39, any gains or losses on the hedging instrument must be taken to profit or loss as and when they occur (if they do satisfy the tests provided in IAS 39, the gains or losses on the hedging instrument will initially be transferred directly to equity to the extent the hedge is deemed to be a cash-flow hedge; amounts transferred to equity are included as part of 'other comprehensive income'). Paragraph 88 of IAS 39 stipulates the requirements for hedge accounting. Among these is the requirement that the financial instrument must be designated a hedging instrument at the initial point of recognition of the hedging instrument. This designation is constituted by documentation being in existence that covers issues associated with:

- the risk management objective and strategy;
- the identification of the *hedging instrument* being used;
- the related transaction or *hedged item*;
- the nature of the risk being hedged; and
- how the entity will assess the *effectiveness* of the hedging instrument in offsetting the exposure to changes in the hedged item's fair value or cash flows attributable to the hedged risk.

Hedges cannot be designated and/or documented on a retrospective basis.

The hedging instrument must also meet certain tests in relation to its effectiveness in hedging the movement in value of the hedged item (the guidance in IAS 39 about hedge effectiveness is extensive). In relation to the requirements pertaining to hedge effectiveness, there are two tests:

1. Prospectively, at the inception of the hedge and throughout the life of the hedge, the hedge must be 'highly effective', which means that the changes in the fair value or cash flows of a hedged item (such as a payable relating to the purchase of inventory) must 'almost fully' offset the changes in the fair value or cash flows of the hedging instrument. If the hedging instrument (for example, a forward-rate agreement with a bank) is only for a small proportion of the amount of the hedged item (for example, an amount payable to an overseas supplier), this test would not be met.

2. Retrospectively, and as measured each financial period, the hedge is deemed to be highly effective so that actual results are in a range of between 80 and 125 per cent. For example, if there is a gain on a hedging instrument of £100 and the loss on the hedged item is £110, the effectiveness of the hedge in terms of off-setting the loss on the hedged item is 100/110, which equals 90.91 per cent. However, if the loss on the hedged item was, say, £200 the test would not be met.

Given the above tests for hedge accounting, it would appear that hedging a small proportion of a hedge will not comply with the requirements for hedge accounting.

The requirements pertaining to how gains and losses on hedging are to be treated depend upon the type of hedge involved (and remember that, as we have noted, IAS 39 identifies three types of hedge).

Fair-value hedge

For a fair-value hedge, paragraph 89 of IAS 39 requires both the *hedged item* and the *hedging instrument* to be valued at fair value, with any gains or losses owing to fair value adjustments to be treated as part of the period's profit or loss. If the gains or losses on the *hedged item* are 'perfectly hedged', the gains or losses on the *hedging instrument* will offset the gains or losses on the hedged item so that the net effect on the period's profit or loss would be £nil.

Worked Example 12.9 provides an example of a fair-value hedge.

Worked Example 12.9 Fair-value hedge

Goldblum plc is a gold producer that has an inventory of gold. It wishes to insulate itself from potential adverse changes in the market price of gold. On 1 July 2014 Goldblum plc enters into a forward contract which is indexed to move with the market price of gold. The gold contract matures on 30 June 2015. There is no requirement to make any upfront payment on the contract. The hedging instrument is deemed to be effective in protecting the entity from adverse movements in the price of gold.

For the six months to 31 December 2014 the fair value of the forward contract has increased by €120,000, whereas the fair value of Goldblum plc's inventory of gold has decreased by €120,000.

In the six months to 30 June 2015 the fair value of the forward contract has increased by €52,000, whereas the fair value of Goldblum plc's inventory of gold has decreased by €55,000.

Required

Provide the journal entries for the year ended 30 June 2015.

Solution

1 July 2014

There is a requirement that a financial asset or financial liability shall initially be measured at fair value (paragraph 5.1.1 of IFRS 9).

There is no entry made on 1 July 2014 as the fair value of the contract is deemed to be zero and no deposits have been made in relation to the contract.

31 December 2014

Dr	Loss on gold inventory (included in profit or loss)	€120,000	
Cr	Gold inventory		€120,000
Dr	Forward contract—gold	€120,000	
Cr	Gain on forward contract (included in profit or loss)		€120,000

▶

◀

30 June 2015			
Dr	Loss on gold inventory (included in profit or loss)	€55,000	
Cr	Gold inventory		€55,000
Dr	Forward contract—gold	€52,000	
Cr	Gain on forward contract (included in profit or loss)		€52,000
Dr	Cash at bank	€172,000	
Cr	Forward contract—gold		€172,000
(the other party to the forward contract settles their debt with Goldblum plc)			

Cash-flow hedge

For a cash-flow hedge, the gain or loss on measuring the *hedged item* at fair value is to be treated as part of the period's profit or loss. If the gains or losses on the hedged item were included in the cost of an asset being acquired, then the amounts initially transferred to equity in relation to the hedging instrument will subsequently be transferred to the cost of the asset being acquired. This is consistent with paragraphs 97 and 98 of IAS 39.

The gain or loss on the *hedging instrument* is initially to be transferred to equity (and thereby included in 'other comprehensive income'—remember, 'other comprehensive income' includes increases and decreases in a variety of equity accounts), but subsequently treated as part of profit or loss as necessary to offset the gains or losses recorded on the hedged item (IAS 39, paragraph 95). At the conclusion of the hedging arrangement, any amount still in equity relating to the *hedging instrument* is to be transferred to profit or loss. Again, if a cash-flow hedge does not satisfy the requirements previously discussed, the gains or losses on the hedging instrument shall go directly to profit or loss.

Worked Example 12.10 provides an example of a cash-flow hedge.

> **Worked Example 12.10** **Cash-flow hedge relating to the purchase of inventory**
>
> Oz plc, a company located in the Republic of Ireland, manufactures electric cars. On 15 June 2014 Oz plc enters into a non-cancellable purchase commitment with Vegas plc for the supply of batteries, with those batteries to be shipped on 30 June 2014. The total contract price was US$2,000,000 and the full amount was due for payment on 30 August 2014.
>
> Because of concerns about movements in foreign exchange rates, on 15 June 2014 Oz plc entered into a forward rate contract on US dollars with a foreign exchange broker so as to receive US$2,000,000 on 30 August 2014 at a forward rate of €1.00 = US$0.80 (meaning €2,500,000 will be payable to the foreign currency broker).
>
> We will assume that Oz plc prepares monthly financial statements and that it elects to treat the hedge as a cash-flow hedge. Further, we will assume that Oz plc elects, pursuant to paragraph 98(b) of IAS 39, to adjust the cost of the inventory as a result of the hedging transaction.
>
> *Other information*
> The respective **spot rates**, with the spot rates being the exchange rates for immediate delivery of currencies to be exchanged, are provided below. The forward rates offered on particular dates, for delivery of US dollars on 30 August 2014, are also provided. It should be noted that on 30 August 2014, the last day of the forward rate contract, the spot rate and the forward rate will be the same.
>
> **spot rates** The exchange rates that apply for immediate delivery of currencies to be exchanged.
>
> | Date | Spot rate | Forward rates for 30 August delivery of US$ |
> |---|---|---|
> | 15 June 2014 | €1.00 = US$0.83 | €1.00 = US$0.80 |
> | 30 June 2014 | €1.00 = US$0.81 | €1.00 = US$0.78 |
> | 31 July 2014 | €1.00 = US$0.80 | €1.00 = US$0.77 |
> | 30 August 2014 | €1.00 = US$0.76 | €1.00 = US$0.76 |

▶

Required

Provide the journal entries to account for the 'hedged item' and the 'hedging instrument' for the months ending 30 June, 31 July and 30 August 2014.

Solution

Given this has been designated as a cash-flow hedge, and it has also been assumed that the hedge is 'effective', then any gains or losses on the hedging instrument shall initially be recognised in equity (and therefore in 'other comprehensive income') and then ultimately transferred to the cost of inventory. It should be noted that this contract is a hedge of a firm commitment and that IAS 39 permits a foreign currency hedge of a committed transaction to be treated either as a cash-flow hedge or a fair-value hedge. In this example, the entity has elected to treat it as a cash-flow hedge.

Gains/losses on the hedged item (the inventory purchase) are calculated as follows:

Date	Spot rate	Amount payable in €	Foreign exchange gain/(loss) in €
15 June 2014	€1.00 = US$0.83	–	–
30 June 2014	€1.00 = US$0.81	€2,469,136	–
31 July 2014	€1.00 = US$0.80	€2,500,000	(30,864)
30 August 2014	€1.00 = US$0.76	€2,631,579	(131,579)
			(162,443)

Note: The purchase is not recognised until such time as the batteries were shipped on 30 June 2014.

Gains/losses on the hedging instrument (the forward rate contract) are calculated as follows:

Date	Fwd rate for delivery of US$ on 30 Aug 2014	Receivable on fwd contract[a]	Amount payable in € on forward contract[b]	Fair value of forward contract[c]	Gain/(loss) on forward contract[d]
15 June 2014	€1.00 = US$0.80	€2,500,000	€2,500,000	0	
30 June 2014	€1.00 = US$0.78	€2,564,103	€2,500,000	€64,103	€64,103
31 July 2014	€1.00 = US$0.77	€2,597,403	€2,500,000	€97,403	€33,300
30 August 2014	€1.00 = US$0.76	€2,631,579	€2,500,000	€131,579	€34,176
					€131,579

Notes:

[a] Determined by dividing $2.0 million by the respective dates' forward rate. This right refers to the amount to be received from the bank, the value of which will fluctuate as the forward rate changes. Although Oz plc has been able to 'lock in' a particular forward rate (being $0.80), because the bank will negotiate different forward rates at different times, the fair value of the receivable will change across time. For example, if the forward rate that was available on 30 June had changed from $0.80 to $0.78, then anybody entering a forward rate on 30 June to receive US$2.0 million on 30 August would need to ultimately pay €2,564,103. This means that the existing forward rate contract has a fair value of €64,103 because it will provide $2.0 million for the 'old' negotiated forward rate of $0.80, which is better than what is currently available (being $0.78). Gains or losses in the value of this receivable will act to offset the gains or losses in the value of the amount payable to the overseas supplier.

[b] The obligation (amount payable) represents the amount that must be paid to the bank using the forward rate negotiated with the bank and is fixed in absolute terms for the contracted party. This amount is fixed regardless of what happens to spot rates, or what forward rates the bank offers on other forward rate contracts.

[c] We have calculated a fair value for the hedging instrument (the hedging instrument being the forward rate contract). It is a requirement of IAS 39 that a fair value be attributed to the hedging instrument (as with all financial instruments). In this situation, the fair value will change as the available forward rate being offered by the bank changes. For example, when the contract is originally negotiated, the bank is assumed to be offering the forward rate of €1.00 = US$0.80 for the delivery of US dollars on 30 August 2014 to any interested parties. Therefore, the contract itself has no fair value. However, if on 30 June 2014 the bank is only prepared to offer a forward rate for delivery of US dollars of €1.00 = US$0.78, then if Oz plc was able to transfer its contract to another party needing US dollars on that date, then, given the other options available to that other party, that party would be prepared to pay up to €64,103

for the contract, which equates to ($2,000,000/0.80) – (€2,000,000/0.78). The fair value of the contract would be deemed to be €64,103. There is also a requirement (paragraph 48A of IAS 39) that the financial instrument—in this case, the forward contract—be measured at the present value of the future cash flows. Because the life of the forward contract is less than 12 months, it has been decided on the basis of materiality not to discount the associated cash flows to present value in this Worked Example. In other examples in this chapter, no discounting will be applied to forward contracts with lives of less than 12 months.

d The gain or loss on the forward rate contract represents the change in the fair value of the forward rate contract.

In the calculations above we have calculated a fair value for the hedging instrument (which, in this case, is the forward contract) at each reporting date. It is a requirement of IAS 39 that a fair value be attributed to the forward contract. The changing fair value represents how much it would cost the entity to take out a forward-rate agreement for the delivery of US$2,000,000. For example, if the entity, or perhaps another entity, was to negotiate the forward-rate agreement at 30 June 2014 it would have cost them €2,564,103 for US$2,000,000 rather than the €2,500,000 they were able to 'lock in' on 15 June 2014. The change in the fair value represents the gain or loss on the forward contract. As we can see from the above table, the amount payable for US$2,000,000 (the commitment) has been locked in at €2,500,000 regardless of what subsequently happens to spot rates and forward rates.

The required journal entries would be as follows:

15 June 2014

No entry is required here as the fair value of the forward-rate agreement is assessed as being zero given that the fair value of the foreign currency receivable is the same as the fair value of the commitment, both being €2,500,000.

30 June 2014

Dr	Forward rate contract (financial asset)	€64,103	
Cr	Cash-flow hedge reserve (would be a gain recorded in other comprehensive income)		€64,103

(to recognise the fair value of the forward contract, which is the difference between the related receivable on the contract and the related commitment)

Dr	Inventory	€2,469,136	
Cr	Foreign currency payable		€2,469,136

(to recognise the acquisition of inventory using the relevant spot rate)

Dr	Cash-flow hedge reserve (gain recorded in other comprehensive income)	€64,103	
Cr	Inventory		€64,103

(to transfer the gain/loss on the forward contract to the cost of inventory as at the date of inventory acquisition)

Following the date of acquisition of the inventory, all gains and losses on the forward rate contract and the foreign currency payable with the supplier are transferred directly to profit or loss just as they would be for a fair-value hedge.

31 July 2014

Dr	Forward rate contract (financial asset)	€33,300	
Cr	Gain on forward contract		€33,300
Dr	Foreign exchange loss	€30,864	
Cr	Foreign currency payable		€30,864

30 August 2014

Dr	Forward rate contract (financial asset)	€34,176	
Cr	Gain on forward contract		€34,176
Dr	Foreign exchange loss	€131,579	
Cr	Foreign currency payable		€131,579
Dr	Cash at bank	€131,579	
Cr	Forward rate contract (financial asset)		€131,579

(in this situation the other party to the forward rate contract has actually lost money on the transaction and therefore provides funds to the entity)

Dr	Foreign currency payable	€2,631,579	
Cr	Cash at bank		€2,631,579

(this represents the amount paid to the overseas battery supplier. As we can see from the above two entries, the net amount paid for the batteries was €2,500,000 (which is €2,631,579 – €131,579), which equates to the amount negotiated in the forward rate contract)

We will consider, in what follows, some financial instruments that may (but need not) be used as hedging instruments. Explanations of the various financial instruments are provided in this chapter; more extensive explanation, including accounting for these instruments (with examples), is provided at www.mcgraw-hill.co.uk/textbooks/deeganward.

futures contract A contract to buy or sell an agreed quantity of a particular item at an agreed price on a specific date.

option Entitles the holder to buy assets at a future time at a prespecified price.

put option Gives its holder the right to sell an asset, at a specified exercise price, on or before a specified date.

call option Provides the holder of the option with the right to buy an asset at a specified exercise price, on or before a specified date.

exercise price/strike price The guaranteed transaction price stipulated in an option contract for an asset that may be bought or sold at some predetermined date in the future.

swap agreement Agreement between borrowers to exchange aspects of their respective loan obligations.

foreign currency swap Agreement under which the obligation relating to a loan denominated in one currency is swapped for a loan denominated in another currency.

Futures contracts

A **futures contract** can be defined simply as a contract to buy or sell an agreed quantity of a particular item, at an agreed price, on a specific *future* date.

Options

Options are another commonly used form of derivative financial instrument. An options contract is the right, with no obligation for the options buyer, to buy or sell a specified amount of an underlying instrument at a fixed price on or before a specified future date. Options can be classified as **put options** or **call options**. A call option on a company's shares entitles the holder to buy shares at a future time for a specified price. This price is usually described as either the **exercise price** or the **strike price**. Once the exercise price is determined it will remain fixed, regardless of variations in the market price of the underlying shares. The option can be traded and its sale price will fluctuate as the value of the underlying shares changes, with an increase in the price of the actual share leading to an increase in the price of the option (and vice versa).

Swaps

Another form of derivative financial instrument is the **swap agreement**. Swaps occur when borrowers exchange aspects of their respective loan obligations. Commonly used swaps are *interest rate swaps*—typically a fixed interest rate obligation is swapped for a variable rate obligation—and **foreign currency swaps**, where the obligation relating to a loan denominated in one currency is swapped for a loan denominated in another currency.

12.7 Disclosure requirements pertaining to financial instruments

Accounting standard IFRS 7 *Financial Instruments: Disclosure* provides the disclosure requirements relating to financial instruments. This standard complements IAS 32 *Financial Instruments* and IFRS 9 *Financial Instruments* and aims to provide users with information that allows them to evaluate the significance of the financial instruments to the entity's reported performance and financial position and to evaluate the nature and extent of the risks associated with the financial instrument, including how the risks are being managed (IFRS 7, paragraphs 1, 2, 7 and 31).

The disclosure requirements within IFRS 7 are extensive. In part, the relatively large number of disclosure requirements is probably a direct consequence of the significant losses many organisations have incurred recently in relation to financial instruments or, more particularly, derivative financial instruments, a notable case being the high profile loss by Société Générale in 2008. Société Générale lost £3.7 billion (€4.9 billion) on Japanese equity index futures as a result of trading undertaken by one of its employees. Such losses make investors wary and inclined to demand greater disclosures about such instruments.

There are numerous disclosure requirements in IFRS 7 and the best way to appreciate their extent is to review the standard itself. Nevertheless, while our intention is not to discuss many of the standard's disclosure requirements, we will briefly consider the disclosures required in relation to 'risks' associated with financial instruments. The disclosures detailed in IFRS 7 include the following:

Qualitative disclosures

33.   *For each type of risk arising from financial instruments, an entity shall disclose:*

(a) the exposures to risk and how they arise;

(b) its objectives, policies and processes for managing the risk and the methods used to measure the risk; and

(c) any changes in (a) or (b) from the previous period.

Quantitative disclosures

34. For each type of risk arising from financial instruments, an entity shall disclose:

(a) summary quantitative data about its exposure to that risk at the end of the reporting period. This disclosure shall be based on the information provided internally to key management personnel of the entity (as defined in IAS 24 Related Party Disclosures), for example the entity's board of directors or chief executive officer;

(b) the disclosures required by paragraphs 36–42, to the extent not provided in (a), unless the risk is not material; and

(c) concentrations of risk if not apparent from (a) and (b).

35. If the quantitative data disclosed as at the end of reporting period are unrepresentative of an entity's exposure to risk during the period, an entity shall provide further information that is representative.

Clearly, the disclosure requirements relating to 'risks' associated with financial instruments are quite extensive. IFRS 7 imposes further detailed disclosure requirements in relation to credit risk (the risk that one party to a financial instrument will cause a financial loss for the other party by failing to discharge an obligation), liquidity risk (the risk that an entity will encounter difficulty in meeting obligations associated with financial liabilities) and market risk (the risk that the fair value or future cash flows of a financial instrument will fluctuate because of changes in market prices). IFRS 7 further explains that market risk comprises three other types of risk, these being currency risk, interest rate risk and other price risk. Disclosures are also required in relation to these components of risk.

SUMMARY

The chapter addressed accounting issues associated with financial instruments. Financial instruments are defined as contracts that give rise to both a financial asset of one entity and a financial liability or equity instrument of another entity. Such a definition, in turn, depends on knowledge of the definitions of a financial asset, a financial liability and an equity instrument, all of which are provided in this chapter.

The term 'financial instruments' encompasses a wide range of items, including cash at bank, bank overdrafts, term deposits, trade receivables and payables, borrowings, loans receivable, notes receivable, notes payable, bonds receivable, options, forward-rate exchange agreements and interest-rate swaps. Financial instruments can be classified as primary financial instruments (such as receivables, payables and equity securities) and derivative financial instruments. There are also compound financial instruments.

Derivative financial instruments create rights and obligations that have the effect of transferring one or more of the financial risks inherent in the underlying primary financial instrument. The value of the derivative contract normally reflects changes in the value of the underlying financial instrument. Derivative financial instruments cause many difficulties for accountants with regard to recognition, measurement and disclosure.

Derivative financial instruments include currency futures, share price index futures, share options, foreign currency swaps and interest-rate swaps. Accounting standard IFRS 7 provides numerous disclosure requirements for financial instruments, some of which relate specifically to derivative financial instruments. For example, an entity is required to disclose its objectives for holding or issuing derivative financial instruments, the context needed to understand its objectives and the entity's strategies for achieving its objectives.

IFRS 9 provides the requirements pertaining to the recognition and measurement of financial instruments (other than for hedges, in which case we need to refer to IAS 39). The requirements incorporated in IFRS 7, IFRS 9, IAS 32 and IAS 39 include the following:

- All derivatives are required to be recognised and measured at fair value. Whether gains and losses on a derivative go directly to profit or loss or to comprehensive income will be dependent upon whether the derivative is used as

a hedging instrument; whether the hedge is a cash-flow hedge or a fair-value hedge; and whether the hedge has been deemed to be 'effective'.

- Where there is a designated cash-flow hedge, the gain or loss on the hedging instrument (for example, a futures contract) is initially recorded in equity (and therefore, the movement is included within other comprehensive income). It can subsequently be transferred to profit or loss so as to offset the impact on profit or loss of any change in value of the hedged item (for example, an amount owing to an overseas supplier).
- Where an item is designated a fair-value hedge, the change in value of the hedged item and the change in value of the hedging instrument are both immediately recognised in profit or loss.
- IAS 32 stipulates requirements for measuring the debt and equity components of a compound financial instrument, with the equity component to be determined as the residual amount after deducting the fair value of the liability component from the fair value of the instrument in its entirety.
- IAS 32 emphasises that a critical feature in distinguishing an equity instrument from a liability is the existence of a contractual obligation. An equity instrument cannot involve a contractual obligation. This requirement caused many financial instruments, such as many preference shares, to be reclassified as debt.
- Following on from the above point, IAS 32 confines its assessment of debt versus equity to the contractual terms of the arrangement. Other known factors that are not included within the terms of a financial instrument (such as the probability that an equity option will be exercised) must be ignored.
- IFRS 7 requires extensive disclosure in relation to the risks associated with financial instruments held or issued by an entity.

KEY TERMS

call option 334	financial instrument 313	option 334
compound financial instrument 317	financial liability 313	put option 334
convertible note 317	foreign currency swap 334	set-off/offsetting 318
derivative financial instrument . 315	forward rate 329	spot rates 331
equity instrument 313	futures contract 334	strike price. 334
exercise price 334	hedge contract 328	swap agreement 334
financial asset 313	hedging 324	

END-OF-CHAPTER EXERCISE

On 1 July 2014 Supertubes plc issues €50 million of convertible bonds to Magnatubes plc. The bonds have a life of three years, a face value of €10.00 each, and they offer interest, payable at the end of each financial year, at a rate of 8 per cent per annum.

The bonds are issued at their face value and each bond can be converted into two ordinary shares in Supertubes plc at any time in the next three years. Organisations of a similar risk profile have recently issued debt with similar terms, but without the option for conversion. The market requires a rate of return of 10 per cent per annum on such securities. It is considered that investors in Supertubes plc are prepared to take a lower return (8 per cent) as a result of the facility to convert the bonds to equity. **LO** 12.3

REQUIRED

Provide the journal entries to account for:

(a) The issue of the above securities.
(b) The payment of the first year's interest.
(c) The conversion of the securities to equity, assuming that the conversion takes place two years after the bonds are issued.

SOLUTION TO END-OF-CHAPTER EXERCISE

(a) Journal entries accounting for the issue of the securities

As discussed in this chapter, the above financial instruments are convertible bonds, which would be classified as compound financial instruments. A compound instrument is a financial instrument that contains both a financial liability and an equity element. In accordance with IAS 32, the debt and equity components of a compound instrument must be accounted for separately.

IAS 32 requires a reporting entity to assign the residual amount to the equity instrument—after deducting from the instrument as a whole the amount separately determined for the liability component. We can identify the present value of the bonds and then allocate to the equity component the difference between the present value of these bonds and the issue price of €50 million.

Present value of bonds at the market rate of debt
Present value of principal discounted at 10 per cent for three years:

€50,000,000 × 0.7513 =	€37,565,000

Present value of interest stream discounted at 10 per cent for three years:

€4,000,000 × 2.4869 =	€9,947,600
Total present value	€47,512,600
Equity component (by deduction)	€2,487,400
Total face value of convertible bonds	€50,000,000

If the convertible bonds did not provide an option to convert to ordinary shares, the bonds would be expected to have been issued at a price of €47,512,600. This is considered to represent the present value of the liability component of the compound instrument.

The accounting entries to account for the above issue would be:

1 July 2014

Dr	Cash at bank	€50,000,000
Cr	Convertible bonds liability	€47,512,600
Cr	Convertible bonds (equity component)	€2,487,400

(to record the issue of the convertible bonds and the recognition of the liability and equity components)

(b) Journal entries accounting for the payment of the first year's interest

30 June 2015

Dr	Interest expense	€4,751,260
Cr	Cash	€4,000,000
Cr	Convertible bonds liability	€751,260

(to recognise the interest expense, where the expense equals the present value of the opening liability multiplied by the market rate of interest—see the table below)

Stream of interest expenses over three-year life of debentures:

Date	Payment (€)	Interest expense (€)	Increase in bond liability (€)	Bond liability (€)
1 July 2014				47,512,600
30 June 2015	4,000,000	4,751,260	751,260	48,263,860
30 June 2016	4,000,000	4,826,386	826,386	49,090,246
30 June 2017	4,000,000	4,909,025	909,025	50,000,000*

* Includes a rounding error of €729 (as present value tables only go to four decimal places)

The stream of interest expenses across three years can be summarised as in the table above, where interest expense for a given year is calculated by multiplying the present value of the liability at the beginning of the period by the market rate of interest, this being 10 per cent.

(c) Journal entries accounting for the conversion of the securities to equity

If the holders of the options elect to convert the options to ordinary shares at the end of the second year of the debentures (after receiving their interest payments), the entries would be:

30 June 2016

Dr	Interest expense	€4,826,386	
Cr	Cash		€4,000,000
Cr	Convertible bonds liability		€826,386

(to recognise interest expense for the period)

Dr	Convertible bonds liability	€49,090,246	
Dr	Convertible bonds (equity component)	€2,487,400	
Cr	Share capital (including share premium)		€51,577,646

(to recognise the conversion of the bonds into shares of Supertubes plc)

REVIEW QUESTIONS

1 Define financial instrument. **LO 12.1**
2 What is a primary financial instrument? Provide some examples. **LO 12.4**
3 What is a derivative financial instrument? Provide some examples. **LO 12.4**
4 What factors influence the value of a derivative financial instrument, and how should changes in the value of derivatives be treated from an accounting perspective? **LO 12.11**
5 Would physical assets (such as inventories, property, plant and equipment) be considered to be financial assets? Why? **LO 12.2**
6 Would prepayments be considered to be financial instruments? Why? **LO 12.2**
7 What is a compound financial instrument? Provide some examples. **LO 12.5**
8 Is there a consequence for reported profit or loss if a particular financial instrument, for example a preference share, is designated as debt rather than equity? Explain the consequence. **LO 12.3**
9 Explain what a set-off of assets and liabilities is. **LO 12.6**
10 What disclosures must be made, pursuant to IAS 32, in the period following a set-off of assets and liabilities? **LO 12.13**
11 Arthur plc has the following statement of financial position:

Statement of financial position before set-off

	€		€
Loans payable	1,000,000	Loans receivable	1,200,000
Shareholders' equity	1,000,000	Non-current assets	800,000
	2,000,000		2,000,000

Assume that Arthur plc has an amount owing to Blayney plc of €300,000 and an amount receivable from Blayney plc of €400,000. **LO 12.6**
Assuming a right of set-off exists, why would Arthur plc want to perform a set-off? What would be the impact on the debt-to-assets ratio?
12 Subsequent to initial measurement, financial assets are to be classified as being measured at either fair value or amortised cost. What is the basis for determining whether fair value or amortised cost shall be used? **LO 12.7**
13 Explain why it is that, when the market's required rate of return is less than the coupon rate being offered on a bond, the price the bond will be sold for (its fair value) will be above its face value. **LO 12.8**
14 IAS 32 requires that, when determining whether a financial instrument is debt or equity, consideration should be given to the *economic substance* of the instrument, rather than simply its *legal form*. What does this mean? **LO 12.8**

15 Contrast the presentation requirements of the IASB Conceptual Framework and of IAS 32 in relation to such instruments as convertible notes, particularly where they concern the probability of conversion. Are you more inclined to agree with the requirements of IAS 32 or the suggestions provided by the IASB Conceptual Framework? Why? **LO** 12.13

16 Should interest on financial liabilities always be treated as an expense? **LO** 12.2

17 Would it ever be appropriate to classify the distributions to holders of preference shares as interest expense rather than dividends? Explain your answer. **LO** 12.3

18 IAS 32 requires the issuing entity to classify a financial instrument, or its component parts, as a liability or as equity in accordance with the economic substance of the instrument at the time of initial recognition. What does this requirement actually mean? **LO** 12.8

19 IFRS 7 is concerned primarily with ensuring extensive disclosure of financial instruments. Why do you think this is the case? **LO** 12.13

20 In the past, a number of organisations have disclosed convertible bonds just below the total of shareholders' equity and therefore have not really disclosed them as debt or equity. **LO** 12.3

   (a) Is the approach described above permitted under IAS 32?

   (b) Would it have been costly for companies to change how they disclose their convertible notes? Explain your answer.

21 Lehman plc sells some printed material to an organisation in the United States on 1 July 2015. The price is denominated in US dollars and is US$500,000. It is to be paid on 1 September 2015. The amount is guaranteed by a local bank, so that payment is deemed to be very certain. The spot rate on the date of the transaction is £1 = US$0.70.

   Worried about fluctuations in the value of sterling, Lehman decides to enter a forward-rate agreement with the bank in which the latter agrees to buy US$500,000 from Lehman plc on 1 September at an agreed forward rate of US$0.72. **LO** 12.10

   (a) Describe how entering a forward-rate agreement will reduce the risk of Lehman plc.

   (b) How much money, in pounds sterling, will Lehman plc ultimately receive from the sale?

CHALLENGING QUESTIONS

22 (a) What is hedge accounting and what are the three types of hedge identified in IAS 39? **LO** 12.11

   (b) What is a 'hedged item' and what is a 'hedging instrument'?

   (c) How are gains and losses on the hedging instrument to be treated for accounting purposes for a fair-value hedge and a cash-flow hedge, respectively?

23 Woodie plc issues £5 million in convertible bonds on 1 July 2015. They are issued at their face value and pay an interest rate of 4 per cent. The interest is paid at the end of each year. The bonds may be converted to ordinary shares in Woodie plc at any time in the next three years. Organisations similar to Woodie plc have recently issued similar debt instruments but without the option for conversion to ordinary shares. These instruments issued by the other entities offer interest at a rate of 6 per cent. **LO** 12.3

   On 1 July 2016 all the holders of the convertible notes decide to convert the bonds to shares in Woodie plc.

   Provide the journal entries to:

   (a) record the issue of the securities on 1 July 2015;

   (b) recognise the interest payment on 30 June 2016; and

   (c) recognise the conversion of the bonds to ordinary shares on 1 July 2016.

24 It has been argued that adoption of global standards will attract international investors. Discuss whether you think analysts and investors across the globe will abstain from investing in companies that do not adopt IFRSs. **LO** 12.12

25 A number of issues were raised in respect of the original introduction of IAS 39, including: **LO** 12.12

   (a) Many hedging contracts would need to be valued at fair value, with any resulting gains and losses having to go to the statement of comprehensive income.

   (b) From 2005 many derivatives were required to appear on the statement of financial position for the first time.

   (c) From 2005 many financial instruments were required to be reclassified from equity to debt.

   (d) From 2005 there were major cuts to corporate profits as a result of the introduction of the accounting standard.

   Explain why the above issues are likely to be of concern to many organisations.

26 On 1 November 2014 Sandy plc issued 10,000 convertible notes with the following features: **LO 12.5**

Face value	€1,000
Term	Four years
Issue price	At face value
Interest	Coupon rate of 10 per cent payable annually in arrears
Conversion option	Each note is convertible into 100 ordinary shares
Market interest rate	12 per cent for similar debt with no conversion option

(a) Prepare the journal entry to record the issue of the convertible notes.

(b) Describe the effect, if any, of the issue of the convertible notes on each of the three components of the statement of financial position, that is, assets, liabilities and equity.

27 Tilburg plc manufactures electric skateboards. On 4 June 2014 Tilburg plc enters into a non-cancellable purchase commitment with Miami plc for the supply of wheels, with the wheels to be shipped on 30 June 2014. The total contract price was US$3,000,000 and the full amount was due for payment on 30 August 2014.

Because of concerns about movements in foreign exchange rates, on 4 June 2014 Tilburg plc entered into a forward rate contract on US dollars with a foreign exchange broker so as to receive US$3,000,000 on 30 August 2014 at a forward rate of £1.00 = US$0.78.

Tilburg plc prepares monthly financial statements and it elects to treat the hedge as a cash-flow hedge. Further, pursuant to paragraph 98(b) of IAS 39, Tilburg plc elects to adjust the cost of the inventory as a result of the hedging transaction. **LO 12.10**

Other information

The respective spot rates are provided below. The forward rates offered on particular dates, for delivery of US dollars on 30 August 2014, are also provided.

Date	Spot rate	Forward rates for 30 August 2014 delivery of US$/£
4 June 2014	£1.00 = US$0.80	£1.00 = US$0.78
30 June 2014	£1.00 = US$0.78	£1.00 = US$0.76
31 July 2014	£1.00 = US$0.75	£1.00 = US$0.74
30 August 2014	£1.00 = US$0.72	£1.00 = US$0.72

Provide the journal entries to account for the 'hedged item' and the 'hedging instrument' for the months ending 30 June, 31 July and 30 August 2014.

Chapter 13

Revenue Recognition Issues

Learning objectives

Upon completing this chapter readers should:

LO1 understand some of the concepts of income and revenue and understand current IASB requirements pertaining to revenue recognition;

LO2 understand the points of an organisation's operating cycle at which income might be recognised;

LO3 appreciate that the amount of income recognised in a particular period will be directly related to the accounting measurement model that has been adopted;

LO4 understand how the existence of particular conditions associated with a sale (such as attached put and call options, or the right of return) will affect the timing of revenue recognition; and

LO5 understand the issues associated with recognising revenues for long-term construction projects.

13.1 New requirements relating to revenue definition

We will commence this chapter by first discussing a joint project being undertaken by the IASB and the US Financial Accounting Standards Board (FASB) in relation to developing a new accounting standard to address revenue derived from contracts with customers. At the time of writing this chapter, the accounting standard has not been finalised and there is an expectation that the standard will not be released before late 2012 or early 2013 and will not be required to be applied until at least 2015. Back in December 2008, and as part of this project to develop a new accounting standard, the IASB released a Discussion Paper entitled *Preliminary Views on Revenue Recognition in Contracts with Customers* (we will refer to this as IASB 2008) and called for interested parties to submit comments and opinions by mid-June 2009. Following this, an Exposure Draft *Revenue from Contracts with Customers* was released in June 2010. Following a review of the submissions received (approximately 1,000), and following many public meetings, it was decided to issue yet another Exposure Draft *Revenue from Contracts with Customers* in November 2011. A good deal of the material provided in this chapter will be based on this November 2011 Exposure Draft and reference to it will be signified by referring to IASB (2011). When the accounting standard is finally released it will replace both IAS 18 *Revenue* and IAS 11 *Construction Contracts*.

In developing the new accounting standard there was a belief that the requirements in IAS 18 and IAS 11 were not consistent with each other in a number of respects, as well as having inconsistencies with the Conceptual Framework. It was also believed that it was preferable to have one accounting standard that would cover issues that are addressed in both standards, as well as other revenue-related issues. According to

IASB (2011, p. 5), the IASB and FASB initiated the joint project to clarify the principles for recognising revenue and to develop a common revenue standard for IFRSs and US GAAP so as to:

(a) *remove inconsistencies and weaknesses in existing revenue requirements;*
(b) *provide a more robust framework for addressing revenue issues;*
(c) *improve comparability of revenue recognition practices across entities, industries, jurisdictions and capital markets;*
(d) *provide more useful information to users of financial statements through improved disclosure requirements; and*
(e) *simplify the preparation of financial statements by reducing the number of requirements to which an entity must refer.*

In considering some of the above points in greater depth, it was argued in IASB (2008) that the recognition of revenue for some transactions, as required by IAS 18 and IAS 11, was inconsistent with the definition and recognition criteria for revenue as provided in the IASB Conceptual Framework. The recognition principles in these standards utilised recognition criteria dependent upon whether the transaction transferred the 'risks and rewards of ownership' of the assets, rather than basing the recognition on the transfer of control. 'Control' is central to the definition of an asset. As paragraph 1.10 of IASB (2008) stated:

> *Some criticise revenue recognition standards in IFRSs because an entity applying those standards might recognise amounts in the financial statements that do not faithfully represent economic phenomena. That can happen because, under existing accounting standards, revenue recognition for the sale of a good depends largely on when the risks and rewards of ownership of the good are transferred to a customer. Therefore, an entity might recognise a good as inventory (because a preponderance of risks and rewards may not have passed yet to the customer) even after the customer has obtained control over the good. That outcome is inconsistent with the IASB's definition of an asset, which depends on control of the good, not the risks and rewards of owning the good.*

Adopting a view that revenue recognition should be consistent with the Conceptual Framework, the IASB and FASB embrace a view, as reflected in IASB (2011), that revenue recognition should be a direct function of whether goods and services have been transferred to the control of the customer (and not be a function of who holds the risks and rewards of ownership of the asset) (IASB 2008, paragraph 6.7).

In providing further explanation of the above view, paragraph 4.8 of IASB (2008) states:

> *In essence, an entity satisfies performance obligations, and recognises revenue, when the customer receives the promised goods and services. Consequently, in the proposed model revenue would reflect the transfer of promised goods and services to customers, and not the activities of the entity in producing those goods and services. Activities that an entity undertakes in fulfilling a contract result in revenue recognition at the time of those activities only if they simultaneously transfer assets to the customer and, hence, satisfy a performance obligation.*

According to IASB (2008), when determining whether an entity has transferred an asset to a customer, it is important to distinguish between the transfer of control of an asset and the transfer of the risks and rewards of owning an asset. In some cases those notions coincide, but in other cases they do not. Paragraphs 4.11 to 4.18 of IASB (2008) provide illustrations to explain when control is transferred and, therefore, when revenue should be recognised under their proposed approach to revenue recognition. These paragraphs state:

> 4.11 *Consider the following example: ToolCo sells power tools. To encourage customers to make purchases, ToolCo allows them to return the tools within 30 days of purchase and to receive a full refund of the purchase price.*
>
> 4.12 *In this example, a customer controls the tool at the point of delivery. In other words, at that time the tool is the customer's asset and ToolCo no longer has enforceable rights to it.*
>
> 4.13 *In contrast, the risks and rewards of owning the tool are not entirely transferred to the customer when the tool is delivered. Although the customer bears some risks of owning the tool, such as the risk of loss or theft, ToolCo bears other risks, such as the risk that the tool will be returned, and the risk that the returned tool will have a reduced value to ToolCo.*
>
> 4.14 *Now consider a slightly different example: ToolCo sells power tools. To encourage customers to make purchases, ToolCo allows them to use the tools on a trial basis for 30 days. ToolCo can take possession of a tool at any time during the trial period and is entitled to full payment if the tool is not returned within 30 days.*
>
> 4.15 *In this example, ToolCo's risks and rewards are similar to those in the first scenario. In both scenarios, ToolCo delivers the tool to the customer at contract inception, and bears the risk that the customer will return it within 30 days and not pay any consideration.*

4.16 However, in the first scenario, ToolCo does not control the tool after the point of delivery (the tool is the customer's asset). In the second, the tool is ToolCo's asset until the expiry of the 30-day trial period—until that time, ToolCo has the enforceable right to the tool. It is not the likelihood of return that determines which entity has the asset (indeed, the likelihood of a return may be the same under either scenario). Rather, the decision is based on which entity controls the tool.

4.17 The fact that the risks of owning the tool are shared by more than one party in the contract makes the risks and rewards notion difficult to apply when determining whether an asset has transferred from one party to another.

4.18 Therefore, the boards think that a focus on control results in more consistent decisions about when assets are transferred. Some may think that this focus is too legalistic and that its use may result in information that is not comparable across different countries and legal jurisdictions. However, the boards note that this concern also applies to the notion of risks and rewards.

In further considering the 'core' requirement that revenue recognition should be directly linked to the transfer of control of the underlying goods and services, paragraph 4.62 of IASB (2008) states:

Consequently, activities that an entity undertakes in fulfilling a contract result in revenue recognition only if they simultaneously transfer assets to the customer. For example, in a contract to construct an asset for a customer, an entity satisfies a performance obligation during construction only if assets are transferred to the customer throughout the construction process. That would be the case if the customer controls the partially constructed asset so that it is the customer's asset as it is being constructed.

The above material hopefully reinforces the perspective that, under current thinking, revenue recognition from contracts with customers is very much linked to the transfer of control of assets and not to the transfer of the risks and rewards of ownership, as has been the accepted position for many years. This is quite a significant shift in thinking and hence why we have dedicated the above material to this topic. We will now move on to consider the definition of income and revenue.

13.2 Definition of income and revenue

According to the IASB Conceptual Framework, 'income' is defined as:

Increases in economic benefits during the accounting period in the form of inflows or enhancements of assets or decreases in liabilities that result in an increase in equity, other than those relating to contributions from equity participants.

As indicated in the IASB Conceptual Framework, income can be subdivided into 'revenues' and 'gains'. Specifically:

The definition of income encompasses both revenues and gains. Revenue arises in the course of the ordinary activities of an entity and is referred to by a variety of different names including sales, fees, interest, dividends, royalties and rent.

In relation to 'gains', the IASB Conceptual Framework provides the following:

■ Gains represent other items that meet the definition of income and may, or may not, arise in the course of the ordinary activities of an entity. Gains represent increases in economic benefits and as such are no different in nature from revenue. Hence they are not regarded as constituting a separate element in this Framework.
■ Gains include, for example, those arising on the disposal of non-current assets. The definition of income also includes unrealised gains, for example those arising on the revaluation of marketable securities and those resulting from increases in the carrying amount of long-term assets. When gains are recognised in the income statement, they are usually displayed separately because knowledge of them is useful for the purpose of making economic decisions. Gains are often reported net of related expenses.

From the above discussion we can see that, generally speaking, revenues relate to the ordinary income-generating activities of an entity—for example, from sales or rental receipts—whereas gains relate to 'other income', which does not necessarily constitute part of the ordinary activities of an entity. The differentiation between revenues and gains is based on some degree of professional judgement, and it is very possible that something that is deemed to be a 'gain' by one accountant might be deemed to be 'revenue' by another (it should be appreciated, however, that the classification of an item as revenue or gain will not affect the amount of total

comprehensive income reported, as total comprehensive income is based on income less expenses, and income incorporates both revenues and gains). Further, because different organisations will be involved in different types of activity, what is an ordinary activity in one business might not be an ordinary activity in another. Hence, an item might be deemed to be revenue in one entity, but a gain within another entity.

13.2.1 Differentiation between revenue and gains

The differentiation between revenue and gains, as presented in the IASB Conceptual Framework, is also embraced within the 2011 Exposure Draft *Revenue from Contracts with Customers*. IASB (2011, Appendix A) defines revenue as:

> *Income arising in the course of an entity's ordinary activities.*

Returning to the broader concept of income (which incorporates both revenues and gains), income can be earned from a variety of transactions or events, including the provision of goods and services; from returns generated from investing in or lending to another entity; from holding and disposing of assets; by receiving non-reciprocal transfers such as grants, donations and bequests; or where liabilities are forgiven. Hence, as already indicated, the recognition of income is not restricted to receiving 'inflows' that relate to the ordinary operating activities of an entity.

To qualify as income, the inflows or other enhancements or the savings in outflows of economic benefits must have the effect of increasing equity. Therefore, transactions such as the purchase of assets, or the issuance of debt, are not considered income because they do not result in an increase in equity. In paragraph 9 of the scope section of the proposed standard—IASB (2011)—four exceptions are stated as they fall within the scope of other standards. These are lease contracts (IAS 17 *Leases*), insurance contracts (IFRS 4 *Insurance Contracts*), contractual rights or obligations (IFRS 9 *Financial Instruments*) and non-monetary exchanges between entities.

Both the objective and the scope of the draft accounting standard make reference to 'contracts' with 'customers'. These terms are defined in the draft accounting standard as follows:

Contract   *An agreement between two or more parties that creates enforceable rights and obligations.*

Customer   *A party that has contracted with an entity to obtain goods or services that are an output of the entity's ordinary activities.*

13.3   Recognition criteria for revenue from contracts with customers

The draft accounting standard (IASB 2011, paragraph 31) states:

> *An entity shall recognise revenue when (or as) the entity satisfies a performance obligation by transferring a promised good or service (ie an asset) to a customer. An asset is transferred when (or as) the customer obtains control of that asset.*

Control is explained in paragraph 32 of IASB (2011):

> *Goods and services are assets, even if only momentarily, when they are received and used (as in the case of many services). Control of an asset refers to the ability to direct the use of and obtain substantially all of the remaining benefits from the asset. Control includes the ability to prevent other entities from directing the use of and obtaining the benefits from an asset. The benefits of an asset are the potential cash flows that can be obtained directly or indirectly in many ways, such as by:*
>
> *(a) using the asset to produce goods or provide services (including public services);*
> *(b) using the asset to enhance the value of other assets;*
> *(c) using the asset to settle liabilities or reduce expenses;*
> *(d) selling or exchanging the asset;*
> *(e) pledging the asset to secure a loan; and*
> *(f) holding the asset.*

Depending upon the nature of the activities of the reporting entity, revenue in relation to particular goods or services might be recognised at a point in time or it might be recognised over a period of time (for example, in relation to a long-term construction contract). Again, we must remember that the transfer of control is a required precondition before revenue shall be recognised at a point in time or over a period of time. In relation to situations where performance obligations are satisfied at a point in time (which might, for example, relate to where an item residing in inventory is sold to a customer), paragraph 37 of IASB (2011) states:

If a performance obligation is not satisfied over time, an entity satisfies the performance obligation at a point in time. To determine the point in time when a customer obtains control of a promised asset and an entity satisfies a performance obligation [therefore enabling the recognition of revenue], the entity shall consider indicators of the transfer of control, which include, but are not limited to, the following:

(a) *The entity has a present right to payment for the asset—if a customer is presently obliged to pay for an asset, then that indicates that the customer has obtained control of the asset in exchange.*

(b) *The customer has legal title to the asset—legal title often indicates which party to a contract has the ability to direct the use of and obtain the benefits from an asset or to restrict the access of other entities to those benefits. Hence, the transfer of legal title of an asset indicates that the customer has obtained control of the asset.*

(c) *The entity has transferred physical possession of the asset—the customer's physical possession of an asset indicates that the customer has the ability to direct the use of and obtain the benefits from the asset or to restrict the access of other entities to those benefits. However, physical possession may not coincide with control of an asset. For example, in some repurchase agreements and in some consignment arrangements, a customer or consignee may have physical possession of an asset that the entity controls.*

(d) *The customer has the significant risks and rewards of ownership of the asset—the transfer of the significant risks and rewards of ownership of an asset to the customer indicates that control of the asset has been transferred. However, when evaluating the risks and rewards of ownership of a promised asset, an entity shall consider any risks that may give rise to a separate performance obligation in addition to the performance obligation to transfer the asset. For example, an entity may have transferred control of an asset to a customer but not yet satisfied an additional separate performance obligation to provide maintenance services related to the transferred asset.*

(e) *The customer has accepted the asset—the customer's acceptance of an asset indicates that it has obtained the ability to direct the use of and obtain the benefits from the asset.*

Again, the above factors are considered in determining whether revenue should be recognised at a point in time. Where performance obligations are satisfied over time (rather than as at a point in time, as above)—for example an organisation might be constructing a building for a customer over a number of years—then paragraph 35 of IASB (2011) permits revenue to be recognised to the extent that the reporting entity's performance creates or enhances an asset (for example, work-in-progress in the form of a building) that the customer controls while the asset is being created or enhanced. If the customer does not control the asset being constructed, then revenue shall not be recognised.

13.4 Measurement of revenue

Where revenue has been recognised, we obviously need to measure it. Paragraph 49 of IASB (2011) states:

When (or as) a performance obligation is satisfied, an entity shall recognise as revenue the amount of the transaction price allocated to that performance obligation. If the amount of consideration to which an entity expects to be entitled is variable, the cumulative amount of revenue an entity recognises to date shall not exceed the amount to which the entity is reasonably assured to be entitled.

The above requirement relating to revenue measurement uses a number of key terms when discussing the measurement of revenue. Of particular relevance is the reference to 'transaction price' and 'reasonably assured'. In relation to 'reasonably assured', paragraph 81 of IASB (2011) states:

If the amount of consideration to which an entity expects to be entitled is variable, the cumulative amount of revenue the entity recognises to date shall not exceed the amount to which the entity is reasonably assured to be entitled. An entity is reasonably assured to be entitled to the amount of consideration allocated to satisfied performance obligations only if both of the following criteria are met:

(a) *the entity has experience with similar types of performance obligations (or has other evidence such as access to the experience of other entities); and*

(b) *the entity's experience (or other evidence) is predictive of the amount of consideration to which the entity will be entitled in exchange for satisfying those performance obligations.*

If no amount is currently considered to be 'reasonably assured' to be entitled, then no revenue shall be recognised. The 'reasonably assured' amount represents that upper limit of the amount to be recognised (IASB 2011, paragraph 84).

The 'transaction price' to be included in revenue is defined in the draft accounting standard as:

The amount of consideration to which an entity expects to be entitled in exchange for transferring promised goods or services to a customer, excluding amounts collected on behalf of third parties (for example, sales taxes).

Paragraph 52 of IASB (2011) further requires:

When determining the transaction price, an entity shall consider the effects of all of the following:

(a) variable consideration;
(b) the time value of money;
(c) non-cash consideration; and
(d) consideration payable to a customer.

In relation to variable consideration (point (a) above), if the promised amount of consideration in a contract is variable, an entity shall estimate the total amount to which the entity will be entitled in exchange for transferring the promised goods or services to a customer. Paragraph 55 of IASB (2011) requires:

To estimate the transaction price, an entity shall use either of the following methods, depending on which method the entity expects to better predict the amount of consideration to which it will be entitled:

(a) The expected value is the sum of probability-weighted amounts in a range of possible consideration amounts. An expected value may be an appropriate estimate of the transaction price if an entity has a large number of contracts with similar characteristics.
(b) The most likely amount is the single most likely amount in a range of possible consideration amounts (ie the single most likely outcome of the contract). The most likely amount may be an appropriate estimate of the transaction price if the contract has only two possible outcomes (for example, an entity either achieves a performance bonus or does not).

If it is clear that there is a financing component in the sale (for example, that the entity has provided settlement terms that include an interest cost), that interest revenue should be accounted for separately. Further, if the transaction price is not expected to be paid for more than a year, then the transaction price must be discounted to recognise the time value of money (IASB 2011, paragraph 58). Where there is no clear finance component within the transaction, and the time between when the entity expects to receive the payment and the time when the goods or services were transferred is less than a year, then discounting can be ignored (IASB 2011, paragraph 60).

When amounts to be received from customers are to be discounted (for example, the amount is to be received beyond 12 months), then the discount rate to be applied should reflect the rate used if the contract were a separate financing transaction and should incorporate the credit characteristics of the customer and any collateral provided (IASB 2011, paragraph 61).

13.4.1 Non-cash consideration

If the contract price is cash, then it is obviously easier to measure the fair value of the consideration relative to the situation where the consideration is in a non-cash form. For example, a customer might pay for a good or service by transferring some land to the reporting entity, rather than paying cash. Where non-cash consideration is received, the consideration shall be measured at fair value (IASB 2011, paragraph 63).

For example, assume that an entity, A plc, provides services to another entity, B plc, in return for receiving an item of plant. The plant has a carrying amount in B plc's financial statements of €80,000, but independent valuations show that the plant has a fair value of €100,000. A plc would recognise revenue of €100,000, being the fair value of the plant.

13.5 Income and revenue recognition points

13.5.1 Current and past practice

As an example of how revenue is affected by a change in the rules governing the measurement of assets, we can consider accounting standard IAS 41 *Agriculture*. This standard addresses how we are to account for biological assets (which are defined as living animals or plants). IAS 41 requires that biological assets, such as forestry assets or livestock, are to be valued on the basis of their fair value, with any increase in value being treated as income. This can be contrasted with the previous practice in the UK whereby many organisations

measured their agricultural assets on the basis of historical cost, with revenue not being recognised until the assets were actually sold. Such a fundamental change in measurement approach can have a significant impact on revenues and reported profits. This is an important point. Put in a slightly different way—it is emphasised that different approaches to measuring assets, and to measuring liabilities, will directly affect reported profits or losses.

The greatest controversy with the new standard lies in the revenue recognition treatment of long-term contracts, as evidenced by the American Accounting Association's response (Colson *et al.* 2010):

> *We support the boards' proposed comprehensive revenue recognition standard based on the following options: (1) the customer consideration approach (based on initial contract price measurement); (2) no recognition of revenue at contract inception (by assigning the initial contract price to performance obligations); and (3) allocation of the transaction price to multiple performance obligations based on the relative stand-alone prices of each performance obligation. We also recommend that the boards carefully consider the following clarifications as they develop the final exposure draft. The formal definition should specify that the contract be an 'enforceable' agreement. The measurement of a performance obligation must be verifiable. While the transfer of an asset to the customer or the acceptance of a service by the customer normally signals the recognition of revenue, we encourage the boards to carefully consider situations (like long-term construction or mining) when the completion of intermediate performance obligations could trigger revenue recognition prior to the transfer of title. Absent special consideration of these situations, companies may be influenced to write contracts in suboptimal ways in an effort to recognize revenue continuously throughout a long-term construction project or in the process of mining or farming. Finally, we highlight difficulties that may arise in allocating the initial transaction price to multiple performance obligation contracts when the individual performance obligations are not normally sold on a stand-alone basis.*

As can be seen from the latter part of the above quote, this area is one that could result in revenue recognition management, something that the IASB does not want to promote, hence the need to have two exposure drafts and extensive discussion on the proposals. After the initial discussion phase the Exposure Draft *Revenue from Contracts with Customers* (IASB 2011) was issued and is now discussed further.

13.5.2 Five steps to recognise revenue according to IASB (2011)

As we have previously indicated, according to the Exposure Draft *Revenue from Contracts with Customers* (2011, paragraph 3):

> *The core principle of this [draft] IFRS is that an entity shall recognise revenue to depict the transfer of promised goods or services to customers in an amount that reflects the consideration to which the entity expects to be entitled in exchange for those goods or services.*

According to paragraph 4 of IASB (2011):

> *To achieve that core principle, an entity shall apply all of the following steps:*
>
> *(a) identify the contract with a customer;*
> *(b) identify the separate performance obligations in the contract;*
> *(c) determine the transaction price;*
> *(d) allocate the transaction price to the separate performance obligations in the contract; and*
> *(e) recognise revenue when (or as) the entity satisfies a performance obligation.*

This sequence of revenue recognition is diagrammatically represented in Figure 13.1.

13.5.3 Income and revenue recognition according to the IASB Conceptual Framework

As we know, pursuant to the IASB Conceptual Framework there are five elements of accounting, these being assets, liabilities, income, expenses and equity. In relation to when an element of accounting, for example income, should be recognised, the Conceptual Framework states:

> *An item that meets the definition of an element should be recognised if:*
>
> *(a) it is probable that any future economic benefit associated with the item will flow to or from the entity; and*
> *(b) the item has a cost or value that can be measured with reliability.*

Figure 13.1 Steps to follow when recognising revenue according to IASB (2011)

Step 1: Identify the contract(s) with the customer

A reporting entity would apply the principles in the accounting standard to the enforceable rights and obligations in each contract that has been agreed with a customer.

Step 2: Identify the separate performance obligations in the contract

A contract includes promises to transfer goods and services to a customer. The promises are called performance obligations. A reporting entity would account separately for performance obligations to transfer goods or services that are distinct.

Step 3: Determine the transaction price

The transaction price is the amount of consideration to which the reporting entity expects to be entitled in exchange for transferring promised goods or services to a customer. The transaction price would be adjusted for the effects of the time value of money. The effects of credit risk (collectability) would not be reflected in the purchase price but would be presented as a separate line item adjacent to revenue.

Step 4: Allocate the transaction price

A reporting entity would typically allocate the transaction price to each separate performance obligation on the basis of the relative stand-alone selling price of each distinct good or service.

Step 5: Recognise revenue when a performance obligation is satisfied

A reporting entity would recognise revenue when, or as, it satisfied a performance obligation by transferring a promised good or service to a customer—which is when the customer obtains control of that good or service. A performance obligation may be satisfied at a point in time or over time.

> **probable** It is generally considered that something is probable if it is more likely than less likely.

As you know from previous chapters, it is generally considered that something is **probable** if it is more likely than less likely. As we now know from this chapter, apart from requirements pertaining to probability and measurability, revenue recognition is also dependent upon whether the entity has satisfied performance obligations and transferred control of the asset to the customer.

Traditionally it was possible for revenue to be recognised during various phases of the revenue cycle. The following discussion considers the recognition of revenue at the completion of production and at the point of ultimate sale. The possibility of recognising revenue during production (and this applies particularly to construction contracts) will be discussed later in this chapter.

Revenue recognition at completion of production

For certain products, such as precious metals or agricultural products, revenue could potentially be recognised at the completion of production, even when no sale has been made. In the past, revenue has been recognised at this point because when these metals were mined or agricultural crops were harvested, the sales price was reasonably assured, the units were interchangeable and no significant costs were involved in distributing the product. It is often the case that statutory bodies have in place an agreement to buy all materials/crops produced by an entity at a specified price, hence the likelihood of not receiving the receipts would be minimal once production is complete. While this was common practice for producers of certain minerals and agricultural products, the contents of the draft accounting standard *Revenue from Contracts with Customers* (IASB 2011) will mean that this practice will probably cease from 2015 as 'control' of the good or service has not been transferred to the customer.

Revenue recognition at the time of sale

The conditions for recognising revenue in relation to the sale of goods are usually met by the time the product or merchandise is delivered or the services are rendered to customers.

Where products require transportation, the revenues from manufacturing and selling activities are commonly recognised at the time of sale, normally determined by the shipping terms. That is, time of sale is commonly interpreted as the time when title passes. If the goods are shipped on terms referred to as **f.o.b. shipping point** (where f.o.b. stands for *free on board*), title passes to the buyer when the seller delivers the goods to a common carrier (the 'shipping point') who acts as an agent for the buyer. Revenue would typically be recognised when the goods reach the carrier. If the goods are shipped **f.o.b. destination**, title does not pass until the buyer receives the goods from the common carrier (that is, at the destination). In this case, revenue would not typically be recognised until the goods reach their destination. 'Shipping point' and 'destination' are frequently designated by a particular location, for example f.o.b. London, which would mean the title passes from the seller to the purchaser when the goods arrive in London.

When revenue is recognised in advance of the actual receipt of cash (or cash substitute), it is common for the entity to recognise an **allowance for doubtful debts**. Logically, if goods are sold or services are provided on credit terms, not all amounts due from the customers will ultimately be collected. To ignore this fact would lead to an overstatement of receivables and, therefore, of assets in the statement of financial position. It would also lead to an overstatement of profit (or an understatement of losses). When the first Exposure Draft *Revenue from Contracts with Customers* was released in June 2010, it was proposed that reporting entities should recognise revenue at the amount of consideration that the company expects to receive from the customer. Thus, it was initially proposed that when determining the 'transaction price' the entity would consider the effect of the customer's credit risk and only record the net expected amount as revenue. This would have represented quite a departure from traditional accounting practice. However, when the second Exposure Draft was released, in November 2011, the requirement was changed back to the traditional approach. That is, a reporting entity shall recognise revenue at the amount of consideration to which the entity considers it is 'entitled'. An entity shall exclude expectations of collectability when determining the amount of the transaction price (and thus the amount to be recognised as revenue). To provide for greater transparency on the relationship between revenue and customer credit risk, the IASB and FASB have proposed that a reporting entity shall present any impairment losses relating to contracts with customers (which could be recognised in the form of a doubtful debts expense) as a separate line item adjacent to the revenue line.

Returning to the issue of **doubtful debts**, the amount recognised for doubtful debts is usually determined on the basis of past experience or, perhaps, of industry averages. As an illustration, assume that an organisation starts operations in January 2014 and by the end of June 2014 it has receivables of €100,000. It is very unlikely that all amounts owing by the credit customers (the receivables) will ultimately be received, and hence some allowance must be made for debts that might not be recovered. Various approaches may be adopted to calculate the allowance. For example, it may be assumed that, on average, 5 per cent of all credit customers within the particular industry will fail to pay their debts. Alternatively, reliance may be placed on an aged receivables listing. For example, an analysis of the amounts owing might show that the debts can be classified by age (see Table 13.1).

> **f.o.b. shipping point** An agreement whereby the price of a purchase typically includes the costs necessary to get the item to a certain transportation point, at which point title passes to the buyer.
>
> **f.o.b. destination** An agreement whereby the price of a purchase typically includes the costs necessary to get the item to a certain destination, at which place title to the goods passes to the buyer.
>
> **allowance for doubtful debts** Account that provides an estimate of the amount of the accounts receivable that will ultimately not be received.
>
> **doubtful debt** When it is considered to be doubtful that credit customers will pay the amounts due, a doubtful debts expense is recognised.

Table 13.1 Outstanding debts classified by age

Age	Amount
Less than one month old	€40,000
Between one month and two months old	€35,000
Between two months and three months old	€10,000
Between three months and four months old	€10,000
More than four months old	€5,000
Total	€100,000

Table 13.2 Calculation of allowance for doubtful debts

Age	Amount	Percentage	Allowance
Less than one month old	€40,000	1	€400
Between one month and two months old	€35,000	2	€700
Between two months and three months old	€10,000	3	€300
Between three months and four months old	€10,000	5	€500
More than four months old	€5,000	15	€750
Total	€100,000		€2,650

Drawing on past experience in the industry, we will assume that outstanding debts are uncollectable at the following percentages: 1 per cent of all debts less than one month old; 2 per cent of those between one month and two months old; 3 per cent of those between two months and three months old; 5 per cent of those between three months and four months old; and 15 per cent of those over four months old. The percentages are based on the general assumption that the longer the receivables have been outstanding the greater the likelihood that the credit customers will ultimately not pay the amounts that are due. With the above information, the allowance for doubtful debts can be calculated as shown in Table 13.2.

The accounting entry to recognise the allowance for doubtful debts and the associated expense as at 30 June 2014 (the year end) would be:

Dr	Doubtful debts expense	€2,650
Cr	Allowance for doubtful debts	€2,650

The allowance for doubtful debts would be shown as an offset against accounts receivable in the statement of financial position. That is, the allowance for doubtful debts is recognised as a **contra asset**. As the above accounting entry shows, when a doubtful debts expense is recognised, with a corresponding increase in the allowance for doubtful debts, there is no adjustment to the **accounts receivable** balance. Consequently, there is also no adjustment made to the accounts receivables' subsidiary ledger. The reason for this is that the allowance is recognised in anticipation of the likely non-recoverability of some of the amounts owing to the entity, although the identity of those who will not pay is unknown. Hence, no adjustment is made to the accounts receivables' control account, or the accounts receivables' subsidiary ledger.

contra asset Account that typically accumulates data from one period to the next, which is shown as a deduction from another related account.

accounts receivable Amounts owed to an entity by external parties generally as a result of the entity providing goods or services.

When it becomes known that a particular credit customer has, for example, become bankrupt and will not pay the amounts owing to the entity, there will be a reduction in the accounts receivable balance (and associated subsidiary ledger account) and the allowance for doubtful debts, since the amount has been anticipated within the allowance for doubtful debts. For example, if such a customer owes €500 when it goes bankrupt, and the likelihood of receiving any payment is considered minimal, the accounting entry would be:

Dr	Allowance for doubtful debts	€500
Cr	Accounts receivable	€500

Within the above entry there is no additional expense recognition, as the expense was recognised at the time the allowance was created or subsequently increased.

Alternatively, if an account receivable (credit customer) is considered unlikely to pay, but the amount has not been anticipated, the entity will recognise a bad debts expense. If such an account receivable owes €5,000 and is deemed unlikely to pay owing to bankruptcy or some similar occurrence, and it is also considered that the allowance for doubtful debts will be sufficient only to cover the other remaining accounts receivable, the accounting entry would be:

Dr	Bad debts expense	€5,000
Cr	Accounts receivable	€5,000

Typically, the bad debts expense account is used when an amount is expensed directly against accounts receivable and the amount has not been previously anticipated as a doubtful debt. As the total of the accounts receivable balance in the ledger account (or control account) must equal the balance of the individual customers' accounts in the accounts receivable subsidiary ledger, when a bad debts expense is recognised there will be a write-off of the amount in the accounts receivable subsidiary ledger. Interestingly, as a general principle, the UK taxation authorities will allow a deduction for taxation purposes only when there is an adjustment against the accounts receivable account, and not when the allowance for doubtful debts is initially credited.

In relation to disclosures of doubtful debts and **bad debts**, the amounts of allowances for doubtful debts (often referred to as provisions for doubtful debts—although this termi-nology is less frequently being used given the meanings now being attributed to provisions in IAS 37 *Provisions, Contingent Liabilities and Contingent Assets*) would be shown as deduc-tions from the classes of assets to which they relate. It would also be common to show separately the net expense in relation to bad and doubtful debts.

> **bad debts** The amount of expense recognised by writing off an amount that was receivable from a credit customer.

13.6   Accounting for sales with associated conditions

Evidence indicates that numerous companies have engaged in innovative transactions to generate revenues, some of which do not initially result in a transfer of economic benefits. With some transactions, considerable professional judgement must be exercised to determine whether revenue should be recognised and, if so, when it should be recognised. Transactions involving the sale of assets with conditions attached should be reviewed to assess whether control has actually passed from the seller to the purchaser and whether it is *probable* that the inflow of economic benefits to the seller will occur. For example, merchandise might be sold subject to reservation of title, whereby a stipulation is placed in the sales contract to the effect that ownership of the goods does not pass to the purchaser until the time of payment. The seller, while possessing legal title to the merchandise and therefore the right to reclaim the merchandise if the buyer defaults, has passed to the purchaser effective control over the future eco-nomic benefits embodied in the transferred merchandise. Recognition of the revenue would appear appropriate.

Goods or other assets might be sold subject to various other conditions, such as the existence of put or call options, a related leaseback or the right to return the assets. We will consider each of these conditions below.

13.6.1 Call and put options

A **call option** provides the holder of the option with the right to buy an asset at a specified **exercise price** on or before a specified date (in Chapter 12 we considered how to account for share options provided to employees—this type of option can be referred to as a call option). The party that writes the call option agrees to deliver a particular asset to the call-option buyer, if that buyer instructs the other party to do so. A call option is considered to have value when the value of the underlying asset exceeds the option's exercise price (when such an option is frequently described as 'being in the money'). Depending on the time period to expiration, an option might also have value even when the exercise price is above the current value of the underlying asset. However, if at exercise date the exercise price is above or equal to the market value of the asset, the option has no value.

> **call option** Provides the holder of the option with the right to buy an asset at a specified exercise price, on or before a specified date.

Therefore, if the market price of the underlying asset exceeds the exercise price at the date of expiration of the option, the buyer of the option would typically exercise the option leading to the delivery of the underlying asset. If the market value of the asset is below the exercise price at expiration of the call option, the buyer will not exercise the call option and the seller has no further liability.

A **put option**, by contrast, operates in the reverse manner to a call option. Its holder has the right to sell an asset at a specified exercise price on or before a specified date. The writer (or seller) of the put option agrees to buy the asset at a future date for the exercise price if the put-option holder (buyer) should request it. The holder of the put option (who may also be in possession of the underlying asset) would typically exercise the option (that is, require the other party to buy the underlying asset) only if the exercise price is above the market price. A put option guarantees holders a minimum price for their assets. These assets might perhaps be the production output of the option holder. If the market price of the underlying assets should fall below the exercise price, the put-option seller will lose the difference between the market value of the asset and the exercise price of the option.

> **exercise price** (or the **strike price**) The guaranteed transaction price stipulated in an option contract for an asset that may be bought or sold at some predetermined date in the future.

> **put option** Gives its holder the right to sell an asset at a specified exercise price on or before a specified date.

Where a transaction involves the concurrent use of a financial instrument such as an option (as discussed above), it is necessary to evaluate the conditions attaching to the transaction to establish whether, in substance, the transaction is a financing arrangement rather than a sale. For example, a purchaser/lender might 'acquire' assets with a call option attached as a means of securing collateral in respect of the 'sales' proceeds/borrowings, rather than by obtaining a mortgage over the assets. In such a case, the transaction constitutes a financing arrangement rather than a sale from the viewpoint of the vendor/borrower and would not give rise to revenue. In these circumstances, the inflow of economic benefits to the vendor/borrower in the form of 'sales' proceeds has resulted from an equivalent increase in liabilities, with the result that equity has not increased.

As an example of the situation described in the previous paragraph, assume that Homeowner plc requires some funds. Homeowner plc 'sells' its building (with a market value of £1,000,000) to The Bank for £800,000 with an attached call option that allows Homeowner plc to reacquire the building at a specified future date for a price of £900,000. As the market price of the building would be expected to exceed £900,000 at the expiration of the option, there is a high likelihood that Homeowner plc will reacquire the asset. In such a situation, it would appear incorrect to recognise the sale. What would probably happen is that Homeowner plc would receive £800,000 from The Bank and would subsequently pay The Bank £900,000—or total interest of £100,000. What some organisations have done in the past (perhaps somewhat *creatively*) is to undertake a transaction such as that described here and simply record the sale and the inflow of cash with no reference to the associated option. If the asset had been acquired some years earlier when the cost was lower than current market values, the entity might also record a profit on sale. Such a practice would be considered misleading as, in substance, what has happened is that Homeowner plc has simply borrowed funds, which it will subsequently repay together with some interest expenses. In reality, there is no 'sale' (and, hence, no profit on sale).

Paragraphs B40 to B42 of the Exposure Draft *Revenue from Contracts with Customers* (IASB 2011) provide guidance which requires that where the original owner of an asset has sold an asset, but also holds a call option that allows it to acquire the asset at a future date at a price less than the original selling price, then no revenue shall be recognised. However, should the option lapse, then revenue can be recognised (IASB 2011, paragraphs B40 to B42). Similarly, if an entity sells an asset to another organisation and the other organisation (customer) has a put option that requires the entity to acquire the asset at a price in excess of the original sale price then no revenue shall be recognised. As paragraphs B46 to B48 of IASB (2011) state:

> B46 *If the repurchase price of the asset exceeds the original selling price and is more than the expected market value of the asset, the contract is in effect a financing arrangement. Hence, an entity shall:*
>
> (a) *continue to recognise the asset; and*
> (b) *recognise a liability that initially shall be measured at the amount of the original selling price of the asset.*
>
> B47 *When comparing the repurchase price with the selling price, an entity shall consider the effects of the time value of money.*
>
> B48 *If the option lapses unexercised, an entity shall derecognise the liability and recognise revenue.*

13.6.2 Revenue recognition when right of return exists

Cash or credit sales present a special problem where there is a 'right of return'. Alternative accounting treatments available when the seller is exposed to the likelihood that assets will be returned could include:

- not recording the sale until all return privileges have expired;
- recording the sale but reducing sales by an estimate of future returns; or
- recording the sale and accounting for the returns as they occur in future periods.

The Exposure Draft *Revenue from Contracts with Customers* (IASB 2011) provides guidance. Paragraph B3 states:

> *To account for the transfer of products with a right of return (and for some services that are provided subject to a refund), an entity shall recognise all of the following:*
>
> (a) *revenue for the transferred products in the amount of consideration to which the entity is reasonably assured to be entitled (considering the products expected to be returned);*
> (b) *a refund liability; and*
> (c) *an asset (and corresponding adjustment to cost of sales) for its right to recover products from customers on settling the refund liability.*

As noted above, the revenue to be recognised is that to which it 'is reasonably assured to be entitled'. See earlier discussion of this term if you require clarification.

Where the entity does not meet the criteria as set out in paragraph 81 (prior experience with similar obligations which enables it to predict the amount of consideration), then no revenue would be recognised. As paragraph B5 of IASB (2011) states:

> *For any amounts to which an entity is not reasonably assured to be entitled, the entity shall not recognise revenue when it transfers products to customers but shall recognise any consideration received as a refund liability. Subsequently, the entity shall update its assessment of amounts to which the entity is reasonably assured to be*

entitled in exchange for the transferred products and shall recognise corresponding adjustments to the amount of revenue recognised.

As noted above, where a sale with a right of return is made, then revenue, a refund liability and an asset relating to the right to recover the product could be recognised. In relation to these assets and liabilities, paragraphs B6 and B7 of IASB (2011) state:

> B6 *An entity shall update the measurement of the refund liability at the end of each reporting period for changes in expectations about the amount of refunds. An entity shall recognise corresponding adjustments as revenue (or reductions of revenue).*

> B7 *An asset recognised for an entity's right to recover products from a customer on settling a refund liability initially shall be measured by reference to the former carrying amount of the inventory less any expected costs to recover those products (including potential decreases in the value to the entity of returned products). Subsequently, an entity shall update the measurement of the asset to correspond with changes in the measurement of the refund liability. An entity shall present the asset separately from the refund liability.*

Worked Example 13.1 provides an illustration of a sale where a right of return exists. This example has been adapted from an illustration provided in IASB (2011).

Worked Example 13.1 — Sale with a right of return

An entity sells 100 products for £100 each. Sales are made for cash, rather than on credit terms. The entity's customary business practice is to allow a customer to return any unused product within 30 days and receive a full refund. The cost of each product is £60. To determine the transaction price, the entity decides that the approach that is most predictive of the amount of consideration to which the entity will be entitled is the most likely amount. Using the most likely amount, the entity estimates that three products will be returned. The entity's experience is predictive of the amount of consideration to which the entity will be entitled. The entity estimates that the costs of recovering the products will be immaterial and expects that the returned products can be resold at a profit.

Required

Provide the accounting entries to record the sale and the subsequent return of the assets, assuming that the returns occur in accordance with expectations.

Solution

Upon transfer of control of the products, the entity would not recognise revenue for the three products that it expects to be returned. Consequently, the entity would recognise:

(a) Revenue of £9,700 (£100 × 97 products expected not to be returned).
(b) A refund liability for £300 (£100 refund × 3 products expected to be returned).
(c) An asset of £180 (£60 × 3 products) for its right to recover products from customers on settling the refund liability. Hence, the amount recognised in cost of sales for 97 products is £5,820 (£60 × 97).

The accounting entries would be:

Dr	Cash	£10,000	
Cr	Revenue		£9,700
Cr	Refund liability		£300
(to recognise the initial sale)			
Dr	Cost of goods sold	£5,820	
Dr	Right to recover	£180	
Cr	Inventory		£6,000
(to recognise the transfer of inventory to the customer)			
Dr	Refund liability	£300	
Cr	Cash		£300
(to recognise the refund provided to the customer when the goods are ultimately returned)			
Dr	Inventory	£180	
Cr	Right to recover		£180
(to place the returned assets back into inventory)			

13.6.3 Sale and leaseback

Entities may enter into transactions whereby non-monetary assets are 'sold' and simultaneously leased back to the vendor, frequently by way of a long-run, non-cancellable lease. The substance of these sale and leaseback transactions is that, although legal ownership of the leased property has been transferred to the purchaser/lessor, the vendor/lessee would normally retain control of the future economic benefits embodied in the leased property by virtue of the lease agreement. Because control of the asset has not been transferred, it would be inappropriate to recognise revenue. The vendor/lessee has, in effect, entered into a financing arrangement whereby the leased property has been used as collateral for a loan. Payments made by the vendor/lessee under the lease will ensure that the purchaser/lessor recoups the investment in the lease and receives an appropriate return on the investment. The transaction does not constitute a sale and does not give rise to revenue, since the inflow of economic benefits in the form of the proceeds from disposal has resulted from an equivalent increase in liabilities (a lease payable), with the result that there has been no increase in equity. Consistent with this, any gain on a sale and leaseback transaction, where the lease is deemed to be a financial lease, should be amortised to the statement of comprehensive income over the term of the lease rather than recognising the profit at the point of sale. Accounting for leases is considered in detail in Chapter 10.

13.7　Interest and dividends

13.7.1 Interest revenue

The recognition of **interest revenue** is usually straightforward, with the revenue being recognised over time, as the borrower has the benefit of the borrowings and the lender establishes claims for interest earned. If the borrower prepays interest, the inflow of future economic benefits represented by the prepayment would not constitute an item of revenue to the lender because the lender has a present obligation (a liability) to the borrower to provide finance for the period to which the prepayment relates. Interest received in advance would be considered to represent a liability.

> **interest revenue**
> Revenue derived as a result of lending resources to another entity.

On occasion, interest revenues are implicit in the terms of a transaction. Where, for example, goods are sold on extended credit, the vendor is effectively financing the purchaser. Arguably, the purchase consideration should be discounted to determine the amount of the sales revenue and the amount of the debt financing on which future interest revenues will be earned. The transaction gives rise to two forms of revenue:

1. sales revenue—the present value of the future payments;
2. interest revenue from financing activities.

To estimate the present value of the proceeds, an applicable interest rate inherent in the agreement must be determined. As already indicated, in relation to interest, IASB (2011, paragraph 61) states:

> To adjust the promised amount of consideration to reflect the time value of money, an entity shall use the discount rate that would be reflected in a separate financing transaction between the entity and its customer at contract inception. That rate would reflect the credit characteristics of the party receiving financing in the contract as well as any collateral or security provided by the customer or the entity, which might include assets transferred in the contract. An entity may be able to determine that rate by identifying the rate that discounts the nominal amount of the promised consideration to the cash selling price of the good or service. After contract inception, an entity shall not update the discount rate for changes in circumstances or interest rates.

Where the gross method is used, it is typical for the unearned interest to be offset, for statement of financial position purposes, against the total of the note receivable, showing it as a contra asset. The net amount for receivables under the gross method thus equates to the amount shown using the net-interest method. Worked Example 13.2 provides an illustration of accounting for interest revenue using the net and gross method.

13.7.2 Dividend revenue

The recognition of dividend revenues is complicated by its discretionary nature. Dividends do not accrue over time, but usually result from a decision of the board of directors or another governing body of the dividend-paying entity. Although a final dividend is usually subject to ratification by the ownership group, the receiving entity should recognise revenues when the inflow of future economic benefits *is considered probable and when it can be measured reliably*. If a dividend needs final approval, perhaps at a meeting of shareholders, then the dividend revenue should not be recognised until such time that the dividend has been approved (or ratified).

Worked Example 13.2 Recognition of interest inherent in a sales transaction

On 1 July 2014 Cassie plc sells a computer to Ted plc. The computer cost Cassie plc €9,000. Rather than selling the item for a cash price or a short-term claim for cash of €12,009, Cassie plc accepts a promissory note that requires Ted plc to make three annual payments of €5,000 each, the first one to be made on 30 June 2015. The difference between the gross receipts and the current sales price represents interest revenue to be earned by Cassie plc over the period of the note. The rate implicit in the arrangement is 12 per cent which is also the rate Cassie plc charges other customers when goods are sold on extended credit terms. (The present value of an annuity of €1 for three years discounted at 12 per cent is €2.4018. Refer to the present value tables provided in Appendix A and Appendix B.)

Required

Provide the journal entries for Cassie plc for the years ended 30 June 2015, 2016 and 2017 using:

(a) the net-interest method
(b) the gross method

Solution

To provide the journal entries, we need to determine the interest component of each €5,000 payment. The easiest way to do this is to draw up a table, as shown below. The interest element is calculated by multiplying the opening liability for a period by the rate of interest implicit in the arrangement (in this case 12 per cent).

Date	Cash payment	Opening liability	Interest revenue at 12%	Principal reduction	Outstanding balance
	€	€	€	€	€
01 July 2014					12,009
30 June 2015	5,000	12,009	1,441	3,559	8,450
30 June 2016	5,000	8,450	1,014	3,986	4,464
30 June 2017	5,000	4,464	536	4,464	0
	15,000		2,991	12,009	

Interest revenue equals the outstanding liability at the beginning of the financial period multiplied by the interest rate implicit in the agreement, which in this example is 12 per cent. This approach is often referred to as the effective-interest method. The reduction in the principal is calculated by subtracting the interest revenue from the cash payment.

(a) Journal entries using the net-interest method

1 July 2014

Dr	Note receivable	€12,009	
Cr	Sales		€12,009

Dr	Cost of sales	€9,000	
Cr	Inventory		€9,000

(to record the initial sale on 1 July 2014)

30 June 2015

Dr	Cash	€5,000	
Cr	Note receivable		€3,559
Cr	Interest revenue		€1,441

(to record the receipt of €5,000 on 30 June 2015)

30 June 2016

Dr	Cash	€5,000	
Cr	Note receivable		€3,986
Cr	Interest revenue		€1,014

(to record the receipt of €5,000 on 30 June 2016)

30 June 2017

Dr	Cash	€5,000	
Cr	Note receivable		€4,464
Cr	Interest revenue		€536

(to record the receipt of €5,000 on 30 June 2017)

(b) Journal entries using the gross method

1 July 2014

Dr	Note receivable	€15,000	
Cr	Sales		€12,009
Cr	Unearned interest		€2,991

Dr	Cost of sales	€9,000	
Cr	Inventory		€9,000

(to record the initial sale on 1 July 2014; unearned interest would be disclosed as a deduction against note receivable)

30 June 2015

Dr	Cash	€5,000	
Cr	Note receivable		€5,000

Dr	Unearned interest	€1,441	
Cr	Interest revenue		€1,441

(to record the receipt of €5,000 on 30 June 2015)

30 June 2016

Dr	Cash	€5,000	
Cr	Note receivable		€5,000

Dr	Unearned interest	€1,014	
Cr	Interest revenue		€1,014

(to record the receipt of €5,000 on 30 June 2016)

30 June 2017

Dr	Cash	€5,000	
Cr	Note receivable		€5,000

Dr	Unearned interest	€536	
Cr	Interest revenue		€536

(to record the receipt of €5,000 on 30 June 2017)

In considering dividends being received, one issue that warrants consideration is whether dividends received out of profits earned by the investee before the investment was made (that is, dividends paid after the investment is made but which are sourced from the pre-acquisition profits of the investee) should be treated as revenue by the investor. Or, alternatively, do we treat dividends paid from pre-acquisition profits as a reduction in the cost of the investment?

A dividend from pre-acquisition profits will typically occur when an investor acquires an interest in another company and the shares have been acquired 'cum div'—the term used to refer to shares being bought with a dividend entitlement. If an entity pays dividends out of profits earned before the acquisition, it is, in effect, returning part of the net assets originally acquired by the acquirer.

An obvious issue is, how do we account for a dividend paid by an investee (which is the organisation in which the reporting entity has shares) out of pre-acquisition profits? Do we treat it as income in the financial statements of the reporting entity or, instead, as a reduction in the cost of the investment?

Under IFRS 9, dividends on investments held for trading, and investments in equity instruments, are recognised when the entity's right to receive the payment of dividend is established. However, IFRS 9 notes that, while the dividends are to be recognised in profit or loss, this will not be the case if the dividend clearly represents a recovery of part of the cost of the investment. Therefore if dividends are received from pre-acquisition earnings, then they shall be treated as a reduction in the cost of the investment. See the support material for this chapter for a discussion of the changes in the accounting treatment of dividend revenue over the past decade.

13.8 Unearned revenue

It is not unusual for entities to receive funds for products or services in advance of actually providing the related goods or services. Common examples would include rent or interest received in advance, or the receipt of consulting fees in advance of the provision of services. Since the services or resources have not been provided to the customer, the receipts have not been *earned* and the customer would not be deemed to be in control of the goods or services. The receipts do not constitute revenue but instead are termed **unearned revenue** and considered liabilities. The entity would be under a present obligation to transfer future economic benefits at a future date. As paragraph 105 of IASB (2011) states:

> **unearned revenue**
> When assets are received by a business for services to be performed at a future date.

> *If a customer pays consideration or an amount of consideration is due before an entity performs by transferring a good or service, the entity shall present the contract as a contract liability. A contract liability is an entity's obligation to transfer goods or services to a customer for which the entity has received consideration from the customer.*

Worked Example 13.3 provides an example of the treatment of revenue received in advance.

Worked Example 13.3 Revenue received in advance

Renter Company rents out some premises to Tenant plc. Tenant plc pays its rent three months in advance and makes the first payment on 1 May 2015. The rent is £2,000 per month. Renter Company has a 30 June reporting date.

Required
Provide the accounting entries to record the receipt of the cash, and the subsequent reporting date adjustment.

Solution
1 May 2015

Dr	Cash at bank	£6,000	
Cr	Rent received in advance (current liability)		£6,000

(to recognise the receipt of the rental income; as the amount has been received in advance, it is credited to the liability account rent received in advance)

30 June 2015

Dr	Rent received in advance	£4,000	
Cr	Rental income		£4,000

(to recognise two months' rent earned in 2015 and to reduce the balance of the liability account rent received in advance; a balance of £2,000 would remain in rent received in advance and would be shown in the statement of financial position as a liability)

13.9 Accounting for construction contracts

Where construction projects such as buildings, ships, major roads, bridges, dams, pipelines and tunnels take several financial periods to complete, a number of accounting issues arise. For example, should revenue be recognised progressively throughout the contract (that is, at point 5 in Figure 13.1) and, if so, how would the quantum of the revenue be determined? It seems reasonable to assume that firms would prefer to recognise revenue throughout the period of a long-term project, rather than having to defer revenue recognition until project completion, which might take many years. If a firm has a small number of long-term contracts, deferral of revenue recognition until the completion of the projects would result in great volatility of reported revenues and related profits or losses. This might be a problem, particularly if the firm has accounting-based contracts in place that rely on such measures as the number of times that interest expense is covered by profits. Further, it could be argued that the results of the period do not reflect the activities and work undertaken if revenues from multi-period contracts are deferred until project completion.

The relevant international accounting standard is IAS 11 *Construction Contracts*. This standard provides rules for determining the reported value of partly completed construction projects and for deciding when the associated revenues and expenses should be recognised. However, as indicated previously in this chapter, when the new accounting standard entitled *Revenue from Contracts with Customers* is finally released—which is expected to happen late in 2012 (and to be applicable after 2015)—both IAS 11 and IAS 18 will be withdrawn. To the extent that a **construction contract** provides the customer with control of the asset under construction, the requirements in the new accounting standard applicable beyond 2015 will generally be consistent with the requirements that have been in place for several years pursuant to IAS 11. However, for those entities that recognise revenue throughout construction-type contracts even though 'ownership rights' are not continuously transferred to the customer—that is, even though the customer does not control the asset being constructed—the accounting requirements proposed in IASB (2011) would preclude the recognition of revenue until the inventory transfers to the customer. For such entities, this might differ significantly from present accounting practice.

> **construction contract**
> Contract relating to the construction of an asset or a combination of assets that are closely interrelated in terms of design, technology, function or use.

The following discussion will be based on the requirements expected to be in place when the new accounting standard *Revenue from Contracts with Customers* is released. Again, to the extent that the customer has control of the asset being constructed, then the new requirements will generally be consistent with the requirements that have been embodied for a number of years within IAS 11 *Construction Contracts*.

In accounting for construction contracts, individual construction contracts would be accounted for separately and the relevant accounting requirements would be applied separately to each contract. If a construction contract carries over across a number of accounting periods, then there will be a need to determine the appropriate revenue and costs to be allocated to each accounting period.

For each separate performance obligation (and the performance obligation might relate to a specific construction) that an entity satisfies over time, an entity shall recognise revenue over time by measuring the progress towards complete satisfaction of that performance obligation. The objective when measuring progress is to depict the transfer of control of goods or services to the customer—that is, to depict an entity's performance. As circumstances change over time, an entity shall update its measure of progress to depict the entity's performance completed to date. Such changes would be accounted for as a change in accounting estimate in accordance with IAS 8 *Accounting Policies, Changes in Accounting Estimates and Errors*.

Pursuant to IASB (2011), and in accordance with the objective of measuring progress towards completing the project, an entity shall exclude from a measure of progress any goods or services for which the entity does not transfer control to the customer. For each separate performance obligation satisfied over time, an entity shall apply a method of measuring progress on the contract. Appropriate methods of measuring progress include output methods and input methods. Paragraphs 41 to 46 of IASB (2011) describe output and input measures of performance:

Output methods

41   *Output methods recognise revenue on the basis of direct measurements of the value to the customer of the goods or services transferred to date (for example, surveys of performance completed to date, appraisals of results achieved, milestones reached or units produced) and can be the most faithful depiction of the entity's performance.*

42   *If an entity has a right to invoice a customer in an amount that corresponds directly with the value to the customer of the entity's performance completed to date (for example, a services contract in which an entity bills a fixed amount for each hour of service provided), the entity shall recognise revenue in the amount to which the entity has a right to invoice.*

43   *A disadvantage of output methods is that they are often not directly observable and the information required to apply them may not be available to the entity without undue cost. Hence, an input method may be necessary.*

Input methods

44   *Input methods recognise revenue on the basis of the entity's efforts or inputs to the satisfaction of a performance obligation (for example, resources consumed, labour hours expended, costs incurred, time lapsed or machine hours used) relative to the total expected inputs to the satisfaction of that performance obligation.*

If the entity's efforts or inputs are expended evenly throughout the performance period, it may be appropriate for an entity to recognise revenue on a straight-line basis.

45   *A shortcoming of input methods is that there may not be a direct relationship between the entity's inputs and the transfer of control of goods or services to the customer because of inefficiencies in the entity's performance or other factors. Hence, when using an input method, an entity shall exclude the effects of any inputs that do not depict the transfer of control of goods or services to the customer (for example, the costs of wasted materials, labour or other resources to fulfil the contract that were not reflected in the price of the contract).*

46   *When applying an input method to a separate performance obligation that includes goods that the customer obtains control of significantly before receiving services related to those goods, the best depiction of the entity's performance may be for the entity to recognise revenue for the transferred goods in an amount equal to the costs of those goods if both of the following conditions are present at contract inception:*

   (a)   the cost of the transferred goods is significant relative to the total expected costs to completely satisfy the performance obligation; and
   (b)   the entity procures the goods from another entity and is not significantly involved in designing and manu-facturing the goods (but the entity is acting as a principal in accordance with paragraphs B16–B19).

IASB (2011) also requires that an entity shall recognise revenue for a performance obligation satisfied over time only if the entity can reasonably measure its progress towards complete satisfaction of the performance obligation. An entity would not be able to reasonably measure its progress towards complete satisfaction of a performance obligation if it lacks reliable information that would be required to apply an appropriate method of measuring progress. Further, in some circumstances (for example, in the early stages of a contract), an entity may not be able to reasonably measure the outcome of a performance obligation, but the entity expects to recover the costs incurred in satisfying the performance obligation. In those circumstances, the entity shall rec-ognise revenue only to the extent of the costs incurred until such time that it can reasonably measure the out-come of the performance obligation.

For a number of years, IAS 11 *Construction Contracts* (which, as we have noted a num-ber of times, is expected to be withdrawn from 2015) has required contractors, if certain criteria are satisfied, to use the **percentage-of-completion method** to account for their construction contracts. With the percentage-of-completion method (also referred to as the **stage-of-completion method**), profit on a construction contract is recognised in proportion to the work performed in each reporting period in which construction occurs. This would reflect an 'input measure' of progress and would be acceptable under the new accounting standard expected to be released in late 2012/early 2013.

Under the percentage-of-completion method, which many organisations within the construction industry use, construction costs plus gross profit earned to date are accu-mulated in an account that might be identified as 'construction-in-progress'. Pursuant to IASB (2011), this would be considered to be a contract asset. When invoices are sent to the customer in accordance with the contract, then part of the construction-in-progress account would be transferred to accounts receivable.

> **percentage-of-completion method (or stage-of-completion method)** Where profits are recognised each period based upon the progress of construction. Represents an input method for measuring the progress towards completing a contract with a customer.

Construction contracts can be of two general types: fixed-price contracts and cost-plus contracts. Fixed-price contracts are contracts in which a price is set (fixed) at the commencement of the project, whereas a cost-plus contract will require the customer to pay the project costs (however determined in the construction contract) plus a percentage on top of that (for example, the contract cost might be 'cost plus 20 per cent'). The type of contract determines the conditions that must be satisfied to use the percentage-of-completion method. The percentage-of-completion method can be used for a fixed-price contract when all of the following conditions are satisfied:

(a)   total contract revenue can be measured reliably;
(b)   it is probable that the economic benefits associated with the contract will flow to the entity;
(c)   both the contract costs to complete the contract and the stage of contract completion at the end of the reporting period can be measured reliably; and
(d)   the contract costs attributable to the contract can be clearly identified and measured reliably so that actual costs incurred can be compared with prior estimates.

For a cost-plus contract, the percentage-of-completion method would be used when both of the following con-ditions are satisfied:

(a)   it is probable that the economic benefits associated with the contract will flow to the entity; and
(b)   the contract costs attributable to the contract, whether or not specifically reimbursable, can be clearly iden-tified and measured reliably.

If the conditions described above are not satisfied, no profit is to be brought to account until they are satisfied. At the extreme, this will mean no profit may be recognised until project completion. Where the outcome of a construction contract cannot be estimated reliably or where the stage of completion cannot be reliably assessed, costs incurred on the contract are to be recognised as expenses and revenue is to be recognised only to the extent that the costs incurred are recoverable.

In order to apply the percentage-of-completion method, the firm must have some basis or standard for measuring the progress towards completion at particular interim dates (such as financial year ends). This is discussed in what follows.

13.9.1 Measuring progress towards completion

The percentage of completion can be measured in a number of ways, for example by:

(a) the proportion that contract costs incurred for work performed to date bear to the estimated total contract costs (an input method);
(b) surveys of work performed (an output method); or
(c) completion of a physical proportion of the contract work (an output method).

Other indicators, such as progress payments made by the customer, would often not reflect the extent of work performed on a contract and hence would not typically be used as a measure of performance.

On the cost basis (option (a) above), the percentage of completion is measured by comparing costs incurred to date with the most recent estimate of the total costs to complete the contract. Care must be taken in recognising when costs are incurred and which costs are attributable to a specific project. When the percentage of contract completion is measured using the cost basis, adjustments have to be made to include only those costs that reflect work performed. When the stage of completion is determined by reference to the contract costs incurred to date, only those contract costs that reflect work performed are included in costs incurred to date. Examples of contract costs that would be excluded are:

(a) contract costs that relate to future activity on the contract, such as costs of materials that have been delivered to a contract site or set aside for use in a contract but not yet installed, used or applied during contract performance, unless the materials have been made specially for the contract; and
(b) payments made to subcontractors in advance of work performed under the subcontract.

The costs incurred on construction contracts can be divided into:
  (i) Costs related directly to a specific contract, such as direct materials, direct labour, depreciation of plant and equipment used on a contract, costs of moving plant and equipment to and from a site, expected warranty costs, costs of design and technical assistance that are directly related to the contract, costs of securing a contract, and costs of hiring plant and equipment used in the construction activity.
  (ii) Costs that are attributable to contract activity in general and are capable of being allocated on a reasonable basis to specific contracts, such as tender preparation, insurance, design and technical assistance, and project overheads.
  (iii) Costs that relate to the activities of the reporting entity generally or that relate to contract activity generally and are not normally related to specific contracts, such as general administrative and selling costs, finance costs, research and development costs that are not directly related to the contract, and depreciation of idle plant and equipment that is not used in the contract concerned.

Costs of the type described in (i) and (ii) above are normally included as part of accumulated contract costs, whereas costs of type (iii) are usually excluded from accumulated contract costs—and treated as costs of the period—because they do not relate to reaching the present stage of completion of a specific contract. Further, any costs that are considered to be 'wasted' would also be excluded from being recognised as part of the contract costs carried forward. As paragraph 93 of IASB (2011) states:

An entity shall recognise the following costs as expenses when incurred:

(a) general and administrative costs (unless those costs are explicitly chargeable to the customer under the contract;
(b) costs of wasted materials, labour or other resources to fulfil the contract that were not reflected in the price of the contract;
(c) costs that relate to satisfied performance obligations (or partially satisfied performance obligations) in the contract (ie costs that relate to past performance); and

(d) costs that relate to remaining performance obligations but that the entity cannot distinguish from costs that relate to satisfied performance obligations.

Under the cost method, the percentage of completion is measured by comparing costs incurred to date—which satisfy the criteria for recognition—with the most recent estimate of the total costs to complete the contract as shown in the following formula:

$$\text{Percentage complete} = \frac{\text{Costs incurred to the end of current period}}{\text{Most recent estimate of total costs}}$$

For example, if it is considered that a contract will cost €10 million to complete (and we exclude costs of the type described in (iii) above) and if the costs incurred to date amount to €8.5 million, using the cost basis the contract would be considered 85 per cent complete.

The percentage represented by 'incurred costs' of total estimated costs is applied to the total revenue or estimated total gross profit on the contract to arrive at the revenue and the gross profit amounts to be recognised to date. The amounts of revenue and gross profit recognised each year are computed using the following formula:

$$\begin{aligned}\text{Current period revenue or gross profit} = \ &(\text{Estimated total revenue or gross profit from the contract}) \\ &\times (\text{Percentage complete}) \\ &- (\text{Total revenue or gross profit recognised in prior periods})\end{aligned}$$

In considering the revenue related to the construction contract, the revenue is to be measured at the fair value of the consideration received or receivable by the contractor. Where the revenue is paid in cash, the revenue will be measured at its face value. Where other goods or services are provided to the contractor in full or partial fulfilment of the contract price, fair values must be determined.

13.9.2 Journal entries for construction contract accounting

When the percentage-of-completion method is used to account for a long-term construction contract, the following journal entries are representative of those that would typically be employed:

Dr Construction-in-progress (also referred to as 'contract asset') €XXX
Cr Materials, cash, payables, accumulated depreciation, etc. €XXX
(to record cost of construction)

Dr Accounts receivable €XXX
Cr Construction-in-progress (contract asset) €XXX
(to record progress billings; billings would be shown as an offset against construction-in-progress)

Dr Cash €XXX
Cr Accounts receivable €XXX
(to record collections of billings)

Dr Construction-in-progress (contract asset) €XXX
Dr Construction expenses (costs incurred) €XXX
Cr Revenue from long-term project €XXX
(to recognise contract revenue and contract expenses)

Because of the uncertainty inherent in estimating costs to complete a project, particularly during the early stages of the work on a contract, it is common practice for entities to carry the project at cost and to adopt the percentage-of-completion method only after the contract has reached a given percentage of completion.

13.9.3 Presentation requirements

When a reporting entity has entered into a contract with a customer—including a long-term construction contract—then when either party to the contract has performed, the reporting entity might present the contract in the statement of financial position as either a *contract liability*, a contract asset or a receivable depending on the relationship between the entity's performance and the customer's payment. In explaining this, and as previously

indicated in this chapter, paragraph 105 of IASB (2011) identifies when a contract liability should be recognised. It states:

> If a customer pays consideration or an amount of consideration is due before an entity performs by transferring a good or service, the entity shall present the contract as a contract liability. A contract liability is an entity's obligation to transfer goods or services to a customer for which the entity has received consideration from the customer.

Therefore, if progress billings exceed the gross amount of construction work-in-progress (the contract asset), the net amount should be shown as a liability; otherwise it is disclosed as an asset. Conversely, if the reporting entity transfers control of an asset to a customer before the customer pays, then an asset shall be recognised which might be either a 'contract asset' or a receivable. Paragraph 106 defines 'contract asset' and 'receivable' in this instance:

(a) A contract asset is an entity's right to consideration in exchange for goods or services that the entity has transferred to a customer, when that right is conditioned on something other than the passage of time (for example, the entity's future performance).
(b) A receivable is an entity's right to consideration that is unconditional. A right to consideration is unconditional if nothing other than the passage of time is required before payment of that consideration is due.

While the above paragraph refers to receivables and contract assets, there is nothing to prohibit an entity from using alternative descriptions in the statement of financial position for those items. If an entity uses an alternative description for a contract asset, the entity shall provide sufficient information for a user of the financial statements to distinguish between unconditional rights to consideration (i.e. receivables) and conditional rights to consideration (i.e. contract assets).

Now that you have read the discussion of the percentage-of-completion method, look at Worked Examples 13.4 and 13.5, which describe the practical application of the method.

Worked Example 13.4 — Percentage-of-completion method

MR plc commences construction of a wave-making machine on 1 July 2014 for Merewether plc. It signs a fixed-price contract for total revenues of €20 million. The project is expected to be completed by the end of 2017. The expected total cost, as estimated at the commencement of construction, is €16 million. The expected costs to complete a construction project can change throughout the project (in this example, they do). The following data relates to the project:

	2015 (€000)	2016 (€000)	2017 (€000)
Costs for the year	4,000	8,000	5,500
Costs incurred to date	4,000	12,000	17,500
Estimated costs to complete	12,000	5,000	–
Progress billings during the year	4,500	8,500	7,000
Cash collected during the year	3,500	7,500	9,000

MR plc uses the percentage-of-completion method to account for its construction contracts. The asset under construction is deemed to be under the control of Merewether plc throughout the period of construction.

Required

(a) Compute the gross profit to be recognised for each of the three years.
(b) Prepare the journal entries for 2015.
(c) Prepare the statement of financial position presentation for 2015 and 2016.

Solution

(a) Computing the gross profit

	2015 (€000)	2016 (€000)	2017 (€000)
Contract price	20,000	20,000	20,000
less Estimated cost:			
– Costs to date	4,000	12,000	17,500
– Estimated costs to complete	12,000	5,000	–
– Estimated total cost	16,000	17,000	17,500
Estimated total gross profit	4,000	3,000	2,500
Percentage complete (%)	25	70.6	100
Gross profit recognised in:			
2015 €4 million × 25 per cent	€1,000		
2016 €3 million × 70.6 per cent		€2,118	
less Gross profit already recognised		(€1,000)	
Gross profit in 2016		€1,118	
2017 €2.5 million × 100 per cent			€2,500
less Gross profit already recognised			(€2,118)
Gross profit in 2017			€382

The sum of the profits recognised in each year equals €2.5 million (€1 million + €1.118 million + €382,000), which is the total profit of the contract (i.e. €20 million less €17.5 million).

(b) Journal entries for 2015

Dr Construction-in-progress (contract asset)   €4,000,000
Cr Materials, cash, payables, accumulated depreciation, etc.   €4,000,000
(to recognise the costs associated with the contract)

Dr Construction-in-progress (contract asset)   €1,000,000
Dr Construction expenses (statement of comprehensive income)   €4,000,000
Cr Revenue from long-term contract (statement of comprehensive income)   €5,000,000
(for the year, and based on the percentage-of-completion 25% of the project has been completed; 25% of the total expected revenue of €20,000,000 is €5,000,000)

Dr Accounts receivable   €4,500,000
Cr Construction-in-progress (contract asset)   €4,500,000
(amount payable unconditionally by the customer. Substitutes an account receivable in place of the contract asset as the entity has transferred control of the contract asset to the customer)

Dr Cash   €3,500,000
Cr Accounts receivable   €3,500,000
(amount received from customer)

(c) Extract from the statement of financial position for 2015 and 2016

	2015 (€000)	2016 (€000)
Current assets		
Accounts receivable	1,000	2,000
Construction-in-progress (contract asset)	500	1,118

| Worked Example 13.5 | Construction contract where outcome cannot be reliably estimated |

Assume the same facts as in Worked Example 13.4, but this time MR plc cannot reliably estimate the outcome of the construction contract.

Required

(a) Compute the gross profit to be recognised for each of the three years.
(b) Prepare the journal entries for 2015.
(c) Prepare the statement of financial position presentation for 2015 and 2016.

Solution

(a) Gross profit for the three years

	2015 (€000)	2016 (€000)	2017 (€000)
Gross profit to be recognised	–	–	2,500

If the stage of completion or the outcome of the construction contract cannot be reliably estimated, profit should be deferred until such time as reliable estimates can be made. At the extreme, profit recognition may be deferred until project completion. Throughout the contract, contract costs would be recognised as an expense when incurred and revenue would be recognised to the extent of the costs incurred.

(b) Journal entries for 2015

Dr	Construction-in-progress (contract asset)	€4,000,000
Cr	Materials, cash, payables, accumulated depreciation, etc.	€4,000,000

(to recognise the costs associated with the contract)

Dr	Construction expenses	€4,000,000
Cr	Revenue from long-term contract	€4,000,000

(because the stage of completion is not clear, revenue recognition is restricted to the amount of cost incurred)

Dr	Accounts receivable	€4,500,000
Cr	Construction-in-progress (contract asset)	€4,500,000

(amount payable unconditionally by the customer)

Dr	Cash	€3,500,000
Cr	Accounts receivable	€3,500,000

(amount received from customer)

Dr	Construction-in-progress (contract asset)	€500,000
Cr	Contract liability—excess of the amount received from the customer over performance completed	€500,000

(this is an adjustment to reclassify the balance of the contract asset to a contract liability given that the amount billed to the customer exceeds the cost of the work completed to date; prior to this entry, the contract asset had a credit balance of €500,000)

(c) Extracts from the statement of financial position for 2015 and 2016

	2015 (€000)	2016 (€000)
Current assets		
Accounts receivable	1,000	2,000
Current liabilities		
Progress billings in excess of costs incurred on construction contracts (contract liability)	500	1,000

13.9.4 Accounting for long-term contract losses

When current estimates of total contract costs and revenues for any contract indicate that a loss is probable, provision should be made immediately for the foreseeable loss on the contract, regardless of the amount of work already performed. The losses should be brought to account as soon as they are foreseeable. Where a contract becomes likely to generate more in costs than it does in revenue, this is now being referred to as an 'onerous performance obligation' (IASB 2011). A performance obligation is considered onerous—and this does not just apply to construction contracts but also to contracts with customers in general—if the lowest cost of settling the performance obligation exceeds the amount of the transaction price allocated to that performance obligation. An entity would recognise a liability and a corresponding expense if the performance obligation is considered to be 'onerous'. In terms of how a reporting entity would measure an onerous performance obligation, paragraph 88 of IASB (2011) states:

> An entity shall initially measure the liability for an onerous performance obligation at the amount by which the lowest cost of settling the remaining performance obligation exceeds the amount of the transaction price allocated to that remaining performance obligation. At each reporting date, an entity shall update the measurement of the liability for an onerous performance obligation for changes in circumstances. An entity shall recognise changes in the measurement of that liability as an expense or as a reduction of an expense. When an entity satisfies an onerous performance obligation, the entity shall derecognise the related liability.

An entity would present a liability for onerous performance obligations separately from contract assets or contract liabilities. Relating some of the above discussion to long-term construction contracts, where there is an expected loss on a contract—when total contract costs exceed total contract revenue—an expense and related liability shall be recognised regardless of:

- whether work has commenced on the project;
- the stage of completion of the activity; or
- the difference between total contract costs and total contract revenue expected to arise from other construction contracts.

Worked Example 13.6 considers recognition of a loss using the percentage-of-completion method.

Worked Example 13.6 Percentage of completion with recognition of a loss

Assume the same facts as in Worked Example 13.4, except that, in this example, it becomes evident at the end of the 2016 financial period that the total costs to complete the project have risen to €21 million, which means that a net loss of €1 million will be incurred. Remember, this is a 'fixed-price' contract. The revised cost data is as follows:

	2015 (€000)	2016 (€000)	2017 (€000)
Costs for the year	4,000	8,000	9,000
Costs incurred to date	4,000	12,000	21,000
Estimated costs to complete	12,000	9,000	–
Progress billings during the year	4,500	8,500	7,000
Cash collected during the year	3,500	7,500	9,000

MR plc uses the percentage-of-completion method to account for its contracts.

Required

(a) Compute the gross profit to be recognised for each of the three years.
(b) Provide the journal entries for 2015 and 2016.

◄ Solution

(a) Gross profits for the three years

	2015 (€000)	2016 (€000)	2017 (€000)
Contract price	20,000	20,000	20,000
less Estimated cost:			
– Costs to date	4,000	12,000	21,000
– Estimated costs to complete	12,000	9,000	–
– Estimated total cost	16,000	21,000	21,000
Estimated total gross profit/(loss)	4,000	(1,000)	(1,000)
Percentage complete (%)	25	57.1	100
Gross profit recognised in:			
2015 €4 million x 25 per cent	1,000		
2016 Expected loss		(1,000)	
less Profit already recognised		(1,000)	
Loss in 2016		(2,000)	
2017 Expected loss			(1,000)
less Profit/(Loss) already recognised in previous years			(1,000)
Profit/Loss in 2017			nil

The sum of the profits/(losses) recognised in each of the three years adds up to (€1 million), which is the total loss incurred on the project. From Worked Example 13.4 we know that, as at the beginning of 2015, there were carried forward debit balances in Construction-in-Progress (contract asset) of €500,000 and in Accounts Receivable of €1,000,000.

(b) Journal entries for 2015 and 2016
(i) Journal entries for 2015 are the same as the 2015 journal entries in Worked Example 13.4(b), as the cost revision did not occur until 2016.
(ii) Journal entries for 2016

Dr	Construction-in-progress (contract asset)	€8,000,000	
Cr	Materials, cash, payables, accumulated depreciation, etc.		€8,000,000

(to recognise the cost of performing work on the contract)

Dr	Accounts receivable	€8,500,000	
Cr	Construction-in-progress (contract asset)		€8,500,000

(once the claim is made against the customer, the contract asset becomes a receivable)

Dr	Cash	€7,500,000	
Cr	Accounts receivable		€7,500,000

(receipt of cash from customer)

Dr	Construction expenses	€1,000,000	
Cr	Onerous liability—construction contract		€1,000,000

(onerous liability recognised because the cost of settling the performance obligation (€21 million) is expected to exceed the amount of the transaction price allocated to that performance obligation (€20 million))

Dr	Construction expenses	€1,000,000	
Cr	Construction-in-progress (contract asset)		€1,000,000

(reversal of profit recognised in the previous year)

Dr	Construction expenses	€6,000,000	
Cr	Revenue from long-term contract		€6,000,000

(recognition of revenues for 2016 and recognition of expenses for the same amount)

►

Note that a total loss of €2 million (represented by the difference between the construction revenue of €6 million and the construction expense of €8 million (which across three sets of journal entries above is made up of €1 million plus €1 million plus €6 million) must be recognised in the year 2016, as the amount is made up of the total expected contract loss of €1 million plus the reversal of the profit of €1 million, which was previously recognised in 2015. If the costs incurred in 2017 are €9 million as expected, in 2017 revenue of €9 million will be shown (giving total revenue of €20 million across the three years), and construction expenses will also be shown as €9 million in 2017.

Following the above entries, at the end of 2016 the Construction in Progress account will have a credit balance of €1,000,000. As such, the following entry might be made:

Dr	Construction-in-progress (contract asset)	€1,000,000
Cr	Contract liability	€1,000,000

13.10 Customer loyalty programmes

Customer loyalty programmes are widespread. Entities such as retailers, airlines, telecommunications operators, hotels and credit card companies use loyalty programmes to provide customers with an incentive to purchase their goods or services. When a customer purchases goods or services, as part of the sales transaction, the customer is rewarded with credits, usually described as 'points' or 'air miles', which can be redeemed at a later date for awards that can include free or discounted goods or services. At issue here is how should these rewards be treated for accounting purposes?

Prior to the issue of IFRC Interpretation 13 *Customer Loyalty Programmes*, many entities treated the cost of redeeming award credits as a marketing expense. The rationale here is that, as the reason for the incentive is to ensure continued customer loyalty, it is a marketing cost. IFRIC 13, however, treats loyalty programmes as multiple element revenue transactions. The fair value of the consideration received for the sale of the goods or services (from which award points are received or receivable) is allocated to:

- the goods or services delivered;
- the awards credit to be redeemed in the future.

Under the multiple element arrangement, the customer has purchased two items—goods, plus the right to receive future goods or services at a discount. This treatment applies irrespective of whether the entity supplies the awards (the discounted goods or services) or if they are supplied by a third party.

According to paragraph 3 of IFRIC 13, the interpretation applies to customer loyalty awards credits that:

(a) *an entity grants to its customers as part of a sales transaction, ie a sale of goods, rendering of services or use by a customer of entity assets; and*

(b) *subject to meeting any further qualifying conditions, the customers can redeem in the future for free or discounted goods or services.*

13.10.1 Accounting treatment

Pursuant to IFRIC 13, the fair value of the consideration received or receivable must be allocated between the award credits and the other components of the sale. The consideration allocated to the award credits is measured by reference to their fair value; that is, the amount for which the award credits could be sold separately. How the awards are accounted for will depend on whether the entity supplies the awards or whether the awards are supplied by a third party. IFRIC 13 clarifies the position as follows:

7. *If the entity supplies the awards itself, it shall recognise the consideration allocated to award credits as revenue when award credits are redeemed and it fulfils its obligations to supply awards. The amount of revenue recognised shall be based on the number of award credits that have been redeemed in exchange for awards, relative to the total number expected to be redeemed.*

8. *If a third party supplies the awards, the entity shall assess whether it is collecting the consideration allocated to the award credits on its own account (ie as the principal in the transaction) or on behalf of the third party (ie as an agent for the third party).*

   (a) *If the entity is collecting the consideration on behalf of the third party, it shall:*

      (i) *measure its revenue as the net amount retained on its own account, ie the difference between the consideration allocated to the award credits and the amount payable to the third party for supplying the awards; and*

> (ii) recognise this net amount as revenue when the third party becomes obliged to supply the awards and entitled to receive consideration for doing so. These events may occur as soon as the award credits are granted. Alternatively, if the customer can choose to claim awards from either the entity or a third party, these events may occur only when the customer chooses to claim awards from the third party.
>
> (b) If the entity is collecting the consideration on its own account, it shall measure its revenue as the gross consideration allocated to the award credits and recognise the revenue when it fulfils its obligations in respect of the awards.

The accounting for awards is considered in Worked Example 13.7, which has been adapted from the illustrative examples accompanying IFRIC 13. It should be noted that, when the accounting standard *Revenue from Contracts with Customers* is ultimately released, it will supersede IFRIC 13—however, it is not anticipated that the accounting requirements will change from those within IFRIC 13.

Worked Example 13.7 — Customer loyalty programmes

(i) *Award supplied by the entity*

Woodwoods plc, a retailer, operates a customer loyalty programme. Programme members are granted loyalty points when they spend a specified amount on groceries in the 2015 financial year. These points can then be redeemed to purchase further goods from the retailer. The points have no expiry date. During the reporting period to 30 June 2015, the retailer grants 100,000 points. The fair value of each loyalty point is estimated to be £1. When the awards scheme was set up, management expected 80 per cent of these points to be redeemed. Management defers the recognition of £100,000 in revenue. By 30 June 2015, customers have redeemed 40,000 points in exchange for goods.

During the reporting period ending 30 June 2016, Woodwoods plc revises its expectations and expects 90 per cent of the points to be redeemed. By the end of the reporting period ending 30 June 2016, a further 41 per cent of the points are redeemed.

During the reporting period ending 30 June 2017, a further 9,000 points are redeemed, taking the total points redeemed to 90,000. Woodwoods plc continues to expect that only 90,000 points will be redeemed. That is, no further points will be redeemed after the reporting period ending 30 June 2017.

Required

Prepare the journal entries to account for the award supplied by Woodwoods plc.

(ii) *Awards supplied by a third party*

Affordable plc is an electrical goods retailer. Affordable plc participates in a customer loyalty programme operated by an airline where programme members are awarded one air travel point for each pound spent on electrical goods. Programme members can redeem the points for air travel with the airline, subject to availability. Affordable plc pays the airline £0.009 for each point.

During the reporting period ending 30 June 2015, the retailer sells electrical goods for consideration totalling £1,000,000 and 1 million points were awarded to programme members. Affordable plc estimates the fair value of each point to be £0.01.

Required

(a) Indicate how Affordable plc would recognise the reward points if it collected the considerations on its own account.

(b) Indicate how Affordable plc would recognise the reward points if it collected the considerations on behalf of the airline.

Solution

(i) *Award supplied by the entity*

As the fair value of each loyalty point is estimated to be £1, at reporting date management defers revenue of £100,000. For the reporting period ending 30 June 2015, Woodwoods plc provides the following journal entry:

30 June 2015

Dr	Revenue	£100,000
Cr	Deferred revenue		£100,000

(recognition of deferred revenue associated with the awarding of reward points)

▶

At the end of the reporting period, 40 per cent of the points have been redeemed by customers, which is half of the total amount expected to be redeemed. Woodwoods plc makes the following entry to recognise £50,000 [which is (£40,000 ÷ £80,000) × £100,000] revenue associated with the awarding of the points.

30 June 2015

Dr	Deferred revenue	£50,000	
Cr	Revenue		£50,000

(recognition of deferred revenue associated with the awarding of reward points)

During the reporting period ending 30 June 2016, a further 41,000 points were redeemed, bringing the total points redeemed to 81,000. The cumulative revenue that Woodwoods plc recognises is £90,000, which equals (81,000 ÷ 90,000) × £100,000. As Woodwoods plc had recognised revenue of £50,000 during the reporting period ending 31 March 2015, £40,000 is recognised in the 2016 reporting period as follows:

30 June 2016

Dr	Deferred revenue	£40,000	
Cr	Revenue		£40,000

(recognition of deferred revenue associated with the awarding of reward points)

During the reporting period ending 30 June 2017, customers redeemed a further 9,000 points. The cumulative revenue recognised to date is £100,000, which is (90,000 ÷ 90,000) × £100,000. As £90,000 has already been recognised in previous reporting periods, £10,000 is recognised in the current year, as follows:

30 June 2017

Dr	Deferred revenue	£10,000	
Cr	Revenue		£10,000

(recognition of deferred revenue associated with the awarding of reward points)

By the end of the 2017 reporting period, all the revenue initially deferred has been recognised.

(ii) *Awards supplied by a third party*
Allocation of consideration to travel points
As Affordable plc estimates the fair value of a point to be £0.01, £10,000 (which is 1,000,000 × £0.01) of the consideration it has received from the sales of its electrical goods is allocated to the points.

Revenue recognition

Having granted the points, Affordable plc has fulfilled its obligations to the customer. The airline is obliged to supply the awards and entitled to receive consideration for doing so. Therefore, the retailer recognises revenue from the points when it sells the electrical goods.

Revenue measurement

(a) If Affordable plc collected the consideration allocated to the points on its own account, it measures its revenue as the gross £10,000 allocated to them. Affordable plc separately recognises the £9,000 paid or payable to the airline as an expense.

(b) If Affordable plc collected the consideration on behalf of the airline, that is, as an agent for the airline, it measures its revenue as the net amount it retains on its own account. This amount of revenue is the difference between the £10,000 consideration allocated to the points and the £9,000 passed on to the airline.

SUMMARY

The chapter considered the recognition of income and revenue—income being comprised of revenues and gains. In relation to the recognition of 'income'—one of the five 'elements of accounting'—reference is required to be made to the IASB Conceptual Framework. The IASB Conceptual Framework requires that for income (and the other elements of accounting) to be recognised, the associated inflow of economic benefits—or the associated reduction in liabilities—must be both probable and measurable with reasonable accuracy. In relation to revenue, we have also learned in this chapter that a new accounting standard pertaining to 'revenue from contracts with customers' is likely to be released in 2012/2013 and one key criterion that will be emphasised when determining whether revenue shall be recognised is whether control of the related good or service has been transferred to the customer.

Sales transactions are often made with associated conditions, such as call and put options, or rights to return the assets. When such conditions exist, it is necessary to consider whether they reduce the probability that the inflow of resources will ultimately occur and whether the conditions have implications for determining whether control of the good or service has been transferred to the customer. If it appears that an option that will reduce the inflow of resources will probably be exercised or that the right of return will be exercised, the revenue should not be recognised by the reporting entity until such time as there is enough certainty that the inflow of economic benefits will in fact occur.

Determining whether revenue should be recognised will also depend on the system of accounting being used. That is, the amount that is recognised as revenue in any period will depend on the particular measurement model being adopted. For example, if historical-cost accounting is used, the increase in the value of marketable securities would not be considered revenue until such time as the securities are sold. However, if a system of accounting based on fair values is used, increased market prices of assets could be treated as part of the period's income.

The chapter also considered how to account for long-term construction contracts. Revenue and expenses relating to a construction contract can be recognised by applying the percentage-of-completion method if the outcome and stage of completion of a construction contract can be reliably estimated and the control of the construction project is held by the customer. Where the percentage-of-completion method is applied, revenue is brought to account on the basis of percentage of completion. Percentage of completion is typically measured by comparing costs incurred to date with the most recent estimate of the total costs to complete the contract. While revenue is recognised throughout the life of the contract, if the percentage-of-completion method is used and it becomes apparent that a loss will be made, the entire loss must be recognised as soon as the loss becomes foreseeable.

KEY TERMS

END-OF-CHAPTER EXERCISE

Sun City plc commences construction of a multi-purpose water park on 1 July 2014 for Pretoria plc. Sun City plc signs a fixed-price contract for total revenues of €50 million. The project is expected to be completed by the end of 2017 and Pretoria plc controls the asset throughout the period of construction. The expected cost as at the commencement of construction is €38 million. The estimated costs of a construction project might change throughout the project—in this example, they do change. The following data relates to the project (the financial years end on 30 June): **LO 13.5**

	2015 (€m)	2016 (€m)	2017 (€m)
Costs for the year	10	18	12
Costs incurred to date	10	28	40
Estimated costs to complete	28	12	–
Progress billings during the year	12	20	18
Cash collected during the year	11	19	20

REQUIRED

(a) Using the above data, compute the gross profit to be recognised for each of the three years, assuming that the outcome of the contract can be reliably estimated.

(b) Prepare the journal entries for the 2015 financial year using the percentage-of-completion method.

(c) Prepare the journal entries for the 2015 financial year, assuming the stage of completion cannot be reliably assessed.

(d) Independently of the above three parts of this exercise, prepare the journal entries for the 2015 and 2016 financial years, assuming that the revised costing data, as shown below, indicates that, overall, the contract will make a loss of €2 million. The revision is due to the fact that, during the year ending 30 June 2016, it becomes apparent that the creation of the water park has damaged the local ecosystem and the damage must be rectified immediately at Sun City plc's expense.

	2016 (€m)
Costs for the year	18
Total costs incurred to date	28
Estimated costs to complete	24
Progress billings during the year	20
Cash collected during the year	19

SOLUTION TO END-OF-CHAPTER EXERCISE

(a) Gross profits for the three years

	2015 (€m)	2016 (€m)	2017 (€m)
Contract price	50	50	50
less Estimated cost:			
– Costs to date	10	28	40
– Estimated costs to complete	28	12	–
– Estimated total cost	38	40	40
Estimated total gross profit	12	10	10
Percentage complete (%)	26.32	70.0	100

Gross profit recognised in:

2015	€12,000,000 × 26.32 per cent	€3,158,400		
2016	€10,000,000 × 70 per cent		€7,000,000	
	less Gross profit already recognised		(€3,158,400)	
	Gross profit in 2016		€3,841,600	
2017	€10,000,000 × 100 per cent			€10,000,000
	less Gross profit already recognised			(€7,000,000)
	Gross profit in 2017			€3,000,000

The sum of the profits recognised in each year equals €10,000,000 (€3,158,400 + €3,841,600 + €3,000,000), which is the total profit of the contract.

(b) Journal entries for 2015 using the percentage-of-completion method

Dr	Construction-in-progress (contract asset)	€10,000,000	
Cr	Materials, cash, payables, accumulated depreciation, etc.		€10,000,000

(to recognise the costs associated with the contract)

Dr	Construction-in-progress (contract asset)	€3,158,400	
Dr	Construction expenses (statement of comprehensive income)	€10,000,000	
Cr	Revenue from long-term contract (statement of comprehensive income)		€13,158,400

(for the year, and based on the percentage of completion, 26.32% of the project has been completed; 26.32% of the total expected revenue of €50,000,000 is €13,158,400)

Dr	Accounts receivable	€12,000,000	
Cr	Construction-in-progress (contract asset)		€12,000,000

(amount payable unconditionally by the customer; part of the contract asset is reclassified to an accounts receivable)

Dr	Cash	€11,000,000	
Cr	Accounts receivable		€11,000,000

(amount received from customer)

(c) The journal entries for the 2015 financial year, assuming that the stage of completion cannot be reliably determined

Dr	Construction-in-progress (contract asset)	€10,000,000	
Cr	Materials, cash, payables, accumulated depreciation, etc.		€10,000,000

(to recognise the costs associated with the contract)

Dr	Construction expenses	€10,000,000	
Cr	Revenue from long-term contract		€10,000,000

(because the stage of completion is not clear, revenue recognition is restricted to the amount of cost incurred)

Dr	Accounts receivable	€12,000,000	
Cr	Construction-in-progress (contract asset)		€12,000,000

(amount payable unconditionally by the customer. Part of the contract asset is reclassified to an accounts receivable. This entry now means that the contract asset will have a credit balance of €2 million, meaning that a subsequent entry will be required to create a contract liability)

Dr	Cash	€11,000,000	
Cr	Accounts receivable		€11,000,000

(amount received from customer)

Dr	Construction-in-progress (contract asset)	€2,000,000	
Cr	Contract liability—excess of the amount received from the customer over performance completed		€2,000,000

(this is an adjustment to reclassify the balance of the contract asset to a contract liability given that the amount billed to the customer exceeds the cost of the work completed to date)

It should be noted that, if the stage of completion cannot be reliably estimated, then in this example the amount invoiced to the customer will exceed the amount of the construction-in-progress (contract asset), thereby making it necessary for a net liability to be disclosed.

(d) Journal entries using revised data that indicates that a loss is foreseeable. When current estimates of future total contract costs and revenues for any contract indicate that a loss is probable, provision should immediately be made for the foreseeable loss on the contract, regardless of the amount of work performed on the contract. That is, losses are to be brought to account as soon as they are foreseeable.

Calculations and journal entries assuming that the percentage-of-completion method was used in 2015 and that a cost revision was made in 2016 but no further revision was required in 2017:

	2015 (€m)	2016 (€m)	2017 (€m)
Contract price	50	50	50
less Estimated cost			
– Costs to date	10	28	52
– Estimated costs to complete	28	24	–
– Estimated total cost	38	52	52
Estimated total gross profit/(loss)	12	(2)	(2)
Percentage complete (%)	26.32	53.85	100

Gross profit recognised in:

2015	€12,000,000 × 26.32 per cent	€3,158,400	
2016	Expected loss		(€2,000,000)
	less Profit already recognised		€3,158,400

	Loss in 2016	(€5,158,400)	
2017	Expected loss		(€2,000,000)
	less Total profit/(loss) already recognised		
	in 2015 plus 2016		(€2,000,000)
	Profit/Loss in 2017		€nil

The sum of the profits/(losses) recognised in each of the three years adds up to (€2,000,000), which is the total loss incurred on the project.

Journal entries for 2015
The 2015 journal entries are the same as the 2015 journal entries shown in part (b) above, since at that stage it was not apparent that a loss would eventuate. At the end of 2015, a contract asset of €1,158,400 was carried forward.

Journal entries for 2016

Dr	Construction-in-progress (contract asset)	€18,000,000	
Cr	Materials, cash, payables, accumulated depreciation, etc.		€18,000,000

(to recognise the cost of performing work on the contract)

Dr	Accounts receivable	€20,000,000	
Cr	Construction-in-progress (contract asset)		€20,000,000

(once the claim is made against the customer, the contract asset becomes a receivable)

Dr	Cash	€19,000,000	
Cr	Accounts receivable		€19,000,000

(receipt of cash from customer)

Dr	Construction expenses	€2,000,000	
Cr	Onerous liability—construction contract		€2,000,000

(onerous liability recognised because the cost of settling the performance obligation (€52 million) is expected to exceed the amount of the transaction price allocated to that performance obligation (€50 million))

Dr	Construction expenses	€3,158,400	
Cr	Construction-in-progress (contract asset)		€3,158,400

Dr	Construction expenses	€12,841,600	
Cr	Revenue from long-term contract		€12,841,600

(recognition of revenues for 2015 and recognition of expenses for the same amount. Revenue is restricted to current costs less overall expected project loss of €2 million less profit already recognised of €3,158,400)

Note that a total loss of €5,158,400 (represented by the difference between the construction revenue of €12,841,600 and the construction expense of €18 million) must be recognised in the year 2016, as the amount is made up of the total expected contract loss of €2 million plus the reversal of the profit of €3,158,400, which was previously recognised in 2015. If the costs incurred in 2017 are €24 million as expected, in 2017 revenue of €24 million will be shown (giving total revenue of €50 million across the three years), and construction expenses will also be shown as €24 million (giving a total expense of €52 million).

Given that there was an opening balance in 'Construction-in-Progress' of €1,158,400 at the beginning of the year, then following the above entries, at the end of 2016 the Construction-in-Progress account will have a credit balance of €4,000,000. As such, the following entry might be made:

Dr	Construction-in-progress (contract asset)	€4,000,000	
Cr	Contract liability		€4,000,000

Journal entries assuming that the percentage-of-completion method was not used in 2015 (because stage of completion could not be determined reliably)

Journal entries for 2015
The 2015 journal entries are the same as the 2015 journal entries shown in (c) above.

Journal entries for 2016

Dr	Construction-in-progress (contract asset)	€18,000,000	
Cr	Materials, cash, payables, accumulated depreciation, etc.		€18,000,000

(to recognise the cost of performing work on the contract)

| Dr | Accounts receivable | €20,000,000 | |
| Cr | Construction-in-progress (contract asset) | | €20,000,000 |

(once the claim is made against the customer, the contract asset becomes a receivable)

| Dr | Cash | €19,000,000 | |
| Cr | Accounts receivable | | €19,000,000 |

(receipt of cash from customer)

| Dr | Construction expenses | €2,000,000 | |
| Cr | Onerous liability—construction contract | | €2,000,000 |

(onerous liability recognised because the cost of settling the performance obligation (€52 million) is expected to exceed the amount of the transaction price allocated to that performance obligation (€50 million))

| Dr | Construction expenses (statement of P&L) | €16,000,000 | |
| Cr | Construction revenue (statement of P&L) | | €16,000,000 |

Note that the entire loss must be recognised in the year in which it becomes apparent. Total revenue to be shown across the life of the contract will be €50 million (€10 million in 2015, €16 million in 2016 and €24 million in 2017). Total expenses to be recorded will be €52 million (€10 million in 2015, €18 million in 2016, and €24 million in 2017).

Following the above entries, at the end of 2016 the Construction-in-Progress (contract asset) account will have a credit balance of €2,000,000. As such, the following entry might be made (and given there was already an opening balance in the liability account of €2 million, this will mean there will be a total balance in the Contract Liability account of €4 million at the end of 2016, which is the difference between costs incurred to date (€28 million) and total billings to date (€32 million):

| Dr | Construction-in-progress (contract asset) | €2,000,000 | |
| Cr | Contract liability | | €2,000,000 |

REVIEW QUESTIONS

1   Would it be appropriate to recognise revenue at completion of production rather than at the point of sale?   **LO** 13.2

2   For several years the IASB and the FASB have been developing an accounting standard entitled *Revenue from Contracts with Customers*. An original Discussion Paper was released in 2008 but it is not anticipated that an ultimate accounting standard will be released until 2012 or 2013. What might be some reasons for the lengthy time period associated with the development of this accounting standard?   **LO** 13.1

3   What is the difference between a bad debt and a doubtful debt?   **LO** 13.1

4   Consider the statement that, 'the measurement model adopted and its underlying concepts of capital and capital maintenance are relevant to the timing of the recognition of revenues'. Explain what this means.   **LO** 13.3

5   If a sale is made 'f.o.b. destination', when should the associated revenue be recognised?   **LO** 13.4

6   If an organisation received non-cash consideration from a customer in return for providing a good or service, then how would the entity determine how much to assign to sales revenue?   **LO** 13.3

7   When organisations sell various goods to customers there is often some uncertainty about the ultimate collectability of the transaction price. Should sales revenue be reduced to take into account the probability that a certain percentage of the sales revenue will never be collected?   **LO** 13.3

8   If an organisation receives a large donation from a particular benefactor, would this donation represent revenue to the organisation? Explain your answer.   **LO** 13.1

9   In accounting for a long-term construction contract, if the billings on a construction-in-progress exceed the costs assigned to the construction-in-progress (contract asset), then how should this be disclosed in the statement of financial position?   **LO** 13.5

10   What are the alternative approaches to determining the percentage-of-completion of a long-term construction project?   **LO** 13.5

11   Sweeney plc owns a pie shop on Hastings Street. The carrying amount of the shop in the financial statements of Sweeney plc is £1.2 million. Because it needs some funds it has decided to sell the shop to Leaseco plc. Leaseco plc

buys the shop for £1.5 million and then immediately leases the shop back to Sweeney plc for the rest of the economic life of the building. How much profit should Sweeney plc show in its financial statements in the year of the sale? **LO** 13.1

12 In the presence of the following contractual arrangements, would you expect the firm to prefer to use the percentage-of-completion method to account for its construction contracts or a method that defers profit recognition until the completion of the contract? **LO** 13.5

(a) A management compensation scheme tied to reported profits.

(b) A debt covenant that is approaching the point of being in technical default.

13 A firm believes that it is subject to scrutiny by particular interest groups because it is earning excessive profits. Do you think that this might influence whether the firm prefers to use the percentage-of-completion method to account for its construction contracts or would prefer to defer profit recognition until the completion of the project? **LO** 13.5

14 Big Construction Company signs a contract on 1 July 2015, agreeing to build a warehouse for Buyer Corporation plc at a contract price of £10 million. Buyer plc will be in control of the asset throughout the construction process. Big Construction Company estimates that construction costs will be as follows:

2015	£2.5 million
2016	£4.0 million
2017	£1.5 million

The contract provides that Buyer Corporation plc will make payments on 31 December each year, as follows:

2015	£2 million
2016	£5 million
2017	£3 million

The contract is completed and accepted on 31 December 2017. Assume that actual costs and cash collections coincide with expectations. Big Construction Company has a financial year ending 31 December. **LO** 13.5

Provide the journal entries for 2015, 2016 and 2017, assuming that:

(a) the stage of completion *can* be reliably estimated.

(b) the stage of completion *cannot* be reliably estimated.

15 Assume the same facts as in Review Question 14, except that in 2016 it becomes apparent that costs to complete the contract will be £5.5 million in 2016 and £3 million in 2017. **LO** 13.5

Provide the journal entries for 2015, 2016 and 2017.

16 XYZ signs a contract on 30 June 2015, agreeing to build a bridge for ABC at a contract price of €40 million. ABC will be in control of the asset throughout the construction process. XYZ estimates that construction costs will be as follows: **LO** 13.5

Year ending	Cost
30 June 2016	€10,000,000
30 June 2017	€16,000,000
30 June 2018	€6,000,000
	€32,000,000

The contract provides that ABC will make payments on 30 June of each year, as follows:

2016	€8,000,000
2017	€20,000,000
2018	€12,000,000
	€40,000,000

The contract is completed as expected on 30 June 2018. Assume that actual costs and cash collections coincide with expectations.

(a) Calculate the income recognised each year.

(b) Provide the journal entries for each year, assuming that stage of completion and the outcome of the construction contract *cannot* be reliably estimated.

(c) Provide the journal entries for each year, assuming that stage of completion and the outcome of the construction contract *can* be reliably estimated.

CHALLENGING QUESTIONS

17 Assume the same facts as in Review Question 16, except that XYZ now estimates at the beginning of the 2017 financial year that construction costs will be as follows: **LO** 13.5

Year ending	Cost
30 June 2016	€10,000,000
30 June 2017	€21,000,000
30 June 2018	€15,000,000
	€46,000,000

REQUIRED

Provide the journal entries for each year, assuming that the percentage-of-completion method is used.

18 On 1 July 2015, Bronzed Scandi plc sells a caravan to Munich plc. The caravan has a normal sales price of £19,019. Rather than selling the item for its normal sales price, Bronzed Scandi plc sells the caravan for four annual payments of £6,000 per year, the first payment to be made on 30 June 2016. The difference between the gross receipts and the current sales price represents interest revenue to be earned by Bronzed Scandi plc over the period of the agreement. **LO** 13.3

(a) Determine what rate of interest is implicit in the agreement.

(b) Provide the journal entries for Bronzed Scandi plc for the years ending 30 June 2016 and 2017, using both the net-interest method and the gross method.

19 An entity sells 3,000 products for £50 each. Sales are made for cash, rather than on credit terms. The entity's customary business practice is to allow a customer to return any unused product within 30 days and receive a full refund. The cost of each product is £20. To determine the transaction price, the entity decides that the approach that is most predictive of the amount of consideration to which the entity will be entitled is the most likely amount. Using the most likely amount, the entity estimates that 50 products will be returned. The entity's experience is predictive of the amount of consideration to which the entity will be entitled. The entity estimates that the costs of recovering the products will be immaterial and expects that the returned products can be resold at a profit. **LO** 13.4

Provide the accounting entries to record the sale, and the subsequent return of the assets, assuming that the returns occur in accordance with expectations.

REFERENCES

COLSON, R.H., BLOOMFIELD, R., CHRISTENSEN, T., JAMAL, K., MOEHRLE, S., ET AL., 'Response to the Financial Accounting Standards Board's and the International Accounting Standards Board's Joint Discussion Paper Entitled Preliminary Views on Revenue Recognition in Contracts with Customers: American Accounting Association's Financial Accounting Standards Committee (AAA FASC), *Accounting Horizons*, vol. 24. no. 4, 2010, pp. 689–702.

INTERNATIONAL ACCOUNTING STANDARDS BOARD, *Discussion Paper: Preliminary Views on Revenue Recognition in Contracts with Customers*, London, International Accounting Standards Board, December 2008.

INTERNATIONAL ACCOUNTING STANDARDS BOARD, *Exposure Draft ED/2011/6: A revision of ED/2010/6 Revenue from Contracts with Customers, Revenue from Contracts with Customers*, London, International Accounting Standards Board, November 2011.

Chapter 14

The Statement of Comprehensive Income and Statement of Changes in Equity (including Share-based Remuneration Payments)

Learning objectives

Upon completing this chapter readers should:

LO1 understand how profit is calculated and how the profit of an organisation should be disclosed in the financial statements of a reporting entity;

LO2 understand the accounting for share-based payments under IFRS 2;

LO3 appreciate that the determination of the profits for a given period is heavily dependent upon both professional judgement and the particular accounting model that has been adopted;

LO4 understand that an entity is required to produce both a statement of comprehensive income and a statement of changes in equity and appreciate that both of these statements need to be read in order to appreciate more fully the financial performance of a reporting entity;

LO5 understand how to account for prior period errors;

LO6 understand how to account for changes in accounting policies and estimates; and

LO7 appreciate that while profit does provide an indication of the financial performance of an organisation, it does not reveal much about other aspects of performance, such as the social and environmental performance of a reporting entity.

14.1 Introduction to the statement of comprehensive income

> **revenues** A class of income relating typically to the ordinary activities of an entity.
>
> **gains** A class of income representing other items that meet the definition of income but need not relate to the ordinary activities of an entity.

A definition of income was provided in Chapter 2. As we learned, income is defined in paragraph 4.25a of the IASB Conceptual Framework as:

increases in economic benefits during the accounting period in the form of inflows or enhancements of assets or decreases of liabilities that result in increases in equity, other than those relating to contributions from equity participants.

As we also know, income is further broken down into **revenues** and **gains**. The general principle is that revenues typically relate to the ordinary activities of the entity and gains come from other activities that may or may not arise from the ordinary activities of the entity (IASB Conceptual Framework, paragraphs 4.29 and 4.30).

To determine the profit or loss of an entity, we need a definition of expenses, as profit is derived by subtracting expenses from income. Expenses are defined in paragraph 4.25b of the IASB Conceptual Framework as:

decreases in economic benefits during the accounting period in the form of outflows or depletions of assets or incurrences of liabilities that result in decreases in equity, other than those relating to distributions to equity participants.

Expenses are not further subdivided into subcomponents in the manner in which income is broken into revenues and gains. Consistent with the recognition criteria that apply to the other elements of financial statements, the recognition of an expense or an item of income relies upon an assessment of the *measurability* of the item, and the *probability* that the item will cause flows of economic benefits from, or to, the entity (IASB Conceptual Framework, paragraph 4.38).

The profit or loss for a period is tied to a determination of how future economic benefits are enhanced or diminished throughout the period. Income represents an inflow of future economic benefits (not including capital contributions), while expenses are consumptions or losses of future economic benefits (not including those that relate to distributions to owners). As indicated in Chapter 13, the determination of income and revenues will be influenced by which measurement model is adopted. Different measurement models are based on historical cost, current cost, fair value, present values and other alternatives. The different models will generate different income and expenses and, in turn, different profits. In recent years there has been a general trend for accounting standard-setters to issue accounting standards that measure assets and liabilities at 'fair value'. Nevertheless, other valuation approaches (for example, historical cost, net realisable value and present value) are required for particular classes of assets and liabilities (as stipulated by particular accounting standards), with the result that we have a 'mixed approach' to measuring financial performance and financial position.

14.1.1 An example: share-based payments

There can be considerable disagreement about how the expense associated with a particular item or event should be measured. For example, there was much debate about how share **options** provided to managers should be valued for accounting purposes. Senior managers or executives are often provided with options to buy shares in the entity that employs them, but they are often not permitted to exercise the options for a number of years. These options are treated as part of the executives' total remuneration, and as the executives cannot exercise the options for a number of years, the options act as a means of encouraging the executives to stay within the organisation (often, the right to exercise the options is lost if an executive leaves the firm before a pre-specified period). A particular accounting issue is identifying the expenses associated with providing the manager or executive with options. That is, how should the options be measured?

> **options** Entitle the holder to buy or sell assets at a future time at a pre-specified price.

Often options are issued with a 'strike price' or 'exercise price' (the amount that must be paid to acquire the shares in question) that is greater than the current share price. For example, a senior manager might be given an option to buy shares in the company at a future point in time for a price of €1.20 per share, when the shares are currently trading on the stock exchange for €1.10. Clearly, the manager would not exercise the option under these conditions, but the argument is that the manager will have an incentive to work hard to increase the value of the company's shares over the time (life) of the options and, therefore, the value of the options they hold. The options are said to have a 'time value'.

In determining the related expense to the organisation, some companies have simply looked at the difference between the exercise price and the current share price. This difference is considered to represent the 'intrinsic value' of the option. If this difference is negative at the time of issue, traditionally the options were considered to be 'out of the money', and no expense was recognised when the options were issued. Conversely, if the difference was positive (there is intrinsic value), the options were considered to be 'in the money', and the difference was recognised by some companies as an expense. However, some other companies considered issues associated with the 'time value' of the option and used various models to determine the cost of options (such as the Black–Scholes model) so that a cost could be assigned to options even when they are 'out of the money'. The point is that, in the absence of any specific rules pertaining to a particular type of expense, different entities will record different expenses and this will have obvious implications for profits. The ability to compare the financial performance of different entities will be eroded where different approaches are taken to account for particular items—such as options.

In recent times the release of IFRS 2 *Share-Based Payment* (initially released in July 2004) has reduced the discretion that companies are able to exercise in relation to placing a cost on share options provided to employees. In general terms, IFRS 2 requires that the fair value of options be determined and this value be deemed to be the cost of the options. However, when it comes to share options granted to employees, in many cases market prices are not available because the options granted are subject to terms and conditions that do not apply to traded options. IFRS 2 requires that, if traded options with similar terms and conditions do not exist, the fair value of the options granted is to be estimated by applying an option pricing model. However, IFRS 2 does not mandate the use of a particular model and hence the choice of model to use will impact on the price attached to the options. Further, as paragraph B6 of IFRS 2 states, a number of factors need to be taken into account—many of which will rely upon professional judgement. The factors to consider include:

- the exercise price of the option;
- the life of the option;
- the current price of the underlying shares;
- the expected volatility of the share price;
- the dividends expected on the shares (if appropriate); and
- the risk-free interest rate for the life of the option.

Where professional judgement is necessary to determine a particular expense, such as the cost to be assigned to share options, an entity should note within its financial statements the assumptions made and the basis for the assumptions. This is a general principle that should be followed. Indeed, in relation to share-based payments, paragraph 46 of IFRS 2 states:

> An entity shall disclose information that enables users of the financial statements to understand how the fair value of the goods or services received, or the fair value of the equity instruments granted, during the period was determined.

While we have looked briefly at determining the expense associated with options, we should appreciate that this is only one of the contentious aspects of how the expense associated with particular transactions and events should be determined, and that the various judgements made will directly affect the profits reported by an entity.

14.1.2 The subjective nature of profits

The IASB Conceptual Framework does not include profit (or loss) as one of its elements of accounting. As noted above, profit is simply the difference between income and expenses, both of which are defined, and hence there is no need for recognition criteria for profits. Without income and/or expenses, there is no profit or loss.

In relation to expenses, the judgement regarding whether or not to recognise assets will have a direct impact upon reported profits. The recognition criteria for **assets** provided in the IASB Conceptual Framework are the same as those required for other elements of accounting and require that it be probable that the future economic benefits embodied in the asset will eventuate. At times, it might not be clear whether or not it is probable that future economic benefits sufficient to absorb the cost of the asset will be derived from an item of expenditure, and thus whether the item of expenditure should be recognised as an expense or an asset. If there is doubt that sufficient future benefits will be derived, the expenditure will be **expensed**. The degree of probability attached to deriving benefits, and

assets Resources controlled by the entity as a result of past events and from which future economic benefits are expected to flow to the entity.

expensed Something is expensed if it is written off.

hence the recognition of an expense, will be a matter of professional judgement. As we know, accounting is not an exact science and so different teams of accountants would be unlikely to calculate the same profit or loss for an entity, even if they were given the same details about all the transactions and events that the entity has entered into or encountered. Potentially, one team of accountants might report a high level of profits, while another team reports losses. This difference will be driven by differences in the assumptions made, and it is very possible that the alternative sets of results generated by the different teams might both be considered to be **true and fair** by the auditors of the reporting entity. For example, a judgement must be made about such things as how many periods should be used to fully depreciate an item of plant and equipment, or whether there has been an impairment loss on a particular asset (which in turn requires judgements to be made about the 'recoverable amount' of an asset).

> **true and fair**
> Disclosures are regarded as giving a true and fair view if they provide all relevant information and comply with applicable standards.

It is obviously important for significant assumptions to be made about the nature and carrying amounts of assets and liabilities (IAS 1, paragraph 125).

While professional judgement is needed in respect of various forms of expenses, the accounting standard-setters have removed all discretion in relation to some expenses by requiring all expenditure on particular items to be expensed. For example, as we learned in Chapter 8, paragraph 54 of IAS 38 *Intangible Assets* stipulates that all expenditure on *research* is to be written off as incurred (development expenditure can be deferred to subsequent periods subject to certain conditions).

The problem with a 'blanket rule' requiring all expenditure of a particular type to be written off as incurred is that it does not enable readers of financial statements to differentiate between entities that have generated future economic benefits from particular activities and entities that have not. For example, in relation to research expenditure, an entity that has spent €10 million on a project that looks like ultimately generating significant economic benefits will be required to treat these expenditures as an expense in the same way as an entity that has spent €10 million researching an idea that turned out to be a 'flop'. Both entities will show an expense of €10 million and neither entity will show an asset pertaining to 'research'.

14.1.3 Stakeholders

As noted in Chapter 3, a firm might have numerous agreements in place that rely upon reported profit, for example dividend constraints, management bonus agreements and interest-coverage clauses incorporated within agreements made with debt holders. Hence the timing of the recognition of income or expenses might also be an important factor to managers of a reporting entity. Different stakeholder groups, such as government, the media, consumers, shareholders, consumer groups and employee groups, might also rely upon reported profits to justify their calls for a firm to take particular actions. For example, if profits are high, an employee group might call for an increase in wage rates, or an environmental group might call for the establishment of a recycling plant. The profitability of an organisation can also be an important factor in attracting additional investment funds into the organisation.

While a great deal of the discussion above refers to 'profits', it should be noted that certain gains and certain expenses will not be taken into consideration in calculating a reporting entity's 'profits'. While this might seem odd, there are a number of accounting standards that specifically stipulate that certain expenses (such as those relating to the correction of prior period accounting errors) and certain gains (such as those relating to asset revaluations) are not to be included in the 'profit or loss' for the reporting period. Hence, we must be careful when referring to the 'profits' of an entity—it does not include *all* expenses and income recognised within the financial period. As we will see within this chapter, a more comprehensive measure of financial performance is provided by a measure known as 'total comprehensive income'. As we will also learn in this chapter, 'total comprehensive income'—which is a relatively recently developed concept—includes both 'profits' and 'other items of comprehensive income'. We will define what we mean by 'other items of comprehensive income' later in this chapter.

14.2 Profit and loss disclosure

Paragraph 88 of IAS 1 requires entities to recognise all items of income and expense of a period in profit or loss *unless* a particular accounting standard requires or permits otherwise. Two specific exceptions to the requirement that all items of income and expense shall be recognised in profit or loss will be considered in this chapter. These are the correction of errors and the effect of changes in accounting policies. It should be noted that other accounting standards may also require or permit components of other comprehensive income that meet the Conceptual Framework's definition of income or expense to be excluded from the calculation of profit or loss. Nevertheless, they would be reflected in a measure of financial performance now

referred to as 'total comprehensive income'. As the name suggests, total comprehensive income, which is comprised of profit or loss plus other gains and losses that are recorded directly in various equity accounts, is presented in a 'statement of comprehensive income'.

The format for disclosing an entity's statement of comprehensive income is prescribed within IAS 1 *Presentation of Financial Statements*. Reporting entities have a choice when presenting information about their financial performance. Effective from 1 January 2012, entities can either present a statement of comprehensive income that provides information about the entity's profit or loss plus 'other items of comprehensive income', or they can separately provide both a statement of profit and loss and a separate statement of other comprehensive income.

14.2.1 Disclosure of profits or losses and disclosure of changes in equity

As we know, the profits or losses, as well as the other comprehensive income, generated by an entity will have a direct impact on the equity of an organisation (with a consequential impact on assets and/or liabilities). Some items of expense and revenue are not included within profit or loss, but rather are adjusted directly against equity (perhaps by way of an increase or decrease in retained earnings). For example, and as explained in Chapter 4, when an error from a prior period is discovered (perhaps the assets recorded last year were valued in excess of their recoverable value) the error is to be corrected retrospectively, as required by IAS 8 *Accounting Policies, Changes in Accounting Estimates, and Errors*. This would require a reduction in assets and a reduction in retained earnings to recognise the asset write-down expense. Although this is an expense that is recognised, it is a case of an expense being recognised directly in equity (retained earnings is an equity account). A number of other accounting standards also require certain income and expense items to be recorded directly in particular equity accounts rather than including them in a period's profit or loss. These items form part of what is now referred to as 'other comprehensive income for the year'. Paragraph 7 of IAS 1 defines 'other comprehensive income' as follows:

> *Other comprehensive income comprises items of income and expense (including reclassification adjustments) that are not recognised in profit or loss as required or permitted by other IFRS.*

According to paragraph 7 of IAS 1, components of 'other comprehensive income' would include:

(a) *changes in revaluation surplus (see IAS 16* Property, Plant and Equipment *and IAS 38* Intangible Assets*);*
(b) *actuarial gains and losses on defined benefit plans recognised in accordance with paragraph 93A of IAS 19* Employee Benefits*;*
(c) *gains and losses arising from translating the financial statements of a foreign operation (see IAS 21* The Effects of Changes in Foreign Exchange Rates*);*
(d) *gains and losses on remeasuring available-for-sale financial assets (see IAS 39* Financial Instruments: Recognition and Measurement*); and*
(e) *the effective portion of gains and losses on hedging instruments in a cash flow hedge (see IAS 39).*

Hence if we were to look only at profit or loss recorded in the statement of comprehensive income (or in a separate statement of profit and loss), we would not get a full picture of all the expenses and income that were recognised in the current period. A joint consideration of the period's profit or loss, plus a consideration of items impacting 'other comprehensive income', allows us to more fully appreciate all the income and expenses of a financial period.

14.2.2 Statement of comprehensive income

As already noted above, IAS 1 requires that all items of income and expense recognised in the period under review and included in the calculation of profit or loss be presented either in a single statement of comprehensive income or in two statements.

IAS 1 deals with the format the statement of comprehensive income should take, as well as identifies those items that are to be disclosed separately in the statement of other comprehensive income, or in the accompanying notes. Specifically, paragraph 82 of IAS 1 requires that the following minimum information be disclosed as line items on the face of the statement of comprehensive income:

(a) *revenue;*
(b) *finance costs;*
(c) *share of the profit or loss of associates and joint ventures accounted for using the equity method;*
(d) *tax expense;*
(e) *a single amount comprising the total of*

      (i) the post-tax profit or loss of discontinued operations and

      (ii) the post-tax gain or loss recognised on the measurement to fair value less costs to sell or on the disposal of the assets or disposal group(s) constituting the discontinued operation;

(f) *profit or loss;*

(g) *each component of other comprehensive income classified by nature (excluding amounts in (h));*

(h) *share of the other comprehensive income of associated and joint ventures accounted for using the equity method; and*

(i) *total comprehensive income.*

In addition, paragraph 83 requires the profit or loss and the total comprehensive income for the period disclosed on the face of the statement of comprehensive income to be disaggregated between the non-controlling interest and the owners of the parent. We will consider issues to do with controlling and non-controlling interests in the chapters of this book that address issues associated with accounting for groups of companies (Chapters 21–23).

The allocation between non-controlling interests and the equity owners must be shown on the face of the statement of comprehensive income. The disclosure on the face of the statement of comprehensive income of additional line items and subtotals is encouraged if this information is relevant to an understanding of an entity's financial performance (IAS 1, paragraph 85).

Regarding the presentation format for the statement of comprehensive income, IAS 1 permits alternative presentation formats to be used, based either upon the *nature of expenses* being incurred or their *function* within the entity. The choice is affected by the need to provide reliable information in the most relevant manner (IAS 1, paragraph 99). In explaining the alternative presentation formats, paragraphs 102 and 103 of IAS 1 state:

102. *The first form of analysis is the 'nature of expense' method. An entity aggregates expenses within profit or loss according to their nature (for example, depreciation, purchases of materials, transport costs, employee benefits and advertising costs), and does not reallocate them among various functions within the entity. This method may be simple to apply because no allocations of expenses to functional classifications are necessary. An example of a classification using the nature of expense method is as follows:*

Revenue	*X*
Other income	*X*
Changes in inventories of finished goods and work-in-progress	*X*
Raw materials and consumables used	*X*
Employee benefits costs	*X*
Depreciation and amortisation expense	*X*
Other expenses	*X*
Total expenses	*(X)*
Profit	*X*

103. *The second form of analysis is the 'function of expense' or 'cost of sales' method and classifies expenses according to their function as part of cost of sales or, for example, the costs of distribution or administrative activities. At a minimum, an entity discloses its cost of sales under this method separately from other expenses. This method can provide more relevant information to users than the classification of expenses by nature, but allocating costs to functions may require arbitrary allocations and involve considerable judgement. An example of a classification using the function of expense method is as follows:*

Revenue	*X*
Cost of sales	*(X)*
Gross profit	*X*
Other income	*X*
Distribution costs	*(X)*
Administrative expenses	*(X)*
Other expenses	*(X)*
Profit	*X*

Again, it should be emphasised that entities have a choice between the two presentation formats described above. In deciding which format to use, paragraph 105 of IAS 1 requires management to select the most relevant and reliable presentation format. For information to be relevant it must be able to influence the economic decisions of users. This is achieved by assisting them to evaluate past, present or future events, and confirm or correct past evaluations. Reliable information, on the other hand, must be free from material error and bias. Users must be able to depend on it to represent faithfully that which it either purports to represent or could reasonably be expected to represent.

While the IASB decided not to provide any illustrations of statements of comprehensive income presented for an entity using both a 'classification of expense by nature' and a 'classification of expenses by function' when it reissued IAS 1 in September 2007, it developed a document entitled *Guidance on Implementing IAS 1 Presentation of Financial Statements*, which it released when the revised IAS 1 was also released. This guidance

---

Exhibit 14.1 | **Single statement of comprehensive income illustrating the classification of expenses by function**

XYZ PLC
Statement of comprehensive income for the year ended 31 December

	2015 (€000)	2014 (€000)
Revenue	390,000	355,000
Cost of sales	(245,000)	(230,000)
Gross profit	145,000	125,000
Other income	20,667	11,300
Distribution costs	(9,000)	(8,700)
Administrative expenses	(20,000)	(21,000)
Other expenses	(2,100)	(1,200)
Finance costs	(8,000)	(7,500)
Share of profits of associates	35,100	30,100
Profit before tax	161,667	128,000
Income tax expense	(40,417)	(32,000)
Profit for the year from continuing operations	121,250	96,000
Loss for the year from discontinued operations	–	(30,500)
Profit for the year	121,250	65,500
Other comprehensive income		
Exchange differences on translating foreign operations	5,334	10,667
Available-for-sale financial assets	(24,000)	26,667
Cash-flow hedges	(667)	(4,000)
Gains on property revaluation	933	3,367
Actuarial gains (losses) on defined benefit pension plans	(667)	1,333
Share of other comprehensive income of associates	400	(700)
Income tax relating to components of other comprehensive income	4,667	(9,334)
Other comprehensive income for the year, net of tax	(14,000)	28,000
Total comprehensive income for the year	107,250	93,500
Profit attributable to:		
Owners of the parent	97,000	52,400
Non-controlling interests	24,250	13,100
	121,250	65,500
Total comprehensive income attributable to:		
Owners of the parent	85,800	74,800
Non-controlling interests	21,450	18,700
	107,250	93,500
Earnings per share		
Basic and diluted	46 cents	30 cents

Source: IAS 1 2008 Guidance on Implementing IAS 1 Presentation of Financial Statements

Exhibit 14.2	Example of note supporting the statement of comprehensive income

XYZ LIMITED
Notes to the 2015 financial statements
Note 10 Disclosure of components of other comprehensive income

	2015		2014	
	(€000)	(€000)	(€000)	(€000)
Other comprehensive income				
Exchange differences on translating foreign operations		5,334		10,667
Available-for-sale financial assets:				
Gains arising during the year	1,333		30,667	
less Reclassification adjustments for gains included in profit or loss	(25,333)	(24,000)	(4,000)	26,667
Cash-flow hedges:				
Gains (losses) arising during the year	(4,667)		(4,000)	
less Reclassification adjustments for gains (losses) included in profit or loss	3,333			–
less Adjustments for amounts transferred to initial carrying amount of hedged items	667	(667)	–	(4,000)
Gains on property revaluation		933		3,367
Actuarial gains (losses) on defined benefit pension plans		(667)		1,333
Share of other comprehensive income of associates		400		(700)
Other comprehensive income		(18,667)		37,334
Income tax relating to components of other comprehensive income		4,667		(9,334)
Other comprehensive income for the year		(14,000)		28,000

Source: IAS 1 2008 *Guidance on Implementing IAS 1 Presentation of Financial Statements*

document provides useful presentation formats which we reproduce in this chapter. A single statement of comprehensive income (classified by function) is reproduced in Exhibit 14.1, while the two-statement format (a separate statement of profit and loss, together with a statement of comprehensive income with expenses classified by nature) is reproduced in Exhibit 14.3. When reviewing the two formats, try to note the differences. At this stage it should be noted that individual items of comprehensive income can be disclosed either on an aggregated basis (Exhibit 14.1) or on a net-of-tax basis (Exhibit 14.3). Again, whichever format is chosen, it should be chosen on the basis of which format is considered by management to be more relevant or reliable. As a general rule, it would be expected that a service provider would disclose its expenses by nature rather than function, whereas a manufacturer would more likely disclose its expenses by function.

Looking at the two formats, one (expenses by function, Exhibit 14.1) separately identifies the cost of sales, whereas the other (expenses by nature, Exhibit 14.3) does not. Arguably, in some industries cost of sales data could be quite sensitive. While this might not be a problem for organisations producing a variety of products, it could well prove to be a controversial disclosure requirement for single-product entities, especially in the manufacturing sector, given the potentially competitive nature of the information involved (Parker and Porter 2000, p. 67). This might cause some entities to select a presentation format for reasons other than relevance and faithful representation. Opportunistic selection of accounting options could result if the choice between particular accounting methods or presentation formats is left to professional judgement. However, this could be limited by ensuring compliance with the detailed disclosure requirements of other accounting standards.

Exhibit 14.3 Two-statement format with expenses classified by nature

XYZ PLC
Statement of profit and loss for the year ended 31 December

	2015 (€000)	2014 (€000)
Revenue	390,000	355,000
Other income	20,667	11,300
Changes in inventories of finished goods and work-in-progress	(115,100)	(107,900)
Work performed by the entity and capitalised	16,000	15,000
Raw material and consumables used	(96,000)	(92,000)
Employee benefits expense	(45,000)	(43,000)
Depreciation and amortisation expense	(19,000)	(17,000)
Impairment of property, plant and equipment	(4,000)	–
Other expenses	(6,000)	(5,500)
Finance costs	(15,000)	(18,000)
Share of profit of associates	35,100	30,100
Profit before tax	161,667	128,000
Income tax expense	(40,417)	(32,000)
Profit for the year from continuing operations	121,250	96,000
Loss for the year from discontinued operations	–	(30,500)
Profit for the year	121,250	65,500
Profit attributable to:		
Owners of the parent	97,000	52,400
Non-controlling interests	24,250	13,100
	121,250	65,500
Earnings per share, basic and diluted	46 cents	30 cents

XYZ PLC
Statement of comprehensive income for the year ended 31 March

	2015 (€000)	2014 (€000)
Profit for the year	121,250	65,500
Other comprehensive income		
Exchange differences on translating foreign operations	5,334	10,667
Available-for-sale financial assets	(24,000)	26,667
Cash-flow hedges	(667)	(4,000)
Gains on property revaluation	933	3,367
Actuarial gains (losses) on defined benefit pension plans	(667)	1,333
Share of other comprehensive income of associates	400	(700)
	(18,667)	37,334
Income tax relating to components of other comprehensive income	4,667	(9,334)
Other comprehensive income for the year, net of tax	(14,000)	28,000
Total comprehensive income for the year	107,250	93,500
Total comprehensive income attributable to:		
Owners of the parent	85,800	74,800
Non-controlling interest	21,450	18,700
	107,250	93,500

Source: IAS 1 2008 *Guidance on Implementing IAS 1 Presentation of Financial Statements*

In the single-statement presentation, all items of income and expense are presented together. Where the two-statement option is chosen, the first statement (statement of profit and loss) presents income and expenses recognised in profit or loss. The second statement (statement of other comprehensive income) begins with the profit or loss (from the statement of profit and loss) and then presents, in addition, the individual components of 'other comprehensive income' (items of income and expense) that accounting standards require or permit to be recognised outside of profit or loss. It is important to remember that the statement of other comprehensive income does not include transactions with owners in their capacity as owners (for example, payment of dividends to shareholders or further capital injections by owners in the form of share purchases). These transactions are presented in the statement of changes in equity, which is discussed later in the chapter.

As indicated in Exhibit 14.1, the statement of comprehensive income provides a total of all income and expenses recognised directly in equity (referred to as 'other comprehensive income'), which is added to profit for the period to give a total referred to as 'total comprehensive income' for the year. At the present time, existing accounting standards do not require all assets and liabilities to be adjusted to fair value. This means that reported measures of financial performance are somewhat incomplete (that is, they are not truly comprehensive). Hence we may argue that the statement of comprehensive income's title and the figure shown for 'total comprehensive income for the period' could potentially be misleading.

14.2.3 Other comprehensive income for the year (taxation)

Paragraph 90 of IAS 1 requires entities to disclose the amount of income tax relating to each component of other comprehensive income, either in the statement of comprehensive income or in the notes to the financial statements. Entities are permitted to present the components of other comprehensive income either before tax effects (gross presentation) or after their related tax effects (net presentation) (IAS 1, paragraph 91).

It should be noted that an alternative presentation of the various components of comprehensive income could be net of tax. When the various components of comprehensive income are shown net of tax, the income tax relating to each component of other comprehensive income must be disclosed in the accompanying financial statement notes in a manner consistent with the presentation in Exhibit 14.4.

Exhibit 14.4 **Required note disclosure when individual components of comprehensive income are shown net of tax**

Note 10 Disclosure of tax effects relating to each component of other comprehensive income

	2015			2014		
	Before tax amount (€000)	Tax (expense)/ benefit (€000)	Net of tax amount (€000)	Before tax amount (€000)	Tax (expense)/ benefit (€000)	Net of tax amount (€000)
Exchange differences on translating foreign operations	5,334	(1,334)	4,000	10,667	(2,667)	8,000
Available-for-sale financial assets	(24,000)	6,000	(18,000)	26,667	(6,667)	20,000
Cash-flow hedges	(667)	167	(500)	(4,000)	1,000	(3,000)
Gains on property revaluation	933	(333)	600	3,367	(667)	2,700
Actuarial gains (losses) on defined benefit pension plans	(667)	167	(500)	1,333	(333)	1,000
Share of other comprehensive income of associates	400	–	400	(700)	–	(700)
Other comprehensive income	(18,667)	4,667	(14,000)	37,334	(9,334)	28,000

Source: IAS 1 2008 Guidance on Implementing IAS 1 Presentation of Financial Statements

14.2.4 Reclassification adjustments

Individual accounting standards specify whether and when amounts previously recognised in 'other comprehensive income' are reclassified to profit or loss (called reclassification adjustments in paragraph 7 of IAS 1, previously described as 'recycling'). IAS 1 requires an entity to disclose reclassification adjustments relating to components of other comprehensive income in the period that the adjustments are reclassified to profit or loss. The purpose is to provide users with information to assess the effect of such reclassifications on profit or loss. Examples of situations giving rise to reclassification adjustments include the disposal of a foreign operation, derecognition of available-for-sale financial assets and when a hedged forecast transaction affects profit or loss. For example, in relation to available-for-sale financial assets (which we addressed more fully in Chapter 12 and which are defined in IAS 39 as 'non-derivative financial assets that are designated as available for sale or that are not classified as loans and receivables, held-to-maturity investments or financial assets at fair value through profit or loss'), paragraph 55 of IAS 39 requires that a gain or loss on an 'available-for-sale financial asset' shall be recognised directly in equity until the financial asset is derecognised, at which time the cumulative gain or loss previously recognised in equity shall be recognised in profit or loss.

The unrealised gains that have previously been recognised in equity (such as the gains or losses on the available-for-sale financial asset) must be deducted from other comprehensive income in the period in which the realised gains are reclassified to profit or loss to avoid double-counting items in total comprehensive income when those items are reclassified to profit or loss. Without this information, users of the financial statements may find it difficult to assess the effect of reclassifications on profit or loss or to calculate the overall gain or loss associated with available-for-sale financial assets and cash-flow hedges, and on translation or disposal of foreign operations.

Paragraph 92 of IAS 1 requires entities to disclose reclassification adjustments relating to components of other comprehensive income. Reclassification adjustments may be disclosed either in the statement of other comprehensive income or in the notes. An entity presenting reclassification adjustments in the notes presents the components of other comprehensive income in the statement of other comprehensive income after any related reclassification adjustments. An illustration of a reclassification adjustment relating to an available for sale investment is detailed in Worked Example 14.1.

Worked Example 14.1   **Reclassification adjustment for available-for-sale investment**

On 31 December 2013 XYZ plc purchased 10,000 equity instruments (shares) at £12.40 per share. On acquisition, XYZ plc classified this investment as 'available-for-sale'. This means that pursuant to IAS 39, gains or losses will be recognised directly in equity until the item is derecognised (sold), at which point the accumulated gain or loss will be transferred to profit or loss. At 31 December 2014, the fair value of the instruments had increased to £18.60. At 31 December 2015, the fair value of the equity instruments had increased to £21.70. All of the instruments were sold on 31 December 2015. No dividends were declared on those instruments during the time that they were held by XYZ plc. At 31 December 2013, the only equity item was paid-up capital of £500,000.
The applicable tax rate is 30 per cent.

Required

Prepare an extract of the statement of comprehensive income and statement of changes in equity for the reporting period ending 31 December 2015 in which the reclassification adjustment for available-for-sale investment is detailed.

Solution

Calculation of gains on available-for-sale investment

	Before Tax (£)	Income Tax (£)	Net of Tax (£)
Gains recognised in other comprehensive income			
Year ended 31 December 2014	62,000	(18,600)	43,400
Year ended 31 December 2015	31,000	(9,300)	21,700
Total gain	93,000	(27,900)	65,100

▶

The amounts will be disclosed in the statement of comprehensive income and statement of changes in equity for the reporting period ending 31 December 2015, as follows:

XYZ plc
Statement of comprehensive income for the year ended 31 December

	2015 (£)	2014 (£)
Profit or loss		
Gain on sale of instruments	93,000	–
Income tax expense	(27,900)	–
Net gain recognised in profit or loss	65,100	–
Other comprehensive income		
Gain on available-for-sale financial assets, net of tax	21,700	43,400
Reclassification adjustment, net of tax	(65,100)	–
Net gain (loss) recognised in other comprehensive income	(43,400)	43,400
Total comprehensive income for the year	21,700	43,400

XYZ plc
Statement of changes in equity for the year ended 31 December 2015

	Share capital (£)	Available-for-sale financial assets (£)	Retained earnings (£)	Total (£)
Balance at 31 December 2013	500,000	–	–	500,000
Changes in equity for 2014				
Total comprehensive income for the year	–	43,400	–	43,400
Balance at 31 December 2014	500,000	43,400	–	543,400
Changes in equity for 2015				
Total comprehensive income for the year	–	21,700	65,100	86,800
Reclassification adjustment for gain included in profit or loss	–	(65,100)	–	(65,100)
	500,000	–	65,100	565,000

Alternatively, components of other comprehensive income may be shown in the statement of comprehensive income gross of tax with a separate line item for tax effects:

XYZ plc
Statement of comprehensive income for the year ended 31 December

	2015 (£)	2014 (£)
Profit or loss		
Gain on sale of instruments	93,000	–
Income tax expense	(27,900)	–
Net gain recognised in profit or loss	65,100	–
Other comprehensive income		
Gain on available-for-sale financial asset	31,000	62,000
Reclassification adjustment	(93,000)	–
Income tax relating to other comprehensive income	18,600	(18,600)
Net gain (loss) recognised in other comprehensive income	(43,400)	43,400
Total comprehensive income for the year	21,700	43,400

While it has been traditional for a profit and loss account to provide a total of profits to which opening retained earnings is added (to give a 'total available for appropriation'), and from which dividends are deducted, this form of presentation is no longer valid under IAS 1. Information about dividends and their impact on retained earnings will now typically be shown in the statement of changes in equity.

14.2.5 Extraordinary items

Under IFRS there is no such thing as extraordinary items. Specifically, paragraph 87 of IAS 1 states:

An entity shall not present any items of income and expense as extraordinary items, in the statement of comprehensive income or the separate income statement (if presented), or in the notes.

Extraordinary items were defined in the UK Financial Reporting Standard FRS 3 as:

Material items possessing a high degree of abnormality which arise from events or transactions that fall outside the ordinary activities of the reporting entity and which are not expected to recur. They do not include exceptional items nor do they include prior period items merely because they relate to a prior period.

An item had to be both outside the ordinary operations of the business and of a non-recurring nature before it was to be classified and disclosed as an extraordinary item. The argument previously accepted was that, if an item was extraordinary (and therefore of an unusual nature and not expected to recur), it should perhaps be separately identified for financial statement users who were trying to assess the future profitability of the business. Hence if a financial statement reader wanted to consider the current and future profitability of a business, it was considered that it would be usual for the user to focus on the profits from ordinary activities after tax, which excluded extraordinary items. By their very nature, extraordinary items were not expected to recur, and hence any consideration of future profitability, or the performance of management, required their exclusion. This perspective, however, is not adopted by IAS 1 and it is open to question whether prohibiting the separate disclosure of extraordinary items, as is now required, will improve international financial reporting. What do you, the reader, think?

While IAS 1 prohibits the disclosure of extraordinary items, the following requirement in paragraph 97 could be used to alert financial report readers to 'unusual' items. Paragraph 97 states:

When items of income and expense are material, an entity shall disclose their nature and amount separately.

This disclosure requirement relies upon professional judgement about the materiality of an item. Under FRS 3 *Reporting Financial Performance* these unusual items were called 'Exceptional items' and are defined as:

Material items which derive from events or transactions that fall within the ordinary activities of the reporting entity and which individually or, if of a similar type, in aggregate, need to be disclosed by virtue of their size or incidence if the financial statements are to give a true and fair view.

This terminology is still being widely used by companies across Europe. For example, a review of the 2010 Annual Report of Nutreco reveals that it uses the terminology 'exceptional items' and it notes that 'Exceptional items consist of non-operational income and/or gains and expenses and/or losses which are not related to the normal course of business'. Exhibit 14.5 reproduces information from Nutreco's 2010 Annual Report.

14.2.6 Non-recurring items

In relation to the separate disclosure of particular items of income and expenses, in addition to relying upon judgements about the materiality of particular income and expense items, IAS 1 also specifically identifies items that would typically warrant separate disclosure. Paragraph 98 of IAS 1 states:

Circumstances that would give rise to the separate disclosure of items of income and expense include:

(a) write-downs of inventories to net realisable value or of property, plant and equipment to recoverable amount, as well as reversals of such write-downs;

(b) restructurings of the activities of an entity and reversals of any provisions for the costs of restructuring;

(c) disposals of items of property, plant and equipment;

(d) disposals of investments;

(e) discontinued operations;

(f) litigation settlements; and

(g) other reversals of provisions.

Nutreco Annual Report 2010
Extract from Note 3 Operating segments

Exceptional items (EUR x million)	Exceptional items	
	2010	2009
Restructuring costs	–20.0*	–11.8
Negative goodwill	–	11.2
Impairment charges	–4.0	–7.5
Acquisition-related costs	–3.0	
Income arising from terms of delivery and alliances	4.7	
Other	–1.0	2.9
Total exceptional items	**–23.3**	**–5.2**

* Restructuring costs of EUR –20.0 million are presented on (i) personnel expenses for an amount of EUR –15.3 million, (ii) other operating expenses for EUR –5.2 million, and (iii) other operating income of EUR 0.5 million.

Exceptional items consist of non-operational income and/or gains and expenses and/or losses which are not related to the normal course of business. These are in general restructuring costs, impairment charges, acquisition-related costs (since 2010) and negative goodwill. The majority of the restructuring costs for 2010 and 2009 are related to the acquisition of the animal nutrition business of Cargill in Spain and Portugal, which closed in 2009.

The negative goodwill in 2009 of EUR 11.2 million is the result of the consideration paid and the fair value of the net identifiable assets and liabilities related to the acquisition of the animal nutrition business in Spain and Portugal. In 2010, the impairment charges of EUR 4.0 million are mainly related to the closures of compound feed factories in Spain (EUR 2.1 million) and a fish feed factory in Ireland (EUR 1.4 million).

The impairment charges in 2009 of EUR 7.5 million were mainly related to the acquired fixed assets of Maple Leaf Animal Nutrition (in 2007) and the animal nutrition business of Cargill in Spain and Portugal. The impairment in Spain and Portugal was a consequence of Nutreco's strategic plans which led to the decision to restructure the business.

The IASB Conceptual Framework also discusses the need to separately disclose particular items. Paragraph 4.27 of the IASB Conceptual Framework states:

Income and expenses may be presented in the income statement in different ways so as to provide information that is relevant for economic decision-making. For example, it is common practice to distinguish between those items of income and expenses that arise in the course of the ordinary activities of the entity and those that do not. This distinction is made on the basis that the source of an item is relevant in evaluating the ability of the entity to generate cash and cash equivalents in the future; for example,... incidental activities such as the disposal of a long-term investment are unlikely to recur on a regular basis. When distinguishing between items in this way consideration needs to be given to the nature of the entity and its operations. Items that arise from the ordinary activities of one entity may be unusual in respect of another.

14.2.7 Changes in accounting estimates

Accounting and, in particular, the preparation of financial statements at the end of the reporting period, relies heavily upon the use of estimates. This is due primarily to the fact that certain information is not available as at the end of the reporting period, and future developments and events cannot be predicted with certainty.

The use of estimates based on specific assumptions and projections concerning future events is, therefore, essential in the preparation of financial statements (paragraph 33 of IAS 8 *Accounting Policies, Changes in Accounting Estimates*). Many estimates must be made in the accounting process in relation to such things as bad debts, inventory obsolescence and useful lives of assets (see paragraph 32 of IAS 8). As the estimation process involves the exercise of professional judgement, it stands to reason that these estimates will require revision as further events occur, more expertise is acquired or additional information is obtained. As new information becomes available, changes in various accounting estimates will be required. Paragraph 5 of IAS 8 defines a change in accounting estimate as:

> *an adjustment of the carrying amount of an asset or a liability, or the amount of the periodic consumption of an asset, that results from the assessment of the present status of, and expected future benefits and obligations associated with, assets and liabilities. Changes in accounting estimates result from new information or new developments and, accordingly, are not corrections of errors.*

The above paragraph makes the point that a change in accounting estimate is not a correction of an error. As we will see shortly, and reflective of this, how we account for a change in accounting estimate is different from how we account for the correction of an error.

One issue we can consider in relation to the use of estimates is whether the use of estimates in the preparation of financial statements undermines the ability of the financial statements to faithfully represent the underlying transactions and events (faithful representation being one of the qualitative characteristics of general purpose financial statements). The fact that estimates have been used in the preparation of financial statements does not in itself undermine the ability of the financial statements to represent faithfully the underlying transactions and events. As indicated in paragraphs 33 and 34 of IAS 8, the use of reasonable estimates is an essential part of the preparation of financial statements and does not undermine their reliability.

Changes in accounting estimates include, but are not limited to:

- changes in the allowance for doubtful debts;
- changes in expected warranty costs on goods sold under guarantee;
- changes in the fair value of financial assets and financial liabilities;
- changes in the expected pattern of consumption of economic benefits of depreciable assets; and
- changes in the provision for inventory obsolescence.

As the estimation process involves judgement based on the latest available information, adjustment is necessary when the circumstances on which the original estimate was based have altered, additional experience has been obtained or there have been subsequent developments.

A change in accounting estimate can affect the current accounting period, or both the current and future accounting periods. Examples of changes in accounting estimates that affect only current accounting periods include bad debts, warranty provisions and inventory obsolescence. The appropriate accounting treatment under these circumstances is to recognise the change immediately. Examples of changes in accounting estimates that affect both the current and future accounting periods include changes in the useful life of an asset and changes in the method used for calculating depreciation (for example, from the straight-line to the sum-of-digits method). Under these circumstances, the appropriate treatment is to recognise the effect of the change in both the current and future periods.

Since a change in estimate arises from new information or developments, does not relate to prior periods and is not the correction of an error, it is not given retrospective effect by restating prior period profit or loss. The reason for this is that the change in estimate is the result of a decision made in the current period and, as a result, should be reflected in the net profit (loss) for the current period (IAS 8, paragraphs 36 and 37).

In relation to the disclosures required for changes in accounting estimates, paragraphs 39 and 40 of IAS 8 state:

> 39. *An entity shall disclose the nature and amount of a change in an accounting estimate that has an effect in the current period or is expected to have an effect in future periods, except for the disclosure of the effect on future periods when it is impracticable to estimate that effect.*
> 40. *If the amount of the effect in future periods is not disclosed because estimating it is impracticable, an entity shall disclose that fact.*

Worked Example 14.2 details how a change in accounting estimate can be accounted for and disclosed in the notes accompanying the statement of comprehensive income.

> **Worked Example 14.2** **Change in accounting estimate (changing the useful life of an asset)**
>
> On 30 June 2015, the end of the current reporting period, Beachley plc made a decision, using the information obtained over the past few years, to revise the useful life of a particular item of manufacturing equipment acquired five years earlier on 1 July 2010 for €300,000. The useful life was revised from 12 years to eight years. The item of manufacturing equipment was originally depreciated on the straight-line basis over its useful life and it was expected that the asset would have no residual value. No depreciation has been provided for in the current period.
>
> **Required**
>
> (a) Prepare the journal entry to account for the change in accounting estimate.
> (b) Assuming that the change in accounting estimate had a material effect on financial performance for the period, prepare an appropriate supporting note.
>
> **Solution**
>
> (a) Journal entry at 30 June 2015
>
>   At the beginning of the current reporting period the net book value of the asset was €200,000. Based on the revised useful life of the asset, the remaining useful life is four years from the beginning of the financial period and not eight years. The book value of €200,000 is to be depreciated over a four-year period so that the remaining depreciation is charged over the useful life of the asset.
>
> | | | |
> |---|---|---|
> | Dr Depreciation | €50,000 | |
> | Cr Accumulated depreciation—manufacturing equipment | | €50,000 |
>
> (b) Supporting note—change in accounting estimate
>
> | | 2015 (€) | 2014 (€) |
> |---|---|---|
> | Profit before tax has been arrived at after taking into account: | | |
> | Depreciation | | |
> | Original | 25,000 | 25,000 |
> | Change in accounting estimate | 25,000 | – |
> | | 50,000 | 25,000 |
>
> As a result of the revision during the year of the estimated useful life of the manufacturing equipment from 12 to eight years, the depreciation charge will increase by €25,000 for the following four years.

14.2.8 Other disclosure issues

Although we have covered a number of the disclosures required by IAS 1 and IAS 8, there are a number of other requirements pertaining to the disclosure of income and expenses. Some of these are identified below.

In relation to dividends, paragraph 107 of IAS 1 requires:

An entity shall disclose, either in the statement of changes in equity, or in the notes, the amount of dividends recognised as distributions to owners during the period, and the related amount per share.

Though not required by IFRS, company law may require disclosures in relation to payments made to auditors. Article 43.1 of the European Directive 78/660/EEC requires that large companies should provide a note in their financial statements disclosing the remuneration paid to auditors for their audit work and separately for other services. Disclosures in relation to non-audit fees paid to auditors have been required in the UK since the amendment to the Companies Act by the Companies (Disclosure of Auditor Remuneration) Regulations 2005. The most recent European directive has been implemented through the Companies (Disclosure of Auditor

Remuneration and Limited Limitation Agreements)(Amendment) Regulations 2011 and requires the disclosures to be provided for each class of non-audit service. The legislation not only requires disclosures on payments due to auditors but also to the auditors' associates. It is interesting to consider possible reasons for regulators believing that readers of financial statements need to know about payments to auditors—why do you think payments to auditors require separate disclosure?

As already noted, many other accounting standards also require the disclosure of information about various items of income and expense. For example, IAS 38 *Intangible Assets* requires the disclosure of various items of expense as they relate to intangible assets, including:

■ impairment losses recognised in profit or loss during the period;
■ impairment losses reversed in profit or loss during the period;
■ any amortisation recognised during the period; and
■ the aggregate amount of research and development expenditure recognised as an expense during the period.

In relation to revenue, IAS 18 *Revenue* requires the separate disclosure of a number of items of revenue. Paragraph 35 of IAS 18 stipulates:

An entity shall disclose:

(a) *the accounting policies adopted for the recognition of revenue including the methods adopted to determine the stage of completion of transactions involving the rendering of services;*
(b) *the amount of each significant category of revenue recognised during the period including revenue arising from:*
  (i) *the sale of goods;*
  (ii) *the rendering of services;*
  (iii) *interest;*
  (iv) *royalties;*
  (v) *dividends; and*
(c) *the amount of revenue arising from exchanges of goods or services included in each significant category of revenue.*

We have mentioned only a limited subset of accounting standards in this discussion. However, the discussion has served to emphasise that there are numerous disclosure requirements pertaining to income and expenses and that these disclosure requirements can be found throughout various accounting standards.

14.3 Statement of changes in equity

In addition to having to present a statement of financial position, a statement of comprehensive income, a statement of cash flows and supporting notes to its financial statements, an entity is also required to produce a statement of changes in equity. The role of the statement of changes in equity is to provide a reconciliation of opening and closing equity, and also to provide details of the various equity accounts that are impacted by the period's total comprehensive income. It also provides information about the effects of transactions with owners in their capacity as owners. In relation to what is to be presented in statement of changes in equity, paragraph 106 of IAS 1 now requires:

An entity shall present a statement of changes in equity showing in the statement:

(a) *total comprehensive income for the period, showing separately the total amounts attributable to owners of the parent and to non-controlling interest;*
(b) *for each component of equity, the effects of retrospective application or retrospective restatement recognised in accordance with IAS 8;*
(c) *the amounts of transactions with owners in their capacity as owners, showing separately contributions by and distributions to owners; and*
(d) *for each component of equity, a reconciliation between the carrying amount at the beginning and the end of the period, separately disclosing each change.*

In relation to dividends, paragraph 107 of IAS 1 states:

> An entity shall present, either in the statement of changes in equity or in the notes, the amount of dividends recognised as distributions to owners during the period, and the related amount per share.

Changes in an entity's equity between the beginning and the end of the reporting period reflect the increase or decrease in its net assets during the period. Paragraph 109 of IAS 1 clarifies this by stating:

> Other than changes resulting from transactions with owners in their capacity as owners (for example equity contributions, reacquisitions of the entity's own equity instruments and dividends) and transaction costs directly related to such transactions, the overall change in equity during a period represents the total amount of income and expense, including gains and losses, generated by the entity's activities during that period.

As shown in Exhibit 14.6, a statement of changes in equity reconciles opening and closing equity, which represents the difference between assets and liabilities, and which will comprise multiple accounts, including share capital, retained earnings, revaluation surplus accounts, and so on. In addition, within the statement of changes in equity, the distribution to and contributions from owners, individual components of total comprehensive income and non-controlling interests are separately disclosed. The statement of changes in equity also provides details of any amounts retained in the revaluation surplus that were transferred to retained earnings when the asset was derecognised. As with other financial statements, comparative information is provided for both the current and preceding financial years.

14.4 Prior period errors

Prior period errors are not addressed by IAS 1. Rather, they are covered by IAS 8 *Accounting Policies, Changes in Accounting Estimates, and Errors*. Paragraph 5 of IAS 8 defines a prior period error as follows:

> Prior period errors are omissions from, and misstatements in, the entity's financial statements for one or more prior periods arising from a failure to use, or misuse of, reliable information that:
>
> (a) was available when the financial statements for those periods were authorised for issue; and
> (b) could reasonably be expected to have been obtained and taken into account in the preparation and presentation of the financial statements.
>
> Such errors include the effects of mathematical mistakes, mistakes in applying accounting policies, oversights or misinterpretations of facts and fraud.

Pursuant to IAS 8, the correction of a prior period error is excluded from the profit or loss of the period in which the error is discovered. The error should be corrected in the period in which it incurred (restatement of comparatives) or as close to it as is practicable (IAS 8, paragraph 46).

IAS 8 requires all errors that relate to prior reporting periods to be corrected by adjusting the opening balance of retained earnings and restating comparative information. For example, if in the year ended 30 June 2015 an entity determined that inventory thought to be on hand at the beginning of the financial year had actually been destroyed in the previous financial period (meaning that there was an error in the previous financial period that resulted in closing inventory of the previous period being overstated and expenses of the previous period being understated), the accounting entry in 2015 would be:

Dr	Retained earnings	X	
Cr	Inventory		X

The implication of the prior period errors being accounted for by making an adjustment against retained earnings is that, if an entity 'forgets' to include an expense in one period and discovers the omission in the next period, then that expense will never appear in the statement of comprehensive income (because the subsequent recognition will be made by virtue of an adjustment against retained earnings). Clearly, this might be a desired outcome for some (less than objective) managers.

The definition of prior period errors excludes changes in accounting estimates and changes in accounting policies. Paragraph 5 of IAS 8 provides the relevant definition:

> A change in accounting estimate is an adjustment of the carrying amount of an asset or a liability or the amount of the periodic consumption of an asset, that results from the assessment of the present status of, and expected future benefits and obligations associated with, assets and liabilities. Changes in accounting estimates result from new information or new developments and, accordingly, are not corrections of errors.

Exhibit 14.6 Statement of changes in equity

XYZ PLC
Statement of changes in equity for the year ended 31 December 2015

	Share capital (€000)	Retained earnings (€000)	Translation of foreign operations (€000)	Available-for-sale financial assets (€000)	Cash-flow hedges (€000)	Re-valuation surplus (€000)	Total (€000)	Non-controlling interest (€000)	Total equity (€000)
Balance at 1 January 2014	600,000	118,100	(4,000)	1,600	2,000	–	717,700	29,800	747,500
Changes in accounting policy	–	400	–	–	–	–	400	100	500
Restated balance	600,000	118,500	(4,000)	1,600	2,000	–	718,100	29,900	748,000
Changes in equity for 2014									
Dividends	–	(10,000)	–	–	–	–	(10,000)	–	(10,000)
Total comprehensive income for the year	–	53,200	6,400	16,000	(2,400)	1,600	74,800	18,700	93,500
Balance at 31 December 2014	600,000	161,700	2,400	17,600	(400)	1,600	782,900	48,600	831,500
Changes in equity for 2015									
Issue of share capital	50,000	–	–	–	–	–	50,000	–	50,000
Dividends	–	(15,000)	–	–	–	–	(15,000)	–	(15,000)
Total comprehensive income for the year	–	96,600	3,200	(14,400)	(400)	800	85,800	21,450	107,250
Transfer to retained earnings	–	200	–	–	–	(200)	–	–	–
Balance at 31 December 2015	650,000	243,500	5,600	3,200	(800)	2,200	903,700	70,050	973,750

Source: IAS 1 2008 *Guidance on Implementing IAS 1 Presentation of Financial Statements*

A change in accounting estimate occurs when different circumstances or assumptions are applied in arriving at a particular estimate.

The difference between a change in accounting estimate and a prior period error is considered in Worked Example 14.3.

Worked Example 14.3 **Difference between a change in accounting estimate and a prior period error**

The following two unrelated scenarios apply to Layne plc, whose financial year ends on 30 June 2015.

Scenario 1: Layne plc has, in the past, always made an allowance for doubtful debts equivalent to 2 per cent of accounts receivable outstanding at year end. As a result of new information obtained by the company during the current year, a decision was made to increase the doubtful debt allowance to 3.5 per cent of accounts receivable outstanding at year end.

Scenario 2: During the preparation of the financial statements it was discovered that an amount of £8,500, incurred in July 2013 and payable to a foreign supplier, was overlooked and not paid or provided for in the financial statements ending 30 June 2014. The amount is considered to be material and will be permitted as a deduction for tax purposes.

Required

Identify which of the two scenarios outlined above is a change in accounting estimate and which is a prior period error.

Solution

Scenario 1 is a change in accounting estimate. The decision to increase the allowance for doubtful debts involves the application of judgement based on the latest information available to management. Changes in the allowance for doubtful debts is a change in estimate.

Scenario 2 is a prior period error. It arose from a material amount not being included when the 2014 financial statements were prepared.

14.4.1 Correction of prior period errors

Material prior period errors are corrected retrospectively in the first set of financial statements authorised for issue after their discovery. In other words, the current year's financial statements are presented as if the error never occurred. Any adjustments are excluded from profit or loss for the period in which the error was discovered. As indicated earlier, this is achieved by adjusting the opening balance of retained earnings and restating the comparative amounts for the prior periods presented. If the error occurred in a period prior to the present period presented, the opening balance of assets, liabilities and equity should be restated for the earliest period presented. Where historical summaries are provided, the amounts relating to prior periods should be restated and this restatement disclosed where practicable.

Using the information contained in Worked Example 14.3, and assuming a tax rate of 30 per cent, the following journal entry would be necessary to correct the financial statements:

30 June 2015

Dr	Retained earnings	£5,950	
Dr	Tax payable	£2,550	
Cr	Accounts payable		£8,500

14.4.2 Disclosing prior period errors

Paragraph 49 of IAS 8 requires the following disclosures to be made in respect of prior period errors:

an entity shall disclose the following:

(a) the nature of the prior period error;

(b) for each prior period presented, to the extent practicable, the amount of the correction:
   (i) for each financial statement line item affected; and
   (ii) if IAS 33 applies to the entity, for basic and diluted earnings per share;
(c) the amount of the correction at the beginning of the earliest prior period presented; and
(d) if retrospective restatement is impracticable for a particular prior period, the circumstances that led to the existence of that condition and a description of how and from when the error has been corrected.

Financial statements of subsequent periods need not repeat these disclosures.

Worked Example 14.4 details how a prior period error should be accounted for and disclosed at the time the error is discovered.

Worked Example 14.4 — Error made in the previous reporting period and discovered in the current reporting period

An extract from the financial statements of Omit plc for the year ended 30 June is provided below:

Omit plc Abridged statement of comprehensive income for the year ended 30 June	2015 (£)	2014 (£)
Profit before tax	9,500	11,800
Income tax expense	(2,850)	(3,540)
Profit for the year	6,650	8,260

Omit plc Statement of changes in equity for the year ended 30 June 2015	Share capital (£)	Retained earnings (£)	Total (£)
Balance at 30 June 2013	1,500	1,520	3,020
Profit for the year	–	8,260	8,260
Distributions	–	(2,000)	(2,000)
Balance at 30 June 2014	1,500	7,780	9,280
Profit for the year ending	–	6,650	6,650
Distributions	–	(2,000)	(2,000)
Balance at 30 June 2015	1,500	12,430	13,930

The following additional information is also available:
During the preparation of the 2015 financial statements, it became apparent that an invoice for purchases of £2,100, due to a foreign supplier for services rendered, had been omitted when the 2014 financial statements were prepared.

The tax authority has indicated that the purchases from the supplier will be permitted as a deduction for tax purposes. The tax rate is 30 per cent. Issued share capital amounted to £1,500. The financial statements above have not incorporated this error.

Required

Prepare the statement of comprehensive income and statement of changes in equity so as to comply with all applicable accounting standards.

►

Solution

Omit plc

Abridged statement of comprehensive income for the year ended 30 June	2015 (£)	2014 (£)
Profit before tax	9,500	9,700
Income tax expense	(2,850)	(2,910)
Profit for the year	6,650	6,790

Omit plc

Statement of changes in equity for the year ended 30 June 2015	Share capital (£)	Retained earnings (£)	Total (£)
Balance at 30 June 2013	1,500	1,520	3,020
Profit for the year as restated	–	6,790	6,790
Distributions		(2,000)	(2,000)
Balance at 30 June 2014	1,500	6,310	7,810
Profit for the year	–	6,650	6,650
Distributions	–	(2,000)	(2,000)
Balance at 30 June 2015	1,500	10,960	12,460

Notes to the financial statements

Note 2 Prior period error

An amount due to a foreign supplier for payment to the foreign supplier for services rendered was omitted during preparation of the 2014 financial statements. The 2014 figures have been restated to take into account the omission. The effect of the restatement on those financial statements is summarised below. There is no effect on 2015 results.

	Effect on 2014 (£)
(Increase) in expenses	(2,100)
Decrease in income tax expense	630
(Decrease) in profit	(1,470)
Increase in accounts payable	(2,100)
Decrease in tax payable	630
(Decrease) in equity reserves	(1,470)

14.5　Changes in accounting policy

One of the essential qualitative characteristics of general purpose financial statements is comparability. Information is considered to be comparable when users of financial statements of an entity are able to identify trends in financial performance and position over a period of time and when they are able to compare the performance of different entities at a point in time. For comparability to apply, users should be able to effectively compare financial statements of different entities. This can only be achieved if users have knowledge of the accounting policies employed in the preparation of the financial statements, together with information about any changes in those policies and the effects of such changes (IAS 8, paragraph 13).

Accounting policies are defined in paragraph 5 of IAS 8 as:

the specific principles, bases, conventions, rules and practices applied by an entity in preparing and presenting financial statements.

Accounting bases are methods developed to apply fundamental accounting concepts to financial transactions and estimates:

■ for determining in which accounting period income and expenses should be recognised in the statement of comprehensive income; and
■ for determining the amounts at which items should be stated in the statement of financial position.

Considerations of comparability would suggest that changes in accounting policy should be infrequent occurrences. Paragraph 14 of IAS 8 identifies two situations when a change in accounting policy is likely to occur. These are where a change in accounting policy is required to comply with an accounting standard or interpretation, or where a decision to change an accounting policy will result in the financial statements providing reliable and more relevant information.

It is often difficult to distinguish between a change in accounting policy and a change in an accounting estimate. For example, the following situations cannot be considered changes in accounting policy:

■ application of an accounting policy for events or transactions that differ in substance from those previously occurring; or
■ application of a new accounting policy for transactions or other events or conditions that did not occur previously or were immaterial.

In Worked Example 14.5, two scenarios are provided. The first, the adoption of a new policy for an event that did not previously exist, is not a change in policy, while the second is clearly a change in accounting policy. At this stage you should make sure you understand what constitutes a change in accounting policy and what constitutes a change in an accounting estimate. You should also understand how to account for changes in accounting policies and changes in accounting estimates.

Further examples of changes in accounting policy would include:

■ changing the basis of providing for deferred tax from the income statement approach to the balance sheet approach; and
■ capitalising borrowing costs incurred in the construction of an asset when borrowing costs were previously expensed.

Worked Example 14.5 — Identifying a change in accounting policy and an instance not considered to be a change in accounting policy

Scenario 1: Racer plc has previously not owned a depreciable building. During the reporting period ended 30 June 2015, a building was constructed. Depreciation was charged for the first time on the building from the 2015 reporting period.

Scenario 2: Racer plc has previously held land at cost. From the 2015 reporting period, the company made the decision to revalue land to its fair value.

Required

Identify, giving reasons, which of the above scenarios is a change in accounting policy and which is not a change in accounting policy.

Solution

Scenario 1 is not a change in accounting policy as no buildings existed previously and, as a consequence, no depreciation charge was necessary.

Scenario 2 is a change in accounting policy. Previously, the policy was to carry the land at its historical cost. The policy is now to hold land at its fair value.

Changes in accounting policy are to be made retrospectively or prospectively, depending upon the background to the change. On initial application of a new accounting policy, and unless a change in accounting policy is being accounted for in accordance with the specific provisions of an accounting standard or interpretation, the effects of the change in accounting policy are to be accounted for retrospectively (IAS 108, paragraph 19).

When a change in accounting policy is made retrospectively, paragraph 22 of IAS 8 requires the opening balance of each affected component of equity to be adjusted for the earliest prior period presented and the other comparative amounts disclosed for each prior period presented, as if the new accounting policy had always been applied. The new policy is applied to both comparative information and historical data for periods as far back as possible.

IAS 8 requires retrospective application to be made for changes in accounting policy, except in those limited circumstances in which it is impracticable to determine either the period-specific effects or the cumulative effect of the change (IAS 8, paragraph 23).

Where it is not possible to determine the period-specific effects of changes in an accounting policy for one or more of the periods presented, paragraph 24 of IAS 8 requires the new policy to be applied to the carrying amounts of assets and liabilities at the beginning of the earliest period for which retrospective application is practicable, which might be the current period. A corresponding adjustment should be made to the opening balance of equity for that period. In noting that retrospective adjustments created by changing accounting policies are typically undertaken by adjusting retained earnings, paragraph 26 of IAS 8 states:

> When an entity applies a new accounting policy retrospectively, it applies the new accounting policy to comparative information for prior periods as far back as is practicable. Retrospective application to a prior period is not practicable unless it is practicable to determine the cumulative effect on the amounts in both the opening and closing balance sheets for that period. The amount of the resulting adjustment relating to periods before those presented in the financial statements is made to the opening balance of each affected component of equity of the earliest prior period presented. Usually the adjustment is made to retained earnings. However, the adjustment may be made to another component of equity (for example, to comply with an IFRS). Any other information about prior periods, such as historical summaries of financial data, is also adjusted as far back as is practicable.

An example of a retrospective change in accounting policy is provided in Worked Example 14.6.

Worked Example 14.6   **Retrospective change in accounting policy**

During 2011 Alpha plc commenced the construction of a geothermal power station outside Maastricht for its own use. During the reporting period ending 30 June 2015, a change in accounting standards means that the directors are required to change the company's treatment of borrowing costs incurred in the construction of assets for its own use. In previous periods Alpha plc expensed such costs, but must now capitalise them as part of the construction cost in line with the requirement of IAS 23 *Borrowing Costs*. As a result of the change, the financial statements of Alpha plc will be more comparable with other entities in the same industry.

The unadjusted statement of comprehensive income and statement of changes in equity for the reporting period ended 30 June 2015 are detailed below.

Alpha plc: Abridged statement of comprehensive income for the year ended 30 June	2015 (€)	2014 (€)
Profit before tax	29,200	28,400
Income tax expense	(8,760)	(8,520)
Profit for the year	20,440	19,880

▶

Alpha plc: Abridged statement of changes in equity for the year ended 30 June 2015	Share capital (€)	Retained earnings (€)	Total (€)
Balance at 1 July 2013	25,000	16,100	41,100
Profit for the year		19,880	19,880
Distributions to shareholders	–	(5,400)	(5,400)
Balance 30 June 2014	25,000	30,580	55,580
Profit for the year	–	20,440	20,440
Distributions to shareholders	–	(7,400)	(7,400)
Balance at 30 June 2015	25,000	43,620	68,620

Alpha plc: Statement of financial position (extract) at 30 June	2015 (€)	2014 (€)	2013 (€)
Qualifying asset under construction	21,400	13,300	8,800
Other assets	47,220	42,280	32,300
	68,620	55,580	41,100
Share capital	25,000	25,000	25,000
Retained earnings	43,620	30,580	16,100
	68,620	55,580	41,100

Additional information

1. In 2015 interest of €2,800 relating to the construction of the geothermal power station was expensed. Interest costs of €4,200 were expensed in 2014, €5,600 was expensed in 2013 and €3,700 was expensed in reporting periods prior to 2013.
2. No depreciation has been charged on the geothermal power station, as it has not yet been commissioned.
3. The tax rate has remained at 30 per cent for the past three years.

Required

Redraft the statement of comprehensive income, statement of changes in equity and statement of financial position (extract) so as to comply with generally accepted accounting practice and all relevant accounting standards.

Solution

Alpha plc: Abridged statement of comprehensive income for the year ended 30 June	2015 (€)	2014 (€)
		Restated
Profit before tax	32,000	32,600
Income tax expense	(9,600)	(9,780)
Profit for the year	22,400	22,820

Alpha plc: Abridged statement of changes in equity for the year ended 30 June 2015	Share capital (€)	Retained earnings (€)	Total (€)
Balance at 1 July 2013 as previously reported	25,000	16,100	41,100
Change in accounting policy resulting from capitalising interest	–	6,510	6,510
Balance at 1 July 2013 as restated	25,000	22,610	47,610
Profit for the year (restated)	–	22,820	22,820
Distributions to shareholders	–	(5,400)	(5,400)
Balance 30 June 2014	25,000	40,030	65,030
Profit for the year	–	22,400	22,400
Distributions to shareholders	–	(7,400)	(7,400)
Balance at 30 June 2015	25,000	55,030	80,030

Alpha plc: Statement of financial position (extract) at 30 June	2015 (€)	2014 (€)	2013 (€)
Qualifying asset under construction	37,700	26,800	18,100
Net assets	47,220	42,280	32,300
Taxation	(4,890)	(4,050)	(2,790)
	80,030	65,030	47,610
Share capital	25,000	25,000	25,000
Retained earnings	55,030	40,030	22,610
	80,030	65,030	47,610

Notes to financial statements

Change in accounting policy

During the year, the accounting policy applicable to borrowing costs for assets constructed for the company's own use was changed. Previously such costs were expensed. However, IAS 23 *Borrowing Costs* now requires borrowing costs attributable to the construction of a qualifying asset to be capitalised as part of the cost of the asset. This policy will provide more relevant and reliable information, as it is consistent with industry practice, making the financial statements more comparable with those of other entities in the same industry. The change in accounting policy has been accounted for retrospectively and the comparative statements for 2014 have been restated. The effect of the change on 2014 is shown below. Opening retained earnings for 2014 is increased by €9,300 (€6,510 after tax), which is the amount of the adjustment relating to periods prior to 2014.

	Effect on 2014 (€)	Effect on periods prior to 2014 (€)
Decrease in interest expense	4,200	9,300
(Increase) in income tax expense	(1,260)	(2,790)
Increase in profit	2,940	6,510
Increase in qualifying assets under construction	13,500	9,300
Increase in tax payable	(4,050)	(2,790)
Increase in retained earnings at 30 June 2014	9,450	6,510

Note that in circumstances where a change in accounting policy or the correction of a prior period error has been made retrospectively, a complete set of financial statements would include a statement of financial position as at the beginning of the earliest comparative period (IAS 1, paragraph 10 (f)). This disclosure requirement is further elaborated by paragraph 39 of IAS 1, which requires:

> *An entity disclosing comparative information shall present, as a minimum, two statements of financial position, two of each of the other statements, and related notes. When an entity applies an accounting policy retrospectively or makes a retrospective restatement of items in its financial statements or when it reclassifies items in its financial statements, it shall present, as a minimum, three statements of financial position, two of each of the other statements, and related notes. An entity presents statements of financial position as at:*
>
> *(a)   the end of the current period;*
> *(b)   the end of the previous period (which is the same as the beginning of the current period); and*
> *(c)   the beginning of the earliest comparative period.*

At the beginning of an accounting period it is, in certain infrequent circumstances, impossible to determine the cumulative effect of applying a new accounting policy to all prior periods. In this situation, the new accounting policy must be applied prospectively from the start of the earliest period possible. A prospective application of a change in accounting policy does not take into account any cumulative adjustments to assets, liabilities and equity that may have arisen before that date. An illustration of a prospective change in accounting policy, based on an example provided in IAS 8, is provided in Worked Example 14.7.

Worked Example 14.7 Prospective change in accounting policy

During the reporting period ending June 2015, the directors of Persuader plc decided to change the company's accounting policy for depreciating property, plant and equipment to the components approach and, at the same time, adopt the revaluation model wherein particular classes of asset will be revalued to fair value. Prior to 2015, the details maintained in the assets register were not sufficiently detailed to apply the components approach fully.

During June 2014 the directors commissioned an engineering survey to provide comprehensive information on the individual components of the various assets, their fair values, useful lives, estimated residual values and depreciable amounts in effect at 1 July 2014, the beginning of the 2015 reporting period. Prior to the reconstruction of the records there was insufficient information to reliably estimate the cost of components that had not been accounted for separately.

Management has determined that it is not practicable to account for the change to the components approach retrospectively or to account for the change prospectively from any earlier date than the start of the 2015 reporting period. In view of this, management has also decided that the change from the cost model to the revaluation model should also be accounted for prospectively, from the start of the 2015 reporting period.

The tax rate for all years is 30 per cent.

The following additional information is available:

Property, plant and equipment at 30 June 2014	£
At cost	160,000
Accumulated depreciation	(89,600)
Carrying amount	70,400
Prospective depreciation expense	9,600

The engineering survey established the following values:

Property, plant and equipment—at valuation	108,800
Estimated residual value	19,200
Remaining asset life	5 years
Depreciation expense on new basis	17,920

Required

Prepare the journal entries that would be made in the records of Persuader plc at 30 June 2015, together with the note that would appear in the 2015 financial statements.

Solution

30 June 2015

Dr	Property, plant and equipment	£38,400	
Cr	Revaluation surplus		£26,880
Cr	Deferred tax liability		£11,520
	(revaluation of plant as per engineering survey)		
Dr	Depreciation	£8,320	
Cr	Accumulated depreciation		£8,320
	(additional depreciation expense for the year)		
Dr	Tax payable	£2,496	
Cr	Income tax expense		£2,496
	(decrease in tax expense for the year)		

Note to the 2015 financial statements
From the start of the 2015 reporting period, Persuader plc changed its accounting policy for depreciating property, plant and equipment to the components approach and, at the same time, adopted the revaluation model. The directors believe that this policy provides reliable and more relevant information because it deals more accurately with the components of property, plant and equipment, and is based on up-to-date values. The policy has been applied prospectively from the start of the 2015 reporting period, as it was not practicable to estimate the effects of applying the policy either retrospectively or prospectively from any earlier date.

> ◄ The adoption of the new policy has no effect on prior years. The effect on the current year is to increase the carrying amount of property, plant and equipment at the start of the year by £38,400; increase the opening deferred tax liability by £11,520; create a revaluation surplus at the start of the year of £26,880; increase depreciation expense by £8,320; and reduce tax expense by £2,496.

14.5.1 Disclosures when changes in accounting policy are made

Understanding the impact that a change in accounting policy has or could have, on the financial performance and position of an entity is only possible if users are aware of the accounting policies employed in the preparation of the financial statements, together with any changes in those policies, and the effects of the changes. To assist users' understanding of the impact that any changes in accounting policy may have, paragraphs 28 to 30 of IAS 8 provides the following extensive disclosures requirements:

28. *When initial application of an IFRS has an effect on the current period or any prior period, would have such an effect except that it is impracticable to determine the amount of the adjustment or might have an effect on future periods, an entity shall disclose:*
    (a) *the title of the IFRS;*
    (b) *when applicable, that the change in accounting policy is made in accordance with its transitional provisions;*
    (c) *the nature of the change in accounting policy;*
    (d) *when applicable, a description of the transitional provisions;*
    (e) *when applicable, the transitional provisions that might have an effect on future periods;*
    (f) *for the current period and each prior period presented, to the extent practicable, the amount of the adjustment:*
        (i) *for each financial statement line item affected; and*
        (ii) *if IAS 33 Earnings per Share applies to the entity, for basic and diluted earnings per share;*
    (g) *the amount of the adjustment relating to periods before those presented, to the extent practicable; and*
    (h) *if retrospective application required by paragraph 19(a) or (b) is impracticable for a particular prior period, or for periods before those presented, the circumstances that led to the existence of that condition and a description of how and from when the change in accounting policy has been applied.*

    Financial statements of subsequent periods need not repeat these disclosures.

29. *When a voluntary change in accounting policy has an effect on the current period or any prior period, would have an effect on that period except that it is impracticable to determine the amount of the adjustment, or might have an effect on future periods, an entity shall disclose:*
    (a) *the nature of the change in accounting policy;*
    (b) *the reasons why applying the new accounting policy provides reliable and more relevant information;*
    (c) *for the current period and each prior period presented, to the extent practicable, the amount of the adjustment:*
        (i) *for each financial statement line item affected; and*
        (ii) *if IAS 33 applies to the entity, for basic and diluted earnings per share;*
    (d) *the amount of the adjustment relating to periods before those presented, to the extent practicable; and*
    (e) *if retrospective application is impracticable for a particular prior period, or for periods before those presented, the circumstances that led to the existence of that condition and a description of how and from when the change in accounting policy has been applied.*

    Financial statements of subsequent periods need not repeat these disclosures.

30. *When an entity has not applied a new IFRS that has been issued but is not yet effective, the entity shall disclose:*
    (a) *this fact; and*
    (b) *known or reasonably estimable information relevant to assessing the possible impact that application of the new IFRS will have on the entity's financial statements in the period of initial application.*

In order to comply with paragraph 30 of IAS 8, an entity should disclose the title of the new accounting standard, the nature of the impending change or changes in accounting policy; the date by which application of the accounting standard is required; the date as at which it plans to apply the accounting standard initially; and either (i) a discussion of the impact that initial application of the accounting standard is expected to have on the entity's financial statements; or (ii) if that impact is not known or reasonably estimable, a statement to that effect.

Lastly, IAS 8 requires all significant changes in accounting policies to be disclosed in the summary of significant accounting policies.

14.6   Profit as a guide to an organisation's success

A central role of accounting is to determine the 'profit or loss' of an organisation (or perhaps, more appropriately these days, we might refer to 'total comprehensive income' rather than profit). As we are aware from media reports, profits often appear to be used as an indicator of the success of an organisation. Similarly, *financial performance* measures such as gross domestic product (GDP) and inflation rates are often used as a measure of the performance or success of a country.

We must remember, however, that *profit* is a measure of financial performance. Hence, non-financial issues such as the *social and environmental performance* of an entity are not directly incorporated within the calculation of financial profit or loss (or comprehensive income). If a company is exploiting its workforce, causing environmental damage or producing potentially unsafe goods, this will not directly impact on profits—although ultimately community support could wane causing demand for the organisation's products to fall. Also, newspaper articles about how a particular company's profits have increased or decreased typically do not mention the accounting methods used to calculate the profit or loss. As we know, the profit figure really only makes sense when considered in the light of the accounting policies adopted and the accounting assumptions made. By not referring to the accounting policies, methods and assumptions, the media tends to treat accounting profits as an objective reality—something we know it is not. The determination of accounting profits is based on many professional judgements, which makes it unlikely that different teams of accountants would calculate the same profit or loss for a particular entity for a given period.

There are various definitions of income in existence (and the term 'income' as used in the economics literature often equates with what an accountant would refer to as 'profit'). Often cited is the one provided by Hicks (1939):

> *The purpose of income calculations in practical affairs is to give people an indication of the amount which they can consume without impoverishing themselves. Following out this idea, it would seem that we ought to define a man's income as the maximum value which he can consume during a week and still expect to be as well-off at the end of the week as he was at the beginning.*

Hicks thus introduced the notion of 'well-offness' to income determination, which would not necessarily have to be restricted to financial wealth. Being well-off could also include factors such as health, happiness, satisfaction and so on. However, for practical purposes the determination of these other components of 'well-offness' would be extremely difficult, and traditional financial accounting, as applied to business entities, typically ignores personal and social issues associated with an entity's performance. Bierman and Davidson (1969) adapted Hicks' definition to argue that the profit of a business entity is 'the dividend which could be paid and leave the firm as well off at the end as it was at the beginning of the period'.

There has been a surge recently of research into social and environmental performance reporting. Many writers have highlighted that, although the economic success of an organisation is typically gauged by using the output of the financial accounting system, this generally ignores environmental and other social consequences unless direct cash flows are incurred such as fines, clean-up costs, investments in recycling plant and so on. An entity can be very successful in financial accounting terms, yet be doing extensive damage to the environment (thereby potentially leaving future generations less 'well-off').

As discussed in previous chapters of this book, there are numerous reasons why traditional financial accounting calculations of profit ignore an organisation's environmental and other social impacts. For example, traditional financial accounting is based on a model that emphasises property rights and market transactions. This means that many 'costs' imposed on society—'social costs' that do not generate cash flows—are ignored because of the role of control in the definition of what constitutes an asset and hence an expense. If an object or resource is not 'controlled' (for example, the air, oceans and waterways), it is excluded from asset recognition. Therefore, if traditional accounting practices are adopted, any diminution in the non-controlled resource's value or quality, such as pollution's adverse effect on air quality, will not be recognised as an expense of the entity.

Let us consider a fairly extreme example. Under traditional financial accounting, if an entity pollutes the water in its local environs, thereby killing all local sea creatures and coastal vegetation, there would be no direct impact on reported profits unless fines or other related cash flows were incurred. No externalities would be recognised and the reported assets/profits of the organisation would not be affected. Under conventional financial reporting practices, the performance of such an organisation could, depending upon the financial transactions undertaken, be portrayed as being very successful. In this regard, Gray and Bebbington (1992, p. 6) note:

> *there is something profoundly wrong about a system of measurement, a system that makes things visible and which guides corporate and national decisions that can signal success in the midst of desecration and destruction.*

Such views can lead us to question how relevant the existing financial reporting frameworks are to environmental and other social performance reporting activities and to recent debates about the need for society (and business entities) to embrace sustainable development. Another point to be stressed is that 'profit' represents the amount that might subsequently be returned to one stakeholder group—the owners—in the form of dividends. Returns to other stakeholders, such as employees, are treated as expenses, yet clearly the payment of salaries generates social benefits. When we commend organisations for high profits we are, perhaps, putting the interests of the investors (the owners) above the interests of other stakeholders. It is not uncommon to see a report in the financial press that a particular company generated a sound profit *despite* increased wage costs. In such a context there is an implication that high returns to one stakeholder (employees) are somehow bad, but gains to other stakeholders (the owners of capital in the form of increased dividends) are good. As Collison (1998, p. 7) states:

> *Financial description of the factors of production in the business media and even in text books, makes clear that profit is an output to be maximised while recompense to labour is a cost to be minimised.* Financial Times *contributors are fond of words like 'ominous' to describe real wage rises: such words are not used to describe profit increases.*

Consider the following extract from an article that appeared on the BBC News website.

Financial Accounting in the News 14.1

FRANCE'S AREVA TO CUT NUCLEAR JOBS AND INVESTMENT

BBC News website, 13 December 2011

Areva has unveiled big cuts to jobs, investments and dividends as it forecast an operating loss of up to 1.6bn euros ($2.1bn, £1.4bn) this year.

The French nuclear giant will shed up to 1,500 workers in Germany—a quarter of its workforce there—after Berlin's decision to phase out nuclear power. French employees will face a wage freeze next year, but no job cuts, while management are forgoing bonuses. Its 2012–16 global investment plans are being cut by 34% to 7.7bn euros. Among the projects being shelved as part of the company's new five-year turnaround plan are:

- a $3bn uranium enrichment plant in the US state of Idaho

- expansion of uranium mines in South Africa, Namibia and the Central African Republic

- expansion of three nuclear plants in France.

Final decisions about the French state-owned firm's investments have yet to be made, according to chief executive Luc Oursel, who took over in June.

Markets responded positively to the details of the plan. The overall thrust of the cuts had been well flagged in advance. Shares rose 1.2% in early trading, outperforming other utility firms. The company's share price remains down more than a third since it first listed on the Paris stock exchange in late May.

Source: www.bbc.co.uk. © BBC 2012

Obviously, reducing available jobs would generate social costs—but such costs are ignored by financial accounting. Similarly, when an organisation spends resources to support local community initiatives (for example, support of educational initiatives), such expenditure is typically treated as an expense (with an adverse impact on profits), even though the expenditure generates social benefits.

The issues associated with recognising the social and environmental implications of an entity's operations are the subject of ongoing debate, but at this stage it is important to recognise that financial performance indicators, such as profits or 'total comprehensive income', are not comprehensive indicators of the overall performance of an organisation. For a comprehensive view of an organisation's performance, financial measures such as profitability should be supplemented with other types of performance-based information, perhaps tied to the social and environmental performance of the entity.

A final point to be made in this chapter concerns government departments. They have recently been required to embrace traditional financial accounting methods. Previously, government departments typically accounted for their operations on a cash basis, with very limited use of accruals and limited attention to profitability. However, greater focus is now being placed on the profitability of government departments. Proponents of this approach argue that it forces managers to be more *accountable* for their departments' performance. However, others argue that it is highly inappropriate for institutions such as government-controlled employment agencies, hospitals, museums, art galleries and national parks to be judged on their ability to generate profits or reduce costs—in fact, focusing on accounting profits distracts them from pursuing the proper goals of their organisations: the provision of necessary social services. Do you consider that traditional financial accounting, as used by private sector, profit-seeking entities, is applicable to government departments? This is an interesting issue.

14.7 Future changes in the requirements pertaining to how we present information about comprehensive income

As noted in Chapter 4, in October 2008 the IASB issued a Discussion Paper entitled *Preliminary Views on Financial Statement Presentation*. The Discussion Paper proposes some significant changes to how financial statements, including the statement of comprehensive income, are to be presented. In particular, the aim is to make the financial statements more cohesive so the reader can follow the flow of information through the various financial statements (IASB 2008).

Pursuant to the proposed approach to presentation, an entity would classify income, expenses and cash flows in the same section and category as the related asset or liability. For example, if an entity classifies inventory in the operating category of the statement of financial position, it would classify changes in inventory in the operating category of the statement of comprehensive income (as part of cost of goods sold) and classify the related cash payments to suppliers in the operating category of the statement of cash flows.

The Discussion Paper proposes that an entity should identify and indicate in the statement of comprehensive income whether the item relates to (or will relate to) an operating activity, investing activity, financing asset or financing liability. It is proposed that the statement of comprehensive income be presented as follows:

- Business
  - Operating income and expenses
  - Investing income and expenses
- Financing
  - Financing asset income
  - Financing liability expenses
- Income taxes
  - On continuing operations (business and financing)
- Discontinued operations
  - Net of tax
- Other comprehensive income
  - Net of tax

According to the Discussion Paper, each entity would decide the order of the sections and categories, but would use the same order in each individual statement. The entity would disclose why it chose those classifications. In explaining the use of the management approach, the Discussion Paper notes that, because functional activities vary from entity to entity, an entity would choose the classification that best reflects management's view of what constitutes its business (operating and investing) and financing activities.

In relation to the presentation format proposed for the statement of comprehensive income, IASB (2008, p. 17) states:

> *The proposed presentation model eliminates the choice an entity currently has of presenting components of income and expense in an income statement and a statement of comprehensive income (two-statement approach). All entities would present a single statement of comprehensive income, with items of other comprehensive income presented in a separate section. This statement would include a subtotal of profit or loss or net income and a total for comprehensive income for the period. Because the statement of comprehensive income would include the same sections and categories used in the other financial statements, it would include more subtotals than are currently presented in an income statement or a statement of comprehensive income. Those additional subtotals will allow for the comparison of effects across the financial statements. For example, users will be able to assess how changes in operating assets and liabilities generate operating income and cash flows.*

In explaining why a single statement of comprehensive income is proposed, rather than the alternative approach whereby a separate income statement is presented, IASB (2008, p. 61) states:

> *when it was first introduced, the concept of comprehensive income was new to both entities and users of their financial statements. Permitting alternative formats for displaying the components of comprehensive income for several years allowed preparers and users of financial statements to become familiar with the new concept. The*

boards concluded that it is time to make the information easier to find and use by requiring it to be presented in a single format that displays all of the components of comprehensive income in the same financial statement.

While the above discussion is only a brief overview of current proposals, it is nevertheless hoped that this discussion provides an indication of the extent of change that might occur in future years, in terms of how we present financial statements. At the time of writing, it is not anticipated that any significant changes in presentation formats would be required before 2015.

SUMMARY

The chapter considered how to construct a statement of comprehensive income and a statement of changes in equity. It is stressed that profit as well as total comprehensive income reflects the recognition of various income and expenses and, as such, is influenced directly by the various asset and liability measurement rules being applied. For example, the valuation of liabilities on the basis of present values rather than face values would have a direct consequence for the expenses that would be recognised. Because profit is the difference between income and expenses, there is no need to have a separate recognition criterion for profits (or losses).

In entities adopting IFRS, the format of the statement of comprehensive income and the statement of changes in equity is governed by IAS 1. The statement of comprehensive income provides details of expenses and income, with such amounts either being incorporated within profit or loss or other comprehensive income. The total income and expenses of the period are then reflected in a measure referred to as total comprehensive income (which is the sum of profit or loss and 'other comprehensive income'). The statement of changes in equity provides information about transactions with owners in their capacity as owners, and also provides a reconciliation of opening and closing equity.

The chapter stressed that profitability is a measure of *financial* performance and as such should not be used as an all-encompassing measure of organisational performance or success. Profit calculations, using traditional financial accounting, typically ignore many social costs and social benefits attributable to an organisation's operations. The chapter also considered the accounting treatment of errors, changes in accounting estimates and changes in accounting policies.

KEY TERMS

assets	379	gains	378	revenues	378
expensed	379	options	378	true and fair	380

END-OF-CHAPTER EXERCISE

If you find you cannot confidently answer the questions that follow, you should go back and reread the relevant sections of the chapter.

1   Does the statement of comprehensive income disclose the income and expense items that were recorded directly in equity?   **LO 14.4**
2   If an entity was to discover that an expense of a prior period was omitted (perhaps as a result of a genuine mistake), should it record the error by increasing the expenses in the period in which the error was discovered or recognise the error by making an adjustment directly to retained earnings?   **LO 14.5**
3   What items must be disclosed on the face of the statement of comprehensive income?   **LO 14.1**
4   What are the two alternative classification bases for the disclosure of expenses in a statement of comprehensive income and what factors should be taken into account when selecting between the two alternative presentation formats?   **LO 14.1**
5   What items must be recorded on the face of the statement of changes in equity?   **LO 14.4**

REVIEW QUESTIONS

1. Within IAS 1 there is a prohibition on disclosing extraordinary items. Provide an assessment of the merits of this prohibition. **LO 14.1**

2. Provide some examples of items that would be adjusted directly against equity rather than being included as part of profit or loss. **LO 14.4**

3. Provide an argument explaining why expenses that were inadvertently omitted in a previous year should be debited directly to retained earnings in the following period in which the error is discovered, rather than recognising them in the profit or loss in the period when the error was discovered. **LO 14.5**

4. How is profit defined for accounting purposes? **LO 14.1**

5. When reviewing the financial statements and supporting notes of a reporting entity, is it possible to find out about all the individual types of expenses and income that the entity has incurred or received? If not, how does management determine which expenses and income should be disclosed? **LO 14.4**

6. List some of the expenses and income that must be disclosed according to IAS 1. Do these items have to be disclosed in the body of the statement of comprehensive income or can they be disclosed in the notes to the statement? **LO 14.4**

7. Does the statement of comprehensive income provide a reconciliation of opening and closing retained earnings? If not, where can such a reconciliation be found? **LO 14.4**

8. When is it permissible for a reporting entity to treat expenses directly as a reduction of retained earnings, rather than including them as part of the period's profit or loss? **LO 14.1**

9. What is the role of the statement of changes in equity and how does it complement the disclosures made within the statement of comprehensive income? **LO 14.4**

10. Do you consider that traditional financial accounting as used by private sector, profit-seeking entities is applicable to government departments? Explain your answer. **LO 14.3**

11. You are to consider the following two scenarios: **LO 14.6**

    Scenario 1: Fishtail plc has changed its basis of calculating doubtful debts from 2.5 per cent of gross accounts receivable to 4.0 per cent of gross accounts receivable.

    Scenario 2: Fishtail plc has previously allocated costs to inventory using a weighted average costing approach. It was decided to change to a first-in, first-out inventory cost flow assumption.

    REQUIRED

    Identify, giving reasons, which of the above scenarios is a change in accounting policy and which is not a change in accounting policy. Further, you are required to describe how the above scenarios are to be accounted for.

12. On 30 June 2015, the end of the current reporting period, Lynch plc made a decision, using the information obtained over the past few years, to revise the useful life of a particular item of its buildings acquired ten years earlier for €2,000,000. The useful life was revised from being a total of 25 years to being a total of 15 years. The building was originally depreciated on the straight-line basis over its useful life and it was expected that the asset would have no residual value. No depreciation has been provided in the current period. **LO 14.6**

    REQUIRED

    (a) Prepare the journal entry to account for the change in accounting estimate.

    (b) Assuming that the change in accounting estimate had a material effect on financial performance for the period, prepare an appropriate supporting note.

13. On 30 June 2013 Southside plc purchased 5,000 shares in ABC plc at €10.00 per share. On acquisition, Southside plc classified this investment as 'available-for-sale'. At 30 June 2014 the fair value of the instruments had increased to €14.00. At 30 June 2015 the fair value of the equity instruments had decreased to €13.00. All of the instruments were sold on 30 June 2015. No dividends were declared on those instruments during the time that they were held by Southside plc. At 30 June 2013 the only equity item was paid-up capital of €100,000. **LO 14.4**
    The applicable tax rate is 30 per cent.

    REQUIRED

    Prepare an extract of the statement of comprehensive income and statement of changes in equity for the reporting period ending 30 June 2015 in which the reclassification adjustment for available for sale investment is detailed.

14. On 30 June 2015, the end of the current reporting period, Helsinki plc made a decision, using the information obtained over the past few years, to revise the useful life of an item of plant acquired three years earlier for €3,000,000.

The useful life was revised from being a total of eight years to being a total of 12 years. The plant was originally depreciated on the straight-line basis over its useful life and it was expected that the asset would have no residual value. No depreciation has been provided in the current period. **LO 14.6**

REQUIRED

(a) Prepare the journal entry to account for the change in accounting estimate.

(b) Assuming that the change in accounting estimate had a material effect on financial performance for the period, prepare an appropriate supporting note.

15 The following two unrelated scenarios apply to Rabbit plc, whose financial year ends on 30 June 2015. **LO 14.7**

Scenario 1: Rabbit plc has, in the past, always depreciated its factory buildings over 25 years. As a result of new information obtained by the company during the current year, a decision was made to reduce the expected useful life of the buildings to 18 years.

Scenario 2: During the preparation of the financial statements it was discovered that a flood occurred in the previous financial year that destroyed some raw materials that were stored off-site and that were expected to have a long useful life. The materials were uninsured. No expense was recorded in the previous year in relation to the flood damage. The material was valued at €75,000 and the expense is considered to be material and will be permitted as a deduction for tax purposes. The tax rate is 30 per cent.

REQUIRED

Identify which of the two scenarios outlined above is a change in accounting estimate and which is a prior period error. Also provide any necessary journal entries.

CHALLENGING QUESTIONS

16 On 30 June 2015, the end of the current reporting period, Kirk plc made a decision, using the information obtained over the past few years, to revise the useful life of its building acquired five years earlier on 1 July 2010 for £1,000,000. The useful life was revised from ten years to 15 years. The building was originally depreciated on the straight-line basis over its useful life and it was expected that the building would have no residual value. No depreciation has been provided in the current period. **LO 14.6**

REQUIRED

(a) Prepare the journal entry to account for the change in accounting estimate.

(b) Assuming that the change in accounting estimate had a material effect on financial performance for the period, prepare an appropriate supporting note.

17 Noosa plc manufactures quality sports clothing. In the 2015 financial year, it reports a profit before tax of £500,000 and an income tax expense of £190,000. **LO 14.1**

REQUIRED

Consider each of the following items of information, and determine their appropriate treatment in the period's statement of comprehensive income. You can assume that each of the items is independent of the others.

(a) As of 1 July 2014 the tax rate increases, resulting in an additional expense to Noosa plc of £5,000.

(b) During recent years, Noosa plc has been developing a long-life wetsuit. The project has been in development for the past five years, with total related expenditure of £400,000 being capitalised as at 30 June 2015. In June 2015 the wetsuits are finally tested. The results are not favourable. The wetsuits act like sponges, absorbing a great deal of water, and a number of the people testing the garments drown. It is decided to abandon the development of the new wetsuits.

(c) On 1 July 2015 an agreement is signed to sell a division of Noosa plc to another organisation. The sale will generate a profit of £300,000. The sale should be finalised before the completion of the 2015 financial statements (financial statements will generally not be completed until two or three months after year end).

(d) Given the influx of tourists into the Noosa area, there has been additional demand for surf clothing in 2015. This has caused wages to increase from £80,000 in 2014 to £170,000 in 2015.

(e) In 2015 Noosa plc sells goods to France and South Africa. The sales to South Africa are denominated in South African currency. A crash in the value of the South African currency results in a foreign exchange loss of £20,000.

18 An extract from the financial statements of Wedding Cake Island plc for the year ended 30 June is provided below.
LO 14.5

Wedding Cake Island plc: Abridged statement of comprehensive income for the year ended 30 June	2015 (€)	2014 (€)
Profit before tax	19,000	23,600
Income tax expense	(5,700)	(7,080)
Profit for the year	13,300	16,520

Wedding Cake Island plc: Statement of changes in equity for the year ended 30 June 2015	Share capital (€)	Retained earnings (€)	Total (€)
Balance at 30 June 2013	3,000	3,040	6,040
Profit for the year	–	16,520	16,520
Distributions	–	(4,000)	(4,000)
Balance at 30 June 2014	3,000	15,560	18,560
Profit for the year ending	–	13,300	13,300
Dividends	–	(4,000)	(4,000)
Balance at 30 June 2015	3,000	24,860	27,860

The following additional information is available:
During the preparation of the 2015 financial statements, it became apparent that electricity expenses of €3,000 had been omitted when the 2014 financial statements were prepared.
The tax authority has indicated that electricity expense will be permitted as a deduction for tax purposes. The tax rate is 30 per cent.

REQUIRED
Prepare the statement of comprehensive income and statement of changes in equity so as to comply with all applicable accounting standards.

19 Fergie plc incurs the following expenses and income for the year ended 30 June 2015:   **LO 14.3**

	€000
Income	
Interest revenue	200
Sales revenue	1,600
Expenses	
Cost of goods sold	550
Administration salaries	170
Depreciation of office equipment	70
Major loss owing to insolvency of customer	110
Damage caused by 'space junk' re-entering atmosphere	65
Interest expense	25
Income tax expense	150
Opening equity	2,460

The income tax expense of €150,000 is calculated after considering a tax deduction of €21,450, which related to the damage caused by the space junk. The tax rate is 33 per cent.

During the year there has also been an increase in the revaluation surplus of €80,000 as a result of a revaluation of land of €80,000. The balance of the revaluation surplus at 1 July 2014 was €nil. A new accounting standard has also been introduced, which has a transitional provision allowing initial write-offs to be recognised as a decrease against retained earnings. The decrease against retained earnings amounts to €50,000. Retained earnings at the beginning

of the financial year were €1,950,000 and dividends of €200,000 were paid during the financial year. Issued share capital at 1 July 2014 and 30 June 2015 was €510,000.

REQUIRED

Prepare a statement of comprehensive income (in a single statement with expenses shown by function) and a statement of changes in equity in conformity with IAS 1. Provide only those notes that can be reasonably determined from the above information.

20 During 2008 Point Addis plc commenced the construction of a windfarm for its own use. During the reporting period ending 30 June 2015, a change in accounting standards means that the directors are required to change the company's treatment of borrowing costs incurred in the construction of assets for its own use. In previous periods, Point Addis plc expensed such costs, but must now capitalise them as part of the construction cost in line with the requirement of IAS 23 *Borrowing Costs*. The unadjusted statement of comprehensive income and statement of changes in equity for the reporting period ended 30 June 2015 are detailed below. **LO 14.4**

Point Addis plc: Abridged statement of comprehensive income for the year ended 30 June	2015 (£)	2014 (£)
Profit before tax	14,600	14,200
Income tax expense	(4,380)	(4,260)
Profit for the year	10,220	9,940

Point Addis plc: Abridged statement of changes in equity for the year ended 30 June 2015	Share capital (£)	Retained earnings (£)	Total (£)
Balance at 1 July 2013	12,500	8,050	20,550
Profit for the year		9,940	9,940
Distributions to shareholders	–	(2,700)	(2,700)
Balance at 30 June 2014	12,500	15,290	27,790
Profit for the year	–	10,220	10,220
Distributions to shareholders	–	(3,700)	(3,700)
Balance at 30 June 2015	12,500	21,810	34,310

Point Addis plc: Statement of financial position (extract) at 30 June	2015 (£)	2014 (£)	2013 (£)
Qualifying asset under construction	10,700	6,650	4,400
Other assets	23,610	21,140	16,150
	34,310	27,790	20,550
Share capital	12,500	12,500	12,500
Retained earnings	21,810	15,290	8,050
	34,310	27,790	20,550

Additional information

1. In 2015 interest of £4,000 relating to the construction of the windfarm was expensed. Interest costs of £3,000 were expensed in 2014, £3,900 was expensed in 2013 and £2,200 was expensed in reporting periods prior to 2013.

2. No depreciation has been charged on the windfarm as it has not yet been commissioned.

3. The tax rate has remained at 30 per cent for the past three years.

REQUIRED

Redraft the statement of comprehensive income, statement of changes in equity and statement of financial position (extract) so as to comply with generally accepted accounting practice and all relevant accounting standards.

REFERENCES

BIERMAN, H. & DAVIDSON, S., 'The Income Concept-Value Increment of Earnings Predictor', *Accounting Review*, April 1969.

COLLISON, D., *Propaganda, Accounting and Finance: An Exploration*, Dundee Discussion Papers, Dundee, Department of Accountancy and Business Finance, University of Dundee, 1998.

GRAY, R. & BEBBINGTON, J., 'Can the Grey Men Go Green?', Discussion paper, Dundee, Centre for Social and Environmental Accounting Research, University of Dundee, 1992.

HICKS, J.R., *Value and Capital*, Oxford, Oxford University Press, 1939.

INTERNATIONAL ACCOUNTING STANDARDS BOARD, *Discussion Paper: Preliminary Views on Financial Statement Presentation*, London, IASB, October 2008.

INTERNATIONAL ACCOUNTING STANDARDS BOARD, *Staff Draft of Exposure Draft IFRS X Financial Statement Presentation*, London, IASB, July 2010.

PARKER, C. & PORTER, B., 'Seeing the Big Picture', *Australian CPA*, December 2000, pp. 67–8.

Chapter 15

Accounting for Income Taxes

Learning objectives

Upon completing this chapter readers should:

LO1 understand that there is typically a difference between an organisation's profit or loss for accounting purposes and its profit or loss for taxation purposes;

LO2 be able to identify some of the types of factor that will cause a difference between profit or loss for accounting purposes and profit or loss for taxation purposes;

LO3 understand how deferred tax assets and deferred tax liabilities arise;

LO4 understand how changes in tax rates will impact on existing deferred tax balance;

LO5 understand how to account for taxation losses incurred by companies and understand how, in certain circumstances, taxation losses can lead to the recognition of assets in the form of deferred tax assets;

LO6 be able to describe how the revaluation of non-current assets should be treated for deferred tax purposes; and

LO7 be able to critically evaluate the *balance sheet approach* to accounting for taxation and the associated asset, deferred tax asset, liability and deferred tax liability.

15.1 Introduction to accounting for income taxes

accounting profit
A measure of profit derived by applying generally accepted accounting principles and accounting standards.

The application of the different accounting rules, typically incorporated within accounting standards, leads to the determination of **accounting profit**. Accounting profit is defined in paragraph 5 of IAS 12 *Income Taxes* as:

profit or loss for a period before deducting tax expense.

Profit for taxation purposes, also known as taxable profit, is, however, determined in accordance with the rules embodied within the income tax legislation of each country and not the rules embodied in accounting standards. There are a number of differences between accounting principles of income and expense recognition and taxation principles of income and expense recognition. The result is that accounting profit (derived using accounting rules as embodied within accounting standards) and taxable profit (using the rules incorporated in the income tax legislation) will generally differ.

In this chapter, the main focus is not on the determination of a company's taxable income or income tax payable. Such a focus would be a subject in itself and would require a detailed analysis of the relevant taxation legislation. Rather, we will be concentrating on the accounting treatment of income tax expense for the purposes of measurement and disclosure in an organisation's general purpose financial statements.

IAS 12 *Income Taxes* is the accounting standard that determines the accounting treatment of income taxes. IAS 12 applies what is known as the 'balance sheet method'. IAS 12 focuses on the recognition of assets and liabilities in the statement of financial position (the balance sheet) to ensure that the correct levels of future tax benefits, and of sacrifices arising from the differences between the accounting and tax values of assets and liabilities, are recognised. The balance sheet approach has been adopted because it is considered to be consistent with the IASB Conceptual Framework, which focuses on the statement of financial position rather than on the statement of comprehensive income (for example, the definition of income and expenses is directly related to changes in assets and liabilities).

Under IAS 12 the approach to accounting for tax is referred to as 'tax-effect accounting'. Pursuant to tax-effect accounting, income tax expense is not only equal to the current income tax payable (as it would be under the **taxes payable method**), but also takes into account the entity's deferred tax assets and deferred tax liabilities. In accounting for income tax, various events impacting the entity and various transactions undertaken by the entity will create two separate effects. There will be current liabilities for income tax payable and there will also be tax consequences beyond the next financial period. These future consequences will give rise to deferred tax assets and deferred tax liabilities—which are both the focus of IAS 12.

> **taxes payable method** A method whereby the amount that is payable to the taxation authorities is also treated as the tax expense of the organisation.

So, at this early stage of the chapter, we emphasise that it needs to be appreciated that the *tax expense* recorded in the statement of comprehensive income will not necessarily equal the amount of tax that has been assessed by a country's taxation authorities in relation to that period's operations. The tax assessed by the relevant taxation authorities, and reflected in the current liability of income tax payable (which appears in an entity's statement of financial position), will be based on the *taxable profit* derived by the entity, and this will be determined by applying the rules stipulated in taxation law, rather than the rules incorporated within accounting standards. From a financial accounting perspective, the liability 'income taxes payable' as appearing in the statement of financial position will be based on what is owed to the taxation authorities, and this liability will be based on the rules incorporated within the income tax legislation.

By contrast, the account 'income tax expense', which will appear in the statement of comprehensive income, will be based on what the organisation earned from a financial accounting perspective—that is, by applying

Table 15.1 Some of the differences between accounting rules and tax rules (these will differ from country to country depending on the taxation legislation)

Item	Generally accepted accounting rule	Tax rule
Many accrued expenses (for example, long-service leave, warranty costs)	An expense when accrued	Recognised as a tax deduction when paid
Depreciation	Treated as an expense when recognised	In some countries (the UK and Ireland, for example) the taxation authorities have their own form of depreciation, called 'Capital Allowances' and the rates of allowable cost can differ across asset type and across years
Entertainment and goodwill impairment	Treated as an expense	Not a tax deduction in current or subsequent periods
Doubtful debts	Treated as an expense when recognised	Treated as a tax deduction when the receivable is actually written off in subsequent period
Development expenditure	Often capitalised and subsequently amortised	Typically a tax deduction when paid for

accounting standards. 'Income tax expense' will typically not be the same as 'income tax payable' and we will refer to the resulting differences as deferred tax assets and deferred tax liabilities. As an example of some of the differences in recognition rules, consider the items in Table 15.1.

15.2   The balance sheet approach to accounting for taxation

The balance sheet approach to accounting for taxation focuses on comparing the *carrying value* of an entity's assets and liabilities (determined in accordance with accounting rules) with the *tax base* for those assets and liabilities. That is, we are comparing the statement of financial position that is derived using accounting rules with the statement of financial position that would be derived if we were to use taxation rules.

When considering how assets and liabilities would be recognised for taxation purposes, we refer to the *tax base* of the relevant asset or liability (also referred to as the 'tax basis'). The *tax base* is defined in IAS 12 as 'the amount that is attributed to an asset or liability for tax purposes'.

Where the carrying amount of an asset or liability (the carrying amount is determined using accounting rules) is different from the tax base, a 'temporary difference' can arise. IAS 12 defines a *temporary difference* as 'the difference between the carrying amount of an asset, liability or other item in the financial statements and its tax basis that the entity expects will affect taxable profit when the carrying amount of the asset or liability is recovered or settled'.

Paragraph 5 of IAS 12 explains that temporary differences may be either:

(a) *taxable temporary differences, which are temporary differences that will result in taxable amounts in determining taxable profit (tax loss) of future periods when the carrying amount of the asset or liability is recovered or settled; or*

(b) *deductible temporary differences, which are temporary differences that will result in amounts that are deductible in determining profit (tax loss) of future periods when the carrying amount of the asset or liability is recovered or settled.*

Using the information in Table 15.1 as a guide, Worked Example 15.1 provides you with an opportunity to calculate and compare taxable profit with accounting profit.

As we can see from the calculations in Worked Example 15.1, there can be reasonably significant differences between the profit we calculate by applying accounting rules (as embodied in accounting standards and generally accepted accounting procedures) and the profit we calculate for tax purposes (applying the tax legislation). In the pages that follow we will learn how to account for these differences.

Returning to paragraph 5 of IAS 12, as just quoted, something that will lead to an increase in taxable profit in future years (a taxable temporary difference) creates a liability—a *deferred tax liability*. Something that will lead to a decrease in taxable profit in future years (a deductible temporary difference) creates an asset—a *deferred tax asset*.

While this might seem confusing at first, the distinctions will become clearer in the illustrations that follow. To illustrate a *taxable temporary difference* that leads to a deferred tax liability, we can consider a depreciable asset—say, a machine. Let us assume that an entity acquires a machine at a cost of €200,000 in 2015. For accounting purposes the asset is expected to have a useful life of five years, after which time it is expected to have no salvage value; the benefits are expected to be derived uniformly, meaning that the straight-line method of depreciation will be used. We will also assume a tax rate of 30 per cent. For tax purposes, the asset can be depreciated on a straight-line basis over four years. Hence after two years we can determine the *carrying amount* (which is the amount calculated by applying accounting standards and other generally accepted accounting principles) and the *tax base* as follows (the determination of the difference between the tax base of a statement of financial position item and its carrying value is *central* to the balance sheet approach for accounting for taxes):

	Carrying amount	Tax base
Cost	€200,000	€200,000
less Accumulated depreciation	€80,000	€100,000
	€120,000	€100,000

In the above situation, what has effectively happened is that the taxation authorities have given the entity a greater deduction relative to the consumption of the economic benefits (as reflected by depreciating the asset

Worked Example 15.1 — Calculating taxable profit and accounting profit

You are provided with the following information from the financial statements of Big Kahuna plc for the year ending 30 June 2015:

Cash sales	£100,000
Cost of goods sold	£40,000
Capital allowances for the year	£5,000
Depreciation charge for the year	£10,000
Entertaining expenses	£1,000
Doubtful debts expenses	£1,000
Amount provided in 2015 for employees' long-service leave entitlements	£3,000

Required

Calculate taxable profit and accounting profit for the year ending 30 June 2015.

Solution

	Accounting profit	Taxable profit
Cash sales	£100,000	£100,000
Cost of goods sold	(£40,000)	(£40,000)
Capital allowances	–	(£5,000)
Depreciation	(£10,000)	–
Entertaining expenses	(£1,000)	–
Doubtful debts costs	(£1,000)	–
Amount provided in 2015 for employees' long-service leave entitlements	(£3,000)	–
	£45,000	£55,000

over its useful life). Further, while the entity is given tax deductions for the first four years, and has effectively reduced the tax that is payable in those years, no deduction will be given in the fifth year, as the cost of the asset will have been fully claimed with the taxation authorities by the end of year 4. Because no deduction will be available for taxation purposes in year 5, the entity has deferred the tax to the fifth year—that is, the entity has a deferred tax liability. A deferred tax liability is defined in IAS 12 as 'the income taxes payable in future reporting periods in respect of temporary differences'.

For example, if it is assumed that the entity with the above asset is going to generate accounting profits of £500,000, £600,000, £650,000, £700,000 and £800,000, respectively, in each of the next five years (before tax, and assuming that there is only one depreciable asset and no other temporary differences) and that the tax rate is 30 per cent, taxable income can be determined as follows:

	2015 (£)	2016 (£)	2017 (£)	2018 (£)	2019 (£)
Accounting profit	500,000	600,000	650,000	700,000	800,000
Add: accounting depreciation	40,000	40,000	40,000	40,000	40,000
Subtract: capital allowances	(50,000)	(50,000)	(50,000)	(50,000)	–
Taxable profit	490,000	590,000	640,000	690,000	840,000
Tax payable (at 30%)	147,000	177,000	192,000	207,000	252,000

Taxable profit is the profit derived by the entity determined by applying the current taxation rules. It will typically be different from accounting profit (which is derived by applying accounting standards). To work out taxable profit, we have to make adjustments to accounting profit so that we remove the effect of differences between accounting rules and tax rules. In this example we are assuming—somewhat simplistically—that the only difference in rules relates to how we are accounting for depreciation (in practice, there will be many differences). As we know, from an accounting perspective an item of property, plant and equipment is to be depreciated over its expected 'useful life' (see Chapter 5). However, from a taxation perspective specific depreciation rates might be stipulated that have no direct relationship to the useful life of an asset (accelerated depreciation rates may be offered by the government to stimulate investment in particular assets). So to determine taxable profit, we will adjust for those items of expense and income that are treated differently by taxation rules and accounting rules. In this example therefore we will add back the depreciation calculated from an accounting perspective (using the principles provided in IAS 16 *Property, Plant and Equipment*), and subtract the amount that would be allowed by the taxation authorities as a deduction to allow us to arrive at taxable profit.

As we can see from the above workings, the excess of the tax depreciation over accounting depreciation in the first four years reduces the taxable profit, and thus the taxes that have to be paid, by a total of £12,000 (which is four years multiplied by the excess of tax depreciation over accounting depreciation of £10,000 multiplied by the tax rate of 30 per cent). However, no depreciation is deductible in the fifth year (for taxation purposes, the asset is fully depreciated at the end of the fourth year and has a tax base of zero), meaning that to determine taxable profit the accounting depreciation has to be added back with no offset of the tax depreciation. Effectively, the entity is given an 'extra' deduction in years 1 to 4, which it will have to give back in year 5. There is in effect a 'timing difference'. A deferred liability is considered to exist throughout the life of the asset. Hence, in year 5 a further £12,000 in taxes will be payable. As we can see, at the end of five years the total depreciation for accounting purposes (£200,000) equals the total depreciation allowed for tax purposes (£200,000). Any differences in total depreciation throughout the five years are of a *temporary nature*. Once the additional taxation of £12,000 is paid in year 5, the deferred tax liability will no longer exist.

Let us now consider in Worked Example 15.2 a more detailed example relating to the depreciation of a non-current asset.

Worked Example 15.2	Temporary differences caused by the depreciation of a non-current asset

Robert August plc commences operations on 1 July 2012. On the same date, it purchases a fibre-glassing machine at a cost of €600,000. The machine is expected to have a useful life of four years, with benefits being uniform throughout its life. It will have no residual value at the end of four years. Hence, for accounting purposes the depreciation expense would be €150,000 per year. For taxation purposes, capital allowances are over three years, straight line—that is, €200,000 per year. The profit before tax of the company for each of the next four years (for years ending 30 June) is €500,000, €600,000, €700,000 and €800,000, respectively. The tax rate is 30 per cent.

Required

Determine the tax expense and taxes payable for the years 2013 to 2016, and provide the necessary accounting journal entries.

Solution

Year 1 (ending 30 June 2013)

	Carrying value (€)	Tax base (€)	Temporary difference (€)
Fibre-glassing machine: cost	600,000	600,000	
Accumulated depreciation	(150,000)	(200,000)	
	450,000	400,000	50,000

As the above calculations show, the carrying amount of the asset exceeds its tax base at the end of year 1, which, according to the definition provided in IAS 12, means that there is a *temporary difference*. Remember, the 'carrying amount' represents the net amount that would be shown in the statement of financial position applying the principles embodied within accounting standards. In this case, the temporary difference is €50,000 and will lead to a deferred tax liability. Effectively, tax is being reduced, or 'saved', in the early years (years 1 to 3), but the additional tax will need

▶

to be paid in year 4 when no deduction for depreciation will be available for tax purposes. The tax payment is being deferred. The excess of the accounting depreciation in years 1 to 3 creates a liability that will accumulate and be paid in year 4. The deferred tax liability at the end of the first year will be determined by multiplying the €50,000 by the tax rate of 30 per cent, giving a deferred tax liability of €15,000—which represents the amount of tax the company will pay when it recovers the balance of the carrying amount of the asset.

Paragraph 16 of IAS 12 explains why a deferred liability is created in situations such as this. It states:

It is inherent in the recognition of an asset that its carrying amount will be recovered in the form of economic benefits that flow to the entity in future periods. When the carrying amount of the asset exceeds its tax base, the amount of taxable economic benefits will exceed the amount that will be allowed as a deduction for tax purposes. This difference is a taxable temporary difference and the obligation to pay the resulting income taxes in future periods is a deferred tax liability. As the entity recovers the carrying amount of the asset, the taxable temporary difference will reverse and the entity will have taxable profit. This makes it probable that economic benefits will flow from the entity in the form of tax payments.

If we look at the calculations for year 1, we see that, in essence, the entity has claimed a €50,000 deduction from the taxation authorities in excess of the asset's recoverable amount. If the asset is sold for its anticipated recoverable amount, this €50,000 would be assessable and €15,000 would consequently be payable (€50,000 × 30 per cent).

However, accepting that the asset has not been sold, the total tax on the company's taxable income would be determined as follows:

Accounting profit before tax	€500,000
Add back accounting depreciation	€150,000
Subtract capital allowances	(€200,000)
Taxable profit	€450,000
Tax at 30 per cent	€135,000

The journal entries at 30 June 2013 would be:

Dr	Income tax expense	€15,000	
Cr	Deferred tax liability		€15,000

(to recognise the tax expense that relates to the temporary difference)

Dr	Income tax expense	€135,000	
Cr	Income tax payable		€135,000

(to recognise the tax expense that relates to the entity's taxable income)

As can be seen from the above journal entries, income tax expense, which will be shown in the statement of comprehensive income, represents the sum of the tax attributable to the taxable profit (as assessed by the taxation authorities) plus or minus any adjustments relating to temporary differences. It also equates to the accounting profit before tax multiplied by the tax rate, which would be €500,000 multiplied by 30 per cent, which equals €150,000. This is consistent with the definition of tax expense provided in IAS 12, which is 'the aggregate amount included in comprehensive income for the period in respect of current tax and deferred tax'.

Year 2 (ending 30 June 2014)

	Carrying value (€)	Tax base (€)	Temporary difference (€)
Fibre-glassing machine: cost	600,000	600,000	
Accumulated depreciation	(300,000)	(400,000)	
	300,000	200,000	100,000

The temporary difference at 30 June 2014 totals €100,000. Applying the tax rate of 30 per cent provides a deferred tax liability of €30,000. Because €15,000 has already been recognised in 2013, an increase (or 'top up') of €15,000 is required.

The tax on the taxable income would be determined as follows:

Accounting profit before tax	€600,000
Add back accounting depreciation	€150,000
Subtract capital allowances	(€200,000)
Taxable profit	€550,000
Tax at 30 per cent	€165,000

The journal entries at 30 June 2014 would be:

Dr Income tax expense	€15,000	
Cr Deferred tax liability		€15,000

(to recognise the tax expense that relates to the temporary difference)

Dr Income tax expense	€165,000	
Cr Income tax payable		€165,000

(to recognise the tax expense that relates to the entity's taxable income)

Year 3 (ending 30 June 2015)

	Carrying value (€)	Tax base (€)	Temporary difference (€)
Fibre-glassing machine: cost	600,000	600,000	
Accumulated depreciation	(450,000)	(600,000)	
	150,000	0	150,000

The temporary difference at 30 June 2015 is €150,000. Applying the tax rate of 30 per cent provides a deferred tax liability of €45,000. Because €30,000 has already been recognised in 2013 and 2014, an increase of €15,000 is required.

The tax on the taxable income would be determined as follows:

Accounting profit before tax	€700,000
Add back accounting depreciation	€150,000
Subtract capital allowances	(€200,000)
Taxable profit	€650,000
Tax at 30 per cent	€195,000

The journal entries at 30 June 2015 would be:

Dr Income tax expense	€15,000	
Cr Deferred tax liability		€15,000

(to recognise the tax expense that relates to the temporary difference)

Dr Income tax expense	€195,000	
Cr Income tax payable		€195,000

(to recognise the tax expense that relates to the entity's taxable income)

Year 4 (ending 30 June 2016)

	Carrying value (€)	Tax base (€)	Temporary difference (€)
Fibre-glassing machine: cost	600,000	600,000	
Accumulated depreciation	(600,000)	(600,000)	
	0	0	0

The temporary difference at 30 June 2016 is €nil, which means that there should be no deferred tax liability or deferred tax asset recorded in relation to this asset. This means the balance accrued in the deferred tax liability must be reversed in 2016.

The tax on the taxable income would be determined as follows:

Accounting profit before tax	€800,000
Add back accounting depreciation	€150,000
Subtract capital allowances	0
Taxable profit	€950,000
Tax at 30 per cent	€285,000

The journal entries at 30 June 2016 would be:

Dr Deferred tax liability	€45,000	
Cr Income tax expense		€45,000

(we credit tax expense because this €45,000 has already been recognised in previous years)

Dr Income tax expense	€285,000	
Cr Income tax payable		€285,000

(to recognise the tax expense that relates to the entity's taxable income)

A review of Worked Example 15.2 indicates that the balance sheet approach to accounting for income tax 'smooths' the tax expenses across the four years, as indicated below:

	Year 1 (€)	Year 2 (€)	Year 3 (€)	Year 4 (€)	Total (€)
Tax expense based on taxable profit	135,000	165,000	195,000	285,000	780,000
Adjustment for 'temporary' difference	15,000	15,000	15,000	(45,000)	–
Total taxation expense as reported in the statement of comprehensive income	150,000	180,000	210,000	240,000	780,000

The whole purpose of deferred taxation is explained clearly by Steve Collings (2009) on the Accountancy Students website:

> Students must understand that the primary intention of deferred tax is to present the estimated actual taxes to be payable in current and future periods as the income tax liability on the statement of financial position. Deferred tax liabilities are the amount of income taxes that are payable in future periods because of taxable temporary differences. Deferred tax is not paid to the tax authorities like (say) corporation tax liabilities are.

15.3 Tax base of assets and liabilities: further consideration

As already noted, *temporary differences* lead to *deferred tax assets* or *deferred tax liabilities*. Temporary differences arise because of differences between the *carrying amount* of an asset and its *tax base*. The tax base represents the amount that an asset or liability would be recorded at if a statement of financial position were prepared applying taxation rules.

Let us further consider the tax base of assets. According to paragraph 7 of IAS 12:

> The tax base of an asset is the amount that will be deductible for tax purposes against any taxable economic benefits that will flow to an entity when it recovers the carrying amount of the asset. If those economic benefits will not be taxable, the tax base of the asset is equal to its carrying amount.

In relation to the tax base of an asset, the following formula can be applied:

Carrying amount + Future amount deductible for tax purposes – Future taxable economic benefits = Tax base

Applying this formula to the depreciable asset in Worked Example 15.2, as at the end of the first year, gives:

€450,000 + €400,000 – €50,000 = €400,000

As we know, the 'carrying amount' of an asset is the amount at which the asset is recorded in the accounting records of an entity as at a particular date. The 'future amount deductible for tax purposes' represents the allowable tax deductions in future years in respect of the asset, and the 'future taxable economic benefits' represents the amount that is expected to be taxed in relation to the asset given existing tax laws and will typically equal the expected cash flows to be generated by the asset, either through use or sale.

Where the carrying amount of an asset exceeds the tax base, there will be a deferred tax liability. This is because the taxation payments have effectively been deferred to future periods (a greater deduction has been given in the early years by the taxation authorities and a smaller deduction, or no deduction, will be given in the later periods of the asset's life). Conversely, if the carrying amount of an asset is less than the tax base, there will be a deferred tax asset. In the above illustration, the deductible amount at the end of year 1 is €400,000 because that is the remaining amount that the taxation authorities will allow as a deduction (the asset cost €600,000, and €200,000 has already been claimed in year 1). Accepting that the carrying amount (€450,000) represents the economic benefits that remain to be derived from the asset, such remaining benefits will be taxable.

It should also be appreciated that, although an asset might be expected to give rise to future taxable amounts that exceed the asset's carrying amount, IAS 12 focuses on the tax consequences of recovering an asset to the extent of its *carrying amount* only. Worked Example 15.3 takes a closer look at determining the tax base of assets.

Worked Example 15.3 Determining the tax base of assets

McTavish plc has the following assets in its statement of financial position as at 30 June 2014.

Machinery

Acquired at a cost of £400,000 on 1 July 2012. It has a useful life for accounting purposes of five years, and no expected salvage value. Its carrying value at 30 June 2014 therefore is £240,000. Capital allowances are at 25 per cent per year (straight-line method).

Interest receivable

McTavish plc has recorded interest receivable (interest earned but not yet received) of £100,000. The taxation authorities will not tax the interest until it is received.

Accounts receivable

McTavish plc has made sales on credit terms amounting to £80,000, and at the end of the reporting period the £80,000 is still to be received. The taxation authorities have already included the £80,000 in taxable income.

Required

Determine the respective tax bases of the above items as at 30 June 2014.

Solution

Machinery

Given the above details, the tax base of the asset is £200,000, which is the cost of £400,000 less two years' capital allowances of £100,000 per year. The carrying amount will be £400,000 − [2 × (£400,000 ÷ 5)], which equals £240,000. This can be reconciled using the following formula:

> Carrying amount + Future amount deductible for tax purposes − Future taxable economic benefits = Tax base

£240,000 + £200,000 − £240,000 = £200,000

In relation to the machinery, £200,000 can be claimed for taxation purposes over the future years (the deductible amount). If the asset is going to generate future economic benefits of £240,000 (through its use or sale)—and this is implied by it having a carrying value of £240,000—the £240,000 will be taxable.

Interest receivable

As the taxation authorities will not tax the interest revenue until it is actually received, from the taxation authorities perspective the asset does not currently exist, and it therefore has a zero tax base. This can be verified using the following formula:

> Carrying amount + Future amount deductible for tax purposes − Future taxable economic benefits = Tax base

£100,000 + £0 − £100,000 = £0

In relation to the interest receivable, there are no related deductions. However, when the interest is actually received in a later period it will be taxable—therefore the future taxable amount is £100,000.

Accounts receivable

Because the sales have already been taxed, no further amounts are taxable. As the taxation authorities have recognised them, the tax base is £80,000. We will assume that no bad or doubtful debts are expected to arise.

This can be verified using the following formula:

> Carrying amount + Future amount deductible for tax purposes − Future taxable economic benefits = Tax base

£80,000 + £0 − £0 = £80,000

Worked Example 15.3 does not consider the issue of doubtful debts. If we assume that, of the credit sales of £80,000 that were made, the recovery of £6,000 is doubtful, the carrying amount of the accounts receivable would be £74,000, with a provision for doubtful debts of £6,000 being raised. For taxation purposes, the amount provided for doubtful debts is not tax-deductible. It is deductible only when the account receivable is actually written off—hence it will be deductible in a future period. As the entire £80,000 has already been taxed, no

further amount will be taxable in the future. The tax base of accounts receivable with a doubtful debt provision of £6,000 would be calculated as follows, with the temporary difference of £6,000 leading to a deferred tax asset:

> Carrying amount + Future amount deductible for tax purposes – Future taxable economic benefits = Tax base

£74,000 + £6,000 – £0 = £80,000

We will now turn our attention to determining the tax base of liabilities (see Worked Example 15.4). According to paragraph 8 of IAS 12, 'The tax base of a liability is its carrying amount, less any amount that will be deductible for tax purposes in respect of that liability in future periods'. If we also consider future taxable amounts, the tax base of a liability can be determined as:

> Carrying amount – Future amount deductible for tax purposes + Future taxable economic benefits = Tax base

IAS 12 provides an exception to the above rule, specifically in relation to revenue received in advance. Paragraph 8 of IAS 12 further states:

> *In the case of revenue which is received in advance, the tax base of the resulting liability is its carrying amount, less any amount of the revenue that will not be taxable in future periods.*

Worked Example 15.4 Determining the tax base of liabilities

Marc Nistelrooy plc has the following liabilities in its statement of financial position as at 30 June 2014.

Revenue received in advance

The company has received €100,000 for interest revenue received in advance. The taxation authorities tax the revenue when it is received by the company.

Accrued expenses

The company has accrued expenses relating to unpaid salaries amounting to €50,000. This is not allowed by the taxation authorities. The amount of the accrual will be tax-deductible when actually paid.

Loan payable

The company has a loan with a carrying value of €40,000. The payment of the loan is not deductible.

Required

Determine the tax base of Marc Nistelrooy plc's liabilities.

Solution

Revenue received in advance

In relation to revenue received in advance, the tax base of a liability that is in the nature of 'revenue received in advance' is equal to the carrying amount of the liability where the 'revenue received in advance' is taxed in a reporting period subsequent to the reporting period in which it is received. It is equal to zero where the 'revenue received in advance' is taxed in the reporting period in which it is received.

Hence the tax base of the interest received in advance is:

Carrying amount	–	Amount of revenue received in advance that will not be subject to tax in future periods	=	Tax base

€100,000 – €100,000 = €0

Accrued expenses

The taxation authorities do not recognise the expense until paid. As such, the tax base is €nil. This can be confirmed as:

> Carrying amount – Future amount deductible for tax purposes + Future taxable economic benefits = Tax base

€50,000 – €50,000 + €0 = €0

Loan payable

As the loan gives rise to no future tax deductions or to any taxable income, the tax base will be €40,000.

> Carrying amount – Future amount deductible for tax purposes + Future taxable economic benefits = Tax base

€40,000 – €0 + €0 = €40,000

15.4 Deferred tax assets and deferred tax liabilities

As we have already stated, *deferred tax assets* and *deferred tax liabilities* occur because of *temporary differences* between the *carrying amount* of an asset or liability in the statement of financial position and the respective *tax bases*. Whether a deferred tax asset or a deferred tax liability will arise is summarised in Table 15.2.

Table 15.2 Overview of when a deferred tax liability or a deferred tax asset will arise

	Deferred tax liability	Deferred tax asset
Assets	Carrying amount > tax base	Carrying amount < tax base
Liabilities	Carrying amount < tax base	Carrying amount > tax base

In the earlier worked examples, we determined the tax base of a number of assets and liabilities. Information about *carrying values* and *tax bases* is necessary before the *deferred tax assets* and *deferred tax liabilities* can be determined. Information about tax rates is also necessary. The general principle applied is that deferred tax liabilities and assets must be measured as:

> *the temporary differences that give rise to recognised deferred tax liabilities and assets and the unused tax losses that can be carried forward and give rise to recognised deferred tax assets*

multiplied by

> *the tax rates that are expected to apply to the reporting period or periods when the liabilities are settled or assets recovered, based on tax rates (and tax laws) that have been enacted or substantively enacted by the reporting date and that will affect the amount of income tax payable (recoverable).*

We can summarise the above with the following formulae:

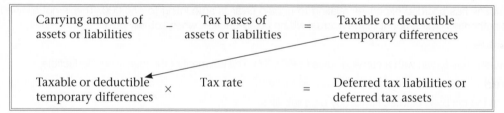

Worked Examples 15.5 and 15.6 further illustrate accounting for temporary differences.

Worked Example 15.5 **Temporary differences and the recognition of a deferred tax liability**

Wingnut plc's statement of financial position shows an item of machinery that cost €150,000 and that has accumulated depreciation of €40,000, giving a carrying amount of €110,000. For taxation purposes the asset has a net value of €90,000. Wingnut plc also has interest receivable of €15,000, which will not be taxed by the taxation authorities until it is received (that is, the taxation authorities do not currently recognise its existence). The tax rate is 30 per cent.

Required

Calculate Wingnut plc's deferred tax liability and provide the relevant journal entries.

Solution

	Carrying value (€)	Tax base (€)	Temporary difference (€)
Machinery—cost	150,000	150,000	
Accumulated depreciation	(40,000)	(60,000)	
	110,000	90,000	20,000
Interest receivable	15,000	0	15,000
			35,000

◀ The respective tax bases can also be confirmed as follows:

For machinery

> Carrying amount + Future amount deductible for tax purposes − Future taxable economic benefits = Tax base

    €110,000 + €90,000 − €110,000 = €90,000

For the interest receivable

> Carrying amount + Future amount deductible for tax purposes − Future taxable economic benefits = Tax base

    €15,000 + €0 − €15,000 = €0

The deferred tax liability is calculated by multiplying the temporary difference of €35,000 by the tax rate of 30 per cent, giving €10,500. The journal entries would be:

Dr Income tax expense	€10,500	
Cr Deferred tax liability		€10,500

Worked Example 15.6	A deductible temporary difference resulting in a deferred tax asset

Kuyt plc's statement of financial position shows that a provision for warranty expenses exists with a balance of €100,000. All of the provision was created in the current financial year, and no amounts have been paid. The warranty expense is not deductible until such time as costs associated with the warranty are actually paid. The tax rate is 30 per cent.

Required

Determine the balance of the deferred tax asset and provide the relevant journal entries.

Solution

The taxation authorities will recognise the expense only when it is paid. Therefore it will not have recognised the warranty expenses, and associated provision, of Kuyt plc, and the tax base is €nil.

	Carrying value (€)	Tax base (€)	Temporary difference (€)
Accrued warranty expense	100,000	0	100,000

The tax base can be confirmed as follows:

> Carrying amount − Future amount deductible for tax purposes + Future taxable economic benefits = Tax base

    €100,000 − €100,000 + €0 = €0

While the taxation authorities will not give a deduction in the current period, it will in future years and the taxable income will consequently be reduced in the future by the amount of €100,000 when the related payments are actually made. This means that future tax payments will be reduced by €30,000 (€100,000 × tax rate of 30 per cent)—this represents a benefit and is a deferred tax asset. The journal entry would be:

Dr Deferred tax asset	€30,000	
Cr Income tax expense		€30,000

When the warranty expense is actually paid in the next year, the above entry will be reversed. This is consistent with the requirement that, when temporary differences reverse, the deferred tax asset or deferred tax liability is removed from the financial statements.

When recognising a deferred tax asset or a deferred tax liability, a number of assumptions are made. A key assumption is that the entity will remain in business (in other words, it is a going concern) and that taxable income will be derived in future years. The recognition criteria for deferred tax assets are the same as those applied to other assets and rely on the 'probable' test. IAS 12 provides the general rule that a deferred tax asset must be recognised for all deductible temporary differences that reflect the future tax consequences of transactions and other events that are recognised in the statement of financial position to the extent that it is probable that future taxable amounts within the entity will be available against which the deductible temporary differences can be utilised (IAS 27, paragraph 27).

Exhibit 15.1 contains the accounting policy for deferred taxation for the Volkswagen Group as per their 2010 annual report.

| **Exhibit 15.1** | **Accounting policy note from the 2010 annual report of Volkswagen** |

ACCOUNTING POLICIES
DEFERRED TAXES

Deferred tax assets are generally recognised for tax-deductible temporary differences between the tax base of assets and their carrying amounts in the consolidated balance sheet, as well as on tax loss carry-forwards and tax-credits provided it is probable that they can be used in future periods. Deferred tax liabilities are generally recognised for all taxable temporary differences between the tax base of liabilities and their carrying amounts in the consolidated balance sheet.

Deferred tax liabilities and assets are recognised in the amount of the expected tax liability or tax benefit, as appropriate, in subsequent fiscal years, based on the expected enacted tax rate at the time of realisation. The tax consequences of dividend payments are not taken into account until the resolution on appropriation of earnings available for distribution has been adopted.

Deferred tax assets that are unlikely to be realised within a clearly predictable period are reduced by valuation allowances. Deferred tax assets and deferred tax liabilities are offset where taxes are levied by the same taxation authority and relate to the same tax period.

15.5 Unused tax losses

Deferred tax assets can also arise as a result of tax losses. Losses incurred in previous years can generally be carried forward to offset taxable income derived in future years (under income tax legislation). That is, tax losses do not result in cash payments being made to the organisation by the government, but they can be carried forward to offset taxes that might be payable in future years. For example, if a company generates a loss for tax purposes of €100,000 in one year, and in the next year it generates a taxable income of €100,000, the prior period tax loss can be used to offset the taxable income and no tax will be payable. Hence generating a taxable loss can generate subsequent benefits in the form of the tax payments that will be saved in a future profitable period. The benefits will equal the unused tax loss multiplied by the tax rate.

Consistent with the test for deferred tax assets generated by temporary differences, deferred tax assets generated as a result of unused tax losses must also be able to satisfy the 'probable' test before they are recognised (see Exhibit 15.1 showing the accounting policy covering this issue)—hence the likelihood of the losses being used to reduce the tax liability in the future must be probable (IAS 12, paragraph 34).

If the company has a history of making losses or there are other doubts about the recoverability of the tax benefit lost, then the company must disclose evidence to support their contention that the entity will be profitable in the future and hence able to offset the unused losses for taxation purposes (IAS 12, paragraphs 35 and 36). A recent case taken by the accounting regulators in the Netherlands, involving the Dutch Authority for the Financial Markets (AFM) and Spyker NV, a Dutch holding company, highlights the controversy that surrounds the application of IAS 12 in respect of the creation of deferred tax assets on the basis of the capability of past losses to reduce potential future tax expenditure. Details of the case are provided in Financial Accounting in the News 15.1.

Financial Accounting In the News 15.1

Spyker NV, a Dutch holding and car company, has been in the news quite often in the last couple of years. The most recent large news item was the bankruptcy of Saab Automobile AB in 2012, which was taken over by Spyker in 2010.[1] Spyker originated in 1880, closed down in 1926, was regenerated in 1999 and went public on Euronext Amsterdam in 2004. The company assembles a limited number of sports cars in Coventry, UK—50 to 100 cars per year. The head office is in Zeewolde, Netherlands.

The annual reporting of Spyker NV was in the news in 2007 with regard to a court case because of assumed errors in the annual report 2006. The Dutch Authority for the Financial Markets (AFM) started a case against Spyker NV on the recognition of deferred tax assets. Spyker reported deferred tax assets of €4,752 million on an asset total of €188,317 million in its annual report 2006. AFM stated that Spyker was not allowed to capitalise carry-forward losses, unless there was evidence on the capability of the company to generate fiscal income to off-set against those losses. IAS 12.35 says deferred tax assets can only be recognised if there is evidence that sufficient future taxable profit will be available.

Until then, the company had never been profitable, except for in 2006. During 2007, the 2006 profit was restated into a loss, because of revaluation of the F1 team. On the issue of the tax assets, AFM stated that the information in the annual report of 2006 did not provide enough evidence for future profits for the deferred tax assets to be recognised. AFM wanted full restatement of the accounts of 2006.

AFM lost the case in 2007 and even started an appeal case at the supreme court in 2008. That case the AFM also lost. The motivation by both courts was the same. A full restatement of the accounts for every disputable item is not necessary. A major issue mentioned by the courts was the different interpretations of 'evidence' between AFM and Spyker. The district court mentions the lack of detailed explanation of 'evidence' in IAS 12, although a bit more is written in IAS 12.82. Spyker's reply: it is the management's task to make estimates of the profitability of the company. The management is aware of insecurity with regard to those estimates, but insecurity as such is no reason to refrain from capitalisation of the tax assets. Spyker's opinion was supported by Ernst & Young. The district court ruled that Spyker could not have known that their future prospects would change dramatically in 2007.[2]

Reuters reported on 29 December 2007: 'Dutch court rules Spyker need not restate figures'[3]. Although they missed the issue of the deferred tax asset, the message was clear: there is no need to restate. But what had happened during 2007? In the annual report 2007, the deferred tax assets were not recognised again, as the management of Spyker states: 'Due to unforeseen adverse developments and resulting deterioration of the results in the second quarter of 2007, management decided to fully write off the deferred tax assets at the end of the second quarter of 2007.'[4]

Source: Compiled, with thanks, by René Orij from various sources.

Consistent with the test for deferred tax assets generated by temporary differences, deferred tax assets generated as a result of unused tax losses must also be able to satisfy the 'probable' test before they are recognised. Paragraph 36 of IAS 12 outlines the criteria that should be used when assessing the probability:

36. *An entity considers the following criteria in assessing the probability that taxable profit will be available against which the unused tax losses or unused tax credits can be utilised:*

   (a) *whether the entity has sufficient taxable temporary differences relating to the same taxation authority and the same taxable entity, which will result in taxable amounts against which the unused tax losses or unused tax credits can be utilised before they expire;*

   (b) *whether it is probable that the entity will have taxable profits before the unused tax losses or unused tax credits expire;*

   (c) *whether the unused tax losses result from identifiable causes which are unlikely to recur; and*

   (d) *whether tax planning opportunities (see paragraph 30) are available to the entity that will create taxable profit in the period in which the unused tax losses or unused tax credits can be utilised.*

   To the extent that it is not probable that taxable profit will be available against which the unused tax losses or unused tax credits can be utilised, the deferred tax asset is not recognised.

As a general principle applicable to all deferred tax assets, whether generated as a result of temporary differences or unused tax losses, it is a requirement that they be reviewed at each reporting date to ensure that the assets are not overstated (IAS 12, paragraph 56).

---

[1]Information from the annual reports of Spyker NV for 2010 and 2011.

[2]Epe (2010).

[3]Reuters, 'Court rules Spyker need not restate figures', 29 December 2007.

[4]Spyker NV, Annual Report 2007, p. 77.

Worked Example 15.7 illustrates the utilisation of unused tax losses.

Worked Example 15.7 Utilisation of unused tax losses

Grommit plc commenced operations in 2015. In the year ending 30 June 2015 it incurred a loss of £1 million. It is expected that the company will not incur losses again and will generate taxable profit in subsequent years.
The profits before tax in the following years are as follows:

Year	Profit before tax
2016	£300,000
2017	£400,000
2018	£600,000

It is assumed that there are no temporary differences between the carrying values of Grommit plc's assets and liabilities and the respective tax bases. The tax rate is 30 per cent.

Required

Provide the journal entries to show the recognition of the asset associated with the tax loss, as well as the journal entries to recognise the use of the loss.

Solution

2015

Accepting that it is probable that the entity will be able to recoup the benefits associated with the tax loss, the entry in 2015 would be:

Dr	Deferred tax asset	£300,000	
Cr	Income tax revenue		£300,000

Effectively, the above entry acts to reduce the size of the loss for accounting purposes from £1 million to £700,000, given the recognition of £300,000 in revenue.
The size of the deferred tax asset that is recognised can be summarised by the following formula:

$$\text{Unused tax loss} \times \text{Tax rate} = \text{Deferred tax asset}$$

2016

In 2016 the entity generates a profit of £300,000. In the absence of a tax loss, £90,000 would be payable. We still recognise tax expense, but rather than crediting *income tax payable*, we credit the deferred tax asset. This will reduce the balance of the *deferred tax asset* account to £210,000, and no amount will be payable to the taxation authorities.

Dr	Income tax expense	£90,000	
Cr	Deferred tax asset		£90,000

2017

In 2017 the entity generates a profit of £400,000. In the absence of a tax loss, £120,000 would be payable. As noted above, we still recognise tax expense, but rather than crediting income tax payable, we credit the deferred tax asset. This will reduce the balance of the deferred tax asset account to £90,000.

Dr	Income tax expense	£120,000	
Cr	Deferred tax asset		£120,000

2018

In 2018 the entity generates a profit of £600,000. In the absence of a tax loss, £180,000 would be payable. We can use the balance of the previously unused tax loss (£90,000) and the remaining amount will then be treated as income tax payable—a current liability.

Dr	Income tax expense	£180,000	
Cr	Deferred tax asset		£90,000
Cr	Income tax payable		£90,000

▶

The statement of comprehensive income for the four years is set out below:

	2018 (£)	2017 (£)	2016 (£)	2015 (£)
Profit/(Loss) before tax	600,000	400,000	300,000	(1,000,000)
Tax revenue/Income tax expense	(180,000)	(120,000)	(90,000)	300,000
Profit/(Loss) after tax	420,000	280,000	210,000	(700,000)

Statement of financial position extract for the four years as at 30 June

	2018 (£)	2017 (£)	2016 (£)	2015 (£)
Assets				
Deferred tax asset	–	90,000	210,000	300,000
Liabilities				
Tax payable	90,000	–	–	–

15.6 Revaluation of non-current assets

As discussed in Chapter 6, reporting entities often revalue their non-current assets to fair value. For an upward revaluation, the general entry is to debit the relevant asset account, and credit the revaluation surplus (unless the revaluation reverses a previous revaluation decrement). Chapter 6 did not discuss the tax implications of asset revaluations, and we will therefore consider them now. According to paragraph 20 of IAS 12, revaluations can create *temporary differences*.

When non-current assets are revalued, the revaluation increment is not deductible for taxation purposes, even though depreciation for accounting purposes will be based on the revalued amount. That is, the tax base is not affected by the revaluation because depreciation for tax purposes will continue to be based on the original cost. However, any increase in the carrying value of a non-current asset through a revaluation undertaken to recognise an increase in fair value implies an expected increase in the future flow of economic benefits. This increase can be taxable and can lead to a deferred tax liability. The rationale for the creation of a deferred tax liability is provided in paragraph 20 of IAS 12, which states:

The revaluation or restatement of an asset does not affect taxable profit in the period of the revaluation or restatement and, consequently, the tax base of the asset is not adjusted. Nevertheless, the future recovery of the carrying amount will result in a taxable flow of economic benefits to the entity and the amount that will be deductible for tax purposes will differ from the amount of those economic benefits. The difference between the carrying amount of a revalued asset and its tax base is a temporary difference and gives rise to a deferred tax liability or asset. This is true even if:

(a) *the entity does not intend to dispose of the asset. In such cases, the revalued carrying amount of the asset will be recovered through use and this will generate taxable income which exceeds the depreciation that will be allowable for tax purposes in future periods; or*

(b) *tax on capital gains is deferred if the proceeds of the disposal of the asset are invested in similar assets. In such cases, the tax will ultimately become payable on sale or use of the similar assets.*

As an example, let us assume that an entity acquires a depreciable non-current asset, say machinery, for a cost of £1 million. It is expected to have a useful life of ten years and no residual value. After using the asset for four years, the entity decides to revalue the asset to its fair value of £780,000. The depreciation expense for accounting purposes will then be £130,000 a year for each of the next six years (£780,000 divided by six). We will assume that, up to the date of the asset revaluation, the capital allowances were the same as depreciation for accounting purposes, that is, £100,000 per year, and we will assume that the tax rate is 30 per cent.

To record the revaluation, the following journal entry would be made:

Dr	Accumulated depreciation	£400,000	
Cr	Machinery		£400,000
Dr	Machinery	£180,000	
Cr	Revaluation surplus		£180,000

We can now consider the carrying amount of the asset and its tax base.

	Carrying amount (£)	Tax base (£)
Fair value/Cost	780,000	1,000,000
less Accumulated depreciation	nil	400,000
	780,000	600,000

Alternatively:

> Carrying amount + Future amount deductible for tax purposes − Future taxable economic benefits = Tax base

£780,000 + £600,000 − £780,000 = £600,000

There is therefore a temporary difference of £180,000. Because the carrying amount is greater than the tax base, this will give rise to a deferred tax liability (as summarised earlier in Table 15.2). However, unlike the previous examples in this chapter where a temporary difference is adjusted against income tax expense, asset revaluations give rise to a special case. IAS 12 requires that, to the extent that the deferred tax relates to amounts that were previously recognised in equity as either direct credits or direct debits (as is the case for upward asset revaluations), the journal entry to recognise the deferred tax asset or liability must also be adjusted against the equity account (IAS 12, paragraph 61).

Given that the revaluation is adjusted against equity (revaluation surplus), the accounting entry to record the recognition of the deferred tax liability would therefore be:

Dr Revaluation surplus	£54,000	
Cr Deferred tax liability		£54,000

(£54,000 = £180,000 x 0.30)

Hence the recognition of the future tax associated with an asset that has a fair value in excess of its cost, as recognised by a revaluation, acts to reduce the amount of the revaluation surplus (and, therefore, the amount of equity).

The above entries assume that the revalued amount of the asset will be recovered by the entity's continued use of the asset. The journal entries to record the deferred tax liability will be different if there is an expectation that the revalued asset will be sold. If a non-current asset is sold, in some countries there is often a 'tax break' given to the organisation, as the tax base is increased by an index that reflects general price increases.

If the tax that will be assessed in the future is to be reduced because of capital gains indexation, the reduction in the amount of tax that would be paid is accounted for by debiting the deferred tax liability and crediting the revaluation surplus. Hence in some countries the tax base of an asset can depend on the manner in which the

capital gains tax A tax that is payable on profits that arise when an asset (typically a non-current asset) is sold at a price in excess of its cost.

entity's management expects to recover the benefits inherent in the asset. **Capital gains tax** concessions, if available in particular countries, are typically provided when the asset is sold, not if it is being used within the organisation. The accounting entries to be made therefore will depend on the intended use of the revalued asset. As paragraph 51A of IAS 12 states:

In some jurisdictions, the manner in which an entity recovers (settles) the carrying amount of an asset (liability) may affect either or both of:

(a) the tax rate applicable when the entity recovers (settles) the carrying amount of the asset (liability); and
(b) the tax base of the asset (liability).

In such cases, an entity measures deferred tax liabilities and deferred tax assets using the tax rate and the tax base that are consistent with the expected manner of recovery or settlement.

Applying an example to the above requirement, let us assume that an item of property, plant and equipment has a carrying amount of €2,000 and a tax base of €1,200. Let us also assume that a tax rate of 20 per cent would apply if the asset was sold and a tax rate of 30 per cent would apply to other income and expenses. The entity would recognise a deferred tax liability of €160 (20 per cent of €800) if it expects to sell the asset without further use and a deferred tax liability of €240 (30 per cent of €800) if it expects to retain the asset and recover its carrying amount through use.

Worked Examples 15.8 and 15.9 examine accounting for a revaluation and Worked Example 15.10 gives a detailed example of accounting for tax.

Worked Example 15.8 — Accounting for a revaluation

Endless Summer plc has a building that has just been revalued to its fair value of €450,000. It was initially acquired at a cost of €300,000. The accumulated depreciation for tax purposes is €24,000. The tax rate is 30 per cent.

Required

(a) Assuming that there is an expectation that the asset will continue to be used by the company, determine the tax base of the asset.
(b) Assuming that there is an expectation that the economic benefits inherent in the asset will be recovered immediately through a sale, determine the tax base of the asset given that the asset was acquired when the index for capital gains tax was 100, while the index at reporting date is 120.

Solution

(a) The tax base can be determined as follows:

> Carrying amount + Future amount deductible for tax purposes – Future taxable economic benefits = Tax base

€450,000 + €276,000 – €450,000 = €276,000

(b) The tax base can be determined as follows:

> Carrying amount + Future amount deductible for tax purposes – Future taxable economic benefits = Tax base

€450,000 + €336,000 – €450,000   = €336,000

The future deductible amount is calculated by multiplying the cost of the asset by the increase in the size of the capital gains index, less the amount of depreciation that has already been claimed, that is, €300,000 × 1.2 – €24,000 = €336,000.

Worked Example 15.9 — Accounting for a revaluation

Winter Swells plc acquired an item of plant with a ten-year useful life, on 1 July 2011, for €200,000. At the end of the item's useful life, the plant will have a €nil residual value. For accounting purposes, the plant was depreciated on a straight-line basis over its useful life while, for tax purposes, the plant is depreciated at 20 per cent per annum on the straight-line basis. On 30 June 2015, which is four years after it was acquired, the plant was revalued to €210,000. The life and residual values remain unchanged. The tax rate is 30 per cent.

Required

(a) Assuming that the asset is expected to continue to be used by Winter Swells plc, determine the tax base of the asset and provide the necessary journal entries at 30 June 2015, assuming the €210,000 is recovered through use.
(b) Assuming that Winter Swells plc continues to use the asset in subsequent reporting periods, provide the journal entries for the depreciation and deferred tax for 30 June 2016 and 30 June 2017.

Solution

(a) *Determining the tax base and journal entries assuming the €210,000 will be recovered through use.*

On 30 June 2015 the journal entries to take account of the revaluation for accounting purposes, assuming the €210,000 will be recovered through use, would be as follows:

30 June 2015

Dr	Accumulated depreciation	€80,000	
Cr	Plant and machinery		€80,000

(eliminating accumulated depreciation on revaluation of asset)

30 June 2015

Dr	Plant and machinery	€90,000
Cr	Revaluation surplus		€90,000
(revaluing asset to fair value)		

> Tax base = Future amount deductible for tax purposes – Future taxable economic benefits of asset + Carrying amount

€40,000 = €40,000 – €210,000 + €210,000

Before the revaluation, the temporary difference was €80,000, which represented the difference between the carrying amount of €120,000 and the tax base of €40,000. A deferred tax liability of €24,000 (€80,000 × 30 per cent) would have appeared in the financial records. After the revaluation, the temporary difference is €170,000 (which is calculated at either €80,000 + €90,000 or €210,000 – €40,000), which would require a total deferred tax liability of €51,000 (€/£170,000 × 30 per cent). As the deferred tax liability already has a balance of €24,000 prior to the revaluation, a further €27,000 must be provided (€90,000 × 30 per cent).

The journal entry to reflect the deferred tax on the revalued amount would be:

30 June 2015

Dr	Revaluation surplus	€27,000
Cr	Deferred tax liability		€27,000
(allocating deferred tax to revaluation surplus)		

Deferred tax is provided on the full increase in value, which includes the amount above the original cost as the carrying amount is expected to be recovered through the generation of taxable profit.

(b) *Provide the journal entries for the depreciation and deferred tax for 30 June 2016 and 30 June 2017.*

30 June 2016

Dr	Depreciation	€35,000
Cr	Accumulated depreciation		€35,000
(depreciation expense for the reporting period ending 30 June 2016 (€35,000 = €210,000 ÷ 6))		

The deferred tax on the increased accounting depreciation must be reversed back to the revaluation surplus, whereas the deferred tax on the depreciation on the original cost will still flow through the statement of comprehensive income. The entries will be as follows:

30 June 2016

Dr	Income tax expense	€6,000
Cr	Revaluation surplus		€4,500
Cr	Deferred tax liability		€1,500
(deferred tax on depreciation for the reporting period ending 30 June 2016)		

The total deferred tax liability will now be €52,500 (€24,000 + €27,000 + €1,500). This amounts to 30 per cent of the total temporary differences of €175,000 at 30 June 2016. At 30 June 2016 the tax base of the asset would be zero as it has been fully depreciated over the five years for tax purposes at €40,000 per annum, which equates to the original cost of €200,000. Once the asset reaches the end of its useful ten-year life, the balance of the revaluation surplus will be €90,000; that is, the tax effect of the original revaluation will be reversed out by way of six annual credit entries to revaluation surplus of €4,500 each [€90,000 = €90,000 – €27,000 + (6 × €4,500)].

30 June 2017

Dr	Depreciation	€35,000
Cr	Accumulated depreciation		€35,000
(depreciation expense for the reporting period ending 30 June 2017)		

The deferred tax on the increased accounting depreciation must be reversed back to the revaluation surplus, whereas the deferred tax on the depreciation on the original cost will still flow through the statement of comprehensive income. The entries will be as follows:

30 June 2017

Dr	Deferred tax liability	€10,500
Cr	Tax expense		€6,000
Cr	Revaluation surplus		€4,500

(deferred tax on depreciation for the reporting period ending 30 June 2017)

The total deferred tax liability will now be €42,000 (€52,500 – €10,500). This amounts to 30 per cent of the total temporary differences of €140,000 at 30 June 2017.

Worked Example 15.10 Detailed example of accounting for tax

First Point plc commences operations on 1 July 2014. One year later, on 30 June 2015, the entity prepares the following information, showing both the *carrying amounts* for accounting purposes, and *tax bases* of the respective assets and liabilities.

	Extract from accounting statement of financial position (£)	Tax bases (£)
Assets		
Cash	50,000	50,000
Accounts receivable (net)	35,000	40,000
Inventory	65,000	65,000
Plant—net	160,000	150,000
Land	400,000	300,000
	710,000	605,000
Liabilities		
Accounts payable	40,000	40,000
Provision for long-service leave	60,000	–
Provision for warranty	70,000	–
Loan payable	350,000	350,000
	520,000	390,000
Net assets	190,000	215,000

Other information
- After adjustments are made for differences between tax rules and accounting rules, it is determined that the taxable profit of First Point plc is £400,000.
- There is a doubtful debt provision of £5,000.
- An item of plant is purchased at a cost of £200,000 on 1 July 2014. For accounting purposes it is expected to have a life of five years; however, for taxation purposes it can be depreciated over four years. It is not expected to have any residual value.
- First Point has some land, which cost £300,000 and which has been revalued to its fair value of £400,000 in accordance with IAS 16.
- None of the amounts accrued in respect of warranty expenses or long service leave has actually been paid.
- The tax rate is 30 per cent.

As demonstrated in the schedule below, given that First Point plc commences operations on 1 July 2014, there are no temporary differences at the commencement of the period. At the end of the period we determine whether there are differences between the carrying values of assets and liabilities (as reflected in the accounting statement of financial position) and their related tax bases. We then determine whether the differences lead to deductible temporary differences, or taxable temporary differences. Table 15.2 is useful for this purpose.

	Extract from accounting SOFP (£)	Tax bases (£)	Deductible temporary differences (£)	Taxable temporary differences (£)	Tax expense (£)	Revaluation surplus (£)	Income tax payable (£)
Assets							
Cash	50,000	50,000					
Accounts receivable net	35,000	40,000	5,000		(5,000)		
Inventory	65,000	65,000					
Plant—net	160,000	150,000		10,000	10,000		
Land	400,000	300,000		100,000		100,000	
	710,000	605,000					
Liabilities							
Accounts payable	40,000	40,000					
Provision for long-service leave	60,000	–	60,000		(60,000)		
Provision for warranty	70,000		70,000		(70,000)		
Loan payment	350,000	350,000					
	520,000	390,000					
Net assets	190,000	215,000					
Temporary differences at period end			135,000	110,000	(125,000)	100,000	
less *Prior period amounts*			–	–	–	–	
Movement for the period			135,000	110,000	(125,000)	100,000	
Tax effected at 30%			40,500	33,000	(37,500)	30,000	
Tax on taxable income, 30% × £400,000			–	–	120,000	–	120,000
Income tax adjustments			40,500	33,000	82,500	30,000	120,000

We then add the differences down the column before multiplying them by the relevant tax rate to determine the balance of deferred tax assets and deferred tax liabilities. The recognition of the deferred tax assets and deferred tax liabilities will also have direct implications for taxation expense, and adjustments to taxation expense will be necessary. The exception to this, however, is where the deferred tax relates to amounts that were previously recognised as direct debits or credits to an equity account. In this case, the adjustment must also be to equity. In this illustration, this exception is relevant to the asset revaluation pertaining to the land.

In the column under tax expense, the negative numbers reflect a decrease (or credit) to tax expense, whereas the positive numbers represent an increase in tax expense (a debit).

The income tax expense pertaining to taxable income is determined by calculating taxable income and multiplying it by the tax rate of 30 per cent, that is, £400,000 multiplied by 30 per cent, which gives £120,000. To this we add the tax effect of the temporary differences, other than that which relates to the asset revaluation. This total adjustment amounts to £37,500.

The required journal entries at 30 June 2015 would be:

Dr	Income tax expense	£82,500	
Dr	Deferred tax asset	£40,500	
Dr	Revaluation surplus	£30,000	
Cr	Deferred tax liability		£33,000
Cr	Income tax payable		£120,000

Because in most cases the tax is payable to the same authority, IAS 12 requires that the deferred tax liabilities and deferred tax assets be set off against one another and that only the net amount be disclosed in the statement of financial position. Hence, for statement of financial position purposes, we would offset the deferred tax liability of £33,000 against the deferred tax asset. The entry on 30 June 2015 would be:

Dr	Deferred tax liability	£33,000	
Cr	Deferred tax asset		£33,000

We can now consider the second year of operations of First Point plc, ending on 30 June 2016. It is expected that the taxable profit for 2016 will be £500,000. The company income tax rate is still 30 per cent. In this year the tax base of accounts receivable is lower than the statement of financial position amount. This might be because some income has been recognised for accounting before it is recognised for tax purposes. The new year-end balances for assets and liabilities are provided in the schedule below:

	Extract from accounting SOFP (£)	Tax bases (£)	Deductible temporary differences (£)	Taxable temporary differences (£)	Tax expense (£)	Revaluation surplus (£)	Current tax payable (£)
Assets							
Cash	80,000	80,000					
Accounts receivable	55,000	45,000		10,000	10,000		
Inventory	85,000	85,000					
Plant—net	120,000	100,000		20,000	20,000		
Land	400,000	300,000		100,000		100,000	
	740,000	610,000					
Liabilities							
Accounts payable	40,000	40,000					
Provision for long-service leave	80,000	–	80,000		(80,000)		
Provision for warranty	85,000		85,000		(85,000)		
Loan payable	535,000	535,000					
	740,000	575,000					
Net assets	–	35,000					
Temporary differences at period end			165,000	130,000	(135,000)	100,000	
less *Prior period amounts*			135,000	110,000	(125,000)	100,000	
Movement for the period			30,000	20,000	(10,000)	0	
Tax effected at 30%			9,000	6,000	(3,000)	0	
Tax on taxable income, 30% × £500,000			–	–	150,000	–	150,000
Income tax adjustments			9,000	6,000	147,000	0	150,000

The tax journal entries for the year to 30 June 2016 are as follows:

Dr	Income tax expense	£147,000
Dr	Deferred tax asset	£9,000
Cr	Deferred tax liability	£6,000
Cr	Income tax payable	£150,000

As we did in the previous year, we set off the deferred tax asset against the deferred tax liability in the statement of financial position presentation:

Dr	Deferred tax liability	£6,000
Cr	Deferred tax asset	£6,000

15.7 Offsetting deferred tax liabilities and deferred tax assets

As indicated in Worked Example 15.10, given that in most cases the tax is payable to the same authority, IAS 12 requires that, if certain conditions are met, then both the current tax liabilities and current tax assets as well as the deferred tax liabilities and deferred tax assets be set off against one another and that only the net amount of each set-off be disclosed in the statement of financial position. In relation to the set-off of current tax assets and current tax liabilities, paragraph 71 of IAS 12 states:

An entity shall offset current tax assets and current tax liabilities if, and only if, the entity:

(a) has a legally enforceable right to set-off the recognised amounts; and

(b) intends either to settle on a net basis, or to realise the asset and settle the liability simultaneously.

As the above paragraph explains, there is a need to have a 'legally enforceable right of set-off'. This is further explained in paragraph 72 of IAS 12:

> An entity will normally have a legally enforceable right to set-off a current tax asset against a current tax liability when they relate to income taxes levied by the same taxation authority and the taxation authority permits the entity to make or receive a single net payment.

The requirements pertaining to offsetting deferred tax assets and deferred tax liabilities are included in paragraph 74 of IAS 12, which states:

> An entity shall offset deferred tax assets and deferred tax liabilities if, and only if:
> (a) the entity has a legally enforceable right to set-off current tax assets against current tax liabilities; and
> (b) the deferred tax assets and the deferred tax liabilities relate to income taxes levied by the same taxation authority on either:
>   (i) the same taxable entity; or
>   (ii) different taxable entities which intend either to settle current tax liabilities and assets on a net basis, or to realise the assets and settle the liabilities simultaneously, in each future period in which significant amounts of deferred tax liabilities or assets are expected to be settled or recovered.

15.8 Change of tax rates

A deferred tax asset or a deferred tax liability is essentially an estimate of a future tax saving or an estimate of a future tax amount owing. As has been shown, the balance on the deferred tax account is calculated by multiplying the temporary difference by the tax rate in existence at the end of the reporting period.

Across time it is likely that governments will change tax rates. Changed tax rates will have implications for the value attributed to pre-existing deferred tax assets and deferred tax liabilities. For example, if an organisation has recognised a deferred tax asset relating to a previous loss for tax purposes and that previous carried-forward tax loss was £1 million, and the tax rate is increased from 30 per cent to 35 per cent, the amount of the deferred tax asset will need to be increased from £300,000 to £350,000. This is because when the organisation subsequently earns a taxable profit of £1,000,000, it will be able to offset the loss against the £350,000 in tax that would otherwise be payable under the revised tax rate. The £50,000 increase in the value of the deferred tax asset (which is calculated as £1,000,000 × [0.35 − 0.30]) would be treated as income, given that the carrying amount of the asset has been increased. Conversely, if the tax rate had been decreased, the value of the asset would be decreased and this would be recognised as an expense.

An increase in tax rates will create an expense where an organisation has deferred tax liabilities, whereas a decrease in tax rates will create income in the presence of deferred tax liabilities. Where there are both deferred tax assets and deferred tax liabilities at the time of a change in tax rate, there will be both gains and losses (there will be a gain on the asset and a loss on the liability, or *vice versa*) and the net amount would be treated as either income or an expense.

Worked Examples 15.11 and 15.12 provide examples of how to account for a change in tax rate.

Worked Example 15.11 Change in tax rates

As at 30 June 2014 the balance of the deferred tax liability account of Huntelaar plc was €660,000 credit. Assume that at 30 June 2015 the tax rate changed from 33 per cent to 30 per cent.

Required

Prepare the journal entries to record the change in tax rates for 2015.

Solution

The accounting entry at 30 June 2015 would be:

Dr	Deferred tax liability	€60,000
Cr	Income tax expense	€60,000

(reduction in tax expense resulting from a decrease in tax rate €660,000 − (€660,000/33 × 30) = €60,000)

Because there has been a downward revision of the deferred tax liability, a corresponding decrease in the income tax expense for the year ending 30 June 2015 will be reported in the statement of comprehensive income.

Worked Example 15.12   Impact of changing tax rates

Gerrard plc has the following deferred tax balances as at 30 June 2015:

Deferred tax asset   £500,000
Deferred tax liability   £300,000

The above balances were calculated when the tax rate was 30 per cent. On 1 August 2015 the government reduced the corporate tax rate to 25 per cent.

Required

Provide the journal entries to adjust the carry-forward balances of the deferred tax asset and deferred tax liability.

Solution

	Balance at 30 June 2015	Balance at 1 August 2015	Change
Deferred tax asset	£500,000	£500,000 × 25/30 = £416,667	(£83,333)
Deferred tax liability	£300,000	£300,000 × 25/30 = £250,000	(£50,000)

The accounting entry at 1 August 2015 would be:

Dr	Deferred tax liability	£50,000	
Dr	Income tax expense	£33,333	
Cr	Deferred tax asset		£83,333

15.9 Evaluation of the assets and liabilities created by IAS 12

Throughout this book we have considered the definitions of the financial elements provided in the IASB Conceptual Framework. At this point, we may consider whether the asset 'deferred tax asset' or the liability 'deferred tax liability' as generated by tax-effect accounting actually meet the definitions provided within the IASB Conceptual Framework.

First, let us consider the deferred tax asset. As we know, an asset is defined as a 'resource controlled by the entity as a result of past events and from which future economic benefits are expected to flow to the entity' (paragraph 4.4(a) of the IASB Conceptual Framework). At the end of the reporting period, the company really has no claim against the government for the value of the deferred tax asset. The realisation of the benefit will arise only if the company earns sufficient revenue in the future and if the relevant taxation legislation does not change. It is questionable whether the benefits are actually *controlled* by the entity at reporting date. There is arguably a contingent element involved.

With respect to the deferred tax liability, a liability is defined in the IASB Conceptual Framework as, 'a present obligation of the entity arising from past events, the settlement of which is expected to result in an outflow from the entity of resources embodying economic benefits'. Where a deferred tax liability exists, the company is not currently obliged to transfer funds of an amount equal to the balance of the account. The funds will be transferred in the future only if the company earns sufficient revenue; that is, there is a dependency on future events, not past events. There is also the assumption that the relevant taxation legislation will not change.

The earlier discussion of issues associated with the revaluation of non-current assets revealed that the amount recorded in the deferred tax liability account will depend upon determining whether management intends for the entity continue to use the asset or whether it intends to sell the asset. If the entity intends to sell the asset, lower tax might be deferred to subsequent periods because of the capital gains allowances that are granted through indexing the cost of the asset. This means that the amount recognised for the liability will be the result of decisions taken by management. To some people it might be inconceivable that a liability is recognised only because management has made a decision to revalue an asset. However, in supporting this treatment under the balance sheet approach, Westwood (2000, p. 318) argues that:

> *The Balance Sheet approach does not necessarily recognise all deferred tax obligations. The basis of the Balance Sheet approach is that deferred tax obligations are recognised to the extent that the underlying assets giving rise*

to the obligations are recognised. The justification is that when an asset revaluation increment is recognised, the equity of the entity has been increased by the future assessable revenues that it is probable that the asset will generate. A corresponding deferred tax obligation must then be recognised at that point to account for the relevant portion of those future assessable revenues that must be paid in tax. This justification assumes that rights (to future revenues) implicit in assets trigger obligations (to future expenses) implicit in liabilities.

As a last general comment, the record-keeping costs associated with applying the balance sheet method are likely to be high, as the accounting is quite complex. Whether this cost is justified in terms of increased usefulness of financial statements is questionable. It will take a very sophisticated reader of financial statements to be able to understand how a deferred tax asset and a deferred tax liability are calculated and what the calculated number actually represents.

SUMMARY

In this chapter we explored how to account for taxes. It was established that *taxable profit* and *accounting profit* will often be different because expense and recognition rules used in accounting are frequently different from those applied for taxation purposes.

IAS 12 applies the balance sheet method for accounting for taxes. This requires a comparison of the *carrying values* and *tax bases* of the entity's assets and liabilities. The comparison of these values is the key to applying the balance sheet method.

The difference between *carrying values* and *tax bases* leads to *deductible temporary differences* or *taxable temporary differences*. Multiplying these differences by the tax rate gives *deferred tax assets* and *deferred tax liabilities*. Generally speaking, if the carrying amount of an asset is greater than its tax base, there will be a deferred tax liability. Conversely, if the carrying value of an asset is less than its tax base, there will be a deferred tax asset. If the carrying value of a liability is greater than its tax base, there will be a deferred tax asset, and if the carrying value of a liability is less than its tax base, there will be a deferred tax liability.

For an entity to recognise deferred tax assets, whether brought about by temporary differences or unused tax losses, there is a requirement that the derivation of the associated economic benefits be probable.

In this chapter it was also established that, when the temporary differences associated with the revaluation of a non-current asset are taken into account, the balance of the revaluation surplus account is reduced.

KEY TERMS

accounting profit . . . . **414**   capital gains tax . . . . **430**   taxes payable method **415**

END-OF-CHAPTER EXERCISE

Wounded Seagull plc commences operations on 1 July 2014 and presents its first statement of comprehensive income and first statement of financial position on 30 June 2015. The statements are prepared before considering taxation. The following information is available: **LO 15.1**

Statement of comprehensive income for the year ended 30 June 2015	(£)	(£)
Gross profit	600,000	
Expenses		
Administration expenses		100,000
Salaries	55,000	
Long-service leave	10,000	
Warranty expenses	20,000	
Depreciation expense—plant	75,000	
Insurance	10,000	270,000
Profit before tax		330,000

Assets and liabilities as disclosed in the statement of financial position as at 30 June 2015	(£)	(£)
Assets		
Cash		30,000
Inventory		80,000
Accounts receivable		90,000
Prepaid insurance		4,000
Plant—cost	300,000	
less Accumulated depreciation	(75,000)	225,000
Total assets		429,000
Liabilities		
Accounts payable		50,000
Provision for warranty expenses		15,000
Loan payable		154,000
Provision for long-service leave expenses		10,000
Total liabilities		229,000
Net assets		200,000

Other information

- All administration and salaries expenses incurred have been paid as at year end.
- None of the long-service leave expense has actually been paid. It is not tax deductible until it is actually paid.
- Warranty expenses were accrued and, at year end, actual payments of £5,000 were made (leaving an accrued balance of £15,000). Tax deductions are available only when the amounts are paid, and not as they are accrued.
- Insurance was initially prepaid to the amount of £14,000. At year end, the unused component of the prepaid insurance amounted to £4,000. Only the actual amounts paid are allowed as a tax deduction.
- Amounts received from sales, including those on credit terms, are taxed at the time the sale is made.
- The plant is depreciated over four years for accounting purposes, but over three years for taxation purposes.
- The tax rate is 30 per cent.

REQUIRED

Provide the journal entries at 30 June 2015 to account for tax in accordance with IAS 12.

SOLUTION TO END-OF-CHAPTER EXERCISE

Our first step will be to determine *taxable income*. We need to know this to determine income tax payable.

	£	£	£
Profit before tax			330,000
(adjust for differences between tax and accounting rules)			
Long-service leave not yet deductible		10,000	
Warranty expenses	20,000		
Warranty expenses paid	(5,000)	15,000	
Accounting depreciation	75,000		
Tax depreciation	(100,000)	(25,000)	
Insurance expense	10,000		
Insurance actually paid	(14,000)	(4,000)	(4,000)
Taxable profit			326,000

	Extract from accounting SOFP (£)	Tax bases (£)	Deductible temporary differences (£)	Taxable temporary differences (£)	Tax expense (£)	Current tax payable (£)
Assets						
Cash	30,000	30,000				
Accounts receivable	90,000	90,000				
Inventory	80,000	80,000				
Prepaid insurance	4,000			4,000	4,000	
Plant—net	225,000	200,000		25,000	25,000	
	429,000	400,000				
Liabilities						
Accounts payable	50,000	50,000				
Provision for warranty	15,000	–	15,000		(15,000)	
Provision for long-service leave	10,000	–	10,000		(10,000)	
Loan	154,000	154,000				
	229,000	204,000				
Net assets	200,000	196,000				
Temporary differences at period end			25,000	29,000	4,000	
less *Prior period amounts*			–	–	–	
Movement for the period			25,000	29,000	4,000	
Tax effected at 30%			7,500	8,700	1,200	
Tax on taxable income 30% × £326,000			–	–	97,800	97,800
Income tax adjustments			7,500	8,700	99,000	97,800

Note 1: Increases to the balance of deductible temporary differences will lead to deferred tax assets after applying the tax rate. They also act to decrease income tax expense.

Note 2: Increases to the balance of taxable temporary differences will lead to deferred tax liabilities after applying the tax rate. They also act to increase income tax expense.

The journal entries for Wounded Seagull plc at year end are:

Dr Income tax expense	£97,800	
Cr Income tax payable		£97,800

(to recognise the tax expense pertaining to taxable income)

Dr Income tax expense	£1,200	
Dr Deferred tax asset	£7,500	
Cr Deferred tax liability		£8,700

(to recognise the additional tax expense pertaining to the temporary differences)

The above entries have given rise to a deferred tax asset and a deferred tax liability. IAS 12 allows these amounts to be offset so that only the net amount is shown (which in this case is a net amount of £1,200, which would be disclosed as a deferred tax liability) so long as certain conditions are present (discussed earlier).

In relation to income tax assessed by the taxation authorities, and assuming that the right of set-off applies, the final offsetting journal entry would be made:

Dr Deferred tax liability	£7,500	
Cr Deferred tax asset		£7,500

In considering the above entries, it should be acknowledged that the tax expense of £99,000 would be shown in the statement of comprehensive income. The net balance of the deferred tax liability, being £1,200 (after offsetting the deferred tax asset of £7,500), would be shown in the statement of financial position as a non-current liability. Income tax payable would be disclosed in the statement of financial position as a current liability.

REVIEW QUESTIONS

1   What is a 'temporary difference' and why does it arise?   **LO 15.2**
2   How is the tax base of an asset determined?   **LO 15.3**
3   How is the tax base of a liability determined?   **LO 15.3**
4   How do you determine the income tax expense of a company for accounting purposes?   **LO 15.1**
5   How does a company calculate its current liability, 'income tax payable'?   **LO 15.2**
6   What is the rationale for recognising a deferred tax asset or a deferred tax liability?   **LO 15.7**
7   What is the justification for recognising a deferred tax asset because an entity has unused tax losses?   **LO 15.5**
8   Explain why a temporary difference relating to an 'employee benefits in relation to long-service leave' account creates a deferred tax asset.   **LO 15.3**
9   Will the existence of unused tax losses always lead to the recognition of a deferred tax asset?   **LO 15.5**
10 How will a change in the tax rate impact on the balances of deferred tax assets and deferred tax liabilities? Should any such change be reflected in the reported profit of the reporting entity?   **LO 15.4**
11 Can deferred tax assets be offset against deferred tax liabilities?   **LO 15.3**
12 Assume that for a particular company the only temporary difference for tax-effect accounting purposes relates to the depreciation of a newly acquired machine. The machine is acquired on 1 July 2011 at a cost of £250,000. Its useful life is considered to be five years, after which time it is expected to have no residual value. For tax purposes it can be fully written off over two years. The tax rate is assumed to be 30 per cent.   **LO 15.3**

    REQUIRED
    (a) Determine whether the depreciation of the machine will lead to a deferred tax asset or a deferred tax liability.
    (b) What would be the balance of the deferred tax asset or deferred tax liability as at 30 June 2014?

13 A company has a depreciable non-current asset that cost €300 and has a carrying amount of €200. For tax purposes, accumulated depreciation amounts to €180.   **LO 15.3**

    REQUIRED
    (a) Assuming that the tax rate is 30 per cent, what is the amount of the temporary difference?
    (b) Does this give rise to a deferred tax asset or a deferred tax liability, and what is the amount of the deferred tax asset/liability?

14 A company has interest receivable with a carrying amount of €400,000. The related revenue will be taxed by the taxation authorities when the amounts are actually received.   **LO 15.3**

    REQUIRED
    (a) Assuming that the tax rate is 30 per cent, what is the amount of the temporary difference?
    (b) Does this give rise to a deferred tax asset or a deferred tax liability and what is the amount of the deferred tax asset/liability?

15 A company has prepaid rent with a carrying value of €400,000. A tax deduction is obtained at the time the rent is paid.   **LO 15.3**

    REQUIRED
    (a) Assuming that the tax rate is 30 per cent, what is the amount of the temporary difference?
    (b) Does this give rise to a deferred tax asset or a deferred tax liability, and what is the amount of the deferred tax asset/liability?

16 A company has a liability for employee benefits (relating to long-service leave) with a carrying value of £500,000, which will be tax deductible when the amounts are actually paid. The company also has accrued wages with a carrying value of £300,000, which have already been claimed as a deduction for tax purposes.   **LO 15.3**

    REQUIRED
    (a) Assuming that the tax rate is 30 per cent, what is the amount of the temporary difference?
    (b) Does this give rise to a deferred tax asset or a deferred tax liability, and what is the amount of the deferred tax asset/liability?

17 A company has interest revenue received in advance with a carrying value of €250,000, which is taxed on a cash basis. It also has a loan payable with a carrying amount of €400,000.   **LO 15.3**

REQUIRED

(a) Assuming that the tax rate is 30 per cent, what is the amount of the temporary difference?

(b) Does this give rise to a deferred tax asset or a deferred tax liability, and what is the amount of the deferred tax asset/liability?

18 Swedish Sands plc has a depreciable asset with a carrying amount of €200,000 and a tax base of €120,000 if the asset were sold immediately (which reflects the effects of indexation for capital gains tax purposes). On the other hand, the asset will have a tax base of €100,000 if its economic benefits were to be recovered through use within the organisation. **LO 15.3**

REQUIRED

Assuming a tax rate of 30 per cent, determine the balance of the deferred tax liability for the scenario of the asset being sold immediately and for the alternative scenario of the asset being retained for use within Swedish Sands plc.

19 Elwood plc has the following deferred tax balances as at 30 June 2015:

Deferred tax asset   €1,000,000
Deferred tax liability   €800,000

The above balances were calculated when the tax rate was 30 per cent. On 1 December 2015 the government raises the corporate tax rate to 35 per cent. **LO 15.5**

REQUIRED

Provide the journal entries to adjust the carry-forward balances of the deferred tax asset and deferred tax liability.

CHALLENGING QUESTIONS

20 Boiling Pot plc commences operations on 1 July 2014. One year after the commencement of its operations (30 June 2015), the entity prepares the following information, showing both the carrying amounts for accounting purposes and the tax bases of the respective assets and liabilities. **LO 15.6**

	Carrying values (€)	Tax bases (€)
Assets		
Cash	60,000	60,000
Accounts receivable (net)	50,000	60,000
Prepaid insurance	20,000	
Inventory	80,000	80,000
Plant—net	450,000	400,000
Land	600,000	400,000
	1,260,000	1,000,000
Liabilities		
Accounts payable	60,000	60,000
Provision for long-service leave	30,000	–
Provision for warranty	40,000	–
Loan payable	400,000	400,000
	530,000	460,000
Net assets	730,000	540,000

Other information

- After adjusting for differences between tax rules and accounting rules, it is determined that the taxable income of Boiling Pot plc is €700,000.
- There is a doubtful debt provision of €10,000.
- An item of plant is purchased at a cost of €600,000 on 1 July 2014. For accounting purposes it is expected to have a life of four years; however, for taxation purposes it can be depreciated over three years. It is not expected to have any residual value.
- Boiling Pot plc has some land, which cost €400,000 and which has been revalued to its fair value of €600,000 in accordance with IAS 16.

- None of the amounts accrued in respect of warranty expenses or long-service leave have actually been paid.
- The tax rate is 30 per cent.

REQUIRED

Prepare the year-end journal entries to account for tax using the balance sheet method.

21 MR plc commences operations on 1 July 2014 and presents its first statement of comprehensive income and first statement of financial position on 30 June 2015. The statements are prepared before considering taxation. The following information is available: **LO 15.2**

Statement of comprehensive income for the year ended 30 June 2015

	€	€
Gross profit		730,000
Expenses		
Administration expenses	80,000	
Salaries	200,000	
Long-service leave	20,000	
Warranty expenses	30,000	
Depreciation expense—plant	80,000	
Insurance	20,000	430,000
Accounting profit before tax		300,000

Assets and liabilities as disclosed in the statement of financial position as at 30 June 2015

	€	€
Assets		
Cash		20,000
Inventory		100,000
Accounts receivable		100,000
Prepaid insurance		10,000
Plant—cost	400,000	
less Accumulated depreciation	(80,000)	320,000
Total assets		550,000
Liabilities		
Accounts payable		80,000
Provision for warranty expenses		20,000
Loan payable		200,000
Provision for long-service leave expenses		20,000
Total liabilities		320,000
Net assets		230,000

Other information

- All administration and salaries expenses incurred have been paid as at year end.
- None of the long-service leave expense has actually been paid. It is not tax deductible until it is actually paid.
- Warranty expenses were accrued and, at year end, actual payments of €10,000 had been made (leaving an accrued balance of €20,000). Assume tax deductions are available only when the amounts are paid and not as they are accrued.
- Insurance was initially prepaid to the amount of €30,000. At year end, the unused component of the prepaid insurance amounted to €10,000. Only the actual amounts paid are allowed as a tax deduction.
- Amounts received from sales, including those on credit terms, are taxed at the time the sale is made.
- The plant is depreciated over five years for accounting purposes, but over four years for taxation purposes.
- The tax rate is 30 per cent.

REQUIRED

Provide the journal entries to account for tax in accordance with IAS 12.

REFERENCES

COLLINGS, S., *Deferred Taxation – The Complications*, Accountancy Students website, http://www.accountancystudents.co.uk/news/read/deferred_tax_-_the_complications/, 2009.

EPE, P., 'Winstbelasting in de bedrijfseconomische jaarrenkenig',

dissertation, van Nyenrode Business University, Belgium, 2010.

WESTWOOD, M., *Financial Accounting in New Zealand*, Auckland, Pearson, 2000.

PART 5

Accounting for the Disclosure of Cash Flows

Part content

Chapter 16

The Statement of Cash Flows

Learning objectives

Upon completing this chapter readers should:

LO1 understand the accounting requirements relating to the disclosure of information about an organisation's cash flows;

LO2 understand how to construct a statement of cash flows in conformity with IAS 7;

LO3 understand how the statement of cash flows provides information that is complementary to the statement of financial position, the statement of changes in equity and the statement of comprehensive income;

LO4 understand how we define 'cash' and 'cash equivalents' for the purposes of a statement of cash flows and appreciate that the definitions mean that statements of cash flows address transactions beyond those simply involving 'cash';

LO5 understand the differences between cash flows from operations, cash flows from investing and cash flows from financing activities; and

LO6 be aware of the various supporting notes that must accompany a statement of cash flows.

16.1 Comparison with other financial statements

The **statement of cash flows** provides a very useful complement to the other statements typically found in a reporting entity's set of financial statements—that is, the statement of financial position, the statement of changes in equity and the statement of comprehensive income. As we know, the statement of financial position shows the assets, liabilities and owners' equity balances as at a certain date (the end of the reporting period). The statement of changes in equity provides a reconciliation of opening and closing equity, as well as details of the various equity accounts that are impacted by the period's total comprehensive income. It also provides information about the effects of transactions with owners in their capacity as owners (distributions and capital contributions). The statement of comprehensive income shows the profit or loss as well as 'other comprehensive income' that has been generated for a period of time, typically a year, adopting the process of **accrual accounting**.

The statement of cash flows, on the other hand, concentrates on the movements in cash and cash equivalents for a given period. As such, it provides a reconciliation of the opening and closing total of cash and cash equivalent balances appearing in the statement of financial position. The statement of cash flows will typically indicate the sources

> **statement of cash flows** A financial statement that provides a reconciliation of opening and closing 'cash', including cash on hand and cash equivalents.
>
> **accrual accounting** A system of accounting in which revenues are recognised when earned and expenses are recognised when incurred, even in the absence of cash flows.

and uses of cash in terms of cash flows from operations, cash flows from investing and cash flows from financing. The information provided in a statement of cash flows may assist in assessing the ability of a company or an economic entity to:

- generate cash flows;
- meet its financial commitments as they fall due, including the servicing of borrowings and the payment of dividends;
- fund changes in the scope and/or nature of its activities; and
- obtain external finance.

As we know, 'profits' or 'losses' are determined by the use of accrual accounting. There are frequently significant differences between cash flows and profits. Profitable firms might actually fail on account of poor cash management. For example, a firm might make sales that are recorded as revenue in the current period; however, the terms of the sale might be that the amount will not be received for, say, three months. Meanwhile wages and many other expenses must be paid. If the collection of the sales revenue is deferred, the organisation might not have sufficient funds to meet its expenses. It might therefore face a liquidity crisis even though its profit, which is determined on an accruals basis, might appear to be sound. An extract from the abstract of Julien Le Maux and Danielle Morin's article in Financial Accounting in the News 16.1 investigates the collapse of Lehman Brothers and discusses the use of statements of cash flows for predicting corporate failure. Armed with knowledge of both cash flows and **accrual profits/losses**, investors should be better able to assess the performance and viability of reporting entities. It is argued (by Le Maux and Morin 2011; Akbar *et al.* 2011; Martin 2010; Tweedie and Whittington 1990; Lee 1981; Lawson 1985, for example) that the data provided within a statement of cash flows is more reliable than profit data—as profit data is typically based on numerous subjective and sometimes 'creative' judgements whereas cash flow data tends to be more 'factual' or 'objective'. Indeed, paragraph 4 of IAS 7 states:

> **accrual profits/ losses** The profits or losses that would be disclosed as a result of applying accrual accounting techniques.

It (the statement of cash flows) also enhances the comparability of the reporting of operating performance by different entities because it eliminates the effects of using different accounting treatments for the same transactions and events.

Financial Accounting in the News 16.1

BLACK AND WHITE AND RED ALL OVER: LEHMAN BROTHERS' INEVITABLE BANKRUPTCY SPLASHED ACROSS ITS FINANCIAL STATEMENTS

Julien Le Maux and Danielle Morin, *International Journal of Business and Social Science*, **vol. 2, no. 20, November 2011**

The purpose of this article is to analyze the statements of cash flows in order to establish whether the failure of Lehman Brothers could have been predicted. Our analysis shows that the following signs of financial distress were detectable in Lehman Brothers' 2005–2007 financial statements:

- Chronic inability to generate cash from operating activities;
- Massive and systematic investments in working capital items, and even more intensive investments in financial instruments;
- Systematic use of external financing (mainly long-term debt) to offset operating deficits;
- Steady deterioration of the cash situation over three consecutive years.

Although Lehman Brothers had $7.286 billion in cash and cash equivalents on November 30, 2007, the analysis of its statement of cash flows signals major dysfunctions in working capital management. This is particularly striking for financial instruments: over a three-year period, they generated net negative cash flows of $161.657 billion. The systematic payment of dividends despite sizeable cash deficits in operating activities, not to mention the financing of dividends through long-term loans, also points to dysfunctional cash management. In conclusion, we argue that Lehman Brothers' statements of cash flows for the years 2005, 2006, and 2007 were very strong predictors of its bankruptcy, which occurred on September 15, 2008. Because they emit clear signals of imminent financial distress starting from 2006, the statements of cash flows are highly informative and are thus of great value to investors and analysts.

Following a similar viewpoint, in an article on DailyFinance.com (by Seth Jayson, 'Is Extreme Networks' Cash Flow Just for Show?, 2012) it was stated that:

> *Although business headlines still tout earnings numbers, many investors have moved past net earnings as a measure of a company's economic output. That's because earnings are very often less trustworthy than cash flow, since earnings are more open to manipulation based on dubious judgement calls.*
>
> *Earnings' unreliability is one of the reasons investors often flip straight past the income statement to check the cash flow statement. In general, by taking a close look at the cash moving in and out of the business, you can better understand whether the last batch of earnings brought money into the company, or merely disguised a cash gusher with a pretty headline.*

Likewise, Walker (1987) claimed that, 'one of the strongest antidotes to creative accounting is a requirement for disclosures of cash flows'. While the above material obviously provides some rather negative perspectives of reported profits and how they may at times be calculated (or manipulated), this is not a view that we necessarily adopt within this book. Rather, we can adopt the perspective that the statement of cash flows is a useful addition to the other information typically provided in a set of financial statements. See also Grady (2010) for a discussion of the benefits of using ratios based on the income statement *and* the statement of cash flows. This article argues for the use of both statements when analysing an entity's debt service coverage ratio.

The usefulness of cash flow data relative to revenue and expense data provided by accrual accounting is a matter for debate. Many consider it to be a true reflection of an entity's performance as it has not been 'manipulated' by accounting adjustments (noted earlier). However, others comment on the fact that it is not as 'white' as it might first seem. For example, the article by Heather Connon reproduced in Financial Accounting in the News 16.2 discusses how the entries in the cash flow statement of WorldCom had been selectively disclosed to 'hoodwink' the reader of the statement. Therefore, we conclude that a balanced view would, as previously noted, perhaps see the statement of cash flows as a useful complement to the statement of financial position and the statement of comprehensive income. Certainly in recent years governments have moved away from cash accounting to accrual accounting because of its perception that accrual-based data generates improved information and enables greater accountability.

In a study of the perceived usefulness of statements of cash flows, Jones and Ratnatunga (1997) undertook a survey of 500 representatives of companies listed on the Australian Securities Exchange. The subjects, 210 of whom

Financial Accounting in the News 16.2

FRAUDS CROWN CASH AS KING

Heather Connon, *The Observer*, 30 June 2002

The thing that worried investors most about the $3.8 billion (£2.5bn) fraud at WorldCom was that it affected cash as well as profits. Not in the strict sense of how much cash there was in the bank—even the most creative accountant finds that impossible to fiddle—but in how the company's cash flow was disclosed in the accounts.

For a brief period during the tech boom, investors were prepared to ignore cashflow today for the sake of bumper profits tomorrow. Now it is clear that the only way companies, at least in the US, were generating any profits—let alone bumper ones—was by making them up, cash has once again become king.

Investors are focusing on what a firm generates in real greenbacks from its sales after paying for labour, raw materials and other direct costs of making its products. WorldCom classified some of these operating expenses as capital investment in long-term projects—which should be ignored when calculating operating cashflow—so making its cash position look better than it really was.

It is not just companies such as WorldCom and Enron that were deluding both themselves and their investors. Richard Burns of fund manager Baillie Gifford points out that a full 17 per cent of last year's profits at General Electric came from credits on its pension fund, which is hardly what it is in business for. That may explain why its shares are at little over half their peak for the year.

Companies have quickly cottoned on to investors' affection for cash. Results statements now give cashflow almost as much prominence as profits and earnings. Vodafone makes much of the fact that, despite reporting the biggest loss in British corporate history, it generated £2.4bn of free cashflow. Everyone from Cable & Wireless down to Fibrenet is cutting spending to conserve its cash.

Source: The Observer. © 2012 Guardian News and Media Limited.

responded, were asked questions about the usefulness of statement of cash flows. The respondents indicated that, on average, they considered the statement of cash flows to be more understandable to users; to give rise to fewer problems with key terms; and to provide greater comparability between companies. Arguably, greater comparability is possible because the compilation of the statement of cash flows relies upon fewer professional judgements. Jones and Ratnatunga also found that many respondents in fact considered cash flows from operations to be a superior performance measure, which avoids the problems of changing price levels that can distort reported earnings and provides a more reliable indicator of operating performance. Apart from the statement of cash flows' perceived ability to provide useful information for performance evaluation, it was also regarded by the respondents, perhaps somewhat predictably, as providing information that is useful in assessing an organisation's liquidity and solvency.

The results of the Jones and Ratnatunga (1997) study can be compared with the apparently contradictory findings of two New Zealand studies. In the first study, Seng (1996) was able to conclude that, overall, cash flows do not provide any incremental information content over and above that contained in accrual data. Seng (pp. 34–5) based his conclusion on the following factors: New Zealand investors rely primarily on financial statements prepared on the accrual basis and they base their decisions on the accrual earnings results owing to their familiarity with this form of profit measurement; and dividend payouts are substantially based on earnings. Findings reported by Dowds (1997) would, however, appear to contradict those of Seng (1996). In a survey of the New Zealand Society of Investment Analysts, Dowds was able to demonstrate that one category of financial statement users, investment analysts, found the statement of cash flows to be almost as useful as the traditional accruals-based statement of comprehensive income and statement of financial position.

Providing a further indication of the potential usefulness, or otherwise, of statements of cash flows, Wilson (1987) found that in the US the public disclosure of information about cash flows did tend to affect share prices.

16.2   Defining 'cash' and 'cash equivalents'

IAS 7 requires the statement of cash flows to provide information about movements in 'cash' and 'cash equivalents'.

IAS 7 defines 'cash flows' as 'inflows and outflows of cash and cash equivalents' and 'cash' as 'cash on hand and demand deposits'. 'Cash equivalents' is defined as 'short-term, highly liquid investments that are readily convertible to known amounts of cash and that are subject to an insignificant risk of change in value'.

Hence, although the statement of cash flows effectively provides a reconciliation of opening and closing 'cash and cash equivalents', 'cash and cash equivalents' as represented in the statement of cash flows might actually relate to the total of a number of accounts shown in the statement of financial position or accompanying notes, rather than a single account, such as cash at bank. These accounts may include cash at bank, bank overdrafts, short-term money market deposits and bank bills. With this in mind, IAS 7 requires that the amount of 'cash' and 'cash equivalents' as at the end of the financial year, as presented in the statement of cash flows, be reconciled—by way of a note to the financial statements—to the related items in the statement of financial position (IAS 7, paragraph 45).

Exhibit 16.1 shows the reconciliation provided in the 30 June 2010 annual report of SAP, along with the other movements that make up its net liquidity.

IAS 7 requires the disclosure of the policy adopted by the organisation for determining which items are classified as 'cash' and 'cash equivalents' in the statement of cash flows. Explicit disclosure of this policy would help users to understand the organisation's statement of cash flows. Importantly, if an entity changes its policy for determining which items are classified as cash in the statement of cash flows, an explanation of the change in policy and the effect of that change would need to be included in the financial report. SAP AG defined cash and cash equivalents as 'highly liquid investments with original maturities of three months or less' (Annual Report 2010, p. 180).

To provide clarity on what exactly constitutes cash equivalents, paragraph 7 of IAS 7 now states:

> *Cash equivalents are held for the purpose of meeting short-term cash commitments rather than for investment or other purposes. For an investment to qualify as a cash equivalent it must be readily convertible to a known amount of cash and be subject to an insignificant risk of changes in value. Therefore, an investment normally qualifies as a cash equivalent only when it has a maturity of, say, three months or less from the date of acquisition.*

Do you think that something that converts into cash in three months is really a 'cash equivalent'?

As noted, for an item to be considered to be a cash equivalent, it must be both highly liquid and be used as part of the cash-management function of the company. This means that a cash equivalent in one entity might not be a cash equivalent in another. It all depends on the respective cash-management programmes adopted. Bank and non-bank bills are proposed as examples of highly liquid investments that would typically meet the definition of cash. As cash equivalents are required to be highly liquid, account items such as accounts receivable, accounts payable, any borrowings subject to a term facility or equity securities would be excluded from the definition of cash equivalents.

| Exhibit 16.1 | Reconciliation of the cash balance of SAP plc as shown in the statement of cash flows to the respective statement of financial position account balances |

22. ADDITIONAL CAPITAL DISCLOSURES

Our net liquidity position is defined as cash, cash equivalents, and current investments, less financial debt, which consists of bank loans, bonds, and private placements. Our goal is to continuously maintain a positive net liquidity position. However, we might deviate from that goal for a limited period of time due to large acquisitions that require us to enter into financing instruments. For example, this is the case as of December 31, 2010, due to the acquisition of Sybase, which we financed with cash on hand and significant financial debt. We structured the maturity profile of the additional financial debt in a balanced way, so that our target of a positive net liquidity position could be reached as quickly as possible given our underlying cash flow planning.

Group Liquidity of SAP Group

€ millions	2010	2009	Change
Cash and cash equivalents	3,518	1,884	1,634
Current investments	10	400	−390
Total group liquidity	3,528	2,284	1,244
Current bank loans	1	4	−3
Net liquidity 1	3,527	2,280	1,247
Non-current bank loans	1,106	2	1,104
Private placement transactions	1,071	697	374
Bonds	2,200	0	2,200
Net liquidity 2	−850	1,581	−2,431

16.3 Classification of cash flows

IAS 7 requires that cash flows be classified into those relating to the following:

- **Operating activities**—defined as 'the principal revenue-producing activities of the entity and other activities that are not investing and financing activities'. Operating activities would be activities that relate to the provision of goods and services, and other activities that are neither investing nor financing activities. Such a definition relies in its turn upon definitions of investing and financing activities.
- **Investing activities**—defined as 'the acquisition and disposal of long-term assets (including property, plant and equipment and other productive assets) and other investments (such as securities) not included in cash equivalents'.
- **Financing activities**—which relate to changing the size and/or composition of the financial structure of the entity, including equity and borrowings not falling within the definition of cash.

In the start-up phase of a business, positive cash flows from financing activities would be likely, as would negative cash flows from both investing and operating activities. Beyond a certain period of time, however, it would be hoped that the majority of cash flows would be generated through the operations of the business, as an entity cannot rely indefinitely on finance from external sources to survive.

Table 16.1 classifies various types of cash flow in terms of whether they would typically be classified as relating to the operating, investing or financing activities of an entity.

operating activities Activities that relate to the provision of goods and services and other activities that are neither investing nor financing activities.

investing activities Activities that relate to the acquisition and/or disposal of non-current assets.

financing activities Activities that relate to changing the size and/or composition of the financial structure of the entity.

Table 16.1   Examples of cash flows that would typically be included in the three classifications of cash flows identified in IAS 7

Operating activities	Investing activities	Financing activities
Cash inflows relating to: • Sales of goods • Provision of services • Commissions received • Royalties received • Dividends received[*1] • Interest received[*1]	*Cash inflows relating to:* • Sale of property, plant and equipment • Sale of intangible assets • Repayment of loans previously advanced by the entity • Sale of equity and other financial instruments of other entities	*Cash inflows relating to:* • Issue of shares or other equity instrument of the entity • Borrowing funds through the issue of secured and unsecured loans
Cash outflows relating to: • Goods and services acquired • Employee benefits paid • Interest paid[*2] • Taxes paid[*3]	*Cash outflows relating to:* • Acquisition of property, plant and equipment • Acquisition of intangible assets • Acquisition of equity and other financial instruments of other entities • Loans made to other entities	*Cash outflows relating to:* • Repayment of borrowed funds (inclusive of various types of debt instruments) • Payment of dividends • Share buybacks

[*1] *Could also be classified as part of investing activities pursuant to paragraph 33 of IAS 7*

[*2] *Could also be classified as part of financing activities pursuant to paragraph 33 of IAS 7*

[*3] *Unless the tax can be specifically identified with investing and financing activities, see paragraph 35 of IAS 7*

16.4   Format of statement of cash flows

Appendix A of IAS 7 provides a suggested format for the statement of cash flows, which is reproduced as Exhibit 16.2. Although no prior year comparatives are shown in Exhibit 16.2, they are required under IAS 7. For a real-life example, see Exhibit 16.3. It is suggested that cash flows from operations be presented first, followed by cash flows from investing and financing, respectively.

Items representing cash flows from investing and financing are shown separately—that is, they are not netted off against each other. Consider the financing example of a debt issue and subsequent repayment, both of which would be shown separately. Similarly, where plant is sold and subsequently replaced (investing activities), the inflow from the sale and the outflow related to the purchase would be shown separately (and typically as part of cash flows relating to investing activities).

A review of Exhibit 16.2 shows that some items, which may ordinarily be considered operating items for statement of comprehensive income purposes, might not be treated the same for cash-flow purposes and vice versa. For example, for cash-flow purposes, interest paid is treated as part of operating activity. However, for income purposes, it would be usual to think of interest paid as being related to the financing operations of the business.

Paragraph 31 of IAS 7 requires cash flows from interest and dividends received and paid to be disclosed separately. These cash flows should be classified in a consistent manner from period to period as operating, investing or financing activities. In addition, paragraph 35 of IAS 7 requires cash flows from taxes on income to be separately disclosed. These are to be classified as cash flows from operating activities unless they can be specifically identified with financing and investing activities.

Paragraph 18 of IAS 7 notes that entities have a choice between using the *direct method* or the *indirect method* to report cash flows from operating activities. Specifically, paragraph 18 states:

An entity shall report cash flows from operating activities using either:

(a) *the direct method, whereby major classes of gross cash receipts and gross cash payments are disclosed; or*

(b) *the indirect method, whereby profit or loss is adjusted for the effects of transactions of a non-cash nature, any deferrals or accruals of past or future operating cash receipts or payments, and items of income or expense associated with investing or financing cash flows.*

Paragraph 19 states that entities are encouraged to report cash flows from operating activities using the direct method because the direct method provides information that may be useful in estimating future cash flows and which is not available under the indirect method.

IAS 7, paragraph 21, also requires an entity to report separately major classes of gross receipts and gross payments arising from investing and financing activities, rather thtan reporting such inflows and outflows as net

	Exhibit 16.2	Illustration of a statement of cash flows—from the Appendix to IAS 7

	€	
Cash flows from operating activities		
Cash receipts from customers	30,150	
Cash paid to suppliers and employees	(27,600)	
Cash generated from operations	2,550	
Interest paid	(270)	
Income taxes paid	(900)	
Net cash used in operating activities		1,380
Cash flows from investing activities		
Acquisition of Subsidiary X, net of cash acquired	(550)	
Purchase of property, plant and equipment	(350)	
Proceeds from sale of equipment	20	
Interest received	200	
Dividends received	200	
Net cash used in investing activities		(480)
Cash flows from financing activities		
Proceeds from issuance of share capital	250	
Proceeds from long-term borrowings	250	
Payment of finance lease liabilities	(90)	
Dividends paid	(1,200)	
Net cash used in financing activities		(790)
Net increase in cash and cash equivalents		**110**
Cash and cash equivalents at beginning of period		**120**
Cash and cash equivalents at end of period		**230**

amounts. There are only a few exceptions to this requirement, and these are provided in paragraphs 22 and 24 of IAS 7.

Table 16.2 provides a sample of the types of item that might give rise to a difference between cash flows from operations and operating profit after tax. Items such as depreciation and amortisation are non-cash flow items; that is, the expense does not relate to a cash flow as these items are allocations of costs that relate to assets that might have been acquired in previous periods. If we start the reconciliation from profit after tax, we would need to add back such non-cash expenses in order to move towards a reconciliation with cash flows from operating activities.

Another example of a reconciling item would be the deduction of any increase in receivables. As we know, sales revenue is brought into account on an accrual basis. It is possible for all sales revenue to be earned initially on credit terms. If some of the customers have not paid, there will be a difference between cash flows from operations and profits after tax.

Table 16.2 Adjustments required to reconcile net profit to cash flows from operations

Operating activities	
Profit/Loss after tax	XX
Add:	
Depreciation expense	XX
Amortisation expense	XX
Loss on sale of plant and equipment	XX
Increase in interest payable	XX
Increase in accrued expenses	XX
Increase in accounts payable	XX
Increase in income taxes payable	XX
Increase in deferred taxes payable	XX
Subtract:	
Gain on sale of plant and equipment	(XX)
Increase in deferred tax benefit	(XX)
Increase in accounts receivable	(XX)
Increase in prepaid expenses	(XX)
Increase in interest receivable	(XX)
Increase in inventories	(XX)
Net cash flows from operating activities	XX

Where items in Table 16.2 move in the opposite direction—that is, they decrease rather than increase—their treatment would be reversed. For example, if accounts receivable decreases, we would add this decrease to net profit or loss, as it would represent a cash inflow of the period (unless the reduction is due to an account write-off), but the change in receivables would not be reflected in that period's earnings.

As an illustration of the reconciliation of net profit to cash flows from operations consider the following, fairly simple, example. As at 1 July 2015, which is the beginning of the financial year, Skipp plc had the following account balances:

	£
Cash at bank	100
Bank overdraft	20
Accounts receivable	60
Accounts payable	40
Accrued expenses	70
Inventory	50

During the year:

1. Skipp plc made £1,000 in sales—all on credit terms. The closing balance of accounts receivable was £80 and there were no bad or doubtful debt expenses. This means that £980 was collected from customers, this being the opening balance of accounts receivable plus total credit sales less the closing balance of accounts receivable, which equals £60 + £1,000 – £80 = £980.
2. Skipp plc acquired £300 of inventory. The accounts payable account in this case is assumed to relate only to inventory purchases. The closing balance of inventory was £80. This means that £270 of inventory was used in the business and is therefore treated as a cost of goods sold expense. Cost of goods sold is determined

by adding the opening balance of inventory to the purchases for the period and subtracting the closing balance of inventory. This equals £50 + £300 − £80 = £270.

3. The closing balance of accounts payable was £80. If £300 of inventory was acquired and the opening balance of accounts payable was £40, and the closing balance was £80, £260 must have been paid to the suppliers of the inventory (that is, to the suppliers represented by accounts payable).

4. Other expenses amounted to £400, and it is assumed that these expenses are initially recorded as accrued expenses. The closing balance of accrued expenses was £50. This means that the actual cash payments made in relation to accrued expenses were £420. This equals £400 + £70 − £50 = £420.

From the above information we can see that profit for the period was £330. This is calculated by subtracting cost of goods sold and other expenses from total sales. This equals £1,000 − £270 − £400 = £330.

Working from the above calculations, the cash flows from operations, calculated using the direct method, would equal:

Cash flows from operating activities	(£)
Cash receipts from customers	980
Cash paid to suppliers and employees	(260)
Cash paid on other expenses	(420)
	300

We can now reconcile net profit to cash flows from operations, calculated using the indirect method as follows:

Reconciliation of net cash provided by operating activities to net profit	(£)
Net profit	330
(Increase) in inventories	(30)
(Increase) in accounts receivable	(20)
Increase in accounts payable	40
Decrease in accrued expenses	(20)
Net cash provided by operating activities	300

Exhibit 16.3 reproduces the statement of cash flows of SAP. As can be seen, they use the indirect method to determine net cash flows from operating activities.

Exhibit 16.3 | **Reconciliation of cash flows from operations to net profit provided by SAP in its 2010 annual report**

Consolidated Statements of Cash Flows of SAP Group as at December 31

€ millions	Note	2010	2009	2008
Profit after tax		1,813	1,750	1,848
Adjustments to reconcile profit after tax to net cash provided by operating activities				
Depreciation and amortization		534	499	539
Income tax expense	(11)	525	685	776
Finance income, net	(10)	67	80	50
Gains/losses on disposals of non-current assets	(7)	−3	−11	11
Decrease/increase in sales and bad debt allowances on trade receivables		−49	64	76
Other adjustments for non-cash items		32	14	52
Decrease/increase in trade receivables		−123	593	−48
Decrease/increase in other assets		−112	205	−12

▶

Consolidated Statements of Cash Flows of SAP Group as at December 31				
Decrease/increase in trade payables, provisions and other liabilities		1,116	−124	−267
Decrease/increase in deferred income		66	48	61
Cash outflows due to TomorrowNow litigation	(24)	−102	−19	−13
Interest paid		−66	−69	−105
Interest received		52	22	72
Income taxes paid, net of refunds		−818	−722	−882
Net cash flows from operating activities		**2,932**	**3,015**	**2,158**
Business combinations, net of cash and cash equivalents acquired	(4)	−4,194	−73	−3,773
Repayment of acquirees' debt in business combinations		0	0	−450
Purchase of intangible assets and property, plant and equipment		−334	−225	−339
Proceeds from sales of intangible assets or property, plant and equipment		44	45	44
Cash transferred to restricted cash		0	0	−448
Use of restricted cash		0	0	1,001
Purchase of equity or debt instruments of other entities		−842	−1,073	−396
Proceeds from sales of equity or debt instruments of other entities		1,332	1,027	595
Net cash flows from investing activities		**−3,994**	**−299**	**−3,766**
Dividends paid	(22)	−594	−594	−594
Purchase of treasury shares	(22)	−220	0	−487
Proceeds from reissuance of treasury shares		127	24	85
Proceeds from issuing shares (share-based compensation)		23	6	20
Proceeds from borrowings		5,380	697	3,859
Repayments of borrowings		−2,196	−2,303	−1,571
Purchase of equity-based derivative instruments		−14	0	−55
Proceeds from the exercise of equity-based derivative financial instruments		4	4	24
Net cash flows from financing activities		**2,510**	**−2,166**	**1,281**
Effect of foreign currency exchange rates on cash and cash equivalents		186	54	−1
Net increase (decrease) in cash and cash equivalents		1,634	604	−328
Cash and cash equivalents at the beginning of the period	(22)	1,884	1,280	1,608
Cash and cash equivalents at the end of the period	(22)	**3,518**	**1,884**	**1,280**

One potential limitation of a statement of cash flows is that the statement obviously does not include details of transactions that are not cash-based but that could nevertheless have a significant impact on the financial structure of the organisation. With this in mind, IAS 7 requires that additional disclosures be made about non-cash financing and investing activities.

16.4.1 Non-cash financing and investing activities

The statement of cash flows reports only transactions that involve cash flows throughout the period. However, there might be numerous non-cash transactions that are part of the investing and financing activities of the reporting entity. For example, the entity might acquire certain non-current assets by issuing additional equity or debt securities. Alternatively, it might convert certain liabilities to equity (convertible notes) or convert certain non-cash assets to other non-cash assets. Paragraph 43 of IAS 7 requires that relevant information about transactions and events that do not result in cash flows during the financial year, but affect assets and liabilities that have been recognised, is to be disclosed in the financial statements or consolidated financial statements where the transactions and other events:

- involve parties external to the entity;
- relate to the financing or investing activities of the entity.

Examples of non-cash financing and investing transactions that are not in the statement of cash flows but should be included in a note supporting the statement of cash flows include:

(a) conversions of liabilities to equity;
(b) conversion of preference shares to ordinary shares;
(c) acquisitions of entities by means of an equity issue;
(d) acquisitions of assets by assumption of directly related liabilities, such as a purchase of a building by incurring a mortgage to the seller;
(e) acquisitions of assets by entering into finance leases;
(f) exchanges of non-cash assets or liabilities for other non-cash assets or liabilities; and
(g) payments of dividends through a share investment scheme rather than through the payment of cash.

Exhibit 16.4 provides the note relating to non-cash financing and investing activities from the 2010 annual report of the Dutch company, Philips Group.

| Exhibit 16.4 | Information relating to non-cash financing and investing activities of Philips Group |

SUPPLEMENTAL DISCLOSURES TO THE CONSOLIDATED STATEMENTS OF CASH FLOWS OF PHILIPS GROUP

	Note	2008	2009	Consolidated 2010
		€m	€m	€m
Non-cash investing and financing activities				
Assets in lieu of cash from the sale of businesses:				
Shares/share options/convertible bonds	27	148	–	3

Note 27 Assets in lieu of cash from sale of businesses

In August 2010, the Company acquired a 49.9% interest in Shapeways Inc. in exchange for the transfer of certain Consumer Lifestyle incubator activities, which represented a value of EUR 3 million at the date of the closing of that transaction.

In 2009, the Company received only cash as consideration in connection with the sale of businesses.
In April 2008, the Company acquired 64.5 million shares in Pace Micro Technology in exchange for the transfer of the Company's Set-Top boxes and Connectivity Solutions activities, which represented a value of EUR 74 million at the date of the closing of that transaction. The Pace shares were sold on April 17, 2009. In August 2008, Philips transferred its 69.5% ownership in MedQuist to CBAY. A part of the consideration was settled through the issuance of a convertible bond by CBAY which represented a fair value of EUR 53 million at the date of the closing of the transaction. The convertible bond, included in Other non-current financial assets, was redeemed on October 15, 2010.

In September 2008, Philips acquired a 33.5% interest in Prime Technology Ventures III in exchange for the transfer of seven incubator activities which represented a value of EUR 21 million at the date of the closing of that transaction.

16.4.2 Disclosure of financing facilities

Apart from requiring the disclosure of cash flows and non-cash financing and investing activities, paragraph 50(a) of IAS 7 suggests—but does not require—that the financial statements (by way of a note) should disclose information about the external financing arrangements of the entity, as at the end of the financial year; for example, details of undrawn borrowing facilities that are available to the company.

Exhibit 16.5 includes information that is considered to be relevant to users for understanding the liquidity of a company. This information is provided as part of Note 26 to the 2010 financial statements of SAP Group.

Exhibit 16.5 **Sample 'additional information' for the proper assessment of the liquidity risk facing SAP Group**

AN EXTRACT FROM THE 2010 ANNUAL REPORT OF SAP Group

26. Financial Risk Management

Liquidity Risk Management

In order to retain high financial flexibility, as at December 15, 2010, SAP AG entered into a €1.5 billion syndicated credit facility agreement with an initial term of five years ending in December 2015, effectively replacing the €1.5 billion syndicated revolving credit facility signed in September 2009. The use of the facility is not restricted by any financial covenants. Borrowings under the facility bear interest of EURIBOR or LIBOR for the respective currency plus a margin of 45 basis points to 75 basis points, depending on the amount drawn. We are also required to pay a commitment fee of 15.75 basis points per annum on the unused available credit. As at December 31, 2010, there were no borrowings outstanding under the facility. Additionally, as at December 31, 2010, and 2009, SAP AG had available lines of credit totalling €545 million and €545 million, respectively. As at December 31, 2010, and 2009, there were no borrowings outstanding under these lines of credit. As at December 31, 2010, and 2009, certain subsidiaries had lines of credit available that allowed them to borrow in local currencies at prevailing interest rates up to €60 million and €51 million, respectively. Total aggregate borrowings under these lines of credit amounted to €1 million and €6 million as at December 31, 2010, and 2009, respectively.

16.5 Calculating cash inflows and outflows

16.5.1 Cash flows from operating activities

As stated previously, cash flows from operating activities are those that relate to the provision of goods and services and other activities that are neither investing nor financing activities.

To determine the cash flows from operations, it might be necessary to reconstruct a number of the entity's ledger accounts. We will demonstrate below how this can be done, using either a t-account approach or an equations approach. The method used is a matter of personal preference.

16.5.2 Receipts from customers

In accrual accounting, revenues are recognised when goods or services are provided, which typically precedes cash collection. To determine cash flows related to sales of goods and services we need to consider any movement in receivables.

Accounts receivable will be affected by such items as sales, discount expenses, the direct recognition of bad debts—that is, where bad debts are offset directly against receivables by a debit to bad debts and a credit to accounts receivable—transfers from provision for doubtful debts and, of course, by cash payments made by customers. Cash flows from customers may be determined by considering the relevant t-accounts, as shown below:

Sales		Accounts receivable			Allowance for doubtful debts		
A/c rec. x	Op. bal. x	Bad debts x	A/c rec. x	Op. bal. x
	Sales x	Prov. d.d. x	Clos. bal. x	D.d. exp. x
		Discounts x		x	x
		Cash x			
		Clos. bal. x			
	x	x			

Alternatively, we can determine the cash flows from customers using an equation, as shown below:

> Cash receipts from customers = Sales + Beginning receivables – Ending receivables
> – Bad debt expense (where bad debts are written off directly against customer accounts)
> – Transfer from provision for doubtful debts (where debts that have previously been considered doubtful have subsequently proved uncollectible)
> – Any discounts that might have been given to customers for early payment

As an illustration of how to compute the cash flows received from customers, consider Worked Example 16.1.

Worked Example 16.1　Calculating cash received from customers

Sneijder plc provides you with the following information:

Sales for the year (all on credit terms)	€600,000
Discounts provided during the year to customers for early payment	€15,000
Doubtful debts expense for the year	€10,000
Opening balance of accounts receivable	€100,000
Closing balance of accounts receivable	€110,000
Opening balance of the provision for doubtful debts	€18,000
Closing balance of the provision for doubtful debts	€20,000

Required

Determine how much cash was received from customers during the year.

Solution

We can use the t-account approach or the equations approach. Using either method, the amount collected from customers was €567,000. Both approaches are shown below. The amounts shown in the t-accounts are in €000.

Sales		Accounts receivable			Provision for doubtful debt		
	A/c rec. 600	Op. bal. 100			A/c rec 8	Op. bal. 18
		Sales 600	Prov. d.d. 8	Clos. bal. 20	D.d. exp. 10
			Discounts 15		28	28
			Cash 567			
			Clos. bal. 110			
		700	700			

Alternatively, we can determine the cash flows from customers using an equation, as shown below:

Cash receipts from customers = €600,000 (sales) + €100,000 (beginning receivables)
　　　　　　　　　　　– €110,000 (ending receivables)
　　　　　　　　　　　– €8,000 (transfer from provision for doubtful debts, which equals opening balance of the provision plus the doubtful debts expense less the closing balance of the provision)
　　　　　　　　　　　– €15,000 (discounts that may have been given for early payment)
　　　　　　　　　　　= €567,000

16.5.3 Interest and dividends received

In relation to interest and dividends received, we first need to determine whether interest and dividends should be treated as operating cash flows, or otherwise. Paragraph 33 of IAS 7 states:

> *Interest paid and interest and dividends received are usually classified as operating cash flows for a financial institution. However, there is no consensus on the classification of these cash flows for other entities. Interest paid and interest and dividends received may be classified as operating cash flows because they enter into the determination of net profit or loss. Alternatively, interest paid and interest and dividends received may be classified as financing cash flows and investing cash flows respectively, because they are costs of obtaining financial resources or returns on investments.*

Hence the accounting standard gives a choice as to where interest paid and dividends and interest received are to be presented. For the purposes of the illustration that follows, we will include them as part of the cash flows from operations. Nevertheless, it is worth noting that Appendix A to IAS 7, which provides an illustration of a statement of cash flows, includes interest paid in the cash flows from operating activities, but also includes interest and dividends received in the cash flows from financing activities. In relation to dividends paid, paragraph 34 also provides an option. It states:

> *Dividends paid may be classified as a financing cash flow because they are a cost of obtaining financial resources. Alternatively, dividends paid may be classified as a component of cash flows from operating activities in order to assist users to determine the ability of an entity to pay dividends out of operating cash flows.*

As with sales, dividend and interest revenue may be recognised within the financial statements before the related cash flow occurs. Interest revenue may be recognised in the statement of comprehensive income, even though the related cash flows may not occur until the next period. For example, an entity purchases the debentures of another entity. Let us assume that the reporting entity acquires debentures with a life of four years and a face value of €1 million. The debentures pay interest yearly. Let us further assume that the coupon rate on the debentures is 10 per cent but the market requires a rate of return of 12 per cent.

The amount that the reporting entity will pay for the debentures can be worked out from the present value tables provided in the appendices to this book. The amount, using a discount rate of 12 per cent, will be:

Present value of the principal	€1,000,000 × 0.6355	= €635,500
Present value of the interest revenue stream	€100,000 × 3.0373	= €303,730
		€939,230

Assuming the debentures are recorded at the net amount of €939,230, the accounting entry to record the acquisition would be as follows:

Dr Debentures	€939,230	
Cr Cash		€939,230

To record the interest one year later, assuming the effective interest method is used to determine interest revenue (whereby the opening balance of the debentures is multiplied by the market rate of interest), the entry would be:

Dr Interest receivable	€100,000	
Dr Debentures	€12,708	
Cr Interest revenue		€112,708

So, to determine the cash flow related to the interest revenue, we would need to deduct, from interest revenue, any increase in interest receivable as well as any increase in the balance of the debentures. In this case, the actual cash, receipt is:

$$€112,708 - €100,000 - €12,708 = 0$$

Had the debentures been acquired at a premium, the reduction in the balance of the debentures would be added back to derive the related cash flows. This can be represented in t-account form as:

Interest receivable			
Op. bal.	x	Debentures	x
Interest rev.	x	Cash	x
Debentures	x	Clos. bal.	x
	x		x

Alternatively, an equation approach can be used, as follows:

> Cash received from interest revenue = Interest revenue + Opening interest receivable
> – Closing interest receivable
> – Increase in debentures + Decrease in debentures

The same analysis can be undertaken for dividends. Using an equation approach, the cash flow from dividend revenue would be:

> Cash received from dividends = Dividend income + Opening dividends receivable
> – Closing dividends receivable

16.5.4 Cash payment of interest

As with interest revenue, we might need to adjust for changes in interest payable, and for any increase or decrease in the value of a bond (or a debenture) as a result of using the effective interest method, to determine the cash flows associated with interest expense. Using a t-account approach, the cash flow may be reconciled as the balancing item.

Interest payable			
Increase in bonds	x	Op. bal.	x
Cash	x	Decrease in bonds	x
Clos. bal.	x	Interest expense	x
	x		x

Alternatively, we can determine cash flows using an equation approach, as follows:

> Interest paid = Interest expense + Opening interest payable – Closing interest payable
> – Increase in bonds + Decrease in bonds

16.5.5 Payment of income taxes

Paragraph 35 of IAS 7 states:

> *Cash flows arising from taxes on income shall be separately disclosed and shall be classified as cash flows from operating activities unless they can be specifically identified with financing and investing activities.*

With the adoption of tax-effect accounting, there might be a number of adjustments that need to be made to determine the cash flows associated with tax expense. For example, assume that a reporting entity has a pre-tax profit of £100,000 and that there are no permanent differences. The tax rate is 30 per cent. Let us further assume that prepayments have increased by £20,000 and that provision for long-service leave has increased by £10,000. There are no other temporary differences.

To determine the tax entries, we need to determine **taxable profit**. In this example, taxable income would be calculated as:

Pre-tax accounting income	£100,000
Temporary differences	
Increase in prepayments	(£20,000)
Increase in provision for long-service leave	£10,000
Taxable profit	£90,000

> **taxable profit** The profit for a period determined in accordance with rules established by the taxation authorities, upon which income taxes are payable.

The accounting entry would be:

Dr	Tax expense	£30,000	
Dr	Deferred tax asset	£3,000	
Cr	Deferred tax liability		£6,000
Cr	Income tax payable		£27,000

Therefore to determine the tax that was actually paid, we would need to add any increase in deferred tax assets (or subtract any decrease) and subtract any increase in deferred tax liabilities (or add any decrease) from/to the tax expense. We would also need to subtract any increase in income taxes payable (closing balance less opening balance). Using a t-account approach, the cash flow related to taxes would be determined as the balancing item.

Taxes payable			
Deferred tax liability	x	Op. bal.	x
Cash	x	Tax expense	x
Clos. bal.	x	Deferred tax asset	x
	x		x

Alternatively, we can determine the cash flows associated with tax expense by using the formula:

Income taxes paid = Income tax expense + Opening income tax payable
– Closing income tax payable + Opening deferred tax liability
– Closing deferred tax liability + Closing deferred tax asset
– Opening deferred tax asset

16.5.6 Payments to suppliers and employees

To determine the cash flows associated with the purchases of inventories, we need to consider such items as cost of goods sold (COGS), changes in inventory levels, changes in accounts payable (also referred to as trade creditors) and any purchase discounts received. If we are using a t-account approach, it is useful to consider the trade payables and inventory accounts together.

If we adopt an equation-method approach, cash payments to suppliers would be determined as:

Trade payables			
Disc. rev.	x	Op. bal.	x
Cash	x	Inventory	x
Clos. bal.	x		
	x		x

Inventory			
Op. bal.	x	COGS	x
Trade payables	x	Inventory w/offs	x
		Clos. bal.	x
	x		x

Cash payments to suppliers = Opening accounts payable – Closing accounts payable
+ Cost of sales + Closing inventory – Opening inventory
– Discounts given by suppliers + Inventory write-offs

For an illustration of how to determine the cash payments made to suppliers, see Worked Example 16.2.

Interest and tax payments must be separately disclosed. To determine the payments for other expenses (apart from interest and tax payments) such as salaries expense, we need to consider which expenses are accrued and which relate to non-cash flow items (for example, depreciation). If an expense is accrued, we need to deduct any increase in the accrued liability to determine the related cash flow (or add any decrease in the accrued liability).

16.5.7 Cash flows from investing activities

Investing activities include the acquisition and disposal of non-current assets (such as property, plant and equipment and other productive assets) and investments (such as securities not falling within the definition of cash).

To determine the proceeds from the sale of non-current assets, specific information about the sale transaction would be required. It is the actual receipt that is recorded in the statement of cash flows, not any gain or loss that might have resulted.

To determine the amount of cash paid for non-current assets, we need to exclude any increase in assets generated by non-cash transactions, such as the acquisition of plant by virtue of a mortgage over the other assets of the business. We also need to deduct from the movement in assets any increases caused by upward asset revaluations. Any assets disposed of need to be considered too. The t-account for non-current assets may be represented as:

Non-current assets			
Op. bal.	x	Disposal	x
Revaluation res.	x	Prov. for deprec.	x
Non-cash trans.	x	Clos. bal.	x
Cash	x		
	x		x

Worked Example 16.2 — Calculating cash payments made to suppliers

Bogus plc has provided you with the following information:

Cost of goods sold for the year	£190,000
Purchases for the year (on credit terms)	£220,000
Discounts received for early payment to suppliers	£7,000
Inventory write-offs owing to water damage caused by global warming	£14,000
Opening balance of trade payables	£50,000
Closing balance of trade payables	£60,000
Opening balance of inventory	£20,000
Closing balance of inventory	£36,000

Required

Determine the cash payments made to suppliers during the year.

Solution

Using the t-account approach, the amount paid to suppliers is £203,000, determined as follows (all amounts are in £000):

Trade payables					Inventory			
Disc. rev.	7	Op. bal.	50	Op. bal.	20	COGS	190
Cash	203	Inventory	220	Trade payables	220	Inventory w/offs	14
Clos. bal.	60					Clos. bal.	36
	270		270		240		240

If we adopt an equation-method approach, cash payments to suppliers would be determined as follows:

Cash payments to suppliers = £50,000 (opening accounts payable)
      − £60,000 (closing accounts payable) + £190,000 (cost of sales)
      + £36,000 (closing inventory) − £20,000 (opening inventory)
      − £7,000 (discounts given by suppliers) + £14,000 (inventory write-offs)
      = £203,000

Using an equation approach, and assuming the assets are not recorded at net values—that is, cost (or revalued amount) less accumulated depreciation—the cash flows associated with the acquisition of non-current assets may be determined as:

> Cash payments = Closing balance of non-current assets − Opening balance of non-current assets
>   + Original cost of assets sold − Assets acquired through non-cash transactions
>   − Revaluation increases + Accumulated depreciation written back to revalued assets

For an illustration of how to determine the cash payments made to suppliers of non-current assets, consider Worked Example 16.3.

Worked Example 16.3 — Calculating cash flows from investing activities

Assume that Seedorf plc provides you with the following information about their holding of plant and equipment:
- Opening balance of plant and equipment is €800,000.
- Closing balance of plant and equipment is €780,000.
- Plant with a carrying value of €100,000 (cost €130,000; accumulated depreciation €30,000) has been revalued during the year to €150,000.

- Shares in the company have been exchanged for plant and equipment with a fair value of €60,000.
- Plant with a carrying value of €50,000 (cost €130,000; accumulated depreciation €80,000) has been sold for €20,000.

Required

Determine the amount of plant and equipment acquired for cash.

Solution

In considering the above data, we should remember (see Chapter 6) that the accounting entries to record the revaluation of plant and equipment would be:

Dr Provision for depreciation	€30,000	
Cr Plant and equipment		€30,000

(to eliminate existing accumulated depreciation in existence at time of revaluation)

Dr Plant and equipment	€50,000	
Cr Revaluation surplus		€50,000

(to revalue the plant and equipment to €150,000)

As explained in Chapter 15, where there is an asset revaluation we also need to consider the related tax implications. As we learned in Chapter 15, a revaluation increment will lead to the recognition of an associated deferred tax liability. Assuming a tax rate of 30 per cent, the entry would be:

Dr Revaluation surplus	€15,000	
Cr Deferred tax liability		€15,000

(€15,000 = €50,000 × 0.30)

With the above in mind, we can reconstruct the t-accounts as follows to show that cash payments for plant and equipment amount to €30,000:

Plant and equipment			
Op. bal.	800	Disposal	130
Revaluation surplus	50	Prov. for deprec.	30
Non-cash trans.	60	Clos. bal.	780
Cash	30		
	940		940

16.5.8 Cash flows from financing activities

financial structure
Refers to how the resources of the entity have been funded, for example how much debt there is relative to equity. Financial structure information can also describe the types of debt and types of equity in existence.

Financing activities relate to changing the size and composition of the **financial structure** of the entity, including equity, and borrowings not falling within the definition of cash.

For many types of debt, it might be easy to determine the cash inflow. It might simply be the difference between the opening and closing liability. For items such as debentures, however, we might need to consider any discount, or premium on issue. Consider our earlier example in Section 16.5.3, where a reporting entity issues debentures with a life of four years and a face value of €1 million. Given that the coupon rate on the debentures is 10 per cent, and the market requires a rate of return of 12 per cent, the issue price is €939,230. So, to determine the cash flow on a debenture issue, we need to deduct any discount from the face value. Conversely, we would add any premium.

To determine the cash flows from the issue of equity securities, we need to consider whether any share issue has been financed out of reserves, such as retained earnings or revaluation surplus. In such cases there would be no related cash flows.

As already discussed, cash payments associated with dividends are required to be treated as part of financing activities. In determining cash payments of dividends, we need to consider the dividend payments, proposed dividends and any increase in dividends payable, determining the associated cash flow as:

> Payment of cash dividends = Dividends paid + Dividends proposed
> + Opening dividends payable − Closing dividends payable

A final point to be made before considering the comprehensive illustration in Worked Example 16.4 is that what we basically need to do in compiling a statement of cash flows is to make sure that we have reconciled the movements in all the non-cash accounts in the statement of financial position to determine which accounts affect cash. Once we have done this, we will have an overview of all cash movements.

Worked Example 16.4   Preparation of a statement of cash flows

The example below uses both the t-account approach and the equation approach. You can use whichever method you prefer. Comparative figures, though required by the standard, are not necessary for this exercise.
   The account details of Cashco plc are shown below.

Cashco plc: Statement of comprehensive income (extract) for the year ended 30 June

	2014 (€000)	2014 (€000)	2015 (€000)	2015 (€000)
Income				
Sales		700		885
Expenses				
Cost of goods sold	200		240	
Depreciation—buildings	20		20	
Depreciation—plant	60		70	
Doubtful debts	30		40	
Electricity and rates	20		45	
Income tax	76		84	
Interest expense	10		11	
Lease rentals	40		70	
Salaries	160	616	200	780
Net profit		84		105

Cashco plc: Statement of financial position as at 30 June

	2014 (€000)	2015 (€000)
ASSETS		
Non-current assets		
Land	100	250
Buildings	400	400
Acc. depreciation—buildings	(40)	(60)
Plant and equipment	400	420
Acc. depreciation—P & E	(40)	(40)
Deferred tax asset	–	4
	820	974
Current assets		
Cash	176	239
Accounts receivable	220	280
Provision for doubtful debts	(30)	(40)
Inventory	90	100
	456	579
Total assets	1,276	1,553

▶

	2014 (€000)	2015 (€000)
EQUITY AND LIABILITIES		
Shareholders' funds		
Share capital	400	500
Revaluation surplus	–	30
Retained earnings	610	715
	1,010	1,245
Non-current liabilities		
Long-term loans	100	110
Deferred tax liability	–	20
	100	130
Current liabilities		
Trade payables	80	70
Accrued expenses	10	20
Income tax payable	76	88
	166	178
Total equity and liabilities	1,276	1,553

Additional information

- There have been no cash sales.
- During the year, €30,000 from provision for doubtful debts has been written off against accounts receivable.
- Land has been revalued upwards by €50,000.
- Land with a fair value of €100,000 has been acquired by the issue of 100,000 fully paid ordinary shares for €1.00 per share.
- Salaries and lease rentals are accrued prior to payment.
- Electricity and rates and interest expense are paid as incurred.
- The trade payables account is used for purchases of inventory.
- During the year, plant that cost €100,000 and that has accumulated depreciation of €70,000 is sold for €30,000 cash.
- For tax purposes, allowable depreciation for the year was:
  - Plant and equipment: €70,000
  - Buildings: no deduction allowable in any year.
- Tax rate is 40 per cent.

Required

Prepare a statement of cash flows for Cashco plc for the year ended 30 June 2015.

Solution

In this example, some expenses (electricity and rates and interest) are accounted for on a cash basis. For the accounts that involve accruals, it may be necessary to reconstruct the accounts to determine relevant cash movements. Note that amounts in all t-accounts in this exercise are shown in €000s.

(a) Cash flows from operating activities
  (i) Receipts from customers

   We need to reconstruct the provision for doubtful debts and accounts receivable.
   The cumulative entry to record sales would be:

Dr	Accounts receivable	€885,000	
Cr	Sales		€885,000

   The entry to record the doubtful debts expense would be:

Dr	Doubtful debts expense	€40,000	
Cr	Provision for doubtful debts		€40,000

As the closing balance of doubtful debts increases by only €10,000, €30,000 must have been written off against accounts receivable. A reconciliation of accounts receivable shows a cash collection of €795,000:

Accounts receivable					Provision for doubtful debts			
Op. bal.	220	Prov. d.d.	30		A/c rec.	30	Op. bal.	30
Sales	885	Cash	795					
		Clos. bal.	280		Clos. bal.	40	D.d exp.	40
	1,105		1,105			70		70

Alternatively, we can determine the cash flow as:

> Cash flow = Sales + Opening accounts receivable − Transfer from provision for doubtful debts (opening balance of provision + Doubtful debts expense − Closing balance of provision) − Closing balance of accounts receivable

$$= €885 + €220 − (€30 + €40 − €40) − €280$$
$$= €795$$

(ii) **Purchases of inventory**

Cashco plc commences the period with €90,000 of inventory. After using €240,000 (COGS), it has a closing balance of €100,000. Given that there are no inventory write-offs, this means that €250,000 of inventory must have been purchased.

Given that trade payables has an opening balance of €80,000, purchases are €250,000 (above) and closing balance is €70,000, €260,000 must have been paid in cash. This is shown in the following t-accounts.

Inventory					Trade payables			
Op. bal.	90	COGS	240		Cash	260	Op. bal.	80
Trade payables	250	Clos. bal.	100		Clos. bal.	70	Inventory	250
	340		340			330		330

In this example, there are no inventory write-downs (for example, due to obsolescence/theft). If there are such write-downs, they would be added to the €260,000 to arrive at the inventory purchases.

Alternatively, we can use the equation method:

> Cash flow = Opening accounts payable − Closing accounts payable + Cost of goods sold + Closing inventory − Opening inventory

$$= €80 − €70 + €240 + €100 − €90$$
$$= €260$$

(iii) **Accrued expenses**

In this example, salary and lease expenses are accrued prior to payment. If the opening balance of accrued expenses is €10,000, salaries and lease expenses total €270,000 and the closing balance is €20,000, then €260,000 must have been paid.

Accrued expenses			
Cash	260	Op. bal.	10
Clos. bal.	20	Sal. & leases	270
	280		280

Alternatively, we can use the equation method:

> Cash flow = Opening balance of accrued expenses + Expenses incurred during the period − Closing balance of accrued expenses

$$= €10 + €270 − €20$$
$$= €260$$

(iv) Taxation

The profit before tax is €189,000. There is €20,000 in permanent differences (building depreciation) and a €10,000 temporary difference (the increase in provision for doubtful debts). Therefore the entry would be (rounded to the nearest €000):

Dr	Income tax expense	€84,000	
Dr	Deferred tax asset	€4,000	
Cr	Income tax payable		€88,000

A reconciliation of income taxes payable would show:

Income tax payable			
Cash	76	Op. bal.	76
Clos. bal.	88	Tax/DTA	88
	164		164

Alternatively, we can use the equation method:

> Cash flow = Income tax expense – Closing income tax payable + Opening income tax payable
> + Opening deferred tax liability – Closing deferred tax liability – Opening deferred tax asset
> + Closing deferred tax asset

$$= €84 - €88 + €76 + €0 - €0 - €0 + €4$$
$$= €76$$

At this stage, we can now calculate the total cash flows from operations as:

	€000
Receipts from customers	795
Payments to suppliers	(260)
Payments for accrued expenses	(260)
Interest payments	(11)
Electricity and rates	(45)
Taxation payments	(76)
	143

(b) Cash flows from investment activities

(i) Land

A reconciliation of the movements in land shows that no land has been acquired for cash. There has been a revaluation, with the related recognition of a deferred tax liability (see Chapter 15), as well as an exchange of shares in the entity for land. The entries would be:

Dr	Land	€50,000	
Cr	Revaluation surplus		€50,000
Dr	Revaluation surplus	€20,000	
Cr	Deferred tax liability		€20,000
Dr	Land	€100,000	
Cr	Share capital		€100,000

Land			
Op. bal.	100		
Share capital	100		
Revaluation surplus	50	Clos. bal.	250
	250		250

Alternatively, the equation method can be used:

> Cash flow = Closing balance of non-current assets – Opening balance of non-current assets
> – Revaluations + Disposals (at cost or revalued amount) – Non-cash acquisitions

$$= €250 - €100 - €50 - €100 = €0$$

(ii) Plant and equipment
The journal entries for the disposal of the plant and equipment can be summarised as:

Dr	Acc. depreciation—plant and equipment	€70,000	
Dr	Cash	€30,000	
Cr	Plant and equipment		€100,000

As plant and equipment increases by €20,000, €120,000 must have been acquired during the period, as reconciled below.

Accumulated depreciation				Plant and equipment			
Disposal	70	Op. bal.	40	Op. bal.	400	Disposal	100
Clos. bal.	40	Deprec. exp.	70	Cash	120	Clos. bal.	420
	110		110		520		520

Alternatively, using the equation method:

> Cash flow = Closing balance of non-current assets
> − Opening balance of non-current assets − Revaluations
> + Disposals (at cost or revalued amount) − Non-cash acquisitions

$$= €420 − €400 − €0 + €100 − €0$$
$$= €120$$

Total cash flows from investing activities	€000
Payment for property, plant and equipment	(120)
Proceeds from sale of equipment	30
	(90)

(c) Cash flows from financing activities
A reconciliation of movements in share capital would show that there have been no issues for cash. The only cash flow from financing relates to €10,000 from long-term loans.

Total cash flows for the period	€000
Opening cash balance	176
Cash from operations	143
Cash from investing	(90)
Cash from financing	10
Closing cash balance	239

We are now able to present a statement of cash flows for Cashco plc (the direct method has been used).

Cashco plc Statement of cash flows for the year ended 30 June 2015	€000
Cash flows from operating activities	
Receipts from customers	795
Payments to suppliers of goods and services, inclusive of labour	(565)
Interest paid	(11)
Income taxes paid	(76)
Net cash provided from operating activities (1)	143

Cashco plc
Statement of cash flows for the year ended 30 June 2015 (cont'd)   €000

Cash flows from investing activities
Payment for property, plant and equipment (2)   (120)
Proceeds from sale of plant   30
Net cash used in investing activities   (90)
Cash flows from financing activities
Proceeds from borrowings   10
Net cash from financing activities   10
Net increase in cash held   63
Cash at the beginning of the financial year   176
Cash at the end of the financial year   239

For Cashco, two notes must accompany the statement of cash flows:

Note 1. Non-cash financing and investing activities

During the financial year the economic entity also acquired land with an aggregate fair value of €100,000 by means of issuing 100,000 fully paid ordinary shares.

Note 2. Were the indirect method to be used the following would be included in the first part of the statement of cash flows:

	€000
Operating profit after tax	105
Depreciation	90
Increase in provision for doubtful debts	10
Increase in income taxes payable	12
Increase in accounts receivable	(60)
Increase in inventories	(10)
Decrease in trade payables	(10)
Increase in accrued expenses	10
Increase in deferred tax asset	(4)
Net cash provided from operating activities	143

16.6 Contractual implications

Cash flows from operations would seem to provide a reasonable guide to the ability of a firm to service debt, perhaps more so than measures such as interest coverage—that is, profit before interest and taxes, divided by interest expense. For example, a debt contract might require the net cash provided by operating activities to exceed total interest obligations by at least five times. Of course, even before the mandatory requirement for large companies to produce statements of cash flows, debt-holders would have been able to require borrowers to provide statements of cash flows as part of the loan agreement.

It could be argued that traditional financial ratios, such as the current ratio—current assets divided by current liabilities—or acid-test ratios, are deficient in monitoring the liquidity of the organisation. As Fadel and Parkinson (1978) indicate, the view that current assets are used to pay current liabilities is false, since these assets 'never become realised . . . and the total current liabilities never become fully paid'. Sharma (1996) argues that cash flows from operating activities divided by current debt might be a more appropriate measure of short-term liquidity. Sharma also proposes that retained cash flows from operations (RCFFO) might be an important indicator of an entity's financial flexibility. He states (p. 40):

> This variable (RCFFO) measures the level of cash retained after meeting all operating costs and priority payments such as interest costs and dividends . . . This variable can therefore be used to assess an entity's debt-paying capacity and its investment power without relying on borrowed funds or the sale of assets . . . Retained cash flows from operations divided by total cash inflows and debt cash inflows divided by total cash flows will indicate the degree to which cash is obtained from sources internal and external to the firm. Where the source of funds is

largely RCFFO, an entity may be in a sound financial position. However, where the source of cash is largely debt, then an entity would be at high financial risk.

Sharma's arguments and findings are generally consistent with those provided in Flanagan and Whittred (1992). In a review of Hooker Corporation Ltd, Flanagan and Whittred documented results that indicate that traditional use of financial ratios pertaining to liquidity, solvency and profitability provided poor guides to the probability of corporate failure. Conversely, however, the analysis of trends in cash flows from operations appeared to provide earlier indications of forthcoming financial distress.

Accepting that parties lending funds to others periodically need to monitor the riskiness of their investments, work such as that of Flanagan and Whittred (1992) and Sharma (1996) would suggest that efficient contracts necessarily include ratios based on the information shown in the statement of cash flows. Grady (2010) examined two methods of calculating the debt service coverage ratio, a profit-based measure and a cash flow-based measure. He concluded that both should be calculated; that analysts should not stop at the traditional profit-based ratio analysis as the cash flow-based ratios can improve the quality of credit analysis.

16.7 Potential future changes to the statement of cash flows

As indicated in earlier chapters of this book, the IASB and US Financial Accounting Standards Board (FASB) are undertaking a joint project investigating the presentation of financial statements. This project led to the release in October 2008 of a Discussion Paper entitled *Preliminary Views on Financial Statement Presentation* followed by a 'staff draft' of an Exposure Draft of a new financial statement presentation accounting standard in July 2010. The Discussion Paper and the 'staff draft' represent the initial steps towards creating a new accounting standard that would ultimately replace IAS 1 and IAS 7 (interested readers should look at the IASB website for further information on the financial statement presentation project). Therefore it is expected that the requirements pertaining to statements of cash flows, as described and explained in this chapter, are likely to change in coming years.

In their work, the IASB and FASB emphasise that the three main financial statements (the statement of financial position, the statement of comprehensive income and the statement of cash flows) should use an account classification scheme that is consistent throughout the financial statements, with the statement of financial position being the dominant statement in terms of determining the account classifications to be used in the other financial statements (IASB 2008, paragraph 2.29).

It is argued that at the present time there is a general lack of 'cohesiveness' in how the various financial statements are presented (IASB 2008, paragraph S7). This in itself is a main reason why the IASB and the FASB have seen the need to embark on the project to revise how financial statements should be presented.

Pursuant to the proposed approach to presentation, an entity would classify income, expenses and cash flows in the same section and category as the related asset or liability. For example, if an entity classifies inventory in the operating category of the statement of financial position, it would classify changes in inventory in the operating category of the statement of comprehensive income (as part of cost of goods sold) and classify the related cash payments to suppliers in the operating category of the statement of cash flows.

The IASB and FASB are also proposing that financial statements should be presented in a more disaggregated manner. In particular, it is proposed that financial statements should be prepared in a way that separates an entity's financing activities from its business and other activities and, further, separates financing activities between transactions with owners in their capacity as owners and all other financing activities. It is proposed that the 'Business' section of the financial statements would include all items related to assets and liabilities that management views as part of its continuing business activities. Business activities are those activities conducted with the intent of creating value, such as producing goods or providing services. It is proposed that the 'Business' section be further disaggregated into an *Operating category* and an *Investing category*. According to the Discussion Paper:

- The *Operating category* would include assets and liabilities that management views as related to the central purpose(s) for which the entity is in business (and changes in those assets and liabilities). An entity uses its operating assets and liabilities in its primary revenue and expense-generating activities.
- The *Investing category* would include all assets and liabilities that management views as unrelated to the central purpose for which the entity is in business (and any changes in those assets and liabilities). An entity would use its investing assets and liabilities to generate a return, but would not use them in its primary revenue and expense-generating activities.
- The *Financing category* would include only financial assets and financial liabilities that management views as part of the financing of the entity's business activities (referred to as 'financing assets and liabilities'). Amounts relating to financing liabilities would be presented in the *financing liabilities category* and amounts relating to financing assets would be presented in the *financing assets category* in each of the financial statements. In determining whether a financial asset or liability should be included in the financing section,

an entity should consider whether the item is interchangeable with other sources of financing and whether the item can be characterised as independent of specific business activities.

Table 16.3 represents the proposed format for presenting information within the financial statements, excluding the notes. (The section names are in *bold italics*; bullet points indicate required categories within sections.)

Table 16.3 Proposed format for the presentation of financial statements

Statement of financial position	Statement of comprehensive income	Statement of cash flows
Business • Operating assets and liabilities • Investing assets and liabilities	*Business* • Operating income and expenses • Investing income and expenses	*Business* • Operating cash flows • Investing cash flows
Financing • Financing assets • Financing liabilities	*Financing* • Financing asset income • Financing liability expenses	*Financing* • Financing asset cash flows • Financing liability cash flows
Income taxes	*Income taxes* On continuing operations (business and financing)	*Income taxes*
Discontinued operations	*Discontinued operations* Net of tax	*Discontinued operations*
	Other comprehensive income Net of tax	
Equity		*Equity*

According to the 2008 IASB Discussion Paper, each entity would decide the order of the sections and categories but would use the same order in each individual statement. Each entity would decide how to classify its assets and liabilities into the sections and categories on the basis of how an item is used (the 'management approach'). The entity would disclose why it chose those classifications. Thus, a manufacturing entity may classify the same asset (or liability) differently from a financial institution because of differences in the businesses in which those entities engage.

The Discussion Paper provides an example of how a statement of cash flows might appear if the contents of the Discussion Paper are ultimately adopted. The proposed format is provided in Exhibit 16.6. As can be seen, this *suggested* format represents a departure from the current disclosure requirements embodied within IAS 7.

Exhibit 16.6 **Proposed format for the statement of cash flows**

TOOLCO STATEMENT OF CASH FLOWS

	For the year ended 31 December	
	2016	2015
BUSINESS		
Operating		
Cash received from wholesale customers	2,108,754	1,928,798
Cash received from retail customers	703,988	643,275
Total cash collected from customers	2,812,742	2,572,073
Cash paid for goods		
Materials purchases	(935,544)	(785,000)
Labour	(418,966)	(475,313)
Overhead—transport	(128,640)	(108,000)

▶

	For the year ended 31 December	
	2016	2015
Pension	(170,100)	(157,500)
Overhead—other	(32,160)	(27,000)
Total cash paid for goods	*(1,685,410)*	*(1,552,813)*
Cash paid for selling activities		
Advertising	(65,000)	(75,000)
Wages, salaries and benefits	(58,655)	(55,453)
Other	(13,500)	(12,500)
Total cash paid for selling activities	*(137,155)*	*(142,953)*
Cash paid for general and administrative activities		
Wages, salaries and benefits	(332,379)	(314,234)
Contributions to pension plan	(170,100)	(157,500)
Capital expenditures	(54,000)	(50,000)
Lease payments	(50,000)	–
Research and development	(8,478)	(7,850)
Settlement of share-based remuneration	(3,602)	(3,335)
Other	(12,960)	(12,000)
Total cash paid for general and administrative activities	*(631,519)*	*(544,919)*
Cash flow before other operating activities	358,658	331,388
Cash from other operating activities		
Disposal of property, plant and equipment	37,650	–
Investment in associate A	–	(120,000)
Sale of receivable	8,000	10,000
Settlement of cash flow hedge	3,401	3,150
Total cash received (paid) for other operating activities	49,051	(106,850)
Net cash from operating activities	**407,709**	**224,538**
Investing		
Purchase of available-for-sale financial assets	–	(130,000)
Sale of available-for-sale financial assets	56,100	51,000
Dividends received	54,000	50,000
Net cash from investing activities	**110,100**	**(29,000)**
NET CASH FROM BUSINESS ACTIVITIES	**517,809**	**195,538**

FINANCING

Interest received on cash	8,619	5,500
Total cash from financing assets	**8,619**	**5,500**
Proceeds from issue of short-term debt	162,000	150,000
Proceeds from issue of long-term debt	–	250,000
Interest paid	(83,514)	(82,688)
Dividends paid	(86,400)	(80,000)
Total cash from financing liabilities	**(7,914)**	**237,312**
NET CASH FROM FINANCING ACTIVITIES	**705**	**242,812**
Change in cash from continuing operations before taxes and equity	*518,514*	*438,350*

INCOME TAXES

Cash taxes paid	(281,221)	(193,786)
Change in cash before discontinued operations and equity	237,293	244,564
DISCONTINUED OPERATIONS		
Cash paid from discontinued operations	(12,582)	(11,650)
NET CASH FROM DISCONTINUED OPERATIONS	**(12,582)**	**(11,650)**
Change in cash before equity	224,711	232,914

EQUITY

Proceeds from reissue of treasury shares	84,240	78,000
NET CASH FROM EQUITY	84,240	78,000
Effect of foreign exchange rates on cash	3,209	1,027
CHANGE IN CASH	312,160	311,941
Beginning cash	861,941	550,000
Ending cash	1,174,101	861,941

In terms of other changes that may occur in the future in regard to the presentation of the statement of cash flows, it has been proposed that 'cash equivalents' no longer be included as part of the statement of cash flows. Specifically, the Discussion Paper states:

> 3.71 *An entity's statement of cash flows should reconcile the beginning and ending amounts of cash.*
>
> 3.72 *Cash in the statement of financial position will no longer include cash equivalents. To be consistent with their preliminary views on presenting cash in the statement of financial position, the boards propose that the statement of cash flows should reconcile the beginning and ending amounts of cash rather than cash and cash equivalents as in present practice.*

The Exposure Draft released by the IASB in 2010 also excludes cash equivalents (paragraphs 117 and 118). The elimination of 'cash equivalents' would represent a major change to existing accounting standards. Obviously, a clear definition of 'cash' will be required. The definition of *cash* used in the 2010 Exposure Draft is 'Cash on hand and demand deposits'.

The Discussion Paper and the Exposure Draft also propose to mandate the use of the direct method of compiling the statement of cash flows (IASB 2008, paragraph 3.75). Under IAS 7, entities have an option to use either the direct method or the indirect method.

Information about cash flows will be important to various stakeholders, including investors and investment analysts. Therefore, as Francis (2010) discusses, any changes to cash flow presentation or measurement will require careful thought by the IASB. Francis undertook a study to investigate whether the proposed approach to presenting a statement of cash flows—as documented in the 2008 Discussion Paper and the 2010 Exposure Draft released by the IASB—provides more or less information content than the approach currently required by IAS 7. One issue considered was the relative information content of the proposed and current (IAS 7) measures for cash flows from operations. Unlike the measure of cash flows from operations currently reported pursuant to IAS 7, the IASB has proposed that cash flows from operations should not include interest paid or received, taxes paid and dividends received. Further, the proposed measure of cash flows from operations would include net capital expenditures, which are cash inflows and outflows associated with retirements and acquisitions of non-current assets used in the operations of the entity. These are not currently included as part of cash flows from operations as determined in accordance with IAS 7. Francis (ibid) reports that the results of his research indicate that the proposed operating cash flow measure has less relative information content than the measure currently prescribed under IAS 7. Francis would therefore question the worth of the new standard. While we would not necessarily question the merit of introducing new accounting standards on the basis of just one study (for example, Francis 2010), if a number of studies were to question the merit of proposed accounting requirements, then it would be hoped that the IASB would take such evidence into consideration. It is costly to create changes in accounting standards (from the perspective of both preparers and readers of financial statements), so the benefits to financial statement users must be perceived as exceeding the related costs associated with introducing new reporting requirements.

SUMMARY

The chapter considered various issues associated with constructing and interpreting a statement of cash flows. The statement of cash flows is described as being a very useful complement to an entity's statement of financial position, statement of comprehensive income and statement of changes in equity. It provides information that is useful for making assessments of such things as an entity's ability to generate cash flows; meet financial commitments as they fall due; finance changes in operating activities; and obtain and service external debt. As the statement of cash flows is not based upon accrual accounting, its compilation is not greatly influenced by professional judgement. While different accountants might not agree on what an entity's profits, assets or liabilities are, they would most likely agree on its cash flows for the purpose of a statement of cash flows. This attribute of the statement of cash flows—the limited professional judgement involved—explains in part why some believe that the statement of cash flows is more credible than the statement of comprehensive income or the statement of financial position.

The statement of cash flows provides a reconciliation of opening and closing cash, with cash being described as cash on hand and cash equivalents. Cash equivalents come in two forms: highly liquid investments with short periods to maturity, readily convertible to cash on hand at the investor's option (typically less than three months to maturity); and borrowings integral to the cash management function of the entity and not subject to a term facility. As the statement of cash flows may relate to a number of accounts (for example, cash on hand, cash at bank, bank overdraft and short-term money market deposits), accounting standard IAS 7 requires a note to the financial statements to be provided reconciling the cash balance to the related statement of financial position items.

Regarding the provision of information on cash flows for a period, the accounting standards require cash flows to be subdivided into operating activities, investing activities and financing activities. This subdivision provides further information about the various facets of an organisation's cash flows. In preparing the statement of cash flows, the direct method, as opposed to the indirect method, is recommended by the accounting standard. Under the direct method, the relevant cash inflows are reported in gross terms, rather than being netted off against one another. For example, rather than showing the net cash received on the movements in an entity's investments, cash inflows from sales of investments are to be shown separately from cash outflows relating to acquisitions of investments. In the UK the approach taken is usually the indirect method.

When financial statements are presented to financial statement users, it is possible that cash flows from operations will be very different from profits after tax. The reason for this is that profits are determined on an accrual basis—that is, revenues are recognised when earned, and expenses are recognised when incurred—and not on a cash basis, as is the case for cash flows from operations.

While the statement of cash flows provides information about the cash flows associated with financing and investing activities, financing and investing activities can occur without the direct transfer of any cash. For example, perhaps some assets are acquired as a result of the exchange of shares in the reporting entity. To help ensure that financial statement users are more fully informed, IAS 7 requires that information about material financing and investing transactions, and events that do not result in or from cash flows during the financial period, be disclosed in the notes accompanying the financial statements.

The chapter described two of the many approaches to preparing a statement of cash flows: the equation approach and the t-account approach. A number of illustrations of both approaches were provided, while stressing that the method that is adopted is a matter of personal preference.

The chapter has also briefly explored work that is being undertaken by the IASB and FASB to develop revised rules pertaining to financial statement presentation. While we cannot be certain at this stage about the exact changes that are likely to be made in terms of how we present statements of cash flows, it does appear somewhat inevitable that some time after 2012 there could be major changes in how we prepare and present a statement of cash flows.

KEY TERMS

accrual accounting 447	financing activities 451	statement of cash flows 447
accrual profits/losses 448	investing activities 451	taxable profit 461
financial structure 464	operating activities 451	

END-OF-CHAPTER EXERCISE

Crescent plc is involved in manufacturing golf clubs, with special emphasis on sand irons. Crescent plc's statements of financial position for the years ended 30 June 2015 and 30 June 2016 are presented below: **LO** 16.2

	2016 (£000)	2015 (£000)
ASSETS		
Non-current assets		
Property, plant and equipment	780	600
Acc. depreciation—property, plant and equipment	(180)	(100)
	600	500
Current assets		
Cash	480	–
Accounts receivable	180	300
Provision for doubtful debts	(60)	(40)
Inventory	460	260
	1,060	520
Total assets	1,660	1,020
EQUITY AND LIABILITIES		
Equity and reserves		
Share capital	700	100
Revaluation surplus	140	40
Retained earnings	80	240
Total equity and reserves	920	380
Non-current liabilities		
Loans	300	–
Current liabilities		
Bank overdraft	–	200
Accounts payable	300	300
Accrued wages	100	80
Provision for annual leave	40	60
	440	640
Total liabilities	740	640
Total equity and liabilities	1,660	1,020

The expenses and revenues of Crescent plc for the year ending 30 June 2016 are:

	2016 (£000)
Revenues	
Sales	300
Interest (no interest receivable at year end)	20
Gain on sale of property (which had a carrying value of £100,000)	40
Expenses	
Cost of goods sold	(200)
Doubtful debts	(40)
Depreciation	(100)
Wages	(100)
Employee entitlements—annual leave	(80)
Net loss for the year	(160)

REQUIRED

Prepare a statement of cash flows for Crescent plc for the year ending 30 June 2016. For the purposes of this exercise, taxation is ignored.

SOLUTION TO END-OF-CHAPTER EXERCISE

(a) Cash flows from operating activities

(i) Cash receipts from customers

Accounts receivable					Provision for doubtful debts			
Op. bal.	300	Cash	400		Accounts receivable	20	Op. bal.	40
Sales	300	Prov. for d.d.	20		Clos. bal.	60	Expense	40
		Clos. bal.	180			80		80
	600		600					

(ii) Cash payments for inventory

Inventory					Accounts payable			
Op. bal.	260	Cost of goods sold	200		Cash	400	Op. bal.	300
Accounts payable	400	Clos. bal.	460		Clos. bal.	300	Inventory	400
	660		660			700		700

(iii) Expense provisions/Accrued expenses

Accrued wages					Accrued employee entitlements (provision for annual leave)			
Cash	80	Op. bal.	80					
Clos. bal.	100	Wages	100		Cash	100	Op. bal.	60
	180		180		Clos. bal.	40	Employee entitlements	80
						140		140

Total cash flows from operating activities	(£000)
From customers	400
Payments to employees (80 + 100)	(180)
Payments to suppliers	(400)
Interest received	20
	(160)

(b) Cash flows from investing activities

Accumulated depreciation					Property, plant and equipment			
Disposal	20	Opening bal.	100		Op. bal.	600	Disposal	120
Clos. bal.	180	Expense	100		Revaluation reserve	100	Clos. bal.	780
	200		200		Cash	200		
						900		900

To determine the original cost of the asset disposed of, we are told that the carrying value of the property is £100,000. From the above t-account analysis, we have determined that the accumulated depreciation related to the disposed asset is £20,000. Therefore its original cost must have been £120,000. As the property has a carrying value of £100,000 and as Crescent plc records a profit on sale of £40,000, it must have received £140,000 from the disposal.

Total cash flows from investing activities	(£000)
From sale of plant	140
Acquisition of plant	(200)
	(60)

(c) Cash flows from financing activities

In the absence of any information to the contrary, it must be assumed that the increase in share capital of £600,000 is received in cash. There are also additional borrowings of £300,000.

Having considered the cash flows associated with the operating, investing and financing activities, we are in a position to compile the statement of cash flows.

Crescent plc Statement of cash flows for the year ended 30 June 2016	(£000)	(£000)
Cash flows from operating activities		
Receipts from customers	400	
Payments to suppliers	(400)	
Payments to employees	(180)	
Interest received	20	
Net cash provided by operating activities (1)		(160)
Cash flows from investing activities		
Proceeds from sale of plant	140	
Acquisition of plant	(200)	
Net cash from investing activities		(60)
Cash flows from financing activities		
Proceeds from share issue	600	
Proceeds from borrowings	300	
Net cash from financing activities		900
Net increase in cash held		680
Cash at the beginning of the year (2)		(200)
Cash at the end of the year		480

To comply with IAS 7, a number of supporting notes, including a reconciliation of the movement in cash and cash equivalents as disclosed in the statement of financial position, are required.

Note 1. Reconciliation statement for cash as shown in statement of cash flows

Cash at the end of the year as shown in the statement of cash flows is reconciled to the related items in the statement of financial position as follows:

	2016 (£000)	2015 (£000)
Cash per statement of financial position	480	–
Bank overdraft per statement of financial position	–	(200)
Cash at year end per statement of cash flows	480	(200)

Note 2. Accounting policy note

In the statement of cash flows, 'cash' includes cash at bank and bank overdraft.

Note 3. Details of credit standby arrangements and used/unused loan facilities

This is a required note. For Crescent plc, there are no such facilities.

Note 4. Details of non-cash financing and investing activities

This is a required note. For Crescent plc, there are no such transactions.

The above solution has been prepared using the direct method. If the indirect method were to be adopted, the following would take the place of the cash flows from the 'operating activities' part of the statement of cash flows.

Reconciliation of net cash provided by operating activities and net profit	£000	£000
Operating profit after tax		(160)
Add/(Subtract):		
Depreciation expense	100	
Increase in receivables	120	
Profit on sale of property, plant and equipment	(40)	
Increase in inventories	(200)	
Decrease in annual leave provision	(20)	
Increase in accrued expenses	20	
Increase in provision for doubtful debts	20	0
Cash flows from operating activities		(160)

REVIEW QUESTIONS

1 Identify and describe the three types of activity that are reported in the statement of cash flows. Why do you think that accounting standard IAS 7 would require such a breakdown?   **LO** 16.5

2 Classify the following cash flows into the respective classifications of operating, financing or investing activity: **LO** 16.5
   (a) dividends received
   (b) dividends paid
   (c) interest paid
   (d) acquisition of plant and equipment
   (e) repayment of borrowings
   (f) borrowing costs
   (g) payments to suppliers
   (h) payments to employees
   (i) receipts from the issue of shares
   (j) payments made to underwriters

3 Define 'cash and cash equivalents' for the purposes of a statement of cash flows.   **LO** 16.4

4 Pursuant to IAS 7, identify which of the following items would be considered to be a 'cash equivalent':   **LO** 16.4
   (a) accounts receivable
   (b) accounts payable
   (c) gold bullion
   (d) deposits that are available at call
   (e) deposits on the money market that are available at two months' notice
   (f) bank overdraft
   (g) a loan that is repayable in two months

5 Is cash-flow data more 'reliable' than profit-related data? Explain your answer.   **LO** 16.3

6 Which form of information is more useful for evaluating the financial performance and position of a reporting entity: cash-flow data or information about accounting profits? Explain your answer.   **LO** 16.3

7 Discuss the practical difficulties in preparing a statement of cash flows pursuant to IAS 7 and critically appraise its value to the statutory accounts.   **LO** 16.3

8 Identify the implications the following have for the preparation of a statement of cash flows and accompanying notes:
   LO 16.1
   (a) the sale of a non-current asset
   (b) an increase in a provision for long-service leave
   (c) the acquisition of land by way of an issue of shares

9 Pursuant to IAS 7, apart from the statement of cash flows, what other disclosures must be made?   **LO** 16.6

10 Fremantle plc provides you with the following information: **LO** 16.5

Sales for the year	£400,000
Discounts provided during the year to customers for early payment	£10,000
Doubtful debts expense for the year	£5,000
Opening balance of accounts receivable	£90,000

Closing balance of accounts receivable	£80,000
Opening balance of the provision for doubtful debts	£9,000
Closing balance of the provision for doubtful debts	£8,000

REQUIRED

Determine how much cash has been received from customers during the year.

11 Rottnest plc has provided you with the following information: **LO 16.5**

Cost of goods sold for the year	€60,000
Purchases for the year (on credit terms)	€80,000
Discounts received for early payment to suppliers	€2,000
Inventory write-offs owing to water damage caused by melting ice in the Arctic	€5,000
Opening balance of trade payables	€40,000
Closing balance of trade payables	€35,000
Opening balance of inventory	€10,000
Closing balance of inventory	€25,000

REQUIRED

You are to determine the cash payments made to suppliers during the year.

12 Bergkamp plc provides you with the following information about its property, plant and equipment: **LO 16.5**

Opening balance of property, plant and equipment	€500,000
Closing balance of property, plant and equipment	€650,000
Depreciation expense for the year	€50,000
Opening balance of accumulated depreciation	€200,000
Closing balance of accumulated depreciation	€210,000
Gain on sale of property, plant and equipment	€20,000
Carrying value of property, plant and equipment that has been disposed of	€90,000

REQUIRED

You are to determine how much cash has been received from the disposal of property, plant and equipment, and how much cash has been used to acquire property, plant and equipment throughout the year.

13 The balances in the accounts of XYZ plc at 30 June 2015 and 30 June 2016 are: **LO 16.2**

	2016 (£000)	2015 (£000)
Revenue (all on credit)	250	350
Cost of goods sold	130	110
Doubtful debts expense	25	30
Interest expense	20	30
Salaries	30	25
Depreciation	10	15
Cash	144	139
Inventory	180	160
Accounts receivable	270	250
Provision for doubtful debts	30	35
Land	150	150
Plant	100	90
Accumulated depreciation	20	30
Bank overdraft	20	19
Accounts payable	200	190
Accrued salaries	22	18
Long-term loan	90	70
Share capital	120	100
Opening retained earnings	307	187

Other information

Share capital is increased by the bonus issue of 20,000 shares for £1.00 each out of retained earnings. Plant is acquired during the period at a cost of £30,000, while plant with a carrying value of £nil (cost of £20,000; accumulated depreciation of £20,000) is scrapped.

REQUIRED

Prepare a statement of cash flows for XYZ plc for the year ending 30 June 2016.

14 Following are extracts from the accounting records of S plc at 30 June 2016: **LO 16.2**

S plc: Proforma statement of financial position as at 30 June	2016 (€000)	2015 (€000)
ASSETS		
Non-current assets		
Land	600	240
Buildings	960	960
Accumulated depreciation—buildings	(144)	(96)
Plant and equipment	1,008	960
Accumulated depreciation—plant and equipment	(96)	(96)
Deferred tax asset	10	–
	2,338	1,968
Current assets		
Cash	574	422
Inventory	240	216
Accounts receivable	672	528
Provision for doubtful debts	(96)	(72)
	1,390	1,094
Total assets	3,728	3,062
EQUITY AND LIABILITIES		
Equity and reserves		
Share capital	1,200	960
Retained earnings	1,728	1,464
Revaluation surplus	72	–
	3,000	2,424
Non-current liabilities		
Long-term loans	264	240
Deferred tax liability	48	–
	312	240
Current liabilities		
Trade payables	168	192
Accrued expenses	30	24
Income tax payable	218	182
	416	398
Total liabilities	728	638
Total liabilities and equity	3,728	3,062

S plc: Statement of comprehensive income (extract) for the year ended 30 June	2016 (€000)	2015 (€000)
Income		
Sales	2,124	1,680
Expenses		
Cost of sales	576	480
Doubtful debts	96	72
Depreciation		
– Buildings	48	48
– Plant and equipment	168	144

S plc: Statement of comprehensive income (extract) for the year ended 30 June (cont'd)	2016 (€000)	2015 (€000)
Interest	26	24
Lease rental	168	96
Rates and electricity	90	48
Salaries	480	384
Income tax	208	182
	1,860	1,478
Net profit	264	202

Additional information

- During the year, land with a fair value of €240,000 is acquired through the issue of 240,000 fully paid shares.
- There is an upward revaluation by €120,000 of land previously held.
- There are no cash sales during the year.
- Trade receivables of €72,000 previously provided for as doubtful were written off during the year.
- The following expenses are paid as incurred:
  - electricity
  - rates
  - interest
- Accruals of lease rentals and salaries are made before payment.
- Depreciation allowable for tax purposes for the year was:
  - Buildings: no allowable tax depreciation
  - Plant and equipment: €168,000 tax depreciation
- Plant costing €240,000 is sold during the year for €72,000. Accumulated depreciation at the time of sale is €168,000.
- The trade payables account is used for inventory purchases.
- Assume a tax rate of 40 per cent.

REQUIRED

Prepare a statement of cash flows for S plc for the year ending 30 June 2016, in accordance with accounting standard IAS 7 (comparative figures are not required).

CHALLENGING QUESTIONS

15 T Pty plc is a manufacturer of tennis equipment and fashion wear. The statement of financial position as at 30 June 2016 and details of expenses and revenues for the year ending 30 June 2016 are as follows: **LO** 16.2

Draft statement of financial position as at 30 June	2016 (£000)	2015 (£000)
ASSETS		
Non-current assets		
Investment—associated company	1,050	0
Investments	1,216	948
Land	1,500	1,750
Buildings	800	800
Accumulated depreciation—buildings	(200)	(160)
Plant and equipment	1,025	768
Accumulated depreciation—plant and equipment	(100)	(548)
Deferred tax asset	312	302
Total non-current assets	5,603	3,860

Current assets		
Cash	135	274
Inventory	2,774	2,486
Prepayments	115	0
Accounts receivable	2,897	2,654
Provision for doubtful debts	(150)	(120)
Total current assets	5,771	5,294
Total assets	11,374	9,154

EQUITY AND LIABILITIES

Shareholders' equity		
Equity share capital	2,750	2,000
Retained earnings	280	130
Revaluation surplus	560	175
Total equity and reserves	3,590	2,305

Non-current liabilities		
Lease liability	15	0
Deferred tax liability	240	75
Borrowings	3,500	3,800
Total non-current liabilities	3,755	3,875

Current liabilities		
Trade payables	1,637	1,483
Accruals	1,575	1,110
Lease liability	5	0
Income tax payable	243	83
Provision for employee entitlements	205	298
Provision for deferred payment (relating to investment in Squash Pty plc)	50	0
Provision for warranty	314	0
Total current liabilities	4,029	2,974
Total liabilities	7,784	6,849
Total equity and liabilities	11,374	9,154

Statement of comprehensive income (extract) for the year ended 30 June	2016 (£000)	2015 (£000)
Income		
Sales	31,394	27,346
Dividends	51	47
Expenses		
Bad debts	(90)	(85)
Cost of sales	(28,205)	(24,611)
Doubtful debts	(35)	(40)
Inventory write-off	(50)	0
Provision for warranty	(314)	0
Depreciation		
– Building	(40)	(40)
– Plant and equipment	(100)	(60)

Interest	(315)	(418)
Rent	(600)	(600)
Salaries and wages	(1,324)	(1,231)
Finance charges	(7)	(90)
Profit before tax	365	218
Income tax	(215)	(90)
Profit after tax	150	128

Statement of changes in equity for the year ended 30 June	2016 (£000)	2015 (£000)
Equity at beginning of the year	2,380	2,002
Profit	150	128
Asset revaluation	550	250
Contributions from owners	750	—
Equity at end of the year	3,830	2,380

Additional information

- An additional investment of £80,000 is acquired for consideration of tennis equipment costing £80,000.
- Land is devalued against a previous increment in the revaluation reserve. The previous increment is fully reversed.
- Plant and equipment with a cost of £700,000 and accumulated depreciation of £500,000 are revalued to £1,000,000 during the year.
- Plant and equipment with a fair value of £25,000 is acquired under a finance lease. The residual is guaranteed by the lessee.
- Plant and equipment is sold for £20,000 cash. Cost is £68,000 and no profit or loss is made on the sale.
- During the year, one line of wooden tennis racquets is scrapped at a loss of £50,000, as there is little demand for this range.
- During the year, an investment is made in an associated company, Squash Pty plc. Consideration is £1,000,000, funded by cash of £250,000 and the balance by the issue of 500,000 shares at £1.50 per share. The purchase agreement includes a clause stating that, if profits exceed £110,000 in the first financial year after purchase, additional amounts are payable. Using the formula, an extra £50,000 is provided.
- Provision for warranty is based on 1 per cent of sales.
- Rent expense of £600,000 is accrued within 'Accruals'.
- Interest expense is paid during the year, and dividends are received.
- Salaries and wages expense includes the expense for employee entitlements.
- The tax rate is 30 per cent.

REQUIRED

Prepare the statement of cash flows in accordance with IAS 7 for the year ending 30 June 2016. Comparatives are not required.

REFERENCES

AKBAR, S., ZULFIQAR ALI SHAH, S., & STARK, A.W., 'The Value Relevance of Cash Flows, Current Accruals, and Non-current Accruals in the UK', *International Review of Financial Analysis*, vol. 20, 2011, pp. 311–19.

DOWDS, J., 'Accrual Versus Cash Flows', *Chartered Accountants Journal*, March 1997, pp. 24–5.

FADEL, H. & PARKINSON, J.M., 'Liquidity Evaluation by Means of Ratio Analysis', *Accounting and Business Research*, Spring 1978, pp. 101–7.

FLANAGAN, J. & WHITTRED, G., 'Hooker Corporation: A Case for Cash Flow Reporting', *Australian Accounting Review*, May 1992, pp. 48–52.

FRANCIS, R., 'The Relative Information Content of Operating and Financing Cash Flow in the Proposed Cash Flow Statement', *Accounting & Finance*, vol. 50, 2010, pp. 829–51.

GRADY, J., 'Debt Service Coverage Ratio: Two Views are Better than One', *RMA Journal*, vol. 92, no. 7, 2010, pp. 52–60.

INTERNATIONAL ACCOUNTING STANDARDS BOARD, *Discussion Paper: Preliminary Views on Financial Statement Presentation*, London, IASB, October 2008.

JONES, S. & RATNATUNGA, J., 'The Decision Usefulness of Cash-flow Statements by Australian Reporting Entities: Some Further Evidence', *British Accounting Review*, vol. 29, 1997, pp. 67–85.

LAWSON, G.H., 'The Measurement of Corporate Performance on a Cash Flow Basis: A Reply to Mr Eglinton', *Accounting and Business Research*, Spring 1985, pp. 85–104.

LE MAUX, J. & MORIN, D., 'Black and White and Red All Over: Lehman Brothers' Inevitable Bankruptcy Splashed across its Financial Statement', *International Journal of Business and Social Science*, vol. 2, no. 20, November 2011, pp. 39–65.

LEE, T.A., 'Reporting Cash Flows and Net Realisable Values', *Accounting and Business Research*, Spring 1981, pp. 163–70.

MARTIN, N. A., 'Watch What They Do With Their Cash', *Barron's*, vol. 90, no.12, 2010, pp. 36–8.

SENG, D., 'Accrual Versus Cash Flows', *Chartered Accountants Journal*, October 1996, pp. 33–5.

SHARMA, D., 'Analysing the Statement of Cash Flows', *Australian Accounting Review*, vol. 6, no. 2, 1996, pp. 37–44.

TWEEDIE, D. & WHITTINGTON, G., 'Financial Reporting: Current Problems and their Implications for Systematic Reform', *Accounting and Business Research*, Winter 1990, pp. 87–102.

WALKER, R.G., 'Cash Flows Tell the Story', *Australian Business*, vol. 8, no. 8, 1987, p. 106.

WILSON, G., 'The Incremental Information Content of the Accruals and Funds Components of Earnings After Controlling for Earnings', *Accounting Review*, April 1987, pp. 293–322.

PART **6**

Disclosure Issues

Part contents

Chapter 17

Events Occurring after the Reporting Date

Learning objectives

Upon completing this chapter readers should:

LO1 understand that, in the time between the end of the reporting period and the date the financial statements are authorised for issue, new information often becomes available that provides additional evidence of conditions that existed at the end of the reporting period or reveals for the first time a condition that existed at the end of the reporting period, and that in such circumstances the new information must be reflected in the financial statements;

LO2 understand that financial statements are often not released for over ten weeks after the end of the reporting period, and to make them more 'relevant' it is sometimes appropriate to add notes giving additional information about material events that have occurred since the end of the reporting period;

LO3 know the difference between an adjusting event after the reporting period, and a non-adjusting event after the reporting period;

LO4 be able to describe how dividends declared after the end of the reporting period should be disclosed;

LO5 understand that an entity should not prepare its financial statements on the going concern basis if events after the reporting period indicate that this basis is inappropriate; and

LO6 be aware of the specific disclosure requirements of IAS 10 *Events After the Reporting Period*.

17.1 What is an 'event after the reporting period'?

Events after the reporting period may sometimes be referred to as 'Events after the Balance Sheet date', 'Post Balance Sheet Events' or 'Subsequent Events'. The international terminology is 'Events after the reporting period' and these are defined in paragraph 3 of IAS 10 as:

> *those events, favourable and unfavourable, that occur between the end of the reporting period and the date when the financial statements are authorised for issue.*

reporting date/ balance sheet date The end of the financial period (typically 12 months).

The end of the reporting period can also be defined as the end of the financial year to which the financial statements relate. It is therefore what we would traditionally have referred to as **reporting date** or **balance sheet date**.

date financial statements are authorised for issue For companies, the date the financial statements/directors' report/declaration by the Legal Representatives is signed, typically the last thing a company's directors do before releasing the financial statements. For other entities it is the date of final approval of the report by the management or governing body of the entity.

event after the reporting period An event or circumstance that has arisen or information that has become available after the end of the reporting period but prior to the time of completion of the report.

The **date when the financial statements are authorised for issue** means, in the case of companies, the date the directors sign off the financial statements. Depending on the company law in different countries, this will require either signatures on the statement of financial position and/or signatures in a bespoke statement. For example, in the UK this involves getting representative signatures on the directors' report, which typically includes a statement of their respective responsibilities, and in Germany a number of signatures are required on the Declaration by the Legal Representatives. Once the directors have signed the financial statements and directors' report, the auditors sign the auditors' report, at which point the reporting process is complete, except for printing and distribution.

The signing-off of the financial statements will occur a number of weeks after the 'end of the reporting period'. For example, Lufthansa has a reporting date of 31 December. Its Declaration by the Legal Representatives was not signed until 9 March 2011, and this date is deemed to be the date upon which the financial statements for the period ended 31 December 2010 were completed. Therefore anything that occurred in the 68-day period between 31 December 2010 and 9 March 2011 would fall into the period covered by IAS 10—a period in which an **event after the reporting period** can occur.

For entities other than companies, the date the financial statements are authorised for issue is the date of final approval of the statements by the management or governing body of the entity, whichever is applicable.

Worked Example 17.1, based on an example provided in IAS 10, illustrates how the date the financial statements are authorised for issue is determined.

To sum up, what IAS 10 addresses is how to treat, for accounting purposes, those events or transactions that occur, or about which information becomes available, between the end of the reporting period and when the financial statements are authorised for issue. This is summarised diagrammatically in Figure 17.1.

As there is usually a time lag of many weeks or even months between the end of the financial period and the date that shareholders and other interested parties receive the financial statements, the data is likely to be out of date by the time it reaches the financial statement users. Many material events could have occurred after the end of the reporting period. The financial statements are *as at* a particular date (for the statement of financial position) or for a period of time to reporting date (for the statement of comprehensive income, statement of changes in equity and statement of cash flows) and it is not correct practice to change the financial statements because of events that have occurred after that date (the only exception to this requirement within the accounting standard—which we will discuss shortly—is the requirement that relates to after-reporting-period changes in the entity's status as a going concern). Nevertheless, the information may be supplemented by notes to the financial statements that document and describe material after-reporting-date events. Failure to disclose material after-reporting-date events can, in effect, make the financial statements misleading. For example, the year-end statement of financial position of a reporting entity might show a

---

| Worked Example 17.1 | **Establishing the date the financial statements are authorised for issue** |

Rugfest plc, whose reporting period ends on 30 June 2015, completes its draft financial statements on 15 September 2015. On 30 September 2015 the board of directors reviews the financial statements, approves them and authorises their issue. Earnings announcements are made on 3 October 2015 and the financial statements are posted to shareholders on 12 October 2015. Rugfest plc's annual general meeting is held on 24 October 2015 and the financial statements are filed with the relevant government body in charge of regulating the registration of companies (Companies House in the UK) on 26 October 2015.

Required

Identify the date the financial statements were authorised for issue and identify the period for which an event would be considered an event occurring after the reporting period for the purposes of IAS 10.

Solution

In this example, the date the financial statements were authorised for issue is 30 September 2015, as this is the date the directors authorised them for issue to shareholders and other interested parties. Transactions or events that occur between 30 June and 30 September would be considered to be 'events after the reporting period'.

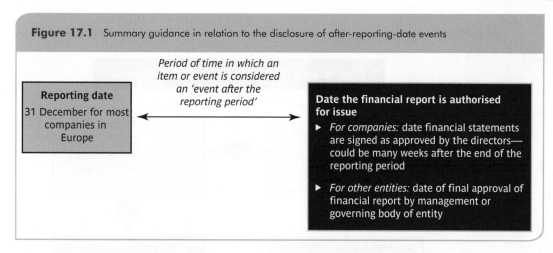

Figure 17.1 Summary guidance in relation to the disclosure of after-reporting-date events

Reporting date	Period of time in which an item or event is considered an 'event after the reporting period'	Date the financial report is authorised for issue

Reporting date
31 December for most companies in Europe

Period of time in which an item or event is considered an 'event after the reporting period'

Date the financial report is authorised for issue

▶ *For companies:* date financial statements are signed as approved by the directors—could be many weeks after the end of the reporting period

▶ *For other entities:* date of final approval of financial report by management or governing body of entity

value for buildings that are an integral part of the entity's operations, and yet they are uninsured. If the buildings are destroyed in the period between the end of the reporting period and the date the financial statements are authorised for issue, the year-end financial statements would not be adjusted (because the statements reflect the assets held at the end of the reporting period), but disclosure of the event in the notes to the financial statements would be required to the extent the loss was material.

The purpose of the accounting standard on events occurring after the reporting period is to require the effect of material events occurring after the end of the reporting period to be included in the financial statements or accompanying notes, so that users entitled to rely on those financial statements are not misled. Again, it is stressed that if the event or transaction does not relate to any conditions that existed at reporting date, it would generally be inappropriate to adjust the financial statements as they are meant to reflect conditions as at the end of the reporting period. Nevertheless, disclosure in the notes to the financial statements might be appropriate, depending on the materiality of the item in question. As we know, a statement of financial position is typically headed, 'Statement of financial position as at 31 December 20XX'. If something material happens after 31 December, it would be inappropriate to alter the 31 December statement of financial position. The transaction or event would be reflected in the next period's financial statements. There is a general requirement that the statement of financial position and the statement of comprehensive income must be prepared on the basis of conditions existing at the end of the reporting period.

Nevertheless, disclosure in the notes to the financial statements might in some circumstances be warranted when the new information pertains to a relevant transaction or event that reflects something that happened in the period after reporting date.

17.2 Events after the reporting date

There are generally two basic types of subsequent event (after-reporting-date events) requiring consideration. First, there are those that relate to events that occurred before the end of the reporting period; and second, there are those that relate to events that occur after the end of the reporting period. These events are referred to as:

1. adjusting events after the reporting period; and
2. non-adjusting events after the reporting period.

As paragraph 3 of IAS 10 states:

Events after the reporting period are those events, favourable and unfavourable, that occur between the end of the reporting period and the date when the financial statements are authorised for issue. Two types of events can be identified:

(a) *those that provide evidence of conditions that existed at the end of the reporting period (adjusting events after the reporting period); and*

(b) *those that are indicative of conditions that arose after the reporting period (non-adjusting events after the reporting period).*

We will consider each of the above types of event in turn. Figure 17.2 provides summary guidance on the treatment of after-reporting-date events.

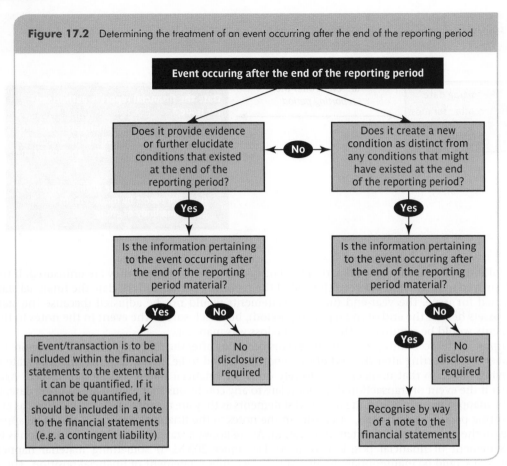

Figure 17.2 Determining the treatment of an event occurring after the end of the reporting period

17.2.1 Events that necessitate adjustments to the financial statements (adjusting events after the reporting period)

'Adjusting events', both favourable and unfavourable, provide additional evidence of, or further elucidate, conditions that existed as at the end of the reporting period (the reporting date). With respect to such 'adjusting events', the accounting standard requires the financial statements to reflect the financial effect of an event occurring after the end of the reporting period that:

■ provides additional evidence of conditions that existed at the end of the reporting period; or
■ reveals for the first time a condition that existed at the end of the reporting period.

Specifically, paragraph 8 of IAS 10 states that:

> An entity shall adjust the amounts recognised in its financial statements to reflect adjusting events after the reporting period.

For example, additional information might become available that enables those in charge of preparing the financial statements to estimate more accurately year-end provisions that are used in preparing financial statements. For instance, there might have been a legal claim outstanding at the end of the reporting period that has subsequently been settled. With this information, the year-end provision for this liability could be recorded reliably. Without the information, the potential obligation might be recorded in the notes to the financial statements as a contingent liability.

Alternatively, new information might come to light that reveals for the first time a condition that existed at the end of the reporting period. For example, it might become apparent before the date the financial statements are authorised for issue that buildings at a remote site were destroyed by flood before year end. In this case, adjustment to the year-end financial statements would be required. Alternatively, it might be discovered that a particular transaction that related to the relevant financial year has been entirely omitted—there might have been a failure in the accounting controls and a liability went unrecorded. The financial statements would require

adjustment in this case too. Further examples of events that necessitate adjustments to the amounts that appear in the financial statements, or adjustments to recognise items that were not previously recognised (assuming they are material individually or in total), are provided in paragraph 9 of IAS 10. These would include:

(a) *the settlement after the reporting period of a court case that confirms that the entity had a present obligation at the end of the reporting period. The entity adjusts any previously recognised provision related to this court case in accordance with IAS 37* Provisions, Contingent Liabilities and Contingent Assets *or recognises a new provision. The entity does not merely disclose a contingent liability because the settlement provides additional evidence that would be considered in accordance with paragraph 16 of IAS 37;*

(b) *the receipt of information after the reporting period indicating that an asset was impaired at the end of the reporting period, or that the amount of a previously recognised impairment loss for that asset needs to be adjusted. For example:*

   (i) *the bankruptcy of a customer that occurs after the reporting period usually confirms that a loss already existed at the end of the reporting period on a trade receivable account and that the entity needs to adjust the carrying amount of the trade receivable; and*

   (ii) *the sale of inventories after the reporting period may give evidence about their net realisable value at the end of the reporting period;*

(c) *the determination after the reporting period of the cost of assets purchased, or the proceeds from assets sold, before the end of the reporting period;*

(d) *the determination after the reporting period of the amount of profit sharing or bonus payments, if the entity had a present legal or constructive obligation at the end of the reporting period to make such payments as a result of events before that date (see IAS 19* Employee Benefits*); and*

(e) *the discovery of fraud or errors that show that the financial statements are incorrect.*

There are two requirements within IAS 10 that represent a change in accounting practice from what was required prior to the 2005 introduction of IAS 10 in many countries. These requirements relate to dividends and the going concern basis for financial statement preparation. These two issues are discussed in turn below.

Dividends declared

In relation to dividends, IAS 10 requires that dividends proposed or declared after the end of the reporting period not be recognised as a liability in the statement of financial position. Specifically, paragraph 12 of the standard requires that:

> *If an entity declares dividends to holders of equity instruments (as defined in IAS 32* Financial Instruments: Presentation*) after the reporting period, the entity shall not recognise those dividends as a liability at the end of the reporting period.*

In explaining the above requirements, paragraph 13 of IAS 10 states:

> *If dividends are declared after the reporting period but before the financial statements are authorised for issue, the dividends are not recognised as a liability at the end of the reporting period because no obligation exists at that time. Such dividends are disclosed in the notes in accordance with IAS 1* Presentation of Financial Statements*.*

Prior to 2005, if dividends were declared after the end of the reporting period they would be included in the liabilities of the reporting entity as at the end of the reporting period. That is, under the former treatment the declaration of dividends would have been treated as an 'adjusting event'. For example, if dividends were declared in July 2014, and the end of the reporting period was 30 June 2014, the dividends declared in July would actually be treated as part of liabilities as at 30 June 2014. The rationale for this treatment was that there would be an expectation that dividends would be paid from 2014 profits, and the decision by the directors as made in July simply allows a quantification of the amount that is payable. However, this treatment is no longer allowed—dividends declared after the end of the reporting period are not to be treated as liabilities as at the end of the reporting period.

Worked Example 17.2 shows how the disclosure of dividends declared after the reporting period shall be made.

Worked Example 17.2 Disclosure of declared dividends

On 18 August 2015 the directors of Alpha plc declared that a dividend of 20 cents per ordinary equity share be paid to shareholders registered on 30 June 2015, the financial year end of the company. The financial statements were authorised for issue on 25 August 2015, while the payment of the dividends is likely to be made on 1 September 2015. An extract of the statement of financial position at 30 June 2015 follows. ▶

	2015 (€m)	2014 (€m)
Equity		
Share capital (20,000,000 ordinary shares on issue)	9,000	9,000
Retained earnings	16,000	10,400
Total equity	25,000	19,400

Required

Illustrate how Alpha plc would disclose the declared dividends.

Solution

The dividend declared after the end of the financial period would be disclosed in the notes to the financial statements as follows:

> *Note xx. Events after the end of the reporting period*
> *Dividends declared*
>
> On 18 August 2015, the directors declared that a dividend of 20 cents per ordinary equity share be paid to shareholders registered on 30 June 2015.

By contrast, if a final dividend of a fixed amount or one based on a percentage of the net profit for the year is declared by the directors before the end of the reporting period and before the financial statements are authorised for issue, this gives rise to a constructive obligation at the end of the reporting period. In this case, the dividend should be accrued. The entry for such a dividend would be:

Dr	Dividend declared (statement of changes in equity)	XXX	
Cr	Dividend payable (statement of financial position)		XXX

Breach of the going concern assumption

In relation to the going concern basis of preparation, IAS 10 requires that, if after the end of the reporting period it becomes apparent that new events or conditions have resulted that indicate that the entity is no longer a going concern, the financial statements are no longer to be prepared on the basis of the going concern assumption. Specifically, paragraph 14 of the standard requires:

> *An entity shall not prepare its financial statements on a going concern basis if management determines after the reporting period either that it intends to liquidate the entity or to cease trading, or that it has no realistic alternative but to do so.*

We should remember that the going concern basis of preparation means that an entity is expected to continue operating for an indefinite period, and not to cease operations in the near future. If an entity is no longer considered to be a going concern, it would mean that assets and liabilities would have to be disclosed in the statement of financial position on a liquidation basis. This could mean very significant write-downs in the measurement of assets.

The determination of whether an entity is a going concern would be dependent upon professional judgement. An entity would not be considered a going concern if it is perceived to be unable to pay its debts as and when they fall due. Failure to be considered a going concern might be the result of a number of factors. For example, there could be major uninsured fire damage; the entity might have lost major customers; or perhaps there are major unhedged overseas borrowings and the relevant exchange rate moves against the entity.

Therefore, and further emphasising the above requirements, an entity might be a going concern at the end of the reporting period (at reporting date). However, if something new happens after the end of the reporting period that brings the going concern of the entity into question, then management is required to go back and change the way the assets are measured. This is an interesting requirement because, as we know, statements of financial position are prepared to represent conditions as at the end of the reporting period. Under IAS 10, if new conditions arise after the reporting period that create a new situation in which the entity is not a going concern, such new events are effectively 'backdated' since we are required to amend the values of assets being shown in the statement of financial position.

17.2.2 Events that necessitate disclosure but no adjustment (non-adjusting events)

The second type of subsequent event (a non-adjusting event) is one that occurs after the end of the reporting period. Such events create new conditions and therefore, as they are outside the financial period being reported on, would not lead to changes to the financial statements themselves. Specifically, paragraph 10 of IAS 10 states that:

An entity shall not adjust the amounts recognised in its financial statements to reflect non-adjusting events after the reporting period.

These events provide evidence, both favourable and unfavourable, about new conditions, as distinct from any that might have existed at the end of the reporting period. If the nature of the event is deemed to be *material*, the event should be disclosed in the notes to the financial statements.

As indicated before in this book, something is deemed to be material if its omission, non-disclosure or mis-statement is likely to affect economic decisions or other evaluations made by users entitled to rely on the financial statements. Again, as the information is new—that is, it does not relate to conditions at the end of the reporting period—it would be inappropriate to adjust the financial statements. Nevertheless, to the extent that the information is deemed to be material, disclosure by way of a note to the financial statements is required.

Paragraph 22 of IAS 10 provides examples of subsequent events that might make note disclosure necessary without adjusting the financial statements. These include:

(a) *a major business combination after the reporting period (IFRS 3* Business Combinations *requires specific disclosures in such cases) or disposing of a major subsidiary;*
(b) *announcing a plan to discontinue an operation;*
(c) *major purchases of assets, classification of assets as held for sale in accordance with IFRS 5* Non-current Assets Held for Sale and Discontinued Operations, *other disposals of operations, or expropriation of major assets by government;*
(d) *the destruction of a major production plant by a fire after the reporting period;*
(e) *announcing, or commencing the implementation of, a major restructuring (see IAS 37);*
(f) *major ordinary share transactions and potential ordinary share transactions after the reporting period (IAS 33* Earnings per Share *requires an entity to disclose a description of such transactions, other than when such transactions involve capitalisation or bonus issues, share splits or reverse share splits (all of which are required to be adjusted under IAS 33));*
(g) *abnormally large changes after the reporting period in asset prices or foreign exchange rates;*
(h) *changes in tax rates or tax laws enacted or announced after the reporting period that have a significant effect on current and deferred tax assets and liabilities (see IAS 12* Income Taxes*);*
(i) *entering into significant commitments or contingent liabilities, for example by issuing significant guarantees; and*
(j) *commencing major litigation arising solely out of events that occurred after the reporting period.*

Having now discussed the difference between an adjusting and a non-adjusting event, we can now consider Worked Example 17.3.

Worked Example 17.3

Distinguishing between an adjusting and a non-adjusting event after the reporting period

Gerry plc owes Lopez plc an amount of €100,000 at 30 June 2015, the end of its reporting period. On 26 July 2015 Lopez plc received a letter from liquidators advising it of the bankruptcy of Gerry plc. The letter indicated that Gerry plc ceased trading in June 2015 and Lopez plc is only likely to receive a liquidation dividend of 15 cents in the euro.

Required

(a) Discuss how the above transaction should be treated.
(b) Provide the journal entry that Lopez plc would make in its records to account for the transaction.
(c) Discuss how the answers to (a) and (b) would differ if a fire on 2 July 2015 destroyed Lopez plc's factory premises.

Solution

(a) This would be considered an adjusting event after the reporting period, as it relates to conditions existing at the end of the reporting period and improves accounting estimates at that date (namely, the solvency and recoverability of the amount owed by Gerry plc).

(b) Lopez plc would, based on the above information, make the following entry to reflect the improved estimate of the accounts receivable at year end:

Dr	Bad debts expense	€85,000	
Cr	Accounts receivable		€85,000

Writing off amount owing by Gerry plc

(c) As the fire that destroyed Lopez plc's premises occurred on 2 July 2015, no adjustments to individual amounts in the financial statements of Lopez plc are required. The reason for this is that the fire was not a condition that existed at the end of the reporting period. Nevertheless, disclosure in the notes to the financial statements would be appropriate.

The impact of the fire might be so great that it might be necessary to establish whether it is still appropriate to prepare Lopez plc's financial statements on the going concern basis. If, as a result of the fire, Lopez plc has no realistic alternative but to cease trading, its assets and liabilities would have to be adjusted to reflect a liquidation basis of accounting.

17.3 Disclosure requirements

It is important for users to know the date the financial statements were authorised for issue since the financial statements and accompanying notes do not reflect events after this date. Further, it is useful for users to know who was responsible for authorising the issue of the financial statements. Accordingly, paragraph 17 of IAS 10 states:

> *An entity shall disclose the date when the financial statements were authorised for issue and who gave that authorisation. If the entity's owners or others have the power to amend the financial statements after issue, the entity shall disclose that fact.*

Consistent with the view that a financial statement (statement of financial position, statement of comprehensive income, statement of changes in equity or statement of cash flows) must be prepared on the basis of conditions existing at the end of the reporting period, an 'adjusting event' (one that provides additional evidence of, or further elucidates, conditions that existed as at the end of the reporting period) would be recognised in the financial statements either by being brought to account, if it relates to an item that would itself be brought to account, or by being included by way of a note, if it relates to an item that would usually be recognised only by way of a note, such as a contingent liability. Paragraph 19 of IAS 10 states:

> *If an entity receives information after the reporting period about conditions that existed at the end of the reporting period, it shall update disclosures that relate to these conditions, in the light of the new information.*

In relation to disclosures that would generally appear in the notes to the financial statements rather than on the face of the financial statements, paragraph 20 states:

> *In some cases, an entity needs to update the disclosures in its financial statements to reflect information received after the reporting period, even when the information does not affect the amounts that it recognises in its financial statements. One example of the need to update disclosures is when evidence becomes available after the reporting period about a contingent liability that existed at the end of the reporting period. In addition to considering whether it should recognise or change a provision under IAS 37 Provisions, Contingent Liabilities and Contingent Assets, an entity updates its disclosures about the contingent liability in the light of that evidence.*

For a material 'non-adjusting' event (an event that occurs after the end of the reporting period and therefore creates new conditions), paragraph 21 of IAS 10 states:

> *If non-adjusting events after the reporting period are material, non-disclosure could influence the economic decisions that users make on the basis of the financial statements. Accordingly, an entity shall disclose the following for each material category of non-adjusting event after the reporting period:*

(a) the nature of the event; and

(b) an estimate of its financial effect, or a statement that such an estimate cannot be made.

Summary guidance in relation to after-reporting-period events is provided in Figure 17.2. Exhibit 17.1 provides a number of examples of the disclosures in a variety of European companies of an after-reporting-event note. In the first example, Air France–KLM, includes a note in its 2010 annual report even though it does not have any 'subsequent events'. In its 2010 annual report, Nutreco disclosed that it had agreed to increase its shareholding in a Russian company. In the final example, Philips reports the acquisition of a private limited company in the US and provides details of the acquisition of a company in India, though this is not yet final as conditions are still outstanding.

Exhibit 17.1 **After-reporting-period event notes from various companies**

After-reporting-period event note from the 2010 annual report of Air France-KLM

17. SUBSEQUENT EVENTS

NONE

After-reporting-period event note from the 2010 annual report of Nutreco

(30) SUBSEQUENT EVENTS

Nutreco has come to an agreement with the non-controlling interest shareholder of Trouw Nutrition Russia B.V. in the segment Premix and Feed Specialties to acquire an additional 15% interest, increasing its ownership from 75 to 90%. The legal transfer of shares is expected to take place in the first quarter of 2011.

The total consideration will be determined after finalising the statutory accounts of 2010 for Trouw Nutrition Russia B.V.

After-reporting-period event note from the 2010 annual report of Philips

(K) SUBSEQUENT EVENTS

Acquisition of Optimum Lighting LLC

On January 5, 2011, Philips announced that it acquired Optimum Lighting LLC, a privately owned company domiciled in the US, specialized in customized energy-efficient lighting solutions for the office, industry and retail segments.

Acquisition of Preethi business

On January 24, 2011, Philips announced that it has agreed to acquire the assets of the Preethi business, a kitchen appliances company in India. Upon closing of this transaction, which is subject to certain contractual and other conditions such as regulatory approval, Preethi will become part of the Domestic Appliances business group within Philips' Consumer Lifestyle sector.

Apart from the general requirements of IAS 10, it should also be acknowledged that company law in some countries, such as the UK and Ireland, may require disclosures of events that occur in the period from the reporting period date to the signing of the financial statements. All large companies in the UK and Ireland have a legal requirement under company law to disclose any material event that arises in the period after the reporting period date in the directors' report even if they have nothing to report, as shown by the extract from Tesco PLC's Director's Report from its 2010 Annual Return, reproduced in Exhibit 17.2. When companies do have material events, they typically do not reiterate the information that is also included in the notes but provide a cross-reference to it. An example of this approach is used by JJB Sport plc and is also reproduced in Exhibit 17.2. This company was selected as, at the time of writing, it was going through a major capital reconstruction which was being reported on by the media in the UK. It was clear that a lot of transactions and deals were being undertaken in the period just after JJB Sport plc's year end.

| Exhibit 17.2 | After-reporting-period event statements |

After-reporting-period event statement in the 2010 Directors' Report of Tesco PLC

Events after the balance sheet date

THERE WERE NO MATERIAL EVENTS AFTER THE BALANCE SHEET DATE

After-reporting-period event statement in the 2011 Directors' Report of JJB Sport plc

EVENTS AFTER THE PERIOD END

Details of important events affecting the Company occurring since the period end are set out in note 44 of the Notes to the Financial Statements.

44. Events after the Statement of financial position date

Since 30 January 2011, there have been the following events.

Changes to the Board

On 2 February 2011, Alan Benzie announced his intention to resign at the 2011 AGM on 8 July.
On 6 April 2011, Richard Manning announced his intention to resign at the 2011 AGM on 8 July.
On 6 May 2011, Richard Bernstein was appointed as a Non-executive Director.
On 17 May 2011, it was announced that Lawrence Christensen would join the Board as a Non-executive Director on 1 November 2011.

First Firm Placing and Placing and Open Offer

On 2 February 2011, the Company published a prospectus detailing a proposal to raise gross proceeds of £31.5 million through a Firm Placing and Placing and Open Offer involving the issue of 630 million new Ordinary Shares at an issue price of 5 pence per new Ordinary Share. The gross proceeds of £31.5 million were received on 25 February 2011. Full details of the First Firm Placing and Placing and Open Offer are contained within the prospectus published on 2 February 2011.

Capital Reorganisation

In conjunction with the First Firm Placing and Placing and Open Offer (see note above), the Directors effected a Capital Reorganisation in order to provide the Company with flexibility in relation to its capital structure in the future and to seek to reduce the impact of the volatility in the Company's share price. Under the Capital Reorganisation, all existing Ordinary Shares were subdivided and reclassified into one new Ordinary Share of 0.1 pence and one deferred share of 4.9 pence and all newly issued Ordinary Shares were issued as a new Ordinary Share of 0.1p. There was then a consolidation such that all Ordinary Shares of 0.1p were consolidated on a 1 for 10 basis into Ordinary Shares of 1 pence each and all deferred shares were consolidated on a 1 for 10 basis into consolidated deferred shares of 49 pence each. Following the Capital Reorganisation, existing shareholders and shareholders participating in the First Firm Placing and Placing and Open Offer held 1 Ordinary Share and (existing shareholders only) 1 consolidated deferred share for every 10 existing Ordinary Shares held.

Warrants

At the same time as the first Firm Placing and Placing and Open Offer (see note above), the Company issued warrants on completion of the process to the firm placee participating in the Firm Placing in lieu of any placing commissions and in consideration for, and pro rata to, their binding agreements to subscribe for shares. On completion of the First Firm Placing and Placing and Open Offer in accordance with its terms, Warrants were issued as follows:
> 9,338,626 Warrants for Harris Associates LP;
> 3,531,413 Warrants for Crystal Amber Fund Limited;
> 1,177,137 Warrants for Bill & Melinda Gates Foundation Trust;
> 1,569,517 Warrants for GoldenPeaks Capital Partners; and
> 9,103,198 Warrants for Invesco Asset Management Limited.

▶

On 22 March 2011, the Company received notification from GoldenPeaks Capital Partners that it had exercised in full its Warrants in respect of 1,569,517 ordinary shares of 1 pence each (the 'Warrant Shares') at an exercise price of 15.25 pence per share. The total subscription proceeds received by the Company as a result were £239,351.

Company Voluntary Arrangement

On 3 March 2011, the Company and its subsidiary, Blane Leisure Limited, launched a proposal to enter into a Company Voluntary Arrangement ('CVA'). On 22 March 2011, the CVA proposals made by the Company and Blane Leisure Limited received the approval of the requisite majority of creditors and members of each Company. On 23 March 2011, the CVA became partially effective, with full implementation conditional on further events. Following the expiry of a 28-day challenge period on 21 April 2011, the CVA proposal was fully implemented upon receipt of the gross proceeds from the Second Firm Placing and Placing and Open Offer on 27 April 2011 (see below).

Full details of the CVA proposal are contained within the Investment circular issued to shareholders on 3 March 2011.

Second Firm Placing and Placing and Open Offer

On 6 April 2011, the Company published a further Prospectus detailing a proposal to raise gross proceeds of £65 million through a Firm Placing and Placing and Open Offer involving the issue of 162.5 million new Ordinary Shares at an issue price of 40 pence per new Ordinary Share. This was dependent on the CVA proposals being approved and proceeds being received by 30 June 2011. As noted above, the CVA proposal was approved and the gross proceeds of £65 million were received on 27 April 2011. Full details of the Second Firm Placing and Placing and Open Offer are contained within the Prospectus published on 6 April 2011.

Transfer to AIM

At a general meeting of the Company held on 22 March 2011, Shareholders approved a resolution to cancel admission of the Ordinary Shares to listing on the premium segment of the Official List and to trading on the London Stock Exchange's main market for listed securities and for an application to be made for admission of those Ordinary Shares to trading on AIM. On 28 April 2011, AIM Admission took place and dealings in Ordinary Shares (including the newly issued Ordinary Shares) started on AIM at 8:00 a.m. on 28 April 2011.

Amendments to banking facilities

On 1 February 2011, the Company and Bank of Scotland ('BoS') agreed an amendment to the existing BoS Facility including the waiver of (i) the fixed charge cover test on the April 2011 Quarter Date and (ii) the clean down test for the period ended 30 January 2011. Further covenants were included within the amendment agreement.

On 15 March 2011 the Company and BoS agreed further amendments to the existing BoS Facility and also agreed an Amended BoS Facility following receipt of proceeds under the Second Firm Placing and Placing and Open Offer (and certain other customary conditions precedent).

The Amended BoS Facility came into effect on 27 April 2011. The key terms of the Amended BoS Facility are as follows:

> The maturity date of the facility was extended to 31 May 2014; and
> An overdraft facility of £7.5 million is contained within the £25 million facility limit.

SUMMARY

The chapter considered various issues associated with accounting for events occurring after the reporting period. In accordance with IAS 10, an event occurring after the reporting period is defined as a circumstance that has arisen or information that has become available after the end of the reporting period but before the date when the financial statements are authorised for issue. For a company, the date the financial statements are authorised for issue would be considered to be the time at which the directors sign off the financial statements.

After-reporting-period events can be classified as either adjusting events or non-adjusting events. An adjusting event is one that provides additional evidence of, or further elucidates, conditions that existed at the end of the reporting period. To the extent that the event would typically be reflected in an entity's financial statements, information about the event must be used to adjust the financial statements (if the effects are material). If it is information of the type that is generally disclosed in the notes to the financial statements (for example, information that comes to light about material contingent liabilities), additional note disclosure is required.

A non-adjusting event is an event occurring after the reporting period and one that therefore creates new conditions. If the information about the non-adjusting event is material, disclosure in the notes to the financial statements is required. Because financial statements are often released a number of months after the end of the reporting period, the note disclosure of non-adjusting events assists in making the financial statements more relevant to financial statement users.

KEY TERMS

END-OF-CHAPTER EXERCISE

After completing this chapter you should ensure that you are able to provide answers to the following questions. (If you are not, you should revisit the appropriate sections of this chapter.)

1 If an event occurs after the reporting period it is considered that the event has occurred between the 'end of the reporting period' and the 'date when the financial statements are authorised for issue'. What is the date when the financial statements are authorised for issue? **LO 17.2**

2 What is the rationale for the inclusion of information pertaining to material after-reporting-period events? **LO 17.1**

3 After-reporting-period events can be classified as either adjusting events or non-adjusting events. Describe each of these types of event and explain the accounting treatment required for each. (For example, for which type of event is note disclosure appropriate?) **LO 17.3**

REVIEW QUESTIONS

1 What are the different types of after-reporting-period event and how should they be disclosed? **LO 17.1**

2 If an event relates to a period after the reporting period, when and why should it be detailed in the notes to the financial statements? **LO 17.6**

3 Determine whether the following events require adjustment to the financial statements or disclosure by way of a note to the financial statements: **LO 17.3**

(a) Loss of a major customer after the end of the reporting period. No amount is owing at the end of the reporting period.

(b) A customer owes a material amount and becomes insolvent after the reporting period.

(c) Flood loss after the end of the reporting period.

(d) Settlement of a negligence claim after the reporting period, which relates to operations undertaken before the end of the financial period.

(e) Declaration of dividends after the end of the reporting period.

4 Torquay plc's financial year ended on June 2015. The following events occurred between the end of the reporting period and the date the directors of Torquay plc expect to authorise the financial statements for issue, namely 15 September 2015. **LO 17.3**

REQUIRED

Classify the following events as either adjusting or non-adjusting events occurring after the reporting period, and indicate (in no more than two sentences) what sort of disclosure is required. Do not provide a detailed note.

(a) Loss of a major customer after the reporting period. The customer owed no amount at the end of the reporting period.

(b) The bankruptcy after the reporting period of a customer who suffered a major loss after the reporting period.

(c) Before the date the financial statements were authorised for issue, judgement against the company was handed down by the court finding the company was in fact liable for damages incurred by a customer that resulted from a faulty product. The court case commenced before the end of the reporting period.

(d) On 31 August 2015 the directors decided to restructure a loss-making division.

5 Indicate how Petersen plc should treat the following events in its financial statements at 30 June 2015. You are not required to draft the financial statement notes. **LO 17.3**

(a) On 15 August Michael plc, a major customer of Petersen plc, indicated that it had found an alternative supplier. At this date, Michael plc owed no amount to Petersen plc.

(b) On 30 June 2015 Lynch plc owed Petersen plc £234,900. On 24 July 2015 Petersen plc received notice that Lynch plc had become insolvent. It had ceased trading in May 2015.

(c) On 31 July 2015 a major flood damaged the premises of Petersen plc. Inventory amounting to £324,600 was destroyed and repairs to office equipment and buildings will amount to a further £564,000.

(d) On 12 August 2015 Petersen plc settled a negligence claim lodged by one of its customers. The claim arose on 7 March 2015, when an employee accidentally removed the customer's ear while shaving him with a sharp razor.

CHALLENGING QUESTIONS

6 You are finalising the 2014 financial statements of Petrol plc, a company involved in the mining, refining and retail distribution of petroleum products. As part of your final review, you have asked the chief executive officer if there are any events that have arisen since the end of the financial year of which you should be made aware. The financial period ends on 30 June 2014. He has advised you of the following events: **LO 17.3**

(a) On 30 August 2014 a meeting of OPEC agreed to increase the Saudi Arabian oil quota by 17 million barrels in 2014–2015. The immediate impact of this decision was to reduce the price of crude oil by €13 a barrel to €56 a barrel. As at 30 June 2014 Petrol plc had 1 million barrels of crude oil in inventory at an average cost of €60 per barrel. The price fluctuation is expected to be permanent given the change in attitude by the OPEC nations.

(b) On 5 July 2014 an oil tanker owned by the company sank in heavy seas off the coast of Spain. The tanker was fully laden and has created an oil spill stretching for 140 km along the Spanish coastline. The tanker was included in the 30 June 2014 financial statements at a carrying amount of €15 million. The oil that the tanker was transporting was being carried in the financial statements at €2 million. An initial evaluation of the cost of the clean-up operation is estimated at €14 million. There is also a strong possibility that the local oyster farmers will take legal action against the firm for inventory losses and related damage to the oyster beds. The risk management team has assessed that the possible costs of litigation could reach €50 million.

(c) Having reviewed the draft financial statements as at 30 June 2014, the directors approved a dividend of €5 per share. There are currently five million fully paid ordinary equity shares on issue. This dividend was declared on 30 September 2014.

(d) For the year ended 30 June 2013, the company had a tax provision of €8.5 million. During the year the company was the subject of a taxation audit, which resulted in an amended assessment of €26 million. The increased liability is in respect of the disputed tax treatment on certain share transactions carried out during the 2013 tax year. During 2014 the company lodged an objection against the revised assessment. The company's tax advisers expected the objection to be successful. As a result the company did not consider it appropriate to recognise a provision in respect of the additional tax. It has, however, included a note explaining the situation and outlining the potential liability in the contingent liability note.

On 1 July 2014, the company received notice from the taxation authorities to the effect that the details of the objection had been considered but that the amended assessment was correct and therefore the objection had

been declined. The company intends to appeal against the decision and take appropriate legal action if necessary. Taxation advisers, however, are not confident that the court will overturn the commissioner's ruling.

(e) In May 2014 the managing director was sacked because of allegations of fraud and theft. He had a five-year employment contract, of which four years remained, and he commenced legal action against the company for wrongful dismissal. The lawsuit is for €4 million but solicitors expect to settle the case out of court for €2 million, the residual value of the employment contract. Legal action began in August 2014. No provision was recognised in the 30 June 2014 financial statements.

(f) At the August 2014 board meeting, the company made a decision to relocate a major oil refinery from Aberdeen to Glasgow. The possibility of such a move was discussed at the March 2014 board meeting, where it was decided that a review should be conducted into the feasibility of the move and that, if the move proved feasible, it should be undertaken. The report that was tabled at the August board meeting was dated 15 June 2014. The report concluded that the move was feasible and arrangements should be made as soon as possible. The report estimated the following costs to be incurred in respect of the move:

- *Loss on sale of property:* The net book value of the property as at 30 June 2014 was €2.5 million. All research indicates that the net market value of the property after selling expenses would be €1.2 million, creating a loss of €1.3 million.
- *Redundancy costs:* These costs for staff are estimated at €600,000.
- *Loss on sale of plant and equipment:* Owing to the specialised nature of the plant and equipment, a loss of €650,000 is expected on its sale.

The report was not tabled at the July board meeting because of the large agenda already planned for that meeting. The chief executive officer agreed that the property, plant and equipment should be put on the market in July, in anticipation of the board's decision.

REQUIRED

Review the information given above, and comment on any adjustments that might need to be made to the financial statements. The financial statements have not been finalised. Also consider the need for any additional disclosures in the financial statements.

7 The 30 June 2014 financial statements of ABC plc have been prepared in draft form. However, the financial statements have not yet been printed and sent to shareholders. Subsequent to the end of the reporting period, the following events occur: **LO 17.3**

(a) A judgment is handed down in the Supreme Court on 15 July 2014 in relation to a 2013 product liability case brought by a customer against the company. This judgment renders the company liable for court costs and compensation totalling €240,000.

(b) On 14 July 2014 the government enacts legislation altering the company income tax rate from 39 per cent to 42 per cent for all income tax returns from 1 July 2014.

(c) On 28 July 2014 the company's country warehouse is destroyed by fire. The total carrying value of the warehouse, which was uninsured, is €350,000.

(d) On 2 August 2014 the financial cost of inventory shipped from overseas is determined. The inventory was received in June 2014 and the cost was estimated for accounting purposes. The revised cost is €900,000 greater than the prior estimate.

(e) On 16 July 2014 the company enters into a contract to purchase 25 per cent of the issued capital of a competitor XYZ plc for €750,000.

Assume all amounts are material for financial statement purposes.

REQUIRED

Discuss the appropriate accounting treatment of the above events.

8 Lombok GmbH is an Austrian entity that makes canoes and associated equipment. The end of its financial period is 30 June 2014. It has compiled a set of draft financial statements, which indicate that its net assets are approximately €4 million and its after-tax profit for the year is €650,000. Before the financial statements are finalised, the following transactions and events come to light. Assume that each event or transaction is independent of the rest. **LO 17.3**

(a) On 30 July 2014 the directors recommend a final dividend of €2 per share.

(b) At a directors' meeting held in May 2014 it is decided that in late July the division that makes flotation devices will be closed, as the demand for such devices has fallen. The costs involved in closing down the division amount to €1.5 million.

(c) On 5 August 2014 the directors become aware that the oars it has been selling since mid-July 2014 tend to fall apart when placed in water for more than 30 minutes. These oars were purchased by Lombok GmbH on 10 July 2014. By 7 August 2014 there have already been claims made against the company by a number of people who were stranded at sea.

(d) Lombok GmbH's main customer, Eco-Friendly Leisure Company, is declared insolvent on 12 July 2014. Apparently it is declared insolvent because it has been unable to pay damages previously awarded against it. The damages relate to an incident in which tour participants were savaged by some rampaging bulls. Eco-Friendly Tours owed Lombok GmbH €600,000 as at 30 June 2014.

(e) In July 2014 an out-of-court settlement has finally been reached with one of Lombok GmbH's material suppliers. Lombok GmbH took action against the supplier two years earlier. The supplier had sold Lombok GmbH canoe paints that tended to wash off when exposed to salt water. Lombok GmbH is expected to receive €1 million in damages.

REQUIRED

Determine how and whether each of the above events or transactions should be disclosed in the financial statements or accompanying notes of Lombok plc for the year ending 30 June 2014.

9   Gunnamatta plc has a financial period ending on 30 June 2014 and is expected to complete its financial statements on 10 September 2014. On 24 August 2014 it loses a major customer that has become insolvent. Also, owing to bad media publicity in August 2014 relating to the private life of its managing director, the demand for Gunnamatta plc's products has plummeted. Both of these events have indicated that, while the entity was a going concern as at 30 June 2014, this appears no longer to be the case.   **LO 17.5**

REQUIRED

(a) Would the reassessment of the entity's going concern basis be an 'adjusting event' or a 'non-adjusting' event?

(b) How would the assessment that the entity is no longer a going concern impact on the preparation of the entity's financial statements?

(c) Do you agree with the treatment required under IAS 10, or do you think that it is a non-adjusting event that should just be disclosed as it does not reflect the position at the reporting period date? Explain your answer.

10   Good Vehicles plc sells tractors. It does not recognise a provision for warranty because warranty claims for the past five years have been immaterial. Good Vehicles plc reported a profit before tax of €500,000 for the year ended 30 June 2015. The company provides the following disclosures in the notes to the financial statements for the year ended 30 June 2015 issued 31 August 2015:   **LO 17.3**

(a) In July 2015 a warranty claim was made for a faulty brake system on 10 tractors sold to a large agricultural business in May 2015. The cost of repairing the tractors was €55,000. This amount has not been recognised in the financial statements for the year ended 30 June 2015.

(b) A negligence lawsuit has been brought against Good Vehicles plc for damages sustained in July 2015 on account of the failure of the braking system in a tractor sold by the company in May 2015. The damages claim is for €400,000, being the cost of replacing a farm shed destroyed by the runaway tractor, but this amount has not been recognised in the financial statements because the event occurred after the reporting period.

(c) In August 2015 Good Vehicles plc was fined €20,000 for breach of noise emission limits at its tractor assembly plant. This expense and liability has not been provided for in the financial statements as at 30 June 2015.

REQUIRED

Discuss whether the note disclosure is adequate for each of the after-reporting-period events reported. Should adjustments have been made to the financial statements for the year ended 30 June 2015? *Hint:* This question integrates your knowledge of the law and its relevance to financial statements. A critical aspect in this case is determining which event gives rise to the obligation in each scenario so that you can determine whether the after-reporting-period event provides evidence of or reveals a condition existing at the end of the reporting period.

11   For each of the following material after-reporting-period events, state whether adjustment or disclosure is required in the 30 June 2015 financial statements. If adjustment is required, state the nature of the adjustment, that is, the effect on elements of the financial statements.   **LO 17.3**

(a) 2 July 2015: directors proposed a dividend of €10,000.

(b) 3 July 2015: the executive directors approved the sale of an off-shore agency to another entity for a profit of €30,000.

(c) 4 July 2015: the company received an invoice from a supplier for €85,000 for goods delivered in June; the goods were included in closing inventory at an estimated cost of €100,000.

(d) 5 July 2015: the company executed a guarantee in favour of the banks for an outstanding loan of €1 million that the bank made to X plc, the company's major supplier, in January of that year; the guarantee was executed because the bank was demanding payment, which would have disrupted inventory supplies.

(e) 6 July 2015: an agreement was signed to take over a production facility in Paris at a cost of €5 million, which will be paid for using a long-term finance lease.

(f) 7 July 2015: the taxation authorities waived fines for the inclusion of incorrect information in the company's 2013 tax return; the adjusted tax return was reflected in the company's financial statements and the fine of €30,000 was recognised as an expense and liability at the end of the reporting period.

(g) 8 July 2015: the government announced an increase in tax rates from 30 per cent to 33 per cent for the year commencing 1 July 2015; the deferred tax asset account is €90,000 and the deferred tax liability account is €60,000.

(h) 9 July 2015: the Remuneration Committee determined the CEO's bonus for the year ended 30 June 2015 as €300,000; the manager is entitled to an annual bonus based on company profits as determined by the Remuneration Committee. No accrual has been made.

Chapter 18

Related-party Disclosures

Learning objectives

Upon completing this chapter readers should:

LO1   understand what a related party is;

LO2   be aware of some of the categories of related parties;

LO3   understand what is meant by a related-party transaction;

LO4   be aware of some of the risks and opportunities that accrue as a result of transactions with related parties;

LO5   understand the rationale behind disclosing extensive information about related-party transactions; and

LO6   understand some of the various disclosure requirements included within IAS 24 *Related Party Disclosures*.

18.1   Introduction to related-party disclosures

The relevant accounting standard for related-party disclosures is IAS 24 *Related Party Disclosures*. IAS 24 applies to all reporting entities, except not-for-profit public sector entities.

In addition to the disclosure requirements in IAS 24, there are reporting requirements pertaining to related parties in company legislation. These differ across countries within Europe, though requirements are laid down in EU directives. For example, the disclosure of related-party transactions in the annual and consolidated accounts of companies is covered by the fourth Directive, specifically in Art 43(1)(76) 78/660/EEC and Art 34 (7b) 83/349/EEC (ECGF 2011). The Directive supports the requirements of IAS 24 and, when IFRSs are not being followed and national standards are being followed (such as IFRS 8 *Related Party Transactions* in the UK and Ireland), the Directive requires disclosure in the notes to the financial statements of transactions entered into by the company with related parties if they are material and have not been concluded under normal market conditions. In brief, the disclosure needs to include the amount of the transaction, the nature of the related-party relationship and other information about the transaction necessary for an understanding of the financial position of the company. In terms of compliance among Member States, the Directive has a number of allowable exclusions from the requirement to disclose related-party transactions, namely, there is an option for Member States: to exempt small companies, to exempt medium-sized companies that are not public companies, to restrict the disclosures required from the latter (public medium-sized companies) and to exempt transactions entered into between two or more members of a group provided that subsidiaries that are party to the transaction are wholly owned. Transparency, including related-party transactions, in reporting in financial statements

is typically promoted by national legislation. Given that the EU Member States are subject to different national legislation, it is no surprise that differences in required disclosures arise. Moscariello (2011), in a study that compared regulation in respect of related-party disclosures in Italy with those of two major Continental European countries (France and Germany), highlights 'the burdensome character of the Italian discipline compared with the French and German regulations'.

18.2   Related-party relationship defined

> **related parties**
> Parties are deemed to be related if one party is able to significantly influence or control the activities of another or where both parties are under the common influence of another party.

For accounting purposes, parties are deemed to be *related* if one party has the ability to *significantly influence* or *control* the activities of another or if both parties are under the *common control* of another party. That is, **related parties** are not considered to be independent of each other. According to paragraph 9 of IAS 24 *Related Party Disclosures*:

A related party is a person or entity that is related to the entity that is preparing its financial statements (in this Standard referred to as the 'reporting entity').

    (a) A person or a close member of that person's family is related to a reporting entity if that person:
        (i) has control or joint control over the reporting entity;
    (ii) has significant influence over the reporting entity; or
    (iii) is a member of the key management personnel of the reporting entity or of a parent of the reporting entity.
  (b) An entity is related to a reporting entity if any of the following conditions applies:
    (i) The entity and the reporting entity are members of the same group (which means that each parent, subsidiary and fellow subsidiary is related to the others).
    (ii) One entity is an associate or joint venture of the other entity (or an associate or joint venture of a member of a group of which the other entity is a member).
    (iii) Both entities are joint ventures of the same third party.
    (iv) One entity is a joint venture of a third entity and the other entity is an associate of the third entity.
    (v) The entity is a post-employment benefit plan for the benefit of employees of either the reporting entity or an entity related to the reporting entity. If the reporting entity is itself such a plan, the sponsoring employers are also related to the reporting entity.
    (vi) The entity is controlled or jointly controlled by a person identified in (a).
    (vii) A person identified in (a)(i) has significant influence over the entity or is a member of the key management personnel of the entity (or of a parent of the entity).

From the above definition of 'related party', we can see that related parties would include organisations (that are controlling or controlled by the entity or are significantly influencing or significantly influenced by the entity) as well as individuals (such as key management personnel or close family members of key management personnel).

A *related-party transaction* is defined in IAS 24 as, 'a transfer of resources, services or obligations between a reporting entity and a related party, regardless of whether a price is charged'.

As we have already indicated, the accounting standard relevant to related-party disclosures is IAS 24 *Related Party Disclosures*.

18.3   IAS 24 *Related Party Disclosures*

In what follows we discuss IAS 24's objectives, materiality guidelines, categories of related parties and disclosure requirements.

18.3.1 Objectives of the standard

Transactions involving related parties cannot be presumed to be carried out on an *arm's length basis*, since the requisite conditions of competitive, free-market dealings might not exist. This could lead to transactions occurring at prices not in accord with fair values. As we know from a number of other standards, fair value is defined as (this definition comes from IFRS 2 *Share-based Payment*):

The amount for which an asset could be exchanged, a liability settled, or an equity instrument granted could be exchanged between knowledgeable, willing parties in an arm's length transaction.

From the above definition of fair value, we can see that a transaction between parties that are not at 'arm's length' will not always result in a transaction occurring at the fair value of the item being transacted. Of course, it is possible for the transaction to be at fair value, but the very presence of related parties will bring this into question.

The existence of a related-party relationship can expose a reporting entity to risks or opportunities that would not have existed in the absence of the relationship. A *related-party relationship* might therefore have a material effect on the performance, financial position and financing and investing activities of a reporting entity. If the performance of an entity and the impact of related-party transactions are to be assessed properly, knowledge of such relationships is necessary. This perspective is consistent with the objectives of IAS 24. As paragraph 1 (the 'Objective' paragraph) of IAS 24 *Related Party Disclosures* states:

> *The objective of this Standard is to ensure that an entity's financial statements contain the disclosures necessary to draw attention to the possibility that its financial position and profit or loss may have been affected by the existence of related parties and by transactions and outstanding balances, including commitments, with such parties.*

Paragraphs 5 to 8 of IAS 24 discuss the 'purpose of related-party disclosures'. According to these:

5. *Related party relationships are a normal feature of commerce and business. For example, entities frequently carry on parts of their activities through subsidiaries, joint ventures and associates. In these circumstances, the entity has the ability to affect the financial and operating policies of the investee through the presence of control, joint control or significant influence.*

6. *A related party relationship could have an effect on the profit or loss and financial position of an entity. Related parties may enter into transactions that unrelated parties would not. For example, an entity that sells goods to its parent at cost might not sell on those terms to another customer. Also, transactions between related parties may not be made at the same amounts as between unrelated parties.*

7. *The profit or loss and financial position of an entity may be affected by a related party relationship even if related party transactions do not occur. The mere existence of the relationship may be sufficient to affect the transactions of the entity with other parties. For example, a subsidiary may terminate relations with a trading partner on acquisition by the parent of a fellow subsidiary engaged in the same activity as the former trading partner. Alternatively, one party may refrain from acting because of the significant influence of another—for example, a subsidiary may be instructed by its parent not to engage in research and development.*

8. *For these reasons, knowledge of an entity's transactions, outstanding balances, including commitments, and relationships with related parties may affect assessments of its operations by users of financial statements, including assessments of the risks and opportunities facing the entity.*

It should be noted at this point that IAS 24 does not take the position that related-party transactions should be restated for disclosure purposes to their fair values if these are different from the amount recorded for the transaction. Rather, the details of actual related-party transactions should be disclosed so that readers of the financial statements can make up their own minds about their possible implications. Working out such implications will not necessarily be an easy exercise.

In extreme cases, **related-party transactions** might be undertaken to defraud other parties with a claim against the firm. For example, a **director** might sell some of the firm's assets to a related entity for a price materially below their market value. Directors might also use their position to pay themselves excessive salaries.

Related-party transactions might also be undertaken to minimise the total taxation payable by a group of related entities. For example, one entity might arrange its activities in such a manner as to allow transfer of profits to a related entity that has carry-forward tax losses or is operating in a country where it is taxed at a low rate.

Related-parties disclosure is highly regulated in Europe. Perhaps one of the driving forces for such regulation has been the occurrence of numerous corporate scandals in Europe (Parmalat), the US (Enron), the United Kingdom (Mirror Group and Maxwell) and Canada (Nortel). We would assume that the majority of transactions initiated within a firm, whether or not with related parties, would be in the interests of the business. However, it is the risk that a minority of transactions might not be in the interests of the organisation that, arguably, has contributed to the extensive disclosure requirements now in place for many European organisations.

related-party transactions Transactions between related parties.

director Directors include anyone who directs an entity in its financial and operating activities independently or with others or anyone occupying or acting in the position of director or directing someone in that position.

18.3.2 Materiality considerations

As with other accounting standards, materiality needs to be considered in determining whether or not to disclose particular related-party transactions. What is interesting in this standard is that different notions of materiality are applied to different parts of IAS 24. The 'usual' notions of materiality apply to paragraphs 1 to 28 of IAS 24. Related-party information is material if its omission, non-disclosure or misstatement has the potential to affect

decisions about the allocation of scarce resources by users of the financial statements and consolidated financial statements, or the discharge of accountability by directors.

A recent European Corporate Governance Forum Statement, issued on 10 March 2011, is recommending that formal levels of materiality be agreed in respect of what materiality is in the context of related parties. This statement is reproduced in Exhibit 18.1.

Exhibit 18.1   **Statement of the European Corporate Governance Forum (ECGF) on Related Party Transactions for Listed Entities**

Transactions with related parties are of vital interest to majority and minority shareholders alike and it is important that the interests of shareholders as a whole are fully protected especially when control of the company or the Board resides with a single party. The Forum recommends that consideration be given to introducing common principles across Europe to address this important area of corporate governance.

The Forum believes strongly that it is for the Directors to provide leadership to companies but this authority is not absolute and should be balanced with a requirement to inform shareholders of important developments and in certain instances to seek authorisation for their actions either from independent agencies or from the shareholders themselves.

In the interest of protecting all categories of shareholders the Forum therefore proposes the following guidelines for all transactions with related parties:[1]

1. Transactions representing less than 1% of assets should be exempted from any special reporting requirements, although the independent Directors should take particular care to satisfy themselves that the transaction is in the best interest of the outside shareholders;
2. Transactions with the same related party (or any of its associates) in any 12 month period that have not been approved by shareholders should be aggregated and if these aggregated transactions exceed 5% of assets then approval should be sought for subsequent transactions;
3. Transactions representing more than 1% but less than 5% of assets should be publicly announced at the time of the transaction, notified to the relevant authority responsible for financial supervision and accompanied by a letter from an independent advisor confirming that the transaction is fair and reasonable from the perspective of the outside shareholders;
4. Transactions representing more than 5% of assets or which have a significant impact on profits or turnover should have the additional requirement of being submitted to a vote by the shareholders in General Meeting but with the related party being precluded from voting;
5. In all instances the related party should abstain from any Board deliberations about the transaction in question.

[1] *The Forum notes that there are existing requirements in EU law for disclosure of related party transactions in the annual and consolidated accounts of companies (Art 43(1)(76) 78/660/EEC and Art 34 (7b) 83/349/EEC). Related party disclosures are also required by IAS 24 as endorsed into EU law.*

What do you think about the recommendations of the ECGF? Are there any instances when their recommended rules would not be appropriate?

Considering what we read in the news media about related-party transactions, we are often left with the feeling that there is something intrinsically bad about such transactions. For example, Parmalat and Enron created special purpose entities and offshore subsidiaries and tunnelled debt and losses into them using accounting transactions. However, these related-party transactions were not disclosed appropriately so the external investor could not obtain a proper assessment of the overall capital structure (debt levels) and performance of the respective companies.

However, there can be benefits associated with many related-party transactions. Perhaps the very reason we deal with related parties is because they provide us with better services and better prices and they are more reliable because of the close association. McCahery and Vermeulen (2005) caution that EU accounting regulation may go too far, that the measures may be counter-productive, rooting out usually efficient related-party transactions. They argue that related-party transactions can be beneficial for a company:

The received wisdom is that related party transactions play an important and legitimate role in a market economy. For firms, trade and foreign investment is often facilitated by inter-company financing transactions. Lower costs of capital and tax savings provide a strong incentive for engaging in these transactions. Indeed, there are many examples of related party transactions that yield benefits for companies. By far the most popular transactions include (1) inter-company loans or guarantees from parent to foreign subsidiary; (2) the sale of receivables to a special purpose entity; and (3) a leasing or licensing agreement between a parent and a foreign subsidiary.

Applying the disclosure requirements for 'related parties' as detailed in IAS 24 *Related Party Disclosures* obviously requires a definition of 'related parties'. As we indicated earlier, IAS 24 provides a relatively broad definition of the term, tying it in with terminology such as 'control', 'significant influence' and 'key management personnel'. We will now consider these terms.

Categories of related party

We will consider the terms 'control', 'significant influence', 'key management personnel' and 'close family member' in turn below. Such terms are used in identifying categories of related parties.

Control

An entity that is controlled by another entity is classified as a subsidiary. **Control** means the power to govern the financial *and* operating policies of an entity so as to obtain benefits from its activities. Because the control of one party by another might affect an entity's financial performance if one party elects to transact with the other (the organisation in the position to exert control could be in a situation to set transaction terms that are favourable to itself), it would appear reasonable that control be used as a criterion for having to provide related-party information.

What should be emphasised is that the definition of control that has been adopted relies on the power to govern—this *power* does not necessarily have to be exercised and perhaps never will be, yet the entity with the power to control another entity would be considered to be related to that entity.

> **control** (organisations) With regard to related parties and other organisations within a group (economic entity), control means the power to govern the financial and operating policies of an entity so as to obtain benefits from its activities.

Significant influence

An entity that is significantly influenced by another entity is referred to as an associate. As indicated above, related-party relationship can also be established through the existence of significant influence by one entity over another. **Significant influence** means the power to participate in the financial and operating policy decisions of an entity, but does not amount to control over those policies. Significant influence is a relationship that falls short of control, but enables one party to substantially affect the policies of another. The most common form of relationship based on significant influence is that between an investor and its associate.

> **significant influence** Capacity of an entity to affect substantially but not control either, or both, the financial and operating policies of another entity.

In Figure 18.1 the percentages represent equity ownership. C plc would be a related party of both A plc and B plc. As both have an equity ownership of 25 per cent, they would most probably be able to exercise significant influence over C plc.

A plc and B plc would not be deemed related to each other, as neither appears to have any direct control or significant influence over the other.

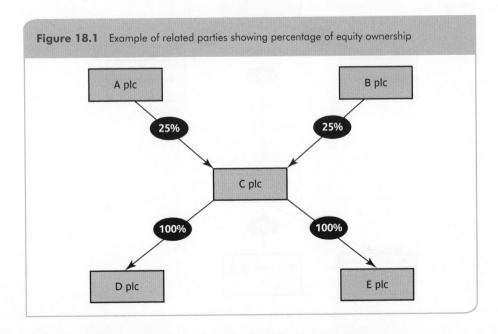

Figure 18.1 Example of related parties showing percentage of equity ownership

D plc and E plc would both be considered related parties of C plc. Being under common control, they would also be considered related to each other. Refer to the definition of related parties provided earlier (from IAS 24).

Key management personnel

> **key management personnel** Persons having authority and responsibility for planning, directing and controlling the activities of an entity, including any director of that entity.

Key management personnel are considered to be related parties. Being closely involved in the operations of the business, they have the ability to initiate numerous transactions. It is possible for some of these transactions not to be at fair value, given that they are not 'arm's length' transactions. Paragraph 9 of IAS 24 defines key management personnel as:

> *those persons having authority and responsibility for planning, directing and controlling the activities of the entity, directly or indirectly, including any director (whether executive or otherwise) of that entity.*

Close family members

As already indicated, a close member of the family of someone who is key management personnel (or of someone who is able to control or significantly influence an entity) is considered to be a related party. 'Close members of the family of an individual' are defined in paragraph 9 of IAS 24 as:

> *those family members who may be expected to influence, or be influenced by, that person in their dealings with the entity and include:*
>
> *(a) that person's children and spouse or domestic partner;*
> *(b) children of that person's spouse or domestic partner; and*
> *(c) dependants of that person or that person's spouse or domestic partner.*

We will now apply the definition of a related party provided in IAS 24 to the example given in Worked Example 18.1.

Worked Example 18.1 **Identification of related parties**

Assume that the figure below represents the structure of some entities in a European group. The percentage ownership is shown, and these percentages are deemed to be representative of voting rights.

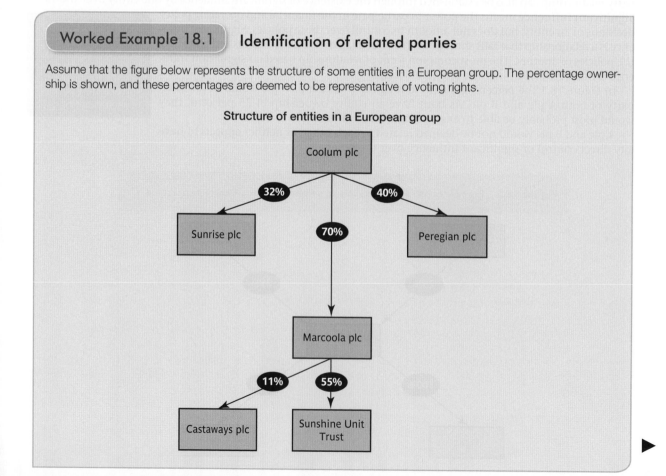

Structure of entities in a European group

The directors of the entities are as follows:

Coolum plc	Smith, Jones
Sunrise plc	Green, Black
Peregian plc	White, Sand
Marcoola plc	Long, Board
Castaways plc	Short, Wax
Sunshine Unit Trust	Reddy, Brown

Required

(a) Identify the related parties of Marcoola plc.
(b) Identify the entities that are not related to Marcoola plc.
(c) Identify the related parties of Peregian plc.
(d) Identify the entities that are not related to Peregian plc.

Solution

To answer this question we need to refer to the definition of related parties provided in IAS 24.

(a) Related parties of Marcoola plc

Sunrise plc would be a related party of Marcoola plc if Coolum plc also controlled Sunrise plc (they would be 'fellow subsidiaries'). It is possible to 'control' another entity with a shareholding of 32 per cent if the balance of the other shareholding is widely dispersed—a condition that must be determined on the basis of additional analysis. However, without sufficient evidence to indicate control, Sunrise plc would not be deemed to be a subsidiary of Coolum plc in the presence of an ownership interest of just 32 per cent. Therefore, Sunrise plc and Marcoola plc would not be 'fellow subsidiaries' and would not be deemed to be related parties.

Peregian plc, as with Sunrise plc, would be a related party of Marcoola plc if Coolum plc also 'controls' Peregian plc. In the absence of evidence to the contrary, an ownership interest of 40 per cent might fall short of constituting control. Hence Peregian would probably not be a 'related party' of Marcoola plc.

Coolum plc is a related party, as it controls Marcoola plc. It would be considered a controlling entity.

Sunshine Unit Trust is controlled by Marcoola plc, and would therefore be considered a controlled entity.

Long and Board are directors of Marcoola plc, and hence would be classed as 'key management personnel'.

Pursuant to IAS 24, only 'key management personnel' of an entity or its parent entity are included as related parties. Hence, we would also include Smith and Jones.

(b) Non-related parties of Marcoola plc

Apart from the entities already discussed, Castaways plc would not be considered a related party as it would probably not be subject to significant influence. Nor would the directors of Castaways plc be considered related parties.

(c) Related parties of Peregian plc

Coolum plc would at the least 'significantly influence' Peregian plc and Peregian plc would be considered an associate of Coolum plc. Hence, Coolum plc is a related party.

Marcoola, as it is controlled by Coolum plc, would be considered to be a related party of Peregian plc only if the 40 per cent ownership held gave control of Peregian plc to Coolum plc (in which case they would be 'fellow subsidiaries'). Under IAS 24, the definition of a related party does not include such entities. Since Coolum plc does not appear to 'control' Peregian plc, Marcoola plc would not be a related party of Peregian plc.

Although it appears that Coolum plc controls (indirectly through its control of Marcoola plc) Sunshine Unit Trust, and Coolum plc significantly influences Peregian plc, Sunshine Unit Trust would not be considered a related party under the definition provided in IAS 24.

The directors of Coolum plc and Peregian plc would be considered to be related parties of Peregian plc.

(d) Non-related parties of Peregian plc

Apart from the entities already discussed, Sunrise plc is not a related party of Peregian plc as Coolum plc only significantly influences Sunrise plc (common significant influence does not constitute related-party status under IAS 24).

Castaways plc is not a related party of Peregian plc, nor is Marcoola plc or Sunshine Unit Trust. The directors of Castaways plc and Sunrise plc would not be considered related parties of Peregian plc.

18.3.3 Disclosure requirements

Up to this point we have been considering how to identify related parties. The next step obviously is to consider the disclosures we must make in relation to related parties. Disclosure is required of transactions between the entity and its related parties, as well as of the general existence of related parties. Broadly speaking, such disclosures would relate to:

- the nature of the relationship;
- the transactions undertaken;
- outstanding balances.

Pursuant to paragraph 19 of IAS 24, related-party disclosures are required to be provided separately in the following categories:

- transactions with the entity's parent entity;
- transactions with entities with joint control or significant influence over the entity;
- subsidiaries;
- associates;
- joint ventures in which the entity is a venturer;
- key management personnel of the entity or its parent; and
- other related parties.

IAS 24 requires various items of disclosure. It requires descriptive information about the relationships between various related parties. In relation to situations where one entity controls another (that is, where there is a parent–subsidiary relationship), paragraph 13 of IAS 24 stipulates:

> *Relationships between a parent and its subsidiaries shall be disclosed irrespective of whether there have been transactions between them. An entity shall disclose the name of its parent and, if different, the ultimate controlling party. If neither the entity's parent nor the ultimate controlling party produces consolidated financial statements available for public use, the name of the next most senior parent that does so shall also be disclosed.*

In explaining the disclosure requirements as they relate to the parent–subsidiary relationship that requires disclosure even in the absence of a transaction, paragraph 14 of IAS 24 states:

> *To enable users of financial statements to form a view about the effects of related party relationships on an entity, it is appropriate to disclose the related party relationship when control exists, irrespective of whether there have been transactions between the related parties.*

There are a number of disclosure requirements in relation to key management personnel. Indeed, this is an area that is heavily regulated in terms of required disclosures. Paragraph 17 of IAS 24 requires the following disclosures at an aggregated level:

> *An entity shall disclose key management personnel compensation in total and for each of the following categories:*
>
> *(a) short-term employee benefits;*
> *(b) post-employment benefits;*
> *(c) other long-term benefits;*
> *(d) termination benefits; and*
> *(e) share-based payment.*

Paragraph 16 just quoted refers to 'compensation'. This word is often used interchangeably with 'remuneration'. The categories of 'compensation' discussed in paragraph 16 are defined in paragraph 9 of IAS 24 as follows:

> *Compensation includes all employee benefits (as defined in IAS 19 Employee Benefits) including employee benefits to which IFRS 2 Share-based Payment applies. Employee benefits are all forms of consideration paid, payable or provided by the entity, or on behalf of the entity, in exchange for services rendered to the entity. It also includes such consideration paid on behalf of a parent of the entity in respect of the entity. Compensation includes:*
>
> *(a) short-term employee benefits, such as wages, salaries and social security contributions, paid annual leave and paid sick leave, profit-sharing and bonuses (if payable within twelve months of the end of the period) and non-monetary benefits (such as medical care, housing, cars and free or subsidised goods or services) for current employees;*
> *(b) post-employment benefits such as pensions, other retirement benefits, post-employment life insurance and post-employment medical care;*

(c) other long-term employee benefits, including long service leave or sabbatical leave, jubilee or other long service benefits, long-term disability benefits and, if they are not payable wholly within twelve months after the end of the period, profit-sharing, bonuses and deferred compensation;

(d) termination benefits; and

(e) share-based payment.

We will return to the detailed disclosures required in respect of key management personnel later in this chapter. Now, we turn our attention away from 'key management personnel' (which includes directors and senior executives) to 'related parties' in general. As we have shown, IAS 24 defines related parties. In relation to the disclosure of information about transactions between related parties, paragraph 18 of IAS 24 requires the following:

If an entity has had related party transactions during the periods covered by the financial statements, it shall disclose the nature of the related party relationship as well as information about those transactions and outstanding balances, including commitments, necessary for users to understand the potential effect of the relationship on the financial statements. These disclosure requirements are in addition to those in paragraph 17. At a minimum disclosures shall include:

(a) the amount of the transactions;

(b) the amount of outstanding balances, including commitments, and:

   (i) their terms and conditions, including whether they are secured, and the nature of the consideration to be provided in settlement; and

   (ii) details of any guarantees given or received;

(c) provisions for doubtful debts related to the amount of outstanding balances; and

(d) the expense recognised during the period in respect of bad or doubtful debts due from related parties.

The disclosures required by paragraph 18 of IAS 24 must be classified by related party. As we have indicated, paragraph 19 of IAS 24 stipulates:

The disclosures required by paragraph 18 shall be made separately for each of the following categories:

(a) the parent;

(b) entities with joint control or significant influence over the entity;

(c) subsidiaries;

(d) associates;

(e) joint ventures in which the entity is a venturer;

(f) key management personnel of the entity or its parent; and

(g) other related parties.

Detailed disclosures of particular transactions with individual related parties would frequently be too voluminous to be easily understood. Accordingly, and as shown above, information would be aggregated by type of transaction, nature of terms and conditions and class of related party. However, disclosure on an individual basis might be more informative when there are significant transactions with specific related parties. IAS 24 provides examples of transactions that should be disclosed. According to paragraph 20 of IAS 24:

The following are examples of transactions that are disclosed if they are with a related party:

(a) purchases or sales of goods (finished or unfinished);

(b) purchases or sales of property and other assets;

(c) rendering or receiving of services;

(d) leases;

(e) transfers of research and development;

(f) transfers under licence agreements;

(g) transfers under finance arrangements (including loans and equity contributions in cash or in kind);

(h) provision of guarantees or collateral;

(i) commitments to do something if a particular event occurs or does not occur in the future, including executory contracts (recognised and unrecognised); and

(j) settlement of liabilities on behalf of the entity or by the entity on behalf of that related party.

In practice, it has often been argued by managers of entities that disclosure of transactions between related parties should not be required if the transactions were made on 'normal business terms'. In this regard, paragraph 23 of IAS 24 further requires that: 'Disclosures that related party transactions were made on terms equivalent to those that prevail in arm's length transactions are made only if such terms can be substantiated.'

IAS 24 provides some relief from the related-party disclosure requirements in relation to transactions with a government. Specifically, paragraph 25 states:

A reporting entity is exempt from the disclosure requirements of paragraph 18 in relation to related party transactions and outstanding balances, including commitments, with:

(a) a government that has control, joint control or significant influence over the reporting entity; and

(b) another entity that is a related party because the same government has control, joint control or significant influence over both the reporting entity and the other entity.

As we have discussed, IAS 24 stipulates a number of disclosures relating to key management personnel. We will now explore these in more detail.

18.4 Key management personnel disclosures under IAS 24

To get a proper idea of the disclosure requirements set by the standard, we really need to review the standard in its entirety. In what follows we identify a number of the main disclosure requirements. Again, it should be noted that IAS 24 requires that, in situations where a *disclosing entity* is the *parent entity* in an *economic entity* and the financial statement of the *parent entity* is presented with the consolidated financial statement of that *economic entity*, the provisions apply only to the consolidated financial statement (this is referred to as 'parent entity relief'). However, should the entity want to provide specific information about the parent entity, it is permitted to do so.

The rewards provided to corporate directors and executives, who are included among 'key management personnel', is a fairly sensitive issue and one in which many stakeholders take a keen interest. Indeed, the public and governments have recently also taken a strong interest in executive and employee compensation, particularly in the financial services industry, as some corporations are widely believed by the public to have contributed to the global and financial downturn that has been affecting Europe since 2008. Financial Accounting in the News 18.1 reproduces an article that reflects the political nature of high executive salaries and the concerns they raise for groups such as regulators and governments. This article focuses on banks operating in London.

Financial Accounting in the News 18.1

WILL PAY REFORM STALL AT THE BANKS?

Jill Treanor, *The Guardian*, 17 January 2012

Disclosures from JP Morgan show its 'code' staff—those taking and managing risk—earned an average of £2.6m in 2010, while at Citigroup the figure was £2m but will the government extend Project Merlin to cover the investment banks?

Slowly but surely, information about secretive City pay deals is being exposed. In the wake of the banking crisis, the Financial Services Authority's first remuneration code found that 2,800 City staff earned more than £1m in 2009.

Then the Merlin agreement between the banks and the coalition shed light on pay practices at the high street banks. For instance, Barclays was forced to admit that it paid five bankers £110m—when performance-related pay deals are included—in 2010. Two of them, Rich Ricci and Jerry del Messier—the co-heads of the Barclays Capital investment bank, got £40m apiece.

A new update to the FSA's code, following the intervention of the EU's banking regulator, also produced other revelations last year. The FSA's code required banks to publish the pay deals of 'code staff'—those taking and managing risks—in aggregation. Barclays admitted it had 231 code staff earning an average of £2.4m while bailed-out Royal Bank of Scotland confessed to 323 code staff taking home an average of £1.1m.

Now, the big US firms with operations in London are also complying with this latest FSA rule in regulatory filings for year-end 2010.

Disclosures by Goldman Sachs imply that its 95 code staff were paid £4m on average in 2010 and bonuses—yet to pay out—worth around $600m (£390m).

Scrutiny of filings by JP Morgan, show that its 82 code staff were paid an average of £2.6m in 2010—with the salary making up £264,000 of the total and a cash bonus amounting to almost £500,000. Some 4,422 of its 11,000 UK staff receive part of their pay in deferred equity. Citigroup has 95 staff who fall within the definition of code staff and were paid an average of £2m. Around £3m is disclosed for guaranteed payments and £2m was used to buy 'code' staff out of arrangements with a previous employer—a signing-on fee which the bank admits can only be used in exceptional circumstances.

All this information relates to 2010 and not 2011, the year for which the current round of bonuses are due, but helps to demonstrate the size of 'average' deals for a very specific set of staff working in the City.

▶

There are still problems, though, with accessing just how big the pay packets of the biggest earners are. The 'code staff' data provides information useful to providing averages—but does not go as far as the recommendations set out for Labour by Sir David Walker who said that banks should provide details of the number of staff earning over £1m. (When asked, the only bank to provide specific numbers for 2010 was HSBC, which said 253 were paid more than £1m that year.)

The Merlin disclosures also present difficulties. The rules allow the banks to select the top five key staff who reported to chief executives to be disclosed, allowing the star traders and other big earners to be excluded. HSBC demonstrated this last year—under Hong Kong rules its five 'highest-paid individuals globally' received a combined £34.3m in salaries, bonuses and pension contributions but under the disclosure required in the UK through Project Merlin, the total of the 'five highest-paid senior executives' was just over £12m.

The government is now consulting on whether the so-called Merlin disclosures should be extended to the top eight—and include not just the high street banks but also the likes of Goldman Sachs. The consultation period runs until mid-February—perilously close to a point when the UK banks might argue they cannot wait for new rules before they publish annual reports where pay is traditionally disclosed.

Despite all the government's pledges to crack down on top pay, it remains to be seen whether it will press on with this disclosure of the top eight, whether it will spread its reach beyond the high street banks, and whether it will demand clear, concise information that can be used for the basis of comparisons. This is something the current system does not allow. For instance, the averages for the code staff need to be worked out manually, while decisions also need to be made about what elements of pay to include in the calculation.

Source: *The Guardian*. © 2012 Guardian News and Media Limited.

A related-party transaction involving key management personnel might in fact be recorded at a low cost because they received the goods at costs below their fair value—so applying materiality thresholds to such disclosures could be problematic.

As already emphasised, the remuneration of 'key management personnel' is an area in which extensive disclosures are required. As we know, paragraph 17 of IAS 24 requires aggregate disclosure of key management personnel compensation.

For the purposes of this requirement, various items—other than cash wages—would also be considered included as part of directors' remuneration, including:

■ private assurance or insurance premiums paid on behalf of the directors;
■ use of a company home by a director;
■ use of an office and secretarial services for private purposes;
■ use of a company-owned holiday home;
■ low-interest-rate loans;
■ motor vehicles for private purposes; and
■ 'golden handcuffs' (amounts paid to directors as sign-on fees).

Once we have determined the items or components of remuneration, we need to measure them. There is a general principle to be applied in determining the 'cost' of a component of remuneration. Basically, each such component should be measured in accordance with the requirements of IAS 19 *Employee Benefits* or, when that standard is silent on a particular item of remuneration, on the basis of the 'cost' to the entity of providing that item.

In relation to costing the components of compensation, one area that has attracted a great deal of attention is the measurement of the 'cost' associated with providing employees, inclusive of senior management, with equity instruments as part of their total remuneration. Until recently, there was relatively little guidance. However, in July 2004 IFRS 2 *Share-based Payment* was released. Equity compensation provided as remuneration by the disclosing entity or any of its subsidiaries must be measured using the fair value of its equity instruments at the grant date, less any amount paid or payable by the recipient for that instrument. The fair value of equity instruments at grant date is:

■ in the case of shares and units, the market price at grant date (or estimated market price if not publicly traded) of an equivalent share or unit (being paid up to the same extent and carrying equivalent entitlements or restrictions);
■ in the case of options and rights that are publicly traded, the market price at grant date; and
■ in the case of options and rights that are not publicly traded over publicly traded shares or units, estimated using an option-pricing model that takes into account, as at grant date, the exercise price and expected life of the instrument, the current price of the underlying share or unit and its expected volatility, expected dividends and the risk-free interest rate for the expected life of the instrument.

In the case of share options and rights, the method of determining the fair value of the equity instrument depends on the circumstances. If an equivalent option or right is quoted on an active and liquid market, the market value at the grant date is used. If an option or right is not traded but the underlying instrument is publicly traded, an accepted option-pricing model, such as the Black–Scholes (modified for dividends) or a binomial model, can be used.

The disclosures required by IAS 24 are to be made in the notes to the financial statements. The disclosures required by company law are typically required in the directors' report. However, it is normally permissible for the directors' report to contain cross-references to the relevant details within the financial statements. Indeed, the information in respect of key management is typically contained in a 'remuneration report'. In some countries, this requirement is recommended under corporate governance guidance or rules. Probably the most controversial and topical related-party transaction, 'executive compensation', is now discussed in more detail.

18.5 Executive remuneration

Executive remuneration is coming under unprecedented public attention as a result of the recent financial crises. This leads to much interest in proper disclosures being presented in financial statements in respect of the packages and incentives that are agreed with executives. The magnitude of executive remuneration packages and arguments for and against shareholders agreeing to such high salary levels are outlined in an article on the London Loves Business website by Rebecca Hobson, reproduced in Financial Accounting in the News 18.2.

Financial Accounting In the News 18.2

WITH NEWS THAT FTSE 100 DIRECTORS HAVE SEEN THEIR EARNINGS INCREASE BY ALMOST 50 PER CENT, HERE'S A ROUND-UP OF WHAT THE WEB THINKS

Rebecca Hobson, *London Loves Business*, 28 October 2011

FTSE 100 directors have seen their total earnings increase by an average of 49 per cent in the last financial year, and are now averaging £2,697,664 per annum reveals the latest research by Incomes Data Services (IDS). IDS says this increase was even higher than the 43 per cent rise in total earnings for CEOs, suggesting, it says, that executive largesse is evenly spread across the board.

The top earning FTSE 350 chief executives

1. Mick Davis (Xstrata) £18,426,105
2. Bart Becht (Reckitt Benkiser) £17,879,000
3. Michael Spencer (ICAP) £13,419,619
4. Sir Terry Leahy (Tesco) £12,038,303
5. Tom Albanese (Rio Tinto) £11,623,162
6. Sir Martin Sorrell (WPP Group) £8,949,985
7. Todd Kozel (Gulf Keystone Petroleum) £8,913,223
8. Don Robert (Experian) £8,601,984
9. Edward Bonham Carter (Jupiter Fund Management) £8,003,641
10. Dame Marjorie Scardino (Pearson) £8,003,641

Martin Sorrell

Speaking on the Today programme and defending directors' pay Martin Sorrell said:

'Look at what chief executives of media companies are paid in other parts of the world. We are a worldwide company, we are the leading company in our industry, the comparison, whether you like it or not, is with other companies in the world.'

Speaking to Sky News, Martin Sorrell said:

'It's also about incentives, both short and long-term incentives and if that's the way the High Pay Commission wants to play it, you will end up with less competitive, less well-run companies who either go elsewhere or go into private equity. If that's what you want, fine, that will be the end result and Britain on the world stage will be even less competitive than it is now. So don't crimp those companies that are trying to build global operations competitively.'

The unions

TUC general secretary Brendan Barber said: 'With the FTSE 100 down on last year and most staff getting pay rises of less than 2%, these bumper settlements prove that chief executive officers' pay bears no resemblance to performance or economic reality.

'Top directors have used tough business conditions to impose real wage cuts, which have hit people's living standards and the wider economy, but have shown no such restraint with their own pay.

►

'Boardroom pay rewards are a brazen stitch-up. Reform should start with employee representation on remuneration committees, which would give directors a much-needed sense of reality.'

General Secretary of the GMB union, Paul Kenny, said: 'This is another shining example of how the elite greedy pigs who run our top companies behave.

'This is in stark contrast with what has happened to average earnings for workers in 294 occupations that cover 90% of the UK workforce that have seen drops in living standards of up to 20%.

'The fall in living standards for the majority means that the Government's strategy for an economic recovery is in tatters as two-thirds of the economy is consumer driven. George Osborne must be the only person who does not get it.'

James Moore, writing in *The Independent*

'It is a system that is clearly broken (if not bent). And as income disparity has been identified as a serious social problem, it is arguably unsustainable.

'One way to bring about change might be to alter the composition of boardrooms, and seek non-executives from more varied backgrounds. This might also result in more and better questions being asked of executives, leading to better run companies.'

Source: www.londonlovesbusiness.com

The UK Treasury Committee that was established to investigate the financial crisis stated that, 'bonus-driven remuneration structures encouraged reckless and excessive risk-taking and that the design of bonus schemes was not aligned with the interests of shareholders and the long-term sustainability of the banks' (House of Commons Treasury Committee 2009). Policy makers seem to believe that executive compensation schemes contributed to the financial crisis and have taken steps to try to align executive and shareholder interests. In an investigation into corporate governance in banks up to and during the financial crisis, Sir David Walker (2009) raised concerns about executive remuneration, recommending that banks should reduce the dependence of executive remuneration on short-term performance. He suggests that this might be achieved 'by increasing the share of total remuneration represented by incentive arrangements that are appropriately and clearly linked to long-term outturns; and to ensure that appropriate adjustment is made if the revenue or other data on which short-term bonus awards were made are seen to have been overstated'. In line with the tenet of the required disclosures in IAS 24, Walker recommends that 'high-end' remuneration be disclosed to shareholders (on a banded basis). Though the Walker Report focuses on banks, the recommendations influenced the content of the UK Corporate Governance Code (2010), which is also relevant for companies quoted on the Irish Stock Exchange. The code recommends that shareholders hold the executives to account for their decisions and actions and recommends that shareholders have an annual opportunity to provide feedback on the performance of the directors prior to the AGM. Indeed, since the financial crisis, shareholders have been more outspoken in raising their objections to executive compensation in AGMs (Hamill *et al.* 2010). They have become more active and have used their power to exercise control over director decision making.

For example, in June 2010 at Tesco's AGM, 47 per cent of shareholders failed to back the remuneration report (Bowers and Finch 2010). Some of the shareholders abstained from the vote but 37 per cent of votes went against the remuneration report. James Thompson writes about the uprising in the article 'Tesco Investors Revolt Against Board Pay Plans' in *The Independent*. The article is reproduced in Financial Accounting in the News 18.3. Figures from PIRC (2010), the UK governance advisory group, show that the number of companies with 10 per cent or more opposition to their remuneration reports jumped from zero in 2000 to 65 in 2009. At a recent British Airways AGM, one disgruntled shareholder got a round of applause when he reportedly told the board, 'you do seem to be feathering your own nests at the expense of the shareholders you are supposed to serve' (Milmo and Agencies 2010).

Financial Accounting In the News 18.3
TESCO INVESTORS REVOLT AGAINST BOARD PAY PLANS

James Thompson, *The Independent*, 3 July 2010

Tesco suffered the biggest blue-chip shareholder rebellion this year after nearly 40 per cent of investors voted against its remuneration report at its annual general meeting yesterday.

Some lobby groups directed particular anger at the £4.3m total pay awarded to Tim Mason, the head of the supermarket's loss-making US business, Fresh & Easy, for the financial year to the end of February.

However, Tesco succeeded in getting the resolution on its remuneration report passed, with 62.3 per cent of the votes in favour. The critical threshold was 50 per cent, with 37 per cent of votes cast against its pay policy.

A spokesman for Tesco said: 'Obviously, some shareholders have expressed their concern and we will be, as you would expect, engaging with them going forward.' The revolt by Tesco investors is the largest this year at a FTSE 100 company – bigger than the 32 per cent of votes cast against the remuneration report of the mining group Xstrata, and 16 per cent against that of the consumer goods company Reckitt Benckiser.

It is the sixth-biggest protest vote over pay in the past decade and puts down a marker for Marks & Spencer's annual meeting later this month. The M&S chief executive, Marc Bolland, could earn up to £14.8m this year.

While the mood at the Tesco AGM was combative when directors were answering questions about its US operations, the chief executive Sir Terry Leahy, who is retiring in March, was given a standing ovation.

Furthermore, all of Tesco's board directors, including Mr Mason, were re-elected and received more than 90 per cent of the votes cast. Several lobbyists expressed concern about the Tesco board's pay in the run-up to yesterday's vote, including the corporate governance company PIRC, the pension-fund adviser Risk Metrics, and CtW Investment Group, a US firm which works with pension funds that have stakes in Tesco.

Michael Garland, the director of value strategies at CtW Investment Group, said: 'The extraordinary opposition vote reflects investor outrage over the excessive pay awarded to Tim Mason, Tesco's second-highest paid executive, despite the dismal performance of the US Fresh & Easy business he oversees.' Mr Mason, who joined Tesco in 1982 and helped to create the company's slogan 'every little helps', will become deputy chief executive in March when Sir Terry retires.

Fresh & Easy made a £165m loss last year, although Tesco said losses had peaked. The chain, which now has more than 150 stores, was launched in November 2007 but has been badly hit by the deep recession in California, Nevada and Arizona.

Tesco said in June that sales at Fresh & Easy rose by 37.8 per cent in the 13 weeks to 30 May. However, it was up against soft comparable sales for the same period last year. David Reid, the Tesco chairman, said: 'In almost every country, you incur losses in the first three years – this is not unusual.'

Tesco also responded robustly to criticism from the floor from a person claiming to act for US shareholders about why it did not engage with unions across the Atlantic. Sir Terry said: 'Your union [in the US] has opposed us from day one and has gone on opposing us, and that is not the basis for a partnership. And we have a good business with motivated staff who don't want to be part of your union.'

Tesco, which operates in 14 countries, including the UK, delivered record underlying pre-tax profits of £3.4bn for the year to 27 February.

Source: The Independent. © independent.co.uk

The intensive shareholder, government and media pressure is starting to have some impact as reflected in Financial Accounting in the News 18.4. In this article, Jill Treanor reports on how the chief executive of Lloyds Banking Group has elected not to claim a £2.4 million bonus, citing the 'tough financial circumstances of the public' as a reason.

Financial Accounting in the News 18.4

LLOYDS BOSS HORTA-OSÓRIO FORGOES £2M BONUS TURNING FOCUS ON BANKING PEERS

Jill Treanor, *The Guardian*, 13 January 2012

Horta-Osório, who started in the job less than a year ago, could have claimed a maximum bonus of £2.4m last year, or 225% of his basic salary

Pressure was mounting today on top bankers to waive their multimillion-pound bonuses after António Horta-Osório, the boss of bailed-out Lloyds Banking Group, announced he would not take a payout that could have been worth £2.4m.

The Portuguese-born banker put his peers in the spotlight by saying he took the decision because of the 'tough financial circumstances of people' as well as the bank's poor performance and his two months' absence following a severe bout of insomnia.

After returning to work on Monday, Horta-Osório had discussed the potential bonus with his family before telling the board of the bank, which is 41% owned by the taxpayer, that he did not want to be considered for a payout.

Treasury sources said George Osborne welcomed the decision, while Lord Oakeshott, the Liberal Democrat peer who resigned as a Treasury spokesman a year ago over the government's soft stance on the banks, urged rivals to follow suit.

The Lloyds board is preparing to discuss bonuses next month. It had made no decision about whether to award Horta-Osório a bonus in light of the 60% fall in the share price and a plunge back into the red after a £3.2bn provision for misselling payment protection insurance.

Horta-Osório's announcement has turned the focus on bosses of other major banks at a time when the government has been calling for restraint, particularly at the bailed out banks – Lloyds and Royal Bank of Scotland – which are expected to be held to the same restrictions as last year when any bonus above £2,000 had to be paid in shares or bonds and not in cash.

Bonuses for 2011 are yet to be finalised but if they were awarded the maximum, Stephen Hester, chief executive of Royal Bank of Scotland, could get £2.4m, Bob Diamond, chief executive of Barclays, as much as £3.4m and Stuart Gulliver, chief executive of HSBC, up to £4.8m.

Horta-Osório had faced questions about his entitlement to a bonus for 2011 after two months off to recover from 'fatigue' following a period last year when he could not sleep for five consecutive days. He checked himself into the Priory to recuperate and pledged to change his intense management style when he returned to work on Monday – defying sceptics who had reckoned his career was in tatters.

'As chief executive, I believe my bonus entitlement should reflect the performance of the group but also the tough financial circumstances that many people are facing. I also acknowledge that my leave of absence has had an impact both inside and outside the bank including for shareholders. On that basis, I have decided to request that the board does not consider me for a 2011 bonus,' he said.

Oakeshott has put pressure not to take bonuses on the bosses of RBS and Barclays – including two bankers at Barclays, Jerry del Missier and Rich Ricci, who a year ago were handed more than £40m each after share deals awarded over the previous five years came to fruition.

'Rejoice. A responsible banker at long last is starting to recognise his customers' pain. It would be unthinkable after this for George Osborne to pay Stephen Hester even a penny bonus at our other state-owned bank. And Bob Diamond's £40m gang of three running Barclays should follow the Horta-Osório example,' said Oakeshott.

Horta-Osório was lured from Spanish bank Santander a year ago with a package of up to £13.4m and in deciding to waive any bonus is still likely to receive millions of pounds as he receives a salary of £1m and other elements from his complex signing-on package.

Lloyds is in the process of trying to claw back a £1.9m bonus handed to Horta-Osório's predecessor Eric Daniels before the bank took the £3.2bn hit for misselling and is braced for a row over the signing-on fee for new finance director George Culmer who might be handed as much as £4.5m to buy him out of deals at his current employer, the insurer RSA.

Source: The Guardian. © 2012 Guardian News and Media Limited

The European Parliament has taken action to curb excessive executive compensation. In June 2010 it approved rules that it hopes will control the bonus culture that has become the norm in banks. The rules include capping upfront cash bonuses at 30 per cent of the total bonus and 20 per cent for particularly large bonuses; deferring between 40 and 60 per cent of any bonus that can be clawed back by the company if investments do not perform as expected and ensuring that at least 50 per cent of the total bonus would be paid as 'contingent capital' (funds to be called upon first in case of bank difficulties). Many countries have taken action to control, or provide a framework for, executive compensation by issuing legislation. For example, in Germany the Appropriateness of Management Board Compensation Act came into force on 5 August 2009 and more rules were introduced in the Regulation on Remuneration in Financial Institutions in 2010.

However, there is opposition to the EU proposals, particularly in London where the British Bankers' Association argued that these rules may be detrimental to London's standing as a leading financial services centre, and that stringent reforms could lead to firms relocating to alternative, more favourable regulatory locations (Hamill *et al.* 2011). As mentioned, the British Bankers' Association is quite opposed to the recommended changes to remuneration packages. Do you think its points of opposition are valid (the members of the British Bankers' Association would typically be senior executives and therefore probably subject to any proposed limits on bonuses and disclosure requirements, so we can speculate on whether 'self-interest' might be motivating some of their opposition)? The comments made by the British Bankers' Association are interesting. They reflect the view that the government is simply reacting to 'current moods' within the public (which raises the point that, if the public expects particular accountability, perhaps it is the role of government to ensure that such accountability is provided). Many executives also question the rights and ability of shareholders to evaluate directors' and executives' remuneration, suggesting that senior corporate management is best placed to determine how much to pay themselves and fellow managers.

18.6 Examples of related-party disclosure notes

Rather than our reproducing here numerous related-party notes as they appear in annual reports, you should consider reviewing a number of annual reports for yourself to see the extent of disclosures made with regard to related-party transactions. As you will see, the disclosures can be quite voluminous and varied depending on the country. For example, in the UK it is normal practice to have a 'Remuneration Report', whereas in Germany a 'Compensation Report' forms part of the Management Report and in Sweden the information on executive remuneration is included in a note to the financial statements. You might like to review the following as examples:

- Sainsbury plc's annual report, which in 2011 had several pages of disclosure relating to directors, senior managers and other related parties, including a ten-page Remuneration Report. In addition, it has a specific related-party transaction note (note 32). The latest annual report can be reviewed at www.sainsburys.co.uk.
- The annual report of Philips, which in 2010 had several notes dedicated to related-party transactions. For example, in note 30 information on significant interests was disclosed, in note 31 six pages of disclosures were provided on remuneration and in note 28 six pages of disclosures in respect of employee benefits were disclosed. The latest annual report can be reviewed at www.philips.com.
- The annual report of Nutreco, which in 2010 had nine pages dedicated to transactions with key management personnel and other related-party transactions (note 24) and a further half a page on other related-party transactions (note 29). The latest annual report can be reviewed at www.nutreco.com.
- The annual report of Deutsche Bank, which in 2010 had a nine-page compensation report dealing with key management personnel remuneration packages and several notes on other related-party transactions, such as note 37 (three pages) on related-party transactions, note 38 (one page) with information on subsidiaries, note 41 (two pages) on Management Board and Supervisory Board details and note 42 (43 pages) on shareholdings. The latest annual report can be reviewed at www.db.com.

SUMMARY

This chapter considered related-party transactions. As demonstrated, related-party transactions are subject to a great deal of disclosure regulation within Europe. The rationale for this is that dealings associated with related parties can expose a reporting entity to risks and can provide opportunities that would otherwise not have existed. As such, the accounting regulators are of the view that a proper assessment of the performance of an entity necessarily requires knowledge of its various related-party transactions.

The accounting standard pertaining to disclosures of related parties and their transactions is IAS 24, though national legislation and corporate governance guidance/recommendations also require/promote the disclosure of certain information about related-party transactions.

Key management personnel-related transactions are subject to the highest degree of required disclosure, reflecting the perceived sensitivity of organisations to director- and executive-related transactions.

To comply with the requirements of the accounting standards and national legislation, listed companies devote many pages of their annual reports to related-party transactions. The cost of preparing and reporting this information would be high—as would that imposed on financial statement readers in their efforts to assimilate and understand the voluminous data—but the regulators obviously consider these costs to be outweighed by the associated benefits. As indicated within this chapter, the extensive regulation of related-party transactions is arguably due to some of the infamous corporate scandals that have occurred in recent decades and the perception that extensive disclosure regulation is necessary to maintain—or perhaps restore—confidence in the European corporate sector.

KEY TERMS

END-OF-CHAPTER EXERCISE

After completing this chapter, you should ensure that you are able to answer the following questions. (If you find you cannot, you should revisit the appropriate sections of this chapter.)

1   For accounting purposes, what is a related party?   **LO** 18.1
2   It is often argued that, to properly assess the performance of an entity, knowledge of related-party transactions is required. What is a possible basis for such an argument?   **LO** 18.4
3   For key management personnel-related transactions, IAS 24 has specific materiality guidelines. According to IAS 24, what types of key management personnel-related transactions are deemed to be material?   **LO** 18.2
4   Key management personnel-related transactions are subject to the highest degree of required disclosure. Why do you think this is the case, and do you think it is justified?   **LO** 18.4
5   IAS 24 provides a definition of related parties. The definition relies upon such terms as *control*, *significant influence*, *key management personnel* and *close family members*. Define these four terms.   **LO** 18.1

REVIEW QUESTIONS

1   What is a related party?   **LO** 18.1
2   Do you consider that disclosure of related-party information is of value to financial statement users? Why?   **LO** 18.5
3   Do you consider that disclosure of related-party information is of value to the organisations making the disclosures? Why?   **LO** 18.5
4   Do you think that an organisation that provides information about its related-party transactions would be more favourably viewed by investors than an organisation that does not provide any such information? Explain your answer.   **LO** 18.5
5   What are the classes of related parties identified in IAS 24?   **LO** 18.2
6   How are 'key management personnel' defined in IAS 24?   **LO** 18.2
7   IAS 24 has many requirements pertaining to key management personnel. Why do you think that part of an accounting standard is dedicated to transactions with key management personnel?   **LO** 18.4
8   In relation to transactions with key management personnel, what materiality guidelines are provided in IAS 24?   **LO** 18.6
9   Briefly identify the types of information that must be disclosed in relation to key management personnel-related transactions.   **LO** 18.2
10 The related-party note provided in the 2000 annual report of Coles Myer stated: 'Options issued to executive directors under the Coles Myer Executive Share Option Plan are deemed to have no remuneration value as the option issue price is set at the market price of CML's shares at date of issue.' Would this treatment, as applied in 2000, be permissible today? Explain your answer.   **LO** 18.5
11 A review of key management personnel disclosure notes will often show that a component of the salary executives are paid is linked to corporate performance. Why do you think organisations would not just pay directors a fixed salary rather than one based on performance?   **LO** 18.5
12 Review the executive and director disclosures made by Tesco PLC in its most recent annual report (you will need to go to the Tesco PLC website) and identify which transactions would cause you most concern. Explain why this is the case.   **LO** 18.4

CHALLENGING QUESTIONS

13 Compare and contrast the views expressed by Martin Sorrell and the unions in Financial Accounting in the News 18.2.   **LO** 18.4
14 Review a number of corporate annual reports for the contents of their related-party disclosures (you are to identify which companies you have reviewed). As you will typically see, the note disclosure is extensive. List the headings of the various related-party disclosures being made. Do you think that the costs involved in making such disclosures would exceed the benefits? What would be some of the costs and what would be some of the benefits?   **LO** 18.6

15 Review the related-party note provided by SAP in its most recent annual report (find it at SAP's website). How many pages are dedicated to related-party disclosures, and what are the various headings of the related-party disclosures? Do you think that this is a case of too much information being provided—a case of information overload? Explain your answer. **LO** 18.6

16 As we indicated in this chapter, shareholders typically have the right under legislation to vote, in a non-binding fashion, on remuneration plans. **LO** 18.4

REQUIRED

Provide arguments for and against shareholders having the right to vote on executive remuneration.

REFERENCES

BOWERS, S. & FINCH, J., 'Shareholders Fight Back over Executive Pay and Bonuses', *Guardian*, 11 July 2010.

ECGF, *Statement of the European Corporate Governance Forum on Related Party Transactions for Listed Entities*, 10 March 2011, http://ec.europa.eu/internal_market/company/docs/ecgforum/ecgf_related_ party_transactions_en.pdf

HAMILL, P.A., WARD, A.M., & WYLIE, J., 'Corporate Governance Policy: New Dawn in Ireland and the UK', *Accountancy Ireland*, vol. 42, no. 6, 2010, pp. 56–9.

HAMILL, P.A., WARD, A.M., & WYLIE, J., 'Corporate Governance: Agency and Executive Compensation', *Accountancy Ireland*, vol. 43, no. 2, 2011, pp. 68–70.

HOUSE OF COMMONS TREASURY COMMITTEE, *Banking Crisis: Reforming Corporate Governance and Pay in the City*, London UK, 2009.

MCCAHERY, J. & VERMEULEN, E., 'Corporate Governance Crises and Related Party Transactions: A Post-Parmalat Agenda' in *Corporate Governance in Context: Corporations, States and Markets in Europe, Japan and the US*, edited by K. HOPT, E. WYMEERSCH, H. KENDA, & H. BAUM, Oxford, Oxford University Press.

MILMO, D. & AGENCIES, 'BA Boss Willie Walsh Heckled at AGM over Strike Claims', *Guardian*, 13 July 2010.

MOSCARIELLO, N., 'Related Party Transactions in Continental European Countries: Evidence from Italy', *International Journal of Disclosure and Governance*, 23 June 2011, http://www.palgrave-journals.com/jdg/journal/vaop/ncurrent/abs/jdg201114a.html.

PIRC, *PIRC Shareholder Voting Guidelines 2010*, 2010, www.pirc.co.uk/publications.

WALKER, D., *A Review of Corporate Governance in UK Banks and other Financial Industry Entities*, London, Walker Review Secretariat, 16 July 2009.

Chapter 19

Earnings Per Share

Learning objectives

Upon completing this chapter readers should:

LO1 be able to define and calculate basic earnings per share;

LO2 know how to adjust the calculation of basic earnings per share to take account of the existence of a bonus or rights entitlement;

LO3 understand what potential ordinary shares are, and be able to determine whether they are dilutive; and

LO4 understand how and why we calculate diluted earnings per share.

19.1 Introduction to earnings per share

IAS 33 *Earnings per Share* was issued in July 2004.

In 2008 the IASB embarked on a project to revise and simplify the requirements of IAS 33. The earnings per share project was part of a wider convergence project between the IASB and the FASB. As noted elsewhere in this book, the purpose of establishing the convergence project was to reduce differences between IFRSs and US GAAP that could be resolved in a relatively short time and could be addressed outside major projects. The objective of the Earnings per Share project is to simplify and converge the calculation of earnings per share according to IAS 33 *Earnings per Share* and SFAS No. 128 *Earnings per Share*. The IASB issued an Exposure Draft of proposed amendments to IAS 33 in August 2008. The Exposure Draft was open for public comment until 5 December 2008. The IASB reviewed a summary of responses to the Exposure Draft at its April 2009 meeting, but in the light of other priorities, the board initially indicated that it would review the responses in more detail and would resume the discussion on the project plan towards the end of 2009. However, a review of the IASB website in late 2011 as it pertained to the earnings per share project revealed the following information:

> *The project is currently paused and will resume; the date is yet to be confirmed.*

Hence, while we can anticipate that some changes will be made to the accounting standard covered in this chapter, the nature and timing of the changes was uncertain at the time this chapter was written.

IAS 33 requires the disclosure of basic earnings per share and diluted earnings per share and typically applies to:

- all listed companies;
- entities that have on issue ordinary shares and are in the process of listing; and
- entities that voluntarily disclose earnings per share.

An entity must disclose earnings per share on the face of the statement of comprehensive income, and it must do so even if the amounts are negative (that is, where there is a loss per share). Earnings per share of the entity for the previous year must also be shown as a basis for comparison. Where an entity is the parent entity in an economic entity and the financial statements of the parent entity are presented with the consolidated financial statements of that economic entity, the standard need only be applied to the consolidated financial statements. Exhibit 19.1 provides an example of the required disclosures in the consolidated income statement from the annual report of Deutsche Bank.

Exhibit 19.1 **Deutsche Bank—Earnings per share disclosures at the bottom of the consolidated income statement**

Earnings per Common Share[1] in €	2010	2009	2008
Basic	3.07	7.21	(6.87)
Diluted[2]	2.92	6.94	(6.87)
Number of shares in million[1]			
Denominator for basic earnings per share – weighted-average shares outstanding	753.3	689.4	558.5
Denominator for diluted earnings per share – adjusted weighted-average shares after assumed conversions	790.8	716.7	558.6

[1] *The number of average basic and diluted shares outstanding has been adjusted for all periods before October 6, 2010 to reflect the effect of the bonus element of the subscription rights issue in connection with the capital increase.*
[2] *Includes numerator effect of assumed conversions. For further detail please see Note 11 'Earnings per Common Share'.*

Before there was any accounting standard requiring disclosure of earnings per share, numerous companies were voluntarily providing details of their earnings per share in the notes to their financial statements. This would appear to signal that such companies' managements considered this information to be of value to financial statement users in their decision making.

As previously indicated in this book, classical finance theory suggests that the value of a firm's securities is a function of the discounted present value of future cash flows. It is conceivable that the higher the firm's earnings, the higher the value of the future cash flows and hence the higher the value of the firm's securities.

Early research on the relationship between earnings and the value of a firm's securities was undertaken by Ball and Brown (1968). They found that when unexpected earnings announcements were made, the value of the firm's securities would change. This was supported on the basis that the unexpected news was not already impounded within the share price. When financial statements are issued—typically a number of months after year end—it is conceivable that the market will already have impounded within the share price the information included in the financial statements. Therefore no additional share price movements will result. For example, the market might have been aware of the firm's profits through preliminary profit announcements.

More recent research by Easton (1990) bears out that accounting earnings affect share prices. If it is accepted that earnings affect share prices, it is not surprising that investors would be interested in information on earnings per share. In this regard it should be noted that the financial press frequently provides summaries of listed companies' earnings per share.

19.2 Computation of basic earnings per share

To compute earnings per share—which is calculated by dividing earnings by the number of shares that have been issued—we need to consider at least two factors:

1. how *earnings* are defined; and
2. how the *number of shares* is determined.

Before any accounting standard on earnings per share existed, companies were employing a multiplicity of ways to compute their **earnings per share (EPS)**. Different firms had different ways of computing earnings and/or the number of shares that had been issued, and such inconsistencies made inter-firm comparisons of EPS difficult. IAS 33 provides guidance on how to compute both *earnings* and the *number of shares*. Hence it would be reasonable to expect that there would now be uniformity in the methods used to calculate EPS.

We must remember, though, that there will continue to be differences in how firms calculate earnings owing to the numerous assumptions accountants must make throughout the accounting process. Therefore care must be taken when comparing EPS, just as it must be when comparing different organisations' earnings. From previous chapters of this book, you will be aware that the accounting process involves many assumptions based on various assessments of probabilities (the recognition criteria of the various elements of accounting rely on considerations of probabilities). You also know that there are a number of alternative accounting techniques that can be applied in accounting for transactions, many of which can have a material effect on profits (relative to the other possible methods). Hence earnings, which directly affect EPS calculations, can be calculated in a number of ways, sometimes depending on who constitutes the team of accountants involved in the accounting process (and, therefore, on the various professional judgements they make).

The standard requires that **basic EPS** and **diluted EPS** must be disclosed on the face of the statement of comprehensive income. Specifically, paragraph 66 of IAS 33 states:

> *An entity shall present in the statement of comprehensive income basic and diluted earnings per share for profit or loss from continuing operations attributable to the ordinary equity holders of the parent entity and for profit or loss attributable to the ordinary equity holders of the parent entity for the period for each class of ordinary shares that has a different right to share in profit for the period. An entity shall present basic and diluted earnings per share with equal prominence for all periods presented.*

Disclosures are required even when EPS is negative. As paragraph 69 of IAS 33 states: 'An entity shall present basic and diluted earnings per share, even if the amounts are negative (i.e. a loss per share).'

Basic EPS is determined by dividing the earnings of the entity for the reporting period by the **weighted-average number of shares** of the entity. Earnings are determined after deducting any preference share dividends appropriated for the financial year to the extent that they have not been treated as expenses of the entity (if preference shares are classified as liabilities, the related 'dividends' would already have been treated as interest expenses and no subsequent adjustment would be necessary). Preference share dividends are deducted to provide 'earnings' on the basis that EPS is calculated from the perspective of ordinary shareholders. That is, EPS relates to earnings per *ordinary* share. The preference share dividends would reduce the amount of earnings that would potentially be available to pay dividends to ordinary shareholders. In a sense, the dividends relating to preference shares are treated from the ordinary shareholders' perspective as a cost of capital (in much the same way as interest is a cost of borrowing funds), and therefore they are treated as an expense and deducted from profits before calculating EPS.

When considering subtracting preference dividends for the purpose of calculating EPS, it is necessary to determine, in periods in which the preference dividend is not paid, whether or not the preference shares are cumulative. The defining characteristic of a **cumulative dividend preference share** is that, where dividends are not paid in a particular year, they must be paid in later years *before* ordinary shareholders are entitled to receive any dividends out of profits. If the preference dividend is not cumulative, and no amount has been appropriated for the year, it may be ignored for the purpose of EPS calculation. As paragraph 14 of IAS 33 states:

> *The after-tax amount of preference dividends that is deducted from profit or loss is:*
>
> *(a) the after-tax amount of any preference dividends on non-cumulative preference shares declared in respect of the period; and*
> *(b) the after-tax amount of the preference dividends for cumulative preference shares required for the period, whether or not the dividends have been declared. The amount of preference*

earnings per share (EPS) Determined by dividing the earnings of the company by the weighted-average number of shares of the company outstanding during the financial year.

basic EPS Determined by dividing the earnings of a company by the weighted-average number of shares of the company outstanding during the financial year after deducting any preference share dividends appropriated for the financial year.

diluted EPS Shows the extent to which the participation of existing shareholders in the company's earnings will likely be reduced as a result of arrangements in place at balance date.

weighted-average number of shares The weighted-average number of ordinary shares outstanding during the period is the number of ordinary shares outstanding at the beginning of the period, adjusted by the number of ordinary shares bought back or issued during the period multiplied by a time-weighting factor.

cumulative dividend preference shares Preference shares with the attribute that if dividends are not paid in a particular year they must be paid in later years before ordinary shareholders receive any dividends.

dividends for the period does not include the amount of any preference dividends for cumulative preference shares paid or declared during the current period in respect of previous periods.

Earnings must be calculated to exclude the following:

- *Any portion attributable to non-controlling interests; and*
- *Any costs of servicing equity, paid or provided for, other than dividends on ordinary shares and partly paid shares.*

The calculation of basic EPS requires the earnings (adjusted as described above) to be divided by the weighted-average number of ordinary shares. An *ordinary share* is defined in paragraph 5 of IAS 33 as an equity instrument that is subordinate to all other classes of equity instruments.

For the purposes of the standard, it does not matter what the shares are called. If they have the above characteristics, they are treated as **ordinary shares**. The standard therefore adopts a **substance-over-form** test.

> **ordinary shares** A class of shares that typically ranks last in terms of any distribution of capital.
>
> **substance over form** Events are accounted for and displayed in accordance with their economic substance rather than their legal form.

In determining the 'weighted-average number of shares' (the denominator when working out EPS), paragraph 20 of IAS 33 states:

Using the weighted average number of ordinary shares outstanding during the period reflects the possibility that the amount of shareholders' capital varied during the period as a result of a larger or smaller number of shares being outstanding at any time. The weighted average number of ordinary shares outstanding during the period is the number of ordinary shares outstanding at the beginning of the period, adjusted by the number of ordinary shares bought back or issued during the period multiplied by a time-weighting factor. The time-weighting factor is the number of days that the shares are outstanding as a proportion of the total number of days in the period; a reasonable approximation of the weighted average is adequate in many circumstances.

For example, if a company has 1,000,000 ordinary shares issued at the beginning of the year (say, 1 July 2014) and it issues 200,000 fully paid shares on 1 March 2015, as well as buying back 100,000 shares on 1 April 2015, the weighted-average number of shares would be calculated as:

Period	Proportion of year	Number of shares outstanding	Weighted average
Fully paid ordinary shares			
1/7/14–28/2/15	243 ÷ 365	1,000,000	665,753
1/3/15–31/3/15	31 ÷ 365	1,200,000	101,918
1/4/15–30/6/15	91 ÷ 365	1,100,000	274,247
	365 days		
Total weighted-average number of ordinary shares			1,041,918

The weighted-average number of ordinary shares, which is the denominator when calculating EPS, also needs to take into account partly paid ordinary shares. However, partly paid shares will be included *only* to the extent that they carry rights to participate in dividends relative to an ordinary share. As paragraph A15 (from the Application Guidance Appendix to the standard) of IAS 33 states:

Where ordinary shares are issued but not fully paid, they are treated in the calculation of basic earnings per share as a fraction of an ordinary share to the extent that they were entitled to participate in dividends during the period relative to a fully paid ordinary share.

Where the partly paid ordinary shares carry no rights to participate in earnings, they would not be included in the weighted-average number of ordinary shares.

Entities might also have on issue mandatorily convertible securities—that is, securities that *must* ultimately be converted to ordinary shares. According to paragraph 23 of IAS 33:

Ordinary shares that will be issued upon the conversion of a mandatorily convertible instrument are included in the calculation of basic earnings per share from the date the contract is entered into.

Worked Example 19.1 considers how to determine basic EPS, which necessarily requires a determination of both *earnings* and the *weighted-average number of shares* that have been issued by the company.

Worked Example 19.1   Calculation of basic EPS

For the year ending 30 June 2014, Kirra plc reports the following:

- net profit after tax of €900,000.

As at 1 July 2013 Kirra plc had 200,000 fully paid ordinary shares. The following issues and purchases were subsequently made during the year:

- 100,000 fully paid ordinary shares issued on 1 September 2013 at the prevailing market price.
- 25,000 fully paid ordinary shares purchased back on 1 February 2014 at the prevailing market price.
- 70,000 partly paid ordinary shares issued on 1 April 2014 at an issue price of €2.00. The shares were partly paid to €1.30. The partly paid shares carry the right to participate in dividends in proportion to the amount paid as a fraction of the issue price.

For the entire financial year Kirra plc had 1 million €1.00 preference shares, which provide dividends at a rate of 10 per cent per year. The dividend rights are cumulative. The preference share dividends were not treated as part of interest expense.

Required

Compute the basic earnings per share amount for 2014.

Solution

Determination of earnings

As previously stated, to determine earnings for EPS purposes we exclude preference dividends. It should be noted that, given that the preference dividends are cumulative, it does not matter whether or not they have been paid as the dividend will still need to be deducted. If they are non-cumulative, the right to the preference dividend would be lost if they have not been declared, and hence for non-cumulative preference shares the dividend will be deducted from earnings when calculating EPS *only* if the dividend has been appropriated. Hence earnings for EPS purposes would be calculated as:

Profit after tax	€900,000
less Preference share dividends	(€100,000)
Earnings for basic EPS	€800,000

It should be noted that, while we have assumed that there are no non-controlling interests in Kirra plc's profit, if there had been this would have been deducted when calculating earnings for basic EPS (non-controlling interests are discussed in Chapter 22).

Determination of the weighted-average number of ordinary shares

Paragraph 19 of IAS 33 requires:

> *For the purpose of calculating basic earnings per share, the number of ordinary shares shall be the weighted average number of ordinary shares outstanding during the period.*

Period	Proportion of year	Shares outstanding	Weighted average
Fully paid ordinary shares			No.
1/7/13–31/8/13	62 ÷ 365	200,000	33,973
1/9/13–31/1/14	153 ÷ 365	300,000	125,753
1/2/14–30/6/14	150 ÷ 365	275,000	113,014
	365 days		
Partly paid ordinary shares			
1/4/14–30/6/14	(91 ÷ 365) × (€1.30 ÷ €2.00)	70,000	11,344
Total weighted-average number of ordinary shares			284,084

Basic EPS therefore is €800,000 ÷ 284,084 = €2.816

19.2.1 Adjustment for the effect of discontinued operations

To address the issues associated with discontinued operations, we need first to consider the contents of IFRS 5 *Non-current Assets Held for Sale and Discontinued Operations*. A discontinued operation is defined in the Appendix to IFRS 5 as:

> *A component of an entity that either has been disposed of or is classified as held for sale and:*
>
> *(a) represents a separate major line of business or geographical area of operations;*
> *(b) is part of a single co-ordinated plan to dispose of a separate major line of business or geographical area of operations; or*
> *(c) is a subsidiary acquired exclusively with a view to resale.*

Pursuant to IFRS 5, in the presence of a discontinued operation, an entity must disclose the profit or loss from continuing operations separately from the profit or loss from discontinued operations. Detailed disclosure requirements relating to the separate disclosure of results for continuing and discontinuing operations are provided in paragraphs 33 to 36 of IFRS 5.

If an entity has a *discontinued operation* this has implications for EPS disclosures (hence the relevance of IFRS 5 to this chapter). If an entity is required to separately disclose results from discontinued operations pursuant to IFRS 5, two EPS figures must be calculated and disclosed pursuant to IAS 33. Specifically, in relation to basic EPS, paragraph 9 of IAS 33 states:

> *An entity shall calculate basic earnings per share amounts for profit or loss attributable to ordinary equity holders of the parent entity and, if presented, profit or loss from continuing operations attributable to those equity holders.*

Hence, IAS 33 requires the disclosure of two basic EPS figures (as well as two diluted EPS figures, as we will see later). The methods to be used to calculate the two basic EPS figures are:

$$\text{Basic EPS} = \frac{\text{Basic earnings, based upon Total profit}}{\text{Basic weighted-average number of ordinary shares}}$$

$$\text{Basic EPS} = \frac{\text{Basic earnings, based upon Profit from continuing operations}}{\text{Basic weighted-average number of ordinary shares}}$$

If there are no discontinued operations, only the top EPS figure needs to be disclosed. Worked Example 19.2 provides an example incorporating discontinued operations.

Worked Example 19.2 — Calculation of basic EPS in the presence of discontinued operations

The statements of comprehensive income of Keet plc and Keet Group (comprising Keet plc and its subsidiaries) for the financial year ending 30 June 2015 are as follows:

Statements of comprehensive income of Keet plc and Keet Group for the year ended 30 June 2015	Keet plc £	Keet plc and its subsidiaries £
Income	95,920,000	483,210,000
Expenses (excluding borrowing costs)	(83,840,000)	(352,890,000)
Borrowing costs	(2,730,000)	(52,470,000)
Profit before income tax expense	9,350,000	77,850,000
Income tax expense	(3,740,000)	(31,140,000)
Profit from continuing operations after income tax expense	5,610,000	46,710,000
Profit (Loss) from discontinuing operations after related income tax	510,000	(1,230,000)
Profit after income tax	6,120,000	45,480,000
Attributable to:		
Owners of the parent		41,220,000
Non-controlling interests		4,260,000
		45,480,000

▶

Notes to and forming part of the financial statements	Keet plc £	Keet plc and its subsidiaries £
Note x: Retained earnings		
Retained earnings—1 July 2014	5,160,000	50,940,000
Profit after income tax	6,120,000	
Profit attributable to members of the parent entity		41,220,000
Interim dividend—ordinary shares	(1,520,000)	(1,520,000)
Final dividend—ordinary shares	(1,640,000)	(1,640,000)
Dividends—preference shares	(900,000)	(900,000)
Retained earnings—30 June 2015	7,220,000	88,100,000

Additional information

(i) On 30 June 2014 the share capital of Keet plc comprised:

Share class	Number of shares on issue	Share capital £
Ordinary	11,500,000	27,630,000
Preference	1,500,000	15,000,000
Total	13,000,000	42,630,000

(ii) During the financial year ending on 30 June 2015, Keet plc made the following share issues:

Date of share issue	Class of share issue	Details relating to share issue
15 September 2014	Ordinary	Private placement of 1,200,000 partly paid shares. The partly paid shares were issued for £7.50, which was the current share price at the time of issue. An amount of £2.80 was payable on allotment, and the balance of £4.70 is payable on 15 September 2016. The partly paid shares rank for (are entitled to participate in) dividends from 15 March 2015. The partly paid shares will entitle shareholders to receive 30 per cent of the dividends received by fully paid ordinary shareholders.
27 November 2014	Ordinary	Public issue of 2,000,000 fully paid shares. The subscription price for the public issue shares was £8.05, which was the current share price at the time of issue.
8 February 2015	Preference	Private placement of 800,000 fully paid shares, issued at the current share price at the time of issue.
12 April 2015	Ordinary	Share buyback of 650,000 fully paid ordinary shares, purchased at the current share price at the time of purchase of £8.30.

(iii) The preference shares entitle shareholders to receive an annual fixed dividend of 12 per cent on share capital, payable in two half-yearly instalments on 31 March and 30 September each year (i.e. 6 per cent on share capital every half year). The preference share dividends are cumulative.

(iv) The dividend due to preference shareholders on 31 March 2015 was not paid.

◀

Required

Calculate basic earnings per share for the financial year ended 30 June 2015, in accordance with the requirements of IAS 33.

Solution

Calculation of basic earnings

Profit attributable to members of the parent entity	41,220,000
less Preference share dividends—30 September 2014	(900,000)
less Cumulative preference dividends not paid or provided for—31 March 2015 (£15,000,000 x 0.06)	(900,000)
Basic earnings, based upon total profit	39,420,000
add Loss from discontinuing operations after related income tax	1,230,000
Basic earnings, based upon profit from continuing operations	40,650,000

Period	Proportion of year	Number of shares outstanding	Weighted average
Fully paid ordinary shares 1/7/14–26/11/14 (shares in place at beginning of year)	149 ÷ 365	11,500,000	4,694,520
27/11/14–11/4/15 (share issue)	137 ÷ 365	13,500,000	5,067,124
12/4/15–30/6/15 (share buy-back)	79 ÷ 365	12,850,000	2,781,233
	365 days		
Partly paid ordinary shares 15/3/15–30/6/15	(108 ÷ 365) x 0.30	1,200,000	106,520
Total weighted-average number of ordinary shares			12,649,397

Calculation of basic EPS, based upon profit from continuing operations

$$\text{Basic EPS} = \frac{\text{Basic earnings, based upon Profit from continuing operations}}{\text{Basic weighted-average number of shares}}$$

$$= \frac{40,650,000}{12,649,397} = £3.21 \text{ per share}$$

Calculation of basic EPS, based upon total profit

$$\text{Basic EPS} = \frac{\text{Basic earnings, based upon Total profit}}{\text{Basic weighted-average number of shares}}$$

$$= \frac{39,420,000}{12,649,397} = £3.12 \text{ per share}$$

In the balance of this chapter we will assume that the entities in our worked examples do not have discontinued operations, and therefore separate figures for EPS based on continuing operations (separate from a figure based on total profits) will not need to be calculated. However, you will need to keep in mind that, if the entity does have discontinued operations, two calculations for basic EPS will be required.

19.2.2 Adjustment for the bonus element in an issue of ordinary shares

A **bonus issue** will have an impact on the weighted-average number of ordinary shares. Assume, for example, that for the year ending 30 June 2015 Greenmount plc has earnings after tax of €500,000. On 1 July 2014 the company has 400,000 shares on issue and on 1 June 2015 it gives a one-for-four bonus issue, funded out of retained earnings. That is, for every four shares held, the shareholder receives one more at no cost. The last sale price of the shares is €3.50.

> **bonus issue** When shareholders are given extra shares at no cost in proportion to their shareholding. A bonus issue is usually funded from retained profits and has no net effect on owners' equity.

The bonus issue does not change total shareholders' funds. It simply involves a transfer from retained earnings to share capital (assuming the bonus share issue is funded from retained earnings). The accounting standard requires for the purposes of calculating EPS that the number of shares outstanding before the bonus issue should be increased as if the bonus had been in place for the entire year (which also has the effect of reducing EPS). As paragraphs 27 and 28 of IAS 33 state:

27. *Ordinary shares may be issued, or the number of ordinary shares outstanding may be reduced, without a corresponding change in resources. Examples include:*

    (a) a capitalisation or bonus issue (sometimes referred to as a stock dividend);
    (b) a bonus element in any other issue, for example a bonus element in a rights issue to existing shareholders;
    (c) a share split; and
    (d) a reverse share split (consolidation of shares).

28. *In a capitalisation or bonus issue or a share split, ordinary shares are issued to existing shareholders for no additional consideration. Therefore, the number of ordinary shares outstanding is increased without an increase in resources. The number of ordinary shares outstanding before the event is adjusted for the proportionate change in the number of ordinary shares outstanding as if the event had occurred at the beginning of the earliest period presented. For example, on a two-for-one bonus issue, the number of ordinary shares outstanding before the issue is multiplied by three to obtain the new total number of ordinary shares, or by two to obtain the number of additional ordinary shares.*

For example, if there is a one-for-one bonus issue (for every share held, the shareholder receives another share at no cost), the number of shares would double. Given that there is no effect on earnings, doubling the number of shares (hence doubling the denominator) will halve the EPS. Prior period comparatives for EPS are also adjusted for the bonus issue so that comparisons are made *as if* the bonus shares had also been issued in the previous period. Otherwise, it could appear that the performance of the entity had worsened.

The adjustment factor for a bonus element is reproduced in Exhibit 19.2.

Exhibit 19.2 **Adjustment factor for EPS in respect of the bonus element in an issue of ordinary shares**

The adjustment factor in respect of a bonus issue or a rights issue in the current financial year is usually determined using the following variables and formulas.

P_0 = last sale price or, if higher, the last bid price cum rights*

N_0 = the number of ordinary shares required for one right

P_r = the subscription price of the right (or the present value of the subscription price in the case of a subscription payable in instalments) plus the present value of dividends forgone in respect of ordinary shares required for one right not presently participating in dividends

$$P_x = \text{theoretical ex-rights price}$$
$$= \frac{(P_0 \times N_0) + P_r}{N_0 + 1}$$

Adjustment factor = $P_x \div P_0$

■ To adjust earnings per share for the current financial year, divide the weighted-average number of ordinary shares prior to the rights or other issue by the adjustment factor.

■ To adjust earnings per share for the prior financial years, multiply the amount of earnings per share by the adjustment factor.

*'bid price cum rights' means the price that would be paid for a share that entitles the holder to participate in the bonus issue.

The formulae assume that prices fully adjust for the bonus issue, so that the shareholders are no better or worse off following the issue. As we know, a bonus issue has no direct effect on the net assets of a company (one owners' equity account—share capital—is increased, while another owners' equity account—typically retained earnings—is decreased), so in a sense it appears reasonable that the value of an individual's investment in the company would not change.

For example, assume that Rob Greenmount has 30,000 shares in Greenmount plc before the bonus issue. Based on the price before the bonus issue, the value of the holding would have been £105,000 (which is 30,000 × £3.50). Following the issue, Rob Greenmount would have held 37,500 shares (which is 30,000 × 5 ÷ 4). The value of Rob's holding using the theoretical price would have been 37,500—multiplied by £2.80, or £105,000. That is, it is the same as it was before the bonus issue. In terms of the total **market capitalisation** of the firm, which is calculated by multiplying the total number of issued shares by their market price, a bonus issue should, according to the formula, have no effect. That is, if there were 400,000 shares on issue before the bonus issue, the market capitalisation should be £1.4 million (400,000 × £3.50). After the bonus issue, there would be 500,000 shares on issue. The market capitalisation of these shares would be assumed to be 500,000 multiplied by £2.80, which also equals £1.4 million.

> **market capitalisation**
> The total value of a firm's securities computed by multiplying the current market value of each security by the number of securities issued by the entity.

If shares are issued at the prevailing market price there is no bonus element and no adjustment would be necessary.

For Greenmount plc, the theoretical ex-bonus issue price would be determined by applying the formula:

$$\frac{(P_0 \times N_0) + P_r}{N_0 + 1}$$

As there is no issue price (that is, they are bonus shares with no required payment), the theoretical price would be:

$$\frac{(£3.50 \times 4) + 0}{4 + 1} = £2.80$$

Note that, as the illustrative examples in IAS 33 show, another way to express the calculation of the theoretical ex-rights price is by using the equation:

$$\frac{\left(\begin{array}{c}\text{Aggregate market price per share} \\ \text{immediately prior to exercise of rights}\end{array}\right) + \left(\begin{array}{c}\text{Proceeds from the} \\ \text{exercise of rights}\end{array}\right)}{\text{Number of shares outstanding after the exercise of rights}}$$

For Greenmount plc, this would equal:

$$[(400,000 \times £3.50) + 0] \div 500,000 = £2.80$$

There is some evidence, however, that the total market capitalisation of a firm might indeed alter following a bonus issue. The reasons for this are not clear. Drawing upon the research of others, Whittred and Zimmer (1992, p. 58) state:

> *The economic reasons for share splits or bonus issues are not well understood. Since neither has any direct implications for a firm's investment policy or future cash flows, such actions should have no effect on a firm's value. After all, the firm's assets are not worth any more after the bonus or split than they were beforehand. Yet, somewhat surprisingly, empirical evidence suggests that a firm's share price increases following both share splits and bonus issues. One possible explanation for this is that, at the same time, firms often announce a dividend increase. For example, the maintenance of the same nominal percentage on an increased number of shares increases total dividends paid. (The evidence in Ball, Brown and Finn (1977) suggests that approximately 92 per cent of bonus issues and 53 per cent of share splits are accompanied by subsequent dividend increases.) Indeed, the evidence also suggests that when these capitalisation changes are not accompanied by dividend increases there is no impact on share price. While this information effect of dividends hypothesis is appealing, the question still arises as to why it is necessary for a dividend increase to be announced in this way.*

Returning to Greenmount plc, the *adjustment factor* would be £2.80 ÷ £3.50 = 0.80. This requires the weighted-average number of shares in place before the issue to be divided by 0.80, thereby inflating the number of shares, and decreasing the EPS. Worked Example 19.3 examines the calculation of EPS in the presence of a bonus issue.

Worked Example 19.3	Calculation of EPS in the presence of a bonus issue

For the year ending 30 June 2015, Redgrave River plc reports a net profit after tax of £700,000.

At the beginning of the year, Redgrave River plc had 500,000 fully paid ordinary shares on issue. It also had 200,000 £1.00, 10 per cent, cumulative preference shares outstanding. The preference shares were classified as equity.

On 1 September 2014 the company issued a further 100,000 fully paid ordinary shares. On 1 May 2015 the company issued another 100,000 fully paid shares on the basis of a one-for-six bonus issue. The last sale price per ordinary share prior to the bonus issue was £4.00.

The basic EPS for the year ending 30 June 2014 was £2.10.

Required

Compute the basic EPS amount for 2015 and provide the adjusted comparative EPS for 2014.

Solution

Earnings calculation

Profit after tax	£700,000
less Preference share dividends	(£20,000)
Profit after tax less preference dividends	£680,000

$$\text{Theoretical ex-bonus price} = \frac{(£4.00)(6) + 0}{6 + 1}$$
$$= £3.4286$$
$$\text{Adjustment factor} = £3.4286 \div 4.00$$
$$= 0.8571$$

Calculation of the weighted-average number of ordinary shares and ordinary share equivalents

Period	Proportion of year	Multiply by number of shares outstanding	Divide by adjustment factor	Weighted average
Fully paid ordinary shares				
1/7/14–31/8/14	62 ÷ 365	500,000	0.8571	99,092
1/9/14–30/4/15	242 ÷ 365	600,000	0.8571	464,133
1/5/15–30/6/15	61 ÷ 365	700,000		116,986
	365			680,211

Basic earnings per share for 2015 would be:

$$£680,000 \div 680,211 = £0.9997$$

The comparative figures for 2014 would be adjusted for the bonus issue. The adjusted figure would be:

$$£2.10 \times 0.8571 = £1.80$$

Failure to adjust previous period's earnings per share would be misleading, as it would appear that the company is not performing as well as it had in the previous period, when in fact the reduction in EPS might be due totally to the bonus issue. Note that, for the current periods in which the bonus issue is made, we adjust the weighted-average number of shares by dividing by the adjustment factor for the period prior to the bonus issue. For the prior financial period, we multiply EPS by the adjustment factor.

19.2.3 Rights issue

Existing shareholders might be provided with rights to acquire additional shares in the company at a price below the current market price of the firm's shares. In a **rights issue**, if the exercise price is less than the market price of the shares, the rights issue includes a *bonus element*. For example, Bombo plc might issue a one-for-three rights issue, which requires the holders of the rights to pay £0.80 to acquire an additional share. If those shares were trading in the market at £1.00 before the rights issue, there would be a bonus element of £0.20. The accounting standard requires that, whenever there is a bonus element, the weighted-average number of shares needs to be adjusted using the formula provided above.

For Bombo plc the theoretical ex-rights price—that is, the value of shares without the rights—would be calculated using the formula:

$$\frac{(P_o \times N_o) + P_r}{N_o + 1}$$

and the theoretical price would be:

$$\frac{(£1.00 \times 3) + 0.80}{3 + 1} = £0.95$$

That is, without a £0.20 bonus element, spread over three shares plus the bonus share, share purchasers would be prepared to pay only £0.95 per share. Worked Example 19.4 looks at calculating EPS in the presence of a rights issue with a bonus element.

> **rights issue** An entitlement provided to shareholders giving them the right or option to buy shares in the entity at a future time at a specific price.

Worked Example 19.4 — Calculation of EPS in the presence of a rights issue with a bonus element

For the year ending 30 June 2015, Sandon plc reports net profit after tax of €500,000.

At the beginning of the year, Sandon plc had 800,000 fully paid ordinary shares. It also had 100,000 €1.00, 10 per cent, cumulative preference shares outstanding. The preference shares were classified as equity. On 1 September 2014 the company issued another 200,000 fully paid ordinary shares by way of a rights issue. The right provided an additional share for each four held, and required the payment of €1.50. The last cum rights share price was €2.00.

The basic EPS for the year ended 30 June 2014 was €1.95.

Required

Compute the basic EPS amount for 2015, and provide the adjusted comparative EPS for 2014.

Solution

Earnings calculation

Profit after tax	€500,000
less Preference share dividends	(€10,000)
Profit after tax less preference dividends	€490,000

$$\text{Theoretical ex-bonus price} = \frac{(€2.00)(4) + €1.50}{4 + 1}$$
$$= €1.90$$
$$\text{Adjustment factor} = €1.90 \div €2.00$$
$$= 0.95$$

Calculation of the weighted-average number of ordinary shares and ordinary share equivalents

Period	Proportion of year	Number of shares outstanding	Adjustment factor	Weighted average
Fully paid ordinary shares				
1/7/14–31/8/14	62 ÷ 365	800,000	0.95	143,043
1/9/14–30/6/15	$\underline{303 \div 365}$	1,000,000		$\underline{830,137}$
	$\underline{365}$			$\underline{973,180}$

Basic earnings per share for 2015 would be:

$$€490,000 \div 973,180 = €0.5035$$

The comparative figures for 2014 would be adjusted for the rights issue. The adjusted figure would be:

$$€1.95 \times 0.95 = €1.853$$

Again, remember that, in calculating the weighted-average number of shares for the period before the rights issue, we divide by the adjustment factor. After the date of the rights issue, no adjustment is necessary. For comparison with the previous year, we multiply the previous EPS figure by the adjustment factor.

19.3 Diluted earnings per share

IAS 33 also requires that diluted EPS should be calculated and disclosed, together with basic EPS, on the face of the statement of comprehensive income. As we indicated earlier in this chapter, paragraph 66 of IAS 33 states:

> *An entity shall present on the face of the statement of comprehensive income basic and diluted earnings per share for profit or loss from continuing operations attributable to the ordinary equity holders of the parent entity and for profit or loss attributable to the ordinary equity holders of the parent entity for the period for each class of ordinary shares that has a different right to share in profit for the period. An entity shall present basic and diluted earnings per share with equal prominence for all periods presented.*

As indicated above, and previously in this chapter, if an entity has *discontinued operations*, disclosure must be made of basic and diluted EPS attributable to profit or loss from continuing operations *as well as* basic and diluted EPS attributable to total profit or loss. In relation to the specific disclosures relating to discontinued operations, paragraph 68 of IAS 33 states:

> *An entity that reports a discontinued operation shall disclose the basic and diluted amounts per share for the discontinued operation either on the face of the statement of comprehensive income or in the notes to the financial statements.*

In the examples that follow we will assume that the entities do not have discontinued operations. However, we should remember that, if they did, two sets of calculations for basic EPS and diluted EPS would need to be made.

IAS 33 requires that diluted EPS be calculated where an *entity* has on issue **potential ordinary shares** that are *dilutive*. Specifically, paragraph 31 of IAS 33 states:

potential ordinary shares An issued security that potentially converts into an ordinary share or results in the calling in of or subscription for ordinary share capital.

> *For the purpose of calculating diluted earnings per share, an entity shall adjust profit or loss attributable to ordinary equity holders of the parent entity, and the weighted average number of shares outstanding, for the effects of all dilutive potential ordinary shares.*

Clearly, we need a definition of 'potential ordinary share' and an indication of when a potential ordinary share can be considered 'dilutive'. A potential ordinary share is defined in paragraph 5 of IAS 33 as, 'a financial instrument or other contract that may entitle its holder to ordinary shares'. According to IAS 33, potential ordinary shares are considered dilutive when and only when the conversion to, calling of or subscription for ordinary shares would decrease (or increase) net profit (or loss) from continuing ordinary operations per share.

The view taken within the accounting standard is that, if there are some securities currently on issue that might be converted to ordinary shares (for example, convertible preference shares, share options or convertible bonds), this will increase the number of ordinary shares on issue, and by increasing the denominator used in determining EPS, this can lead to a decrease in EPS. It is considered that users of financial statements need to know about this potential reduction (or dilution) in EPS. The calculation referred to as 'diluted earnings per share' will show how EPS would fall *if* the potential ordinary shares were actually converted to ordinary shares. That is, diluted EPS is a 'what if' measure in the sense that it shows the extent to which basic EPS would be diluted *if* potential ordinary shares were actually converted to ordinary shares. This helps to inform investors about how EPS *could* conceivably be affected in the future.

To determine diluted EPS, the weighted-average number of shares is determined in accordance with the calculations provided above for basic EPS, with the inclusion of an additional factor based on the weighted-average number of *potential ordinary shares* that the company had on issue throughout all or part of the financial year.

There is a general rule that, if a potential ordinary share issue would increase EPS (that is, it is 'antidilutive'), it is not considered to be *dilutive* and would be excluded from the calculation of diluted EPS. Each type of potential ordinary share (for example, convertible preference shares, convertible notes and share options) must be considered separately. Consideration must also be given to the probability of conversion. If the conversion is at the option of the entity, and the conversion is probable, the potential ordinary shares must be included in the diluted EPS calculation, even if their inclusion does not dilute EPS. It should be noted that, if conversion of the potential ordinary shares to ordinary shares is mandatory, they must already have been included in the calculation of basic EPS.

We will now consider how to determine *earnings* and the *weighted-average number of shares* for the purpose of calculating diluted EPS. As we will see, there are differences relative to the earnings and weighted-average number of ordinary shares used to calculate basic EPS.

19.3.1 Calculation of 'earnings' for diluted EPS

In calculating earnings for diluted EPS, we have to consider the effects on earnings in the event of those *potential ordinary shares* that are *dilutive* being converted to ordinary shares. We work out revised earnings *as if* the conversion of the potential ordinary shares had actually occurred. Paragraph 33 of IAS 33 requires that, for the purposes of calculating diluted EPS, we start with basic EPS and make adjustments for the after-tax effect of:

(a) *any dividends or other items related to dilutive potential ordinary shares deducted in arriving at profit or loss attributable to ordinary equity holders of the parent entity as calculated in accordance with paragraph 12;*
(b) *any interest recognised in the period related to dilutive potential ordinary shares; and*
(c) *any other changes in income or expense that would result from the conversion of the dilutive potential ordinary shares.*

As paragraph 32 of IAS 33 explains:

The object of diluted earnings per share is consistent with that of basic earnings per share, to provide a measure of the interest of each ordinary share in the performance of an entity, while giving effect to all dilutive potential ordinary shares outstanding during the period. As a result:

(a) *profit or loss attributable to ordinary equity holders of the parent entity is increased by the after-tax amount of dividends and interest recognised in the period in respect of the dilutive potential ordinary shares and is adjusted for any other changes in income or expense that would result from the conversion of the dilutive potential ordinary shares; and*
(b) *the weighted average number of ordinary shares outstanding is increased by the weighted average number of additional ordinary shares that would have been outstanding assuming the conversion of all dilutive potential ordinary shares.*

The conversion of potential ordinary shares might also have a number of flow-on effects. As paragraph 35 of IAS 33 states:

The conversion of potential ordinary shares may lead to consequential changes in income or expenses. For example, the reduction of interest expense related to potential ordinary shares and the resulting increase in profit or reduction in loss may lead to an increase in the expense related to a non-discretionary employee profit-sharing plan. For the purpose of calculating diluted earnings per share, profit or loss attributable to ordinary equity holders of the parent entity is adjusted for any such consequential changes in income or expense.

19.3.2 Calculating the weighted-average number of shares for diluted EPS

IAS 33 requires that, in determining the weighted-average number of shares for diluted EPS, we start with the number used to calculate basic EPS and proceed by making adjustments to this number. Specifically, we add the following:

- the weighted-average number of shares deemed to be issued for no consideration; and
- the weighted-average number of shares that are contingently issued.

The dilutive potential ordinary shares are weighted by the number of days they were outstanding. Dilutive potential ordinary shares that have been issued since the beginning of the reporting period and remain outstanding at the end of the reporting period are weighted by reference to the number of days from their date of issue to the end of the reporting period. Further explanation is necessary in relation to the two adjustment steps just listed.

Shares deemed to be issued for no consideration

Shares would be deemed to be issued for no consideration if the price to be paid for the shares is less than the market price. If the price to be paid is greater than the market price, rational investors would not be expected to make the payment (they would simply buy the share directly from the market) and the potential ordinary shares can be ignored for determining diluted EPS. Their conversion would not be probable. In relation to shares deemed to be issued for no consideration, paragraphs 46 and 47 of IAS 33 state:

46. *Options and warrants are dilutive when they would result in the issue of ordinary shares for less than the average market price of ordinary shares during the period. The amount of the dilution is the average market price of ordinary shares during the period minus the issue price. Therefore, to calculate diluted earnings per share, potential ordinary shares are treated as consisting of both the following:*
    (a) *a contract to issue a certain number of the ordinary shares at their average market price during the period. Such ordinary shares are assumed to be fairly priced and to be neither dilutive nor antidilutive. They are ignored in the calculation of diluted earnings per share; and*
    (b) *a contract to issue the remaining ordinary shares for no consideration. Such ordinary shares generate no proceeds and have no effect on profit or loss attributable to ordinary shares outstanding. Therefore, such shares are dilutive and are added to the number of ordinary shares outstanding in the calculation of diluted earnings per share.*
47. *Options and warrants have a dilutive effect only when the average market price of ordinary shares during the period exceeds the exercise price of the options or warrants (i.e. they are 'in-the-money'). Previously reported earnings per share are not retroactively adjusted to reflect changes in prices of ordinary shares.*

If an entity has issued options, the option holders will pay the exercise price only if they are effectively getting some shares for no consideration. Assume, for example, that a company has issued 1,000 options that have an exercise price of €2 each. If we assume the market price of the shares subsequently increases to €2.50 per share, the exercise price is less than the market price (the options are referred to as being 'in the money') and the options would be expected to be exercised. The option holders would pay 1,000 × €2, which equals €2,000, and receive 1,000 shares. The number of shares that they would have acquired for €2,000 if they had paid the market price of €2.50 would be 800. Effectively, the number of shares issued for no consideration is 200. This number is added to the number of ordinary shares (to the denominator) in the computation of EPS. Any assumed earnings from the inflow of the €2,000 are not added to the numerator (that is, any such amount is not added to earnings).

We also need to consider partly paid shares. As we know, if partly paid shares are entitled to participate in dividends in proportion to their paid-up amount, they would already be included in the weighted-average number of shares used to calculate basic EPS. Paragraph A16 of IAS 33 requires that:

To the extent that partly paid shares are not entitled to participate in dividends during the period they are treated as the equivalent of warrants or options in the calculation of diluted earnings per share. The unpaid balance is assumed to represent proceeds used to purchase ordinary shares. The number of shares included in diluted earnings per share is the difference between the number of shares subscribed and the number of shares assumed to be purchased.

Contingently issuable shares

According to paragraph 5 of IAS 33, contingently issuable ordinary shares are ordinary shares issuable for little or no cash or other consideration upon the satisfaction of specified conditions in a contingent share agreement. A contingent share agreement is an agreement to issue shares that is dependent upon the satisfaction of specified conditions. For example, Company A might have acquired Company B, with the consideration for B's shares being shares in Company A. There might be an agreement to issue further shares in Company A if the share price of Company B exceeds a certain level for a specified period (perhaps a few months) before a specified time (within two years of the acquisition of Company B perhaps). If the price of Company B's shares exceeds this price at year end, the shares would be included in the denominator, provided that the price is

expected to remain above the minimum threshold for the required period of time. As paragraph 52 of IAS 33 states:

> *As in the calculation of basic earnings per share, contingently issuable ordinary shares are treated as outstanding and included in the calculation of diluted earnings per share if the conditions are satisfied (i.e. the events have occurred). Contingently issuable shares are included from the beginning of the period (or from the date of the contingent share agreement, if later). If the conditions are not satisfied, the number of contingently issuable shares included in the diluted earnings per share calculation is based on the number of shares that would be issuable if the end of the period were the end of the contingency period. Restatement is not permitted if the conditions are not met when the contingency period expires.*

Worked Example 19.5 considers an example of calculating diluted EPS.

Worked Example 19.5 — Calculation of basic and diluted EPS

For the year ending 30 June 2015, Lennox plc earns a profit after tax of €1.05 million. Dividends on 400,000 convertible, cumulative preference shares amount to €200,000. The preference dividends are not treated as expenses in the financial statements of Lennox plc (the preference shares have been disclosed as equity in the statement of financial position). As at 1 July 2014 there were 500,000 fully paid ordinary shares. There were no additional share issues during the year.

As at 1 July 2014 there were also:

- €250,000 in convertible debentures, which paid interest at a rate of 10 per cent per year, and which could be converted to 125,000 ordinary shares, at the option of the debenture holder;
- 20,000 share options currently on issue, with an exercise price of €2.00; and
- the 400,000 convertible, cumulative preference shares, which were issued in 2013 and are convertible into 120,000 ordinary shares at the option of the preference shareholders.
  Assume the tax rate is 33 per cent and that the average market price for ordinary shares during the year was €5.

Required

Calculate Lennox plc's:

(a) basic EPS
(b) diluted EPS

Solution

(a) Basic EPS for Lennox plc

Profit after tax	€1,050,000
less Preference dividends	(€200,000)
Profit after tax and preference dividends	€850,000

Basic EPS = €850,000 ÷ 500,000
          = €1.70 per share

(b) Diluted EPS for Lennox plc

We need to consider the securities that are potential ordinary shares. The convertible debentures, options and convertible preference shares are potentially dilutive. Each security must be considered separately.

Convertible debentures

If the debentures are converted to ordinary shares, the pre-tax earnings would be increased by €25,000 (the interest expense that would no longer be payable = €250,000 x 10%). This would lead to an after-tax increase in earnings of €16,750, which is €25,000 x (1 − 0.33).

As an additional 125,000 shares would be created, the increase in earnings attributable to ordinary shareholders on conversion of the convertible debentures would, on an incremental share basis, be:

$$€16,750 ÷ 125,000 = €0.134$$

Share options

As the options have been on issue for the entire year, we treat them as potentially dilutive as of the beginning of the year. If the options had been exercised, the company would have received €40,000. Obviously such a fund inflow could have earned a return for the company. Should this be factored into a consideration of any increase in earnings? IAS 33 does not consider such earnings—that is, it does not consider *notional earnings* on fund inflows. With such returns ignored, the exercise of the options will not cause any increase in earnings. The standard requires that we consider the number of shares that would effectively be issued for *no consideration* if these options are exercised. To determine this we perform the following calculation:

Number of shares issuable	20,000
Number of shares that would be issued at market price for the actual proceeds of €40,000 = €40,000 ÷ €5	8,000
Number of shares deemed issued for no consideration	12,000

Given that there is no adjustment to earnings recognised in relation to the options, the earnings per incremental share are €nil. Twelve thousand shares will be added to the denominator to calculate diluted EPS.

Convertible, cumulative preference shares

If the preference shares are converted, dividends of €200,000 would be saved. Their conversion would lead to an increase in ordinary shares by 120,000. The increase in earnings per incremental share (because the preference share dividends were initially excluded when calculating EPS) would be €200,000/120,000 = €1.667.

Ranking the potential ordinary shares from greatest to least dilution

IAS 33 requires that, when we consider whether potential ordinary shares are dilutive, each issue or series of potential ordinary shares must be considered separately, rather than in aggregate. Each issue or series of potential ordinary shares must be considered in sequence from the most dilutive (smallest earnings per incremental share) to the least dilutive (largest earnings per incremental share). As paragraph 44 of IAS 33 states:

> *In determining whether potential ordinary shares are dilutive or antidilutive, each issue or series of potential ordinary shares is considered separately rather than in aggregate. The sequence in which potential ordinary shares are considered may affect whether they are dilutive. Therefore, to maximise the dilution of basic earnings per share, each issue or series of potential ordinary shares is considered in sequence from the most dilutive to the least dilutive, that is, dilutive potential ordinary shares with the lowest 'earnings per incremental share' are included in the diluted earnings per share calculation before those with a higher earnings per incremental share. Options and warrants are generally included first because they do not affect the numerator of the calculation.*

In this example, the order from most dilutive to least dilutive is:

	Increase in shares	Earnings per incremental share
Options	12,000	€nil
Convertible debentures	125,000	€0.134
Convertible preference shares	120,000	€1.667

The sequence in which potential ordinary shares are considered might affect whether or not they are dilutive. If potential ordinary shares are not dilutive, the standard generally requires that they be ignored when calculating diluted EPS.

Determining the 'trigger test'

IAS 33 includes a 'trigger test' to determine whether potential ordinary shares are dilutive. If the shares cause EPS to decrease from the initial amount determined for the trigger test, they are considered dilutive. The

standard uses profit or loss from *continuing operations* attributable to the parent entity as the initial amount for the trigger test to determine whether potential ordinary shares are dilutive.

The profit or loss from *continuing operations* attributable to the parent entity is defined as excluding amounts relating to discontinuing operations.

Profit used to calculate basic EPS	€850,000
less Adjustments	€nil
Net profit from *continuing operations* for the trigger test	€850,000

€850,000 ÷ 500,000 = €1.70

As previously noted, IAS 33 requires that diluted EPS be presented on the face of the statement of comprehensive income. It must be disclosed with the same prominence as basic EPS.

Applying the 'trigger test'

We have already determined the order in which to include potential ordinary shares in the calculation of diluted EPS.

	Profit and adjustments	Ordinary shares	EPS	Dilutive?
Net profit from continuing operations	€850,000	500,000	€1.70	
Options	Nil	12,000		
	€850,000	512,000	€1.6602	Yes
Convertible debentures	€16,750	125,000		
	€866,750	637,000	€1.3607	Yes
Convertible preference shares	€200,000	120,000		
	€1,066,750	757,000	€1.4092	No*

*EPS from continuing operations increases from €1.3607 to €1.4092 when the convertible preference shares are included, so they are not dilutive.

In the above calculation, profit or loss from continuing operations is the starting point in the trigger test. After this point, each potential ordinary share is considered in order of smallest earnings per incremental share to largest earnings per incremental share. If a particular security does not dilute EPS, it is not to be included when calculating diluted EPS.

Calculation of diluted EPS

While net profit from *continuing operations* is used to assess whether or not potential ordinary shares are dilutive, IAS 33 requires that net profit or loss be used in the calculation of diluted EPS. As noted above, the earnings figure used in the actual calculation of diluted EPS includes discontinuing operations, adjustments for changes in accounting policies and corrections of material errors. As with basic EPS, the preference dividends paid are excluded.

	Profit	Ordinary shares
As reported for basic EPS	€850,000	500,000
Options	€nil	12,000
Convertible debentures	€16,750	125,000
	€866,750	637,000

Diluted EPS = €866,750 ÷ 637,000 = €1.3607.

Again, as the preference shares are not dilutive, they are not included in the calculation of diluted EPS.

In Exhibit 19.3, note 11 from the annual report of Deutsche Bank is provided. This note shows the calculations made to determine the bank's basic and diluted earnings per share.

Exhibit 19.3 Deutsche Bank – Note on Earnings Per Share

11– Earnings per Common Share

Basic earnings per common share amounts are computed by dividing net income (loss) attributable to Deutsche Bank shareholders by the average number of common shares outstanding during the year. The average number of common shares outstanding is defined as the average number of common shares issued, reduced by the average number of shares in treasury and by the average number of shares that will be acquired under physically-settled forward purchase contracts, and increased by undistributed vested shares awarded under deferred share plans.

Diluted earnings per share assumes the conversion into common shares of outstanding securities or other contracts to issue common stock, such as share options, convertible debt, unvested deferred share awards and forward contracts. The aforementioned instruments are only included in the calculation of diluted earnings per share if they are dilutive in the respective reporting period.

In December 2008, the Group decided to amend existing forward purchase contracts covering 33.6 million Deutsche Bank common shares from physical to net-cash settlement and these instruments are no longer included in the computation of basic and diluted earnings per share.

The following table presents the computation of basic and diluted earnings per share for the years ended December 31, 2010, 2009 and 2008, respectively.

in € m.	2010	2009	2008
Net income (loss) attributable to Deutsche Bank shareholders – numerator for basic earnings per share	**2,310**	**4,973**	**(3,835)**
Effect of dilutive securities			
Forwards and options	–	–	–
Convertible debt	3	2	(1)
Net income (loss) attributable to Deutsche Bank shareholders after assumed conversions – numerator for diluted earnings per share	**2,313**	**4,975**	**(3,836)**
Number of shares in m.			
Weighted-average shares outstanding – denominator for basic earnings per share	**753.3**	**689.4**	**558.5**
Effect of dilutive securities			
Forwards	0.0	0.0	0.0
Employee stock compensation options	0.0	0.1	0.0
Convertible debt	2.1	0.7	0.1
Deferred shares	35.4	26.4	0.0
Other (including trading options)	0.0	0.1	0.0
Dilutive potential common shares	37.5	27.3	0.1

▶

◄

Adjusted weighted-average shares after assumed conversions – denominator for diluted earnings per share	790.8	716.7	558.6
in €	2010	2009	2008
Basic earnings per share	3.07	7.21	(6.87)
Diluted earnings per share	2.92	6.94	(6.87)

On October 6, 2010, Deutsche Bank AG completed a capital increase with subscription rights. As the subscription price of the new shares was lower than the market price of the existing shares, the capital increase included a bonus element. According to IAS 33, the bonus element is the result of an implicit change in the number of shares outstanding for all periods prior to the capital increase without a fully proportionate change in resources. As a consequence, the weighted average number of shares outstanding has been adjusted retrospectively for all periods before October 6, 2010.

Due to the net loss situation, potentially dilutive instruments were generally not considered for the calculation of diluted earnings per share for the year ended December 31, 2008, because to do so would have been antidilutive. Under a net income situation however, the number of adjusted weighted-average shares after assumed conversions for the year ended December 31, 2008 would have increased by 31.2 million shares.

As of December 31, 2010, 2009 and 2008, the following instruments were outstanding and were not included in the calculation of diluted earnings per share, because to do so would have been antidilutive.

Number of shares in m.	2010	2009	2008
Forward purchase contracts	0.0	0.0	0.0
Put options sold	0.0	0.0	0.1
Call options sold	0.0	0.0	0.3
Employee stock compensation options	0.4	0.3	1.8
Deferred shares	0.0	0.0	26.9

SUMMARY

In this chapter we considered various aspects of the calculation and disclosure of earnings per share (EPS). In most countries in Europe listed entities and those in the process of listing are required, pursuant to IAS 33, to disclose information about their EPS within their annual reports. EPS is calculated from the perspective of ordinary shareholders and is determined by dividing the earnings of the company by the weighted-average number of ordinary shares outstanding during the year. In determining earnings for the purposes of calculating EPS, preference share dividends are to be excluded (and if they are cumulative, they are excluded whether or not they are paid).

A number of examples are given of calculating basic EPS, including cases where there is a bonus issue of shares and/or a rights issue. We also considered how to calculate diluted EPS, which is to be disclosed, together with basic EPS, on the face of the statement of comprehensive income. In calculating diluted EPS, the adjusted earnings (calculated on the notional basis that the various securities have actually been converted to ordinary shares) are to be divided by the weighted-average number of ordinary and potential ordinary dilutive shares. Each type of potential ordinary share must be considered separately when calculating diluted EPS. If a particular type of potential ordinary share, for example convertible notes, convertible preference shares or options, is not considered to be dilutive, it should be excluded from the calculation of diluted EPS.

The chapter stressed that care must be taken when comparing various entities' basic and diluted EPS. Given that the calculations are based directly on accounting profits and that accounting profits themselves are heavily dependent upon professional judgement, if different entities employ different accounting recognition and measurement rules, comparison of EPS can be misleading.

KEY TERMS

END-OF-CHAPTER EXERCISE

For the year ending 30 June 2016, Green Island plc reports a net profit after tax of £1,800,000.

At the beginning of the financial year Green Island plc had 500,000 fully paid ordinary shares outstanding. Green Island plc also had 100,000 partly paid shares. These shares were partly paid to 90p and had an original issue price of £2.00. The partly paid shares carry the rights to dividends in proportion to the amount paid relative to the total issue price. They were still partly paid at year end. **LO 19.4**

Apart from the above, Green Island plc also has the following securities outstanding:

- £1 million of 10 per cent debentures issued on 1 August 2015. The debentures have a life of five years and give holders the right to convert the debentures into 400,000 fully paid ordinary shares.
- In 2014 employees were provided with options, at no initial cost, which gave them the right to acquire 250,000 shares at an exercise price of £2.30. The options expire five years after their original issue date. Given the time period to option expiry, the directors believe it is probable that the options will be exercised.
- In 2014 Green Island plc issued 200,000 10 per cent, cumulative dividend preference shares. They were issued at £1.00 each and provide the shareholders with the right to convert each two preference shares into one fully paid ordinary share.

Other information

- The company tax rate is 40 per cent.
- The average market price of the ordinary shares for the financial year is £2.50.

REQUIRED

Compute the amounts for 2016 of Green Island plc's:

(a) basic earnings per share
(b) diluted earnings per share

SOLUTION TO END-OF-CHAPTER EXERCISE

(a) Basic earnings per share for Green Island plc

Profit after tax	£1,800,000
less Preference share dividends	(£20,000)
Profit after tax less preference dividends	£1,780,000

Determining the weighted-average number of ordinary shares

Period	Proportion of year	Number of shares outstanding	Weighted average
Fully paid ordinary shares			
1/7/15–30/6/16	365 ÷ 365	500,000	500,000
Partly paid ordinary shares			
1/7/15–30/6/16	365 ÷ 365	100,000 (£0.90 ÷ £2.00)	45,000
Total weighted-average number of ordinary shares			545,000

Basic earnings per share therefore is £1,780,000 ÷ 545,000 = £3.266

(b) Diluted earnings per share for Green Island plc

As we have noted in this chapter, we need to consider each issue/series separately.

Step 1: Determine earnings per incremental share from the potential ordinary shares

Partly paid shares

Number of ordinary share equivalents issuable (100,000)(£1.10) ÷ £2.00	55,000
Number of shares that would be issued with the proceeds given the average market price (100,000)(£1.10) ÷ £2.50	(44,000)
Number of shares deemed issued for no consideration	11,000

There is no adjustment to earnings for the capital inflow associated with the partly paid shares, and hence the earnings per incremental share are considered to be £nil.

Convertible debentures

If the debentures had been converted, Green Island plc would have saved paying £100,000 in interest. As the debentures were issued during the year, the weighted-average potential ordinary shares will need to be weighted by the number of days in the financial year for which they were issued.

Had the debentures been converted, Green Island plc would have had an after-tax saving of:

$(1,000,000)(10 \text{ per cent})(334 ÷ 365)(1 - 0.40) = £54,904$

Had the conversion been undertaken, the weighted-average ordinary shares from conversion of debentures would have been:

$(400,000)(334 ÷ 365) = 366,027$

The earnings per incremental share is:

$£54,904 ÷ 366,027 = £0.1500$

Options

Number of shares issuable	250,000
Number of shares that would be issued with the proceeds given the average market price (250,000)(£2.30) ÷ £2.50	230,000
Number of shares deemed issued for no consideration	20,000

There is no adjustment to earnings for the capital inflow associated with the partly paid shares, and hence the earnings per incremental share are considered to be £nil.

Convertible preference shares

Had the preference shares been converted, the preference dividend (£20,000) would no longer have been paid. As the preference shares were outstanding for the entire year, the potential ordinary shares will be weighted for the whole year. Earnings per incremental share is:

$£20,000 ÷ 100,000 = £0.20$

Step 2: Rank the potential ordinary shares from greatest dilution (lowest earnings per incremental share) to least dilution (greatest earnings per incremental share)

	Increase in shares	Earnings per incremental share
Options	20,000	£nil
Partly paid shares	11,000	£nil
Convertible debentures	366,027	£0.1500
Convertible preference shares	100,000	£0.2000

Step 3: Compute profit to be used in the trigger test

The profit from continuing operations is used for the trigger test.

Earnings used when calculating basic EPS	£1,780,000
add Adjustments	£nil
Net profit from *continuing operations* to be used for the purpose of the trigger test	£1,780,000

Step 4: Perform the trigger test

	Profit and adjustments (£)	Ordinary shares No.	EPS (£)	Dilutive?
Net profit from continuing operations	1,780,000	545,000	3.2661	
Options	Nil	20,000		
	1,780,000	565,000	3.1504	Yes
Partly paid shares	Nil	11,000		
	1,780,000	576,000	3.0903	Yes
Convertible debentures	54,904	366,027		
	1,834,904	942,027	1.9478	Yes
Convertible preference shares	20,000	100,000		
	1,854,904	1,042,027	1.7801	Yes

Step 5: Compute diluted earnings per share

	Profit (£)	Ordinary shares No.
As reported for basic EPS	1,780,000	545,000
Options	0	20,000
Convertible debentures	54,904	366,027
Convertible preference shares	20,000	100,000
Partly paid shares	0	11,000
	1,854,904	1,042,027

Diluted EPS = £1,854,904 ÷ 1,042,027

= £1.7801

REVIEW QUESTIONS

1 How do we determine: **LO** 19.4
 (a) basic earnings per share?
 (b) diluted earnings per share?

2   How would you determine whether *potential ordinary shares* are dilutive?   **LO 19.3**

3   If there were a 'share split' in the current period, would any adjustment be necessary for the prior period comparative EPS? If so, how would the adjustment be calculated?   **LO 19.2**

4   When should both basic and diluted EPS be disclosed?   **LO 19.4**

5   If there has been a bonus issue in a particular year, do we need to adjust the previous period's EPS for comparative purposes? If so, *how* do we adjust the previous period's EPS?   **LO 19.2**

6   For the year ending 30 June 2016, Granite plc reports the following: **LO 19.1**

   (a) Net profit after tax of £1.2 million.

   (b) Granite plc commenced the year with 400,000 fully paid ordinary shares. During the year the company:
   - issued 80,000 fully paid ordinary shares on 1 November 2015 at the prevailing market price;
   - purchased back 50,000 fully paid ordinary shares on 1 March 2016 at the prevailing market price; and
   - issued 100,000 partly paid ordinary shares on 1 June 2016 at an issue price of £2.00. The shares were partly paid to £1.00. The partly paid shares carry the right to participate in dividends in proportion to the amount paid as a fraction of the issue price.

   (c) For the entire year, Granite plc had 500,000 £1.00 preference shares, which provide dividends at a rate of 10 per cent per year. The dividend rights are cumulative. The preference shares were disclosed as equity.

   REQUIRED

   Compute the basic earnings per share for Granite plc for 2016.

7   For the year ending 30 June 2015, A-Bay plc reports net profit after tax of €1 million.

   At the beginning of the year, A-Bay plc had 600,000 fully paid ordinary shares on issue. It also had 100,000 €1.00, 6 per cent, cumulative preference shares outstanding. On 1 October 2014 the company issued another 150,000 fully paid ordinary shares. On 1 May 2015 the company issued further fully paid shares on the basis of a one-for-five bonus issue. The last sale price per ordinary share before the bonus issue was €3.00.

   The basic EPS for the year ended 30 June 2014 was €2.30.   **LO 19.1**

   REQUIRED

   Compute the basic earnings per share amount for 2015 and provide the adjusted comparative EPS for 2014.

8   X plc has earnings for the year ending 30 June 2015 of €410 million. Outstanding ordinary shares as at 1 July 2014 were 100 million fully paid ordinary shares.   **LO 19.1**

   During the year the company issued 15 million partly paid shares. The information relating to the issue is shown below:

Issue price	€2.00
Paid	€0.50
Closing date	31 May 2015

   REQUIRED

   Calculate the basic earnings per share for the year ending 30 June 2015.

9   You are given the following information for Y plc for the year ending 30 June 2015:

Net profit before tax	€1,455,000
Income tax expense	(€655,000)
Profit after tax	€800,000
Non-controlling interest	(€100,000)
Dividends:	
– Preference	(€100,000)
– Ordinary	(€300,000)
Increase in retained earnings	€300,000

   The company has 2.4 million fully paid ordinary shares on issue at July 2014 and 2 million, 5 per cent, €1.00 preference shares.   **LO 19.1**

On 1 January 2015 the company issued a further 600,000 ordinary shares at full market price and on 1 May 2015 the company made a one-for-three bonus issue. The last sale price before the issue was €1.50.

REQUIRED

Calculate the basic earnings per share of Y plc for the year ending 30 June 2015.

10 Z plc has on issue 2 million ordinary shares and 1 million convertible preference shares of €0.50 each. The holders of the preference shares have the right to convert into ordinary shares at the rate of two preference shares for one ordinary share at a future date. The following figures have been extracted from the statement of comprehensive income of Z plc for the year ending 30 June 2016: **LO 19.4**

Profit after income tax	€290,000
Dividends:	
– Ordinary	(€160,000)
– Preference	(€20,000)
Increase in retained earnings	€110,000

REQUIRED

Calculate the diluted earnings per share for Z plc for the year ending 30 June 2016.

11 Outline the requirements in respect of the disclosure of both basic and fully diluted EPS in the financial statements of listed public companies. Discuss the advantages and disadvantages of such disclosure. **LO 19.4**

12 P plc is an Italian listed company. Its results for the financial year ending 30 June 2015 have exceeded expectations — profit before tax is €5.597 million and income tax expense is €1.847 million. As at 30 June 2014 there were 9.75 million ordinary shares on issue. On 11 May 2015, 3.25 million further ordinary shares were issued at a price of €2.30 — paid to €2.00. The partly paid shares carry rights to dividends in proportion to the amount paid relative to the total issue price. **LO 19.1**

REQUIRED

Calculate the basic EPS for P plc for the year ending 30 June 2015.

13 C S.A. is a Spanish listed company. **LO 19.4**

Results for the year are as follows:

	6 months ended 31/12/14	12 months ended 30/6/15
Profit	€7,035,800	€17,500,000
Income tax expense	€1,756,000	€5,500,000

Year-end price of the shares is €2.40.

Shares

Number of fully paid ordinary shares	
At 1/7/14	5,000,000
At 30/6/15	5,000,000

Ten million options were issued by the company on 15 September 2014. These are exercisable by the holder at €2.50 per option on or before 22 November 2017.

One million options were also issued by the company on 15 March 2015. These are exercisable by the holder at €2.00 per option on or before 11 May 2019.

Other information

Average share price for the year	€2.20
Company tax rate	33 per cent

REQUIRED

Calculate the basic earnings per share and diluted earnings per share for C S.A. for the year ending 30 June 2015.

CHALLENGING QUESTIONS

14 XYZ plc is a public company listed on the London Stock Exchange. You are provided with the following information about XYZ: **LO 19.1**

	£
Earnings (profit after tax) for six months ended 31 December 2015	10,000,000
Earnings (profit after tax) for six months ended 30 June 2016	13,000,000
	23,000,000
Fully paid ordinary shares as at 30 June 2015	90,000,000
Outstanding partly paid shares as at 30 June 2015	
– Number	10,000,000
– Issue price	£2.00
– Paid to	£1.00

These shares were issued on 1 January 2015 and are payable over the following three years.

- The allotment of shares pursuant to the Dividend Reinvestment Plan was 1,000,000. 'Dividend declared to shareholders registered in the books of the company at the close of business on 31 March 2016. The company will post the dividend on 15 April 2016.'
- Call of partly paid shares during the year:
  - Previously paid to   £1.00
  - Call of   £0.50
  - Closing date   28 February 2016
- The current share price at reporting date is £2.50.
- The average share price for the year is £2.50.
- Ten million options were issued on 1 January 2014, exercisable at £2.60 on or before 31 December 2018.
- Ten million options were issued on 30 June 2014, exercisable at £2.10 on or before 30 June 2017.
- The company income tax rate is 40 per cent.

REQUIRED

Calculate basic earnings per share and diluted earnings per share as at 30 June 2016.

15 You are given the following information in respect of XYZ plc for the year ending 30 June 2014. **LO 19.4**

Earnings for the year ending 30 June 2014   £70,000,000
Fully paid ordinary shares at 1 July 2013   75,000,000

Ten million options were issued on 30 June 2009, exercisable at £2.00 per option on or before 30 June 2016. The holder of each option has the right to purchase one share.

At July 2013 there are 2 million, 10 per cent, convertible notes on issue at face value (also called 'par'). The face value is £2.50. Interest is paid on 1 September and 1 March each year. Each convertible note is convertible into one fully paid ordinary share on 1 May 2016 and 1 May 2017.

On 1 May 2014 there is a rights issue of one-for-three ordinary fully paid shares. The price of the rights is £1.00. The last cum rights share price was £2.50. New shares issued do not participate in the interim dividend of 3.5 per share. The average share price for the year was £2.50.

The company income tax rate is 40 per cent.

REQUIRED

Calculate the basic and fully diluted earnings per share for XYZ plc for the year ending 30 June 2014.

16 The statements of comprehensive income of PK plc, and PK Group (comprising PK plc and its subsidiaries), for the financial year ending 30 June 2015 are as follows: **LO 19.1**

Statements of comprehensive income of PK plc and PK Group for the year ended 30 June 2015

	PK plc (£)	PK plc and its subsidiaries (£)
Income	38,368,000	193,284,000
Expenses (excluding borrowing costs)	(33,536,000)	(141,156,000)
Borrowing costs	(1,092,000)	(20,988,000)
Profit before income tax expense	3,740,000	31,140,000
Income tax expense	(1,496,000)	(12,456,000)
Profit from continuing operations after income tax expense	2,244,000	18,684,000
Profit (Loss) from discontinuing operations after related income tax	204,000	(492,000)
Profit after income tax	2,448,000	18,192,000
Profit attributable to non-controlling interest		1,704,000
Profit attributable to members of the parent entity		16,488,000

Notes to and forming part of the financial statements

	PK plc (£)	PK plc and its subsidiaries (£)
Note x: Retained earnings		
Retained earnings—1 July 2014	2,064,000	20,376,000
Profit after income tax	2,448,000	
Profit attributable to members of the parent entity		16,488,000
Interim dividend—ordinary shares	(608,000)	(608,000)
Final dividend—ordinary shares	(656,000)	(656,000)
Dividends—preference shares	(360,000)	(360,000)
Retained earnings—30 June 2015	2,888,000	35,240,000

Additional information

(i) On 30 June 2014 the share capital of PK plc comprised:

Share class	Number of shares on issue	Share capital (£)
Ordinary	4,600,000	11,052,000
Preference	600,000	6,000,000
Total	5,200,000	17,052,000

(ii) During the financial year ending on 30 June 2015, PK plc made the following share issues:

Date of share issue	Class of share issue	Details relating to share issue
1 October 2014	Ordinary	Private placement of 480,000 partly paid shares. The partly paid shares were issued for £3.00, which was the current share price at the time of issue. An amount of £1.12 was payable on allotment, and the balance of £1.88 is payable on 1 October 2016. The partly paid shares rank for (are entitled to participate in) dividends from 1 April 2015. The partly paid shares will entitle shareholders to receive 30 per cent of the dividends received by fully paid ordinary shareholders.
1 December 2014	Ordinary	Public issue of 8,000,000 fully paid shares. The subscription price for the public issue shares was £3.22, which was the current share price at the time of issue.
1 March 2015	Preference	Private placement of 320,000 fully paid shares, issued at the current share price at the time of issue.
1 May 2015	Ordinary	Share buyback of 260,000 fully paid ordinary shares, purchased at the current share price at the time of purchase of £3.32.

(iii) The preference shares entitle shareholders to receive an annual fixed dividend of 12 per cent on share capital, payable in two half-yearly instalments on 31 March and 30 September each year (that is 6 per cent on share capital every half year). The preference share dividends are cumulative.

(iv) The dividend due to preference shareholders on 31 March 2015 was not paid.

REQUIRED

Calculate basic earnings per share for the financial year ended 30 June 2015 in accordance with the requirements of IAS 33.

REFERENCES

BALL, R. & BROWN, P., 'An Empirical Evaluation of Accounting Income Numbers', *Journal of Accounting Research*, Autumn 1968, pp. 159–78.

EASTON, S., 'The Impact of the Disclosure of Extraordinary Items on Returns on Equity', *Accounting and Finance*, November 1990, pp. 1–13.

WHITTRED, G. & ZIMMER, I., *Financial Accounting: Incentive Effects and Economic Consequences*, 3rd edn, Sydney, Holt, Rinehart and Winston, 1992.

PART 7

Accounting for Equity Interests in other Entities

Chapter 20

Accounting for Group Structures

Learning objectives

Upon completing this chapter readers should:

LO1 understand the reasons for preparing consolidated financial statements;

LO2 understand the alternative consolidation concepts;

LO3 understand the basics involved in preparing consolidated financial statements;

LO4 be able to use a consolidation worksheet to perform relatively simple consolidations;

LO5 understand that *control*, and not *legal form*, is the criterion for determining whether or not to consolidate an entity;

LO6 be able to explain what *control* means, and be able to explain what factors should be considered in determining the existence of control;

LO7 be able to provide the journal entries necessary to account for any goodwill that arises on consolidation; and

LO8 have acquired the necessary basic knowledge of the consolidation process on which to base an understanding of the further consolidation issues addressed in Chapters 21, 22 and 23.

20.1 Introduction to accounting for group structures

In this and the next three chapters we will consider how to account for groups of entities. Specifically, we will consider how to consolidate (or combine) the financial statements of a parent entity and its subsidiaries. In doing so, we will need to make reference to a number of accounting standards. Of particular relevance to our discussion will be the following accounting standards:

- IFRS 3 *Business Combinations*
- IFRS 10 *Consolidated Financial Statements*
- IFRS 11 *Joint Arrangements*
- IFRS 12 *Disclosure of Interests in Other Entities*
- IFRS 13 *Fair Value Measurement*

These accounting standards are relatively new, with IFRS 10, 11 and 12 being issued in late 2011 and being applicable for annual reporting periods beginning on or after 1 January 2013.

It is common in Europe, and elsewhere, for groups of companies to combine in the pursuit of common goals. For example, a company might gain a controlling equity ownership in another company, with the intention of increasing the total assets and, relatedly, the profits of the **group** (the 'group' would comprise the parent entity and its subsidiaries). Where a reporting entity *controls* another entity, IFRS 10 *Consolidated Financial Statements* requires that consolidated financial statements be prepared. In this chapter we will consider issues relating to the **consolidation** process, including:

> **group** Typically a group of entities comprising the parent entity and each of its subsidiaries.
>
> **consolidation** The aggregation of the accounts of a number of separate legal entities.

- the rationale for presenting consolidated financial statements;
- the importance of *control* to the decision to consolidate an entity; and
- the basic mechanics of the consolidation process, together with a consideration of how to account for any goodwill or gain on bargain purchase that might arise on consolidation.

Chapters 21, 22 and 23 will consider consolidation issues relating to intragroup transactions, non-controlling interests and indirect interests. Accounting for changes in the degree of ownership of subsidiaries is also covered in WebChapter 7.

There are a number of key terms used in this chapter. We will briefly introduce some key terms now, which we will revisit throughout this and the next three chapters. In defining these key terms we will rely upon definitions provided in IFRS 10 *Consolidated Financial Statements*. Consolidation accounting key terms that we will use include:

- *consolidated financial statements*, which are the financial statements of a group presented as those of a single economic entity;
- a *parent*, which is an entity that controls one or more entities known as subsidiaries;
- a *subsidiary*, which is an entity, typically a company but would also include an unincorporated entity such as a partnership or a trust, that is *controlled* by another entity (known as the parent); and
- *control over an investee*, which is defined in IFRS 10 as being in existence 'when the investor is exposed, or has rights, to variable returns from its involvement with the investee and has the ability to affect those returns through its power over the investee'.

As we can see from the above definitions, an entity must 'control' an organisation before the organisation is considered to be a subsidiary of the investor.

Consolidated financial statements provide information about the financial performance and position of an entity that exists in an economic, but not a legal, sense. The 'legal entities' are the separate organisations within the group. As a simple example of a 'group'—or an economic entity as it is also called—we can consider Figure 20.1.

In Figure 20.1, Company A holds all the issued capital—and voting rights—in Company B. Company A and Company B would each be considered to be separate legal entities. Company A would be considered to be the 'parent' and, because Company B is controlled by Company A, Company B would be considered to be the subsidiary of Company A. Company A and Company B together would be considered to represent a 'group', and

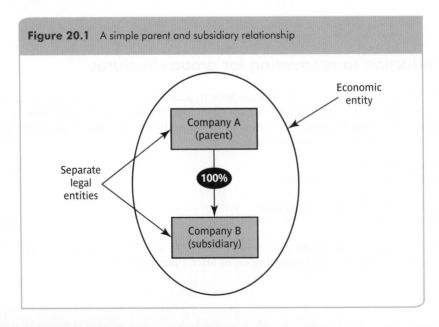

Figure 20.1 A simple parent and subsidiary relationship

while Company A and Company B might be considered to be separate legal entities, Company A and Company B together would constitute a single economic entity.

20.2 Rationale for consolidating the financial statements of different legal entities

Virtually every company listed on a recognised Securities Exchange, such as the London Stock Exchange or the Frankfurt Stock Exchange, has subsidiaries. Therefore, investors in a parent entity (which has subsidiaries) have effectively invested in the group comprising the parent entity and its subsidiaries. A large number of entities may be controlled by a particular parent entity. For example, consider note 42 of the 2010 financial statements prepared by Deutsche Bank. When we talk about the results of Deutsche Bank, we are actually talking about the combined results and financial positions of many entities all consolidated together. Indeed, a review of note 42 reveals that Deutsche Bank controlled, 2,012 separate legal entities respectively, all of which are incorporated within the consolidated financial statements. Therefore, when we are talking about Deutsche Bank's performance as a whole (as reflected in the consolidated financial statements) we are aggregating the results of a large number of entities. If investors in Deutsche Bank wish to review the operations of the group under the control of the parent entity concerned, it would be extremely confusing for them to have to study hundreds of separate financial statements, each prepared separately for each entity making up the group. The purpose of providing consolidated financial statements is to show the results and financial position of a group of organisations as if they are operating as a single economic entity. The consolidated financial statements represent the combination of the financial statements of all the entities within the group, with the 'group' comprising the parent entity and all of its subsidiaries. When consolidated financial statements are prepared, we get one set of financial statements (plus supporting notes) that cover the entire group. That is, we get:

- one consolidated statement of comprehensive income covering the group;
- one consolidated statement of financial position covering the group;
- one consolidated statement of changes in equity covering the group; and
- one consolidated statement of cash flows covering the group.

In terms of the act of preparing consolidated financial statements, paragraph B86 of IFRS 10 states (paragraphs commencing with B are part of the *Application Guidance*, which is attached to IFRS 10):

> *Consolidated financial statements combine like items of assets, liabilities, equity, income, expenses and cash flows of the parent with those of its subsidiaries.*

For example, if Company A and Company B, as shown in Figure 20.1, have cash of €500,000 and €400,000, respectively, the consolidated financial statements would show cash of €900,000 being controlled by the economic entity. As we will see in this and the next three chapters, the process of aggregating items will also often involve undertaking various eliminations and adjustments. As will be stressed in this and the following chapter, the consolidation process does not involve any adjustments to the financial statements of the individual entities making up the group. The effect of previous consolidation adjustments will also not be reflected in the opening balances of the ledger accounts of any entities within the group. Supplementary worksheets are utilised to perform the consolidation, and we will call these 'consolidation worksheets'. The preparation of consolidated financial statements will not obviate the need for separate entities to prepare their own, separate financial statements.

Following the consolidation process, the **consolidated statement of comprehensive income** will show the result derived from operations with parties external to the group of entities. The effects of all intragroup transactions—in other words, the transactions between organisations within the economic entity—are eliminated, since from the economic entity's perspective (that is, the controlling or parent entity and its controlled entities) income will not be derived as a result of transactions within the group, only from transactions with external parties.

The **consolidated statement of financial position** will show the total assets controlled by the economic entity and the total liabilities owed to parties outside the economic entity. Liabilities owing to organisations within the group (that is, within

consolidated statement of comprehensive income A statement of comprehensive income that combines, with various eliminations and adjustments, the statements of comprehensive income of the various entities within the economic entity.

consolidated statement of financial position Shows the assets of the economic entity and all liabilities owing to parties external to the economic entity.

the economic entity) by other group members will be eliminated in the consolidation process, and so will not be shown in the consolidated statement of financial position.

Consolidated financial statements must be read with care. They provide details of the aggregated financial position and financial performance of a large number of entities that are involved in many different industries and localities. Some organisations within an economic entity might have performed very well, while others might have performed poorly. This information will be lost in the consolidation process. Also, the consolidated statement of financial position represents the consolidation of many entities, which conceivably have vastly different financial structures. As such, it is possible that the consolidated statement of financial position might not be representative of the statements of financial position of individual legal entities. Hence, where consolidated financial data is provided, it is essential that it is supplemented by segment data (that provides information about the different operating segments in the economic entity).

While 'control' of another entity is a central requirement for that entity to be included in the consolidation process, IFRS 10 requires that, even where control is only temporary, the consolidated statements should incorporate the results of a subsidiary (which as we know is defined as an entity that is controlled by a parent entity) during the time in which control existed, even though this might have been for only a small part of the year. If control is lost during the period, the income and expenses of a subsidiary shall be included in the consolidated financial statements until the date on which the parent ceases to control the subsidiary.

As part of the ongoing evolution in how consolidated financial statements are to be prepared, in August 2011 IAS 27 *Consolidated and Separate Financial Statements* was superseded by the release of IFRS 10 *Consolidated Financial Statements*. There was also a change in the focus of IAS 27, with the revised standard now being entitled IAS 27 *Separate Financial Statements*. Both of the new standards are operative for annual reporting periods beginning on or after 1 January 2013. The objective of IFRS 10 is to establish principles for the presentation and preparation of consolidated financial statements when an entity controls one or more other entities, whereas the objective of the revised IAS 27 is now to prescribe the accounting and disclosure requirements for investments in subsidiaries, joint ventures and associates when an entity prepares separate financial statements (rather than consolidated financial statements).

20.3 Alternative consolidation concepts

Generally speaking, there are three main consolidation concepts that have been discussed over time by researchers as being relevant to the consolidation process. These three alternative concepts are:

1. the entity concept;
2. the proprietary concept; and
3. the parent-entity concept.

IFRS 10 adopts the entity concept (as did its predecessor, IAS 27). Pursuant to the entity concept, the entire group is viewed as a single economic entity, which incorporates all the assets and liabilities of the parent entity and its subsidiaries (subject to the elimination of the impacts of intragroup transactions). The consolidated financial statements reflect the financial position and financial performance of the economic entity as if it were operating as a single economic unit under common managerial control—the control emanating from the management group of the ultimate parent organisation. The consolidated statement of comprehensive income reflects the profit or loss and other items of comprehensive income that arise from transactions with parties external to the economic entity. The consolidated statement of financial position shows the assets of the economic entity (and, remember, the 'economic entity' means the parent entity and all of its subsidiaries) and all liabilities owing to parties external to the economic entity. No liabilities owing to any member of the economic entity by another member will be shown in the consolidated statement of financial position. What this means is that transactions between the individual entities making up the economic entity, for example, sales and purchases, dividends paid and received, and receivables and payables, must be eliminated as part of the consolidation process (IFRS 10, paragraph B86(a)).

Pursuant to the entity concept of consolidation, non-controlling interests are treated as part of consolidated equity. Non-controlling interests are defined in Appendix A of IFRS 10 as, 'equity in a subsidiary not attributable, directly or indirectly, to a parent' (sometimes called 'minority interests').

For example, if Company A owned 80 per cent of Company B (with Company A therefore being considered to be the 'parent entity') and the remaining 20 per cent of the shareholding was owned by an unrelated entity, the non-controlling interest in Company B is 20 per cent.

By contrast, under the proprietary concept of consolidation, all assets and liabilities of the parent entity and only a proportionate share of the subsidiaries' assets and liabilities are included in the consolidation process.

Non-controlling interest is not included if the proprietary concept is embraced by virtue of the view that any non-controlling interest is external to the consolidated group. This would mean that, if the parent entity holds 70 per cent of the shares in the subsidiary, it would include 70 per cent of the assets, liabilities, revenues and expenses in the consolidation process (and not 100 per cent of the assets and liabilities, as would be the case under the entity concept) even though the parent entity would effectively be able to control all the subsidiary's assets.

Under the final concept—the parent-entity concept—all assets and liabilities of the parent and its subsidiaries are included. The non-controlling interest is treated as a liability, rather than as part of equity.

As just indicated, IFRS 10 requires the adoption of the entity concept. In rejecting the parent-entity concept, the accounting standard-setters considered that it was inappropriate to classify the interests of outside shareholders, that is, the non-controlling interests, as liabilities because their claim on the net assets of a subsidiary is not of the nature of a liability (IFRS 10, paragraph BCZ157). This is explained in paragraphs BCZ158 and 159 of the *Basis for Conclusions on IFRS 10*:

> BCZ158 *Paragraph 49(b) of the Framework (now paragraph 4.4(b) of the Conceptual Framework) stated that a liability is a present obligation of the entity arising from past events, the settlement of which is expected to result in an outflow from the entity of resources embodying economic benefits. Paragraph 60 of the Framework (now paragraph 4.15 of the Conceptual Framework) explained that an essential characteristic of a liability is that the entity has a present obligation and that an obligation is a duty or responsibility to act or perform in a particular way. The Board noted that the existence of a non-controlling interest in the net assets of a subsidiary does not give rise to a present obligation, the settlement of which is expected to result in an outflow of economic benefits from the group.*

> BCZ159 *Instead, the Board noted that non-controlling interests represent the residual interest in the net assets of those subsidiaries held by some of the shareholders of the subsidiaries within the group, and therefore met the Framework's definition of equity. Paragraph 49(c) of the Framework (now paragraph 4.4(c) of the Conceptual Framework) stated that equity is the residual interest in the assets of the entity after deducting all its liabilities.*

Therefore, the view is that non-controlling interests are to be disclosed as part of owners' equity. Non-controlling interests will be explored in depth within Chapter 22.

20.4 The concept of control

As we should now appreciate, the definitions of 'control' and 'subsidiary' are central to determining the entities to be consolidated and the nature of the group. Paragraph 20 of IFRS 10 requires that:

> *Consolidation of an investee shall begin from the date the investor obtains control of the investee and cease when the investor loses control of the investee.*

When IFRS 10 was released in August 2011 (thereby replacing IAS 27 as the accounting standard relevant to consolidations) it more clearly articulated the principle of 'control' relative to the guidance provided formerly in IAS 27. IFRS 10 defines control as requiring three elements, these being:

- power;
- exposure to variable returns; and
- the investor's ability to use power to affect its amount of variable returns.

Specifically, 'control of an investee' is defined in IFRS 10 as:

> *An investor controls an investee when the investor is **exposed, or has rights, to variable returns** from its involvement with the investee and **has the ability to affect those returns** through **its power over the investee.*** (emphasis added)

The above definition can be contrasted with the definition of control previously provided in IAS 27, which was:

> *the power to govern the financial and operating policies of an entity so as to obtain benefits from its activities.*

The three elements of control are explained in some detail throughout IFRS 10 and in the associated *Application Guidance* that accompanies IFRS 10. For control to be deemed to exist, all three elements—just identified—must be present (IFRS 10, paragraph 7).

Having 'power' over the investee is essential for there to be 'control' over the investee. Paragraph 10 of IFRS 10 states that:

an investor has power over an investee when the investor has existing rights that give it the current ability to direct the relevant activities, i.e. the activities that significantly affect the investee's returns.

Determining the existence of 'power' will not always be a straightforward exercise such as countable voting rights but may be complex, with several factors influencing the overall relationship such as contractual arrangements (IFRS 10, paragraph 11).

In deciding whether an entity is a subsidiary, it is not necessary that the investor has actually exercised its power. Rather, it is necessary to show it has the *capacity* to exercise power (IFRS 10, paragraph 12). Where control is considered to exist, the amount of returns to be derived from the interest in the investee would be expected to vary depending upon the efforts and performance of both the investee and the investor (IFRS 10, paragraph 17).

In much of the discussion above we are using the terms 'investor' and 'investee'. If the investor controls the investee, then the investor would also be the 'parent' and the investee would be the 'subsidiary'.

In further considering the link between power and returns, paragraph BC68 of IFRS 10 states:

To have control, an investor must have power and exposure or rights to variable returns and be able to use that power to affect its own returns from its involvement with the investee. Thus, power and the returns to which an investor is exposed, or has rights to, must be linked. The link between power and returns does not mean that the proportion of returns accruing to an investor needs to be perfectly correlated with the amount of power that the investor has. The Board noted that many parties can have the right to receive variable returns from an investee (e.g. shareholders, debt providers and agents), but only one party can control an investee.

The above paragraph raises the important point that only one party can be in 'control' of an entity before that controlling entity can be considered to be the parent entity. If an entity 'jointly controls' another entity, then that entity cannot be considered to be a subsidiary, and rather than applying IFRS 10, another standard—IFRS 11 *Joint Arrangements* (released in August 2011)—needs to be applied (and this standard does not allow consolidation for jointly controlled entities). As paragraph BC83 of the *Basis for Conclusions* to IFRS 10 states:

IFRS 11 Joint Arrangements *defines joint control as the contractually agreed sharing of control of an arrangement. Joint control exists only when decisions about the relevant activities require the unanimous consent of the parties sharing control. When two or more parties have joint control of an investee, no single party controls that investee and, accordingly, the investee is not consolidated. IFRS 11 is applicable to all investees for which two or more parties have joint control.*

The *Basis for Conclusions* that accompanied the release of IFRS 10 addressed a number of situations that could lead to control, these being:

- where a majority of voting rights are held by the investor;
- where less than a majority of the voting rights are held by the investor (but perhaps where the balance of the voting rights are widely dispersed among many different owners); and
- where the investor holds some potential voting rights in the investee.

We will consider these attributes of 'control' in more detail below.

20.4.1 Majority of voting rights

It is generally understood that, in most circumstances, if the investor holds the majority of the voting rights (for example, over half of the ordinary shares in a company), then that should provide the investor with control over the investee unless there is a contractual arrangement in place which assigns power to another entity (*Basis for Conclusions* to IFRS 10, paragraph BC97).

20.4.2 Less than the majority of voting rights

It is quite common that an investor can control an investee even if it does not hold the majority of the voting rights. This may happen when one party has a large share of the voting rights and the other shareholdings are widely dispersed with shareholders who do not actively exercise their votes (*Basis for Conclusions* to IFRS 10, paragraph BC99). Further clarification was provided in paragraphs BC99, BC107 and BC108 of the *Basis for Conclusions* to IFRS 10.

20.4.3 Potential voting rights

Another factor that requires consideration when determining whether an investor might control an investee is the existence of *potential voting rights*. Potential voting rights are financial instruments that do not in themselves have voting rights but they can potentially be converted into other financial instruments—such as ordinary shares—that would then provide voting rights. For example, the investor might hold share options or preference shares that in themselves do not have voting rights, but they can potentially be converted to ordinary shares that would provide voting rights. An increase in voting rights would increase the potential for an investor to control the investee. Therefore, where the 'potential voting rights' are currently exercisable, they should be taken into account when assessing the existence of 'control' (see paragraphs BC120, 121 and 124 of the *Basis for Conclusions* to IFRS 10). In particular, BC124 provides guidance on concerns raised about the potential for fluctuations in what can be construed as control. It states:

> BC124 *Some constituents were concerned about whether the proposed model would lead to frequent changes in the control assessment solely because of changes in market conditions—would an investor consolidate and deconsolidate an investee if potential voting rights moved in and out of the money? In response to those comments, the Board noted that determining whether a potential voting right is substantive is not based solely on a comparison of the strike or conversion price of the instrument and the then current market price of its underlying share. Although the strike or conversion price is one factor to consider, determining whether potential voting rights are substantive requires a holistic approach, considering a variety of factors. This includes assessing the purpose and design of the instrument, considering whether the investor can benefit for other reasons such as by realising synergies between the investor and the investee, and determining whether there are any barriers (financial or otherwise) that would prevent the holder of potential voting rights from exercising or converting those rights. Accordingly, the Board believes that a change in market conditions (i.e. the market price of the underlying shares) alone would not typically result in a change in the consolidation conclusion.*

As we can see from the above paragraph, as with control generally, professional judgement needs to be employed to determine whether the existence of potential voting rights impacts the assessment of whether an entity has control over another entity.

Worked Example 20.1 provides a number of scenarios adapted from the *Implementation Guidance* accompanying IFRS 10 that illustrate individual aspects of potential voting rights.

Worked Example 20.1 — Consideration of potential voting rights

Part A

Options are out of the money

A plc and B plc own 70 per cent and 30 per cent, respectively, of the ordinary contributed equity that carries voting rights in C plc. A plc sells 70 per cent of its interest in C plc to D plc. At the same time, A plc purchases call options (right to buy) from D plc that are exercisable at any time at a premium to the market price when issued. If the options are exercised, they give A plc its original 70 per cent ownership interest and voting rights in C plc.

Part B

Possibility of exercise or conversion

A plc, B plc and C plc own 40 per cent, 30 per cent and 30 per cent, respectively, of the ordinary contributed equity that carries voting rights in D plc. A plc also owns call options that are exercisable at any time at the fair value of the underlying shares. If the options are exercised, A plc receives an extra 20 per cent of the voting rights in D plc, while B plc and C plc's interests are reduced to 20 per cent each.

Part C

Management intention

A plc, B plc and C plc each own 33.33 per cent of the ordinary contributed equity that carries voting rights in D plc. A plc, B plc and C plc each have the right to appoint two directors to the Board of D plc. A plc also owns call options that are exercisable at a fixed price at any time and, if exercised, would give it all the voting rights in D plc. The management of A plc does not intend to exercise the call options, even if B plc and C plc do not vote along the same lines as A plc.

Part D

Financial ability

A plc and B plc own 55 per cent and 45 per cent, respectively, of the ordinary contributed equity that carries voting rights in C plc. B plc also holds debt instruments that are convertible into ordinary shares of C plc. The debt can be converted at a substantial price, in comparison with B plc's net assets, at any time. If the debt instruments were

▶

converted, B plc would be required to borrow additional funds to make the payment. Should the debt be converted, B plc would hold 70 per cent of the voting rights and A plc's interest would reduce to 30 per cent.

Required

Taking the potential voting rights into consideration in each of the above scenarios, explain which entity has control over the other.

Solution

Part A

In this scenario, the options are out of the money. However, because A plc can exercise its options now (they are currently exercisable), A plc has the power to continue to set the operating and financial policies of C plc. The existence of the potential voting rights means that A plc controls C plc.

Part B

If the options are exercised, A plc will have control over more than one-half of the voting rights over D plc. The existence of the potential voting rights means that A plc controls D plc.

Part C

The existence of the potential voting rights means that A plc controls D plc. The intention of A plc's management does not influence the assessment of control.

Part D

Although the debt instruments are convertible at a substantial price, they are currently convertible. This conversion feature gives B plc the power to set the operating and financial policies of C plc. The existence of the potential voting rights means that it is B plc and not A plc that controls C plc. The financial ability of B plc to pay the conversion price does not influence the assessment of control.

A real-life example of what is considered to amount to control is provided by Deutsche Bank in its annual report for 2010. This is reproduced in Exhibit 20.1. This accounting policy is very comprehensive and covers many areas relating to consolidation, though only the policies in relation to subsidiaries (not special purpose entities or business combinations) are included here. To view the full accounting policy, access their annual report from their website.

| Exhibit 20.1 | Control as interpreted by Deutsche Bank in its Significant Accounting Policies (Annual Report 2010) |

Principles of Consolidation

The financial information in the consolidated financial statements includes that for the parent company, Deutsche Bank AG, together with its subsidiaries, including certain special purpose entities ('SPEs'), presented as a single economic unit.

Subsidiaries

The Group's subsidiaries are those entities which it controls. The Group controls entities when it has the power to govern the financial and operating policies of the entity, generally accompanying a shareholding, either directly or indirectly, of more than one half of the voting rights. The existence and effect of potential voting rights that are currently exercisable or convertible are considered in assessing whether the Group controls an entity.

Subsidiaries are consolidated from the date on which control is transferred to the Group and are no longer consolidated from the date that control ceases. The Group reassesses consolidation status at least at every quarterly reporting date. Therefore, any changes in structure are considered when they occur. This includes changes to any contractual arrangements the Group has, including those newly executed with the entity, and is not only limited to changes in ownership.

All intercompany transactions, balances and unrealized gains on transactions between Group companies are eliminated on consolidation. Consistent accounting policies are applied throughout the Group for the purposes of consolidation. Issuances of a subsidiary's stock to third parties are treated as non-controlling interests.

At the date that control of a subsidiary is lost, the Group a) derecognizes the assets (including any goodwill) and liabilities of the subsidiary at their carrying amounts, b) derecognizes the carrying amount of any non-controlling interests in the former subsidiary (including any components in accumulated other comprehensive income attributable to the subsidiary), c) recognizes the fair value of the consideration received and any distribution of the shares of the subsidiary, d) recognizes any investment retained in the former subsidiary at its fair value and e) recognizes any resulting difference of the above items as a gain or loss in the income statement. Any amounts recognized in prior periods in other comprehensive income in relation to that subsidiary would be reclassified to the consolidated statement of income at the date that control is lost.

Assets held in an agency or fiduciary capacity are not assets of the Group and are not included in the Group's consolidated balance sheet.

20.4.4 Delegated power (agency relationships)

Pursuant to IFRS 10, another factor to consider in determining whether to consolidate an entity is whether any power to be exerted over the entity is being done in the context of an agency relationship or whether the power is being exercised to benefit the investor directly. In defining an 'agency relationship', paragraph BC129 of the *Basis for Conclusions* to IFRS 10 states:

> The Board decided to base its principal/agent guidance on the thinking developed in agency theory. Jensen and Meckling (1976) define an agency relationship as 'a contractual relationship in which one or more persons (the principal) engage another person (the agent) to perform some service on their behalf which involves delegating some decision-making authority to the agent.

If an entity has power, but is acting under the direction of another entity—perhaps as an 'agent' of that other entity—then control would not be deemed to exist and the entity would not be required to consolidate the entity over which it had power. As paragraph 18 of IFRS 10 states:

> Thus, an investor with decision-making rights shall determine whether it is a principal or an agent. An investor that is an agent in accordance with paragraphs B58–B72 does not control an investee when it exercises decision-making rights delegated to it.

In explaining the above requirement, paragraph BC133 of the *Basis for Conclusions* to IFRS 10 states:

> The Board concluded that the guidance in IFRS 10 that addresses control should apply to agency relationships, i.e. when assessing control, a decision maker should consider whether it has the current ability to direct the relevant activities of an investee that it manages to affect the returns it receives, or whether it uses the decision-making authority delegated to it primarily for the benefit of other parties.

In relation to the various factors to consider in determining whether decision-making authority has been delegated to an agent, paragraph B60 of IFRS 10 states:

> A decision maker shall consider the overall relationship between itself, the investee being managed and other parties involved with the investee, in particular all the factors below, in determining whether it is an agent:
>
> (a) the scope of its decision-making authority over the investee (paragraphs B62 and B63).
> (b) the rights held by other parties (paragraphs B64–B67).
> (c) the remuneration to which it is entitled in accordance with the remuneration agreement(s) (paragraphs B68–B70).
> (d) the decision maker's exposure to variability of returns from other interests that it holds in the investee (paragraphs B71 and B72).
>
> Different weightings shall be applied to each of the factors on the basis of particular facts and circumstances.

So, in summarising some of the above discussion on 'agency relationships', if an organisation has power over another entity but it is acting as an agent, then the agent is not to consolidate the financial statements of the controlled entity.

As stated earlier, it is possible for control to be passive—that is, it might be possible to exert control over another entity, even though the option to exert such control might never have been exercised. Nevertheless, **capacity to control** a subsidiary is sufficient to require consolidation of that subsidiary. Where control is 'passive', and perhaps another entity is formulating the policies of the subsidiary, a particular entity would nevertheless be considered to be in 'control' to the extent it ultimately has the ability to modify or change the policies being applied by another entity if it deems it necessary to step in and make such a change.

> **capacity to control**
> Capacity to control exists where it is possible to exert control over another entity, even though the option to exert such control might never have been exercised.

As emphasised earlier in this chapter, by adopting the criterion of control (and not legal form) as the basis for determining the necessity to consolidate, the economic entity may include organisations of a corporate and non-corporate form. That is, adoption of the criterion of control will enable a complete economic entity to be reflected in consolidated financial statements even though, for example, some of the subsidiaries might be in the form of partnerships or trusts. Including entities such as trusts and partnerships in the consolidation process prevents entities from opportunistically omitting certain key (non-corporate) entities from the consolidation process.

As we have noted, another necessary attribute of control (see paragraph 15 of IFRS 10) is that there is an expectation that the investor will be exposed to variable returns from its involvement with the investee.

This requirement means that parties such as receivers and managers of financially troubled organisations, as well as trustees, would not be required to consolidate a controlled entity's financial statements with their own statements because, apart from the professional fees being received, those concerned would not be managing such organisations for their own benefit but on behalf of owners and creditors.

20.4.5 Loss of control

As we noted earlier in this chapter, just as control can be established, it can also be lost. That is, a parent entity might subsequently lose control over its subsidiary. It is not necessary for a change in the level of ownership to occur for control to be lost. Once an entity has lost control, the consolidated statement of comprehensive income is only to include the results of the subsidiary for the period during which control existed.

An excerpt from an article on The Financial Express website by Aditya V Lodha in Financial Accounting in the News 20.1 was published as the first accounting standard on consolidations was released in India. It notes some of the benefits associated with compiling consolidated financial statements, many of which we have already discussed. While this article is quite dated, it is useful in understanding some of the issues associated with the development of accounting for economic entities. It also provides an interesting historical perspective on the practice of consolidation accounting.

Financial Accounting in the News 20.1
SHOULD CONSOLIDATED ACCOUNTS BE MANDATORY?

Aditya V Lodha, *The Financial Express*,
8 November 2004

It'll help give a company's true financial picture

Consolidation of subsidiaries/associates in the financial statements is an important and critical component in the process of qualitative improvement. It is widely recognised that consolidated financial statements provide meaningful representation of the financial position and results of operations of controlled or closely related groups of entities, for all stakeholders.

Business enterprises have been conducting a diverse range of activities through complex financial structures. Independent subsidiaries/special purpose vehicles (SPVs)

are being increasingly formed for the purposes of risk mitigation, fiscal planning, cross-border acquisitions or specific partnerships/alliances.

Consolidation would result in depicting the true financial position of the group in contrast to stand-alone results that do not necessarily reflect the actual performance of such investments in the parent enterprise.

It would also ensure that financial statements reflect the overall financial position of the entity without having to sift through the individual financials. Moreover, owing to the fact that all the financial statements of the group entity are

▶

prepared using uniform accounting principles, the consolidation process also ensures consistency in the form of comparable reporting.

Considering that the consolidation requirement is at present restricted to listed companies only, there is an inconsistent system since non-listed companies can use subsidiaries/associates in a creative manner not in keeping with the desire to enhance transparency. Mandatory consolidation would ensure consistency across the system, would curb inappropriate creativity, and would make sure that users of financial statements can be assured of the true financial position of the entity. It would bring about greater transparency—the statements would conform to WYSIWYG (what you see is what you get).

The combined group strength reflected in the consolidated accounts would also facilitate greater resource mobilisation, domestically and internationally. World capital markets recognise and appreciate high-quality financial information, and consolidated statements help provide much greater confidence to potential fund providers/investors.

Apart from the accounting benefits, mandatory consolidation could slowly help build a suitable platform for introduction of tax consolidation. Under this mechanism, the parent files a single tax return for the entire group. The advantages and resultant efficiencies arising from tax consolidation could be a significant boon for industry and allow it to work in a more efficient environment.

Source: www.financialexpress.com. © 2012 The Indian Express Limited

20.5 Direct and indirect control

A number of scenarios are possible to illustrate the concept of *control*. Control can exist by virtue of direct ownership interests, indirect ownership interests, or perhaps a combination of the two. Consider Figure 20.2, which provides an illustration of direct control—in this case, Company A's ownership (and voting) interest in Company B. Company A owns 70 per cent of the issued capital of Company B. This would be expected to lead to Company A having control of B directly. Company A's 70 per cent voting interest in Company B will also amount to a 70 per cent *beneficial interest* in the profits being generated by Company B. For example, with a 70 per cent ownership interest in Company B, for each £1 of dividends paid by Company B, 70 pence will go to Company A, while 30 pence will go to non-controlling interests. The voting interest and beneficial interest will not always be the same, as some of the examples that follow will demonstrate.

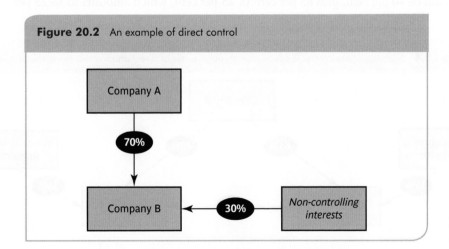

Figure 20.2 An example of direct control

If we turn our attention to Figure 20.3, we may contemplate the case in which Company A has control of Company C by virtue of its control of Company B. This form of control would be considered to be indirect control. Because Company B is considered to control Company C, and because Company A controls Company B, Company A therefore effectively controls Company C even though it has no direct shareholding in Company C. The beneficial interest of Company A in Company C's profits will equate to 0.75×0.60, which equals 45 per cent. That means that, for every pound of dividends paid by Company C, 45 pence will find its way back to Company A. This can be explained as follows: when Company C pays a dividend, 60 per cent of the dividend

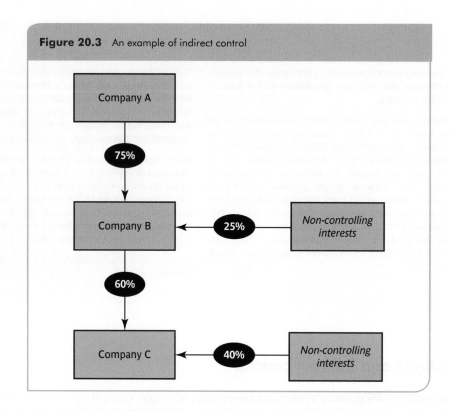

Figure 20.3 An example of indirect control

will flow to Company B. Hence, for every pound of dividends paid by Company C, 60 pence goes to Company B. If Company B in turn pays this amount to its shareholders, 75 per cent (or 45 pence) will go to Company A, and 25 per cent (or 15 pence) will go to those parties holding the non-controlling interest in Company B.

Moving on to Figure 20.4, we can see that control of another entity may also be achieved in a combination of direct and indirect ownership interests. Company A has direct voting interests in Company C of 40 per cent, as well as indirectly controlling 25 per cent of the voting interests through its control of Company B. The economic entity would be considered to be constituted by all three companies. Company A's beneficial interest in Company C would be 40 per cent, plus 65 per cent of 25 per cent, which amounts to 56.25 per cent in total.

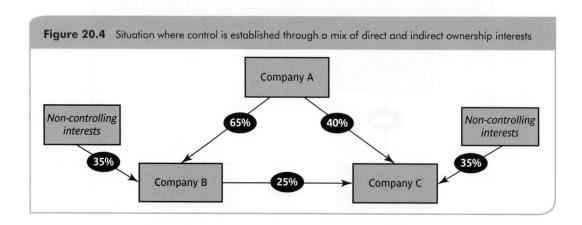

Figure 20.4 Situation where control is established through a mix of direct and indirect ownership interests

20.6 Accounting for business combinations

According to IFRS 3, a 'business combination' is defined as:

A transaction or other event in which an acquirer obtains control of one or more businesses. Transactions sometimes referred to as 'true mergers' or 'mergers of equals' are also business combinations as that term is used in this Standard.

IFRS 3 *Business Combinations* and IFRS 10 *Consolidated Financial Statements* must both be considered when compiling and presenting consolidated financial statements. As a central requirement, IFRS 3 requires an entity to determine whether a transaction or other event is a business combination, as defined above. When we consolidate other entities, we are consolidating businesses and we can recognise the goodwill of the business being acquired. This requires that the assets acquired and liabilities assumed constitute a business. Guidance on what constitutes a business is provided in the *Application Guidance* accompanying IFRS 3. According to paragraph B7 of IFRS 3:

> *A business consists of inputs and processes applied to those inputs that have the ability to create outputs. Although businesses usually have outputs, outputs are not required for an integrated set to qualify as a business. The three elements of a business are defined as follows:*
>
> (a) **Input**: *Any economic resource that creates, or has the ability to create, outputs when one or more processes are applied to it. Examples include non-current assets (including intangible assets or rights to use non-current assets), intellectual property, the ability to obtain access to necessary materials or rights and employees.*
>
> (b) **Process**: *Any system, standard, protocol, convention or rule that when applied to an input or inputs, creates or has the ability to create outputs. Examples include strategic management processes, operational processes and resource management processes. These processes typically are documented, but an organised workforce having the necessary skills and experience following rules and conventions may provide the necessary processes that are capable of being applied to inputs to create outputs. (Accounting, billing, payroll and other administrative systems typically are not processes used to create outputs.)*
>
> (c) **Output**: *The result of inputs and processes applied to those inputs that provide or have the ability to provide a return in the form of dividends, lower costs or other economic benefits directly to investors or other owners, members or participants.*

If the assets acquired do not fit the description of business considered above, the transaction shall represent the acquisition of a group of assets and the appropriate accounting treatment would be covered by IAS 16 *Property, Plant and Equipment*, and IAS 38 *Intangible Assets* rather than IFRS 3 *Business Combinations*. If we are not acquiring a business, then we would not recognise goodwill.

IFRS 3 requires entities to account for business combinations using what is referred to as the *acquisition method*. The acquisition method requires four steps to be taken:

1. identifying the acquirer;
2. determining the acquisition date;
3. recognising and measuring the identifiable assets acquired, the liabilities assumed and any non-controlling interest in the acquiree; and
4. recognising and measuring goodwill or a gain from a bargain purchase.

These four steps will be considered in turn below.

20.6.1 Identifying the acquirer

An acquirer might obtain *control* of an acquiree in a variety of ways. These include:

- transferring cash, cash equivalents or other assets (including net assets that constitute a business);
- incurring liabilities;
- issuing equity interests;
- providing more than one type of consideration; and
- without transferring consideration, including by contract alone.

In a business combination, the acquirer is usually the entity that transfers the cash, cash equivalents or other assets, incurs the liabilities or issues the equity interests. There are, however, occasions where, in some business combinations, known as 'reverse acquisitions', the issuing entity is the acquiree. Determining the acquirer in a business combination involving more than two entities shall include a consideration of, among other things, which of the combining entities initiated the combination, as well as the relative size of the combining entities. Where the relative size (measured in, for example, assets, revenues or profit) of one entity is significantly greater than that of the other combining entity or entities, the acquirer is usually the combining entity whose relative size is the greater.

20.6.2 Determining the acquisition date

Paragraph 8 of IFRS 3 identifies the acquisition date as the date on which the acquirer obtains control of the acquiree. This is usually the date on which the acquirer legally transfers the consideration, acquires the assets and assumes the liabilities of the acquiree—the closing date. However, IFRS 3 acknowledges that the acquirer may obtain control on a date other than the closing date.

20.6.3 Recognising and measuring the identifiable assets acquired and the liabilities assumed

At the *acquisition date*, the *acquirer* is required to recognise:

- goodwill separately from the identifiable assets acquired;
- the liabilities assumed; and
- any non-controlling interest in the acquiree.

To qualify for recognition as part of applying the acquisition method, at the acquisition date the identifiable assets acquired and liabilities assumed must meet the definitions of assets and liabilities in the IASB Conceptual Framework.

By applying the recognition principles contained in IFRS 3, it is possible for the acquirer to recognise assets and liabilities that the acquiree had not previously recognised in its own financial statements. Examples of assets that may be recognised by the acquirer, but not previously by the acquiree, would include acquired identifiable intangible assets, such as a brand name, a patent, publishing titles, customer lists, and so forth. These assets may not have been recognised by the acquiree in its financial statements because it developed them internally and expensed the related costs in the statement of comprehensive income in the period in which they were incurred, in compliance with IAS 38 *Intangible Assets*, as explained in Chapter 8 of this book. However, should another entity (the acquirer) acquire the business of another entity (the acquiree), then the acquirer is permitted to recognise such assets at their fair value. To the acquiring entity such assets would not have been 'internally generated'; rather, they would have been acquired.

The general rule for measuring the identifiable assets acquired and the liabilities assumed is provided by IFRS 3. Under paragraph 18, the acquirer measures each identifiable asset acquired (including identifiable intangible assets) and liability assumed, at their acquisition-date fair values. 'Fair value' is defined in IFRS 3 (and in other accounting standards) as:

> the price that would be received to sell an asset or paid to transfer a liability in an orderly transaction between market participants at the measurement date. (See IFRS 13 for detailed coverage of how to determine fair values.)

The above definition makes use of two key terms in determining fair value: 'orderly transaction' and 'market participants'. If certain conditions do not exist, then the resulting transaction cannot be deemed to have been at fair value. In relation to the expectations relating to an 'orderly transaction', IFRS 13 defines an orderly transaction as:

> A transaction that assumes exposure to the market for a period before the measurement date to allow for marketing activities that are usual and customary for transactions involving such assets or liabilities; it is not a forced transaction (e.g. a forced liquidation or distress sale).

In relation to the attributes of the 'market participants' that must exist before a transaction can be deemed to have taken place at 'fair value', IFRS 13 defines market participants as:

> Buyers and sellers in the principal (or most advantageous) market for the asset or liability that have all of the following characteristics:
>
> (a) They are independent of each other, ie they are not related parties as defined in IAS 24, although the price in a related party transaction may be used as an input to a fair value measurement if the entity has evidence that the transaction was entered into at market terms.
> (b) They are knowledgeable, having a reasonable understanding about the asset or liability and the transaction using all available information, including information that might be obtained through due diligence efforts that are usual and customary.
> (c) They are able to enter into a transaction for the asset or liability.
> (d) They are willing to enter into a transaction for the asset or liability, ie they are motivated but not forced or otherwise compelled to do so.

Prior to the release of IFRS 13 *Fair Value Measurement* in August 2011, fair value had been defined in the accounting standards as, 'the amount for which an asset could be exchanged between a knowledgeable, willing buyer and a knowledgeable, willing seller in an arm's length transaction'. This 'old' definition is generally consistent with the new definition provided above.

An exception to the recognition principle is contingent liabilities (see Chapter 9 for details of contingent liabilities).

As indicated in paragraph 23 of IFRS 3, the requirements in IAS 37 do not apply in determining which contingent liabilities to recognise at the acquisition date. On acquisition date, a contingent liability in a business

combination is recognised if it is a present obligation that arises from past events and its fair value can be measured reliably. In other words, a contingent liability is recognised at the acquisition date even if it is not probable that an outflow of resources embodying economic benefits will be required to settle the obligation.

20.6.4 Recognising and measuring goodwill

Goodwill is defined in IFRS 3 *Business Combinations* as:

> *An asset representing future economic benefits arising from assets acquired in a business combination that are not individually identified and separately recognised.*

In the context of business combinations, IFRS 3, paragraph 32, requires that:

> *The acquirer shall recognise goodwill as of the acquisition date measured as the excess of (a) over (b) below:*
>
> *(a)   the aggregate of:*
> *(i)   the consideration transferred measured in accordance with this Standard, which generally requires acquisition-date fair value (see paragraph 37);*
> *(ii)   the amount of any non-controlling interest in the acquiree measured in accordance with this Standard; and*
> *(iii)   in a business combination achieved in stages (see paragraphs 41 and 42), the acquisition-date fair value of the acquirer's previously held equity interest in the acquiree.*
> *(b)   the net of the acquisition-date amounts of the identifiable assets acquired and the liabilities assumed measured in accordance with this Standard.*

This can be simplified as follows:

FAIR VALUE OF CONSIDERATION TRANSFERRED	XXX
plus Amount of non-controlling interest	XXX
plus Fair value of any previously held equity interest in the acquiree	XXX
	XXX
less Fair value of identifiable assets acquired and liabilities assumed	XXX
GOODWILL ON ACQUISITION DATE	XXX

Calculated in the manner shown above, the net figure for goodwill will be a positive number. If the number is negative, then rather than it being considered as goodwill, the amount would be considered as a gain on bargain purchase and would be recognised in profit or loss at the acquisition date by the acquirer (IFRS 3, paragraph 34). According to the *Basis for Conclusions* in paragraph BC134 of IAS 36 *Impairment of Assets*, goodwill acquired in a business combination represents:

> *a payment made by the acquirer in anticipation of future economic benefits from assets that are not capable of being individually identified and separately recognised. Goodwill does not generate cash flows independently of other assets or groups of assets and therefore cannot be measured directly. Instead, it is measured as a residual amount, being the excess of the cost of a business combination over the acquirer's interest in the net fair value of the acquiree's identifiable assets, liabilities and contingent liabilities. Moreover, goodwill acquired in a business combination and goodwill generated after that business combination cannot be separately identified, because they contribute jointly to the same cash flows.*

In determining goodwill, the fair value of both the assets acquired and the liabilities assumed, and the purchase consideration given in exchange must be considered.

Consideration transferred

In a business combination, the consideration transferred is measured at fair value. Paragraph 37 of IFRS 3 expands on this requirement. It states that the fair value of consideration transferred is calculated as:

> *the sum of the acquisition-date fair values of the assets transferred by the acquirer, the liabilities incurred by the acquirer to former owners of the acquiree and the equity interests issued by the acquirer.*

Forms of consideration include cash, other assets, a business or a subsidiary of the acquirer, contingent consideration, ordinary or preference equity instruments, options, warrants and member interests of mutual entities.

The calculation of goodwill in line with the requirements of paragraph 32 of IFRS 3 is detailed in Worked Example 20.2.

Worked Example 20.2   Calculation of goodwill on acquisition

On 1 July 2015 Ying plc acquired for cash all the issued share capital of Yang plc for an amount of €650,000. On the date of the acquisition, the assets, liabilities and contingent liabilities of Yang plc are as follows:

	Carrying amount (€)	Fair value (€)
Cash	15,000	15,000
Accounts receivable	68,000	68,000
Inventory	112,000	131,000
Land	360,000	420,000
Plant	220,000	240,000
Loans payable	(170,000)	(170,000)
Accounts payable	(58,000)	(58,000)
Contingent liabilities	—	(46,000)

Required

Calculate the goodwill on acquisition. Ignore any deferred tax considerations.

Solution

The difference between the fair value of the identifiable assets acquired and the liabilities assumed, and the consideration transferred is the goodwill. From the information provided, the goodwill on acquisition date is calculated as follows:

	(€)	(€)
Fair value of consideration transferred		650,000
less Fair value of identifiable assets acquired and liabilities assumed		
Cash	15,000	
Accounts receivable	68,000	
Inventory	131,000	
Land	420,000	
Plant	240,000	
Loans payable	(170,000)	
Accounts payable	(58,000)	
Contingent liabilities	(46,000)	
Total fair value of net assets acquired		600,000
Goodwill on acquisition date		50,000

As Ying plc paid cash for the equity interest in Yang plc, the fair value of the purchase consideration is easily determined as the amount of cash given in exchange. Based on the fair value of the assets of Yang plc, the goodwill acquired by Ying plc would be €50,000.

Consistent with the requirements of paragraph 48 of IAS 38 *Intangible Assets* that internally generated goodwill not be recognised as an asset, no goodwill would be brought to account by Yang plc (the acquiree) in Worked Example 20.2 as only purchased goodwill, and not internally generated goodwill, is recognised for accounting purposes. The purchased goodwill may be brought to account by Ying plc as part of the consolidation process. The view taken is that, although the acquiree might not be able to reliably measure the value of internally generated goodwill, another entity that acquires the entity (the acquirer) is able to attribute reliably a value to goodwill being acquired. In the above example, Yang plc (the acquirer) was able to attribute a cost of €50,000 to the goodwill.

Unlike internally generated goodwill, which may not be brought to account in the separate financial statements of a reporting entity or in the consolidated financial statements, purchased goodwill is to be brought to account in the consolidation process. The goodwill acquired in a business combination is not amortised. Rather, after its initial recognition, goodwill should be measured at cost less any accumulated impairment losses. Impairment testing should be conducted at least annually, but can be performed more frequently if events or changes in circumstances indicate that the goodwill might be impaired. See Chapter 4 for details of accounting for the impairment of assets. Unlike other assets, goodwill cannot be revalued. Therefore, impairment losses must be recognised immediately in profit and loss. Paragraphs 80 to 99 of IAS 36 provide guidance on impairment testing of goodwill.

According to IFRS 3, only the goodwill acquired by the parent entity is recognised on consolidation. Where the parent acquires all of the shares of the subsidiary, all of the goodwill of the subsidiary is shown in the consolidated financial statements. However, where the parent does not acquire all the shares—that is, there is a non-controlling interest in the subsidiary (perhaps the parent entity acquired 80 per cent of the issued capital of the subsidiary meaning that the non-controlling interest is 20 per cent)—then IFRS 3 permits a parent to recognise either its share of the goodwill only or to recognise the total goodwill in the consolidated financial statements. That is, a parent has a choice as to whether to disclose goodwill attributable to non-controlling interests. This matter will be considered more fully in Chapter 22, which focuses on various aspects of accounting for non-controlling interests. At this point, it should simply be appreciated that parent entities have a choice regarding how to account for goodwill on acquisition—a choice that was not available within the accounting standards prior to amendments made in 2008.

To undertake the consolidation of the parent's and subsidiaries' financial statements, a worksheet is typically used (as will be shown in Worked Example 20.3). It is usual to set up the worksheet so that the entities to be consolidated are arranged side by side in the left-hand columns. To the right, there are debit and credit columns for the consolidation adjustment entries. A final column on the right-hand side of the worksheet will provide the consolidated figures to then be used to compile the consolidated financial statements.

What should also be noted is that the individual account balances included within the ledgers of the separate legal entities are not adjusted as a result of consolidating the financial statements of the various entities within the group. The consolidation entries are made outside of their individual ledgers. The consolidation journal entries are written into a consolidation journal and are then typically posted to a consolidation worksheet. A new worksheet is prepared each time consolidated financial statements are required. As indicated, the consolidation worksheet provides the numbers that are used directly to construct the consolidated financial statements.

Group members to use consistent accounting policies

When consolidated financial statements are being prepared, they are required to be prepared on the basis that all entities within the group are adopting the same accounting policies. Where separate entities do not apply the same accounting methods, adjustments are necessary on consolidation to remove the impacts of different accounting policies (paragraphs 19 and B87 of IFRS 10).

The ends of the reporting periods of all the entities in the group are also expected to be the same. Where this is not possible, adjustments for the effect of significant transactions or events that occurred between the two reporting period dates will be required on consolidation. However, adjustments are only possible if the different ends of reporting periods are reasonably close together, for example no more than three months apart (IFRS 10, paragraphs B92 and B93).

Eliminating parent's investment in subsidiary

The first step in the consolidation process is substituting the assets and liabilities of the subsidiary for the investment account that currently exists in the parent company. Where the fair value of the net assets (inclusive of an amount being attributed to contingent liabilities) does not equal the fair value of the investment, this will lead to a difference on consolidation. This difference will either be goodwill or a bargain gain on purchase (in Worked Example 20.3 it will lead to a difference of €20,000, this being the goodwill acquired).

The investment account is eliminated in full against the pre-acquisition equity of the subsidiary. This avoids double-counting assets, liabilities and equity of Subsidiary plc. IFRS 10 details a number of the procedures required in preparing consolidated financial statements (some, but not all, of which will be considered in this chapter). Paragraphs B86–B99 set out guidance for the preparation of consolidated financial statements. Some of these paragraphs, to the extent they are relevant to the material covered in this chapter, are reproduced below:

B86 Consolidated financial statements:

(a) combine like items of assets, liabilities, equity, income, expenses and cash flows of the parent with those of its subsidiaries.

(b) offset (eliminate) the carrying amount of the parent's investment in each subsidiary and the parent's portion of equity of each subsidiary (IFRS 3 explains how to account for any related goodwill).

(c) eliminate in full intragroup assets and liabilities, equity, income, expenses and cash flows relating to transactions between entities of the group (profits or losses resulting from intragroup transactions that are recognised in assets, such as inventory and fixed assets, are eliminated in full). Intragroup losses may indicate an impairment that requires recognition in the consolidated financial statements. IAS 12 Income Taxes applies to temporary differences that arise from the elimination of profits and losses resulting from intragroup transactions.

B88 An entity includes the income and expenses of a subsidiary in the consolidated financial statements from the date it gains control until the date when the entity ceases to control the subsidiary. Income and expenses of the subsidiary are based on the amounts of the assets and liabilities recognised in the consolidated financial statements at the acquisition date. For example, depreciation expense recognised in the consolidated statement of comprehensive income after the acquisition date is based on the fair values of the related depreciable assets recognised in the consolidated financial statements at the acquisition date.

We start our consolidation illustrations with a simple case in which one company acquires a 100 per cent interest in another company, and the consolidation is undertaken immediately subsequent to the share acquisition. This is shown in Worked Example 20.3.

Worked Example 20.3　A simple consolidation

Parent plc acquires all the issued capital of Subsidiary plc for a cash payment of €500,000 on 30 June 2015. The statements of financial position of both entities immediately following the purchase are:

	Parent plc (€000)	Subsidiary plc (€000)
ASSETS		
Non-current assets		
Plant	800	500
Land	200	100
Investment in Subsidiary plc	500	–
	1,500	600
Current assets		
Accounts receivable	150	55
Cash	10	5
	160	60
Total assets	1,660	660
EQUITY AND LIABILITIES		
Equity and reserves		
Share capital	1,000	200
Retained earnings	200	280
	1,200	480
Non-current liabilities		
Loans	400	150
Current liabilities		
Accounts payable	60	30
Total liabilities	460	180
Total equity and liabilities	1,660	660

Required
Provide the consolidated statement of financial position for Parent plc and Subsidiary plc as at 30 June 2015.

▶

Solution

Determination of goodwill

As this is a simple consolidation at the date of acquisition, and as the parent has acquired 100 per cent of the subsidiary, there is no need to consider the amount of the non-controlling interest and the fair value of any previously held equity interest in the acquiree. These issues will be considered in the chapters that follow.

In determining the amount of goodwill acquired, consideration needs to be given to the fair value of the assets acquired. We must consider the fair value of both the assets acquired and the purchase consideration given in exchange. For example, as Parent plc pays cash for the equity interest in Subsidiary plc, the fair value of the purchase consideration is easily determined as the amount of cash given in exchange. If we assume that the assets in Subsidiary plc are fairly valued, and there are no contingent liabilities to consider, then goodwill acquired by Parent plc would be determined as:

Fair value of purchase consideration	€500,000
less Fair value of identifiable assets acquired and liabilities assumed	€480,000
Goodwill on acquisition	€20,000

As we know from previous discussions in this chapter, and in Chapter 8, goodwill cannot be brought to account by Subsidiary plc, as only **purchased goodwill** and not **internally generated goodwill** is permitted to be recognised for accounting purposes. However, it *may* be brought to account by Parent plc as part of the consolidation process. That is, the consolidated statement of financial position will show goodwill of €20,000.

To undertake the consolidation of the parent and subsidiaries' financial statements, a consolidation worksheet is typically used and consolidation journal entries record the adjustments.

The consolidation entry to eliminate the investment in Subsidiary plc would be:

Dr	Share capital	€200,000	
Dr	Retained earnings	€280,000	
Dr	Goodwill	€20,000	
Cr	Investment in Subsidiary plc		€500,000

(to eliminate the investment in Subsidiary plc and to recognise the goodwill on acquisition)

purchased goodwill Goodwill that has been acquired through a transaction with an external party, as opposed to goodwill that is generated by the reporting entity itself. Purchased goodwill is shown as an asset of the reporting entity.

internally generated goodwill Goodwill that is generated by the reporting entity itself, not purchased from an external entity.

The above entry would be posted to the consolidation worksheet and the final column of the worksheet would provide the information to present the consolidated statement of financial position. The above entry is not made in the journal of either Parent plc or Subsidiary plc, but rather in a separate consolidation journal, which is then posted to the consolidation worksheet. A review of the following consolidation worksheet reveals the following points about the worksheet:

- The first column provides the names of the accounts that will be recognised in the consolidation process.
- The second and third columns represent the account balances of the individual entities. There are only two columns here because there are only two entities involved in the group. Additional columns would be required for each additional subsidiary in the group.
- The following two columns are then provided for the consolidation eliminations and adjustments. These adjustments will be in journal entry form, with the journal entries often being made in a separate consolidation journal. Because the adjustments are not recorded in the accounts of the individual entities, where consolidated financial statements are prepared over a number of periods there will be a need every year to repeat certain consolidation adjustments and eliminations, such as the entry that eliminates pre-acquisition share capital and reserves of the subsidiaries.
- The final column on the right-hand side of the worksheet represents the information that will be used directly to construct the consolidated financial statements. The numbers are derived by working across the worksheet and taking account of the various eliminations and adjustments.

Again, it should be emphasised that the consolidated financial statements are drawn up from the worksheet. There is no ledger as there would be for the separate entities in the group.

Consolidation worksheet for Parent plc and its controlled entity for the period ending 30 June 2015

	Parent plc	Subsidiary plc	Eliminations and adjustments Dr	Cr	Consolidated statement
ASSETS	(€000)	(€000)	(€000)	(€000)	(€000)
Non-current assets					
Plant	800	500			1,300
Land	200	100			300
Investment in Subsidiary plc	500	—		500	—
Goodwill on acquisition	—	—	20		20
	1,500	600			1,620
Current assets					
Accounts receivable	150	55			205
Cash	10	5			15
	160	60			220
Total assets	1,660	660			1,840
EQUITY AND LIABILITIES					
Equity and reserves					
Share capital	1,000	200	200		1,000
Retained earnings	200	280	280		200
	1,200	480			1,200
Non-current liabilities					
Loans	400	150			550
Current liabilities					
Accounts payable	60	30			90
Total liabilities	460	180			640
TOTAL EQUITY AND LIABILITIES	1,660	660	500	500	1,840

A review of the data to be included in the consolidated statement of financial position (the right-hand column) provides some useful information. It reveals that the economic entity controls assets with a total value of €1.84 million and that it has liabilities to parties external to the group totalling €640,000. The consolidated statement of financial position would appear as follows:

Consolidated statement of financial position
for Parent plc and its controlled entity as at 30 June 2015

	Parent entity (€000)	Group (€000)
ASSETS		
Non-current assets		
Plant	800	1,300
Land	200	300
Investment in Subsidiary plc	500	—
Goodwill	—	20
	1,500	1,620
Current assets		
Accounts receivable	150	205
Cash	10	15
	160	220
Total assets	1,660	1,840

EQUITY AND LIABILITIES		
Equity and reserves		
Equity share capital	1,000	1,000
Retained earnings	200	200
	1,200	1,200
Non-current liabilities		
Loans	400	550
Current liabilities		
Accounts payable	60	90
Total liabilities	460	640
Total equity and liabilities	1,660	1,840

Because the consolidated statement of financial position is prepared immediately after the acquisition, it does not include any share capital or reserves of the subsidiary given that all pre-acquisition share capital and reserves were eliminated on consolidation. Only the parent's pre-acquisition share capital and reserves will be shown. In subsequent periods the consolidated retained earnings will include the post-acquisition earnings of the subsidiary.

20.7   Gain on bargain purchase

Although not common, it is possible for a company to gain control of an entity for an amount less than the fair value of the proportional share of the identifiable assets acquired and the liabilities assumed. Bargain purchases are considered to be anomalous transactions because business entities and their owners generally do not knowingly and willingly sell assets or businesses at prices below their fair values. However a number of circumstances exist where bargain purchases occur. These include a forced liquidation or distress sale (for example, after the death of a founder or key manager) in which owners need to sell a business quickly, which may result in a price less than fair value.

A gain arising from a bargain purchase occurs when the acquisition-date fair values of the identifiable assets acquired and liabilities assumed *exceeds* the acquisition-date fair value of the consideration transferred *plus* the amount of any non-controlling interest in the acquiree *plus* the acquisition-date fair value of the acquiree's previously held equity interest in the acquiree. When a bargain purchase occurs, the acquirer recognises a gain in the profit or loss on the acquisition date. Before a gain on a bargain purchase is recognised, paragraph 36 of IFRS 3 requires that:

the acquirer shall reassess whether it has correctly identified all of the assets acquired and all of the liabilities assumed and shall recognise any additional assets or liabilities that are identified in that review. The acquirer shall then review the procedures used to measure the amounts this Standard requires to be recognised at the acquisition date for all of the following:

(a) the identifiable assets acquired and liabilities assumed;
(b) the non-controlling interest in the acquiree, if any;
(c) for a business combination achieved in stages, the acquirer's previously held equity interest in the acquiree; and
(d) the consideration transferred.

The objective of the review is to ensure that the measurements appropriately reflect consideration of all available information as of the acquisition date.

An example of a gain on bargain purchase is provided in Worked Example 20.4.

Worked Example 20.4   Acquisition of a subsidiary at a discount

Assume the same information as in Worked Example 20.3, except that this time Parent plc acquires Subsidiary plc for €400,000.

Fair value of purchase consideration	€400,000
Fair value of net assets acquired	€480,000
Gain on bargain purchase	€80,000

◀ **Required**

Provide the consolidation worksheet for Parent plc and its controlled entity for the year ending 30 June 2015.

Solution

Where Parent plc has acquired Subsidiary plc for €400,000, the elimination of the investment in Subsidiary plc would be recorded as:

Dr	Share capital	€200,000	
Dr	Retained earnings	€280,000	
Cr	Gain on bargain purchase (P&L)		€80,000
Cr	Investment in Subsidiary plc		€400,000

(to eliminate the investment in Subsidiary plc and to recognise the bargain purchase on acquisition)

Consolidation worksheet for Parent plc and its controlled entity for the year ending 30 June 2015

	Parent plc (€000)	Subsidiary plc (€000)	Eliminations and adjustments Dr (€000)	Eliminations and adjustments Cr (€000)	Consolidated statement (€000)
ASSETS					
Non-current assets					
Plant	800	500			1,300
Land	200	100			300
Investment in					
Subsidiary plc	400	—		400	—
	1,400	600			1,600
Current Assets					
Accounts receivable	150	55			205
Cash	110	5			115
	260	60			320
Total assets	1,660	660			1,920
EQUITY AND LIABILITIES					
Equity and reserves					
Share capital	1,000	200	200		1,000
Retained earnings	200	280	280	80	280
	1,200	480			1,280
Non-current liabilities					
Loans	400	150			550
Current liabilities					
Accounts payable	60	30			90
Total liabilities	460	180			640
Total equity and liabilities	1,660	660	480	480	1,920

Note 1: When completing a consolidation worksheet, the aggregate of the debits in the eliminations and adjustments columns should equal the aggregate of the credits.

Note 2: In this worked example, the gain has been taken directly to retained earnings in the absence of a consolidated statement of comprehensive income.

20.8 Subsidiary's assets not recorded at fair values

Frequently, a subsidiary's assets are not recorded at fair value (perhaps the subsidiary uses the cost model to account for its property, plant and equipment), hence adjustments will be required so that a reliable figure for goodwill (or the bargain on a purchase) can be calculated. As IFRS 3 indicates, if at acquisition the subsidiary's

assets are not recorded at fair value we can either revalue the identifiable assets in the accounting records of the subsidiary before consolidation or we can recognise the necessary adjustments on consolidation. In undertaking the revaluations we would need to consider the requirements pertaining to revaluations as stipulated in IAS 16 *Property, Plant and Equipment* and IAS 38 *Intangible Assets*. As we know from Chapter 8, there are some major restrictions in relation to upward revaluations of intangible assets.

A further consideration is that, where non-current assets are revalued upwards, an adjustment for deferred tax should also be made. Further details in respect of this can be found in Chapter 15.

With the first approach, all the non-current assets of the subsidiary would be revalued to their fair values in the accounting records of the subsidiary in accordance with IAS 16 and IAS 38. This would require the following entry to be made in the accounting records of the subsidiary (which would need some co-operation from the subsidiary, which might not always be forthcoming prior to acquisition):

Dr	Non-current assets	XX	
Cr	Revaluation surplus		XX
Cr	Deferred tax liability		XX

(revaluing assets to fair value and recognising deferred tax)

With the second approach—where we recognise the increment in the value of the assets in the consolidation process rather than in the accounts of the subsidiary—the above entry would be made in the consolidation worksheet.

Following the entries to recognise the fair value of the non-current assets (either in the books of the subsidiary or in the consolidation worksheet), a consolidation entry would be processed to eliminate the investment and the corresponding equity in the subsidiary. The equity in the subsidiary would include the revaluation surplus, that is, it would be treated the same as other pre-acquisition capital and reserve accounts. This might require the following entries on consolidation:

Dr	Share capital	XX	
Dr	Retained earnings	XX	
Dr	Revaluation surplus	XX	
Dr	Goodwill	XX	
Cr	Investment in subsidiary		XX

(eliminating the investment in subsidiary, as well as the revaluation surplus created in the previous entry)

Worked Example 20.5 provides the entries necessary to account for the assets of a subsidiary when those assets are not recorded at fair value at the date of acquisition.

Worked Example 20.5 **Consolidation where subsidiary's assets are not recorded at fair value**

Assume the same information as provided in Worked Example 20.3, except this time Parent plc acquires Subsidiary plc for €550,000. At this date, all assets were fairly valued except for land, which had a fair value of €130,000. The tax rate is 30 per cent.

Required

Provide the journal entries necessary to consolidate Parent plc and its controlled entity for the year ended 30 June 2015, assuming:

(a) Subsidiary plc revalued its land
(b) Subsidiary plc did not revalue its land

Solution

(a) As we explained in Chapter 15, an entity revaluing its non-current assets creates a tax effect, which needs to be recognised in accordance with IAS 12 *Income Taxes* (you may need to go back and read Chapter 15 if you have forgotten the requirements of tax-effect accounting). The revaluation creates a difference between the *carrying amount* and the *tax base* of the asset, which in turn creates a deferred tax difference.

If Subsidiary plc revalued its land at the date of its acquisition by Parent plc, the journal entry in the books of Subsidiary plc would have been:

30 June 2015

Dr	Land	€30,000	
Cr	Revaluation surplus		€21,000
Cr	Deferred tax liability		€9,000

(revaluing the asset to fair value and recognising the associated deferred tax liability)

As the revaluation surplus is part of pre-acquisition reserves of the subsidiary, it needs to be taken into account when calculating goodwill. Goodwill is calculated to be €49,000, determined as follows:

Share capital	€200,000
Retained earnings	€280,000
Revaluation surplus	€21,000
Total pre-acquisition capital and reserves	€501,000
Fair value of consideration	€550,000
Goodwill	€49,000

From the above workings, the consolidation entry to eliminate the investment in Subsidiary plc would be:

30 June 2015

Dr	Share capital	€200,000	
Dr	Retained earnings	€280,000	
Dr	Revaluation surplus	€21,000	
Dr	Goodwill	€49,000	
Cr	Investment in Subsidiary plc		€550,000

It should be noted that, when a consolidation adjustment is made to depreciable assets, a consolidation journal entry is required to adjust future depreciation expenses. This is considered in more detail in Chapter 21.

(b) Had Subsidiary plc chosen not to revalue its land when it was acquired by Parent plc, Parent plc would still have needed to make an adjustment to recognise the actual value of land purchased by it when the equity was acquired. What would have been necessary would have been for the revaluation to have been made as a consolidation adjustment prior to the elimination of the pre-acquisition share capital and reserves of Subsidiary plc. This would create a revaluation surplus in the consolidation worksheet, which would be treated as a pre-acquisition reserve of the subsidiary. The above entry would be required.

20.8.1 Subsidiary's assets not recorded at fair value at date of acquisition together with a gain on bargain purchase

It is possible, even if the assets of the subsidiary are recognised at their fair value at the date of acquisition, for a gain to result on acquisition. Where there is a gain on bargain purchase, this shall be recognised as a gain in the statement of comprehensive income.

Any depreciable non-monetary assets should be depreciated at their cost to the economic entity. A comparison of the depreciation charge in the books of the subsidiary with the amount required in the consolidated financial statements will provide the amount of the adjustment.

In Worked Example 20.6 we consider the joint situation where a gain on bargain purchase is calculated following a fair value adjustment being undertaken in relation to a subsidiary's assets.

Worked Example 20.6	**Revaluation to fair value with a resulting discount on acquisition**

On 30 June 2015 Kite plc acquired 100 per cent of the issued capital of Surfer plc for £3,920,000. At that date, the statement of financial position of Surfer plc showed share capital and reserves of:

Share capital	£2,500,000
Retained earnings	£900,000
Total share capital and reserves	£3,400,000

At the date of acquisition, the statements of financial position of Kite plc and Surfer plc were as follows:

	Kite plc (£000)	Surfer plc (£000)
ASSETS		
Non-current assets		
Land	2,890	2,700
Plant and equipment	1,905	900
Investment in Surfer plc	3,920	—
	8,715	3,600
Current assets		
Accounts receivable	175	64
Cash	15	6
	190	70
Total assets	8,905	3,670
EQUITY AND LIABILITIES		
Equity and reserves		
Equity share capital	5,500	2,500
Retained earnings	2,120	900
	7,620	3,400
Non-current liabilities		
Loans	1,145	215
Current liabilities		
Accounts payable	140	55
Total liabilities	1,285	270
Total equity and liabilities	8,905	3,670

Additional information
- At the date of acquisition, all the assets acquired and the liabilities assumed were valued at fair value except certain non-monetary assets, which have the following fair values:

	Carrying amount	Fair value
Land	2,700,000	3,200,000
Plant at cost	3,700,000	1,300,000
Accumulated depreciation	(2,800,000)	
	900,000	

- The plant and equipment of Surfer plc is expected to have a remaining useful life of four years and no residual value.
- The tax rate is 30 per cent.

Required

(a) Prepare the consolidation journal entries necessary to consolidate Kite plc and Surfer plc at 30 June 2015 assuming that Surfer plc did not revalue its non-monetary assets in its own financial statements as at the date of the acquisition. Prepare the consolidated statement of financial position.
(b) Assuming that the plant will be depreciated on the straight-line basis over its remaining useful life of four years, prepare the consolidation journal entries at 30 June 2016.

Solution

(a) Consolidation journal entries

30 June 2015

(i)	Dr	Land	£500,000	
	Cr	Revaluation surplus		£350,000
	Cr	Deferred tax liability		£150,000

| (ii) | Dr | Accumulated depreciation | £2,800,000 | |
| | Cr | Plant | | £2,800,000 |

(iii)	Dr	Plant	£400,000	
	Cr	Revaluation surplus		£280,000
	Cr	Deferred tax liability		£120,000

Having revalued the assets, and therefore having restated the pre-acquisition reserves of the subsidiary, we can determine the goodwill or gain on bargain purchase as follows:

Share capital	£2,500,000
Retained earnings	£900,000
Revaluation surplus	£630,000
Total pre-acquisition capital and reserves	£4,030,000
Cost of investment in Surfer plc	£3,920,000
Gain on bargain purchase	£110,000

(iv)	Dr	Share capital	£2,500,000	
	Dr	Retained earnings	£900,000	
	Dr	Revaluation surplus	£630,000	
	Cr	Gain on bargain purchase of Surfer plc (P&L)		£110,000
	Cr	Investment in Surfer plc		£3,920,000

Consolidation worksheet for Kite plc and its controlled entity for the period ending 30 June 2015

	Kite plc (£000)	Surfer plc (£000)	Eliminations and adjustments		Consolidated SOFP (£000)
			Dr (£000)	Cr (£000)	
Retained earnings	2,120	900	900(d)	110(d)	2,230
Share capital	5,500	2,500	2,500(d)		
			630(d)	350(a), 280(c)	5,500
Revaluation surplus					—
Current liabilities					
Accounts payable	140	55			195
Non-current liabilities					
Deferred tax liability				150(a), 120(c)	270
Loans	1,145	215			1,360
	8,905	3,670			9,555
Current assets					
Cash	15	6			21
Accounts receivable	175	64			239
Non-current assets					
Plant	4,000	3,700	400(c)	2,800(b)	5,300
Accumulated depreciation	(2,095)	(2,800)	2,800(b)		(2,095)
Land	2,890	2,700	500(a)		6,090
Investment in Surfer plc	3,920	—		3,920(d)	—
	8,905	3,670	7,730	7,730	9,555

(b) Additional depreciation expense adjustment at 30 June 2016 (one year later)

While the carrying amount of the asset in the financial statements of Surfer plc was £900,000 (with remaining depreciation of £225,000 per year), the asset is measured at its fair value of £1,300,000 in the consolidated financial statements (which means a related depreciation of £325,000 per year). Hence, from the group's perspective we need to increase depreciation by £100,000 per year.

Fair value of plant acquired	£1,300,000
Carrying value of plant in accounting records of Surfer plc	£900,000
Additional depreciation to be recognised in total over next 4 years	£400,000
Additional depreciation per year	£100,000

30 June 2016 — consolidation journal entries to recognise additional depreciation expense

Dr	Depreciation expense	£100,000	
Cr	Accumulated depreciation—plant		£100,000
Dr	Deferred tax liability	£30,000	
Cr	Income tax expense		£30,000

The additional depreciation charge results from the additional amount paid by the economic entity for the item of plant. As the value of the asset is recovered through use, the deferred tax liability recognised at the date of acquisition, 30 June 2015, which was £120,000, is reversed. At the end of four years, the remaining useful life of the item of plant, the balance of the deferred tax liability, will be £nil (it will be reduced by £30,000 each year).

20.9   Previously unrecognised identifiable intangible assets

In the above examples we assumed that the subsidiary did not have any other assets that existed at acquisition but were precluded from being recognised in the subsidiary's financial statements. As we know, many internally generated intangible assets are not permitted to be recognised by the entity creating the asset; however, they can be recognised at fair value on consolidation. Any excess of the fair value of the purchase consideration over the fair value of the net assets acquired (including the fair value of the identifiable intangible asset, for example a publishing title) would then be considered to be of the nature of goodwill. Consider Worked Example 20.7.

Worked Example 20.7   Recognition on consolidation of previously unrecognised identifiable intangible assets

On 30 June 2015 Cameron plc acquired 100 per cent of the issued capital of Blair plc for £4,000,000. At that date, the statement of financial position of Blair plc showed share capital and reserves of:

Share capital	£3,000,000
Retained earnings	£400,000
Total share capital and reserves	£3,400,000

At the date of acquisition, the statements of financial position of Cameron plc and Blair plc were as follows:

	Cameron plc (£000)	Blair plc (£000)
ASSETS		
Non-current assets		
Land	3,500	3,000
Plant and equipment	1,700	600
Investment in Blair plc	4,000	—
	9,200	3,600
Current assets		
Accounts receivable	200	45
Cash	100	25
	300	70
Total assets	9,500	3,670

	Cameron plc (£000)	Blair plc (£000)
EQUITY AND LIABILITIES		
Equity and reserves		
Share capital	5,500	3,000
Retained earnings	2,500	400
	8,000	3,400
Non-current liabilities		
Loans	1,400	220
Current liabilities		
Accounts payable	100	50
Total liabilities	1,500	270
Total equity and liabilities	9,500	3,670

Additional information
- At the date of acquisition, all the assets acquired and the liabilities assumed were valued at fair value.
- Blair plc had a successful publishing title which had a fair value of £400,000 at 30 June 2015 but which had been internally developed and therefore not recognised in its statement of financial position.

Required

Prepare the consolidation journal entries necessary to consolidate Cameron plc and Blair plc at 30 June 2015. Prepare the consolidated statement of financial position.

Solution

Determination of goodwill	£
Share capital	3,000,000
Retained earnings	400,000
Total pre-acquisition capital and reserves	3,400,000
Cost of investment in Surfer plc	4,000,000
	600,000
Less: Fair value of publishing title	400,000
Goodwill	200,000

Consolidation journal entries

Dr	Share capital	£3,000,000	
Dr	Retained earnings	£400,000	
Dr	Publishing title	£400,000	
Dr	Goodwill	£200,000	
Cr	Investment in Blair plc		£4,000,000

Consolidation worksheet for Cameron plc and its controlled entity for the period ending 30 June 2015

	Cameron plc (£000)	Blair plc (£000)	Eliminations and adjustments		Consolidated SOFP (£000)
			Dr (£000)	Cr (£000)	
Retained earnings	2,500	400	400		2,500
Share capital	5,500	3,000	3,000		5,500
Current liabilities					
Accounts payable	100	50			150
Non-current liabilities					
Loans	1,400	220			1,620
	9,500	3,670			9,770

Current assets					
Cash	100	25			125
Accounts receivable	200	45			245
Non-current assets					
Plant	1,700	600			2,300
Land	3,500	3,000			6,500
Publishing title			400		400
Goodwill			200		200
Investment in Surfer plc	4,000	—	—	4,000	—
	9,500	3,670	4,000	4,000	9,770

20.10 Consolidation after date of acquisition

As we have noted, the **pre-acquisition shareholders' funds** of the subsidiary are eliminated on consolidation against the investment in the subsidiary. This then typically provides goodwill on consolidation (which is, in effect, a balancing item). Occasionally it will result in a gain on bargain purchase.

In the period following acquisition, the subsidiary will generate profits or losses. To the extent that these results have been generated in the period after acquisition, and therefore reflect, in part, the efforts of the management team of the parent entity, they should be reflected in the results of the economic entity. That is, unlike pre-acquisition earnings, post-acquisition earnings of the subsidiary are considered to be part of the earnings of the economic entity and are not eliminated on consolidation. Accounting post-acquisition is examined more closely in Worked Example 20.8.

> **pre-acquisition shareholders' funds** Shareholders' funds that were in existence within an organisation before an entity acquired an ownership interest in that organisation.

Worked Example 20.8 — Consolidation in a period subsequent to the acquisition of the subsidiary

Assume the same facts as in Worked Example 20.3, in which Parent plc acquires all the shares in Subsidiary plc for €500,000 on 30 June 2015, leading to goodwill of €20,000 being recognised. We will assume that there is no tax to be paid, and that there are no intragroup transactions.

The financial statements for Parent plc and Subsidiary plc at 30 June 2016 (one year after acquisition) are provided here.

Reconciliation of opening and closing retained earnings	Parent plc (€000)	Subsidiary plc (€000)
Sales revenue	300	100
Cost of goods sold	(100)	(40)
Other expenses	(60)	(30)
Profit	140	30
Retained earnings opening balance	200	280
Retained earnings—30 June 2016	340	310

Statements of financial position	Parent plc (€000)	Subsidiary plc (€000)
ASSETS		
Non-current assets		
Land	200	100
Plant	1,000	600
Investment in Subsidiary plc	500	—
	1,700	700

Statements of financial position	Parent plc (€000)	Subsidiary plc (€000)
CURRENT ASSETS		
Accounts receivable	250	75
Cash	50	25
	300	100
Total assets	2,000	800
EQUITY AND LIABILITIES		
Equity and reserves		
Retained earnings	340	310
Share capital	1,000	200
	1,340	510
Non-current liabilities		
Loans	600	250
Current liabilities		
Accounts payable	60	40
Total liabilities	660	290
Total equity and liabilities	2,000	800

Additional information
Directors have determined that goodwill acquired in 2015 has been impaired by €5,000, so that its value at 30 June 2016 is €15,000. There are no intragroup transactions.

Required

Prepare the consolidation worksheet for Parent plc and its controlled entity as at 30 June 2016.

Solution

There are three parts to preparing the consolidation worksheet for Parent plc and Subsidiary plc.
(a) Elimination of investment
    We need to perform the same entry to eliminate the investment as we did in the previous year. Remember, the effects of past consolidation adjustments and eliminations are not incorporated in any opening balances and need to be replicated across successive years.

Dr	Share capital	€200,000	
Dr	Retained earnings	€280,000	
Dr	Goodwill	€20,000	
Cr	Investment in Subsidiary plc		€500,000

(to eliminate the investment in Subsidiary plc and to recognise the goodwill on acquisition)

(b) Impairment of goodwill
    IAS 36 requires us to consider whether goodwill acquired is subsequently impaired. In this illustration we have assumed that goodwill is the subject of an impairment loss, hence the adjusting entries for goodwill are:

Dr	Impairment loss — goodwill (P&L)	€5,000	
Cr	Goodwill		€5,000

(to recognise the impairment loss recognised for 2016)

(c) Preparation of worksheet
    As can be seen from the below worksheet, the consolidated retained earnings balance at the end of the 2016 financial year will equal the parent entity's retained earnings, plus the post-acquisition earnings of the controlled entity. You will notice the letter markers next to the adjusting entries. These allow us to trace the journal entries back to the consolidation journal. The above worksheet then provides the data necessary to produce the required consolidated financial statements in accordance with IFRS 3, IFRS 10, IAS 12 and IAS 1.

Consolidation worksheet for Parent plc and its controlled entity for the period ending 30 June 2016

	Parent plc (€000)	Subsidiary plc (€000)	Eliminations and adjustments Dr (€000)	Eliminations and adjustments Cr (€000)	Consolidated statement (€000)
Reconciliation of opening and closing retained earnings					
Sales revenue	300	100			400
Cost of goods sold	(100)	(40)			(140)
Other expenses	(60)	(30)	5(b)		(95)
Profit	140	30			165
Retained earnings opening balance	200	280	280(a)		200
Retained earnings closing balance	340	310			365
Statements of financial position					
Retained earnings—30 June 2016	340	310			365
Share capital	1,000	200	200(a)		1,000
Current liabilities					
Accounts payable	60	40			100
Non-current liabilities					
Loans	600	250			850
Total equity and liabilities	2,000	800			2,315
Current assets					
Cash	50	25			75
Accounts receivable	250	75			325
Non-current assets					
Plant	1,000	600			1,600
Land	200	100			300
Investment in Subsidiary plc	500	–		500(a)	–
Goodwill on acquisition	–	–	20(a)	5(b)	15
	2,000	800	505	505	2,315

20.11 Disclosure requirements

While IFRS 10 stipulates the accounting procedures to be adopted in consolidating the financial statements of a parent and its subsidiaries, we need to look to IFRS 12 *Disclosure of Interests in Other Entities* (issued August 2011) for the disclosures required in relation to interests in subsidiaries. This can be contrasted to the prior situation (before implementation of IFRS 12) wherein the accounting procedures and related disclosure requirements were incorporated in one accounting standard: IAS 27.

20.11.1 Interests in subsidiaries

Regarding interests in subsidiaries, paragraphs 10 and 11 of IFRS 12 require the following:

10. *An entity shall disclose information that enables users of its consolidated financial statements*

   (a) to understand:
     (i) the composition of the group; and
     (ii) the interest that non-controlling interests have in the group's activities and cash flows (paragraph 12); and
   (b) to evaluate:
     (i) the nature and extent of significant restrictions on its ability to access or use assets, and settle liabilities, of the group (paragraph 13);

    (ii) *the nature of, and changes in, the risks associated with its interests in consolidated structured entities (paragraphs 14–17);*

    (iii) *the consequences of changes in its ownership interest in a subsidiary that do not result in a loss of control (paragraph 18); and*

    (iv) *the consequences of losing control of a subsidiary during the reporting period (paragraph 19).*

11.   *When the financial statements of a subsidiary used in the preparation of consolidated financial statements are as of a date or for a period that is different from that of the consolidated financial statements (see paragraphs B92 and B93 of IFRS 10), an entity shall disclose:*

    (a) *the date of the end of the reporting period of the financial statements of that subsidiary; and*

    (b) *the reason for using a different date or period.*

20.11.2 The interest that non-controlling interests have in the group's activities and cash flows

Paragraph IFRS 12 requires the following disclosures:

12. *An entity shall disclose for each of its subsidiaries that have non-controlling interests that are material to the reporting entity:*

    (a) *the name of the subsidiary.*

    (b) *the principal place of business (and country of incorporation if different from the principal place of business) of the subsidiary.*

    (c) *the proportion of ownership interests held by non-controlling interests.*

    (d) *the proportion of voting rights held by non-controlling interests, if different from the proportion of ownership interests held.*

    (e) *the profit or loss allocated to non-controlling interests of the subsidiary during the reporting period.*

    (f) *accumulated non-controlling interests of the subsidiary at the end of the reporting period.*

    (g) *summarised financial information about the subsidiary (see paragraph B10).*

IFRS 12 also stipulates a number of disclosure requirements in relation to:

■ the nature and extent of significant restrictions (see paragraph 13);
■ the nature of the risks associated with an entity's interests in consolidated structured entities (see paragraphs 14–17);
■ the consequences of changes in a parent's ownership interest in a subsidiary that do not result in a loss of control (see paragraph 18); and
■ the consequences of losing control of a subsidiary during the reporting period (paragraph 19).

20.12 Control, joint control and significant influence

An investor can have various degrees of influence over an investee. For example, an investor might control an investee, in which case the investee would be considered to be a subsidiary. Alternatively, it might have joint control or significant influence over an investee. Lastly, its level of influence might fall short of significant influence. The degree of influence or power over an investee has direct implications for how the investor shall account for the investment.

    As we know from reading this chapter, if an investor controls an investee, then it must consolidate the investee in accordance with IFRS 10. It must also make disclosures in accordance with IFRS 12. This is reflected in Figure 20.5. We have also learned in this chapter that, if an organisation is jointly controlled, then the financial statements of that jointly controlled organisation are not to be incorporated within the consolidated financial statements.

    A summarised overview of how the degree of influence or power over an investee influences how an investor accounts for an equity investment is provided in Figure 20.5. As Figure 20.5 indicates, if there is deemed to be joint control, then such a situation would be referred to as a 'joint arrangement'. Joint arrangements are addressed in WebChapter 6. As WebChapter 6 explains, joint arrangements will be classified as either 'joint operations' or 'joint ventures'. The classification depends upon the rights and obligations of the parties to the arrangement.

Figure 20.5 Accounting for investments in which the investee has control, joint control or significant influence over the investee

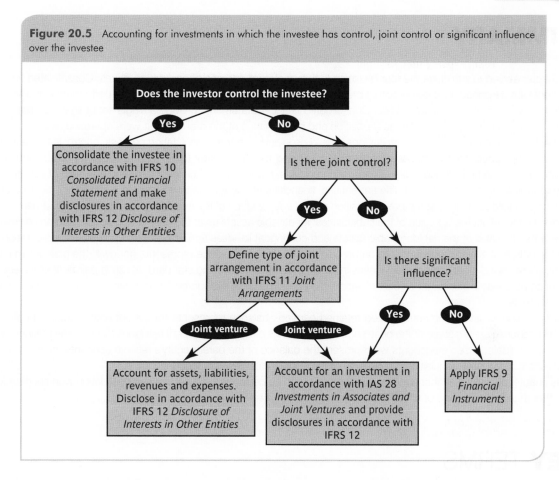

A joint operation is defined in paragraph 15 of IFRS 11 *Joint Arrangements* as:

a joint arrangement whereby the parties that have joint control of the arrangement have rights to the assets, and obligations for the liabilities, relating to the arrangement. Those parties are called joint operators.

By contrast, a joint venture is defined in paragraph 16 of IFRS 11 as:

a joint arrangement whereby the parties that have joint control of the arrangement have rights to the net assets of the arrangement. Those parties are called joint venturers.

The classification as a 'joint operation' or 'joint venture' in turn impacts how the investor accounts for its interest in the investee. If the investment is deemed to be a joint operation, then the investor's interest in the respective assets, liabilities, expenses and revenues will be recognised in the consolidated financial statements (IFRS 11, paragraph 21). By contrast, if the investment is deemed to be a joint venture, then the equity method of accounting (IFRS 11, paragraph 24)—which is explained in Chapter 24—is to be used to account for the investment.

If an investee is not controlled or subject to joint control, but is significantly influenced (which is defined in IAS 28 *Investments in Associates and Joint Ventures* as influence which falls short of control, or joint control, but is the power to participate in the financial and operating policy decisions of the investee), then the investee would be classified as an 'associate' and the equity method of accounting is to be employed to account for the investment.

Where an investor does not have control, joint control or significant influence over an investee—and therefore does not even have the power to *participate* in the financial and operating policy decisions of the investee—then the interest in the investee is to be accounted for in accordance with IFRS 9 *Financial Instruments*. IFRS 9 is considered in depth in Chapter 12.

SUMMARY

This chapter served to introduce the four chapters in this book that address consolidation issues. Consolidated financial statements are described as statements that present aggregated information about the financial performance and financial positions of various separate legal entities. Consolidated financial statements provide a single set of financial statements that are prepared to represent the financial position and performance of the group as if it were operating as a single economic entity. In determining which organisations should be included in the consolidation process, *control* is the determining factor. The group itself comprises the parent entity and its subsidiaries (controlled entities). IFRS 10 requires all controlled entities to be included in the consolidation process, regardless of their legal form and their field of activities.

In performing the consolidation of different entities' financial statements, the investment in a subsidiary must be eliminated, on consolidation, against the pre-acquisition capital and reserves of the subsidiary. Any required adjustment has to be made first to reflect the fair value of the subsidiaries' identifiable assets as at the date of acquisition, and any difference between the fair value of the net identifiable assets and contingent liabilities acquired and the purchase consideration will be of the nature of either goodwill or gain on bargain purchase. If the balance represents goodwill, the goodwill must be periodically reviewed for any impairment losses in accordance with accounting standard IAS 36 *Impairment of Assets*. If a bargain on purchase is calculated on consolidation, the bargain is to be accounted for as a gain in the consolidated financial statements.

Following consolidation, the consolidated retained earnings balance represents the parent entity's retained earnings, plus the economic entity's share of the post-acquisition earnings of the controlled entities (subsidiaries). The balance in the various consolidated reserve accounts will represent the balance of the parent entity's reserve accounts, plus the parent entity's share of the post-acquisition movements of the subsidiaries' reserve accounts.

This chapter also stresses that consolidation entries are to be performed in a separate consolidation worksheet or journal, rather than in the journals of any of the entities within the group.

KEY TERMS

END-OF-CHAPTER EXERCISE

Stubbs plc acquires all the shares in Billa plc on 30 June 2014. The financial statements for Stubbs plc and Billa plc at 30 June 2015 (one year after acquisition) are provided below. **LO 20.4**

Reconciliation of opening and closing retained earnings

	Stubbs plc (€000)	Billa plc (€000)
Sales revenue	2,000	610
Cost of goods sold	(800)	(240)
Other expenses	(300)	(70)
Profit	900	300
Retained earnings opening balance	1,100	500
Retained earnings at 30 June 2015	2,000	800

Statements of financial position

	Stubbs plc (€000)	Billa plc (€000)
ASSETS		
Non-current assets		
Land	1,200	750
Plant	2,600	1,000
Accumulated depreciation — plant	(600)	(200)
Investment in Billa plc	1,100	–
	4,300	1,550
Current assets		
Accounts receivable	450	250
Cash	150	200
	600	450
Total assets	4,900	2,000
EQUITY AND LIABILITIES		
Equity and reserves		
Equity share capital	1,100	350
Retained earnings	2,000	800
	3,100	1,150
Non-current liabilities		
Loans	1,100	700
Current liabilities		
Accounts payable	700	150
Total liabilities	1,800	850
Total equity and liabilities	4,900	2,000

Additional information

- Stubbs plc acquires Billa plc on 1 July 2014 for €1.1 million in cash.
- The directors of Stubbs plc consider that, in the year to 30 June 2015, the value of goodwill has been impaired by an amount of €20,000.
- There are no intragroup transactions.
- The tax rate is 30 per cent.
- On the date at which Stubbs plc acquires Billa plc, the carrying value and fair value of the assets of Billa plc are:

	Carrying value (€000)	Fair value (€000)
Cash	150	150
Accounts receivable	200	200
Land	750	800
Plant (cost of €1,000,000, accumulated depreciation of €200,000)	800	900
	1,900	2,050

- No revaluations are undertaken in Billa plc's financial statements before consolidation.
- At the date of acquisition of Billa plc, Billa plc's liabilities amount to €1.050 million and there are no contingent liabilities.
- The plant in Billa plc is expected to have a remaining useful life of ten years from 30 June 2014, and no residual value.

REQUIRED

Provide the consolidated financial statements of Stubbs plc and Billa plc as at 30 June 2015.

SOLUTION TO END-OF-CHAPTER EXERCISE

We need to determine goodwill (the difference between the fair value of the net assets acquired and the fair value of the purchase consideration).

Fair value of purchase consideration		€1,100,000
Carrying value of net assets acquired:		
Carrying value of assets	€1,900,000	
Carrying value of liabilities	(€1,050,000)	€850,000
Fair value adjustment:		
Excess of fair value of land over carrying value	€50,000	
Excess of fair value of plant over carrying value	€100,000	
	€150,000	
Tax effect of revaluation (deferred tax liability)		
€150,000 × 0.30	(€45,000)	€105,000
Fair value of net assets acquired		€955,000
Goodwill acquired		€145,000

The consolidation journal entries would be as follows:

(a) To revalue the assets of Billa plc so that goodwill can subsequently be accounted for

Dr	Land	€50,000	
Cr	Revaluation surplus		€35,000
Cr	Deferred tax liability		€15,000
Dr	Accumulated depreciation	€200,000	
Cr	Plant		€200,000
Dr	Plant	€100,000	
Cr	Revaluation surplus		€70,000
Cr	Deferred tax liability		€30,000

(b) To eliminate the investment in Billa plc and the pre-acquisition capital and reserves of Billa plc

Dr	Share capital	€350,000	
Dr	Retained earnings	€500,000	
Dr	Revaluation surplus	€105,000	
Dr	Goodwill	€145,000	
Cr	Investment in Billa plc		€1,100,000

(c) To recognise impairment of goodwill

In this illustration there is a €20,000 impairment of goodwill and hence the adjusting entry required is:

Dr	Impairment loss—goodwill	€20,000	
Cr	Goodwill		€20,000

(d) Additional depreciation

From the perspective of the group, the plant in Billa plc has a carrying value of €900,000, which needs to be depreciated over its useful life. To recognise the depreciation of the fair value of adjustment of €100,000 over the remaining useful life of ten years, the following adjusting entry is necessary:

Dr	Depreciation	€10,000	
Cr	Accumulated depreciation		€10,000
Dr	Deferred tax liability	€3,000	
Cr	Income tax expense		€3,000

Consolidation worksheet for Stubbs plc and its controlled entity for the period ending 30 June 2015

	Stubbs plc (€000)	Billa plc (€000)	Eliminations and adjustments Dr (€000)	Eliminations and adjustments Cr (€000)	Consolidated statement (€000)
Reconciliation of opening and closing retained earnings					
Sales revenue	2,000	610			2,610
Cost of goods sold	(800)	(240)			(1,040)
Other expenses	(300)	(70)	10(d), 20(c)	3(d)	(397)
Profit	900	300			1,173
Retained earnings—30 June 2014	1,100	500	500(b)	–	1,100
Retained earnings—30 June 2015	2,000	800			2,273
Statements of financial position					
Shareholders' equity					
Retained earnings	2,000	800			2,273
Share capital	1,100	350	350(b)		1,100
Revaluation surplus	–	–	105(b)	70(a), 35(a)	–
Current liabilities					
Accounts payable	700	150			850
Non-current liabilities					
Loans	1,100	700			1,800
Deferred tax liability	–	–	3(d)	15(a), 30(b)	42
Total equity and liabilities	4,900	2,000			6,065
Current assets					
Cash	150	280			430
Accounts receivable	450	250			700
Non-current assets					
Land	1,200	750	50(a)		2,000
Plant	2,600	1,000	100(a)	200(a)	3,500
Accumulated depreciation	(600)	(280)	200(a)	10(d)	(690)
Goodwill			145(b)	20(c)	125
Investment in Billa plc	1,100	–		1,100(b)	–
	4,900	2,000	1,483	1,483	6,065

The consolidated statement of financial position of the Stubbs group can now be provided as follows:

Consolidated statement of financial position for Stubbs plc and its controlled entity as at 30 June 2015

	Stubbs plc (€000)	Group (€000)
ASSETS		
Non-current assets		
Land	1,200	2,000
Plant	2,600	3,500
Accumulated depreciation	(600)	(690)
Goodwill	–	125
Investment in Billa plc	1,100	–
	4,300	4,935
Current assets		
Accounts receivable	450	700
Cash	150	430
	600	1,130
Total assets	4,900	6,065
EQUITY AND LIABILITIES		
Equity and reserves		
Retained earnings	2,000	2,273
Share capital	1,100	1,100
	3,100	3,373
Non-current liabilities		
Loans	1,100	1,800
Deferred tax liability	–	42
	1,100	1,842
Current liabilities		
Accounts payable	700	850
Total liabilities	1,800	2,692
Total equity and liabilities	4,900	6,065

REVIEW QUESTIONS

1. What is the role of consolidated financial statements? **LO 20.1**
2. There is one asset that appears in the consolidated statement of financial position, but probably does not appear in the parent entity's or subsidiaries' separate financial statements, and there is also one asset that will appear in the statement of financial position of the parent entity, but will not appear in the consolidated financial statements. What accounts would these be? **LO 20.7**
3. Define: **LO 20.3**
    (a) a legal entity
    (b) an economic entity
    (c) a parent entity
    (d) a subsidiary
4. On consolidation, how is the goodwill on acquisition or the bargain gain on purchase determined? **LO 20.7**
5. What is 'fair value' and why is it relevant to consolidation accounting? **LO 20.3**

6   If a parent entity acquires a controlling interest in a subsidiary, and the subsidiary's assets are not measured at fair value, there is a requirement to make an adjusting entry to record the assets at fair value. Why do we need to do this adjusting entry? What would be the implications if we do not do the adjusting entry?   **LO** 20.8

7   On consolidation, we need to eliminate the investments in controlled entities. Against what accounts do we eliminate these investments?   **LO** 20.3

8   What is the primary criterion for determining whether or not to consolidate an entity?   **LO** 20.5

9   What are 'potential voting rights', and what part do they play in determining whether an entity is under the control of another entity?   **LO** 20.5

10 If Rip plc controls Curl plc, but is acting as agent for Quik plc in relation to its dealings with Curl plc, would Rip plc be required to include Curl plc's financial statements within its consolidated financial statements?   **LO** 20.6

11 What is the rationale for including the post-acquisition movements in retained earnings and other reserves of a subsidiary in the consolidated financial statements?   **LO** 20.1

12 The management of one of your clients has told you that they intend not to consolidate the financial statements of one of their subsidiaries because it is involved in mining, whereas all the other organisations in the group are involved in service industries. How would you respond to this position?   **LO** 20.3

13 What forms of entity may be consolidated (for example, partnerships, trusts, companies)? Has this requirement changed in recent years?   **LO** 20.3

14 According to IFRS 3, how should a bargain gain on purchase arising on consolidation be treated?   **LO** 20.7

15 Explain what 'control' means in the context of consolidation.   **LO** 20.6

16 Biggin plc acquires 100 per cent of the shares of Smallin plc on 1 July 2014 for a consideration of €730,000. The share capital and reserves of Smallin plc at the date of acquisition are: **LO** 20.4

Share capital	€200,000
Retained earnings	€100,000
Revaluation reserve account	€150,000
	€450,000

There are no transactions between the entities and all assets are fairly valued at the date of acquisition. The financial statements of Biggin plc and Smallin plc at 30 June 2015 (one year after acquisition) are:

	Biggin plc (€000)	Smallin plc (€000)
Reconciliation of opening and closing retained earnings		
Profit before tax	300	100
Tax	(100)	(30)
Profit after tax	200	70
Retained earnings—1 July 2014	200	100
Retained earnings—30 June 2015	400	170
Statements of financial positions		
ASSETS		
Non-current assets		
Land	200	120
Plant	1,000	600
Investment in Smallin plc	730	—
	1,930	720
Current assets		
Accounts receivable	350	95
Cash	80	45
	430	140
Total assets	2,360	860

	Biggin plc (€000)	Smallin plc (€000)
EQUITY AND LIABILITIES		
Equity and reserves		
Retained earnings	400	170
Share capital	1,000	200
Revaluation surplus	300	200
	1,700	570
Non-current liabilities		
Loans	600	250
Current liabilities		
Accounts payable	60	40
Total liabilities	660	290
Total equity and liabilities	2,360	860

REQUIRED

Prepare the consolidated financial statements for Biggin plc and Smallin plc as at 30 June 2015.

17 Michael plc acquires all the issued capital of McKee plc for a cash payment of £600,000 on 30 June 2015. The statements of financial position of both entities immediately following the purchase are: **LO 20.4**

	Michael plc (£000)	McKee plc (£000)
ASSETS		
Non-current assets		
Plant	700	500
Land	200	100
Investment in Subsidiary plc	600	–
	1,500	600
Current assets		
Cash	10	5
Accounts receivable	150	55
	160	60
Total assets	1,660	660
TOTAL EQUITY AND LIABILITIES		
Equity and reserves		
Share capital	1,000	200
Retained earnings	200	280
	1,200	480
Current liabilities		
Accounts payable	60	30
Non-current liabilities		
Loans	400	150
Total liabilities	460	180
Total equity and liabilities	1,660	660

Additional information
- All assets of McKee appearing in the 30 June 2015 statement of financial position are fairly valued.
- At 30 June 2015 McKee had two internally developed identifiable intangible assets with the following fair values:

	Fair value (£000)
Patent	100
Publishing title	25

REQUIRED

Provide the consolidated statement of financial position for Michael plc and McKee plc as at 30 June 2015.

18 Whopper plc acquires 100 per cent of the shares of Weenie plc on 1 July 2014 for a consideration of £1.25 million. The share capital and reserves of Weenie plc at the date of acquisition are: **LO 20.4**

Share capital	£750,000
Retained earnings	£375,000
Revaluation reserve	£375,000
	£1,500,000

Additional information

There are no transactions between the entities and all assets are fairly valued at the date of acquisition. No land or plant is acquired or sold by Weenie plc in the year to 30 June 2015. The financial statements of Whopper plc and Weenie plc at 30 June 2015 (one year after acquisition) are:

	Whopper plc (£000)	Weenie plc (£000)
Reconciliation of opening and closing retained earnings		
Profit before tax	750	375
Tax	(250)	(125)
Profit after tax	500	250
Retained earnings at 30 June 2014	1,000	375
Retained earnings at 30 June 2015	1,500	625
Statements of financial position		
ASSETS		
Non-current assets		
Land	1,750	750
Plant	2,875	1,500
Investment in Weenie plc	1,250	–
	5,875	2,250
Current assets		
Accounts receivable	875	300
Cash	250	200
	1,125	500
Total assets	7,000	2,750

	Whopper plc (£000)	Weenie plc (£000)
EQUITY AND LIABILITIES		
Equity and reserves		
Equity share capital	3,000	750
Retained earnings	1,500	625
Revaluation surplus	750	500
	5,250	1,875
Non-current liabilities		
Loans	1,500	625
Current liabilities		
Accounts payable	250	250
Total liabilities	1,750	875
Total equity and liabilities	7,000	2,750

REQUIRED

Prepare the consolidated accounts for Whopper plc and Weenie plc as at 30 June 2015.

CHALLENGING QUESTIONS

19 P plc is a public company that is listed on the London Stock Exchange. P plc has numerous small shareholders. P plc owns 35 per cent of the issued ordinary shares of B plc. The remaining shares of B plc are widely distributed among numerous small shareholders, none of which owns more than 4 per cent of B plc. B plc's constitution provides that, at general meetings of the company, ordinary shareholders are entitled to vote on resolutions and elect directors, on the basis of one vote per ordinary share.

At general meetings of B plc, resolutions proposed by P plc are invariably passed, and candidates for directorships nominated by P plc are invariably elected, because many small shareholders in B plc do not exercise their right to attend general meetings and vote.

P plc does not own any investments in other entities. **LO 20.6**

REQUIRED

Advise P plc whether it is required to produce consolidated financial statements. Give reasons for your answer.

20 FXL Pty Ltd (FXL) is a private company with many strategic investments. The finance director is concerned that he might be required to consolidate some of these investments, pursuant to IFRS 10. Details of the investment relationships are as follows: **LO 20.6**

(a) FXL has a 25 per cent interest in the share capital of LBX Pty Limited (LBX), which is a company involved in the same industry as FXL. The remaining 75 per cent of the share capital is owned by LBX's founders, Mr and Mrs T. Mr and Mrs T are unfamiliar with the industry and so have given FXL three out of the five seats available on the board of directors. FXL takes the lead on all decisions but the business is closely monitored by Mr and Mrs T, who hold the other two board positions.

(b) FXL has a substantial loan receivable from BBT Pty plc (BBT). BBT, as a result of the current economic climate, has experienced significant trading problems. BBT has failed to make its regular payments under the loan agreement. FXL has become concerned about the recoverability of the loan and has reached an agreement with the management of BBT that FXL executives will take control of the company's finances for a period of five years. An executive of FXL has been given control of BBT's cheque book and makes all payments. FXL has not gained any seats on BBT's board of directors, which is still dominated by BBT shareholders.

(c) FXL owns 50 per cent of A Pty plc (A), with the other 50 per cent being owned by B Pty plc (B). Both companies have equal voting rights and an equal share of seats on the board of directors. Under an agreement with B, FXL supplies the finance to the company on normal commercial terms. The loan is fully secured against the assets of the company. B provides the management and entrepreneurial flair to A. Under the agreement forged, B will receive a management fee in respect of the net profits of A after allowing for interest payments on the FXL loan. In times of no profits, the interest payments will still be met, but B will not receive any remuneration.

(d) FXL operates as the trustee company for the FXL trading trust. The trust is a discretionary trust, with the nominated beneficiaries being the directors of FXL. These directors are Mr F, Mrs X and Mr L. Over the years, the trust has distributed its income in the following proportions:

Mr F	70%
Mrs X	20%
Mr L	10%

Under the terms of the trust deed, FXL has complete control over the operating and financing decisions of the trust.

(e) FXL holds a 75 per cent interest in JIB Pty Ltd (JIB). The interest was created when FXL converted a substantial loan it made to JIB into equity at the invitation of JIB when JIB began to trade poorly and recovery of the loan seemed uncertain. JIB has a large deficiency in net assets and has been consolidated for many years. FXL is a passive investor, having no seats on the board of directors and no say in the financing or operating decisions of JIB.

REQUIRED

Advise the finance director of FXL of the requirements of IFRS 10 in respect of the control criterion. For each of the above investments, indicate where the control rests and whether or not consolidation will be required.

21 On 30 June 2014 Bells plc acquired all the issued capital of Winkipop plc for a cost of €950,000. At the date of acquisition, the acquired shares had the right to share in a dividend that had been declared on 30 June, the total amount of the dividend being €200,000. Bells plc will not recognise the dividend until it is received. It was ultimately received on 1 February 2015. The statement of financial position of Winkipop plc at 30 June 2014 was as follows: **LO 20.4**

Statement of financial position of Winkipop plc as at 30 June 2014	€000
ASSETS	
Non-current assets	
Plant and equipment	720
Accumulated depreciation—plant and equipment	(120)
Land	800
	1,400
Current assets	
Inventory	110
Accounts receivable	40
Cash	50
	200
Total assets	1,600
EQUITY AND LIABILITIES	
Equity and reserves	
Share capital	700
Retained earnings	200
Revaluation surplus	100
	1,000
Non-current liabilities	
Loan	500
Current liabilities	
Accounts payable	100
Total liabilities	600
Total equity and liabilities	1,600

Additional information

- The plant and equipment of Winkipop plc has a fair value of €750,000.
- The tax rate is 30 per cent.

REQUIRED

Prepare the consolidation worksheet journal entries immediately after the above acquisition.

22 Slowsilver plc is listed on the London Stock Exchange and has a large number of shareholders, each with relatively small parcels of shares. Slowsilver holds shares in one other entity, this being Quickgold plc. Slowsilver owns 30 per cent of the issued ordinary shares of Quickgold plc. The remaining 70 per cent of shares in Quickgold plc are dispersed among a large number of shareholders, none of whom has an ownership interest of more than 3 per cent of Quickgold plc. Each share in Quickgold plc and Slowsilver plc entitles the shareholder to one vote at annual general meetings. **LO 20.5**

REQUIRED

Determine whether Slowsilver plc would be required to prepare consolidated financial statements.

23 Sandy plc acquired 100 per cent of the issued capital of Beach plc on 30 June 2014 for £900,000, when the statement of financial position of Beach plc was as follows: **LO 20.4**

Statement of financial position of Beach plc as at 30 June 2014 (working sheet)

	£000		£000
Assets		*Liabilities*	
Accounts receivable	70	Loan	300
Inventory	100		
Land	400	*Shareholders' equity*	
Property, plant and equipment	700	Share capital	500
Accumulated depreciation	(270)	Retained earnings	200
	1,000		1,000

Additional information

- The tax rate is 30 per cent.
- As at the date of acquisition, all assets of Beach plc were at fair value, other than the property, plant and equipment, which had a fair value of £530,000. Beach plc adopts the cost model for measuring its property, plant and equipment. The property, plant and equipment is expected to have a remaining useful life of ten years, and no residual value.
- One year following acquisition, it was considered that Beach plc's goodwill had a recoverable amount of £60,000.
- Beach plc declared a dividend of £40,000 on 10 July 2014, with the dividends being paid from pre-acquisition retained earnings.
- The statements of financial position and statements of comprehensive income of Sandy plc and Beach plc one year after acquisition are as follows:

Statements of financial position of Sandy plc and Beach plc as at 30 June 2015

	Sandy plc (£000)	Beach plc (£000)
ASSETS		
Non-current assets		
Land	600	400
Property, plant and equipment	900	700
Accumulated depreciation	(300)	(313)
Investment in Beach plc	900	–
	2,100	787
Current assets		
Inventory	140	123
Accounts receivable	50	50
Cash	80	40
	270	213
Total assets	2,370	1,000
EQUITY AND LIABILITIES		
Equity and reserves		
Share capital	1,000	500
Retained earnings	500	300
	1,500	800
Non-current liabilities		
Loan	670	140
Liabilities		
Accounts payable	100	10
Dividends payable	100	50
	200	60
Total liabilities	870	200
Total equity and liabilities	2,370	1,000

Reconciliation of opening and closing retained earnings

Profit after tax	400	190
Retained earnings—30 June 2014	300	200
Interim dividend	(90)	(40)
Final dividend	(110)	(50)
Retained earnings—30 June 2015	500	300

REQUIRED

Prepare the consolidated statement of financial position for the above entities as at 30 June 2015.

Chapter **21**

Further Consolidation Issues I: Accounting for Intragroup Transactions

Learning objectives

Upon completing this chapter readers should understand:

LO1 the nature of intragroup transactions;

LO2 why and how to eliminate intragroup dividends on consolidation from both post-acquisition and pre-acquisition earnings;

LO3 how to account for intragroup sales of inventory inclusive of the related tax expense effects; and

LO4 how to account for intragroup sales of non-current assets inclusive of the related tax expense effects.

21.1 Introduction to accounting for intragroup transactions

During the financial period it is common for separate legal entities within an economic entity (group) to transact with each other. In preparing consolidated financial statements, the effects of all transactions between entities within the economic entity—which we refer to as intragroup transactions—are eliminated in full, even where the parent entity holds only a fraction of the issued equity (IFRS 10, paragraph B86c). Remember, in rare circumstances it might be necessary to consolidate an entity even when no equity is owned if it is determined that there is a capacity to *control* the other organisation.

Intragroup transactions include:

- the payment of dividends to group members;
- the payment of management fees or interest costs to a group member;
- the transfer of tax losses between entities with or without consideration;
- intragroup sales of inventory;
- intragroup sales of non-current assets; and
- intragroup loans.

> **Intragroup transaction**
> Transaction undertaken between separate legal entities within an economic entity.

In performing the consolidation adjustments for intragroup transactions, within the consolidation worksheet we would typically eliminate these intragroup transactions by reversing the original accounting entries made to recognise the transactions in the financial statements of the separate legal entities. In the discussion that follows, we will consider how to account for various intragroup transactions.

21.2   Dividend payments from pre- and post-acquisition earnings

In the consolidation process it is necessary to eliminate all dividends paid/payable to other entities within the group, and all intragroup dividends received/receivable from other entities within the group. Even though the separate legal entities in the group might be paying dividends to each other, it does not make sense for such dividends to be shown when we consider the group as a *single economic entity*. That is, you cannot pay 'dividends' to yourself. The only dividends that should be shown in the consolidated financial statements would be dividends paid to parties external to the group—that is, to the shareholders of the parent entity and to the non-controlling interests. We will discuss non-controlling interests in depth in the next chapter.

21.2.1 Dividends out of post-acquisition profits

In Figure 21.1, for example, we see that the subsidiary, which we will say is 100 per cent owned by Parent Entity, pays €1,000 in dividends to Parent Entity and Parent Entity pays €4,000 in dividends to its shareholders. The only dividends being paid externally (that is, which leave the 'boundary' of the economic entity), and hence the only dividends to be shown in the consolidated financial statements, will be the dividends paid to the shareholders of Parent Entity; that is, the €4,000 in dividends. The dividends paid to the parent entity by the 100 per cent-owned subsidiary will be eliminated on consolidation.

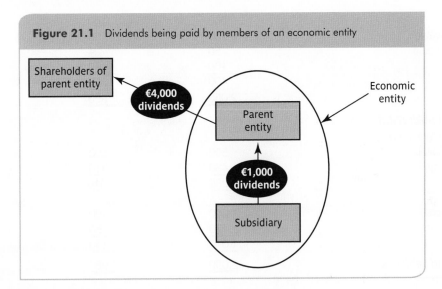

Figure 21.1   Dividends being paid by members of an economic entity

Worked Example 21.1 illustrates the consolidation of accounts when a dividend has been paid by a subsidiary company after acquisition.

Worked Example 21.1	**Dividend payments to a subsidiary out of post-acquisition earnings**

Company A owns all the issued capital of Company B. Company A acquired its 100 per cent interest in Company B on 1 July 2014 for a cost of €800,000. The share capital and reserves of Company B on the date of acquisition are:

Share capital	€500,000
Retained earnings	€300,000
	€800,000

Dividends of €50,000 paid by Company B come from profits earned since 1 July 2014 (that is, they are paid from post-acquisition earnings). It is considered that the assets of Company B are fairly stated at the date that Company A acquires its shares, and therefore there is no goodwill to be recognised on consolidation. Company A recognises dividend income when it is declared by the investee (that is, by Company B). The financial statements of Company A and Company B as at 30 June 2015 reveal the following:

	Company A (€000)	Company B (€000)
Reconciliation of opening and closing retained earnings		
Profit before tax	200	100
Tax expense	(50)	(40)
Profit after tax	150	60
Opening retained earnings—1 July 2014	400	300
	550	360
Dividends proposed	(70)	(50)
Closing retained earnings—30 June 2015	480	310
Statement of financial position		
ASSETS		
Non-current assets		
Plant and equipment	850	600
Investment in Company B	800	–
	1,650	600
Current assets		
Inventory	200	160
Accounts receivable	50	130
Dividends receivable	50	–
Cash	100	70
	400	360
Total assets	2,050	960
EQUITY AND LIABILITIES		
Equity shareholders' funds		
Equity share capital	500	500
Retained earnings	480	310
	980	810
Liabilities		
Accounts payable	1,000	100
Dividends payable	70	50
	1,070	150
Total equity and liabilities	2,050	960

Required

(a) Provide the journal entries that would have appeared in the separate accounts of Company A and Company B to account for the dividends proposed by Company B.

(b) Prepare the consolidation worksheet for Company A and its controlled entity.

Solution

(a) Journal entries to account for dividends
The entry in Company B's journal would be:

Dr	Dividend declared (statement of changes in equity)	€50,000	
Cr	Dividend payable (statement of financial position)		€50,000

As Company A recognises dividend income when the dividend is declared by the investee, it would have the following entry in its own accounts:

Dr	Dividend receivable (statement of financial position)	€50,000	
Cr	Dividend income (statement of comprehensive income)		€50,000

As it does not make sense to retain the intercompany payables and receivables in the consolidated financial statements (from the group's perspective, you cannot owe money to yourself), these will be eliminated on consolidation.

(b) Consolidation worksheet for Company A and its controlled entity

From the economic entity's perspective, no dividends have been paid by Company B to external parties. So they will also need to be removed. The elimination entries to be made as part of the consolidation process, which would be the reverse of those shown above, would be:

(i) *Elimination entry for dividends proposed by Company B*

Dr	Dividend payable (statement of financial position)	€50,000
Cr	Dividend declared (statement of changes in equity)	€50,000

(ii) *Elimination entry for dividends receivable by Company A*

Dr	Dividend income (statement of comprehensive income)	€50,000
Cr	Dividend receivable (statement of financial position)	€50,000

Consolidation journal entries are written not in the individual journals of either company but in a separate consolidation journal, which are then posted to the consolidation worksheet.

We would also need to eliminate the investment in Company B. The elimination entry would be:

(iii) *Consolidation entry to eliminate investment in Company B*

Dr	Share capital	€500,000
Dr	Retained earnings	€300,000
Cr	Investment in Company B	€800,000

The consolidation worksheet can now be presented as follows:

Consolidation worksheet for Company A and its controlled entity

	Company A (€000)	Company B (€000)	Eliminations and adjustments Dr (€000)	Eliminations and adjustments Cr (€000)	Consolidated statements (€000)
Reconciliation of opening and closing retained earnings					
Profit before tax	200	100	50(b)		250
Tax expense	(50)	(40)			(90)
Profit after tax	150	60			160
Opening retained earnings	400	300	300(c)		400
	550	360			560
Dividends declared	(70)	(50)		50(a)	(70)
Closing retained earnings	480	310			490
Statement of financial position					
ASSETS					
Plant and equipment	850	600			1,450
Investment in Company B	800	–		800(c)	–
Inventory	200	160			360
Dividends receivable	50	–		50(b)	–
Accounts receivable	50	130			180
Cash	100	70			170
Total assets	2,050	960			2,160
EQUITY AND LIABILITIES					
Equity shareholders' funds					
Retained earnings	480	310			490
Share capital	500	500	500(c)		500
Liabilities					
Accounts payable	1,000	100			1,100
Dividends payable	70	50	50(a)		70
Total equity and liabilities	2,050	960	900	900	2,160

A review of the retained earnings balance provided in the consolidated financial statements reveals a balance of €490,000 as at 30 June 2015. This balance represents the retained earnings of Company A (€480,000) plus the increment in retained earnings of Company B (€10,000) after the acquisition of Company B (the post-acquisition increment).

21.2.2 Dividends out of pre-acquisition profits

In the situation illustrated in Worked Example 21.1, the dividends are paid out of post-acquisition profits. By contrast, a dividend from pre-acquisition profits will typically occur when an investor acquires an interest in another company and the shares have been acquired 'cum div'—the term used to refer to shares being bought with a dividend entitlement. If an entity pays dividends out of profits earned before the acquisition, it is, in effect, returning part of the net assets originally acquired by the acquirer.

An obvious issue is how do we account for the dividend paid by a subsidiary out of pre-acquisition profits? Do we treat it as income in the financial statements of the parent entity, or instead, within the financial statements of the parent entity, do we treat it as a reduction in the cost of the investment in the subsidiary?

Prior to amendments to accounting standards released by the IASB in 2008, the correct treatment was to treat dividends paid by a subsidiary, which were sourced from pre-acquisition profits of the subsidiary, as a return of part of the cost of the original investment. Under this approach, which had been acceptable for decades, in the parent entity's accounts there would have been a debit entry to cash (or dividends receivable), and a credit entry against the investment in the subsidiary (thereby reducing the cost of the investment).

Many people would consider that the above treatment is logical as, if we were to acquire an investment today and then the next day we received a dividend payment, then we were in effect receiving back some of the investment we had just acquired, and hence it seemed very reasonable for the dividend that is paid out of earnings made before the investment was acquired to be treated as a return of part of the cost of that investment.

However, in July 2008 the treatment was changed. Paragraph 12 of IAS 27 *Separate Financial Statements* now requires that:

> *An entity shall recognise a dividend from a subsidiary, a joint venture or an associate in profit or loss in its separate financial statements when its right to receive the dividend is established.*

Therefore, the situation now is that dividends paid by a subsidiary are recorded as dividend revenue in the parent entity's financial statements, regardless of whether they are paid out of:

(a) pre-acquisition profits/equity (that is, paid out of profits earned by the subsidiary prior to the purchase by the parent of the interest in the subsidiary); or

(b) post-acquisition profits/equity (that is, paid out of profits earned by the subsidiary after the purchase by the parent entity of the interest in the subsidiary).

Once a subsidiary makes a dividend payment out of pre-acquisition earnings, this raises another issue to consider. If a payment is made out of pre-acquisition profits of the subsidiary, then this in itself may have implications for the value of the parent's investment in the subsidiary. The dividend payment will have the effect of reducing the net assets of the subsidiary. This in turn may provide an indication that the parent entity's investment in the subsidiary may thereafter have a value which may be below the original cost of the investment; that is, the investment in the subsidiary may be impaired.

Therefore, in accordance with an amendment made to IAS 36 *Impairment of Assets* in mid-2008, paragraph 12(h) now states that the payment of a dividend by a subsidiary is treated as an indication that the parent's investment in a subsidiary may be impaired, if:

(i) *the carrying amount of the investment in the separate financial statements exceeds the carrying amounts in the consolidated financial statements of the investee's net assets, including associated goodwill; or*

(ii) *the dividend exceeds the total comprehensive income of the subsidiary, jointly controlled entity or associate in the period the dividend is declared.*

If the parent's investment in the subsidiary is impaired as a result of the subsidiary making a dividend payment out of pre-acquisition earnings, the investment in the subsidiary in the parent's own accounts must be written down to its recoverable amount by recognising an impairment loss expense. In the parent's accounts the entries would be:

Dr	Impairment loss—investment in subsidiary	XX
Cr	Accumulated impairment loss—investment in subsidiary	XX

In the consolidation worksheet, the impairment losses relating to the parent's investment in the subsidiary would be reinstated to both the investment in subsidiary account, and to the subsidiary's equity by virtue of the following entries:

Dr	Accumulated impairment loss—investment in subsidiary	XX
Cr	Impairment loss—investment in subsidiary	XX

(The above credit entry might instead be to opening retained earnings if the impairment loss was recognised in a previous financial year.)

The reinstatement of the investment in the above entry acts to restore the investment in subsidiary account back to the original purchase price paid by the parent, and adjusts the equity of the subsidiary to include the entire equity of the subsidiary at acquisition date. This reinstatement enables the original purchase price/investment in subsidiary account to be eliminated against the parent's proportionate share of the subsidiary's equity, at acquisition date.

It should be noted that, if the parent's investment in subsidiary is impaired, it does not necessarily follow that the goodwill relating to the subsidiary in the consolidated financial statements is also impaired (especially if the impairment of the investment in subsidiary account is due to dividends paid out of pre-acquisition profits/equity).

Dividends paid out of pre-acquisition earnings are considered in Worked Example 21.2.

Worked Example 21.2   Dividends paid out of pre-acquisition earnings

Sunshine plc acquires all the issued capital of Sunrise plc for a cash payment of £500,000 on 30 June 2015. The statements of financial position of both entities immediately following the purchase are:

	Sunshine plc (£000)	Sunrise plc (£000)
ASSETS		
Non-current assets		
Plant	1,480	600
Investment in Sunrise plc	500	
Accumulated impairment loss—investment in Sunrise plc	(200)	–
	1,780	600
Current assets		
Accounts receivable	300	45
Dividend receivable	200	–
Cash	20	15
	520	60
Total assets	2,300	660
EQUITY AND LIABILITIES		
Equity and reserves		
Share capital	1,000	200
Retained earnings	400	50
	1,400	250
Non-current liabilities		
Loans	800	180
Current liabilities		
Accounts payable	100	30
Dividend payable	–	200
	100	230
Total liabilities	900	410
Total equity and liabilities	2,300	660

Immediately following the acquisition (that is, on the same day), a dividend of £200,000 is proposed by Sunrise plc. The financial statements provided above reflect this dividend (the dividend receivable was treated as a dividend income in the financial statements of Sunshine plc).

Required

Provide the consolidated statement of financial position of Sunshine plc and Sunrise plc as at 30 June 2015.

Solution

Before making any adjusting entries in the consolidation worksheet, it is useful to consider how the parent entity and subsidiary accounted for particular transactions in their own accounts.

▶

Recognition of the dividend in the accounts of Sunrise plc

Prior to completing its financial statements, Sunrise plc would have recorded the dividend payable to Sunshine plc by means of the following journal entry:

Dr	Dividend declared (reduces retained earnings)	£200,000	
Cr	Dividend payable		£200,000

Recognition of the dividend in the accounts of Sunshine plc

Sunshine plc would have recorded the dividend received out of pre-acquisition profits of Sunrise plc in the following way:

Dr	Dividend receivable	£200,000	
Cr	Dividend income		£200,000

Again, and as we have just noted, dividends out of pre-acquisition profits are to be treated no differently in the accounts of the investor than dividends paid by an investee out of post-acquisition profits. In both cases, dividends are to be treated as dividend income in the investor's accounts. Given that the dividends have been paid out of pre-acquisition earnings, and the payment was made on the same day as acquisition and represented 40 per cent of the investment cost, then there is a high probability that the value of the investment in Sunrise plc has been impaired. We will assume that the amount of the dividend payment equates to the amount of the impairment and, as such, the following entry would have been made in the accounts of Sunshine plc:

Dr	Impairment loss—investment in Sunrise plc	£200,000	
Cr	Accumulated impairment loss—investment in Sunrise plc		£200,000

Again, it is emphasised that the above three lots of journal entries (unlike the consolidation entries provided below) were made in the journals of the respective companies.

Consolidation journal entries

(a) *Reinstatement of impairment loss*

In the consolidation worksheet, impairment losses relating to Sunshine plc's investment in Sunrise plc are reinstated:

Dr	Accumulated impairment loss —investment in Sunrise plc	£200,000	
Cr	impairment loss—Sunrise plc		£200,000

The above reinstatement enables the original purchase price to be eliminated against the parent's proportionate share of the subsidiary's equity as at acquisition date. If the parent entity had not recognised an impairment loss on the investment, then this reversing entry would not be required. As already noted, if the parent entity's investment is impaired because the subsidiary paid dividends out of pre-acquisition earnings (perhaps there was surplus cash), then it does not necessarily follow that the asset goodwill is also impaired within the consolidated financial statements.

(b) *Journal entries to eliminate intragroup dividends income and dividend payment from pre-acquisition earnings*

Dr	Dividend income (retained earnings—Sunshine)	£200,000	
Cr	Dividend declared (retained earnings—Sunrise)		£200,000

(c) *Journal entries to eliminate intragroup receivable and payable*

We would also need to eliminate the intercompany payables and receivables as, from the group perspective, the group cannot owe itself any money.

Dr	Dividend payable	£200,000	
Cr	Dividend receivable		£200,000

(d) *Elimination of investment in Sunrise plc*

To determine the acquired goodwill that will be recognised on consolidation, we can perform the following calculation:

	(£)
Share capital of Sunrise plc at acquisition	200,000
Retained earnings of Sunrise plc at acquisition	250,000
	450,000
Cost of investment in Sunrise plc	500,000
Goodwill	50,000

Dr	Share capital	£200,000	
Dr	Retained earnings	£250,000	
Dr	Goodwill	£50,000	
Cr	investment in Sunrise plc		£500,000

The consolidated statement of financial position can then be prepared as follows:

Consolidation worksheet for Sunshine plc and its controlled entity for the period ending 30 June 2015

	Sunshine plc (£000)	Sunrise plc (£000)	Eliminations and adjustments Dr (£000)	Eliminations and adjustments Cr (£000)	Consolidated statements (£000)
ASSETS					
Non-current assets					
Plant	1,480	600			2,080
Investment in Sunrise plc	500	–		500(d)	–
Accumulated impairment loss—investment in Sunrise plc	(200)		200(a)		
Goodwill	–	–	50(d)		50
Current assets					
Accounts receivable	300	45			345
Dividend receivable	200			200(c)	–
Cash	20	15			35
Total assets	2,300	660			2,510
EQUITY AND LIABILITIES					
Equity and reserves					
Share capital	1,000	200	200(d)		1,000
Retained earnings	400	50	250(d) 200(b)	200(a) 200(b)	400
Non-current liabilities					
Loans	800	180			980
Current liabilities					
Accounts payable	100	30			130
Dividend payable		200	200(c)		–
Total equity and liabilities	2,300	660	1,100	1,100	2,510

The consolidated statement of financial position would be as follows:

Consolidated statement of financial position of Sunshine Plc and its controlled entities as at 30 June 2015

	Sunshine plc (£000)	Economic entity (£000)
ASSETS		
Non-current assets		
Plant	1,480	2,080
Investment in Sunrise plc (net)	300	–
Goodwill	–	50
	1,780	2,130
Current assets		
Accounts receivable	300	345
Dividend receivable	200	–
Cash	20	35
	520	380
Total assets	2,300	2,510

	Sunshine plc (£000)	Economic entity (£000)
EQUITY AND LIABILITIES		
Equity and reserves		
Share capital	1,000	1,000
Retained earnings	400	400
	1,400	1,400
Non-current liabilities		
Loans	800	980
Current liabilities		
Accounts payable	100	130
Total liabilities	900	1,110
Total equity and liabilities	2,300	2,510

21.3 Intragroup sale of inventory

Entities that are related often sell inventory to one another in what is known as an intragroup sale of inventory. From the group's perspective, revenues should not be recognised until an external sale of inventory has taken place, that is, when inventory has been sold to parties outside the group (IFRS 10, paragraph B86c). For example, Company A might sell €100,000 of inventory to Company B, which, in turn, sells it to a party outside the economic entity for an amount of €150,000 (see Figure 21.2). If we simply aggregate the sales of Company A and Company B in the consolidation process, it would appear that the economic entity's total sales are €250,000. From the economic entity's perspective, this would be incorrect. The only sales that should appear in the consolidated statements are those made to parties external to the group, in this case one sale of €150,000.

It is possible at year end for some, or all, of the inventory sold within the group to still be on hand. Let us assume that half of the inventory sold by Company A to Company B is still on hand at year end and, further, that the total amount of inventory transferred from Company A to Company B at a sales price of €100,000 actually cost Company A €70,000 to manufacture.

With half of the inventory still on hand, this would mean that effectively there is inventory on hand in Company B's accounts, at a cost to Company B of €50,000, which cost the group only €35,000 to manufacture. As we know, pursuant to international accounting standards, an entity is to record inventory at the lower of cost and net realisable value (see Chapter 7 for an explanation of how to measure inventory), so the inventory needs to be written down by €15,000 for the purposes of the consolidated financial statements (which have as their focus the economic entity). In the financial statements of Company B, as a separate legal entity, it would be correct to leave the inventory at its cost to Company B, that is, €50,000.

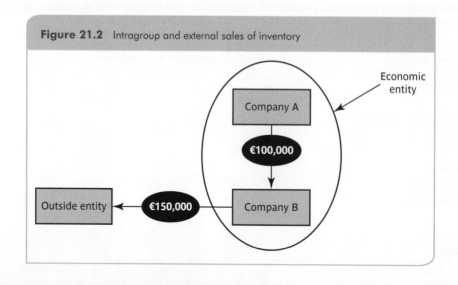

Figure 21.2 Intragroup and external sales of inventory

What we must remember is that, although we are eliminating unrealised profits from the consolidated financial statements, from Company A's perspective the profits have been earned, leading to a liability for taxation. The economic entity does not necessarily pay tax on a collective basis if the group has not notified the taxation authorities that it wants to be treated as a 'tax consolidated entity' (see Chapter 15 for details of how companies might elect to be taxed on a group basis, rather than as separate entities). If the companies have not notified the taxation authorities that they want to be treated as a single entity for tax purposes, the individual legal entities pay tax on their own account. For the balance of this chapter it will be assumed that the companies have not elected to be taxed as a group, and therefore the taxation authorities would assess profits earned by the separate legal entities without any consideration of consolidation adjustments. Returning to the inventory discussed above, from the group's perspective, an amount of profit related to the sale has not been realised and should not be included in the economic entity's profits. Therefore, if tax has been paid by one of the separate legal entities (for example, Company A), from the group's perspective this represents a prepayment of tax (a deferred tax asset), as this income will not be earned by the economic entity until the inventory is sold outside the group. Worked Example 21.3 considers how to account for unrealised profit in closing inventory.

Worked Example 21.3   Unrealised profit in closing inventory

Big plc owns 100 per cent of the shares of Little plc. These shares are acquired on 1 July 2014 for £1 million when the shareholders' funds of Little plc are:

Share capital	£500,000
Retained earnings	£400,000
	£900,000

All assets of Little plc are fairly stated at acquisition date. The directors believe that, during the financial year ending 30 June 2015, the value of goodwill has been impaired by an amount of £10,000.

During the 2015 financial year Little plc sells inventory to Big plc at a sales price of £200,000. The inventory cost Little plc £120,000 to produce. At 30 June 2015 half of the inventory is still on hand with Big plc. The tax rate is assumed to be 33 per cent.

The financial statements of Big plc and Little plc at 30 June 2015 are as follows:

	Big plc (£000)	Little plc (£000)
Reconciliation of opening and closing retained earnings		
Sales revenue	1,200	400
Cost of goods sold	(500)	(140)
Other expenses	(60)	(30)
Other revenue	70	25
Profit	710	255
Tax expense	(200)	(100)
Profit after tax	510	155
Retained earnings—30 June 2014	1,000	400
	1,510	555
Dividends paid	(200)	(40)
Retained earnings—30 June 2015	1,310	515

	Big plc (£000)	Little plc (£000)
Statement of financial position		
ASSETS		
Non-current assets		
Land	1,440	400
Plant	2,470	400
Investment in Little plc	1,000	–
Deferred tax asset	100	50
	5,010	850

	Big plc (£000)	Little plc (£000)
Current assets		
Inventory	600	300
Accounts receivable	150	175
Cash	250	25
	1,000	500
Total assets	6,010	1,350
EQUITY AND LIABILITIES		
Equity and reserves		
Share capital	4,000	500
Retained earnings	1,310	515
	5,310	1,015
Non-current liabilities		
Loans	600	250
Current liabilities		
Accounts payable	100	85
Total liabilities	700	335
Total equity and liabilities	6,010	1,350

Required

Provide the consolidated statement of financial position and statement of comprehensive income, together with a note reconciling opening and closing retained earnings for Big plc and its controlled entities, for the year ended 2015.

Solution

Determination of goodwill

At date of acquisition:	£
Share capital of Little plc	500,000
Retained earnings	400,000
	900,000
Cost of investment in Little plc	1,000,000
Goodwill on acquisition	100,000

Consolidation journal entries

(a) *Elimination of investment in controlled entity*

Dr	Share capital	£500,000	
Dr	Retained earnings	£400,000	
Dr	Goodwill	£100,000	
Cr	Investment in Little plc		£1,000,000

(b) *Recognition of the impairment of goodwill*

As we know, pursuant to IFRS 3 *Business Combinations* there is a prohibition on the amortisation of goodwill acquired in a business combination. Rather, IFRS 3 requires such goodwill to be tested for impairment annually, or more frequently if events or changes in circumstance indicate that the asset might be impaired, in accordance with IAS 36 *Impairment of Assets*. The journal entry to record the impairment of goodwill would be:

Dr	Impairment loss—goodwill	£10,000	
Cr	Accumulated impairment losses—goodwill		£10,000

In relation to changes in the carrying amount of goodwill, which would be brought about by the recognition of impairment losses, paragraph 61 of IFRS 3 states:

> *An entity shall disclose information that enables users of its financial statements to evaluate the financial effects of adjustments recognised in the current reporting period that relate to business combinations that occurred in the period or previous reporting periods.*

With regard to operationalising the requirements of paragraph 61 above, paragraph B67(d) of IFRS 3 requires:

a reconciliation of the carrying amount of goodwill at the beginning and end of the reporting period showing separately:

(i) *the gross amount and accumulated impairment losses at the beginning of the reporting period.*

(ii) *additional goodwill recognised during the reporting period, except goodwill included in a disposal group that, on acquisition, meets the criteria to be classified as held for sale in accordance with IFRS 5 Non-current Assets Held for Sale and Discontinued Operations.*

(iii) *adjustments resulting from the subsequent recognition of deferred tax assets during the reporting period in accordance with paragraph 67.*

(iv) *goodwill included in a disposal group classified as held for sale in accordance with IFRS 5 and goodwill derecognised during the reporting period without having previously been included in a disposal group classified as held for sale.*

(v) *impairment losses recognised during the reporting period in accordance with IAS 36. (IAS 36 requires disclosure of information about the recoverable amount and impairment of goodwill in addition to this requirement.)*

(vi) *net exchange rate differences arising during the reporting period in accordance with IAS 21 The Effects of Changes in Foreign Exchange Rates.*

(vii) *any other changes in the carrying amount during the reporting period.*

(viii) *the gross amount and accumulated impairment losses at the end of the reporting period.*

(c) *Elimination of intragroup sales*

We need to eliminate the intragroup sales because, from the perspective of the economic entity, no sales have in fact occurred. This will ensure that we do not overstate the turnover of the economic entity.

Dr	Sales revenue	£200,000	
Cr	Cost of goods sold		£200,000

Under a periodic inventory system, the above credit entry would be to purchases, which would ultimately lead to a reduction in cost of goods sold. (Cost of goods sold equals opening inventory plus purchases less closing inventory—so any reduction in purchases leads to a reduction in cost of goods sold.)

(d) *Elimination of unrealised profit in closing inventory*

The total profit earned by Little plc on the sale of the inventory is £80,000. Since some of this inventory remains in the economic entity, this amount has not been fully earned from the perspective of the group. In this case, half of the inventory is still on hand, so unrealised profit amounts to £40,000. In accordance with IAS 2 *Inventories*, we must value the inventory at the *lower of cost and net realisable value*. Hence, on consolidation we must reduce the value of recorded inventory, as the amount shown in the accounts of Big plc exceeds what the inventory cost the economic entity (that is, we must remove the profit element).

Dr	Cost of goods sold	£40,000	
Cr	Inventory		£40,000

Under a periodic inventory system, the above debit entry would be to closing inventory—profit and loss. We would increase cost of goods sold by the unrealised profit in closing inventory because reducing closing inventory effectively increases cost of goods sold. The effect of the above entries is to adjust the value of inventory so that it reflects the cost of the inventory to the group.

(e) *Consideration of the tax paid on the sale of inventory that is still held within the group*

From the group's perspective, £40,000 has not been earned. However, from Little plc's individual perspective (as a separate legal entity), the full amount of the sale has been earned. This will attract a tax liability in Little plc's accounts of £26,400 (33 per cent of £80,000). However, from the group's perspective, some of this will represent a prepayment of tax as the full amount has not been earned by the group even if Little plc is obliged to pay the tax. Specifically, the tax paid on the unrealised profit component is considered to be a prepayment.

Dr	Deferred tax asset	£13,200	
Cr	Income tax expense		£13,200
	(£40,000 x 33 per cent)		

(f) *Elimination of intercompany dividends*

As we know, any intragroup dividends must be eliminated on consolidation.

Dr	Dividend income	£40,000	
Cr	Dividends paid		£40,000

◀

Consolidation worksheet for Big plc and its controlled entity for the year ending 30 June 2015

	Big plc (£000)	Little plc (£000)	Eliminations and adjustments Dr (£000)	Cr (£000)	Consolidated statements (£000)
Reconciliation of opening and closing retained earnings					
Sales revenue	1,200	400	200(c)		1,400
Cost of goods sold	(500)	(140)	40(d)	200(c)	(480)
Other expenses	(60)	(30)	10(b)		(100)
Other revenue	70	25	40(f)		55
Profit	710	255			875
Tax expense	(200)	(100)		13.2(e)	(286.8)
Profit after tax	510	155			588.2
Retained earnings—30 June 2014	1,000	400	400(a)		1,000
	1,510	555			1,588.2
Dividends paid	(200)	(40)		40(f)	(200)
Statement of financial position					
Shareholders' equity					
Retained earnings—30 June 2015	1,310	515			1,388.2
Share capital	4,000	500	500(a)		4,000
Current liabilities					
Accounts payable	100	85			185
Non-current liabilities					
Loans	600	250			850
	6,010	1,350			6,423.2
Current assets					
Cash	250	25			275
Accounts receivable	150	175			325
Inventory	600	300		40(d)	860
Non-current assets					
Land	1,440	400			1,840
Plant	2,470	400			2,870
investment in Little plc	1,000	–		1,000(a)	–
Deferred tax asset	100	50	13.2(e)		163.2
Goodwill	–	–	100(a)		100
Accumulated impairment loss				10(b)	(10)
	6,010	1,350	1,303.2	1,303.2	6,423.2

Consolidated statement of comprehensive income of Big plc and its controlled entities for the year ended 30 June 2015

	The Group (£)	Big plc (£)
Sales	1,400,000	1,200,000
Cost of goods sold	(480,000)	(500,000)
Gross profit	920,000	700,000
Other revenue	55,000	70,000
Other expenses	(100,000)	(60,000)
Profit before tax	875,000	710,000
Income tax expense	(286,800)	(200,000)
Profit for the year	588,200	510,000
Other comprehensive income	–	–
Total comprehensive income for the year	588,200	510,000

▶

Big plc and its controlled entity: Consolidated statement of changes in equity for the year ended 30 June 2015	Share capital (£)	Group retained earnings (£)	Group total equity (£)
Balance at 1 July 2014	4,000,000	1,000,000	5,000,000
Total comprehensive income for the year	–	588,200	588,200
Distributions—dividends	–	(200,000)	(200,000)
Balance at 30 June 2015	4,000,000	1,388,200	5,388,200

Big plc: Statement of changes in equity for the year ended 30 June 2015	Share capital (£)	Retained earnings (£)	Total equity (£)
Balance at 1 July 2014	4,000,000	1,000,000	5,000,000
Total comprehensive income for the year	–	510,000	510,000
Distributions—dividends	–	(200,000)	(200,000)
Balance at 30 June 2015	4,000,000	1,310,000	5,310,000

Consolidated statement of financial position of Big plc and its controlled entities as at 30 June 2015	The Group (£)	Big plc (£)
ASSETS		
Non-current assets		
Land	1,840,000	1,440,000
Plant and equipment	2,870,000	2,470,000
Investment in Little plc	–	1,000,000
Goodwill	100,000	–
Accumulated impairment loss	(10,000)	–
Deferred tax asset	163,200	100,000
	4,963,200	5,010,000
Current assets		
Inventory	860,000	600,000
Accounts receivable	325,000	150,000
Cash	275,000	250,000
	1,460,000	1,000,000
Total assets	6,423,200	6,010,000
EQUITY AND LIABILITIES		
Equity and reserves		
Share capital	4,000,000	4,000,000
Retained earnings	1,388,200	1,310,000
Total equity and reserves	5,388,200	5,310,000
Non-current liabilities		
Loans	850,000	600,000
Current liabilities		
Accounts payable	185,000	100,000
Total liabilities	1,035,000	700,000
Total equity and liabilities	6,423,200	6,010,000

21.3.1 Unrealised profit in opening inventory

Given that there were unrealised profits in the closing inventory of Big plc at 30 June 2015, when it is time to do the consolidation adjustments at the end of the next financial year for Big plc and its controlled entity (from Worked Example 21.3 earlier), there will be unrealised profits in opening inventory. Remember that the consolidation journal entries do not affect the accounts of the individual legal entities and hence do not carry forward, and therefore the cost of the opening inventory held by one of the entities within the group will be overstated, from the group's perspective, as at the beginning of the financial period.

The closing retained earnings of Little plc in the last year (opening retained earnings this year) will also be overstated from the group's perspective as it will include a gain on the intragroup sale of inventory. In the consolidation adjustments, we need to shift the income from the previous period, in which the inventory was still on hand, to the period in which the inventory will ultimately be sold to parties external to the economic entity. The inventory is assumed to be sold in the following period. Hence the consolidation adjustment entries at the end of the following year—that is, at 30 June 2016—would be:

Dr	Opening retained earnings—1 July 2015	£40,000	
Cr	Cost of goods sold		£40,000

Remember that reducing the value of opening inventory will reduce cost of goods sold. This entry will effectively shift the income from 2015 to 2016 (the period in which the sale to an external party actually occurs). With higher profits, this will lead to a higher tax expense, which, as we know, is based upon accounting profits with the adoption of tax-effect accounting.

Dr	Income tax expense	£13,200	
Cr	Opening retained earnings—1 July 2015		£13,200

Any profits in closing inventory in 2016 will also need to be accounted for. You will note in the above that we have not reversed the deferred tax asset account of £13,200 raised in the previous year. Have we made a mistake? No! Remember that all consolidation adjustments are undertaken on a worksheet, which is started 'fresh' each year. Prior adjustments do not accumulate in any ledger accounts. So in 2016 there is no amount residing in a deferred tax asset account that needs to be reversed. The treatment of unrealised profit in opening inventory is shown in Worked Example 21.4.

Worked Example 21.4 Unrealised profit in opening inventory

This worked example is a continuation of Worked Example 21.3. During the 2016 financial year, Little plc sold £220,000 worth of inventory to Big plc. The inventory cost Little plc £160,000 to produce. At 30 June 2016 Big plc had inventory worth £55,000 on hand that had been purchased from Little plc. In addition, the directors believe that at 30 June 2016 goodwill has been impaired by a further £20,000.

The financial statements of Big plc and Little plc at 30 June 2016 are as follows:

	Big plc (£000)	Little plc (£000)
Reconciliation of opening and closing retained earnings		
Sales revenue	1,500	550
Cost of goods sold	(800)	(180)
Other expenses	(70)	(40)
Other revenue	90	30
Profit	720	360
Tax expense	(320)	(130)
Profit after tax	400	230
Retained earnings—30 June 2015	1,310	515
	1,710	745
Dividends paid	(200)	(50)
Retained earnings—30 June 2016	1,510	695

►

Statement of financial position

ASSETS

Non-current assets

Land	1,440	400
Plant	2,450	390
investment in Little plc	1,000	–
Deferred tax asset	110	55
	5,000	845

Current assets

Inventory	750	455
Accounts receivable	220	190
Cash	270	35
	1,240	680
Total assets	6,240	1,525

EQUITY AND LIABILITIES

Equity and reserves

Share capital	4,000	500
Retained earnings	1,510	695
	5,510	1,195

Non-current liabilities

Loans	590	240
Current liabilities		
Accounts payable	140	90
Total liabilities	730	330
Total equity and liabilities	6,240	1,525

Required

Provide the consolidated worksheet for Big plc and its controlled entity for the year ended 30 June 2016.

Solution

(a) *Elimination of investment in controlled entity*

Dr	Share capital	£500,000	
Dr	Retained earnings	£400,000	
Dr	Goodwill	£100,000	
Cr	Investment in Little plc		£1,000,000

(b) *Recognition of the impairment of goodwill*

The entry below recognises the goodwill impairment loss for the period. Note that the cumulative effect of previous goodwill impairment losses must also be taken into account—as we know, the effects of previous consolidation entries do not carry forward. To make the adjustment, we will debit opening retained earnings with the cumulative goodwill impairment losses to the beginning of the current financial period:

Dr	Impairment loss—goodwill	£20,000	
Dr	Retained earnings—1 July 2015	£10,000	
Cr	Accumulated impairment losses—goodwill		£30,000

(c) *Elimination of intercompany sales*

We need to eliminate the intercompany sales because, from the perspective of the economic entity, no sales have in fact occurred. This will ensure that we do not overstate the turnover of the economic entity.

Dr	Sales revenue	£220,000	
Cr	Cost of goods sold		£220,000

(d) *Eliminating unrealised profit in opening inventory*

Remember, from the previous worked example, that there were unrealised profits in closing inventory. Therefore, in the consolidation adjustments, we need to shift the income from the previous period, in which the inventory was still on hand, to the period in which the inventory will ultimately be sold to parties external to the economic entity. The effect of reducing cost of goods sold is to increase profits in the current year.

Dr	Opening retained earnings—1 July 2015	£40,000	
Cr	Cost of goods sold		£40,000

(e) *Consideration of the tax on the sale of inventory held within the group at the beginning of the reporting period*
Reducing the value of opening inventory will reduce the cost of goods sold. This entry will effectively shift the income from 2015 to 2016 (the period in which the sale to an external party actually occurs). Higher profits will lead to a higher tax expense, which, as we know, is based upon accounting profits with the adoption of tax-effect accounting.

Dr	Income tax expense	£13,200	
Cr	Retained earnings—1 July 2015		£13,200

(f) *Elimination of unrealised profit in closing inventory*
The total profit earned by Little plc on the sale to Big plc of the £220,000 inventory is £60,000. Since 25 per cent of this inventory (£55,000 of £220,000)—or £55,000—remains in the economic entity, this amount has not been fully earned. In this case, the unrealised profit amounts to £15,000. Hence, on consolidation we must reduce the value of recorded inventory, as the amount shown in the accounts of Big plc exceeds what the inventory cost the economic entity.

Dr	Cost of goods sold	£15,000	
Cr	Inventory		£15,000

(g) *Consideration of the tax paid on the sale of inventory that is still held within the group*
From the group's perspective, £15,000 has not been earned. However, from Little plc's individual perspective (as a separate legal entity), the full amount of the sale has been earned. This will attract a tax liability in Little plc's accounts of £4,950 (33 per cent of £15,000). However, from the group's perspective, some of this will represent a prepayment of tax, as the full amount has not been earned by the group even if Little plc is obliged to pay the tax.

Dr	Deferred tax asset	£4,950	
Cr	Income tax expense		£4,950
	(£15,000 x 33 per cent)		

(h) *Elimination of intercompany dividends*
As we know, any intragroup dividends must be eliminated on consolidation (as an entity cannot pay itself a dividend).

Dr	Dividend income (statement of comprehensive income)	£50,000	
Cr	Dividends paid (statement of changes in equity)		£50,000

Consolidation worksheet for Big plc and its controlled entity for the year ending 30 June 2016

	Big plc (£000)	Little plc (£000)	Eliminations and adjustments Dr (£000)	Eliminations and adjustments Cr (£000)	Consolidated statements (£000)
Reconciliation of opening and closing retained earnings					
Sales revenue	1,500	550	220(c)		1,830
Cost of goods sold	(800)	(180)	15(f)	40(d)	
				220(c)	(735)
Other expenses	(70)	(40)	20(b)		(130)
Other revenue	90	30	50(h)		70
Profit before tax	720	360			1,035
Tax expense	(320)	(130)	13.2(e)	4.95(g)	(458.25)
Profit after tax	400	230			576.75
Retained earnings – 30 June 2015	1,310	515	400(a) 10(b) 40(d)	13.2(e)	1,388.2
	1,710	745			1,964.95
Dividends paid	(200)	(50)		50(h)	(200)
Retained earnings – 30 June 2016	1,510	695			1,764.95

Consolidation worksheet for Big plc and its controlled entity for the year ending 30 June 2016 (cont'd)					
			Eliminations and adjustments		
	Big plc (£000)	Little plc (£000)	Dr (£000)	Cr (£000)	Consolidated statements (£000)
Statement of financial position					
Shareholders' equity					
Retained earnings—					
30 June 2016	1,510	695			1,764.95
Share capital	4,000	500	500(a)		4,000
Current liabilities					
Accounts payable	140	90			230
Non-current liabilities					
Loans	590	240			830
	6,240	1,525			6,824.95
Current assets					
Inventory	750	455		15(f)	1,190
Accounts receivable	220	190			410
Cash	270	35			305
Non-current assets					
Land	1,440	400			1,840
Plant	2,450	390			2,840
Investment in Little plc	1,000	–		1,000(a)	–
Deferred tax asset	110	55	4.95(g)		169.95
Goodwill	–	–	100(a)		100
Accumulated impairment loss				30(b)	(30)
	6,240	1,525	1,373.15	1,373.15	6,824.95

21.4 Sale of non-current assets within the group

Intragroup sales are not limited to the sale of inventory. It is common for non-current assets to be sold within a group. As with inventory, for the purposes of preparing the consolidated financial statements for the economic entity, we need to value the assets as if any intragroup sale had not occurred. This means that we will need to reinstate non-current assets to their original cost or revalued amount. Any unrealised gains on the sale will need to be eliminated.

Because the separate entity that acquires the asset would be depreciating the asset on the basis of the cost to itself, which might be more or less than the cost to the economic entity, there will also be a need for adjustments to depreciation as a result of intragroup sales of non-current assets. Further, from the economic entity's perspective, no gain or loss on sale should be recorded in the financial statements—in the consolidated financial statements there should be no tax expense relating to any gain on the sale. In the separate legal entity's financial statements, however, there will be tax implications. Hence temporary differences pertaining to tax expense can also arise as a result of intercompany sales of non-current assets. In Worked Example 21.5 we discuss the intragroup sale of a non-current asset (again, this discussion of tax effects assumes that you are familiar with the requirements of tax-effect accounting as described in Chapter 15).

Worked Example 21.5   Intragroup sale of a non-current asset

On 1 July 2014 Eddie plc acquired a 100 per cent interest in Sandy plc for £850,000, when the equity of Sandy plc was as follows:

Share capital	£500,000
Retained earnings	£300,000
	£800,000

All assets of Sandy plc were fairly stated at acquisition date. On 1 July 2014 Eddie plc sells an item of plant to Sandy plc for £780,000. This plant cost Eddie plc £1 million, is four years old and has accumulated depreciation of £400,000 at the date of the sale. The remaining useful life of the plant is assessed as six years, and the tax rate is 30 per cent. At 30 June 2015 it was estimated that goodwill acquired in Sandy plc had been impaired by £5,000. The financial statements of Eddie plc and Sandy plc at 30 June 2015 provided the following information:

	Eddie plc (£000)	Sandy plc (£000)
Reconciliation of opening and closing retained earnings		
Sales revenue	2,000	900
Cost of goods sold	(1,400)	(350)
Gross profit	600	550
Other income		
Gain on sale of fixed asset	180	–
Expenses		
Depreciation	–	(130)
Other expenses	(280)	(100)
Profit before tax	500	320
Tax expense	(150)	(96)
Profit after tax	350	224
Retained earnings—1 July 2014	400	300
Retained earnings—30 June 2015	750	524

	Eddie plc (£000)	Sandy plc (£000)
Statement of financial position		
ASSETS		
Non-current assets		
Land	730	320
Plant, at cost	–	780
Plant—accumulated depreciation	–	(130)
investment in Sandy plc	850	–
	1,580	970
Current assets		
Inventory	420	220
Accounts receivable	300	180
	720	400
Total assets	2,300	1,370
EQUITY AND LIABILITIES		
Equity and reserves		
Share capital	1,000	500
Retained earnings	750	524
	1,750	1,024
Non-current liabilities		
Loans	400	250
Current liabilities		
Tax payable	150	96
Total liabilities	550	346
Total equity and liabilities	2,300	1,370

Required

Provide the consolidated worksheet of Eddie plc and its controlled entity for the years ended 30 June 2015 and 30 June 2016.

Solution

Consolidated financial statements for 2015

(a) *Elimination of investment in controlled entity*

Dr Share capital	£500,000	
Dr Retained earnings	£300,000	
Dr Goodwill	£50,000	
Cr Investment in Sandy plc		£850,000

(b) *Reversal of gain recognised on sale of asset and reinstatement of cost and accumulated depreciation*

The result of the sale of the item of plant to Sandy plc is that the gain of £180,000—the difference between the sales proceeds of £780,000 and the carrying amount of £600,000—will be shown in Eddie plc's financial statements. However, from the economic entity's perspective there has been no sale and therefore no gain on sale given that there has been no transaction with a party external to the group. The following entry is necessary so that the financial statements reflect the balances that would have applied had the intragroup sale not occurred.

Dr Gain on sale of plant (P&L)	£180,000	
Dr Plant	£220,000	
Cr Accumulated depreciation		£400,000

The result of this entry is that the intragroup gain is removed and the asset and accumulated depreciation accounts revert to reflecting no sales transaction. The gain of £180,000 will be recognised progressively in the consolidated financial statements of the economic entity by adjustments to the amounts of depreciation charged by Sandy plc in its financial statements. As the service potential or economic benefits embodied in the asset are consumed, the £180,000 gain will be progressively recognised from the economic entity's perspective. This is shown in journal entry (d).

(c) *Impact of tax on gain on sale of item of plant*

From Eddie plc's individual perspective it would have made a gain of £180,000 on the sale of the plant and this gain would have been taxable. At a tax rate of 30 per cent, £54,000 would be payable in tax by Eddie plc and £54,000 would similarly have been included in the income tax expense account. However, from the economic entity's perspective, no gain has been made, which means that the related 'tax expense' must be reversed and a related deferred tax benefit recognised. A deferred tax asset is recognised because, from the economic entity's perspective, the amount paid to the taxation authorities represents a prepayment of tax.

Dr Deferred tax asset	£54,000	
Cr Income tax expense		£54,000

(d) *Reinstating accumulated depreciation in the statement of financial position*

Sandy plc would be depreciating the asset on the basis of the cost it incurred to acquire the asset. Its depreciation charge would be £780,000 ÷ 6 = £130,000. From the economic entity's perspective, the asset had a carrying value of £600,000, which was to be allocated over the next six years, giving a depreciation charge of £600,000 ÷ 6 = £100,000. An adjustment of £30,000 is therefore required.

Dr Accumulated depreciation	£30,000	
Cr Depreciation expense		£30,000

(e) *Consideration of the tax effect of the reduction in depreciation expense*

The increase in the tax expense from the perspective of the economic entity is due to the reduction in the depreciation expense. The additional tax expense is £9,000, which is £30,000 × 30 per cent. This entry represents a partial reversal of the deferred tax asset of £54,000 recognised in the earlier entry. After six years, the balance of the deferred tax asset relating to the sale of the item of plant will be £nil.

Dr Income tax expense	£9,000	
Cr Deferred tax asset		£9,000

(f) *Recognition of the impairment of goodwill*

This entry recognises the goodwill impairment loss for the period.

Dr Impairment loss—goodwill	£5,000	
Cr Accumulated impairment losses—goodwill		£5,000

	Eddie plc (£000)	Sandy plc (£000)	Eliminations and adjustments Dr (£000)	Eliminations and adjustments Cr (£000)	Consolidated statement (£000)
Detailed reconciliation of opening and closing retained earnings					
Sales revenue	2,000	900			2,900
Cost of goods sold	(1,400)	(350)			1,750
Gross profit	600	550			1,150
Other income					
Gain on sale of fixed asset	180	–	180(b)		–
Total income	780	550			1,150
Expenses					
Depreciation	–	(130)		30(d)	(100)
Other expenses	(280)	(100)	5(f)		(385)
Profit before tax	500	320			665
Tax expense	(150)	(96)	9(e)	54(c)	(201)
Profit after tax	350	224			464
Retained earnings—1 July 2014	400	300	300(a)		400
Retained earnings—30 June 2015	750	524			864
Statement of financial position					
Shareholders' equity					
Retained earnings	750	524			864
Share capital	1,000	500	500(a)		1,000
Current liabilities					
Tax payable	150	96			246
Non-current liabilities					
Loans	400	250			650
	2,300	1,370			2,760
Current assets					
Accounts receivable	300	180			480
Inventory	420	220			640
Non-current assets					
Land	730	320			1,050
Plant, at cost	–	780	220(b)		1,000
Plant—accumulated depreciation	–	(130)	30(d)	400(b)	(500)
Investment in Sandy plc	850	–		850(a)	–
Deferred tax asset	–	–	54(c)	9(e)	45
Goodwill—at cost	–	–	50(a)		50
Goodwill—accum. impairment loss	–	–		5(f)	(5)
	2,300	1,370	1,348	1,348	2,760

To ensure that we know how to take account of prior period adjustments (such as adjustments relating to a prior period sale of a non-current asset) when we undertake a consolidation in periods subsequent to the first consolidation, in Worked Example 21.6 we undertake the consolidation of Eddie plc and its controlled entity as at 30 June 2016—that is two years after control of the subsidiary was established.

| | Worked Example 21.6 | **Consolidation two years after acquisition in the presence of a prior period intragroup sale of a non-current asset** |

The financial statements of Eddie plc and its controlled entity, Sandy plc, at 30 June 2016 are as follows:

	Eddie plc (£000)	Sandy plc (£000)
Detailed reconciliation of opening and closing retained earnings		
Sales revenue	2,700	1,100
Cost of goods sold	(1,550)	(440)
Gross profit	1,150	660
Expenses		
Depreciation	–	(130)
Other expenses	(410)	(120)
Profit before tax	740	410
Tax expense	(222)	(123)
Profit after tax	518	287
Retained earnings—1 July 2015	750	524
Retained earnings—30 June 2016	1,268	811

	Eddie plc (£000)	Sandy plc (£000)
Statement of financial position		
ASSETS		
Non-current assets		
Land	910	320
Plant, at cost	–	780
Plant—accumulated depreciation	–	(260)
investment in Sandy plc	850	–
	1,760	840
Current assets		
Inventory	820	559
Accounts receivable	300	280
	1,120	839
Total assets	2,880	1,679
EQUITY AND LIABILITIES		
Equity and reserves		
Equity share capital	1,000	500
Retained earnings	1,268	811
	2,268	1,311
Non-current liabilities		
Loans	390	245
Current liabilities		
Tax payable	222	123
Total liabilities	612	368
Total equity and liabilities	2,880	1,679

Required

Prepare the consolidated statement of financial position and statement of comprehensive income of Eddie plc and its controlled entity for the year ended 30 June 2016, assuming that the directors believe that goodwill on acquisition has been impaired by a further £5,000.

In undertaking the consolidation you will need to take account of the sale of plant made in the prior period, as discussed in Worked Example 21.5.

Solution

(a) *Elimination of investment in controlled entity*

Dr	Share capital	£500,000	
Dr	Retained earnings	£300,000	
Dr	Goodwill	£50,000	
Cr	investment in Sandy plc		£850,000

(b) *Reversal of gain recognised in prior period on sale of asset and reinstatement of cost and accumulated depreciation*

Dr	Retained earnings	£126,000	
Dr	Deferred tax asset	£54,000	
Dr	Plant	£220,000	
Cr	Accumulated depreciation		£400,000

(c) *Reinstating accumulated depreciation in the statement of financial position*

Dr	Accumulated depreciation	£60,000	
Cr	Depreciation expense		£30,000
Cr	Retained earnings		£30,000

(d) *Consideration of the tax effect of current and previous period's depreciation*

Dr	Income tax expense	£9,000	
Dr	Retained earnings	£9,000	
Cr	Deferred tax asset		£18,000

(e) *Recognition of the impairment of goodwill in current and previous period*

Dr	Impairment loss—goodwill	£5,000	
Dr	Retained earnings	£5,000	
Cr	Accumulated impairment losses—goodwill		£10,000

The consolidated financial statements can be prepared from the following worksheet:

	Eddie plc (£000)	Sandy plc (£000)	Eliminations and adjustments Dr (£000)	Eliminations and adjustments Cr (£000)	Consolidated statement (£000)
Detailed reconciliation of opening and closing retained earnings					
Sales revenue	2,700	1,100			3,800
Cost of goods sold	(1,550)	(440)			1,990
Gross profit	1,150	660			1,810
Expenses					
Depreciation	–	(130)		30(c)	(100)
Other expenses	(410)	(120)	5(e)		(535)
Profit before tax	740	410			1,175
Tax expense	(222)	(123)	9(d)		(354)
Profit after tax	518	287			821
Retained earnings—1 July 2015	750	524	300(a) 126(b) 9(d) 5(e)	30(c)	864
Retained earnings—30 June 2016	1,268	811			1,685

Statement of financial position

	Eddie plc (£000)	Sandy plc (£000)	Eliminations and adjustments Dr (£000)	Eliminations and adjustments Cr (£000)	Consolidated statement (£000)
Shareholders' equity					
Retained earnings	1,268	811			1,685
Share capital	1,000	500	500(a)		1,000
Current liabilities					
Tax payable	222	123			345
Non-current liabilities					
Loans	390	245			635
	2,880	1,679			3,665
Current assets					
Accounts receivable	300	280			580
Inventory	820	559			1,379
Non-current assets					
Land	910	320			1,230
Plant, at cost	–	780	220(b)		1,000
Plant—accumulated depreciation	–	(260)	60(c)	400(b)	(600)
Investment in Sandy plc	850	–		850(a)	–
Deferred tax asset	–	–	54(b)	18(d)	36
Goodwill—at cost	–	–	50(a)		50
Goodwill—accum. impairment loss	–	–		10(e)	(10)
	2,880	1,679	1,338	1,338	3,665

Consolidated statement of comprehensive income of Eddie plc and its controlled entity for the year ended 30 June 2016	The Group (£)	Eddie plc (£)
Sales	3,800,000	2,700,000
Cost of goods sold	(1,990,000)	(1,550,000)
Gross profit	1,810,000	1,150,000
Depreciation	(100,000)	–
Other expenses	(535,000)	(410,000)
Profit before tax	1,175,000	740,000
Income tax expense	(354,000)	(222,000)
Profit after tax	821,000	518,000
Other comprehensive income	–	–
Total comprehensive income for the year	821,000	518,000

Eddie plc and its controlled entity (Group) Statement of changes in equity for the year ended 30 June 2016	Share capital (£)	Group retained earnings (£)	Group total equity (£)
Balance at 1 July 2015	1,000,000	864,000	1,864,000
Total comprehensive income for the year		821,000	821,000
Distributions—dividends		–	–
Balance at 30 June 2016	1,000,000	1,685,000	2,685,000

Eddie plc: Statement of changes in equity for the year ended 30 June 2016

	Share capital (£)	Retained earnings (£)	Total equity (£)
Balance at 1 July 2015	1,000,000	750,000	1,750,000
Total comprehensive income for the year	–	518,000	518,000
Distributions—dividends	–	–	–
Balance at 30 June 2016	1,000,000	1,268,000	2,268,000

*Consolidated statement of financial position
of Eddie plc and its controlled entity as at 30 June 2016*

	The Group (£)	Eddie plc (£)
ASSETS		
Non-current assets		
Land	1,230,000	910,000
Plant and equipment	1,000,000	–
Accumulated depreciation	(600,000)	–
Investment in Sandy plc		850,000
Deferred tax asset	36,000	–
Goodwill	50,000	–
Accumulated impairment loss	(10,000)	–
	1,706,000	1,760,000
Current assets		
Inventory	1,379,000	820,000
Accounts receivable	580,000	300,000
	1,959,000	1,120,000
Total assets	3,665,000	2,880,000
EQUITY AND LIABILITIES		
Equity and reserves		
Share capital	1,000,000	1,000,000
Retained earnings	1,685,000	1,268,000
Total equity and reserves	2,685,000	2,268,000
Non-current liabilities		
Loan	635,000	390,000
Current liabilities		
Tax payable	345,000	222,000
Total liabilities	980,000	612,000
Total equity and liabilities	3,665,000	2,880,000

SUMMARY

The chapter considered the consolidation process and, in particular, how to account for intragroup transactions—that is, intragroup dividend payments, sales of inventory and sales of non-current assets.

Only dividends paid externally should be shown in the consolidated financial statements, so that intragroup dividends paid by one entity within the group are offset against dividend revenue recorded in another entity. Further, for intragroup dividends, the liability associated with dividends payable is to be offset against the asset dividend receivable, as recorded by other entities within the group.

Individual entities within a group often provide goods and services to one another at a profit. From the economic entity's perspective, however, revenue related to the sale of goods and services should be shown only where the inflow of economic benefits has come from parties external to the group. As a result, on consolidation it is often necessary to provide adjusting entries, which eliminate the effects of the intragroup sales. Where there have been intragroup sales and some of the inventory is still on hand within the group at year end, consolidation adjustments will need to be made, which reduce the consolidated balance of closing inventory. This is required to ensure that the consolidated financial statements measure inventory at the lower of cost and net realisable value from the group's perspective (consistent with IAS 2 *Inventories*).

Where there is a sale of non-current assets within the group, consolidation adjustments are to be made to eliminate any intragroup gain on the sale of the assets and to adjust the cost of the asset to reflect its cost to the economic entity. Where there are intragroup sales of non-current assets, there is also typically a requirement to adjust depreciation as part of the consolidation process.

KEY TERM

intragroup transaction **598**

END-OF-CHAPTER EXERCISE

PART A

After completing this chapter, you should ensure that you are able to answer the following questions. (If you find you cannot provide appropriate answers, you should revisit the relevant sections of the chapter.)

1   Following consolidation, should dividends paid to the parent entity by its subsidiaries be shown in the economic entity's financial statements?   **LO** **21.2**

2   Will dividends paid by subsidiaries out of their pre-acquisition earnings affect the amount of goodwill that will be calculated on consolidation?   **LO** **21.2**

3   If a subsidiary sells inventory to the parent entity and some of the inventory is still on hand at year end, what adjustments are necessary at year end? Will adjustments be required to restate the balance of opening inventory as at the beginning of the next financial period?   **LO** **21.3**

PART B

The following financial statements of Mungo plc and its subsidiary Barry plc have been extracted from their financial records at 30 June 2015.   **LO** **21.3**

	Mungo plc (€000)	Barry plc (€000)
Detailed reconciliation of opening and closing retained earnings		
Sales revenue	1,380	1,160
Cost of goods sold	(928)	(476)
Gross profit	452	684
Dividends received from Barry plc	186	–
Management fee revenue	53	–
Gain on sale of plant	70	–
Expenses		
Administrative expenses	(98.8)	(77.4)
Depreciation	(49)	(113.6)
Management fee expense	–	(53)
Other expenses	(202.2)	(154)
Profit before tax	411	286
Tax expense	(123)	(84.4)
Profit for the year	288	201.6
Retained earnings—30 June 2014	638.8	478.4
	926.8	680
Dividends paid	(274.8)	(186)
Retained earnings—30 June 2015	652	494

	Mungo plc (€000)	Barry plc (€000)
Statement of financial position		
ASSETS		
Non-current assets		
Land and buildings	448	652
Plant—at cost	599.7	711.6
Accumulated depreciation	(171.5)	(277.6)
Investment in Barry plc	712	–
	1,588.2	1,086
Current assets		
Inventory	184	58
Accounts receivable	118.8	124.6
	302.8	182.6
Total assets	1,891	1,268.6
EQUITY AND LIABILITIES		
Equity and reserves		
Equity share capital	700	400
Retained earnings	652	494
	1,352	894
Non-current liabilities		
Loans	347	232
Current liabilities		
Accounts payable	109.4	92.6
Tax payable	82.6	50
	192	142.6
Total liabilities	539	374.6
Total equity and liabilities	1,891	1,268.6

Other information

- Mungo plc acquired its 100 per cent interest in Barry plc on 1 July 2011, that is, four years earlier. At that date the capital and reserves of Barry plc were:

Share capital	€400,000
Retained earnings	€250,000
	€650,000

At the date of acquisition all assets were considered to be fairly valued.

- During the year Mungo plc made total sales to Barry plc of €130,000, while Barry plc sold €104,000 in inventory to Mungo plc.
- The opening inventory in Mungo plc as at 1 July 2014 included inventory acquired from Barry plc for €84,000 that had cost Barry plc €70,000 to produce.
- The closing inventory in Mungo plc includes inventory acquired from Barry plc at a cost of €67,200. This cost Barry plc €52,000 to produce.
- The closing inventory of Barry plc includes inventory acquired from Mungo plc at a cost of €24,000. This cost Mungo plc €19,200 to produce.
- The management of Mungo plc believe that goodwill acquired was impaired by €5,000 in the current financial year. Previous impairments of goodwill amounted to €10,000.
- On 1 July 2014 Mungo plc sold an item of plant to Barry plc for €100,000 when its carrying value in Mungo plc's financial statements was €80,000 (cost €120,000, accumulated depreciation €40,000). This plant is assessed as having a remaining useful life of six years from the date of sale.
- Barry plc paid €20,000 in management fees to Mungo plc.
- The tax rate is 30 per cent.

REQUIRED

Provide the consolidated financial statements of Mungo plc and Barry plc as at 30 June 2015.

SOLUTION TO END-OF-CHAPTER EXERCISE

Elimination of the investment in Barry plc and the recognition of goodwill on consolidation

	Barry plc (€)
Share capital at acquisition date—1 July 2011	400,000
Retained earnings at acquisition date—1 July 2011	250,000
	650,000
Investment in Barry plc	712,000
Goodwill on consolidation	62,000

As shown above, the net assets of Barry plc are €650,000 at acquisition date. As €712,000 is paid for the investment, the goodwill amounts to €62,000. The consolidation entry to eliminate the investment is:

(a)

Dr	Share capital	€400,000	
Dr	Retained earnings	€250,000	
Dr	Goodwill	€62,000	
Cr	investment in Barry plc		€712,000

Elimination of intercompany sales

We need to eliminate the intragroup sales because, from the perspective of the economic entity, no sales have in fact occurred.

(b) *Sale of inventory from Barry plc to Mungo plc*

Dr	Sales revenue	€104,000	
Cr	Cost of goods sold		€104,000

(c) *Elimination of the unrealised profit in the closing inventory of Mungo plc*

In this case, the unrealised profit in closing inventory amounts to €15,200. This must be removed.

Dr	Cost of goods sold	€15,200	
Cr	Inventory		€15,200

(d) *Consideration of the tax paid or payable on the sale of inventory that is still held within the group*

From Barry plc's individual perspective (as a separate legal entity), the full amount of the sale has been earned. This will attract a tax liability in Barry plc's accounts of €4,560 (30 per cent of €15,200). However, from the group's perspective some of this will represent a prepayment of tax as the full amount has not been earned by the group even if Barry plc is obliged to pay the tax.

Dr	Deferred tax asset	€4,560	
Cr	Income tax expense		€4,560

(€15,200 × 30 per cent)

(e) *Sale of inventory from Mungo plc to Barry plc*

During the current financial period Mungo plc sold inventory to Barry plc at a price of €130,000. The unrealised profit component is €4,800.

Dr	Sales	€130,000	
Cr	Cost of goods sold		€130,000

(eliminating intragroup sales)

(f) *Elimination of unrealised profits in the closing inventory of Barry plc*

In this case, the unrealised profit in closing inventory amounts to €4,800. To remove:

Dr	Cost of goods sold	€4,800	
Cr	Inventory		€4,800

(eliminating unrealised profit in closing inventory)

(g) *Consideration of the tax paid on the sale of the inventory that is still held within the group*
Tax recorded in Mungo plc's financial statements of €1,440, which is 30 per cent of €4,880, also needs to be adjusted. From the group's perspective, this will represent a prepayment of tax, as the full amount has not been earned by the group even though Mungo plc is obliged to pay the tax.

Dr	Deferred tax asset	€1,440	
Cr	Income tax expense		€1,440

(€4,800 × 30 per cent)

(h) *Unrealised profit in opening inventory*
At the end of the preceding financial year, Mungo plc had €84,000 of inventory on hand, which had been purchased from Barry plc. The inventory had cost Barry plc €70,000 to produce. Assume that the inventory has been sold to an external party in the current period and is therefore realised—so there is no need to adjust the closing balance of inventory.

Dr	Retained earnings—30 June 2014	€9,800	
Dr	Income tax expense	€4,200	
Cr	Cost of sales		€14,000

Adjustments for intragroup sale of plant
On 1 July 2014 Mungo plc sold an item of plant to Barry plc for €100,000 when its carrying value in Barry plc's financial statements was €80,000 (cost of €120,000 and accumulated depreciation of €40,000). This item of plant was being depreciated over a further six years from acquisition date, with no expected residual value.

(i) *Reversal of gain recognised on sale of asset and reinstatement of cost and accumulated depreciation*
The result of the sale of the item of plant to Barry plc is that the gain on sale of €20,000—the difference between the sales proceeds of €100,000 and the carrying amount of €80,000—will be shown in Mungo plc's financial statements. However, from the economic entity's perspective there has been no sale and, therefore, no gain on sale given that there has been no transaction with a party external to the group. The following entry is necessary for the accounts to reflect the balances that would have applied had the intragroup sale not occurred.

Dr	Gain on sale of plant	€20,000	
Dr	Plant	€20,000	
Cr	Accumulated depreciation		€40,000

The result of this entry is that the intragroup gain on sale is removed and the asset and accumulated depreciation accounts revert to reflecting no sales transaction. The gain of €20,000 will be recognised progressively in the consolidated financial report of the economic entity by adjustments to the amounts of depreciation charged by Barry plc in its financial statements. As the service potential or economic benefits embodied in the asset are consumed, the €20,000 gain will be progressively recognised from the economic entity's perspective. This is shown in journal entry (k).

(j) *Effect of tax on profit on sale of item of plant*
From Mungo plc's individual perspective, it would have made a gain of €20,000 on the sale of the plant and this gain would have been taxable. At a tax rate of 30 per cent, €6,000 would then be payable by Mungo plc. However, from the economic entity's perspective, no gain has been made, which means that the related 'tax expense' must be reversed and a related deferred tax benefit be recognised. A deferred tax asset is recognised because, from the economic entity's perspective, the amount paid to the taxation authorities represents a prepayment of tax.

Dr	Deferred tax asset	€6,000	
Cr	Income tax expense		€6,000

(k) *Reinstating accumulated depreciation in the statement of financial position*
Mungo plc would be depreciating the asset on the basis of the cost it incurred to acquire the asset. Its depreciation charge would be €100,000 ÷ 6 = €16,667. From the economic entity's perspective, the asset had a carrying value of €80,000, which was to be allocated over the next six years, giving a depreciation charge of €80,000 ÷ 6 = €13,333. An adjustment of €3,334 is therefore required.

Dr	Accumulated depreciation	€3,334	
Cr	Depreciation expense		€3,334

(l) *Consideration of the tax effect of the reduction in depreciation expense*

The increase in the tax expense from the perspective of the economic entity is due to the reduction in the depreciation expense. The additional tax expense is €1,000, which is €3,334 x 30 per cent. This entry represents a partial reversal of the deferred tax asset of €6,000 recognised in an earlier entry. After six years the balance of the deferred tax asset relating to the sale of the item of plant will be €nil.

Dr	Income tax expense	€1,000	
Cr	Deferred tax asset		€1,000

(m) *Impairment of goodwill*

Dr	Retained earnings	€10,000	
Dr	Impairment loss—goodwill	€5,000	
Cr	Accumulated impairment losses—goodwill		€15,000

(n) *Elimination of intragroup transactions—management fees*

All of the management fees paid within the group will need to be eliminated on consolidation.

Dr	Management fee revenue	€20,000	
Cr	Management fee expense		€20,000

(o) *Dividends paid*

We eliminate dividends paid within the group. Only dividends paid to parties outside the entity (non-controlling interests) are to be shown in the consolidated financial statements.

Dr	Dividend revenue	€186,000	
Cr	Dividend paid		€186,000

We can now post the consolidation journal entries to the consolidation worksheet.

	Mungo plc (€000)	Barry plc (€000)	Eliminations and adjustments Dr (€000)	Eliminations and adjustments Cr (€000)	Consolidated statement (€000)
Detailed reconciliation of opening and closing retained earnings					
Sales revenue	1,380	1,160	104(b) 130(e)		2,306
Cost of goods sold	(928)	(476)	15.2(c) 4.8(f)	104(b) 130(e) 14(h)	1,176
Gross profit	452	684			1,130
Other revenue					–
Dividends received from Barry plc	186	–	186(o)		–
Management fee revenue	53		20(n)		33
Gain on sale of plant	70		20(i)		50
Expenses					
Administrative expenses	(98.8)	(77.4)			(176.2)
Depreciation	(49)	(113.6)		3.34(k)	(159.26)
Management fee expense	–	(53)		20(n)	(33)
Other expenses	(202.2)	(154)	5(m)		(361.2)
Profit before tax	411	286			483.34
Tax expense	(123)	(84.4)	4.2(h) 1(l)	4.56(d) 1.44(g) 6(j)	(200.6)
Profit for the year	288	201.6			282.74
Retained earnings—30 June 2014	638.8	478.4	250(a) 9.8(h) 10(m)		847.4
	926.8	680			1,130.14
Dividends paid	(274.8)	(186)		186(o)	(274.8)
Retained earnings—30 June 2015	652	494			855.34

	Mungo plc (€000)	Barry plc (€000)	Eliminations and adjustments		Consolidated statement (€000)
			Dr (€000)	Cr (€000)	
Statement of financial position					
Shareholders' equity					
Retained earnings	652	494			855.34
Share capital	700	400	400(a)		700
Current liabilities					
Accounts payable	109.4	92.6			202
Tax payable	82.6	50			132.6
Non-current liabilities					
Loans	347	232			579
	1,891	1,268.6			2,468.94
Current assets					
Accounts receivable	118.8	124.6			243.4
Inventory	184	58		15.2(c) 4.8(f)	222
Non-current assets					
Deferred tax asset			4.56(d) 1.44(g) 6(j)	1(l)	11
Land and buildings	448	652			1,100
Plant—at cost	599.7	711.6	20(i)		1,331.3
Accumulated depreciation	(171.5)	(277.6)	3.34(k)	40(i)	(485.76)
Investment in Barry plc	712	–		712(a)	–
Goodwill	–	–	62(a)		62
Accumulated amortisation		–		15(m)	(15)
	1,891	1,268.6	1,257.34	1,257.34	2,468.94

The next step would be to present the consolidated financial statements. A suggested format for the consolidated financial statements would be as follows (prior year comparatives for the financial statements of the parent entity, both of which would be required in practice, have not been provided).

Consolidated statement of comprehensive income of Mungo plc and its subsidiaries for the year ended 30 June 2015

	The Group (€)	Mungo plc (€)
Sales	2,306,000	1,380,000
Cost of goods sold	(1,176,000)	(928,000)
Gross profit	1,130,000	452,000
Dividend income	–	186,000
Management fee revenue	33,000	53,000
Gain on sale of plant	50,000	70,000
Administrative expenses	(176,200)	(98,800)
Depreciation	(159,266)	(49,000)
Goodwill amortisation	(5,000)	–
Management fee expense	(33,000)	–
Other expenses	(356,200)	(202,200)
Profit before income tax expense	483,334	411,000
Income tax expense	(200,600)	(123,000)
Profit after tax	282,734	288,000
Other comprehensive income	–	–
Total comprehensive income	282,734	288,000

Mungo plc and its controlled entity: Statement of changes in equity for the year ended 30 June 2015	Share capital (£)	Group retained earnings (£)	Group total equity (£)
Balance at 1 July 2014	700,000	847,400	1,547,400
Total comprehensive income for the year	–	282,734	282,734
Distributions—dividends	–	(274,800)	(274,800)
Balance at 30 June 2015	700,000	855,334	1,555,334

Mungo plc: Statement of changes in equity for the year ended 30 June 2015	Share capital (£)	Retained earnings (£)	Total equity (£)
Balance at 1 July 2014	700,000	638,800	1,338,800
Total comprehensive income for the year		288,000	288,000
Distributions—dividends		(274,800)	(274,800)
Balance at 30 June 2015	700,000	652,000	1,352,000

Consolidated statement of financial position of Mungo plc and its subsidiaries as at 30 June 2015

	The Group (£)	Mungo Plc (£)
ASSETS		
Non-current assets		
Land and buildings	1,100,000	448,000
Plant and equipment	1,331,300	599,700
Accumulated depreciation	(485,766)	(171,500)
Investment in Barry plc		712,000
Goodwill	62,000	–
Accumulated impairment loss	(15,000)	–
Deferred tax asset	11,000	–
	2,003,534	1,588,200
Current assets		
Inventory	222,000	184,000
Accounts receivable	243,400	118,800
	465,400	302,800
Total assets	2,468,934	1,891,000
EQUITY AND LIABILITIES		
Equity and reserves		
Share capital	700,000	700,000
Retained earnings	855,334	652,000
Total equity and reserves	1,555,334	1,352,000
Non-current liabilities		
Loan	579,000	347,000
Current liabilities		
Accounts payable	202,000	109,400
Tax payable	132,600	82,600
	334,600	192,000
Total liabilities	913,600	539,000
Total equity and liabilities	2,468,934	1,891,000

REVIEW QUESTIONS

1 What is an intragroup transaction and why do we need to know about them? **LO 21.1**
2 When does an intragroup inventory transaction require us to perform a consolidation adjustment to tax expense? **LO 21.3**
3 In the consolidated financial statements, which dividends are to be shown as paid, declared, payable and receivable? **LO 21.2**
4 How would dividends that have been paid out of pre-acquisition earnings of a subsidiary be treated in the financial statements of the parent entity? **LO 21.2**
5 What effect, if any, would the payment of dividends by a controlled entity, out of its pre-acquisition earnings, have on the amount of goodwill that would be recognised on consolidation? **LO 21.2**
6 If one entity sells inventory to another entity, which is 80 per cent owned, what percentage of the sales revenue needs to be eliminated in the consolidation process? **LO 21.3**
7 A plc owns 100 per cent of B plc, which in turn owns 100 per cent of C plc. During the financial year A plc sells inventory to B plc at a sales price of £150,000. The inventory cost A plc £100,000 to produce.

Within the same financial year, B plc subsequently sells the same inventory to C plc for £200,000 without incurring any additional costs. At the end of the financial year, C plc has sold half of this inventory to companies outside the group for a sales price of £180,000. At year end C plc still has half the inventory on hand. **LO 21.3**

REQUIRED

From the economic entity's perspective (that is, the group's perspective), determine:
(a) the sales revenue for the financial year
(b) the value of closing inventory.

8 Big Company owns all the issued capital of Small Company. Big Company acquires its 100 per cent interest in Small Company on 1 July 2014 for a cost of £2,000. All assets are fairly stated at acquisition date. The share capital and reserves of Small Company on the date of acquisition are: **LO 21.2**

	£
Share capital	1,250
Retained earnings	750
	2,000

The reconciliation of retained earnings and statement of financial positions of Big Company and Small Company, as at 30 June 2015, are as follows:

	Big Company (£)	Small Company (£)
Reconciliation of opening and closing retained earnings		
Profit before tax	500	250
Tax	(125)	(100)
Profit after tax	375	150
Opening retained earnings	1,000	750
	1,375	900
Dividends declared	(175)	(125)
Closing retained earnings	1,200	775
Statement of financial position (Draft)		
Shareholders' funds		
Retained earnings	1,200	775
Share capital	1,250	1,250
Liabilities		
Accounts payable	2,500	250
Dividends payable	175	125
	5,125	2,400

	Big Company (£)	Small Company (£)
Assets		
Cash	250	175
Accounts receivable	125	325
Dividends receivable	250	–
Inventory	375	400
Plant and equipment	2,125	1,500
investment in Small Company	2,000	–
	5,125	2,400

REQUIRED

Provide the consolidated statement of comprehensive income, statement of financial position and statement of changes in equity for Big Company and its controlled entity for the year ending 30 June 2015.

9 Bernie Boffin plc owns 100 per cent of Computer plc. On 1 July 2013 Bernie Boffin plc sells an item of plant to Computer plc for £3.6 million. This plant cost Bernie Boffin plc £4.5 million and had accumulated depreciation of £1.8 million at the date of the sale. The remaining useful life of the plant is assessed as 12 years and the tax rate is 33 per cent. **LO 21.2**

REQUIRED

Provide the consolidation journal entries for 30 June 2014 and 30 June 2015 to adjust for the above sale.

10 Bigger Company owns all the issued capital of Smaller Company. The financial statements of Bigger Company and Smaller Company at 30 June 2015 are as follows: **LO 21.3**

	Bigger Company (£)	Smaller Company (£)
Reconciliation of opening and closing retained earnings		
Profit before tax	500	500
Tax	(125)	(200)
Profit after tax	375	300
Opening retained earnings	4,000	1,500
	4,375	1,800
Dividends declared	(175)	(250)
Closing retained earnings	4,200	1,550
Statement of financial position		
ASSETS		
Non-current assets		
Plant and equipment	2,125	3,000
Investment in Smaller Company	5,000	–
	7,125	3,000
Current assets		
Inventory	375	800
Accounts receivable	125	650
Dividends receivable	250	–
Cash	250	350
	1,000	1,800
Total assets	8,125	4,800
EQUITY AND LIABILITIES		
Equity and reserves		
Equity share capital	1,250	2,500
Retained earnings	4,200	1,550
	5,450	4,050
Liabilities		
Accounts payable	2,500	500
Dividends payable	175	250
Total liabilities	2,675	750
Total equity and liabilities	8,125	4,800

Bigger Company acquired its 100 per cent interest in Smaller Company on 1 July 2014 for a cost of £5,000. The share capital and reserves of Smaller Company on the date of acquisition are:

	£
Share capital	2,500
Retained earnings	1,500
	4,000

The directors believe that goodwill has been impaired by 20 per cent in the year to 2015.

The dividends represent interim dividends that had been agreed before the year end but were not paid by 30 June 2015.

REQUIRED

Provide the consolidated statement of comprehensive income and statement of financial position for Bigger Company and its controlled entity for the year ending 30 June 2015.

11 Nat plc acquires all the issued capital of Midget plc for a cash payment of €1.5 million on 30 June 2015. The statements of financial position of both entities immediately following the purchase are: **LO 21.2**

	Nat plc (€000)	Midget plc (€000)
ASSETS		
Non-current assets		
Plant	4,440	1,800
Investment in Midget plc	1,500	–
	5,940	1,800
Current assets		
Accounts receivable	900	135
Cash	60	45
	960	180
Total assets	6,900	1,980
EQUITY AND LIABILITIES		
Equity and reserves		
Share capital	3,000	600
Retained earnings	1,200	750
	4,200	1,350
Non-current liabilities		
Loans	2,400	540
Current liabilities		
Accounts payable	300	90
Total liabilities	2,700	630
Total equity and liabilities	6,900	1,980

Additional Information

Immediately following the acquisition, a dividend of €600,000 is declared by Midget Plc. The financial statements provided here do not reflect this dividend payment.

REQUIRED

Provide the consolidated statement of financial position of Nat plc and Midget plc as at 30 June 2015.

CHALLENGING QUESTIONS

12 Jacko plc owns 100 per cent of the shares of Jackson plc, acquired on 1 July 2014 for €3.5 million when the shareholders' funds of Jackson plc were: **LO 21.3**

	€
Share capital	1,750,000
Retained earnings	1,400,000
	3,150,000

All assets of Jackson plc are fairly stated at acquisition date. The directors believe that there has been an impairment loss on the goodwill of €35,000 for the year ended 30 June 2015.

During the 2015 financial year, Jackson plc sells inventory to Jacko plc at a sales price of €700,000. The inventory cost Jackson plc €420,000 to produce. At 30 June 2015 half of the inventory is still on hand with Jacko plc. The tax rate is 33 per cent.

The financial statements of Jacko plc and Jackson plc at 30 June 2015 are as follows:

	Jacko plc (€000)	Jackson plc (€000)
Reconciliation of opening and closing retained earnings		
Sales revenue	4,200	1,400
Cost of goods sold	(1,750)	(490)
Other expenses	(210)	(105)
Other revenue	245	87.5
Profit	2,485	892.5
Tax expense	(700)	(350)
Profit after tax	1,785	542.5
Retained earnings—1 July 2014	3,500	1,400
	5,285	1,942.5
Dividends paid	(700)	(140)
Retained earnings—30 June 2015	4,585	1,802.5
Statement of financial position		
ASSETS		
Non-current assets		
Land	5,040	1,400
Plant	8,645	1,400
Investment in Jackson plc	3,500	–
Future income tax benefit	350	175
Goodwill	–	–
	17,535	2,975
Current assets		
Inventory	2,100	1,050
Accounts receivable	525	612.5
Cash	875	87.5
	3,500	1,750
Total assets	21,035	4,725
EQUITY AND LIABILITIES		
Equity and reserves		
Equity share capital	14,000	1,750
Retained earnings	4,585	1,802.5
	18,585	3,552.5
Non-current liabilities		
Loans	2,100	875
Current liabilities		
Accounts payable	350	297.5
Total liabilities	2,450	1,172.5
Total equity and liabilities	21,035	4,725

REQUIRED

Provide the consolidated financial statements for Jacko Plc and its controlled entity for 2015.

13 The following financial statements of Andy plc and its subsidiary Irons plc have been extracted from their financial records at 30 June 2015. **LO 21.4**

	Andy plc (€)	Irons plc (€)
Statement of profit and loss		
Sales revenue	839,250	725,000
Cost of goods sold	(580,000)	(297,500)
Gross profit	259,250	427,500
Dividends received from Irons plc	116,250	–
Management fee revenue	33,125	–
Gain on sale of plant	43,750	–
Expenses		
Administrative expenses	(38,500)	(48,375)
Depreciation	(30,625)	(71,000)
Management fee expense	–	(33,125)
Other expenses	(126,375)	(96,250)
Profit before tax	256,875	178,750
Tax expense	(76,875)	(52,750)
Profit for the year	180,000	126,000
Statement of financial position		
ASSETS		
Non-current assets		
Land and buildings	198,750	407,500
Plant—at cost	400,000	444,750
Accumulated depreciation	(107,000)	(173,500)
Investment in Irons plc	500,000	–
	991,750	678,750
Current assets		
Inventory	115,000	36,250
Accounts receivable	74,250	77,875
	189,250	114,125
Total assets	1,181,000	792,875
EQUITY AND LIABILITIES		
Equity and reserves		
Share capital	437,500	250,000
Retained earnings	407,500	308,750
	845,000	558,750
Non-current liabilities		
Loans	236,000	145,000
Current liabilities		
Accounts payable	–	57,875
Tax payable	100,000	31,250
	100,000	89,125
Total liabilities	336,000	234,125
Total equity and liabilities	1,181,000	792,875

Other information

- Andy plc had opening retained earnings of €399,250 and paid €171,750 in dividends in the year. Irons plc had opening retained earnings of €299,000 and paid €116,250 in dividends in the year.

- Andy plc acquired its 100 per cent interest in Irons plc on 1 July 2008—that is, seven years earlier. The cost of the investment was €500,000. At that date the capital and reserves of Irons plc were:

	€
Share capital	250,000
Retained earnings	200,000
	450,000

At the date of acquisition all assets were considered to be fairly valued.

- During the year Andy plc made total sales to Irons plc of €81,250, while Irons plc sold €65,000 in inventory to Andy plc.
- The opening inventory in Andy plc as at 1 July 2014 included inventory acquired from Irons plc for €52,500 that cost Irons plc €43,750 to produce.
- The closing inventory in Andy plc includes inventory acquired from Irons plc at a cost of €42,000. This cost Irons plc €35,000 to produce.
- The closing inventory of Irons plc includes inventory acquired from Andy plc at a cost of €15,000. This cost Andy plc €12,000 to produce.
- The management of Andy plc believe that goodwill acquired was impaired by €3,750 in the current financial year. Previous impairments of goodwill amounted to €20,000.
- On 1 July 2014 Andy plc sold an item of plant to Irons plc for €145,000 when its carrying value in Andy plc's financial statements was €101,250 (cost €168,750, accumulated depreciation €67,500). This plant is assessed as having a remaining useful life of six years.
- Andy plc paid €33,125 in management fees to Irons plc.
- The tax rate is 30 per cent.

REQUIRED

Prepare the consolidated statement of financial position and statement of comprehensive income of Andy plc and Irons plc as at 30 June 2015. Also provide a statement of changes in equity.

Chapter 22

Further Consolidation Issues II: Accounting for Non-controlling Interests

Learning objectives

Upon completing this chapter readers should:

LO1 be aware of the meaning and nature of non-controlling interests;

LO2 be aware of how to calculate the non-controlling interests' share in share capital and reserves, and current period profit;

LO3 be aware of how to calculate goodwill or bargain gain on purchase in the presence of non-controlling interests; and

LO4 be aware of how to disclose non-controlling interests within consolidated financial statements.

22.1 Introduction to accounting for non-controlling interests

In Chapters 20 and 21 we performed consolidations in cases where one entity, the parent entity, owned all of the share capital of the other entity—the subsidiary. In this chapter we introduce the accounting procedures required where the parent entity holds less than 100 per cent of the share capital of the subsidiary. The equity interests in the subsidiary that are not held by the parent entity are referred to as the non-controlling interests (they were previously referred to as *minority interests* or *outside equity interests*).

22.2 What is a non-controlling interest?

As we noted in Chapters 20 and 21, the requirement to consolidate an entity is based on the criterion of *control*. One entity can control another with less than 100 per cent ownership. This is illustrated in Figure 22.1.

parent entity An entity that controls another entity.

In Figure 22.1, Big Company owns 75 per cent of Little Company. Big Company is referred to as the **parent entity**. The remaining 25 per cent is held by investors who are

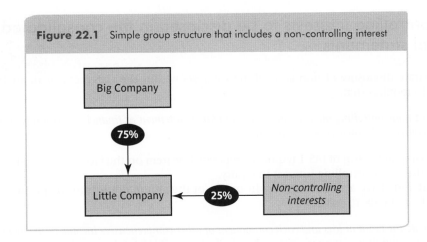

Figure 22.1 Simple group structure that includes a non-controlling interest

Big Company

75%

Little Company ← 25% ← *Non-controlling interests*

not part of the economic entity. These outside investors—who could be numerous—are called 'non-controlling interests'. A non-controlling interest exists when a subsidiary is partly owned by the parent entity. Accounting standard IFRS 10 *Consolidated Financial Statements* defines a non-controlling interest as 'the equity in a subsidiary not attributable, directly or indirectly, to a parent'.

The holders of the non-controlling interest have an entitlement to share in the net assets and profit of the subsidiary and their share is determined by their percentage ownership of the share capital of the subsidiary. For disclosure purposes, the amount of profits and net assets that are attributable to the non-controlling interest is required to be measured. We determine the non-controlling interest in three stages:

1. the non-controlling interest in the current period's profit or loss;
2. the non-controlling interest in share capital and reserves at the date of the acquisition of the subsidiary by the parent entity; and
3. the non-controlling interest in post-acquisition changes in share capital and reserves.

The term 'non-controlling interests' can sometimes be a little confusing. A parent entity does not have to hold 50 per cent or more of the equity capital of a subsidiary to control it. Hence, the non-controlling interest, which includes all the shareholders of the subsidiary other than the parent entity, might actually represent more than 50 per cent (that is, the majority) of the shareholding of the subsidiary.

The concept that is applied to the consolidation process under IFRS 10 is the entity concept. This means the subsidiary is consolidated in full with the non-controlling interests being disclosed separately but with the parent entity's interest as the non-controlling interests are considered to be contributors of equity capital to the economic entity.

The argument for this approach stems from the view that, when a parent entity controls a subsidiary, it controls all the assets even though it does not have a 100 per cent ownership interest in the subsidiary. Therefore, it is appropriate for the consolidated financial statements to show all the assets under the control of the parent entity, and how profitably those assets have been used by the parent entity's management.

In Chapters 20 and 21 we considered various consolidation journal entries. Even though those journal entries were made in cases where the parent entity owned 100 per cent of the subsidiary, all such journal entries would remain the same in the presence of non-controlling interests, except for the following:

- We eliminate only the parent's share of the subsidiaries' pre-acquisition share capital and reserves against the investment in the subsidiary. Hence, the non-controlling interest in share capital and reserves will be included in the statement of financial position.
- In relation to the dividends paid and declared by the subsidiary, only the parent's share of such dividends is treated as intragroup transactions and therefore eliminated as part of the consolidation process. The dividends paid, or payable, to non-controlling interests are shown in the consolidated financial statements (as are the dividends paid and payable by the parent entity).
- In relation to dividends payable by subsidiaries, only those payable to the parent entity are eliminated against the dividends receivable in the accounts of the parent entity. Dividends payable by the subsidiary to non-controlling interests are included within the consolidated financial statements (as are the dividends payable by the parent entity to its shareholders).

22.3	Non-controlling interests to be disclosed in the consolidated financial statements

In relation to the separate disclosure of non-controlling interests within the statement of financial position, paragraph 22 of IFRS 10 requires that:

> *A parent shall present non-controlling interests in the consolidated statement of financial position within equity, separately from the equity of the owners of the parent.*

Consistent with this, paragraph 54(q) of IAS 1 requires a separate line item on the face of the statement of financial position showing the non-controlling interest in equity.

Non-controlling interests have a share in the profit or loss of the group, not just in the profit or loss of the subsidiary. Paragraph B94 of IFRS 10 states:

> *An entity shall attribute the profit or loss and each component of other comprehensive income to the owners of the parent and to the non-controlling interests. The entity shall also attribute total comprehensive income to the owners of the parent and to the non-controlling interests even if this results in the non-controlling interests having a deficit balance.*

IAS 1 *Presentation of Financial Statements* includes a number of disclosure requirements relating to non-controlling interests. These are consistent with the requirements of IFRS 10. Paragraph 83 of IAS 1 requires:

> *An entity shall disclose the following items in the statement of comprehensive income as allocations of profit or loss for the period:*
>
> (a) *profit or loss for the period attributable to:*
>   (i) *non-controlling interest; and*
>   (ii) *owners of the parent; and*
>
> (b) *total comprehensive income for the period attributable to:*
>   (i) *non-controlling interest; and*
>   (ii) *owners of the parent.*

Exhibit 22.1 shows the suggested disclosures in the equity component of the statement of financial position, while Exhibits 22.2 and 22.3 provide suggested disclosures in relation to the statement of comprehensive income and statement of changes in equity, respectively. All these suggestions are adapted from the previous version of IAS 1 (not in the current version).

Exhibit 22.1	Non-controlling interest disclosures in statement of financial position

XYZ GROUP PLC

Statement of financial position as at 30 June 2015 (extract)

	The Group		Parent	
	2015 (€000)	2014 (€000)	2015 (€000)	2014 (€000)
Equity and Reserves				
Equity share capital	X	X	X	X
Other reserves	X	X	X	X
Retained earnings	X	X	X	X
Total equity	X	X	X	X
Parent interest	X	X	X	X
Non-controlling interest	X	X	–	–
Total equity	X	X	X	X

Exhibit 22.2 — Non-controlling interest disclosures in the statement of comprehensive income

XYZ GROUP PLC
Statement of comprehensive income for the year ended 30 June

	The Group		Parent	
	2015 (€000)	2014 (€000)	2015 (€000)	2014 (€000)
Revenue	XXX	XXX	XXX	XXX
Expenses	(XXX)	(XXX)	(XXX)	(XXX)
Profit before income tax	XXX	XXX	XXX	XXX
Income tax expense	(XXX)	(XXX)	(XXX)	(XXX)
Profit for the period	XXX	XXX	XXX	XXX
Other comprehensive income				
Exchange differences on translating foreign operations	XXX	XXX	XXX	XXX
Gains on property revaluation	XXX	XXX	XXX	XXX
Other comprehensive income for the year	XXX	XXX	XXX	XXX
Total comprehensive income for the year	XXX	XXX	XXX	XXX
Profit attributable to:				
Owners of the parent entity	XXX	XXX	XXX	XXX
Non-controlling interest	XXX	XXX	–	–
	XXX	XXX	XXX	XXX
Total comprehensive income attributable to:				
Owners of the parent entity	XXX	XXX	XXX	XXX
Non-controlling entity	XXX	XXX	–	–
	XXX	XXX	XXX	XXX

Exhibit 22.2 gives an example of a consolidated statement of comprehensive income. As can be seen, the non-controlling interests are not allocated on a 'line-by-line' basis throughout the statement of comprehensive income. A separate allocation of individual reserves in the statement of financial position is also not required. Rather, only the consolidated aggregate balance is apportioned to the shareholders of the parent entity, and to the non-controlling interests. The calculation of non-controlling interests will be considered shortly.

Paragraph 106(a) of IAS 1 requires the statement of changes in equity to disclose—not on a line-by-line basis, but on an aggregated basis, as shown in Exhibit 22.3—total comprehensive income for the period, showing separately the total amounts attributable to owners of the parent and to non-controlling interests.

22.4 Calculating non-controlling interests

As non-controlling interests require separate disclosure, a key step in preparing consolidated financial statements is working out the amounts to be attributed to non-controlling interests. However, the first step is to combine *all* the assets, liabilities, equity, income and expenses of the entities of the parent and the subsidiaries even in the presence of non-controlling interests and to eliminate the parent's investment in the subsidiary account and intragroup transactions and the related tax effects (IFRS 10, paragraph B86). The only exception to this is where the assets, liabilities, equity, income or assets have been impacted by transactions within the group, in which case the effects need to be eliminated in full. When eliminating the investment in subsidiaries we only

Exhibit 22.3　**Non-controlling interest disclosures in the statement of changes in equity**

XYZ GROUP PLC: Statement of changes in equity for the year ended 30 June 2015

	Attributable to owners of the parent					Non-controlling interest (€000)	Total equity (€000)
	Share capital (€000)	Retained earnings (€000)	Translation of foreign operations (€000)	Revaluation surplus (€000)	Total (€000)		
Balance at 1 July 2014	XXX	XXX	(XXX)	XXX	**XXX**	XXX	**XXX**
Changes in accounting policy	–	XXX	–	–	**XXX**	XXX	**XXX**
Restated balance	XXX	XXX	(XXX)	XXX	**XXX**	XXX	**XXX**
Changes in equity for 2015							
Issue of share capital	XXX	–	–	–	**XXX**	–	**XXX**
Dividends	–	(XXX)	–	–	**(XXX)**	(XXX)	**(XXX)**
Total comprehensive income for the year	–	XXX	XXX	XXX	**XXX**	XXX	**XXX**
Transfer to retained earnings	–	XXX	–	XXX	–	–	–
Balance at 30 June 2015	XXX	XXX	(XXX)	XXX	**XXX**	XXX	**XXX**

---

eliminate the parent entity's interest in each subsidiary's equity accounts. The remaining amounts of the subsidiaries' equity accounts will relate to the non-controlling interests in the economic entity. The non-controlling interests are identified but not eliminated as part of the consolidation process. They are identified for disclosure purposes. Non-controlling interest is calculated by taking three elements into account:

1. *Non-controlling interests' share in the net assets (equity) of subsidiaries at the dates the parent entity acquired the subsidiaries.* This requires the non-controlling interests' share of the pre-acquisition balances of contributed equity, retained earnings and reserves to be determined.
2. *Non-controlling interests' share in the changes in equity since acquisition date.* This is achieved through calculating the non-controlling interests' share of the post-acquisition movements in retained earnings and reserves.
3. *Non-controlling interests' share in the profit or loss of the subsidiaries in the current period.* At the end of the reporting period the non-controlling interests' share in profit for the year, distributions and transfers made, and movements in reserves for the year must be determined.

Apart from the above calculations, IFRS 3 provides preparers of financial statements with a choice in the measurement of non-controlling interest. The choice relates to the amount of goodwill in the subsidiary we allocate to the non-controlling interests. According to paragraph 19 of IFRS 3, for each business combination the acquirer shall measure any non-controlling interest in the acquiree either at fair value (including non-controlling interests' share of goodwill) or at the non-controlling interests' proportionate share of the acquiree's identifiable net assets (excluding non-controlling interests' share of goodwill). Specifically, paragraphs 18 and 19 of IFRS 3 state:

18. *The acquirer shall measure the identifiable assets acquired and the liabilities assumed at their acquisition-date fair values.*
19. *For each business combination, the acquirer shall measure at the acquisition date components of non-controlling interests in the acquiree that are present ownership interests and entitle their holders to a proportionate share of the entity's net assets in the event of liquidation at either:*
    (a) fair value; or
    (b) the present ownership instruments' proportionate share in the recognised amounts of the acquiree's identifiable net assets.

All other components of non-controlling interests shall be measured at their acquisition-date fair values, unless another measurement basis is required by International Financial Reporting Standards.

Again, it is emphasised that preparers of financial statements have the choice of which measure to use in each business combination. For example, reporting entities can use 'fair value' for one business combination and the 'proportionate share of the acquiree's identifiable net assets' for another business combination. This provides reporting entities with significant flexibility when accounting for business combinations, particularly where further acquisitions of ownership interests are expected to be acquired.

If the non-controlling interests are calculated on the basis of the fair value of the subsidiary, then an amount representing the non-controlling interest's share of goodwill will be calculated. This will be in addition to the amount of goodwill allocated to the parent entity's interest. This means, in effect, that the full amount of the goodwill of the subsidiary is being recognised, which is in basic accordance with the entity concept of consolidation. This approach is referred to by some people as the 'full goodwill method'. Pursuant to the entity concept of consolidation, all the assets and liabilities of the subsidiary are included within the consolidated financial statements.

By contrast, if the parent entity elects to account for the non-controlling interest in accordance with the second option—this being the non-controlling interest's proportionate share of the acquiree's identifiable net assets—then no goodwill will be calculated as being attributable to the non-controlling interests (which is perhaps somewhat obvious given that this second option explicitly refers to the non-controlling interest's proportionate share of *identifiable* net assets, which explicitly excludes goodwill given that goodwill is an *unidentifiable* intangible asset). Hence, if this option is taken, then only a portion of the subsidiary's goodwill—the amount attributable to the parent entity's interest—will be reflected in the consolidated financial statements, which is not consistent with a 'pure' application of the entity concept of consolidation. This is often referred to as the 'partial goodwill method'. Therefore, when we said in Chapter 20 that IFRS 10 adopts the entity principle of consolidation, this is correct, with the specific exception in relation to goodwill if the non-controlling interest in the subsidiary is measured as their proportionate share in the subsidiary's identifiable net assets.

In relation to the choice between using the 'full goodwill method' and the 'partial goodwill method', it is interesting to consider how the joint work being undertaken by the IASB and the US Financial Accounting Standards Board (FASB) ultimately led to this option being available within IFRS 3.

The reasoning behind this change can be found in the *Basis for Conclusions* that was released with IFRS 3. Paragraph BC 210 states:

> BC210 *Introducing a choice of measurement basis for non-controlling interests was not the IASB's first preference. In general, the IASB believes that alternative accounting methods reduce the comparability of financial statements. However, the IASB was not able to agree on a single measurement basis for non-controlling interests because neither of the alternatives considered (fair value and proportionate share of the acquiree's identifiable net assets) was supported by enough board members to enable a revised business combinations standard to be issued. The IASB decided to permit a choice of measurement basis for non-controlling interests because it concluded that the benefits of the other improvements to, and the convergence of, the accounting for business combinations developed in this project outweigh the disadvantages of allowing this particular option.*

Hence, the choice of two options within the IASB standard was the outcome of a political exercise to make sure the standard was approved, rather than on the basis that the approach was conceptually sound. We really have to ponder the impacts such decisions have on the ultimate quality of financial information being generated in compliance with accounting standards. In considering the differences in final outcomes that will arise as a result of allowing either option to be used, the *Basis for Conclusions* to IFRS 3 stated:

> BC217 *The IASB noted that there are likely to be three main differences in outcome that occur when the non-controlling interest is measured as its proportionate share of the acquiree's identifiable net assets, rather than at fair value. First, the amounts recognised in a business combination for non-controlling interests and goodwill are likely to be lower (and these should be the only two items affected on initial recognition). Second, if a cash-generating unit is subsequently impaired, any resulting impairment of goodwill recognised through income is likely to be lower than it would have been if the non-controlling interest had been measured at fair value (although it does not affect the impairment loss attributable to the controlling interest).*

Paragraph BC218 provides insights into a third difference—but this difference goes beyond issues addressed in this book, so we will not further complicate our discussion by detailing it.

This book uses consolidation journal entries to account for the non-controlling interest. These consolidation journal entries are posted to the consolidation worksheet in the same way as the consolidation journal entries considered earlier. This ensures that the whole consolidation worksheet takes into account the consolidation workings, line-by-line combinations of assets, liabilities, equity, income and expenses. In addition, making use of consolidation journals to account for non-controlling interests consolidates all adjustments into a one-line statement of financial position total (see Exhibit 22.1).

Turning our attention to dividends, in the presence of non-controlling interests, the dividends received by the parent from the subsidiary are eliminated against the parent's share of the subsidiary's dividend distributions. The dividends paid by the subsidiary to the non-controlling interests are to be shown in the consolidated financial statements, as are the dividends paid to the shareholders of the parent entity. These dividends will flow from the economic entity, as illustrated in Figure 22.2 and would not be considered to be intragroup transactions. Likewise, dividends receivable by the parent entity will be eliminated against the parent entity's share of the subsidiary's dividend payable as part of the usual consolidation adjustments. The balance of dividends payable by the subsidiary to the non-controlling interest will be included within the consolidated financial statements. Dividends paid or payable to non-controlling interests will act to reduce their interest in the net assets of the subsidiary.

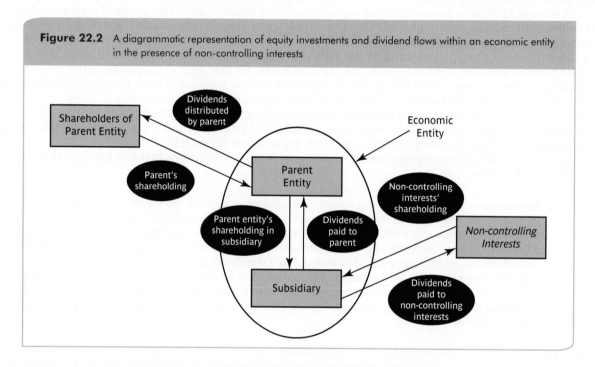

Figure 22.2 A diagrammatic representation of equity investments and dividend flows within an economic entity in the presence of non-controlling interests

The non-controlling interest is determined as the non-controlling interest's proportion of the fair value of the recognised identifiable assets, liabilities and contingent liabilities at the date of the original acquisition. Post-acquisition non-controlling interest in the identifiable assets and liabilities of a subsidiary comprises the non-controlling interest's share of movements in equity since the date of the original controlling acquisition, after eliminating intragroup transactions.

As we know, where there are intragroup transactions any related profit or loss should be eliminated in the consolidation process, not merely the percentage of the profit or loss equal to the parent entity's interest in the subsidiary.

When we calculate the non-controlling interest, it is necessary first to determine the subsidiary's contribution to the profit and equity of the group. In doing so, we must adjust the reported profit and equity of the subsidiary for any unrealised profits or losses, as they relate to the subsidiary.

22.4.1 Elimination of pre-acquisition share capital and reserves in the presence of non-controlling interests

In Chapters 20 and 21 we learned that the carrying values of subsidiaries' assets must be adjusted to fair value prior to the elimination of the parent entity's investment. This is necessary to prevent the amount of goodwill acquired by the parent entity from being wrongly stated, as would be the case if the equity (net assets) of the subsidiary were undervalued. The existence of non-controlling interests does not change the requirement for the assets and liabilities of a subsidiary to be measured at fair value as at acquisition date.

Again, reiterating an earlier important point, as far as the non-controlling interest is concerned, paragraph 19 of IFRS 3 provides the acquirer with two alternative measurements for non-controlling interests in the acquiree. As previously mentioned, non-controlling interests can either be measured at the non-controlling interest's proportionate share of the acquiree's identifiable net assets (Worked Example 22.1) or at fair value (Worked Example 22.2). The main difference is in the amount of goodwill recognised, and the total amount attributed to the non-controlling interest. It should be noted that the choice is available for each business combination. Again, this means that the entity can use fair value for one business combination and the proportionate share of the acquiree's net identifiable assets for another. This means that reporting entities will have a significant amount of flexibility when accounting for business combinations, particularly where further acquisitions of ownership interests are expected. The calculation of non-controlling interests is detailed in Worked Examples 22.1 and 22.2.

Worked Example 22.1 — Non-controlling interest in pre-acquisition capital and reserves

On 1 July 2015 Parent Entity acquired 70 per cent of the share capital of Subsidiary plc for €800,000, which represented the fair value of the consideration paid, when the share capital and reserves of Subsidiary plc were:

Share capital	€700,000
Revaluation surplus	€200,000
Retained earnings	€100,000
	€1,000,000

All assets of Subsidiary plc were recorded at fair value at acquisition date, except for some plant that had a fair value €50,000 greater than its carrying amount. The cost of the plant was €250,000 and it had accumulated depreciation of €180,000. The tax rate is 30 per cent.

Required

Prepare the consolidation eliminations and adjustments to recognise the pre-acquisition capital and reserves of Subsidiary plc, assuming that the non-controlling interest was measured at the proportionate share of the acquiree's identifiable net assets.

Solution

The elimination of the investment in Subsidiary plc and recognition of goodwill on acquisition date is determined as follows:

Elimination of investment in Subsidiary plc	Subsidiary plc (€)	Parent Entity's 70% interest (€)	30% non-controlling interest (€)
Fair value of consideration transferred		800,000	
less Fair value of identifiable assets acquired and liabilities assumed:			
Share capital on acquisition date	700,000	490,000	210,000
Revaluation surplus on acquisition date	200,000	140,000	60,000
Retained earnings on acquisition date	100,000	70,000	30,000
Fair value adjustment (€50,000 × (1 – tax rate))	35,000	24,500	10,500
	1,035,000	724,500	
Goodwill on acquisition date		75,500	
Non-controlling interest			310,500

▶

The same answer can be derived by an alternative method of calculating goodwill on acquisition, which focuses on the net fair value of the identifiable assets and liabilities acquired as follows:

Share capital and reserves	€1,000,000
Fair value adjustment (after tax)	€35,000
	€1,035,000
Proportional interest at 70 per cent	€724,500
Cost of investment	€800,000
Goodwill acquired	€75,500

What should be appreciated from Worked Example 22.1 is that the calculation of goodwill on acquisition is determined by comparing the fair value of the consideration paid or transferred with the proportional interest in the net value of the identifiable assets, liabilities and contingent liabilities acquired in the subsidiary. This provides the parent entity's share of the subsidiary's goodwill. As in this example, when the non-controlling interest is measured at the proportionate share of the acquiree's identifiable net assets, any share of goodwill attributable to the non-controlling interest's share is not recognised. In a sense, therefore, the consolidated financial statements will understate the value of goodwill being controlled by the parent entity.

The consolidation journal entries for Parent Entity and its controlled entities to eliminate Parent Entity's share of pre-acquisition capital and reserves of Subsidiary plc would be:

Dr	Accumulated depreciation—plant	€180,000	
Cr	Plant		€180,000

(to close off accumulated depreciation in accordance with the net method of asset revaluation)

Dr	Plant	€50,000	
Cr	Revaluation surplus		€35,000
Cr	Deferred tax liability		€15,000

(to recognise the revaluation increment after tax)

Dr	Share capital (70% of €700,000)	€490,000	
Dr	Revaluation reserve (70% of €235,000)	€164,500	
Dr	Retained earnings (70% of €100,000)	€70,000	
Dr	Goodwill	€75,500	
Cr	Investment in Subsidiary plc		€800,000

(to recognise the goodwill acquired by Parent Entity and to eliminate the parent's interest in pre-acquisition capital and reserves)

Dr	Share capital	€210,000	
Dr	Revaluation surplus	€70,500	
Dr	Retained earnings	€30,000	
Cr	Non-controlling interest		€310,500

(to recognise the non-controlling interest in contributed equity and reserves at date of acquisition; this entry acts to eliminate the entire balance of the pre-acquisition capital and reserves of the subsidiary and to allocate the proportion—30 per cent—to the non-controlling interest)

Following the above entries, the consolidated financial statements would include Parent Entity's share capital and reserves, plus the non-controlling interest's share of Subsidiary plc's pre-acquisition share capital and reserves (which have not been eliminated as part of the consolidation process).

22.4.2 Adjustments for intragroup transactions

IFRS 10 requires the elimination of the effects of all intragroup transactions before the consolidated financial statements are presented (IFRS 10, paragraph B86(c)). The requirement to eliminate the effects of intragroup transactions holds whether or not there are non-controlling interests, as IFRS 10 requires the effects of intragroup transactions to be eliminated 'in full'. We will now consider various intragroup transactions and their related treatments.

Worked Example 22.2	Non-controlling interest in Subsidiary plc measured at fair value

Assume the same information as in Worked Example 22.1, except this time we will apply the other option available within the accounting standard and value the non-controlling interest in the acquiree at fair value.

Required

Prepare the consolidation journal entry to recognise the non-controlling interests in the pre-acquisition capital and reserves of Subsidiary plc, assuming that the non-controlling interest is measured at the fair value.

Solution

The recognition of goodwill on acquisition and its allocation between Parent Entity and Subsidiary plc can be calculated as follows:

Elimination of investment in Subsidiary plc	Subsidiary plc (€)	Parent Entity's 70% interest (€)	30% non-controlling interest (€)
Fair value of consideration transferred	800,000	800,000	
plus Non-controlling interest measured at fair value (€800,000 × 30/70)	342,857		342,857
	1,142,857		
less Fair value of identifiable assets acquired and liabilities assumed			
Share capital on acquisition date	700,000	490,000	210,000
Revaluation surplus on acquisition date	200,000	140,000	60,000
Retained earnings on acquisition date	100,000	70,000	30,000
Fair value adjustment (€50,000 × (1 – tax rate))	35,000	24,500	10,500
	1,035,000	724,500	310,500
GOODWILL ON ACQUISITION DATE	107,857	75,500	32,357

Journal entry

Dr	Share capital	€210,000	
Dr	Revaluation surplus (€60,000 + €10,500)	€70,500	
Dr	Retained earnings	€30,000	
Dr	Goodwill	€32,357	
Cr	Non-controlling interest		€342,857

(to recognise non-controlling interest in contributed equity, reserves and goodwill at date of acquisition)

The entry to eliminate the parent entity's interest would be the same as shown in Worked Example 22.1, and would be:

Dr	Share capital (70% of €700,000)	€490,000	
Dr	Revaluation reserve (70% of €235,000)	€164,500	
Dr	Retained earnings (70% of €100,000)	€70,000	
Dr	Goodwill	€75,500	
Cr	Investment in Subsidiary plc		€800,000

(to recognise the goodwill acquired by Parent Entity and to eliminate the parent's interest in pre-acquisition capital and reserves)

22.4.3 Intragroup payment of dividends

In relation to dividends paid by a subsidiary, the consolidation worksheet journal entries will eliminate the proportion of the dividends that relates to the parent entity's entitlement. The non-controlling interest's share of the dividends paid by the subsidiary will not be eliminated and will be shown in the consolidated financial statements. This is appropriate because the dividends paid to the non-controlling interests represent a flow of resources away from the group, as indicated in Figure 22.2. The dividends distributed to the non-controlling interests will act to reduce the non-controlling interests' share in the equity of the subsidiary. The consolidated statement of financial position will show any dividends payable to the non-controlling interests as a liability (no liability will be shown in the consolidated financial statements for dividends payable to the parent entity).

For example, let us assume that Subsidiary plc declares a dividend of €1,000 and that Parent Entity (from Worked Example 22.1) recognises dividend income when it is declared by its investees. In this case, the consolidation adjusting entries would be:

Dr	Dividend income—statement of comprehensive income	€700	
Cr	Dividend receivable—statement of financial position		€700
Dr	Dividend payable—statement of financial position	€700	
Cr	Dividend declared—statement of changes in equity		€700

22.4.4 Intragroup sale of inventory

When we calculate the non-controlling interest's share of the profits of the subsidiary, we need to calculate the subsidiary's profit after adjustments to eliminate income and expenses of the subsidiary that are unrealised from the economic entity's perspective.

If the gains or losses have been *realised*, no adjustment is necessary when calculating non-controlling interest. For example, if a subsidiary sold inventory to the parent at a gain, and the parent entity has in turn sold all the inventory to external parties, the non-controlling interest's share of profit would not need to be reduced as the related gain would be deemed to have been realised from the perspective of the group. For example, let us assume that Subsidiary plc sold inventory to Parent Entity for €1,000 when Subsidiary plc had a related cost of sales of €700. Let us further assume that Parent Entity then sold all the inventory to an external customer for €1,500. Subsidiary plc would record a profit on sale of €300 and Parent Entity would record a profit on sale of €500 in their individual accounts. The total profit to the economic entity would be €800 (€1,500 less €700) and therefore all profits would be realised. An adjustment only needs to be made to the extent that the asset sold within the economic entity, such as inventory, is still on hand at the end of the reporting period (that is, where profits recorded in the individual accounts of a group member have not been realised from the perspective of the economic entity).

Our remarks so far relate to sales made in the current reporting period by the subsidiary. If there are unrealised profits in closing inventory, this will mean that in the next financial period there will be unrealised profits in opening inventory. In the next financial period we would need to adjust the non-controlling interest's share of opening retained earnings (by reducing it) and provide a corresponding increase in the non-controlling interest's share of that period's profits.

22.4.5 Intragroup sale of non-current assets

As with inventory, if a subsidiary sells a non-current asset, such as an item of property, plant and equipment, to another entity within the group, to the extent that the asset stays within the group, the gain or loss on sale has not been recognised from the group's perspective and the non-controlling interests' share of profits will need to be adjusted. However, the gain or loss is considered to be realised across the life of the asset as the asset is used up, that is, as it is depreciated. As the assets, such as plant, are used, perhaps to produce inventory, the intragroup profit is considered to be realised as the service potential of the plant becomes embodied in goods produced by the plant, for example, in inventory. Therefore, if a subsidiary sold an item of plant to another entity at the beginning of the financial year at a gain of £1,000 and if that asset is to be depreciated over ten years, only £100 of the gain could be recognised in the first year and £900 would be deemed to be unrealised. It would be realised over the next nine years.

22.4.6 Intragroup service and interest payments

There will also be other intragroup transactions that affect the profit or loss of the subsidiary, for example management fees and interest payments. To the extent that there is no related asset that is retained in the economic entity upon which any profit has accrued, no adjustments are necessary in calculating the non-controlling interest in the subsidiary's profit (of course, consolidation adjustments will still be required but this discussion is about calculating the non-controlling interest's share of profits for presentation purposes and not for the purpose of

generating consolidation journal adjustments). If we assume that any related profits have been realised immediately, we need not go to the lengths required to determine when such profits should be adjusted. There is no adjustment for such things as management fees when we are determining non-controlling interests—they are considered to be *realised*. This is consistent with paragraph B86 of IFRS 10.

22.4.7 Intragroup transaction that creates gains or losses in parent entity

In calculating non-controlling interests, we do not need to adjust for gains or losses in the parent entity's accounts that are unrealised as non-controlling interests have an interest only in the subsidiary's profit contribution. As we know, it is only the unrealised intragroup profits or losses accruing *to the subsidiary* that need to be eliminated before we calculate non-controlling interests. Hence, if a subsidiary has acquired inventory from the parent entity, no adjustment is required if the inventory is still on hand (and hence the profit is unrealised from the perspective of the economic entity) when calculating non-controlling interests, as the purchase of inventory has no implications for the equity of the subsidiary—it is simply acquiring one asset in exchange for another (if paid for by cash) or acquiring one asset by incurring a liability (accounts payable)—in either case, the equity of the subsidiary does not change. The related profit is in the financial statements of the parent entity.

22.4.8 Summary of some general principles for calculating non-controlling interests in profits or losses

From the discussion so far we can summarise some rules to use when calculating non-controlling interests in profits or losses. We apply these rules in Worked Example 22.3 that follows. The general principles are:

- We only need to make adjustments to non-controlling interests' share of profits where an intragroup transaction affects the *subsidiary's* profit or loss.
- We make adjustments for profits or losses made by the subsidiary to the extent they are *unrealised* from the economic entity's perspective, that is, the respective asset is still on hand at the end of the reporting period.
- For profits relating to transactions that do not involve the transfer of assets, such as those relating to interest, management fees and so forth, no adjustments are necessary. The related profits are deemed to be realised at the point of the transaction.
- We do not need to make adjustments for unrealised gains or losses made by the *parent entity* when calculating the non-controlling interest in profits. If the non-controlling interest in the acquiree is measured at the proportionate share of the subsidiary's identifiable net assets, only the parent entity's share of goodwill is recognised on consolidation. No goodwill is recognised in relation to the non-controlling interest in the subsidiary. In this situation no goodwill impairment losses are recognised in relation to a non-controlling interest in goodwill when the non-controlling interest in profits is calculated.
- If the non-controlling interest in a subsidiary is measured at fair value (the other adoption available under paragraph 19 of IFRS 3), then the goodwill attributable to both the parent and non-controlling interest is recognised on consolidation. Any goodwill impairment losses are allocated between the parent and the non-controlling interest on the same basis as that on which profit or loss is allocated.

We consider how to present consolidated financial statements in the presence of non-controlling interests in Worked Example 22.3. This quite detailed example demonstrates a number of issues that we face when calculating non-controlling interests.

Worked Example 22.3   **Consolidated financial statement presentation in the presence of non-controlling interests**

On 1 July 2014 Bells plc acquires 80 per cent of the equity capital of Torquay plc at a cost of £2 million. All assets of Torquay plc were fairly stated, and the total shareholders' funds of Torquay plc were £2.2 million, as follows:

Share capital	£1,500,000
Retained earnings	£700,000
	£2,200,000

As at 30 June 2016 (that is, two years after the date of acquisition) the financial statements of the two companies are as follows:

	Bells plc (£000)	Torquay plc (£000)
Detailed reconciliation of opening and closing retained earnings		
Sales revenue	480	115
Cost of goods sold	(100)	(40)
Other expenses	(80)	(15)
Other revenue	70	25
Profit before tax	370	85
Tax expense	(60)	(30)
Profit for the year	310	55
Retained earnings—30 June 2015	1,000	800
	1,310	855
Dividends paid	(160)	(30)
Dividend declared before year end	(40)	(10)
Retained earnings—30 June 2016	1,110	815

	Bells plc (£000)	Torquay plc (£000)
Statement of financial position		
ASSETS		
Non-current assets		
Land	1,400	1,105
Plant	1,870	1,300
Accumulated depreciation	(400)	(300)
Investment in Torquay plc	2,000	–
	4,870	2,105
Current assets		
Inventory	500	300
Accounts receivable	242	175
Dividends receivable	8	–
Cash	150	25
	900	500
Total assets	5,770	2,605
EQUITY AND LIABILITIES		
Equity and reserves		
Equity share capital	4,000	1,500
Retained earnings	1,110	815
	5,110	2,315
Non-current liabilities		
Loans	600	250
Current liabilities		
Accounts payable	20	30
Dividends payable	40	10
	60	40
Total liabilities	660	290
Total liabilities and equity	5,770	2,605

Other information

- The management of Bells plc values any non-controlling interest in Torquay plc at fair value.
- During the current financial year Torquay plc pays management fees of £10,000 to Bells plc. This item is included in 'other' expenses and income.

- During the current financial year Bells plc sold inventory to Torquay plc at a price of £30,000. The inventory cost Bells £22,000 to produce. Fifty per cent of this inventory is still on hand with Torquay plc at the end of the financial year (*Hint: as this unrealised profit relates to sales made by Bells plc, then no adjustments are necessary when calculating non-controlling interests in Torquay plc*).
- During the current financial year Torquay plc sold inventory to Bells plc at a price of £20,000. The inventory cost Torquay plc £14,000 to produce. Forty per cent of this inventory is still on hand with Bells plc at the end of the financial year (*Hint: as this unrealised profit relates to sales made by Torquay plc, then adjustments will be necessary when calculating non-controlling interests in Torquay plc*).
- In the preceding financial year, Torquay plc sold inventory to Bells plc at a price of £11,000. The inventory cost Torquay plc £8,000 to produce. At 30 June 2015, 20 per cent of this inventory was still held by Bells plc (*Hint: this information will be used to create an adjustment to non-controlling interests in Torquay plc*).
- The management of Bells plc believe that goodwill acquired has subsequently been impaired. It was impaired by £12,000 in the year to 30 June 2015, and by a further £12,000 in the year to 30 June 2016 (*Hint: because the non-controlling interest in Torquay is being valued at fair value, then this will mean that the non-controlling interests will incorporate a proportional share of goodwill; therefore, any impairment in goodwill will impact the non-controlling interests in Torquay plc*).
- On 1 July 2015 Torquay plc sold an item of plant to Bells plc for a price of £45,000 when its carrying value in Torquay plc's financial statements was £25,000 (cost £50,000, accumulated depreciation £25,000). This item of plant was being depreciated over a further ten years, with no expected residual value (*Hint: as this unrealised profit relates to a sale of plant made by Torquay plc, then adjustments will be necessary when calculating non-controlling interests in Torquay plc*).
- On 30 June 2016 the directors of Torquay plc declared and communicated to their shareholders that they would pay a final dividend amounting to £10,000 (*Hint: dividends paid by Torquay plc will act to reduce the non-controlling interests in Torquay plc*).
- The tax rate is 30 per cent.

Required

Prepare the consolidated financial statements of Bells plc and its controlled entity for the reporting period ending 30 June 2016.

Solution

Workings to eliminate the investment in the subsidiary and recognise goodwill on acquisition date.

(a) *Elimination of the investment in Torquay plc and recognition of goodwill on acquisition date*

Elimination of investment in Torquay plc	Torquay plc (£)	Bells plc's 80% interest (£)	20% non-controlling interest (£)
Fair value of consideration transferred	2,000,000	2,000,000	
plus Non-controlling interest at fair value			
(£2,000,000 × 20/80)	500,000		500,000
	2,500,000		
less Fair value of identifiable assets acquired and liabilities assumed			
Share capital on acquisition date	1,500,000	1,200,000	300,000
Retained earnings on acquisition date	700,000	560,000	140,000
	2,200,000	1,760,000	440,000
Goodwill on acquisition date	300,000	240,000	60,000

The entry to eliminate Bells plc's investment in Torquay plc at acquisition date is:

Dr	Share capital	£1,200,000	
Dr	Retained earnings	£560,000	
Dr	Goodwill	£240,000	
Cr	Investment in Torquay plc		£2,000,000

(eliminating investment in Torquay plc and recognising goodwill on acquisition)

Elimination of intercompany sales

We need to provide consolidation journal entries to eliminate the intercompany sales because, from the perspective of the economic entity, the sales did not involve external parties. This will ensure that we do not overstate the total sales of the economic entity.

(b) *Sale of inventory from Torquay plc to Bells plc*

Dr	Sales revenue	£20,000	
Cr	Cost of goods sold		£20,000

Under the periodic inventory system, the above credit entry would be to purchases, which would ultimately lead to a reduction in cost of goods sold.

(c) *Elimination of unrealised profit in closing inventory*

We are told that the total profit earned by Torquay plc on the sale of the inventory is £6,000. Since some of this inventory remains in the economic entity, this amount has not been fully earned. In this case, 40 per cent of the inventory is still on hand, so the unrealised profit amounts to £6,000 × 0.4, which equals £2,400. In accordance with IAS 2 *Inventories*, we must value inventory at the *lower of cost and net realisable value*. So, on consolidation we must reduce the value of inventory, as the amount shown in the financial statements of Bells plc exceeds what the inventory cost the economic entity. It should be noted that the entire amount of the unrealised profit must be eliminated on consolidation regardless of the level of equity ownership of the non-controlling interests. As we have already learned, paragraph B86 of IFRS 10 stipulates that intragroup balances, transactions, income and expenses shall be eliminated in full.

Dr	Cost of goods sold	£2,400	
Cr	Inventory		£2,400

Under the periodic inventory system, the above consolidation debit entry would be to closing inventory—profit and loss. We increase cost of goods sold by the unrealised profit in closing inventory because reducing closing inventory effectively increases cost of goods sold. (Remember, cost of goods sold equals opening inventory plus purchases less closing inventory.) The effect of the above entries is to adjust the value of inventory so that it reflects the cost of the inventory to the group.

(d) *Consideration of the tax paid or payable on the sale of inventory that is still held within the group*

From the group's perspective, £2,400 has not been earned. However, from Torquay plc's individual perspective (as a separate legal entity), the full amount of the sale has been earned. This will attract a tax liability in Torquay plc's accounts of £720 (30 per cent of £2,400). However, from the group's perspective, some of this will represent a prepayment of tax, as the full amount has not been earned by the group even if Torquay plc is obliged to pay the tax.

Dr	Deferred tax asset	£720	
Cr	Income tax expense		£720
	(£2,400 × 30 per cent)		

(e) *Sale of inventory from Bells plc to Torquay plc*

During the current financial period Bells plc sold inventory to Torquay plc at a price of £30,000. The inventory cost Bells plc £22,000 to produce. We are informed that 50 per cent of this inventory is still on hand with Torquay plc at the end of the financial year. The respective consolidation adjustment journal entries are:

Dr	Sales revenue	£30,000	
Cr	Cost of goods sold		£30,000

(f) *Elimination of unrealised profit in closing inventory*

The total profit earned by Bells plc on the sale of the inventory is £8,000. Since some of this inventory remains in the economic entity, this amount has not been fully earned from the group's perspective. In this case, 50 per cent of the inventory is still on hand, so the unrealised profit amounts to £8,000 × 50 per cent, which equals £4,000.

Dr	Cost of goods sold	£4,000	
Cr	Inventory		£4,000

(g) *Consideration of the tax paid or payable on the sale of inventory that is still held within the group*

The tax consequences will also have to be adjusted for in line with (c) above, therefore the sale of inventory will attract a tax liability in Bells of £1,200 (30 per cent of £4,000). This represents a prepayment of tax from the group's perspective.

| Dr | Deferred tax asset | £1,200 | |
| Cr | Income tax expense | | £1,200 |

Subsequently, when we calculate non-controlling interests we will need to remember that, in relation to the above consolidation adjustments (e), (f) and (g), even though the profit has not been recognised from the perspective of the economic entity, the unrealised profits were recorded in the books of the parent entity and not the subsidiary. In calculating the non-controlling interest in group profits, we will not make adjustments for unrealised profits made by the parent entity.

(h) *Unrealised profit in opening inventory*
We are told that, in the preceding financial year, Torquay plc sold inventory to Bells plc at a price of £11,000. The inventory cost Torquay plc £8,000 to produce. At the beginning of the financial year (1 July 2015) 20 per cent of this inventory was still held by Bells plc. Therefore, the unrealised profit component at the end of the previous financial year was (£11,000 – £8,000) × 0.20 = £600. Therefore, in the preceding year we would have taken through entries like those provided above, which would have had the impact of reducing closing retained earnings at 30 June 2015 and reducing income tax expense for the 2015 financial year. It is assumed that the inventory has been sold to an external party in the current period and is therefore realised—so there is no need to adjust closing balance of inventory. However, we will transfer an amount from opening retained earnings to current period profits.

Dr	Retained earnings—30 June 2015	£420	
Dr	Income tax expense	£180	
Cr	Cost of sales		£600

Adjustments for intragroup sale of plant and associated depreciation adjustments
On 1 July 2015 Torquay plc sold an item of plant to Bells plc for £45,000 when its carrying value in Torquay plc's financial statements was £25,000 (cost of £50,000 and accumulated depreciation of £25,000). This item of plant was being depreciated over a further ten years, with no expected residual value.

(i) *Reversal of profit recognised on sale of asset and reinstatement of cost and accumulated depreciation*
The result of the sale of the item of plant to Bells plc is that the gain of £20,000—the difference between the sales proceeds of £45,000 and the carrying amount of £25,000—will be shown in Torquay plc's financial statements. However, from the economic entity's perspective there has been no sale and, therefore, no gain on sale given that there has been no transaction with a party external to the group. The following consolidation entry is necessary in the consolidation worksheet so that the consolidated financial statements will reflect the balances that would have applied had the intragroup sale not occurred.

Dr	Gain on sale of plant	£20,000	
Dr	Plant	£5,000	
Cr	Accumulated depreciation		£25,000

The result of this entry is that the intragroup gain on sale of the non-current asset is removed and the asset and accumulated depreciation account reverts to reflecting no intragroup sales transaction. The gain of £20,000 will be recognised progressively in the consolidated financial statements of the economic entity by adjustments to the amounts of depreciation expensed by Bells plc in its financial statements. As the service potential or economic benefits embodied in the asset are consumed, the £20,000 gain will be progressively recognised from the economic entity's perspective. This is shown in journal entry (k).

(j) *Tax implications of the intragroup sale of plant*
From Torquay plc's individual perspective, it would have made a gain of £20,000 on the sale of the plant and this gain would have been taxable. At a tax rate of 30 per cent, £6,000 would be payable by Torquay plc. However, from the economic entity's perspective, no gain has been made, which means that the related 'tax expense' must be reversed and a related deferred tax benefit be recognised. A deferred tax asset is recognised because, from the economic entity's perspective, the amount paid to the tax authority represents a prepayment of tax.

| Dr | Deferred tax asset | £6,000 | |
| Cr | Income tax expense | | £6,000 |

(k) *Reinstating accumulated depreciation in the statement of financial position*
Bells plc would be depreciating the asset on the basis of the cost it incurred to acquire the asset. Its depreciation charge would be £45,000 divided by 10, which equals £4,500. From the economic entity's perspective, the asset had a carrying value of £25,000, which was to be allocated over the next ten years, giving a depreciation charge of £25,000 divided by 10, which equals £2,500. An adjustment of £2,000 is therefore required.

Dr	Accumulated depreciation	£2,000	
Cr	Depreciation expense		£2,000

(l) *Consideration of the tax effect of the reduction in depreciation expense*

The increase in the tax expense from the perspective of the economic entity is due to the reduction in the depreciation expense. The additional tax expense is £600, which is £2,000 × 30 per cent. This entry represents a partial reversal of the deferred tax asset of £6,000 recognised in an earlier entry. After ten years the balance of the deferred tax asset relating to the sale of the item of plant will be £nil.

Dr	Income tax expense	£600	
Cr	Deferred tax asset		£600

(m) *Impairment of goodwill—Torquay plc*

As Bells plc measures the non-controlling interest in Torquay plc at fair value, goodwill of £300,000 was recognised, £60,000 of which has been allocated to the non-controlling interest (see earlier calculation). Where goodwill has been impaired, paragraph 6 of Appendix C to IAS 36 requires goodwill impairment losses to be allocated between the parent and the non-controlling interest on the same basis as that on which profit or loss is allocated.

Two years have elapsed since the original acquisition. In each reporting period an impairment loss of £12,000 is recognised by Bells plc, with £2,400 (20 per cent of £12,000) allocated to the non-controlling interest. (See calculation of non-controlling interest in Torquay plc. The impact of the allocation of the impairment has been taken into account in journal entries (s) and (t) below.) Had Bells plc valued any non-controlling interest at the proportionate share of Torquay plc's identifiable net assets, there would be no necessity to allocate any goodwill impairment expense between the parent and the non-controlling interest as the goodwill impairment would only relate to goodwill attributed to the parent's interest.

Dr	Retained earnings—1 July 2015	£12,000	
Dr	Other expenses—impairment goodwill	£12,000	
Cr	Accumulated impairment losses—goodwill		£24,000

(recognising current and previous years' impairment of goodwill expense)

(n) *Elimination of intragroup transactions—management fees*

All of the management fees paid within the group will need to be eliminated on consolidation.

Dr	Management fee revenue	£10,000	
Cr	Management fee expense		£10,000

It is not necessary to make any adjustments to non-controlling interest in profits, as the related profits or losses associated with the payment of management fees are assumed to be realised from the perspective of the economic entity.

(o) *Dividends paid*

We eliminate the dividends paid within the group. Only the dividends paid to parties outside the entity (to the shareholders of the parent entity and to the non-controlling interests) are to be shown in the consolidated accounts.

Dr	Dividend revenue	£24,000	
Cr	Dividend paid		£24,000

(p) *Dividend declared*

Dr	Dividend payable	£8,000	
Cr	Dividend declared		£8,000

(q) | Dr | Dividend revenue | £8,000 | |
|---|---|---|---|
| Cr | Dividend receivable | | £8,000 |

Recognising non-controlling interest in contributed equity, reserves and earnings

It must be remembered that, in order to recognise the non-controlling interest's share in contributed equity and reserves at the end of the reporting period, three calculations need to be made:

  (i) The non-controlling interests on acquisition date.

  (ii) The non-controlling interest in movements in contributed equity and reserves between the date of the parent entity's acquisition and the beginning of the current reporting period.

  (iii) The non-controlling interest in the current period's profit, as well as movements in reserves in the current period. In determining the non-controlling interest's share of current period profit or loss, gains and losses of the subsidiary that are unrealised from the economic entity's perspective will need to be adjusted for.

The steps above are used to calculate the non-controlling interest.

The calculations below are completed so that the relative proportions of consolidated profits and consolidated share capital and reserves that are attributable to parent entity interests and non-controlling interests can be journalised in the consolidation worksheet and subsequently disclosed in the consolidated financial statements. Earlier in the chapter some possible formats for the disclosure of non-controlling interests (see Exhibits 22.1 to 22.3) were provided.

Calculation of non-controlling interests in Torquay plc	Torquay plc (£)	20% non-controlling interest (£)
(i) Non-controlling interests and goodwill on acquisition date		
Share capital	1,500,000	300,000
Retained earnings—on acquisition	700,000	140,000
Goodwill on acquisition	–	60,000
	2,200,000	500,000
(ii) Non-controlling interest in movements in share capital and reserves between the date of the parent entity's acquisition and the beginning of the current reporting period:		
Retained earnings		
since acquisition (£800,000 – £700,000)	100,000	
Unrealised profits in inventory—1 July 2015	(600)	
Tax effect on unrealised profits	180	
Goodwill impairment—2015	(12,000)	
	87,580	17,516
(iii) Non-controlling interest in the current period's profit and movements in reserves in the current period		
Profit for the year	55,000	
add Unrealised profit in inventory—1 July 2015 now realised	600	
Tax effect on unrealised profit now realised	(180)	
less Unrealised profits in inventory—30 June 2016	(2,400)	
Tax effect on unrealised profit	720	
less Unrealised profit on sale of non-current asset	(20,000)	
Tax effect on unrealised profit	6,000	
add Depreciation	2,000	
Tax effect on depreciation	(600)	
Goodwill impairment—2016	(12,000)	
Profit Torquay plc contributed to the economic entity	29,140	5,828
Dividends paid by Torquay plc	(30,000)	(6,000)
Dividends declared by Torquay plc	(10,000)	(2,000)
		515,344

(r) *Non-controlling interests and goodwill on acquisition date*
The non-controlling interest in the equity share capital and reserves of Torquay plc is transferred to non-controlling interest. The non-controlling interest will be disclosed as part of total equity in the consolidated statement of financial position (IFRS 10, paragraph 22).

Dr	Share capital	£300,000	
Dr	Retained earnings	£140,000	
Dr	Goodwill	£60,000	
Cr	Non-controlling interest		£500,000

(recognising non-controlling interests and goodwill on acquisition date)

(s) *Non-controlling interest in movements in contributed equity and reserves between the date of the parent entity's acquisition and the beginning of the current reporting period*

The retained earnings at the date of acquisition is deducted from the retained earnings at the beginning of the current reporting period (£800,000 − £700,000). A number of adjustments may need to be made to this figure.

In this worked example, the unrealised profit on the sale of inventory at 1 July 2015 amounted to £600. The reduction in profits will lead to a lower tax expense. At a tax rate of 30 per cent an adjustment of £180 (£600 × 30 per cent), the tax effect on the unrealised profits, must be made. An adjustment for the 2015 goodwill impairment allocated to the non-controlling interest needs to be made. The 20 per cent non-controlling interest share in interest in movements in contributed equity, reserves and for goodwill impairment between the date of the parent entity's acquisition and the beginning of the current reporting period amounted to £17,516, as shown in calculations provided earlier.

Dr Retained earnings	£17,516	
Cr Non-controlling interest		£17,516

(recognising non-controlling interest and non-controlling interest in earnings)

(t) *Non-controlling interest in the current period's profit and movements in reserves in the current period*
The profit of the subsidiary for the current reporting period as reported in the financial statements of the subsidiary is £55,000. This is the starting point, which will subsequently be adjusted for unrealised profits and losses. A number of adjustments are then made to take account of any unrealised components—from the perspective of the subsidiary's profits—that are included within the £55,000.

Unrealised profit in opening inventory on 1 July 2015 now realised
At 1 July 2015 the profit on sale of the inventory in the previous period was considered unrealised from the perspective of the non-controlling interest. However, from the economic entity's perspective, it is considered realised in the current period. This requires the adjustments made in the previous period to be reversed in the current period.

Unrealised profit in inventory—30 June 2016
This sale was made by the subsidiary and is unrealised (the related assets are still on hand within the group) and therefore requires the non-controlling interest's share of current period profits to be adjusted. The unrealised profit on the sale of inventory at 30 June 2016 amounted to £2,400. The reduction in profits will lead to a lower tax expense. At a tax rate of 30 per cent an adjustment of £720 (£2,400 × 30 per cent), the tax effect on the unrealised profits, must be made.

Intragroup sale of a non-current asset
As there had been no transaction with a party outside the economic entity, the intragroup gain of £20,000 on the sale of the plant must be reversed. This gain was recognised in the financial statements of the subsidiary and, from the perspective of the economic entity, is unrealised at the end of the reporting period. As no gain has been made, a tax expense of £6,000 (£20,000 × 30 per cent) must be reversed.

As the depreciation expense charged by Bells plc would be greater than that charged by Torquay plc, the additional depreciation charge of £2,000 (£4,500 − £2,500) should be adjusted for. The decrease in depreciation results in an increase in profits. This would lead to an increase in tax of £600 (£2,000 × 30 per cent).

An adjustment for the 2016 goodwill impairment allocated to the non-controlling interest must be made. This amounts to £12,000 for 2016.

The 20 per cent non-controlling interest in the current period's profit and movements in reserves in the current period amounted to £5,828, as shown in the calculations provided earlier.

Dr Non-controlling interest in earnings	£5,828	
Cr Non-controlling interest		£5,828

(non-controlling interest in the current period's profit and movements in reserves in the current period)

(u) *Dividends paid by Torquay plc*
The impact of the dividends on non-controlling interests needs to be considered. The payment and declaration of dividends by the subsidiary act to reduce the interest of the non-controlling entity/entities in the subsidiary's closing retained earnings.

30 June 2016

Dr Non-controlling interest	£8,000	
Cr Dividends paid		£6,000
Cr Dividends declared		£2,000

(dividends attributable to non-controlling interest)

Next we transfer the above consolidation journal entries to the consolidation worksheet. As we see from the four sets of consolidation journal entries above, the total amount of the non-controlling interest in Torquay plc is £515,344 (which equals £500,000 + £17,516 + £5,828 − £8,000, and which is the total amount shown in the table provided earlier).

Bells plc and its controlled entity
Consolidation worksheet for the year ending 30 June 2016

	Bells plc (£000)	Torquay plc (£000)	Eliminations and adjustments Dr (£000)	Cr (£000)	Consolidated statements (£000)
Reconciliation of opening and closing retained earnings					
Revenue	480	115	20(b) 30(e)		545
Cost of goods sold	(100)	(40)	2.4(c) 4(f)	20(b) 30(e) 0.6(h)	(95.8)
Other expenses	(80)	(15)	12(m)	2(k) 10(n)	(95)
Other income	70	25	20(i) 10(n) 24(o) 8(q)		33
Profit before tax	370	85			387.2
Income tax expense	(60)	(30)	0.18(h) 0.6(l)	0.72(d) 1.2(g) 6(j)	(82.86)
Profit for the year	310	55			304.34
Non-controlling interest in earnings			5.828(t)		(5.828)
Retained earnings—1 July 2015	1,000	800	560(a) 0.42(h) 12(m) 140(r) 17.516(s)		1,070.064
	1,310	855			1,368.576
Dividends paid	(160)	(30)		24(o) 6(u)	(160)
Dividend declared	(40)	(10)		8(p) 2(u)	(40)
Retained earnings 30 June 2016	1,110	815			1,168.576
Statement of financial position					
Equity					
Share capital	4,000	1,500	1,200(a) 300(r)		4,000
Retained earnings b/d	1,110	815			1,168.576
Non-controlling interest			8(u)	500(r) 17.516(s) 5.828(t)	515.344
Current liabilities					
Accounts payable	20	30			50
Dividends payable	40	10	8(p)		42
Non-current liabilities					
Loans	600	250			850
	5,770	2,605			6,625.92

	Bells plc (£000)	Torquay plc (£000)	Eliminations and adjustments		Consolidated statements (£000)
			Dr (£000)	Cr (£000)	
Current assets					
Cash	150	25			175
Accounts receivable	242	175			417
Dividend receivable	8	–		8(q)	–
Inventory	500	300		2.4(c)	
				4(f) }	793.6
Non-current assets					
Deferred tax asset			0.72(d)	0.6(l)	
			1.2(g) }		
			6(j)		7.32
Land	1,400	1,105			2,505
Plant	1,870	1,300	5(i)		3,175
Accumulated depreciation	(400)	(300)	2(k)	25(i)	(723)
Investment in Torquay plc	2,000	–		2,000(a)	–
Goodwill	–	–	240(a)		
			60(r)		300
Accumulated impairment loss—goodwill				24(m)	(24)
	5,770	2,605	2,697.864	2,697.864	6,625.92

The above worksheet provides the data for the consolidated statement of comprehensive income and consolidated statement of financial position. As can be seen, the Bells plc dividend paid and declared totals £200,000. In the consolidated financial statements, dividends payable amount to £208,000 (£200,000 by Bells plc, and 20 per cent of the £40,000 paid and declared by Torquay plc).

The consolidated financial statements can now be presented. A suggested format for the consolidated financial statements would be as follows (prior-year comparatives for the financial statements of the parent entity and the group, both of which would be required in practice, have not been provided):

Bells plc and its controlled entity: Consolidated statement of comprehensive income for the year ended 30 June 2016

	Group (£)	Bells plc (£)
Revenue	545,000	480,000
Cost of goods sold	(95,800)	(100,000)
Gross profit	449,200	380,000
Other income	33,000	70,000
	482,200	450,000
Other expenses	(95,000)	(80,000)
Profit before tax	387,200	370,000
Income tax expense	(82,860)	(60,000)
Profit for the year	304,340	310,000
Other comprehensive income	–	–
Total comprehensive income	304,340	310,000

Bells plc and its controlled entity: Consolidated statement of comprehensive income for the year ended 30 June 2016 (cont'd)

	Group (£)	Bells plc (£)
Profit attributable to:		
Owners of the parent	298,512	310,000
Non-controlling interest	5,828	–
	304,340	310,000
Total comprehensive income attributable to:		
Owners of the parent	298,512	310,000
Non-controlling interest	5,828	–
	304,340	310,000

Bells plc and its controlled entity
Consolidated statement of changes in equity for the year ended 30 June 2016

	Attributable to owners of the parent			Non-controlling interest (£)	Total equity (£)
	Share capital (£)	Retained earnings (£)	Total (£)		
Balance at 1 July 2015	4,000,000	1,070,064	5,070,064	517,516	5,587,180
Total comprehensive income for the year	–	298,512	298,512	5,828	304,340
Dividends	–	(200,000)	(200,000)	(8,000)	(208,000)
Balance at 30 June 2016	4,000,000	1,168,576	5,168,576	515,344	5,683,920

Bells plc: Statement of changes in equity for the year ended 30 June 2016

	Share capital (£)	Retained earnings (£)	Total equity (£)
Balance at 1 July 2015	4,000,000	1,000,000	5,000,000
Total comprehensive income for the year		310,000	310,000
Distributions		(200,000)	(200,000)
Balance at 30 June 2016	4,000,000	1,110,000	5,110,000

Bells plc and its controlled entity
Consolidated statement of financial position at 30 June 2016

	Group (£000)	Bells plc (£000)
ASSETS		
Non-current assets		
Land	2,505,000	1,400,000
Plant and equipment	3,175,000	1,870,000
Accumulated depreciation	(723,000)	(400,000)
Goodwill	300,000	–
Accumulated impairment loss	(24,000)	–
Investment in Torquay plc	–	2,000,000
Deferred tax asset	7,320	–
Total non-current assets	5,240,320	4,870,000

Bells plc and its controlled entity
Consolidated statement of financial position at 30 June 2016 (cont'd)

	Group (£000)	Bells plc (£000)
Current assets		
Inventory	793,600	500,000
Accounts receivable	417,000	242,000
Dividends receivable	–	8,000
Cash	175,000	150,000
Total current assets	1,385,600	900,000
Total assets	6,625,920	5,770,000
EQUITY AND LIABILITIES		
Equity and reserves		
Share capital	4,000,000	4,000,000
Retained earnings	1,168,576	1,110,000
	5,168,576	5,110,000
Non-controlling interest	515,344	–
Total equity	5,683,920	5,110,000
Non-current liabilities		
Loans	850,000	600,000
Total non-current liabilities	850,000	600,000
Current liabilities		
Accounts payable	50,000	20,000
Dividends payable	42,000	40,000
Total current liabilities	92,000	60,000
Total liabilities	942,000	660,000
Total equity and liabilities	6,625,920	5,770,000

SUMMARY

In this chapter we learned about how to calculate and disclose non-controlling interests in the profits and capital and reserves of an economic entity. Non-controlling interests are defined as, 'that portion of the profit or loss and net assets of a subsidiary attributable to equity interests that are not owned, directly or indirectly through subsidiaries, by the parent'. IFRS 10 and IAS 1 require us to separately disclose the amount of profit attributable to non-controlling interests and parent interests. There is also a requirement to separately disclose parent entity interests and non-controlling interests in share capital and reserves of the economic entity.

We learned that, in calculating non-controlling interests in the profits of the economic entity, we start with the reported after-tax profit of the subsidiary and calculate a proportionate share in this unadjusted amount. We then make adjustments for profits made in the financial statements of the subsidiary that are unrealised at year end from the perspective of the economic entity. In calculating non-controlling interests, we do not make any adjustments for unrealised profits that were recorded in the accounts of the parent entity.

Following the consolidation process we will see that the dividends included in the consolidated financial statements show the dividends paid and declared by the parent entity, as well as the non-controlling interests in the dividends paid and declared by the subsidiary. The parent entity's interest in the dividends paid and declared by the subsidiaries is eliminated as part of the consolidation process and therefore will not be shown in the consolidated financial statements.

In relation to share capital and reserves, the consolidated financial statements will include, within total share capital and reserves, the parent entity's share capital and reserves, as well as the share capital and reserves of the subsidiary that are attributable to the non-controlling interest. The parent entity's interest in pre-acquisition share capital and reserves will be eliminated on consolidation.

KEY TERM

parent entity 636

END-OF-CHAPTER EXERCISE

After completing this chapter you should ensure that you are able to answer the following questions. (If you find you cannot provide appropriate answers, you should revisit the relevant sections of the chapter.)

PART A

1   What is a non-controlling interest and how should it be disclosed in the financial statements?   **LO** 22.1
2   If there is a purchase transaction between the parent entity and a 60 per cent-owned subsidiary, which generates a payable in the financial statements of the parent entity and a receivable in the financial statements of the controlled entity, what percentage of the intragroup payable and receivable should be eliminated on consolidation?   **LO** 22.2
3   If less than 100 per cent of a subsidiary is owned by the parent entity, will less than 100 per cent of the assets and liabilities of the subsidiary be included within the consolidated financial statements?   **LO** 22.2

PART B

The following financial statements of Hogwarts plc and its subsidiary Gryffindor plc have been extracted from their financial records at 30 June 2015.   **LO** 22.4

	Hogwarts plc (£000)	Gryffindor plc (£000)
Detailed reconciliation of opening and closing retained earnings		
Sales revenue	690	580
Cost of goods sold	(464)	(238)
Gross profit	226	342
Dividends received—from Gryffindor	74.4	–
Management fee revenue	26.5	–
Profit on sale of plant	35	–
Expenses		
Administrative expenses	(30.8)	(38.7)
Depreciation	(24.5)	(56.8)
Management fee expense	–	(26.5)
Other expenses	(101.1)	(77)
Profit before tax	205.5	143
Tax expense	(61.5)	(42.2)
Profit for the year	144	100.8
Retained earnings—30 June 2014	319.4	239.2
	463.4	340
Dividends paid	(137.4)	(93)
Retained earnings—30 June 2015	326	247

	Hogwarts plc (£000)	Gryffindor plc (£000)
Statement of financial position		
ASSETS		
Non-current assets		
Land and buildings	224	326
Plant—at cost	299.85	355.8
Accumulated depreciation	(85.75)	(138.8)
Investment in Gryffindor plc	356	–
	794.1	543
Current assets		
Inventory	92	29
Accounts receivable	59.4	62.3
	151.4	91.3
Total assets	945.5	634.3
EQUITY AND LIABILITIES		
Equity and reserves		
Equity share capital	350	200
Retained earnings	326	247
	676	447
Non-current liabilities		
Loans	173.5	116
Current liabilities		
Accounts payable	54.7	46.3
Tax payable	41.3	25
	96	71.3
Total liabilities	269.5	187.3
Total equity and liabilities	945.5	634.3

Other information
- Hogwarts plc had acquired its 80 per cent interest in Gryffindor plc on 1 July 2006, that is, nine years earlier. At that date the capital and reserves of Gryffindor plc were:

Equity share capital	£200,000
Retained earnings	£170,000
	£370,000

At the date of acquisition all assets were considered to be fairly valued.
- The management of Hogwarts plc values any non-controlling interest at the proportionate share of Gryffindor plc's identifiable net assets (*Hint: this means that, unlike Worked Example 22.3, in this worked example no goodwill in the subsidiary will be attributed to the non-controlling interest*).
- During the year Hogwarts plc made total sales to Gryffindor plc of £65,000, while Gryffindor plc sold £52,000 in inventory to Hogwarts plc.
- The opening inventory in Hogwarts plc as at 1 July 2014 included inventory acquired from Gryffindor plc for £42,000 that had cost Gryffindor plc £35,000 to produce.
- The closing inventory in Hogwarts plc includes inventory acquired from Gryffindor plc at a cost of £33,600. This cost Gryffindor plc £28,000 to produce.
- The closing inventory of Gryffindor plc includes inventory acquired from Hogwarts plc at a cost of £12,000. This cost Hogwarts plc £9,600 to produce.
- The management of Hogwarts plc believe that goodwill acquired was impaired by £3,000 in the current financial year. Previous impairments of goodwill amounted to £22,500.
- On 1 July 2014 Hogwarts plc sold an item of plant to Gryffindor plc for £116,000 when its carrying value in Hogwarts plc's financial statements was £81,000 (cost of £135,000, accumulated depreciation of £54,000). This plant is assessed as having a remaining useful life of six years.

- Gryffindor plc paid £26,500 in management fees to Hogwarts plc.
- The tax rate is 30 per cent.

REQUIRED

Provide the consolidated financial statements of Hogwarts plc and Gryffindor plc for the reporting period ending 30 June 2015.

SOLUTION TO END-OF-CHAPTER EXERCISE

(a) *Eliminating the investment in Gryffindor plc and recognising goodwill on acquisition date*

Elimination of investment in Gryffindor plc	Gryffindor plc (£)	Hogwarts plc's 80% interest (£)	20% non-controlling interest (£)
Fair value of consideration transferred		356,000	
less Fair value of identifiable assets acquired and liabilities assumed			
Share capital on acquisition date	200,000	160,000	40,000
Retained earnings on acquisition date	170,000	136,000	34,000
	370,000	296,000	
Goodwill on acquisition date		60,000	–
Non-controlling interest at date of acquisition			74,000

As shown, the net assets of Gryffindor plc are £370,000 at acquisition date. The parent entity's proportional interest acquired in these net assets (80 per cent) amounts to £296,000. As £356,000 is paid for the investment, the goodwill amounts to £60,000. As we know, this represents only the portion of goodwill acquired by Hogwarts plc and not the entire goodwill of Gryffindor plc at acquisition date.

The consolidation entry to eliminate the investment is:

Dr Share capital	£160,000	
Dr Retained earnings	£136,000	
Dr Goodwill	£60,000	
Cr Investment in Gryffindor plc		£356,000

What should be noted at this point is that, because we have been told that the management of Hogwarts plc values any non-controlling interest at the proportionate share of Gryffindor plc's identifiable net assets, this means only the goodwill that has been purchased by Hogwarts plc is recognised. However, had the non-controlling interest been measured at fair value, this would have amounted to £89,000 (£356,000 × 20 ÷ 80). The goodwill attributable to the non-controlling interest would have amounted to £15,000 (£89,000 – £74,000). Because no amount of goodwill has been attributed to the non-controlling interest, this also means that no portion of any subsequent impairment of goodwill will be attributed to (deducted from) the non-controlling interests.

Elimination of intragroup sales of inventory

We need to eliminate the intragroup sales because, from the perspective of the economic entity, no sales have in fact occurred. This will ensure that we do not overstate the turnover of the economic entity.

(b) *Sale of inventory from Gryffindor plc to Hogwarts plc*

Dr Sales revenue	£52,000	
Cr Cost of goods sold		£52,000

(c) *Elimination of unrealised profit in closing inventory*

In this case, the unrealised profit in closing inventory amounts to £5,600. Hence on consolidation we must reduce the value of recorded inventory, as the amount shown in the accounts of Hogwarts plc exceeds what the inventory cost the economic entity.

Dr Cost of goods sold	£5,600	
Cr Inventory		£5,600

(d) *Consideration of the tax paid or payable on the sale of inventory that is still held within the group*

From the group's perspective, £5,600 has not been earned. However, from Gryffindor plc's individual perspective (as a separate legal entity), the full amount of the sale has been earned. This will attract a tax liability in Gryffindor plc's financial statements of £1,680 (30 per cent of £5,600). However, from the group's perspective, some of this will represent a prepayment of tax, as the full amount has not been earned by the group even if Gryffindor plc is obliged to pay the tax.

Dr Deferred tax asset	£1,680	
Cr Income tax expense		£1,680

(e) *Eliminating sale of inventory from Hogwarts plc to Gryffindor plc*

During the current financial period Hogwarts plc sold inventory to Gryffindor plc at a price of £65,000.

Dr Sales revenue	£65,000	
Cr Cost of goods sold		£65,000

At year end Gryffindor plc has £12,000 of this inventory on hand, which cost Hogwarts plc £9,600 to produce.

(f) *Unrealised profit in closing inventory held by Gryffindor plc*

In this case, the unrealised profit in closing inventory amounting to £2,400 (£12,000 × 25 ÷ 125) needs to be eliminated.

Dr Cost of goods sold	£2,400	
Cr Inventory		£2,400

(g) *Tax attributable to unrealised profit in closing inventory held by Gryffindor plc*

The tax charge relating to the unrealised profit has to be reversed and a prepayment of £720 (£2,400 × 30 per cent) created.

Dr Deferred tax asset	£720	
Cr Income tax expense		£720

We do not need to make any adjustments to non-controlling interests as profit was not recorded in the financial statements of the subsidiary.

(h) *Unrealised profit in opening inventory*

If unrealised profit in opening inventory is not eliminated, opening inventory will be overstated from the group perspective. At the end of the preceding financial year, Hogwarts plc had £42,000 of inventory on hand, which had been purchased from Gryffindor plc. The inventory cost Gryffindor plc £35,000 to produce.

It is assumed that the inventory has been sold to an external party in the current period and hence is realised—so there is no need to adjust closing balance of inventory.

Dr Retained earnings—30 June 2014	£4,900	
Dr Income tax expense	£2,100	
Cr Cost of sales		£7,000

Adjustments for intragroup sale of plant

On 1 July 2014 Hogwarts plc sold an item of plant to Gryffindor plc for £116,000 when its carrying value in Gryffindor plc's financial statements was £81,000 (cost of £135,000 and accumulated depreciation of £54,000). This item of plant was being depreciated over ten years, with no expected residual value.

(i) *Reversal of gain recognised on sale of asset and reinstatement of cost and accumulated depreciation*

The result of the sale of the item of plant to Gryffindor plc is that the gain of £35,000—the difference between the sales proceeds of £116,000 and the carrying amount of £81,000—will be shown in Hogwarts plc's financial statements. However, from the economic entity's perspective there has been no sale and, therefore, no gain on sale given that there has been no transaction with a party external to the group. The following entry is necessary so that the financial statements will reflect the balances that would have been in place had the intragroup sale not occurred.

Dr Gain on sale of plant	£35,000	
Dr Plant	£19,000	
Cr Accumulated depreciation		£54,000

The result of this entry is that the intragroup gain is removed and the asset and accumulated depreciation accounts revert to reflecting no sales transaction. As the service potential or economic benefits embodied in the asset are consumed, the £35,000 gain will be progressively recognised from the economic entity's perspective by adjustment to the amount of depreciation charged by Gryffindor plc in its financial statements. This is shown in journal entry (k).

(j) *Impact of tax on gain on sale of item of plant*
From Gryffindor plc's individual perspective it would have made a gain of £35,000 on the sale of the plant and this gain would have been taxable. At a tax rate of 30 per cent, £10,500 would be payable by Hogwarts plc. However, from the economic entity's perspective no gain has been made, which means that the related 'tax expense' must be reversed and a related deferred tax benefit recognised. A deferred tax asset is recognised because, from the economic entity's perspective, the amount paid to the taxation authorities represents a prepayment of tax.

Dr Deferred tax asset	£10,500	
Cr Income tax expense		£10,500

(k) *Reinstating accumulated depreciation in the statement of financial position*
Hogwarts plc would be depreciating the asset on the basis of the cost it incurred to acquire the asset. Its depreciation charge would be £116,000 ÷ 6 = £19,333. From the economic entity's perspective, the asset had a carrying value of £81,000, which was to be allocated over the next six years, giving a depreciation charge of £81,000 ÷ 6 = £13,500. An adjustment of £5,833 is therefore required.

Dr Accumulated depreciation	£5,833	
Cr Depreciation expense		£5,833

(l) *Consideration of the tax effect of the reduction in depreciation expense*
The increase in the tax expense from the perspective of the economic entity is due to the reduction in the depreciation expense. The additional tax expense is £1,750, which is £5,833 × 30 per cent. This entry represents a partial reversal of the deferred tax asset of £10,500 recognised in the earlier entry. After six years the balance of the deferred tax asset relating to the sale of the item of plant will be £nil.

Dr Income tax expense	£1,750	
Cr Deferred tax asset		£1,750

(m) *Impairment of goodwill*
The total impairment of goodwill amounts to £25,500. Of this amount, £3,000 must be recognised in the current period, with £22,500 relating to a previous period's impairment being offset against opening retained earnings.

Dr Retained earnings—30 June 2014	£22,500	
Dr Impairment loss—goodwill	£3,000	
Cr Accumulated impairment losses—goodwill		£25,500

As Hogwarts plc values the non-controlling interest at the proportionate share of Gryffindor plc's identifiable assets, there is no necessity to allocate any goodwill impairment expense between the parent and the non-controlling interest. There are no implications for non-controlling interest as this only relates to the parent entity's share.

(n) *Elimination of intragroup transactions—management fees*
All of the management fees paid within the group will need to be eliminated on consolidation.

Dr Management fee revenue	£26,500	
Cr Management fee expense		£26,500

Implications for non-controlling interests: Intragroup payment of management fees
It is not necessary to make any adjustments to non-controlling interest of profits as the profits associated with the management are deemed to be realised.

(o) *Dividends paid*
We eliminate the dividends paid within the group. Only the dividends paid to parties outside the entity (the non-controlling interests) are to be shown in the consolidated financial statements.

Dr Dividend revenue	£74,400	
Cr Dividend paid		£74,400

Recognising non-controlling interest in contributed equity and earnings
It must be remembered that, in order to recognise the non-controlling interest's share in contributed equity and reserves at the end of the reporting period, three calculations need to be made:
(i) The non-controlling interests on acquisition date.
(ii) The non-controlling interest in movements in contributed equity and reserves between the date of the parent entity's acquisition and the beginning of the current reporting period.

(iii) The non-controlling interest in the current period's profit, as well as movements in reserves in the current period. In determining the non-controlling interest's share of current period profit or loss, gains and losses of the subsidiary that are unrealised from the economic entity's perspective will need to be adjusted for.

The steps above are used to calculate the non-controlling interest.

Calculation of non-controlling interest in Gryffindor plc	Gryffindor plc (£)	20% non-controlling interest (£)
(i) *Non-controlling interests on acquisition date*		
Share capital	200,000	40,000
Retained earnings—on acquisition	170,000	34,000
	340,000	74,000
(ii) *Non-controlling interest in movements in share capital and reserves between*		
the date of the parent entity's acquisition and the beginning of the current reporting period		
Retained earnings—since acquisition (£239,200 – £170,000)	69,200	
less Unrealised profits in inventory—1 July 2014	(7,000)	
Tax effect on unrealised profits	2,100	
	64,300	12,860
(iii) *Non-controlling interest in the current period's profit and movements*		
in reserves in the current period		
Profit for the year	100,800	
add Unrealised profit in inventory—1 July 2014—now realised	7,000	
Tax effect on unrealised profit now realised	(2,100)	
less Unrealised profits in inventory—30 June 2015	(5,600)	
Tax effect on unrealised profit	1,680	
Profit Gryffindor contributed to the economic entity	101,780	20,356
Dividends paid by Gryffindor plc	(93,000)	(18,600)
		88,616

In the above calculation of non-controlling interests, the subsidiary's profits have not been reduced by any amount related to goodwill impairment. As indicated earlier, only the parent entity's share of goodwill is brought to account given that the management of Hogwarts plc values any non-controlling interest at the proportionate share of Gryffindor plc's identifiable assets. It would therefore be inappropriate to allocate any goodwill impairment expense against the profits of the subsidiary.

(p) *Non-controlling interests on acquisition date*
The non-controlling interest in contributed equity and reserves is transferred to non-controlling interest.

Dr	Share capital	£40,000	
Dr	Retained earnings	£34,000	
Cr	Non-controlling interest		£74,000

(recognising non-controlling interests on acquisition date)

(q) *Non-controlling interest in movements in retained earnings between the date of the parent entity's acquisition and the beginning of the current reporting period*
The retained earnings at the date of acquisition is deducted from the retained earnings at the beginning of the current reporting period (£239,200 – £170,000).

In this end-of-chapter exercise, the unrealised profit on the sale of inventory at 1 July 2014 amounted to £7,000. The reduction in profits will lead to a lower tax expense. At a tax rate of 30 per cent, an adjustment of £2,100 (£7,000 × 30 per cent), the tax effect on the unrealised profits, must be made. The 20 per cent non-controlling share in interest in movements in contributed equity and reserves between the date of the parent entity's acquisition and the beginning of the current reporting period amounted to £12,860.

| Dr | Retained earnings | £12,860 | |
| Cr | Non-controlling interest | | £12,860 |

(recognising non-controlling interest in movements in retained earnings between the date of the parent entity's acquisition and the beginning of the current reporting period)

(r) *Non-controlling interest in the current period's profit and movements in reserves in the current period*

The profit of the subsidiary for the current reporting period as reported in the financial statements of the subsidiary is £100,800. This is the starting point, which will subsequently be adjusted for unrealised profits and losses. A number of adjustments are then made to take account of any unrealised components—from the perspective of the subsidiary's profits—that are included within the £100,800.

Unrealised profit in opening inventory—1 July 2014 now realised

At 1 July 2014 the profit on sale of the inventory in the previous period was considered unrealised from the perspective of the non-controlling interest. However, from the economic entity's perspective it is considered realised in the current period. This requires the adjustments made in the previous period to be reversed in the current period.

Unrealised profit in inventory—30 June 2015

This sale was made by the subsidiary and is unrealised (the related assets are still on hand within the group) and therefore requires the non-controlling interest's share of current period profits to be adjusted. The unrealised profit on the sale of inventory at 30 June 2015 amounted to £5,600. The reduction in profits will lead to a lower tax expense. At a tax rate of 30 per cent an adjustment of £1,680 (£5,600 × 30 per cent), the tax effect on the unrealised profits, must be made.

The 20 per cent non-controlling interest in the current period's profit and movements in reserves in the current period amounted to £20,356.

Dr   Non-controlling interest in earnings   £20,356
Cr   Non-controlling interest   £20,356
(recognising non-controlling interest in the current period's profit and movements in reserves in the current period)

(s) *Dividends paid by Gryffindor plc*

The impact of the dividends on non-controlling interests needs to be considered. The payment and declaration of dividends by the subsidiary reduces the interest of the non-controlling entity/entities in the subsidiary's closing retained earnings.

Dr   Non-controlling interest   £18,600
Cr   Dividends paid   £18,600
(recognising dividends paid by Gryffindor plc)

Now we can post the consolidation journal entries to the consolidation worksheet.

	Hogwarts plc (£000)	Gryffindor plc (£000)	Eliminations and adjustments Dr (£000)	Eliminations and adjustments Cr (£000)	Consolidated statements (£000)
Detailed reconciliation of opening and closing retained earnings					
Sales revenue	690	580	52(b) 65(e)		1,153
Cost of goods sold	(464)	(238)	5.6(c) 2.4(f)	52(b) 65(e) 7(h)	586
Gross profit	226	342			567
Other revenue					
Dividends received—from Gryffindor	74.4	–	74.4(o)		–
Management fee revenue	26.5	–	26.5(n)		–
Gain on sale of plant	35	–	35(i)		–
Expenses					
Administrative expenses	(30.8)	(38.7)			(69.5)
Depreciation	(24.5)	(56.8)		5.833(k)	(75.467)
Management fee expense	–	(26.5)		26.5(n)	–
Other expenses	(101.1)	(77)	3(m)		(181.1)
Profit before tax	205.5	143			240.933

	Hogwarts plc (£000)	Gryffindor plc (£000)	Eliminations and adjustments Dr (£000)	Cr (£000)	Consolidated statements (£000)
Profit before tax (c'twd)	205.5	143			240.933
Tax expense	(61.5)	(42.2)	2.1(h) 1.75(l)	1.68(d) 0.72(g) 10.5(j)	(94.65)
Profit for the year	144	100.8			146.283
Non-controlling interest in profit after tax			20.356(r)		(20.356)
Parent entity interest in profits after tax					125.927
Retained earnings—30 June 2014	319.4	239.2	136(a) 4.9(h) 22.5(m) 34(p) 12.86(q)		348.34
	463.4	340			474.267
Dividends paid	(137.4)	(93)		74.4(o) 18.6(s)	(137.4)
Retained earnings—30 June 2015	326	247			336.867
Statement of financial position					
Shareholders' equity					
Retained earnings	326	247			336.867
Share capital	350	200	160(a) 40(p)		350
Non-controlling interest			18.6(s)	74(p) 12.86(q) 20.356(r)	88.616
Current liabilities					
Accounts payable	54.7	46.3			101
Tax payable	41.30	25			66.3
Non-current liabilities					
Loans	173.5	116			289.5
	945.5	634.3			1,232.283
Current assets					
Accounts receivable	59.4	62.3			121.7
Inventory	92	29		5.6(c) 2.4(f)	113
Non-current assets					
Deferred tax asset			1.68(d) 0.72(g) 10.5(j)	1.75(l)	11.15
Land and buildings	224	326			550
Plant—at cost	299.85	355.8	19(i)	–	674.65
Accumulated depreciation	(85.75)	(138.8)	5.833(k)	54(i)	(272.717)
Investment in Gryffindor plc	356	–	–	356(a)	–
Goodwill	–	–	60(a)	–	60
Accumulated impairment loss	–	–	–	25.5(m)	(25.5)
	945.5	634.3	814.699	814.699	1,232.283

Summary of non-controlling interest

		20% non-controlling interest	
Profit			
Profit of Gryffindor plc	100,800	20,160	
Adjustments			
Unrealised profit in opening inventory	4,900	980	
Unrealised profit in closing inventory	(3,920)	(784)	20,356
Opening retained earnings			
Opening retained earnings of Gryffindor plc	239,200	47,840	
Unrealised profit in opening inventory	(4,900)	(980)	46,860
Dividends			
Paid by Gryffindor plc	(93,000)	(18,600)	(18,600)
Non-controlling interest in closing retained earnings			48,616
Non-controlling interest in share capital	200,000	40,000	40,000
Total non-controlling interest			88,616

We are now in a position to present the consolidated financial statements. A suggested format for the consolidated financial statements would be as follows:

Consolidated statement of comprehensive income of Hogwarts plc and its subsidiaries for the year ended 30 June 2015

	The Group (£)	Hogwarts plc (£)
Sales revenue	1,153,000	690,000
Cost of goods sold	(586,000)	(464,000)
Gross profit	567,000	226,000
Dividend revenue		74,400
Management fee revenue		26,500
Gain on sale of plant		35,000
Administrative expenses	(69,500)	(30,800)
Depreciation	(75,467)	(24,500)
Other expenses	(181,100)	(101,100)
Profit before income tax expense	240,933	205,500
Income tax expense	(94,650)	(61,500)
Profit after income tax expense	146,283	144,000
Other comprehensive income	–	–
Total comprehensive income	146,283	144,000
Profit after income tax attributable to:		
Owners of the parent	125,927	144,000
Non-controlling interest	20,356	–
	146,283	144,000

Consolidated statement of financial position of Hogwarts plc and its subsidiaries as at 30 June 2015

	The Group (£)	Hogwarts plc (£)
ASSETS		
Non-current assets		
Land and buildings	550,000	224,000
Plant and equipment	674,650	299,850
less Accumulated depreciation	(272,717)	(85,750)
Goodwill	60,000	–
Accumulated impairment loss	(25,500)	–
Investment in Gryffindor plc	–	356,000
Deferred tax asset	11,150	–
	997,583	794,100
Current assets		
Inventory	113,000	92,000
Accounts receivable	121,700	59,400
	234,700	151,400
Total assets	1,232,283	945,500
EQUITY AND LIABILITIES		
Equity and reserves		
Equity share capital	350,000	350,000
Retained earnings	336,867	326,000
Total parent entity interest in equity	686,867	676,000
Non-controlling interest in equity	88,616	–
Total equity and reserves	775,483	676,000
Non-current liabilities		
Loan	289,500	173,500
Current liabilities		
Accounts payable	101,000	54,700
Tax payable	66,300	41,300
	167,300	96,000
Total liabilities	456,800	269,500
Total equity and liabilities	1,232,283	945,500

Hogwarts plc and its controlled entity
Consolidated statement of changes in equity for the year ended 30 June 2015

	Attributable to owners of the parent				
	Share capital (£)	Retained earnings (£)	Total (£)	Non-controlling interest (£)	Total equity (£)
Balance at 1 July 2014	350,000	348,340	698,340	86,860	785,200
Total comprehensive income for the year	–	125,927	125,927	20,356	146,283
Distributions	–	(137,400)	(137,400)	(18,600)	(156,000)
Balance at 30 June 2015	350,000	336,867	686,867	88,616	775,483

Hogwarts plc
Statement of changes in equity for the year ended 30 June 2015

	Share capital (£)	Retained earnings (£)	Total equity (£)
Balance at 1 July 2014	350,000	319,400	669,400
Total comprehensive income for the year	–	144,000	144,000
Distributions	–	(137,400)	(137,400)
Balance at 30 June 2015	350,000	326,000	676,000

REVIEW QUESTIONS

1 Where only a proportion of a subsidiary's shares are owned by a parent entity, what proportion of the intragroup transactions between the parent entity and the subsidiary will need to be eliminated on consolidation? **LO 22.2**

2 What is a non-controlling interest, and how should it be disclosed? **LO 22.1**

3 How are non-controlling interests affected by intragroup transactions? **LO 22.1**

4 In working out the non-controlling interest in current period profits, we start with the reported profit of the subsidiary and then make a number of adjustments. What sorts of things do we need to make adjustments for? **LO 22.1**

5 Assume that Company A acquires 70 per cent of Company B for a cash price of €10 million when the share capital and reserves of Company B are: **LO 22.3**

Share capital   €8 million
Retained earnings   €2 million
                €10 million

(a) What amount will be shown in the consolidated statement of financial position for goodwill, pursuant to IFRS 3, assuming that any non-controlling interest in the acquirer is measured at fair value?

(b) What amount will be shown in the consolidated statement of financial position for goodwill, pursuant to IFRS 3, assuming that any non-controlling interest in the acquirer is measured at the non-controlling interest's proportionate share of the acquiree's identifiable net assets?

(c) What are some of the implications of allowing the group to have two options in accounting for goodwill on consolidation?

6 Backbeach plc acquired a 70 per cent interest in another entity, Frontbeach plc, in 2008 for a cost of €5 million. There was no goodwill or bargain gain on purchase. The consolidated worksheet for Backbeach plc and its controlled entity as at 30 June 2015 included the following: **LO 22.2**

	Parent (€000)	Consolidated (€000)
Revenue	2,000	5,000
Cost of goods sold	400	1,500
Dividend revenue	1,000	200
Interest expense	50	100
Depreciation expense	100	50
Other expenses	50	10

Prepare a consolidated statement of comprehensive income for Backbeach plc and its controlled entities that conforms with the disclosure requirements of IAS 1 *Presentation of Financial Statements*.

7   Kelly plc acquired 70 per cent of the share capital of Slater plc on 1 July 2014 for a cost of £300,000. At the date of acquisition all assets were fairly valued, and the balance of share capital and reserves was as follows: **LO 22.2**

	£
Share capital	180,000
Retained earnings	50,000
Revaluation surplus	60,000
	290,000

On 15 August 2014 Slater plc paid a £50,000 dividend out of pre-acquisition earnings to all shareholders that held shares at 10 July 2014. Non-controlling interest in the acquirer is measured at fair value.

Using the above information, prepare the consolidation adjustments and eliminations required for the year ended 30 June 2015.

8   Layne plc acquired 90 per cent of the share capital of Beachly plc on 1 July 2014 for a cost of £500,000. As at the date of acquisition all assets of Beachly plc were fairly valued, other than land that had a carrying amount £50,000 less than its fair value. The recorded balances of equity in Beachly plc as at 1 July 2014 were: **LO 22.2**

	£
Share capital	350,000
Retained earnings	100,000
	450,000

Additional information
- The management of Layne plc values any non-controlling interest at the proportionate share of Beachly plc's identifiable net assets.
- Beachly plc had a profit after tax of £70,000 for the year ended 30 June 2015.
- During the financial year to 30 June 2015 Beachly plc sold inventory to Layne plc for a price of £60,000. The inventory cost Beachly plc £30,000 to produce, and 25 per cent of this inventory was still on hand with Layne plc as at 30 June 2015.
- During the year Beachly plc paid £10,000 in management fees to Layne plc.
- On 1 July 2014 Beachly plc sold an item of plant to Layne plc for £40,000 when it had a carrying amount of £30,000 (cost of £50,000, accumulated depreciation of £20,000). At the date of sale it was expected that the plant had a remaining useful life of four years, and no residual value.
- The tax rate is 30 per cent.

Prepare the consolidation adjustments for the year ended 30 June 2015 and, based on the information provided above, calculate the non-controlling interests in the 2015 profits.

9   On 1 July 2013 Anderson plc acquires 70 per cent of the equity capital of Thruster plc at a cost of €4 million. At the date of acquisition all assets of Thruster plc are fairly stated, and the total shareholders' funds of Thruster plc are €4.4 million, consisting of: **LO 22.4**

Share capital	€3,000,000
Retained earnings	€1,400,000
	€4,400,000

As at 30 June 2015 (two years after the date of acquisition) the financial statements of the two companies are as follows:

	Anderson plc (€000)	Thruster plc (€000)
Detailed reconciliation of opening and closing retained earnings		
Sales revenue	800	200
Cost of goods sold	(200)	(80)
Other expenses	(120)	(60)
Other revenue	310	85
Profit	790	145
Tax	(170)	(35)
Profit after tax	620	110
Retained earnings—30 June 2014	2,000	1,600
	2,620	1,710
Dividends paid	(400)	(80)
Retained earnings—30 June 2015	2,220	1,630
Statement of financial position		
ASSETS		
Non-current assets		
Land	2,800	2,210
Plant	2,940	2,000
Investment in Thruster plc	4,000	–
	9,740	4,210
Current assets		
Inventory	1,000	600
Accounts receivable	500	350
Cash	300	50
	1,800	1,000
Total assets	11,540	5,210
EQUITY AND LIABILITIES		
Equity and reserves		
Equity share capital	8,000	3,000
Retained earnings	2,220	1,630
	10,220	4,630
Non-current liabilities		
Loans	1,200	500
Current liabilities		
Accounts payable	120	80
Total liabilities	1,320	580
Total equity and liabilities	11,540	5,210

Additional information

- The management of Anderson plc measures any non-controlling interest in Thruster plc at fair value.
- During the 2015 financial year Thruster plc sells €45,000 of inventory to Anderson plc. At year end, Anderson plc has sold all this inventory.
- The tax rate is 30 per cent.

REQUIRED

Prepare the consolidated statement of financial position, consolidated statement of comprehensive income and consolidated statement of changes in equity for Anderson plc and its controlled entity.

CHALLENGING QUESTIONS

10 On 1 July 2013 Borris plc purchased 80 per cent of the shares of Natasha plc for £8 million. On 1 July 2013 the shareholders' funds of Natasha plc were: **LO 22.4**

Share capital	£5,500,000
Retained earnings	£3,500,000
	£9,000,000

Additional information
- The management of Borris plc measures any non-controlling interest in Natasha plc at fair value.
- At acquisition date all assets of Natasha plc were fairly stated, except land that had a fair value £225,000 in excess of its book value.
- On 30 June 2015 the recoverable amount of goodwill of Borris plc was assessed to be £500,000. There had been no previous impairment losses recognised in relation to goodwill.
- During the financial year ending 30 June 2015 Natasha plc sold inventory to Borris plc at a sale price of £290,000. The inventory cost Natasha plc £200,000 to produce. At 30 June 2015 half of this inventory had been sold by Borris plc.
- On 1 July 2014 Natasha plc sold an item of plant to Borris plc for £250,000 when it had a carrying amount of £200,000 (cost of £400,000, accumulated depreciation of £200,000). The item of plant was expected to have a remaining useful life of five years from the date of sale.
- Natasha plc pays £30,000 per year in management fees to Borris plc.
- The income tax rate is 30 per cent.

Statement of comprehensive income of Borris plc and Natasha plc
for the year ended 30 June 2015

	Borris plc (£)	Natasha plc (£)
Sales revenue	5,200,000	1,550,000
Cost of goods sold	(3,000,000)	(500,000)
Gross profit	2,200,000	1,050,000
Other revenues	200,000	150,000
Other expenses	(400,000)	(200,000)
Profit before income tax expense	2,000,000	1,000,000
Income tax expense	(500,000)	(350,000)
Profit after income tax expense	1,500,000	650,000

Statement of financial positions of Borris plc and Natasha plc
as at 30 June 2015

	Borris plc (£)	Natasha plc (£)
ASSETS		
Non-current assets		
Land	4,910,000	3,450,000
Plant	7,500,000	5,000,000
Accumulated depreciation	(1,500,000)	(1,000,000)
Investment in Natasha plc	8,000,000	–
Deferred tax assets	250,000	1,100,000
	19,160,000	8,550,000

	Borris plc (£)	Natasha plc (£)
Current assets		
Inventory	2,800,000	1,200,000
Accounts receivable	650,000	250,000
Dividends receivable	40,000	–
Cash	250,000	300,000
	3,740,000	1,750,000
Total assets	22,900,000	10,300,000
EQUITY AND LIABILITIES		
Equity and reserves		
Equity share capital	15,000,000	5,500,000
Retained earnings	7,000,000	4,500,000
Total equity and reserves	22,000,000	10,000,000
Non-current liabilities		
Loans	650,000	150,000
Current liabilities		
Accounts payable	250,000	100,000
Dividends payable	–	50,000
	250,000	150,000
Total liabilities	900,000	300,000
Total equity and liabilities	22,900,000	10,300,000

Borris plc
Statement of changes in equity for the year ended 30 June 2015

	Share capital (£)	Retained earnings (£)	Total (£)
Balance at 1 July 2014	15,000,000	6,000,000	21,000,000
Total comprehensive income for the year	–	1,500,000	1,500,000
Distributions—interim	–	(500,000)	(500,000)
Balance at 30 June 2015	15,000,000	7,000,000	22,000,000

Natasha plc
Statement of changes in equity for the year ended 30 June 2015

	Share capital (£)	Retained earnings (£)	Total (£)
Balance at 1 July 2014	5,500,000	4,000,000	9,500,000
Total comprehensive income for the year	–	650,000	650,000
Distributions—interim	–	(100,000)	(100,000)
Distributions—final	–	(50,000)	(50,000)
Balance at 30 June 2015	5,500,000	4,500,000	10,000,000

(a) Prepare the consolidation worksheet journal entries for Borris plc and its controlled entity as at 30 June 2015 and post them to a consolidation worksheet.

(b) Calculate the non-controlling interest in profit and equity as at 30 June 2015.

(c) Prepare the consolidated statement of financial position, consolidated statement of comprehensive income and consolidated statement of changes in equity for Borris plc and its controlled entities clearly showing non-controlling interests.

11 The following financial statements of Mark plc and its subsidiary Richards plc have been extracted from their financial records at 30 June 2015. **LO 22.4**

	Mark plc (£)	Richards plc (£)
Detailed reconciliation of opening and closing retained earnings		
Sales revenue	1,725,000	1,450,000
Cost of goods sold	(1,160,000)	(595,000)
Gross profit	565,000	855,000
Dividend revenue—from Richards plc	186,000	–
Management fee revenue	66,250	–
Profit on sale of plant	87,500	–
Expenses		
Administrative expenses	(77,000)	(96,750)
Depreciation	(61,250)	(142,000)
Management fee expense	–	(66,250)
Other expenses	(252,750)	(192,500)
Profit before tax	513,750	357,500
Tax expense	(153,750)	(105,500)
Profit for the year	360,000	252,000
Retained earnings—1 July 2014	798,500	598,000
	1,158,500	850,000
Dividends paid	(343,500)	(232,500)
Retained earnings—30 June 2015	815,000	617,500
Statement of financial position		
ASSETS		
Non-current assets		
Land and buildings	560,000	815,000
Plant—at cost	749,625	889,500
Accumulated depreciation	(214,375)	(347,000)
Investment in Richards plc	890,000	–
	1,985,250	1,357,500
Current assets		
Inventory	230,000	72,500
Accounts receivable	148,500	155,750
	378,500	228,250
Total assets	2,363,750	1,585,750
EQUITY AND LIABILITIES		
Equity and reserves		
Share capital	875,000	500,000
Retained earnings	815,000	617,500
	1,690,000	1,117,500
Non-current liabilities		
Loans	433,750	290,000
Current liabilities		
Accounts payable	136,750	115,750
Tax payable	103,250	62,500
	240,000	178,250
Total liabilities	673,750	468,250
Total equity and liabilities	2,363,750	1,585,750

Other information

- Mark plc had acquired its 80 per cent interest in Richards plc on 1 July 2006, that is, nine years earlier. At that date the capital and reserves of Richards plc were:

Equity share capital	£500,000
Retained earnings	£425,000
	£925,000

At the date of acquisition all assets were considered to be fairly valued.

- The management of Mark plc measures any non-controlling interest at the proportionate share of Richards plc's identifiable net assets.
- During the year Mark plc made total sales to Richards plc of £162,500, while Richards plc sold £130,000 in inventory to Mark plc.
- The opening inventory in Mark plc as at 1 July 2014 included inventory acquired from Richards plc of £105,000 that had cost Richards plc £87,500 to produce.
- The closing inventory in Mark plc includes inventory acquired from Richards plc at a cost of £84,000. This had cost Richards plc £70,000 to produce.
- The closing inventory of Richards plc includes inventory acquired from Mark plc at a cost of £30,000. This had cost Mark plc £24,000 to produce.
- The management of Mark plc believe that goodwill acquired was impaired by £7,500 in the current financial year. Previous impairments of goodwill amounted to £56,250.
- On 1 July 2014 Mark plc sold an item of plant to Richards plc for £290,000 when its carrying value in Mark plc's financial statements was £202,500 (cost of £337,500, accumulated depreciation of £135,000). This plant is assessed as having a remaining useful life of six years.
- Richards plc paid £66,250 in management fees to Mark plc.
- The tax rate is 30 per cent.

REQUIRED

Provide the consolidated statement of financial position, consolidated statement of comprehensive income and consolidated statement of changes in equity of Mark plc and Richards plc as at 30 June 2015.

Chapter 23

Further Consolidation Issues III: Accounting for Indirect Ownership Interests

Learning objectives

Upon completing this chapter readers should:

LO1 be aware of what an indirect equity ownership interest represents and how it is calculated;

LO2 be aware that the determination of the total ownership interest in a subsidiary must take account of both direct and indirect ownership interests;

LO3 be aware that the parent entity's interest in the post-acquisition movements of a subsidiary's retained earnings and other reserves will be based on the sum of the direct and indirect ownership interests; and

LO4 be aware that, even in the presence of indirect ownership interests, the pre-acquisition capital and reserves of a subsidiary will be eliminated on consolidation on the basis of only the direct ownership interests.

23.1 Introduction to accounting for indirect ownership interests

In the previous three chapters we explored the process of consolidation where there are only two organisations within the economic entity. In this chapter we look at economic entities with more than one subsidiary and create situations in which a parent entity controls a subsidiary indirectly; in other words, we consider situations in which a parent entity controls another entity by virtue of its control of an intermediate entity. As we will see, if a subsidiary that is controlled by the parent entity in turn has ownership interests in another entity, this creates what we will refer to as 'indirect ownership interests'. These ownership interests are held by parent entities as well as by non-controlling interests. So in this chapter we consider not only how to consolidate the financial statements of more than two separate entities within an economic entity, but also how to calculate parent entity interests, and non-controlling interests, in the presence of indirect ownership interests.

23.2   Indirect ownership interests

As we know from previous chapters, 'control' is the criterion for determining whether an entity is a subsidiary (discussed in Chapter 21).

'Control' can be exercised even in the absence of any direct ownership interest—it can arise through indirect ownership interests. That is, if an entity has a controlling ownership in one entity, it effectively has control over the other entities controlled by that entity. That is, it is possible for one entity to **control** another entity without any direct ownership interest. For example, in Figure 23.1 the parent entity controls A plc as a result of a direct ownership interest of 70 per cent. Through its control of A plc, the parent entity can, in turn, control B plc, even though no investments have been made directly in B plc. The control is exercised through an indirect ownership interest (that is, via its direct ownership interest in A plc). In Figure 23.1 the indirect interests are depicted by broken-line arrows and the direct ownership interests by solid lines.

In this example, the parent entity's indirect interest in B plc would be 42 per cent, that is, 70 per cent of 60 per cent. What this means is that, if B plc pays a dividend of €1,000, €600 would be paid to A plc and €400 would be paid to the direct **non-controlling interests** in B plc. If A plc receives the €600 and decides in turn to pay out the entire receipts as dividends, 70 per cent (€420) of the €600 would find its way to the parent entity (or 42 per cent of the original €1,000 dividend payment made by B plc). The remaining €180 would go to the non-controlling interests of A plc. That is, the non-controlling interests in A plc have an indirect ownership interest (indirect non-controlling interest) in B plc of 18 per cent. The ownership interests are summarised in Table 23.1.

control (organisations) With regards to related parties and other organisations within a group (economic entity), control means the power to govern the financial and operating policies of an entity so as to obtain benefits from its activities.

non-controlling interests That portion of the profit or loss and net assets of a subsidiary attributable to equity interests that are not owned by the parent.

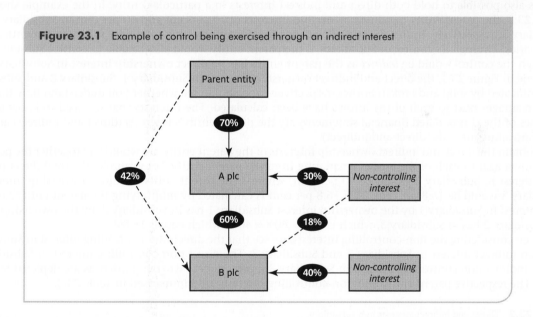

Figure 23.1   Example of control being exercised through an indirect interest

Table 23.1   Ownership interests in A and B plc

	A plc (% interest)	B plc (% interest)
Parent entity interest		
Direct	70	–
Indirect	–	42
Non-controlling interest		
Direct	30	40
Indirect	–	18
	100	100

Figure 23.2 Where a parent entity holds both a direct and an indirect interest in a subsidiary

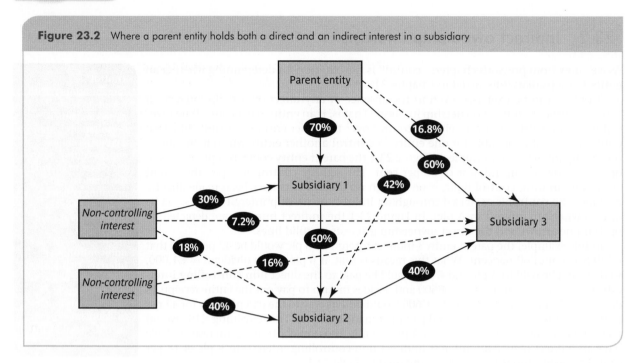

It is also possible to hold both direct and indirect interests in a particular entity. In the example shown in Figure 23.2, the parent entity has direct ownership interests of 70 per cent and 60 per cent in Subsidiary 1 and Subsidiary 3, respectively. In the absence of evidence to the contrary, this should be sufficient to control both subsidiaries. Through its control of Subsidiary 1, the parent entity would also be able to control Subsidiary 2—although the control would be *indirect* as the parent entity has no direct ownership interest in Subsidiary 2. As was done in Figure 23.1, the direct and indirect ownership interests in Subsidiary 1, Subsidiary 2 and Subsidiary 3 are indicated by solid and broken arrows, respectively. You should see whether you understand how the various percentages next to each of the arrows have been calculated. The interests that we need to know for the purposes of the consolidated financial statements are the parent entity's interests (direct and indirect) and the non-controlling interests (direct and indirect).

To obtain the direct and indirect ownership interests of the parent entity, we would add together the percentages shown against each of the arrows emanating from the parent entity. For example, the total direct ownership interest in Subsidiary 3 would be 60 per cent, whereas the parent entity's indirect ownership interest in Subsidiary 3 would be 16.8 per cent. This 16.8 per cent is calculated by multiplying the parent entity's ownership interest in Subsidiary 1 by the ownership interest Subsidiary 1 has in Subsidiary 2, by the ownership interest Subsidiary 2 has in Subsidiary 3, which is 70% × 60% × 40%, which equals 16.8%.

When considering the non-controlling interests, we see that the direct non-controlling interest in Subsidiary 1 has an indirect interest in Subsidiary 2 and Subsidiary 3. The direct non-controlling interest in Subsidiary 2 has an indirect non-controlling interest in Subsidiary 3 (again, direct ownership interests are depicted by solid lines). The respective parent entity and non-controlling interests are summarised in Table 23.2.

Table 23.2 Direct and indirect interests in a subsidiary

	Subsidiary 1 (% interest)	Subsidiary 2 (% interest)	Subsidiary 3 (% interest)
Parent entity interest			
Direct	70	–	60
Indirect	–	42	16.8*
Non-controlling interest			
Direct	30	40	–
Indirect	–	18	23.2**
	100	100	100

* 16.8 = 100 × 0.7 × 0.6 × 0.4
**23.2 = 100 × ((0.3 × 0.6 × 0.4) + (0.4 × 0.4))

As we can see in Figure 23.2, the direct ownership interests (which include the direct parent entity interests and the direct non-controlling interests)—represented by solid lines—add up to 100 per cent for all the subsidiaries. As stated above, to determine the parent entity interest in all subsidiaries we only look at the arrows emanating from the parent entity box. So, looking at Subsidiary 2, we can see that the parent entity interest is indirect and is 42 per cent. The non-controlling interest will be direct (40 per cent) and indirect (18 per cent), giving a total non-controlling interest of 58 per cent. Adding the total parent entity interest (direct and indirect) to the total non-controlling interest (direct and indirect) must give 100 per cent. Similarly, for Subsidiary 3, the parent entity has a mixture of both direct and indirect ownership interests, which add up to 76.8 per cent in total, while the non-controlling interests, also a mix of direct and indirect interests, total 23.2 per cent. But why are we spending all this time working out direct and indirect parent entity interests and direct and indirect non-controlling interests? After all, it does seem to require a lot of effort. As we will see, we need to have these details to determine the non-controlling interests in profits and capital and reserves, which will need to be disclosed in the economic entity's financial statements. For example, as we will learn shortly:

- the elimination of the parent entity's investment in a subsidiary will be done by eliminating the investment against the parent entity's *direct* ownership interest in pre-acquisition share capital and reserves;
- the parent entity interest in post-acquisition profits and post-acquisition movements in reserves will be based on the combined total of the parent entity's *direct* and *indirect* interests;
- the non-controlling interest in pre-acquisition capital and reserves will be based on *direct* non-controlling interest; and
- the non-controlling interest in post-acquisition movement in reserves and post-acquisition profits will be based on the combined sum of both *direct* non-controlling interest and *indirect* non-controlling interest.

In Worked Example 23.1 we will consider, in more detail, the consolidation process in the presence of indirect interests.

Worked Example 23.1   Consolidation in the presence of indirect interests

Assume that on 1 July 2014 Burridge plc acquires 70 per cent of the issued capital of Anderson plc and, on the same date, Anderson plc acquires 60 per cent of the issued capital of Menser plc. The group's structure would appear as shown in the figure below.

Group structure of Burridge plc and its controlled entities

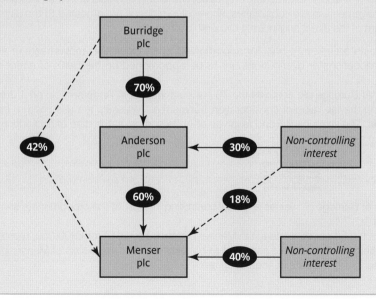

▶

Burridge plc has no direct ownership interest in Menser plc. Burridge plc's ownership interest (indirect) in Menser plc would be 42 per cent (70 per cent of 60 per cent). Because we have assumed that Anderson plc's 60 per cent direct ownership of Menser plc allows Anderson plc to control Menser plc, Burridge plc controls Menser plc indirectly through its control of Anderson plc. That is, even in the absence of direct shareholding, Menser plc would be considered a subsidiary of Burridge plc. This is consistent with the definition of 'subsidiary' provided earlier. Burridge plc would be described as the *ultimate parent entity of the group*, as well as the *immediate parent entity* of Anderson plc. Anderson plc would be described as the immediate parent entity of Menser plc.

The direct and indirect interests in Anderson plc and Menser plc can be represented as in the following table.

Direct and indirect interests in Anderson plc and Menser plc

	Anderson plc (% interest)	Menser plc (% interest)
Burridge plc's interest		
Direct	70	–
Indirect	–	42
Non-controlling interest		
Direct	30	40
Indirect	–	18
	100	100

Note that the indirect non-controlling interest in Menser plc of 18 per cent is derived by multiplying the 30 per cent non-controlling interest in Anderson plc by the ownership interest Anderson plc has in Menser plc (60 per cent).

There is a choice between two methods when performing the consolidation. The first method is the sequential-consolidation approach, which, if there are numerous subsidiaries, would be time consuming and rather messy as consolidation of each separate legal entity with its controlled entities would be performed sequentially. Adopting the sequential-consolidation method, it would be necessary first to consolidate Anderson plc with Menser plc, and then sequentially consolidate Burridge plc with the Anderson–Menser group (working backwards from the most distant subsidiary).

Alternatively, we could adopt a multiple-consolidation approach, which is the method advocated in this book. When using the multiple-consolidation approach, the following general principles should be followed:

- In eliminating the investments held by the immediate parent entities (the investments as they would appear in the separate legal entities' financial statements), only direct ownership interests are taken into account.
- Post-acquisition movements in the subsidiaries' shareholders' funds are allocated to the ultimate parent entity on the basis of the sum of the direct and indirect ownership interests.

Hence, indirect interests are relevant only for apportioning post-acquisition movements in shareholders' funds. Any pre-acquisition allocations or distributions are to be apportioned on the basis of direct ownership interests only.

We will assume that Burridge plc acquires the 70 per cent interest in Anderson plc on 1 July 2014 for a cost of €1 million, representing the fair value of consideration transferred. All assets are assumed to be fairly valued in the books of Anderson plc. The share capital and reserves of Anderson plc at the date of acquisition are:

Share capital	€1,000,000
Retained earnings	€300,000
	€1,300,000

The management of Burridge plc values any non-controlling interest at the proportionate share of Anderson plc's identifiable net assets.

Anderson acquires the 60 per cent interest in Menser plc on 1 July 2014 for €800,000, representing the fair value of consideration transferred. All assets are assumed to be fairly valued in the books of Menser plc. The share capital and reserves of Menser plc at the date of acquisition are:

Share capital	€800,000
Retained earnings	€400,000
	€1,200,000

The non-controlling interest in Menser plc is valued at fair value.

As noted above, in the consolidation process the elimination of the investment will be based on the direct ownership interests of the immediate parent entity, whereas the allocation of post-acquisition profits and movements in reserves will be based on the ultimate parent entity's direct and indirect interests. Similarly, the non-controlling interest in pre-acquisition capital and reserves will be based on the non-controlling interest's direct ownership interest, whereas the allocation of the non-controlling interest share in post-acquisition profits and movements in reserves will be based on the total of the direct and indirect non-controlling interests.

It must be remembered that preparers of financial statements have a choice about how to measure the non-controlling interests at acquisition in each business combination. For example, and as we have already indicated in previous chapters, reporting entities can use fair value for one business combination and the proportionate share of the acquiree's net identifiable assets for another business combination. As the information in this worked example has already indicated:

■ The non-controlling interest in Anderson plc at acquisition is to be measured at the non-controlling interest's proportionate share of Anderson plc's identifiable net assets.
■ The non-controlling interest in Menser plc at acquisition is to be measured at fair value.

An extract of the income statements, statements of changes in equity and statements of financial position of the entities at 30 June 2015 (one year after the acquisition) are as follows:

	Burridge plc (€000)	Anderson plc (€000)	Menser plc (€000)
Extract from income statement			
Profit before tax	500	80	100
Tax	(270)	(25)	(40)
Profit after tax	230	55	60
Statement of changes in equity (extract)			
Retained earnings—30 June 2014	1,000	300	400
Profit after tax	230	55	60
	1,230	355	460
Dividends declared	(200)	(50)	(30)
Retained earnings—30 June 2015	1,030	305	430
Statement of financial position			
ASSETS			
Non-current assets			
Land	2,350	–	200
Plant	1,500	315	360
Investment in Anderson plc	1,000	–	–
Investment in Menser plc	–	800	–
	4,850	1,115	560
Current assets			
Inventory	500	300	400
Accounts receivable	250	175	200
Dividends receivable	35	18	–
Cash	165	37	100
	950	530	700
Total assets	5,800	1,645	1,260

	Burridge plc (€000)	Anderson plc (€000)	Menser plc (€000)
EQUITY AND LIABILITIES			
Equity and reserves			
Equity share capital	4,000	1,000	800
Retained earnings	1,030	305	430
	5,030	1,305	1,230
Non-current liabilities			
Loans	400	250	–
Current liabilities			
Accounts payable	170	40	–
Dividends payable	200	50	30
	370	90	30
Total liabilities	770	340	30
Total equity and liabilities	5,800	1,645	1,260

Additional information

It is assumed that, in the year to 30 June 2015, there have been impairment losses in relation to the goodwill acquired in Anderson plc. The goodwill has been deemed to have been impaired by an amount of 10 per cent of its original balance. Similarly, the goodwill in Menser plc is considered to have been impaired by €13,333 in the year to 30 June 2015. All dividends were declared on 30 June 2015 and the decision to pay them communicated to shareholders on that date.

For the purposes of this illustration we will assume that, apart from the dividends, there are no intragroup transactions (this assumption will not apply in the next worked example).

Required

Present a consolidated statement of financial position, a consolidated statement of comprehensive income and a consolidated statement of changes in equity for Burridge plc and its controlled entities as at 30 June 2015.

Solution

Elimination of the cost of the investment and recognition of goodwill
When eliminating the investment against the pre-acquisition capital and reserves of the subsidiaries, we consider only direct ownership interests.

Elimination of investment in Anderson plc	Anderson plc (€)	Burridge plc's 70% interest (€)	30% non-controlling interest (€)
Fair value of consideration transferred		1,000,000	
less Fair value of identifiable assets acquired and liabilities assumed			
Share capital on acquisition date	1,000,000	700,000	300,000
Retained earnings on acquisition date	300,000	210,000	90,000
	1,300,000	910,000	
Goodwill on acquisition date		90,000	
Non-controlling interest at date of acquisition			390,000

Elimination of investment in Menser plc	Menser plc (€)	Anderson plc's 60% interest (€)	40% non-controlling interest (€)
Fair value of consideration transferred	800,000	800,000	
plus Non-controlling interest at fair value (€800,000 × 40/60)	533,333		533,333
	1,333,333		
less Fair value of identifiable assets acquired and liabilities assumed			
Share capital on acquisition date	800,000	480,000	320,000
Retained earnings on acquisition date	400,000	240,000	160,000
	1,200,000	720,000	480,000
Goodwill on acquisition date	133,333	80,000	53,333

Again, it should be noted that the approach to determining goodwill on acquisition will depend upon whether:

- the non-controlling interest at acquisition date is measured at the non-controlling interest's proportionate share of the acquiree's identifiable net assets (which means no goodwill will be attributed to the non-controlling interest, as in the case of Burridge plc's investment in Anderson plc above, as it was decided by management that the non-controlling interest in Anderson plc would be measured at the non-controlling interest's proportionate share of Anderson plc's identifiable assets); or
- the non-controlling interest at acquisition date is measured at fair value (which means goodwill will be attributed to the non-controlling interest, as in the case of Anderson's investment in Menser plc above, as it was decided by management that the non-controlling interest in Menser plc would be measured at fair value at acquisition date).

Consolidation worksheet entries

(a) *To eliminate Burridge plc's investment in Anderson plc*

Dr Share capital	€700,000	
Dr Retained earnings	€210,000	
Dr Goodwill	€90,000	
Cr Investment in Anderson plc		€1,000,000

(b) *To eliminate Anderson plc's investment in Menser plc*

Dr Share capital	€480,000	
Dr Retained earnings	€240,000	
Dr Goodwill	€80,000	
Cr Investment in Menser plc		€800,000

As we can see in the tables above, the total goodwill in Menser plc of €133,333 also includes an amount attributed to the non-controlling interest, this being €53,333. This amount will be recognised subsequently when we recognise the non-controlling interest in the net assets of Menser plc. At this stage we are only recognising the parent entity's share of goodwill at acquisition date.

Goodwill impairment

(c) *Impairment of the goodwill associated with the acquisition of Anderson plc*

Dr Impairment expense—goodwill	€9,000	
Cr Accumulated impairment losses—goodwill		€9,000

(d) *Impairment of the goodwill associated with the acquisition of Menser plc*

Dr Impairment expense—goodwill	€13,333	
Cr Accumulated impairment losses—goodwill		€13,333

It should be noted that the above impairment losses relate to the total amount of goodwill recognised on acquisition (see the above tables).

An issue we will need to address subsequently is that, when we subsequently calculate the non-controlling interest in profits or losses, which entities will we attribute any goodwill impairments to? Possible treatments would be to:

1. Attribute the goodwill impairment losses to the ultimate parent entity in the group (in this case, Burridge plc).
2. Attribute the goodwill impairment losses to the immediate parent entity of the subsidiary (in this case, Anderson plc would be the immediate parent entity of Menser plc).
3. Attribute the goodwill impairment losses to the subsidiary itself.

While the accounting standards do not provide any clear guidelines, a choice between the three options above nevertheless has to be made. It is the opinion of the authors that the appropriate treatment of goodwill impairment losses relating to an investment in a subsidiary depends upon how the non-controlling interest is measured. We know there are two options in terms of how the non-controlling interest can be measured.

If it has been decided to adopt the option that allows the acquirer to measure any non-controlling interest in the acquiree (the subsidiary) at the acquisition-date fair values, then:

- As we know, the goodwill acquired by the acquirer (the immediate parent), as well as the direct non-controlling interests' share of goodwill at acquisition, will be recognised (referred to as the 'full goodwill method').

- Therefore, if events have occurred which have created an impairment in goodwill, then both the immediate parent's share of goodwill, and the direct non-controlling interests' share of goodwill will be impacted.
- As such, when working out the non-controlling interests' share of the profit or loss of the subsidiary, the amount of the impairment should be subtracted from the subsidiary's profit or loss before the non-controlling interests' share of profit is determined. This impairment will then be proportionally allocated to both the direct parent entity and the non-controlling interest on the basis of the respective ownership interests. This will have the effect of reducing the non-controlling interest in the subsidiary's profits.

If it has been decided to adopt the other option that allows the acquirer (the immediate parent entity) to measure the non-controlling interest in the subsidiary at the non-controlling interest's proportionate share of the subsidiary's identifiable net assets, then:

- As we know, only the goodwill acquired by the acquirer (the immediate parent), will be recognised (referred to as the 'partial goodwill method', as explained in Chapter 22). No goodwill will be recognised in relation to the non-controlling interest.
- Therefore, if events have occurred which have created an impairment in the value of goodwill, then it is only the immediate parent's share of goodwill that will be impacted.
- As such, when working out the non-controlling interests' share of the profit or loss of the subsidiary, no adjustment is necessary in relation to goodwill impairment. Any impairment in goodwill will only relate to goodwill that has been attributed to the immediate parent entity's interest in the subsidiary. As such, any goodwill impairment will be recognised as a consolidation adjustment, but will not be considered when determining the non-controlling interest in the subsidiary's profit or loss.

Elimination of intercompany dividends
As discussed in previous chapters, all intercompany dividends should be eliminated on consolidation.

(e) *To eliminate dividends payable and receivable within the group*

Dr Dividend payable (statement of financial position)	€35,000
Cr Dividend receivable (statement of financial position)	€35,000

(to take account of Burridge plc's direct interest of 70 per cent in Anderson plc's dividends of €50,000)

(f) *To eliminate dividend income and dividends declared within the group*

Dr Dividend revenue	€35,000
Cr Dividend declared (statement of changes in equity)	€35,000

(elimination of dividends declared by Menser plc)

(g)
Dr Dividend payable (statement of financial position)	€18,000
Cr Dividend receivable (statement of financial position)	€18,000

(to take account of Anderson plc's direct interest of 60 per cent in Menser plc's dividends of €30,000)

(h)
Dr Dividend revenue	€18,000
Cr Dividend declared (statement of changes in equity)	€18,000

Up to this point we have not introduced any journal entries that were not already explained in the previous chapters on consolidation. Even in the presence of indirect interests we still eliminate the pre-acquisition capital and reserves against the direct investment and we eliminate all the intragroup transactions before we construct the consolidated financial statements. As we will see shortly, the indirect interests affect how we apportion the total consolidated share-holder funds and consolidated profits between the parent and non-controlling interests.

Recognising non-controlling interest in share capital, reserves and earnings

(i) *Non-controlling interest in Anderson plc*

Calculation of non-controlling interests in Anderson plc	Anderson plc (€)	30% non-controlling interest (€)
Non-controlling interests and goodwill on acquisition date		
Share capital	1,000,000	300,000
Retained earnings—on acquisition	300,000	90,000
	1,300,000	390,000

Non-controlling interest in the current period's profit and movements in reserves in the current period

Profit for the year	55,000	
Dividends received from entity within group*	(18,000)	
Impairment of goodwill in Menser plc*	–	
	37,000	11,100
Dividends paid by Anderson plc	(50,000)	(15,000)
Non-controlling interests		386,100

* Explanations for these adjustments are provided below

Dr	Share capital (1,000,000 × 30 per cent)	€300,000	
Dr	Retained earnings—1 July 2014 (€300,000 × 30 per cent)	€90,000	
Dr	Non-controlling interest in earnings	€11,100	
Cr	Dividend declared (€50,000 × 30 per cent)		€15,000
Cr	Non-controlling interest		€386,100

Recognising non-controlling interest and non-controlling interest in earnings of Anderson plc
Explanation for adjustments

If the above calculations of the non-controlling interest in current period profits are reviewed, it is apparent that adjustments for the intragroup dividends have been made, but no adjustments have been made for any goodwill impairment. Why?

First, in relation to dividends, of the dividends declared by Menser plc, which totalled €30,000, €18,000 (60 per cent) went to Anderson plc and €12,000 (40 per cent) went to the direct non-controlling interests in Menser plc. The dividend paid to Anderson plc will be included in Anderson plc's profits, in which the direct non-controlling interests (30 per cent) will have a share. The indirect non-controlling interests in Menser plc—who are the same parties as the direct non-controlling interests in Anderson plc (see Figure 23.3 provided earlier)—will be allocated a share in the profits of Menser plc (through their 18 per cent indirect interest). The dividends paid by Menser plc to Anderson plc represent a distribution of these profits. The non-controlling interests in Anderson plc (who are the same investors as the indirect non-controlling interests in Menser plc) should not get a share of these profits yet again (it would be double-counting), so before the non-controlling interest in the profits of Anderson plc are calculated, the dividends paid to Anderson plc by Menser plc are subtracted. The general rule here is that intragroup dividends paid to an 'intermediate parent' from a subsidiary are subtracted from the profits of that intermediate parent before the non-controlling interest in profits of that organisation is calculated.

In relation to why neither the impairment of Menser plc's goodwill nor Anderson plc's goodwill impairment is deducted from Anderson plc's profit before the non-controlling interest is determined, we can refer back to the general principles provided earlier, these being:

■ If the non-controlling interest is valued at fair value at acquisition date, the goodwill impairment loss relating to the purchase of a subsidiary should be attributed to that subsidiary.

■ If the non-controlling interest is valued at the non-controlling interests' proportionate share of the subsidiary's identifiable net assets at acquisition date, then the goodwill impairment loss relating to the purchase of a subsidiary should be attributed to the immediate parent entity of the subsidiary because it is only the immediate parent entity's share of goodwill which has been recognised.

Because the non-controlling interest in Menser at acquisition date was determined on the basis of fair value, then the goodwill impairment will be attributed to Menser plc (see below). Further, as the non-controlling interest in Anderson plc at acquisition date was determined on the basis of the non-controlling interests' proportionate share of the identifiable net assets of the subsidiary at acquisition date, then the impairment of the goodwill in Anderson plc will be attributed to Burridge plc. Hence, for Anderson plc, there are no goodwill impairment adjustments when calculating the non-controlling interest in current period profits.

(j) *Non-controlling interest in Menser plc*

Calculation of non-controlling interests in Menser plc	Menser plc (€)	40% non-controlling interest (€)
Non-controlling interests and goodwill on acquisition date		
Share capital	800,000	320,000
Retained earnings—on acquisition	400,000	160,000
Goodwill on acquisition	–	53,333
	1,200,000	533,333

Non-controlling interest in the current period's profit and movements in reserves in the current period

Profit for the year	60,000	
Goodwill impairment	(13,333)	
	46,667	18,667
Dividend declared by Menser plc	(30,000)	(12,000)
		540,000

Dr	Share capital	€320,000	
Dr	Retained earnings—1 July 2014	€160,000	
Dr	Goodwill	€53,333	
Dr	Non-controlling interest in earnings	€18,667	
Cr	Dividend declared		€12,000
Cr	Non-controlling interest		€540,000

(recognising non-controlling interest and non-controlling interest in earnings of Menser plc)

(k) *Indirect non-controlling interest in Menser plc*

Calculation of indirect non-controlling interest in Menser plc	Menser plc (€)	18% indirect non-controlling interest (€)
Profit for the year	60,000	
Impairment of goodwill acquired in Menser plc	(13,333)	
	46,667	8,400

Dr	Non-controlling interest in earnings	€8,400	
Cr	Non-controlling interest		€8,400

(recognising indirect non-controlling interest in earnings of Menser plc)

The above consolidation journal entries can now be posted to the consolidation worksheet.

Consolidation worksheet for Burridge plc and its controlled entities for the year ending 30 June 2015

	Burridge plc (€000)	Anderson plc (€000)	Menser plc (€000)	Eliminations and adjustments Dr (€000)	Cr (€000)	Consolidated statements (€000)
Abbreviated statement of comprehensive income						
Profit before tax	500	80	100	9(c)		
				13.333(d)		
				35(f)		
				18(h)		604.667
Tax expense	(270)	(25)	(40)			(335)
Profit after tax	230	55	60			269.667
Non-controlling interest in earnings				11.1(i)		
				18.667(j)		
				8.4(k)		(38.167)
Statement of changes in equity						
Profit after tax	230	55	60			
Retained earnings— 1 July 2014	1,000	300	400	210(a)		
				90(i)		
				240(b)		1,000
				160(j)		
	1,230	355	460			1,231.5
Dividends declared	(200)	(50)	(30)		18(h)	
					15(i)	
					35(f)	(200)
					12(j)	
Retained earnings— 30 June 2015	1,030	305	430			1,031.5

	Burridge plc (€000)	Anderson plc (€000)	Menser plc (€000)	Eliminations and adjustments		Consolidated statements (€000)
				Dr (€000)	Cr (€000)	
Statement of financial position						
Shareholders' equity						
Retained earnings	1,030	305	430			1,031.5
Share capital	4,000	1,000	800	700(a)		
				480(b)		
				300(i)		
				320(k)		4,000
Non-controlling interest					386.1(i)	
					540(j)	
					8.4(k)	934.5
Current liabilities						
Accounts payable	170	40				210
Dividends payable	200	50	30	35(e)		
				18(g)		227
Non-current liabilities						
Loans	400	250	–			650
	5,800	1,645	1,260			7,053
Current assets						
Cash	165	37	100			302
Accounts receivable	250	175	200			625
Dividends receivable	35	18			35(e)	
					18(g)	–
Inventory	500	300	400			1,200
Non-current assets						
Land	2,350	–	200			2,550
Plant	1,500	315	360			2,175
Investment in Anderson plc	1,000	–			1,000(a)	–
Investment in Menser plc		800			800(b)	–
Goodwill				90(a)		
	–	–	–	80(b)		223.333
				53.333(j)		
Accumulated impairment losses—goodwill	–	–	–	–	9(c)	(22.333)
					13.333(d)	
	5,800	1,645	1,260	2,889.833	2,889.833	7,053

Before the consolidated statement of financial position, the consolidated statement of changes in equity and the consolidated statement of comprehensive income can be presented, the non-controlling interest needs to be considered. As was established in Chapter 22, the non-controlling interest must be disclosed separately within equity within the financial statements (IFRS 10, paragraph 22).

In addition, non-controlling interests in the profit or loss of the group shall also be separately disclosed (IFRS 10, paragraph B94). Exhibits 22.1, 22.2 and 22.3 (detailed in Chapter 22) show the suggested disclosures for non-controlling interests in the equity component of the statement of financial position, the statement of comprehensive income and statement of changes in equity.

Burridge plc and its controlled entities: Consolidated statement of comprehensive income for the year ending 30 June 2015

	The Group (€)	Burridge plc (€)
Profit before tax	604,667	500,000
Income tax expense	(335,000)	(270,000)
Profit for the year	269,667	230,000
Other comprehensive income	–	–
Total comprehensive income	269,667	230,000
Attributable to:		
Owners of the parent	231,500	
Non-controlling interest	38,167	
	269,667	

Burridge plc and its controlled entities

Consolidated statement of changes in equity for the year ending 30 June 2015

	Attributable to owners of the parent			Non-controlling interest (€)	Total equity (€)
	Share capital (€)	Retained earnings (€)	Total (€)		
Balance at 1 July 2014	4,000,000	1,000,000	5,000,000	923,333	5,923,333
Total comprehensive income for the year	–	231,500	231,500	38,167	269,667
Dividends	–	(200,000)	(200,000)	(27,000)	(227,000)
Balance at 30 June 2015	4,000,000	1,031,500	5,031,500	934,500	5,966,000

Burridge plc statement of changes in equity for the year ending 30 June 2015

	Share capital (€)	Retained earnings (€)	Total equity (€)
Balance at 1 July 2014	4,000,000	1,000,000	5,000,000
Total comprehensive income for the year	–	230,000	230,000
Dividends	–	(200,000)	(200,000)
Balance at 30 June 2015	4,000,000	1,030,000	5,030,000

Burridge plc and its controlled entities: Consolidated statement of financial position at 30 June 2015

	The Group (€)	Burridge plc (€)
ASSETS		
Non-current assets		
Property, plant and equipment	4,725,000	3,850,000
Goodwill	223,333	–
Accumulated impairment losses	(22,333)	
Investment in Anderson plc	–	1,000,000
Total non-current assets	4,926,000	4,850,000
Current assets		
Inventories	1,200,000	500,000
Accounts receivable	625,000	250,000
Dividends receivable	–	35,000
Cash	302,000	165,000
Total current assets	2,127,000	950,000
Total assets	7,053,000	5,800,000
EQUITY AND LIABILITIES		
Equity and reserves		
Equity share capital	4,000,000	4,000,000
Retained earnings	1,031,500	1,030,000
	5,031,000	5,030,000
Non-controlling interest	934,500	–
Total equity and reserves	5,966,000	5,030,000
Non-current liabilities		
Loans	650,000	400,000
Total non-current liabilities	650,000	400,000
Current liabilities		
Accounts payable	210,000	170,000
Dividends payable	227,000	200,000
Total current liabilities	437,000	370,000
Total liabilities	1,087,000	770,000
Total equity and liabilities	7,053,000	5,800,000

In Worked Example 23.2 we introduce intragroup transactions into the consolidation process.

Worked Example 23.2	Consolidation in the presence of indirect ownership interests and intragroup transactions

On 30 June 2011 Big plc purchased 70 per cent of the shares of Medium plc for £660,000 cash. On the same date, Medium plc purchased 60 per cent of the shares of Small plc for £420,000 cash.

The statements of financial position of Medium plc and Small plc immediately before the investments were as follows:

Statements of financial position of Medium plc and Small plc as at 30 June 2011

	Medium plc (£)	Small plc (£)
ASSETS		
Non-current assets		
Land	105,000	210,000
Factory buildings	1,000,000	360,000
Accumulated depreciation	(700,000)	(72,000)
	405,000	498,000

	Medium plc (£)	Small plc (£)
Current assets		
Inventory	200,000	130,000
Accounts receivable	180,000	80,000
Cash	465,000	30,000
	845,000	240,000
Total assets	1,250,000	738,000
EQUITY AND LIABILITIES		
Equity and reserves		
Share capital	560,000	160,000
Retained earnings	240,000	320,000
Total equity and reserves	800,000	480,000
Liabilities		
Accounts payable	450,000	258,000
Total equity and liabilities	1,250,000	738,000

Additional information

(i) The non-controlling interest in Medium plc is measured at fair value, while the non-controlling interest in Small plc is measured at the proportionate share of its identifiable net assets *(Hint: as we should now appreciate, the choice of either of these two options for measuring the non-controlling interest at acquisition will have implications for the amount of goodwill recognised on acquisition and how any goodwill impairment expenses will be allocated between the separate legal entities).*

(ii) At the date of investment, all the identifiable net assets of Medium plc and Small plc were considered to be recorded at fair value in the respective statements of financial position of Medium plc and Small plc, except Small plc's factory buildings, which had a fair value of £416,000, and a carrying value of £288,000 (cost of £360,000, accumulated depreciation of £72,000). Small plc did not revalue its buildings at the date of investment. At 30 June 2011 the factory buildings had a remaining useful life of 16 years.

(iii) On 1 July 2014 the recoverable amount of the goodwill relating to the purchase of Small plc by Medium plc was assessed to be £40,000 (reflecting an accumulated impairment loss of £38,240, as we will see shortly). This impairment loss of £38,240 was recognised in the first year following acquisition, that is, in the year to 30 June 2012. During the year to 30 June 2015 it was considered that the goodwill in Small plc had been further impaired by an amount of £5,000 to provide a recoverable amount at 30 June 2015 of £35,000.

(iv) On 30 June 2015 the recoverable amount of the goodwill relating to the purchase of Medium plc by Big plc was assessed to be £110,000 and it was considered that all the impairment occurred in the 2015 financial year.

(v) During the 2015 financial year Small plc sold goods to Big plc for £2,000,000. These goods had originally cost Small plc £1,600,000. On 30 June 2015, 35 per cent of these goods remained in Big plc's closing inventory.

(vi) Small plc's opening inventory included goods purchased from Medium plc for £570,000. These goods had originally cost Medium plc £490,000.

(vii) On 30 June 2015 Big plc sold a factory building to Medium plc for £800,000. Big plc had originally purchased the factory building for £900,000, on 1 July 2009. The original estimated useful life of the factory building was 20 years.

(viii) On 31 November 2014 Big plc paid an interim dividend of £125,000, while Small plc paid an interim dividend of £110,000.

(ix) On 30 June 2015, Big plc declared a final dividend of £260,000, while Medium plc declared a final dividend of £90,000. The decision to pay these dividends was communicated to shareholders on this date.

(x) The income tax rate is 30 per cent.

The financial statements of Big plc, Medium plc and Small plc revealed the following balances as at 30 June 2015:

Statements of comprehensive income of Big plc, Medium plc and Small plc, for the year ended 30 June 2015

	Big plc (£)	Medium plc (£)	Small plc (£)
Sales	7,500,000	4,000,000	3,500,000
Cost of goods sold	(6,100,000)	(3,260,000)	(2,900,000)
Gross profit	1,400,000	740,000	600,000
Depreciation expense	(130,000)	(50,000)	(18,000)
Other expenses	(743,000)	(476,000)	(262,000)
Dividend revenue	63,000	66,000	–

Gain on sale of factory building	170,000	–	–
Profit before income tax	760,000	280,000	320,000
Income tax expense	(304,000)	(112,000)	(128,000)
Profit after income tax	456,000	168,000	192,000
Other comprehensive income	–	–	–
Total comprehensive income	456,000	168,000	192,000

Statements of financial position of Big plc, Medium plc and Small plc as at 30 June 2015

	Big plc (£)	Medium plc (£)	Small plc (£)
ASSETS			
Non-current assets			
Land	720,000	105,000	210,000
Factory buildings	2,600,000	1,800,000	360,000
Accumulated depreciation	(130,000)	(900,000)	(144,000)
Investment in Medium plc	660,000	–	–
Investment in Small plc	–	420,000	–
	3,850,000	1,425,000	426,000
Current assets			
Inventory	1,100,000	440,000	700,000
Accounts receivable	172,000	52,000	68,000
Dividends receivable	63,000	–	–
Cash	76,000	6,000	37,000
	1,411,000	498,000	805,000
Total assets	5,261,000	1,923,000	1,231,000
EQUITY AND LIABILITIES			
Equity and reserves			
Share capital	3,300,000	560,000	160,000
Retained earnings	791,000	558,000	752,000
	4,091,000	1,118,000	912,000
Liabilities			
Accounts payable	910,000	715,000	319,000
Dividends payable	260,000	90,000	–
	1,170,000	805,000	319,000
Total equity and liabilities	5,261,000	1,923,000	1,231,000

Big plc: Statement of changes in equity for the year ending 30 June 2015

	Share capital (£)	Retained earnings (£)	Total equity (£)
Balance at 1 July 2014	3,300,000	720,000	4,020,000
Total comprehensive income for the year	–	456,000	456,000
Dividends paid and declared	–	(385,000)	(385,000)
Balance at 30 June 2015	3,300,000	791,000	4,091,000

Medium plc: Statement of changes in equity for the year ending 30 June 2015

	Share capital (£)	Retained earnings (£)	Total equity (£)
Balance at 1 July 2014	560,000	480,000	1,040,000
Total comprehensive income for the year	–	168,000	168,000
Dividends paid and declared	–	(90,000)	(90,000)
Balance at 30 June 2015	560,000	558,000	1,118,000

Small plc: Statement of changes in equity for the year ending 30 June 2015

	Contributed equity (£)	Retained earnings (£)	Total equity (£)
Balance at 1 July 2014	160,000	670,000	830,000
Total comprehensive income for the year	–	192,000	192,000
Dividends paid and declared	–	(110,000)	(110,000)
Balance at 30 June 2015	160,000	752,000	912,000

Required

Prepare a consolidated statement of comprehensive income, a consolidated statement of financial position and a consolidated statement of changes in equity for the year ended 30 June 2015.

Solution

As we know from previous chapters, there are a number of steps to take. We need to:

1. provide the consolidation worksheet journal entries;
2. calculate non-controlling interests;
3. post the consolidation journal entries to the worksheet; and
4. prepare the consolidated financial statements from the consolidation worksheet and utilise the calculation of non-controlling interests to disclose the non-controlling interests' contribution to profits, and the non-controlling interests in share capital and reserves.

Consolidation worksheet journal entries

Recognition of the fair value adjustment

At the date of Medium plc's acquisition of Small plc the carrying amount of the factory buildings was less than their fair value. So that we can correctly calculate goodwill on acquisition, we must put through a revaluation adjustment as at the date of acquisition before we eliminate the investment against the pre-acquisition capital and reserves of the acquired subsidiary. As we explained in Chapter 15, when an entity revalues its non-current assets a tax effect is created, which needs to be recognised in accordance with IAS 12 *Income Taxes*.

(a) Dr Factory buildings (£416,000 – £360,000)   £56,000
    Dr Accumulated depreciation (to close off balance before revaluation) £72,000
    Cr Revaluation surplus   £128,000

(b) Dr Revaluation surplus   £38,400
    Cr Deferred tax liability (£128,000 × 0.3)   £38,400

Adjusting the carrying amount of the buildings will have implications for depreciation expense. The depreciation expense will be based on the revised measure. Because the subsidiary was acquired four years ago, and the fair value adjustment was initially made four years ago, then four years' adjustment to depreciation must be made. Three years' depreciation will be adjusted against opening retained earnings.

(c) Dr Depreciation expense (£128,000/16 for the current year)   £8,000
    Dr Retained earnings—1 July 2014
        (£128,000/16 × 3 for the previous 3 years)   £24,000
    Cr Accumulated depreciation (£128,000/16 × 4 years)   £32,000

(d) Dr Deferred tax liability (£32,000 × 0.3)   £9,600
    Cr Income tax expense (£8,000 × 0.3 for the current year)   £2,400
    Cr Retained earnings—1 July 2014 (£24,000 × 0.3 for the previous 3 years)   £7,200

Elimination of the fair value of consideration transferred and recognition of goodwill

Because the non-controlling interest in Medium plc at acquisition is to be measured at fair value, this means goodwill will be attributed to the non-controlling interest in Medium plc.

Elimination of investment in Medium plc	Medium plc (£)	Big plc's 70% interest (£)	30% non-controlling interest (£)
Fair value of consideration transferred	660,000	660,000	
plus Non-controlling interest at fair value (£660,000 × 30/70)	282,857		
	942,857		
less Fair value of identifiable assets acquired and liabilities assumed			
Share capital on acquisition date	560,000	392,000	168,000
Retained earnings on acquisition date	240,000	168,000	72,000
	800,000	560,000	
Goodwill on acquisition date	142,857	100,000	42,857
Non-controlling interest on acquisition date			282,857

(e) *Elimination of investment in Small plc*
Because the non-controlling interest in Small plc at acquisition is to be measured at the proportionate share of the fair value of the identifiable net assets of Small plc, this means no goodwill will be attributed to the non-controlling interest in Medium plc.

	Small plc (£)	Medium plc's 60% interest (£)	40% non-controlling interest (£)
Fair value of consideration transferred		420,000	
less Fair value of identifiable assets acquired and liabilities assumed			
Share capital on acquisition date	160,000	96,000	64,000
Retained earnings on acquisition date	320,000	192,000	128,000
Revaluation surplus on acquisition date	89,600	53,760	35,840
	569,600	341,760	
Goodwill on acquisition date		78,240	
Non-controlling interest at date of acquisition			227,840

Dr Share capital		£392,000	
Dr Retained earnings—1 July 2014		£168,000	
Dr Goodwill		£100,000	
Cr Investment in Medium plc			£660,000

(f)
Dr Share capital		£96,000	
Dr Retained earnings—1 July 2014		£192,000	
Dr Revaluation surplus		£53,760	
Dr Goodwill		£78,240	
Cr Investment in Small plc			£420,000

(g) *Impairment of goodwill (relating to purchase of Small plc by Medium plc)*
Dr Retained earnings—1 July 2014 (previous years' accumulated impairment)		£38,240	
Cr Accumulated impairment losses—goodwill			£38,240

(h)
Dr Impairment loss—goodwill (the impairment loss recognised in 2012)		£5,000	
Cr Accumulated impairment losses—goodwill			£5,000

(i) *Impairment of goodwill in 2012 (relating to purchase of Medium plc by Big plc)*
Dr Impairment loss—goodwill (£142,857 − £110,000)		£32,857	
Cr Accumulated impairment losses—goodwill			£32,857

(j) *Elimination of intercompany sales*
As part of the consolidation adjustments and eliminations we need to eliminate the intragroup sales because, from the perspective of the economic entity, no sales have in fact occurred. This will ensure that we do not over-state the turnover of the economic entity.

Sale of inventory from Small plc to Big plc

Dr	Sales revenue	£2,000,000
Cr	Cost of goods sold	£2,000,000

Under the periodic inventory system, the above credit entry would be to purchases, which would ultimately lead to a reduction in cost of goods sold.

(k) *Elimination of unrealised profit in closing inventory*

In this case, the unrealised profit in closing inventory amounts to £140,000, which represents the profit on the total sales multiplied by the proportion of sales still on hand, that is, (£2,000,000 – £1,600,000) × 35 per cent. In accordance with IAS 2 *Inventories*, we must value the inventory at the *lower of cost and net realisable value*. Hence on consolidation we must reduce the value of recorded inventory, as the amount shown in the financial statements of Big plc exceeds what the inventory cost the economic entity.

Dr	Cost of goods sold	£140,000
Cr	Inventory	£140,000

Under the periodic inventory system, the above debit entry would be to closing inventory—profit and loss. We increase cost of goods sold by the unrealised profit in closing inventory because reducing closing inventory effectively increases cost of goods sold. The effect of the above entries is to adjust the value of inventory so that it reflects the cost of the inventory to the group.

(l) *Consideration of the tax paid or payable on the sale of inventory that is still held within the group*

From the group's perspective, £140,000 has not been earned. However, from Small plc's individual perspective (as a separate legal entity), the full amount of the sale has been earned. This will attract a tax liability in Small plc's financial statements of £42,000 (30 per cent of £140,000). However, from the group's perspective, some of this will represent a prepayment of tax, as the full amount has not been earned by the group even if Small plc is obliged to pay the tax.

Dr	Deferred tax asset	£42,000
Cr	Income tax expense (£140,000 × 30 per cent)	£42,000

(m) *Unrealised profit in opening inventory*

At the end of the preceding financial year, Small plc had £570,000 of inventory on hand, which had been purchased from Medium plc. The inventory had cost Medium plc £490,000 to produce.

Dr	Retained earnings—1 July 2014	£56,000
Dr	Income tax expense	£24,000
Cr	Cost of sales	£80,000

Adjustments for intragroup sale of factory building

On 30 June 2015, Big plc sold a factory building to Medium plc for £800,000 when its carrying value in Big plc's financial statements was £630,000 (cost of £900,000, accumulated depreciation of £270,000). The building was being depreciated over a further 14 years, with no expected residual value.

(n) *Reversal of gain recognised on sale of asset and reinstatement of cost and accumulated depreciation*

The result of the sale of the factory building to Medium plc is that the profit of £170,000—the difference between the sales proceeds of £800,000 and the carrying amount of £630,000—will be shown in Big plc's financial statements. However, from the economic entity's perspective there has been no sale and, therefore, no gain on sale given that there has been no transaction with a party external to the group. The following entry is necessary so that the financial statements will reflect the balances that would have applied had the intragroup sale not occurred.

Dr	Gain on sale of building	£170,000
Dr	Building	£100,000
Cr	Accumulated depreciation	£270,000

The result of this entry is that the intragroup profit is removed and the asset and accumulated depreciation account reverts to reflecting no sales transaction. The profit of £170,000 will be recognised progressively in the consolidated financial statements of the economic entity by adjustments to the amounts of depreciation charged by Medium plc in its financial statements. As the service potential or economic benefits embodied in the asset are consumed, the £170,000 profit will be progressively recognised from the economic entity's perspective.

(o) *Impact of tax on gain on sale of factory building*

From Big plc's individual perspective it would have made a profit of £170,000 on the sale of the building and this gain would have been taxable. At a tax rate of 30 per cent, £51,000 would be payable by Big plc. However, from the economic entity's perspective, no gain has been made, which means that the related 'tax expense' must be reversed and a related deferred tax benefit be recognised. A deferred tax asset is recognised because, from the economic entity's perspective, the amount paid to the taxation authorities represents a prepayment of tax.

Dr	Deferred tax asset	£51,000	
Cr	Income tax expense		£51,000

As the sale of the factory building occurred on consolidation date, there are no consolidation worksheet journal entries required to adjust the depreciation of the factory building.

Dividends paid and declared
We eliminate the dividends paid and payable within the group. Only the dividends paid and payable to parties outside the entity (to the investors in the parent entity and to the direct non-controlling interests) are to be shown in the consolidated financial statements.

(p) *Elimination of interim dividend (paid by Small plc to Medium plc)*

Dr	Dividend revenue (£110,000 × 0.6)	£66,000	
Cr	Interim dividend		£66,000

(q) *Elimination of final dividend (declared by Medium plc to Big plc)*

Dr	Dividend revenue (£90,000 × 0.7)	£63,000	
Cr	Final dividend		£63,000

(r) *Elimination of intragroup debt: Big plc's share of Medium plc's declared final dividend*

Dr	Dividend payable (£90,000 × 0.7)	£63,000	
Cr	Dividend receivable		£63,000

Having completed the consolidation adjustments and eliminations, we can now calculate the non-controlling interests in current period's profits and in share capital and reserves. We will need to consider direct and indirect ownership interests. These are reflected in the figure below and then summarised in the table.

Group structure of Big plc and its controlled entities

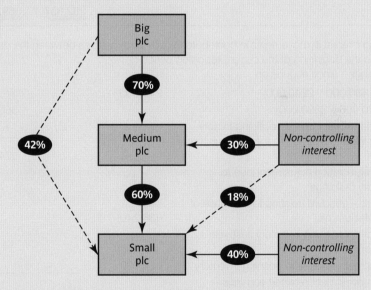

Calculation of direct and indirect interests in Medium plc and Small plc:

	Medium plc (%)	Small plc (%)
Parent entity interest		
Direct	70	–
Indirect [0.70 × 0.60]	–	42
Non-controlling interest		
Direct	30	40
Indirect [0.30 × 0.60]	–	18
	100	100

Recognising non-controlling interest in share capital, reserves and earnings

It must be remembered that, in order to recognise the non-controlling interest's share in share capital and reserves at the end of the reporting period, three calculations need to be made:

(i) The non-controlling interests on acquisition date.

(ii) The non-controlling interest in movements in contributed equity and reserves between the date of the parent entity's acquisition and the beginning of the current reporting period.

(iii) The non-controlling interest in the current period's profit, as well as movements in reserves in the current period. In determining the non-controlling interest's share of current period profit or loss, gains and losses of the subsidiary that are unrealised from the economic entity's perspective will need to be adjusted for.

As we also know, where the non-controlling interest at acquisition date is to be valued at fair value, then goodwill will be attributed to the non-controlling interest. We also need to apply the general rules about which legal entity should be allocated amounts attributable to any goodwill impairment.

Calculation of non-controlling interests in Medium plc and Small plc	Medium plc (£)	30% non-controlling interest (£)	Small plc (£)	40% non-controlling interest (£)
(i) Non-controlling interests on acquisition date				
Share capital on acquisition date	560,000	168,000	160,000	64,000
Retained earnings on acquisition date	240,000	72,000	320,000	128,000
	800,000			
Revaluation surplus on acquisition date	–	–	89,600	35,840
Goodwill		42,857	–	–
		282,857	569,600	227,840

(ii) Non-controlling interest in movements in contributed equity and reserves between the date of the parent entity's acquisition and the beginning of the current reporting period
Retained earnings — since acquisition

Medium plc (£480,000 – £240,000)	240,000			
Small plc (£670,000 – £320,000)			350,000	
Depreciation adjustment due to revaluing factory building to fair value (in relation to the previous three years)			(24,000)	
Tax effect of depreciation adjustment due to revaluing factory buildings			7,200	
Impairment loss — goodwill (relating to purchase of Small plc by Medium plc)	(38,240)		–	
Unrealised profit in opening inventory (last year's closing inventory)	(80,000)		–	
Tax effect of unrealised profit in opening inventory	24,000	–	–	–
Adjusted post-investment retained earnings — 1 July 2014	145,760	43,728	333,200	133,280

(iii) Non-controlling interest in the current period's profit and movements in reserves in the current period

Profit for the year	168,000		192,000	
Adjustment relating to inventory				
Unrealised profit in opening inventory	80,000			

Calculation of non-controlling interests in Medium plc and Small plc	Medium plc (£)	30% non-controlling interest (£)	Small plc (£)	40% non-controlling interest (£)
Tax effect of unrealised profit in opening inventory	(24,000)			
Unrealised profit in closing inventory			(140,000)	
Tax effect of unrealised profit in closing inventory			42,000	
Fair value adjustment				
Depreciation adjustment due to revaluing factory buildings to fair value			(8,000)	
Tax effect of depreciation adjustment due to revaluing factory buildings			2,400	
Intragroup dividends				
Dividend revenue from within the group (paid by Small plc to Medium plc)	(66,000)			
Goodwill impairment in organisation controlled by intermediate subsidiary	(5,000)			
Goodwill impairment—2015	(32,857)	–	–	–
Adjusted profit for the year	120,143	36,043	88,400	35,360
Dividends paid and declared	(90,000)	(27,000)	(110,000)	(44,000)
		335,628		352,480

(s) *Recognising non-controlling interest in contributed equity, reserves and earnings in Medium plc*

Dr	Share capital	£168,000	
Dr	Retained earnings—1 July 2014 (£72,000 + £43,728)	£115,728	
Dr	Goodwill	£42,857	
Dr	Non-controlling interest in earnings	£36,043	
Cr	Final dividend		£27,000
Cr	Non-controlling interest		£335,628

(t) *Recognising non-controlling interest in contributed equity, reserves and earnings in Small plc*

Dr	Share capital	£64,000	
Dr	Retained earnings—1 July 2014 (£128,000 + £133,280)	£261,280	
Dr	Revaluation surplus	£35,840	
Dr	Non-controlling interest in earnings	£35,360	
Cr	Interim dividend		£44,000
Cr	Non-controlling interest		£352,480

(u) *Indirect non-controlling interest in Small plc*
This entry recognised the indirect non-controlling interest in Small plc

Calculation of indirect non-controlling interest in Small plc	Small plc (£)	18% indirect non-controlling interest (£)
Indirect non-controlling interest in movements in share capital and reserves between the date of the parent entity's acquisition and the beginning of the current reporting period	333,200	59,976
Indirect non-controlling interest in the current period's profit for the year	88,400	15,912
	421,600	75,888

Dr	Retained earnings—1 July 2014	£59,976	
Dr	Non-controlling interest in earnings	£15,912	
Cr	Non-controlling interest		£75,888

Recognising indirect non-controlling interest in earnings of Small plc

Looking at the above calculations, it can be seen that they are the same form of adjustments as were made in Chapter 22, which concentrated on non-controlling interests. The only difference is that an adjustment has been made for the dividends received by Medium plc from Small plc, and adjustments have also been made for the impairment loss pertaining to the goodwill acquired in Small plc (which is adjusted against the profits of Medium plc, as Medium plc acquired the goodwill in Small plc). Explanations for these adjustments were provided in Worked Example 23.1.

A review of the above calculations reinforces the following:

- Pre-acquisition balances of reserves (in this example, retained earnings and revaluation surplus) are allocated on the basis of direct ownership interests only.
- Post-acquisition movements in reserves are allocated on the basis of the sum of direct and indirect ownership interests.
- Current period profits are allocated using the sum of direct and indirect ownership interests.
- Dividends are allocated on the basis of direct ownership interests only.

Consolidation worksheet as at 30 June 2015

	Big plc	Medium plc	Small plc	Eliminations and adjustments Dr	Eliminations and adjustments Cr	Consolidated
Sales	7,500,000	4,000,000	3,500,000	2,000,000(j)		13,000,000
Cost of goods sold	6,100,000	3,260,000	2,900,000	140,000(k)	2,000,000(j) 80,000(m)	10,320,000
Gross profit	1,400,000	740,000	600,000			2,680,000
Depreciation expense	(130,000)	(50,000)	(18,000)	8,000(c) 5,000(h)		(206,000)
	–	–	–			
Impairment loss—goodwill				32,857(i)		(37,857)
Other expenses	(743,000)	(476,000)	(262,000)			(1,481,000)
Dividend revenue	63,000	66,000	–	66,000(p) 63,000(q)		–
Gain on sale of factory	170,000	–	–	170,000(n)		–
Profit before tax	760,000	280,000	320,000			955,143
Income tax expense	(304,000)	(112,000)	(128,000)	24,000(m)	2,400(d) 42,000(l) 51,000(o)	(472,600)
Profit after tax	456,000	168,000	192,000			482,543
Non-controlling interest in earnings				36,043(s) 35,360(t) 15,912(u)		(87,315)
Retained earnings— 1 July 2014	720,000	480,000	670,000	24,000(c) 192,000(f) 38,240(g) 168,000(e) 56,000(m) 115,728(s) 261,280(t) 59,976(u)	7,200(d)	961,976
						1,357,204
Interim dividend	(125,000)	–	(110,000)		66,000(p) 44,000(t)	(125,000)
Final dividend	(260,000)	(90,000)	–		63,000(q) 27,000(s)	(260,000)
Retained earnings— 30 June 2015	791,000	558,000	752,000			972,204
Share capital	3,300,000	560,000	160,000	96,000(f) 392,000(e) 168,000(s) 64,000(t)		3,300,000

	Big plc	Medium plc	Small plc	Eliminations and adjustments Dr	Eliminations and adjustments Cr	Consolidated
Revaluation surplus	–	–	–	38,400(b) 53,760(f) 35,840(t)	128,000(a) ⎫ ⎬ ⎭	–
Non-controlling interest					335,628(s) ⎫ 352,480(t) ⎬ 75,888(u) ⎭	763,996
Total shareholders' equity	4,091,000	1,118,000	912,000			5,036,200
Accounts payable	910,000	715,000	319,000			1,944,000
Dividends payable	260,000	90,000	–	63,000(r)		287,000
Deferred tax liability	–	–	–	9,600(d)	38,400(b)	28,800
Total equity and liabilities	5,261,000	1,923,000	1,231,000			7,296,000
Cash	76,000	6,000	37,000			119,000
Accounts receivable	172,000	52,000	68,000			292,000
Dividends receivable	63,000	–	–		63,000(r)	–
Inventory	1,100,000	440,000	700,000		140,000(k)	2,100,000
Land	720,000	105,000	210,000			1,035,000
Factory buildings	2,600,000	1,800,000	360,000	56,000(a) 100,000(n)	⎫ ⎬ ⎭	4,916,000
Accum. depreciation	(130,000)	(900,000)	(144,000)	72,000(a)	32,000(c) ⎫ 270,000(n) ⎭	(1,404,000)
Investment in Medium plc	660,000	–	–		660,000(e)	–
Investment in Small plc	–	420,000	–		420,000(f)	–
Goodwill	–	–	–	78,240(f) 100,000(e) 42,857(s)	⎫ ⎬ ⎭	221,097
Accum. impairment loss					38,240(g) ⎫ 5,000(h) ⎬ 32,857(i) ⎭	(76,097)
Deferred tax asset	–	–	–	42,000(l) 51,000(o)	⎫ ⎬ ⎭	93,000
Total assets	5,261,000	1,923,000	1,231,000	4,974,093	4,974,093	7,296,000

We can now prepare the consolidated financial statements.

Consolidated statement of comprehensive income of Big plc and its subsidiaries for the year ended 30 June 2015

	The Group (£)	Big plc (£)
Sales revenue	13,000,000	7,500,000
Cost of goods sold	(10,320,000)	(6,100,000)
Gross profit	2,680,000	1,400,000
Depreciation expense	(206,000)	(130,000)
Impairment loss—goodwill	(37,857)	–
Dividend revenue	–	63,000
Gain on sale of factory	–	170,000
Other expenses	(1,481,000)	(743,000)
Profit before income tax expense	955,143	760,000
Income tax expense	(472,600)	(304,000)
Profit after income tax expense	482,543	456,000
Other comprehensive income	–	–
Total comprehensive income	482,543	456,000
Profit after income tax attributable to non-controlling interest	87,315	
Profit after income tax attributable to parent entity interest	395,228	
	482,543	

Big plc and its controlled entities: Consolidated statement of changes in equity for the year ending 30 June 2015

	Attributable to owners of the parent				
	Share capital (£)	Retained earnings (£)	Total (£)	Non-controlling interest (£)	Total equity (£)
Balance at 1 July 2014	3,300,000	961,976	4,261,976	747,681	5,009,657
Total comprehensive income for the year	–	395,228	395,228	87,315	482,543
Dividends	–	(385,000)	(385,000)	(71,000)	(456,000)
Balance at 30 June 2015	3,300,000	972,204	4,272,204	763,996	5,036,200

Big plc: Statement of changes in equity for the year ending 30 June 2015

	Share capital (£)	Retained earnings (£)	Total equity (£)
Balance at 1 July 2014	3,300,000	720,000	4,020,000
Total comprehensive income for the year	–	456,000	456,000
Distributions—interim dividend	–	(125,000)	(125,000)
Distributions—final dividend	–	(260,000)	(260,000)
Balance at 30 June 2015	3,300,000	791,000	4,091,000

Consolidated statement of financial position of Big plc and its subsidiaries as at 30 June 2015

	The Group (£)	Big plc (£)
ASSETS		
Non-current assets		
Land	1,035,000	720,000
Factory buildings	4,916,000	2,600,000
Accumulated depreciation	(1,404,000)	(130,000)
Goodwill	221,097	–
Accumulated impairment losses	(76,097)	–
Investment in Medium plc	–	660,000
Deferred tax asset	93,000	–
Total non-current assets	4,785,000	3,850,000
Current assets		
Inventory	2,100,000	1,100,000
Dividends receivable	–	63,000
Accounts receivable	292,000	172,000
Cash	119,000	76,000
Total current assets	2,511,000	1,411,000
Total assets	7,296,000	5,261,000
EQUITY AND LIABILITIES		
Equity and reserves		
Share capital	3,300,000	3,300,000
Retained earnings	972,204	791,000
Parent entity interest	4,272,204	4,091,000
Non-controlling interest	763,996	–
Total equity and reserves	5,036,200	4,091,000
Non-current liabilities		
Deferred tax liability	28,800	–
Current liabilities		
Accounts payable	1,944,000	910,000
Dividends payable	287,000	260,000
	2,231,000	1,170,000
Total liabilities	2,259,800	1,170,000
Total equity and liabilities	7,296,000	5,261,000

In the examples provided so far in this chapter the acquisitions have all occurred on the same date. That is, the ultimate parent entity acquired the intermediate subsidiary at the same time as the intermediate subsidiary acquired the controlling interest in the other entity. The next section will consider the situation where the acquisitions occur on different dates.

23.3 Sequential and non-sequential acquisitions

Although up to now it has suited our purposes to confine our examples to cases in which all acquisitions occur on the same date, this will not always be the case in practice. Acquisitions could also occur in the following ways:

■ The parent acquires its interest in the intermediate subsidiary *before* the intermediate subsidiary acquires its interest in the other subsidiary (this is referred to as sequential acquisition and is represented in Figure 23.3).

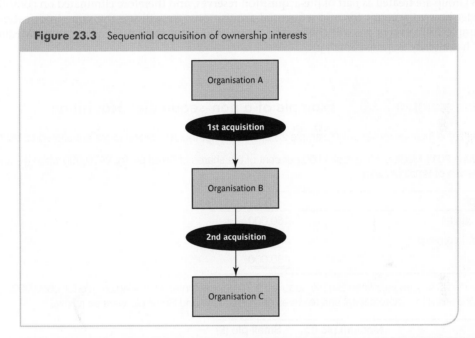

Figure 23.3 Sequential acquisition of ownership interests

■ The parent acquires its interest in the intermediate subsidiary *after* the intermediate subsidiary acquires its interest in the other subsidiary (this is referred to as non-sequential acquisition and is represented in Figure 23.4).

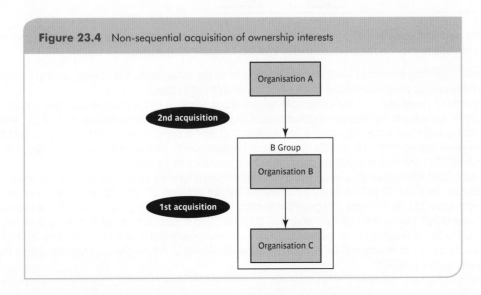

Figure 23.4 Non-sequential acquisition of ownership interests

In a sequential acquisition, as depicted in Figure 23.3, the consolidated financial statements will be accounted for in the same manner as when acquisitions occur simultaneously. Since we have considered simultaneous acquisitions up to now in this book, we will have no trouble accounting for sequential transactions.

Figure 23.4 depicts a non-sequential acquisition—the situation where by the parent entity acquires its control of the intermediate subsidiary *after* the intermediate subsidiary acquired its interest in another subsidiary. Effectively, what is happening is that the ultimate parent entity—which we will refer to as Organisation A—is acquiring an interest in the B Group, rather than solely in Organisation B. Hence, in determining the fair value of the assets acquired in Organisation B, which is necessary for our consolidation entry that eliminates the investment in Organisation B against the pre-acquisition capital and reserves of Organisation B, we need to consider the value of both Organisation B and Organisation C. The value of Organisation B's investment in Organisation C will be affected by post-acquisition profits and reserve movements in Organisation C. Therefore, Organisation A's investment in Organisation B must be eliminated against Organisation A's share of the owners' equity of the B Group (Organisation B plus Organisation C) as at the date of Organisation A's investment. The profits earned by Organisation C, after Organisation B acquired its interest in Organisation C, but prior to Organisation A's acquisition of the B Group are treated as part of pre-acquisition reserves, and therefore eliminated on consolidation.

To consider how to account for non-sequential acquisitions, we will use the same information as that in Worked Example 23.2, except we will change the acquisition dates so that Big plc acquires Medium plc after Medium plc has already acquired Small plc.

Worked Example 23.3   Example of a non-sequential acquisition

Assume the same facts as for Worked Example 23.2, except that the acquisition dates are altered as follows:

■ On 30 June 2011 Medium plc acquired 60 per cent of the shares of Small plc for £420,000 when the share capital and reserves of Small plc were:

Small plc	(£)
Share capital	160,000
Retained earnings	320,000
	480,000

■ On 30 June 2012 (one year later) Big plc acquired a 70 per cent interest in Medium plc for £660,000. At 30 June 2012 the share capital and reserves of Medium plc and Small plc were as follows:

	Medium plc (£)	Small plc (£)
Share capital	560,000	160,000
Retained earnings	340,000	370,000
	900,000	530,000

The amounts paid for the equity in Big plc and Medium plc represented the fair value of consideration transferred. The remaining information below is the same as that in Worked Example 23.2 above.

(i) Any non-controlling interest in Medium plc is measured at fair value, while the non-controlling interest in Small plc is measured at the proportionate share of its identifiable net assets.

(ii) At the date of investment, all the identifiable net assets of Medium plc and Small plc were considered to be recorded at fair value in the respective statements of financial position of Medium plc and Small plc, except Small plc's factory buildings, which had a fair value of £416,000, and a carrying value of £288,000 (cost of £360,000, accumulated depreciation of £72,000). Small plc did not revalue its factory buildings at the date of investment. At 30 June 2011 the factory buildings had a remaining useful life of 16 years.

(iii) On 1 June 2014 the recoverable amount of the goodwill relating to the purchase of Small plc by Medium plc was assessed to be £40,000 (reflecting an accumulated impairment loss of £38,240, as will be seen shortly). This impairment loss of £38,240 was recognised in the first year following acquisition, that is, in the reporting period to 30 June 2012. During the reporting period to 30 June 2015 it was considered that the goodwill in Small plc had been further impaired by an amount of £5,000 to provide a recoverable amount at 30 June 2015 of £35,000.

(iv) On 30 June 2015 the recoverable amount of the goodwill relating to the purchase of Medium plc by Big plc was assessed to be £110,000.

▶

(v) During the 2015 reporting period Small plc sold goods to Big plc for £2,000,000. These goods had originally cost Small plc £1,600,000. On 30 June 2015, 35 per cent of these goods remained in Big plc's closing inventory.

(vi) Small plc's opening inventory included goods purchased from Medium plc for £570,000. These goods had originally cost Medium plc £490,000.

(vii) On 30 June 2015 Big plc sold a factory building to Medium plc for £800,000. Big plc had originally purchased the factory building for £900,000, on 1 July 2009. The original estimated useful life of the factory building was 20 years.

(viii) On 31 December 2014 Big plc paid an interim dividend of £125,000, while Small plc paid an interim dividend of £110,000.

(ix) On 30 June 2015 Big plc declared a final dividend of £260,000, while Medium plc declared a final dividend of £90,000. The decision to pay these dividends was communicated to shareholders on that date.

(x) The income tax rate is 30 per cent.

The financial statements of Big plc, Medium plc and Small plc revealed the following balances at 30 June 2015.

Big plc, Medium plc and Small plc
Statements of comprehensive income for the year ended 30 June 2015

	Big plc (£)	Medium plc (£)	Small plc (£)
Sales revenue	7,500,000	4,000,000	3,500,000
Cost of goods sold	(6,100,000)	(3,260,000)	(2,900,000)
Gross profit	1,400,000	740,000	600,000
Depreciation expense	(130,000)	(50,000)	(18,000)
Other expenses	(743,000)	(476,000)	(262,000)
Dividend revenue	63,000	66,000	–
Gain on sale of factory building	170,000	–	–
Profit before tax	760,000	280,000	320,000
Income tax expense	(304,000)	(112,000)	(128,000)
Profit for the year	456,000	168,000	192,000

Big plc, Medium plc and Small plc: Statements of financial position at 30 June 2015

	Big plc (£)	Medium plc (£)	Small plc (£)
ASSETS			
Non-current assets			
Land	720,000	105,000	210,000
Factory buildings	2,600,000	1,800,000	360,000
Accumulated depreciation	(130,000)	(900,000)	(144,000)
Investment in Medium plc	660,000	–	–
Investment in Small plc	–	420,000	–
	3,850,000	1,425,000	426,000
Current assets			
Inventory	1,100,000	440,000	700,000
Accounts receivable	172,000	52,000	68,000
Dividends receivable	63,000	–	–
Cash	76,000	6,000	37,000
	1,411,000	498,000	805,000
Total assets	5,261,000	1,923,000	1,231,000
EQUITY AND LIABILITIES			
Equity and reserves			
Share capital	3,300,000	560,000	160,000
Retained earnings	791,000	558,000	752,000
	4,091,000	1,118,000	912,000
Liabilities			
Accounts payable	910,000	715,000	319,000
Dividends payable	260,000	90,000	–
	1,170,000	805,000	319,000
Total equity and liabilities	5,261,000	1,923,000	1,231,000

Big plc: Statement of changes in equity for the year ending 30 June 2015

	Share capital (£)	Retained earnings (£)	Total (£)
Balance at 1 July 2014	3,300,000	720,000	4,020,000
Total comprehensive income for the year	–	456,000	456,000
Distributions paid and declared	–	(385,000)	(385,000)
Balance at 30 June 2015	3,300,000	791,000	4,091,000

Medium plc: Statement of changes in equity for the year ending 30 June 2015

	Share capital (£)	Retained earnings (£)	Total (£)
Balance at 1 July 2014	560,000	480,000	1,040,000
Total comprehensive income for the year	–	168,000	168,000
Distributions paid and declared	–	(90,000)	(90,000)
Balance at 30 June 2015	560,000	558,000	1,118,000

Small plc: Statement of changes in equity for the year ending 30 June 2015

	Contributed equity (£)	Retained earnings (£)	Total (£)
Balance at 1 July 2014	160,000	670,000	830,000
Total comprehensive income for the year	–	192,000	192,000
Distributions paid and declared	–	(110,000)	(110,000)
Balance at 30 June 2015	160,000	752,000	912,000

Required

Prepare a consolidated statement of comprehensive income, a consolidated statement of financial position and a consolidated statement of changes in equity for Big plc and its controlled entities as at 30 June 2015.

Solution

The consolidation journal entries required to revalue the building of Small plc at the date of Medium plc's acquisition (the same date as that used in Worked Example 23.2) will be the same as those provided at entries (a) to (d). The consolidation journal entry required to eliminate Medium plc's investment in Small plc is the same as provided in entry (f), while the entry to recognise the impairment loss will be the same as provided in entries (m) and (n). As a number of entries are the same as those in Worked Example 23.2 above, the explanations are not repeated here. However, explanations are provided in relation to the elimination of Big plc's investment in Medium plc.

(a) *Revaluation of factory balance to fair value*

Dr Factory buildings (£416,000 – £360,000)	£56,000	
Dr Accumulated depreciation (to close off balance before revaluation)	£72,000	
Cr Revaluation surplus		£128,000

(b) *Deferred tax liability arising on revaluation of factory building*

Dr Revaluation surplus	£38,400	
Cr Deferred tax liability (£128,000 × 0.30)		£38,400

(c) *Recognition of additional depreciation expense for the current reporting period and accumulated depreciation for previous three reporting periods*

Dr Depreciation expense (£128,000/16 for the current year)	£8,000	
Dr Retained earnings—1 July 2014 (£128,000/16 × 3 for the previous 3 years)	£24,000	
Cr Accumulated depreciation (£128,000/16 × 4 years)		£32,000

(d) *Adjustments to current tax expense and deferred tax liability arising from additional depreciation expense*

Dr Deferred tax liability (£32,000 × 0.3)	£9,600	
Cr Income tax expense (£8,000 × 0.3 for the current year)		£2,400
Cr Retained earnings—1 July 2014 (£24,000 × 0.3 for the previous 3 years)		£7,200

◀

Eliminate investment in Medium plc against Big plc's share of Medium plc's owners' equity on acquisition date
Of critical importance in this worked example is how any goodwill or bargain purchase on acquisition is measured in relation to Big plc's acquisition of the economic entity, Medium plc and its controlled entity (Small plc). It should be noted that, in calculating the goodwill or the bargain gain on the purchase associated with Big plc's acquisition of Medium plc and its subsidiary, Big plc has acquired interests in the net assets of the whole economic entity, not only of Medium plc. In other words, Big plc has acquired an interest in the net assets of the economic entity attributable to the owners of Medium plc.

Big plc's acquisition of the economic entity (Medium plc and its controlled entity, Small plc) comprises:

- seventy per cent of the equity (contributed capital and reserves) of Medium plc; and
- sixty per cent of the post-acquisition reserves of Small plc from the date of Medium plc's acquisition of Small plc to the date of Big plc's acquisition of Medium plc.

Calculation of non-controlling interests in Medium plc

	Medium plc (£)	Big plc's 70% interest (£)	30% non-controlling interest (£)
Fair value of consideration transferred	660,000	660,000	
plus Non-controlling interest at fair value			
(£660,000 × 30/70)	282,857		
	942,857		
less Fair value of identifiable assets acquired and liabilities assumed			
Share capital on acquisition date	560,000	392,000	168,000
Retained earnings on acquisition date	340,000	238,000	102,000
	900,000	630,000	
Share of post-acquisition retained earnings of Small plc attributable to Medium plc prior to Big plc's acquisition of Medium plc			
Increase in retained earnings of Small plc from 30 June 2008 to 30 June 2012 = (£370,000 – £320,000) × 60 per cent	30,000	21,000	9,000
Goodwill impairment in Small plc to 30 June 2012	(38,240)	(26,768)	(11,472)
	891,760	624,232	267,528
Goodwill on acquisition date	51,097	35,768	15,329
Non-controlling interest on acquisition date			282,857

(e) *Eliminating Big plc's investment in Medium plc and recognition of goodwill*

Dr	Share capital	£392,000	
Dr	Retained earnings (Medium plc)—1 July 2014	£238,000	
Dr	Goodwill	£35,768	
Cr	Retained earnings (Small plc)—1 July 2014		£5,768
Cr	Investment in Medium plc		£660,000

(f) *Eliminating Medium plc's investment in Small plc and recognition of goodwill*

Dr	Share capital	£96,000	
Dr	Retained earnings—1 July 2014	£192,000	
Dr	Revaluation surplus	£53,760	
Dr	Goodwill	£78,240	
Cr	Investment in Small plc		£420,000

Eliminating intragroup sales of inventory

(g) *Elimination of intragroup sales inventory from Small plc to Big plc*

Dr	Sales revenue	£2,000,000	
Cr	Cost of goods sold		£2,000,000

(h) *Elimination of unrealised profit in closing inventory*

Dr	Cost of goods sold	£140,000	
Cr	Inventory (statement of financial position)		£140,000

(i) *Consideration of the tax paid or payable on the sale of inventory that is still held within the group*

Dr	Deferred tax asset	£42,000	
Cr	Income tax expense		£42,000

(recognising tax effect on unrealised profit in inventory (£140,000 × 30 per cent))

▶

(j) *Unrealised profit in opening inventory*

Dr	Retained earnings—1 July 2014	£56,000	
Dr	Income tax expense	£24,000	
Cr	Cost of goods sold		£80,000

Eliminating intragroup sale of non-current asset and associated depreciation adjustments

(k) *Reversal of gain recognised on sale of asset and reinstatement of cost and accumulated depreciation*

Dr	Gain on sale of building	£170,000	
Dr	Factory building	£100,000	
Cr	Accumulated depreciation		£270,000

(l) *Impact of tax on gain on sale of factory building*

Dr	Deferred tax asset	£51,000	
Cr	Income tax expense		£51,000

Recognise impairment of goodwill (relating to purchase of Small plc by Medium plc)

(m) *Impairment of goodwill in prior periods*

Dr	Retained earnings—1 July 2014 (previous years' accumulated impairment)	£38,240	
Cr	Accumulated impairment loss—goodwill		£38,240

(n) *Impairment of goodwill in current period*

Dr	Impairment loss—goodwill (the impairment loss recognised in 2015)	£5,000	
Cr	Accumulated impairment loss—goodwill		£5,000

As Medium plc valued the non-controlling interest at the proportionate share of Small plc's identifiable assets, there is no necessity to allocate any goodwill impairment expense between the parent and the non-controlling interest either in the current or previous reporting periods.

In the previous worked example, an impairment loss on the goodwill acquired by Big plc in Medium plc was recognised because the carrying amount of goodwill was greater than its recoverable amount. However, in this example, because the recoverable amount of goodwill at 30 June 2015 is deemed to be £110,000, which is greater than its carrying amount, no consolidation entry is required to recognise an impairment loss.

Dividends paid and declared

(o) *Elimination of interim dividend (paid by Small plc to Medium plc)*

Dr	Dividend revenue (£110,000 × 0.60)	£66,000	
Cr	Interim dividend		£66,000

(p) *Elimination of final dividend (declared by Medium plc to Big plc)*

Dr	Dividend revenue (£90,000 × 0.7)	£63,000	
Cr	Final dividend		£63,000

(q) *Elimination of intragroup debt: Big plc's share of Medium plc's declared final dividend*

Dr	Dividend payable (£90,000 × 0.7)	£63,000	
Cr	Dividend receivable		£63,000

Recognising non-controlling interest in contributed equity, reserves and earnings

As was established earlier, it is necessary to calculate the non-controlling interests' share in profits and capital and reserves. The calculations undertaken in Worked Example 23.2 for the non-controlling interests' share of current period's profits, contributed equity and dividends apply equally here. However, the non-controlling interests' share of retained earnings at 1 July 2015 (that is, opening retained earnings) will need to be recalculated.

Calculation of non-controlling interests in Medium plc and Small plc	Medium plc (£)	30% non-controlling interest (£)	Small plc (£)	40% non-controlling interest (£)
(i) *Non-controlling interests on acquisition date*				
Share capital on acquisition date	560,000	168,000	160,000	64,000
Retained earnings on acquisition date	340,000	102,000	320,000	128,000
Post acquisition retained earnings Small plc (£370,000 − £320,000) × 0.6	30,000			

Calculation of non-controlling interests in Medium plc and Small plc	Medium plc (£)	30% non-controlling interest (£)	Small plc (£)	40% non-controlling interest (£)
Impairment loss—goodwill (relating to purchase of Small plc by Medium plc), being £78,240 – £40,000	(38,240)			
	(8,240)	(2,472)		
Revaluation surplus on acquisition date (£128,000 – £38,400)	–	–	89,600	35,840
	891,760	267,528		
Goodwill (see calculation provided earlier)		15,329		
		282,857	569,600	227,840

(ii) *Non-controlling interest in movements in contributed equity and reserves between the date of the parent entity's acquisition and the beginning of the current reporting period*

	Medium plc (£)	30% non-controlling interest (£)	Small plc (£)	40% non-controlling interest (£)
Retained earnings—since acquisition				
Medium plc (£480,000 – £340,000)	140,000			
Small plc (£670,000 – £320,000)			350,000	
Depreciation adjustment due to revaluing factory building to fair value (in relation to the previous three years)			(24,000)	
Tax effect of depreciation adjustment due to revaluing factory buildings			7,200	
Unrealised profit in opening inventory (last year's closing inventory)	(80,000)		–	
Tax effect of unrealised profit in opening inventory	24,000		–	
Adjusted post-investment retained earnings—1 July 2014	84,000	25,200	333,200	133,280

(iii) *Non-controlling interest in the current period's profit and movements in reserves in the current period*

	Medium plc (£)	30% non-controlling interest (£)	Small plc (£)	40% non-controlling interest (£)
Profit for the year	168,000		192,000	
Adjustment relating to inventory				
Unrealised profit in opening inventory	80,000			
Tax effect of unrealised profit in opening inventory	(24,000)			
Unrealised profit in closing inventory			(140,000)	
Tax effect of unrealised profit in closing inventory			42,000	
Fair value adjustment				
Depreciation adjustment due to revaluing factory buildings to fair value			(8,000)	
Tax effect of depreciation adjustment due to revaluing factory buildings			2,400	
Intragroup dividends				
Dividend revenue from within the group (paid by Small plc to Medium plc)	(66,000)			
Goodwill impairment in organisation controlled by intermediate subsidiary	(5,000)		–	
Adjusted profit for the year	153,000	45,900	88,400	35,360
Dividends paid and declared	(90,000)	(27,000)	(110,000)	(44,000)
		326,957		352,480

(r) *Recognising non-controlling interest in contributed equity, reserves and earnings in Medium plc on acquisition date*

Dr	Share capital	£168,000	
Dr	Retained earnings (Medium plc)—1 July 2014 (£102,000 + £25,200)	£127,200	
Dr	Goodwill	£15,329	
Dr	Non-controlling interest in earnings	£45,900	
Cr	Retained earnings (Small plc)—1 July 2014		£2,472
Cr	Final dividend		£27,000
Cr	Non-controlling interest		£326,957

(s) *Recognising non-controlling interest in contributed equity, reserves and earnings in Small plc*

Dr	Share capital	£64,000
Dr	Retained earnings—1 July 2014 (£128,000 + £133,280)	£261,280
Dr	Revaluation surplus	£35,840
Dr	Non-controlling interest in earnings	£35,360
Cr	Interim dividend		£44,000
Cr	Non-controlling interest		£352,480

(t) *Indirect non-controlling interest in Small plc*

Calculation of indirect non-controlling interest in Small plc	Small plc (£)	18% indirect non-controlling interest (£)
Indirect non-controlling interest in movements in contributed equity and reserves between the date of the parent entity's acquisition and the beginning of the current reporting period	333,200	59,976
Indirect non-controlling interest in the current period's profit for the year	88,400	15,912
	421,600	75,888

Dr	Retained earnings—1 July 2014	£59,976
Dr	Non-controlling interest in earnings	£15,912
Cr	Non-controlling interest	£75,888

(recognising indirect non-controlling interest in earnings of Small plc)

Consolidation worksheet as at 30 June 2015

	Big plc (£)	Medium plc (£)	Small plc (£)	Eliminations and adjustments Dr (£)	Eliminations and adjustments Cr (£)	Consolidated statements (£)
Sales revenue	7,500,000	4,000,000	3,500,000	2,000,000(g)		13,000,000
Cost of goods sold	(6,100,000)	(3,260,000)	(2,900,000)	140,000(h)	2,000,000(g) 80,000(j)	(10,320,000)
Gross profit	1,400,000	740,000	600,000			2,680,000
Depreciation expense	(130,000)	(50,000)	(18,000)	8,000(c)		(206,000)
Impairment loss—goodwill	–	–	–	5,000(n)		(5,000)
Other expenses	(743,000)	(476,000)	(262,000)			(1,481,000)
Dividend revenue	63,000	66,000	–	66,000(o) 63,000(p)	}	–
Gain on sale of factory	170,000	–	–	170,000(k)		–
Profit before tax	760,000	280,000	320,000			988,000
Income tax expense	(304,000)	(112,000)	(128,000)	24,000(j)	2,400(d) 42,000(i) 51,000(l) }	(472,600)
Profit for the year	456,000	168,000	192,000			515,400
Non-controlling interest in earnings				45,900(r) 35,360(s) 15,912(t) }		(97,172)
Retained earnings— 1 July 2014	720,000	480,000	670,000	24,000(c) 238,000(e) 192,000(f) 56,000(j) 38,240(m)	7,200(d) 5,768(e) 2,472(r) }	888,744

	Big plc (£)	Medium plc (£)	Small plc (£)	Eliminations and adjustments Dr (£)	Cr (£)	Consolidated statements (£)
Interim dividend	(125,000)	–	(110,000)	127,200(r) 261,280(s) 59,976(t)	66,000(o) 44,000(s)	(125,000)
Final dividend	(260,000)	(90,000)	–		63,000(p) 27,000(r)	(260,000)
Retained earnings— 30 June 2015	791,000	558,000	752,000			921,972
Share capital	3,300,000	560,000	160,000	392,000(e) 96,000(f) 168,000(r) 64,000(s)		3,300,000
Revaluation surplus	–	–	–	38,400(b) 53,760(f) 35,840(s)	128,000(a)	–
Non-controlling interest	–	–	–		326,957(r) 352,480(s) 75,888(t)	755,325
Total equity	4,091,000	1,118,000	912,000			4,977,297
Accounts payable	910,000	715,000	319,000			1 944,000
Dividends payable	260,000	90,000	–	63,000(q)		287,000
Deferred tax liability	–	–	–	9,600(d)	38,400(b)	28,800
Total equity	5,261,000	1,923,000	1,231,000			7,237,097
ASSETS						
Cash	76,000	6,000	37,000			119,000
Accounts receivable	172,000	52,000	68,000			292,000
Dividends receivable	63,000	–	–		63,000(q)	–
Inventory	1,100,000	440,000	700,000		140,000(h)	2,100,000
Land	720,000	105,000	210,000			1,035,000
Factory buildings	2,600,000	1,800,000	360,000	56,000(a) 100,000(k)		4,916,000
Accumulated depreciation	(130,000)	(900,000)	(144,000)	72,000(a)	32,000(c) 270,000(k)	(1,404,000)
Investment—Medium plc	660,000	–	–		660,000(e)	–
Investment—Small plc	–	420,000	–		420,000(f)	–
Goodwill	–	–	–	35,768(e) 78,240(f) 15,329(r)		129,337
Accumulated impairment loss					38,240(m) 5,000(n)	(43,240)
Deferred tax asset	–	–	–	42,000(i) 51,000(l)		93,000
Total assets	5,261,000	1,923,000	1,231,000	4,940,805	4,940,805	7,237,097

Big plc and its controlled entities
Consolidated statement of comprehensive income for the year ending 30 June 2015

	The Group (£)	Big plc (£)
Sales	13,000,000	7,500,000
Cost of goods sold	(10,320,000)	(6,100,000)
Gross profit	2,680,000	1,400,000
Dividend revenue	–	63,000
Gain on sale of factory	–	170,000
Depreciation expense	(206,000)	(130,000)
Impairment loss—goodwill	(5,000)	–
Other expenses	(1,481,000)	(743,000)
Profit before tax	988,000	760,000
Income tax expense	(472,600)	(304,000)
Profit for the year	515,400	456,000
Other comprehensive income	–	–
Total comprehensive income	515,400	456,000
Attributable to:		
Owners of the parent	418,228	
Non-controlling interest	97,172	
	515,400	

Big plc and its controlled entities
Consolidated statement of changes in equity for the year ending 30 June 2015

	Attributable to owners of the parent			Non-controlling interest (£)	Total equity (£)
	Share capital (£)	Retained earnings (£)	Total (£)		
Balance—1 July 2014	3,300,000	888,744	4,188,744	729,153	4,917,897
Comprehensive income for the year					
	–	418,228	418,228	97,172	515,400
Dividends	–	(385,000)	(385,000)	(71,000)	(456,000)
Balance—30 June 2015	3,300,000	921,972	4,221,972	755,325	4,977,297

Big plc: Statement of changes in equity for the year ending 30 June 2015

	Share capital (£)	Retained earnings (£)	Total equity (£)
Balance—1 July 2014	3,300,000	720,000	4,020,000
Comprehensive income for the year	–	456,000	456,000
Dividends	–	(385,000)	(385,000)
Balance—30 June 2015	3,300,000	791,000	4,091,000

Big plc and its controlled entities
Consolidated statement of financial position at 31 March 2015

	The Group (£)	Big plc (£)
ASSETS		
Non-current assets		
Land	1,035,000	720,000
Factory buildings	4,916,000	2,600,000
Accumulated depreciation	(1,404,000)	(130,000)
Goodwill	129,337	–
Accumulated impairment losses	(43,240)	–
Investment in Medium plc	–	660,000
Deferred tax asset	93,000	–
Total non-current assets	4,726,097	3,850,000

◀

	The Group (£)	Big plc (£)
Current assets		
Inventory	2,100,000	1,100,000
Accounts receivable	292,000	172,000
Dividend receivable	–	63,000
Cash	119,000	76,000
Total current assets	2,511,000	1,411,000
Total assets	7,237,097	5,261,000
EQUITY AND LIABILITIES		
Equity and reserves		
Share capital	3,300,000	3,300,000
Retained earnings	921,972	791,000
	4,221,972	4,091,000
Non-controlling interest	755,325	–
Total equity	4,977,297	4,091,000
Non-current liabilities		
Deferred tax liability	28,800	–
Total non-current liabilities	28,800	–
Current liabilities		
Accounts payable	1,944,000	910,000
Dividends payable	287,000	260,000
Total current liabilities	2,231,000	1,170,000
Total liabilities	2,259,800	1,170,000
Total equity and liabilities	7,237,097	5,261,000

SUMMARY

This chapter, like the three before it, considered issues associated with preparing consolidated financial statements—specifically, how to account for indirect interests.

The chapter showed that it is possible to control another entity—and therefore be required to consolidate it—without necessarily having any direct ownership in that separate legal entity. The control can be established through an indirect ownership interest, that is, through an interest established by *controlling* another entity that in turn *controls* the entity in question. When consolidating in the presence of indirect interests, the elimination of the investments held by the immediate parent entities is to be undertaken on the basis of the direct ownership interest. The economic entity's interest in the post-acquisition profits of subsidiaries, however, will be based on the sum of both the direct ownership interests and the indirect ownership interests.

KEY TERMS

END-OF-CHAPTER EXERCISE

After completing this chapter you should ensure that you are able to answer the following questions. (If you find you cannot provide appropriate answers, you should revisit the relevant sections of the chapter.)

1   What is an indirect ownership interest?   **LO 23.1**

2   Can an entity be considered a controlled entity (that is, a subsidiary) of another entity even if that other entity has no direct ownership interest?   **LO 23.1**

3   On consolidation, when we eliminate the investment in the subsidiary against the pre-acquisition capital and reserves of the subsidiary, do we take account of only the direct ownership interests or both the direct and indirect ownership interests?   **LO 23.2**

4   On consolidation, post-acquisition movements in the reserves and retained earnings of a subsidiary will be included in the consolidated financial statements. However, they will need to be apportioned between the parent entity's interest and the non-controlling interests. In undertaking this apportionment, should we take account of only the direct ownership interests or both the direct and indirect ownership interests?   **LO 23.3**

5   If an intermediate parent acquires a subsidiary and, in doing so, purchases goodwill, how will any impairment of that goodwill be treated when working out the non-controlling interest in profits and retained earnings?   **LO 23.2**

REVIEW QUESTIONS

1   What is a direct equity interest and what is an indirect equity interest?   **LO 23.1**

2   Why do we need to know which part of non-controlling interest is direct and which part is indirect?   **LO 23.2**

3   Where in the statement of financial position would indirect non-controlling interests be disclosed?   **LO 23.3**

4   What is the difference in the consolidation accounting used for sequential and non-sequential acquisitions?   **LO 23.1**

5   If an intermediate parent acquires a subsidiary and, in doing so, purchases goodwill, how will any impairment of that goodwill be treated when working out the non-controlling interest in profits and retained earnings?   **LO 23.3**

6   A plc has a 60 per cent interest in B plc and B plc has an 80 per cent interest in C plc. Both acquisitions were made in 2012. During the financial year ended 30 June 2015, A plc paid a dividend of €300,000, B plc paid a dividend of €200,000 and C plc paid a dividend of €100,000. What amount of dividends paid would be shown in the consolidated financial statements of A plc and its controlled entities for the year ending 30 June 2015?   **LO 23.3**

7   Consider the example in the figure below and assume that ownership interest (the percentages shown) is representative of the capacity to control the various entities.   **LO 23.3**

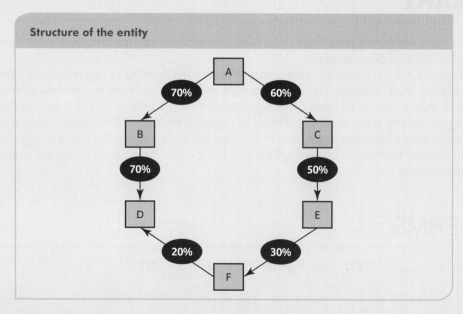

Structure of the entity

Determine which of the entities would constitute the economic entity.

8   Maroubra plc holds 70 per cent of the ownership equity of Coogee plc and Coogee plc holds 80 per cent of the ownership equity of Clovelly plc. During the financial year the following dividends are paid by the respective companies:
Maroubra plc   £120,000
Coogee plc   £80,000
Clovelly plc   £60,000
What amount of dividend payments would be shown in the consolidated financial statements?   **LO 23.3**

9   When eliminating the pre-acquisition capital and reserves of a subsidiary for the purposes of presenting consolidated financial statements, should both direct and indirect ownership interests be considered?   **LO 23.4**

10 Consider the corporate structure represented in the figure below.   **LO 23.1**

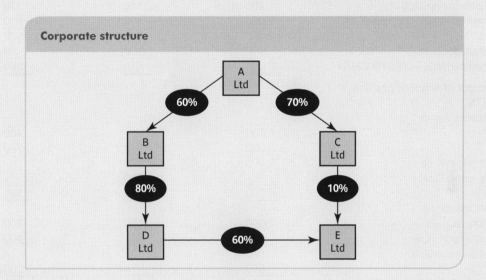

Corporate structure

Determine A plc's interest (direct and indirect) and the non-controlling interest in the separate legal entities under the control of A plc.

CHALLENGING QUESTIONS

11 A plc acquires a 60 per cent interest in B plc on 1 July 2014 for a cost of €2 million, representing the fair value of consideration transferred. The management of A plc values any non-controlling interest at acquisition date at the proportionate share of B plc's net identifiable assets at acquisition date. All assets are assumed to be fairly valued in the books of B plc. The share capital and reserves of B plc at the date of acquisition are: **LO 23.3**

Share capital   €2,000,000
Retained earnings   €600,000
                            €2,600,000

B plc acquires a 60 per cent interest in C plc on 1 July 2014 for €1.6 million, representing the fair value of consideration transferred. Any non-controlling interest in C plc at acquisition date is based on fair value. The share capital and reserves of C plc at the date of acquisition are:

Share capital   €1,600,000
Retained earnings   €800,000
                            €2,400,000

The statements of comprehensive income and statements of financial position of the entities at 30 June 2015 (one year after the acquisition) are as follows:

	A plc (€000)	B plc (€000)	C plc (€000)
Abbreviated statement of comprehensive income			
Retained earnings			
Profit before tax	1,000	160	200
Tax expense	(540)	(50)	(80)
Profit after tax	460	110	120
Statement of changes in equity			
Profit after tax (extract)	460	110	120
Retained earnings—30 June 2014	2,000	600	800
	2,460	710	920
Dividends declared	(400)	(100)	(60)
Retained earnings—30 June 2015	2,060	610	860
Statement of financial position			
ASSETS			
Non-current assets			
Land	4,700	–	400
Plant	3,000	630	720
Investment in B plc	2,000	–	
Investment in C plc	–	1,600	–
	9,700	2,230	1,120
Current assets			
Inventory	1,000	600	800
Accounts receivable	250	350	400
Dividends receivable	60	36	–
Cash	590	74	200
	1,900	1,060	1,400
Total assets	11,600	3,290	2,520
EQUITY AND LIABILITIES			
Equity and reserves			
Equity share capital	8,000	2,000	1,600
Retained earnings	2,060	610	860
	10,060	2,610	2,460
Non-current liabilities			
Loans	800	500	–
Current liabilities			
Accounts payable	340	80	
Dividends payable	400	100	60
	740	180	60
Total liabilities	1,540	680	60
Total equity and liabilities	11,600	3,290	2,520

Additional information

It is assumed that goodwill acquired has been subject to an impairment loss of 20 per cent of the original goodwill value.

REQUIRED

Present consolidated financial statements for A plc and its controlled entities as at 30 June 2015.

12 On 1 July 2012 Anglesea acquired a 70 per cent interest in Bells plc at a cost of €1,000,000, and Bells plc acquired an 80 per cent interest in Torquay plc at a cost of €750,000. Both payments represent the fair value of consideration transferred. All assets are assumed to be recorded at their fair value. At the date of acquisition the equity share capital and reserves of Bells plc and Torquay plc were as follows: **LO 23.3**

	Bells plc (€)	Torquay plc (€)
Equity share capital	500,000	400,000
Revaluation surplus	150,000	100,000
Retained earnings	250,000	100,000
	900,000	600,000

For the year ending 30 June 2015 Bells plc and Torquay plc generated the following results:

	Bells plc (€)	Torquay plc (€)
Profit before tax	250,000	100,000
Tax expense	(100,000)	(40,000)
Profit after tax	150,000	60,000
Retained earnings—1 July 2014	280,000	130,000
	430,000	190,000
Dividends paid	(30,000)	(10,000)
Retained earnings—30 June 2015	400,000	180,000

Non-controlling interests are measured at the non-controlling interest's proportionate share of the acquiree's identifiable net assets. In relation to goodwill, the recoverable amount of the goodwill acquired in Bells plc was assessed as being €250,000 at 30 June 2015, with €15,000 of the accumulated impairment occurring in the 2015 financial year. The goodwill acquired in Torquay plc was assessed as having a recoverable amount of €150,000 as at 30 June 2015 with €10,000 of the total impairment occurring in the year ending 30 June 2015.

REQUIRED

Determine the total non-controlling interest in closing retained earnings as at 30 June 2015.

PART 8

Foreign Currency

Part contents

Chapter 24

Accounting for Foreign Currency Transactions

Learning objectives

Upon completing this chapter readers should:

LO1 understand why it is necessary to translate transactions that are denominated in foreign currencies;

LO2 understand that all transactions denominated in overseas currencies must initially be translated at the exchange rate in place as at the date of the transaction (the transaction date's spot rate) using the entity's 'functional currency';

LO3 understand that at the end of the reporting period all foreign currency monetary items must be translated at the reporting date spot rate;

LO4 understand the difference between a functional currency and a presentation currency;

LO5 understand what a qualifying asset is and be able to provide the appropriate accounting entries relating to a qualifying asset;

LO6 understand the difference between a fair-value hedge and a cash-flow hedge, and be able to provide the appropriate accounting entries in respect of both; and

LO7 understand what a foreign currency swap is and why it might be undertaken, and be able to provide the relevant journal entries to account for a foreign currency swap.

24.1 Introduction to accounting for foreign currency transactions

The accounting standard on foreign currency transactions is IAS 21 *The Effects of Changes in Foreign Exchange Rates*. A number of other accounting standards are also relevant when accounting for foreign currency transactions, in particular IFRS 9 *Financial Instruments*, IAS 23 *Borrowing Costs* and IAS 39 *Financial Instruments: Recognition and Measurement*.

In considering foreign currency translations, reporting entities must consider two general issues. First, business entities frequently transact with overseas entities in currencies other than their domestic currency. Where debts, receivables or other monetary items are denominated in currencies other than the domestic currency, there is an obvious need to convert the transactions into a single currency. Unless the transactions are converted into a common currency, financial statements would include account balances denominated in a number of different currencies, and the totals of such balances would be meaningless.

Second, where an entity controls a foreign subsidiary, there is a need to translate the financial statements of that subsidiary into a common currency before the consolidation process. We will defer a discussion of the translation of foreign subsidiaries' financial statements until Chapter 25.

24.2   Foreign currency transactions

IAS 21 defines an **exchange rate** as 'the ratio of exchange for two currencies'. Exchange rates for major currencies typically change throughout the day, with the changes being driven by many factors, including the demand for,

> **exchange rate**
> The rate at which one currency can be exchanged for another.

and supply of, a particular currency. For example, the value of sterling, relative to the euro fell on 30 December 2008 to approximately £1.00 = €1.022. That is, for every sterling pound we would receive about €1.022. A *fall* in the value of a currency, for example sterling relative to the euro, has many implications. People from the UK travelling to Europe found that they were typically able to buy far less for a given amount of sterling. The costs for imports from Europe also rose, while the relative prices of exports fell.

Parties that had borrowed in Europe, with the debt denominated in euros, found that the amount of the debt, when translated to sterling, increased significantly. When the value of a currency such as sterling *increases* the situation is the opposite. For example, on 6 January 2012 the exchange rate was approximately £1.00 = €1.21. In this situation, those parties with debts denominated in the euro found it relatively less expensive to repay debts (especially compared with when the exchange rate was at €1.022 in 2008). For example, if such parties had to repay €1,000,000 in 2008 at the exchange rates previously mentioned, it would have cost them £978,474 (which is €1,000,000 ÷ 1.022). However, to repay €1,000,000 on 6 January 2012 would have cost £826,446 (which is €1,000,000 ÷ 1.21). Assuming that the debt was still outstanding, the amount of the debt when converted to sterling is much less than it originally was. An accounting issue here would be whether this reduction in debt value should be included within profit or loss as income. This will be an issue we address shortly.

People often question whether a currency is correctly valued, but it is very difficult to provide any evidence to prove that a currency is over- or undervalued. The relative prices of various currencies (as reflected in exchange

> **translation of foreign currency transactions**
> Translation of transactions denominated or requiring settlement in a currency other than the functional currency of the entity.

rates) will fluctuate across time for a variety of reasons, many of which are sometimes hard to explain. An interesting index that has been used for over two decades now is the *Big Mac index* (see the article about this index reproduced in Financial Accounting in the News 24.1). This article provides a graph to show how several currencies, including sterling and the euro, are performing relative to the other currencies in the Big Mac index in 2010.

We will not pay any further attention to considering whether exchange rates are appropriate or how they are determined. Such issues are more appropriately addressed in a course on economics. Rather, we will concentrate on how to account for movements in exchange rates. As an illustration of some of the issues relating to the **translation of foreign currency transactions**, consider Worked Example 24.1.

Worked Example 24.1   **Acquisition of goods from a foreign supplier where the transaction is denominated in a foreign currency**

On 1 June 2014 Michaela plc, a company located in England, acquires goods on credit from a supplier in the Republic of Ireland. The goods are shipped FOB Dublin on 1 June 2014. (FOB is the abbreviation for 'free on board' and signifies the point at which title passes from the seller to the purchaser. Once title passes, the purchaser has an obligation that must be recorded.) The cost of the goods is €100,000 and this amount remains unpaid at 30 June 2014.

On 1 June 2014 the exchange rate is £1.00 = €1.10. On 30 June 2014 it is £1.00 = €1.20. So the value of sterling has risen relative to the euro.

Required

Determine the amount of the debt, denominated in sterling, as at:

(a) 1 June 2014
(b) 30 June 2014

Solution

(a) As at 1 June 2014 the debt would be equal to £90,909 (€100,000 ÷ 1.10). That is, if the debt is paid on 1 June, the required payment, in sterling, would be £90,909.

(b) As at 30 June 2014 the debt would be equal to £83,333 (€100,000 ÷ 1.20). Because of the movement in foreign exchange rates, Michaela plc has made a foreign exchange gain due to the fact that the entity has to pay less for the goods following the exchange rate movement.

Financial Accounting in the News 24.1
THE BIG MAC INDEX: CURRENCY COMPARISONS, TO GO

The Economist, 28 July 2011

A beefed-up version of the Big Mac index suggests that the Chinese yuan is now close to its fair value against the dollar.

Our new improved recipe

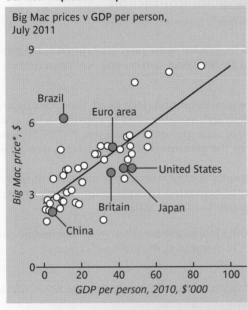

Big Mac prices v GDP per person, July 2011

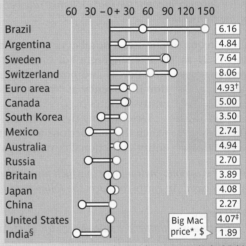

Big Mac index, local currency under(–)/over(+) valuation against the dollar, %

○ Raw index ○ Adjusted for GDP per person

Country	Big Mac price*, $
Brazil	6.16
Argentina	4.84
Sweden	7.64
Switzerland	8.06
Euro area	4.93†
Canada	5.00
South Korea	3.50
Mexico	2.74
Australia	4.94
Russia	2.70
Britain	3.89
Japan	4.08
China	2.27
United States	4.07‡
India§	1.89

*At market exchange rate (July 25th)
†Average of member countries
‡Average of four cities §Maharaja Mac

The Economist's Big Mac index is a fun guide to whether currencies are at their 'correct' level. It is based on the theory of purchasing-power parity (PPP), the notion that in the long run exchange rates should move towards the rate that would equalise the prices of a basket of goods and services around the world. At market exchange rates, a burger is 44% cheaper in China than in America. In other words, the raw Big Mac index suggests that the yuan is 44% undervalued against the dollar. But we have long warned that cheap burgers in China do not prove that the yuan is massively undervalued. Average prices should be lower in poor countries than in rich ones because labour costs are lower. The chart above shows a strong positive relationship between the dollar price of a Big Mac and GDP per person.

PPP signals where exchange rates should move in the long run. To estimate the current fair value of a currency we use the 'line of best fit' between Big Mac prices and GDP per person. The difference between the price predicted for each country, given its average income, and its actual price offers a better guide to currency under- and overvaluation than the 'raw' index. The beefed-up index suggests that the Brazilian real is the most overvalued currency in the world; the euro is also overvalued. But the yuan now appears to be close to its fair value against the dollar—something for American politicians to chew over.

Source: www.economist.com. © The Economist Newspaper Limited 2012

In Worked Example 24.1, the value of the obligation, as denominated in sterling, has fallen by £7,576, although it clearly has not changed when denominated in euro. The UK entity is better off.

A number of issues arise in relation to such a reduction in a liability. For example, should the £7,576 be treated as a gain or should the cost of the inventory be adjusted downwards? As we know from previous chapters, the IASB Conceptual Framework suggests that, if the value of a liability decreases other than through repayment, the reduction in the liability may be recognised as income.

For example, if a debt is forgiven, the value of the debt that is no longer payable will be treated as income. If services or goods are supplied to another entity in return for the extinguishment of a liability, the value of the liability would typically be treated as income. Where exchange gains arise on translation of loans denominated in a foreign currency, these gains would also traditionally be treated as part of income. As we know, however, where there is an accounting standard that addresses a particular issue, such as foreign currency translations, that accounting standard will take precedence over guidance presented in documents such as the IASB Conceptual Framework. In the discussion that follows, we consider whether or not a movement in the value of a foreign currency obligation such as that in Worked Example 24.1 should be treated as part of the profit or loss of the financial period.

24.2.1 Accounting entry at the date of the original transaction

Paragraph 21 of IAS 21 *The Effects of Changes in Foreign Exchange Rates* requires that:

A foreign currency transaction shall be recorded, on initial recognition in the functional currency, by applying to the foreign currency amount the spot exchange rate between the functional currency and the foreign currency at the date of the transaction.

The above requirement uses a number of terms that require definition. First of all, the spot exchange rate is defined in IAS 21 as 'the exchange rate for immediate delivery'. We also need to consider what a 'functional currency' is and how this differs from the 'presentation currency'. IAS 21 defines **functional currency** as 'the currency of the primary economic environment in which the entity operates'.

> **functional currency**
> The currency of the primary economic environment in which the entity operates.

Determining the functional currency is important as this identifies the currency into which the transactions will initially be converted. In explanation of how to determine an entity's functional currency, paragraph 9 of IAS 21 states:

The primary economic environment in which an entity operates is normally the one in which it primarily generates and expends cash. An entity considers the following factors in determining its functional currency:

(a) *the currency:*
  (i) *that mainly influences sales prices for goods and services (this will often be the currency in which sales prices for its goods and services are denominated and settled); and*
  (ii) *of the country whose competitive forces and regulations mainly determine the sales price of its goods and services;*
(b) *the currency that mainly influences labour, material and other costs of providing goods or services (this will often be the currency in which such costs are denominated and settled).*

Should the functional currency not be apparent even after considering the above factors, paragraph 10 of IAS 21 suggests that the following additional indicators can be utilised by management to assist them in the determination of the entity's functional currency:

(a) *the currency in which funds from financing activities (i.e. issuing debt and equity instruments) are generated; and*
(b) *the currency in which receipts from operating activities are usually retained.*

Apart from determining the functional currency of the reporting entity itself, there will also be a necessity to determine the functional currency of entities that are controlled or significantly influenced by the entity. In this regard, paragraph 11 of IAS 21 states:

The following additional factors are considered in determining the functional currency of a foreign operation, and whether its functional currency is the same as that of the reporting entity (the reporting entity, in this context, being the entity that has the foreign operation as its subsidiary, branch, associate or joint venture):

(a) *whether the activities of the foreign operation are carried out as an extension of the reporting entity, rather than being carried out with a significant degree of autonomy. An example of the former is when the foreign operation only sells goods imported from the reporting entity and remits the proceeds to it. An example of the latter is when the operation accumulates cash and other monetary items, incurs expenses, generates income and arranges borrowings, all substantially in its local currency;*
(b) *whether transactions with the reporting entity are a high or low proportion of the foreign operation's activities;*

(c) whether cash flows from the activities of the foreign operation directly affect the cash flows of the reporting entity and are readily available for remittance to it;

(d) whether cash flows from the activities of the foreign operation are sufficient to service existing and normally expected debt obligations without funds being made available by the reporting entity.

In situations where the functional currency is not obvious IAS 21, paragraph 12, requires management to use its judgement in determining the functional currency that best represents the economic effects of the underlying transactions, events and conditions and paragraph 13 requires the functional currency to be applied consistently unless there is a change in the underlying transactions, events and conditions that support change.

Therefore, to this point we have provided factors that can be used to determine the functional currency, which is the currency in which transactions are initially recorded. However, we then need to determine the presentation currency, which may or may not be the same as the functional currency. If the presentation currency is different from the functional currency, then further adjustments will be necessary.

presentation currency The currency in which the financial statements are presented.

Presentation currency is defined in IAS 21 as 'the currency in which the financial statements are presented'. In relation to the determination of the presentation currency, paragraph 38 of IAS 21 states:

An entity may present its financial statements in any currency (or currencies). If the presentation currency differs from the entity's functional currency, it translates its results and financial position into the presentation currency. For example, when a group contains individual entities with different functional currencies, the results and financial position of each entity are expressed in a common currency so that the consolidated financial statements may be presented.

Regarding the selection of a presentation currency, it is interesting to note that BP plc presents its financial statements using US dollars rather than sterling as its presentation currency, though its head office is situated in London. This choice is noted in the accounting policy note in the 2010 annual report of BP plc as outlined in Exhibit 24.1.

Exhibit 24.1 | BP plc

Significant Accounting Policies (extract)
Foreign currency translation

Functional currency is the currency of the primary economic environment in which an entity operates and is normally the currency in which the entity primarily generates and expends cash.

In individual companies, transactions in foreign currencies are initially recorded in the functional currency by applying the rate of exchange ruling at the date of the transaction. Monetary assets and liabilities denominated in foreign currencies are retranslated into the functional currency at the rate of exchange ruling at the balance sheet date. Any resulting exchange differences are included in the income statement. Non-monetary assets and liabilities, other than those measured at fair value, are not retranslated subsequent to initial recognition.

In the consolidated financial statements, the assets and liabilities of non-US dollar functional currency subsidiaries, jointly controlled entities and associates, including related goodwill, are translated into US dollars at the rate of exchange ruling at the balance sheet date. The results and cash flows of non-US dollar functional currency subsidiaries, jointly controlled entities and associates are translated into US dollars using average rates of exchange. Exchange adjustments arising when the opening net assets and the profits for the year retained by non-US dollar functional currency subsidiaries, jointly controlled entities and associates are translated into US dollars are taken to a separate component of equity and reported in the statement of comprehensive income. Exchange gains and losses arising on long-term intragroup foreign currency borrowings used to finance the group's non-US dollar investments are also taken to equity. On disposal of a non-US dollar functional currency subsidiary, jointly controlled entity or associate, the deferred cumulative amount of exchange gains and losses recognized in equity relating to that particular non-US dollar operation is reclassified to the income statement.

Returning to Worked Example 24.1, for Michaela plc the initial entry on 1 June 2014 would be:

Dr	Inventory	£90,909
Cr	Accounts payable	£90,909

24.2.2 Adjustments at the end of the reporting period

Paragraph 23 of IAS 21 requires that, at the end of each reporting period, foreign currency monetary items are to be translated using the *closing rate*. Closing rate is defined in IAS 21 as 'the spot exchange rate at the end of the reporting period'. Foreign currency monetary items would include accounts payable and accounts receivable, as well as cash, interest receivable, notes receivable, loans receivable, dividends receivable, bank overdraft, income taxes payable, wages payable, notes payable and/or debentures payable. In the case of Michaela plc, this would mean that the obligation would need to be restated to £83,333.

The entity effectively owes £7,576 less than it did at the date of the original transaction owing to the fluctuation in the exchange rate. Of course, the exchange rate could have moved in the opposite direction. As we will show, to insulate themselves from potentially unfavourable foreign currency fluctuations, firms frequently enter into hedging arrangements.

An exception to the above rule (that foreign currency monetary items outstanding at the end of the reporting period must be translated at the spot rate in existence at the end of the reporting period) would be those few cases where, according to a contractual arrangement, the exchange rate has been fixed for a particular transaction. A general principle applied is that the exchange differences relating to monetary items are to be recognised as part of profit or loss in the reporting period in which the exchange rates change (IAS 21, paragraph 28). There are some exceptions to this general rule, which we will address shortly (to do with 'qualifying assets' and certain hedges), although these exceptions would not apply to Michaela plc.

For Michaela plc, the entry on 30 June 2014 would be:

Dr	Accounts payable	£7,576
Cr	Foreign exchange gain	£7,576

The amount of the liability is increased to take account of a change in the foreign exchange rate. The reduction in the sterling equivalent of the foreign debt is treated as part of the period's profit or loss (as an expense) and not as an increase in the cost of the inventory.

24.3   Determination of functional currency and presentation currency

In the discussion so far we have considered the difference between functional currency and presentation currency. As we noted, there are a number of factors to consider in determining the appropriate functional currency. The functional currency is the currency of the primary economic environment in which the entity operates. Paragraph 9 of IAS 21 (referred to above) provides a number of factors to consider in determining the functional currency.

In determining the presentation currency, consideration needs to be given to the currency in which the general purpose financial statements are to be prepared. If the entity's shareholders primarily reside within the UK there would be an expectation that the presentation currency would be sterling. As already indicated, the presentation currency might not be the same as the functional currency. This might happen, for example, when a parent company residing within the UK controls a subsidiary company that resides in a foreign country, for example the US. If the subsidiary operates within the US, and sells its goods and purchases its factors of production in US dollars, its functional currency is US dollars. However, for the purposes of translating the results for UK use, the presentation currency would be sterling. The US entity's financial statements would be translated from the functional currency (US dollars) into the economic entity's presentation currency (sterling) prior to consolidation. The difference between functional currency and presentation currency is considered in Worked Example 24.2.

24.4   Longer-term receivables and payables

The transactions of Michaela plc, introduced in Worked Example 24.1 and referred to since, led to the recognition of a short-term payable. Reporting entities can also have long-term monetary items, many of which might be denominated in a foreign currency. According to IAS 21, at the end of the reporting period, all

Worked Example 24.2 — Determination of functional currency and presentation currency

Shamrock plc is an Irish company that is listed on the Irish and London stock exchanges. The company has established a number of sportswear factories in the Philippines, Indonesia, Vietnam, China, Great Britain and Republic of Ireland. Materials and labour are typically acquired in the local currencies; however, all acquisitions of plant and machinery are denominated in UK pounds. All sales of clothing are denominated in UK pounds and all borrowing tends to be done in UK pounds and come from UK-based banks. Most equity capital has been raised within Ireland, although in recent years there has been a trend towards issuing new shares on the London Stock Exchange.

In terms of current shareholding, 82 per cent of issued shares are held by Irish shareholders. The balance is held by UK residents (12 per cent) and Chinese residents (6 per cent).

Required

(a) Determine the functional currency of Shamrock plc.
(b) Determine the presentation currency of Shamrock plc.

Solution

(a) Determination of functional currency

It would be expected that the functional currency would be UK pounds. Factors to support this decision would be the following:

- Sales are denominated in UK pounds.
- Plant and machinery are acquired in UK pounds.
- Bank finance is denominated in UK pounds.
- Recent share issues have been undertaken within the UK.

Given the above facts, it would appear that the UK is the primary economic environment in which the entity operates.

(b) Determination of presentation currency

IAS 21 does not provide much guidance on determining the presentation currency. We need to determine the currency in which the financial statements would, or should, be presented. Given that most shares are held by Irish residents and that employees are dispersed throughout the world (with no one group of employees dominating), it would seem appropriate for the presentation currency to be the euro. While most borrowing comes from UK organisations, the banks would be expected to be able to demand financial statements to satisfy their own requirements and so would not be dependent upon general purpose financial statements for their information needs.

Hence, even though all transactions would initially be recorded in sterling, which would in turn mean that the financial statements would initially be prepared in sterling, it will be necessary for the financial statements to be translated from sterling into euro. The next chapter, Chapter 25, concentrates on the translation of financial statements from one currency to another—the presentation currency. Therefore we will defer further issues associated with translating financial statements to the next chapter. In this chapter we concentrate on the accounting entries made in an entity's functional currency.

---

monetary items must be translated using the reporting-date **spot rates**. The exchange gain or loss that results from translating both current and non-current payables and receivables at reporting-date spot rates must be included in the profit or loss for the financial period (subject to a limited number of exceptions, as briefly mentioned above).

spot rate The exchange rate for immediate delivery of currencies to be exchanged.

Across time, the requirement to recognise the gains or losses that result from exchange rate movements as part of profit or loss has been quite unpopular with many reporting entities, particularly as it relates to non-current monetary items. Companies have argued that the recognition of a profit or loss on the translation of non-current monetary items at the end of each reporting period is inappropriate, since the exchange rate fluctuates in the long term and there is significant doubt about whether the unrealised profit or loss will ever be realised. If the long-term monetary items are translated at the end of each reporting period, it has been argued that we should establish a deferred account that would be amortised into operating profit or loss over the term of the long-term monetary asset or liability. This view has not been endorsed by the accounting standard-setters. In Worked Example 24.3 we consider the translation of a non-current liability from a foreign currency into the euro.

Worked Example 24.3 **Translation of a non-current liability**

On 1 July 2014 Noosa plc enters into an agreement to borrow £500,000 from Fistral plc (UK). Fistral plc sends the loan money to Noosa plc's Spanish bank account. The loan is for five years and requires the payment of interest at the rate of 10 per cent on 30 June each year. Noosa plc's reporting date is 30 June. The relevant exchange rates are:

| 1 July 2014 | €1.00 = £0.90 |
| 30 June 2015 | €1.00 = £0.80 |

Required

Provide the journal entries in the books of Noosa plc for the year ending 30 June 2015 to account for the above transaction.

Solution

1 July 2014

| Dr | Cash | €555,555 | |
| Cr | Loan payable | | €555,555 |

(to recognise the foreign currency loan at the 1 July 2014 spot rate: €555,555 = £500,000 ÷ 0.90; remember that throughout the period the transactions are recorded in the entity's functional currency)

30 June 2015

| Dr | Interest expense | €62,500 | |
| Cr | Cash | | €62,500 |

(to recognise year-end interest payment €62,500 = (£500,000 × 10 per cent) ÷ 0.80)

| Dr | Foreign exchange loss | €69,445 | |
| Cr | Loan payable | | €69,445 |

(to recognise the effect of retranslation of the loan at the 30 June 2015 spot rates; the increase in the amount of the loan payable is to be treated as an expense in the period in which the exchange rate moves)

Balance of payable at 1 July 2014: £500,000 ÷ 0.90	€555,555
Balance of payable at 30 June 2015: £500,000 ÷ 0.80	€625,000
Increase in loan payable	€69,445

24.5 Translation of other monetary assets such as cash deposits

In Worked Example 24.3 we translated a foreign currency payable. The same principles apply to other monetary items such as cash, money market deposits and the like, as we will see in Worked Example 24.4.

Worked Example 24.4 **Translation of cash denominated in a foreign currency**

On 1 July 2014 Peregian plc, a German company, provides some consulting advice to Oxford Co., a UK organisation, for an agreed fee of £400,000. The amount is paid into the UK bank account of Peregian plc on 1 July 2014. Peregian plc has left the amount in the UK bank account, which pays interest each year on 30 June at a rate of 12 per cent. The relevant exchange rates are:

| 1 July 2014 | €1.00 = £0.75 |
| 30 June 2015 | €1.00 = £0.80 |

Required

Provide the journal entries in the books of Peregian plc for the year ending 30 June 2015 to account for the above transaction.

▶

Solution

The accounting entries in the books of Peregian plc would be:

1 July 2014

Dr	Cash	€533,333	
Cr	Consulting revenue		€533,333

(to recognise consulting revenue at the 1 July 2014 spot rate: €533,000 = £400,000 ÷ 0.75)

30 June 2015

Dr	Cash	€60,000	
Cr	Interest revenue		€60,000

(to recognise the interest revenue at the 30 June 2015 spot rate: €60,000 = (£400,000 × 12%) ÷ 0.80)

Dr	Foreign exchange loss	€33,333	
Cr	Cash		€33,333

(to adjust for the change in the euro equivalent of the overseas bank deposit using the 30 June 2015 spot rates)

Balance of cash at 1 July 2014: £400,000 ÷ 0.75	€533,333
Balance of cash at 30 June 2015: £400,000 ÷ 0.80	€500,000
Reduction in cash	€33,333

24.6 Qualifying assets

As we have noted, there is a general rule within IAS 21 that exchange differences relating to monetary items (both current and non-current) are to be brought to account as expenses or income in the period in which the exchange rate changes. One exception to the above rule relates to exchange differences for monetary items that relate to **qualifying assets**. In determining how to account for qualifying assets, we must refer to another accounting standard: IAS 23 *Borrowing Costs*. A 'qualifying asset' is defined in IAS 23 as 'an asset that necessarily takes a substantial period of time to get ready for its intended use or sale'. IAS 23 does not provide guidance on what constitutes a 'substantial period of time', although it is generally accepted that it would be a period greater than 12 months.

> **qualifying asset** Asset under construction or otherwise being made ready for future productive use of the company or for the use of another entity under a contract.

Qualifying assets would include inventories that require a substantial period of time to bring to a saleable condition, assets resulting from development and construction activities in the extractive industries, manufacturing plants, power generation facilities and investment properties. Other investments, and inventories that are routinely manufactured or mass-produced in a short period of time, are not qualifying assets. Nor are assets that are ready for their intended use or sale when acquired. As paragraph 7 of IAS 23 states:

> *Depending on the circumstances, any of the following may be qualifying assets:*
>
> *(a) inventories*
> *(b) manufacturing plants*
> *(c) power generation facilities*
> *(d) intangible assets*
> *(e) investment properties.*
>
> *Financial assets, and inventories that are manufactured, or otherwise produced, over a short period of time, are not qualifying assets. Assets that are ready for their intended use or sale when acquired are not qualifying assets.*

Exchange differences arising from foreign currency borrowings to the extent that they are regarded as an adjustment to interest costs are considered to be borrowing costs under IAS 23. For qualifying assets, the core principle contained in IAS 23, paragraph 1, is detailed as follows:

> *Borrowing costs that are directly attributable to the acquisition, construction or production of a qualifying asset form part of the cost of that asset. Other borrowing costs are recognised as an expense.*

In relation to the borrowing costs, IAS 23 provides their accounting treatment. Paragraph 8 of IAS 23 stipulates that, 'An entity shall capitalise borrowing costs that are directly attributable to the acquisition, construction or

production of a qualifying asset as part of the cost of that asset'. All other borrowing costs should be recognised as an expense in the period in which they are incurred.

There is a general requirement that the capitalisation of such borrowing costs as part of the cost of the asset is allowed only when it is probable that such costs will result in future economic benefits to the entity and the costs can be measured reliably. As noted above, exchange rate differences would be included as part of borrowing costs and hence can be included in the cost of a qualifying asset. An asset ceases to be a qualifying asset when its construction has been completed, even if the associated liability has not been paid. According to paragraph 22 of IAS 23, the capitalisation of borrowing costs 'shall cease when substantially all the activities necessary to prepare the qualifying asset for its intended use or sale are complete'.

The exchange differences included in the cost of qualifying assets for the financial year are the amounts that would otherwise have been credited/debited to profit or loss. The amount capitalised as the cost of the asset is not to exceed the recoverable amount of the asset. If exchange differences cause the recoverable amount of a qualifying asset to be exceeded, the excess should be written off to profit or loss (IAS 23, paragraph 16). Worked Example 24.5 provides an illustration of how to account for exchange differences that arise while an asset is considered to be a qualifying asset.

Worked Example 24.5	**Foreign currency transaction relating to a qualifying asset**

On 1 March 2014 Greenough plc, a French company, enters into a binding agreement with a Singaporean company to construct an item of machinery that manufactures spoons. The cost of the machinery is S$250,000. The construction of the machinery is completed on 1 June 2014 and shipped FOB Singapore on that date. The debt is unpaid at 30 June 2014, which is also Greenough plc's end of reporting period. The exchange rates at the relevant dates are:

1 March 2014	€1.00 = S$1.10
1 June 2014	€1.00 = S$1.02
30 June 2014	€1.00 = S$1.00

Required

Provide the required journal entries for the year ending 30 June 2014.

Solution

Being under construction, the item would appear to be a qualifying asset under IAS 23 for the period from 1 March 2014 to 1 June 2014. Therefore, the movement in exchange rates to 1 June 2014 shall be incorporated in the cost of the asset. Once an asset ceases to be a qualifying asset, any subsequent movements would be treated as an expense or income and be included as part of the period's profit or loss.

1 March 2014

| Dr Machinery | €227,273 | |
| Cr Accounts payable | | €227,273 |

(to recognise the cost of the asset on 1 March 2014: S$250,000 ÷ 1.10)

1 June 2014

| Dr Machinery | €17,825 | |
| Cr Accounts payable | | €17,825 |

(to recognise the change in the euro equivalent of the foreign currency monetary item during the period in which the asset is a qualifying asset: (S$250,000 ÷ 1.02) − €227,273)

30 June 2014

| Dr Foreign exchange loss | €4,902 | |
| Cr Accounts payable | | €4,902 |

(to recognise the change in the euro equivalent of the foreign currency monetary item in the period after which the asset ceases to be a qualifying asset: (S$250,000 ÷ 1.00) − (€227,273 + €17,825))

24.7 Hedging transactions

As shown above, where amounts are owed to or owed by entities in foreign currencies, it is possible that exchange rates will vary, leading to a change in the euro value of the receivable/payable. That is, the reporting entity will be exposed to the risk of losses (and also possible gains) that might be generated owing to movements in exchange rates.

To minimise the risk associated with foreign currency monetary items, an entity can enter into a **hedge contract**. By entering into an agreement that assumes a position opposite to the original transaction, an entity can minimise its exposure to foreign currency movements. Although IAS 21 relates to foreign currency transactions, it does not address foreign currency hedges. As paragraph 5 of IAS 21 explains: 'This Standard does not apply to hedge accounting for foreign currency items, including the hedging of a net investment in a foreign operation. IAS 39 applies to hedge accounting.'

> **hedge contract** Arrangement with another party in which that other party accepts the risks associated with changing commodity prices, cash flows or exchange rates.

Hence, for foreign currency hedges, we must refer to IAS 39 *Financial Instruments: Recognition and Measurement* (again, as indicated earlier, this means that within Europe when accounting for foreign currency, we now need to refer to three accounting standards: IAS 21, IAS 23 and IAS 39). As explained in Chapter 12, the IASB embarked on a project to improve the usefulness for users of financial statements by simplifying the classifications and measurement requirements for financial instruments. IFRS 9 *Financial Instruments*, which focuses on the classification and measurement of financial instruments, is to replace IAS 39. At the time of writing, the relevant requirements for hedge accounting are in IAS 39, hence this is the standard that we refer to. However, it needs to be appreciated that the rules will likely change in the near future, with the new requirements ultimately being incorporated in a revised IFRS 9.

A foreign currency hedge occurs when action is taken, whether by entering a foreign currency contract or otherwise, with the objective of avoiding or mitigating possible adverse financial effects of movements in exchange rates.

To illustrate a **hedge** agreement, let us assume that an Italian company orders some inventory from a US supplier on 1 May 2014 for US$200,000 (when the exchange rate is €1.00 = US$0.75) at a cost in euro of €266,667 (US$200,000 ÷ 0.75). The goods are to be supplied and paid for on 30 June 2014. To safeguard against exchange rate fluctuations, on the date it placed the order the company also entered into a forward exchange-rate contract to buy US$200,000 on 30 June 2014 from another party (typically a bank) at a **forward rate** of €1.00 = US$0.72.

> **hedge** Action taken to minimise possible adverse financial effects of movements in exchange rates or other market values.
>
> **forward rate** The exchange rate that is currently offered for the future acquisition or sale of a specific currency.

A forward rate is the exchange rate for delivery of a currency at a specified date in the future. It is a guaranteed rate of exchange that will be provided at a future date. With this forward-rate agreement, the entity has locked in the price of the goods to €277,778 (which is US$200,000 ÷ 0.72). The entity has contracted to buy a specified number of US dollars at a future date (probably from a bank) at a predetermined rate. This is sometimes referred to as a 'buy hedge'.

Let us assume that the euro decreases in value relative to the US dollar so that €1.00 buys only US$0.60 on 30 June 2014. In the absence of a forward-rate agreement, the entity would pay the US supplier €333,333 (US$200,000 ÷ 0.60). This is €66,666 more than the original euro obligation. However, given the forward exchange-rate agreement, the entity can obtain US$200,000 at an agreed cost of €277,778. The supplier of the US currency is a different party from the overseas inventory supplier and, as the other party to the forward-rate agreement bears the cost of the currency fluctuation, it would have received the gains if the exchange rate had moved in the opposite direction.

The above hedging arrangement involves a situation where a third party agrees to sell a fixed amount of a particular overseas currency on a fixed future date (or during a period expiring on a fixed future date) at the rate of exchange quoted in the contract (the forward rate). This is simply referred to as a 'forward contract'. Conversely, it is also possible to enter into an arrangement called a 'sell hedge' to sell an overseas currency to another entity, on or before a particular date, at an agreed rate. This could be particularly useful to an entity that sells goods overseas with the sales price denominated in foreign currencies. The European entity can lock in at the outset the amount of euros it will ultimately receive from the sale.

To illustrate a 'sell hedge', let us assume that an Austrian entity agrees on 1 January 2014 to sell some plant (to be constructed) to a UK company at a price of £500,000, payable on 30 June 2014. The exchange rate on 1 January 2014 is €1.00 = £0.46. At the same date it signs the contract with the UK organisation, the Austrian entity also enters into a forward-rate contract with a bank in which it agrees to sell £500,000 to the bank at an exchange rate of €1.00 = £0.50. The bank charges a premium, in this case equal to €86,957 [(£500,000 ÷ 0.46) – (£500,000 ÷ 0.50)], to compensate it for the risk it will be exposed to as a result of the agreement.

In effect the company has locked in the amount in euros it will receive for the sale. It will receive €1 million (£500,000 ÷ 0.50) regardless of what the exchange rate does. The company will deliver £500,000 to the bank, which has agreed by way of a forward-rate contract to convert the amount to €1 million. With the hedge, the value of the sales receipts is certain and the Austrian entity is prepared to pay (or forgo) the €86,957 to create this certainty and therefore insulate itself from possible adverse impacts of foreign exchange rate movements.

Of course, if the entity does not hedge the sale it could earn a greater amount of euros. For example, if the exchange rate drops to £0.40, the entity would receive €1.25 million. Conversely, if the exchange rate moves in the opposite direction, the receipts in euros would be less. To shield themselves from the risk of adverse exchange-rate movements, entities frequently hedge the foreign currency payable or receivable through a contract with a bank.

Where there is a hedge, the foreign exchange gains or losses on one transaction (for example, the hedge contract) will be offset by gains or losses on another (for example, on a transaction with a purchaser of the entity's inventory). This is the very reason for the entity to enter the hedge agreement. For the above sales transaction, if the exchange rate falls—that is, sterling pounds buy more euros or, alternatively, euros buy fewer sterling pounds—the entity will make gains on the sales contract with the overseas purchaser, which is denominated in sterling pounds that have increased in value when translated to euros, but will make losses on the contract with the bank. The loss is made on the contract with the bank because the overseas currency has increased in value, but the entity has already agreed to a forward rate with the bank, which is based on a previous exchange rate. If the exchange rate rises, the opposite holds. Where the hedge arrangement completely eliminates the consequences of adverse exchange-rate fluctuations, the purchase or sales arrangement is considered to be *perfectly hedged*. Otherwise, it is considered to be *partially hedged*.

24.7.1 Accounting for hedging transactions

As noted above, the relevant accounting standard in relation to hedges of foreign currency payables or receivables is IAS 39. In due course, and as mentioned previously, it will be IFRS 9.

According to paragraph 85 of IAS 39, the purpose of 'hedge accounting' is to recognise 'the offsetting effects on profit or loss of changes in the fair values of the hedging instrument and the hedged item'. The above definition refers to a 'hedging instrument' and a 'hedged item' and is therefore important to our discussion. These terms are defined in paragraph 9 of IAS 39 as follows:

> A hedging instrument *is a designated derivative or (for a hedge of the risk of changes in foreign currency exchange rates only) a designated non-derivative financial asset or non-derivative financial liability whose fair value or cash flows are expected to offset changes in the fair value or cash flows of a designated hedged item (paragraphs 72–77 and Appendix A paragraphs AG94–AG97 elaborate on the definition of a hedging instrument).*

Hedging instruments would include such things as forward foreign currency exchange contracts (forward contracts) and interest rate swaps.

> A hedged item *is an asset, liability, firm commitment, highly probable forecast transaction or net investment in a foreign operation that (a) exposes the entity to risk of changes in fair value or future cash flows and (b) is designated as being hedged (paragraphs 78–84 and Appendix A paragraphs AG98–AG101 elaborate on the definition of hedged items).*

The above definition of a hedged item makes reference to a 'highly probably forecast transaction'. This would include an anticipated future transaction that is currently uncommitted. A 'firm commitment' (also referred to in the above definition) would include, for example, a purchase order to buy an item of machinery in, say, four months.

Hedge accounting attempts to match the timing of profit or loss recognition on the hedging instrument with the profit or loss on the hedged item—but only when the hedging instrument meets specific requirements. To classify an arrangement as a hedge, and therefore to apply 'hedge accounting', IAS 39 strictly requires five conditions to be met. If a transaction is designated as a cash-flow hedge (and, as we will see, there are three general classifications of hedges, cash-flow hedges being one such classification), gains and losses on the hedging instrument will not generally need to be included within profit or loss until such time as the underlying transaction (for example, the sale or purchase of goods) occurs. If it is not designated as a cash-flow hedge, the gains and losses on both the hedged item and the hedging instrument would generally be required to be included as part of the period's profit or loss with the effects of one (for example, the hedged item) fully or partially offsetting the other (for example, the hedging instrument). The five conditions requiring to be met in order to apply 'hedge accounting' are contained in paragraph 88 of IAS 39 and summarised in Figure 24.1.

If the conditions are not met, hedge accounting as described in IAS 39 is not to be applied (this does not mean that an entity cannot account for its hedges, it simply means that the treatment allowed under IAS 39 is

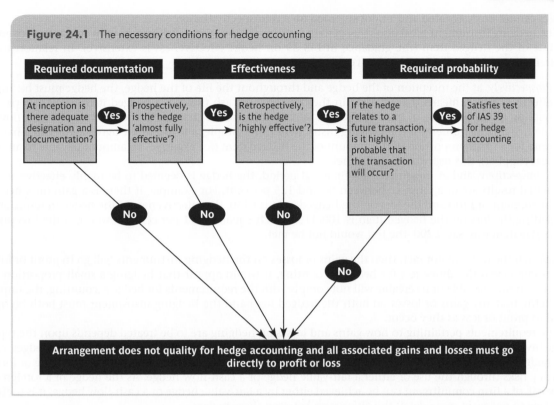

Figure 24.1 The necessary conditions for hedge accounting

not available). Rather, it would mean that gains or losses on the hedging instrument associated with the hedge would go to profit or loss as such gains or losses occur.

According to paragraph 86 of IAS 39, there are three principal types of hedge:

1. fair-value hedges;
2. cash-flow hedges; and
3. hedges of net investments in a foreign operation.

The most common forms of hedge are fair-value hedges and cash-flow hedges. Such hedges—which were discussed in Chapter 12—could be undertaken to mitigate risks associated with movements in foreign currency exchange rates; however, hedging arrangements can also be used to mitigate against price or value changes that are unrelated to foreign currency exchange rate movements. For example, fair-value hedges could be used to hedge the value of particular assets or liabilities—for example, to hedge the value of a share portfolio (the value of a share portfolio might be hedged by acquiring share price index (SPI) futures as a hedging instrument), and this hedging arrangement might have nothing to do with foreign currency exchange rates. A cash-flow hedge, on the other hand, could be used to hedge a future expected cash flow—for example, to hedge an amount that is payable to a foreign supplier, where that amount is denominated in US dollars and, hence, might fluctuate as foreign exchange rates fluctuate. We discussed such a hedge earlier in this chapter.

If a hedging instrument does not satisfy certain strict requirements identified in IAS 39, any gains or losses on the hedging instrument associated with a cash-flow hedge must be taken to profit or loss as and when they occur (if they do satisfy the tests provided in IAS 39, the gains or losses will initially be transferred directly to equity, perhaps accumulated in an account referred to as a 'hedging reserve' or similar). Paragraph 89 of IAS 39 stipulates the requirements for hedge accounting. Among these, as noted above, is the requirement for the financial instrument to be designated a hedging instrument at the initial point of recognition of the hedging instrument. This designation is constituted by documentation being in existence that covers matters associated with:

- the risk management objective and strategy;
- the identification of the *hedging instrument* being used;
- the related transaction or *hedged item*;
- the nature of the risk being hedged; and
- how the entity will assess the *effectiveness* of the hedging instrument.

Hedges cannot be designated and/or documented on a retrospective basis.

The hedging instrument must also meet certain tests in relation to its effectiveness in hedging the movement in value of the hedged item (the guidance in IAS 39 on hedge effectiveness is extensive). In relation to the requirements pertaining to hedge effectiveness, there are two tests:

1. *Prospectively*, at the inception of the hedge and throughout the life of the hedge, the hedge must be 'highly effective', which means that changes in the fair value or cash flows of a hedged item (such as a payable relating to the purchase of inventory) must 'almost fully' offset changes in the fair value or cash flows of the hedging instrument. If the hedging instrument (for example, a forward-rate agreement with a bank) is only for a small proportion of the amount of the hedged item (for example, an amount payable to an overseas supplier), this test would not be met.
2. *Retrospectively*, and as measured each financial period, the hedge is deemed to be highly effective so that actual results are in a range of between 80 and 125 per cent. For example, if there is a gain on a hedging instrument of £100 and the loss on the hedged item is £110, the effectiveness of the hedge in terms of offsetting the loss on the hedged item is 100/110, which equals 90.91 per cent. However, if the loss on the hedge item was, say, £200, the test would not be met.

Again, if the tests are not met, then the gains or losses on the hedging instruments will go to profit or loss as they occur. Given the above test for hedge accounting, it would appear that hedging a small proportion of a foreign currency payable or receivable will not comply with the requirements for hedge accounting, the implication being that any gains or losses on both the hedged item and the hedging instrument must both be transferred to profit or loss as they occur.

The requirements pertaining to how gains and losses on hedging are to be treated depends upon the type of hedge involved. Although three different types of hedge are identified by IAS 39, namely fair-value hedges, cash-flow hedges and hedges of net investments in foreign operations, this chapter deals with the hedging of foreign currency risks through the use of either a fair-value hedge or a cash-flow hedge. As the hedge of a foreign currency risk of a firm commitment can be achieved either by a fair-value hedge or a cash-flow hedge, it is useful at this stage to review in more detail the differences between these hedges.

Fair-value hedge

For a fair-value hedge (which might be undertaken to mitigate the risks associated with changes in the fair values of particular assets, such as an entity's share portfolio), paragraph 89 of IAS 39 requires both the *hedged item* and the *hedging instrument* to be valued at fair value, with any gains or losses owing to fair value adjustments to be treated as part of the period's profit or loss. If the gains or losses on the *hedged item* are 'perfectly hedged', the gains or losses on the *hedging instrument* will offset the gains or losses on the hedged item so that the net effect on the period's profit or loss could be £nil.

With a fair-value hedge, the risk being hedged is a change in the fair value of an asset or liability that will result in a gain or loss being recognised. Such changes in fair value can come about through changes in interest rates, foreign exchange rates, equity or commodity prices (IAS 39, paragraph 86).

An example of a fair-value hedge is the hedge of a fixed-rate bond with an interest rate swap, changing the interest rate from fixed to floating. A further example is the hedge of the changes in value of inventory using commodity forwards.

A fair-value hedge, then, is a hedge of exposure to changes in the fair value of a recognised asset or liability or an unrecognised firm commitment. For a fair-value hedge to be effective, it must create a risk exposure in the opposite direction from the risk of exposure of the hedged item. A recognised asset or liability is one that is shown in the statement of financial position, for example inventory or accounts payable. The risk exposure with these items is that they will be subject to an unfavourable change in value.

A firm commitment is defined in paragraph 9 of IAS 39 as a 'binding agreement for the exchange of a specified quantity of resources at a specified price on a specified future date or dates'. So an unrecognised firm commitment is a contractual obligation not yet recognised in the statement of financial position. In other words, there is no recorded asset or liability. The unrecognised firm commitment will, however, be recorded as an asset or liability that has risk exposure at some future date. An example of an unrecognised firm commitment would be a non-cancellable purchase order.

A further term that requires mention at this stage is 'forecast transaction'. A forecast transaction is defined in paragraph 9 of IAS 39 as 'an uncommitted but anticipated future transaction'.

Cash-flow hedges

In a cash-flow hedge, the risk being hedged is potential volatility in future cash flows. The cash flows might relate to a particular asset or liability, for example future expected sales in a foreign currency or future floating interest payments on a recognised liability. This is confirmed by paragraph 86 of IAS 39, which defines a cash-flow hedge as:

> *a hedge of the exposure to variability in cash flows that (i) is attributable to a particular risk associated with a recognised asset or liability (such as all or some future interest payments on variable rate debt) or a highly probable forecast transaction and (ii) could affect profit or loss.*

Any gain or loss that is determined to be associated with an effective hedge is recognised in equity. This ensures that any volatility in the profit or loss is avoided in the period during which the gains or losses are not yet recognised in the entity's profit or loss. The ineffective part of the hedge is recognised in profit or loss. In order to match the gains or losses of the hedged item and the hedging instrument, the changes in the fair value of the hedging instrument recognised in equity are removed from equity and recognised in the entity's profit or loss at the same time as the cash flows from the hedged item are recognised in profit or loss.

Therefore a cash-flow hedge is a hedge of the variability of cash flows relating to a future transaction. An effective cash-flow hedge will ensure any changes in cash flows from the hedging instrument are offset by changes in the cash flows of the hedged item. The hedged item might be a contractual cash flow relating to an existing asset or liability (for example, interest received or paid relating to an existing investment) or it might relate to a forecast transaction, including anticipated sales or purchases in a foreign currency that are not yet the subject of a contract (for example, forecast purchases or sales). Potential volatility results from changes in interest rates, exchange rates or commodity prices. Clearly the main distinction between a fair-value hedge and a cash-flow hedge is the fact that the former deals with changes in fair value while the latter deals with changes in cash flows.

For hedge accounting, forward contracts must be recognised as an asset or liability on the commitment date rather than on the date on which the settlement takes place. Further guidance is provided by paragraph AG35(c) of IAS 39, which states that:

> *When an entity becomes a party to a forward contract, the fair values of the rights and obligations are often equal, so that the net fair value of the forward is zero. If the net fair value of the right and obligation is not zero, the contract is recognised as an asset or liability.*

Again, reiterating some of the above points, for a cash-flow hedge (which might be undertaken to minimise the risk that a future expected cash flow, such as a payable denominated in a foreign currency, might fluctuate in a manner unfavourable to the entity), the gain or loss on measuring the *hedged item* at fair value is to be treated as part of the period's profit or loss. The gain or loss on the *hedging instrument* is initially to be transferred to equity, but subsequently transferred to profit or loss as necessary to offset the gains or losses recorded on the hedged item. At the conclusion of the hedging arrangement, any amount still in equity relating to the *hedging instrument* is to be transferred to profit or loss.

It is necessary to account separately for the hedging transaction (typically a forward-rate agreement with a bank, which would be designated as the 'hedging instrument') and the transaction that led to the need for the hedge—that is, the original purchase or sales arrangement with the overseas entity (the foreign currency receivable or payable would be the 'hedged item').

24.7.2 Accounting for fair-value hedges

For a fair-value hedge (which might be undertaken to mitigate the risks associated with changes in the fair values of particular assets, such as an entity's share portfolio), paragraph 89 of IAS 39 requires both the *hedged item* and the *hedging instrument* to be valued at fair value, with any gains or losses owing to fair value adjustments to be treated as part of the period's profit or loss. If the gains or losses on the *hedged item* are 'perfectly hedged', the gains or losses on the *hedging instrument* will offset the gains or losses on the hedged item so that the net effect on the period's profit or loss could be €nil.

For example, if there is a gain of €110 on a hedging instrument (say, a forward contract to buy foreign currency) and a loss of €100 on the hedged item (say, accounts payable denominated in foreign currency), the accounting entries for a fair-value hedge would be:

Dr	Forward contract	€110	
Cr	Profit or loss		€110
Dr	Profit or loss	€100	
Cr	Accounts payable		€100

Where an entity enters into a firm commitment to acquire an asset or assume a liability that is a hedged item in a fair-value hedge, paragraph 94 of IAS 39 requires the initial carrying amount of the asset or liability that results from the entity meeting the firm commitment to be adjusted to include the cumulative changes in the fair value of the firm commitment attributable to the hedged risk that was recognised in the statement of financial position.

In a firm commitment, the hedge relates to the price of particular goods or services to be purchased or sold. The gain or loss on that fair value hedging transaction up to the date of purchase or sale and any costs or gains arising at the time of entering into that transaction are, according to paragraph 94 of IAS 39, to be deferred by recognising the amounts directly in a hedge asset or liability account. When the underlying transaction is recognised in the accounts (for example, when inventory is actually acquired or a sale transaction is completed), the amounts are removed from the hedge asset or liability account and included in the measurement of the purchase price, or as part of the sale transaction. However, exchange differences relating to a hedge contract after the date of the underlying transaction are treated as part of profit or loss. The date of the hedge transaction is critical. An example of a fair-value hedge is provided in Worked Example 24.6.

Worked Example 24.6

Adoption of a hedge contract for a firm commitment to purchase goods where the hedge relates specifically to the purchase transaction

On 1 November 2014, Bonza plc, a Greek entity, entered a contract for US$3 million worth of inventory with Beattie Incorporated, a US supplier. The goods will be purchased FOB Philadelphia. A decision is made to take out a foreign exchange contract for US$3 million on 1 November 2014 with NYC Bank in which NYC Bank agrees to supply Bonza plc with US$3 million on 30 June 2015 at a cost of €4,411,764 (which is US$3.0m ÷ 0.68 with €1.00 = US$0.68 being the agreed forward rate). The goods are shipped on 1 April 2015 and are paid for on 30 June 2015. Bonza plc uses fair-value hedge accounting.

Additional information on exchange rates
The relevant exchange rates are provided below. The forward rates offered on particular dates, for delivery of US dollars on 30 June 2015, are provided. It should be noted that, on 30 June 2015, the last day of the forward rate contract, the spot rate and the forward rate will be the same.

Date	Spot rate US $	Forward rate US $
1 November 2014	0.70	0.68
31 December 2014	0.65	0.63
1 April 2015	0.60	0.58
30 June 2015	0.55	0.55

As we can see from the above information, the negotiated forward rate is lower than the prevailing spot rate. Bonza plc's end of reporting period is 31 December.

Required

Provide the necessary journal entries for Bonza plc to account for both the purchase transaction with Beattie Incorporated and the forward-rate contract with NYC Bank.

Solution

It is assumed that the hedge arrangement meets the five conditions (IAS 39, paragraph 88) necessary to permit the entity to apply hedge accounting. The hedge contract was entered into before the date of purchase and relates specifically to the purchase of the inventory. It is a hedge of a firm commitment. This means the exchange differences on the firm commitment, to the extent that they occur up to the date of the purchase, and the costs arising at the time of entering the transaction are to be deferred and included in the measurement of the purchase price of the inventory (consistent with paragraph 94 of IAS 39).

Gains or losses on the hedging instrument (forward contract) are calculated using the following information:

▶

Date	Spot rate US$	Forward rate US$	Receivable on forward contract[a] €	Amount payable on forward contract[b] €	Fair value of forward contract[c] €	Gain/(loss) on forward contract[d] €
1 November 2014	0.70	0.68	4,411,764	4,411,764	–	–
31 December 2014	0.65	0.63	4,761,905	4,411,764	350,141	350,141
1 April 2015	0.60	0.58	5,172,414	4,411,764	760,650	410,509
30 June 2015	0.55	0.55	5,454,545	4,411,764	1,042,781	282,131

Notes to the above table

[a] Determined by dividing US$3.0m by the respective dates' forward rate. This right refers to the amount to be received from the bank, the value of which will fluctuate as the forward rate changes. Although Bonza plc has been able to 'lock in' a particular forward rate (being 0.68), because the bank will negotiate different forward rates at different times the fair value of the receivable will change across time. For example, if the forward rate that was available in December was 0.63, then anybody entering a forward rate on that date would ultimately receive €4,761,905 on 30 June 2015. Gains or losses in the value of this receivable will act to offset the gains or losses in the value of the amount payable to the overseas supplier.

[b] The obligation (amount payable) represents the amount that must be paid to the bank using the forward rate negotiated with the bank and is fixed in absolute terms for the contracted party. This amount is fixed regardless of what happens to spot rates, or what forward rates the bank offers on other forward-rate contracts.

[c] We have calculated a fair value for the hedging instrument (the hedging instrument being the forward-rate contract). It is a requirement of IAS 39 that a fair value be attributed to the hedging instrument. According to IAS 39, the fair value represents the amount for which an asset could be exchanged, or a liability settled, between knowledgeable, willing parties in an arm's length transaction. In this situation, the fair value will change as the available forward rate being offered by the bank changes. For example, when the contract is originally negotiated, the bank is assumed to be offering the forward rate of €1.00 = US$0.68 for the delivery of US dollars on 30 June 2015 to any interested parties. Therefore, the contract itself has no fair value. However, if on 31 December the bank is only prepared to offer a forward rate for delivery of US dollars at €1.00 = US$0.63, then if Bonza plc was able to transfer its contract to another party needing US dollars on that date then, given the other options available to that other party, that party would be prepared to pay up to €350,141 for the contract, which equates to (US$3,000,000 ÷ 0.63) – (US$3,000,000 ÷ 0.68). The fair value of the contract would be deemed to be €350,141. There is also a requirement (paragraph 48A of IAS 39) that the financial instrument—in this case, the forward contract—be measured at the present value of the future cash flows. Because the life of the forward contract is less than 12 months, it has been decided on the basis of materiality not to discount the associated cash flows to present value in this worked example. In other examples in this chapter, no discounting will be applied to forward contracts with lives of less than 12 months.

[d] The gain or loss on the forward-rate contract represents the change in the fair value of the forward-rate contract.

1 November 2014
No entry is required here as the fair value of the forward-rate contract agreement is assessed as being zero as is the value of the firm commitment.

31 December 2014

Dr Forward contract (asset)	€350,141	
Cr Gain on forward contract (included in profit or loss)		€350,141

(to record changes in the fair value of forward contract)

31 December 2014

Dr Loss on firm commitment (included in profit or loss)	€329,671	
Cr Firm commitment (liability)		€329,671

(to record changes in the value of the firm commitment)

Because Bonza plc has entered a contract to buy inventory, there is considered to be a 'firm commitment' in terms of the requirements of IAS 39. The amount of the firm commitment will fluctuate as spot rates fluctuate on particular dates.

Value of firm commitment as at 1 November 2014: US$3,000,000 ÷ 0.70 = €4,285,714
Value of firm commitment as at 31 December 2014: US$3,000,000 ÷ 0.65 = €4,615,385
Increase in value of firm commitment €329,671

1 April 2015

Dr Forward contract (asset)	€410,509	
Cr Gain on forward contract (included in profit or loss)		€410,509

(to record change in fair value of forward contract)

1 April 2015

Dr	Loss on firm commitment (included in profit or loss)	€384,615	
Cr	Firm commitment (liability)		€384,615

(to record changes in value of firm commitment)

Value of firm commitment as at 1 November 2014: US$3,000,000 ÷ 0.65 =	€4,615,385
Value of firm commitment as at 31 December 2014: US$3,000,000 ÷ 0.60 =	€5,000,000
Increase in value of firm commitment	€384,615

1 April 2015

Dr	Firm commitment (asset)	€714,286	
Cr	Inventory (asset)		€714,286

(including cumulative loss on the 'firm commitment' in inventory up to the date of purchase, in accordance with paragraph 94 of IAS 39)

1 April 2015

Dr	Inventory	€5,000,000	
Cr	Accounts payable		€5,000,000

(recording purchase of inventory at the purchase date's spot rate (US$3,000,000 ÷ 0.60 = €5,000,000))

30 June 2015

Dr	Forward contract	€282,131	
Cr	Gain from forward contract (included in profit or loss)		€282,131

(recording gain from change in fair value of forward contract.)

30 June 2015

Dr	Foreign exchange loss (included in profit or loss)	€454,545	
Cr	Accounts payable		€454,545

(recording foreign exchange loss on accounts payable)

Value of accounts payable as at 30 June 2015: US$3,000,000 ÷ 0.55 =	€5,454,545
Value of firm commitment as at 1 April 2015: US$3,000,000 ÷ 0.60 =	€5,000,000
	€454,545

30 June 2015

Dr	Accounts payable	€5,454,545	
Cr	Forward contract		€1,042,781
Cr	Cash		€4,411,764

(to settle accounts payable. In this example, the other party to the forward-rate agreement—the bank—has actually made a loss on the transaction given the direction the exchange rates have moved. The total amount of cash ultimately paid by Bonza plc equals the amount that was originally negotiated in the forward-rate contract with the bank. The above entry assumes that the bank will transfer €1,042,781 to the overseas supplier.)

24.7.3 Accounting for cash-flow hedges

A cash-flow hedge (which might be undertaken to minimise the risk that a future expected cash flow, such as a payable denominated in a foreign currency, might fluctuate in a manner unfavourable to the entity) that meets the conditions of paragraph 88 of IAS 39 considered earlier is initially accounted for as follows. Paragraph 95 of IAS 39 requires the portion of the gain or loss on the *hedging instrument* determined to be an effective hedge to be recognised in equity, while the ineffective portion of the gain or loss on the hedging instrument is recognised in profit or loss. Specifically, guidelines for accounting for cash-flow hedges are provided by paragraph 96 of IAS 39 as follows:

(a) *the separate component of equity associated with the hedged item is adjusted to the lesser of the following (in absolute amounts):*
   (i) *the cumulative gain or loss on the hedging instrument from inception of the hedge; and*
   (ii) *the cumulative change in fair value (present value) of the expected future cash flows on the hedged item from inception of the hedge;*

(b) any remaining gain or loss on the hedging instrument or designated component of it (that is not an effective hedge) is recognised in profit or loss; and

(c) if an entity's documented risk management strategy for a particular hedging relationship excludes from the assessment of hedge effectiveness a specific component of the gain or loss or related cash flows on the hedging instrument (see paragraphs 74, 75 and 88(a)), that excluded component of gain or loss is recognised in accordance with paragraph 55.

For example, if there is a gain of £110 on a hedging instrument (say, a forward contract to buy foreign currency) and a loss of £100 on the hedged item (say, accounts payable denominated in foreign currency), the accounting entries for a cash-flow hedge are:

Dr	Forward contract	£110	
Cr	Hedging reserve (included in other comprehensive income)		£100
Cr	Foreign exchange gain		£10
Dr	Foreign exchange loss	£100	
Cr	Accounts payable		£100

In the case of a firm commitment and a cash-flow hedge there are two alternatives for the recording of gains and losses arising from fluctuations in exchange rates:

1. reclassify the gains and losses that were recognised directly in equity into profit or loss in the same period or periods during which the asset acquired or liability assumed affects profit or loss (IAS 39, paragraph 98(a)); or
2. remove the gains and losses that were recognised directly in equity and include them in the carrying value of the asset or liability.

If cash-flow hedge accounting were used in Worked Example 24.6, the journal entries for 31 December 2014 and 1 April 2015 would be recorded as follows:

31 Dec 2014

Dr	Forward contract	€350,141	
Cr	Hedging reserve (included in other comprehensive income)		€350,141

(recording changes in the fair value of forward contract)

1 April 2015

Dr	Inventory	€5,000,000	
Cr	Accounts payable		€5,000,000

(recording purchase of inventory (US$3,000,000 ÷ 0.60 = €5,000,000))

1 April 2015

Dr	Forward contract	€410,509	
Cr	Hedging reserve (included in other comprehensive income)		€410,509

(recording change in fair value of forward contract)

1 April 2015

Dr	Hedging reserve (included in other comprehensive income)	€760,650	
Cr	Gain on forward contract (included in profit or loss)		€760,650

(reclassifying cumulative gain on forward contract in profit and loss)

With alternative 2, the first three entries are the same as those provided under alternative 1. The fourth entry would be recorded as follows:

1 April 2015

Dr	Hedging reserve (included in other comprehensive income)	€760,650	
Cr	Inventory		€760,650

(including cumulative gain on forward contract in inventory)

The journal entries for 30 June 2015 are the same as those for fair-value hedge accounting because, according to paragraphs 97 and 100 of IAS 39, amounts that have been recognised directly in equity are included in profit

and loss in the same periods or in periods during which the forecast transaction affects profit and loss. This means that all gains and losses after this point are recognised directly in profit and loss.

In Worked Example 24.6, the hedge contract is entered into before the date of the purchase transaction. However, some companies might enter into a forward contract after the purchase or sale of goods but before payments are made or received. When such transactions occur, the accounting treatment is the same for fair-value hedge and cash-flow hedge accounting; in other words, gains and losses from changes in fair value of the forward contract are immediately recognised in profit or loss. This is in accordance with paragraph 89 (for fair-value hedge accounting) and paragraph 100 (for cash-flow hedge accounting) of IAS 39. An example of the adoption of a hedge contract after the date of purchase of goods is provided in Worked Example 24.7.

Worked Example 24.7 — Adoption of a hedge contract after the date of the purchase of goods

On 1 March 2015 Koala plc, a Bulgarian entity, purchases £1.2 million of inventory from Nigel Incorporated, a UK entity. The amount is payable on 1 August 2015. A forward exchange contract for the delivery of £1.2 million is taken out with ABC Bank on 1 May 2015. ABC Bank requires delivery of the foreign currency on 1 August 2015. Koala plc has a 30 June end.

Additional information
The relevant exchange rates are as follows:

Date	Spot rate	Forward rate
01 March 2015	0.40	
01 May 2015	0.37	0.35
30 June 2015	0.36	0.34
01 August 2015	0.32	0.32

Required

Prepare the journal entries for Koala plc to account for the hedge and provide evidence of whether or not hedge accounting in the above situation was beneficial.

Solution

The solution assumes that the hedge arrangement meets the conditions necessary to permit Koala plc to apply hedge accounting.

Date	Spot rate £	Forward rate £	Receivable on forward contract BGN	Amount payable on forward contract BGN	Fair value of forward contract BGN	Gain/(loss) on forward contract BGN
01 March 2015	0.40		–	–	–	–
01 May 2015	0.37	0.35	3,428,571	3,428,571	–	–
30 June 2015	0.36	0.34	3,529,412	3,428,571	100,840	100,840
01 August 2015	0.32	0.32	3,750,000	3,428,571	321,429	220,589

1 March 2015

Dr	Inventory	BGN3,000,000
Cr	Accounts payable	BGN3,000,000

(recording purchase of inventory (£1,200,000 ÷ 0.40))

1 May 2015

Dr	Foreign exchange loss	BGN243,243
Cr	Accounts payable	BGN243,243

(recording foreign exchange loss on accounts payable)
[(£1,200,000 ÷ 0.37) – (£1,200,000 ÷ 0.40) = BGN243,243]

▶

◄

30 June 2015

Dr Forward contract	BGN100,840	
Cr Gain on forward contract		BGN100,840

(recording gain on forward contract)

30 June 2015

Dr Foreign exchange loss	BGN90,090	
Cr Accounts payable		BGN90,090

(recording foreign exchange loss)
[(£1,200,000 ÷ 0.37) – (£1,200,000 ÷ 0.36) = BGN90,090; Test BGN90,090 ÷ BGN100,840 = 89%]

1 August 2015

Dr Forward contract	BGN220,589	
Cr Gain on forward contract		BGN220,589

(recording gain on forward contract)

1 August 2015

Dr Foreign exchange loss	BGN416,667	
Cr Accounts payable		BGN416,667

(recording foreign exchange loss) [(£1,200,000 ÷ 0.36) – (£1,200,000 ÷ 0.32) = BGN416,667]

1 August 2015

Dr Accounts payable	BGN3,750,000	
Cr Forward contract		BGN321,429
Cr Cash		BGN3,428,571

(settlement of forward-rate contract and accounts payable)

Foreign exchange loss incurred

	BGN
Amount paid on 1 August 2015	3,428,571
Accounts payable as at 1 March 2015 (date of purchase)	3,000,000
Total foreign exchange loss	(428,571)

Foreign exchange loss recorded

	BGN
For reporting period ending 30 June 2015	
Foreign exchange loss on accounts payable on 1 May 2015	(243,243)
Foreign exchange gain on forward contract on 30 June 2015	100,840
Foreign exchange loss on accounts payable on 30 June 2015	(90,090)
	(232,493)
For year ending 30 June 2016	
Foreign exchange gain on forward contract on 1 August 2015	220,589
Foreign exchange loss on accounts payable on 1 August5	(416,667)
	(196,078)
Total foreign exchange loss recorded	(428,571)

If the purchase was not hedged:

	BGN
Amount paid on 1 August 2015 (£1,200,000 ÷ 0.32)	3,750,000
Accounts payable as at 1 March 2015 (date of purchase)	3,000,000
Total foreign exchange loss	750,000

Hedging is therefore beneficial in this case.

Up to this point, hedging transactions relating to purchases of goods and services have been discussed. The same general principles apply to sales transactions. If a hedge contract is entered into before the date of sale, the contract relates to a particular sale and, if the required conditions for hedge accounting are met, any gains or costs at the date of entering the hedge (these gains or losses would include brokerage fees) and any gains or losses on the hedging instrument up to and including the date of sale are initially to be transferred to the hedged asset or liability (in fair-value hedge accounting) or to hedge reserve (in cash-flow hedge accounting) and then, when the underlying transaction occurs, transferred out and adjusted against the sales price of the goods or services. Subsequent gains or losses are included in profit or loss in the period in which the exchange rate fluctuation occurs. Worked Example 24.8 illustrates the adoption of a hedge contract prior to the date of sale of goods in a firm commitment.

| Worked Example 24.8 | Adoption of a hedge contract before the date of a sale of goods (a firm commitment) |

Cornish plc exports surfboards to Newquay (UK) plc. Newquay (UK) plc placed the order on 1 April 2015. The consignment of surfboards was sold FOB Calais (France) on 1 May 2015. The sales price was £1 million payable on 1 August 2015.

A sell-hedge forward-rate contract was entered into on 1 April 2015 (before the date of the sale) with ABC Bank for the delivery of euros in exchange for £1 million on 1 August 2015. The forward rate of the contract is €1.00 = £0.40 on 1 April 2015. Cornish plc uses cash-flow hedge accounting. Cornish plc's end of reporting period is 30 June.

Additional information

Date	Spot rate £	Forward rate £
01 April 2015	0.35	0.40
01 May 2015	0.30	0.36
30 June 2015	0.25	0.29
01 August 2015	0.37	0.37

Required

Prepare the journal entries for Cornish plc.

Solution

The solution assumes that the hedge arrangement meets the conditions necessary to permit Cornish plc to apply hedge accounting.

Date	Spot rate £	Forward rate £	Receivable on forward contract €	Amount payable on forward contract €	Fair value of forward contract €	Gain/(loss) on forward contract €
1 April 2015	0.35	0.40	2,500,000	2,500,000	–	–
1 May 2015	0.30	0.36	2,500,000	2,777,778	(277,778)	(277,778)
30 June 2015	0.25	0.29	2,500,000	3,448,276	(948,276)	(670,498)
1 August 2015	0.37	0.37	2,500,000	2,702,702	(202,702)	745,574

1 April 2015 No journal entries because right and obligation are the same

1 May 2015

Dr	Accounts receivable	€3,333,333	
Cr	Sales revenue		€3,333,333

(recording sales revenue (£1,000,000 ÷ 0.30))

1 May 2015

Dr	Hedging reserve (included in other comprehensive income)	€277,778	
Cr	Forward contract		€277,778

(recording loss on accounts receivable; the forward contract would represent a liability rather than an asset)

▶

1 May 2015

| Dr | Sales revenue | €277,778 | |
| Cr | Hedging reserve (included in other comprehensive income) | | €277,778 |

(transferring hedge reserve to sales revenue account)

On 30 June 2015 an effectiveness test is conducted. The foreign exchange gain on accounts receivable = (£1,000,000 ÷ 0.30 = €3,333,333) − (£1,000,000 ÷ 0.25 = €4,000,000) = €666,667 and loss on forward contract = €670,498 so the effectiveness is €670,498 ÷ €666,667 = 100.6 per cent, which is between the 80 to 125 per cent range required by paragraph AG105 of IAS 39. Therefore the forward contract is effective in hedging the accounts receivable and hedge accounting may be continued.

30 June 2015

| Dr | Accounts receivable | €666,667 | |
| Cr | Foreign exchange gain | | €666,667 |

[(£1,000,000 ÷ 0.30 = €3,333,333) − (£1,000,000 ÷ 0.25 = €4,000,000) = €666,667]

30 June 2015

| Dr | Loss on forward contract | €670,498 | |
| Cr | Forward contract | | €670,498 |

(recording loss on forward contract)

1 August 2015

| Dr | Foreign exchange loss | €1,297,297 | |
| Cr | Accounts receivable | | €1,297,297 |

(recording loss on accounts receivable)
[(£1,000,000 ÷ 0.37 = €2,702,702) − (£1,000,000 ÷ 0.25 = €4,000,000) = €1,297,297]

1 August 2015

| Dr | Forward contract | €745,574 | |
| Cr | Gain from forward contract | | €745,574 |

(recording change in fair value of forward contract)

1 August 2015

Dr	Cash	€2,500,000	
Dr	Forward contract	€202,702	
Cr	Accounts receivable		€2,702,702

(receiving payments and fulfilling forward contract)

In this example, the sales proceeds of £1.0 million have been fully hedged. As the forward-rate contract was entered into before the date of the sale, any costs or gains associated with the hedge contract are adjusted against the sales price. It is assumed that all five conditions necessary for hedge accounting are satisfied. Further, any exchange gains or losses on the forward-rate contract, after the date of sale, will be recognised in profit and loss. Ultimately, the entity receives the amount it had locked in with the bank, this being €2,500,000. Effectively, the entity is receiving €2,702,702 from the overseas customer, of which €202,702 goes to the bank. The amount that is paid to the bank at the end of the contract represents the difference between £1.0 million divided by the negotiated forward rate (£1,000,000 ÷ 0.40) and £1.0 million divided by the spot rate on 1 August 2015 (£1,000,000 ÷ 0.37).

If the hedge of the sales transaction occurs after the date of the sales transaction any costs or gains from entering the hedge are to be taken to profit or loss in the period they arise. In Worked Example 24.9 accounting for hedge contracts adopted after the date of a sale of goods is considered.

Worked Example 24.9	Adoption of a hedge contract after the date of a sale of goods

Energy plc exports modified Holden cars to Detroit Incorporated. All sales contracts are in US dollars. Sales of US$2.5 million are made on 1 May 2015, FOB Belfast (UK). The amount is due for payment by Detroit Incorporated on 30 September 2015. A sell-hedge contract—that is, an agreed rate at which Energy plc can sell the foreign currency at a future date—for US$2.5 million is taken out on 1 June 2015 with US Bank in which US Bank agrees to exchange US$2.5 million on 30 September 2015 at a forward rate of £1.00 = US$1.59. Energy plc's end of reporting period is 30 June.

Additional information
The relevant exchange rates are as follows:

Date	Spot rate US$	Forward rate US$
1 May 2015	1.60	
1 June 2015	1.57	1.59
30 June 2015	1.54	1.56
30 September 2015	1.52	1.52

Required
Prepare the journal entries for Energy plc.

Solution
The solution assumes that the hedge arrangement meets the conditions necessary to permit Energy plc to apply hedge accounting.

Date	Spot rate US$	Forward rate US$	Receivable on forward contract £	Amount payable on forward contract £	Fair value of forward contract £	Gain/(loss) on forward contract £
01 May 2015	1.60					
01 June 2015	1.57	1.59	1,572,327	1,572,327	–	–
30 June 2015	1.54	1.56	1,572,327	1,602,564	30,237	30,237
30 September 2015	1.52	1.52	1,572,327	1,644,737	72,410	42,173

1 May 2015

Dr	Accounts receivable	£1,562,500	
Cr	Sales revenue		£1,562,500

(recording sale: US$2,500,000 ÷ 1.60 = £1,562,500)

1 June 2015 No journal entries for recording forward contract as fair values of rights and obligations are the same

1 June 2015

Dr	Accounts receivable	£29,857	
Cr	Foreign exchange gain		£29,857

(recording loss on accounts receivable due to movements in foreign exchange rates)
[(US$2,500,000 ÷ 1.60) – (US$2,500,000 ÷ 1.57) = £29,857]

An effectiveness test is conducted on 30 June 2015. The gain on accounts receivable due to movements in foreign exchange rates is (US$2,500,000 ÷ 1.57) – (US$2,500,000 ÷ 1.54) = £31,020. Loss on forward contract owing to changes in fair value of forward contract = £30,237 and therefore the effectiveness = £30,237 ÷ £31,020 = 97 per cent, which is within the 80 to 125 per cent range. Therefore the forward contract is effective in hedging the accounts receivable and hedge accounting may be continued. If it is not, then gains or losses would go to profit or loss as they occur.

30 June 2015

Dr	Accounts receivable	£31,020	
Cr	Foreign exchange gain		£31,020

(recording gains on accounts receivable due to movements in foreign exchange rates)
[(US$2,500,000 ÷ 1.57) – (US$2,500,000 ÷ 1.54) = £31,020]

30 June 2015

Dr	Loss on forward contract	£30,237	
Cr	Forward contract		£30,237

(recording changes in fair value of forward contract)

30 Sept 2015

Dr	Accounts receivable	£21,360	
Cr	Foreign exchange gain		£21,360

(recording gains on accounts receivable due to movements in foreign exchange rates)
[(US$2,500,000 ÷ 1.52) – (US$2,500,000 ÷ 1.54) = £21,360]

30 Sept 2015

Dr	Loss on forward contract	£42,173	
Cr	Forward contract		£42,173

(recording changes in fair value of forward contract)

30 Sept 2015

Dr	Cash	£1,572,327	
Dr	Forward contract	£72,410	
Cr	Accounts receivable		£1,644,737

(receiving payments and fulfilling forward contract)

The net amount received is the amount agreed to with the bank. Effectively, £1,644,737 is received from the overseas customer (US$2,500,000 ÷ 1.52) and an amount of £72,410 is transferred to the bank (which represents the difference between US$2,500,000 divided by the agreed forward rate and US$2,500,000 divided by the closing spot rate).

Note that an effectiveness test is not conducted on 30 September 2015 because it is the settlement date.

24.7.4 Discontinuing hedge accounting

IAS 39 provides for the discontinuation of hedge accounting—in paragraph 91 for fair-value hedges, and in paragraph 101 for cash-flow hedges. In both cases discontinuation is to be done prospectively.

Discontinuing fair-value hedge accounting

The discontinuation of fair-value hedge accounting is to be done prospectively should any of the following situations arise:

- the hedging instrument expires, is sold, terminated or exercised;
- the hedge no longer meets the criteria for hedge accounting (considered earlier); or
- the entity revokes the designation.

If the fair-value hedge is discontinued because it no longer meets the hedge effectiveness criteria, according to paragraph AG113 of IAS 39, the discontinuation occurs from 'the last date on which compliance with hedge accounting was demonstrated'. However, if hedge accounting is discontinued as a result of changes in circumstances that result in the hedging relationship no longer meeting the effectiveness criteria, assuming that the hedge was effective before the change in circumstances, hedge accounting should be discontinued from the date the circumstances changed.

Discontinuing cash-flow hedge accounting

Like fair-value hedge accounting, cash-flow hedge accounting should be discontinued prospectively in the event of any of the following circumstances:

- the hedging instrument expires, is sold, terminated or exercised;
- the hedge no longer meets the criteria for hedge accounting (considered earlier);

- the forecast transaction is no longer expected to occur; or
- the entity revokes the designation.

Where cash-flow hedge accounting has been discontinued, entities are faced with the question of how to deal with any balances in equity. Where the hedging instrument is replaced or rolled over into another hedging instrument as part of the entity's documented hedging strategy, this is not considered to be an expiration or termination of a cash-flow hedge. As such, any amounts recognised in equity prior to the replacement or rollover, assuming the hedge was effective, remain in equity until the forecast transaction occurs.

When the forecast transaction is no longer expected to occur, any amounts previously recognised in equity are transferred to profit or loss. If the hedge designation is revoked by the entity, any balance in equity should remain in equity until the forecast transaction occurs or is no longer expected to occur. If the transaction is no longer expected to occur, the balance recognised directly in equity should be transferred to profit or loss.

24.8 Foreign currency swaps

Swaps occur when borrowers exchange aspects of their respective loan obligations. Commonly used swaps are:

- interest-rate swaps (typically a fixed-interest-rate obligation is swapped for a variable-rate obligation); and
- **foreign currency swaps** (where the obligation related to a loan denominated in one currency is swapped for a loan denominated in another currency).

> **foreign currency swap** Agreement under which the obligation relating to a loan denominated in one currency is swapped for a loan denominated in another currency.

In this section we will be looking at foreign currency swaps. The rules already discussed in this chapter apply generally to swap arrangements.

Let us look first, however, at why organisations would want to swap a loan denominated in one currency for a loan denominated in another. As we know, if we have receivables and payables that are both denominated in a particular foreign currency, changes in the spot rates will create gains on one and losses on the other. To the extent that the receivables and payables are for the same amount and denominated in the same currency, the losses on one monetary item (perhaps the foreign currency payable) will be offset by gains on the other monetary item (perhaps the foreign currency receivable).

If a particular organisation has a number of receivables that are denominated in a foreign currency, changes in spot rates can potentially create sizeable foreign currency gains or losses. If that same organisation is able to convert some of its domestic loans into foreign currency loans of the same denomination as its receivables, it will effectively insulate or hedge itself against the effects of changes in spot rates. Such an organisation might try to find another entity that is prepared to swap its foreign currency loans for the organisation's domestic loans, as shown in Worked Example 24.10.

Worked Example 24.10 **Foreign currency swap**

On 1 July 2014 Lennox plc, a European company, borrows £1 million in sterling from a UK company at a rate of 10 per cent, repayable in sterling. The loan is for a period of three years. The loan is on more favourable terms than Lennox plc is able to obtain within Europe. Lennox plc trades predominantly within Europe and therefore does not have any receivables that are denominated in sterling.

At the same time, Angourie plc, also a European company, borrows €1.25 million from a European bank at a fixed rate of 10 per cent. The loan is also for a period of three years. Angourie plc also has a number of receivables denominated in sterling. To insulate itself from foreign currency movements, it would prefer to have some payables denominated in sterling.

As a result of perceived benefits to both parties, Lennox plc and Angourie plc decide to swap their interest and principal obligations on the same date that they take out the loans, this being 1 July 2014. Under the swap terms, each party agrees to take control of the other party's principal and interest obligations.

▶

The relevant exchange rates are:

01 July 2014	€1.00 = £0.80
30 June 2015	€1.00 = £0.70
30 June 2016	€1.00 = £0.68
30 June 2017	€1.00 = £0.76

We will assume that the required market rates on both loans are equal to the coupon rates, that is, they are also 10 per cent (meaning there is no discount or premium on the loans), and we will further assume that the market rates remain at 10 per cent throughout the terms of the loans. Cash payments related to each loan are to be made on 30 June of each year.

Required

Provide the journal entries in the books of Lennox plc and Angourie plc to account for the above swap for the year ending 30 June 2015.

Solution

We use the following table to determine the fair value of the swap from Lennox plc's perspective.

Date	Fair value of foreign currency receivable component of swap	Fair value of the European payable component of swap*(€)	Fair value of swap (€)	Gain/(loss) on hedge (€)
01 July 2014	[(£1,000,000 ÷ 0.8) × 0.10 × 2.487 + [(£1,000,000 ÷ 0.8) × 0.7513] = €1,250,000	€1,250,000	–	–
30 June 2015	[(£1,000,000 ÷ 0.70) × 0.10 × 1.7355] + [(£1,000,000 ÷ 0.70) × 0.8264] = €1,428,571	€1,250,000	178,571	178,571
30 June 2016	[(£1,000,000 ÷ 0.68) × 0.10 × 0.9091] + [(£1,000,000 ÷ 0.68) × 0.9091] = €1,470,588	€1,250,000	220,588	42,017
30 June 2014	£1,000,000 ÷ 0.75 = €1,333,333	€1,250,000	83,333	(137,255)

*Because the interest paid on the European loan (the coupon rate) is 10 per cent, which also matches the required market rate, the face value of the loan also equates to the present value—that is, there is no premium or discount on the loan.

Accounting entries in the books of Lennox plc

1 July 2014

| Dr | Cash | €1,250,000 | |
| Cr | Foreign loan | | €1,250,000 |

(to recognise, at the 1 July 2014 spot rate, the initial loan received from the European company (€1,250,000 = £1,000,000 ÷ 0.80))

There is no entry to recognise the swap as the fair value of the swap agreement is deemed to be zero on 1 July 2014, as shown in the table above. The effect of entering the swap means that Lennox plc is insulated from any foreign currency gains or losses that might result from changes in the exchange rates.

30 June 2015

| Dr | Foreign exchange loss | €178,571 | |
| Cr | Foreign loan | | €178,571 |

Value of loan as at 1 July 2014 (£1,000,000 ÷ 0.80)	€1,250,000
Value of loan as at 30 June 2015 (£1,000,000 ÷ 0.70)	€1,428,571
Increase in the value of the loan	€178,571

◀

Dr	Swap	€178,571
Cr	Gain on swap contract	€178,571

(to recognise the gain on the swap contract negotiated with Angourie plc—see table above; the swap would be considered to represent a financial asset)

Dr	Interest expense	€142,857
Cr	Cash	€142,857

[€142,857 = (£1,000,000 × 0.10) ÷ 0.7]

Dr	Cash	€17,857
Cr	Interest expense	€17,857

(€142,857 − (€1,250,000 × 10 per cent) = €17,857)

Lennox initially has to make the payment to the European company for the funds it borrows. That is, even in the presence of the agreement with Angourie, Lennox will still comply with its contractual commitment with the overseas capital supplier. However, Angourie has agreed to take responsibility for the overseas loan, while Lennox plc has agreed to take responsibility for Angourie plc's domestic loan. The interest payment on the domestic loan is €125,000 (that is €1,250,000 × 10 per cent). Lennox plc will receive €17,857 from Angourie plc, so that Lennox plc's total interest expense (€142,857 − €17,857) is that payable on the domestic loan (€125,000)—the loan for which it has agreed to take responsibility.

Accounting entries in the books of Angourie plc

1 July 2014

Dr	Cash	€1,250,000
Cr	Loan	€1,250,000

(to recognise the domestic loan taken out by Angourie plc)

Remember that other parties to such loans, such as the overseas and domestic financial institutions in this example, might not know about swap arrangements such as the one negotiated between Angourie plc and Lennox plc. The contractual relationship between each company and its lending institution remains unchanged as a result of the swap arrangement. Should one party to the swap default on the arrangement, the obligation for repayment vests with the primary borrower. Generally, the interest and principal repayments will be made by the party that entered the initial contract with the financial institution. Cash adjustments will then be made between the parties to the swap.

There is no entry to recognise the swap as the fair value of the swap agreement is deemed to be zero on 1 July 2014, as shown in the table above.

30 June 2015

Dr	Loss on swap contract	€178,571
Cr	Swap	€178,571

Angourie plc records a loss as a result of entering the swap contract (the swap itself would be considered to be a financial liability). But, as indicated earlier, the reason Angourie plc has entered the swap contract is that it has receivables denominated in sterling. Adjustments to the value of these receivables (not shown in this example owing to lack of information) will offset, fully or partially, the losses on the swap contract.

Dr	Interest expense	€125,000
Cr	Cash	€125,000

(to recognise the interest payment made by Angourie plc on the domestic loan: €125,000 = €1,250,000 × 10 per cent)

As per the swap agreement, however, Lennox will take responsibility for the domestic loan commitments.

Dr	Interest expense	€17,857
Cr	Cash	€17,857

An adjustment payment between Angourie plc and Lennox plc is made so that, in total, Angourie plc will make payments equivalent only to the interest on the overseas loan (the loan it has taken responsibility for as part of the swap).

Cash flows associated with domestic loan (€1,250,000 × 10 per cent)	€125,000
Cash flows associated with overseas loan (£1,000,000 × 10 per cent) ÷ 0.70	€142,857
Amount to be transferred from Angourie to Lennox	€17,857

SUMMARY

In this chapter we considered various aspects of the translation of transactions that are denominated in a foreign currency. We learned that we need to refer to three accounting standards: IAS 21 *The Effects of Changes in Foreign Exchange Rates*, IAS 23 *Borrowing Costs* and IAS 39 *Financial Instruments: Recognition and Measurement*.

In terms of specific requirements, we learned the following:

- Foreign currency transactions should initially be translated at the spot rate in place at the date of the transaction using the functional currency as the basis of the translation.
- The functional currency might be different from the presentation currency.
- Any changes in the functional currency equivalents of foreign currency monetary amounts (such as foreign currency receivables, foreign currency payables and foreign currency monetary deposits) are, with some limited exceptions, to be recognised as part of the profit or loss as disclosed in the statement of comprehensive income, whether or not the amounts have been realised.
- Gains or losses on foreign currency receivables and payables are not to be offset against related purchases or sales amounts.
- We need to ascertain whether a foreign currency movement relates to a qualifying asset. If the movement relates to a qualifying asset, IAS 23 requires the movement to be adjusted against the cost of the asset. The foreign currency movements will be adjusted against the cost of the asset only as long as the asset's adjusted book value does not exceed its recoverable amount. Once an asset ceases to be a qualifying asset, all movements in related monetary items are to go to the statement of comprehensive income.
- Where hedge contracts have been entered into, the forward-rate contracts and the purchase or sales transactions must be accounted for separately. With a fair-value hedge, the risk being hedged is any change in the fair value of an asset or liability that will have an effect on profit or loss. Provided a fair-value hedge satisfies the five conditions necessary for hedge accounting, any gain or loss arising from remeasuring the hedging instrument at fair value and any gain or loss on the hedged item attributable to the hedged risk is recognised in profit or loss.
- In a cash-flow hedge the risk being hedged is the potential volatility in future cash flows. If a cash-flow hedge meets the five conditions for hedge accounting, the portion of the gain or loss on the hedging instrument deemed to be an effective hedge is recognised directly in equity. The ineffective portion of the gain or loss on the hedging instrument is recognised directly in profit or loss.
- Foreign currency swaps may be undertaken as a form of hedging. Where a swap occurs, the primary borrower will still have a commitment to the primary lender should the other party to the swap default on the swap arrangement. Hence, it is not correct practice to eliminate a loan from the accounts once a swap arrangement has been negotiated.

KEY TERMS

END-OF-CHAPTER EXERCISE

On 1 March 2015 Narrabeen plc, a German company, enters a purchase transaction with Huntington plc (UK) for the supply of £1 million in inventory. The goods are purchased FOB Holyhead on 1 March 2015. The amount is payable on 1 August 2015. To cover this exposure and other related foreign exchange exposures, a forward-exchange contract for the delivery of £1 million is taken out with The Bank on 1 May 2015. It requires delivery of the sterling on 1 August 2015. Narrabeen plc uses fair-value hedge accounting and the applicable discount rate is 6 per cent. Narrabeen plc's year end is 30 June. The relevant exchange rates are: **LO** 24.6

Date	Spot rate £	Forward rate £
01 March 2015	0.75	
01 May 2015	0.70	0.67
30 June 2015	0.65	0.63
01 August 2015	0.60	0.60

REQUIRED

Provide the necessary accounting journal entries to record the above transactions from 1 March 2015 to 1 August 2015, inclusive. Provide evidence of whether or not hedge accounting was effective in the above situation.

SOLUTION TO END-OF-CHAPTER EXERCISE

The solution assumes that the hedge arrangement meets the conditions necessary to permit Narrabeen plc to apply hedge accounting.

Date	Spot rate £	Forward rate £	Receivable on forward contract €	Amount payable on forward contract €	Fair value of forward contract €	Gain/(loss) on forward contract €
01 March 2015	0.75					
01 May 2015	0.70	0.67	1,492,537	1,492,537	0	
30 June 2015	0.65	0.63	1,587,302	1,492,537	94,765	94,765
01 August 2015	0.60	0.60	1,666,667	1,492,537	174,130	79,365

1 March 2015

Dr	Inventory	€1,333,333	
Cr	Accounts Payable		€1,333,333

(recording purchase of inventory (£1,000,000 ÷ 0.75))

1 May 2015

Dr	Foreign exchange loss	€95,238	
Cr	Accounts payable		€95,238

(recording foreign exchange loss on accounts payable)
[(£1,000,000 ÷ 0.75 = €1,333,333) − (£1,000,000 ÷ 0.70 = €1,428,571) = €95,238]

1 May 2015 No journal entries for forward contract because right and obligation are the same

At the end of the reporting period of 30 June 2015, the effectiveness test showed that the hedge was 85 per cent effective, determined as follows: (£1,000,000 ÷ 0.70 = €1,428,571) − (£1,000,000 ÷ 0.65 = €1,538,462) = €109,891. The gains from forward contract = €94,765. The effectiveness is calculated as €94,765 ÷ €109,891 = 86 per cent, which is within the range of 80 to 125 per cent, with the result that hedge accounting may be continued.

30 June 2015

Dr	Forward contract	€94,765	
Cr	Gain on forward contract		€94,765

(recording gain on forward contract)

30 June 2015

Dr	Foreign exchange loss	€109,891	
Cr	Accounts payable		€109,891

(recording loss on accounts payable denominated in foreign currency)
[(£1,000,000 ÷ 0.70 = €1,428,571) − (£1,000,000 ÷ 0.65 = €1,538,462) = €109,891]

1 August 2015

Dr	Forward contract	€79,365	
Cr	Gain on forward contract		€79,365

(recording loss on forward contract)

1 August 2015

Dr	Foreign exchange loss	€128,205	
Cr	Accounts payable		€128,205

(recording loss on accounts payable denominated in foreign currency)
[(£1,000,000 ÷ 0.60 = €1,666,667) – (£1,000,000 ÷ 0.65 = €1,538,462) = €128,205]

1 August 2015

Dr	Accounts payable	€1,666,667	
Cr	Forward contract		€174,130
Cr	Bank		€1,492,537

(settlement of forward-rate contract and accounts payable)

Foreign exchange loss incurred	€
Amount paid on 1 August 2015	1,492,537
Accounts payable as at 1 March 2015 (date of purchase)	1,333,333
Total foreign exchange loss	(159,204)

Foreign exchange loss recorded	€
For year ending 30 June 2015	
Foreign exchange loss on accounts payable on 1 May 2015	(95,238)
Foreign exchange gain on forward contract on 30 June 2015	94,765
Foreign exchange loss on accounts payable on 30 June 2015	(109,891)
	(110,364)
For year ending 30 June 2016	
Foreign exchange gain on forward contract on 1 August 2015	79,365
Foreign exchange loss on accounts payable on 1 August 2015	(128,205)
	(48,840)
Total foreign exchange loss recorded	(159,204)

If the purchase was not hedged:	€
Amount paid on 1 August 2015 (£1,000,000 ÷ 0.60)	1,666,667
Accounts payable as at 1 March 2015 (date of purchase)	1,333,333
Total foreign exchange loss	333,334

Hedging is therefore beneficial in this case.

REVIEW QUESTIONS

1   Explain why it is necessary to translate foreign currency transactions into the euro (or sterling if you are a UK student). **LO** 24.1

2   At the reporting date of a reporting entity, are any adjustments necessary in relation to the reporting entity's foreign currency monetary items? How should any adjustments (if necessary) be treated for statement of comprehensive income purposes? **LO** 24.3

3   When initially recognising a transaction that is denominated in a foreign currency, what exchange rates should be used to translate the transaction to euros (or sterling if you are a UK student)? **LO** 24.2

4   Some inventory is acquired from an overseas supplier with the debt denominated in a foreign currency. In the absence of a hedge arrangement, if the exchange rate moves against the euro (or sterling if you are a UK student) while the debt is outstanding, how should this movement be treated for accounting purposes? **LO** 24.3

5   What is a qualifying asset and how do we treat exchange rate differences relating to the acquisition of qualifying assets? Contrast this with the treatment for assets that are not qualifying assets. **LO** 24.5

6 What is a hedge transaction and how does it reduce foreign currency risk exposure? **LO 24.6**

7 When is a foreign currency monetary item considered to be perfectly hedged? **LO 24.6**

8 Why are the definitions of a hedging instrument and a hedged item important? **LO 24.6**

9 What are foreign currency swaps and why are they undertaken? **LO 24.7**

10 On 5 June 2014 Paris plc acquires goods on credit from a supplier in London. The goods are shipped FOB London on 5 June 2014. The cost of the goods is £250,000 and the debt remains unpaid at 30 June 2014. On 5 June 2014 the exchange rate is €1.00 = £0.46. On 30 June 2014 it is €1.00 = £0.44. Hence the value of the euro has decreased relative to sterling. Paris plc's reporting date is 30 June. **LO 24.2**

Provide the accounting entries necessary to account for the above purchase transaction for the year ending 30 June 2014.

11 On 1 July 2014 Double Island plc, a Finnish company, enters into an agreement to borrow £2 million from Point plc (UK). Point plc sends the loan money to Double Island plc's bank account in Finland. The loan is for four years and requires the payment of interest at the rate of 8 per cent on 30 June each year. Double Island plc's reporting date is 30 June. The relevant exchange rates are: **LO 24.3**

01 July 2014	€1.00 = £0.48
30 June 2015	€1.00 = £0.50

REQUIRED

Provide the necessary journal entries that would be made in the books of Double Island plc to account for the above transaction for the year ending 30 June 2015.

12 On 10 July 2014 Coolum plc, an Italian company, provides some consulting advice to Birmingham plc (UK) for an agreed fee of €1 million. The amount is paid into the UK bank account of Coolum plc on 10 July 2014. Coolum plc elects to leave the amount in the UK bank account, which pays interest each year on 30 June at a rate of 10 per cent. The relevant exchange rates are: **LO 24.3**

10 July 2014	€1.00 = £0.78
30 June 2015	€1.00 = £0.75

REQUIRED

Provide the journal entries that would need to be made in the books of Coolum plc to account for the above transaction for the year ending 30 June 2015.

13 On 1 March 2014 Drouyn plc, a Scottish company, enters into a binding agreement with a Spanish company, which requires the Spanish company to construct an item of machinery for Drouyn plc. The cost of the machinery is €750,000. The machinery is completed on 1 June 2014 and shipped FOB Barcelona on that date. The debt is unpaid at 30 June 2014, which is also Drouyn plc's reporting date. **LO 24.3**

The exchange rates at the relevant dates are:

01 March 2014	£1.00 = €1.20
01 June 2014	£1.00 = €1.30
30 June 2014	£1.00 = €1.25

REQUIRED

Provide the required journal entries of Drouyn plc for the year ending 30 June 2014.

14 On 1 March 2014 Possum plc, an entity located in Luxembourg, purchases £1.5 million of inventory from Liverpool plc, a UK entity. The amount is payable on 1 August 2014. A forward-exchange contract for the delivery of £1 million is taken out with The Bank on 1 May 2014. It requires delivery of the foreign currency to Possum plc on 1 August 2014. Possum plc has a 30 June financial year end. **LO 24.3**

Additional information

Date	Spot rate	Forward rate
01 March 2014	£0.70	
01 May 2014	£0.75	£0.73
30 June 2014	£0.72	£0.70
01 August 2014	£0.70	£0.70

Prepare the journal entries for Possum plc to account for the above transaction.

15 On 1 March 2014 Kanga plc, a Turkish entity, places an order for £1.5 million of inventory with Ferrett plc, a UK supplier. The goods will be purchased FOB Liverpool. A decision is made to take out a foreign exchange forward-rate contract for £1.5 million on 1 March 2014 with The Bank, in which The Bank agrees to supply Kanga plc with £1.5 million on 1 August 2014. The goods are shipped on 1 June 2014 and are paid for on 1 August 2014. **LO 24.6**

Additional information

Date	Spot rate	Forward rate
01 March 2014	£0.45	£0.42
01 June 2014	£0.43	£0.40
30 June 2014	£0.39	£0.36
01 August 2014	£0.41	£0.41

REQUIRED

Assuming that the hedging arrangement satisfies the requirements for hedge accounting as stipulated in IAS 39, and the management of Kanga plc adopts cash-flow hedge accounting, provide the necessary journal entries for Kanga plc to account for both the purchase transaction with Ferrett plc and the forward-rate contract with The Bank.

16 Platypus plc, a UK company exports goods to France plc. All sales contracts are denominated in euros. Sales of €5 million are made on 1 May 2014, FOB Lyon. The amount is due for payment by France plc on 1 September 2014. A sell-hedge contract for €5 million is taken out on 1 June 2014 with The Bank. It matures on 1 September 2014. Platypus plc's reporting date is 30 June. **LO 24.6**

Additional information

Date	Spot rate	Forward rate
01 May 2014	£0.84	–
01 June 2014	£0.82	£0.84
30 June 2014	£0.85	£0.87
01 September 2014	£0.86	£0.86

REQUIRED

Prepare the journal entries for Platypus plc to account for the above transaction.

17 On 1 July 2014 Crescent plc, a Belgian company, borrows £15 million at a rate of 8 per cent from a UK company, repayable in sterling. The loan is for a period of five years. The loan is on more favourable terms than Crescent plc is able to obtain within Belgium. Crescent plc trades predominantly within Europe.

At the same time, Plummer plc, also a Belgian company, borrows €18.75 million from a European bank at a fixed rate of 8 per cent. The loan is for a period of five years. Plummer plc also has a number of receivables denominated in sterling.

As a result of perceived benefits to both parties, Crescent plc and Plummer plc decide to swap their interest and principal obligations on the same date that they take out the loans, that is, 1 July 2014. Under the swap terms, each party agrees to take control of the other party's principal and interest obligations. The required market rates of return on both loans is assumed to be 8 per cent and these market rates remain at 8 per cent throughout the terms of the loans. **LO 24.7**

The relevant exchange rates are:

01 July 2014 €1.00 = £0.80
30 June 2015 €1.00 = £0.70

REQUIRED

Provide the journal entries for the year ending 30 June 2015 in the books of Crescent plc and Plummer plc to account for the above swap.

CHALLENGING QUESTIONS

18 You are the finance director of ME plc. The company specialises in importing classic foreign vehicles from overseas countries and then selling these vehicles cheaply on the open market. The company's financial year ends on 30 June 2014. The company enters into the following transactions during the year: **LO 24.5**

(a) The company purchases inventories from Denmark for DKK300,000. The order is placed on 22 April 2014, with delivery due by 30 April 2014. Under the conditions of the contract, title to the goods passes to the company on delivery. Payment in respect of these inventories is due in equal instalments on 30 May 2014, 30 June 2014 and a final payment on 31 July 2014. The following exchange rates are applicable:

22 April 2014	DKK8.00 = £1.00
30 April 2014	DKK8.50 = £1.00
31 May 2014	DKK8.56 = £1.00
30 June 2014	DKK8.59 = £1.00
31 July 2014	DKK8.94 = £1.00

(b) The company enters into a long-term construction contract with a Japanese company. Under the terms of the contract the Japanese firm will manufacture an engine diagnosis machine, which can be used on all classic cars. The contract is entered into on 30 April 2013 for a fixed price of ¥5 million. The equipment is delivered on 31 May 2014, subject to a two-month credit period after the date of delivery to ensure that the company is satisfied with the equipment. Payment falls due on 31 July 2014. The following exchange rates are applicable:

30 April 2013	¥160 = £1.00
31 May 2014	¥240 = £1.00
30 June 2014	¥245 = £1.00
31 July 2014	¥260 = £1.00

(c) The company arranges a US-dollar interest-only loan on 1 January 2014 for US$20 million. The loan is for a ten-year period at an interest rate of 11.5 per cent per annum. Interest is payable annually. Concerned about the volatility of sterling against the US dollar, the company takes out a hedge contract on the loan, payable on 1 January 2014. The hedge contract covers the first two years' interest payments. The hedge rate is set at £1.00 = US$1.65. The following exchange rates are applicable:

Date	Spot rate	Forward rate
01 January 2014	$US1.69	$US1.65
30 June 2014	$US1.64	$US1.60

(d) The company has agreed to purchase ten new hand-made sports cars from a Sporta supplier. The official order for the vehicles is placed on 31 January 2014. The contract price is established at Sp$350,000 and delivery takes place on 30 May 2014, as agreed. Payment is due in respect of these vehicles on 31 August 2014. In anticipation of the contract on 31 January 2014, the company enters into a foreign currency contract to receive Sp$350,000 at a forward rate of Sp$0.45 = £1.00. The following exchange rates are applicable:

Date	Spot rate	Forward rate
31 January 2014	Sp$0.49 = £1.00	Sp$0.46 = £1.00
31 May 2014	Sp$0.47 = £1.00	Sp$0.44 = £1.00
30 June 2014	Sp$0.43 = £1.00	Sp$0.40 = £1.00
31 August 2014	Sp$0.40 = £1.00	Sp$0.40 = £1.00

REQUIRED

Prepare the journal entries to reflect the effects of the above transactions in accordance with IAS 21, IAS 23 and IAS 39. Explain the treatment adopted in respect of each of the above transactions.

19 ABC Pty plc, a Bulgarian company, purchases inventory from DEF plc, a listed British company. Relevant events and the spot rates at each date are shown as follows: **LO** 24.6

Date	Event	Spot rate
15 March 2014	Order £300,000 of inventory	BGN1.00 = 37p
11 May 2014	Purchase takes place as inventory is shipped to ABC plc (FOB)	BGN1.00 = 41p
30 June 2014	End of financial year	BGN1.00 = 43p
02 July 2014	Inventory arrives at warehouse	BGN1.00 = 42p
14 August 2014	Payment of £300,000 to supplier	BGN1.00 = 39p

(a) Prepare appropriate journal entries for each relevant event.

(b) Assume that, instead of inventory, the purchase is plant and equipment, which is installed ready for use on 15 July 2014 when the rate is still BGN1.00 = 42p. Prepare appropriate journal entries for each relevant event.

(c) Assume that the inventory purchase prompts the taking out of a forward-rate contract on 15 March 2014 to purchase £300,000 on 14 August 2014 at an agreed rate of BGN1.00 = 34p. Prepare appropriate journal entries for each relevant event.

The forward rates applicable at each of the dates are:

Date	Forward rate
15 March 2014	BGN1.00 = £0.34
11 May 2014	BGN1.00 = £0.38
30 June 2014	BGN1.00 = £0.40
2 July 2014	BGN1.00 = £0.38
14 August 2014	BGN1.00 = £0.39

(d) Explain the effect of an 'effective' hedge contract on ABC Pty plc's profit or loss.

You can assume a discount rate of 12 per cent per annum.

Chapter 25

Translating the Financial Statements of Foreign Operations

Learning objectives

Upon completing this chapter readers should:

LO1 understand why it is necessary to translate the financial statements of foreign subsidiaries to a specific presentation currency before the consolidation process is performed;

LO2 be able to translate the financial statements of a foreign operation into a particular functional currency;

LO3 be able to translate the financial statements of a foreign operation into a particular presentation currency; and

LO4 understand what exchange rates to use when translating the financial statements of a foreign operation.

25.1 Introduction to translating the financial statements of foreign operations

In the consolidation process we combine the financial statements of a parent entity (defined in IFRS 10 as an entity that has one or more subsidiaries) and its controlled entities (or subsidiaries, which are defined in IFRS 10 as entities, including unincorporated entities such as partnerships, that are controlled by another entity), subject to a number of adjustments and eliminations. If some of the controlled entities are foreign entities with account balances denominated in foreign currencies, it would be necessary to translate these accounts to a given presentation currency (euro or sterling, for example) before the consolidation process is undertaken. It would not make sense to consolidate financial statements that are in different currencies. As paragraph 38 of IAS 21 states:

> An entity may present its financial statements in any currency (or currencies). If the presentation currency differs from the entity's functional currency, it translates its results and financial position into the presentation currency. For example, when a group contains individual entities with different functional currencies, the results and financial position of each entity are expressed in a common currency so that the consolidated financial statements may be presented.

The issue of how to translate these foreign entities' financial statements is addressed in this chapter. The accounting standard pertaining to the translation of foreign subsidiaries is IAS 21 *The Effects of Changes in Foreign Exchange Rates*. As we saw in Chapter 24, this accounting standard also provides rules for translating foreign currency transactions.

In this chapter we will consider how to translate the financial statements from a particular local currency into a particular functional currency, and we will also consider how to translate the financial statements from a particular functional currency into a specific presentation currency.

From the preceding sentence, reference was made to three different types of currency, these being local currency, functional currency and presentation currency. These currencies can be defined as follows:

- *Local currency*: the currency used in the country in which the foreign operation is located.
- *Functional currency*: Paragraph 8 of IAS 21 defines functional currency as 'the currency of the primary economic environment in which the entity operates'.
- *Presentation currency*: Paragraph 8 of IAS 21 defines the presentation currency as 'the currency in which the financial statements are presented'.

A detailed discussion of the factors management needs to consider when determining the functional currency of an entity and of how to establish its presentation currency is provided in Chapter 24. We now consider how to translate the accounts of a foreign operation in accordance with the requirements of IAS 21.

25.2   Reporting foreign currency transactions in the functional currency

In this chapter we will consider two situations. First, we will consider translating the financial statements of an entity into a particular functional currency. Next, we will consider how to translate the financial statements of an entity from a particular functional currency into a particular presentation currency.

This section reviews how transactions undertaken in a **foreign currency** are translated into an entity's functional currency. If the functional currency is the same as the local currency, then there will be no need to translate the financial statements of the foreign operation into the functional currency, as the financial statements prepared in the local currency will already have been prepared in the functional currency. In such circumstances we will only need to translate the foreign operation's financial statements into the group's presentation currency (that is, we could ignore the requirements detailed in this section and move directly to Section 25.3).

> **foreign currency**
> A currency other than the functional currency of the entity.

As noted above, the functional currency of an entity is, according to IAS 21, 'the currency of the primary economic environment in which the entity operates'. According to paragraph 12 of IAS 21, management uses its judgement 'to determine the functional currency that most faithfully represents the economic effects of the underlying transactions, events and conditions'. Paragraph 12 of IAS 21 further states:

> *As part of this approach [to determining the functional currency], management gives priority to the primary indicators in paragraph 9 before considering the indicators in paragraphs 10 and 11, which are designed to provide additional supporting evidence to determine an entity's functional currency.*

Paragraphs 9, 10 and 11 of IAS 21 state the following (and remember, from the above paragraph, that management is required to give priority to paragraph 9 when determining an entity's functional currency):

9. *The primary economic environment in which an entity operates is normally the one in which it primarily generates and expends cash. An entity considers the following factors in determining its functional currency:*
   (a) *the currency:*
      (i) *that mainly influences sales prices for goods and services (this will often be the currency in which sales prices for its goods and services are denominated and settled); and*
      (ii) *of the country whose competitive forces and regulations mainly determine the sales price of its goods and services;*
   (b) *the currency that mainly influences labour, material and other costs of providing goods or services (this will often be the currency in which such costs are denominated and settled).*
10. *The following factors may also provide evidence of an entity's functional currency:*
    (a) *the currency in which funds from financing activities (i.e. issuing debt and equity instruments) are generated;*
    (b) *the currency in which receipts from operating activities are usually retained.*
11. *The following additional factors are considered in determining the functional currency of a foreign operation, and whether its functional currency is the same as that of the reporting entity (the reporting entity, in this context, being the entity that has the foreign operation as its subsidiary, branch, associate or joint venture):*
    (a) *whether the activities of the foreign operation are carried out as an extension of the reporting entity, rather than being carried out with a significant degree of autonomy. An example of the former is when the foreign operation only sells goods imported from the reporting entity and remits the proceeds to it. An example of the latter is when the operation accumulates cash and other monetary items, incurs expenses, generates income and arranges borrowings, all substantially in its local currency;*

(b) *whether transactions with the reporting entity are a high or low proportion of the foreign operation's activities;*

(c) *whether cash flows from the activities of the foreign operation directly affect the cash flows of the reporting entity and are readily available for remittance to it;*

(d) *whether cash flows from the activities of the foreign operation are sufficient to service existing and normally expected debt obligations without funds being made available by the reporting entity.*

Therefore, if a parent entity has a subsidiary located in another country, then the first task to be undertaken prior to the consolidation process is to determine the functional currency of the overseas subsidiary. For example, if a UK parent has a subsidiary that is located in Ireland, then it is likely that the subsidiary would maintain its financial statements in the local currency, which is euros. However, the functional currency of that subsidiary would probably be either sterling or the euro. For the functional currency of the subsidiary to be sterling there would be an expectation that there is a high degree of dependence between the subsidiary and the parent entity such that the subsidiary is effectively operating as a direct branch of the UK operation. Perhaps the entity acquires products directly from the parent entity and sells the products at prices based on sterling. If the functional currency is determined to be sterling, then there will be a need to translate the Irish subsidiary's financial statements from euros into sterling. In contrast, if the subsidiary operates quite independently from the UK parent, perhaps because it produces the goods locally, and sells its products at prices based on the euro, then the functional currency might be the same as the local currency of the subsidiary, in this case, the euro. In this example, financial statements prepared in euros are automatically also presented in the functional currency.

A parent entity may have many subsidiaries in many different countries, many of which have different functional currencies. The more subsidiaries that operate independently of the parent entity, the more likely there will be various functional currencies used by the subsidiaries. Following on from the above discussion, if it is determined that the functional currency of the subsidiary located in Ireland is euros, then the financial statements of the subsidiary would already be presented in the functional currency. However, if the functional currency of the subsidiary in Ireland is deemed to be sterling, then the financial statements of the Irish subsidiary will need to be translated into the functional currency of sterling.

Paragraphs 21 and 23 of IAS 21 provide the rules for translating one currency into another currency. In relation to items included within the statement of comprehensive income, paragraph 21 states:

A foreign currency transaction shall be recorded, on initial recognition in the functional currency, by applying to the foreign currency amount the spot exchange rate between the functional currency and the foreign currency at the date of the transaction.

From the above paragraph we can see that there is a general requirement that each item of expense and revenue shall be translated at the spot exchange rate between the functional currency and the local currency on the dates the respective transactions took place. However, this would be an extremely time-consuming and difficult task and, as such, IAS 21 allows average rates to be used. For example, an average exchange rate between the local currency and the functional currency for a month may be used to translate transactions that occurred within that month. As paragraph 22 of IAS 21 states:

For practical reasons, a rate that approximates the actual rate at the date of the transaction is often used; for example, an average rate for a week or a month might be used for all transactions in each foreign currency occurring during that period. However, if exchange rates fluctuate significantly, the use of the average rate for a period is inappropriate.

The above requirements relate to accounts contained within the statement of comprehensive income. In relation to accounts that would generally be presented within the statement of financial position, paragraph 23 of IAS 21 states:

At each reporting date:

(a) *foreign currency monetary items shall be translated using the closing rate;*

(b) *non-monetary items that are measured in terms of historical cost in a foreign currency shall be translated using the exchange rate at the date of the transaction; and*

(c) *non-monetary items that are measured at fair value in a foreign currency shall be translated using the exchange rates at the date when the fair value was determined.*

The above paragraph makes reference to monetary items. Monetary items are defined in paragraph 8 of IAS 21 as:

units of currency held and assets and liabilities to be received or paid in a fixed or determinable number of units of currency.

In relation to monetary assets, paragraph 16 of IAS 21 also states:

> *The essential feature of a monetary item is a right to receive (or an obligation to deliver) a fixed or determinable number of units of currency. Examples include: pensions and other employee benefits to be paid in cash; provisions that are to be settled in cash; and cash dividends that are recognised as a liability. Similarly, a contract to receive (or deliver) a variable number of the entity's own equity instruments or a variable amount of assets in which the fair value to be received (or delivered) equals a fixed or determinable number of units of currency is a monetary item. Conversely, the essential feature of a non-monetary item is the absence of a right to receive (or an obligation to deliver) a fixed or determinable number of units of currency. Examples include: amounts prepaid for goods and services (e.g. prepaid rent); goodwill; intangible assets; inventories; property, plant and equipment; and provisions that are to be settled by the delivery of a non-monetary asset.*

In relation to non-monetary assets, such as plant and equipment, IAS 16 *Property, Plant and Equipment* allows that either cost or fair value is used as the basis of measurement. If the cost basis is used, and consistent with paragraph 23 reproduced above, the rate to be used to translate the local currency to the functional currency is the spot rate as at the date the asset was originally recognised by the subsidiary. If fair values are used by way of undertaking revaluations, then the exchange rate to be used between the foreign currency and the functional currency will be the exchange rate in place when the valuation was made.

The rates to be used to translate financial statements into a given functional currency are summarised in Table 25.1.

Table 25.1 Summary of rates used when translating financial statements into the functional currency

Category	Rate
Assets	
Monetary	Translate at the spot exchange rate at reporting rate (that is, at the closing rate)
Non-monetary—held at historical cost	Translate at the spot rate at the day the asset was recorded by the subsidiary
Non-monetary—fair value	Translate at the exchange rate at the date of valuation
Liabilities	
Monetary	Translate at the closing rate
Non-monetary	Translate at the exchange rate at the date of valuation
Equity	
Contributed equity—at acquisition	Translated at the rate when the investment was acquired
Reserves—at acquisition	Translated at the rate when the investment was acquired
Reserves—post-acquisition	If the transfer to the reserves is the result of, say, a revaluation of property, plant and equipment, the rate used is the rate at the date of revaluation
Retained earnings—at acquisition	Translated at the rate when the investment was acquired
Revenues and expenses	
Revenue and expenses	Translated at the rate of the transaction. For practical purposes, a rate that approximates the actual rate of the transaction can be used
Non-monetary-related expenses, e.g. depreciation	Translated at the rate used to translate the related non-monetary item
Distributions	
Dividends paid	Translated at the current rate at the date of payment
Dividends declared	Translated at the current rate at the date the dividends are declared

Applying the rates in Table 25.1 to the translation of the foreign operation's financial statements into the functional currency results in exchange differences. These arise because the foreign operation's monetary items are translated at the closing rate, while statement of comprehensive income items (sales, purchases and other expenses) are translated at the spot exchange rate at the date of the transaction or, for practical purposes, at a rate (average rate) that approximates the actual rate. The translation of non-monetary items does not give rise to exchange differences as the spot exchange rate at the date of the transaction is used from year to year. Paragraph 28 of IAS 21 explains this as follows:

> *Exchange differences arising on the settlement of monetary items or on translating monetary items at rates different from those at which they were translated on initial recognition during the period or in previous financial statements shall be recognised in profit or loss in the period in which they arise, except as described in paragraph 32.*

Applying the requirements of IAS 21 as they relate to translating the financial statements from a local currency to a particular functional currency means that the final financial statements, after translation, will reflect amounts that would be recorded had the transactions or events been originally recorded in the functional currency. As paragraph 34 of IAS 21 states:

> *When an entity keeps its books and records in a currency other than its functional currency, at the time the entity prepares its financial statements, all amounts are translated into the functional currency in accordance with paragraphs 20–26. This produces the same amounts in the functional currency as would have occurred had the items been recorded initially in the functional currency. For example, monetary items are translated into the functional currency using the closing rate, and non-monetary items that are measured on a historical cost basis are translated using the exchange rate at the date of the transaction that resulted in their recognition.*

The translation from a foreign currency into a functional currency is explored in Worked Example 25.1.

| Worked Example 25.1 | Translation from a foreign currency into a functional currency |

On 1 July 2014 Berlin, a German company whose shares are listed on the German Securities Exchange, acquired all the equity in Bulldog plc, a company incorporated in England. Because of the high level of dependence of Bulldog plc on Berlin, the functional currency is deemed to be the euro.
The exchange rates for the reporting period ending 30 June 2015 are shown below.

1 July 2014	£1 = €1.00
Average rate for the year	£1 = €1.05
Ending inventory (acquired before year end)	£1 = €1.10
30 June 2015	£1 = €1.15

The statement of comprehensive income and statement of financial position of Bulldog plc, stated in UK pounds, are detailed below.

Bulldog plc

Statement of comprehensive income and details of closing retained earnings for the year ended 30 June 2015

	£000
Sales revenue	2,500
Cost of sales:	
– Inventory—1 July 2014	(500)
– Purchases	(2,000)
– Inventory—30 June 2015	450
Administration expenses	(75)
Depreciation expense	(100)
Profit before tax	275
Income tax expense	(125)
Profit for the year	150
Retained earnings—1 July 2014	150
Retained earnings—30 June 2015	300

▶

Bulldog plc
Statement of financial position as at 30 June 2015

	1 July 2014 £000	30 June 2015 £000
ASSETS		
Property, plant and equipment	1,050	950
Cash and trade receivables	100	800
Inventory	500	450
Total assets	1,650	2,200
EQUITY AND LIABILITIES		
Equity		
Share capital	500	500
Retained earnings	150	300
	650	800
Liabilities		
Bank loan	1,000	1,000
Trade payables	–	400
Total liabilities	1,000	1,400
Total equity and liabilities	1,650	2,200

Required

Translate the financial statements of Bulldog plc into the functional currency.

Solution

Bulldog plc
Statement of comprehensive income for the year ending 30 June 2015

	£000	Exchange rate	€000
Sales revenue	2,500	1.05	2,625.0
Cost of sales:			
– Inventory – 1 July 2014	(500)	1.00	(500.0)
– Purchases	(2,000)	1.05	(2,100.0)
– Inventory – 30 June 2015	450	1.10	495.0
Administration expenses	(75)	1.05	(78.75)
Depreciation expense	(100)	1.00	(100.0)
Foreign exchange loss	–		(105.0)
Profit before tax	275		236.25
Income tax expense	(125)	1.05	(131.25)
Profit for the year	150		105.0
Retained earnings – 1 July 2014	150	1.00	150.0
Retained earnings – 30 June 2015	300		255.0

◀ **Bulldog plc**
Statement of financial position as at 30 June 2015

	£000	Exchange rate	€000
ASSETS			
Property, plant and equipment	950	1.00	950
Cash and receivables	800	1.15	920
Inventory	450	1.10	495
Total assets	2,200		2,365
EQUITY AND LIABILITIES			
Equity and reserves			
Share capital	500	1.00	500
Retained earnings	300		255
	800		755
Liabilities			
Bank loan	1,000	1.15	1,150
Trade payables	400	1.15	460
Total liabilities	1,400		1,610
Total equity and liabilities	2,200		2,365

In this worked example the exchange differences have arisen, in the main, from the translation of the foreign operation's monetary items at current rates in the same way as for the foreign currency monetary items of the entity. The non-monetary items, for example property, plant, equipment and inventory, are translated at the spot rate at the day the asset was recorded by the subsidiary. This rate will be used in subsequent years unless the item is sold, in which case an exchange difference will arise.

Statement of comprehensive income items, for example sales and purchases, give rise to monetary items in the form of cash, accounts receivable and accounts payable. The exchange differences are established by comparing the changes in the monetary items for the reporting period. This is achieved by comparing the difference between the exchange rate used in the translation process and the closing rate at the end of the reporting period.

	£000	£000	Current rate less rate applied	Gain/(loss) €000
Net monetary assets at 1 July 2014				
– Bank loan	(1,000)			
– Cash and trade receivables	100	(900)	(1.15 – 1.00)	(135)
Increases in monetary assets—sales		2,500	(1.15 – 1.05)	250
Decreases in monetary assets resulting from:				
– Purchases		(2,000)	(1.15 – 1.05)	(200)
– Cash expenses		(75)	(1.15 – 1.05)	(7.5)
– Income tax expense		(125)	(1.15 – 1.05)	(12.5)
		(600)		(105)

Reconciled to net monetary items at 30 June 2015 as follows:

	£000
Bank loan	(1,000)
Trade payables	(400)
Cash and trade receivables	800
	(600)

The result of translating the financial statements maintained in UK pounds into the functional currency, the euro, is that the same result is obtained as would have been the case if Bulldog plc had maintained its books and records in euros.

25.3 Translating the financial statements of foreign operations into the presentation currency

As an example, a subsidiary of a UK company might prepare its financial statements in a functional currency that is different from the parent entity's presentation currency. Indeed, there might be many subsidiaries using a variety of functional currencies. Before consolidating the financial statements of the parent entity and its subsidiaries it will be necessary to convert the financial statements of the various foreign subsidiaries from their respective functional currencies into the presentation currency of the parent entity. That is, we will need to ensure that prior to consolidation all the financial statements of the entities within the group are presented in the one currency, which will be the group's presentation currency.

Under the approach required by IAS 21, all assets and liabilities of a foreign operation are to be translated from the functional currency to the presentation currency using the **spot rate** applicable at the end of the reporting period. Income and expenses are translated at the exchange rates in place at the dates of the various transactions. If expense and revenue transactions are considered to occur uniformly throughout the period, average rates may be used. Any resulting translation gains or losses are taken directly to reserves (rather than to profit or loss, which was the case when we translated the financial statements from a local currency to the functional currency). Specifically, paragraph 39 of IAS 21 states:

> **spot rate** The exchange rate for immediate delivery of currencies to be exchanged.

> *The results and financial position of an entity whose functional currency is not the currency of a hyperinflationary economy shall be translated into a different presentation currency using the following procedures:*
>
> *(a) assets and liabilities for each statement of financial position presented (i.e. including comparatives) shall be translated at the closing rate at the date of that statement of financial position;*
> *(b) income and expenses for each statement of comprehensive income (i.e. including comparatives) shall be translated at exchange rates at the dates of the transactions; and*
> *(c) all resulting exchange differences shall be recognised in other comprehensive income.*

Note from part (c) above that the exchange differences are not to be treated as part of profit or loss but are to be transferred to a reserve—a foreign currency translation reserve—and the increase or decrease in this reserve is included as part of 'other comprehensive income', and therefore included within 'total comprehensive income' (rather than in profit or loss).

With reference to the requirement in paragraph 39(b) above, it would obviously be very difficult and time-consuming to determine the rates for each and every transaction. This being so, and as indicated earlier in relation to translations to a particular functional currency, average rates are often used.

With regard to the requirement in paragraph 39(c) above that all exchange differences are to go to equity (rather than be included as part of the profit or loss of the financial period), paragraph 41 of IAS 21 states:

> *These exchange differences are not recognised in profit or loss because the changes in exchange rates have little or no direct effect on the present and future cash flows from operations. The cumulative amount of the exchange differences is presented in a separate component of equity until disposal of the foreign operation.*

To illustrate simplistically the use of the required method for translating foreign operation financial statements, let us assume that a foreign operation has assets of €1,500,000 and liabilities of €1,000,000 at the beginning of a financial period and, further, that it does not trade during the financial period. We will also assume that, during the financial period, the value of sterling moves from €1.00 = £0.80 to €1.00 = £0.90.

Using the method of translation required by IAS 21, the translation gain on holding the assets would be £150,000, which is €1,500,000 × (£0.90 − £0.80). There would be a loss on the liabilities amounting to £100,000, which is €1,000,000 × (£0.90 − £0.80). That is, in terms of sterling, the foreign operation owes a greater amount in sterling because of the devaluation of sterling. What we must remember, however, is that the foreign operation could operate independently, in which case sterling would not be used to pay the debt and therefore the loss would not be treated as being realised. The net gain of £50,000 would be transferred to a foreign currency translation reserve and not be treated as an income or expense of the period. In a sense, the net amount of £50,000, which is the difference between £150,000 and £100,000, is the balancing item—that is, the difference between the respective gain and loss.

The foreign exchange exposure of the parent entity in relation to its foreign operations relates only to its net investment in the operation—that is, to the net assets of the foreign operation. In the above example, the net gain is simply calculated as:

$$(\text{€}1,500,000 - \text{€}1,000,000) \times (\text{£}0.90 - \text{£}0.80) = \text{£}50,000$$

This example demonstrates that, if the assets of the foreign operation exceed its liabilities (which means that shareholders' funds are positive) and if the value of sterling falls relative to the currency of the foreign operation, there will be a credit to the foreign currency translation reserve (assuming the company is a UK company and the functional currency is sterling). Otherwise, there will be a debit to the foreign currency translation reserve.

While paragraph 39 of IAS 21 (provided earlier) does outline the method for translating the assets, liabilities, income and expenses of a foreign entity, the standard is silent on the translation of:

- equity at the date of the investment, that is, pre-acquisition capital and reserves;
- post-acquisition movements in equity other than retained earnings or accumulated losses; and
- distributions from retained earnings.

In relation to all financial statements (including those covered by paragraph 39 of IAS 21), the approach to translating the financial statements of a foreign subsidiary from a particular functional currency to a particular presentation currency is as follows:

(a) Assets and liabilities are translated at the exchange rate current at the end of the reporting period.
(b) Equity at the date of the investment, including in the case of a corporation, share capital at acquisition and pre-acquisition reserves, is translated at the exchange rate current at that date of investment.
(c) Post-acquisition movements in equity, other than retained earnings (surplus) or accumulated losses (deficiency), are translated at the exchange rates current at the dates of those movements, except that, where a movement represents a transfer between items within equity, the movement is translated at the exchange rate current at the date that the amount transferred or returned was first included in equity.
(d) Distributions from retained earnings (that is, dividends paid or declared, or their equivalent) are translated at the exchange rates current at the dates when the distributions were first declared.
(e) Revenue and expense items are translated at the exchange rates current at the applicable transaction dates.

Table 25.2 summarises the approach to translating the accounts of a foreign subsidiary.

Table 25.2 Summary of the method to be applied for translating financial statements from a given functional currency to a specific presentation currency

Item	Rate
Assets	
Monetary assets	Translated at closing rate
Non-monetary assets—measured at historical cost	Translated at closing rate
Non-monetary assets—measured at fair value	Translated at closing rate
Liabilities	
Monetary	Translated at closing rate
Non-monetary	Translated at closing rate
Equity	
Share capital and reserves at date of acquisition	Translated at spot rate when investment acquired
Post-acquisition movements in share capital and reserves (excluding retained earnings/accumulated losses)	Translated at the spot rate at the date they were recognised in the financial statements
Post-acquisition retained earnings	Amount determined from translating the statement of comprehensive income

▶

Table 25.2 Summary of the method to be applied for translating financial statements from a given functional currency to a specific presentation currency *(Continued)*

Item	Rate
Revenues and expenses	
Revenues	Translated at the rate in place as at the time of the transaction. For practical reasons, however, it is acceptable to use a rate that approximates the rate in place when the transactions took place (for example, to use an average rate for the year)
Expenses (apart from the amortisation or depreciation of non-current assets)	Translated at the rate in place as at the time of the transaction. For practical reasons, however, it is acceptable to use a rate that approximates the rate in place when the transactions took place (for example, to use an average rate for the year)
Depreciation/Amortisation	Translated at the average rate for the year
Income tax expense	Translated at the average rate for the year
Distributions	
Dividends paid/declared	Translated at the spot rate when paid/declared

Worked Example 25.2 provides an illustration of the translation of a foreign subsidiary's financial statements.

Note that the exchange rate has moved against the euro in Worked Example 25.2. In such a case, a gain would arise on the assets and a loss would arise on the liabilities. Since the assets of Nigel plc exceed its liabilities, a net gain would be credited to the foreign currency translation reserve. The movement in the foreign currency translation reserve will be included as part of 'other comprehensive income' in the consolidated statement of comprehensive income.

Worked Example 25.2

Translation of a foreign operation's financial statements from a functional currency into a presentation currency

On 1 July 2014 Bruce, a French company, acquires all the issued shares in Nigel plc, a company incorporated in England. Exchange rates for the year ending 30 June 2015 are as follows:

1 July 2014	£1.00 = €2.00
Average rate for year	£1.00 = €2.10
Inventory acquired (before year end)	£1.00 = €2.20
30 June 2015	£1.00 = €2.30

The statement of comprehensive income and statement of financial position of Nigel plc are shown below. The financial statements are stated in £, which is Nigel plc's functional currency.

▶

*Abbreviated statement of comprehensive income for
Nigel plc for the year ending 30 June 2015 and details of closing retained earnings*

	£
Sales revenue	2,500
Cost of sales	
– Inventory—1 July 2014	(500)
– Purchases	(2,000)
– Inventory—30 June 2015	450
Administration expense	(75)
Depreciation expense	(100)
Profit	275
Income tax expense	(125)
Profit after tax	150
Retained earnings—1 July 2014	150
Retained earnings—30 June 2015	300

Statement of financial position for Nigel plc as at 30 June 2015

	1 July 2014 (£)	30 June 2015 (£)
ASSETS		
Plant and equipment	1,050	950
Cash and trade receivables	100	800
Inventory	500	450
Total assets	1,650	2,200
EQUITY AND LIABILITIES		
Equity and reserves		
Equity share capital	500	500
Retained earnings	150	300
	650	800
Liabilities		
Bank loan	1,000	1,000
Trade payables	–	400
Total liabilities	1,000	1,400
Total equity and liabilities	1,650	2,200

Required

Translate the financial statements of the foreign operation from the functional currency of the subsidiary into the presentation currency of the group.

Solution

To determine which rates should be used for the various items, we can refer to Table 25.2.

*Statement of comprehensive income and reconciliation of retained earnings
for Nigel plc for the year ending 30 June 2015*

	(£)	(Rate)	(€)
Sales revenue	2,500	2.10	5,250
Cost of sales			
– Inventory—1 July 2014	(500)	2.00	(1,000)
– Purchases	(2,000)	2.10	(4,200)
– Inventory—30 June 2015	450	2.20	990

	(£)	(Rate)	(€)
Administration expense	(75)	2.10	(157.5)
Depreciation expense	(100)	2.10	(210)
Profit	275		672.5
Income tax expense	(125)	2.10	(262.5)
Profit after tax	150		410
Retained earnings—1 July 2014	150	2.00	300
Retained earnings—30 June 2015	300		710

Statement of financial position for Nigel plc as at 30 June 2015

	1 July 2014 (£)	30 June 2015 (£)	(Rate)	(€)
ASSETS				
Plant and equipment	1,050	950	2.30	2,185
Cash and receivables	100	800	2.30	1,840
Inventory	500	450	2.30	1,035
Total assets	1,650	2,200		5,060
EQUITY AND LIABILITIES				
Equity and reserves				
Equity share capital	500	500	2.00	1,000
Foreign currency translation reserve				130*
Retained earnings	150	300		710**
	650	800		1,840
Liabilities				
Bank loan	1,000	1,000	2.30	2,300
Trade payables	–	400	2.30	920
Total liabilities	1,000	1,400		3,220
Total equity and liabilities	1,650	2,200		5,060

*See calculation provided.
**See statement of comprehensive income.

Foreign currency translation reserve

As we have noted, all assets and liabilities of the foreign subsidiary are translated at the spot rate in place at the end of the reporting period. Because we know that assets less liabilities equals owners' equity, it follows that in effect the total of owners' equity is translated at the reporting date spot rate. However, the individual components of owners' equity will be translated differently. The share capital will be translated using the rate in place when the investment was acquired. Retained earnings will be the balance provided from the statement of comprehensive income (which might use a variety of rates). The translation gain, which does not go to the statement of comprehensive income but remains part of equity, is in effect the balancing item. When the foreign operation is ultimately disposed of, the amount accumulated in equity as the foreign currency translation reserve will be treated as part of profits.

The transfer to the foreign currency translation reserve is determined as follows:

Net assets at 30 June 2015 at closing rate (£800 × €2.30)	€1,840
less Components of net assets at their historical rates	
– Share capital £500 × €2.00	(€1,000)
– Retained earnings from statement of comprehensive income	(€710)
Translation gain—to foreign currency translation reserve	€130

25.4 Consolidation subsequent to translation

Having translated the foreign subsidiary's financial statements into the presentation currency, we can consolidate these financial statements, adopting normal consolidation principles (as explained in Chapters 21 to 23). Paragraph 45 of IAS 21, however, explains that when intragroup monetary items, assets or liabilities are eliminated against the corresponding intragroup asset or liability, the resulting currency fluctuations are shown in the financial statements. Paragraph 45 of IAS 21 explains the reason for this, as follows:

> *The incorporation of the results and financial position of a foreign operation with those of the reporting entity follows normal consolidation procedures, such as the elimination of intragroup balances and intragroup transactions of a subsidiary (see IAS 27 and IAS 31 Interests in Joint Ventures). However, an intragroup monetary asset (or liability), whether short-term or long-term, cannot be eliminated against the corresponding intragroup liability (or asset) without showing the results of currency fluctuations in the consolidated financial statements. This is because the monetary item represents a commitment to convert one currency into another and exposes the reporting entity to a gain or loss through currency fluctuations. Accordingly, in the consolidated financial statements of the reporting entity, such an exchange difference is recognised in profit or loss or, if it arises from the circumstances described in paragraph 32, it is recognised in other comprehensive income and accumulated in a separate component of equity until the disposal of the foreign operation.*

As with consolidations generally, the cost of the investment is eliminated against the pre-acquisition capital and reserves of the controlled entities, with a resultant goodwill or bargain purchase on acquisition being recognised. Paragraph 47 of IAS 21 requires goodwill on the acquisition of a foreign subsidiary and any fair value adjustments in the carrying value of assets and liabilities arising on the acquisition of a foreign operation to be treated as assets and liabilities of the foreign operation. Specifically, paragraph 47 states:

> *Any goodwill arising on the acquisition of a foreign operation and any fair value adjustments to the carrying amounts of assets and liabilities arising on the acquisition of that foreign operation shall be treated as assets and liabilities of the foreign operation. Thus they shall be expressed in the functional currency of the foreign operation and shall be translated at the closing rate in accordance with paragraphs 39 and 42.*

The above requirement means that they must be translated at the closing rate at the end of the reporting period. How this should occur is detailed in Worked Example 25.3.

Worked Example 25.3 — Accounting treatment of goodwill arising on acquisition

On 1 July 2013 Manly plc, a UK entity, acquired 100 per cent of the equity of Jeffreys Bay, a Turkish company. At that date, the equity of Jeffreys Bay was as follows:

	TRY
Equity share capital	4,800,000
Retained earnings	800,000
	5,600,000

At the date of acquisition, all the assets and liabilities were valued at fair value except for land, which was as follows:

	Carrying amount TRY	Fair value TRY
Land	2,800,000	3,400,000

The relevant exchange rates are as follows:

- 01 July 2013   £1 = TRY4
- 30 June 2014   £1 = TRY5

Jeffreys Bay's functional currency is the Turkish Lira (TRY), while the presentation currency is sterling. The tax rate in the UK is 30 per cent, while the tax rate in Turkey is 40 per cent.

▶

Required

Prepare the consolidation journal entries at 1 July 2013 and 30 June 2014.

Solution

Elimination of investment in Jeffreys Bay

	Jeffreys Bay Limited (£)	Eliminate parent 100% (£)
Share capital (TRY4,800,000 ÷ 4)	1,200,000	1,200,000
Retained earnings—at acquisition (TRY800,000 ÷ 4)	200,000	200,000
Revaluation surplus (TRY600,000 ÷ 4 = £150,000 net of deferred tax at 40% of £60,000)	90,000	90,000
		1,490,000
Investment in Jeffreys Bay		1,550,000
Goodwill on acquisition		60,000

From the above workings, the consolidation entry to eliminate the investment in Jeffreys Bay would be:

1 July 2013

Dr	Equity share capital	£1,200,000	
Dr	Retained earnings	£200,000	
Dr	Revaluation surplus	£90,000	
Dr	Goodwill on acquisition	£60,000	
Cr	Investment in Jeffreys Bay		£1,550,000

(eliminating the investment in Jeffreys Bay and recognising goodwill at date of acquisition)

At 30 June 2014, the exchange rate had moved to £1 = TRY5. The revaluation surplus and other equity items are translated at the rate at acquisition, while goodwill is translated at the closing rate at reporting date. The following additional entry should be made at 30 June 2014.

30 June 2014

Dr	Foreign currency translation reserve	£12,000	
Cr	Goodwill on acquisition		£12,000

(recognising decrease in value of goodwill resulting from movements in exchange rate)

At 1 July 2013 goodwill expressed in Turkish Lira amounted to TRY240,000 (£60,000 × 4). At 30 June 2014 the goodwill translated at the closing rate amounted to £48,000 (TRY240,000 ÷ 5). The difference is allocated to the foreign currency translation reserve.

The non-controlling interests will be determined following the translation of the financial statements. A foreign currency translation reserve will reside in the subsidiaries' statement of financial positions before the consolidation adjustments and the non-controlling interests will be allocated a proportion of this reserve.

As indicated in Chapter 21, on consolidation we need to eliminate inter-entity sales of inventory. If the foreign operation has acquired inventory from the parent entity, the inventory (as with all assets) is translated at the exchange rate in place at the end of the reporting period, which might lead to an adjustment to the foreign currency translation reserve. As the inventory on hand at year end has to be recorded as though no inter-entity transaction has occurred, if we assume that the value of foreign currency has increased relative to the domestic currency, a journal entry of the following form would be required to eliminate the adjustment to inventory:

Dr	Foreign currency translation reserve	X	
Cr	Inventory		X

SUMMARY

In this chapter we considered why and how we translate the financial statements of foreign operations. We learned how to translate financial statements into a particular functional currency and we also learned how to translate financial statements from a particular functional currency into a presentation currency.

If the financial statements of a foreign operation are translated into the functional currency, which is the currency of the primary economic environment in which the entity operates, any gain or loss on translation is treated as part of the entity's profit or loss for the period and disclosed in the statement of comprehensive income. We also learned that, where the financial statements of the foreign operation are translated from its functional currency into the presentation currency, the net exchange difference on translation is treated as part of equity. The equity account has been referred to as a foreign currency translation reserve (although the accounting standard does not actually give the reserve a name).

KEY TERMS

foreign currency. . . . . **755**   spot rate **761**

END-OF-CHAPTER EXERCISE

On 1 July 2014 Barry plc, a US company, acquires all the issued shares in Chuck plc, a company incorporated in the UK. The presentation currency is the US dollar. Exchange rates for the year ending 30 June 2015 are as follows:

1 July 2014	£1.00 = US$1.40
Average rate for year	£1.00 = US$1.50
Ending inventory acquired (before year end)	£1.00 = US$1.55
30 June 2015	£1.00 = US$1.60

The statement of comprehensive income and statement of financial position of Chuck plc are shown below. The financial statements are stated in sterling, which is the functional currency of Chuck plc.   **LO 25.3**

Statement of comprehensive income for Chuck plc for the year ending 30 June 2015,
with a reconciliation of opening and closing retained earnings

	£000
Sales revenue	5,000
Cost of sales	
– Inventory—1 July 2014	(1,000)
– Purchases	(4,000)
– Inventory—30 June 2015	900
Administration expense	(150)
Depreciation expense	(200)
Profit	550
Income tax expense	(250)
Profit after tax	300
Retained earnings—1 July 2014	300
Retained earnings—30 June 2015	600

Statement of financial position for Chuck plc as at 30 June 2015

	1 July 2014 (£000)	30 June 2015 (£000)
ASSETS		
Plant and equipment	2,100	1,900
Cash and receivables	200	1,600
Inventory	1,000	900
Total assets	3,300	4,400
EQUITY AND LIABILITIES		
Equity and reserves		
Equity share capital	1,000	1,000
Retained earnings	300	600
	1,300	1,600
Liabilities		
Bank loan	2,000	2,000
Trade payables	–	800
Total liabilities	2,000	2,800
Total equity and liabilities	3,300	4,400

REQUIRED

Translate the financial statements of Chuck plc into US dollars.

SOLUTION TO END-OF-CHAPTER EXERCISE

We can refer to Table 25.1 (on p. 757) for a summary of which rates to use for the various items.

Statement of comprehensive income for Chuck plc for the year ending 30 June 2015,
with a reconciliation of opening and closing retained earnings

	(£000)	Rate	(US$000)
Sales revenue	5,000	1.50	7,500
Cost of sales			
– Inventory—1 July 2014	(1,000)	1.40	(1,400)
– Purchases	(4,000)	1.50	(6,000)
– Inventory—30 June 2015	900	1.55	1,395
Administration expense	(150)	1.50	(225)
Depreciation expense	(200)	1.50	(300)
Profit	550		970
Income tax expense	(250)	1.50	(375)
Profit after tax	300		595
Retained earnings—1 July 2014	300	1.40	420
Retained earnings—30 June 2015	600		1,015

Statement of financial position for Chuck plc as at 30 June 2015

	1 July 2014 (£000)	30 June 2015 (£000)	(Rate)	(US$000)
ASSETS				
Plant and equipment	2,100	1,900	1.60	3,040
Cash and receivables	200	1,600	1.60	2,560
Inventory	1,000	900	1.60	1,440
Total assets	3,300	4,400		7,040
EQUITY AND LIABILITIES				
Equity and reserves				
Equity share capital	1,000	1,000	1.40	1,400
Foreign currency translation reserve				145*
Retained earnings	300	600		1,015**
	1,300	1,600		2,560
Liabilities				
Bank loan	2,000	2,000	1.60	3,200
Trade payables	–	800	1.60	1,280
Total liabilities	2,000	2,800		4,480
Total equity and liabilities	3,300	4,400		7,040

*See calculation provided below.
**From statement of comprehensive income.

Foreign currency translation reserve
The transfer to the foreign currency translation reserve is determined as follows:

Net assets at 30 June 2015 at closing rate (£1,600 × US$1.60)	US$2,560
Components of net assets at their historical rates: share capital (£1,000 × US$1.40)	(US$1,400)
Retained earnings from the statement of comprehensive income	(US$1,015)
Translation gain—to foreign currency translation reserve	US$145

REVIEW QUESTIONS

1 Why do we need to translate the financial statements of a foreign operation? **LO** 25.1
2 Explain why foreign currency gains or losses in relation to the translation of the financial statements of a foreign opera-tion into a particular presentation currency are not treated as part of the period's profit or loss, but instead are trans-ferred to an equity account referred to as the foreign currency translation reserve. **LO** 25.4
3 What is the difference between the presentation currency and the functional currency and how would an organisation determine the appropriate presentation currency? **LO** 25.4
4 Explain what rates should be used for the assets, liabilities and equity items of a foreign entity when translating the financial statements from a functional currency to a particular presentation currency. **LO** 25.4
5 What rates should be used to translate the expense and income items of a foreign entity's financial statements? When would average rates be acceptable? **LO** 25.4

CHALLENGING QUESTIONS

6 On 1 July 2014 Milano, an Italian company, acquires all the issued shares in Felicity plc, a company incorporated in England. Exchange rates for the year ending 30 June 2015 are as follows:

1 July 2014	£1.00 = €2.00
Average rate for year	£1.00 = €2.10
Ending inventory acquired (before year end)	£1.00 = €2.20
30 June 2015	£1.00 = €2.30

The statement of comprehensive income and statement of financial position of Felicity plc are shown below. The accounts are stated in £. **LO** **25.3**

Statement of comprehensive income for Felicity plc for the year ending 30 June 2015, together with information reconciling opening and closing retained earnings

	(£)
Sales revenue	5,000
Cost of sales	
– Inventory—1 July 2014	(1,000)
– Purchases	(4,000)
– Inventory—30 June 2015	900
Administration expense	(150)
Depreciation expense	(200)
Profit	550
Income tax expense	(250)
Profit after tax	300
Retained earnings—1 July 2014	300
Retained earnings—30 June 2015	600

Statement of financial position for Felicity plc as at 30 June 2015

	1 July 2014 (£)	30 June 2015 (£)
ASSETS		
Plant and equipment	2,100	1,900
Cash and receivables	200	1,600
Inventory	1,000	900
Total assets	3,300	4,400
EQUITY AND LIABILITIES		
Equity and reserves		
Share capital	1,000	1,000
Retained earnings	300	600
	1,300	1,600
Current liabilities		
Bank loan	2,000	2,000
Trade payables	–	800
Total liabilities	2,000	2,800
Total equity and liabilities	3,300	4,400

REQUIRED

Translate the financial statements of the foreign operation, assuming:

(a) The euro is the functional currency of Felicity plc and the euro is also the presentation currency of the group.

(b) UK pounds are the functional currency of Felicity plc and the euro is the presentation currency of the group.

7 Bazza plc, an Irish company, acquires all the shares of Ching, a Polish company, on 1 July 2014. Ching had a złzero balance in retained earnings as at the date of acquisition. The financial statements of Ching are presented below:
LO 25.2

Statement of comprehensive income for Ching for the year ending 30 June 2015, together with a reconciliation of opening and closing retained earnings

	(zł)	(zł)
Sales revenue		250,000
Cost of sales		
– Inventory—1 July 2014	(25,000)	
– Cost of goods manufactured	(152,500)	
– Inventory—30 June 2015	27,500	(150,000)
Gross profit		100,000
Selling and administrative expenses		(20,000)
Depreciation		(30,000)
Profit before tax		50,000
Income tax expense (20 per cent)		(10,000)
Profit after tax		40,000
Dividends proposed—30 June 2015		(10,000)
Retained earnings—30 June 2015		30,000

Statement of financial position for Ching as at 30 June 2015

	(zł)
ASSETS	
Non-current assets	
Plant and equipment	125,000
Accumulated depreciation	(30,000)
Land	50,000
	145,000
Current assets	
Inventory (cost)	27,500
Accounts receivable	46,000
Cash	34,000
	107,500
Total assets	252,500
EQUITY AND LIABILITIES	
Equity and reserves	
Share capital	150,000
Retained earnings	30,000
	180,000
Non-current liabilities	
Long-term bonds	50,000
Current liabilities	22,500
Total liabilities	72,500
Total equity and liabilities	252,500

Additional information
• Relevant exchange rates are:

1 July 2014	€1.00 = zł4.00
Plant, equipment and inventory acquired	€1.00 = zł4.00
Long-term bonds issued	€1.00 = zł3.50
Land acquired	€1.00 = zł3.50
Average rate for 2015 financial year	€1.00 = zł3.00
Average rate for June 2015 quarter	€1.00 = zł2.25
30 June 2015	€1.00 = zł2.00

- Plant, equipment and inventory are acquired on 1 July 2014. There were no monetary assets or liabilities at the commencement of business.
- Long-term bonds are issued on 1 August 2014, with the principal to be repaid in full in five years. The bonds are issued in exchange for land, which is to be developed as a factory site.
- Inventory on hand at the end of the financial year has been manufactured throughout the June 2015 quarter.
- All revenue and expense items are incurred evenly throughout the year.

REQUIRED

Translate the financial statements of Ching into euros in preparation for group consolidation in accordance with IAS 21 assuming that the Polish Zloty (zł) is the functional currency of Ching and the euro is the presentation currency of the group.

PART 9

Corporate Social Responsibility Reporting

Part content

Chapter 26

Accounting for Corporate Social Responsibility

Learning objectives

Upon completing this chapter readers should:

LO1   understand alternative perceptions about the accountability and social responsibility of business;

LO2   know what social responsibility reporting is;

LO3   understand how social responsibility reporting relates to financial reporting;

LO4   understand the possible linkages between social and environmental performance and financial performance;

LO5   recognise the linkage between social and environmental risk and business risk;

LO6   know the regulatory requirements for the disclosure of social and environmental performance;

LO7   recognise the trends in relation to sustainability reporting;

LO8   understand the extent to which European organisations currently disclose information about their social and environmental performance;

LO9   recognise user demand and market responses to the disclosure of social performance and environmental performance information;

LO10 understand theoretical perspectives on what motivates organisations to present social and environmental information;

LO11 recognise some of the limitations of conventional financial accounting in relation to the recognition of social and environmental costs and benefits;

LO12 recognise some of the various frameworks for social performance and environmental performance reporting; and

26.1   Introduction to social responsibility reporting

So far in this book we have focused on financial performance reporting. In this chapter we will consider a number of issues associated with corporate social and environmental reporting, as well as what is commonly

social responsibility reporting The provision of information about the performance of an organisation with regard to its interaction with its physical and social environment.

stakeholder Any group or individual who can affect or is affected by the achievement of a firm's objectives.

becoming known as sustainability reporting. First, we will define corporate **social responsibility reporting** and the associated terms *social reporting* and *environmental reporting*. We will consider different views about the responsibilities of business entities and whether such *responsibilities* are considered to encompass the entity's social and environmental performance, and also whether they include the responsibility to publicly disclose information about the entity's social and environmental performance.

Traditionally, it has been considered that business entities are responsible for their financial performance and that their principal stakeholders are the owners of the entity (for a company, its shareholders). However, such views are changing, and it is becoming accepted that organisations have responsibilities to a broader group of **stakeholders** extending beyond their shareholders (this broader group of stakeholders might include local communities, customers, suppliers, employees, creditors, government and per-haps even future generations) for their *social* and *environmental performance*, as well as their *financial performance*. The following statements made by representatives of three well-known companies reflect this view:

I believe strongly that a sustainable business is a good business. That's where Plan A comes in. Plan A is about securing the future success of Marks & Spencer, its shareholders, employees and suppliers.

(Robert Swannell, Chairman, Marks and Spencer, Your M&S How We Do Business Report, 2011)

Our mission is to be admired as a diverse ethical company, operating responsibly and providing services that enable a more sustainable society for our customers by being the leading communications company for:

■ *Responsible, ethical and honest behaviour*
■ *Eco-efficiency – doing more for customers with less*
■ *Creating sustainable societies.*

(Vodafone Group, Sustainability Report for the year ended 31 March 2011)

The objectives of the Shell group are to engage efficiently, responsibly and profitably in oil, oil products, gas, chemicals and other selected businesses and to participate in the search for and development of other sources of energy to meet evolving customer needs and the world's growing demand for energy.

We believe that oil and gas will be integral to the global energy needs for economic development for many decades to come. Our role is to ensure that we extract and deliver them profitably and in environmentally and socially responsible ways.

We seek a high standard of performance, maintaining a strong long-term and growing position in the competitive environments in which we choose to operate.

We aim to work closely with our customers, our partners and policymakers to advance more efficient and sustainable use of energy and natural resources.

(Shell: http://www.shell.com/home/content/aboutshell/who_we_are/our_purpose/)

In this chapter we will consider the regulation and guidance relating to public social and environmental reporting, and we will see that the accounting profession and those bodies in charge of regulating accounting disclosures have been relatively silent on formulating guidelines or standards for social and environmental reporting. We will see that existing generally accepted accounting principles, as embodied within accounting standards and conceptual frameworks, typically act to exclude from measurement many social and environ-

social cost Cost imposed on society as a result of the operations or activities of a particular entity. Often referred to as 'externalities', and typically ignored by conventional accounting procedures.

mental costs and benefits generated by a business entity. Existing accounting standards tend to focus on providing information about financial performance within a frame-work that emphasises property rights and market transactions. Hence moves to provide social and environmental information require an entity to go *outside* conventional financial accounting practices. We will specifically consider the limitations of tradi-tional financial accounting with respect to providing information about an entity's social and environmental performance. As we will see, traditional financial accounting has treated environmental goods (for example, air and water) as being in infinite sup-ply and *free*, with the consequence that the use or *abuse* of the environment is not reflected in accounting performance indicators such as 'profits' (unless fines or other penalties are imposed). However, environmental goods are all too finite. Also, traditional financial accounting practices have tended to ignore the **social costs** that an entity might have imposed upon the societies with which it interacts. For example, while retrenching thousands of people from a workforce can actually have positive effects on accounting profits (as has been the case for a number of financial institutions in recent years), there are associated *social costs* that are ignored by the organisation when calculating profits.

Although this chapter establishes that there are limited formal provisions requiring organisations to publicly disclose information about their social and environmental performance, it will be shown that many organisations are producing such information and, increasingly, this information is being provided in stand-alone social and environmental reports—often quite extensive in length and typically available on corporate websites. Because there is a general lack of regulation in this area of reporting, there is much variation in how the reporting is being done. Some reporting approaches represent quite radical changes from how financial accounting has traditionally been practised. As will be seen, some approaches (these are in the minority) attempt to put a 'cost' on the social and environmental **externalities** caused by business entities (such externalities are typically ignored by financial accountants). Related to the practice of social reporting is the practice of **social auditing**, which we will also briefly consider. Social auditing is now being undertaken by many large multinational companies, and typically provides the basis for information to be included in a social report, or the social performance section of a social responsibility or sustainability report.

There have been noticeable trends in social and environmental reporting, which we will discuss. In the early 1990s environmental reporting came to greater prominence, initially more as a public relations exercise (such reports were often referred to as *greenwash*). Throughout the 1990s the quality of reporting appeared to improve and organisations started to seek verification of the information (just as financial information is verified by an independent external party, it is common now to find that the information in a sustainability report or corporate social responsibility report is also subject to some form of independent verification or assurance). In the late 1990s social reporting tended to increase, with a trend through the early 2000s of *sustainability reporting* (which provides information about the financial, social and environmental performance of an entity).

Because social and **environmental accounting** is predominantly voluntary, there has been a great deal of research exploring the *motivations* for such disclosure. We will consider some of the motivations, and related theoretical perspectives, which have been suggested as driving the practice of social and environmental reporting. We will also consider evidence of how different stakeholder groups react to social and environmental information. The chapter will also consider the linkages between corporate social and environmental performance and financial performance. The linkage between social risk, environmental risk and financial risk will also be considered. The chapter will conclude with some discussion of the perceived future of social and environmental reporting.

It is hoped that the material provided in this chapter emphasises the current focus on areas of performance that have, until the mid-1990s, received relatively scant attention. We are starting to see new 'breeds' of accountant—*environmental accountants* and *social accountants*—who work alongside 'traditional' financial accountants. Because this area of reporting is continually evolving, it is a very exciting area for accountants to be involved in and, because of the environmental problems confronting the planet, it is an area in which greater accountability is urgently required.

> **externality** An impact that an entity has on parties external to the organisation. Externalities can be viewed as positive externalities (benefits) or negative externalities (costs).
>
> **social auditing** A process whereby an enterprise can account for its performance against its social objectives and report on that performance to evaluate observance of the principles of accountability.
>
> **environmental accounting** Environmental accounting focuses on the identification of the cost of environmental conservation during the normal course of business, identifying the benefits to be gained from such activities, providing the best possible means of quantitative measurement (in monetary value or physical units) and supporting the communication of results.[1]

26.2 Social and environmental reporting defined

Environmental reporting and social reporting are considered to represent components of the broader form of reporting commonly known as social responsibility reporting. So, what is 'corporate social responsibility'? There really is no consensus, but obviously it is central to the content and focus of this chapter. A definition requires consideration of, and perhaps consensus on, the actual social responsibilities of organisations. The *Financial Times* Lexicon (accessed 2012) provides the following explanation of corporate social responsibility:

> *Movement aimed at encouraging companies to be more aware of the impact of their business on the rest of society, including their own stakeholders and the environment.*

---

[1] Ministry of the Environment, Japan, *Environmental Accounting Guidelines*, 2005, http://www.env.go.jp., p/en/policy/ssee/eag05.pdf, p. 3.

Corporate social responsibility (CSR) is a business approach that contributes to sustainable development by delivering economic, social and environmental benefits for all stakeholders. CSR is a concept with many definitions and practices. The way it is understood and implemented differs greatly for each company and country. Moreover, CSR is a very broad concept that addresses many and various topics such as human rights, corporate governance, health and safety, environmental effects, working conditions and contribution to economic development. Whatever the definition is, the purpose of CSR is to drive change towards sustainability.

Although some companies may achieve remarkable efforts with unique CSR initiatives, it is difficult to be on the forefront on all aspects of CSR. Considering this, the example below provides good practices on one aspect of CSR – environmental sustainability.

Example

Unilever is a multinational corporation, in the food and beverage sector, with a comprehensive CSR strategy. The company has been ranked 'Food Industry leader' in the Dow Jones Sustainability World Indexes for 11 consecutive years and ranked 7th in the 'Global 100 Most Sustainable Corporations in the World'.

One of the major and unique initiatives is the 'sustainable tea' programme. On a partnership-based model with the Rainforest Alliance (an NGO), Unilever aims to source all of its Lipton and PG Tips tea bags from Rainforest Alliance Certified™ farms by 2015. The Rainforest Alliance Certification offers farms a way to differentiate their products as being socially, economically and environmentally sustainable.

(*Source*: *Financial Times* Lexicon. © The Financial Times Ltd 2012)

The above quotation highlights the fact that the definition of corporate social responsibility typically extends the responsibilities of corporations beyond their shareholders alone, and incorporates activities over and above those relating to the usual provision of goods and services. Corporate social responsibilities also relate to measures of economic, social and environmental performance. One generally accepted definition of corporate social responsibility, and one that is consistent with the perspective adopted within this chapter, was provided by the Commission of European Communities (2001, p. 6) in which it stated that CSR is:

a concept whereby companies integrate social and environmental concerns in their business operations and in their interaction with their stakeholders on a voluntary basis. Being socially responsible means not only fulfilling legal expectations, but also going beyond compliance and investing more into human capital, the environment and the relations with stakeholders.

Corporate social responsibility reporting, perhaps somewhat obviously, provides information about how an organisation has addressed its corporate social responsibilities. Once we start discussing organisations' choice to disclose information about their social and environmental performance, we accept, at least implicitly, that organisations have a responsibility, and associated accountability, not only for their financial performance but also their environmental and social performance. The perceived responsibilities of organisations will conceivably differ from individual to individual within the community and, again, from culture to culture and period to period. Nevertheless, we will define social responsibility reporting as the provision of information about the performance of an organisation in relation to its interaction with its physical and social environment. This would include such factors as an organisation's:

- interaction with the local community;
- level of support for community projects;
- level of support for developing countries;
- health and safety record;
- training, employment and education programmes; and
- environmental performance.

triple-bottom-line reporting Reporting that provides information about the economic, environmental and social performance of an entity.

Social reporting, which is a component of corporate social responsibility reporting, provides information about an organisation's interaction with, and associated impacts on, particular societies. It would include the first five points just listed.

In the mid to late 1990s, more and more corporations throughout the world started discussing aspects of what has commonly become termed **triple-bottom-line reporting**. This term is still frequently used today. Triple-bottom-line reporting has been defined by Elkington (1997) as reporting that provides information about the economic, environmental and social performance of an entity. At the time it represented a departure from previous 'bottom line' perspectives, which had traditionally focused solely on an entity's financial or economic performance. The notion of reporting against the three components (or 'bottom lines') of economic, environmental and social performance is tied directly to the concept and goal of **sustainable development**—something that from the beginning of the 1990s began to appear on the agenda of many countries and large corporations. According to Elkington (1997, p. 397):

> *Sustainable development involves the simultaneous pursuit of economic prosperity, environmental quality and social equity. Companies aiming for sustainability need to perform not against a single financial bottom line, but against the triple bottom line.*

sustainable development Development that meets the needs of the present world without compromising the ability of future generations to meet their own needs.

26.2.1 Sustainability

The above definition of triple-bottom-line reporting makes reference to sustainability. There are various definitions of sustainable development, but the one most commonly cited is 'development that meets the needs of the present world without compromising the ability of future generations to meet their own needs' (World Commission on Environment and Development 1987—the Brundtland Report).

Triple-bottom-line reporting, as well as sustainability reporting, will, if properly implemented, provide information that enables report readers to assess how sustainable an organisation's or a community's operations are. The perspective taken is that, for an organisation (or a community) to be sustainable (a long-term perspective), it must be financially secure (as evidenced through such measures as profitability); it must minimise (or, ideally, eliminate) its negative environmental impacts; and it must act in conformity with societal expectations or else lose its 'community licence to operate'. These three factors are obviously highly interrelated.

It is a relatively recent phenomenon for companies to embrace the 'sustainability agenda', and different organisations appear to define sustainability in different ways, some of which represent departures from the definition provided above (definition from the Brundtland Report). Consider, for example, the following quotations:

> *Sustainable development for Shell means considering both short- and long-term interests, and integrating economic, environmental and social considerations into our decision-making.*

(Shell Sustainability Report, 2010)

For InterGen, a global power generation company headquartered in the US with power plants located in the UK, the Netherlands, Mexico, the Philippines and Australia, sustainable development is a key objective. To achieve sustainable development the global player has identified 11 areas that it considers are important to the company's overall success:

- *Sustainable Development. InterGen seeks to integrate the economic, environmental and societal aspects of its business to achieve sustained financial success, safeguard the environment and develop the Company's reputation as a respected corporate citizen. InterGen will take active steps to ensure that this Sustainable Development policy is implemented in the development, construction and operation of its facilities worldwide. A systematic approach will be employed to achieve this integration in the following areas:*
- *Corporate Commitment. The Company will establish, implement and monitor policies, programs and best practices for conducting its development, construction and operations in a manner that is consistent with this policy. Moreover, the Company will pursue a process of continuous improvement with regard to the sustainable development of its facilities.*
- *Integrated Management. The Company will integrate this sustainable development policy, and associated programs and standards fully in all activities and all functions as an essential element of management. InterGen will create an environment where a genuine concern for sustainable development is fostered through example and involvement. The implementation of these policies will be considered when taking into account performance at all levels.*
- *Communications. The Company will establish and maintain communications with its employees, residents in communities hosting its facilities and other appropriate stakeholders, to keep them fully informed of the Company's activities and its facilities' development, construction and operations.*
- *Environmental Stewardship. When constructing and operating its facilities, the Company will respect biodiversity and utilize proven, environmentally responsible technology.*
- *Impact Mitigation. The Company will work with communities to anticipate and manage the impact of its plant construction and operations upon the local community.*
- *Use of Natural Resources. The Company will seek to effectively and efficiently utilize natural resources in the construction and operation of its projects.*

- **Economic Development.** *The Company will actively seek to create and promote local economic opportunities associated with the development, construction and operations of its projects.*
- **Employment.** *The Company will actively seek to create a safe and healthy environment for its employees. The Company will also proactively encourage the hiring of local personnel for both the construction and operations of its projects.*
- **Community Development.** *The Company will provide support, financial or otherwise, for local community development initiatives; depending on the circumstance of each project. This could include assistance with social, educational, health or other similar activities.*
- **Human Rights.** *The Company will respect the human rights of employees and members of the communities in which it operates.*
- **Cultural Sensitivity.** *The Company will respect the rights of local cultures and indigenous peoples and proactively seek to support cultural identity initiatives.*

    By addressing these issues and impacts related to its business, InterGen will be in a better position to achieve sustained financial success.

As this chapter will demonstrate, social and environmental reporting, or sustainability reporting, are quite new forms of reporting when compared with financial reporting. There are generally accepted frameworks for general purpose financial reporting, which are supported by conceptual framework projects and a multitude of accounting standards. However, while there are numerous guidance documents for social and environmental reporting (and sustainability reporting), to date there is no uniform approach that is generally adopted by all organisations. There is no conceptual framework for social and environmental reporting (although the *Sustainability Reporting Guidelines* developed by the Global Reporting Initiative—which we will discuss later in this chapter—are attracting widespread acceptance on an international basis), which means that there is limited consensus on such issues as the *objectives*, required *qualitative characteristics*, appropriate *formats* and the *audience* of social and environmental reporting. Hence there is much variation in how entities are providing social and environmental information—with obvious implications for comparing different entities' performance.

We will consider some of the various approaches to disclosing social and environmental information later in this chapter. At this point it is again emphasised that there is great variability in reporting approaches and terms such as *corporate social reporting*, *social responsibility reporting*, *triple-bottom-line reporting* and *sustainability reporting* all seem to be used interchangeably. Indeed, when defining sustainability reporting, the Global Reporting Initiative (2011, p. 3), noted:

> *Sustainability reporting is the practice of measuring, disclosing, and being accountable to internal and external stakeholders for organizational performance towards the goal of sustainable development. 'Sustainability reporting' is a broad term considered synonymous with others used to describe reporting on economic, environmental, and social impacts (e.g., triple bottom line, corporate responsibility reporting, etc.). A sustainability report should provide a balanced and reasonable representation of the sustainability performance of a reporting organisation—including both positive and negative contributions.*

Now we will examine the responsibilities of business and whether these responsibilities can reasonably be expected to extend to providing information about social and environmental performance.

26.3 What are the responsibilities of business (to whom and for what)?

The issue of corporate social responsibility has become very topical.

While in the past many corporate managers might have given little direct consideration to stakeholders other than shareholders, this seems to have changed. There has long been much discussion about what information organisations *should* provide in relation to the various facets (for example, financial, social and environmental implications) of their performance. Many arguments are tied to subjective opinions about stakeholders' *rights to know* (which, if they are to carry any weight, would seem to require some identification of the *stakeholders* involved) and associated opinions on the extent of an organisation's accountability.

Indeed, once we open a debate about the information that an entity *should* disclose, we are, in effect, entering a debate about the responsibilities and associated accountabilities of organisations. Is the sole function of a company to make a profit or do companies have wider responsibilities to the societies in which they operate, and that allow them to exist? What do you, the reader, think? As we can see from some of the discussion so far, views seem to be changing about the importance of embracing corporate social responsibility.

If we believe a company is responsible only for its financial performance and for providing financial returns to its shareholders, we might accept that it is inappropriate and indeed wasteful to provide social and environmental information—unless doing so is expected to enhance the profitability of the organisation.

There are many views on the responsibilities of business. At one extreme are the views of the famous economist Milton Friedman. In his widely cited book *Capitalism and Freedom*, Friedman rejects the view that corporate managers have any *moral* obligations or responsibilities. He notes (1962, p. 133) that such a view:

> shows a fundamental misconception of the character and nature of a free economy. In such an economy, there is one and only one social responsibility of business – to use its resources and engage in activities designed to increase its profits as long as it stays within the rules of the game, which is to say, engages in open and free competition, without deception or fraud.

At the other end of the 'responsibility spectrum' are those who hold the view that managers should manage the organisation for the benefit of *all* stakeholders, not just those with control over scarce resources. Taking a broader perspective on the responsibilities of business, an entity's stakeholders have been defined by Freeman and Reed (1983, p. 91) as 'any identifiable group or individual who can affect the achievement of an organisation's objectives, or is affected by the achievement of an organisation's objectives'. Interestingly, this is very similar to the definition provided by BP in its Sustainability Review 2010 and Vodafone in its Sustainability Report 2011. These companies respectively state:

> We talk with stakeholders in many ways and at many levels, from the queries that reach us via our website to face-to-face meetings with investors, governments and regulators, customers, employees, community groups and others.

> (BP, Sustainability Review, 2010)

> We are committed to acting responsibly in all our activities to maintain the trust of our customers, our employees and other stakeholders.

> (Vodafone, Sustainability Report for the year ended 31 March 2011)

Divergent views on the responsibilities of business are nothing new, as captured by the following article by Joel Makower which evaluates Friedman's famous essay on the role of business in society—several decades on.

Financial Accounting in the News 26.1

MILTON FRIEDMAN AND THE SOCIAL RESPONSIBILITY OF BUSINESS

Joel Makower, Worldchanging website, 19 November 2006

In a 1970 *Times* magazine article, the economist Milton Friedman argued that businesses' sole purpose is to generate profit for shareholders. Moreover, he maintained, companies that did adopt 'responsible' attitudes would be faced with more binding constraints than companies that did not, rendering them less competitive...

'What does it mean to say that the corporate executive has a "social responsibility" in his capacity as businessman?' asked Friedman in his 1970 article.

'If this statement is not pure rhetoric, it must mean that he is to act in some way that is not in the interest of his employers. For example, that he is to refrain from increasing the price of the product in order to contribute to the social objective of pre-venting inflation, even though a price increase would be in the best interests of the corporation. Or that he is to make expenditures on reducing pollution beyond the amount that is in the best interests of the corporation or that is required by law in order to contribute to the social objective of improving the environment. Or that, at the expense of corporate profits, he is to hire "hardcore" unemployed instead of better-qualified available workmen to contribute to the social objective of reducing poverty.

'In each of these cases, the corporate executive would be spending someone else's money for a general social interest. Insofar as his actions in accord with his "social responsibility" reduce returns to stockholders, he is spending their money. Insofar

◀

as his actions raise the price to customers, he is spending the customers' money. Insofar as his actions lower the wages of some employees, he is spending their money.'

Friedman argued that such actions in effect turned executives into public employees or civil servants, levying "taxes" (in the form of corporate money allocated to social causes) and making "expenditures"—a part of "the socialist view that political mechanisms, not market mechanisms, are the appropriate way to determine the allocation of scarce resources to alternative uses".

Friedman concluded:

'The difficulty of exercising "social responsibility" illustrates, of course, the great virtue of private competitive enterprise—it forces people to be responsible for their own actions and makes it difficult for them to "exploit" other people for either selfish or unselfish purposes. They can do good—but only at their own expense.'

We know better now. For example, we understand that ignoring environmental and social issues can be bad for business. Companies that pollute their local communities risk poisoning their customers. Ignoring the state of the local school system risks depleting the pool of qualified workers. Abusing workers risks higher turnover and training costs, not to mention greater difficulty attracting the most qualified candidates.

It's never that simple, of course. In a globalised world, companies are free to exploit or pollute a local community, then move on to the next place. Unfettered markets and exploitation-friendly tax schemes reward companies for

acting in their own interests in the name of economic growth and competitiveness. So, Friedman's philosophy still reigns supreme.

Friedman's philosophy is far from universally shared, even in the business community. In 1979, for example, Quaker Oats president Kenneth Mason, writing in *Businessweek*, declared Friedman's profits-are-everything philosophy 'a dreary and demeaning view of the role of business and business leaders in our society.' Wrote Mason: 'Making a profit is no more the purpose of a corporation than getting enough to eat is the purpose of life. Getting enough to eat is a requirement of life; life's purpose, one would hope, is somewhat broader and more challenging. Likewise with business and profit.'

Mason went on:

'The moral imperative all of us share in this world is that of getting the best return we can on whatever assets we are privileged to employ. What American business leaders too often forget is that this means all the assets employed—not just the financial assets but also the brains employed, the labour employed, the materials employed, and the land, air, and water employed'.

He urged readers to 'encourage, not evade, discussion of those problems that arise when the activities of business conflict with the needs and concerns of society'.

But these were largely just well-intentioned words. Action, and even discussion, on some of these issues would be decades in coming. Even when it did take place, the discussion involved only big companies. The social responsibility of smaller firms is just now entering the conversation.

Financial Accounting in the News 26.2 provides further insight into the debates that rage with respect to the extent to which organisations have responsibilities to groups other than shareholders.

Financial Accounting in the News 26.2
COPPING FLAK OVER CORPORATE SOCIALISM
Leela de Kretser, *Herald-Sun*, 29 January 2008

With the world's financial markets in freefall, the United States economy grinding to a halt and a French trader forcing his bank to bring out the begging bowls, who would've thought a five-minute speech about corporate socialism could cause an uproar in the press?

But that's exactly what Microsoft genius Bill Gates faces at home after suggesting to his fellow billionaires at Davos that the free market is failing the world's poor—and that it's time to introduce a little bit of creative capitalism.

According to the one-time richest man on the planet, it's possible for a business to make profits and also improve the lives of others who don't necessarily benefit from market forces.

But—and with all good speeches the 'but' often contains the main point—Gates said profits are not always possible when business tries to serve the very poor.

In such cases, there needs to be another incentive, and that incentive is recognition.

We must appreciate the link between perceived corporate responsibilities and associated accountabilities. If an entity is not considered to have a responsibility in relation to a particular aspect of its performance, it would not be expected to provide an account of that performance. If an organisation adopts a broad perspective in identifying its stakeholders (as opposed to a narrow perspective, which might include only shareholders), this will normally mean that it will choose to provide information about quite a diverse range of the organisation's activities in order to satisfy the information needs and expectations of the various stakeholder groups. By contrast, if an entity has a narrow perspective on identifying its stakeholders, it might produce a limited amount of performance information.

The range of definitions of stakeholders provided by companies do indicate that some companies define their stakeholders quite broadly. The view that it would be *bad business* not to consider the concerns of a broad group of stakeholders is reflected in an extract from Simon Goodley's article reproduced in Financial Accounting in the News 26.3. In this article, Goodley discusses a book that has been published by David Jones, an advisor to David Cameron on his election campaign and the current head of Kofi Annan's 'tck tck tck' campaign, which aims to raise awareness of climate change. In his book, Jones argues that 'good business is better business' and good business is business that is responsible. This approach to business, he argues, will reap better financial returns for an entity.

Financial Accounting in the News 26.3

DAVID JONES, HAVAS CHIEF, HAS SEEN THE FUTURE— AND IT'S CSR

Simon Goodley, *The Guardian*, 1 January 2012

Now Jones is plugging his latest project, a book on corporate social responsibility (CSR) called *Who Cares Wins: Why Good Business Is Better Business*. It does exactly what it says on the tin, arguing that the worlds of social responsibility and social media have become fused and that there is a commercial benefit for companies that behave themselves.

'Social media has taken CSR from a silo to putting it in the profit and loss account,' he says in a tidily prepared soundbite. 'The price of doing well is doing good.'

To illustrate this point, the book identifies an 'age of image', from 1990 to 2000, that was focused on altering the reputation of a business in a consumer's mind, rather than genuinely changing how it did things; an 'age of advantage',

from 2000 to 2010, when a few companies realised they could gain an edge by delivering on promises made; and an 'age of damage', from 2010 onwards, when businesses that are not socially responsible will suffer as a result.

Transparency

'If I had to pick one word to use as the guideline for running a business in this new era, it would be "transparency"', Jones writes in his book. 'And the research among business leaders, where 67% believe that business success is based in corporate transparency, supports this.'

Source: The Guardian. © 2012 Guardian News and Media Limited

However, not all segments of the community embrace broad perspectives on corporate responsibility. For example, we could be excused for thinking that many individuals working within the contemporary financial press hold the same view as Friedman (a restricted view of responsibilities, as noted above). The financial press continues to praise companies for increased profitability and to criticise companies who are subject to falling profitability. They often do this with little or no regard to the social costs or **social benefits** (which are not directly incorporated within reported profit) generated by the operations of the entities concerned.

> **social benefits**
> Benefits generated by an entity for society, or a segment thereof, such as provision of education, clean water, safe products and health care.

Examine your own opinions: what sort of information do you think organisations *should* disclose, and to whom should they make the disclosures (who are the stakeholders)? Do you think your views about organisations' accountabilities would be the same as those of your fellow students? Perhaps ask them. It is easy to see just how subjective such assessments are.

Somewhat surprisingly, many students of accounting complete their accounting qualifications without ever considering issues associated with the *accountability of business*. But the practice of accounting, which, at a fairly simplistic level, can be defined as the provision of information about the performance of an entity to a particular group of report readers (or stakeholders), cannot be divorced from a consideration of the extent of an entity's responsibility and accountability. This linkage should always be considered. If we accept that an entity has a responsibility for its social and environmental performance, we, as accountants, should accept a duty to provide

> **accountability** The duty to provide an account or reckoning of those actions for which one can be held responsible.

an account of an organisation's social and environmental performance. If we don't accept this, we won't feel obliged to provide such an account.

At this point it would be useful to consider a definition of **accountability**. Let us adopt the definition of accountability provided by Gray *et al.* (1996, p. 38): the 'duty to provide an account (by no means necessarily a financial account) or reckoning of those actions for which one is held responsible'. According to Gray *et al.*, accountability involves two responsibilities or duties:

1. The responsibility to undertake certain actions (or to refrain from taking certain actions).
2. The responsibility to provide an account of those actions.

Accepting the above definition, we can again see that perceptions of accountability depend on subjective perceptions of the extent of an organisation's responsibility. Are businesses responsible to their direct owners (shareholders) alone or do they owe a duty to the wider community in which they operate? Certainly, many organisations are currently making public statements to the effect that they consider that they do have responsibilities to parties other than just their shareholders. Another issue is whether the responsibility of business is restricted to current generations, or whether the implications for future generations should be factored into current management decisions. If sustainability is embraced, our current production patterns should not compromise the ability of future generations to satisfy their own needs.

Whether these public positions actually inform decision making within the firm is another matter—we clearly cannot be sure. The articles reproduced in Financial Accounting in the News 26.4 and 26.5 support the view that business organisations do have social responsibilities and are becoming more active in being accountable for those responsibilities. By contrast, the article reproduced in Financial Accounting in the News 26.6 perhaps reflects a more 'dated' view wherein organisations have one main and over-riding responsibility, this being to maximise shareholder value. In this case, it involves banks charging persons who are regarded as financially marginalised for services that were once free to all. Read the articles and consider which of the perspectives you would be more inclined to agree with. This is very much a subjective decision.

Financial Accounting In the News 26.4

HALF TOP COMPANIES REPORT ON ENVIRONMENTAL CONDUCT: CORPORATE RESPONSIBILITY

Alison Maitland, *Financial Times*, 9 September 2003

More than half the top 250 companies now produce reports on environmental, social or ethical performance, demonstrating how non-financial disclosure has become mainstream.

A new study found that 132 of the FTSE 250 companies report. All of those covered the environment and 100 also covered social and ethical issues. This compares with 30 that produced non-financial reports five years ago and six 10 years ago.

Reports are also appearing in sectors not traditionally targeted by campaigners, such as media and telecommunications.

'Corporate social responsibility reporting in the UK is reaching critical mass,' said Simon Propper, managing

director of Context, the CSR consultancy that carried out the Directions study with SalterBaxter, a corporate identity and communications firm. 'In most sectors, it's only a small minority who don't report. Unless you're a maverick, this is an uncomfortable place for any company to be.'

However Nigel Salter, of SalterBaxter, said some reports reflected genuine CSR efforts while others could be merely 'a fine coat of worthy gloss paint'. This is underlined by a survey showing that, despite the emphasis on CSR, 74 per cent of employees believe they do not have enough opportunities to get involved with charities at work.

(www.econtext.co.uk www.strip4shelter.org.uk www.bitc.org.uk)

Source: Financial Times. © The Financial Times Ltd 2012

Financial Accounting in the News 26.5

THE HEARTS ARE WON BUT NOT THE MINDS

Alison Maitland, *Financial Times*, 18 June 2002

Europe's corporate leaders are convinced that responsible business practice leads to greater innovation, competitiveness and profitability….

…A wide range of leading companies took part in the survey, including Adecco, Anglo American, British Telecommunications, Cable & Wireless, GlaxoSmithKline, Levi Strauss, Morgan Stanley Dean Witter, Norsk Hydro, Renault and Telefonica.

For these business leaders, the top issues that will affect performance in the next five years are attracting and retaining talented staff, ability to innovate and corporate reputation. Their concern with reputation, together with involvement in corporate social responsibility, is driven primarily by the views and expectations of customers. About half regard environmental issues as important to performance but only 13 per cent are worried about the impact of protests against globalisation and capitalism.

They give strong backing to the idea that responsible social and environmental behaviour pays dividends, especially if it is a mainstream part of business activities. Nearly 80 per cent agree that companies that integrate responsible practices will be more competitive; and 73 per cent accept that 'sustained social and environmental engagement can significantly improve profitability'. Seventy-six per cent agree that innovation and creativity are helped by responsible business practices. 'It is an interest for our potential customers and future markets,' says one respondent. 'We can refer to it a lot when planning innovations.'

Just over half say that the benefits to businesses of corporate social and environmental responsibility are not exaggerated, although this is strongly weighted towards the UK, where 74 per cent of leaders take this view compared with 47 per cent in the rest of Europe.

When it comes to integrating responsible behaviour into all aspects of the business, however, it is another story. The majority of companies have boardroom statements or codes of conduct but fewer than a third have assessed the risks and opportunities presented by environmental, ethical and social issues. Only half are setting targets for their performance in these areas.

It seems that some business leaders, at least, are aware there is a discrepancy here. Nearly half agree that companies do not pay enough attention to the value that social and environmental initiatives can bring them, even though almost all accept it as the responsibility of top management to push these programmes forward.

The study reveals disagreement between business leaders in the UK and the rest of Europe about who in the company should take charge of corporate social responsibility. While 43 per cent of UK directors believe all departments should be involved, this view is shared by just 10 per cent of top executives elsewhere in Europe.

Source: Financial Times. © The Financial Times Ltd 2012

Financial Accounting in the News 26.6

WHY ATM CHARGES PROVE FINANCIAL INCLUSION IS OUT OF FASHION

Faisel Rahman, *The Guardian*, 20 September 2011

The basic account was introduced by banks almost a decade ago after coming under pressure from the Labour government to give financially excluded people access to banking services. It is a no-frills account without overdraft facilities that allows people to have their wages paid into a bank account and to set up direct debits to pay bills.

The Treasury estimates that between 2002 and 2008, nearly half of the 2.2 million people without bank accounts in the UK signed up to opening one—the vast majority, to

basic accounts. Of these, 1.1 million—more than half— were from the lowest income quintile.

The short-term financial benefits of having a basic account have turned out to be limited, as savings made by moving to electronic banking have been offset by penalty payment charges if a direct debit bounces or the account goes into the red—basic bank account customers are not able to negotiate an agreed overdraft. But the longer term benefits of improved financial stability, security, inclusion, convenience and greater financial savings are not in doubt.

▶

> ... We cannot stop banks charging what they want and, as they are not charities, they of course need to cover their costs. However, charging poor people to help rebuild their balance sheets seems like a bad choice. It is estimated that more than a million people are still without a bank account. Making it more expensive to have one will only add to this number.
>
> Source: The Guardian. © 2012 Guardian News and Media Limited

Reflecting different perspectives about the accountabilities of business organisations, a study of 'sustainability reporting' undertaken by Gray *et al.* (1995) reported that sustainability reports by UK companies typically addressed four groups of stakeholder, in order of importance (as measured by volume of disclosures): employees (the greatest coverage), the community, the environment and customers. A more recent study, by Idowu and Towler (2004), reported progress in the volume and type of information being reported and the higher incidence of separate bespoke CSR reports that typically focused on four main areas: the workplace, the environment, the community and the marketplace.

26.4   Regulation of public social and environmental reporting

In 2007 the British government made amendments to the Companies Act 2006 to require that quoted companies provide an extended directors' report. This report was to provide information on environmental, employment, social, community and other issues likely to impact on a company's future. This requirement was mandated for reports relating to financial years beginning on or after 1 October 2007.

26.4.1 Reporting requirements within accounting standards

In Europe, reporting on social and environmental issues within a company's annual report remains predominantly voluntary. A specific international requirement for companies to provide environmental information in their annual reports is to be found in IAS 16 *Property, Plant and Equipment*, which requires the cost of an item of property, plant and equipment to include the initial estimate of the costs of dismantling and removing the item and restoring the site on which it is located, the obligation for which an entity incurs either when the item is acquired or as a consequence of having used the item during a particular period for purposes other than to produce inventories during the period.

A further accounting standard that has some relevance to accounting for the environment is IAS 37 *Provisions, Contingent Liabilities and Contingent Assets*. Obligations relating to environmental performance could be considered to be included in either 'provisions' or 'contingent liabilities', depending upon the circumstances. Appendix C to IAS 37 provides an example of an environment-related liability. It is reproduced in Exhibit 26.1.

Exhibit 26.1   **Example of how IAS 37 is applied to environment-related liabilities**

An entity operates an offshore oilfield where its licensing agreement requires it to remove the oil rig at the end of production and restore the seabed. Ninety per cent of the eventual costs relate to the removal of the oil rig and restoration of damage caused by building it, and 10 per cent arise through the extraction of oil. At the end of the reporting period, the rig has been constructed but no oil has been extracted.

Present obligation as a result of a past obligating event: The construction of the oil rig creates a legal obligation under the terms of the licence to remove the rig and restore the seabed and is thus an obligating event. At the end of the reporting period, however, there is no obligation to rectify the damage that will be caused by extraction of the oil.

An outflow of resources embodying economic benefits in settlement: Probable.

Conclusion: A provision is recognised for the best estimate of 90 per cent of the eventual costs that relate to the removal of the oil rig and restoration of damage caused by building it (see paragraph 14 of IAS 37). These costs are included as part of the cost of the oil rig. The 10 per cent of costs that arise through the extraction of oil are recognised as a liability when the oil is extracted.

IAS 37 *Provisions, Contingent Liabilities and Contingent Assets* also states that 'constructive obligations' will often require recognition in an entity's financial statements. Paragraph 10 of IAS 37 defines constructive obligations, while paragraph 21 provides some discussion of constructive obligations:

> 10. *A constructive obligation is an obligation that derives from an entity's actions where:*
>   (a) *by an established pattern of past practice, published policies or a sufficiently specific current statement, the entity has indicated to other parties that it will accept certain responsibilities; and*
>   (b) *as a result, the entity has created a valid expectation on the part of those other parties that it will discharge those responsibilities.*
> 21. *An event that does not give rise to an obligation immediately may do so at a later date, because of changes in the law or because an act (for example, a sufficiently specific public statement) by the entity gives rise to a constructive obligation. For example, when environmental damage is caused there may be no obligation to remedy the consequences. However, the causing of the damage will become an obligating event when a new law requires the existing damage to be rectified or when the entity publicly accepts responsibility for rectification in a way that creates a constructive obligation.*

While there is limited coverage of environmental issues in accounting standards—as detailed above—what coverage there is, is restricted to the financial consequences of various actions, rather than being driven by a desire to provide readers with information about the social and environmental performance of a reporting entity.

26.4.2 Corporate law disclosure requirements

The UK government's policy, for the past ten years or more, is to encourage voluntary environmental reporting. This policy is considered to have been successful in other countries; for example, in a study of 822 financial statements of Norwegian companies, Fallan and Fallan (2009) support the claim of voluntarism that companies will meet the heterogeneous requirements of their stakeholders without any governmental regulations. They argue that 'no statutory regulations are needed to make the companies increase and adapt their environmental disclosure'. They found that the regulation approach has 'a significant, immediate effect on mandatory environmental disclosure only, and that companies do not fully comply with such statutory regulations'.

In contrast to this, the UK Environment Agency argues that the UK's voluntary approach has not worked, as their research (see http://www.environment-agency.gov.uk/business/topics/performance/32348.aspx) found that only 24 per cent (136 out of 570) of the FTSE All-Share companies disclose quantified information on their environmental risks, impact or performance, and they reported no consistency or comparability in the disclosures examined. They argue that legislation should direct companies to disclose their environmental KPIs in line with the Defra Environmental Key Performance Indicators—reporting guidelines for UK business. They argue the case for unambiguous reporting requirements as these provide clarity, comparability and comprehensive information for both writers and users (Environment Agency 2006).

Though not providing detailed legislation on the disclosure of environmental factors that impact on a company, there are several laws that companies must comply with, so the sector is not lawless. For example, the Clean Air Act (1993), the Environment Act (1995) and the Pollution Prevention and Control Act (1999) in the UK provide rules on air quality. Many of the sections have been included as a result of European law.

The UK sector is not without guidance in respect of disclosures, either. The Department for Environment, Food and Rural Affairs (DEFRA) issued a report entitled 'Guidance on Reporting on Greenhouse Gas Emissions' in September 2009. This report provides detail on the disclosures that are deemed to reflect good practice. The report incorporates the GreenHouse Gas (GHG) protocol—the internationally recognised standard for corporate accounting and reporting of GHG emissions. In its appendix it also provides an example of the type of disclosures that are recommended for a small company, suggesting that the guidance is for all companies regardless of size.

While disclosures are required by a variety of regulatory regimes (for example, the EU Emissions Trading System and the Climate Change Agreement), organisations are not compelled to disclose the information in their own annual reports, sustainability reports, or on their websites. While the information is publicly accessible, it would be reasonable to argue that many people would be unaware of the various databases available. The idea behind establishing these sites is that public reporting will create public pressure on organisations to change if their performance appears to be relatively poor—but this obviously requires that the public actually know about these websites in the first place.

As with environmental performance, organisations are generally not required to publicly disclose in their annual reports information about their social performance. For example, there is no requirement for a company to disclose information about its support of local communities, its employment or education policies or its support of charitable organisations. Companies *are* required to disclose quite extensive information about

payments to directors and executives, but such requirements are arguably a reaction to the corporate excesses of recent decades, when numerous directors were deemed to be paid excessive amounts.

26.4.3 Corporate governance principles

If we consider existing mandatory corporate reporting frameworks as constituted by accounting standards, company law reporting requirements and securities exchange reporting requirements, it would appear that external reporting requirements have focused predominantly on providing financial performance information to parties with a financial stake in the corporation. Developments in disclosure requirements pertaining to corporate governance issues (for example, the UK Corporate Governance Code), though recognising the needs of several stakeholders, have tended to focus on the information needs of shareholders rather than taking a broader 'stakeholder' perspective.

However, while the corporate governance recommendations do seem to indicate an acceptance of broader corporate responsibilities, a review of the listing requirements of the London Stock Exchange (which are mandatory for organisations listed on the LSE) does overwhelmingly seem to indicate that extremely limited attention has been given to requiring listed organisations to provide information to a group of stakeholders that extends beyond shareholders (that is, accountability seems to be restricted to shareholders).

Such a narrow approach to accountability by UK regulators, according to which attention is primarily focused on the needs and expectations of shareholders (rather than stakeholders generally), is commonly referred to as the 'shareholder primacy' view of corporate reporting. This approach to reporting is found in many other countries too. The shareholder primacy approach generally adopted within the UK is being challenged increasingly by various interest groups. Up till now, however, government has tended to leave corporations, their industry bodies and 'the market' to determine the extent of corporate social and environmental disclosure.

26.4.4 Examples of overseas reporting requirements

The UK position on reporting on social and environmental performance can be contrasted with that of some other countries. Briefly, some of the disclosure requirements in other countries are as follows:

- *France.* Pursuant to the French Economic Regulations Law (NRE), there is a legal obligation for French corporations to provide information within their annual reports about their social and environmental performance. Such disclosures are to include information about use of energy, water and raw materials; levels of emissions to air, land and water; development of environmental management systems; and details of certifications and compliances with standards. Information pertaining to specific qualitative and quantitative indicators is to be disclosed. From 2003, French companies listed on the 'premier marché' (those with the largest market capitalisation) are also to include in their annual report 'information on how the company takes into account the social and environmental consequences of its activities'.
- *Sweden.* The Swedish Financial Accounts Act (1999) requires that specific companies (for example, those requiring an environmental permit) must make certain disclosures within the directors' report section of their annual reports. The Act requires disclosures mainly to show that licence or permit conditions have been satisfied.
- *Canada.* Public corporations are required to report how environmental protection requirements will impact on current and future operations.
- *The Netherlands.* The Environmental Protection Act (1997) requires more than 300 companies to publicly release reports that provide specific information about their environmental performance.
- *Denmark.* In 2001 the Law on Accounts was introduced, which requires disclosures to be made in the annual report about 'environmental issues' associated with the organisation's operations. Particular disclosures are to be made about the organisation's impact on the external environment and what measures have been taken to remedy this impact. Within Denmark there is also a requirement for companies to produce 'green accounts' pursuant to the Green Accounting Law (1995). This law affects approximately 3,000 companies.
- *Norway.* The Accounting Act 1999 requires specific disclosures to be made in the directors' report that is included in the annual report. Information must be disclosed about the organisation's impact on the environment (for example, through the use of particular resources), together with activities that have been undertaken to reduce the impact of the organisation upon the environment. A detailed list of social and environmental indicators is provided.
- *Belgium.* VLAREM II (1995) requires that specific companies must issue an annual environmental report.
- *The United States.* The Securities Exchange Commission has a joint agreement with the US Environmental Protection Agency (EPA) in which the SEC is provided by the EPA with information on companies identified as potentially responsible parties on hazardous waste sites; companies subject to clean-up requirements under the Resource Conservation and Recovery Act; and companies named in criminal and civil proceedings under environmental laws. This information is, potentially, used by the SEC to ensure that corporations

properly disclose their environmental obligations. The US also has requirements for corporations to make disclosures in filings with the SEC about material financial effects of environmental compliance (Reg. S-K, Item 101).

■ *South Africa*. Companies listed on the Johannesburg Stock Exchange have, since 2003, been required to report annually on their social and environmental performance using the Global Reporting Initiative *Sustainability Reporting Guidelines*.

In contrast with overseas requirements, it is interesting to speculate on why UK regulators have appeared loathe to introduce specific sustainability-related disclosure requirements in corporate annual reports.

Although there is a general lack of statutory requirement within the UK, many organisations nevertheless do publicly disclose social and environmental information. However, as disclosure is voluntary, it is sometimes claimed that organisations tend to exclude information portraying them in a negative light. In addition, as reported in an article reproduced in Financial Accounting in the News 26.7, there is some concern about the quality of information being disclosed.

Financial Accounting in the News 26.7

HOWLERS AND OMISSIONS EXPOSED IN A WORLD OF CORPORATE SOCIAL RESPONSIBILITY

Juliette Jowit, *The Guardian*, 24 November 2011

Environment reports by some of the world's biggest companies are routinely including wrong statistics and leaving out vital information, according to the most comprehensive study yet carried out. The examination of more than 4,000 corporate social responsibility (CSR) reports and company surveys by a team at Leeds University found 'irrelevant data, unsubstantiated claims, gaps in data and inaccurate figures'—a finding that will cast serious doubt over the burgeoning sector.

Among the most colourful mistakes and omissions made by some of the world's biggest corporations were a company whose carbon footprint was four times that for the whole world and a car maker and power group which both, entirely legally, managed to excise a huge coal plant from their pollution record. More regular problems included companies ignoring data from individual countries or subsidiaries in their group—including many in China and Brazil—two of the world's biggest economies. Failing to collect or ignoring data from multiple sources was so endemic that BT, which has won awards for its CSR reporting, highlighted zero energy and water use, waste and transport for many of its international operations in 2007; the following year the company did not claim they were zero but left more than half the table blank. In total, fewer than one in six of the companies surveyed reported greenhouse gases for all their operations, said the academics, and many more did not make it clear which activities were covered.

The Leeds study, carried out jointly with Euromed Management School in Marseille, France, comes just weeks after a major report by the consultancy and accountants KPMG, who found nearly two-thirds of the biggest companies in the 34 countries they studied were producing CSR reports, and that Britain was leading the world with a 100% reporting rate. Previous studies of CSR have also praised some of the world's most reviled companies, raising doubts over the value of the practice. 'The quality of environmental data in sustainability reports remains appalling at times, even today,' said Dr Ralf Barkemeyer, a lecturer in CSR at Leeds and one of the team leaders. 'In financial reporting to leave out an undisclosed part of the company in the calculation of profits would be a scandal. In sustainability reporting it is common practice. Put provocatively, companies get points for knowing where they want to go, but nobody seems to check whether this is where they are heading. Aspiration replaces performance.'

BT: The telecoms operator apparently generated more than 99% of its waste from overseas operations in the relatively small country of Belgium in 2007 and 2008

Volkswagen and E.ON: The German carmaker and power company both decided not to include a massive coal plant in Germany in their emissions records: VW because it was owned by E.ON, E.ON because it was run by VW

Enel: The Italian energy company reported in 2009 that its total carbon dioxide emissions were 122,089m tonnes – four times the global total that year

BP: The oil and gas group long ago branded itself Beyond Petroleum, but as well as still being a mainly fossil fuel producer its carbon emissions are the size of Finland's

Ford: The US carmaker said in 2004 that it generated more mineral waste in North America than in the whole world, including North America

ABB: The Swiss power and engineering group overstated its sulphur emissions from power stations by 1,000 times in three successive reports from 2003 to 2005

Source: The Guardian. © 2012 Guardian News and Media Limited

> **traditional financial accounting practices**
> Practices that have been applied for a long time and are considered to be generally accepted by the majority of accountants. Would emphasise measures associated with historical costs.

Errors and omissions as highlighted in Financial Accounting in the News 26.7 have fuelled calls for more regulation (which have been largely ignored). However, when more regulation is proposed there are often protests from industry. Because social and environmental disclosures are predominantly voluntary, many researchers have been interested in the *motivation* behind such disclosures. We will consider some of the possible motivations later in this chapter. We will also consider various industry initiatives that encourage (voluntary) disclosure. However, at this point it would be worth considering how **traditional financial accounting practices** act to limit the extent of social and environmental disclosures being made. In the past, the 'traditions' of general purpose financial reporting caused many accountants to question the relevance of the *environment* and *society* to the functions of accounting—however, attitudes have changed dramatically in recent years.

26.5 Limitations of traditional financial accounting

Financial accounting, which is what this book has focused on, is often criticised on the basis that it ignores many of the *externalities* caused by reporting entities. Externalities can be defined as impacts that an entity has on parties (not necessarily restricted to human beings) that are external to the organisation, parties that typically have no direct relationship with the organisation. Some of these effects or impacts relate to the social and environmental implications of the reporting entity's operations and include such things as the adverse health effects of pollution produced by the entity, or injuries caused to consumers by the entity's products, or the adverse social effects of retrenchment of part of a workforce. Some of the perceived limitations of traditional financial accounting, which acts to exclude these externalities, will be considered briefly below. Specifically, financial accounting:

- tends to focus on the information needs of stakeholders with a financial interest;
- applies the concept of 'materiality';
- adopts the practice of discounting liabilities;
- applies the 'entity assumption';
- excludes from expenses the impacts on resources not *controlled* by the entity; and
- applies the recognition criteria of 'measurability' and 'probability'.

Because accounting standards and the conceptual framework dictate the contents of a great deal of an annual report, it would seem important that you understand the limitations of such standards when it comes to requiring organisations to be more accountable for their social and environmental performance.

26.5.1 Focusing on the information needs of stakeholders with a financial interest

Financial accounting focuses on the information needs of parties involved in making resource allocation decisions. That is, the focus tends to be restricted to stakeholders with a financial interest in the entity, and the information that is provided tends consequently to be primarily of a financial or economic nature. In the *Conceptual Framework for Financial Reporting* the objective of general purpose financial reporting is identified as being:

> *to provide financial information about the reporting entity that is useful to existing and potential investors, lenders and other creditors in making decisions about providing resources to the entity.*

Such a definition has the effect of denying or restricting access to information by those parties or individuals who are affected in any way that is not *financial*. However, as we can appreciate, companies may elect voluntarily to provide social and environmental information. Publications such as *The Corporate Report* (issued in 1975 by the Accounting Standards Steering Committee of the Institute of Chartered Accountants in England and Wales) have clearly indicated that information about corporate performance (including information of a non-financial nature) should be provided to a wider group than simply those with a financial interest. As paragraph 25 of *The Corporate Report* states:

> *The public's right to information arises not from a direct financial or human relationship with the reporting entity but from the general role played in our society by economic entities. Such organisations, which exist with*

the general consent of the community, are afforded special legal and operational privileges, they compete for resources of manpower, materials and energy and they make use of community owned assets such as roads and harbours.

26.5.2 The concept of 'materiality'

'Materiality' is an issue involving the exercise of a great deal of professional judgement. If something is not considered to be material, it does not need to be disclosed in the financial statements or supporting notes. Unfortunately, this has meant that, if something cannot be quantified (as is the case for many social and environmental externalities), it is generally not considered to be 'material' and therefore does not warrant separate disclosure. This obviously implies that 'materiality'—as used by accountants—might not be a relevant criterion for the disclosure of environmental performance data.

Social performance and environmental performance are quite different from financial performance. Yet many accountants have been conditioned through their education and training to adopt the *materiality* criterion to decide whether information should be disclosed. In a review of British companies, Gray *et al.* (1998) indicate that companies frequently provide little or no information about environmental expenses (however defined) because individually the expenditure is not considered to be *material*.

'Materiality' is indeed something that can be interpreted very subjectively. The 2000 version of the Global Reporting Initiative's *Sustainability Reporting Guidelines* provided a useful comment on materiality:

> *The application of the materiality concept to economic, environmental, and social reporting is more complex than in financial reporting. In contrast to financial reporting, percentage-based or other precise quantitative materiality yardsticks will seldom be appropriate for determining materiality [for sustainability reporting purposes]. Instead, materiality is heavily dependent upon the nature and circumstances of an item or event, as well as its scale or magnitude. For example, in environmental terms, the carrying capacity of the receiving environment (such as a watershed or airshed) will be just one among several factors in the materiality of the release of one tonne or one kilogram of waste, air emissions, or effluent. Similarly, health and safety information is likely to be of considerable interest to sustainability report users despite its typical insignificance in traditional financial accounting terms.*

However, while 'materiality' considerations are overarching, specific accounting standards can be developed that provide an override to the traditional 'materiality test', requiring disclosure of particular items regardless of the quantum involved.

Environmental and social impacts that are significant are those that are of considerable importance to the environment, the organisation or its stakeholders. Determining what is significant is a dynamic and subjective process. It is the organisation's responsibility to determine (in a consistent and systematic way) what is significant and to apply this assessment to potential impacts as well as to actual impacts. Relevant considerations in determining what is significant include the type and existing condition of the environment, prevailing culture and community values, relevant legislation, financial impacts and public image. Stakeholders' expectations are also important in determining what is significant. A factor in such considerations is identifying the stakeholders with greatest interest (or 'stake') in the environmental impacts of an organisation. Further, a determination needs to be made of whether these stakeholders are different from those envisaged in the concept of financial materiality.

26.5.3 The practice of discounting liabilities

As highlighted in Gray *et al.* (1996), another issue when it comes to the limitations of traditional financial accounting is that reporting entities frequently discount liabilities to their present value, particularly those liabilities that will not be settled for many years. This practice tends to make future expenditure less significant in the present period. For example, imagine that we are an organisation whose current activities are creating a need for future environmental expenditure of a remedial nature, but that work will not be undertaken for many years. As a result of discounting, we will recognise little or no cost now (which appears to be at odds with the sustainability agenda). For example, if we were anticipating that our activities would lead to a clean-up bill of £100 million in 30 years' time, and if we accept that our normal earnings rate is 10 per cent, the current expenses to be recognised in our financial statements under generally accepted accounting principles would be £5.73 million.

While discounting makes good *economic* sense (as opposed to good *ecological* sense), Gray *et al.* (1996) argue that it does tend at the same time to downplay the importance of the future clean-up, and perhaps to encourage the entity to undertake activities that will damage the environment but that will not need to be remedied for

many years. In a sense, the practice of discounting encourages us to *shift* problems of a social or environmental nature onto future generations—again, something that is arguably not consistent with the sustainability agenda. This view is consistent with that of Perks (1993, p. 100), who suggests that the use of costing approaches that rely upon such factors as present values has had the effect of hindering the introduction of renewable energy and other sources of 'cleaner' energy.

Within the UK, and at a more general level, there is no accounting standard that relates specifically to environment-related liabilities. However, apart from the general guidance provided within the Conceptual Framework, we have accounting standard IAS 37 *Provisions, Contingent Liabilities and Contingent Assets*. Obligations relating to environmental performance could be considered to be either provisions or contingent liabilities, depending upon the circumstances.

In relation to the measurement of a provision, IAS 37 states that the carrying amount of the provision must be the present value at the end of the reporting period of the expected cash flows. Paragraph 47 of IAS 37 requires the discount rate to be a pre-tax rate that reflects current market assessments of the time value of money and the risks specific to the liability. Clearly, professional judgement is called for in determining the discount rate applicable to the organisation. Further, as noted previously, discounting a future obligation to its present value can, depending upon the discount rate chosen and the assumptions about advances in technology, tend to make the amount less than 'material' at the present time. If something is deemed not to be material it might be decided that no disclosure is warranted.

Take, for example, the clean-up bill for an oil rig or a quarry. Apart from the issue of the need for legislation to compel organisations to remediate contaminated land/sea (or to allow government to compulsorily acquire such sites), we can consider how an organisation might account for the 'obligation' associated with cleaning up such a site. Arguably, an organisation should account for remediation costs throughout the life of an operation. In doing so, it would recognise a periodic expense (remediation costs) and incrementally increase (credit) a liability account, perhaps entitled 'Provision for remediation'. This liability would remain in the financial statements and increase across time as operations continued and until such time as remediation works were undertaken. Such a liability should be recognised not only when there is a legal requirement to remediate a site, but also when usual prudent business practices would suggest that such remediation should be undertaken. While this would be 'proper' accounting procedure, it does appear that many organisations are not recognising such liabilities. At issue, obviously, is whether financial statements that fail to show material liabilities relating to expected clean-ups are misleading. Arguably, they are.

26.5.4 The entity assumption

Financial accounting adopts the 'entity assumption', which requires an organisation to be treated as an entity distinct from its owners, other organisations and other stakeholders. The entity assumption or concept is typically taught to students of accounting at the introductory stages. According to this concept, an organisation is treated as an *accounting unit* that is quite distinct and separate from the owners and other organisations, and the accountant must define the organisation's area of interest in such a way as to limit the events and transactions to be included in the financial statements. The organisation and the stakeholders of that organisation are treated as separate accounting entities.

The entity assumption allows the accountant to measure the financial performance and position of each entity, independent of all other entities. According to the entity assumption, if a transaction or event does not directly affect the entity, the transaction or event is to be ignored for accounting purposes. This means that the externalities caused by reporting entities will typically be ignored, and that performance measures (such as profitability) are incomplete from a broader societal (as opposed to a 'discrete entity') perspective.

We can relate the entity principle to the profits that might be reported by a tobacco manufacturer. It is generally accepted that cigarettes cause many health problems, yet externalities that relate to the products of a reporting entity are ignored for financial reporting purposes. That is, reported profits are not affected by such externalities. In a similar vein, recent legislative changes in the UK have resulted in a growth of casinos and online gambling sites. See http://www.nebusiness.co.uk/business-news/ for a discussion of the growth of Aspers, a casino chain located in the UK. The increased profit achieved by Aspers ignores the social costs gambling creates within the community, and how the actions of these companies in providing gambling opportunities contribute to such social costs. Arguably, any moves towards accounting for sustainability would require a modification to, or a move away from, the *entity assumption*.

A related area in which our traditional financial accounting system generates a rather strange outcome is that of the treatment of tradeable pollution permits. In a number of countries, certain organisations are provided with permits, often free of charge, that allow the holder to release a pre-specified amount of a particular pollutant. If the original recipient of the permit is not going to emit as much pollution as the licence allows, that party

is allowed to sell the permit to another party. What happens in some jurisdictions is that some organisations treat tradeable pollution permits as assets. This might make sense from an 'economic' perspective—but it is questionable whether something that allows an organisation to pollute is an asset from a broader 'societal' perspective.

26.5.5 Exclusion from expenses of any impacts on resources not 'controlled' by the entity

Expenses are defined by the Conceptual Framework so as to exclude the recognition of any impacts on resources that are not *controlled* by the entity (such as the environment) unless fines or other cash flows result.

Environmental resources such as air and water are *shared* and not controlled by the organisation and hence cannot be considered to be assets. Therefore, their use and/or abuse is not considered an expense. It should be emphasised that this is a significant limitation of financial accounting as it pertains to reporting information about social and environmental performance.

As discussed in Deegan (1996), and using a rather extreme example, imagine that an entity destroys the quality of water in its local environment, thereby killing all local sea creatures and coastal vegetation. Under conventional financial accounting, if the entity incurs no fines or other related cash flows as a result of its actions, no externalities would be recognised. Reported profits, calculated by applying generally accepted accounting principles, would not be directly affected, nor would reported assets. The reason no expenses would be recognised is that resources such as the local waterways are not controlled by the reporting entity, and therefore they would not be recognised as the entity's assets. Thus the use (or abuse) of resources would go unrecognised. If conventional financial reporting practices were followed, the performance of such an organisation could, depending on the financial transactions undertaken, be portrayed as very successful. In this regard, Gray and Bebbington (1992, p. 6) provide the following opinion of traditional financial accounting:

> there is something profoundly wrong about a system of measurement, a system that makes things visible and which guides corporate and national decisions that can signal success in the midst of desecration and destruction.

Motivated by their concern about the limitations of traditional financial accounting, Gray and Bebbington have sought to develop alternative methods of accounting—methods that embrace the sustainability agenda and that calculate a notional *sustainable cost*, which is subtracted from accounting profits to provide a measure of performance known as *sustainable profits*.

As an example of how accounting profits ignore social and environmental costs, consider the article reproduced in Financial Accounting in the News 26.8, which documents how an organisation will 'slash 5,300 jobs in a bid to cut costs'. This perspective ignores the obvious *social costs* associated with the thousands of unemployed people that will result from the organisation's decisions. It also emphasises the perceived relative importance attributed to maximising returns to investors rather than to other stakeholders.

Financial Accounting in the News 26.8

CREDIT SUISSE BOOST

Scott Murdoch, *The Australian*, 24 July 2009

Swiss banking giant Credit Suisse posted its second consecutive quarterly profits yesterday, reporting a 29 per cent leap in earnings as it turns a page on the massive full-year losses of last year.

The second-quarter earnings of 1.571 billion francs followed a profit of Sfr2bn in the first quarter—a sharp contrast to the full-year loss of Sfr8.2bn last year.

The bank's chief executive, Brady Dougan, said the global economic climate was expected to 'remain challenging and uneven business conditions' should persist.

'However, if markets continue to improve we expect to see further momentum across our businesses, and if markets become more difficult we believe Credit Suisse is positioned to perform well,' he said.

The bank has been hurt by the financial crisis and said in December it would slash 5,300 jobs in a bid to cut costs.

However, it ended a losing streak this year and even its investment bank unit, which was blamed for incurring massive losses during the financial crisis, has been profitable for two consecutive quarters.

In the second quarter, the investment bank's profit before taxes reached Sfr1.655bn, up 444 per cent against the same period last year.

Its asset management outfit turned profitable in the second quarter, with an income of Sfr55million, reversing a Sfr490m first-quarter loss.

As another example of the difference between the externalities caused by an organisation and the costs (expenses) that it actually recognises, we can consider the *just-in-time* (JIT) approach to acquiring raw materials and other inventory (this method is typically taught in undergraduate management accounting courses). Under this approach, an organisation may acquire its inventories by way of many deliveries rather than ordering in large quantities and having high average amounts of inventory on hand. Many deliveries means greater use of the roads and fuel, as well as greater levels of pollution. However, the costs associated with traffic congestion, pollution and so forth are not recognised by the organisation (they are treated as 'free goods') and, hence, they are encouraged to embrace JIT because of the savings it creates in terms of reducing warehousing costs, insurance costs, stock obsolescence costs and so forth. If we were to incorporate the unrecognised costs into profit calculations, then perhaps we might question how cost-effective the JIT system really is.

It is argued by many that the failure to place a cost on the externalities created by organisations is one of the contributing factors to current problems associated with climate change. Until recently, carbon emissions have not been incorporated in the production costs of organisations, and hence there has not been great motivation for organisations to reduce carbon emissions. The advent of emissions trading schemes (such as the 'cap and trade' approach) and carbon taxes will mean that carbon emissions will be priced, typically, on the basis of tonnes of emissions. Pricing the emissions will then effectively turn an unrecorded externality into an internal recognised cost. This will lead to incentives for firms to reduce their emissions, and therefore their emission-related costs. Emission trading schemes will create winners and losers within the marketplace. The threats that emission trading and carbon taxes create for many carbon-intensive industries is one of the reasons that the introduction of emissions trading schemes and taxes has been so contentious internationally. Also, if the introduction of emission trading schemes, or tax regimes, is not internationally uniform, then production will become more expensive in some countries, and this may lead to those countries no longer being internationally competitive from a price perspective.

26.5.6 The recognition criteria of 'measurability' and 'probability'

We have already considered how the definitions of two elements of financial reporting (assets and expenses) act to preclude the inclusion of various 'externalities'. The Conceptual Framework also provides recognition criteria for the elements of financial reporting (these being Assets, Liabilities, Equity, Expenses and Income) whereby:

An item that meets the definition of an element should be recognised if:

(a) it is probable that any future economic benefit associated with the item will flow to or from the entity; and
(b) the item has a cost or value that can be measured with reliability.

Hence, for all five elements of financial accounting, both *probability* and *measurability* are key considerations. Evidence suggests that many liabilities—particularly those related to the environment—are ignored, often on the basis that they are too difficult to measure reliably and therefore do not satisfy the recognition criteria. This argument was used by a number of large Australian companies that were known to have some significantly contaminated land sites under their control for failing to disclose information about liabilities associated with remediating (cleaning up) the contaminated sites (Ji and Deegan 2011). If the liabilities are not recognised on the basis of an inability to measure the liabilities with reasonable accuracy, then the associated expenses will also not be recognised.

Ji and Deegan (ibid) also reported that the companies failed to recognise provisions in relation to contaminated sites despite the fact that 'provisions' are to be created in situations where there is some uncertainty about the ultimate payment. Indeed, the defining characteristic of a 'provision', as opposed to other 'liabilities', is that the timing of the ultimate payment, and perhaps the amount of the ultimate payment, is uncertain (IAS 37, paragraph 11). The accounting standard makes it explicit that some uncertainty about timing and amount is acceptable when recognising a provision. Paragraph 25 of IAS 37 notes that:

> *The use of estimates is an essential part of the preparation of financial statements and does not undermine their reliability. This is especially true in the case of provisions, which by their nature are more uncertain than most other statements of financial position items. Except in extremely rare cases, an entity will be able to determine a range of possible outcomes and can therefore make an estimate of the obligation that is sufficiently reliable to use in recognising a provision.*

Therefore, if a present obligation exists in relation to a contaminated site, only with exceptions 'in extremely rare cases' should the obligation not be recognised as a provision and, therefore, not recognised in the statement of financial position. Therefore, and based on the above reporting requirements, Ji and Deegan expected to find that the companies identified from publicly available information as having significant obligations associated with remediating contaminated sites would recognise and disclose associated provisions for remediation—again, a failure to do so should only occur in 'extremely rare cases'. Nevertheless, the companies in question used the issue of 'measurability' in a number of situations as a rationale for non-disclosure. Indeed, some organisations used this as the basis for not recognising a provision in relation to numerous sites known to be contaminated. This could be interpreted as a clear lack of accountability by these sample firms.

Yankelovich (1972, p.72) also addressed the 'measurement issue' and his opinion is still pertinent today. He described a four-step hypothetical decision process that may be faced by an accountant in attempting to report a variety of environmental issues:

> *The first step is to measure whatever can be easily measured. This is OK as far as it goes. The second step is to disregard that which can't be easily measured or give it an arbitrary quantitative value. This is artificial and misleading. The third step is to presume that what can't be measured easily really isn't important. This is blindness. The fourth step is to say that what can't be easily measured really doesn't exist. This is suicide.*

If it is accepted that an organisation is *accountable* for its social and environmental performance, arguably we need to take action to redefine how financial accounting is undertaken. This is consistent with calls from a number of corporations. For example, in its report released in 1998, entitled *Profits and Principles—Does There Have to Be a Choice?* (available on its website at www.shell.com), Shell states:

> *If sustainable development is to become a global reality rather than remain a seductive mirage, governments, communities, companies and individuals must work together to improve their 'triple-bottom-line' (economic, social and environmental) performance. To this end, we not only need new forms of accountability but also new forms of accounting.*

Shell believes necessary, professional accounting bodies would need to publicly support new forms of accounting that embrace social and environmental issues. Of concern to many is the fact that the IASB does not have social or environmental reporting issues on its agenda. What appears to be necessary is for accountancy bodies to start a debate on the relevance of social and environmental issues to general purpose financial statements. That is, there needs to be debate about whether non-financial information comes within the scope of general purpose financial statements. If accountants do not take the lead in this area of reporting, it is not clear what body of professionals will fill the void.

Thankfully, in response to the increasing demand in Europe for information about social and environmental performance, a number of universities are running modules on social and environmental reporting/accounting issues within their undergraduate accounting courses. However, such universities still tend to be in the minority, with many academic staff denying the relevance of environmental and social performance to accounting. Perhaps they need to consider more carefully the relationship between *accountability* and *accounting*. Universities that fixate on teaching material relating to calculating and reporting information about financial performance are, at least implicitly, embracing a view that the only accountability of organisations relates to financial performance.

While the accounting profession and many educational institutions might not have fully embraced social and environmental issues as part of accounting, a number of industry and government bodies *have* accepted their relevance, and have released guidance documents relating to such issues. We will now consider some of these documents.

26.6 Industry and government initiatives

While the accounting profession in general has been fairly silent on developing reporting guides, a number of industry and government bodies have developed:

- a range of reporting guidance documents;
- listings of potential sustainability performance indicators; and
- social and environmental ratings indices.

We will consider some of these releases in brief in this section.

26.6.1 Reporting guidance documents

The UK government has provided guidance on sustainability and environmental reporting and the UK professional accountancy bodies have supported research on environmental reporting. HM Treasury hosts a website with links to reports on good practice and provides examples of good disclosure practice (see http//www.hm-treasury.gov.uk/frem_sustainability.htm).

Starting in 2010 a yearly report has been published by the government that provides guidance on sustainability reporting for public sector bodies:

Overview of Requirements

1. *From 2011–12, all bodies that are required to produce a sustainability report (see Section 1 paragraphs 5–6) in accordance with the* Government Financial Reporting Manual (FReM) *are required to include a discrete section in their Annual Report covering their performance on sustainability during the year. The section in the Annual Report must include: A simple overview commentary covering their performance in the reported year along with an overview of forward plans; and a comparison of financial and non-financial information covering the organisation's emissions, waste and finite resource consumption. Details of an illustrative format for a table, and guidance supporting its population, are included within this Guidance (see pages 12–16).*
2. *The key principles of such reporting are that it should provide both transparency, in terms of clarity and openness, consistency for comparative purposes and accuracy.*
3. *The requirements for minimum reporting as part of 2011–12 HM Treasury Sustainability Reporting are fully consistent with non-financial information requirements laid down under the Greening Government commitments (GGC) (including the transparency requirements).*
4. *The following table provides an overview of the minimum requirements in each of the three main reporting areas:*

Area	Type	Non-Financial Information	Financial Information
Greenhouse Gas Emissions	*Scope 1 (Direct) GHG Emissions*	*All Scope 1 emissions must be accounted for. These occur from sources owned or controlled by the organisation. Examples include emissions as a result of combustion in boilers owned or controlled by the organisation and fugitive emissions from equipment such as air conditioning units. This includes emissions from organisation-owned fleet vehicles (including vehicles on finance leases). An analysis of related gas consumption, in Kwh, should also be included.*	*Gross expenditure on the purchase of energy, expenditure on the CRC Energy Efficiency Scheme, expenditure on accredited offset purchases, total expenditure on official business travel and expenditure on reported areas of energy use.*

Area	Type	Non-Financial Information	Financial Information
	Scope 2 (Energy Indirect) Emissions	*All Scope 2 emissions must be accounted for. These result from energy consumed which is supplied by another party (e.g. electricity supply in buildings or outstations), and purchased heat, steam and cooling. An analysis of related energy consumption, in Kwh, should also be included.*	
	Scope 3 Official Business Travel Emissions.	*Scope 3 emissions relating to official business travel directly paid for by an organisation (i.e. not business travel re-charged by contractors) must be accounted for. Minimum requirements do not include international air or rail travel in line with GGC.*	
Waste Minimisation and Management		*The minimum requirement is to report absolute values for waste from the organisation's estate (administrative and operational – operational construction waste is not a minimum requirement) against the following categories: (a) total waste arising, (b) waste sent to landfill (e.g. residual waste), (c) waste recycled / reused (recycled, composted, internal or external re-used), and (d) waste incinerated / energy from waste (e.g. food waste).*	*Total expenditure on waste disposal (incl waste disposal contracts, specialist waste arising and the purchase of licenses for waste) and expenditure against each of the additional three categories (b) to (d) opposite.*
Finite Resource Consumption		*As a minimum public sector bodies must report on estates' water consumption in cubic metres. Public sector bodies must also consider reporting their consumption of any other finite resources where their use is material.*	*Total expenditure on purchase of related finite resources including purchase of licenses.*
Biodiversity Action Planning		*The commentary section must cover any biodiversity action plans and the organisation's performance against them in line with GGC. This requirement applies only to those organisations subject to the GGC.*	*Not required.*
Sustainable Procurement		*The commentary must explain progress in achieving more sustainable procurement methods, in line with GGC.*	*Not required*

5. *Expenditure information should be collected through normal financial systems developing the financial systems accounts coding to ensure clarity of cost capture in alignment with audited year-end financial accounts. This will also provide internal visibility for in-year monitoring purposes and will assist in development of any future performance management targets in expenditure areas.*

Minimum Non-Financial Reporting Requirements

6. *The minimum non-financial reporting requirements are detailed in the table above. Emissions are defined under three different scopes by the Greenhouse Gas (GHG) Protocol: www.ghgprotocol.org.*

7. *Organisations should, wherever possible, make use of their normal accounting and environmental management systems to regularise the collection of such information throughout the year. This may require additions/ changes to existing systems (e.g. fields to capture quantitative information, additional subjective codes in financial systems etc.) or processes; these should be identified as early as possible so that the necessary changes can be made to capture the required information.*

The HM Treasury report requires that the sustainability report contains three years' comparatives and a commentary in each of the key areas of performance against key performance indicators, including the impact (direct and indirect). The entity's strategy in each of the areas outlined in the table should be disclosed, with more detail being provided on its website. The report should have a cross-reference to this site. This report provides the minimum requirements and public sector bodies are encouraged to provide additional information.

A pro forma example of what to disclose is provided in the appendix to the report, reproduced in Exhibit 26.2. The guidance report is 75 pages long and this is just an extract of the main suggested disclosures for sustainability performance.

Exhibit 26.2   **EXAMPLE 1: Public Sector Sustainability Reporting Format**

Example Commentary on Sustainability Performance; Department/Agency Yellow

1. Initial narrative setting out the reasons behind undertaking sustainability reporting. Explain that it conforms to the public sector requirements and where the requirements are laid down (e.g. FReM and website for guidance).

Summary of Performance

2. Provide a brief explanation of the effectiveness of the programmes set up to improve sustainability in the organisation and its impacts externally.

3. Provide a high level discussion of the targets and direction of the organisation in terms of performance. Essentially it sets the scene for the information that follows and puts it into context for the reader. This could include any references to external verification etc. Provide the reader with a quick summary of the information on the pages that follow. The exact areas shown would be defined by their relevance to the specific reporting entity. The following table is an example of how this may be reported:

Area	2011–12 Performance		
		Actual	Target
Greenhouse Gas emissions (Scopes 1, 2 & 3 Business Travel including/ [excluding] international air/rail travel)		x,xxx tCO$_2$e	[Insert target]
Estate Energy	Consumption	xx.x million kWh	[Insert target]
	Expenditure	£xxx,xxx	[Insert budget]
Estate Waste	Amount	xxx tonnes	[Insert target]
	Expenditure	£xxx,xxx	–
Estate Water	Consumption	xx,xxx m³	[Insert target]
	Expenditure	£xxx,xxx	–

▶

- Include a summary of normalised performance (ref Section 2, para 20).
- Industry or sector benchmarks should be referred to where available.

Summary of Future Strategy

4. Provide an overview of the organisation's future strategy to improve performance.

GHG Emissions

5. Provide a high level discussion of the targets and direction of the organisation in terms of performance.

Waste

6. Provide a high level discussion of the targets and direction of the organisation in terms of performance.

Use of Resources

7. Provide a high level discussion of the targets and direction of the organisation in terms of performance against the consumption of natural resources.

Climate Change Adaptation and Mitigation

8. Provide a high level discussion of the direction of the organisation in terms of performance (or refer to the section of the Annual Report where it is covered).

Biodiversity and Natural Environment

9. Provide a high level discussion of the direction of the organisation in terms of performance (or refer to the section of the Annual Report where it is covered). It is recognised that this will not apply to many organisations.

Sustainable Procurement including Food

10. Provide a high level discussion of the targets and direction of the organisation in terms of performance (or refer to the section of the Annual Report where it is covered).

Sustainable Construction

11. In line with the transparency requirements of the Greening Government commitments, the organisation should give an overview of the management of construction waste to best practice standards, the application of BRE's Environmental Assessment Methodology, and the extent to which standards used at the London 2012 Games are being applied/exceeded.

People

12. Including, for example, reporting on social and environmental assessment of office re-locations, and action taken to promote staff wellbeing.

Environmental Management System (EMS)

13. Provide a high level overview of any EMS in place for the organisation.

Governance

14. Explain the governance processes in place to support management of sustainability performance. For example, whether it is managed as part of the organisation's standard performance management regime, such as through a balanced scorecard, and how the information is used to support corporate decision making.
15. This should include a brief outline of the systems and methods used for collecting the data, and how assurance is gained to ensure that it is robust. Organisations are responsible for applying appropriate data quality standards, and collecting and presenting data that conforms to the prescribed definitions in the guidance. Organisations are also responsible for introducing arrangements to satisfy themselves that information in sustainability reports is reliable (see Audit and Scrutiny, paragraph 39).
16. Organisations already have a responsibility to report on their internal assurance arrangements in the annual Statement of Internal Control, and this should cover the arrangements for sustainability reporting.

As mentioned previously, in the UK DEFRA provides environmental reporting guidelines on key performance indicators and the Environment Agency has undertaken extensive research on environmental disclosures in the annual reports of all companies in the FTSE All-Share index.

The professional accountancy bodies have also actively encouraged research on environmental reporting practices and since 1991 the Association of Chartered Certified Accountants (ACCA) has sponsored the Sustainability Reporting Reward. This reward highlights organisations that have demonstrated good practice, encourage improved reporting in this area and raise awareness of the importance of corporate transparency. The awards aim to 'give recognition to organisations which report and disclose environmental, social or full sustainability information' (discussed later). A similar award run by PWC for public sector bodies, called 'Building Public Trust Awards', recognises good reporting practice in relation to environmental issues. A report backed by the Environmental Agency of the findings of the 2005 award is available and provides examples of good practice. The Chartered Institute of Public Finance and Accountants (CIPFA) has a sustainability microsite that includes current developments and relevant information for reporting. CIPFA hopes that this site will raise awareness of sustainability reporting among its members. The Institute of Chartered Accountants in England and Wales (ICAEW) also covers corporate responsibility on its website and has a link to its report 'Sustainability: The Role of Accountants'. In conjunction with the UN and governments across the globe, the International Federation of Accountants (IFAC) has produced global guidance on Environmental Management Accounting (EMA). This guidance is meant to provide a framework and set of definitions that is comprehensive and consistent with other existing environmental accounting frameworks.

Many industries provide specific guidance on issues facing their industry and typically try to be consistent with the global bodies. For example, in Europe in the electricity industry, an organisation—Euroelectric—has been established to provide guidance on sustainability within the industry. The 27 EU countries are members and six non-EU members have also joined. In the UK, guidance is communicated within the industry through Ofgem, the industry government regulator (http://www.ofgem.gov.uk) via a website and a 'Sustainable Development Focus' document produced each year. The construction industry in the UK also actively promotes CSR and an academic study by Jones *et al.* (2006) reported that the majority of major UK construction companies do report on their CSR activities and expenditures but considerable variation exists in the nature and extent of the information provided. In general, they found that most companies reported on the environment, health and safety, and human resources. Supply chain management, customers and communities received more selective and limited treatment, and ethics and governance received even less attention.

26.6.2 The Global Reporting Initiative

At an international level, one source of reporting guidance that has assumed a dominant position in the social and environmental reporting domain is the Global Reporting Initiative's *Sustainability Reporting Guidelines*[2]. Many organisations in Europe embrace these guidelines. See www.globalreporting.org for details of the reporting guidelines. According to the GRI's website, the vision and mission of the GRI are:

Vision: *A sustainable global economy where organizations manage their economic, environmental, social and governance performance and impacts responsibly, and report transparently.*

Mission: *To make sustainability reporting standard practice by providing guidance and support to organizations.*

The GRI guidelines are generally accepted as representing current 'best practice' reporting. Many organisations worldwide are using the *Sustainability Reporting Guidelines* as the basis for their social and environmental (and sustainability) reporting. Various industry codes that require periodic reporting also refer signatories to the GRI Guidelines. The GRI Guidelines—which are available online—are now in their third version (commonly referred to as G3; the G3 Guidelines were released in late 2006). In 2011 amendments were made to the G3 Guidelines and the revised guidelines are now referred to as the G3.1 Guidelines. The guidelines are divided into two main parts:

---

[2] The GRI was originally convened by the US-based Coalition for Environmentally Responsible Economies (CERES is a non-profit non-governmental organisation based in Boston) in partnership with the United Nations Environmental Programme (UNEP's website is at www.unep.org), with subsequent inputs from the Association of Chartered Certified Accountants (UK), the Tellus Institute, the World Business Council for Sustainable Development, the World Resources Institute, the Canadian Institute of Chartered Accountants, the Institute of Social and Ethical Accountability (UK), the Council on Economic Priorities (US) and other organisations and corporate bodies from around the world. Given its representation, the initiative is clearly 'global' in nature.

1. Defining report content, quality, and boundary.
2. Standard disclosures.

In the section of the guidelines entitled '1.1 Defining Report Content', reference is made to the following reporting principles:

- **Materiality**—*The information in a report should cover topics and indicators that reflect the organization's significant economic, environmental, and social impacts or that would substantively influence the assessments and decisions of stakeholders.*
- **Stakeholder Inclusiveness**—*The reporting organization should identify its stakeholders and explain in the report how it has responded to their reasonable expectations and interests.*
- **Sustainability Context**—*The reporting organization should present the organization's performance in the wider context of sustainability.*
- **Completeness**—*Coverage of the material topics and indicators, and definition of the report boundary should be sufficient to reflect significant economic, environmental, and social impacts and enable stakeholders to assess the reporting organization's performance in the reporting period.*

In the section entitled '1.2 Reporting Principles for Defining Quality', reference is made to the qualitative attributes of reliability, clarity, balance, comparability, accuracy and timeliness. These are explained as follows:

- **Balance** *The report should reflect positive and negative aspects of the organization's performance to enable a reasoned assessment of overall performance.*
- **Comparability** *Issues and information should be selected, compiled and reported consistently. Reported information should be presented in a manner that enables stakeholders to analyze changes in the organization's performance over time, and could support analysis relative to other organizations.*
- **Accuracy** *The reported information should be sufficiently accurate and detailed for stakeholders to assess the reporting organization's performance.*
- **Timeliness** *Reporting occurs on a regular schedule and information is available for stakeholders to make informed decisions.*
- **Clarity** *Information should be made available in a manner that is understandable and accessible to stakeholders using the report.*
- **Reliability** *Information and processes used in the preparation of a report should be gathered, recorded, compiled, analyzed and disclosed in a way that could be subject to examination and that establishes the quality and materiality of the information.*

As we can start to see, there does appear to be a large degree of overlap between the qualitative characteristics identified in the GRI Guidelines and those provided in the IASB *Conceptual Framework for Financial Reporting*. This overlap becomes particularly apparent when we consider '1.3 Reporting Guidance for Boundary Setting'. In this section it is stated:

In parallel with defining the content of a report, an organization must determine which entities' (e.g., subsidiaries and joint ventures) performance will be represented by the report. The Sustainability Report Boundary should include the entities over which the reporting organization exercises control or significant influence both in and through its relationships with various entities upstream (e.g., supply chain) and downstream (e.g., distribution and customers).

For the purpose of setting boundaries, the following definitions should apply:

- **Control:** *the power to govern the financial and operating policies of an enterprise so as to obtain benefits from its activities.*
- **Significant influence:** *the power to participate in the financial and operating policy decisions of the entity but not the power to control those policies.*

The guidance on setting the Report Boundary pertains to the report as a whole as well as setting the boundary for individual Performance Indicators.

As we can see from the above, the definitions of 'significant influence' and 'control' have been extracted from financial reporting standards. Whether it is appropriate to use these concepts, which were developed for financial reporting, for the purposes of sustainability reporting is an interesting point to ponder. The G3 Guidelines provide a diagram to use when setting the boundary of a report. It is reproduced in Figure 26.1. As we can see,

control seems to be the criterion that determines whether we provide performance data (in consolidation accounting, control is the criterion used to determine whether we consolidate other entities' reports with those of the parent entity).

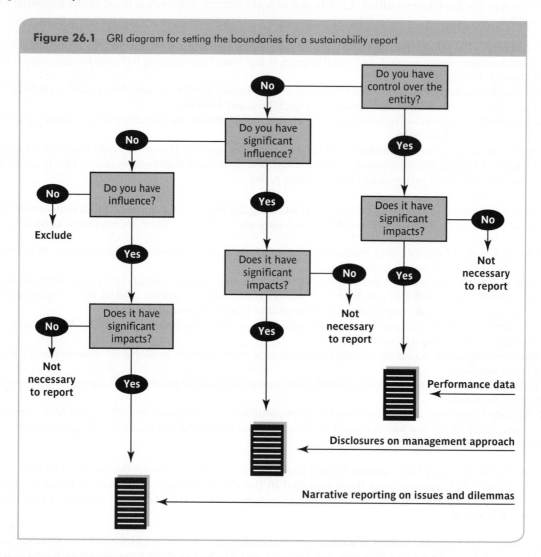

Figure 26.1   GRI diagram for setting the boundaries for a sustainability report

In Part 2 of the Guidelines (Standard Disclosures) is a section entitled 'Profile', which is subdivided into five parts, including: Strategy and Analysis (which requires a statement from the most senior decision maker of the organisation about the relevance of sustainability to the organisation and its strategy, as well as a description of key impacts, risks and opportunities); Organisational Profile; Report Parameters; and Governance, Commitments, and Engagement.

The fifth part of the 'Profile' section is entitled 'Management Approach and Performance Indicators' (which covers such things as policies, responsibilities and goals). This section contains 84 performance indicators, relating to the following domains (the numbers in brackets refer to the number of respective indicators):

- economic (9)
- environment (30)
- social performance (broken down into four components)

  1. labour practices and decent work (15)
  2. social practice: human rights (11)
  3. social performance: society (10)
  4. social performance: product responsibility (9)

(Interested readers should go to the GRI Guidelines (www.globalreporting.org) to review the details of the specific indicators.)

The last section of the G3 Guidelines relates to 'sector supplements', which provide additional reporting guidance for specific industry sectors.

While the GRI Guidelines have brought about improvement in environmental reporting, it should be acknowledged that, since they are not mandatory, many companies, while being selective about the indicators they choose to use in their reporting, nonetheless gain the 'legitimacy' that is associated with using them. The GRI Guidelines could be used as a basis for mandatory reporting if mandatory social and environmental (and sustainability) reporting were introduced within a particular jurisdiction. For example, the *King Report on Corporate Governance for South Africa* (Institute of Directors in South Africa 2001), which was endorsed in 2002 by the Johannesburg Stock Exchange, requires listed companies to adopt the GRI Guidelines.

Finally, in determining how to disclose social and environmental information, some organisations also refer to reports that have been acknowledged as representing *best reporting practice*—perhaps by winning an award. The criteria for such awards can themselves be used as guidance in determining what and how to report. For example, some organisations refer to the judging criteria used in the Association of Chartered Certified Accountants' (ACCA) Sustainability Reporting Awards as a guide to determining what should be included in a *good* report. As mentioned earlier, this award, which originated in the UK and which has been operating for a number of years, has been developed to give positive recognition to organisations that are attempting to report on the sustainability of their operations. The ACCA judging criteria are grouped around three key report characteristics (completeness, credibility and communication). The criteria for the 2011 awards are provided in Table 26.1.

Table 26.1 ACCA Sustainability Reporting Awards judging criteria

Report characteristic	Key element	Indicator
Completeness An excellent sustainability (or equivalent) report should enable the reader to form a complete view of that organisation's operations and impacts. In summary, what is being sought in a report is for the reader to be able to develop a complete mental picture of the organisation: what it does, the extent of its operations and the scope of the report in conjunction with its entire activities. Once the completeness of the reporting entity has been established, the credibility of the information presented then becomes important. Completeness covers four broad areas: materiality (i.e. significance of information disclosed), stakeholder inclusion (i.e. identification of audience and stakeholders as well as processes followed), strategy (the level of integration and thus commitment of the organisation to SD) and organisational context (general information and placing activities in context of SD). *SD-Sustainable Development*	Materiality	1.01 Key (direct and indirect) economic/social/environmental impacts and issues of business identified, considered and explained 1.02 Process and rationale behind choice of key impacts and issues identified and indicators used in report explained
	Stakeholder inclusion	1.03 Report audience identified 1.04 Organisational stakeholders identified including an indication of relative levels of importance 1.05 Process and description of stakeholder identification and consultation
	Strategy	1.06 Detail and clarity of social/environmental/SD policy (including upstream responsibility, i.e. supply chain) and management commitment 1.07 Product or service stewardship (e.g. design, LCA, disposal policies, social and/or economic impact of product) 1.08 Inclusion of targets (short, medium and long-term) and objectives 1.09 Description of process (approaches to measurement, reporting and accounting) 1.10 Reporting period, scope of the report (by entity) and clear rationale for reporting 1.11 Demonstration of SD integrated into core business strategy 1.12 Evidence of coherent and collective management of SD strategy and issues 1.13 Overview of public policy strategy, description of activities undertaken and views/statements disclosed

►

Table 26.1 ACCA Sustainability Reporting Awards judging criteria (*Continued*)

Report characteristic	Key element	Indicator

	Organisational context	1.14 Corporate context, e.g.
		    • major products and/or services
		    • financial performance
		    • geographical location(s)
		    • employment information
		1.15 A clear and credible articulation of the meaning of SD, consideration of what implications arise for the organisation as it pursues SD, tensions which emerge and unresolved complexities and dilemmas
		1.16 Placing organisational activity in the context of the wider societal and environmental systems within which the organisation operates
		1.17 Placing of social/environmental/SD reporting in context of other reporting undertaken

Credibility From the report, one would be seeking assurance (from the presentation of evidence) that there are organisational structures, processes and controls in place to enable the organisation to accurately present information on its impacts. This includes having policies, appropriate personnel in place, information-gathering systems, management systems and having targets which are designed to achieve sustainable development. Report users would be seeking to identify the extent to which there is evidence that, where appropriate, the internal systems and information have been tested and the views of external parties have been incorporated into the report. Credibility covers five broad areas: management process (the way the organisation is managed), stakeholder inclusion (how feedback is used and how it influences organisational functioning), governance (senior management style and involvement), performance (data) and assurance (both internal and external).	Managerial process	2.01 Management systems and their integration into the business process 2.02 Application of guidance and/or standards (e.g. GRI, Investors in People, ISO/EMAS), including providing reasons for their use 2.03 Contact name and details for person in charge of report
	Stakeholder inclusion	2.04 Identification and description of stakeholder feedback and interests in the organisation's impacts and operations and process for selecting these views (as being the most important) for disclosure. 2.05 Use of stakeholder feedback (e.g. from engagement or external campaigns) to impact strategy, influence policy and operations and alter report content (i.e. to demonstrate learning), or conversely disclosing, with reasons, where stakeholder feedback has not been used.
	Governance	2.06 Governance system explained, including named board member responsible for SD issues 2.07 Description of how incentivisation of staff and managers is linked to sustainability performance and achievement of targets 2.08 Description of risk identification and management processes and disclosure of actual risks identified and discussion of opportunities resulting from this 2.09 Consistency of management commitment to SD—review of annual report and accounts (if applicable)

▶

Table 26.1 ACCA Sustainability Reporting Awards judging criteria (*Continued*)

Report characteristic	Key element	Indicator
	Performance	2.10 Economic/social/environmental performance and impact data (showing absolute and normalised data with trends over time and within sector) on material issues 2.11 Identification of and accounting for social/environmental/SD externalities 2.12 Compliance/non-compliance record with legislation 2.13 Headline achievements in current period
	Assurance	2.14 Internal audit/assurance processes 2.15 External assurance statement. Factors the panel will bear in mind include: • independence and impartiality • remit, clarity and scope • indication of methodology (including reference to standards and guidance used, e.g. AA1000AS, ISAE3000) • depth of investigation—site visits and site-specific testing • interpretation of data/performance reported • identification of any data/information omitted that could/should have been included • independent comment on corporate targets set and impacts identified • shortcomings and recommendations
Communication Communication is the extent to which the sustainability (or equivalent) report communicates to the declared target audiences. This is, at least in part, an assessment of the media by which communication has been attempted. Communication covers three broad areas: presentation (how the report looks), stakeholder inclusion (how the report is made available to users) and structure (the style of reporting).	Presentation	3.01 Layout and appearance 3.02 Comprehensibility, readability and appropriateness of length 3.03 Innovative approaches 3.04 Appropriateness of graphs, illustrations and photos
	Stakeholder inclusion	3.05 Accessibility (e.g. Braille/large print, electronic format on accessible website, available in language(s) relevant to audience, printed version available) 3.06 Communication and feedback mechanisms for report-users to provide/send comments to reporter
	Structure	3.07 Availability of a summary report and/or executive summary 3.08 Comprehensive navigation through report and signposting and links to other reporting 3.09 Reference to website and use of internet

In concluding this discussion of industry and government initiatives in the field of social and environmental performance and reporting, it should be stressed that there are still many issues to resolve before we come anywhere near a unified approach to reporting. Details of other international initiatives that can assist recording and reporting on corporate social and environmental performance include the Global Compact (www.unglobalcompact.org), the Equator Principles (www.equator-principles.com/), the International Organisation for Standardisation (ISO; www.iso.org); the Carbon Disclosure Project (CDP; www.cdproject.net), Account Ability AA1000 series (www.accountability.org/standards/aa1000aps.html) and the Greenhouse Gas Protocol (www.ghgprotocol.org).

26.7 Evidence of social and environmental reporting

As already noted in this chapter, the dominant focus for external corporate reporting has traditionally been financial reporting. Financial reporting is heavily regulated, and rules within companies legislation and accounting standards must be followed by corporations (securities exchange disclosure requirements must also be followed by listed companies).

Since the early 1990s many European companies have increased their output of public information on their environmental performance. Initially, this information was voluntarily included within annual reports. However, from the mid-1990s many European companies began producing stand-alone environmental/social reports and, more recently, companies have been producing publicly available sustainability reports (also commonly referred to as corporate social responsibility (CSR) reports). While reports in the early 1990s were typically not subject to any independent verification, it is now becoming common for corporate social responsibility reports to be subject to some form of verification or assurance. However, as with the reporting itself, there is much variation in what the verification, or audit, reports actually do and say.

In a study on sustainability reporting in Europe, Van Wensen *et al.* (2011) found variant compliance depending on the industry:

> With regard to differences among sectors, in general, it can be stated that in the last decade, the most polluting companies traditionally have been most active in sustainability reporting (Kolk 2010). In global industries, with a relatively small number of large firms, competitors closely watch one another, and 'follow the leader' (ibid). More specific research among the G250 on reporting and verification, indicates the following sector dynamics, considering the firm patterns: (ibid)

> - *Reporting has become common in the automotive industry, but verification has not, just until recently.*
> - *In the oil and gas industry, reporting as well as verification is rather common.*
> - *Companies in utilities are less internationalised, but, since 2002 reporting has become common. Verification has only become common by European firms in this sector.*
> - *Companies in the chemical and pharmaceutical industry started reporting very early, already before 1998; verification is being done by European firms, not by US firms.*
> - *Reporting is prevalent in electronics/computers. The late adopters in this sector come from Asia.*
> - *In banking, reporting took off relatively late (large number of late adopters). Especially some banks from the Netherlands and the United Kingdom adopted verification later than reporting.*

> The data of GRI and UN Global Compact show that the highest reporting figures are to be found in the sectors financial and/or supporting services, construction and energy, although these figures are not corrected for the total number of companies per sector.

There have been a number of studies on corporate social and environmental reporting. For example, Guthrie and Parker (1989) performed a study of the social disclosure practices of BHP Ltd for the 100 years between 1885 and 1985. In their study, they investigated whether an association existed between social disclosures (classified into environment, energy, human resources, products, community involvement and 'other') and major corporate events (as evidenced by a number of available studies of BHP's history), which could be explained in terms of Legitimacy Theory (we considered Legitimacy Theory in Chapter 3). Guthrie and Parker examined the hypothesis, generated from Legitimacy Theory, that corporate disclosures are made in reaction to environmental pressures (economic, social and political) and in order to legitimise the corporation's existence and actions. They sought concurrence in the timing of disclosures and related activities and events (p. 348). Apart from environmental disclosures, the findings of Guthrie and Parker failed to support Legitimacy Theory. However, and by the researchers' own admission, the data might have excluded a number of significant events or activities. Further, the matching of peak disclosure levels with periods of significant social, economic or political events ignores potential lags in reporting behaviour. Also, as with any case-study analysis, using only one subject has its limitations. Guthrie and Parker found that environmental disclosures were totally absent until about 1950. Disclosures recurred in the early 1970s and 1980s but remained at a relatively low level. Environmental disclosures peaked in the 1970s, and Guthrie and Parker associated this peak with a time when the mining, steel and oil industries became targets for criticism by conservationists.

More recently, Brown and Deegan (1999) conducted research that drew upon both Legitimacy Theory and Media Agenda-Setting Theory, reporting that increased community concern about environmental issues, driven by increased media attention, was matched by increased disclosure (consistent with Legitimacy Theory, disclosure policies are a function of community concern). Briefly, Media Agenda-Setting Theory posits a relationship between the relative emphasis given by the media to various topics and the degree of salience these

topics have for the general public (Ader 1995, p. 300). In terms of causality, increased media attention is believed to lead to increased community concern about a particular issue. The media is not seen as mirroring public priorities; rather, it is seen as shaping them. Brown and Deegan's results were also consistent with those of O'Donovan (1999).

Guthrie and Parker (1990) undertook a comparative international analysis of corporate social disclosure practices in the US, the UK and Australia for 1983. They reviewed and documented disclosures relating to the environment, energy, human resources, products, community involvement and 'other'. They found that corporate social disclosures in the UK, as measured by number of pages within the annual report, was high relative to Australia and the US. They reported that 98 per cent of UK companies examined, reported some form of social disclosure compared with 56 per cent of Australian companies and 85 per cent of US companies. In all three countries, corporations appeared to have the same priorities about the types of social disclosure made. Human resource disclosures were the most evident, followed by community involvement and then environment-related disclosures.

In relation to environmental disclosures, Guthrie and Parker found that companies rarely provided 'bad news' about their activities. The authors view this behaviour as possibly part of a disclosure strategy to counter criticisms of their activities. Guthrie and Parker consider that a sizeable proportion of social disclosures appear to be a reactive response to various social pressures exerted on the firm. They propose that corporate social disclosures can be explained as an attempt to respond to demands for social impact information from particular interest groups. To specifically test this theory, Deegan and Rankin (1996) empirically tested the disclosures of 20 companies that had been successfully prosecuted in relation to environmental issues. Consistent with the findings of Guthrie and Parker (1990), they found that the organisations voluntarily disclosed particularly 'favourable' information and suggested that a motivation for this is to deflect attention away from other potentially damaging news.

As readers of annual reports would have a general awareness of the potentially harmful activities that companies undertake, it is arguable that they would be cynical about a firm that publishes positive information without admitting to any environmentally harmful activities. Consistent with this view, it may be expected that firms would have an incentive to disclose negative information, if it exists, in order to establish credibility with the public. As KPMG (1993, p. 16) states:

> Disclosing the bad news as well as good is very important if companies want to gain credibility for their reports. Otherwise, the reports can appear biased and akin to public relations tools. Even if there is considerable data, an otherwise 'good' report will invite suspicion on all its disclosures if companies are not 'up front' about the problems they are facing, including fines and prosecutions.

If we consider Positive Accounting Theory (PAT; discussed in Chapter 3), we see that the *political-cost hypothesis* yields predictions that are consistent with some of those made by Guthrie and Parker (although the PAT predictions are derived from a different philosophical perspective). The political-cost hypothesis proposes that a company's management will adopt particular strategies to minimise the likelihood of any negative wealth transfers (that is, increased taxes, calls for additional wages and so on) if it perceives that the company is subject to political scrutiny, which can come from government, consumers, employee groups, conservation groups and the like. Although most researchers adopting the political-cost hypothesis argue that a company should reduce its reported income to reduce the likelihood of adverse wealth transfers, some researchers operating within the PAT paradigm argue that voluntary disclosure of information, such as social responsibility information, might also be used to reduce political costs. Ness and Mirza (1991), for example, adopted the political-cost hypothesis to explain why UK mining companies provided environmental disclosures. The research studies discussed above support the view that annual reports can provide inaccurate representations of corporate environmental performance. In previous research on US corporate annual reports, such as that reported in Wiseman (1982) and Rockness (1985), the evidence indicates that firms providing the greatest amount of positive or favourable environmental news are typically poorer environmental performers. A similar finding was reported by Kolk (2010) for other global regions, including Europe. This is consistent with the view that such disclosures are made in an effort to deflect attention away from the negative aspects of an organisation's performance.

The common concern of these studies is that biased or misleading information is causing individuals and organisations to support companies that they might not support if balanced information was being provided. This concern is premised on the assumption that annual report users consider information about environmental performance to play a part in their decision-making processes.

In another study, using Australian companies, Deegan *et al.* (2000) reviewed the annual reports of a sample of companies within the mining, oil transport and production, and chemical industries, which were considered to be facing threats to their legitimacy as a result of a major incident or disaster. Corporations in the related industries were found to provide significantly greater levels of *total* and *positive* incident-related disclosures after the incident than before the incident. Similar findings were reported by Islam and Deegan (2010), when they inves-

tigated the social and environmental disclosure practices of two large multinational companies, specifically Nike and Hennes & Mauritz. When the two entities experienced industry-related social and environmental issues that attracted the greatest amount of negative media attention, they reacted by providing positive social and environmental disclosures. The results were particularly significant in relation to labour practices in developing countries—the issue attracting the greatest amount of negative media attention for the companies in question.

Patten (1992) argued that an environmental issue in one company can influence the environmental reporting of companies in that particular industry. Patton focused on the change in the extent of environmental disclosure made by North American oil companies, in addition to ExxonMobil, both before and after the *Exxon Valdez* incident in Alaska in 1989. He argued that, if the Alaskan oil spill resulted in a threat to the legitimacy of the petroleum industry, and not just to Exxon, Legitimacy Theory would suggest that companies operating within that industry would immediately respond by increasing the amount of environmental disclosure in their annual reports. Patten's results indicate that there were, indeed, increased environmental disclosures by the petroleum companies for the post-1989 period, consistent with a legitimation perspective. This disclosure reaction took place across the industry, even though the incident itself directly concerned one oil company. It would seem therefore that companies appear to change their disclosure policies around the time of major company and/or industry-related events. The disclosure appears to be a reaction to the incident, rather than to social or environmental issues generally.

This raises the question: do people actually use or rely upon the environmental performance information provided in annual reports? This issue was studied by Deegan and Rankin (1997). The groups studied were shareholders, stockbrokers and research analysts, accounting academics, representatives of financial institutions, and a number of organisations performing a general review or oversight function. Their study undertook, by means of a questionnaire, to determine:

- the materiality of environmental issues to certain groups in society who use annual reports to gain information;
- whether environmental information is sought from annual reports; and
- how important environmental information is to the decision-making process compared with other social responsibility information and information about the organisation's financial performance and position.

Deegan and Rankin (1997) found, at statistically significant levels, that shareholders and individuals within organisations with a review or oversight function—these included consumer associations, employee groups, industry associations and environmental groups—consider that environmental performance information is material to the decisions they make. In addition, shareholders, accounting academics and individuals from organisations with a review or oversight function were found to seek environmental information from annual reports to assist in making their various decisions. The annual report was perceived by the total group of respondents to be significantly more important than any other source of information concerning an organisation's interaction with the environment.

Although our discussion so far in this chapter has indicated that the practice of social and environmental performance reporting appears deficient historically, and apparently tied to a legitimisation motive, the quality of reporting in relation to social and environmental performance has improved significantly in recent years.

Although some of the research studies considered here indicate that companies are not likely to provide negative information about their social or environmental performance, this trend seems to be changing and companies do now appear to be producing more balanced information. At an international level, evidence shows that organisations show as increasing propensity to report. In the KPMG *International Survey of Corporate Responsibility Reporting 2011*, they found (p. 12):

- *Ninety-five per cent of the 250 largest companies in the world (G250 companies) now report on their corporate responsibility (CR) activities.*
- *Traditional CR reporting nations in Europe continue to see the highest reporting rates, but the Americas and the Middle East and Africa region are quickly gaining ground. Only around half of Asia Pacific companies report on their CR activities.*
- *For the 100 largest companies in each of the 34 countries studied (N100 companies), CR reporting by the consumer markets, pharmaceuticals and construction industries more than doubled since KPMG's last survey in 2008, but overall numbers in some sectors—such as trade and retail and transportation—continue to lag stubbornly behind.*
- *Of the N100 companies, 69 per cent of publicly traded companies conduct CR reporting, compared to just 36 per cent of family-owned enterprises and close to 45 per cent for both cooperatives and companies owned by professional investors such as private equity firms.*
- *Around the world, corporate responsibility reporting has become a fundamental imperative for businesses. Our survey finds that—almost across the board—companies are demonstrating an increasing willingness to account for their behavior on key societal issues.*

■ *The number of companies now reporting on CR has continued to rise since KPMG's 2008 CR study. Indeed, where CR reporting was once merely considered an 'optional but nice' activity, it now seems to have become virtually mandatory for most multinational companies, almost regardless of where they operate around the world.*

In the 2011 KPMG study, the UK ranked first out of 34 countries surveyed (compared to second out of the 22 countries surveyed in 2008), with 100 per cent of the top 100 companies in the sample producing a stand-alone corporate responsibility report (up from 91 per cent in 2008).

26.8 Social accounting and social auditing

Consideration of social-based issues for external reporting purposes is often referred to as **social accounting** (which we can contrast with financial accounting and environmental accounting). According to Elkington (1997, p. 87):

> *Social accounting aims to assess the impact of an organisation or company on people both inside and outside. Issues often covered are community relations, product safety, training and education initiatives, sponsorship, charitable donations of money and time, and employment of disadvantaged groups.*

social accounting A practice that aims to assess an entity's impact on people—both inside and outside the organisation—by examining its performance in areas such as community relations, product safety and training initiatives.

The practice of social reporting was widely promoted in the 1970s but lost prominence in the 1980s. In the early 1990s attention was devoted to environmental reporting from an eco-efficiency perspective. Social reporting did not appear to re-emerge until the mid- to late 1990s. As Gray *et al.* (1998, p. 303) state:

> *There are many reasons for this renewal of interest. The increasing concern with stakeholders, growing anxiety about business ethics and corporate social responsibilities and the increasing importance of ethical investment have all raised the need for new accounting and accounting methods through which organisations and their participants can address such matters. But probably the most important of all the influences has been the dawning realisation that environmental issues—especially when examined within the framework of sustainability—cannot be separated from social issues and the accompanying questions of justice, distribution, poverty, and so forth. Social accounting, in all its guises, is designed to deal exactly with these issues.*

As we appreciate from reading this chapter, social information is now typically included in a sustainability report, which also provides information about an entity's environmental and economic performance.

Closely linked to social accounting is the practice of *social auditing*. According to Elkington (p. 88), the purpose of social auditing is to enable organisations to assess their performance in relation to society's requirements and expectations. Highlands and Islands Enterprise commissioned Graham Boyd of Alana Albee Consultants and Associates to produce a short article for its website on social auditing and its relevance to Community Land initiatives. On the website (http://www.caledonia.org.uk/socialland/social.htm) social auditing is defined as:

■ *a process that enables an organisation to assess and demonstrate its social, economic, and environmental benefits and limitations. It is a way of measuring the extent to which an organisation lives up to the shared values and objectives it has committed itself to.*
■ *Social auditing provides an assessment of the impact of an organisation's non-financial objectives through systematically and regularly monitoring its performance and the views of its stakeholders.*
■ *Social auditing requires the involvement of stakeholders. This may include employees, clients, volunteers, funders, contractors, suppliers and local residents interested in the organisation. Stakeholders are defined as those persons or organisations who have an interest in, or who have invested resources in, the organisation.*
■ *Social audits are generated by the organisation themselves and those directly involved. A person or panel of people external to the organisation undertakes verification of the social audit's accuracy and objectivity.*

The results of a social audit often form the basis of an entity's publicly released social annual report (thereby increasing the apparent transparency of the organisation), and the outcomes of social audits can be considered an important part of the ongoing dialogue with various stakeholder groups. A social audit might involve the analysis of questionnaires distributed to a cross-section of an entity's stakeholders in an effort to form opinions on how the organisation operates and whether it may be deemed to be a good corporate citizen.

A social audit provides details of where improvements are necessary from the perspective of stakeholders. A review of an organisation's actual social performance and, importantly, stakeholders' expectations about its

performance can be undertaken in the belief that it is preferable to anticipate potential stakeholder backlash before a given activity is undertaken. Undertaking social audits on a periodic basis is becoming accepted as a necessary part of a well-functioning management system. For example, recently the BBC *Panorama* programme reported that child labour was being used in the supply chain for chocolate that possibly ends up being used in Nestlé, Cadbury and Fairtrade products. This controversial documentary resulted in investigations being performed by the large companies, highlighting the role that the media has when it comes to policing corporate social responsibility. An extract of the official response from the companies is provided in Financial Accounting in the News 26.9.

Financial Accounting in the News 26.9

CHOCOLATE INDUSTRY COMMENTS TO *PANORAMA*

Panorama, 24 March 2010

CADBURY

Cadbury's response in relation to this issue of child labour:

Cadbury takes the issue of child labour very seriously, and is wholly committed to eliminating it. Through our investment in the Cadbury Cocoa Partnership and our partnership with Fairtrade, our aim is to enable farmers to live and work in thriving cocoa communities for the long term. This means supporting farmers to increase their incomes from cocoa and other crops, to improve life in cocoa villages and to tackle issues including child labour. We are investing £45 million over 10 years into cocoa sustainability and one of the key themes for our investment is to eliminate child labour. We are also strong supporters and funders of the International Cocoa Initiative, who have been leaders in developing best practice to tackle the root causes of child labour in West Africa.

Cadbury's response in relation to the Kuapa Kokoo suspension:

Although investigation has determined that Cadbury's Fairtrade cocoa beans have not been sourced from any of the implicated societies (either prior to or during the suspension), Cadbury is clear that any instances of child labour are unacceptable and supports the suspension process instigated by Fairtrade and the requirement for immediate corrective actions. In Cadbury's view the audit, suspension and subsequent remediation actions provide strong evidence that the Fairtrade system is functioning effectively.

NESTLÉ UK

Panorama has been unable to provide us with any evidence whatsoever of child labour being used to produce cocoa beans purchased by Nestlé. In addition, *Panorama* has been unable to provide Nestlé with sufficient details to investigate the areas where they have raised other concerns and Nestlé has therefore been unable to address these in any detail.

Nestlé has been working in the Ivory Coast, one of the poorest countries in the world, for over 50 years and there is certainly more to be done. There are many challenges in cocoa farming and the chocolate industry shares a long-term commitment to improving conditions for Ivory Coast farmers and their families.... All Nestlé suppliers are required to comply with Nestlé's Supplier Code, which prohibits the use of forced or compulsory labour, and the use of child labour (meaning work that is mentally, physically, socially or morally dangerous or harmful to children, or improperly interferes with their schooling needs).

If any instance of child exploitation were to be found on any of the farms from which Nestlé cocoa is sourced, they would be fully investigated and immediate action taken.

Source: www.bbc.co.uk

26.9 Assurance of social and environmental reports

As we have noted, a trend exists in relation to subjecting social and environmental reports (or sustainability or triple-bottom-line reports) to some form of independent third-party review—although many organisations still do not have their sustainability reports independently reviewed. As KPMG (2011, p. 28) states:

> *It is surprising that only 46 per cent of the 250 largest companies in the world (G250 companies) and 38 per cent of the 100 largest companies in each of the 34 countries we studied (N100 companies) currently use assurance as*